3e

Physics Galaxy

Volume II

Thermodynamics, Oscillation & Waves

Ashish Arora
Mentor & Founder

PHYSICSGALAXY.COM

World's largest encyclopedia of online video courses on High School Students preparing for

JEE Main * JEE Advanced * NEET * NSEP/INPhO/IPhO

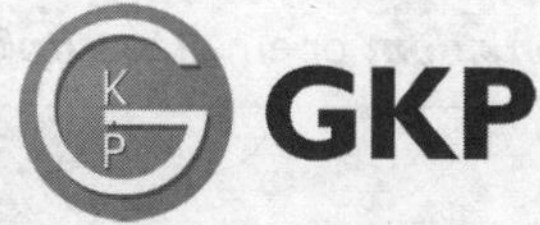

First Edition : December, 2000

Second Edition : May, 2016

Revised Edition : April, 2023

Title : Physics Galaxy : Vol.II - Thermodynamics, Oscillation & Waves (3e)

Language : English

Author's Name : Ashish Arora

Typeset & Published by :

Career Launcher Infrastructure (P) Ltd.

A-45, Mohan Cooperative Industrial Area, Near Mohan Estate Metro Station, New Delhi - 110044

Marketed by :

G.K. Publications (A Unit of CL Educate)

14/4, Mathura Road, Faridabad, Haryana, 121003

ISBN : **978-93-95101-00-4**

Printer's Details: Printed in India, New Delhi.

For product information :

Visit ***www.gkpublications.com*** or email to ***gkp@gkpublications.com***

Dedicated

to

My Parents, Son, Daughter

and

My beloved wife

In his teaching career since 1992 Ashish Arora personally mentored more than 10000 IITians and students who reached global heights in various career and profession chosen. It is his helping attitude toward students with which all his students remember him in life for his contribution in their success and keep connections with him live. Below is the list of some of the successful students in International Olympiad personally taught by him.

NAVNEET LOIWAL	***International GOLD Medal in IPhO-2000 at LONDON***, Also secured **AIR-4** in **IIT JEE 2000**
	PROUD FOR INDIA : Navneet Loiwal was the first Indian Student who won first International GOLD Medal for our country in International Physics Olympiad.
DUNGRA RAM CHOUDHARY	**AIR-1** in **IIT JEE 2002**
HARSHIT CHOPRA	***National Gold Medal in INPhO-2002*** and got **AIR-2** in **IIT JEE-2002**
KUNTAL LOYA	A Girl Student got position **AIR-8** in **IIT JEE 2002**
LUV KUMAR	***National Gold Medal in INPhO-2003*** and got **AIR-3** in **IIT JEE-2003**
RAJHANS SAMDANI	***National Gold Medal in INPhO-2003*** and got **AIR-5** in **IIT JEE-2003**
SHANTANU BHARDWAJ	***International SILVER Medal in IPhO-2002 at INDONESIA***
SHALEEN HARLALKA	***International GOLD Medal in IPhO-2003 at CHINA*** and got **AIR-46** in **IIT JEE-2003**
TARUN GUPTA	***National GOLD Medal in INPhO-2005***
APEKSHA KHANDELWAL	***National GOLD Medal in INPhO-2005***
ABHINAV SINHA	***Hon'ble Mension Award in APhO-2006*** at ***KAZAKHSTAN***
RAMAN SHARMA	***International GOLD Medal in IPhO-2007*** at ***IRAN*** and got **AIR-20** in **IIT JEE-2007**
PRATYUSH PANDEY	***International SILVER Medal in IPhO-2007*** at ***IRAN*** and got **AIR-85 in IIT JEE-2007**
GARVIT JUNIWAL	***International GOLD Medal in IPhO-2008*** at ***VIETNAM*** and got **AIR-10** in **IIT JEE-2008**
ANKIT PARASHAR	***National GOLD Medal in INPhO-2008***
HEMANT NOVAL	***National GOLD Medal in INPhO-2008*** and got **AIR-25** in **IIT JEE-2008**
ABHISHEK MITRUKA	***National GOLD Medal in INPhO-2009***
SARTHAK KALANI	***National GOLD Medal in INPhO-2009***
ASTHA AGARWAL	***International SILVER Medal in IJSO-2009*** at ***AZERBAIJAN***
RAHUL GURNANI	***International SILVER Medal in IJSO-2009*** at ***AZERBAIJAN***
AYUSH SINGHAL	***International SILVER Medal in IJSO-2009*** at ***AZERBAIJAN***
MEHUL KUMAR	***International SILVER Medal in IPhO-2010*** at ***CROATIA*** and got **AIR-19** in **IIT JEE-2010**
ABHIROOP BHATNAGAR	***National GOLD Medal in INPhO-2010***
AYUSH SHARMA	***International Double GOLD Medal in IJSO-2010*** at ***NIGERIA***
AASTHA AGRAWAL	***Hon'ble Mension Award in APhO-2011*** at ***ISRAEL*** and got **AIR-93** in **IIT JEE 2011**
ABHISHEK BANSAL	***National GOLD Medal in INPhO-2011***
SAMYAK DAGA	***National GOLD Medal in INPhO-2011***
SHREY GOYAL	***National GOLD Medal in INPhO-2012*** and secured **AIR-24** in **IIT JEE 2012**
RAHUL GURNANI	***National GOLD Medal in INPhO-2012***
JASPREET SINGH JHEETA	***National GOLD Medal in INPhO-2012***
DIVYANSHU MUND	***National GOLD Medal in INPhO-2012***
SHESHANSH AGARWAL	***International SILVER Medal in IAO-2012 at KOREA***
SWATI GUPTA	***International SILVER Medal in IJSO-2012 at IRAN***
PRATYUSH RAJPUT	***International SILVER Medal in IJSO-2012 at IRAN***
SHESHANSH AGARWAL	***International BRONZE Medal in IOAA-2013 at GREECE***
SHESHANSH AGARWAL	***International GOLD Medal in IOAA-2014 at ROMANIA***
SHESHANSH AGARWAL	***International SILVER Medal in IPhO-2015 at INDIA*** and secured **AIR-58** in **JEE(Advanced)-2015**
VIDUSHI VARSHNEY	***International SILVER Medal in IJSO-2015 at SOUTH KOREA***
AMAN BANSAL	**AIR-1 in JEE Advanced 2016**
KUNAL GOYAL	**AIR-3 in JEE Advanced 2016**
GOURAV DIDWANIA	**AIR-9 in JEE Advanced 2016**
DIVYANSH GARG	***International SILVER Medal in IPhO-2016 at SWITZERLAND***
NALIN KHANDELWAL	**AIR-1 in NEET 2019**
MRIDUL AGARWAL	**AIR-1 in JEE Advanced 2021**

ABOUT THE AUTHOR

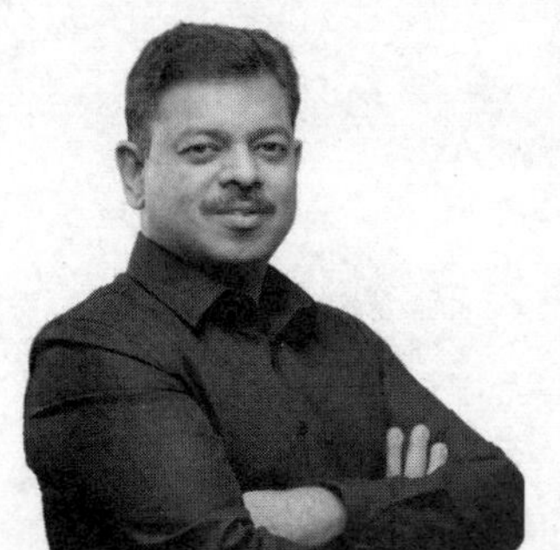

The complexities of Physics have given nightmares to many, but the homegrown genius of Jaipur- Ashish Arora has helped millions of students to live their dreams by decoding it.

Newton Law of Gravitation and Faraday's Magnetic induction force apply perfectly well with this unassuming genius. A Pied Piper of students, his webportal https://www.physicsgalaxy.com, The world's largest encyclopedia of video lectures on high school Physics possesses strong gravitational pull and magnetic attraction for students who want to make it big in life.

Ashish Arora, gifted with rare ability to train masterminds, has mentored over 10,000 IITians and Medicos in his past over three decades of teaching sojourn including lots of students made it to Top 100 in IIT-JEE/JEE(Advance) including multiple times AIR-1 and many in Top-10. Apart from that, he has also groomed hundreds of students for cracking International Physics Olympiad. No wonder his student Navneet Loiwal brought laurel to the country by becoming the first Indian to win a Gold medal at the 2000 - International Physics Olympiad in London (UK).

His special ability to simplify the toughest of the Physics theorems and applications rates him as one among the best Physics teachers in the world. With this, Arora simply defies the logic that perfection comes with age. Even at 18 when he started teaching Physics while pursuing engineering, he was as engaging as he is now. Experience, besides graying his hair, has just widened his horizon.

Now after encountering all tribes of students - some brilliant and some not-so-intelligent - this celebrated teacher has embarked upon a noble mission to make the entire galaxy of Physics inform of his webportal PHYSICSGALAXY.COM to serve and help global students in the subject. Today students from 183 countries are connected with this webportal. On any topic of physics students can post their queries in INTERACT tab of the webportal on which many global experts with Ashish Arora reply to several queries posted online by students.

Dedicated to global students of middle and high school level, his website *www.physicsgalaxy.com* also has teaching sessions dubbed in American accent and subtitles in 87 languages. For students in India preparing for JEE & NEET, his online courses will be available soon on PHYSICSGALAXY.COM.

FOREWORD

It has been pleasure for me to follow the progress Er. Ashish Arora has made in teaching and professional career. In the last about three decades he has actively contributed in developing several new techniques for teaching & learning of Physics and driven important contribution to Science domain through nurturing young students and budding scientists. Physics Galaxy is one such example of numerous efforts he has undertaken.

The third edition of Physics Galaxy provides a good coverage of various topics of Mechanics, Thermodynamics and Waves, Optics & Modern Physics and Electricity & Magnetism through dedicated volumes and many new questions included. It would be an important resource for students appearing in competitive examination for seeking admission in engineering and medical streams.

The structure of book is logical and the presentation is innovative. Importantly the book covers some of the concepts on the basis of realistic experiments and examples. The book has been written in an informal style to help students learn faster and more interactively with better diagrams and visual appeal of the content. Each chapter has variety of theoretical and numerical problems to test the knowledge acquired by students. The book also includes solution to all practice exercises with several new illustrations and problems for deeper learning.

I am sure the book will widen the horizons of knowledge in Physics and will be found very useful by the students for developing in-depth understanding of the subject.

Prof. Sandeep Sancheti
Ph. D. (U.K.), B.Tech. FIETE, FIE (I), SMIEEE

Vice-Chancellor (Provost) Marwadi University, Rajkot
Member Executive Council, Association of Commonwealth Universities, London
Former President, AIU, New Delhi
Former Vice-Chancellor, SRMIST, Chennai
Former President, Manipal University, Jaipur
Former-Director NIT Surathkal, NIT New Delhi, NIT Trichy,
NIT Calicut, SPA Delhi; Former-Mentor Director NIT Goa,
NIT Sikkim, NIT Puducherry
Former-Member JEE Apex Board (JAB), MHRD, GoI
Former-Chairman, Central Counselling Board (CCB), AIEEE, MHRD, GoI
Former-Chairman, Direct Admission of Students Abroad (DASA), MHRD, GoI

PREFACE

For a science student, Physics is the most important subject, unlike to other subjects it requires logical reasoning and high imagination of brain. Without improving the level of physics it is very difficult to achieve a goal in the present age of competitions. To score better, one does not require hard working at least in physics. It just requires a simple understanding and approach to think a physical situation. Actually physics is the surrounding of our everyday life. All the six parts of general physics-Mechanics, Heat, Sound, Light, Electromagnetism and Modern Physics are the constituents of our surroundings. If you wish to make the concepts of physics strong, you should try to understand core concepts of physics in practical approach rather than theoretical. Whenever you try to solve a physics problem, first create a hypothetical approach rather than theoretical. Whenever you try to solve a physics problem, first create a hypothetical world in your imagination about the problem and try to think psychologically, what the next step should be, the best answer would be given by your brain psychology. For making physics strong in all respects and you should try to merge and understand all the concepts with the brain psychologically.

The book PHYSICS GALAXY is designed in a totally different and friendly approach to develop the physics concepts psychologically. The book is presented in five volumes, which covers almost all the core branches of general physics. This part of book, volume 2 covers Thermal Properties of Matter, Kinetic Theory of Gases, Thermodynamic Laws, Specific Heats of Gases, Oscillations & Waves. These are one of the critical topics for building fundamental base in Physics. The things you will learn in this book will help in building your overall strength in the branch of thermal physics, oscillations and waves. In this book every chapter is explained in a simple, interactive and experimental way. The book is divided in the two major chapters, first chapters is covering all the applications of basic thermal physics. Third chapter involves the thermodynamic processes governed by laws of thermodynamics. In this chapter mainly gaseous systems are analyzed at different levels of understanding. Fourth chapter includes the applications of heat transfer through modes of conduction, convection and radiation with several applications including conduction before steady state and analysis of solar constant. Last two chapter at the end covers the major applications of oscillations and waves that includes the whole branch of wave applications for sound waves and waves on a string.

The best way of understanding physics is the experiments and this methodology I am using in my lectures and I found that it helps students a lot in concept visualization. In this book I have tried to translate the things as I used in lectures. After every important section there are several solved examples included with simple and interactive explanations. It might help a student in a way that the student does not require to consult any thing with the teacher. Everything is self explanatory and in simple language.

One important factor in preparation of physics I wish to highlight that most of the student after reading the theory of a concept start working out the numerical problems. This is not the efficient way of developing concepts in brain. To get the maximum benefit of the book students should read carefully the whole chapter at least three or four times with all the illustrative examples and with more stress on some illustrative examples included in the chapter. Practice exercises included after every theory section in each chapter is for the purpose of in-depth understanding of the applications of concepts covered. Illustrative examples are explaining some theoretical concept in the form of an example. After a thorough reading of the chapter students can start thinking on discussion questions and start working on numerical problems.

Exercises given at the end of each chapter are for circulation of all the concepts in mind. There are two sections, first is the discussion questions, which are theoretical and help in understanding the concepts at root level. Second section is of conceptual MCQs which helps in enhancing the theoretical thinking of students and building logical skills in the chapter. Third section of numerical MCQs helps in the developing scientific and analytical application of concepts. Fourth section of advance MCQs with one or more options correct type questions is for developing advance and comprehensive thoughts. Last section is the Unsolved Numerical Problems which includes some simple problems and some tough problems which require the building fundamentals of physics from basics to advance level problems which are useful in preparation of NSEP, INPhO or IPhO.

In this third edition of the book I have included many new questions and solutions in different exercises at practice, conceptual, numerical and advance MCQs to support students who are dependent on their self study and not getting access to teachers for their preparation.

This book has taken a shape just because of motivational inspiration by my mother in 1997 when I just thought to write something for my students. She always motivated and was on my side whenever I thought to develop some new learning methodology for my students.

I don't have words for my best friend my wife Anuja for always being together with me to complete this book in the unique style and format.

I would like to pay my gratitude to Sh. Dayashankar Prajapati in assisting me to complete the task in Design Labs of PHYSICSGALAXY.COM and presenting the book in totally new format of third edition.

At last but the most important person, my father who has devoted his valuable time in finally presenting the book in such a format and a simple language, thanks is a very small word for his dedication in building the base structure of this book.

In this third edition I have tried my best to make this book error free but owing to the nature of work, inadvertently, there is possibility of errors left untouched. I shall be grateful to the readers, if they point out me regarding errors and oblige me by giving their valuable and constructive suggestions via emails for further improvement of the book.

Ashish Arora

PHYSICSGALAXY.COM
B-80, Model Town, Malviya Nagar, Jaipur-302017
e-mails: ashisharora@physicsgalaxy.com
ashash12345@gmail.com

CONTENTS

Chapter 1 ***Heat and Thermal Expansion*** **1-48**

1.1 Heat and Temperature 2
1.1.1 Thermal Partitions 2
1.2 Temperature and States of Matter 2
1.3 Thermometry 3
1.4 Thermal Equilibrium 5
1.5 Thermal Expansion 6
1.5.1 Linear Expansion 6
1.5.2 Stress in Objects Due to Thermal Expansion 7
1.5.3 Variation in Time Period of Pendulum Clocks by Thermal Expansion 8
1.5.4 Superficial Expansion 15
1.5.5 Cubical or Volume Expansion 15
1.5.6 Variation in Density of a Substance 15
1.5.7 Weight Thermometer 15
1.5.8 Isotropic and Anisotropic Expansion 16
1.6 Calorimetry 20
1.6.1 Specific Heat and Absorption of Heat 21
1.6.2 Mechanical Equivalent of Heat 21
1.6.3 Water Equivalent of a Substance 21
1.6.4 Phase Transformation 24
DISCUSSION QUESTION 28
CONCEPTUAL MCQS SINGLE OPTION CORRECT 30
NUMERICAL MCQS SINGLE OPTIONS CORRECT 32
ADVANCE MCQS WITH ONE OR MORE OPTIONS CORRECT 39
UNSOLVED NUMERICAL PROBLEMS FOR PREPARATION OF NSEP, INPHO & IPHO 42

Chapter 2 ***Kinetic Theory of Gases and Gas Laws*** **49-91**

2.1 Postulates of Kinetic Theory of Gases 50
2.2 Gas Laws 50
2.2.1 Boyle's Law 50
2.2.2 Charles and Gay-Lussac's Law 51
2.2.3 Ideal Gas Law 52
2.2.4 Avogadro's Number and Avogadro Hypothesis 52
2.2.5 Dalton's Law of Partial Pressures 53
2.2.6 Different Forms of Ideal Gas Law 53
2.2.7 Real Gases and Change of Phase 53
2.3 Pressure of Air 57
2.3.1 Barometric Relation 57
2.4 Distribution of Molecular Speeds 62
2.4.1 Different Speeds For Molecules of a Gas 63
2.5 Pressure Exerted by a Gas 64
2.6 Kinetic Energy of Gas Molecules 65
2.7 Microscopic Interpretation of Temperature 66
2.8 Degrees of Freedom and Equipartition of Energy 70
2.9 Internal Energy of a Gas 70
2.9.1 Degrees of Freedom and Internal Energy For Different Types of Gases 70
2.9.2 Equivalent Degrees of Freedom For a Gaseous Mixture 72
2.9.3 Mixing of Gases at Constant Volume 72

2.10 Path of Molecules and Mean Free Path 76
2.11 Vander Walls Gas Equation 76
2.12 Diffusion 77
DISCUSSION QUESTION 78
CONCEPTUAL MCQS SINGLE OPTION CORRECT 79
NUMERICAL MCQS SINGLE OPTIONS CORRECT 82
ADVANCE MCQS WITH ONE OR MORE OPTIONS CORRECT 85
UNSOLVED NUMERICAL PROBLEMS FOR PREPARATION OF NSEP, INPHO & IPHO 87

Chapter 3 ***Thermodynamics Laws & Specific Heats of Gases*** **92-168**

3.1 Thermal Equilibrium and Zeroth Law of Thermodynamics 93
3.2 First Law of Thermodynamics 93
3.2.1 Specific Heat Capacities of Gases 93
3.2.2 Heating of a Gaseous System and Work done by a Gas 94
3.2.3 Change in Internal Energy of a Gas on Heating 94
3.3 State of a Gas and Indicator Diagram 97
3.3.1 Properties of an Indicator Diagram 97
3.3.2 State Variable and Path Variables 98
3.3.3 Cyclic Processes 98
3.3.4 Positive and Negative Cycles 99
3.4 Molar Specific Heats of a Gas 105
3.4.1 Molar Heat Capacity at Constant Volume (CV) 105
3.4.2 Molar Heat Capacity at Constant Pressure (CP) 106
3.4.3 Ratio of Heat Capacities of a Gas 107
3.4.4 Ratio of Specific Heats for a Mixture of Gases 107
3.5 Different Type of Thermodynamic Processes 112
3.5.1 Isochoric or Isometric Process 112
3.5.2 Isobaric Process 113
3.5.3 Isothermal Process 114
3.5.4 Adiabatic Process 116
3.6 Free Expansion of a Gas 121
3.7 Polytropic Process 127
3.7.1 Standard Processes as a Special Case of Polytropic Process 128
3.7.2 Indicator Diagram For a Polytropic Process 129
3.8 Second Law of Thermodynamics 134
3.8.1 Reversible Processes 134
3.8.2 Heat Engines 135
3.8.3 Thermal Efficiency of a Heat Engine 135
3.8.4 Refrigerators 136
3.8.5 Statement of Second Law of Thermodynamics 136
3.8.6 Carnot Cycle 136
DISCUSSION QUESTION 144
CONCEPTUAL MCQS SINGLE OPTION CORRECT 146
NUMERICAL MCQS SINGLE OPTIONS CORRECT 152
ADVANCE MCQS WITH ONE OR MORE OPTIONS CORRECT 156
UNSOLVED NUMERICAL PROBLEMS FOR PREPARATION OF NSEP, INPHO & IPHO 159

Chapter 4 ***Heat Transfer*** **169-216**

4.1 Conduction of Heat 170
4.1.1 Analysis of Heat Conduction in Steady State 171

4.1.2 *Heat Transfer Before Steady State* 172
4.1.3 *Thermal Resistance and Ohm's Law in Thermal Conduction* 172
4.2 *Convection of Heat* **180**
4.3 *Radiation of Heat* **182**
4.3.1 *Prevost Theory* 182
4.3.2 *Kirchhoff's Law* 182
4.3.3 *Stefan Boltzmann Law* 183
4.3.4 *Solar Constant* 183
4.4 *Newton's Law of Cooling* **187**
4.4.1 *Average Form of Newton's Law of Cooling* 188
4.5 *Black Body Radiation Spectrum* **192**
4.5.1 *Plank's Radiation Theory as a Proof of Wein's Law and Stefan Boltzmann's Law* 193
4.5.2 *Practical Applications of Kirchhoff's Law* 194
DISCUSSION QUESTION 196
CONCEPTUAL MCQS SINGLE OPTION CORRECT 197
NUMERICAL MCQS SINGLE OPTIONS CORRECT 200
ADVANCE MCQS WITH ONE OR MORE OPTIONS CORRECT 208
UNSOLVED NUMERICAL PROBLEMS FOR PREPARATION OF NSEP, INPHO & IPHO 211

Chapter 5 ***Oscillation and Simple Harmonic Motion*** **217-291**

5.1 *Periodic Motion and Oscillations* **218**
5.1.1 *Types of Oscillations* 218
5.2 *Simple Harmonic Motion* **218**
5.2.1 *Representation of SHM* 218
5.2.2 *Equation of SHM* 219
5.2.3 *General Equation of SHM* 219
5.2.4 *Velocity and Acceleration of a Particle in SHM* 220
5.3 *Superpositions of Simple Harmonic Motions* **223**
5.3.1 *Superposition of Same Frequency SHMs* 223
5.3.2 *Superposition of Different Frequency SHMs* 224
5.4 *Analysis of Angular SHM* **224**
5.5 *How to Find Time Period of SHM* **225**
5.5.1 *Steps to Find Angular Frequency or Time Period of SHM* 225
5.6 *Different Types of Pendulums* **226**
5.6.1 *Simple Pendulum* 226
5.6.2 *Spring Block Pendulum* 227
5.6.3 *Compound Pendulum* 227
5.6.4 *Torsional Pendulum* 227
5.6.5 *Equivalent Length of a Simple Pendulum* 228
5.7 *Phase Analysis of a Particle in SHM* **234**
5.7.1 *Phase Difference in Two SHM* 234
5.7.2 *Same Phase and Opposite Phase SHMs* 235
5.8 *Energy of a Particle in SHM* **244**
5.8.1 *Energy of Oscillation in Angular SHM* 245
5.9 *Energy Method to Find Frequency of SHM* **245**
5.10 *Taylor's Method to Find Angular Frequency of a Particle in SHM* **252**
5.11 *Equation of SHM With Shifting of Origin* **254**
5.12 *SHM of Free Bodies in Absence of External Forces* **256**
DISCUSSION QUESTION 261
CONCEPTUAL MCQS SINGLE OPTION CORRECT 262
NUMERICAL MCQS SINGLE OPTIONS CORRECT 265
ADVANCE MCQS WITH ONE OR MORE OPTIONS CORRECT 274
UNSOLVED NUMERICAL PROBLEMS FOR PREPARATION OF NSEP, INPHO & IPHO 279

Chapter 6 Waves 292-394

6.1 Properties of a Mechanical Wave 293
6.1.1 Different Types of Mechanical Waves 293
6.2 Equation of a Simple Harmonic Wave 293
6.2.1 Velocity and Acceleration of a Medium Particle in Wave Propagation 295
6.2.2 Phase Difference and Path Difference of Medium Particles in Simple Harmonic Wave 295
6.3 Sound Waves 296
6.4 Velocity of a Wave 301
6.4.1 Wave Speed of Transverse Waves on a Stretched String 301
6.4.2 Wave Speed on a Stretched String from Newton's Second Law 302
6.4.3 Velocity of Sound/Longitudinal Waves in Solids 302
6.4.4 Wave Velocity of Longitudinal Waves in Fluid/Gas 303
6.4.5 Newton's Formula for Velocity of Sound in Gases 303
6.4.6 Laplace Correction 304
6.4.7 Effect of Temperature on Velocity of Sound 305
6.4.8 Effect of Pressure on Velocity of Sound 305
6.4.9 Effect of Humidity on Velocity of Sound 305
6.4.10 Effect of Wind on Velocity of Sound 305
6.4.11 Velocity of Longitudinal Waves in a Slinky Spring 305
6.4.12 Velocity of Torsional Waves in a Rod 306
6.4.13 Surface Waves in a Liquid 306
6.5 Principle of Superposition 310
6.5.1 Application of Principle of Superposition of Waves 311
6.6 Interference of Waves 311
6.6.1 Analytical Treatment of Interference of Waves 312
6.6.2 Interference of two Coherent Waves of Same Amplitude 312
6.6.3 Condition on path difference at the point of interference 313
6.7 Intensity of Wave 313
6.7.1 Wave Intensity in Interference 314
6.7.2 Power of a Wave and Wave Energy Density of a Transverse Wave 314
6.7.3 Quincke's Tube 316
6.7.4 Seebeck's Tube 316
6.8 Compression Waves 322
6.9 Spherical and Cylindrical Waves 323
6.9.1 Intensity of Spherical and Cylindrical Waves 323
6.9.2 Equation of Spherical and Cylindrical Waves 324
6.10 Measurements of Sound Levels 324
6.10.1 Comparison of Loudness Levels 325
6.11 Stationary Waves 327
6.11.1 Different Equations for a Stationary Wave 329
6.11.2 Velocity and Acceleration of Medium Particle in Stationary Wave 330
6.12 Standing Waves on Clamped String 331
6.12.1 Normal Modes of Oscillations of a Clamped String 332
6.13 Wave Resonance 333
6.13.1 Resonance in Clamped String Oscillations 333
6.13.2 Sonometer 334
6.13.3 Vibrations of Composite Strings 335
6.13.4 Melde's Experiment 335
6.13.5 Energy Associated with the Medium Particles in a Stationary Wave on a String 336
6.14 Vibrations of Clamped Rod 336
6.15 Waves in a Vibrating air Column 344
6.15.1 Vibration of Air in a Closed Organ Pipe 344
6.15.2 Vibration of Air in Open Organ Pipe 345

6.15.3 Natural Oscillations of Organ Pipes 345
6.15.4 Kundt's Tube 345
6.15.5 Resonance Tube 346
6.15.6 End Correction in Organ Pipes 347
6.16 Beats **353**
6.16.1 Echo 354
6.17 Doppler's Effect **358**
6.17.1 Stationary Source and Stationary Observer 359
6.17.2 Stationary Source and Moving Observer 359
6.17.3 Moving Source and Stationary Observer 359
6.17.4 Moving Source and Moving Observer 360
6.17.5 Doppler Effect in Reflected Sound 360
6.17.6 Doppler's Effect for Accelerated Motion 361
6.17.7 Doppler's Effect when Source and Observer are not in Same Line of Motion 361
6.17.8 Doppler's Effect in Light 361
6.17.9 Applications of Doppler Effect in Light 362
6.18 Shock Waves **367**
6.19 Reflection and Refraction of Waves **369**
6.19.1 Reflection of a Wave Pulse in a Stretched String 370
DISCUSSION QUESTION 371
CONCEPTUAL MCQS SINGLE OPTION CORRECT 373
NUMERICAL MCQS SINGLE OPTIONS CORRECT 376
ADVANCE MCQS WITH ONE OR MORE OPTIONS CORRECT 384
UNSOLVED NUMERICAL PROBLEMS FOR PREPARATION OF NSEP, INPHO & IPHO 387

ANSWERS & SOLUTIONS

Chapter 1 **Heat and Thermal Expansion** 395 - 412
Chapter 2 **Kinetic Theory of Gases and Gas Laws** 413 - 423
Chapter 3 **Thermodynamics Laws & Specific Heats of Gases** 424 - 441
Chapter 4 **Heat Transfer** 442 - 460
Chapter 5 **Oscillation and Simple Harmonic Motion** 461 - 486
Chapter 6 **Waves** 487 - 510

Heat and Thermal Expansion

1

FEW WORDS FOR STUDENTS

Thermal Physics is the branch of Physics which deals with the theory and application of thermal energy. In this chapter we'll mainly deal with the measurement of temperature and the different effects which takes place on changing the temperature of body or due to supply of thermal energy. In next chapters we'll discuss some fundamental laws of thermal physics related to heat exchange between bodies, called thermodynamic laws. This chapter gives you a thorough understanding of basic ideas needed in understanding thermodynamic laws in depth.

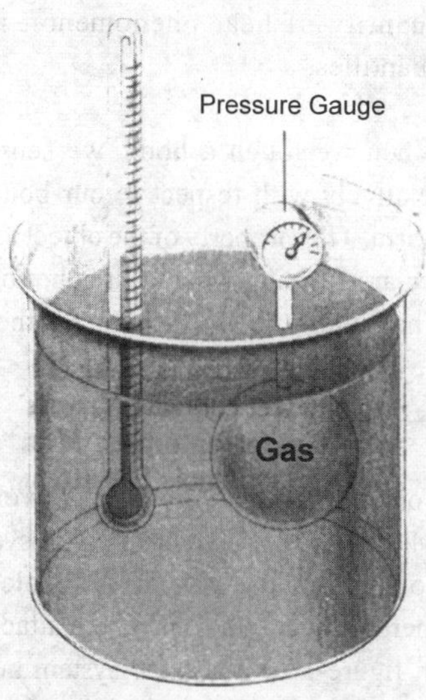

CHAPTER CONTENTS

1.1 *Heat and Temperature*

1.2 *Temperature and States of Matter*

1.3 *Thermometry*

1.4 *Thermal Equilibrium*

1.5 *Thermal Expansion*

1.6 *Calorimetry*

COVER APPLICATION

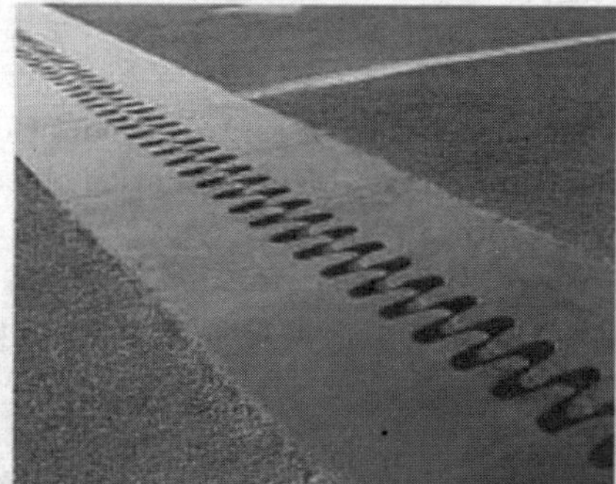

Figure (a)

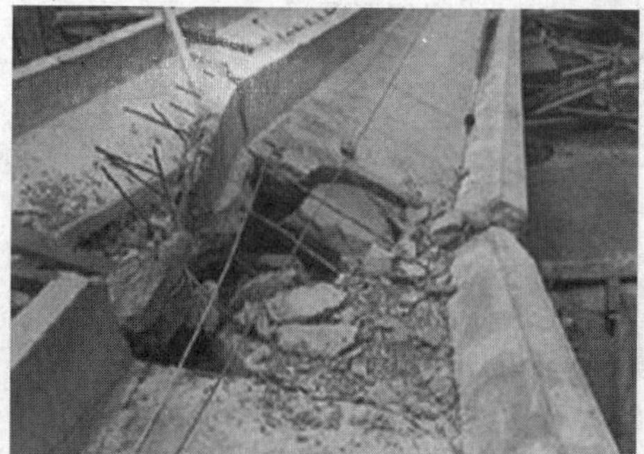

Figure (b)

To avoid damage in over-bridges caused by thermal expansion as shown in figure-(b), during construction steel girders with slots are fitted leaving gap between these as shown in figure-(a). In summers due to expansion this gap decreases and keeps the bridge safe.

In previous chapters till now we have discussed only three fundamental quantities i.e. length, mass and time. All other mechanical quantities such as force, energy, momentum can be expressed in terms of these quantities. We now start another phenomena, the heat phenomenon which requires a fourth fundamental quantity called temperature to express a physical quantity of heat phenomenon in terms of fundamental quantities.

When we touch a body, we sense its coldness or hotness relatively with respect to our body and we say it is cool or warm. This property of the object as well as our body by which we are revising whether it is hot or cold, called temperature. The hotter it feels, the higher is the temperature.

1.1 Heat and Temperature

To define temperature quantitatively some systems are used in which a measurable property of system varies with hotness or coldness of the system. A simple example is a liquid (like mercury or alcohol) in a bulb attached to a thin tube as shown in figure-1.1. When the system becomes hot due to thermal expansion the volume of liquid increases and the length of liquid in the tube increases. The scale used to measure length of liquid column can be calibrated from an arbitrarily fixed point for measurement of temperature. Another simple system is quantity of gas in a constant volume container as shown in figure-1.2. the pressure of the gas measured by a pressure gauge or by a manometer increases or decreases as the gas becomes hot or colder. Another example of such a system is an electrical resistance R of a wire, which also varies with hotness or coldness of surrounding. In each of these examples, the quantity describing the varying state of the system, such as the length, the pressure or the resistance R is called a state coordinate of the system. Such systems which are used to measure temperature are called thermometers.

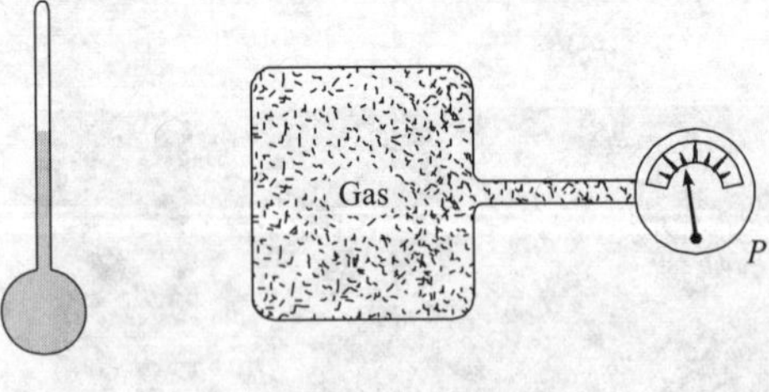

Figure 1.1 Figure 1.2

1.1.1 Thermal Partitions

When two bodies A and B with thermometers T_A and T_B attached to them as shown in figure-1.3(a) at different hotness level are placed in contact as shown in figure-1.3(b). Their state coordinates changes due to different energy content of the bodies. The one which is hotter than other is said to have more energy content and will start loosing this extra energy to the colder body, hence state coordinates of the bodies start changing as they come in contact depending on the relative hotness or coldness level. Qualitatively, we say that initially one is hotter then the other and each system changes the state of the other.

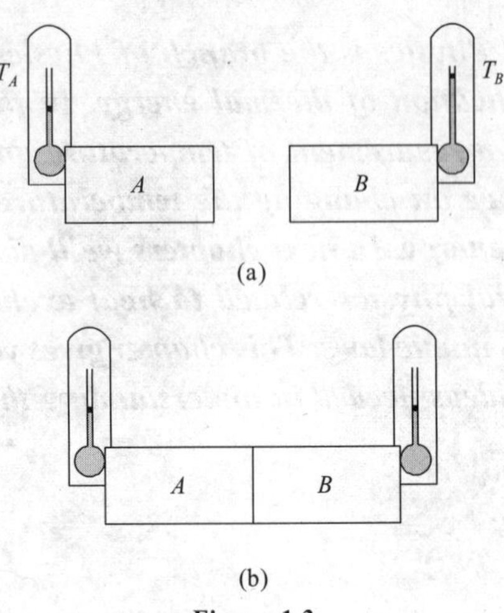

Figure 1.3

If the two system (bodies A and B) are separated by an insulating material such as wood, plastic foam or fibre glass, they influence each other much more slowly. Such a separator or an insulating wall through which the energy content of a body, which we call thermal energy or heat, can not flow is called an adiabatic separator or an adiabatic wall. Due to such a separator the state coordinates of both the system vary independently of each other. Such a partition is an idealized model which can be only approximately realized in real world.

The opposite of an adiabatic wall is a partition that does allow the two systems on opposite sides to influence each other or which allows the heat to flow through it, such a wall is called a diathermic wall or a diathermic separator.

1.2 Temperature and States of Matter

If we talk about water, we know it can exist in form of ice (solid), water (liquid) or steam (gas). Many other material can exist as solid, liquid or gases. Such distinct forms or states of matter are called phases. The change from one state or phase to another, such as melting of ice, is usually caused by a transfer of thermal energy.

The molecules of a gas move about freely, except when they collide with other gas molecules or the walls of the container. The average separation between molecules is large compared with their own size, and as a result, a gas has no definite volume.

Consequently a gas may be compressed or expanded and will fill a container of any shape or size. In a liquid, the average separation between molecules is comparable to their own diameters. Individual molecules are free to move about, but because of the forces between them they move so that the average separation between the neighbouring molecules remains same. As a result, a liquid is virtually incompressible and has a definite volume, although its shape can change to match the shape of its container. In solids the separation between molecules are comparable to that in liquids but binding forces are so strong that the atoms in a solid are not free to move about fixed positions. Thus a solid has not only a definite volume but a definite shape as well.

In every state of matter with the motion of molecules of the matter some energy is associated. What we've discussed in previous article about temperature is that it gives us a feeling for how hot or cold the object is depending on its temperature and temperature of an object can be measured by a device called thermometer. Changes in temperature, changes the energy associated with the different types of motion (linear, rotation and vibrational) depending on the state of matter (solid, liquid or gas). Changes in one state to another are also the changes in energy of the atoms and molecules that compose the material. The energy of molecules of a body can be measured quantitatively as dependent on temperature. But it doesn't mean the two different bodies at same temperature have same energy content in their molecules. What we can say for one body is, if we increase its temperature, total energy associated with its molecule will increase. If kinetic energy of molecules increases then it means the temperature of body increases. If the phase of substance is changing, it is due to change in potential energy of the molecules, which exist due to inter molecular forces of the body.

As we've discussed that thermometers are used to measure temperature of a body quantitatively what a human body can feel qualitatively. But range of measurement of thermometers can be extended for beyond the sense of touch. The range of thermometers extends from temperature low enough to freeze the gases of air to the enormous temperature at the interior of sun.

1.3 Thermometry

The science and measurement of temperature is thermometry. The basis of thermometry is that some physical properties vary with temperature in a quantitative and repeatable fashion. Some of these thermometric properties are the volume of a gas or liquid, the length of a metallic strip, the electric resistance of a conductor and the light transmitting properties of a crystal. Some crystal has their transmission coefficient or light dependent on their temperature thus as temperature of crystal changes, the amount of light transmitted through it changes. Any physical system whose properties change with temperature can be used as a thermometer. The choice of thermometer depends primarily on range of temperature to be measured. We measure the change in some property, say the length of a column of liquid, and there associate the change in temperature with our measurement of the change in length of liquid column.

The most popular thermometer is liquid in glass thermometer. In this thermometer a liquid is sealed into a glass capillary tube having a glass bulb at one end. When temperature increases, both the volume of the glass bulb and the volume of liquid increases. If the liquid expended at the same rate as that of glass, we would observe no change. But as liquid expands at a greater rate then glass does, the liquid will rise in the capillary connected to bulb as the temperature increases. By using a large bulb and a narrow tube, it is possible to make a thermometer that we can read easily from a scale scribed on the glass. The common fever thermometer is made this way.

As discussed, some thermometers determine temperature by measuring the amount of light transmitted by a crystal as shown in figure-1.4. The amount of light transmitted by the crystal depends on the temperature and is reproducible. This type of thermometer is used in medical applications that require a small, remotely readable thermometer.

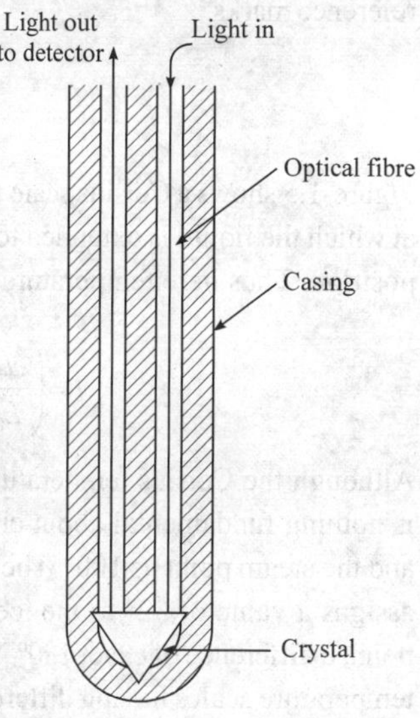

Figure 1.4

Any thermometer, whether liquid in glass or one that depends on other thermal properties, must be calibrated to make it a useful instrument. While calibrating the scale marked on thermometer it must be having the range of temperatures to measure temperature between standard or reference temperatures.

For example in case of liquid in glass thermometer temperature between reference marks are interpreted as proportional to the length of liquid column. There are so many temperature scales are defined for measurement of temperatures for thermometers. First we discuss the most common one-

Celsius temperature scale. The two fixed points lower and upper for references of measurement are chosen as ice point and steam point of water. The ice point is defined as the equilibrium temperature of a mixture of ice and water at a pressure of one atmosphere and the steam point is defined as the equilibrium temperature of water and steam at a pressure of one atmosphere. The numbers assigned to these point in the Celsius scale are arbitrarily chosen as 0 for the ice point and 100 for the steam point.

Assuming the cross-section of the thermometer capillary is uniform and rate of expansion of the liquid with change in temperature is constant then we can mark the distance between ice point and steam point into 100 equal parts and each part we call degree. At any temperature we can easily compare the level of the liquid to the nearest mark. This scale was originally known as the centigrade scale because it has one hundred divisions between the principal reference marks.

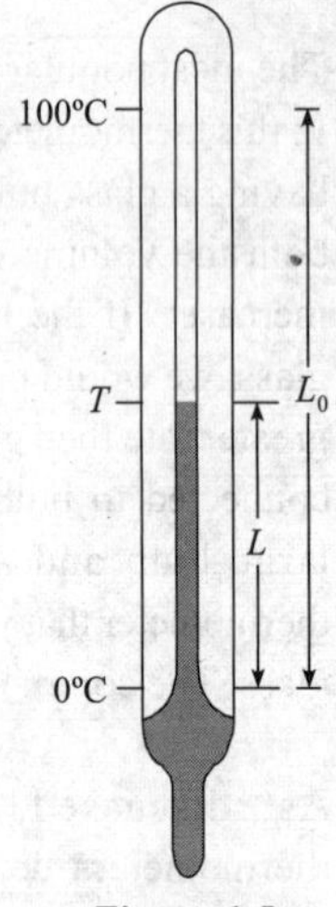

Figure 1.5

Figure-1.5 shows a Celsius scale thermometer at temperature T, at which the liquid is extended to a distance L beyond the zero position. Thus here temperature can be calculated by

$$T = \left(\frac{L}{L_0}\right) \times 100 \qquad \ldots(1.1)$$

Although the Celsius temperature scale is widely used, there is nothing fundamental about choosing the ice point to be 0° and the steam point as 100°. The Fahrenheit temperature scale assigns a value of 32° to the ice point and 212° to the steam point, a difference of exact 180°. Similarly there can be so many temperature scales having different numerical values assigned for ice point and steam point respectively. It is easy to transform temperature in one system into temperatures in the other system. The general transformation formula used for this is

$$\frac{\text{Temperature in X Scale} - \text{ice point in X Scale}}{\text{Steam point in X Scale} - \text{ice point in X Scale}}$$

= constant for all temperature Scales

The above formula, if we use to transform a temperature T_C in Celsius scale to its value T_F in Fahrenheit scale, we have

$$\frac{T_C - 0}{100 - 0} = \frac{T_F - 32}{212 - 32} \qquad \ldots(1.2)$$

or $$T_F = \frac{9}{5}\, T_C + 32 \qquad \ldots(1.3)$$

In both the Fahrenheit and Celsius temperature scale, the assignment of the zero point is arbitrary. We can readily achieve temperatures below these zero points. However, one temperature scale has more fundamental choice of zero point. This was given by Lord Kelvin from the study of gases. Kelvin scale uses intervals equal to those of the Celsius degree but with zero set at the lowest theoretical temperature that a gas can reach. The scale is based on the fact that a gas at 0°C will lose $1/273.15$ of its volume for a 1°C drop in temperature. If this reduction in volume were to continue with decreasing temperature and if the gas did not liquefy, the volume would become zero at –273.15°C. This is a temperature called absolute zero. The temperature scale based on this zero is the Kelvin temperature scale. If we use equation-(1.2) to establish a relation in temperatures measured in Celsius scale T_C and Kelvin Scale T_K, we have

$$\frac{T_C - 0}{100 - 0} = \frac{T_K - 273.15}{373.15 - 273.15}$$

or $$T_K = T_C + 273.15 \qquad \ldots(1.4)$$

This temperature in Kelvin scale is used with a unit of Kelvin (K) and it is not written with a degree sign. The temperature in Kelvin is called absolute temperature.

Illustrative Example 1.1

What are the following temperature on the Kelvin scale :
(a) 37°C, (b) 80° F, (c) – 196°C ?

Solution

(a) Temperature on Kelvin scale T_k is related to temperature T_c on Celsius scale as

$$T_k = T_c + 273$$

or $$T_k = 37 + 273$$

or $$T_k = 310\,\text{K}$$

(b) Temperature T_K on Kelvin scale and T_F on Fahrenheit scale are related as

$$\frac{T_K - 273}{373 - 273} = \frac{T_F - 32}{212 - 32}$$

$$\frac{T_K - 273}{100} = \frac{T_F - 32}{180}$$

$$T_K = \frac{5}{9}(T_F - 32) + 273$$

Here $T_f = 80°\ F$ thus

$$T_K = \frac{5}{9}(80 - 32) + 273$$

or $$T_K = 299.66\,\text{K}$$

(c) Again from relation used in part (a)

$$T_K = T_c + 273$$

or $$T_K = -196 + 273$$

or $$T_K = 77\text{ K}$$

Illustrative Example 1.2

Typical temperatures in the interior of the earth and sun are about 4 × 10^3 °C and 1.5 × 10^7 °C, respectively. (a) What are these temperature in Kelvins ? (b) What percentage error is made in each case if a person forgets to change °C to K ?

Solution

(a) Temperature on Kelvin scale are

$$T_K = T_c + 273$$

For T_c = 4000°C, we have $T_K = 4000 + 273 = 4273$ K and for T_c = 1.5 × 10^7 °C we have

$$T_K = (1.5 \times 10^7 + 273)\text{ K}$$

(b) Percentage error can be given as

$$\%\text{ error} = \frac{T_K - T_c}{T_c} \times 100 = \frac{273}{T_c} \times 100$$

For T_c = 4000°C, we have

$$\%\text{ error} = \frac{273}{4000} \times 100 = 6.825\%$$

For T_c = 1.5 × 10^7 °C we have

$$\%\text{ error} = \frac{273}{1.5 \times 10^7} \times 100$$

or $$\%\text{ error} = 1.82 \times 10^{-3}\ \%$$

Web Reference at www.physicsgalaxy.com

Age Group - High School Physics | Age 17-19 Years
Section - HEAT & THERMODYNAMICS
Topic - Thermal Expansion & Thermometry
Module Number - 2

Practice Exercise 1.1

(i) (a) "Room temperature" is often taken to be 68° F; what will it be on Celsius scale ? (b) The temperature of the filament in a light bulb is about 1800°C; what will it be on Fahrenheit scale ?

[(a) 20°C, (b) 3272°F]

(ii) If a temperature scale defined the freezing point of water as 100° and the boiling point as 0°. What temperature on this scale corresponds to 25°C ?

[75°]

(iii) In an alcohol-in-glass thermometer, the alcohol column has length 12.45 cm at 0.0°C and length 21.30 cm at 100.0°C. What is the temperature if the column has length (a) 15.10 cm, and (b) 22.95 cm.

[(a) 29.94°C, (b) 118.64°C]

(iv) At what temperature will the Fahrenheit and Centigrade scales yield the same numerical value ?

[– 40°]

1.4 Thermal Equilibrium

When two different system at different temperatures are kept in contact for a long duration or connected through a diathermic wall for a long duration till all the changes in their temperature are ceased, this situation is called thermal equilibrium.

The condition of thermal equilibrium can be simply related by the temperature of respective bodies. Earlier we've discussed that temperature of a body determines the total kinetic energy of all the molecules of the body. When two bodies at different temperature are connected by a heat conducting material, thermal energy starts flowing from a high temperature body to the body at lower temperature. This energy which flows from one body to another due to its thermal properties, is called heat. Remember the word "heat" is only used for the energy which is being transferred or energy in flow from or to a body due to its thermal properties. The word "heat" can never be used for energy stored in a body whether or not due to its thermal properties.

As stated above when two bodies at different temperatures are connected by a diathermic material, heat starts flowing between them from high temperature body to the lower temperature body till their temperature becomes equal and after that no net heat flow takes place between them. They are now said to be in thermal equilibrium. Thus we can state that when two bodies in thermal equilibrium (at same temperatures) are connected, no net heat flow takes place between them. On the basis of this concept a law is defined called zeroth law of thermodynamics and is stated as

"When two different bodies are in thermal equilibrium with a third body independently then both of these are also in thermal equilibrium."

1.5 Thermal Expansion

When a body is heated, its temperature rises and as we've discussed that on increasing temperature total kinetic energy of its molecules increases. In a solid, molecules can only have thermal agitation (random vibrations). As temperature of a body increases, the vibrations of molecules will become fast and due to this the rate of collision among neighbouring molecules increases. As the collisions between neighbouring molecules increases, it develops a thermal stress in the body and due to this the intermolecular separation increases which results in thermal expansion of body. In the similar way the block diagram shown in figure-1.6 explains the way how thermal expansion takes place.

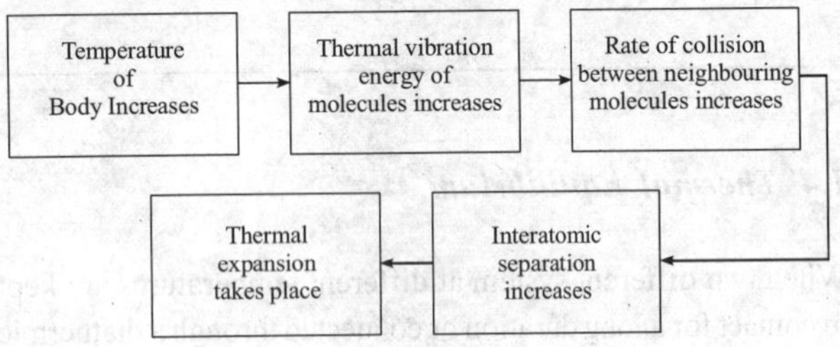

Figure 1.6

Thermal expansion of a substance can be classified in three broad categories, these are (i) Linear Expansion (ii) Superficial Expansion and (iii) Cubical Expansion or Volume Expansion

1.5.1 Linear Expansion

This is expansion in dimension of length of a solid body. It takes place only in solids. To explain linear expansion we take a simple example of a ruler scale. Figure-1.7 shows a ruler scale of length L at temperature T. If the temperature of scale increases, due to thermal expansion, its length also increase. It is observed that on increasing temperature by ΔT, the expansion in its length ΔL is directly proportional to the rise in temperature ΔT as

$$\Delta L \propto \Delta T \quad \ldots(1.5)$$

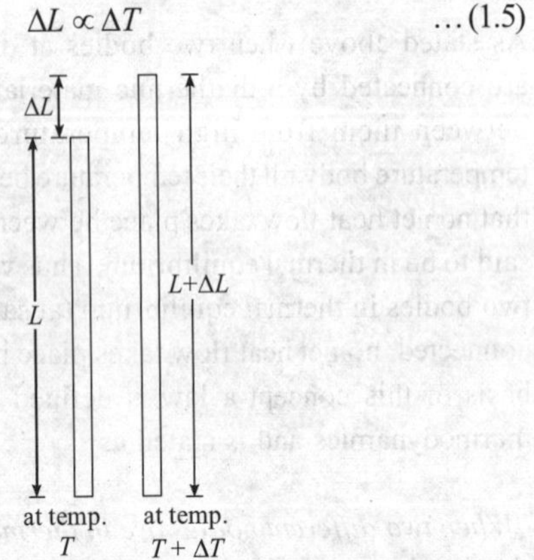

Figure 1.7

It is also observed that expansion of large object is more due to more number of molecule and equal increase in all intermolecular spacing increases the dimensions proportionally, thus we can say that the expansion in its length ΔL is also proportional to the initial length of the scale as

$$\Delta L \propto L \quad \ldots(1.6)$$

From equation-(1.5) and (1.6), we have

$$\Delta L \propto L\Delta T$$

or

$$\Delta L = \alpha L\Delta T \quad \ldots(1.7)$$

Thus the final length at higher temperature can be given as

$$L_f = L + \Delta L$$

or

$$L_f = L(1 + \alpha\Delta T) \quad \ldots(1.8)$$

Here α is the proportionality constant which depends on the material of the body in simple cases, and is called coefficient of linear expansion. Theoretically α is supposed to be a constant but practically it is seen that the value of α varies with temperature and its relation also changes with temperature depending on the range of temperatures. But for a short range of temperature α can be taken as a constant.

The above relation given by equation-(1.8) is not only valid for the length of an object but it can also be used to obtain the enclosed length of an object or distance between two points on an object. For example consider the disc of radius R shown in figure-1.8. If temperature of this disc increases, its size will also increase, as we have discussed, any change in length due to temperature variation can be given by equation-(1.8), we can use the same result to find the final radius of the disc as

$$R' = R(1 + \alpha\Delta T) \quad \ldots(1.9)$$

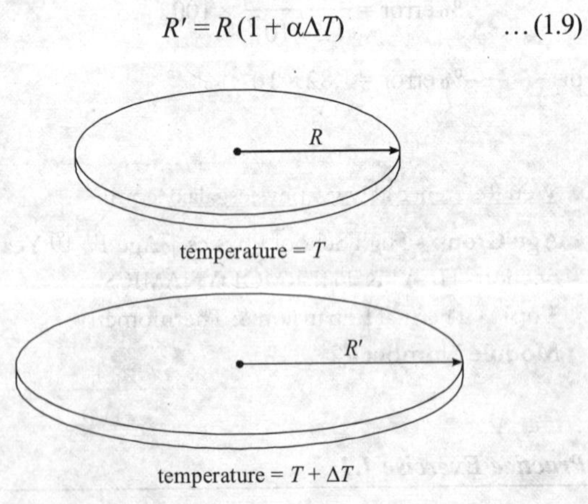

Figure 1.8

Similarly this expression can also be used to find the distance between any two points on a body. For example figure-1.9 shows a copper rod bent in the form of a semicircle. We consider two points on it marked as A and B. Let the separation between the two is l at a temperature T. If the temperature of rod is increased by ΔT. It will expand and hence the length l will also increase and become l'. As here A & B are the points on a body made of similar molecules and one lattice structure, the separation between A and B follows the similar law of linear expansion. Thus l' can be gives as

$$l' = l(1 + \alpha\Delta T) \qquad \ldots(1.10)$$

Where α is the coefficient of linear expansion of material of rod.

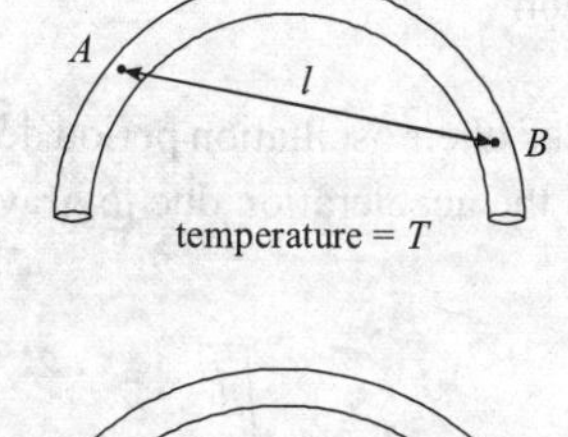

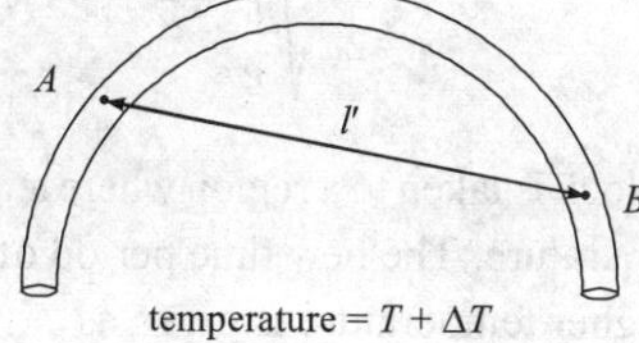

Figure 1.9

Similarly the same result can also be used for lengths and dimensions of an object enclosed by a material like radius of a hole in a disc or radius of a spherical cavity in a solid object. While applying the concept of linear expansion in such cases actually the length is that of air section but we use the coefficient of linear expansion for the material enclosing this air section. Now we take some examples for understanding the linear expansion in detail.

1.5.2 Stress in Objects Due to Thermal Expansion

In thermal expansion the inter molecular separation between molecules of an object increases. It results several applications. For example consider a metal wire of length l, just taut between two rigid clamps at same separation l as shown in figure-1.10(a). If the temperature of surrounding increases, the length of wire will increase due to thermal expansion and there will be a sag in the wire as shown in figure-1.10(b). If the temperature of wire will decrease, it will tend to contract but due to clamps at the ends, it is not allowed to contract. If due to fall in temperature ΔT, its contraction would be $\Delta L = \alpha L\Delta T$ then this change in length will be balanced by the elastic strain in the wire. As temperature starts decreasing, intermolecular spacing between molecules of wire tend to decrease but due to clamps, a tension starts developing in the wire which stretches the wire by the same amount to keep its length constant. If total drop in temperature is ΔT, change in length due to thermal expansion can be written as

$$\Delta L = \alpha L\Delta T \qquad \ldots(1.11)$$

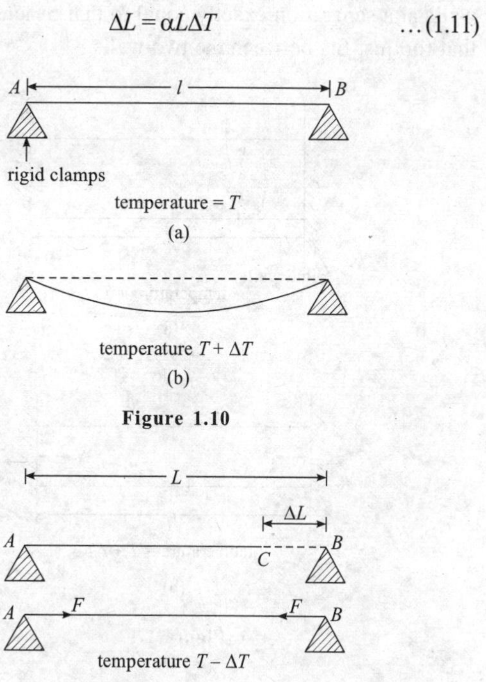

Figure 1.10

Figure 1.11

As shown in figure-1.11 if wire is not clamped at end B, its new length should become AC which is $L - \Delta L$. If it is externally stretched and the end C is tied to clamp B, this ΔL will be the extension in string length due to its elasticity. If cross-sectional area of wire is S and F be the tension developed in wire due to stretching. Thus the stress developed in the wire due to this tension F is given as

$$\text{stress} = \frac{F}{S} \qquad \ldots(1.12)$$

Strain produced in wire due to its elastic properties is

$$\text{strain} = \frac{\Delta L}{L} = \alpha\Delta T \qquad \ldots(1.13)$$

If Young's modulus of the material of wire is Y, we have

$$Y = \frac{\text{stress}}{\text{strain}}$$

or

$$Y = \frac{F/S}{\alpha\Delta T}$$

or

$$F = YS\alpha\Delta T \qquad \ldots(1.14)$$

Equation-(1.14) gives the expression for tension in the wire due to decrease in its temperature by ΔT. This result gives the tension in wire if initially wire is just taught between clamps. If it already has some tension in it then this expression will give the increment in tension in the wire.

Figure-1.12(a) shows another similar example. A rod of cross sectional area S and length L is supported between two rigid walls at a separation exactly equal to that of length of rod so that rod just fits between the two walls.

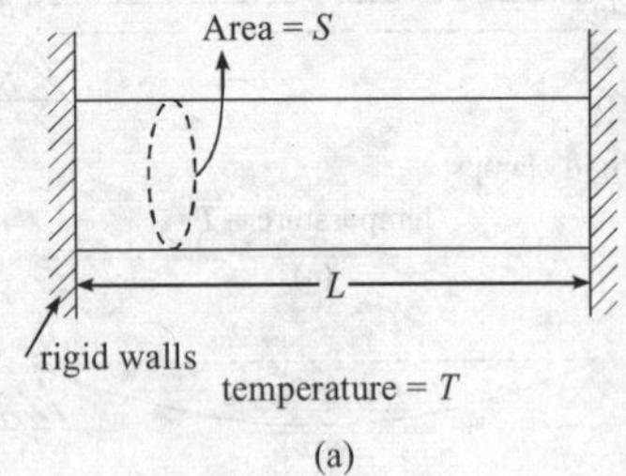

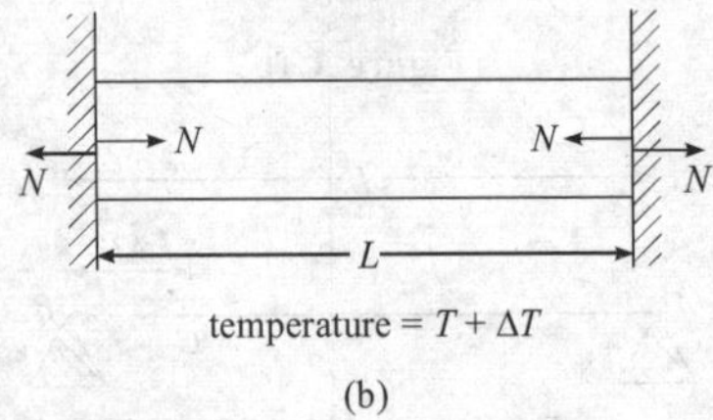

Figure 1.12

If surrounding temperature decreases, the rod contracts and it will fall down as the separation between the wall does not change. But if temperature of surrounding increase, the rod will tend to expand and start pushing the two walls with a normal force as shown in figure-1.12(b) and as temperature of system increases, the magnitude of normal force between walls and rod is also increased. As rigid walls do not allow rod to expand from its original length L, as temperature increases, N will increase to produce an elastic strain in it due to which at any higher temperature the increment in length of rod due to thermal expansion is exactly compensated by the elastic compression in the rod due to normal reaction acting on it by the walls.

If temperature of surrounding increases by ΔT, the natural increase in length due to thermal expansion is given as

$$\Delta L = \alpha L \Delta T$$

If N is the normal reaction on rod's cross-section then due to walls, elastic stress on rod is

$$\text{stress} = \frac{N}{S} \qquad \ldots(1.15)$$

As length of rod remains constant, this implies that due to the normal reaction on rod, it is elastically compressed by exactly the same amount by which it would thermally expand. Thus elastic strain in rod is given as

$$\text{strain} = \frac{\Delta L}{L} = \alpha \Delta T \qquad \ldots(1.16)$$

If Y is the Young's modulus of the material of rod then from equation-(1.15) & (1.16), we have

$$Y = \frac{\text{stress}}{\text{strain}} = \frac{N/S}{\Delta L/L}$$

or
$$N = YS\alpha\Delta T \qquad \ldots(1.17)$$

Similar to the previous case the expression in equation-(1.17) gives us increment in normal reaction between walls and rod if initially some normal force between the two exists.

1.5.3 Variation in Time Period of Pendulum Clocks by Thermal Expansion

In pendulum clocks, their oscillation period depends on length of pendulum and the acceleration due to gravity and is given as

$$t = 2\pi\sqrt{\frac{l}{g}} \qquad \ldots(1.18)$$

If a pendulum clock is taken to a region where temperature is Δt above this temperature. The new time period of oscillation of pendulum at higher temperature is given as

$$t' = 2\pi\sqrt{\frac{l'}{g}}$$

or
$$t' = 2\pi\sqrt{\frac{l(1+\alpha_0\Delta T)}{g}}$$

[If α_0 is the coefficient of linear expansion of material of pendulum rod]

or
$$t' = t(1+\alpha_0\Delta T)^{1/2}$$

or
$$t' = t\left(1+\frac{1}{2}\alpha_0\Delta T\right)$$

[As α_0 is very small $(1+\alpha_0\Delta T)^{1/2} \simeq (1+\frac{1}{2}\alpha_0\Delta T)$]

Change in period of oscillation can be given as

$$t' - t = \frac{1}{2}\alpha_0 t\Delta T \qquad \ldots(1.19)$$

Equation-(1.19) gives the increase in period of oscillation of the pendulum and we can see that the increase in time period depends on the rise in temperature as well as the initial time period of oscillations.

Here if we find the change in time per second, we get

$$\frac{t'-t}{t} = \frac{1}{2}\alpha_0\Delta T \qquad \ldots(1.20)$$

Equation-(1.20) gives the time lost per second by the pendulum clock. If ΔT is the fall in temperature, same equation will give the time gained by the clock per second as its oscillation will become faster due to reduction in its length.

Now we take some numerical examples to understand the applications of thermal expansion in a better way.

Illustrative Example 1.3

In an aluminium sheet there is a hole of diameter 2 m and is horizontally mounted on a stand. Onto this hole an iron sphere of diameter 2.004 m is resting. Initial temperature of this system is 25°C. Find at what temperature, the iron sphere will fall down through the hole in sheet. The coefficients of linear expansion for aluminium and iron are 2.4×10^{-5} and 1.2×10^{-5} respectively.

Solution

As value of coefficient of linear expansion for aluminium is more than that for iron, it expends faster then iron. So at some higher temperature when diameter of hole will exactly become equal to that of iron sphere, the sphere will pass through the hole. Let it happen at some higher temperature T. Thus we have at this temperature T,

$$(\text{diameter of hole})_{Al} = (\text{diameter of sphere})_{\text{iron}}$$

$$2[1+\alpha_{Al}(T-25)] = 2.004\,[1+\alpha_{\text{iron}}(T-25)]$$

$$2\alpha_{Al}(T-25) = 0.004 + 2.004\,\alpha_{\text{iron}}(T-25)$$

or $$T = \left(\frac{0.004}{2\alpha_{Al} - 2.004\alpha_{\text{iron}}} + 25\right)\ °\text{C}$$

or $$T = \frac{0.004}{2\times 2.4\times 10^{-5} - 2.004\times 1.2\times 10^{-5}} + 25$$

or $$T = 191.7°\text{C}$$

Illustrative Example 1.4

A metal rod A of 25 cm length expends by 0.05 cm when its temperature is raised from 0°C to 100°C. Another rod B of a different metal of length 40 cm expands by 0.04 cm for the same rise in temperature. A third rod C of 50 cm length is made up of pieces of rods A and B placed end to end expands by 0.03 cm on heating from 0°C to 50°C. Find the length of each portion of composite rod C.

Solution

From the given data for rod A, we have

$$\Delta L = \alpha_A L \Delta T$$

or $$\alpha_A = \frac{\Delta L}{L\Delta L} = \frac{0.05}{25\times 100}$$

$$= 2\times 10^{-5}\ °\text{C}^{-1}$$

For rod B, we have $\Delta L = \alpha_B L\Delta T$

or $$\alpha_B = \frac{\Delta L}{L\Delta L} = \frac{0.04}{40\times 100}$$

$$= 10^{-5}\ °\text{C}^{-1}$$

If rod C is made of segments of rod A and B of lengths l_1 and l_2 respectively then we have at °C

$$l_1 + l_2 = 50\ \text{cm} \qquad \ldots(1.21)$$

At $$T = 50°\text{C}$$

$$l_1' + l_2' = 50.03\ \text{cm}$$

Thus $$\alpha_A l_1 \Delta T + \alpha_B l_2 \Delta T = 0.03\ \text{cm}$$

or $$2\times 10^{-5}\times l_1\times 50 + 10^{-5}\times l_2\times 50 = 0.03\ \text{cm}$$

or $$2l_1 + l_2 = \frac{0.03}{50}\times 10^5 = 60\ \text{cm} \qquad \ldots(1.22)$$

Solving-(1.21) and (1.22) we get $l_1 = 10$ cm and $l_2 = 40$ cm

Illustrative Example 1.5

Two straight thin bars, one of brass and the other of steel are joined together side by side by short steel cross-pieces at 0°C, one cm long, the centre lines of the bars being one cm apart. When heated to 100°C, the composite bar becomes bent into the arc of a circle. Calculate the radius of this circle.

$$\alpha \text{ for brass} = 19\times 10^{-6}\ \text{per °C},$$

and $$\alpha \text{ for steel} = 11\times 10^{-6}\ \text{per °C}.$$

Solution

As the expansion of brass is greater and hence the combination will bend with brass rod outside as shown in figure-1.13.

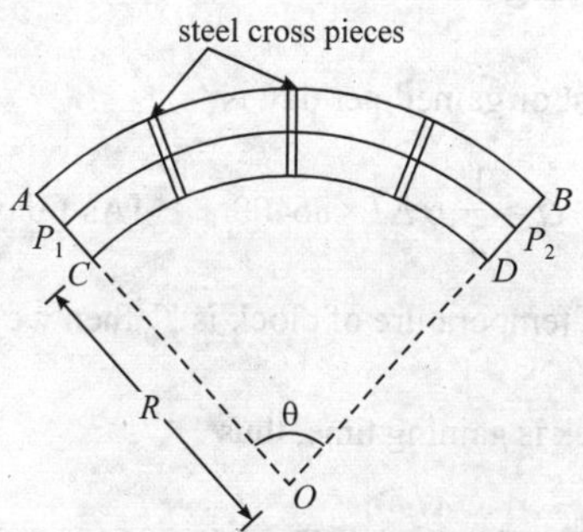

Figure 1.13

In figure, AB is brass bar and CD is steel bar.

Let $OC = R$ and $\angle COD = \theta$.

Length of steel cross pieces at 100 °C

$$= 1(1 + 11 \times 10^{-6} \times 100) = 1.0011 \text{ cm}$$

Now $$OA = (R + 1.0011) \text{ cm}$$

and $$CD = R\theta \qquad \ldots(1.23)$$

and $$AB = (R + 1.0011)\theta \qquad \ldots(1.24)$$

Also, $$AB = L_0(1 + 19 \times 10^{-6} \times 100) \qquad \ldots(1.25)$$

and $$CD = L_0(1 + 11 \times 10^{-6} \times 100) \qquad \ldots(1.26)$$

From equation-(1.23), (1.24), (1.25) and (1.26), we have

$$\frac{AB}{CD} = \frac{R + 1.0011}{R} = \frac{(1 + 19 \times 10^{-6} \times 100)}{(1 + 11 \times 10^{-6} \times 100)}$$

or $$1 + \frac{1.001}{R} = \frac{1 + 19 \times 10^{-4}}{1 + 11 \times 10^{-4}} \frac{1.0011}{R} = \frac{8 \times 10^{-4}}{1 + 11 \times 10^{-4}}$$

or $$R = (1.0011)\frac{(1 + 11 \times 10^{-4})}{8 \times 10^{-4}}$$

$$= 1252.8 \text{ cm}$$

Illustrative Example 1.6

A clock with a metallic pendulum is 5 seconds fast each day at a temperature of 15ºC and 10 seconds slow each day at a temperature of 30ºC. Find coefficient of linear expansion for the metal.

Solution

We've discussed that time lost or gained per second by a pendulum clock is given by

$$\delta t = \frac{1}{2}\alpha\Delta T$$

Here temperature is higher then graduation temperature thus clock will loose time and if it is lower then graduation temperature will gain time.

Thus time lost or gained per day is

$$\delta t = \frac{1}{2}\alpha\Delta T \times 86400 \qquad [\text{As 1 day} = 86400 \text{ s.}]$$

If graduation temperature of clock is T_0 then we have

At 15ºC, clock is gaining time, thus

$$5 = \frac{1}{2} \cdot \alpha \cdot (T_0 - 15) \times 86400 \qquad \ldots(1.27)$$

At 30º clock is loosing time, thus

$$10 = \frac{1}{2}\alpha(30 - T_0) \times 86400 \qquad \ldots(1.28)$$

Dividing equation-(1.28) by (1.27), we get

$$2(T_0 - 15) = (30 - T_0)$$

or $$T_0 = 20ºC$$

Thus from equation-(1.27)

$$5 = \frac{1}{2} \times \alpha \times [20 - 15] \times 86400\alpha$$

$$= 2.31 \times 10^{-5} \, ºC^{-1}$$

Illustrative Example 1.7

What should be the lengths of steel and copper rod so that the length of steel rod is 5 cm longer then the copper rod at all the temperatures. Coefficients of linear expansion for copper and steel are

$$\alpha_{Cu} = 1.7 \times 10^{-5} \, ºC^{-1} \text{ and } \alpha_{steel} = 1.1 \times 10^{-5} \, ºC^{-1}$$

Solution

It is given that the difference in length of the two rods is always 5 cm. Thus the expansion in both the rods must be same for all temperature differences. Thus we can say that at all temperature differences, we have

$$\Delta L_{Cu} = \Delta L_{steel}$$

or $$\alpha_{Cu} l_1 \Delta T = \alpha_{st} l_2 \Delta T$$

[If l_1 and l_2 are the initial lengths of Cu and steel rods]

or $$\alpha_{Cu} l_1 = \alpha_{st} l_2$$

or $$1.7 l_1 = 1.1 l_2 \qquad \ldots(1.29)$$

It is given that $$l_2 - l_1 = 5 \text{ cm} \qquad \ldots(1.30)$$

From equations-(1.29) and (1.30) we have

$$\left(\frac{1.7}{1.1} - 1\right) l_1 = 5 \text{ cm}$$

or $$l_1 = \frac{5 \times 1.1}{0.6} = 9.17 \text{ cm}$$

Now from equation-(1.30)

$$l_2 = 14.17 \text{ cm}$$

Illustrative Example 1.8

A steel wire of cross-sectional area 0.5 mm² is held between two rigid clamps so that it is just taut at 20ºC. Find the tension in the wire at 0ºC. Given that Young's Modulus of steel is $Y_{st} = 2.1 \times 10^{12}$ dynes/cm² and coefficient of linear expansion of steel is $\alpha_{st} = 1.1 \times 10^{-5}$ ºC^{-1}.

Solution

We know that due to drop in temperature, the tension increment in a clamped wire is

$$T = YA\,\alpha\Delta T$$

$$= 2.1 \times 10^{12} \times 0.5 \times 10^{-2} \times 1.1 \times 10^{-5} \times 20$$

$$= 2.31 \times 10^{-6} \text{ dynes}$$

Illustrative Example 1.9

Three rods A, B and C, having identical shape and size, are hinged together at ends to form an equilateral triangle. Rods A and B are made of same material having coefficient of linear thermal expansion α_1 while that of material of rod C is α_2. By how many kelvin should the system of rods be heated to increase the angle opposite to rod C by $\Delta\theta$.

Solution

When the system is heated, the rods expand and the triangle does not remain equilateral. Let lengths of rods A, B and C be l_1, l_2 and l_3 respectively. Then

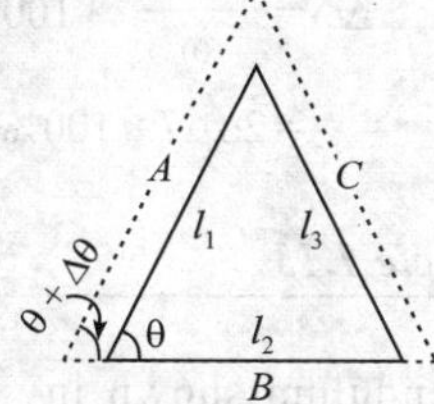

Figure 1.14

$$\cos\theta = \frac{l_1^2 + l_2^2 - l_3^2}{2\,l_1\,l_2}$$

or $$2\,l_1\,l_2\cos\theta = l_1^2 + l_2^2 - l_3^2 \quad \ldots(1.31)$$

Differentiating equation-(1.30), we get

$$2\,l_1\cos\theta\,dl_2 + 2\,l_1\cos\theta\,dl_1 - 2\,l_1\,l_2\sin\theta\,d\theta$$

$$= 2\,l_1\,dl_1 + 2\,l_2\,dl_2 - 2\,l_3\,dl_3 \quad \ldots(1.32)$$

Let the temperature of the system be increased by ΔT. Then

$$dl_1 = l_1\,\alpha_1\,\Delta T$$

$$dl_2 = l_2\,\alpha_1\,\Delta T \quad \ldots(1.33)$$

and $$dl_3 = l_3\,\alpha_2\,\Delta T$$

In case of equilateral triangle $l_1 = l_2 = l_3 = l$ (say) and $\theta = 60º$ and for small change in angle $d\theta = \Delta\theta$

From equation-(1.32) and (1.33), we get

$$2\,l^2\cos(60º)\,\alpha_1\,\Delta T + 2\,l^2\cos(60º)\,\alpha_1\,\Delta T - 2\,l^2\sin(60º)\,\Delta\theta$$

$$= 2\,l^2\,\alpha_1\,\Delta T + 2\,l^2\,\alpha_1\,\Delta T - 2\,l^2\,\alpha_2\,\Delta T$$

$$\frac{\alpha_1}{2}\,\Delta T + \frac{\alpha_1}{2}\,\Delta T - \frac{\sqrt{3}}{2}\,\Delta\theta$$

$$= \alpha_1\,\Delta T + \alpha_1\,\Delta T - \alpha_2\,\Delta T$$

$$\alpha_1\,\Delta T - \frac{\sqrt{3}}{2}\,\Delta\theta = 2\,\alpha_1\,\Delta T - \alpha_2\,\Delta T$$

$$(\alpha_2 - \alpha_1)\,\Delta T = \frac{\sqrt{3}}{2}\,\Delta\theta$$

$$\Delta T = \frac{\sqrt{3}\,\Delta\theta}{2(\alpha_2 - \alpha_1)}$$

Illustrative Example 1.10

A pendulum clock and a digital clock both are synchronized to beep correct time at temperature 20ºC in the morning on 1st March, 2003. At 12:00 noon temperature increases to 40ºC and remains constant for three months. Now on 1st June, 2003, at 12:00 noon temperature drops to 10ºC and remains constant for a very long duration. Find the date and time on which both the clocks will again be synchronized for a moment.

Solution

As a digital clock (if ideal) always keeps correct time. But on increasing temperature on 1st March 12:00 noon, the pendulum clock slows down and start loosing time. We know that time lost by a pendulum clock per second is given as

$$\delta t = \frac{1}{2}\,\alpha\Delta T$$

[If α is the coefficient of linear expansion for the material of pendulum]

$$= \frac{1}{2}\,\alpha(20)$$

In three months (March + April + May = 92 days) it looses time

$$\delta t_{92\text{ days}} = \frac{1}{2} \times \alpha \times 20 \times 92 \times 86400$$

On 1st June, 12:00 noon, temperature drops to 10ºC which is 10º less then the temperature at which clock keeps correct time, thus now clock starts gaining time and if after N days it gains exactly the time lost during previous three months, it shows right time again for a moment. Thus time gained by the clock in N days is

$$\delta t_{N\text{ days}} = \frac{1}{2}\alpha(10) \times N \times 86400$$

We have $\delta t_{92\text{ days}}(\text{lost}) = \delta t_{N\text{ days}}(\text{gained})$

or $$\frac{1}{2} \times \alpha \times 20 \times 92 \times 86400 = \frac{1}{2} \times \alpha \times 10 \times N \times 86400$$

or $$N = 184 \text{ days}$$

Thus after 184 days from 1st June 2003, pendulum clock will show correct time and both the clocks will be in synchronization for a moment and after 184 days means the date is 2nd Dec. 2003 and time is 12:00 noon.

Illustrative Example 1.11

At room temperature (25°C) the length of a steel rod is measured using a brass centimeter scale. The measured length is 20 cm. If the scale is calibrated to read accurately at temperature 0°C. Find the actual length of steel rod at room temperature

Solution

The brass scale is calibrated to read accurately at 0°C, this means at 0°C, each division of scale has exact 1 cm length. Thus at higher temperature the division length of scale will be more than 1 cm due to thermal expansion. Thus at higher temperatures the scale reading for length measurement is not appropriate and as at higher temperature the division length is more, the length this scale reads will be lesser than the actual length to be measured. For example in this case the length of each division on brass scale at 25°C is

$$l_{1\,div} = (1\text{ cm})[1 + \alpha_{br}(25 - 0)]$$
$$= 1 + \alpha_{br}(25)$$

It is given that at 25°C the length of steel rod measured is 20 cm. Actually it is not 20 cm, it is 20 divisions on the brass scale. Now we can find the actual length of the steel rod at 25°C as

$$l_{25°C} = (20\text{ cm}) \times l_{1\,div}$$

or $$l_{active} = 20[1 + \alpha_{br}(25)] \qquad \ldots(1.34)$$

The above expression is a general relation using which you can find the actual lengths of the objects of which lengths are measured by a metallic scale at some temperature other than the graduation temperature of the scale.

Illustrative Example 1.12

A rod AB of length l is pivoted at an end A and freely rotated in a horizontal plane at an angular speed ω about a vertical axis passing through A. If coefficient of linear expansion of material of rod is α, find the percentage change in its angular velocity if temperature of system is increased by ΔT.

Solution

If temperature of surrounding increases by ΔT, the new length of rod becomes

$$l' = l(1 + \alpha\Delta T)$$

Due to change in length, moment of inertia of rod also changes and it is about an end A and is given as $I'_A = \frac{Ml'^2}{3}$

As no external force or torque is acting on rod thus its angular momentum remains constant during heating thus we have

$$I_A\omega = I'_A\omega'$$

[If ω' is the final angular velocity of rod after heating]

or $$\frac{Ml^2}{3}\omega = \frac{Ml^2(1+\alpha\Delta T)^2}{3}\omega'$$

or $$\omega' = \omega(1 - 2\alpha\Delta T)$$

[Using binomial expansion for small α]

Thus percentage change in angular velocity of rod due to heating can be given as

$$\Delta\omega = \frac{\omega - \omega'}{\omega} \times 100\%$$
$$= 2\alpha\Delta T \times 100\%$$

Illustrative Example 1.13

A compensated pendulum shown in figure-1.15 is in the form of an isosceles triangle of base length l_1 = 5 cm and coefficient of linear expansion α_1 = 18 × 10^{-6} and side length l_2 and coefficient of linear expansion α_2 = 12 × 10^{-6}. Find l_2 so that the distance of centre of mass of the bob from suspension centre O may remain the same at all the temperature.

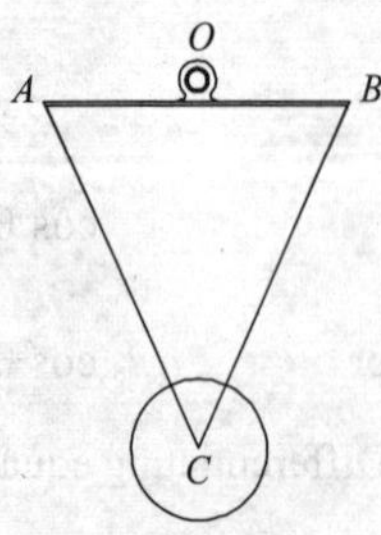

Figure 1.15

Solution

First we must know what is a compensated pendulum. We've discussed that due to change in temperature the time period of a pendulum clock changes. Due to this in pendulum clocks, to make a pendulum some specific metals are used which have very low coefficient of expansion so that the error introduced in their time is very small. The other alternative of minimizing the error in time measurement, is to use compensated pendulum. This is a pendulum made up of two or more metals of such an arrangement in which the effective length of centre of mass of the whole body remains unchanged. Such a situation is given in figure-1.15.

In this case the distance of centre of mass from suspension point O is

$$h = \sqrt{l_2^2 - \frac{l_1^2}{4}}$$

At some higher temperature Δt, new value of h will become

$$h' = \sqrt{l_2^2(1+\alpha_2\Delta t)^2 + \frac{l_1^2}{4}(1+\alpha_1\Delta t)^2}$$

As we require $h = h'$, we have

$$l_2^2 \frac{l_1^2}{4} = l_2^2(1+2\alpha_2\Delta t) - \frac{l_1^2}{4}(1+2\alpha_1\Delta t)$$

or $$2\alpha_2 l_2^2 = \frac{l_1^2}{4}\alpha_1$$

or $$l_2 = \frac{l_1}{2}\sqrt{\frac{\alpha_1}{\alpha_2}}$$

Illustrative Example 1.14

Two same length rods of brass and steel of equal cross-sectional area are joined end to end as shown in figure-1.16 and supported between two rigid vertical walls. Initially the rods are unstrained. If the temperature of system is raised by Δt. Find the displacement of the junction of two rods. Given that the coefficients of linear expansion and young's modulus of brass and steel are α_b, α_s ($\alpha_b > \alpha_s$), Y_b and Y_s respectively.

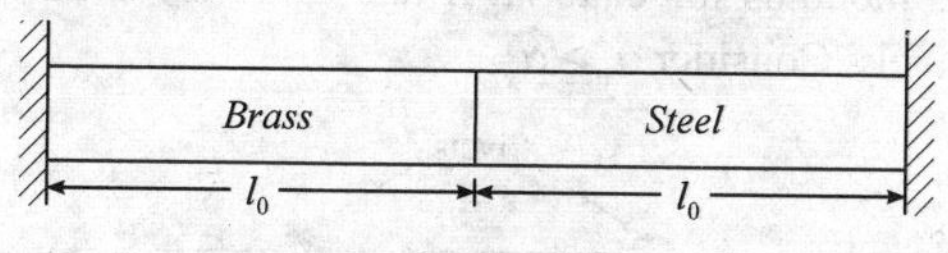

Figure 1.16

Solution

Here the initial lengths of the two rods are l_0 and as $\alpha_b > \alpha_s$, we can directly state that the junction of the two rods is displaced toward right. Due to this brass rod is some what expanded but less as compared to free expansion and steel is overall compressed due to the stress developed between the two rods.

Figure-1.17 shows the final situation of rods at higher temperature Δt. In figure, A is the initial position of junction and B is its final position.

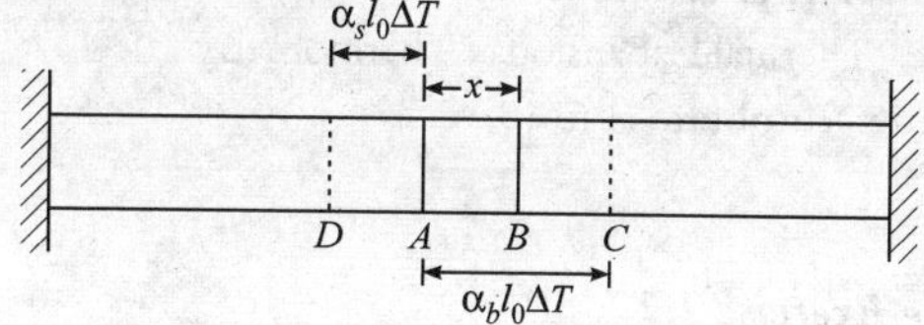

Figure 1.17

If only brass rod is present, expansion in it due to increase in temperature by ΔT is

$$\Delta l_b = \alpha_b l_0 \Delta T$$

Which is equal to AC in figure-1.17. But finally the rod is expanded by x, thus the elastic compression in the rod due to stress between the two rods is BC, which is given as

$$BC = \alpha_b l_0 \Delta T - x$$

Thus elastic strain in brass rod is

$$(Strain)_{brass} = \frac{\alpha_b l_0 \Delta T - x}{l_0} \quad [\text{As } \alpha_b l_0 \Delta T \text{ is small}]$$

Similarly if steel rod alone is there, it would have been expanded by

$$\Delta l_s = \alpha_s l_0 \Delta T$$

Which is equal to AD in figure-1.17. But finally steel rod is compressed by x, thus the elastic compression in steel rod due to stress between the two rods is BD, which is given as

$$BD = \alpha_s l_0 \Delta T + x$$

Thus elastic strain in steel rod is

$$(Strain)_{steel} = \frac{\alpha_s l_0 \Delta T - x}{l_0} \quad [\text{As } \alpha_s l_0 \Delta T \text{ is small}]$$

As the two rods are in contact, stress developed in the two rods must be equal thus we have

$$(Stress)_{brass} = (Stress)_{steel}$$

or $$Y_b \times (Strain)_{brass} = Y_s \times (Strain)_{steel}$$

or $$Y_b\left[\frac{\alpha_b l_b \Delta T - x}{l_0}\right] = Y_s\left[\frac{\alpha_s l_0 \Delta T + x}{l_0}\right]$$

or $$x = \frac{(Y_b\alpha_b - Y_s\alpha_s)\, l_0 \Delta T}{(Y_b + Y_s)}$$

Web Reference at www.physicsgalaxy.com

Age Group - High School Physics | Age 17-19 Years
Section - HEAT & THERMODYNAMICS
Topic - Thermal Expansion & Thermometry
Module Numbers - 1 to 10

Practice Exercise 1.2

(i) A steel tape measures the length of a copper rod as 90.0 cm and when both are at 10°C, which is the graduation temperature of the tape. What would the tape read for the length of the rod when both are at 30°C. Given that coefficient of linear expansion of steel is 1.2×10^{-5} °C^{-1} and that of copper is 1.7×10^{-5} °C^{-1}.

[90.01 cm]

(ii) In the construction of a flyover, steel girders of length 12 m are used to place one after another. How much gap should be left between the two at their junction so that in summers when peak temperature is about 48°C, there should not be any compression. Given that the construction is done in peak winters when temperature is 18°C. Given that the coefficient of linear expansion of steel is 1.1×10^{-5} °C^{-1}.

[3.96×10^{-3} m]

(iii) A steel rod is clamped between two rigid supports at 20°C. If the temperature of rod increases to 50°C, find the strain developed in the rod due to this. Given that the coefficient of linear expansion of steel is 1.2×10^{-5}°C^{-1}.

[-3.6×10^{-4}]

(iv) Figure-1.18 shows a steel rod of cross sectional area 2×10^{-6} m^2 is fixed between two vertical walls. Initially at 20°C, there is no force between the ends of the rod and the walls. Find the force which the rod will exert on walls at 100°C. Given that the coefficient of linear expansion of steel is 1.2×10^{-5} °C^{-1} and its Young's modulus is 2×10^{11} N/m^2.

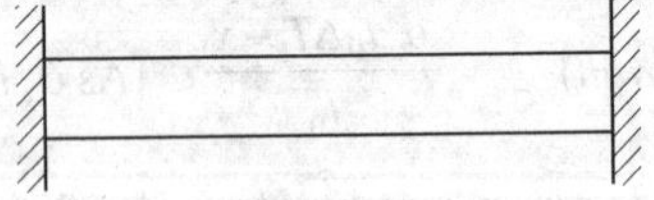

Figure 1.18

[384 N]

(v) A glass window is to be fitted in an aluminium frame. The temperature on the working day is 40°C and the size of the glass piece is a rectangle of sides 20 cm and 30 cm. What should be the dimensions of the aluminium frame so that in winters glass does not experience any stress when temperature drops to 0°C. Given that the coefficients of linear expansion for glass is 9×10^{-6} °C^{-1} and that for aluminium is 2.4×10^{-5}°C^{-1}.

[20.012 cm and 30.018 cm]

(vi) A cylindrical steel component machined on an engine lathe is heated to temperature of 80°C. The diameter of the component should be 5 cm at temperature of 10°C and the permissible error should not exceed 10 microns from the specified dimension. Do we need corrections for the thermal expansion component be introduced during the process of machining ? If so, what diameter should be prepared ? Take : $\alpha_{steel} = 12 \times 10^{-6}$ °C^{-1}.

[Yes, 5.0052 cm]

(vii) At a certain temperature the pendulum of a clock keeps correct time. The coefficient of linear expansion for the pendulum material is $\alpha = 1.85 \times 10^{-5}$ K^{-1}. How much will the clock gain or lose in 24 hours if the ambient temperature is 10°C higher ?

[7.992 s]

(viii) A clock pendulum made of invar has a period of 0.5 s at 20°C. If the clock is used in a climate where average temperature is 30°C, what correction may be necessary at the end of 30 days. $\alpha_{invar} = 7 \times 10^{-7}$ (°C)$^{-1}$.

[9 s (to be added)]

(ix) The time period of a physical pendulum is given by $T = 2\pi\sqrt{\dfrac{I}{mgl}}$ where m = mass of the pendulum, I = moment of inertia about the axis of suspension, l = distance of centre of mass of bob from the centre of suspension. Calculate the change in time period when temperature changes by ΔT. The coefficient of linear expansion of the material of pendulum is α.

[$\pi\, \alpha\Delta T\sqrt{\dfrac{I}{mgl}}$]

(x) Two rods of material X sandwich another rod of material Y as shown in figure-1.19. At temperature T, the three rods are in a state of zero strain and of length L and riveted to each other in this state. If the temperature of the system increases to $T + \Delta T$, find the final length of the system of the three rods. Given that the coefficients of linear expansions of the rods and their Young's modulus for material X and Y are α_x, α_y, Y_x and Y_y respectively. Consider $\alpha_y > \alpha_x$.

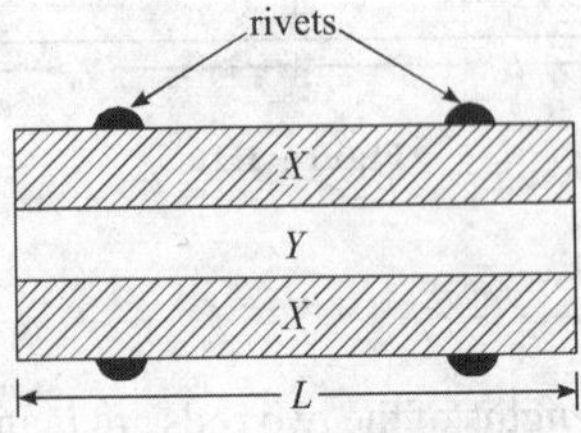

Figure 1.19

[$L\left[1 + \dfrac{\alpha_y Y_y + 2\alpha_x Y_x}{Y_y + 2Y_x}\Delta T\right]$]

1.5.4 Superficial Expansion

This is expansion in surface of a body or two dimensional expansion of an object. Figure-1.20 shows a rectangular plate of size $l \times b$, when its temperature increases from T to $T+\Delta T$, both of its length and width increases as thermal expansion takes place uniformly in all direction in a material. If α be the coefficient of linear expansion for the material of plate, its final length and width at higher temperature can be given as

$$l' = l(1+\alpha\Delta T) \quad \ldots(1.35)$$

$$b' = b(1+\alpha\Delta T) \quad \ldots(1.36)$$

Figure 1.20

Final area of plate is

$$A' = l'\,b' = l\,b\,(1+\alpha\Delta T)^2$$

or $$A' = A\,(1+1\,\alpha\Delta T)^2 \quad \text{[Initial area } A = l\,b]$$

or $$A' = A\,(1+2\,\alpha\Delta T)$$

[As $\alpha\Delta T << 1$, using binomial expansion]

or $$A' = A\,(1+\beta\Delta T) \quad \ldots(1.37)$$

Here $\beta = 2\alpha$ is called coefficient of superficial expansion for the material of object. In some objects if linear expansion coefficient α is not very small (which is very rare), we can not use $\beta = 2\alpha$ for that material as binomial expansion can not be used and value of β can only be experimentally evaluated.

From equation-(1.37) it can be seen that temperature of a body if decreases, its final area at lower temperature can be given as

$$A_f = \frac{A}{(1+\beta\Delta T)}$$

For small β we can write this expression as

$$A_f = A\,(1-\beta\Delta T)^{-1} = A\,(1-\beta\Delta T) \quad \ldots(1.38)$$

1.5.5 Cubical or Volume Expansion

As we know when temperature of a body increases, thermal expansion takes place uniformly in all directions. Due to this volume of body also increases. Consider a box of length, width and height $l \times b \times h$. If its temperature increases by ΔT, and the coefficient of linear expansion for the material of box is α, the final volume of box will be given as

$$V_f = l\,b\,h\,(1+\alpha\Delta T)^3$$

or $$V_f = V_i\,(1+3\alpha\Delta T)$$

[Where $V_i = lbh$ and for $\alpha\Delta T << 1$]

or $$V_f = V_i\,(1+\gamma\Delta T) \quad \ldots(1.39)$$

Here $\gamma = 3\alpha$ is called coefficient of volume or cubical expansion of the material of body. In case of expansion of liquids, length and area do not have any significance and so for a liquid we can only define coefficient of volume expansion. In liquids molecules are more mobile as compared to solid thus expansion of liquids is always more than that of solids, thus the value of γ is also higher for liquids than solids.

1.5.6 Variation in Density of a Substance

We know volume of a substance increases with rise in temperature. Thus we can obviously state that the density of object decreases with rise in temperature as its mass is a constant. For example if a body of mass m has density ρ_1 and volume V_1 at temperature T, then at some higher temperature $T+\Delta[T$ the volume of body V_2 can be given as

$$V_2 = V_1\,(1+\gamma\Delta T) \quad \ldots(1.40)$$

If the density of body now becomes ρ_2 then it can be given as

$$\rho_2 = \frac{m}{V_2} = \frac{\rho_1 V_1}{V_1(1+\gamma\Delta T)}$$

or $$\rho_2 = \frac{\rho_1}{1+\gamma\Delta T} \quad \ldots(1.41)$$

or $$\rho_2 = \rho_1\,(1+\gamma\Delta T)^{-1} = \rho_1(1-\gamma\Delta T) \quad \ldots(1.42)$$

[As for $\gamma\Delta T << 1$]

We have discussed that with temperature expansion rate of liquids is faster than solids thus some times in case of liquids when coefficient of expansion γ is not a very small value, above equation-(1.42) will not be valid, as we can not use binomial approximation as $\gamma\Delta T$ is not very less than 1. Then variation of density of such liquids is given by equation-(1.41) only.

1.5.7 Weight Thermometer

This is a very good application of thermal expansion. In ancient times this device was used to measure surrounding temperature of a region. In it a liquid is taken in a container as shown in figure-1.21. Initially the liquid is filled to completely fill up the container and both have initial volume V_0. If temperature of region [container] is increased by ΔT, final volume of liquid and container will become V_l & V_c respectively. If γ_l and γ_c are the coefficient of volume expansion of liquid and container then V_l and V_c are given as

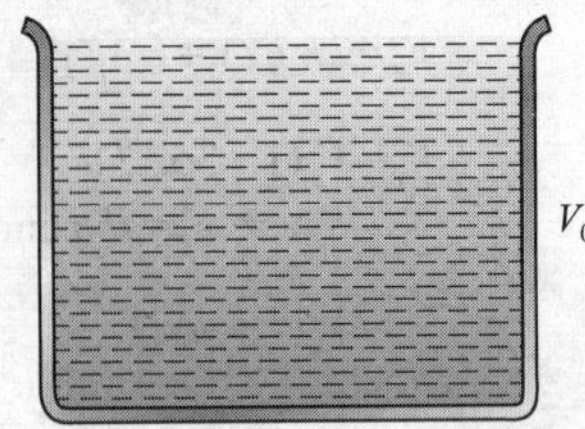

Figure 1.21

$$V_l = V_0(1+\gamma_l \Delta T) \qquad \ldots(1.43)$$

and
$$V_c = V_0(1+\gamma_c \Delta T) \qquad \ldots(1.44)$$

As $\gamma_l > \gamma_c$, liquid will expand more than container and some liquid will expel from the container. The volume of overflow liquid can be given as

$$\Delta V = V_l - V_c$$
$$= V_0(\gamma_l - \gamma_c)\Delta T \qquad \ldots(1.45)$$

Here this volume ΔV can be taken as apparent expansion of liquid relative to container and the term $(\gamma_l - \gamma_c)$ is called as coefficient of apparent expansion of liquid with respect to glass and can also be denoted by γ_{lc}, thus we can write the volume of liquid overflow is

$$\Delta V = V_0 \gamma_{lc} \Delta T \qquad \ldots(1.46)$$

The density of liquid at this higher temperature is given as

$$\rho_l' = \frac{\rho_l}{(1+\gamma_l \Delta T)}$$

Mass of liquid overflow is $\Delta m = \Delta V \times \rho_l'$

$$\Delta m = \frac{V_0(\gamma_l - \gamma_c)\Delta T \rho_l}{1+\gamma_l \Delta T}$$

or
$$\Delta m + \gamma_l \Delta m \Delta T = V_0(\gamma_l - \gamma_c)\Delta T \rho_l$$

or
$$\Delta T = \left[\frac{\Delta m}{V_0(\gamma_l - \gamma_c) - \Delta m \gamma_l}\right]\frac{1}{\rho_l} \qquad \ldots(1.47)$$

If we weight the mass of liquid overflown, then using this in expression of equation-(1.47) we can find the rise in temperature.

1.5.8 Isotropic and Anisotropic Expansion

We've discussed that when a substance is heated, its temperature rises and thermal expansion takes place uniformly in all direction. But this is not always true, the expansion of a body in different direction depends on the lattice structure of the material of body. In most of the solids, atoms are arranged at uniform interatomic distances thus expansion takes place uniformly in all directions. But in some solids interatomic separations in different dimensions are different. For example in graphite, the separation of carbon atoms in layers is different then the separation between layers as shown in figure-1.22. Thus when graphite is heated and its temperature increases, the expansion in the plane of layers of carbon atoms is uniform but only in two dimensional plane but the expansion along z direction in figure-1.22 i.e. in the direction normal to layers the expansion is different. If a cube made of graphite is heated, we can conclusively state that at some higher temperature two opposite faces of the cube out of six remains expanded squares, other four faces become rectangular.

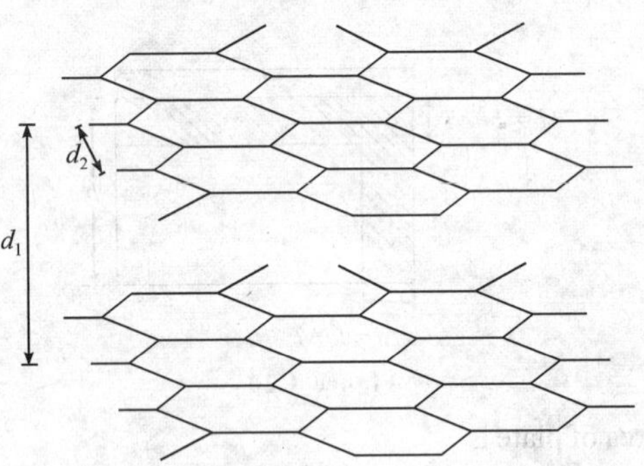

Figure 1.22

Thus when a solid expands uniformly in all three dimensions, this is called isotropic expansion of solid. In isotropic expansion the coefficient of linear expansion α remains same in all three dimension and thus the volume coefficient of thermal expansion can be written as

$$\gamma = 3\alpha \qquad \ldots(1.48)$$

When expansion of solid is different in the three dimensions due to atomic arrangement in solid lattice structure, this is termed as anisotropic expansion of solids. In anisotropic expansion the coefficient of linear expansion of solid is different in different dimensions of solid. For example in a piece of graphite if α_1 is the linear expansion coefficient in x and y direction (along the plane of carbon layers) and α_2 is the linear expansion coefficient in z direction (normal to graphite layers) then the coefficient of cubical expansion of solid is given as

$$\gamma = 2\alpha_1 + \alpha_2 \qquad \ldots(1.49)$$

Some times the value of α is different in all three dimensions in a solid say α_1, α_2 and α_3 then in that case the value of γ is given as

$$\gamma = \alpha_1 + \alpha_2 + \alpha_3 \qquad \ldots(1.50)$$

As we've observed the anisotropic expansion is due to the properties of a lattice structure in atomic arrangement, it can be seen only in solids not in liquids or gases.

Now we take some examples to discuss thermal expansion in detail.

Illustrative Example 1.15

A one litre closed flask contains some mercury. It is found that at different temperatures the volume of air inside the flask remains the same. What is the volume of mercury in flask ? Given coefficient of linear expansion of glass = $9 \times 10^{-6}\,°C^{-1}$. Coefficient of volume expansion of Hg = $1.8 \times 10^{-4}\,°C^{-1}$.

Solution

Here the volume of air in the flask remains the same. This is only possible when the expansion of flask is exactly the same as the expansion of mercury in the flask.

Here coefficient of cubical expansion of glass is

$$\gamma_g = 3\,\alpha = 3 \times 9 \times 10^{-6} = 27 \times 10^{-6}\,°C^{-1}$$

Here to keep the volume of air in flask constant, we have

Expansion of flask = Expansion of mercury

$$(1000)\gamma_g \Delta T = x \,.\, \gamma_m \Delta T$$

[Let x be the volume of mercury in the flask]

or $$x = V \,.\, \frac{\gamma_g}{\gamma_m}$$

$$= 1000 \times \frac{27 \times 10^{-6}}{1.8 \times 10^{-4}} = 150\ \text{cm}^3$$

Illustrative Example 1.16

A sphere of radius 3.5 cm and mass 250 gm floats in a liquid at 20ºC. As the temperature is raised, the sphere just begin to sink at a temperature of 35ºC. If the density of liquid at 0ºC is 1.527 gm/cm³, find the coefficient of cubical expansion of the liquid. Neglect expansion of the sphere.

Solution

It is given that at 20ºC, sphere is floating in liquid but at 35ºC it begins to sink as on increasing temperature liquid expands and its density decreases. At 35ºC, its density becomes equal to that of sphere and then the buoyancy force on sphere is just equal to the weight of sphere and it is fully submerged in the liquid.

Given that density of sphere is

$$\rho_s = \frac{m}{\frac{4}{3}\pi r^3}$$

$$= \frac{250}{\frac{4}{3} \times 3.14 \times (3.5)^3} = 1.396\ \text{gm/cm}^3$$

It is given that density of liquid at 0ºC is $\rho_0 = 1.527$ gm/cm³ if γ is the coefficient of cubical expansion of liquid then its density at 35ºC is given as

$$\rho_{35} = \frac{\rho_0}{1 + \gamma(35)}$$

At 35ºC, as sphere begins to sink, we have

density of sphere = density of liquid

$$1.396 = \frac{1.527}{1 + \gamma(35)}$$

[As sphere does not expand, its density remains constant.]

or $$\gamma = \left(\frac{1.527}{1.396} - 1\right) \times \frac{1}{35}$$

$$= 2.681 \times 10^{-3}\,°C^{-1}$$

Illustrative Example 1.17

A piece of metal weighs 46 gm in air. When it is immersed in a liquid of specific gravity 1.24 at 27 ºC, it weighs 30 gm. When the temperature of the liquid is raised to 42 ºC, the metal piece weighs 30.5 gm. The specific gravity of the liquid at 42 ºC is 1.20. Calculate the coefficient of linear expansion of the metal.

Solution

Here we first calculate the volume of the metal piece at 27 ºC as well as the volume of metal piece at 42 ºC. It is given that

Weight of the piece of metal in air = 46 gm

Weight of the piece of metal in liquid at 27 ºC = 30 gm

Thus loss of the weight of the piece of metal in liquid = 46 – 30 = 16 gm = weight of liquid displaced

Thus the volume of metal piece at 27ºC is

$$= \frac{\text{weight of liquid displaced}}{\text{density}} = \frac{16}{1.24}\ \text{cm}^3$$

$$V_1 = \frac{16}{1.24}\ \text{cm}^3$$

Similarly, the volume of the piece of metal at 42 °C can be calculated in the following way :

Weight of the piece of metal in air = 46 gm

Weight of the piece of metal in liquid at 42 °C = 30.5 gm

Loss of the weight of the piece of metal = 46 – 30.5 = 15.5 gm

Weight of the volume displaced of liquid at 42 °C = 15.5 gm
Now the volume of the liquid displaced

$$= \frac{\text{weight of the liquid displaced}}{\text{density}}$$

$$= \frac{15.5}{1.20}\ \text{cm}^3$$

Thus the volume of piece of metal at 42 °C

$$V_2 = \frac{15.5}{1.20}\ \text{cm}^3$$

Applying the formula $V_2 = V_1(1+\gamma\Delta T)$, we have

$$\frac{15.5}{1.20} = \frac{16}{1.24}(1+\gamma . 15) \qquad [\text{As } \Delta T = 42-27 = 15]$$

$$\Rightarrow \quad 1+15\gamma = \frac{15.5}{1.20} \times \frac{1.24}{16}$$

or $$\gamma = \frac{1}{15}\left[\frac{15.5}{1.20}\times\frac{1.24}{16} - 1\right] = \frac{1}{15}\times\frac{1}{960}$$

$$\Rightarrow \quad \alpha = \frac{1}{3\times 15\times 960} = 2.315\times 10^{-5}\ {}^{\circ}\text{C}^{-1}$$

Illustrative Example 1.18

A sinker of weight W_0 has an apparent weight W_1 when weighed in a liquid at a temperature T_1 and W_2 when weighed in the same liquid at a temperature T_2. The coefficient of cubical expansion of the material of the sinker is β. What is the coefficient of volume expansion of the liquid ?

Solution

Here, weight of sinker in air = W_0

Weight of sinker in liquid at temperature $T_1 = W_1$

Weight of sinker in liquid at temperature $T_2 = W_2$

(i) *At temperature T_1*

Loss of weight of the sinker in liquid = $W_0 - W_1$

Weight of the liquid displaced = $W_0 - W_1$

Volume of liquid displaced

$$V_{T_1} = \frac{\text{weight of liquid displaced}}{\text{density}}$$

$$V_{T_1} = \frac{(W_0 - W_1)}{d_1} \qquad \ldots(1.51)$$

Where d_1 is the density of the liquid at temperature T_1.

(ii) *At temperature T_2*

Similarly, we can calculate the volume of liquid displaced V_{T_2} at temperature T_2.

$$V_{T_2} = \frac{(W_0 - W_2)}{d_2} \qquad \ldots(1.52)$$

Where d_2 is the density of the liquid at temperature T_2

We know that

$$V_{T_2} = V_{T_1}[1+\gamma(T_2 - T_1)]$$

Where γ is the coefficient of cubical expansion of sinker

According to the given problem γ = β, thus

$$V_{T_2} = V_{T_1}[1+\beta(T_2 - T_1)] \qquad \ldots(1.53)$$

Substituting the value of V_{T_2} and V_{T_1}, we have

$$\left(\frac{(W_0 - W_2)}{d_2}\right) = \left(\frac{(W_0 - W_1)}{d_1}\right)[1+\beta(T_2 - T_1)] \qquad \ldots(1.54)$$

But $$\frac{d_1}{d_2} = \frac{M/V_{T_1}}{M/V_{T_2}} = \frac{V_{T_2}}{V_{T_1}} = \frac{V_{T_1}[1+\gamma_L(T_2 - T_1)]}{V_{T_1}}$$

or $$\frac{d_1}{d_2} = [1+\gamma_L(T_2 - T_1)] \qquad \ldots(1.55)$$

Where γ_L is the coefficient of cubical expansion of the liquid.

From equations-(1.54) and (1.55), we have

$$[1+\gamma_L(T_2 - T_1)] = \left(\frac{W_0 - W_1}{W_0 - W_2}\right)[1+\beta(T_2 - T_1)]$$

Solving we have

$$\gamma_L = \frac{(W_2 - W_1) + \beta(W_0 - W_1)(T_2 - T_1)}{(W_0 - W_2)(T_2 - T_1)}$$

Illustrative Example 1.19

A barometer reads 75 cm on a steel scale. The room temperature is 30ºC. The scale is correctly graduated for 0ºC. Find the correct atmospheric pressure. Given that coefficient of linear expansion of steel is $1.1 \times 10^{-5}\ ^\circ C^{-1}$ and that of cubical expansion of mercury is $1.8 \times 10^{-4}\ ^\circ C^{-1}$. Neglect expansion of glass tube.

Solution

For steel scale at 30ºC, length of 1 cm division will become

$$l_{1\text{ cm at }30^\circ C} = (1\text{ cm})\,[1 + \alpha_{st} \times (30)]$$

$$= 1 + 1.1 \times 10^{-5} \times 30$$

$$= 1.00033\text{ cm}$$

Thus actual length of mercury column at 30ºC will be

$$l_{Hg\text{ at }30^\circ C} = 1.00033 \times 75 = 75.02\text{ cm}$$

If area of cross section of capillary tube is A length of mercury column at 0ºC can be given as

$$l_{Hg\text{ at }30^\circ C} \times A = l_{Hg\text{ at }30^\circ C} \times A \times [1 + \gamma_{Hg}(30)]$$

[Given that A does not change with temperature]

or $$l_{Hg\text{ at }0^\circ C} = \frac{75.024}{(1 + 1.8 \times 10^{-4} \times 30)} = 74.62\text{ cm}$$

Atmospheric pressure is measured in terms of length of mercury column at 0ºC thus the correct barometric pressure is 74.62 cm.

Illustrative Example 1.20

A cylindrical Can can made up of aluminium contains 500 cm^3 of beer. The area of cross-section of Can is 125 cm^3 at 10ºC. Find the rise in level of beer if temperature of Can increases to 80ºC. Given that coefficients of linear expansion of aluminium is $\alpha_{Al} = 2.3 \times 10^{-5}\ ^\circ C^{-1}$ and that for cubical expansion of beer is $\gamma_{Beer} = 3.2 \times 10^{-4}\ ^\circ C^{-1}$.

Solution

It is given that at 10 ºC, volume of beer is 500 cm^3 and the area of cross section of Can is 125 cm^2. Thus height of bear level is

$$h = \frac{500}{125} = 4\text{ cm}$$

Now at 80º, volume of beer becomes

$$V_{80^\circ C} = 500\,(1 + \gamma_{Beer} \times 70)$$

$$= 500\,(1 + 3.2 \times 10^{-4} \times 70)$$

$$= 511.2\text{ cm}^3$$

At 80º, area of cross-section of Can becomes

$$A_{80^\circ C} = 125\,[1 + 2\alpha_{Al} \times 70]$$

$$= 125\,[1 + 2 \times 2.3 \times 10^{-5} \times 70]$$

$$= 125.402\text{ cm}^2$$

Thus new height of beer level at 80ºC is

$$h' = \frac{V_{80^\circ C}}{A_{80^\circ C}} = \frac{511.2}{125.402} = 4.076\text{ cm}$$

Thus rise in level of beer is

$$\Delta h = h' - h$$

$$= 4.076 - 4.0$$

$$= 0.076\text{ cm}$$

Illustrative Example 1.21

A steel ball initially at a pressure of 10^5 Pa is heated from 20ºC to 120ºC keeping its volume constant. Find the final pressure inside the ball. Given that coefficient of linear expansion of steel is $1.1 \times 10^{-5}\ ^\circ C^{-1}$ and Bulk modulus of steel is $1.6 \times 10^{11}\ N/m^2$.

Solution

On increasing temperature of ball by 100ºC (from 20ºC to 120ºC), the thermal expansion in its volume can be given as

$$\Delta V = \gamma_{st}\, V \Delta T$$

$$= 3\,\alpha_{st}\, V \Delta T \qquad \ldots(1.56)$$

Here it is given that no change is volume is allowed. This implies that the volume increment by thermal expansion is compressed elastically by external pressure. Thus elastic compression in the sphere must be equal to that given in equation-(1.56). Bulk modulus of a material is defined as

$$B = \frac{\text{increase in pressure}}{\text{volume strain}} = \frac{\Delta P}{\Delta V / V}$$

Here the externally applied pressure to keep the volume of ball constant is given as

$$\Delta P = B \times \frac{\Delta V}{V} = B\,(3\alpha_{st} \Delta T)$$

$$= 1.6 \times 10^{11} \times 3 \times 1.1 \times 10^{-5} \times 100$$

$$= 5.28 \times 10^{8}\ N/m^2$$

$$= 5.28 \times 10^{8}\ Pa$$

Thus this must be the excess pressure inside the ball at 120ºC to keep its volume constant during heating.

Web Reference at www.physicsgalaxy.com

Age Group - High School Physics | Age 17-19 Years
Section - HEAT & THERMODYNAMICS
Topic - Thermal Expansion & Thermometry
Module Numbers - 11 to 19

Practice Exercise 1.3

(i) In a mercury in glass thermometer the cross-section of the capillary is A_0 and volume of the bulb is V_0 at 0ºC. If mercury just fills the bulb at 0ºC, find that the length of mercury in the capillary at temperature t ºC. Given that β = coefficient of cubical expansion of mercury and α = coefficient of linear expansion of glass.

$[\frac{V_0(\beta-3\alpha)t}{A_0(1+2\alpha t)}]$

(ii) The volume of glass vessel is 1000 cc at 20°C. What volume of mercury in cc should be poured into it at this temperature so that the volume of the remaining space does not change with temperature. Coefficient of cubical expansion of mercury and glass are 1.8×10^{-4}/°C and 9.0×10^{-6}/°C respectively.

[50 cc]

(iii) Some steel balls are fixed at the bottom of a silica bulb of negligible expansivity. The bulb holds 340 gm of mercury at 0ºC when filled, in the absence of the steel balls and 255 gm of mercury, when the steel balls are inside. On heating the bulb and its contents (steel balls and mercury) to 100ºC, 4.8 gm of mercury overflows. Find the coefficient of linear expansion of steel. $\gamma_{Hg} = 180 \times 10^{-6}$ ºC^{-1}.

[11.76×10^{-6} ºC^{-1}]

(iv) If a liquid is contained in a long narrow rigid vessel so it an expand in essentially one direction only, show that the effective coefficient of linear expansion α of liquid is approximately equal to the coefficient of volume expansion β of liquid.

(v) In observing the real expansion of a liquid a certain part of glass vessel is to be filled with a liquid of volume expansion $\gamma = 18 \times 10^{-5}$ in order to exclude the effect of the change in remaining volume of the vessel during heating. What fraction of the vessel should be filled with the liquid ? The coefficient of linear expansion of glass is $\alpha = 9.0 \times 10^{-6}$.

[$3/20$]

(vi) A clock with a metallic pendulum gains 6 seconds each day when the temperature is 20°C and loses 6 second when the temperature is 40°C. Find the coefficient of linear expansion of the metal.

[$\alpha = 1.4 \times 10^{-5}$ ºC^{-1}]

(vii) The coefficient of apparent expansion of a liquid when determined using two different vessels A and B are γ_1 and γ_2 respectively. If the coefficient of linear expansion of the vessel A is α_1, Find the coefficient of linear expansion of the vessel B.

$[\frac{\gamma_1-\gamma_2+3\alpha_1}{3}]$

(viii) A solid whose volume does not change with temperature floats in a liquid. For two different temperatures T_1 and T_2 of the liquid, fractions f_1 and f_2 of the volume of the solid remain submerged in the liquid. Find the coefficient of volume expansion of the liquid.

$[\frac{f_2-f_1}{f_1T_2-f_2T_1}]$

(ix) A small quantity of a liquid which does not mix with water sinks to the bottom at 20ºC, the densities of the liquid and water at that temperature being 1021 and 998 kg m^{-3}, respectively. To what temperature must the mixture be uniformly heated in order that the liquid form globules which just float on water ? The coefficient of cubical expansion of the liquid and water over the temperature ranges are 85×10^{-5} ºC^{-1} and 45×10^{-5} ºC^{-1}, respectively.

[79.15ºC]

1.6 Calorimetry

The process of measurements of heat exchanges between bodies and system is known as calorimetry in early ages some chemists of the time found that when a hot object such as an iron ball, was immersed in a water bath, the resulting change in temperature of the water depend on both the mass and initial temperature of the ball. The temperature change was interpreted as a measure of the heat contained in the object. Further experiments showed that when two similar iron blocks at the same initial temperature were immersed in identical water baths, the more massive block caused a greater temperature change. Similarly for two identical blocks at different temperatures, the hotter block gave rise to a greater temperature change in the bath. Finally, for blocks of same mass and same initial temperature, the change in temperature of both was different for different materials. Thus the amount of heat supplied by a body depends on its mass, initial temperature and its material. Lets discuss the things in details and in scientific terms.

1.6.1 Specific Heat and Absorption of Heat

When heat is supplied to a substance it increases the energy of its molecule and hence its temperature increases. The rise in temperature of substance is proportional to heat supplied to it and also depends on the mass and material of the substance. If ΔQ is the amount of heat supplied to a body of mass m and due to this if its temperature increases by ΔT, then this heat supplied ΔQ and the rise in temperature ΔT are related as

$$\Delta Q = ms\Delta T \quad \ldots(1.57)$$

Where s is a constant for material of body known as specific heat of the material of body, from above expression in equation-(1.57), if m = 1 gm and $\Delta T = 1°C$ then $s = \Delta Q$ thus specific heat of a material is defined as "*the amount of heat for unit mass of a body to raise its temperature by 1°C.*" Thus material with a high specific heat requires a lot of heat to change its temperature, while a material with a low specific heat requires little heat to change its temperature. If an object cools, then the temperature change is taken negative and heat ΔQ is given by the object. The units of specific heat are cal/gm °C or J/kg °C. Specific heats of some common materials used in general life are given in the lists shown in table-1.1

Table -1.1

Substance	*Specific heat J/kg °C*	*Specific heat Cal/gm °C*
Water	4187	1.00
Ice	2090	0.50
Steam	2010	0.48
Wood	1700	0.40
Aluminium	900	0.215
Glass	840	0.200
Iron	448	0.107
Copper	390	0.092
Lead	128	0.0305

In the expression shown in equation-(1.57), the term *ms*, the product of mass of body and specific heat of its material is described as the heat capacity of the body which is the *amount of heat required to change an objects temperature by 1°C.* Thus bodies of the same material but of different masses have heat capacities proportional to their mass.

In most of the materials, with temperature their specific heat varies slightly but for short temperature ranges we can take it to a constant. All the specific heats given in Table -1.1 are at temperature 25°C.

1.6.2 Mechanical Equivalent of Heat

At the time of discovery of heat and temperature, the distinction between the two was not clear and the two were often confused. At that time it was generally taught that heat was some kind of fluid, which could be added to or taken away from a substance to make it hot or cold. We know that heat is a form of "Energy Transfer" that occurs when there is a temperature difference between objects. A common example of the distinction between heat and temperature is taken by comparing a candle flame and a warm hot water radiator in a cool room. The candle flame is at a much higher temperature then the radiator but we can not expect it to appreciably warm the room. Although the radiator is at much lower temperature then the candle but enough heat flows from it to keep the whole room warm. In both cases energy (Heat) is transferred from an object at a higher temperature to surrounding at a lower temperature.

In year 1842 Julius Mayer suggested that heat and mechanical work were equivalent and that one could be transformed into the other, he also showed that the temperature of water could be raised by 1°C or more by mechanical agitation alone. But he failed to determine the amount of work required for such a change.

The conclusive relation between heat flow and work was demonstrated by James Prescott Joule in 1843.

He demonstrated by his experiments that mechanical energy can be directly converted into thermal energy and he also measured the numerical factor relating mechanical units to thermal units. A common unit of energy was devised and given name in the honor of Joule's contribution to science. This unit joule is equal to roughly one fourth the size of calorie as

$$1 \text{ calorie} = 4.187 \text{ joules}$$

This relation is called "*Mechanical equivalent of heat*" and denoted by '*J*'. The calorie is not accepted unit of energy as SI units. The appropriated SI unit for energy is joule. But calorie is still used in several practical applications. Therefore we use both wants in our examples.

1.6.3 Water Equivalent of a Substance

Water equivalent of a substance is defined as the quantity of water which requires the same amount of heat which the substance requires for same rise in temperature. For example if a body of mass m and specific heat s is heated from temperature T_1 to T_2 then the amount of heat required for the purpose is

$$Q = ms(T_2 - T_1) \quad \ldots(1.58)$$

If m_ω is the mass of water which requires the same heat given in equation-(1.58), to range its temperature from T_1 to T_2 then we have

$$Q = ms(T_2 - T_1) = m_\omega s_\omega (T_2 - T_1)$$

or $$m_\omega = \frac{ms}{s_\omega} \quad \ldots(1.59)$$

Equation-(1.59) gives the water equivalent of the body. Now we take some examples to understand the heat flow and variation in temperature of different bodies.

Illustrative Example 1.22

A lead ball at 25°C is dropped from a height of 2 km. It is heated due to air resistance and it is assumed that all of its kinetic energy is used in increasing the temperature of ball. If specific heat of lead is s = 126 Joule/kg °C, find the final temperature of ball.

Solution

If there is no air resistance, velocity of ball on reaching ground is

$$V = \sqrt{2gh} = \sqrt{2 \times 10 \times 2000} = 200 \text{ m/s}$$

Kinetic energy of ball is

$$K = \frac{1}{2}mv^2$$

$$= \frac{1}{2} \times m \times (200)^2 = 2 \times 10^4 \times \text{m Joule}$$

[If mass m is in kg]

If all the kinetic energy is absorbed by the ball as heat and due to this temperature of ball is increased by ΔT, we have

$$K = ms\Delta T$$

or $$2 \times 10^4 \times m = m \times 126 \times \Delta T$$

or $$\Delta T = \frac{2 \times 10^4}{126} = 158.73\,°\text{C}$$

Illustrative Example 1.23

The temperature of equal masses of three different liquids A, B and C are 15°C, 20°C and 30°C respectively. When A and B are mixed, their equilibrium temperature is 18°C. When B and C are mixed, it is 22°C. What will be the equilibrium temperature when liquids A and C are mixed.

Solution

Let specific heats of liquids are s_A, s_B and s_C respectively. Then for mixing of liquids A and B, we have

heat lost by B = heat gained by A

or $$m \times s_B \times (20 - 18) = m \times s_A \times (18 - 15)$$

$$2s_B = 3s_A \quad \ldots(1.60)$$

For mixing of liquids B and C, we have

heat lost by C = heat gained by B

$$m \times s_C \times (30 - 22) = m \times s_B \times (22 - 20)$$

$$8s_C = 2s_B$$

or $$s_B = 4s_C \quad \ldots(1.61)$$

From equation-(1.60) and (1.61), we get

$$8s_C = 3s_A \quad \ldots(1.62)$$

Now if liquids A and C are mixed, let their equilibrium temperature in T_e then we have

Heat lost by C = heat gained by A

$$m \times s_C \times (30 - T_e) = m \times s_A \times (T_e - 15)$$

or $$\frac{3s_A}{8} \times (30 - T_e) = s_A \times (T_e - 15)$$

or $$90 - 3T_e = 8T_e - 120$$

or $$11T_e = 210$$

or $$T_e = \frac{210}{11} = 19.09\,°\text{C}$$

Illustrative Example 1.24

A metal block of density 5000 kg/m³ and mass 2 kg is suspended by a spring of force constant 200 Nt/m. The spring block system is submerged in a water vessel. Total mass of water in it is 300 g and in equilibrium the block is at a height 40 cm above the bottom of vessel. If the support is broken. Find the rise in temperature of water. Specific heat of the material of block is 250 J/kg K and that of water is 4200 J/kg K. Neglect the heat capacities of the vessel and the spring.

Solution

When the block is in equilibrium in the water and spring is stretched by a distance x and the spring force balances the effective weight of block i.e. weight of block minus the buoyant force on block. Thus for equilibrium of block in water, we have kx + weight of liquid displaced = weight of block

$$200\,x+\frac{2}{5000}\times 1000\times 10=2\times 10$$

or $$x=\frac{20-4}{200}=\frac{16}{200}=0.08\text{ m}=8\text{ cm}$$

Thus in equilibrium, energy stored in spring is

$$U=\frac{1}{2}kx^2$$

$$=\frac{1}{2}\times 200\times(0.08)^2=0.64\text{ Joule}$$

When the support is broken, the mass fall down to the bottom of vessel and the potential energy stored in spring and the gravitational potential energy of block is released and used in heating the water and block. Thus we have

$$0.64+mg\,(0.4)=m_\omega\times s_\omega\times\Delta T+m_B\times s_B\times\Delta T$$

or $$0.64+2\times 10\times 0.4=[0.3\times 4200+2\times 250]\,\Delta T$$

or $$\Delta T=\frac{8.64}{1760}=0.0049°\text{C}$$

Illustrative Example 1.25

A copper cube of mass 200 gm slides down on a rough inclined plane of inclination 37° at a constant speed. Assume that any loss in mechanical energy goes into the block as thermal energy. Find the increase in temperature of block as it slides down through 60 cm. Given that specific heat of copper is 420 J/kg.K.

Solution

As block slides at constant speed, friction on block exactly balances the gravitational pull on it, $mg\sin\theta$. Thus

$$f=mg\sin\theta=0.2\times 10\times\sin 37°$$

$$=2\times\frac{3}{5}=1.2\text{ N}$$

As block slides 60 cm distance, work done by it against friction is

$$W=f\cdot l$$

$$=1.2\times 0.6=0.72\text{ J}$$

This energy is only used in increasing the temperature of copper block, thus

$$0.72=m.s.\,\Delta T$$

or $$\Delta T=\frac{0.72}{ms}$$

$$=\frac{0.72}{0.2\times 420}=0.00857°\text{C}$$

Illustrative Example 1.26

A metal container of mass 500 gm contains 200 gm of water at 20°C. A block of iron also of mass 200 gm at 100°C is dropped into water. Find the equilibrium temperature of the water. Given that specific heats of metal of container and iron and that of water are 910 J/kg K, 470 J/kg K and 4200 J/kg K respectively.

Solution

Here container and water are at 20°C, thus when iron block is dropped into water it will loose energy to it and its temperature will fall. If equilibrium temperature is T_0, then we have

heat lost by iron block = heat gained by water plus container

$$m_i\times s_i\,(100-T_0)=m_\omega\times s_\omega\,(T_0-20)+m_c+s_c\,(T_0-20)$$

or $$T_0=\frac{m_is_i(100)+m_\omega s_\omega(20+m_cs_c(20)}{m_is_i+m_\omega s_\omega+m_cs_c}$$

$$=\frac{0.2\times 470\times 100+0.2\times 4200\times 20+0.5\times 910\times 20}{0.2\times 470+0.2\times 4200+0.5\times 910}$$

$$=\frac{9400+16800+9100}{94+840+455}$$

$$=\frac{35300}{1329}=26.56\,°\text{C}$$

Web Reference at www.physicsgalaxy.com
Age Group - High School Physics | Age 17-19 Years
Section - HEAT & THERMODYNAMICS
Topic - Calorimetry
Module Numbers - 1 to 6

Practice Exercise 1.4

(i) A can of water of volume 0.5 m^3 at a temperature 30°C is cooled to 15°C. Neglect heat capacity of the can. If the amount of heat released by water is used to lift a box of weight 10 kg, find the height to which it can be lifted. Given that specific heat of water is 4200 J/kg °C. Take $g=10$ m/s^2.

[3.15 × 10^5 m]

(ii) Equal masses of three liquids have temperatures 10°C, 25°C and 40°C respectively. If First two liquids are mixed, the mixture has a temperature of 15°C. If second and third are mixed, the equilibrium temperature is 30°C. Find the final temperature if first and third liquids are mixed.

[16°C]

(iii) A water heater can generate 8500 kcal/hr. How much water can it heat from 10°C to 60°C per hour ? Use specific heat of water 4200 J/kg°C.

[170 kg/hr]

(iv) When a 290 gm piece of iron at 180°C is placed in a 100 gm aluminium calorimeter cup containing 250 gm of glycerin at 10°C, the final temperature is observed to be 38°C. What is the specific heat of glycerin ? Use specific heat of iron 470 J/kg K and that of aluminium is 900 J/kg K.

[2405 J/kg K]

(v) The specific heat of many solids at low temperatures varies with absolute temperature T according to the relation $s = aT^3$, where a is a constant. Find the heat energy required to raise the temperature of a mass m of such a solid from 0 to 20K.

[4×10^4 *ma*]

(vi) A certain calorimeter has a water equivalent of 4.9 gm. That is, in heat exchanges, the calorimeter behaves like 4.9 gm of water. It contains 40 gm of oil at 50.0°C. When 100 gm of lead at 30.0°C is added, the final temperature is 48.0°C. What is the specific heat capacity of the oil ?
[Take $S_{water} = 1$ cal/gm°C, $S_{lead} = 0.305$ cal/gm°C]

[0.563 cal/gm°C]

1.6.4 Phase Transformation

When heat is supplied to a substance, its temperature increases and simultaneously the agitation (vibration energy) of its molecules also increases. If the substance is a solid, we have discussed that in a solid intermolecular forces are strong enough to make the position of molecule fixed in the lattice and the substance has a definite shape unlike to liquid or gases. When thermal agitation of molecules increases with rise in temperature, molecules start exerting an additional force onto each other and with temperature this force also increases. When temperature of a substance attains a value at which this force due to thermal agitation exceeds the cohesive force due to which molecules are bounded to each other, the molecules start becoming free and the heat energy due to which temperature of body was increasing will be now used in breaking the molecules from the lattice and further supply of heat will break more molecules from the lattice and this phenomenon is called melting of solid and during melting temperature of substance do not increase with further supply of heat. During melting supplied energy is used to break the bonds between molecules to melt the substance. Thus no temperature rise take place until the whole substance is melt. The amount of heat required to melt a given mass of a solid substance is measured in terms of Latent Heat which is characteristic property of a solid substance. It is defined as *the amount of heat required to melt a unit mass of solid*, denoted by L_f and termed as latent heat of fusion. If Q is the heat, which melt a mass m of a solid substance with latent heat of fusion L_f, then we have

$$Q = mL_f \qquad \ldots(1.63)$$

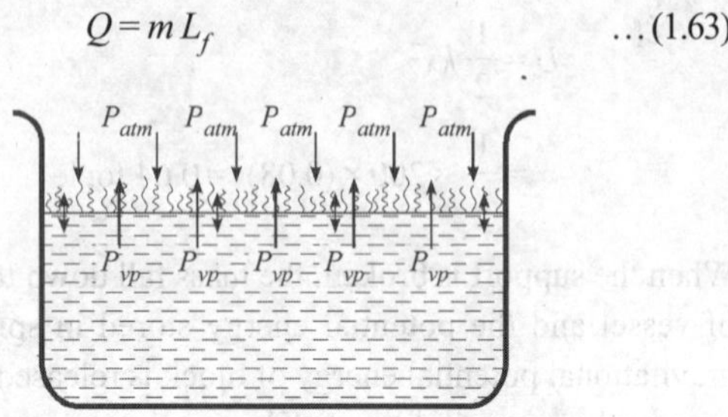

Figure 1.23

A similar phenomenon vaporization can also be defined, for transformation of a liquid to vapour. Figure-1.23 shows some liquid in a container, we have already discussed that at a temperature every molecule has some thermal agitation energy which is proportional to the absolute temperature of substance. Due to this, molecules on the surface of liquid are in continuous random oscillations as shown in figure-1.23. Some surface molecules randomly jumps in atmosphere from the surface but due to atmospheric pressure comes back to liquid surface. Due to thermal agitation the surface molecules repeatedly bounce from the surface and exert a pressure on atmosphere above the liquid surface, this pressure is called vapoure pressure of the liquid which is exerted by those molecules which leave the surface of liquid for a short time randomly and repeatedly which may be treated as the vapour of liquid for the time these are in air. This vapour just above the liquid surface exerts a upward pressure on atmospheric air molecules as shown in figure-1.23. As temperature of liquid increases, due to increase in thermal agitation its vapour pressure will also increase. When vapour pressure of liquid exceeds atmospheric pressure, liquid molecules start escaping from surface to atmospheric air. This is called vaporization of liquid. At this stage if heat is supplied to the liquid, its temperature would not increase and the amount of energy supplied is taken by molecules on liquid surface in vapourization. *The amount of heat required to vapourize unit mass of a liquid is called as latent heat of vapourization of the liquid* and is denoted by L_v. The amount of heat required to vapourize a liquid of mass m is

$$Q = mL_v \qquad \ldots(1.64)$$

To understand the application of latent heat of fusion and vapourization, we take few examples.

Illustrative Example 1.27

Find the result of mixing 0.5 kg ice at 0ºC with 2 kg water at 30ºC. Given that latent heat of ice is $L = 3.36 \times 10^5$ J kg^{-1} and specific heat of water is 4200 Joule kg^{-1} k^{-1}.

Solution

In such mixing problems, it is advisable to first convert all the phases of mixing substance into a single phase at a common temperature and keep the excess or required heat for this aside and finally supply or extract that amount of heat to get the final equilibrium temperature of the mixture.

As in this problem 0.5 kg of ice is given at 0ºC. To convert it into water at 0ºC if we require Q_1 amount of heat, the we have

$$Q_1 = -mL_f = -0.5 \times 3.36 \times 10^5$$

$$= -1.68 \times 10^5 \text{ Joule[– ve sign for heat required]}$$

The water 2 kg is available at 30ºC, to convert it into 0ºC, it release some heat say Q_2, then we have

$$Q_2 = ms\Delta T$$

$$= 2 \times 4200 \times 30 = 2.52 \times 10^5 \text{ Joule}$$

Thus we have the final mixture as

$$\text{Final mixture} = 2.5 \text{ kg water at } 0^\circ + 2.52 \times 10^5 \text{ J} - 1.68 \times 10^5 \text{ J}$$

$$= 2.5 \text{ kg water at } 0^\circ + 8.4 \times 10^4 \text{ J}$$

Thus finally we can supply the available heat to the 2.5 kg water at 0ºC to get the final temperature of mixture as

$$2.5 \times 4200 \times (T_g - 0) = 8.4 \times 10^4$$

or $$T_f = 8^\circ\text{C}$$

Thus final result is 8ºC of 2.5 kg water after mixing.

Illustrative Example 1.28

When 2 kg block of copper at 100ºC is put in an ice container with 0.75 kg of ice at 0ºC, find the equilibrium temperature and final composition of the mixture. Given that specific heat of copper is 378 J/kg K and that of water is 4200 J/kg K and the latent heat of fusion of ice is 3.36×10^5 J/kg.

Solution

Here in the given mixture initially we have

Mixture = 2 kg copper at 100ºC + 0.75 kg of ice at 0ºC

Now heat released by copper to attain 0ºC is

$$Q_1 = 2 \times 378 \times 100 = 7.56 \times 10^4 \text{ Joule}$$

Heat gained by ice to melt is

$$Q_2 = -0.75 \times 3.36 \times 10^5 = -25.2 \times 10^4 \text{ Joule}$$

Thus mixture contains

Mixture = 2 kg copper at 0ºC + 0.75 kg

water at 0ºC + 7.56×10^4 J – 25.2×10^4 J

= 2 kg copper at 0ºC + 0.75 kg water at 0ºC – 17.64×10^4 J

Here the available heat is negative which implies that whole ice will not melt here we can freeze the available water at 0ºC upto the extent when the available negative heat is balanced. 17.64×10^4 J heat is released when m mass of water is frozen thus m is given as

$$m = \frac{17.64 \times 10^4}{3.36 \times 10^5} = 0.525 \text{ kg}$$

Thus final mixture contains

Mixture = 2 kg copper at 0ºC + 0.525 kg

ice at 0ºC + 0.225 kg water at 0ºC

Thus it is obvious that the equilibrium temperature is 0ºC.

Illustrative Example 1.29

How should 1 kg of water at 50ºC is divided in two parts so that if one part is turned into ice at 0ºC, it would release sufficient amount of heat to vaporize the other part. Given that latent heat of fusion of ice is 3.36×10^5 J/kg, latent heat of vapourization of water is 22.5×10^5 J/kg and specific heat of water is 4200 J/kg K.

Solution

Let x kg of water is frozen then the amount of heat it releases is

$$Q_1 = x \times 4200 \times 50 + x \times 3.36 \times 10^5 \text{ Joule}$$

$$= x \times 5.46 \times 10^5 \text{ Joule}$$

The heat required to vapourize the $(1 - x)$ kg of water from 50ºC is

$$Q_2 = (1 - x) \times 22.5 \times 10^5$$

Here we've taken heat required to vapourize the water as only mass × latent heat of vapourization and not the heat required to first raise the temperature of $(1 - x)$ kg of water from 50º to 100º plus the mass × latent heat similar as when heat is supplied to water from an external source, it first reaches 100ºC then its vaporization starts but when heat is taken by water itself it vapourize (evaporation) at 50ºC as in this case. The similar case we see in our general life in cooling of water in a pitcher, drying of cloths hanging in open air etc.

Thus heat Q_2 must be provided by first part of water, we have

$$Q_2 = Q_1$$

$$(1-x) \times 22.5 \times 10^5 = x \times 5.46 \times 10^5$$

or $$22.5 - 22.5\,x = 5.46\,x$$

or $$x = \frac{22.5}{27.96} = 0.805 \text{ kg}$$

Illustrative Example 1.30

In a pitcher when water is filled some water comes to outer surface slowly through its porous walls and gets evaporated. Most of the latent heat needed for evaporation is taken from water inside and hence this water is cooled down. If 10 kg water is taken in the pitcher and 12 gm water comes out and evaporated per minute. Neglect heat transfer by convection and radiation to surrounding, find the time in which the temperature of water in pitcher decreases by 5°C.

Solution

It is given that 12 gm water is evaporated per minute, thus heat required per minute for it is

$$Q = mL_v$$

$$= 12 \times 540 = 6480 \text{ cal/min}$$

After time t, mass of inside water is

$$m = 10000 - 12\,t$$

If in further time dt, dm = 12 dt, mass is vapourized, and the temperature of inside water falls by dT, we have

$$(10000 - 12\,t) \times 1 \times dT = 12\,dt\,540$$

or $$dT = 12 \times 540 \frac{dt}{10000 - 12t}$$

Integrating the above expression in proper limits, we get,

$$\int_{T_0}^{T_0 - 5} dT = 12 \times 540 \times \int_0^t \frac{dt}{10000 - 12t}$$

$$5 = 540\, ln \left(\frac{10000}{10000 - 12t}\right)$$

or $$e^{5/540} = \frac{10000}{10000 - 12t}$$

or $$t = \frac{10000}{12}\,[e^{1/108} - 1]$$

$$= 7.737 \text{ minutes}$$

Alternative method

As here the amount of water vaporized is very small, we can assume that the quantity of water inside remains constant. Thus to reduce the temperature of inside water, amount of heat to be rejected is

$$Q = m^3\,\Delta T$$

$$= 10000 \times 1 \times 5$$

$$= 50{,}000 \text{ calories}$$

As obtained from the given data that 6480 calories of heat is required per minute to vapourize 12 gm water thus if in time t minutes, temperature of inside water falls by 5°C, we have

$$50000 = 6480\,t$$

or $$t = \frac{50000}{6480}$$

$$= 7.716 \text{ minutes}$$

Which is approximately same as obtained earlier. But students should note that this method will give the correct answer if the mass of inside water actually remains constant *i.e.* when the rate of evaporation is very very low.

Web Reference at www.physicsgalaxy.com

Age Group - High School Physics | Age 17-19 Years
Section - HEAT & THERMODYNAMICS
Topic - Calorimetry
Module Numbers - 7 to 11

Practice Exercise 1.5

(i) 5g ice at 0°C is mixed with 5g of steam at 100°C. What is the final temperature?

[100°C]

(ii) A block of ice of mass M = 50 kg slides on a horizontal surface. It starts with a speed v = 5.0 m/s and finally stops after moving a distance s = 30 m. What is the mass of ice that has melted due to friction between block and surface ? Latent heat of fusion of ice is L_f = 80 cal/g.

[1.86 g]

(iii) The temperature of a body rises by 44°C when a certain amount of heat is given to it. The same heat when supplied to 22 g of ice at – 8°C, raises its temperature to 16°C. Find the water equivalent of the body.
[Given : s_{water} = 1 cal/g°C & L_f = 80 cal/g, s_{ice} = 0.5 cal/g°C]

[50g]

(iv) In a mixture of 35 g of ice and 35 g of water in equilibrium, 4 gm steam is passed. The whole mixture is in a copper calorimeter of mass 50 g. Find the equilibrium temperature of the mixture. Given that specific heat of water is 4200 J/kgK and that of copper is 420 J/kgK and latent heat of fusion of ice is 3.36×10^5 J/kg and latent heat of vaporization of water is 2.25×10^6 J/kg.

[0°C, mixture = 3.22 g of ice + 70.78 g water]

(v) A lead bullet melts when stopped by a wall. Assuming that 25% of the energy is absorbed and distributed in the wall. Find the velocity of the bullet if its temperature first rises by 300K and then it melts. Given that the specific heat of lead is 0.03 cal/gm°C and latent heat of fusion of lead is 6000 cal/kg.

[409.87 m/s]

(vi) An aluminium container of mass 100 g contains 200 g of ice at – 20°C. Heat is added to the system at the rate 100 calories per second. What is temperature of the system after four minutes ? Specific heat of ice = 0.5 cal/g °C^{-1} and latent heat of fusion of ice = 80 cal/gm g and specific heat of aluminium is 0.215 cal/g °C^{-1}.

[27.08°C]

(vii) 1 kg of ice at 0°C is mixed with 1 kg of steam at 100°C. Find the equilibrium temperature and the final composition of the mixture. Given that latent heat of fusion of ice is 3.36×10^5 J/kg and latent heat of vaporization of water is 2.27×10^6 J/kg. Specific heat of water is 4200 J/kg°C^{-1}.

[100°C, mixture = 1335 g water + 665 g steam]

(viii) When a block of metal of specific heat 0.1 cal/g °C and weighing 110 gm is heated to 100°C and then quickly transferred to a calorimefer containing 200 g of liquid at 10°C, the resulting temperature is 18°C. On repeating the experiment with 400 g of same liquid in the same calorimeter at the same initial temperature, the resulting temperature is 14.5°C. Find :

(i) specific heat of the liquid

(ii) the water equivalent of the calorimeter.

[S_L = 0.481 cal g^{-1} °C^{-1}; W_c = 16.55 g]

(ix) A pitcher contains 10 kg of water at 20°C. Water comes to its outer surface through its porus walls and gets evaporated. The latent heat required for evaporation is taken from the water inside the pitcher, thus the inside water is cooled down. It is given that the rate of evaporation is 0.2 g/s. Calculate the time in which the temperature of the water inside drops to 15°C. Given that the specific heat of water is 4200 J/kg°C and latent heat of vaporization of water is 2.27×10^6 J/kg.

[Approx. 462 s]

(x) A pitcher contains 1 kg water at 40°C. It is given that the rate of evaporation of water from the surface of pitcher is 50 gm/s. Find the time it will take to cool down the water inside to 30°C. Given that latent heat of vaporization of water is 540 cal/g and specific heat of water is 1 cal/g °C.

[20 $(1 - e^{-1/54})$ s]

* * * * *

Discussion Question

Q1-1 Explain why some rubber-like substances contract with increase in temperature.

Q1-2 Two thermometers are constructed in the same way except that one has a spherical bulb and the other has a cylindrical bulb of same radius. Which one will respond faster to temperature changes.

Q1-3 Two large holes are cut in a metal sheet. If this sheet is heated, what will happen to the distance between the centres of the two holes.

Q1-4 A long metal rod is bent to form a ring with a small gap left between two ends of the rod. If this rod is heated what will happen to this gap.

Q1-5 Temperature of a body is increasing, is it necessarily absorbing heat.

Q1-6 Why a small gap is left between rails at the time of installation.

Q1-7 A tightened glass stopper can be taken out easily by pouring hot water around the neck of the bottle. Why it is so ?

Q1-8 "The coefficient of linear expansion is proportional to the heat capacity of a substance." Explain.

Q1-9 The latent heat of fusion of a substance is always less than the latent heat of vaporization or latent heat of sublimation of the same substance. Explain.

Q1-10 Equal quantities of a salt are dissolved in two identical vessels filled with water. In one vessel, the salt is in the form of powder and in other it is in form of a crystal of same mass. In which vessel will the temperature of the solution be higher after the salt is completely dissolved.

Q1-11 Does evaporation cause cooling. Explain.

Q1-12 Is boiling of a liquid is possible without suppling heat ?

Q1-13 Why an ice block melt at the bottom first ?

Q1-14 On a planet if there is no atmosphere can we find water on it ? Water vapour on it ?

Q1-15 In summers the air is hot than how fans are used in summer to produce a cooling effect ?

Q1-16 On moon if ice cubes are placed what will happen to it.

Q1-17 In summers water kept in a pitcher is cooler as compared to water kept in a brass vessel but in rainy season water kept in brass vessel is cooler as compared to that in pitcher. Why ?

Q1-18 Wet clothes dry faster on a winter day than on a summer day. Explain.

Q1-19 Why does fog generally disappears before noon ?

Q1-20 Why does it take longer to cook food in the mountains than in the plains ?

Q1-21 A flat uniform cylinder of lead floats in mercury at 0°C. Will the lead float higher or lower when the temperature is raised ?

Q1-22 The Pyrex glass is having very low coefficient of linear expansion. It is also used as a very good transparent heat resistor as compared to ordinary glass. Explain ?

Q1-23 Alcohol evaporates more quickly than water at room temperature. Why ?

Q1-24 The heating system such as radiators uses some substance with large specific heat like water. Explain.

Q1-25 Why does water in a steel container stay cooler if a cloth jacket surrounding the container is kept moist ?

Q1-26 Explain why burns caused by steam on the skin is more severe than that by boiling water.

Q1-27 A thermometer is laid out in direct sunlight. Does it measure the temperature of the air, or that of sun or what it measures ?

Q1-28 Thermometers sometimes contain red or blue liquid, which is often ethanol. What advantages and disadvantages does this have compared to mercury.

Q1-29 Coolants are used in automobiles to cool engine. What can you say about the specific heat of material used for coolant high or low.

Q1-30 Water coolers used to cool room by blowing air in room through a water soaked dry grass filter. How does this work. Would it work well in a high humidity climate ?

Q1-31 Why do frozen water pipes burst ?

Q1-32 Glasses containing alcoholic drinks sometimes form frost on the outside. How does this happen?

Q1-33 A solid material is supplied with heat at a constant rate. The temperature of the material is changing with the heat input as shown in figure-1.24. Study the graph carefully and answer the following questions :

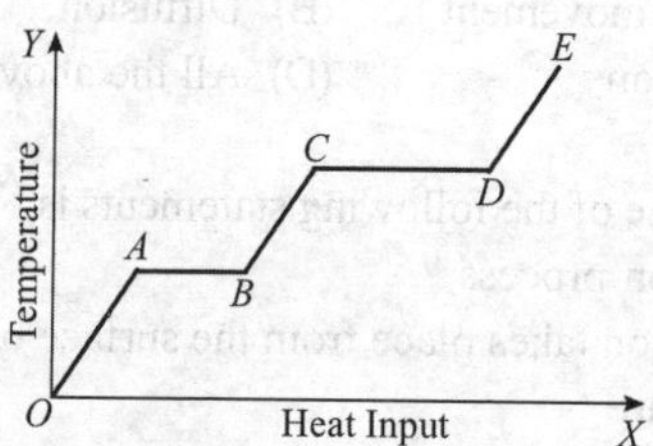

Figure 1.24

(i) What do the horizontal regions AC and CD represent ?

(ii) If $CD = 2\,BA$, what do you infer ?

(iii) What does slope DE represent ?

(iv) The slope of OA > the slope of BC. What does this indicate ?

* * * * *

Conceptual MCQs Single Option Correct

1-1 A vertical glass jar is filled with water at 10°C. It has one thermometer at the top and another at the bottom. The central region of the jar is gradually cooled. It is found that the bottom thermometer reads 4°C earlier than the top thermometer. And the top thermometer reads 0°C earlier than the bottom thermometer. This happens because :
(A) The top thermometer is faulty
(B) The bottom thermometer is faulty
(C) Density of water is maximum at 4°C
(D) Density of water is minimum at 0°C

1-2 Two spheres are made of same metal and have same mass. One is solid and the other is hollow. When heated to the same temperature, which of the following statements is correct about the percentage increase in their diameters ?
(A) It will be more for hollow sphere
(B) It will be more for solid sphere
(C) It will be same for both spheres
(D) It may be more or less depending on the ratio of the diameters of the two spheres

1-3 If water at 0°C, kept in a container with an open top, is placed in a large evacuated chamber :
(A) All the water will vaporize
(B) All the water will freeze
(C) Part of the water will vaporize and the rest will freeze
(D) Ice, water and water vapour will be formed and reach equilibrium at the triple point

1-4 What determines the ratio of specific heat capacity to molar heat capacity of a compound ?
(A) Universal gas constant
(B) Mass of the compound
(C) Molecular weight of the compound
(D) None of the above

1-5 A bimetal made of copper and iron strips welded together is straight at room temperature. It is held vertically in the hand so that iron strip is towards the left hand and copper strip is towards the right hand side. This bimetal is then heated by flame. Given that the coefficient of thermal expansion of copper if it is more than that of iron. The bimetal strip will :
(A) Remain straight (B) Bend towards right
(C) Bend towards left (D) No change

1-6 When a copper sphere is heated percentage change :
(A) Is maximum in radius
(B) Is maximum in area
(C) Is maximum in density
(D) Is equal in radius, area and density

1-7 A metal ball immersed in water weighs W_1 at 0°C and W_2 at 50°C. The coefficient of cubical expansion of metal is less than that of water. Then :
(A) $W_1 > W_2$ (B) $W_1 < W_2$
(C) $W_1 = W_2$ (D) Data is insufficient

1-8 Which of the following phenomena gives evidence of the molecular structure of matter ?
(A) Brownian movement (B) Diffusion
(C) Evaporation (D) All the above

1-9 Which one of the following statements is NOT true about the evaporation process ?
(A) Evaporation takes place from the surface of a liquid at all temperature
(B) The rate of evaporation depends upon the area of the exposed surface of the liquid, nature of the liquid and its temperature
(C) The rate of evaporation is independent of the pressure to which the liquid is subjected
(D) The cooling produced in evaporation is a consequence of the face that a liquid has latent heat

1-10 Two spheres of same metal have the same volume. But one is solid and the other is hollow. When the change in temperature of both of them is same, which of the following statements about the change in their diameters is true ?
(A) More for solid sphere (B) More for hollow sphere
(C) Same for both spheres (D) It cannot be predicted

1-11 A source of heat supplies heat at a constant rate to a solid cube. The variation of the temperature of the cube with heat supplied is shown in figure-1.25. The portion DE of the graph represents conversion of :

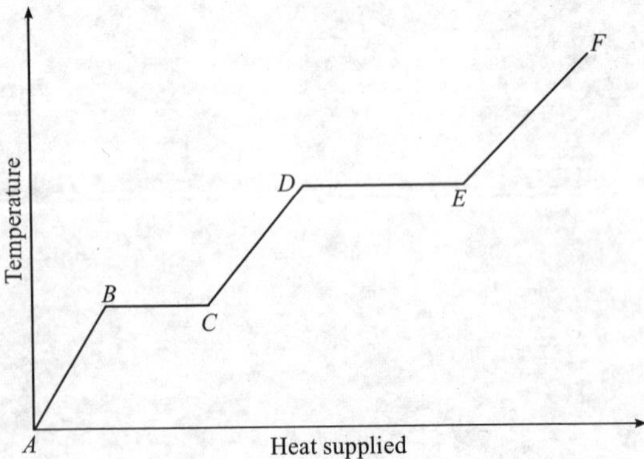

Figure 1.25

(A) Solid into liquid (B) Liquid into vapour
(C) Solid into vapour (D) Vapour into liquid

1-12 A bimetallic strip is made of two strips A and B, having co-efficient of linear expansion as α_A and α_B. If $\alpha_A > \alpha_B$, which of the following describes the behaviour of the metallic strip when heated ?

(A) It will bend but will not elongate

(B) It will bend the metal A s the outer side

(C) It will bend with metal B as the outer side

(D) It will bend only when

1-13 In a cylindrical glass container a solid silica cylinder is placed vertically at its bottom and remaining space is filled with mercury upto the top level of the silica cylinder as shown in the figure-1.26. Assume that the volume of the silica remains unchanged due to variation in temperature. The coefficient of cubical expansion of mercury is γ and coefficient of linear expansion of glass is α. If the top surface of silica and mercury level remain at the same level with the variation in temperature then the ratio of volume of silica to the volume of mercury is equal to :

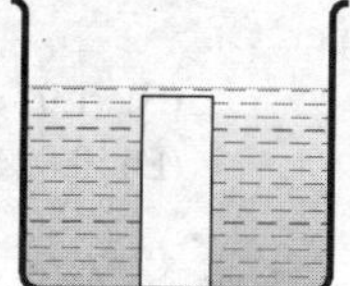

Figure 1.26

(A) $\frac{\gamma}{2\alpha}$ (B) $\frac{\gamma}{3\alpha}$

(C) $\frac{\gamma}{2\alpha}-1$ (D) $\frac{\gamma}{3\alpha}-1$

1-14 The heat (Q) supplied to a solid, which is otherwise thermally isolated from its surroundings, is plotted as a function of its absolute temperature, θ. It is found that they are related by the equation, $Q = a\theta^2 + b\theta^4$. ($a$, b are constants). The heat capacity of the solid is :

(A) $a\frac{\theta^3}{3}+b\frac{\theta^5}{5}$ (B) $a\theta + b\theta^3$

(C) $a\frac{\theta}{3}+b\frac{\theta^5}{5}$ (D) $2a\theta + 4b\theta^3$

1-15 The coefficient of linear expansion of an inhomogeneous rod changes linearly from α_1 to α_2 from one end to the other end of the rod. The effective coefficient of linear expansion of rod is :

(A) $\alpha_1 + \alpha_2$ (B) $\frac{\alpha_1+\alpha_2}{2}$

(C) $\sqrt{\alpha_1\alpha_2}$ (D) $\alpha_1 - \alpha_2$

1-16 A graph between the temperature read on the Celsius Scale and that on the Fahrenheit Scale, when plotted, gives the following :

(A)
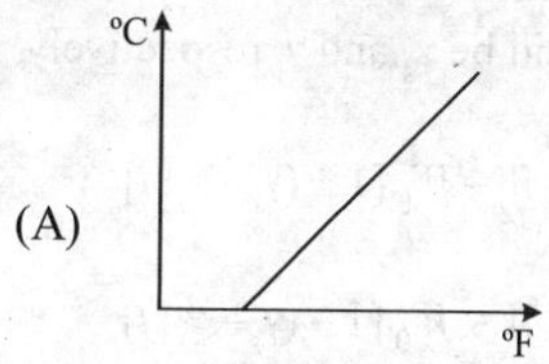

(B)
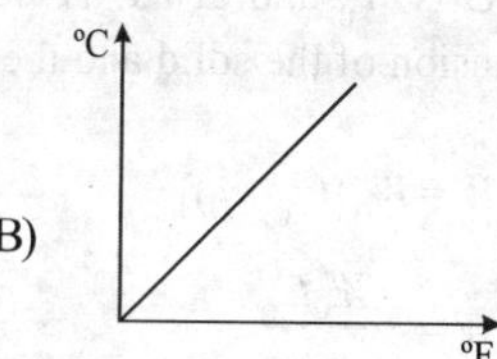

(C)
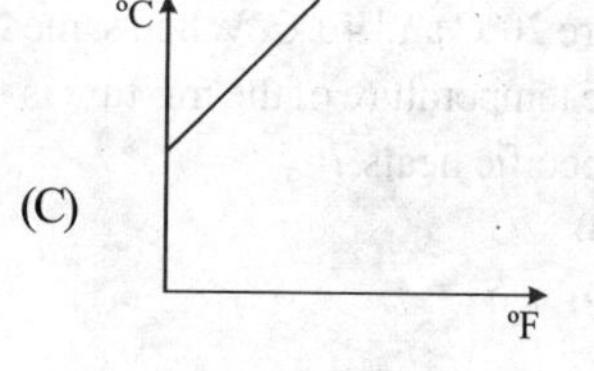

(D)
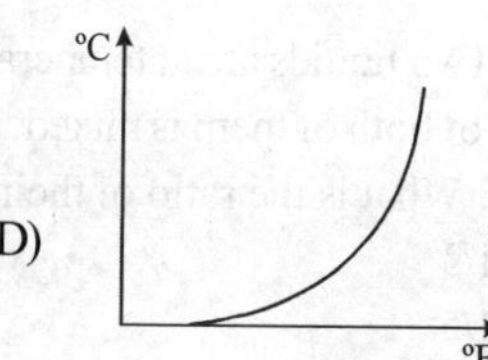

* * * * *

Numerical MCQs Single Options Correct

1-1 Two rods, one hollow and the other solid, made of the same material have the same length of 20 cm and radius of 2 cm. When their temperature is increased through the same amount of 50°C, their expansion ratio $E_h : E_s$ will be :

(A) 1 : 8 (B) 1 : 4
(C) 1 : 1 (D) 1 : 2

1-2 Two rods of lengths l_1 and l_2 are made of materials whose coefficients of linear expansion are α_1 and α_2 respectively. If the difference between the two lengths is independent of temperature, then :

(A) $\frac{l_1}{l_2} = \frac{\alpha_2}{\alpha_1}$ (B) $l_1^2 \alpha_2 = l_2^2 \alpha_1$
(C) $\frac{l_1}{l_2} = \frac{\alpha_1}{\alpha_2}$ (D) $\alpha_2^2 l_1 = \alpha_1^2 l_2$

1-3 The loss in weight of a solid when immersed in a liquid at 0°C is W_0 and at t°C is W. If the coefficients of volume expansion of the solid and the liquid be γ_s and γ_l respectively, then :

(A) $W = W_0 [(\gamma_s - \gamma_l)]$ (B) $W = W_0 [1 + (\gamma_s - \gamma_l) t]$
(C) $W = \frac{W_0 t}{\gamma_l - \gamma_s}$ (D) $W = W_0 [1 - (\gamma_s - \gamma_l) t]$

1-4 Two liquids are at temperature 20°C and 40°C. When same mass of both of them is mixed, the temperature of the mixture is 32°C. What is the ratio of their specific heats ?

(A) 1/3 (B) 2/3
(C) 1/5 (D) 2/5

1-5 The densities of two materials X and Y are in the ratio 1 : 3. Their specific heats are in the ratio 3 : 1. If we take same volumes of the two substances, the ratio of their thermal capacities will be :

(A) 1 : 1 (B) 1 : 3
(C) 1 : 6 (D) 1 : 9

1-6 Given that the specific heat in cal/g is $c = 0.6\, t^2$, where t is the temperature on the celsius scale. If the temperature of 10 g of water is raised through 15° C, what is the amount of heat required ?

(A) 60 cal (B) 200 cal
(C) 0.6 kcal (D) 6750 cal

1-7 A metallic container is completely filled with liquid. The coefficient of linear expansion of the metal is 2.0×10^{-6} per °C and the coefficient of cubical expansion of the liquid is 6.0×10^{-6} per °C. On heating the vessel :

(A) The liquid will overflow
(B) The level of the liquid will fall
(C) The level of the liquid will remain unchanged
(D) The level of liquid will rise or fall depending on the nature of the metal and of the liquid

1-8 At 40°C, a brass rod has a length 50 cm and a diameter 3.0 mm. it is joined to a steel rod of the same length and diameter at the same temperature. What is the change in the length of the composite rod when it is heated to 240°C ? The coefficients of linear expansion of brass and steel are 2.0×10^{-5} °C^{-1} and 1.2×10^{-5} °C^{-1} respectively :

(A) 0.28 cm (B) 0.30 cm
(C) 0.32 cm (D) 0.34 cm

1-9 A uniform solid brass sphere is rotating with angular speed ω_0 about a diameter. If its temperature is now increased by 100°C. What will be its new angular speed. (Given $\alpha_B = 2.0 \times 10^{-5}$ per° C)

(A) $1.1\, \omega_0$ (B) $1.01\, \omega_0$
(C) $0.996\, \omega_0$ (D) $0.824\, \omega_0$

1-10 An aluminium measuring rod, which is correct at 5°C measures the length of a line as 80 cm at 45°C. If thermal coefficient of linear expansion of aluminium is 2.50×10^{-5} per °C. The correct length of the line is :

(A) 80.08 cm (B) 79.92 cm
(C) 81.12 cm (D) 79.62 cm

1-11 A thin copper wire of length l increases in length by 1% when heated from 0°C to 100°C. If a thin copper plate of area $2l \times l$ is heated from 0°C to 100°C, the percentage increase in its area will be :

(A) 1% (B) 2%
(C) 3% (D) 4%

1-12 Which one of the following would raise the temperature of 20 gm of water at 30°C most when mixed with :

(A) 20 gm of water at 40°C (B) 40 gm of water at 35°C
(C) 10 gm of water at 50°C (D) 4 gm of water at 80°C

1-13 The lower and upper fixed points of a faulty thermometer are 5° and 99° respectively. If the reading of the thermometer is 52°, the temperature on the Fahrenheit scale is :

(A) 132°F (B) 122°F
(C) 154°F (D) 151°F

1-14 A constant volume gas thermometer shows pressure reading of 50 cm and 90 cm of mercury at 0°C and 100°C respectively. When the pressure reading is 60 cm of mercury, the temperature is :

(A) 25ºC (B) 40ºC
(C) 15ºC (D) 12.5ºC

1-15 The temperature of a body on Kelvin scale is found to be x K. When it is measured by a Fahrenheit thermometer, it is found to be xºF. Then x is :
(A) 301.25 (B) 588.45
(C) 313 (D) 40

1-16 A simple seconds pendulum is constructed out of a very thin string of thermal coefficient of linear expansion $\alpha = 20 \times 10^{-4}$ / °C and a heavy particle attached to one end. The free end of the string is suspended from the ceiling of an elevator at rest. The pendulum keeps correct time at 0°C. When the temperature rises to 50°C, the elevator operator of mass 60 kg being a student of Physics accelerates the elevator vertically, to have the pendulum correct time. The apparent weight of the operator when the pendulum keeps correct time at 50°C is. (Take $g = 10$ m/s^2)
(A) 600 N (B) 720 N
(C) 660 N (D) 330 N

1-17 The readings of air thermometer at 0°C and 100°C are 50 cm and 75 cm of mercury column respectively. The temperature at which its reading is 80 cm of mercury column is :
(A) 105ºC (B) 110ºC
(C) 115ºC (D) 120ºC

1-18 A wire of cross-sectional area A at temperature T is held taut with negligible tension between two rigid supports. If the wire is cooled to a temperature $(T - \Delta T)$, what tension is developed in the wire ? The coefficient of linear expansion is α and the Young's modulus of the wire is Y :

(A) $YA\alpha\Delta T$ (B) $\frac{Y\alpha\Delta T}{A}$

(C) $\frac{A\alpha\Delta T}{Y}$ (D) $\frac{YA}{\alpha\Delta T}$

1-19 A drilling machine of power P watts is used to drill a hole in copper block of mass M kg. If the specific heat of copper is s J kg^{-1} °C^{-1} and 40% of the power is lost due to heating of the machine, the rise in the temperature of the block in T seconds will be (in °C) :

(A) $\frac{0.6PT}{Ms}$ (B) $\frac{0.6P}{MsT}$

(C) $\frac{0.4PT}{Ms}$ (D) $\frac{0.4P}{MsT}$

1-20 A copper block of mass 2 kg is heated to a temperature of 500°C and then placed in a large block of ice at 0°C. What is the maximum amount of ice that can melt ? The specific heat of copper is 400 J kg^{-1} °C^{-1} and latent heat of fusion of water is 3.5×10^5 J kg^{-1} :

(A) $\frac{4}{3}$ kg (B) $\frac{6}{5}$ kg

(C) $\frac{8}{7}$ kg (D) $\frac{10}{9}$ kg

1-21 5 g of steam at 100°C is passed into 6 g of ice at 0°C. If the latent heats of steam and ice are 540 cal/g and 80 cal/g, then the final temperature is :
(A) 0ºC (B) 50ºC
(C) 30ºC (D) 100ºC

1-22 A water fall is 84 m high. Assuming that half the kinetic energy of falling water get converted to heat, the rise in temperature of water is :
(A) 0.098ºC (B) 0.98ºC
(C) 98ºC (D) 0.0098ºC

1-23 The density of a liquid of coefficient of cubical expansion γ is ρ at 0 °C. When the liquid is heated to a temperature T, the change in density will be :

(A) $-\frac{\rho\gamma T}{(1+\gamma T)}$ (B) $\frac{\rho\gamma T}{(1+\gamma T)}$

(C) $-\frac{\rho(1+\gamma T)}{\gamma T}$ (D) $\frac{\rho(1+\gamma T)}{\gamma T}$

1-24 Two rods of different materials having coefficients of thermal expansion α_1 and α_2 and Young's modulii Y_1 and Y_2 are fixed between two rigid and massive walls. The rods are heated to the same temperature. If there is no bending of the rods, the thermal stresses developed in them are equal provided :

(A) $\frac{Y_1}{Y_2} = \sqrt{\frac{\alpha_1}{\alpha_2}}$ (B) $\frac{Y_1}{Y_2} = \sqrt{\frac{\alpha_2}{\alpha_1}}$

(C) $\frac{Y_1}{Y_2} = \frac{\alpha_1}{\alpha_2}$ (D) $\frac{Y_1}{Y_2} = \frac{\alpha_2}{\alpha_1}$

1-25 A glass flask of volume 1000 cm^3 is completely filled with mercury at 0ºC. The co-efficient of cubical expansion of mercury is 182×10^{-6}/ °C and that of glass is 30×10^{-6}/ °C, how much mercury will over flow ? "When heated to 100°C."
(A) 30 cm^3 (B) 18.2 cm^3
(C) 15.2 cm^3 (D) 3 cm^2

1-26 The density of water at 20ºC is 998 kg m^{-3} and that at 40ºC is 992 kg m^{-3}. The co-efficient of cubical expansion of water is :

(A) $0.2 \times 10^{-4}\,°C^{-1}$ (B) $0.4 \times 10^{-4}\,°C^{-1}$
(C) $0.6 \times 10^{-4}\,°C^{-1}$ (D) None of the above

1-27 A metal ball-bearing of specific heat capacity c, moving with speed v, is brought to rest. All its kinetic energy is converted into thermal energy which it absorbs, causing a temperature rise $\Delta\theta$. What was the value of v :

(A) $\frac{1}{2}\, c\,\Delta\theta$ (B) $2\,c\,\Delta\theta$
(C) $\sqrt{c\,\Delta\theta}$ (D) $\sqrt{2c\,\Delta\theta}$

1-28 When x grams of steam is mixed with y grams of ice at 0°C, we obtain $(x + y)$ grams of water at 100°C. What is the ratio y/x ?
(A) 1 (B) 2
(C) 3 (D) 4

1-29 Heat required to convert 1 g of ice at 0°C into steam at 100°C is (Latent heat of steam = 536 cal g^{-1})
(A) 100 cal (B) 0.01 kcal
(C) 716 cal (D) 1 kcal

1-30 A piece of metal floats on mercury. The coefficients of volume expansion of the metal and mercury are γ_1 and γ_2 respectively. If their temperature is increased by ΔT, the fraction of the volume of metal submerged in mercury changes by a factor :

(A) $\left(\frac{1+\gamma_2\Delta T}{1+\gamma_1\Delta T}\right)$ (B) $\left(\frac{1+\gamma_2\Delta T}{1-\gamma_1\Delta T}\right)$

(C) $\left(\frac{1-\gamma_2\Delta T}{1+\gamma_1\Delta T}\right)$ (D) $\frac{\gamma_2}{\gamma_1}$

1-31 Heat required to melt 1 g of ice is 80 cal. A man melts 60 g of ice by chewing in one minute. His power is :
(A) 4800 W (B) 336 W
(C) 1.33 W (D) 0.75 W

1-32 A rod of length 20 cm made of a metal A expands by 0.075 cm wen its temperature is raised from 0°C to 100°C. Another rod of a different metal B having the same length expands by 0.045 cm for the same change in temperature. A third rod of the same length is composed of two parts, one of metal A and the other of metal B. This rod expands by 0.060 cm for the same change in temperature. The portion made of metal A has length :
(A) 20 cm (B) 10 cm
(C) 15 cm (D) 18 cm

1-33 When a metallic bar is heated from 0°C to 100°C, its length increases by 0.05%. What is the coefficient of linear expansion of the metal ?
(A) $5 \times 10^{-3}\,°C^{-1}$ (B) $5 \times 10^{-4}\,°C^{-1}$
(C) $5 \times 10^{-5}\,°C^{-1}$ (D) $5 \times 10^{-6}\,°C^{-1}$

1-34 In Q. No. 1-33 above, what is the percentage increase in the volume of the bar ?
(A) 0.1% (B) 0.15%
(C) 0.2% (D) 0.25%

1-35 A thin metal square plate has length l. When it is heated from 0°C to 100°C, its length increases by 1%. What is the percentage increase in the area of the plate ?
(A) 2.00% (B) 2.02%
(C) 2.03% (D) 2.01%

1-36 How many grams of ice at 0°C should be mixed with 240 g of water at 40°C so that the ice completely melts and the final temperature is of 0°C ?
(A) 120 g (B) 240 g
(C) 360 g (D) 480 g

1-37 Three liquids with masses m_1, m_2, m_3 are thoroughly mixed. If their specific heats are s_1, s_2, s_3 and their temperatures are θ_1, θ_2, θ_3 respectively, then the temperature of the mixture is :

(A) $\frac{s_1\theta_1 + s_2\theta_2 + s_3\theta_3}{m_1s_1 + m_2s_2 + m_3s_3}$ (B) $\frac{m_1s_1\theta_1 + m_2s_2\theta_2 + m_3s_3\theta_3}{m_1s_1 + m_2s_2 + m_3s_3}$

(C) $\frac{m_1\theta_1 + m_2\theta_2 + m_3\theta_3}{s_1\theta_1 + s_2\theta_2 + s_3\theta_3}$ (D) $\frac{m_1\theta_1 + m_2\theta_2 + m_3\theta_3}{s_1\theta_1 + s_2\theta_2 + s_3\theta_3}$

1-38 An electric kettle contains 1.5 kg of water at 100°C and is powered by a 2.0 kW electric element. If the thermostat of the kettle fails to operate, approximately how long will the kettle take to boil dry ? (Take the specific latent heat of vaporisation of water as 2000 kJ kg^{-1}) :
(A) 500 s (B) 1000 s
(C) 1500 s (D) 3000 s

1-39 Celsius and a Fahrenheit thermometer are put in hot water. The reading of the Fahrenheit thermometer is three times that of the Celsius thermometer. What is the reading of Fahrenheit thermometer ?
(A) 80/3 (B) 80
(C) 160/3 (D) 160

1-40 The fundamental interval, that is the number of divisions between *LFP* & *UFP* on the two scales X and Y are 50 and 150 respectively. The ice point on both the scales is at 0°. If the temperature on the X-scale is 15°, then what is the temperature on the Y-scale ?
(A) 30° (B) 45°
(C) 60° (D) 75°

1-41 A cylinder of diameter exactly 1 cm at 30°C is to be inserted into a hole in a steel plate. The hole has a diameter of 0.99967 cm at 30°C. If α for steel is $1.1 \times 10^{-5}\,°C^{-1}$, to what temperature must

the plate be heated ?

(A) 40°C (B) 50°C
(C) 60°C (D) 70°C

1-42 A linear accelerator consists of a hundred brass discs tightly fitted into a steel tube. At 40°C the diameter of each disc is 10.02 cm. The system is assembled by cooling the discs in dry ice at – 60°C to enable them to slide into the close fitting tube. If the coefficient of expansion of brass is 2×10^{-5} °C^{-1}, the diameter of each disc in dry ice will be :

(A) 9.94 cm (B) 9.96 cm
(C) 9.98 cm (D) 10.00 cm

1-43 At the top of the mountain the temperature is – 13°C and the barometer reads 68 cm of Hg. At the bottom the temperature is 27°C and the barometer reads 70 cm of Hg. What is the ratio of the densities of the air at the mountain to that at the sea level ?

(A) 1.03 (B) 1.12
(C) 1.15 (D) 1.24

1-44 A new scale of temperature called X-scale is defined with ice point as – 10°X and steam point as 90°X. What temperature on the X-scale will correspond to 40°C ?

(A) 20°X (B) 30°X
(C) 40°X (D) 50°X

1-45 300 g of water at 25°C is added to 100 g of ice at 0°C. The final temperature of the mixture is :

(A) $-\frac{5}{3}$°C (B) $-\frac{5}{2}$°C
(C) –5°C (D) 0°C

1-46 100 g of ice at 0°C is mixed with 100 g of water 80°C. The final temperature of the mixture will be :

(A) 0°C (B) 20°C
(C) 40°C (D) 60°C

1-47 Thermocouples are used to measure temperature in the linear parts of the emf versus temperature graph with cold junction at 0°C. The thermoelectric power of Pt, Ni thermocouple are – 4 and – 20 microvolt per °C respectively. What will be the magnitudes of emfs of the thermocouple when the cold junction is at 0° C and the hot junction is at 100°C ?

(A) 4mV (B) 2mV
(C) 3.2 mV (D) 1.6 mV

1-48 When a platinum resistance thermometer is put in contact with ice, steam and a liquid, the resistances of platinum wire recorded are 2.56 ohm, 3.56 ohm and 5.06 ohm respectively. The temperature of the liquid is :

(A) 100°C (B) 250°C
(C) 40°C (D) 25°C

1-49 When a Celsius thermometer reads 90°C, a faulty Fahrenheit thermometer reads 190°F. The correction to be made in the latter scale is :

(A) +2°F (B) – 2°F
(C) – 4°F (D) +4°F

1-50 The upper and lower fixed points of a faulty mercury thermometer are 210°F and 34°F respectively. What temperature read by this thermometer would be correct ?

(A) 22°F (B) 80°F
(C) 100°F (D) 122°F

1-51 Two straight metallic strips each of thickness t and length l are riveted together. Their coefficients of linear expansions are α_1 and α_2. If they are heated through temperature ΔT, the bimetallic strip will bend to form an arc of radius :

(A) $t/(\alpha_1 + \alpha_2)$ (B) $t/(\alpha_1 - \alpha_2)\,\Delta T$
(D) $t(\alpha_1 + \alpha_2)\,\Delta T$ (D) $t(\alpha_1 - \alpha_2)\,\Delta T$

1-52 A metal cube of length 10.0 mm at 0°C is heated to 200°C. Given : its coefficient of linear expansion is 2×10^{-5} K^{-1}. The percent change of its volume is :

(A) 0.1 (B) 0.2
(C) 0.4 (D) 1.2

1-53 Two thermometers x and y have fundamental intervals of 80° and 120°. When immersed in ice, they show the readings of 20° and 30°. If y measures the temperature of a body as 120°, the reading of x is :

(A) 55° (B) 65°
(C) 75° (D) 80°

1-54 Which of the following temperatures is the highest ?

(A) 100 K (B) – 13°F
(C) – 20°C (D) – 23°C

1-55 A difference of temperature of 25°C is equivalent to a difference of :

(A) 45°F (B) 72°F
(C) 32°F (D) 25°F

1-56 A thermometer has wrong calibration (of course at equal distances and the capillary is of uniform diameter). It reads the melting point of ice as – 10°C. It reads 60°C in place of 50°. The temperature of boiling point of water on this scale is :

(A) 100°C (B) 130°C
(C) 110°C (D) 120°C

1-57 A fixed mass of an ideal gas is maintained at constant volume. The pressure of the gas at the triple point of water is p_{tr}. What is the thermodynamic temperature of the gas when its

pressure is p ?

(A) $273.16\left(\frac{p_{tr}}{p}\right)$ K (B) $273.16\left(\frac{p}{p_{tr}}\right)$ K

(C) $273.16\left(\frac{p-P_{tr}}{p_{tr}}\right)$ K (D) $273.16\left(\frac{p-P_{tr}}{p}\right)$ K

1-58 A graph is plotted between the temperature of a copper cube in °C versus °F. The sine of the angle made by the graph with °F axis is :

(A) $\frac{2}{\sqrt{106}}$ (B) $\frac{3}{\sqrt{106}}$

(C) $\frac{4}{\sqrt{106}}$ (D) $\frac{5}{\sqrt{106}}$

1-59 At what temperature do the Kelvin and Reaumur scales agree ?

(A) 0° (B) 3°
(C) –9° (D) They never agree

1-60 The upper fixed point and lower fixed point of a thermometer are wrongly marked as 96°C and –2°C respectively. The reading of this thermometer is (correct thermometer reads 50°C):

(A) 37°C (B) 40°C
(C) 42°C (D) 47°C

1-61 The resistance of the platinum resistance thermometer at the triple point of water is 15.00 Ω and that when put inside the furnace is found to be 30.00 Ω. What is the temperature of the furnace ?

(A) 136.58 K (B) 273.16 K
(C) 409.74 K (D) 546.32 K

1-62 An iron metre rod is allowed an error of 1 part per million. If the coefficient of linear expansion of iron is 1×10^{-5}°C^{-1}, what is the maximum variation in temperature that the rod could have ?

(A) ±0.01 K (B) ±0.10 K
(C) ±1.00 K (D) ±10.0 K

1-63 On a hypothetical scale X, the ice point is 40° and the steam point is 120°. For another scale Y, the ice point and steam point are – 30° and 130° respectively. If X reads 50°, then Y would read :

(A) – 5° (B) – 8°
(C) – 10° (D) – 12°

1-64 A Fahrenheit thermometer reads 113°F while a faulty Celsius thermometer reads 44°C. The correction required to be applied to the Celsius thermometer is :

(A) – 1°C (B) + 1°C
(C) + 2°C (D) – 2°C

1-65 A steel scale measures the length of a copper rod as L cm when both are at 20°C, the calibration temperature for the scale. If the coefficients of linear expansion for steel and copper are α_s and α_c respectively, what would be the scale reading (in cm) when both are at 21°C ?

(A) $L\frac{(1+\alpha_c)}{(1+\alpha_s)}$ (B) $L\frac{\alpha_c}{\alpha_s}$

(C) $L\frac{\alpha_s}{\alpha_c}$ (D) L

1-66 If temperature of a pendulum clock changes from θ_1 to θ_2, the fractional change in the period of a pendulum clock is :

(A) $\frac{1}{2}\alpha(\theta_2-\theta_1)^2$ (B) $2\alpha(\theta_2-\theta_1)$

(C) $\frac{1}{2}\alpha(\theta_2-\theta_1)$ (D) $2\alpha(\theta_2-\theta_1)^2$

1-67 The density of a substance at 0°C is 10 g cm^{-3} and at 100°C, its density is 9.7 g cm^{-3}. The coefficient of linear expansion of substance is :

(A) 0.0001 °C^{-1} (B) 0.001 °C^{-1}
(C) 0.00001 °C^{-1} (D) 0.1 °C^{-1}

1-68 A sphere made of iron is rotating about its diameter as axis. $\alpha = 1 \times 10^{-5}$ °C^{-1}. If the temperature rises by 100°C, the percentage increase in its moment of inertia is :

(A) 0.1% (B) 0.2%
(C) 0.5% (D) 0.002%

1-69 A solid occupies 1000 cm^3 at 20°C. Its volume becomes 1016.2 cm^3 at 320°C. Coefficient of linear expansion of the material is :

(A) 18×10^{-6} °C^{-1} (B) 16×10^{-6} °C^{-1}
(C) 12×10^{-6} °C^{-1} (D) 36×10^{-6} °C^{-1}

1-70 A clock with a metal pendulum beating seconds keeps correct time at 0°C. If it loses 10 second a day at 20°C, the coefficient of linear expansion of metal of pendulum is :

(A) $\frac{1}{43200}$ °C^{-1} (B) $\frac{1}{86400}$ °C^{-1}

(C) $\frac{1}{64800}$ °C^{-1} (D) 16×10^{-6} °C^{-1}

1-71 A clock which keeps correct time at 25°C has a pendulum made of a metal. The temperature falls to 0°C. If the coefficient of linear expansion of the metal is 1.9×10^{-5} per °C, then number

of second the clock gains per day is :
(A) 10.25 s (B) 20.52 s
(C) 30.75 s (D) 41 s

1-72 A faulty thermometer has its fixed points marked 5° and 95°. This thermometer reads the temperature of a body as 59°. Then correct temperature on Celsius scale is :
(A) 59° (B) 48.6°
(C) 60° (D) 58°

1-73 At what temperature, the Fahrenheit and Celsius scales will give numerically equal (but opposite in sign) values :
(A) – 40° F and 40°C (B) 11.43° F and – 11.43°C
(C) – 11.43°F and +11.43°C (D) +40° F and – 40°C

1-74 0.93 watt-hour of energy is supplied to a block of ice weighing 10 g. It is found that :
(A) Half of the block melts
(B) The entire block melts and the water attains a temperature of 4°C
(C) The entire block just melts
(D) The block remains unchanged

1-75 The coefficient of linear expansion of iron is 0.000011°K. An iron rod is 10 metre long at 27°C. The length of the rod will be decreased by 1.1 mm when the temperature of the rod changes to :
(A) 0°C (B) 10°C
(C) 17°C (D) 20°C

1-76 A uniform metal rod of 2 mm^2 cross-section is heated from 0°C to 20°C. The coefficient of linear expansion of the rod is 12×10^{-6} per °C, Y = 10^{11} N/m^2. The energy stored per unit volume of the rod is :
(A) 1440 J/m^3 (B) 1500 J/m^3
(C) 2880 J/m^3 (D) 5760 J/m^3

1-77 A beaker contains 200 g of water. The heat capacity of beaker is equal to that of 20 g of water. The initial temperature of water in the beaker is 20°C. If 440 g of hot water at 92°C is poured in, the final temperature, neglecting radiation loss, will be :
(A) 58°C (B) 68°C
(C) 73°C (D) 78°C

1-78 A sphere of diameter 7 cm and mass 266.5 g floats in a bath of liquid. As the temperature is raised, the sphere is about to sink at 35°C. If the density of liquid is 1.527 g cm^{-3} at 0°C, the coefficient of cubical expansion of the liquid will be (neglect the expansion of sphere)
(A) 8.486×10^{-3} °C (B) 8.48×10^{-4} °C
(C) 8.486×10^{-5} °C (D) 8.486×10^{-6} °C

1-79 The real coefficient of volume expansion of glycerine is 0,000597 per °C and the linear coefficient of expansion of glass is 0.000009 per °C. Then the apparent volume coefficient of expansion of glycerine in glass will be :
(A) 0.000606 per °C (B) 0.000588 per °C
(C) 0.00057 per °C (D) 0.00027 per °C

1-80 10 g of ice at – 20°C is added to 10 g of water at 50°C. The amount of ice in the mixture at resulting temperature is (Specific heat of ice = 0.5 cal g^{-1} °C^{-1} and latent heat of ice = 80 cal g^{-1})
(A) 10 g (B) 5 g
(C) 0 g (D) 20 g

1-81 10 g of ice cubes at 0°C is released in a tumbler containing water (water equivalent 55 g) at 40°C. Assuming that negligible heat is taken from surroundings, the temperature of water in the tumbler becomes (L = 80 cal g^{-1}) :
(A) 31°C (B) 21.5°C
(C) 19°C (D) 15°C

1-82 Steam at 100°C is passed into 1.1 kg of water contained in a calorimeter of water equivalent 0.02 kg at 15°C, till the temperature of the calorimeter and its contents rises to 80°C. The mass of steam condensed (in kg) is (Take latent heat of steam = 540 cal g^{-1}) :
(A) 0.130 (B) 0.065
(C) 0.260 (D) 0.135

1-83 The temperature of equal masses of three different liquids A, B and C are 12°C, 19°C and 28°C respectively. The temperature when A and B are mixed is 16°C and when B and C are mixed is 23°C. The temperature when A and C are mixed is :
(A) 18.2°C (B) 20.3°
(C) 22.2°C (D) 24.2°C

1-84 Hailstone at 0°C falls from a height of 1 km on an insulating surface converting whole of its kinetic energy into heat. What part of it will melt ? (Given : g = 10 m s^{-2}) :
(A) $\frac{1}{33}$ (B) $\frac{1}{8}$
(C) $\frac{1}{33} \times 10^{-4}$ (D) All of it will melt

1-85 If the reading of the Reaumur scale is numerically less than that of Celsius scale by 3, then the reading of the Celsius scale is :
(A) 5° (B) 10°
(C) 15° (D) 20°

1-86 5 g of water at 30°C and 5 g of ice at –20°C are mixed together in a calorimeter. Neglect the water equivalent of the

calorimeter. The final temperature of the mixture is (Specific heat of ice = 0.5 cal $g^{-1}\,{}^{\circ}C^{-1}$)

(A) 0ºC (B) – 20ºC
(C) – 10ºC (D) + 1.2ºC

1-87 In Q. No. 1-86, the amount of ice melted is :

(A) 0 g (B) 0.25 g
(C) 0.50 g (D) 1.25 g

1-88 One gram of ice at 0ºC is added to 5 gram of water at 10ºC. If the latent heat of ice be 80 cal/g, then the final temperature of the mixture is :

(A) 5ºC (B) 0ºC
(C) – 5ºC (D) None of these

1-89 One gram of ice is mixed with one gram of steam. After thermal equilibrium, the temperature of the mixture is :

(A) 0ºC (B) 100ºC
(C) 55ºC (D) 80ºC

* * * * *

Advance MCQs with One or More Options Correct

1-1 Which of the following statements are not true ?
(A) Size of degree is smallest on Celsius scale
(B) Size of degree is smallest on Fahrenheit scale
(C) Size of degree is equal on Fahrenheit and Kelvin scale
(D) Size of degree is equal on Celsius and Kelvin scale

1-2 Which of the following statements are true ?
(A) Rubber contracts on heating
(B) Water expands on freezing
(C) Water contracts on heating from 0°C to 4°C
(D) Water expands on heating from 4°C to 100°C

1-3 A metallic circular disc having a circular hole at its centre rotates about an axis passing through its centre and perpendicular to its plane. When the disc is heated :
(A) Its angular speed will decrease
(B) Its diameter will decrease
(C) Its moment of inertia will increase
(D) Its angular speed will increase

1-4 Due to thermal expansion, with rise in temperature :
(A) Metallic scale reading becomes lesser than true value
(B) Pendulum clock becomes fast
(C) A floating body sinks a little more
(D) The weight of a body in a liquid increases

1-5 Two identical beakers are filled with water to the same level at 4°C. If one say A is heated while the other B is cooled, then :
(A) Water level in A will rise (B) Water level in B will rise
(C) Water level in A will fall (D) Water level in B will fall

1-6 Thermal capacity of a body depends on :
(A) The heat supplied
(B) The temperature raised of body
(C) The mass of the body
(D) The material of the body

1-7 Specific heat of a substance can be :
(A) Finite (B) Infinite
(C) Zero (D) Negative

1-8 When two samples of finite specific heats at different temperatures are mixed the temperature of the mixture may be :
(A) Lesser than lower or greater than higher temperature
(B) Equal to lower or higher temperature
(C) Greater than lower but lesser than higher temperature
(D) Average of lower and higher temperatures

1-9 Which of the following statements are true ?
(A) Water in a test tube can be made to boil by placing it in a bath of boiling water
(B) Heat cannot be stored in a body
(C) With increase in pressure melting point decreases
(D) Vapour can be directly converted into solid

1-10 A metal rod is shaped into a ring with a small gap. If this is heated :
(A) The length of the rod will increase
(B) The gap will decrease
(C) The gap will increase
(D) The diameter of the ring will increase in the same ratio as the length of the rod

1-11 Heat is supplied to a certain homogenous sample of matter, at a uniform rate. Its temperature is plotted against time, as shown. Which of the following conclusions can be drawn ?

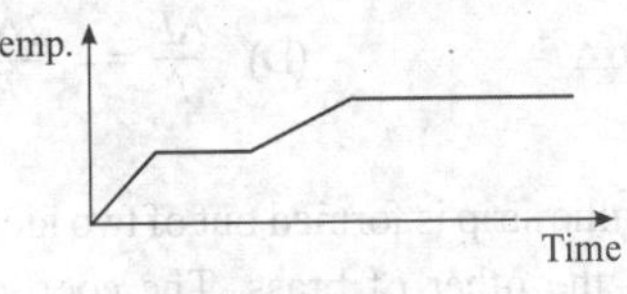

Figure 1.27

(A) Its specific heat capacity is greater in the solid state than in the liquid state
(B) Its specific heat capacity is greater in the liquid state than in the solid state
(C) Its latent heat of vaporization is greater than its latent heat of fusion
(D) Its latent heat of vaporization is smaller than its latent heat of fusion

1-12 Two rods of length L_1 and L_2 are made of materials of coefficients of linear expansions α_1 and α_2 respectively such that $L_1\alpha_1 = L_2\alpha_2$. The temperature of the rods is increased by ΔT and correspondingly the change in their respective lengths be ΔL_1 and ΔL_2:
(A) $\Delta L_1 \neq \Delta L_2$
(B) $\Delta L_1 = \Delta L_2$
(C) Difference in length $(L_1 - L_2)$ is a constant and is independent of rise of temperature
(D) Data is insufficient to arrive at a conclusion

1-13 A bimetallic strip is made up of two metals with different α :
(A) On heating, it bends towards the metal with high α
(B) On heating, it bends towards the metal with low α
(C) On cooling, it bends towards the metal with high α
(D) On cooling, it bends towards the metal with low α

1-14 A bolt is passed through a pipe and a nut is just tightened. Coefficients of linear expansion for bolt and pipe material are α_b and α_p respectively. If the assembly is heated then :

(A) A tensile stress will be induced in the bolt if $\alpha_b < \alpha_p$

(B) A compressive stress will be induced in the bolt if $\alpha_b < \alpha_p$

(C) A compressive stress will be induced in the bolt is $\alpha_b = \alpha_p$

(D) No stress will be induced in the bolt if $\alpha_b > \alpha_p$

1-15 A uniform cylinder of steel of mass M, radius R is placed on frictionless bearings and set to rotate about its vertical axis with angular velocity ω_0. After the cylinder has reached the specified state of rotation it is heated without any mechanical contact from temperature T_0 to $T_0 + \Delta T$. If $\frac{\Delta I}{I}$ is the fractional change in moment of inertia of the cylinder and $\frac{\Delta\omega}{\omega_0}$ be the fractional change in the angular velocity of the cylinder and α be the coefficient of linear expansion, then :

(A) $\frac{\Delta I}{I} = \frac{2\Delta R}{R}$ (B) $\frac{\Delta I}{I} = \frac{\Delta\omega}{\omega_0}$

(C) $\frac{\Delta\omega}{\omega_0} = -2\alpha\Delta T$ (D) $\frac{\Delta I}{I} = -\frac{2\Delta R}{R}$

1-16 A bimetallic strip is formed out of two identical strips one of copper and the other of brass. The coefficients of linear expansions of the two metals are α_C and α_B respectively. On heating, the temperature of the strip goes up by ΔT and the strip bends to form an arc of radius of curvature R. Then R is :

(A) Proportional to ΔT

(B) Inversely proportional to ΔT

(C) Proportional to $|\alpha_B - \alpha_C|$

(D) Inversely proportional to $|\alpha_B - \alpha_C|$

1-17 A body of mass m has gram specific heat c :

(A) Heat capacity of the body is mc

(B) Water equivalent of the body is m

(C) Water equivalent of the body is mc

(D) Heat capacity of the body is c

1-18 A thermos bottle contains coffee. The thermos bottle is vigorously shaken. Consider the coffee as the system. Choose the correct statement (s) :

(A) Its temperature would rise

(B) Heat has been added to it

(C) Work has been done on it

(D) Its internal energy has changed

1-19 When m gram of water at 100°C is mixed with m gram of ice at 0°C, which of the following statements are false ? Take specific heat of water 1 cal/gm°C and latent heat of ice is 80 cal/gm.

(A) The temperature of the system will be given by the equation $m \times 80 + m \times 1 \times (T - 0) = m \times 1 \times (100 - T)$

(B) Whole of ice will melt and temperature will be more than 0°C but lesser than 100°C

(C) Whole of ice will melt and temperature will be 10°C

(D) Whole of ice will not melt and temperature will be 0°C

1-20 The temperature of an isotropic cubical solid of length L, density d and coefficient of linear expansion α per degree Kelvin, is raised by 10°C. then, at this temperature, to a good approximation :

(A) Length is $L(1 + 10\alpha)$

(B) Total surface area is $L^2(1 + 20\alpha)$

(C) Density is $d(1 + 30\alpha)$

(D) Density is $d/(1 + 30\alpha)$

1-21 A metal sphere of radius R and specific heat C is rotated about an axis passing through its centre at a speed n rps. It is suddenly stopped and 50% of its energy is used in increasing its temperature, then choose the correct statement (s) from the following ?

(A) Kinetic energy used to raise the temperature of the sphere is $\frac{2\pi^2 n^2}{5} MR^2$

(B) Kinetic energy used to raise the temperature of the sphere is $\frac{5\pi^2 n}{3} MR$

(C) The rise in the temperature of the sphere is $\frac{4\pi^2 n^2 R^2}{5C}$

(D) The rise in the temperature of the sphere is $\frac{2\pi^2 n^2 R^2}{5C}$

1-22 5g of steam at 100°C is mixed with 10g of ice at 0°C. Choose correct alternative/s) : (Given s_{water} = 1 cal/g°C, L_F = 80 cal/g, L_V = 540 cal/g)

(A) Equilibrium temperature of mixture is 160°C

(B) Equilibrium temperature of mixture is 100°C

(C) At equilibrium, mixture contain $13\frac{1}{3}$ g of water

(D) At equilibrium, mixture contain $1\frac{2}{3}$ g of steam

1-23 The temperature of an isotropic cubical solid of length l_0, density ρ_0 and coefficient of linear expansion α is increased by 20°C. Then at higher temperature, to a good approximation :

(A) Length is $l_0(1+20\alpha)$

(B) Total surface area is $l_0^2(1 + 40\alpha)$

(C) Total volume is $l_0^3(1 + 60\alpha)$

(D) Density is $\frac{\rho_0}{1 + 60\alpha}$

1-24 In a pressure cooker the cooking is fast because :

(A) The boiling point of water is raised by the increased pressure inside the cooker

(B) The boiling point of water is lowered by pressure

(C) More steam is available to cook the food at 100°C

(D) None of these

1-25 There is a rectangular metal plate in which two cavities in the shape of rectangle and circle are made, as shown with dimensions. P and Q are centres of these cavities. On heating the plate, which of the following quantities increase ?

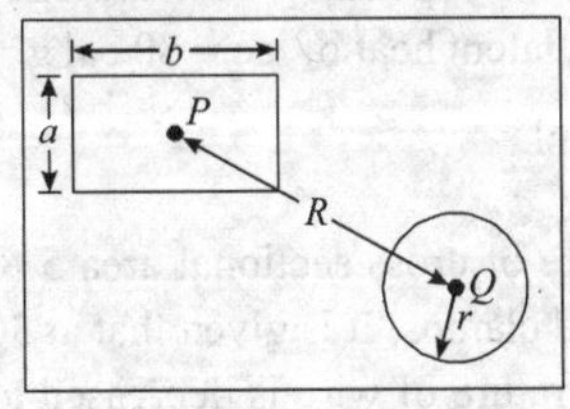

Figure 1.28

(A) πr^2 (B) ab

(C) R (D) b

1-26 A temperature T is measured by a constant volume gas thermometer :

(A) T is independent of the gas used for all pressures

(B) T is independent of the gas used only at low pressure

(C) The ideal gas scale agrees with the absolute scale of temperature

(D) The ideal gas scale does not agree with the absolute scale of temperature

* * * * *

Unsolved Numerical Problems for Preparation of NSEP, INPhO & IPhO

For detailed preparation of INPhO and IPhO students can refer advance study material on www.physicsgalaxy.com

1-1 In a vertical U-tube containing a liquid, the two arms are maintained at different temperatures, T_1 and T_2. The liquid columns in the two arms have heights l_1 and l_2 respectively as shown in figure-1.29. Find the coefficient of volume expansion of the liquid.

Figure 1.29

Ans. $\left[\dfrac{l_1 - l_2}{l_1(T_2 - T_1)}\right]$

1-2 How many kilograms of copper will experience the same temperature rise as 10 kg of water when the same amount of heat is absorbed ? ($s_{cu} = 0.09$ cal/g °C)

Ans. [1.11×10^2 kg]

1-3 If coal gives off 7000 kcal/kg when it is burnt, how much coal will be needed to heat a house that requires 4.2×10^7 kcal for the whole winter ? Assume that an additional 30 percent of the heat is lost up the chimney.

Ans. [7.8×10^3 kg]

1-4 How much water would have to evaporate from the skin per minute to take away all the heat generated by the basal metabolism (60 kcal/h) of a 65 kg person ?

Ans. [1.85 g/min]

1-5 During exercise, a person may give off 180 kcal of heat in 30 min by evaporation of water from the skin. How much water has been lost ? Given that latent heat of vaporization of water is 540 cal/gm.

Ans. [333.34 gm]

1-6 A 55.0 kg ice skater moving at 8.5 m/s glides to a stop. Assuming the ice is at 0°C and that 50 percent of the heat generated by friction is absorbed by the ice, how much ice melts ?

Ans. [2.95 gm]

1-7 The design of some physical instrument requires that there be a constant difference in length of 10 cm between an iron rod and a copper cylinder laid side by side at all temperature. Find their lengths. Given that coefficient of linear expansion of iron is 1.1×10^{-5} °C^{-1} and that of copper is 1.67×10^{-5} °C^{-1}.

Ans. [$l_1 = 29.4$ cm, $l_2 = 19.4$ cm]

1-8 A steel rod 25 cm long has a cross-sectional area of 0.8 cm^2. What force would be required to stretch this rod by the same amount as the expansion produced by heating it by 10°C ? Given that for steel coefficient of linear expansion and Young's modulus are given as $\alpha = 1.1 \times 10^{-5}$ °C^{-1} and $Y = 2 \times 10^{11}$ N m^{-2}

Ans. [1.76×10^3 N]

1-9 How should 1 kg of water at 5°C be divided into two parts so that if one part turned into ice at 0°C, it would release enough heat to vaporize the other part ? Latent heat of steam = 540 cal g^{-1} and latent heat of ice = 80 cal g^{-1}.

Ans. [864 g + 136 g]

1-10 A steel wire of cross sectional area 5×10^{-7} m^2 is tied between two rigid clamps. It is given that at 30°C, wire is just taut. If the temperature of wire is decreased to 10°C, find the tension in the wire. Given that the coefficient of linear expansion of steel is 1.1×10^{-5} °C^{-1} and its Young's modulus is 2×10^{11} N/m^2.

Ans. [30 N]

1-11 A box measured with a vernier caliper is found to be 180 mm long. The temperature during the measurement is 10°C. What will the measurement error be if the scale of the vernier caliper has been graduated at a temperature of 20°C ? The coefficient of linear expansion of the material of vernier = 11×10^{-6} °C^{-1}.

Ans. [0.0198 mm]

1-12 The brass scale of a mercury barometer has been graduated at 0°C. At 18°C the barometer shows a pressure of 760 mm. Reduce the reading of the barometer to 0°C. The coefficient of linear expansion of brass = 1.9×10^{-5} = 1 and the coefficient of volume expansion of mercury $\gamma = 1.8 \times 10^{-4}$ °C^{-1}.

Ans. [757.3 mm]

1-13 At 0°C, three metal rod form an equilateral triangle. Two rods are of the same material, but the third is made of invar (its expansion is negligible). When the triangle is heated upto 100°C, the angle formed between the two metal rods of the same material is $\dfrac{\pi}{3} - \theta$. Calculate the coefficient of linear expansion of the two metal rods in terms of θ.

Ans. [$\alpha = \dfrac{\sqrt{3}}{200}\theta$]

1-14 Calculate the percentage increase in the moment of inertia of a ring of iron. Given that $\alpha_{iron} = 11 \times 10^{-6}$ °C^{-1} and rise in temperature is 20°C.

Ans. [0.044%]

1-15 A gas heated geyser consumes $V_0 = 1.8\ m^3$ of methane (CH_4) in an hour. Find the temperature of the water heated by the geyser if the water flows out at the rate of $v = 50$ cm/s. The diameter of the stream $D = 1$ cm, the initial temperature of the water and the gas is $t_1 = 11°C$ and the calorific value of methane is $q_0 = 13$ kcal/g. The gas in the tube is under a pressure of 1.2 atm. The efficiency of the heater is $\eta = 60\%$.

Ans. [93°C]

1-16 A mixture of 250 g of water and 200 g of ice at 0°C is kept in a calorimeter which has a water equivalent of 50 g. If 200 g of steam at 100°C is passed through this mixture, calculate the final temperature and the weight of the contents of the calorimeter. Latent heat of fusion of ice = 80 cal/g and latent heat of vaporisation of = 540 cal/g.

Ans. [100°C, 572.2 g]

1-17 An earthenware vessel loses 1 g of water per second due to evaporation. The water equivalent of the vessel is 0.5 kg and the vessel contains 9.5 kg of water. Find the time required for the water in the vessel to cool to 28°C from 30°C. Neglect radiation losses. Latent heat of vaporisation of water in this range of temperature is 540 cal/g.

Ans. [≃ 37.5 sec]

1-18 A steel rule is calibrated at 22°C against a standard so that the distance between numbered divisions is 10.00 mm. (a) What is the distance between these divisions when the rule is at – 5°C ? (b) If a nominal length of 1 m is measured with the rule at this lower temperature, what percent error is made ? (c) What absolute error is made for a 100 m length ?
[$\alpha_{st} = 1.1 \times 10^{-5}\ °C^{-1}$]

Ans. [(a) 9.997 mm; (b) 3%; (c) 3 cm]

1-19 An iron cube floats in a bowl of liquid mercury at 0°C. (a) If the temperature is raised to 30°C, will the cube float higher or lower in the mercury ? (b) By what percent will the fraction of volume submerged change ?

Ans. [(a) More of the cube is submerged, (b) 0.54%]

1-20 A precise steel tape measure has been calibrated at 20°C. At 40°C, (a) will it read high or low, and (b) what will be the percentage error ?

Ans. [(a) low, (b) 0.024%]

1-21 An 18-g ice cube (at 0°C) is dropped into a glass containing 200 g of water at 25°C. If there is negligible heat exchange with the glass, what is the temperature after the ice melts ?

Ans. [16.33°C]

1-22 A bimetallic strip consists of two metal strips with different coefficients of linear expansion α_1 and α_2, each of small thickness d and length L_0 at T_0. They are bonded together and, with a change in temperature ΔT, will curve in a circular arc, as shown in figure-1.30. Show that the radius of curvature R is given approximately by

$$R = \frac{d}{(\alpha_2 - \alpha_1)\,\Delta T}$$

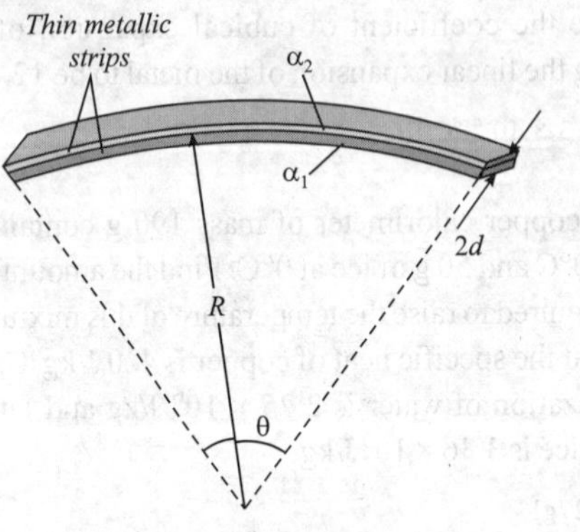

Figure 1.30

1-23 A thin smooth tube of length 2 m containing a small pallet of mercury in it is rapidly inverted 50 times. If capillary effect is neglected find the approximate increase in temperature of the mercury. Given that the specific heat of mercury is 30 cal/kgK.

Ans. [7.8°C]

1-24 From what height must a block of ice fall to just melt by the impact, if 50% of the heat generated is absorbed by the ice. Given that latent heat of fusion of ice is 80 cal/gm.

Ans. [68570 m]

1-25 A hole is drilled into a block of lead of mass 10 kg by a drill machine. The drill machine is operated at 30 rpm and the torque exerted by the electric motor on drill is 10 N-m. Calculate the rise in temperature of the lead block in 10 minutes. Given that specific heat of lead is 0.03 cal/gm°C and that of water is 1 cal/gm°C.

Ans. [14.96°C]

1-26 A mercury thermometer is to be made with glass tubing of internal bore 0.5 mm diameter and the distance between the fixed points is to be 20 cm. Estimate the volume of the bulb below the lower fixed point, given that the coefficient of cubical expansion of mercury is 0.00018 $°C^{-1}$ and the coefficient of linear expansion of glass is 0.000009 $°C^{-1}$

Ans. [2.57 cm^3]

1-27 A lump of ice of 0.1 kg at – 10°C is put in 0.15 kg of water at 20°C. How much water and ice will be found in the mixture when it has reached thermal equilibrium ? Specific heat of ice = 0.5 kcal kg^{-1} $°C^{-1}$ and its latent heat of melting = 80 kcal kg^{-1}.

Ans. [Final temperature is 0°C with 0.07 kg of ice and 0.18 kg of water]

1-28 A metallic bob weighs 50 g in air. If it is immersed in a liquid at a temperature of 25°C its weighs 45 g. When the temperature of the liquid is raised to 100°C, it weighs 45.1 g. Calculate the coefficient of cubical expansion of the liquid assuming the linear expansion of the metal to be $12 \times 10^{-6}\,°C^{-1}$.

Ans. [$\gamma_1 = 3 \times 10^{-4}\,°C^{-1}$]

1-29 A copper calorimeter of mass 190 g contains 300 g of water at 0°C and 50 g of ice at 0°C. Find the amount of steam at 100°C required to raise the temperature of this mixture by 10°C. Given that the specific heat of copper is 420 J/kg°C, latent heat of vaporization of water is 2.25×10^6 J/kg and latent heat of fusion of ice is 3.36×10^5 J/kg.

Ans. [12.27g]

1-30 Using a condenser coil 10 kg of water is to be heated from 20°C to 80°C per hour. For the purpose, steam at 150°C is passed from the condenser which is immersed in water and steam condenses in the coil and comes out at 90°C. Find the amount of steam required per hour for this purpose. Given that specific heat of water is 4200 J/kg°C and latent heat of steam is 2.25×10^6 J/kg.

Ans. [1 kg]

1-31 In the past, it was practice to measure temperature using so called 'weight thermometer' which consists of a glass sphere having a narrow flow-out tube. Such a certain weight thermometer is completely filled with 14.578 g of liquid at 15°C. It is found that 1.232 g of liquid overflows when the temperature is raised to 100°C. How much more liquid will overflow when the temperature is further raised to 200°C ?

Ans. [1.449 g]

1-32 A barometer having a brass scale reads 77.24 cm at a temperature of 20°C. The scale is graduated to be accurate at 0°C. What would be the reading at 0°C ? Coefficient of cubical expansion of mercury = $18 \times 10^{-5}\,°C^{-1}$ and linear expansion of brass = $19 \times 10^{-6}\,°C^{-1}$.

Ans. [76.99 cm]

1-33 A horizontal thin copper ring has a diameter exactly 1.00000 inch at temperature 0°C and is fixed to a non-conducting stand. An aluminium sphere of diameter exactly 1.00200 inch at 100°C is placed on the top of the ring. When the two attain temperature equilibrium, the sphere just passes through the ring. Assuming that the whole heat energy remains within the ring-sphere system, find :
($\alpha_{Cu} = 1.67 \times 10^{-5}\,°C^{-1}$; $\alpha_{Al} = 2.4 \times 10^{-5}\,°C^{-1}$)

(i) the final equilibrium temperature

(ii) the ratio of the mass of the ring to that of the sphere.

Ans. [57.14°C, 1.643]

1-34 Aniline is a liquid which does not mix with water. When a small quantity of it is poured into a beaker of water at 20°C, it sinks to the bottom. The densities of aniline and water at 20°C are 1021 kg m^{-3} and 998 kg m^{-3} respectively. Find the minimum temperature to which the mixture is to be heated so that aniline will form a globule and just starts floating. $\gamma_{aniline} = 85 \times 10^{-5}\,°C^{-1}$; $\gamma_{water} = 45 \times 10^{-5}\,°C^{-1}$.

Ans. [79.15°C]

1-35 During light activity, a 70 kg person may generate 200 kcal/hr. Assuming that 20 percent of this goes into useful work and the other 80 percent is converted to heat, calculate the temperature rise of the body after 1.00 if none of this heat is transferred to the environment. Assume specific heat of the human body is 450 cal/kg°C.

Ans. [5.08°C]

1-36 A "*makki ki roti*" has 100 kcal of thermal energy. What a man of 60 kg eats five such roti, how many meters can he climb by using this energy. Given that the working efficiency of man is 30% of the total energy gain by eating.

Ans. [1.072 km]

1-37 A copper calorimeter of negligible thermal capacity is filled with a liquid. The mass of the liquid is 250 gm. A heating element of negligible thermal capacity is immersed in the liquid. It is found that the temperature of the calorimeter and its contents rises from 25°C to 30°C in 5 minutes when a current of 2.05 A is passed through it at a potential difference of 5 volts. The liquid is thrown off and the heater is switched on again. It is now found that the temperature of the calorimeter alone remains constant at 32°C when the current through the heater is 0.7 A at the potential difference 6 volts. Calculate the specific heat capacity of the liquid. The temperature of the surrounding is 25°C.

Ans. [2100 J/kgK]

1-38 A long horizontal glass capillary tube open at both ends contains a mercury thread 1 m long at 0°C. Find its length at 100°C. A scale is etched (marked) on the glass tube. This scale is correct at 0°C. Find the length of the mercury thread, as read on this scale, at 100°C. Given that the coefficient of volume expansion of mercury is $1.8 \times 10^{-4}\,°C^{-1}$ and the coefficient of linear expansion of glass is $8.5 \times 10^{-6}\,°C^{-1}$.

Ans. [1.0154 m]

1-39 Ice of mass 600 g and at temperature – 10°C is placed into a copper vessel heated to 350°C. As a result, the vessel now contains 550 g ice mixed with water. Find the mass of the vessel. The specific heat of copper $c = 0.1$ cal/gm°C. Specific latent heat of ice = 80 cal g^{-1}, specific heat of ice = 0.5 cal/g°C.

Ans. [200 g]

1-40 A metal rod of length 5 m is placed on a smooth table. Given that Young's modulus of the material of the rod is 1.6×10^{11} N/m^2 and the its coefficient of linear expansion is 1.2×10^{-5} °C^{-1}. If temperature of rod is changed from 20°C to 80°C, find the elastic stress developed in the rod.

Ans. [0]

1-41 An ice block of volume 3.2×10^{-5} m^3 and at temperature 0°C is put in 200 gm water at 10°C. Find the temperature and composition of mixture when thermal equilibrium is attained. Given that density of ice is 900 kg/m^3, specific heat of water is 4200 J/kg°C and latent heat of fusion of ice is 3.4×10^5 J/kg.

Ans. [0°C, mixture = 4.1g ice + 224.7g water]

1-42 A body made up of an alloy (40% copper + 60% nickel) of mass 0.1 kg is placed in a container of water equivalent 10 gm which contains 90 g of water at 10°C. If the equilibrium temperature is 20°C, find the initial temperature of the body. Given that specific heat of water is 4200 J/kg°C and that of copper is 420 J/kg°C and that of nickel is 460 J/kg°C.

Ans. [114.6°C]

1-43 A block of 10 kg mass is thrown on a rough surface having friction coefficient 0.3 with an initial speed of 5 m/s. Find the amount by which the internal energy of the block and the surface will increase. If this block is seen from a frame moving at a speed of 5 m/s in the direction of its velocity then it is observed that the block is gently put on the rough surface moving in opposite direction at speed 5 m/s. Find the gain in kinetic energy of the block as seen from this frame.

Ans. [125J, 125J]

1-44 A glass container is filled with 500 g of water and 1 kg mercury. When 21200 cal of heat is given to it, 3.52 g of water overflows. Calculate the coefficient of volume expansion of mercury. Given that the coefficient of volume expansion of water is 1.5×10^{-4} °C^{-1}, relative density of mercury is 13.6 and specific heat of mercury is 0.03 cal/g °C^{-1} and that of water is 1 cal/g °C^{-1}. Neglect the expansion of glass.

Ans. [1.7×10^{4} °C^{-1}]

1-45 When a certain quantity of liquid bismuth at its melting point of 271°C is transferred to a calorimeter containing oil, the temperature of oil rises from 13.4°C to 28.5°C. When the experiment is repeated under identical conditions except that bismuth is in solid form, the temperature of oil rises to 19°C. If the specific heat of bismuth is 0.134 J g^{-1} °C^{-1}, find the latent heat of fusion of bismuth.

Ans. [58.56 J g^{-1}]

1-46 An iron plug is to be placed in a ring made of brass. At room temperature 28°C the diameter of the plug is 9.114 cm and that of the inside of the ring is 9.097 cm. To what common temperature these both be brought in order to fit ? Given that coefficient of linear expansion of iron is 1.1×10^{-5} °C^{-1} and that of brass is 1.9×10^{-5} °C^{-1}.

Ans. [262.2°C]

1-47 The 0.50 kg head of a hammer has a speed of 5.0 m/s just before it strikes a nail and is brought to rest. Estimate the temperature rise of a 15 g iron nail generated by ten such hammer blows done in quick succession. Assume the nail absorbs all the "*heat*."

Ans. [9.3°C]

1-48 Two metal spheres (10 kg and 30 kg) moving towards each other at speeds 10 m/s and 20 m/s respectively. They collide inelastically. What is the rise in temperature of the combined body after collision if all the energy lost appears in the form of heat. Given that specific heat of the metal of spheres is 0.03 cal/g°C.

Ans. [0.65°C]

1-49 A 25 g lead bullet traveling at 400 m/s passes through a thin iron wall and emerges at a speed of 250 m/s. If the bullet absorbs 50 percent of the heat generated, (a) what will be the temperature rise of the bullet ? (b) If the ambient temperature is 20°C, will the bullet melt, and if so, how much ? Given that specific heat of lead is 0.03 cal/gm°C and latent heat of fusion of lead is 6000 cal/kg. It is also given that melting point of lead is 320°C.

Ans. [194.38°C, No]

1-50 About 5 g water at 30°C and 5 g ice at – 20°C are mixed in a container of negligible heat capacity. Find the final temperature and composition of the mixture. Given that specific heat of water is 4200 J/kg°C and that of ice is 2100 J/kg°C and latent heat of ice is 3.36×10^5 J/kg.

Ans. [0°C, 3.75 g ice + 6.25 g water]

1-51 A brass pipe that is 10 cm in diameter and has a wall thickness of 0.25 cm carries steam at 100°C through a vat of circulating water at 20°C. How much heat is lost per meter of pipe in 1 s ?

Ans. [1.06 MJ]

1-52 (a) The tube of a mercury thermometer has an inside diameter of 0.120 mm. The bulb has a volume of 0.250 cm^3. How far will the thread of mercury move when the temperature changes from 10.0°C to 20.0°C ? Take into account expansion of the glass (Pyrex). (b) Determine a formula for the length of the mercury column in terms of relevant variables.

Ans. [(a) 3.78 cm; (b) (approx) $(\beta_{Hg} - \beta_{gl})\Delta T\, V_{bulb}/\pi r^2_{tube}$]

1-53 200 g of water and equal volume of another liquid of mass 250 g are placed in turn in the same calorimeter of mass 100 g and specific heat capacity 420 J/kgK. The liquids which are constantly stirred are found to cool from 60°C to 20°C in 3 minutes and 2 minutes 20 seconds, respectively. Find the specific heat capacity of the liquid. The temperature of the surroundings is 20°C.

Ans. [2576 J/kgK]

1-54 Figure-1.31 shows a wheel pivoted at its center in a water tank containing 1 kg water. A light string is wound on the shaft of the wheel and its other end is connected to a hanging block of mass 12 kg as shown. It is observed that the block falls slowly by a distance 0.7 m. Find the rise in temperature of the water. Also find the amount of heat supplied to the water. Given that the specific heat of water is 4200 J/kg°C and that of wheel is negligible.

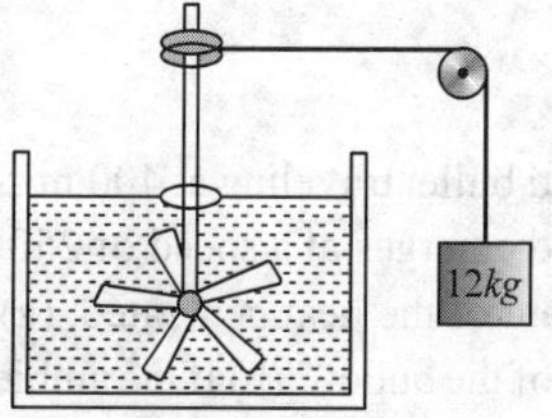

Figure 1.31

Ans. [0.02°C, 0]

1-55 0.6 kg of ice at – 10°C is place in a copper calorimeter at 350°C. After some time when thermal equilibrium is attained, calorimeter contains 550 g of ice with some water. Find the water equivalent of the calorimeter. Given that the specific heat of copper is 420 J/kgK, and that of ice is 2100 J/kg°C and latent heat of ice is 3.32 × 10^{-5} J/kg.

Ans. [83.42 g]

1-56 Two pendulum clocks, one having an iron pendulum and the other having a brass pendulum are keeping correct time at 5°C. How much per day will they differ at 25°C ? $\alpha_{iron} = 12 \times 10^{-6}\,°C^{-1}$, $\alpha_{brass} = 18.7 \times 10^{-6}\,°C^{-1}$.

Ans. [5.79 s]

1-57 A 12.4 kg solid iron cylindrical wheel of radius 0.45 m is rotating about its axle in frictionless bearings with angular velocity ω = 32.8 rad/s. If its temperature is now raised from 20°C to 80°C, what is the fractional change in ω ? Given that coefficient of linear expansion of iron is 1.1 × 10^{-5} °C^{-1}.

Ans. [1.32 × 10^{-3}]

1-58 When a man does exercise on a treadmill machine, work done by him is supplied in the form of heat to an ice bath. Find how much work he has to do to convert a piece of 5 gm of ice at –3°C to steam at 100°C. Given that the specific heat of ice is 0.5 cal/gm°C, latent heat of fusion of ice is 80 cal/gm and latent heat of vaporization of water is 540 cal/gm.

Ans. [15079.35 J]

1-59 A steel ball, of mass 10 g and specific heat 100 cal/kg°C, is pushed out after being heated inside a furnace. It is quickly caught inside a thick copper vessel of mass 200 g and relative specific heat 0.09 at 50°C and the vessel is dropped into a calorimeter of water equivalent 20 g containing 180 g of water at 20°C. The thermometer in the calorimeter shows a maximum temperature of 26°C. Calculate the temperature of the furnace and find by calculation whether there was any local boiling in the calorimeter.

Ans. [794°C]

1-60 At a temperature of 20°C, the volume of a certain glass flask, up to a reference mark on the cylindrical stem of the flask is exactly 100 cm^3. The flask is filled to this point with a liquid of coefficient of cubical expansion 120 × 10^{-5} °C^{-1}, when both the flask and the liquid are at 20°C. The cross-section of the stem is 1 mm^2 and the coefficient of linear expansion of glass is 8 × 10^{-6} °C^{-1}. Find the rise or fall of the liquid level in the stem, when the temperature is raised to 40°C.

Ans. [235.12 cm]

1-61 Find the final temperature and composition of the mixture of 1 kg of ice at 0°C and 1.5 kg of water at 45°C. Given that specific heat of water is 4200 J/kgK and latent heat of fusion of ice is 3.36 × 10^5 J/kg.

Ans. [0°C, mixture = 156.25 g ice + 2.343 kg of water]

1-62 A solid substance of mass 10 g at – 10°C was heated to – 2°C (still in the solid state). The heat required was 64 calories. Another 880 calories was required to raise the temperature of the substance (now in the liquid state) to 1°C, while 900 calories was required to raise the temperature from – 2°C to 3°C. Calculate the specific heat capacities of the substance in the solid and liquid state in calories per kilogram per kelvin.

Ans. [0.8 cal/g °C, 1 cal/g °C]

1-63 The volume of a mixture of ice and water is found to decrease by 1.25×10^{-7} m^3 without change in temperature when a small metal block of mass 10 gm and at temperature 100°C is put into it. The density of ice is 917 kg/m^3. Find the specific heat of the metal block.

Ans. [464 J/kgK]

1-64 Water in a fall falls through $h = 1.0$ km considering this as a thermodynamical process, calculate the difference in temperature of water at the top and bottom of the fall. Specific heat of water $c = 1000$ cal/kg°C and $J = 4.2$ J/cal.

Ans. [2.3°C]

1-65 A calorimeter of specific heat 0.42 J/gm°C and weighing 40 g contains 50 g of water mixed with 50 g of ice. Dry steam at 100°C is passed into the mixture until the temperature rises to 20°C. Find the mass of steam condensed.

Ans. [9.8 g]

1-66 How much steam at 100°C is needed to change 40 g of ice at – 10°C to water at 20°C if the ice is in a 50 g copper can ? Assume that the can maintains the same temperature as the ice and water. Given that specific heat of copper is $s_{Cu} = 0.09$ cal/gm °C and specific heat of ice is $s_{ice} = 0.5$ cal/gm °C.

Ans. [7.01 g]

1-67 A vertical, steel I-beam at the base of a building is 6.0 m tall, has a mass of 300 kg, and supports a load of 3.0×10^5 N. If the beam's temperature decreases by 4.0°C, calculate the change in its internal energy using the facts that for steel c_p is 0.11 kcal/kg °C and the coefficient of linear expansion is 11×10^{-6} °C^{-1}.

Ans. [– 5.5×10^5 J]

1-68 A heavy brass bar has projections at its ends as shown in the figure-1.32. Two fine steel wires, fastened between the projections, are just taut (zero tension) when the whole system is at 0°C. What is the tensile stress in the steel wires when the temperature of the system is raised to 300°C ? Make simplifying assumptions that you think are justified, but state what they are.

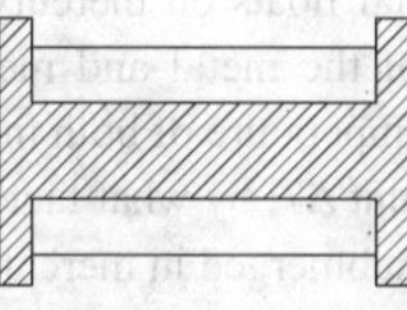

Figure 1.32

Given that

$$\alpha_{brass} = 20 \times 10^{-6}\,°C^{-1}$$

$$\alpha_{steel} = 12 \times 10^{-6}\,°C^{-1}$$

$$Y_{steel} = 2 \times 10^{11}\ \text{N m}^{-2}$$

Ans. [48×10^7 Nm^{-2}]

1-69 Find the final temperature and composition of the mixture of 1 kg of ice at – 10°C and 4.4 kg of water at 30°C. Given that specific heat of water is 4200 J/kg°C and that of ice is 2100 J/kg°C and latent heat of fusion of ice is 3.36×10^5 J/kg.

Ans. [mixture = 5.4 kg water at 8.7°C]

1-70 Suppose that 40 g of solid mercury at its freezing point (– 39°C) is dropped into a mixture of water and ice at 0°C. After equilibrium is achieved, the mercury – ice – water mixture is still at 0°C. How much additional ice is produced by the addition of the mercury ?

Ans. [2.04 g]

1-71 Some ice is put in a calorimeter. Determine the heat capacity of the calorimeter as 2.1 kJ of heat is required to heat it together with its contents form 270 K to 272 K, and 69.72 kJ of heat is required to raise its temperature of 272 K to 274 K. Latent heat of fusion of ice is 3.36×10^5 J/kg and specific heat capacity of ice is 2100 J/kg.

Ans. [630 J/K]

1-72 A steel drill making 180 revolutions per minute is used to drill a hole in a block of steel. The mass of the steel block and drill is 180 g. If the entire mechanical work is used up in producing heat and the rate of rise of temperature of the block is 0.5°C per second, find

(a) The rate of working of the drill in watts and

(b) The torque required to drive the drill.

(Specific heat of steel = 0.1 cal g^{-1} °C^{-1}).

Ans. [(a) 37.8 W; (b) 2 Nm]

1-73 A substance is in the solid form at 0°C. The amount of heat added to this substance and its temperature are plotted in the following graph.

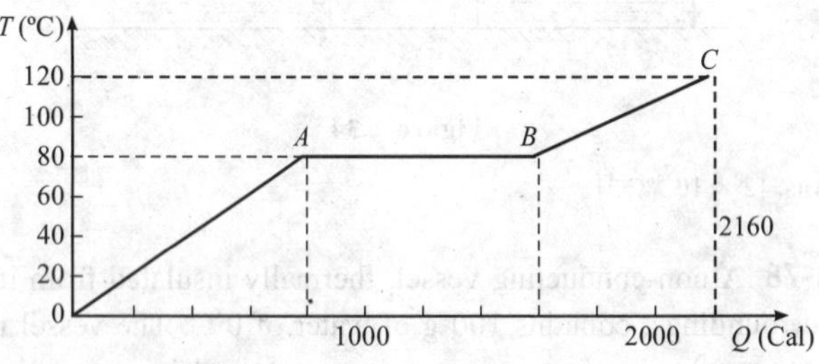

Figure 1.33

If the relative specific heat capacity of the solid substance is 0.5, find from the graph (i) the mass of the substance; (ii) the specific latent heat of the melting process, and (iii) the specific heat of the substance in the liquid state.

Ans. [(i) 0.02 kg, (ii) 4000 cal kg^{-1}, (iii) 700 cal kg^{-1} K^{-1}]

1-74 Steam at 100°C is passed into a calorimeter of water equivalent 10 mg containing 74 cc of water and 10 g of ice at 0°C. If the temperature of the calorimeter and its contents rises to 5°C, calculate the amount of steam passed. Latent heat of steam = 540 kcal/kg, latent heat of fusion = 80 kcal/kg.

Ans. [2 g]

1-75 An electron beam travelling at a speed of 10^7 m/s strikes a metal target and absorbed by it. If the mass of the target is 0.5 g and its specific heat is 100 cal/kg°C, find the rate at which its temperature rises. Given that the electron beam current is 0.048 A.

Ans. [65°C/s]

1-76 Some water at 0°C is placed in a large insulated enclosure (vessel). The water vapour formed is pumped out continuously. What fraction of the water will ultimately freeze, if the latent heat of vaporization is seven times the latent heat of fusion ?

Ans. [7/8]

1-77 The apparatus shown in the figure-1.34 consists of four glass columns connected by horizontal sections. The height of two central columns *B* and *C* are 49 cm each. The two outer columns *A* and *D* are open to atmosphere. *A* and *C* are maintained at a temperature of 95°C while the columns *B* and *D* are maintained at 5°C. The height of the liquid in *A* and *D* measured from the base line are 52.8 cm and 51 cm respectively. Determine the coefficient of cubical expansion of the liquid.

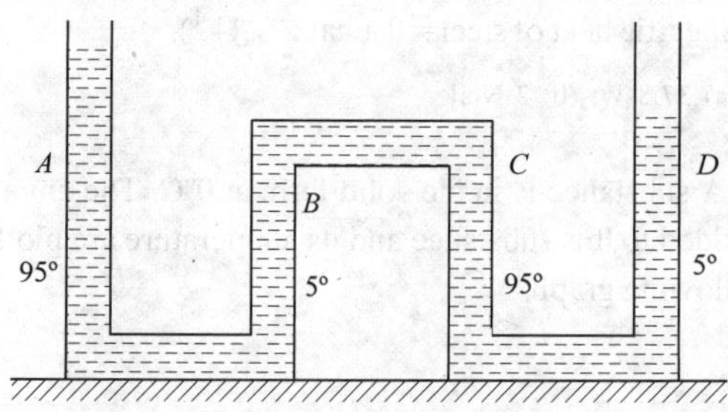

Figure 1.34

Ans. [2×10^{-4}°C^{-1}]

1-78 A non-conducting vessel, thermally insulated from its surroundings, contains 100 g of water of 0°C. The vessel is connected to a vacuum pump to pump out water vapour. As a result of this, some water is frozen. If the removal of water vapour is continued, what is the maximum amount of water that can be frozen in this manner ? Latent heat of vaporisation of water = 22.5×10^5 J kg^{-1} and latent heat of fusion of ice = 3.36×10^5 J kg^{-1}.

Ans. [87 g]

1-79 A mercury-in-glass thermometer has a stem of internal diameter 0.06 cm and contains 43 gm of mercury. The mercury thread expands by 10 cm when the temperature changes from 0°C to 50°C. Find the coefficient of cubical expansion of mercury. Relative density of mercury = 13.6 and $\alpha_{glass} = 9.0 \times 10^{-6}$ °C^{-1}.

Ans. [1.9×10^{-4}]

1-80 A loaded and completely sealed glass bulb weighs 156.25 gm in air at 15°C, 57.5 gm when completely immersed in a liquid at 15°C and 58.57 gm when completely immersed at 52°C. Calculate the mean coefficient of real expansion of the liquid between 15°C and 52°C. $\alpha_{glass} = 9 \times 10^{-6}$ °C^{-1}.

Ans. [32.335×10^{-5} °C^{-1}]

1-81 A certain amount of ice is supplied heat at a constant rate for 7 minutes. For the first 1 minute, the temperature rises uniformly with time, then it remains constant for the next 4 minutes and again rises at a uniform rate for the last 2 minutes. Explain qualitatively these observations and calculate the final temperature. L_f of ice = 336×10^3 J kg^{-1} and $s_{water} = 4200$ J kg^{-1} K^{-1}.

Ans. [40°C]

1-82 Two cylinders of equal masses, one made of aluminium and the other of copper, with their lateral surfaces thermally insulated, are heated to 50°C and placed on two large blocks of ice at 0°C. If both the cylinders have the same height, find the ratio of their depths of penetration in the ice. Assume that no heat is lost to the surroundings. Given that

$$s_{Al} = 0.22 \text{ cal gm}^{-1}\,°\text{C}^{-1},\ \rho_{Al} = 2.7 \text{ gm cm}^{-3}$$

$$s_{Cu} = 0.1 \text{ cal gm}^{-1}\,°\text{C}^{-1},\ \rho_{Cu} = 8.9 \text{ gm cm}^{-3}$$

Ans. [$\frac{1}{1.498}$]

1-83 A piece of metal floats on mercury. The coefficient of volume expansion of the metal and mercury are γ_1 and γ_2 respectively. If the temperature of both mercury and metal are increased by an amount ΔT, by what factor the fraction of the volume of the metal submerged in mercury changes?

Ans. [$(\gamma_2 - \gamma_1)\,\Delta T$]

* * * * *

Kinetic Theory of Gases and Gas Laws 2

FEW WORDS FOR STUDENTS

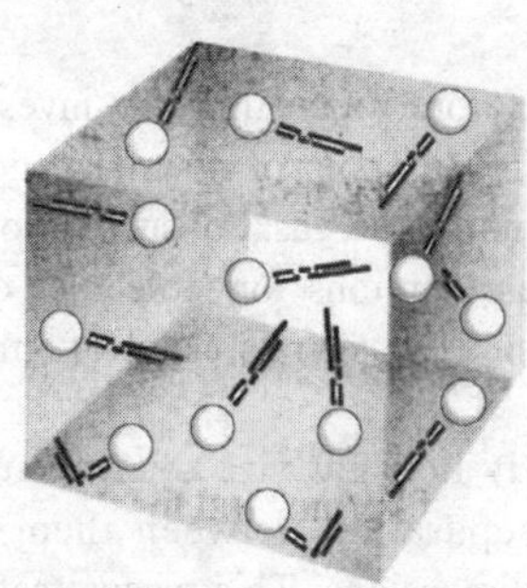

In this chapter we'll discuss about the general behaviour of gases. We use the basic ideas that we've discussed in previous chapter and some concept of mechanics to understand the gas behaviour. Mainly how a gas exerts pressure and its relation with volume and temperature of gas and the total energy possessed by gas and its relation to the temperature of gas.

CHAPTER CONTENTS

2.1 *Postulates of Kinetic Theory of Gases*

2.2 *Gas Laws*

2.3 *Pressure of Air*

2.4 *Distribution of Molecular Speeds*

2.5 *Pressure Exerted by a Gas*

2.6 *Kinetic Energy of Gas Molecules*

2.7 *Microscopic Interpretation of Temperature*

2.8 *Degrees of Freedom and Equipartition of Energy*

2.9 *Internal Energy of a Gas*

2.10 *Path of Molecules and Mean Free Path*

2.11 *Vander Walls Gas Equation*

2.12 *Diffusion*

COVER APPLICATION

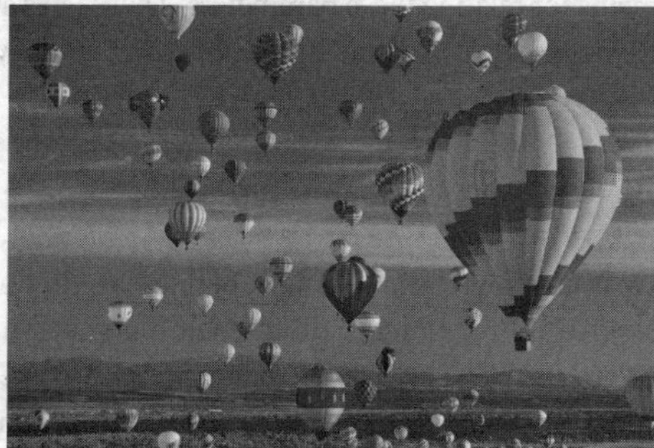

Figure (a)

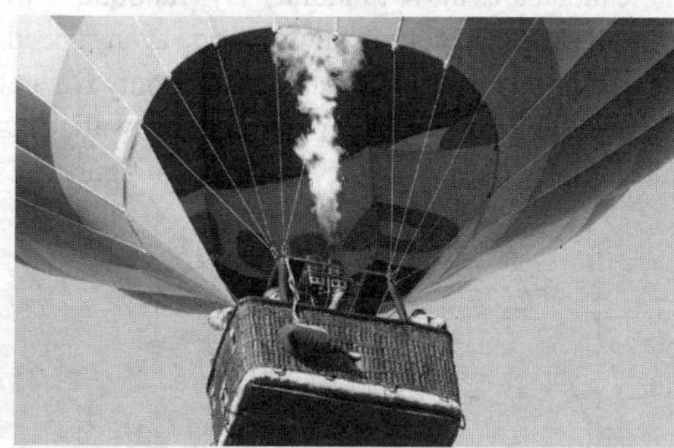

Figure (b)

Warmer air rises in cooler air is the basis of how hot air balloon works. This is because hot air is lighter than cool air as it has lower density. The actual balloon (called an envelope) has to be so large as it can take a large amount of heated air to lift it off the ground. For example, to lift 1000 pounds worth of weight you would need almost 65,000 cubic feet of heated air! To help keep the balloon in the air and rising, hot air needs to be propelled upwards into the envelope using the burner (see separate section on burners for more information.)

In this chapter, mainly we'll deal with the behaviour of gases. In fact a gas is composed of large number of molecules in random motion. Characteristics of a gas depends on the properties of the motion of these molecules. The analysis of a gas at such a microscopic level is called kinetic theory of gases.

2.1 Postulates of Kinetic Theory of Gases

Before proceeding for investigations on properties of a gas from the point of view of kinetic theory, we first define an idealized model of a gas. For such a model of an ideal gas we make some assumptions for molecules of a gas. These assumptions are called basic postulates of kinetic theory of gases. These are :

(i) In a gas size of molecules is negligible or the average separation between them is large compared with their dimensions. This means that the volume of the molecules is negligible when compared with the volume of the container.

(ii) Each molecule is considered to be a hard sphere and collide elastically with the other molecules and container walls. The pressure that a gas exerts on the walls of its container is a consequence of the repeated collisions of the gas molecules with the walls.

(iii) It is assumed that molecules obey Newton's Laws of motion but during motion they do not interact each other except during collisions and these are not deformed during collisions thus forces between molecules are short range forces which only acts during collisions.

(iv) As during motion molecules do not interact, the total energy of a gas can be considered as the sum of kinetic energies of all of its molecules and hence a gas contain zero potential energy.

(v) During collision the time of contact is negligible compared to the time between two successive collision of a gas molecule, which is called relaxation time.

(vi) As a whole molecules move randomly. By "randomly" we mean that any molecule can move in any direction at any speed. The direction of motion of gas molecules changes only when it collides with the other gas molecule or the container wall. This results a random zigzag path of a molecule shown in figure-2.1.

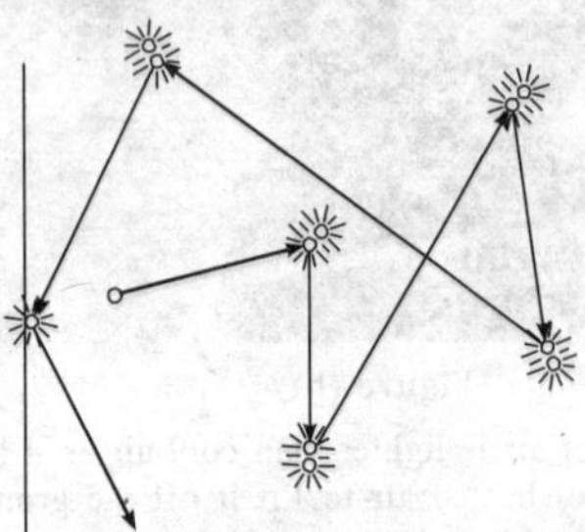

Figure 2.1

This type of random motion is termed "Brownian Motion". We also assume that the distribution of speeds does not change in time, despite the collisions between molecules. That is at any given moment, a certain percentage of molecules move at high speeds, a certain percentage move at low speeds and so on.

(vii) The gas under consideration is assumed a pure substance. That is, all of its molecules are identical.

(viii) Effect of gravity on gas molecules in a container is neglected. That is in a container we assume throughout its volume density of gas is same.

(ix) At all temperature and pressures, all gases obey ideal gas law which relates the microscope characteristics of a gas i.e. pressure, volume and temperature. The ideal gas law is stated as

$$PV = nRT \qquad \dots(2.1)$$

Here n are the number of moles of a gas and R is universal gas constant. In next sections of the chapter we'll discuss gas law in details.

Generally real gases obey ideal gas law $PV = nRT$ only at very high temperature and very low pressure as at very high temperature kinetic energy of the gas molecules is so high that even if some interaction between molecules is present, it will not contribute any energy and at very low pressure, separation between molecule is very large thus reduces their interaction. So we can say that at high temperature and low pressure, real gases behave like ideal gases.

2.2 Gas Laws

In mathematical analysis and behaviour of gases, three parameters are important in describing the properties of a gas. These are pressure, volume and temperature. Several experiments are done for analysis of a gas and to relate these parameters. Some laws are established on the basis of these experiments for relating these parameters. These laws are known as gas laws. Now we'll discuss these laws in details with some examples.

2.2.1 Boyle's Law

This law is an experimental result obtained by Boyle between the pressure and the volume of an enclosed gas at a constant temperature. Boyle's Law states that the pressure exerted by a gas at constant temperature is inversely proportional to the volume in which it is enclosed. Thus Boyle's law is written as

$$P \propto \frac{1}{V}$$

or

$$PV = \text{constant} \qquad \dots(2.2)$$

Where P is the gas pressure, V its volume and the value of constant depends on the gas temperature and its quantity. The complete statement of Boyle's law includes the condition that both the temperature and the amount of gas must be held constant.

Alternatively Boyle's law may be written as

$$P_1V_1 = P_2V_2 \qquad \dots (2.3)$$

Where the subscripts 1 and 2 refer to different physical states of the same sample of gas with the temperature held constant. The variation of pressure and volume of gas at constant temperature is shown in graph in figure-2.2.

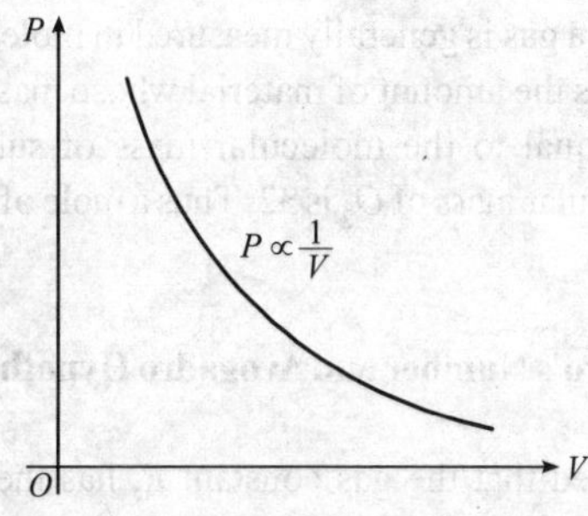

Figure 2.2

Another important point about Boyle's law is to be noted that while Boyle's law is applicable over a wide range of pressure but it does not always apply. For example, if the temperature is low enough, a sample of gas will be condensed to a liquid at sufficiently high pressure. In further sections we'll discuss about liquefaction of gases in detail.

If we find the volume of one mole molecules of gas using gas law, at standard pressure 1 atm and standard temperature 273 K, we get

$$PV = nRT$$

or $$V = \frac{1 \times 8.314 \times 273}{1.013 \times 10^5}$$

$$= 2.2406 \times 10^{-2}\ m^3$$

$$= 22406\ cm^3$$

$$= 22.4\ litre$$

Thus we can state that one mole of all gases occupy a volume of 22.4 litre at standard pressure and temperature.

2.2.2 Charles and Gay-Lussac's Law

Boyle's law relates the pressure and the volume of a gas at constant temperature. However, we can also investigate the effect of temperature change on the volume of a gas at constant pressure. The apparatus for such an experiment is shown in figure-2.3.

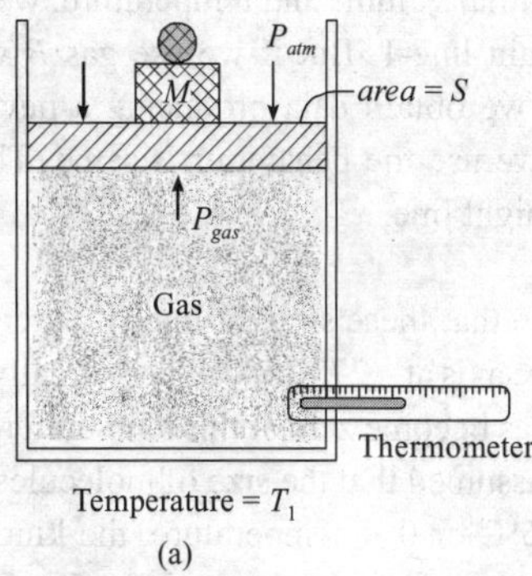

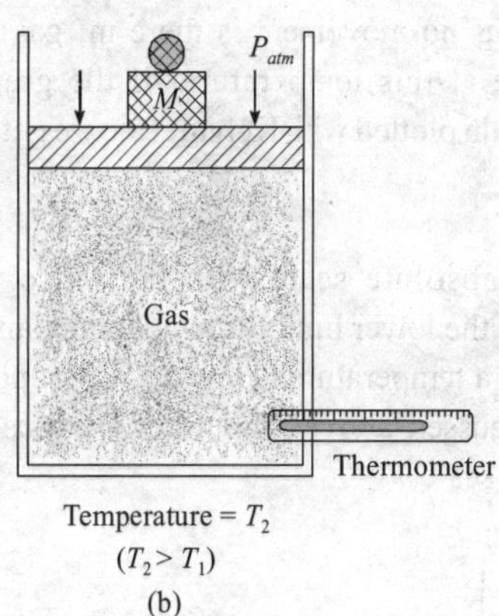

Figure 2.3

We introduced a gas into a cylinder and place a weight on the piston of mass M. This arrangement if in equilibrium at a temperature T_1 as shown in figure-2.3(a) develops a constant pressure in the gas. For equilibrium of piston, the gas pressure can be given as

$$P_{gas} = P_{atm} + \frac{Mg}{S} \qquad \dots (2.4)$$

If gas is heated this pressure remains constant as for equilibrium the gas expands to maintain the pressure. Now after heating the gas to different temperatures and recording its data for temperature and corresponding volume, we plot a graph. The respective graph is shown in figure-2.4.

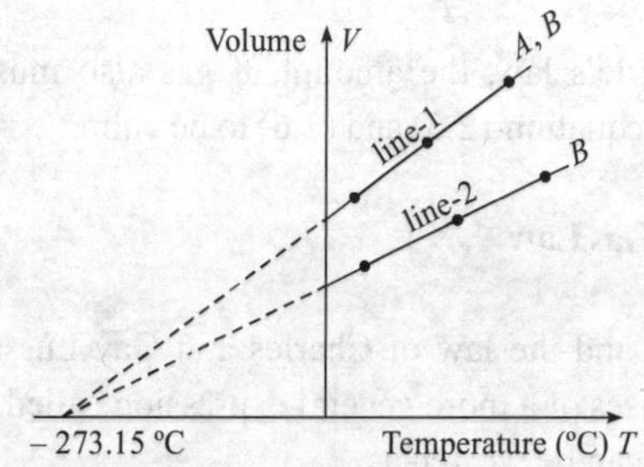

Figure 2.4

If the data is recorded for a gas A we get line-1 shown in figure-2.4 and if we repeat the experiment with another gas B, with the same initial volume and temperature, we get the same results and obtain line-1. But if we use gas B with different initial volume, we obtain data producing a new line, line-2. Whatever gas we use the behaviour is same. The graph will always be a straight line.

Here we can see that these straight lines if extended intersect with temperature axis at – 273.15ºC. Theoretically it shows that the volume of gas become zero at this temperature. The reason already we've assumed that the size of molecules is negligible and at – 273.15ºC or 0 K temperature, the kinetic energy of molecules become zero or all motions are frozen at 0 K temperature thus no movement is there in gas molecules of negligible size at this temperature. If the graph shown in figure-2.4 is again plotted with Kelvin scale we get one as shown in figure-2.5.

This scale is absolute scale with the sense that its zero (– 273.15ºC) is the lower limit for temperature and in practical nature to attain a temperature below this is not possible due to the reason discussed above. In further analysis of gases we will use Kelvin scale.

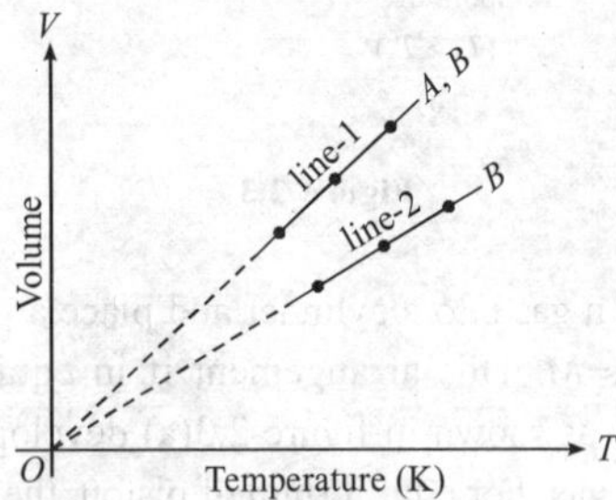

Figure 2.5

Thus if temperature is expressed in Kelvins, we find that when the pressure is held constant, the volume is proportional to the temperature. This statement in the law of Charles and Gay-Lussac. This can be expressed mathematically as

$$\frac{V_1}{V_2} = \frac{T_1}{T_2} \quad \ldots(2.5)$$

or

$$\frac{V}{T} = \text{constant} \quad \ldots(2.6)$$

As with Boyle's law, the amount of gas also must be held constant for equation-(2.5) and (2.6) to be valid.

2.2.3 Ideal Gas Law

Boyle's law and the law of Charles and Gay-Lussac are the Particular cases of a more general expression called the "*ideal gas law*". It can be written as

$$PV = nRT \quad \ldots(2.7)$$

Here, P V and T stand for pressure, volume and temperature respectively and R is a constant that is same for all gases and so is called the universal gas constant and n are the number of moles of gas. If pressure is measured in SI units of units of pascal, volume in cubic meters, and temperature in kelvins, then R has a value 8.314 Joule/mole-K. If in a state gas pressure, volume and temperature are P_1, V_1 and T_1 and after some experiment on same sample of gas if its pressure, volume and temperature are P_2, V_2 and T_2, then from equation-(2.7) we have

$$\frac{P_1V_1}{T_1} = \frac{P_2V_2}{T_2} \quad \ldots(2.8)$$

As number of moles in initial and final state are equal.

The amount of a gas is generally measured in moles, given as n. A mole (mol) is the amount of material whose mass in grams is numerically equal to the molecular mass of substance. For example molecular mass of O_2 is 32, Thus a mole of oxygen is 32 grams.

2.2.4 Avogadro's Number and Avogadro Hypothesis

We've discussed that the gas constant R, has the same value for all gases. This fact was first recognised in a slightly different form, by an Italian Scientist Amedeo Avogadro. Avogadro stated that equal volumes of gas at the same pressure and temperature contain equal numbers of molecules. This statement is called Avogadro's hypothesis. We can see that this statement is consistent with R being the same for all gases.

The number of molecule in a mole is known as Avogadro's number, N_A. Although Avogadro was not able to actually determine the value of N_A, several methods have been devised to measure N_A and the acceptable value found is

$$N_A = 6.023 \times 10^{23} \text{ molecules/mole}$$

Thus in n moles of a gas total number of molecules of the gas are

$$N = nN_A \quad \ldots(2.9)$$

or number of moles of a gas can be given as

$$n = \frac{N}{N_A} = \frac{m'N}{m'N_A} = \frac{m}{M} \quad \ldots(2.10)$$

Here m' is the mass of each molecule, m is the total mass of gas and M is the mass of 1 mole of molecules of gas *i.e.* its molecular mass.

From gas law, we have

$$PV = nRT$$

or

$$PV = \frac{N}{N_A}RT = \frac{m}{M}RT$$

or

$$PV = NkT \quad \ldots(2.11)$$

Where $k = \dfrac{R}{N_{AV}}$ is the Boltzmann's constant and has the value

$k = 1.38 \times 10^{-23}$ J/K

This equation-(2.11) is another form of ideal gas law which is in terms of total number of molecules of gas N instead of moles n.

2.2.5 Dalton's Law of Partial Pressures

This law states that the total pressure of a mixture of gases is equal to the sum of the partial pressures of the gases in the mixture. In a container of volume V if n different gases are taken at a common temperature independently at pressure $P_1, P_2, \ldots P_n$, then on mixing all these gases in the same container at the same temperature, the total pressure of the mixture is given by

$$P_T = P_1 + P_2 + \cdots\cdots P_n \qquad \ldots(2.12)$$

2.2.6 Different Forms of Ideal Gas Law

As discussed the pressure volume and temperature of a gas in a state related by ideal gas law given as

$$PV = nRT \qquad \ldots(2.13)$$

Where n are the number of moles of gas in the enclosed volume V. If m mass of a gas (molecular mass = M) is taken in the container of volume V, we have number of moles of gas as

$$n = \frac{m}{M} \qquad \ldots(2.14)$$

Now from equation-(2.13)

$$PV = \frac{m}{M} RT$$

or $$P = \frac{m}{VM} RT$$

or $$P = \frac{\rho RT}{M} \qquad \ldots(2.15)$$

Equation-(2.15) is a modified form of ideal gas law which relates gas pressure, its density and temperature in a physical state. Equation-(2.13) is termed as container form of Gas Law as it is generally used when a gas is enclosed in a container and equation-(2.15) is termed as atmospheric form of gas law as it relates density of gas with the pressure and temperature and is used widely for open atmosphere or in a region where gas is not enclosed.

2.2.7 Real Gases and Change of Phase

The ideal gas law $PV = nRT$ gives the behaviour of a gas as long as its pressure is not too high, as discussed earlier. To discuss this in depth look at PV graph shown in figure-2.6 for a given amount of gas. These curves shows how pressure of gas varies with the change in volume at constant temperatures. Here the dotted curves represent the behaviour of an ideal gas at PV = Constant. The solid curve represents the behaviour of a real gas at the same temperature. Notice that at high pressure the volume in a real gas is less than that predicted by the ideal gas law and the deviation is more when gas is about to liquefy.

Students should also note that at high pressure, the molecules of the gas are close together, particularly at lower temperatures, the potential energy associated with the attractive forces between molecules, which we ignore (assumptions of KTG) are now no longer negligible compared to the low kinetic energy of molecules. These attractive forces tend to pull the molecules close together so that at a given pressure the volume of gas is less then expected from ideal gas law. If we see at further lower temperatures, these forces cause liquefaction of the gas.

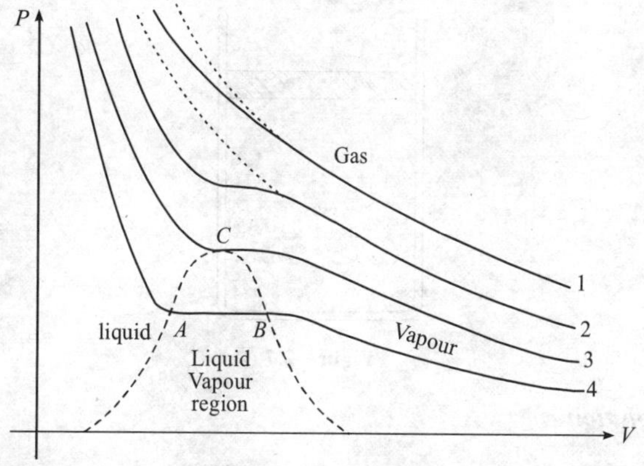

Figure 2.6

In figure-2.6, curve-4 represents the situation when liquefaction occurs. At low pressure on curve-4, the substance is a gas and occupies large volume. As the pressure is increased, the volume decreases till point B. Beyond point B, the volume decreases without change in pressure. In this region the gas is gradually changing to liquid upto point A. At point A gas is completely liquefied. Further if we increase the pressure, volume changes slightly as liquids are almost incompressible so here curve is very steep. The region, where gas and liquid phase exist together in equilibrium.

If we carefully look on curve-3, we can see that at point C, curve is almost horizontal and it happens only at this point. This point C is called critical point and the gas temperature of curve-3 is called critical temperature of the gas. Critical temperature of a gas is defined as - "*A gas will change to liquid phase if its temperature is less then critical temperature if sufficient pressure is applied on the gas*". Above critical temperature, no matters whatever be the amount of pressure applied, the gas can not be liquefied. As pressure is increased, gas becomes denser and denser and acquires the properties resembling to a liquid but does not condense. A distinction is made between "*gas*" and "*vapour*", students should keep in mind that a substance below its critical temperature in gaseous state is called "*vapour*" (which can be liquefied on applying sufficient pressure on it) and a substance above its critical temperature in gaseous state is called "*gas*" (which can not be liquefied).

Illustrative Example 2.1

A cylindrical container is shown in figure-2.7 in which a gas is enclosed. Its initial volume is V and temperature is T. As no external pressure is applied on the light piston shown, gas pressure must be equal to the atmospheric pressure. If gas temperature is doubled, find its final volume. In its final state if piston is clamped and temperature is again doubled, find the final pressure of the gas.

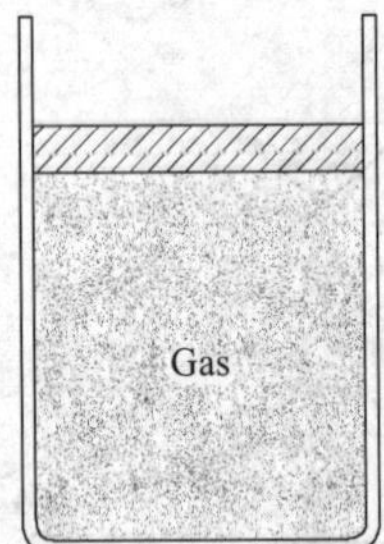

Figure 2.7

Solution

In the initial state the pressure, volume and temperature of gas P_0 V and T respectively if P_0 is the atmospheric pressure.

It is given that temperature of gas is increased to double its value i.e. up to $2T$. As in initial and final state pressure of gas remains constant as initially as well as finally the piston is exposed to atmospheric pressure. Thus we have from Charles and Gay Lussac Law

$$\frac{V_1}{T_1} = \frac{V_2}{T_2}$$

Here $$V_2 = \frac{V_1 T_2}{T_1} = 2V$$

$$[\text{As } V_1 = V, T_1 = T \text{ and } T_2 = 2T]$$

Thus after increasing the gas temperature to $2T$, its volume becomes $2V$. Now the piston is clamped that means, now the volume of gas remains constant. Again its temperature is doubled from $2T$ to $4T$, let the pressure changes from P_0 to P'. Thus we have

$$\frac{P_1}{T_1} = \frac{P_2}{T_2}$$

or $$P_2 = P' = \frac{P_1 T_2}{T_1} = 2P_0$$

$$[\text{As } P_1 = P_0, T_1 = 2T \text{ and } T_2 = 4T]$$

Thus in final state gas pressure becomes $2P_0$.

Illustrative Example 2.2

Two glass bulbs of equal volume are connected by a narrow tube and are filled with a gas at 0°C and a pressure of 76 cm of mercury. One of the bulbs is then placed in melting ice and the other is placed in water bath maintained at 62°C. What is the new value of the pressure inside the bulbs ? The volume of the connecting tube is negligible.

Solution

If we assume the volume of each bulbs is V, the number of moles present in each bulb initially is

$$n = \frac{PV}{RT} = \frac{(76\text{cm})V}{R(273)}$$

Thus total number of moles in the two connected bulbs is $2n = \frac{2\times(76cm)V}{R(273)}$ when one bulbs is placed in melting ice (273 K) and other is placed in water at 62°C (62 + 273 = 335 K) still total number of moles in the two bulbs will be equal to the initial moles i.e. $2n$. If P_f be the final pressure in the two bulbs we have

$$\frac{P_i(2V)}{T_i} = \frac{P_f V}{T_{f_1}} + \frac{P_f V}{T_{f_2}}$$

$$\frac{(76\text{cm})(2V)}{273} = \frac{P_f V}{273} + \frac{P_f V}{335}$$

or $$P_f = \frac{2\times 76}{273} \times \frac{273\times 335}{608}$$

$$= 83.75 \text{ cm of } Hg$$

Illustrative Example 2.3

Two closed containers of equal volume of air are initially at 1.05×10^5 Pa, and 300 K temperature. If the containers are connected by a narrow tube and one container is maintained at 300 K temperature and other at 400 K temperature. Find the final pressure in the containers.

Solution

Similar to previous example final pressure in both the containers remain same as they are connected. If initial pressure volume and temperatures of the two containers are denoted by P_0 V_0 and T_0 and P_f, V_0 T_1 and $P_f V_0$ T_2 are the final pressure volume and temperature in the two containers then according to gas law and constant number of moles, we have

$$\frac{P_0(2V_0)}{T_0} = \frac{P_fV_0}{T_1} + \frac{P_fV_0}{T_2}$$

or
$$P_f = \frac{2P_0}{T_0}\left(\frac{T_1T_2}{T_1+T_2}\right)$$

Here it is given that P_0 = 105 k Pa, T_0 = 300 k, T_1 = 300 K, T_2 = 400 k, then we get

$$P_f = \frac{2\times105\times10^3\times400}{300+400} = 120\text{ kPa}$$

Illustrative Example 2.4

Equal masses of a gas are sealed in two vessels, one of volume V_0 and other of volume $2V_0$. If the first vessel is at temperature 300 K and the other is at 600 K. Find the ratio of pressures in the two vessels.

Solution

As number of moles in the two vessels are equal, we have

$$\frac{P_1V_1}{T_1} = \frac{P_2V_2}{T_2}$$

It is given that $V_1 = V_0$, $V_2 = 2V_0$ and T_1 = 300 K, T_2 = 600 K
Thus we have

$$\frac{P_1V_0}{300} = \frac{P_2(2V_0)}{600}$$

or
$$P_1 = P_2$$

or
$$\frac{P_1}{P_2} = 1$$

Illustrative Example 2.5

A glass container encloses a gas at a pressure of 8×10^5 Pa and 300 K temperature. The container walls can bear a maximum pressure of 10^6 Pa. If the temperature of container is gradually increased, find the temperature at which container will break.

Solution

From gas law, we have for a constant volume container

$$\frac{P_1}{T_1} = \frac{P_2}{T_2}$$

or
$$T_2 = \left(\frac{P_2}{P_1}\right)T_1$$

Given that $P_1 = 8\times10^5\ Pa$, T_1 = 300 K,
$P_2 = 10^6$ Pa, then we have

$$T_2 = \frac{10^6}{8\times10^5}\times300 = 375\text{ K}$$

Illustrative Example 2.6

Find the minimum attainable pressure of one mole of an ideal gas if during its expansion its temperature and volume are related as $T = T_0 + \alpha V^2$ where T_0 and α are positive constants.

Solution

Given that one mole of gas is used, thus from gas law, we have

$$PV = RT$$

or
$$P = \frac{RT}{V} = \frac{R}{V}(T_0+\alpha V^2)$$

[As $T = T_0 + \alpha V^2$]

Here pressure P will be minimum when

$$\frac{dP}{dV} = 0$$

or
$$\frac{dP}{dV} = -\frac{RT_0}{V^2} + \alpha R = 0$$

or
$$V = \sqrt{\frac{T_0}{\alpha}}$$

Thus pressure of gas is minimum when its volume is $V = \sqrt{\frac{T_0}{\alpha}}$

and at this volume its temperature is given as

$$T = T_0 + \alpha V^2$$

$$T = T_0 + \alpha\left(\sqrt{\frac{T_0}{\alpha}}\right)^2 = 2\,T_0$$

Thus minimum value of pressure is

$$P_{min} = \frac{RT}{V} = \frac{R(2T_0)}{\sqrt{T_0/\alpha}} = 2R\sqrt{T_0\alpha}$$

Illustrative Example 2.7

A smooth vertical tube having two different cross section is open from both the ends but closed by two sliding pistons as shown in figure-2.8 and tied with an inextensible string. One mole of an ideal gas is enclosed between the pistons. The difference in cross-sectional areas of the two pistons is given ΔS. The masses of piston are m_1 and m_2 for larger and smaller one respectively. Find the temperature by which tube is raised so that the pistons will be displaced by a distance l. Take atmospheric pressure equal to P_0.

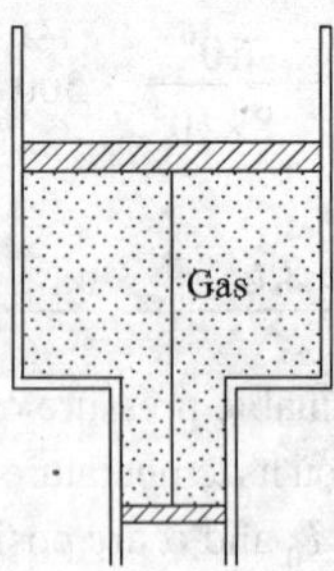

Figure 2.8

Solution

If initial pressure of gas is P and let S_1 and S_2 are the cross-sectional areas of the larger and smaller piston then for equilibrium of the two pistons we have

For larger piston

$$P_0S_1 + m_1g + T = PS_1$$

[If T is the tension in string] ...(2.16)

For smaller piston

$$PS_2 + m_2g = T + P_0S_2 \qquad \text{...(2.17)}$$

Adding equation-(2.16) and-(2.17), we get

$$P_0(S_1 - S_2) + m_1g + m_2g = P(S_1 - S_2)$$

or $$P_0 + \left(\frac{m_1 + m_2}{\Delta S}\right)g = P \qquad \text{...(2.18)}$$

If gas temperature is increased from T_1 to T_2 the volume of gas increases from V to $V + l\Delta S$ as l is the displacement of pistons, then from gas law we must have

$$P \cdot V = RT_1 \qquad \text{[For initial state]} \quad \text{...(2.19)}$$

$$P(V + l\Delta S) = RT_2 \qquad \text{[For final state]} \quad \text{...(2.20)}$$

According to equation-(2.18)

Pressure of gas does not change as it does not depend on temperature

From equation-(2.19) and (2.20), if we subtract these equation, we get

$$P \cdot l\Delta S = R(T_2 - T_1)$$

or $$T_2 - T_1 = \frac{Pl\Delta S}{R}$$

$$= \left(P_0 + \frac{(m_1 + m_2)}{\Delta S}g\right)\frac{l\Delta S}{R}$$

$$= [P_0\Delta S + (m_1 + m_2)g]\,\frac{l}{R}$$

Web Reference at www.physicsgalaxy.com
Age Group - High School Physics | Age 17-19 Years
Section - HEAT & THERMODYNAMICS
Topic - Kinetic Theory of Gases
Module Number - 1 to 13

Practice Exercise 2.1

(i) A rubber balloon is filled with air at 2×10^5 N/m^2 pressure at a temperature 20°C. When its temperature is increased to 40°C, the volume of balloon is increased by 2%. Find the final air pressure inside the balloon at 40°C.

[2.095×10^5 N/m^2]

(ii) There are two containers, each of volume V containing ideal gases. The pressure and temperature of the gases in the two vessels are p_1, T_1 and p_2, T_2 respectively. If the vessels are now connected by a thin long tube of negligible volume, the final temperature of the two after mixing is T. Find the final pressure of the gas.

[$\frac{T}{2}\left(\frac{p_1}{T_1} + \frac{p_2}{T_2}\right)$]

(iii) A vessel of volume $V = 20$ litre contains a mixture of H_2 and Heat 20°C and pressure $P = 2$ atm. The mass of the mixture is $m = 5$ g. Find the ratio of masses m_1/m_2 where m_1 = mass of H_2 and m_2 = mass of He.

[$\frac{1}{2}$]

(iv) The temperature of a gas contained in a closed vessel increases by 1°C when pressure of the gas is increased by 1%. Find the initial temperature of the gas.

[100 K]

(v) A vessel contains a mixture of nitrogen ($m_1 = 7\ g$) and carbon dioxide ($m_2 = 11\ g$) at a temperature $T = 290$ K and pressure $p_0 = 1$ atm. Find the density of this mixture, assuming the gases to be ideal.

[1.494 kg m^{-3}]

(vi) A vessel of volume $V = 30$ litre is separated into 3 equal parts by stationary semipermeable partitions. The left, middle and right parts are filled with $m_1 = 30$ g of hydrogen (H_2), $m_2 = 160$ g of oxygen (O_2), and $m_3 = 70$ g of nitrogen (N_2) respectively. The left partition lets only hydrogen, while the right partition lets through hydrogen and nitrogen. What will be the pressure in each part of the vessel after the equilibrium has been set in if the vessel is kept at a constant temperature $T = 300$ K?

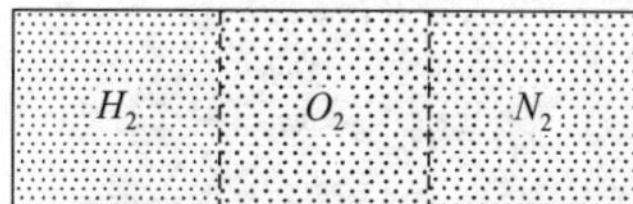

Figure 2.9

[$P_1 = 12.471 \times 10^5$ Pa, $P_2 = 28.06 \times 10^5$ Pa, $P_3 = 15.589 \times 10^5$ Pa]

(vii) A vessel of volume 30 litres contains ideal gas at a temperature 63°C. After a portion of the gas has been let out, the pressure in the vessel decreased by 0.415 bar. If density of gas at STP is 1.3 gm/ltr, find the mass of gas released from the vessel.

[13.14 g]

(viii) A vessel of volume 8.3 litres contains a mixture of ideal gases at temperature 300 K, 0.1 mol of nitrogen, 0.2 mol of oxygen and 0.3 mol of carbon dioxide. Find the pressure and molecular weight of the mixture.

[1.8×10^5 Pa; 37.33]

(ix) Two glass bulbs of volume 3 litres and 1 litre, respectively, are connected by a capillary tube. Air at a pressure of 76 cm of mercury at 30°C is contained in the apparatus which is then hermetically sealed. If the 3 litre bulb is immersed in steam at 100°C, the other remaining at 30°C, what would be the pressure of the air in the bulbs ? Neglect expansion of the 3 litre bulb.

[88.45 cm of *Hg*]

(x) A freely moving piston divides a vertical cylinder, closed at both ends, into two parts each containing 1 mole of air. In equilibrium, at $T = 300$ K, volume of the upper part is $\eta = 4$ times greater than the lower part. At what temperature will the ratio of these volumes be equal to $\eta' = 2$?

[750 K]

2.3 Pressure of Air

Figure-2.10 shows a Torricellian tube, the principle of today's barometer. If a glass tube, closed at one end, is completely filled with mercury and then inverted into a bowl of mercury, the column of mercury in the tube drops until it reaches a height of about 76 cm above the lower surface as shown in figure-2.10 this is what Torricelli predicted before experiment. According to Pascal's principle, the pressure of the atmosphere on the surface of the mercury in the bowl at point *A* is equal to the pressure due to the weight of mercury in the tube at point *B* if this were not so, the mercury would flow because it would not be in static equilibrium. The space between the top of liquid and the end of the tube contains no air and was named the Torricellian vacuum.

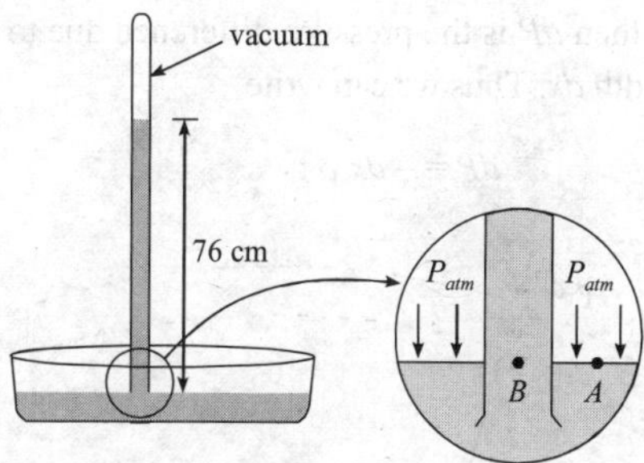

Figure 2.10

This is how barometer works and the height of mercury column in the tube gives the atmospheric pressure of air. If cross-sectional area of tube is A then the weight of mercury column is

$$W = h A \rho g$$

Thus pressure at its bottom is given as

$$p = \frac{W}{A} = h \rho g \quad \ldots(2.21)$$

In general the height of mercury column in open atmosphere in standard conditions is about 76 cm, thus atmospheric pressure of air is given as

$$p = h \rho g$$

$$= (0.76) \times (13.6 \times 10^3) \times (9.81)\ \text{W/m}^2$$

$$= 1.01 \times 10^5\ \text{N/m}^2$$

$$p_{air} = 1.01 \times 10^5\ Pa = 1\ \text{atm}$$

This pressure is atmospheric pressure. An atmosphere (1 atm) is a unit of pressure equal to the pressure of the earth's atmosphere at sea level.

2.3.1 Barometric Relation

After Torricelli's experiments, pascal suggested that the atmosphere is like a big ocean of air, in which pressure is greater at the bottom than at higher altitudes. This assumption was verified and confirmed when a Torricellian tube was carried from sea level to a mountain top and the mercury column was observed to be shorter at higher elevations.

Maxwell developed a relation to find atmospheric pressure as a function of height from ground level (more precisely sea level). The relation is named Barometric Relation. We first derive the relation mathematically and than we'll discuss some uses and applications of this relation.

We consider an atmospheric layer of width dx at a height x above the earth surface as shown in figure-2.11. According to Pascal's assumption as we go up in air, pressure decreases thus if just below this elemental layer if pressure is P and just above it is $P-dP$, then dP is the pressure difference due to this small layer of width dx. Thus we can write

$$dP = -dx\,\rho\,g \qquad \ldots(2.22)$$

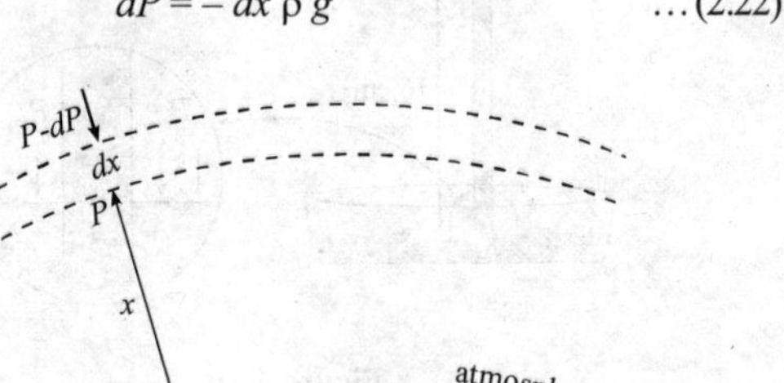

Figure 2.11

Here minus sign indicates that the pressure decreases as altitude increases where ρ is the air density in the elemental layer at a height dx. According to gas law the pressure at this layer P is given as

$$P = \rho\frac{RT}{M} \qquad \ldots(2.23)$$

From equation-(2.22) and (2.23)

$$dP = -dx\,\frac{PM}{RT}g$$

or
$$\frac{dP}{P} = -\frac{Mg}{RT}dx$$

Integrating this expression within proper limits, gives

$$\int_{P_0}^{P}\frac{dP}{P} = -\int_{0}^{h}\frac{Mg}{RT}dx \qquad \ldots(2.24)$$

or
$$ln\,\frac{P}{P_0} = -\frac{Mgh}{RT}$$

[Assuming throughout the atmosphere temperature T = constant]

or
$$P = P_0 e^{-\frac{Mgh}{RT}} \qquad \ldots(2.25)$$

Here P_0 is the atmospheric pressure on ground-level or sea-level and equation-(2.25) gives the pressure of atmospheric air at a height h above the earth surface and is called as Barometric formula. Using this we can also find the atmospheric air density at a height h above the ground level.

Using equation-(2.23) we have

$$\rho = \frac{PM}{RT}$$

or
$$\rho = \frac{P_0 M}{RT}\,e^{-\frac{Mgh}{RT}}$$

or
$$\rho = \rho_0\,e^{-\frac{Mgh}{RT}} \qquad \ldots(2.26)$$

Here $\rho_0 = \frac{P_0 M}{RT}$ can be taken as atmosphere air density at the ground level. Another form of Barometric formula can be written in terms of number of molecules per unit volume or the molecular density in atmosphere and can be given as

$$n = n_0 e^{-\frac{Mgh}{RT}} \qquad \ldots(2.27)$$

Above equation-(2.25), (2.26) and (2.27) are used with the assumption that the atmospheric temperature T and the acceleration due to gravity g remains constant within the limits of integration of expression in equation-(2.24). If in some region temperature gradient (dT/dh) exist then the above formula can be modified while integrating the expression in equation-(2.24).

 # Illustrative Example 2.8

A vertical cylinder of height 100 cm contains air at a constant temperature and its top is closed by a frictionless piston at atmospheric pressure (76 cm of *Hg*) as shown in figure-2.12. If mercury is slowly poured on the piston, due to its weight air is compressed. Find the maximum height of the mercury column which can be put on the piston.

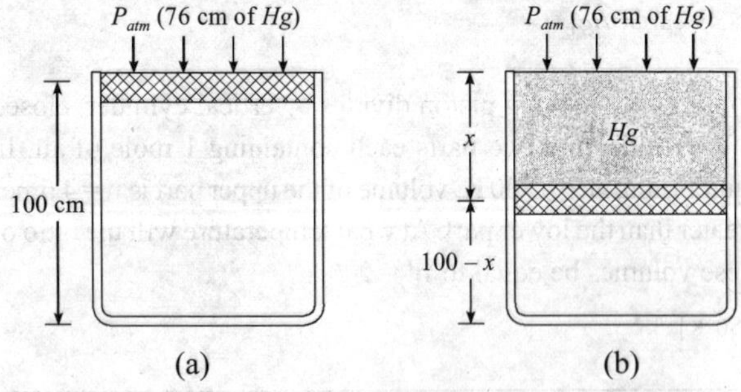

Figure 2.12

Solution

When mercury is poured on the top of the piston, due to increase in pressure, the volume of air will decrease according to Boyle's

Law. If final mercury column of height x is poured on the piston then gas pressure in equilibrium can be given as

$$P_f = (76 + x)\text{ cm of } Hg$$

As atmospheric pressure is equivalent to the pressure due to a mercury column of height 76 cm. If A be the area of cross section of cylinder then we have according to Boyle's Law

$$P_1V_1 = P_2V_2$$

or $$(76\text{ cm})(100\text{A}) = (76 + x)(100 - x)\text{A}$$

or $$7600 = 7600 + 24x - x^2$$

or $$x = 24\text{ cm}$$

Illustrative Example 2.9

A vertical hollow cylinder of height 1.52 m is fitted with a movable piston of negligible mass and thickness. The lower part of cylinder contains an ideal gas and the upper part is filled with mercury as shown in figure-2.13. Initially the temperature of system is 300 K and the lengths of gas and mercury columns are equal. Find the temperature to which system is raised so that half of mercury overflows. Take atmospheric pressure is 76 cm of Hg and neglect thermal expansion of mercury.

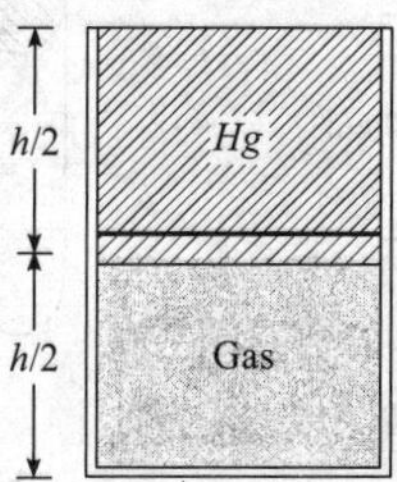

Figure 2.13

Solution

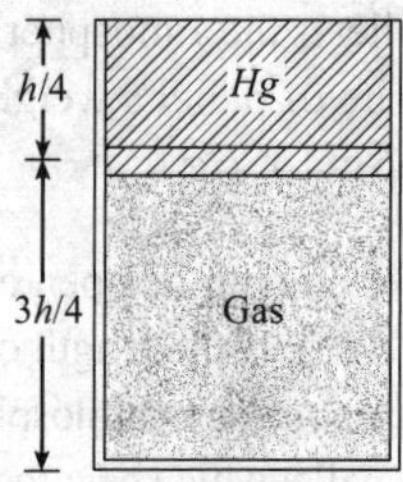

Figure 2.14

Final state of gas is shown in figure-2.14 after half of mercury overflows. Let this temperature be T. Then from gas law for initial and final state of gas we have

$$\frac{P_1V_1}{T_1} = \frac{P_2V_2}{T_2}$$

Here initial pressure, volume and temperature of gas are

$$P_1 = 76 + \frac{h}{2} = 76 + 76 = 152\text{ cm of } Hg$$

$$V_1 = \frac{h}{2}A = 76\text{A}$$

$$T_1 = 300\text{ K}$$

Similarly after heating pressure, volume and temperature of gas are

$$P_2 = 76 + \frac{h}{4} = 76 + 38 = 114\text{ cm of } Hg$$

$$V_2 = \frac{3h}{4}A = 114A$$

Thus from gas law, we have

$$\frac{152 \times 76A}{300} = \frac{114 \times 114A}{T_2}$$

or $$T_2 = 337.5\text{ K}$$

Illustrative Example 2.10

A very tall cylindrical vessel with an ideal gas of molar mass M, filled in it is placed in a uniform gravitational field. It is given that the temperature of gas varies with height in such a manner that its density remains same throughout the container. Find the temperature gradient in the container dT/dh.

Solution

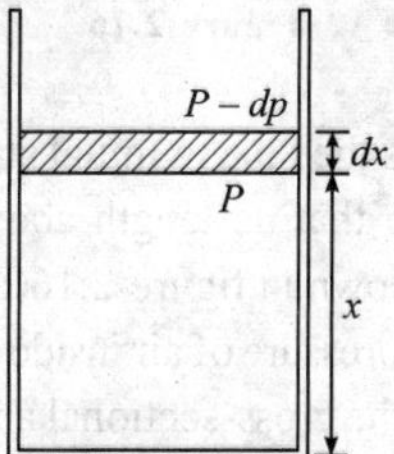

Figure 2.15

In the container shown in figure-2.15, consider a layer of width dx at a height x above its bottom. If P is the pressure just below this layer then just above this layer, we can consider pressure to be P-dP. Here dP is the pressure due to the gas layer of width dx which can be given as

$$dP = -dx\,\rho g$$

[If ρ is the density. of gas] ...(2.28)

From open atmospheric form of gas law, we have

$$P = \frac{\rho RT}{M}$$

As it is given that density of gas is constant, we have

$$dP = \frac{\rho R}{M} dT \quad \ldots (2.29)$$

From (2.28) and (2.29) we have

$$\frac{\rho R}{M} dT = -dx\, \rho g$$

or $$\frac{dT}{dx} = -\frac{Mg}{R}$$

Illustrative Example 2.11

An open glass tube is immersed in mercury in such a way that the length of 8 cm extends above the mercury level. Now the open end of the tube is closed by a finger and raised by further by 44 cm. What will be the length of air column above mercury in the tube. Take atmospheric pressure to be 76 cm of mercury. Neglect capillary effect.

Solution

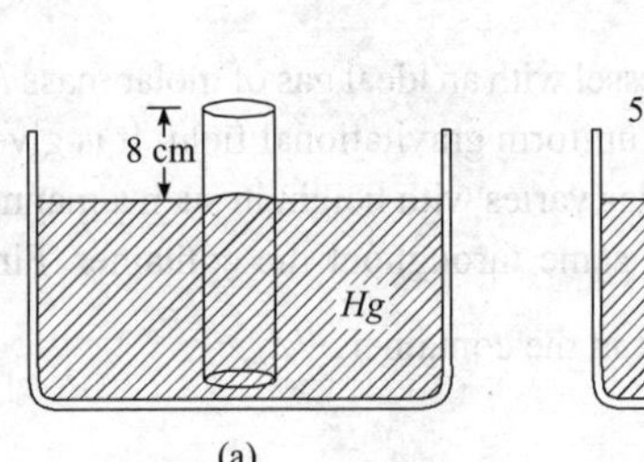

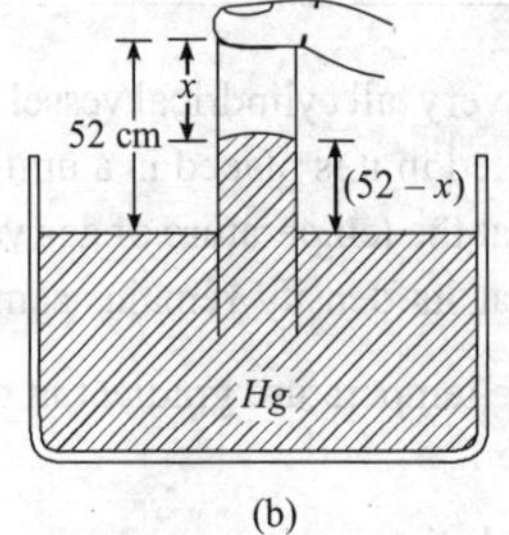

Figure 2.16

Figure-2.16(a) shows the tube in initial state then it is closed at top and raised up so that its length above mercury becomes 8 + 44 = 52 cm as shown in figure-2.16(b). As initially tube is open to atmosphere, pressure of air inside is 76 cm of *Hg* and its volume is 8*A* if *A* is the cross-sectional area of the tube.

When its upper end is closed and raised up, situation is shown in figure-2.16(b). Let the air column be of length *x* then its final volume will be *xA*. Pressure at the mercury level in the container is equal to atmospheric pressure 76 cm of *Hg* and the air column is separated by another mercury column of height 52-*x* above this level which will oppose the atmospheric pressure thus pressure inside the column will be $76-(52-x)=(24+x)$ cm of mercury.

As during the process temperature of system remains constant, thus we can use Boyle's law for the initial and final states as

$$P_1V_1 = P_2V_2$$

or $$76 \times 8A = (24+x) \times xA$$

or $$608 = 24x + x^2$$

or $$x^2 + 24x - 608 = 0$$

On solving, we get $x = 15.4$ cm or $x = -39.4$ cm

Thus the acceptable value of final air column is 15.4 cm.

Illustrative Example 2.12

A uniform tube closed at one end, contains a pallet of mercury 10 cm long. When the tube is kept vertically with the closed end of tube upward, the length of air column trapped by mercury and the closed end of the tube is 20 cm. If the tube is inverted so that its open end becomes upward. Find the final length of the air column trapped. Take atmospheric pressure to be 76 cm of *Hg*.

Solution

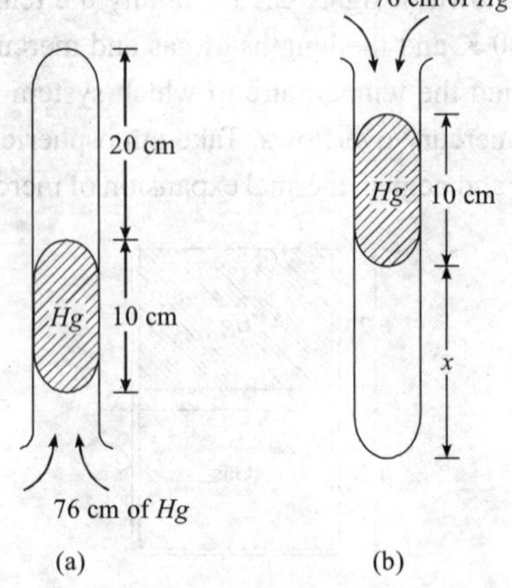

Figure 2.17

Figure-2.17(a) shows the initial state of the tube. Here pressure below the mercury pallet is the atmospheric pressure. 76 cm of *Hg* and due to opposite of pallet's weight the pressure of air column is $76 - 10 = 66$ cm of *Hg*.

When the tube is inverted with its open end upward, situation is shown in figure-2.17(b). If the length of air column is *x* and the pressure on this air column is atmospheric pressure planes the weight of mercury pallet which becomes 76 + 10 = 86 cm of *Hg*, then according to Boyle's Law we have

$$P_1V_1 = P_2V_2$$

$$66 \times 20A = 86 \times xA$$

[If *A* is the cross sectional area of tube]

or $$x = 15.35 \text{ cm}$$

Illustrative Example 2.13

Figure-2.18 shows a horizontal cylindrical container of length 30 cm, which is partitioned by a tight fitting separator. The separator is diathermic but conducts heat very slowly. Initially the separator is in the state shown in figure-2.18. The temperature of left part of cylinder is 100 K and that on right part is 400 K. Initially the separator is in equilibrium. As heat is conducted from right to left part, separator displaces to the right. Find the displacement of separator after a long two when gases on the parts of cylinder are in thermal equilibrium.

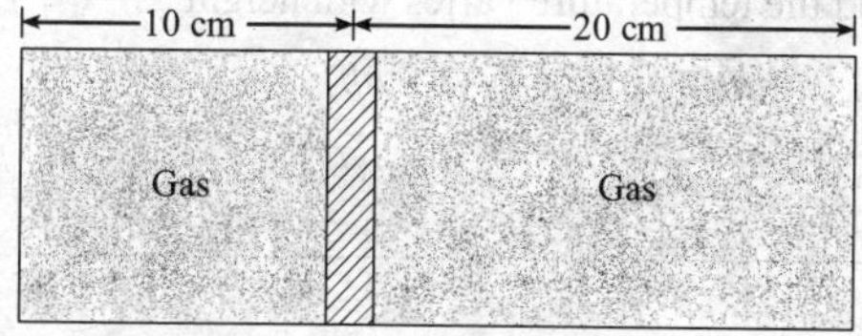

Figure 2.18

Solution

It is given that initially the separator is in equilibrium thus pressure on both sides of gas are equal say, it is P_i. If A be the area of cross-section of cylinder, number of moles of gas in left and right part n_1 and n_2 can be given as

$$n_1 = \frac{P_i(10A)}{R(100)} \quad \text{and} \quad n_2 = \frac{P_i(20A)}{R(400)}$$

Finally if separator is displaced to right by a distance x, we have

$$n_1 = \frac{P_f(10+x)A}{RT_f} \quad \text{and} \quad n_2 = \frac{P_f(20-x)A}{RT_f}$$

If P_f and T_f be the final pressure and temperature on both sides after a long time.

Now if we equate the ratio of moles $^{n_1}/_{n_2}$ in initial and final state we get

$$\frac{n_1}{n_2} = \frac{\left(\frac{10A}{100}\right)}{\left(\frac{20A}{400}\right)} = \frac{(10+x)A}{(20-x)A}$$

or $\qquad 2(20-x) = 10+x$

or $\qquad x = 10\text{ cm}$

Thus in final state when gases in both parts are in thermal equilibrium, the piston is displaced to 10 cm right from its initial position.

Web Reference at www.physicsgalaxy.com
Age Group - High School Physics | Age 17-19 Years
Section - HEAT & THERMODYNAMICS
Topic - Kinetic Theory of Gases
Module Number - 14 to 17

Practice Exercise 2.2

(i) A glass tube, which is closed at one end, is completely submerged with open end downward in a vessel of mercury, so that air column of length l = 10 cm is entrapped inside the tube. To what height must the upper end of the tube be raised above the level of mercury in the vessel so that the level of mercury in the tube coincides with that in the vessel ? Also calculate the mass of the air if the temperature remains constant at = 27°C. The area of cross-section of the tube is α = 1.0 cm^2. Given that atmospheric pressure $p_0 = 1.013 \times 10^5$ Pa = 76 cm of Hg, molecular weight of air = 29.

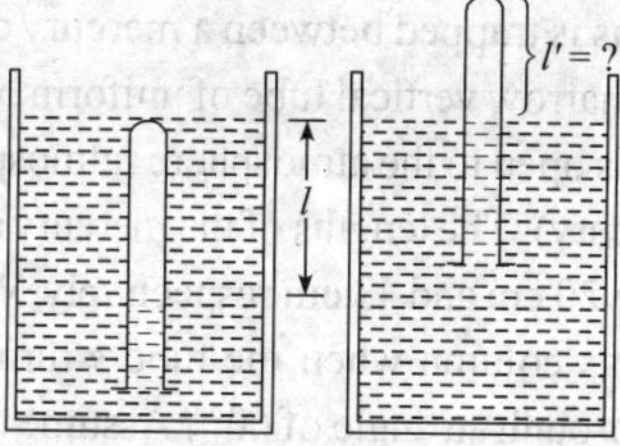

Figure 2.19

[l' = 11.315 cm, m = 13.32 mg]

(ii) An ideal gas is enclosed in a tube and is held in the vertical position with the closed end upward. The length of the pellet of mercury entrapping the gas is h = 10 cm and the length of the tube occupied by gas is l = 40 cm. Calculate the length occupied by the gas when it is turned through θ = 60° and 90°. Atmospheric pressure, H = 76 cm of mercury.

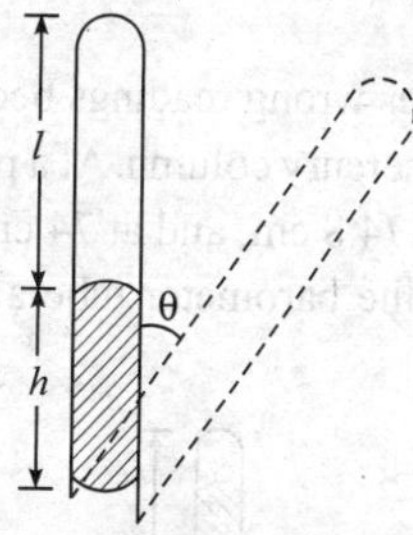

Figure 2.20

[37.18 cm, 34.73 cm]

(iii) A glass tube of length l = 50 cm and cross-section A = 0.5 cm^2 is sealed at one end and submerged into water as shown in the figure-2.21. What force should be applied to hold the tube under the water if the distance from the surface of the water to the closed end is $h = 20$ cm and the atmospheric pressure is 10^5 Pa ? The weight of the tube is 15 gm.

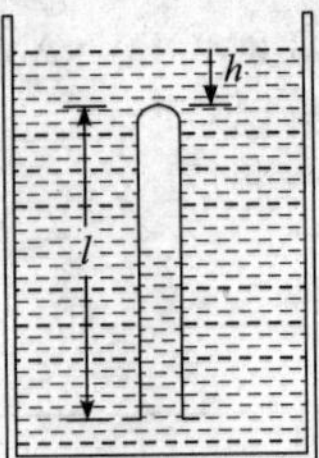

Figure 2.21

[0.084 N]

(iv) An ideal gas of molar mass M is contained in a tall vertical cylindrical vessel whose base area is S and height h. The temperature of the gas is T, its pressure on the bottom base is p_0. Assuming the temperature and the free-fall acceleration g to be independent of the height, find the mass of gas in the vessel.

[$m = (1 - e^{-Mgh/RT})\ p_0\ S/g$]

(v) An ideal gas is trapped between a mercury column and the closed end of a narrow vertical tube of uniform bore. The upper end of the tube is open to the atmosphere (atmospheric pressure = 76 cm of mercury). The lengths of the mercury and the trapped gas columns are 20 cm and 43 cm respectively. What will be the length of the gas column when the tube s turned slowly in a vertical plane through an angle of 60° ? Assume the temperature to be constant

[48 cm]

(vi) An ideal gas of molar mass M is contained in a very tall vertical cylindrical vessel in the uniform gravitational field in which the free-fall acceleration equals g. Assuming the gas temperature to be the same and equal to T, find the height at which the centre of gravity of the gas is located.

[RT/Mg]

(vii) A barometer gives wrong readings because of some air in the space above the mercury column. At a pressure 75.5 cm Hg the barometer shows 74.8 cm, and at 74 cm it shows 73.6 cm. Find the length l of the barometer tube above the surface of mercury.

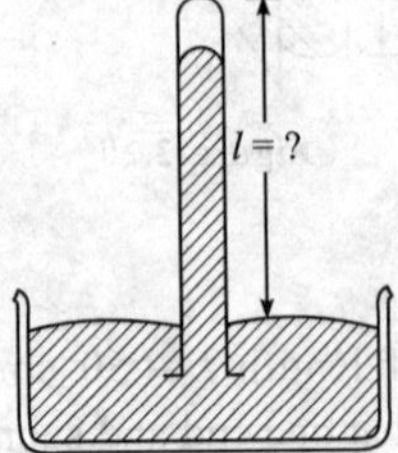

Figure 2.22

[94.1 cm]

(viii) A horizontal cylinder closed from one end is rotated with a constant angular velocity ω about a vertical axis passing through the open end of the cylinder. The outside air pressure is equal to p_0, the temperature to T, and the molar mass of air to M. Find the air pressure as a function of the distance r from the rotation axis. The molar mass is assumed to be independent of r.

[$p = p_0\ e^{M\omega^2 r^2/2RT}$]

(ix) An ideal gas of molar mass M is located in the uniform gravitational field in which the free-fall acceleration is equal to g. Find the gas pressure as a function of height h, if $p = p_0$ at $h = 0$, and the temperature varies with height as

(a) $T = T_0(1 - ah)$; (b) $T = T_0(1 + ah)$

[(a) $p = p_0\ (1 - ah)^n$, $h < 1/a$; (b) $p = p_0 / (1 + ah)^n$. Here $n = Mg/aRT_0$]

2.4 Distribution of Molecular Speeds

The molecules in a gas are assumed to be in random motion, which means that many molecules have speeds less then the average speed and others have speeds greater than the average. On the basis of kinetic theory and experiments Maxwell plotted a graph of variation of speeds with relative number of molecules as shown in figure-2.23. The graph shows how the speeds of molecules in a gas are distributed. This is known as Maxwell distribution of speeds. The speeds vary from zero up to many times the average speed, but as can be seen from the graph, most molecules have speeds that are not far from the average.

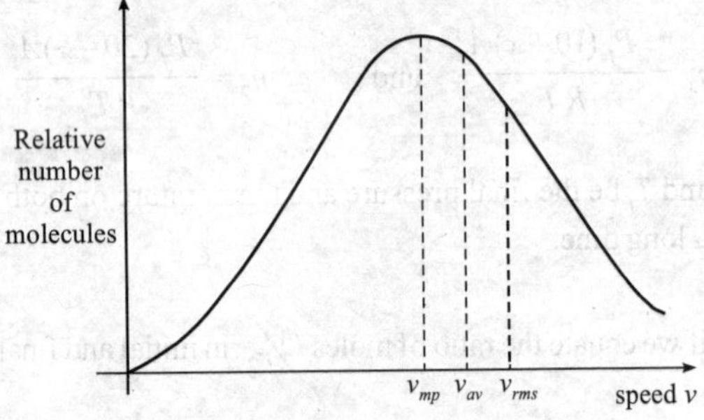

Figure 2.23

The exact distribution of speeds is described by a distribution function by Maxwell, who defined a function named probability distribution function $f(v)$, so that, of the N molecules in a gaseous system, the number dN molecules which have range of speeds between v and $v + dv$ or in the very short neighbourhood of v is given by

$$dN = f(v)\ dv \qquad \text{...(2.30)}$$

Thus $f(v)$ is the number of molecules per unit range of speeds. As we have discussed that the speeds of molecules vary in a wide range from zero to infinity, from equation-(2.30), we can write for total number of molecules as

$$N = \int_0^{\infty} f(v)\, dv \qquad \ldots(2.31)$$

The distribution function $f(v)$ was obtained by statical analysis and found out as

$$f(v) = 4\pi N v^2 \left[\frac{M}{2\pi RT}\right]^{3/2} e^{-\frac{Mv^2}{2RT}} \qquad \ldots(2.32)$$

Where R is universal gas constant and M is the molar mass, using equation-(2.32) we can write

$$f(v)\, dv = 4\pi N v^2 \left[\frac{M}{2\pi RT}\right]^{3/2} e^{-\frac{Mv^2}{2RT}}\, dv \qquad \ldots(2.33)$$

Here $f(v)\, dv$ is the number of molecules that have speeds between v and $v + dv$ and this equation-(2.33) is called as analytical Maxwell Boltzmann distribution function. Figure-2.24(a) shows the function computed for oxygen, neon and helium gases at 300 K temperature.

Here we can observe that the peak of each curve represents the speed, the maximum number of molecules have and it is called the most probable speed for that gas at particular temperature. This most probable speed is exhibited by large number of molecules of a gas at a given temperature.

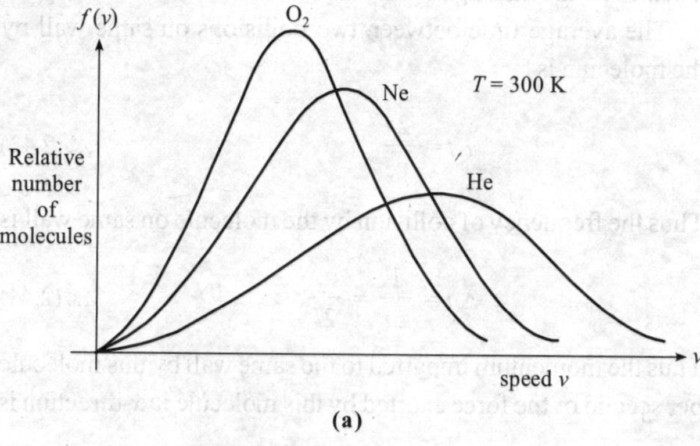

(a)

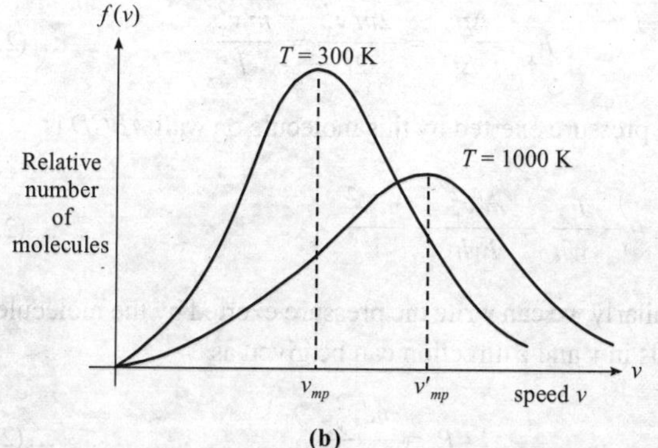

(b)

Figure 2.24

It can also be seen from figure-2.24(a) that more massive molecules have lower most probable speed. For a given gas, the most probable molecular speed becomes greater with increase in temperature as shown in figure-2.24(b). It can also be seen that more molecules have high speeds and fewer molecule have lower speeds throughout the range of speeds.

2.4.1 Different Speeds For Molecules of a Gas

(i) Average velocity of Gas Molecules

Initially we've discussed that all molecules of a gas in a container are in Brownian motion, thus due to randomness the directions of motion of different molecules are random and continuously changing due to repeated collisions randomly. If $\vec{v}_1$, $\vec{v}_2$ ...... $\vec{v}_N$ are the instantaneous velocity vectors of all N molecules of a gas, the average velocity vector of these N molecules can be written as

$$<\vec{v}> = \frac{\vec{v}_1 + \vec{v}_2 + \ldots\ldots + \vec{v}_N}{N} = 0 \qquad \ldots(2.34)$$

It is obvious that as all vectors are randomly scattered in space thus their sum i.e. the numerator of expression in equation-(2.34) can be approximated to zero. Thus the average velocity vector of molecules in a gas is always taken as zero.

(ii) Root-Mean-Square Velocity of Gas Molecules

As the name implies this is the square root of mean of squares of velocities of all the molecules of a gas. Mean of squares can be simply written as

$$<v^2> = \left(\frac{|\vec{v}_1|^2 + |\vec{v}_2|^2 + \ldots\ldots |\vec{v}_N|^2}{N}\right)$$

and $$v_{rms} = \sqrt{<v^2>}$$

$$= \sqrt{\left(\frac{|\vec{v}_1|^2 + |\vec{v}_2|^2 + \ldots\ldots |\vec{v}_N|^2}{N}\right)} \qquad \ldots(2.35)$$

Mathematically its value can be calculated by using the distribution function and taking the average of the square of the speed. Since $f(v)\, dv$ is the number of molecules with speed v in the range dv, the mean square speed can be given as

$$<v^2> = \frac{\int_0^{\infty} v^2 f(v) dv}{N} \qquad \ldots(2.36)$$

Integrating the expression in equation-(2.36), we finally get

$$<v^2> = \frac{3RT}{M}$$

So that rms speed can be given as

$$v_{rms} = \sqrt{\frac{3RT}{M}} \quad \ldots(2.37)$$

In most of numeric calculation and analysis of kinetic theory we use rms velocity for gas molecules.

(iii) Mean Speed of Gas Molecules

We have discussed that due to randomness average velocity vector of all the molecules of a gas comes out zero. But it is not same in case of mean or average speed. We obtain the mean speed by averaging the speed of the molecules. If can be simply defined as

$$\langle v \rangle = \frac{|\vec{v}_1| + |\vec{v}_2| + \ldots\ldots |\vec{v}_N|}{N} \quad \ldots(2.38)$$

Using distribution function we can calculate the mean speed as

$$\langle v \rangle = \frac{\int_0^{\infty} v\, f(v) dv}{N} \quad \ldots(2.39)$$

Integrating expression in equation-(2.39) results

$$v_{mean} = \sqrt{\frac{8RT}{\pi M}} \quad \ldots(2.40)$$

We can see on comparing equation-(2.37) and equation-(2.40)

$$v_{mean} < v_{rms}$$

(iv) Most Probable Speed of Gas Molecules

As discussed this is the speed maximum number of molecules have, and this is the speed corresponding to which distribution function has maximum or peak value, It's value can be obtained by differentiating the distribution function $f(v)$ and setting the derivative equal to zero. The final result obtained is

$$v_{mp} = \sqrt{\frac{2RT}{M}} \quad \ldots(2.41)$$

Comparing equation-(2.37), (2.40) and (2.41) we can see

$$v_{mp} < v_{mean} < v_{rms}$$

2.5 Pressure Exerted by a Gas

When a gas is enclosed in a rigid container, we have discussed that the molecules of gas are in Brownian motion and randomly collide with each other and container walls. All these collisions are assumed to be perfectly elastic. Due to these continuous collisions of large number of gas molecules with container walls, a pressure is exerted on the walls. Now we calculate this pressure analytically. Consider N molecules of a gas enclosed in a container as shown in figure-2.25. The length, width and height of container are l, w and h respectively along x, y and z direction. Out of several molecules, we consider one gas molecule of mass m' which is moving at an instant with a velocity v. This velocity has three components v_x, v_y and v_z along x, y and z directions respectively.

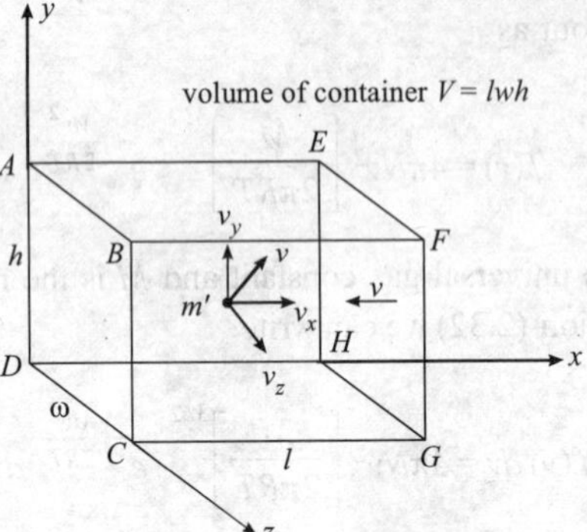

Figure 2.25

Let us first consider the motion of this molecule in x direction only. If it is moving with a velocity v_x towards the wall $EFGH$. It collides with the wall elastically and rebonds with the same speed v_x. Now it is travelling towards the wall $ABCD$. During a collision the momentum imparted to the wall by the molecule is

$$\Delta p_x = 2\, m' v_x \quad \ldots(2.42)$$

Now the molecule strikes the wall $ABCD$ after travelling a distance l and strike again onto the wall $EFGH$ with same speed v_x. The average time between two collisions on same wall by the molecule is

$$\Delta t = \frac{2l}{v_x} \quad \ldots(2.43)$$

Thus the frequency of collision by the molecule on same wall is

$$\Delta n = \frac{1}{\Delta t} = \frac{v_x}{2l} \quad \ldots(2.44)$$

Thus the momentum imparted to the same wall by this molecule per second or the force exerted by this molecule in x-direction is

$$F_x = \frac{\Delta p_x}{\Delta t} = \frac{2m'v_x^2}{2l} = \frac{m'v_x^2}{l} \quad \ldots(2.45)$$

The pressure exerted by this molecule on wall $ABCD$ is

$$P_x = \frac{F_x}{wh} = \frac{m'v_x^2}{lwh} = \frac{m'v_x^2}{V} \quad \ldots(2.46)$$

Similarly we can write the pressure exerted by the molecule on walls in y and z direction can be given as

$$P_y = \frac{m'v_y^2}{V} \quad \ldots(2.47)$$

and $$P_z = \frac{m'v_z^2}{V} \quad \ldots(2.48)$$

The average pressure by the molecule on container walls is

$$P = \frac{1}{3}(P_x + P_y + P_z)$$

or $$P = \frac{1}{3}\frac{m'}{v}(v_x^2 + v_y^2 + v_z^2)$$

or $$P = \frac{1}{3}\frac{m'}{v}v^2 \quad \ldots(2.49)$$

Where $v^2 = v_x^2 + v_y^2 + v_z^2$ is the root mean square (rms) velocity of a gas molecule we've already discussed. Equation-(2.49) gives the average pressure on container walls due to motion of only one molecule. There are total N molecules of gas enclosed in the container. Thus total average pressure exerted by a gas on its container walls is

$$P = \frac{1}{3}\frac{m'}{v}v^2 \times N$$

or $$P = \frac{1}{3}\frac{m}{v}v^2$$

[Where $m = m'N$ is the total mass of gas]

or $$P = \frac{1}{3}\rho v^2$$

[Where $\rho = \frac{m}{v}$ is the density of gas] ...(2.50)

Here we can also write

$$P = \frac{2}{3}\left(\frac{1}{2}\rho v^2\right) = \frac{2}{3}e \quad \ldots(2.51)$$

Here e represents the average kinetic energy of gas per unit volume or average kinetic energy density of gas pressure of a gas in a container can also be derived in another way as shown in figure-2.26. Figure shows a container wall and the gas molecules in its neighbourhood. If total number of molecules in the container are N, then the molecular density n_0 can be given as

$$n_0 = \frac{N}{V} \quad \ldots(2.52)$$

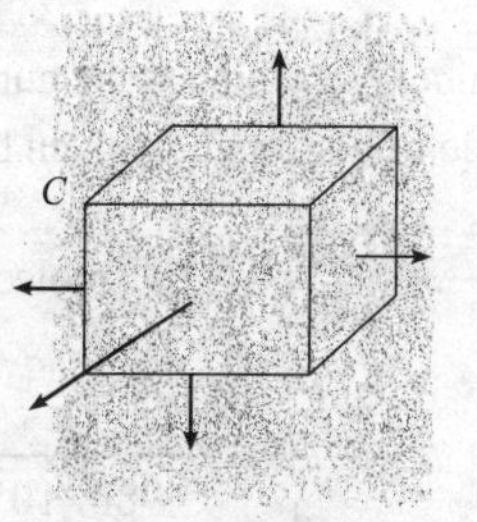

Figure 2.26

We consider a cube C of unit volume 1 m^3 near the wall shown. Total number of molecules in this cube are n_0 (molecular density) and each molecule is assumed to be moving in a random direction with the rms speed v. Due to randomness it can be assumed that toward every face of the cube $n/6$ molecules are moving with this speed. Thus number of collisions with a container wall per second per square meter of its surface can be written as

$$N_c = \frac{n_0}{6}v \quad \ldots(2.53)$$

Equation-(2.53) gives the number of collision per unit area of container wall in contact with a gas. As collisions are elastic, the momentum transferred to wall in each collision by a molecule is

$$\Delta p = 2m'v$$ [If m' is the mass of each molecule]

Thus momentum transferred to a container wall per second per unit of its surface area or average pressure can be given as

$$P = \frac{n_0 v}{6} \times 2m'v = \frac{1}{3}\rho v^2 \quad \ldots(2.54)$$

[As $n_0 \cdot m' = \rho$ density of gas]

Thus we can see that equation-(2.54) is identical with equation-(2.50). Equation-(2.50) was derived for a box shaped container but in derivation of equation-(2.54) we haven't taken any specific shape of container. Thus, this relation of average pressure always remains same irrespective of the shape of container.

Web Reference at www.physicsgalaxy.com

Age Group - High School Physics | Age 17-19 Years
Section - HEAT & THERMODYNAMICS
Topic - Kinetic Theory of Gases
Module Number - 18 to 20

2.6 Kinetic Energy of Gas Molecules

We've discussed that all gas molecules in a container are in continuous random motion repeatedly colliding with neighbouring molecules and container walls elastically. As all collisions are considered to be perfectly elastic we can assume that the total kinetic energy of all the gas molecules remains constant and all molecules are assumed to be always moving with their rms velocity. In this situation kinetic energy of a gas molecule of mass m' can be given as

$$E_K = \frac{1}{2}m'v_{rms}^2$$

or $$E_K = \frac{1}{2}m'\left(\frac{3RT}{M}\right) \quad \ldots(2.55)$$

By definition, the molecular mass of a gas molecule can be given as

$$M = m' N_{AV} \quad [N_{AV} = \text{Avogadro Number}] \quad \ldots(2.56)$$

From equation-(2.55) and (2.56)

$$E_K = \frac{1}{2} m' \left(\frac{3RT}{m' N_{AV}}\right) = \frac{3}{2} \frac{R}{N_{AV}} T = \frac{3}{2} kT \quad \ldots(2.57)$$

Here $k = R/N_{AV} = 1.38 \times 10^{-23}$ Joule/molecule, k is a universal constant called Boltzmann's constant. This equation-(2.57) gives the kinetic energy of a moving gas molecule in a gas at absolute temperature T. If we find the total kinetic energy of all the molecules of a gas, it is given as

$$E_T = \frac{3}{2} kT \times N$$

[If N are the total no. of gas molecules in a container]

If n moles of gas are there in a container, we have

$$N = n \times N_{AV}$$

Thus $$E_T = \frac{3}{2} \left(\frac{R}{N_{AV}}\right) T \times n \times N_{AV}$$

or $$E_T = \frac{3}{2} nRT \quad \ldots(2.58)$$

As we've discussed that total energy of a gas is the sum of kinetic energy of all of its molecules. Equation-(2.58) thus gives the total energy of a gas in its molecular motion or the expression in equation-(2.58) gives the total translational energy of all the gas molecules at absolute temperature T.

2.7 *Microscopic Interpretation of Temperature*

In previous section we've discussed that the average molecular translational kinetic energy and absolute temperature are proportional. The higher the temperature of a system. The greater, proportionally, is the average translational kinetic energy of the molecules of that system. Thus in terms of average kinetic energy of a gas molecule E_T, the temperature can be given by equation-(2.57) as

$$T = \frac{2}{3} \frac{E_T}{k} \quad \ldots(2.59)$$

Thus the average translational kinetic energy of gas molecules in an ideal gas depends only on the temperature, not on the pressure or type of gas. Thus equation-(2.58) shows that temperature is a measure of kinetic energies of molecules or temperature is a large-scale manifestation of motion at the molecular level of gases, liquids and solids.

Now we take few example to understand the molecular speeds and their kinetic energy in detail.

 # Illustrative Example 2.14

(a) Calculate (i) root mean square speed and (ii) the mean kinetic energy of one mole of hydrogen at S.T.P. (Given that density of hydrogen is 0.09 kg/m^3).

(b) Given that the mass of a molecule of hydrogen is 3.34×10^{-27} kg. Calculate Avogadro's number.

(c) Calculate Boltzmann's constant.

Solution

(a) (i) We know that the pressure of a gas is given as

$$P = \frac{1}{3} \rho v_{rms}^2$$

$$v_{rms} = \sqrt{\left(\frac{3P}{\rho}\right)}$$

$$v_{rms} = \sqrt{\left(\frac{3 \times 0.76 \times 13.6 \times 10^3 \times 9.8}{0.09}\right)}$$

$$= 1837 \text{ m/sec} = 1.837 \text{ km/sec}$$

(ii) Kinetic energy $= \frac{1}{2} m v_{rms}^2$

Here $M = 2 \text{ gm} = 2 \times 10^{-3}$ kg.

or $$\text{K.E.} = \frac{1}{2} \times 2 \times 10^{-3} \times (1837)^2$$

$$= 3374.56 \text{ joules}$$

(b) Mass of one molecule of $H_2 = 3.34 \times 10^{-27}$ kg

Molecular mass of hydrogen $= 2 \times 10^{-3}$ kg

The Avogadro's number N_A, which is the number of molecules in one gram molecule of hydrogen is given by

$$N_A = \frac{2 \times 10^{-3}}{3.34 \times 10^{-27}} = 5.988 \times 10^{23} \text{ molecules.}$$

(c) We know that $k = \dfrac{R}{N_A} = \dfrac{8.3}{5.988 \times 10^{23}}$

$$= 1.37 \times 10^{-23} \text{ J/mol.K}$$

Illustrative Example 2.15

Calculate the number of molecules in 1 cm^3 of an ideal gas at 27°C and a pressure of 10 mm of mercury. Mean kinetic energy of a molecule at 27°C is 4×10^{-14} erg; the density of mercury is 13.6 gm/c.c.

Solution

The pressure exerted by a gas is given by

$$P = \frac{2}{3} \text{ (K.E. per unit volume)}$$

or $$\text{K.E.} = \frac{3}{2} P$$

Here $P = 10$ mm of mercury = 1 cm of mercury,

$$= 1 \times 13.6 \times 980 = 1.33 \times 10^4 \text{ dynes/cm}^2$$

Thus, we have $$\text{K.E.} = \frac{3}{2} \times 1.33 \times 10^4 \times 1 = 1.99 \times 10^4 \text{ ergs}$$

As mean kinetic energy per molecule is 4×10^{-14} ergs, the number of molecule will be

$$\frac{1.99 \times 10^4}{4 \times 10^{-14}} = 4.9 \times 10^{17} \approx 5 \times 10^{17} \text{ molecules.}$$

Illustrative Example 2.16

A parallel beam of nitrogen molecules moving with velocity $v = 400$ m/s impinges on a wall at an angle $\theta = 30°$ to its normal. The concentration of molecules in the beam $n_0 = 0.9 \times 10^{19}$ cm^{-3}. Find the pressure exerted by the beam on the wall assuming the collisions of molecules with the wall are perfectly elastic.

Solution

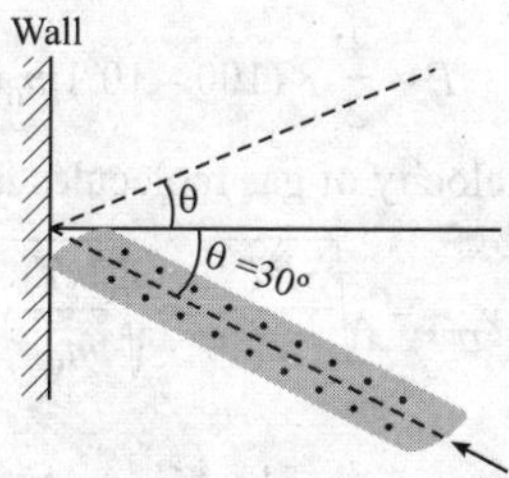

Figure 2.27

Figure-2.27 shows a beam of molecules in cylindrical form striking the wall. According to elastic collision, each molecule is reflected from the wall at the same angle of incidence as shown with same speed. If m_0 is the mass of each nitrogen molecule, momentum of each molecule is

$$P_0 = m_0 v$$

During collision change in momentum of each molecule or momentum imparted to wall by each molecule is

$$\Delta P_0 = 2m_0 v \cos\theta$$

If S is the cross-sectional area of beam and v be the velocity of molecules in the beam then number of molecules incident on wall per second are

$$N = n_0 v S \qquad [n_0 = \text{molecular density}]$$

Thus total momentum imparted to the wall per second by the beam or the force exerted on wall is

$$F = \frac{\Delta P_0}{\Delta t} = 2m_0 v \cos\theta \times n_0 v S \qquad \dots(2.60)$$

As equation-(2.60) gives that total momentum imparted to the wall per second, this is the net force exerted by beam on wall. Thus the pressure on wall by beam is

$$P = \frac{F}{S} = 2\, m_0 v^2 \cos\theta .\, n_0$$

$$= 2 \times \frac{28 \times 10^{-3}}{6.023 \times 10^{23}} \times 9 \times 10^{24} \times (400)^2 \times \cos^2(30°)$$

$$= 10^5\, Pa \cong 1 \text{ atm}$$

Illustrative Example 2.17

Calculate the temperature at which rms velocity of a gas molecule is same as that of a molecule of another gas at 47°C. Molecular weight of first and second gases are 64 and 32 respectively.

Solution

We know rms speed of a gas molecule is given as

$$v = \sqrt{\frac{3RT}{M}}$$

For first and second gas if temperature are T_1 and T_2 respectively, we have

$$v_{\text{rms1}} = v_{\text{rms2}}$$

or $$\frac{T_1}{M_1} = \frac{T_2}{M_2}$$

or $$\frac{T_1}{64 \times 10^{-3}} = \frac{320}{32} \qquad [\text{As } T_2 = 47 + 273 = 320 \text{ K}]$$

or $$T_1 = 640 \text{ K}$$

Illustrative Example 2.18

Figure-2.28 shows a cylindrical container which is divided in two equal parts by a clamped diathermic piston. Different ideal gases are filled in the two parts. It is found that the rms speed of molecules in the lower part is equal to the mean speed of molecules in the upper part. Find the ratio of mass of molecule of gas in lower part to that of the gas in upper part.

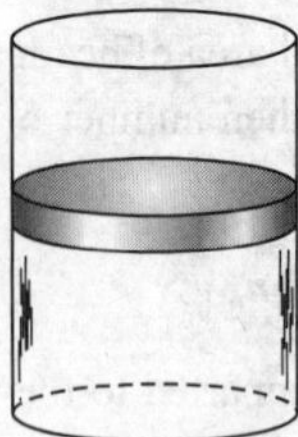

Figure 2.28

Solution

As piston is diathermic the two gases must be in thermal equilibrium. If M_1 and M_2 be the molecular masses of the gases filled in lower and upper part of the container, the rms speed of gas molecules in lower part is

$$v_{rms} = \sqrt{\frac{3RT}{M_1}} \qquad \ldots(2.61)$$

The mean speed of gas molecules in upper part is

$$v_{mean} = \sqrt{\frac{8RT}{\pi M_2}} \qquad \ldots(2.62)$$

From equation-(2.61) and (2.62), according to the given situation, we have

$$v_{rms} = v_{mean}$$

or $$\sqrt{\frac{3RT}{M_1}} = \sqrt{\frac{8RT}{\pi M_2}}$$

or $$\frac{M_1}{M_2} = \frac{3\pi}{8} = 1.178$$

As ratio of masses of molecules and that of molecular masses is same, it is 1.178.

Illustrative Example 2.19

In a closed container of volume 10^{-3} m^3, O_2 gas is filled at temperature 400 K and pressure 1.5 atm. A small hole is made in the container from which gas leaks out to open atmosphere. After some time the temperature and pressure of container become equals to that of surrounding. Find the mass of gas that leaks out from the container. (Atmospheric temperature = 300 K)

Solution

If initially there is m_1 mass of O_2 gas in the container, from gas law we have

$$PV = \frac{m_1}{32} RT$$

or $$m_1 = \frac{32PV}{RT} = \frac{32 \times 1.5 \times 10^5 \times 10^{-3}}{8.314 \times 400}$$

$$= 1.443 \text{ gm}$$

Finally if m_2 mass of O_2 is left in the container, from gas law we have

$$PV = \frac{m_2}{32} RT$$

or $$m_2 = \frac{32PV}{RT}$$

$$= \frac{32 \times 10^5 \times 10^{-3}}{8.314 \times 300} = 1.283 \text{ gm}$$

Thus mass of gas leaked out is

$$\Delta m = m_1 - m_2$$

$$= 1.443 - 1.283 = 0.16 \text{ gm}$$

Illustrative Example 2.20

In a certain region of outer space there are only 100 molecules per cm^3 on an average. The temperature there is about 3 K. What is the average pressure of this very dilute gas.

Solution

We know that the gas pressure is given as

$$P = \frac{1}{3} \rho v_{rms}^2$$

Now we can write the density of gas as $\rho = m_0 N$, where m_0 is the mass of the gas molecule and N is the number of molecules in 1 m^3 of the gas.

In the present case

$$N = 100 \times 10^6$$

or $$P = \frac{1}{3} \times (100 \times 10^6)\, m_0 v_{rms}^2$$

As we know rms velocity of gas molecules is given as

$$v_{rms} = \sqrt{\frac{3RT}{M}} = \sqrt{\frac{3kT}{m_0}}$$

$$\left[\text{As } M = m_0 N_{AV} \text{ and } \frac{R}{N_{AV}} = k\right]$$

So, we have $$P = \frac{1}{3} \times (100 \times 10^6) \times 3kT$$

$$= (100 \times 10^6) kT$$

$$= (100 \times 10^6)(1.38 \times 10^{-23})(3) \quad [\text{As } T = 3 \text{ K}]$$

$$= 41.4 \times 10^{-16}$$

$$= 4.14 \times 10^{-15}\, Pa$$

Illustrative Example 2.21

One gram-mole of oxygen at 27°C and one atmospheric pressure is enclosed in a vessel. Assuming the molecules to be moving with v_{rms}, find the number of collisions per second which the molecules makes with one square meter area of the vessel wall.

Solution

From gas law we have

$$PV = \frac{m}{M} RT$$

or $$PV = \frac{m'N}{m'N_{AV}} RT$$

[If m' = Mass of one molecule and N = total number of molecules]

or $$PV = NkT \qquad \left[\text{As } \frac{R}{N_{AV}} = k\right]$$

or $$P = n_0 kT \qquad \ldots(2.63)$$

Here $n_0 = N/V$ the number of molecules per unit volume of gas. Students should note that equation (2.63) relates the gas pressure, temperature and molecular density. This expression can be used as a standard equation in several numerical cases as an alternative form of gas law.

Thus here molecular density is given as

$$n_0 = \frac{P}{kT}$$

$$= \frac{(1\,\text{atm})}{(1.38\times10^{-23})\times(300)}$$

$$= \frac{10^5}{1.38\times10^{-23}\times300} = 2.44\times10^{25}\,\text{m}^{-3}$$

The rms speed of gas molecules is given as

$$v_{rms} = \sqrt{\frac{3RT}{M}}$$

$$= \sqrt{\frac{3\times8.314\times300}{32\times10^{-3}}} = 483.4\,\text{m/s}$$

Now number of collision per square metre of vessel wall is given as

$$N = \frac{n_0 v_{rms}}{6} = \frac{2.44\times10^{25}\times433.4}{6}$$

$$= 1.97\times10^{27}\,\text{m}^{-2}$$

Web Reference at www.physicsgalaxy.com

Age Group - High School Physics | Age 17-19 Years
Section - HEAT & THERMODYNAMICS
Topic - Kinetic Theory of Gases
Module Number - 21 to 25

Practice Exercise 2.3

(i) The rms velocity of hydrogen molecules at a certain temperature is 300 m/s. If the temperature is doubled and hydrogen gas dissociates into atomic hydrogen. Find the rms speed of the gas molecules now.

[600 m/s]

(ii) In a container, the molecular density of an enclosed gas is 10^{26} molecules/m^3, each of mass 3×10^{-27} kg. If rms velocity of the gas molecules is 2000 m/s, find the number of molecules hitting per square meter of the container wall every second and the pressure exerted on the walls of container by the molecules.

[3.33×10^{28} s^{-1}, 4×10^5 N/m^2]

(iii) An ideal gas is enclosed between the closed end of a uniform cross-sectional tube and a pellet of mercury of length h = 10 cm. The length of the tube occupied by the gas when held vertical with the closed end upward is l_1 = 40 cm. When it is turned through θ = 60° the length occupied by the gas is only l_2 = 38 cm. Calculate the frictional force between the wall of the tube and mercury pellet. The radius of the tube is r = 2 mm. Take g = 10 m/s^2 and density of mercury 13600 kg/m^3.

[0.026 N]

(iv) The average translational kinetic energy of O_2 at a particular temperature is 0.048 eV. Find the average translational kinetic energy of N_2 molecules in eV at the same temperature.

[0.048 eV]

(v) Find the number of molecules per unit volume of air at temperature 0°C and a pressure of $p = 1.013\times10^5$ Pa and the average distance between molecules. Boltzmann constant is $k = 1.38\times10^{-23}$ J/K.

[2.688×10^{25} m^{-3}, 3.31×10^{-9} m]

(vi) Evaluate the speeds v_{mp}, $\langle v \rangle$, v_{rms} for (a) H_2 at 300 K and (b) O_2 at 300 K.

[(a) 1579.3 m/s, 1782.5 m/s, 1934.25 m/s (b) 394.83 m/s, 445.63 m/s, 483.56 m/s]

(vii) Twelve molecules have the following speeds, given in arbitrary units : 5, 2, 2, 6, 0, 4, 1, 3, 5, 1, 7, 3,. Calculate (a) the mean speed and (b) the rms speed.

[(a) 3.25 m/s, (b) 3.86 m/s]

(viii) What is the rms speed of nitrogen molecules contained in an 8.0 m^{-3} volume at 2.1 atm if the total amount of nitrogen is 1300 mol?

[374.68 m/s]

2.8 *Degrees of Freedom and Equipartition of Energy*

In previous section we've derived a relation among temperature and average translational kinetic energy of a gas molecule as

$$E_T = \frac{1}{2} m' v_{rms}^2 = \frac{3}{2} kT$$

Initially we have discussed that if a molecule has v_x, v_y and v_z, average velocity components in three dimensional co-ordinate system,

We have

$$v_{rms}^2 = v_x^2 + v_y^2 + v_z^2$$

As for a single molecule in space the three directions x, y and z are identical in all respect, we can assume that the average values of v_x, v_y and v_z must be same, hence

$$v_x^2 = v_y^2 = v_z^2 = \frac{v_{rms}^2}{3}$$

Thus, the average kinetic energies of a gas molecule in the three directions respectively can be given as

$$\frac{1}{2} mv_x^2 = \frac{1}{2} mv_y^2 = \frac{1}{2} mv_z^2 = \frac{1}{2} \text{kT} \quad \text{...(2.64)}$$

The three kinetic energies in expression of equation-(2.64) are the three parts of total kinetic energy of a gas molecule used corresponding to the three velocity components in the three directions in space.

Thus *a* gas molecule uses its total translational kinetic energy in three ways of translations. These ways are called translational degrees of freedom. Here each degree of freedom corresponds to the ability of a molecule to participate in a one dimensional motion which contributes to the total mechanical energy of that molecule. Since there are three spatial directions in which the molecule can move, a gas molecule has three translational degrees of freedom and from equation-(2.64) it can be seen that energy associated with each degree of freedom is $\frac{1}{2}\, kT$. It is further observed that energy associated with each degree of freedom whether it is due to translational motion, rotational motion or any type of motion is always $\frac{1}{2}\, kT$, irrespective of type of motion. This is called as law of equipartition of energy, stated as

"The total energy of an ideal gas molecule is distributed equally among all of its degrees of freedom and energy associated with each degree of freedom is $\frac{1}{2}\, kT$."

2.9 *Internal Energy of a Gas*

Law of equipartition of energy states that the total energy of a gas molecule is equally divided among all of its degrees of freedom or the number of ways in which the molecule can contribute to its mechanical energy, and energy in each contribution type is $\frac{1}{2}\, kT$.

Thus if a gas molecule has *f* degrees of freedom or it can move in *f* number of ways, the total energy of that molecule can be given as

$$E = f \times \frac{1}{2} kT = \frac{f}{2} kT \quad \text{...(2.65)}$$

If an ideal gas having *f* degrees of freedom and have *n* moles in a container than total energy of this gas is given as

$$U = \frac{f}{2} kT \times n \times N_{AV}$$

or

$$U = \frac{f}{2} nRT \quad [\text{As } kN_{AV} = R] \quad \text{...(2.66)}$$

The expression in equation-(2.66) gives the sum of total kinetic energies of all types of motion of all the molecules of a gas, called as *total internal energy* of a gas. Our initial assumption for an ideal gas was, its molecules do not interact thus no potential energy exist for gas molecules thus energy given by equation-(2.66) is the net amount of energy a gas can contain i.e. the internal energy of gas and it depends only on absolute temperature of the gas.

2.9.1 Degrees of Freedom and Internal Energy For Different Types of Gases

Monoatomic Gases

The molecule of a monoatomic gas is just a single atom. It can have several types of motion shown in figure-2.29.

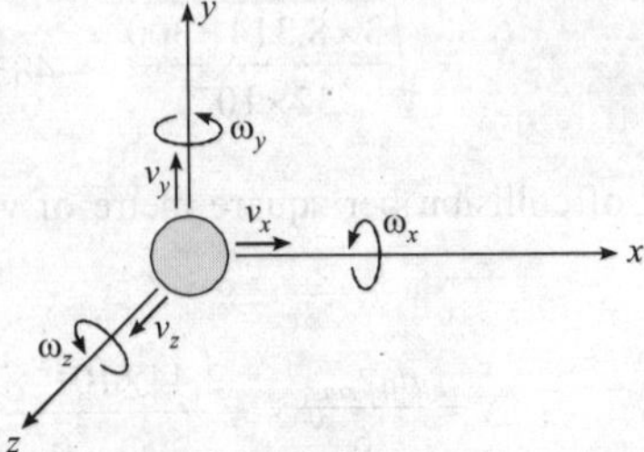

Figure 2.29

A single atom, can translate in x, y and z direction with speeds v_x, v_y, and v_z respectively as discussed earlier and hence has three translational degrees of freedom and energies in these three degrees of freedom can be written as $\frac{1}{2}mv_x^2$, $\frac{1}{2}mv_y^2$ and $\frac{1}{2}mv_z^2$ respectively. Similar to this translational motion the atom can also spin about the three co-ordinate axes as shown with respective angular speeds ω_x, ω_y and ω_z. Thus this gas molecule must also has three rotational degrees of freedom and energy in these three degrees of freedom can be given as $\frac{1}{2}I\omega_x^2$, $\frac{1}{2}I\omega_y^2$ and $\frac{1}{2}I\omega_z^2$. Here I is the moment of inertia of the gas molecule. According to our initial assumption for an ideal gas, we neglect the size of a gas molecule. If size or radius of an atom is neglected, we must take its moment of inertia negligible which is proportional to the square of its radius. Thus in a monoatomic gas molecule we can consider that no energy is contributed by its rotational motion hence a monoatomic gas molecule has only three degrees of freedom and all these are called translational degrees of freedom.

Thus total internal energy of n moles of a monoatomic gas at a temperature T is given as

$$U = \frac{f}{2}\,nRT = \frac{3}{2}\,nRT \qquad \ldots(2.67)$$

Diatomic Gases

The molecule of a diatomic gas consists of two atoms connected by a bond or interatomic forces between the two atoms. Figure-2.30 shows a rough sketch of such an atom. In free space this atom is free to move in the three dimensional co-ordinate system, hence has three velocity components along the three axes shown in figure-2.30 thus it has three translational degrees of freedom. In fact all type of molecules, irrespective of its atomic configuration has three translational degrees of freedom in space. Here also if we consider the rotational motion of the molecule about x, y and z axis from figure-2.30 we can see that the rotation of this molecule about y and z axis in this situation is significant as the bond length between the two atoms can not be neglected however, we are ignoring the radii of individual atoms. Masses of individual atoms are concentrated at their position thus moment of inertia of this molecule about y and z axis is a significant value but when we consider the rotation of this molecule about x-axis in the coordinate system shown in figure-2.30, its moment of inertia is again negligible thus rotation of the molecule about x-axis does not contribute any energy to the total energy of molecule so here we can state that a diatomic gas molecule has two rotational degrees of freedom in addition to three translational degrees of freedom. Thus in general, a diatomic gas molecule has five degrees of freedom.

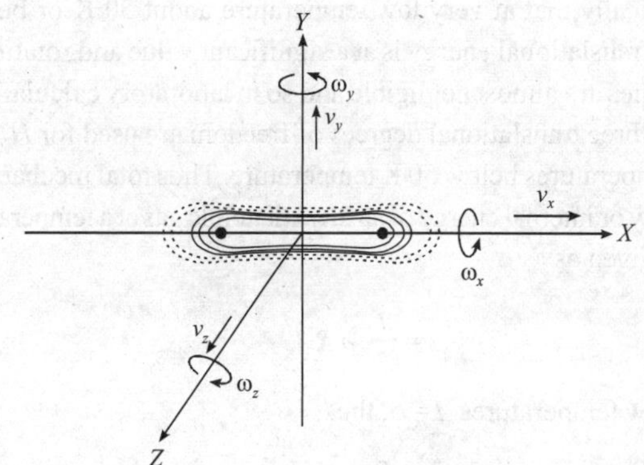

Figure 2.30

Some times vibrational motion of molecules can also contribute to the total mechanical energy of a gas molecule as the molecular bonds are not rigid, they can stretch bend, may behave like a spring as shown in figure-2.30. This result lead to additional degrees of freedom and as well as energy. For most diatomic gases, however the vibrational motion does not contribute appreciably to the total energy of a gas molecule. The reason for this involves the concept of quantum mechanics and beyond the scope of this book. Briefly, vibrational energy of an atom can change only in some finite steps in a quantized manner. If the energy change of the first step is much larger then the energy possessed by most molecules, then nearly all the molecules remain in the minimum energy state of motion and so at low temperature, changing the temperature does not change their average vibrational energy appreciable and do not contribute any energy change to the total mechanical energy of a gas molecule. At low temperature the vibrational degrees of freedom are said to be frozen out and not included in total energy calculation and changes of energy. But at very high temperatures like 5000 K and above the atoms of the diatomic gas starts vibrating at their local position appreciably and bond behaves like a spring as shown in figure-2.31 and then after we include two additional vibrational degrees of freedom for a diatomic gas.

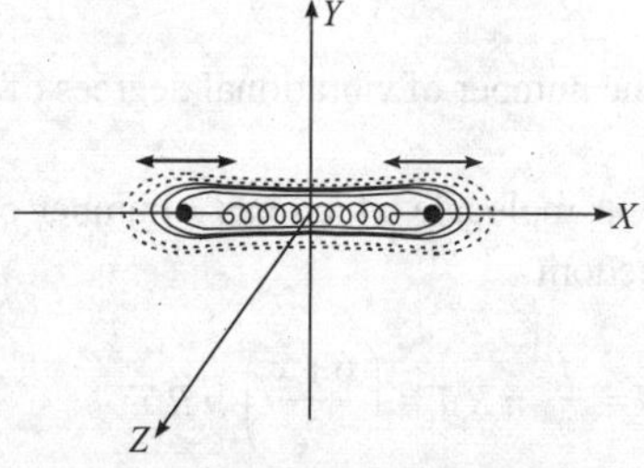

Figure 2.31

According to quantum mechanical properties, rotational energy of a molecule also changes in finite steps, but these steps are usually very small. Thus the freezing out of rotational degrees of freedom is very rare for example in hydrogen gas it is observed practically that at very low temperature about 50 K or below only translational energy is at a significant value and rotational energies are almost negligible and so in laboratory calculations only three translational degrees of freedom are used for H_2 gas at temperatures below 50 K temperature. Thus total mechanical energy or internal energy of an ideal diatomic gas at a temperature T is given as

$$U = \frac{f}{2} nRT$$

At low temperatures $f = 5$, thus

$$U = \frac{5}{2} nRT \qquad \dots(2.68)$$

At very high temperatures $f = 7$, thus

$$U = \frac{7}{2} nRT \qquad \dots(2.69)$$

Polyatomic Gases

A polyatomic gas molecule should also have three translational degrees of freedom and the number of rotational degrees of freedom depending on the geometry of the molecule. If the molecule is a linear one like CO_2 then it has only two rotational degrees of freedom due to the obvious reason discussed in previous section, and if it is a non linear molecule like H_2O, CH_4 etc. then it has three rotational degrees of freedom as about all three co-ordinate axes, some significant moment of inertia exists. Number of vibrational degrees of freedom in complex polyatomic molecules varies in different ways. There is no simple theoretical way to calculate the exact number of active vibrational degrees of freedom in a polyatomic molecule.

Thus the total internal energy of n moles of a polyatomic gas at a temperature T is given as

For a linear molecule

$$U = \frac{f}{2} nRT = \left(\frac{5+x}{2}\right) nRT \qquad \dots(2.70)$$

Where x are the number of vibrational degrees of freedoms

For a non linear molecule which has x number of vibrational degrees of freedom

$$U = \frac{f}{2} nRT = \left(\frac{6+x}{2}\right) nRT \qquad \dots(2.71)$$

2.9.2 Equivalent Degrees of Freedom For a Gaseous Mixture

We know if two substances at same temperature are connected or mixed, they do not exchange any thermal energy and the temperature of mixture remains same.

If N gases with degrees of freedom $f_1, f_2, f_3 \dots f_N$ are mixed with $n_1, n_2, n_3 \dots n_N$ moles at same temperature T then their total internal energy before mixing can be given as

$$U_i = \frac{f_1}{2} n_1RT + \frac{f_2}{2} n_2RT + \dots + \frac{f_N}{2} n_NRT \qquad \dots(2.72)$$

If after homogeneous mixing, for analytical purpose we assume f_{eq} are the number of degrees of freedom for the mixture then after mixing the internal energy of this mixture can be given as

$$U_f = \frac{f_{eq}}{2} (n_1 + n_2 + \dots n_N) RT \qquad \dots(2.73)$$

As no energy loss is taking place during mixing of gases, we have from equation-(2.72) and (2.73)

$$U_i = U_f$$

or $$\frac{f_1}{2} n_1RT + \frac{f_2}{2} n_2RT + \dots + \frac{f_N}{2} n_NRT$$

$$= \frac{f_{eq}}{2} (n_1 + n_2 + \dots n_N) RT$$

or $$f_{eq} = \frac{f_1n_1 + f_2n_2 + \cdots f_Nn_N}{n_1 + n_2 + \cdots n_N} \qquad \dots(2.74)$$

2.9.3 Mixing of Gases at Constant Volume

When some gases at different temperature are mixed at constant volume in a thermally insulated vessel, the total internal energy of all the gases remains constant. For example if N gases with $n_1, n_2, \dots n_N$ moles at temperature $T_1, T_2 \dots T_N$ are mixed in a container and if the gases have degrees of freedom $f_1, f_2, \dots f_N$, then the total internal energy of gases before mixing is

$$U_i = \frac{f_1}{2} n_1RT_1 + \frac{f_2}{2} n_2RT_2 + \dots\dots + \frac{f_N}{2} n_NRT_N \dots(2.75)$$

If after mixing temperature of mixture become T_f then the total internal energy of gas after mixing of gases is

$$U_f = \frac{f_1}{2} n_1RT_f + \frac{f_2}{2} n_2RT_f + \dots\dots + \frac{f_N}{2} n_NRT_f \dots(2.76)$$

As total internal energy of the gaseous mixture must remains constant thus we have from equation-(2.75) and (2.76),

$$U_i = U_f$$

or $$\frac{f_1}{2} n_1RT_f + \frac{f_2}{2} n_2RT_f + \dots\dots + \frac{f_N}{2} n_NRT_f$$

$$= \frac{f_1}{2} n_1RT_1 + \frac{f_2}{2} n_2RT_2 + \dots\dots + \frac{f_N}{2} n_NRT_N$$

or $$T_f = \frac{f_1n_1T_1 + f_2n_2T_2 + \cdots f_Nn_NT_N}{f_1n_1 + f_2n_2 + \cdots f_Nn_N} \qquad \dots(2.77)$$

Here equation-(2.77) can be used to find the final temperature of a gaseous mixture of different gases after mixing in a thermally insulated container.

Illustrative Example 2.22

Calculate (a) the average kinetic energy of translation of an oxygen molecule at 27ºC, (b) the total kinetic energy of an oxygen molecule at 27ºC, (c) the total kinetic energy in joule of one mole of oxygen at 27ºC. Given Avogadro number = 6.02 × 10^23 and Boltzmann's constant = 1.38 × 10^–23 J/molecule-K.

Solution

(a) An oxygen molecule has three translational degrees of freedom, thus the average translational kinetic energy of an oxygen molecule at 27ºC is given as

$$E_T = \frac{3}{2}kT = \frac{3}{2} \times 1.38 \times 10^{-23} \times 300$$

$$= 6.21 \times 10^{-21} \text{ J/mole}$$

(b) An oxygen molecule has total five degrees of freedom, hence its total kinetic energy is given as

$$E_T = \frac{5}{2}kT = \frac{5}{2} \times 1.38 \times 10^{-23} \times 300$$

$$= 10.35 \times 10^{-21} \text{ J/mole}$$

(c) Total kinetic energy of one mole of oxygen is its internal energy, which can be given as

$$U = \frac{5}{2}nRT$$

$$= \frac{5}{2} \times 1 \times 8.314 \times 300$$

$$= 6235.5 \text{ J/mole}$$

Illustrative Example 2.23

15 gm of nitrogen is enclosed in a vessel at temperature $T = 300$ K. Find the amount of heat required to double the root mean square velocity of these molecules.

Solution

We know rms speed of gas molecules is given as

$$v_{rms} = \sqrt{\frac{3RT}{M}}$$

As v_{rms} is directly proportional to $\sqrt{T}$, to double rms speed, temperature must be raised four times to $T_f = 1200$ K

As the gas is enclosed in a container, it can not expand or it can not loose any energy to external system. Its initial internal energy is given as

$$U_i = \frac{f}{2}nRT = \frac{5}{2}nRT \text{ [As for a diatomic gas } f = 5]$$

$$= \frac{5}{2} \times \frac{15}{28} \times 8.314 \times 300$$

$$= 3340.45 \text{ joule}$$

Finally when gas temperature is raised to 1200 K, its internal energy is given as

$$U_f = \frac{5}{2}nRT_f$$

$$= \frac{5}{2} \times \frac{15}{28} \times 8.314 \times 1200$$

$$= 13361.6 \text{ joule}$$

Increase in internal energy or amount of heat supplied is

$$\Delta Q = U_f - U_i = 10021.35 \text{ joule}$$

Illustrative Example 2.24

1 gm of helium having rms velocity of molecules 1000 m/s and 4 gm of oxygen having rms velocity of molecules 1000 m/s are mixed in a container which is thermally isolated. What are the rms velocities of helium and oxygen molecules after equilibrium is attained ?

Solution

Given that rms velocity of He molecules is 1000 m/s. If gas is at temperature T, we have

$$v_{rms} = \sqrt{\frac{3RT}{M_1}}$$

or $$1000 = \sqrt{\frac{3 \times 8.314 \times T_1}{2 \times 10^{-3}}}$$

or $$T_1 = \frac{2 \times 10^{-3} \times 10^6}{3 \times 8.314} = 80.186 \text{ K}$$

It is given that rms velocity of oxygen molecules is also 1000 m/s. If temperature of this gas is T_2, we have

$$v_{rms} = \sqrt{\frac{3RT_2}{M_2}}$$

or $$1000 = \sqrt{\frac{3\times8.314\times T_2}{32\times10^{-3}}}$$

or $$T_2 = \frac{32\times10^{-3}\times10^6}{3\times8.314} = 1282.976\,\text{K}$$

It is given that 1 gm of He and 4 gm of O_2 is mixed. If their number of moles are n_1 and n_2 then

$$n_1 = \frac{1}{2} \text{ and } n_2 = \frac{4}{32} = \frac{1}{8}$$

We know that gases at different temperature are mixed at constant volume (or in a container), the total internal energy of system remains constant before and after mixing. If in this case final temperature of mixture is T_f, then we have

$$T_f = \frac{f_1n_1T_1 + f_2n_2T_2}{f_1n_1 + f_2n_2}$$

Here we have $f_1 = 3$, $f_2 = 5$, $n_1 = \frac{1}{2}$, $n_2 = \frac{1}{8}$, T_1 80.186 and $T_2 = 1282.76$

Thus final temperature of mixture is given as

$$T_f = \frac{3\times\frac{1}{2}\times80.186 + 5\times\frac{1}{8}\times1282.76}{3\times\frac{1}{2}+5\times\frac{1}{8}}$$

$$= \frac{120.28\times801.725}{2.125} = 433.89\,\text{K}$$

Thus final rms velocity of *He* gas molecules is

$$v_{\text{rms}} = \sqrt{\frac{3RT_f}{M_1}}$$

$$= \sqrt{\frac{3\times8.314\times433.89}{2\times10^{-3}}} = 2326.17\,\text{m/s}$$

Final rms velocity of O_2 gas molecules is

$$v_{rms} = \sqrt{\frac{3RT_f}{M_2}}$$

$$= \sqrt{\frac{3\times8.314\times433.89}{32\times10^{-3}}} = 581.54\,\text{m/s}$$

Illustrative Example 2.25

A cubical vessel of side 1 m contains one mole of nitrogen at a temperature of 300 K. If the molecules are assuming to move with the rms velocity (a) find the number of collisions per second which the molecules may make with the wall of the vessel, (b) further if the vessel now thermally insulated moved with a constant speed v and then suddenly stopped and this results in rise of temperature by 2°C, find v.

Solution

Given that volume of container = 1 m^2

Temperature of gas = 300 K

Amount of gas = 1 mole

(a) If n_0 be the number of molecules per unit volume, we have

$$n_0 = 1 \text{ mole}$$

$$= 6.023 \times 10^{23}\,\text{m}^{-3}$$

The rms velocity of molecules at 300 K temperature is

$$v_{rms} = \sqrt{\frac{3RT}{M}}$$

$$= \sqrt{\frac{3\times3.314\times300}{28\times10^{-3}}}$$

$$= 516.75\,\text{m/s}$$

We know that number of collisions per second per square meter of wall is given by

$$N = \frac{n_0v}{6}$$

$$= \frac{6.023\times10^{23}\times516.75}{6}$$

$$= 5.187 \times 10^{25}\,\text{s}^{-1}\,\text{m}^{-1}$$

(b) When container is moving at speed v, the kinetic energy in the nitrogen molecules is

$$E_k = \frac{1}{2}Mv^2$$

$$= \frac{1}{2} \times 28 \times 10^{-3} \times v^2$$

[Mass of 1 mole of gas = 28×10^{-3} kg]

When the container is suddenly stopped, this kinetic energy is transformed into thermal energy and increases the internal energy of gas as container is insulated. If temperature increment of gas is ΔT, rise in its internal energy is

$$\Delta U = \frac{f}{2}\,nR\Delta T$$

or $$\Delta U = \frac{5}{2}\,nR\,\Delta T$$

or $$= \frac{5}{2} \times 1 \times 8.314 \times 2$$

or $$= 41.57\,\text{joule}$$

From energy conservation, we have

$$\frac{1}{2}\times 28\times 10^{-3}\times v^2 = 41.57$$

or
$$v = \sqrt{\frac{41.57\times 2}{28\times 10^{-3}}}$$

$$= 54.5 \text{ m/s}$$

Illustrative Example 2.26

An adiabatic vessel contains $n_1 = 3$ mole of a diatomic gas. Moment of inertia of each molecule is $I = 2.76 \times 10^{-46}$ kg m^2 and root mean square angular velocity is $\omega_0 = 5 \times 10^{12}$ rad/sec. Another adiabatic vessel contains $n_2 = 5$ mole of a monatomic gas at a temperature 470 K. Assume gases to be ideal, calculate root mean square angular velocity of diatomic molecules when the two vessels are connected by a thin tube of negligible volume. Boltzmann constant $k = 1.38 \times 10^{-23}$ J/molecule.

Solution

We know according to law of equipartition of energy, each gas molecule has $\frac{1}{2} kT$ energy associated with each of its degrees of freedom. As a diatomic gas molecule has two rotational degrees of freedom, its total rotational energy must be $2 \times \frac{1}{2} kT = kT$.

If initial temperature of diatomic gas is T_1, we have

$$\frac{1}{2} I\omega^2_{rms} = kT_1$$

or
$$T_1 = \frac{I\omega^2_{rms}}{2k}$$

$$= \frac{(2.76\times 10^{-46})(5\times 10^{12})^2}{2\times 1.38\times 10^{-23}}$$

$$T_1 = 250\text{ K}$$

When the two vessels containing diatomic and monoatomic gases are connected, these gases exchange this thermal energy but no energy is lost to surrounding as vessels are adiabatic. Thus this mixing of gases tables place at constant volume, total internal energy of system remains constant. If T_f be the final temperature of the system, we have

$$T_f = \frac{f_1 n_1 T_1 + f_2 n_2 T_2}{f_1 n_1 + f_2 n_2} \quad \dots(2.78)$$

Here for diatomic gas

$$f_1 = 5,\ n = 3 \text{ and } T_1 = 250\text{ K}$$

For monoatomic gas

$$f_2 = 3,\ n_2 = 5 \text{ and } T_2 = 470\text{ K}$$

Thus from equation-(2.78)

or
$$T_f = \frac{5\times 3\times 250 + 3\times 5\times 470}{5\times 3 + 3\times 5}$$

$$T_f = 360\text{ K}$$

Thus final mixture of the two gases is at temperature 360 K. If final rms angular velocity of diatomic gas molecules is $\omega_{rms\,f}$, according to law of equipartition of energy, we have

$$\frac{1}{2} I\omega^2_{rms\,f} = kT$$

or
$$\omega_{rms\,f} = \sqrt{\frac{2kT}{I}}$$

$$\omega_{rms\,f} = \sqrt{\frac{2\times 1.38\times 10^{-23}\times 360}{2.76\times 10^{-46}}}$$

$$\omega_{rms\,f} = 6\times 10^{12}\text{ rad/s}$$

Web Reference at www.physicsgalaxy.com

Age Group - High School Physics | Age 17-19 Years
Section - HEAT & THERMODYNAMICS
Topic - Kinetic Theory of Gases
Module Number - 26 to 32

Practice Exercise 2.4

(i) The ratio of translational and rotational kinetic energy at 100K temperature is 3 : 2. Find the internal energy of one mole gas at this temperature.

[2075 J]

(ii) The temperature of a gas consisting of rigid diatomic molecules is $T = 300$ K. Calculate the angular root mean square velocity of a rotating molecule if its moment of inertia is equal to $I = 2.1 \times 10^{-39}$ kgm^2.

[1.985×10^9 rad/s]

(iii) A nonlinear polyatomic gas at 650 K has molecules with 12 active degrees of freedom. (a) Evaluate the average molecular mechanical energy. (b) What is the value of v_{rms} ? Take mass of one molecule of gas $m = 1.3 \times 10^{-25}$ kg. (c) How many vibrational degrees of freedom are active ?

[(a) 5.382×10^{-20} J (b) 455.03 m/s (c) 6]

(iv) The first allowed excited state of hydrogen atom is 10.2 eV above its lowest energy (ground) state. To what temperature should hydrogen gas be raised so that inelastic collisions may excite an appreciable number of atoms to their first excited state ?

[7.88×10^4 K]

(v) A cylindrical container of volume V is divided in two equal parts by a fixed diathermic partition. Identical gas is filled in the two parts at initial pressure and temperature p_1, T_1 and p_2, T_2 ($T_2 > T_1$) respectively. After a long time when the two gases are in thermal equilibrium, find the final temperature and pressure of the gases in the two parts.

$$\left[\frac{p_1T_2(p_1+p_2)}{p_1T_2+p_2T_1}, \frac{p_2T_1(p_1+p_2)}{p_1T_2+p_2T_1}, \frac{T_1T_2(p_1+p_2)}{p_1T_2+p_2T_1}\right]$$

(vi) Find the amount of heat supplied by gas in one part to that in other part in previous question if gas taken is monoatomic.

$$\left[\frac{3p_1p_2(T_2-T_1)V}{2(p_1T_2+p_2T_1)}\right]$$

2.10 Path of Molecules and Mean Free Path

If we find the mean speed of a molecules of air at room temperature 25°C, we get

$$v_{av} = \sqrt{\frac{8RT}{\pi M}} = \sqrt{\frac{8\times 8.314\times 298}{3.14\times 29\times 10^{-3}}}$$

$$= 466.54 \text{ m/s}$$

It shows that in general average speed of a common gas molecule or air molecules is comparable or more than the speed of sound. In this situation a question arises, why the smell of a scent appears to spread in a room at much slower then this. If the speed of the molecules of the scent were of the order of about 500 m/s then the molecules of the scent should have taken almost no time to reach any corner of the room. The reason behind this is the explanation of pressure by kinetic theory assumptions. In assumptions of kinetic theory for an ideal gas we've ignored the size of gas molecules. If all the molecules of a gas are assumed point sized, they will never collide during their motion but in fact molecules are finite in size so they repeatedly collide with the neighbouring molecules randomly.

A molecule in its path undergoes a number of collisions so the path traversed by it is not a straight line but somewhat zigzag as shown in figure-2.32. As a result of this zigzag motion, its net displacement per unit time is comparatively small. So the scent takes more time to reach a place then the time predicted by kinetic theory. Between two successive collisions a molecule however travels in a straight line with uniform velocity. As shown in figure-2.32, the motion is random thus the distance travelled by the molecule between two successive collisions are not always equal. Due to this we use a parameter to describe this random motion. This is mean free path of the molecules, denoted by λ. As the name implies it is the average distance traversed by a molecule between two successive collisions. We expect λ to vary inversely with the molecular density N/V, the number of molecules per unit volume. The larger the molecular density is, the more collisions there should be in the dense gas and the smaller the mean free path. We also expect λ to vary inversely with the size of molecules. If the molecules were point sized, they would never collide and the mean free path would be infinite. Thus the larger the molecules are, the smaller the mean free path.

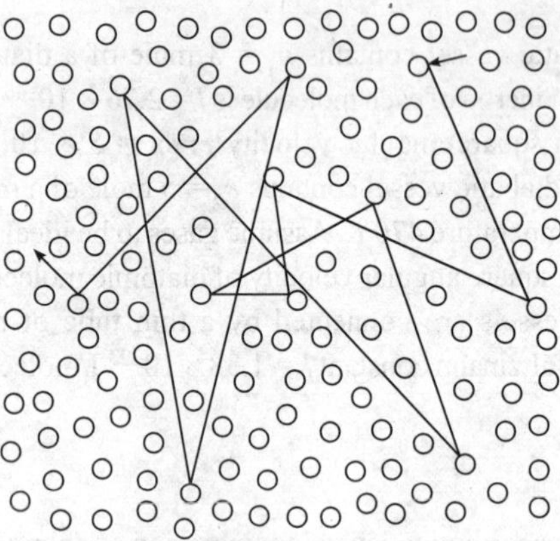

Figure 2.32

The exact expression for mean free path is turned out to be

$$\lambda = \frac{1}{\sqrt{2}md^2(N/V)} \qquad \ldots(2.79)$$

Here m is the mass of molecules and d is the molecular diameter. From gas law we have $PV = nRT$ or $PV = NkT$ as $\frac{R}{N_{AV}} = k$ if N are the total number of molecules in a gas, thus equation-(2.79) now become

$$\lambda = \frac{kT}{\sqrt{2}md^2P} \qquad \ldots(2.80)$$

2.11 Vander Walls Gas Equation

In the beginning of chapter we've discussed the assumptions of kinetic theory for ideal gases. In these assumptions the volume of gas molecules as well as the interaction between them are neglected. But in practical or real gases this is not true. Due to the size of the gas molecules, actual volume available for motion of molecules is less than the container in which gas is enclosed. Similarly the pressure which the molecules exert on container walls, we've derived in equation-(2.50) should also be different due to the interaction between the neighbouring molecules during their collisions.

The ideal gas equation in equation-(2.7) can be used for different ideal gases but not for real gases due to the above reason. This ideal gas law can be modified for real gases and by introducing some appropriate corrections, we can develop another equation of state for a real gas. This equation was developed by Dutch physicist J.D. Vander Walls. The equation is named vander walls gas equation after him and is given as

$$\left(P+\frac{an^2}{V^2}\right)(V-nb)=nRT \quad ...(2.81)$$

Here a and b are empirical constants, different for different gases. Roughly b is the volume of one mole of molecules, thus the total volume of molecules in n moles of a gas is then nb, and the total volume available for the molecules to move around in the gas is $(V - n\,b)$. The constant a depends on the attractive intermolecular forces, which reduces the pressure of gas for given values of n, V and T by pulling the molecules together as they push the walls of container during collisions. The decrease in pressure is proportional to the number of molecules per unit volume in a layer near the wall which are colliding and exerting pressure on walls and is also proportional to the number per unit volume in the next layer beyond the wall which are attracting the first layer molecules. Hence the decrease in pressure due to intermolecular forces is proportional to n^2/V^2.

When a gas is at very low pressure, (n/V) for the gas is very small or we can say that the gas is dilute, the separation between the gas molecules is large, the correlations in the vander walls equation become insignificant and equation-(2.81) reduces to ideal gas equation. Some times at very high temperature when kinetic energy of gas molecules is very high, the effect of molecular interaction is negligible. Thus we can say that at very low pressure or at very high temperature real gases may behave like ideal gases.

2.12 Diffusion

If we care fully place a drop of ink in a glass of water, we'll find that the ink colour spreads throughout the water. After a long time eventually the colour will become uniform. This mixing occurs because of the random movement of the molecules and is called diffusion. Diffusion also occurs in gases. Common examples of diffusion is the spreading of smell of a perfume in a room or smoke diffusing in air, although convection often plays a greater role in this spreading then does diffusion. In all cases the diffusing substance moves from a region where its concentration is high to one where its concentration is low.

The simplest explanation of diffusion is on the basis of kinetic theory and the random motion of molecules. We take a simple example to understand this. Consider a long tube of cross-sectional area A as shown in figure-2.33. Containing molecules in a higher concentration on the left than on the right. According to the kinetic theory molecules are in Brownian motion. If we consider a small elemental length Δx of the tube then molecules from both regions left and right cross into this section of length Δx due to their random motion. Since there is higher concentration on left side, more molecules cross into this elemental section from left side then to the right side. Thus there is a net flow of molecules from left to right, from high concentration toward low concentration. When after sometime the two side concentration become equal, the flow still continues but equal from both the sides thus there is no net flow of molecules from either side when concentration on both sides become equal.

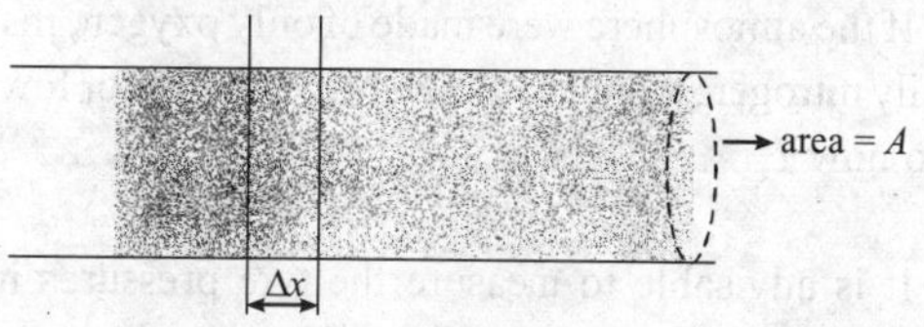

Figure 2.33

Detailed mathematical analysis of diffusion is beyond the scope of this book. At elementary level we discuss the Adolf formula which gives the average rate of diffusion from one region of concentration C_1 to another region of concentration C_2 separated by a central section of width Δx, as discussed in figure-2.33, is given as

$$J=DA\,\frac{C_1-C_2}{\Delta x} \quad ...(2.82)$$

Here $(C_1 - C_2)/\Delta x$ is the change in concentration per unit distance and some times written as dC/dx for mathematical analysis, and is called as concentration gradient.

Here D is the proportionality constant called diffusion constant and the above equation-(2.82) is called as "*Adolf formula*" or "*Adolf Fick's Law of Diffusion*". Above equation is not only valid for a gas diffusing in itself called self diffusion but also applicable for a gas diffusing in a second gas. If the concentrations C_1 and C_2 here are in mole/m^3 then J is the number of moles passing a given area per second. The diffusion constant D will depend on the properties of the substances involved, and also on the temperature and the external pressure.

* * * * *

Discussion Question

Q2-1 Two balloons of the same volume are filled with gases at the same pressure, one with hydrogen and the other with helium. Which of the two has the greater buoyancy and what is the ratio of the two buoyancies.

Q2-2 Among hydrogen, helium, nitrogen and oxygen, which is the most ideal as a thermometric substance.

Q2-3 Why is the climate of coastal cities milder than that of cities in the midst of large land areas ?

Q2-4 What would happen if we take a barometer to the bottom of a swimming pool ? What would happen if we take it to the moon ?

Q2-5 If the atmosphere were made of only oxygen, instead of primarily nitrogen, would barometers read higher or lower than they do now ?

Q2-6 It is advisable to measure the tyre pressures in a car before going for a long drive. What difference would it make if the pressure were measured after driving several miles at speed.

Q2-7 In the assumptions of kinetic theory of gases we consider elastic collisions between gas molecules. What difference would be there on our kinetic theory model of a gas if collisions are assumed inelastic.

Q2-8 At high altitude, the ratio of nitrogen to oxygen in the atmosphere increases above the ratio at sea level. Why ?

Q2-9 In an open room at atmospheric pressure, the total kinetic energy of all the air molecules is more when the room is warm than the total kinetic energy of the molecules in the same room when it is cool. Justify this statement.

Q2-10 Some potatoes are put in container with water. If pressure in the container is reduced, potatoes will cook faster.

Q2-11 Why does food cook faster in a pressure cooker than in boiling water ?

Q2-12 In the ideal gas equation, could Celsius temperature be used instead of Kelvin if an appropriate numerical value of the gas constant R is used ?

Q2-13 "Desert areas often have exceptionally large day-night temperature variations" Comment on this statement.

Q2-14 Helium gas found in nature is a mixture of two isotopes having atomic weights 3 and 4, which atom move faster on average and why ?

Q2-15 When two gases are mixed and if they are in thermal equilibrium, they must have the same average molecular speed. Justify this statement.

Q2-16 We know according the kinetic theory model of a gas the temperature of an ideal gas is directly proportional to the average kinetic energy of its molecules. If a container of ideal gas is moving at a speed of 2500 m/s, is the temperature of the gas higher than it would be if the contain were at rest. Explain.

Q2-17 In the chemistry lab when you are standing at one corner and at the other end of the lab, the lab assistant opens the valve of a gas container, you can hear the sound of the escaping gas almost immediately, but it takes several seconds before you can smell the gas. Why ?

Q2-18 A flask is closed by a stop valve. The valve allows only those air molecules that are moving faster than a certain speed to move out of the flask and allows only air molecules that are moving slower than that speed to enter the flask from outside. What effect would this filter have on the temperature of the air in the flask.

Q2-19 If a gas is made up entirely of free electrons. Would the temperature of such a gas rise, fall or remains same if it undergoes free expansion.

Q2-20 An ideal diatomic gas, without vibrations loses heat Q to a system in a process. Is the resulting decrease in the internal energy of the gas greater if the loss occurs in isochoric process or in isobaric process.

Q2-21 We know the mechanical energy of a body is a frame dependent property. Is temperature of a substance is also a frame dependent property.

Q2-22 "For a constant volume gas thermometer, the gas should be filled in it at low pressure and high temperature". Justify this statement.

Q2-23 LPG gas is filled in a cooking gas cylinder in compressed form. When it is used the pressure of gas remains same but starts falling when it is becoming empty. Why ?

Q2-24 What we can say about the specific heat of a boiling water or melting ice.

* * * * *

Conceptual MCQs Single Option Correct

2-1 The following four gases are at the same temperature. In which gas do the molecules have the maximum root mean square speed ?

(A) Hydrogen (B) Oxygen
(C) Nitrogen (D) Carbon dioxide

2-2 Cooking vegetables and other food in a pressure cooker saves time and fuel because :

(A) Under increased pressure, water can be made to boil at a temperature much higher than 100°C
(B) Under increased pressure, water can be made to boil at a temperature much lower than 100°C
(C) Heat losses are reduced to a minimum
(D) Condensation of steam is prevented

2-3 On increasing temperature of a gas, the number of molecules having most probable speed will :

(A) Decrease (B) Increase
(C) May increase or decrease (D) Remains same

2-4 If water at 0°C, kept in a container with an open top, is placed in a large evacuated chamber :

(A) All the water will vaporize
(B) All the water will freeze
(C) Part of the water will vaporize and the rest will freeze
(D) Ice, water and water vapour will be formed and reach equilibrium at the triple point

2-5 Which of the following is correct for the molecules of a gas in equilibrium temperature?

(A) All have the same speed
(B) Molecules have different speed distribution of which average remain constant
(C) They have a certain constant average speed
(D) They do not collide with one another

2-6 When amount of gas in a closed container is increased at a given temperature, the pressure of gas increases because of :

(A) Increase in momentum transfer per molecule only
(B) Increase in frequency of collision only
(C) Both (A) and (B)
(D) Increase in non-ideal behaviour

2-7 E_0 and E_h respectively represent the average kinetic energy of a molecule of oxygen and hydrogen. If the two gases are at the same temperature, which of the following statements is true ?

(A) $E_0 > E_h$
(B) $E_0 = E_h$
(C) $E_0 < E_h$
(D) Nothing can be said about the magnitude of E_0 and E_h as the information given is insufficient

2-8 N molecules of an ideal gas at temperature T_1 and pressure P_1 are contained in a closed box. If the molecules in the box gets doubled keeping total kinetic energy same. If new pressure is P_2 and temperature is T_2, then :

(A) $P_2 = P, T_2 = T_1$ (B) $P_2 = P_1, T_2 = T_1/2$
(C) $P_2 = 2P_1, T_2 = T_1$ (D) $P_2 = 2P_1, T_2 = T_1/2$

2-9 Three closed vessels A, B and C at the same temperature T and contain gases which obey the Maxwellian distribution of velocities. Vessel A contains only O_2, B only N_2 and C a mixture of equal quantities of O_2 and N_2. If the average speed of the O_2 molecules in vessel A is v_1, that of the N_2 molecules in vessel B is v_2, the average speed of O_2 molecules in vessel C is : (Take M is the mass of an oxygen molecule)

(A) $(v_1 + v_2)/2$ (B) v_1
(C) $(v_1 - v_2)^{1/2}$ (D) $\sqrt{3kT/M}$

2-10 The pressure p of a gas is plotted against its absolute temperature T for two different constant volumes V_1 and V_2, where $V_1 > V_2$. p is plotted on the y-axis and T on the x-axis :

(A) The curve for V_1 has greater slope than the curve for V_2
(B) The curve for V_2 has greater slope than the curve for V_1
(C) The curves must intersect at some point other than $T = 0$
(D) The curves have the same slope and do not intersect

2-11 Pressure versus temperature graph of an ideal gas of equal number of moles of different volumes are plotted as shown in figure-2.34. Choose the correct alternative :

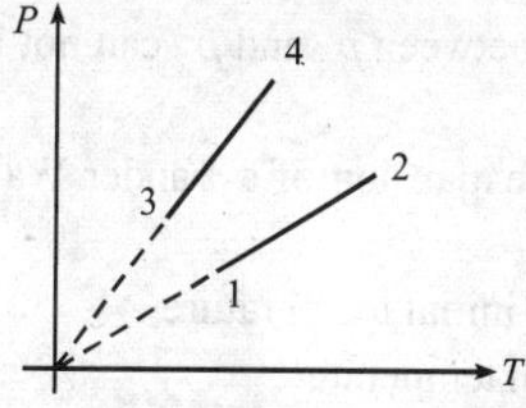

Figure 2.34

(A) $V_1 = V_2, V_3 = V_4$ and $V_2 > V_3$
(B) $V_1 = V_2, V_3 = V_4$ and $V_2 < V_3$
(C) $V_1 = V_2 = V_3 = V_4$
(D) $V_4 > V_3 > V_2 > V_1$

2-12 A gas is contained in a metallic cylinder fitted with a piston. The piston is suddenly moved in to compress the gas and is maintained at this position. As time passes the pressure of the gas in the cylinder :

(A) Increases
(B) Decreases
(C) Remains constant
(D) Increases or decreases depending on the nature of the gas

2-13 The absolute zero is the temperature at which :
(A) water Freezes
(B) all substances exist in solid state
(C) molecular motion ceases
(D) none of the above

2-14 A graph is plotted with $\frac{PV}{T}$ on y-axis and mass of the gas along x-axis for different gases. The graph is :
(A) A straight line parallel to x-axis for all the gases
(B) A straight line passing through origin with a slope having a constant value for all the gases
(C) A straight line passing through origin with a slope having different values for different gases
(D) A straight line parallel to y-axis for all the gases

2-15 Volume V of air is saturated with water vapours. The pressure exerted by the moist air is p. If the volume of the mixture is reduced to $V/2$ isothermally, what will be the pressure exerted by the air now ?
(A) More than $2p$ (B) Less than $2p$
(C) Equal to $2p$ (D) Equal to p

2-16 Two sample A and B are initially kept in the same state. The sample A is expanded through an adiabatic process and the sample B through an isothermal process to the same final volume. The final pressures in samples A and B are p_A and p_B respectively, then :
(A) $p_A > p_B$
(B) $p_A = p_B$
(C) $p_A < p_B$
(D) The relation between p_A and p_B can not be deduced.

2-17 In the free expansion of a Vander Wall's gas, the final temperature is :
(A) Less than the initial temperature
(B) Same as initial temperature
(C) More than the initial temperature
(D) More or less than initial temperature depending upon the nature of gas

2-18 A horizontal cylinder has two sections of unequal cross-sections, in which two pistons can move freely. The pistons are joined by a string. Some gas is trapped between the pistons. If this gas is heated, the pistons will :

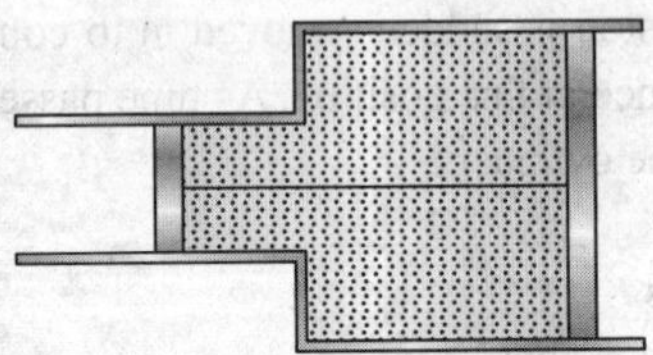
Figure 2.35

(A) Move to the left
(B) Move to the right
(C) Remain stationary
(D) Either (A) or (B) depending on the initial pressure of the gas

2-19 Helium filled balloon bursts at great height because :
(A) Helium catches fire
(B) Air has large velocities at high altitudes
(C) The inside pressure very is large than the outside pressure
(D) The inside pressure is very small than the pressure outside

2-20 Pressure versus temperature graph of an ideal gas is as shown in figure-2.36. Density of the gas at point A is ρ_0. Density at B will be :

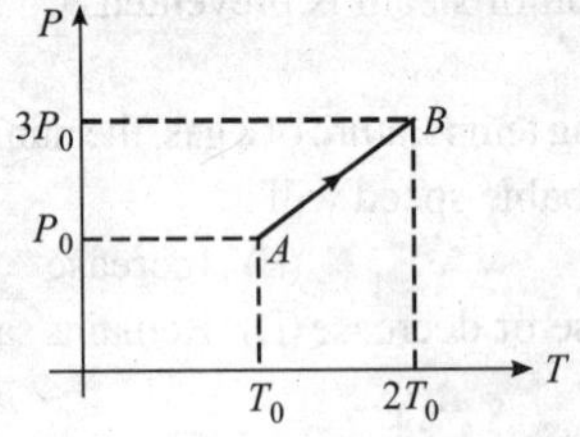

Figure 2.36

(A) $\frac{3}{4}\rho_0$ (B) $\frac{3}{2}\rho_0$
(C) $\frac{4}{3}\rho_0$ (D) $2\rho_0$

2-21 The quantity $\frac{PV}{kT}$ (k = Boltzmann's constant) represents :
(A) Number of moles of the gas
(B) Total mass of the gas
(C) Number of molecules in the gas
(D) Density of the gas

2-22 The equation of state for a real gas such as hydrogen, oxygen, etc. is called the Van der Waal's equation which reads

$$\left(P+\frac{a}{V^2}\right)(V-b)=nRT,$$

where a and b are constants of the gas. The dimensional formula of constant a is :
(A) ML^5T^{-2}
(B) ML^5T^{-1}
(C) $ML^{-1}T^{-1}$
(D) a being a constant, is dimensionless

2-23 A stationary vertical cylindrical container of very large height filled with a gas of molar mass M at constant Temperature. The pressure at the bottom is P_1 and at the top is P_2. If the acceleration due to gravity is assumed to be constant for the whole cylinder, which is equal to g. Then the height of the cylinder is :

(A) $\frac{RT}{Mg}\ln\frac{P_1}{P_2}$ (B) $\frac{RT}{2Mg}\ln\frac{P_1}{P_2}$

(C) $\frac{2RT}{Mg}\ln\frac{P_1}{P_2}$ (D) $\frac{RT}{3Mg}\ln\frac{P_1}{P_2}$

2-24 The conversion of ideal gas into solids is :
(A) Possible only at low pressure
(B) Possible only at low temperature
(C) Possible only at low volume
(D) Not possible

2-25 If a small hole is made in a cylinder full of a gas at atmospheric temperature, then :
(A) The temperature of gas remains constant
(B) The rate of collision with the wall of cylinder increases
(C) The rms velocity of gas molecules will decrease
(D) rms velocity of gas molecules will increase

2-26 For matter to exist simultaneously in gas and liquid phases :
(A) The temperature must be 0 K
(B) The temperature must be less than 0°C
(C) The temperature must be less than the critical temperature
(D) The temperature must be less than the reduced temperature

2-27 P-T graphs of an ideal gas are as shown in figures-2.37 below. Choose the wrong statement from the options given:

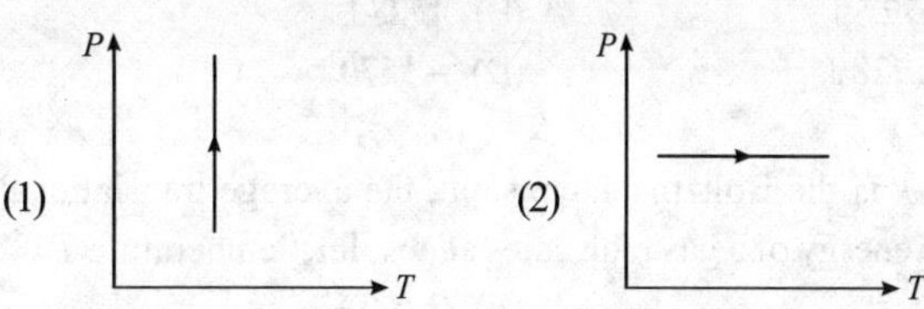

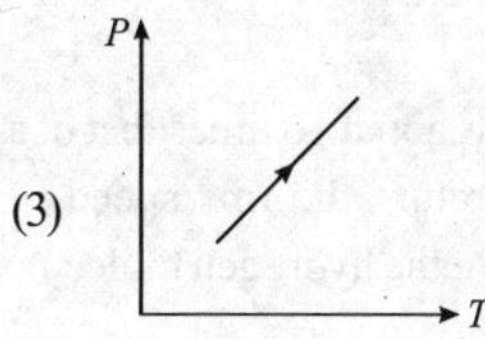

Figure 2.37

(A) Density of gas is increasing in graph (1)
(B) Density of gas decreasing in graph (2)
(C) Density of gas is constant in graph (3)
(D) None of the above

* * * * *

Numerical MCQs Single Options Correct

2-1 One mole of O_2 gas having a volume equal to 22.4 litre at 0°C and 1 atmospheric pressure is compressed isothermally so that its volume reduces to 11.2 litre. The work done in this process is nearly :

(A) 1672.5 J (B) 1728 J

(C) – 1728 J (D) – 1570 J

2-2 If k is the Boltzmann constant, the average translational kinetic energy of a gas molecules at absolute temperature T is :

(A) $kT/2$ (B) $3kT/4$

(C) kT (D) $3kT/2$

2-3 The mass of an oxygen molecule is about 16 times that of a hydrogen molecule. At room temperature the rms speed of oxygen molecules is v. The rms speed of the hydrogen molecule at the same temperature will be :

(A) $v/16$ (B) $v/4$

(C) $4v$ (D) $16v$

2-4 The average kinetic energy of hydrogen molecules at 300 K is E. At the same temperature, the average kinetic energy of oxygen molecules will be :

(A) $E/16$ (B) $E/4$

(C) E (D) $4E$

2-5 A jar contains gas G_1 ar pressure p, volume V and temperature T. Another jar contains gas G_2 at pressure $2p$, volume $V/2$ and temperature $2T$. What is the ratio of the number of molecules of G_1 to that of G_2 ?

(A) 1 (B) 2

(C) 3 (D) 4

2-6 It 2 moles of an ideal monoatomic gas at temperature T_0 is mixed with 4 moles of another ideal monoatomic gas at temperature $2T_0$, then the temperature of the mixture is :

(A) $\frac{5}{3}T_0$ (B) $\frac{3}{2}T_0$

(C) $\frac{4}{3}T_0$ (D) $\frac{5}{4}T_0$

2-7 A vessel contains a mixture of 1 mole of oxygen and two moles of nitrogen at 300 K. The ratio of the rotational kinetic energy per O_2 molecule to that per N_2 molecule is :

(A) 1 : 1

(B) 1 : 2

(C) 2 : 1

(D) Depends on the moment of inertia of the two molecules

2-8 The equation of state of a gas is

$$\left(P+\frac{aT^2}{V}\right)\times V^c=(RT+b)$$

where a, b, c and R are constants. The isotherms can be represented by

$$P=AV^m-BV^n$$

where A and B depend only on temperature and

(A) $m=-c, n=-1$ (B) $m=c, n=1$

(C) $m=-c, n=1$ (D) $m=c, n=-1$

2-9 The rms speed of hydrogen at 27°C is v. What will be the rms speed of oxygen at 300 K ?

(A) $4v$ (B) $2v$

(C) $v/2$ (D) $v/4$

2-10 Same volumes of hydrogen and oxygen at the same temperature and pressure are mixed together so that the volume of the mixture is same as the initial volume of the either gas. If the initial pressure be p, then the pressure of the mixture will be :

(A) $4p$ (B) $2p$

(C) $p/2$ (D) $p/4$

2-11 2 m³ of hydrogen and 2 m³ of oxygen are at the same temperature. If the pressure of hydrogen be p, then that of oxygen will be :

(A) $2p$ (B) $4p$

(C) $8p$ (D) $1p$

2-12 A flask contains hydrogen and helium gases in the ratio 1 : 3 at temperature 300 K. The masses of helium and hydrogen molecule are in the ratio 2 : 1. What will be the ratio of the average kinetic energies of these molecules at 600 K ?

(A) 6 (B) 3

(C) 2 (D) 1

2-13 The mean rotational kinetic energy of a diatomic molecule at temperature T is :

(A) $\frac{1}{2}kT$ (B) kT

(C) $2kT$ (D) $\frac{5}{2}kT$

2-14 An ideal gas undergoes a process in which $T=T_0+aV^3$, where T_0 and "a" are positive constants and V is molar volume. The volume for which pressure will be minimum is :

(A) $\left(\frac{T_0}{2a}\right)^{1/3}$ (B) $\left(\frac{T_0}{3a}\right)^{1/3}$

(C) $\left(\frac{a}{2T_0}\right)^{2/3}$ (D) $\left(\frac{a}{3T_0}\right)^{2/3}$

2-15 In above question, minimum pressure attainable is :

(A) $\frac{3}{4}(a^{5/3}R^{2/3}T_0^{2/3})2^{1/3}$ (B) $\frac{3}{2}(a^{2/3}R\,T_0^{2/3})3^{1/2}$

(C) $\frac{3}{2}(a^{1/2}R^{2/3}T_0^{3/4})4^{1/3}$ (D) $\frac{3}{2}(a^{1/3}R\,T_0^{2/3})2^{1/3}$

2-16 If a gas f degrees of freedom, the ratio C_p/C_v of the gas is :

(A) $\frac{1+f}{2}$ (B) $1+\frac{f}{2}$

(C) $\frac{1}{2}+f$ (D) $1+\frac{2}{f}$

2-17 A gas at pressure P_0 is contained in a vessel. If the masses of all the molecules are halved and their speeds doubled, the resulting pressure would be :

(A) $4P_0$ (B) $2P_0$

(C) P_0 (D) $\frac{P_0}{2}$

2-18 The root mean square speed of the molecules of an enclosed gas is v. What will be the root mean square speed if the pressure is doubled, the temperature remaining the same ?

(A) $v/2$ (B) v

(C) $2v$ (D) $4v$

2-19 Two containers of equal volume contain the same gas at pressures p_1 and p_2 and absolute temperatures T_1 and T_2 respectively. On joining the vessels, the gas reaches a common pressure p and a common temperature T. The ratio p/T is equal to :

(A) $\frac{p_1}{T_1}+\frac{p_2}{T_2}$ (B) $\frac{1}{2}\left[\frac{p_1}{T_1}+\frac{p_2}{T_2}\right]$

(C) $\frac{p_1T_2+p_2T_1}{T_1+T_2}$ (D) $\frac{p_1T_2-p_2T_1}{T_1-T_2}$

2-20 The root mean square speed of the molecules of a gas at absolute temperature T is proportional to :

(A) $1/T$ (B) $\sqrt{T}$

(C) T (D) T^2

2-21 At the middle of the mercury barometer tube there is a little column of air with the length l_0 as shown in figure-2.38 below and there is vacuum at the top. Under normal atmospheric pressure and the temperature of 300 K, l_0 = 10 cm. Neglect expansion of the tube and evaporation of mercury. Calculate the length of the air column if the temperature rises to 330 K.

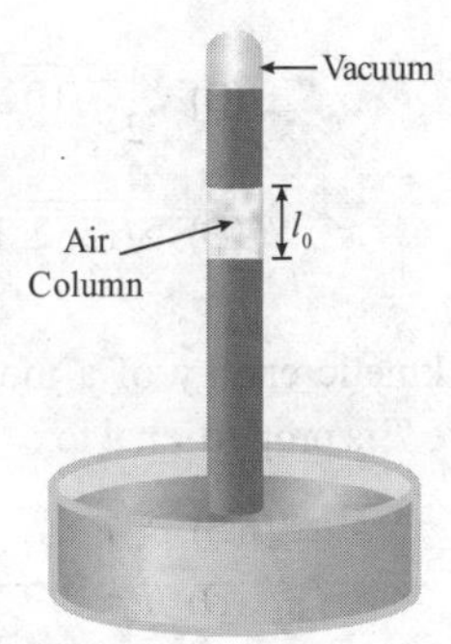

Figure 2.38

(A) $\frac{100}{11}$ cm (B) 11 cm

(C) 10 cm (D) 12 cm

2-22 Three moles of oxygen is mixed with two moles of helium. What will be the ratio of specific heats at constant pressure and constant volume of the mixture ?

(A) 1.67 (B) 1.5

(C) 1.4 (D) None of the above

2-23 The weight of a person is 60 kg. If he gets 10^5 calories of heat through food and the efficiency of his body is 28%, then upto how much height he can climb ? Take $g = 10$ m s^{-2} :

(A) 100 m (B) 196 m

(C) 400 m (D) 1000 m

2-24 Two identical containers joined by a small pipe initially contain the same gas at pressure p_0 and absolute temperature T_0. One container is now maintained at the same temperature while the other is heated to $2T_0$. The common pressure of the gases will be :

(A) $\frac{3}{2}p_0$ (B) $\frac{4}{3}p_0$

(C) $\frac{5}{3}p_0$ (D) $2p_0$

2-25 In the previous question, let V_0 be the volume of each container. All other details remain he same. The number of moles of gas in the container at temperature $2T_0$ will be :

(A) $\frac{p_0V_0}{2RT_0}$ (B) $\frac{p_0V_0}{RT_0}$

(C) $\frac{2p_0V_0}{3RT_0}$ (D) $\frac{p_0V_0}{3RT_0}$

2-26 Four molecules of a gas have speeds 1, 2, 3 and 4 km s^{-1}. The value of the root mean square speed of the gas molecule is :

(A) $\frac{1}{2}\sqrt{15}$ km s^{-1} (B) $\frac{1}{2}\sqrt{10}$ km s^{-1}

(C) 2.5 km s^{-1} (D) $\sqrt{15/2}$ km s^{-1}

2-27 The average kinetic energy of a molecule of a gas at absolute temperature T is proportional to :

(A) $1/T$ (B) $\sqrt{T}$

(C) T (D) T^2

2-28 A bubble rises from bed of a lake to its surface. The depth of lake is 10^3 times the value by which radius of the bubble increase in size. If the atmospheric pressure is equal to pressure due to a column of water of 10 m, find the value by which bubble increases in size (approximately) :

(A) 100 (B) 10

(C) $10\sqrt{2}$ (D) $10\sqrt{3}$

2-29 The equation of state of n moles of an ideal gas is $PV = nRT$, where R is a constant. The SI unit for R is :

(A) J kg^{-1} K^{-1} (B) J g^{-1} K^{-1}

(C) J K^{-1} mol^{-1} (D) J K^{-1} per molecule

2-30 The reading of a barometer containing some air above the mercury column is 73 cm while that of a correct one is 76 cm. If the tube of the faulty barometer is pushed down into mercury until volume of air in it is reduced to half, the reading shown by it will be :

(A) 70 cm (B) 72 cm

(C) 74 cm (D) 76 cm

Paragraph for Question No. 31 to 33

In a cylindrical container of sufficiently large height, two easily moving pistons enclose certain amount of same ideal gas in two chambers as shown in the figure-2.39.

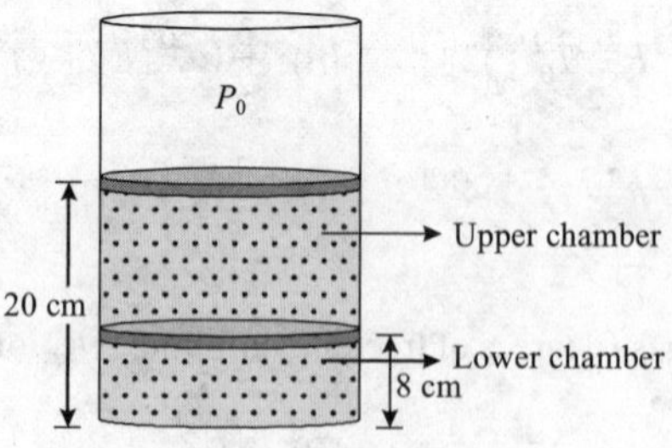

Figure 2.39

The upper piston is at a height 20 cm from the bottom and lower piston is at a height 8 cm from the bottom. The mass of each piston is m kg and cross sectional area of each piston is A m^2, where $\frac{mg}{A} = P_0$ and P_0 is the atmospheric pressure $= 1 \times 10^5$ N/m^2.

The cylindrical container and pistons are made of conducting material. Initially the temperature of gas is 27°C and whole system is in equilibrium. Now if the upper piston is slowly lifted by 16 cm and held in that position with the help of some external force. As a result, the lower piston rises slowly by l cm.

2-31 The value of l is :

(A) 2 cm (B) 4 cm

(C) 8 cm (D) 6 cm

2-32 Find the ratio of volume of gas in upper chamber to that of in lower chamber in final state :

(A) 2 : 1 (B) 1 : 2

(C) 4 : 1 (D) 1 : 4

2-33 Find the pressure of gas in lower chamber in final state :

(A) 1.0×10^5 N/m^2 (B) 2.0×10^5 N/m^2

(C) 3.0×10^5 N/m^2 (D) 4.0×10^5 N/m^2

* * * * *

Advance MCQs with One or More Options Correct

2-1 Choose the INCORRECT statement(s) from the following:
(A) The pressure of a gas is equal to the total kinetic energy of the molecules in a unit volume of the gas
(B) The product of pressure and volume of a gas is always constant
(C) The average kinetic energy of molecules of a gas is proportional to its absolute temperature
(D) The average kinetic energy of molecules of a gas is proportional to the square root of its absolute temperature

2-2 A closed vessel contains a mixture of two diatomic gases *A* and *B*. Molar mass of *A* is 16 times that of *B* and mass of gas *A* contained in the vessel is 2 times that of *B*. Which of the following statements are true?
(A) Average kinetic energy per molecule of *A* is equal to that of *B*
(B) Root mean square value of translational velocity of *B* is four times that of *A*
(C) Pressure exerted by *B* is eight times of that exerted by *A*
(D) Number of molecules of *B* in the cylinder is eight times that of *A*

2-3 The quantity $\frac{mkT}{V}$ of an ideal gas depends on (m = mass of the gas)
(A) Temperature of the gas (B) Volume of the gas
(C) Pressure of the gas (D) Nature of the gas

2-4 Which of the following quantities is/are independent of the nature of the gas at same temperature :
(A) The number of molecules in 1 mole
(B) The number of molecules in equal volume
(C) The translational kinetic energy of 1 mole
(D) The kinetic energy of unit mass

2-5 During experiment, an ideal gas is found to obey a condition P^2/ρ = constant [ρ = density of the gas]. The gas is initially at temperature T, pressure P and density ρ. The gas expands such that density changes to $\rho/2$:
(A) The pressure of the gas changes to $\sqrt{2}P$
(B) The temperature of the gas changes to $\sqrt{2}T$
(C) The graph of the above process on the P–T diagram is parabola
(D) The graph of the above process on the P–T diagram is hyperbola

2-6 Pick the correct statements (s) :
(A) The rms translational speed for all ideal-gas molecules at the same temperature is not the same but it depends on the mass.
(B) Each particle in a gas has average translational kinetic energy and the equation $\frac{1}{2}mv_{rms}^2 = \frac{3}{2}kT$ establishes the relationship between the average translational kinetic energy per particle and temperature of an ideal gas. It can be concluded that single particle has a temperature.
(C) Temperature of an ideal gas is doubled from 100°C to 200°C. The average kinetic energy of each particle is also doubled.
(D) It is possible for both the pressure and volume of a monoatomic ideal gas to change simultaneously without causing the internal energy of the gas to change.

2-7 From the following statements, concerning ideal gas at any given temperature T, select the correct one(s) :
(A) The coefficient of volume expansion at constant pressure is same for all ideal gases
(B) The average translational kinetic energy per molecule of oxygen gas is 3 KT (K being Boltzmann constant)
(C) In a gaseous mixture, the average translational kinetic energy of the molecules of each component is same
(D) The mean free path of molecules increases with the decrease in pressure

2-8 A gas in container *A* is in thermal equilibrium with another gas in container *B*, both contain equal masses of the two gases in the respective containers. Which of the following can be true :
(A) $P_AV_A = P_BV_B$ (B) $P_A = P_B, V_A \neq V_B$
(C) $P_A \neq P_B, V_A = V_B$ (D) $\frac{P_A}{V_A} = \frac{P_B}{V_B}$

2-9 Graph shows a hypothetical speed distribution for a sample of N gas particle (for $V > V_0$; $\frac{dN}{dV} = 0$)

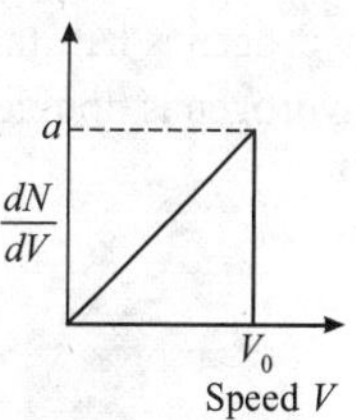

Figure 2.40

(A) The value of V_0 is 2 N
(B) The ratio V_{avg}/V_0 is equal to 2/3
(C) The ratio V_{rms}/V_0 is equal to $1/\sqrt{2}$
(D) Three fourth of the total particle has a speed between 0.5 V_0 and V_0

2-10 A piston of mass m can move without friction in a uniform cylinder, closed at one end. A gas is enclosed in it. Then :
(A) Pressure of the gas will be equal to that of the surrounding if axis is not horizontal
(B) Pressure of the gas may be equal to that of surrounding if axis of the cylinder is not horizontal
(C) Pressure of the gas may be less than that of surrounding if axis of the cylinder is not horizontal
(D) Pressure of the gas cannot be less than that of the surrounding, if axis of the cylinder is not horizontal

2-11 A vessel contains H_2 and He in thermal equilibrium. Which of the following is correct :
(A) Molecules of both gases have same average translational kinetic energy
(B) The molecules of gases have same average energy
(C) Hydrogen molecules have greater average energy than Helium molecules
(D) Molecules of both gases have same average speed

2-12 Which of the following statements is (are) correct ?
(A) A real gas behaves as an ideal gas at high temperature and low pressure
(B) Liquid state of an ideal gas is impossible
(C) An ideal gas obeys Boyle's and Charle's laws at all temperature
(D) The molecules of a real gas do no exert any force on one another

2-13 The *RMS* speed of the molecules of a given mass of an ideal gas will increase by increasing the :
(A) Pressure keeping the volume constant
(B) Pressure keeping the temperature constant
(C) Temperature keeping the volume constant
(D) Temperature keeping the pressure constant

2-14 Two tanks of equal volumes contain equal masses of hydrogen and helium at the same temperature. Then :
(A) The pressure of hydrogen is half that of helium
(B) The pressure of hydrogen is double that of helium
(C) The translational kinetic energy of all the molecules of hydrogen is double of that of all the molecules of helium
(D) The total kinetic energy of all the molecules of hydrogen is more than double of that of all the molecules of helium

2-15 A container holds 10^{26} molecule/m^3, each of mass 3×10^{-27} kg. Assume that $\frac{1}{6}$ of the molecules move with velocity 2000 ms^{-1} directly toward one wall of the container while the remaining $\frac{5}{6}$ of the molecules move either away from the wall or in perpendicular direction, and all collisions of the molecules with the wall are elastic :
(A) Number of molecules hitting 1 m^2 of the wall every second is $\frac{1}{3} \times 10^{29}$
(B) Number of molecules hitting 1 m^2 of the wall every second is 2×10^{29}
(C) Pressure exerted on the wall by molecules is 24×10^5 Nm^{-2}
(D) Pressure exerted on the wall by molecules is 4×10^5 Nm^{-2}

2-16 Consider a collision between one oxygen molecule and a hydrogen molecule in a mixture of oxygen and hydrogen kept at room temperature. Which of the following are possible ?
(A) The kinetic energies of both the molecules increase.
(B) The kinetic energies of both the molecules decrease.
(C) The kinetic energy of the oxygen molecule increases and that of the hydrogen molecules decreases.
(D) The kinetic energy of the hydrogen molecules increases and that of the oxygen molecule decreases.

2-17 An ideal gas can be expanded from an initial state to a certain volume through two different processes
(i) PV^2 = constant and
(ii) $P = KV^2$ where K is a positive constant. Then:
(A) Final temperature in (i) will be greater than in (ii)
(B) Final temperature in (ii) will be greater than in (i)
(C) Total heat given to the gas in (i) case is greater than in (ii)
(D) Total heat given to the gas in (ii) case is greater than in (i)

* * * * *

Unsolved Numerical Problems for Preparation of NSEP, INPhO & IPhO

For detailed preparation of INPhO and IPhO students can refer advance study material on www.physicsgalaxy.com

2-1 An electron tube was sealed off during manufacture at a pressure of 1.2×10^{-7} mm of mercury at 27°C. Its volume is 100 cm^3. What is the number of molecules that remain the tube ?

Ans. [3.814×10^{11}]

2-2 The mass of a hydrogen molecule is 3.23×10^{-27} kg. If 10^{23} hydrogen molecules strike 2 cm^2 of a wall per second at an angle of 45° with the normal when moving with a speed of 10^5 cm s^{-1}, what pressure do they exert on the wall ?

Ans. [2.284×10^3 N m^{-2}]

2-3 A lamp of volume 50 cc was sealed off during manufacture at a pressure 0.1 newton per square metre at 27°C. Calculate the mass of the gas enclosed in the lamp. Molecular weight of the gas = 10 and $R = 8.3$ J mol^{-1} K^{-1}.

Ans. [2×10^{-11} kg]

2-4 An electric bulb of 250 cc was sealed off during manufacture at a pressure of 10^{-3} mm of *Hg* and at 27°C. Compute the number of air molecules in the bulb. (Avogadro constant = 6×10^{23} mol^{-1} and $R = 8.3$ J mol^{-1} K^{-1}). Calculate the mean distance between the molecules at this pressure.

Ans. [8.05×10^{15}, 3.1×10^{-7} m]

2-5 Calculate the kinetic energy of translation of the molecules of 20 g of CO_2 at 27°C.

Ans. [1700.6 J]

2-6 A cubic box of volume 8.0×10^{-3} m^3 is filled with air at atmospheric pressure at 20°C. The box is closed and heated to 150°C. What is the net force on each side of the box ?

Ans. [5774.7 N]

2-7 Calculate the number of molecules/m^3 in an ideal gas at STP.

Ans. [2.69×10^{25} molecules/m^3]

2-8 The lowest pressure attainable using the best available vacuum techniques is about 10^{-12} N/m^2. At such a pressure, how many molecules are there per cm^3 at 0°C ?

Ans. [2.6×10^2 molecules/cm^3]

2-9 In outer space the density of matter is about one atom per cm^3, mainly hydrogen atoms, and the temperature is about 3.4 K. Calculate the average speed of these hydrogen atoms, and the pressure (in atmospheres).

Ans. [$v_{rms} \approx 300$ m/s. P $\approx 5 \times 10^{-22}$ atm]

2-10 Calculate the density of oxygen at STP using the ideal gas law.

Ans. [1.41 kg/m^3]

2-11 A tank contains 28.0 kg of O_2 gas at a gauge pressure of 6.80 atm. If the oxygen is replaced by helium, how many kg of the latter will be needed to produce a gauge pressure of 8.25 atm ?

Ans. [4.246 kg]

2-12 A house has a volume of 600 m^3. (a) What is the total mass of air inside the house at 0°C ? (b) If the temperature rises to 25°C, what mass of air enters or leaves the house ?

Ans. [(a) 774 kg, (b) 65 kg leaves]

2-13 A tire is filled with air at 15°C to a gauge pressure of 1.9×10^5 Pa. If the tire reaches a temperature of 40°C, what fraction of the original air must be removed if the original pressure of 1.9×10^5 Pa is to be maintained ?

Ans. [0.080 (8.0%)]

2-14 An electric bulb of volume 250 cm^3 was sealed off during manufacture at pressure 10^{-3} mm of the *Hg* at 27°C. Compute the number of air molecules in the bulb.

Ans. [8.02×10^{15}]

2-15 A column of mercury of 10 cm in length is contained in the middle of a narrow horizontal 1 m along tube which is closed at both ends. Both the ends contain air at a pressure of 76 cm of mercury. By what distance will the column of mercury be displaced if the tube is held vertically ?

Ans. [3 cm]

2-16 Two chambers containing m_1 and m_2 of an ideal gas at pressure P_1 and P_2 are put into communication. What will be the pressure of the mixture ?

Ans. [$\dfrac{(m_1 + m_2)P_1 P_2}{m_1 P_2 + m_2 P_1}$]

2-17 In a toy truck the volume of its tyre tube is 2000 cm^3 in which air is filled at a pressure of 2×10^5 N/m^2. When the tube gets punctured, its volume reduces to 500 cm^3. Find the number of moles of air leaked out in the puncture. Given that the atmospheric pressure is 1×10^5 N/m^2 and atmospheric temperature is 27°C.

Ans. [0.14 moles]

2-18 The volume expansion coefficient of an ideal gas at a constant pressure is observed as $\gamma \propto \frac{1}{T^n}$. Find the value of n.

Ans. [1]

2-19 The temperature of a room of volume V rise from T_1 to T_2. How much will the mass of the air in the room changes if the atmospheric pressure is p_0. The molecular weight of the air is M.

Ans. [$\Delta m = \frac{p_0 MV}{R}\left(\frac{1}{T_1} - \frac{1}{T_2}\right)$]

2-20 When the bulb of a constant volume air thermometer is immersed in ice, the mercury level in the open tube is 15 cm higher than the fixed index. When the bulb is immersed in boiling water the difference in the two levels increases to 48.3 cm. When the bulb is immersed in a hot liquid, the difference in levels decreases to 21 cm. What is the temperature of the hot liquid ?

Ans. [18°C]

2-21 The pressure in a helium gas cylinder is initially 30 atmospheres. After many balloons have been blown up, the pressure has decreased to 6 atm. What fraction of the original gas remains in the cylinder ?

Ans. [0.2]

2-22 In figure-2.41, a uniform tube with an open stopcock is lowered into mercury so that 12 cm of the tube remains unfilled. After the stopcock is closed, the tube is lifted 8 cm. What is the height y of the mercury in the tube ? Assume standard atmospheric conditions. In standard condition atmospheric pressure is 76 cm of Hg.

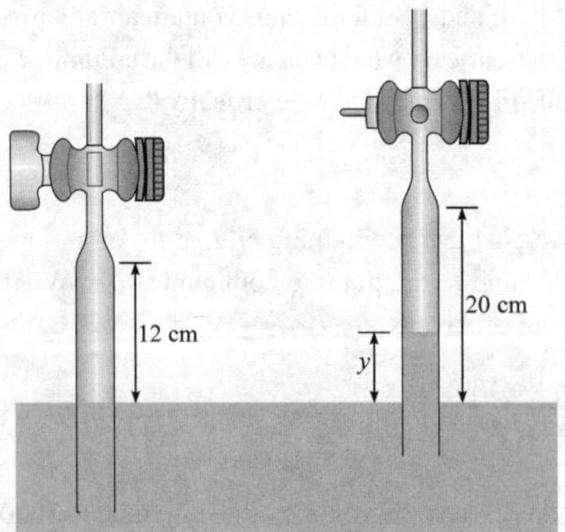

Figure 2.41

Ans. [6.82 cm]

2-23 A beam of particles, each of mass m_0 and speed v, is directed along the x axis. The beam strikes an area 1 mm square, with 1×10^{15} particles striking per second. Find the pressure on the area due to the beam if the particles stick to the area when they hit. Evaluate for an electron beam in a television tube, where $m_0 = 9.11 \times 10^{-31}$ kg and $v = 8 \times 10^7$ m/s.

Ans. [$10^{21}\ m_0 v$; 0.0729 Pa]

2-24 A cylinder of length 42 cm is divided into chambers of equal volumes and each half contains a gas of equal mass at temperature 27°C. The separator is a frictionless piston of insulating material. Calculate the distance by which the piston will be displaced if the temperature of one half is increased to 57°C.

Ans. [1 cm]

2-25 Two identical vessels are connected by a tube with a valve letting the gas pass from one vessel into the other if the pressure difference is ΔP. Initially there was a vacuum in one vessel while the other contained ideal gas at a temperature T_1 and pressure P_1. Then both vessels were heated to a temperature T_2. Up to what value will the pressure in the first vessel (which had vaccum initially) increase ?

Ans. [$P = \frac{1}{2}(P_1 T_2 / T_1 - \Delta P)$]

2-26 A chamber of volume V is evacuated by a pump whose evacuation rate equals C. How soon will the pressure in the chamber decrease by η ($\eta > 1$)?

Ans. [$t = (V/C) \ln \eta$]

2-27 A vertical cylinder closed from both ends is equipped with an easily moving piston dividing the volume into two parts, each containing one mole of air. In equilibrium at T_0 the volume of the upper part is η times greater than that of the lower part. At what temperature will the ratio of these volumes be equal to η' ($\eta' > \eta$) ?

Ans. [$T = T_0 \eta' (\eta^2 - 1) / \eta (\eta'^2 - 1)$]

2-28 Suppose the pressure p and the density ρ of air are related as p/ρ^n = constant regardless of height (n is a constant here). Find the corresponding temperature gradient.

Ans. [$dT/dh = -Mg(n-1)/nR$]

2-29 A vessel of volume $V = 5.01$ contains $m = 1.4$ g of nitrogen at a temperature $T = 1800$ K. Find the gas pressure, taking into account that $\eta = 30\%$ of molecules are disassociated into atoms at this temperature.

Ans. [1.9 atm]

2-30 Under standard conditions the density of the helium and nitrogen mixture equals $\rho = 0.60$ g/l. Find the concentration of helium atoms in the given mixture.

Ans. [1.6×10^{19} cm^{-3}]

2-31 A glass bulb of volume 100 cm^3 is connected by a narrow tube of negligible volume to another bulb of volume 300 cm^3. The apparatus is filled with air at a pressure of 76 cm of mercury and a temperature of 12°C, and then sealed. The smaller bulb is then immersed in melting ice whilst the larger bulb is placed in boiling water. Calculate the fraction of the total mass of air in the larger bulb, ignoring the expansion of the bulbs.

Ans. [0.69]

2-32 A horizontal cylinder closed at both ends is divided into two parts by a thermally insulated piston. Both halves of the cylinder contain equal masses of a gas at a temperature of 27°C and a pressure of 1 atm. What distance from the centre of the cylinder will the piston move if the gas in one section is heated to 57°C ? What will be the final pressure in each section of the cylinder ? The initial length of each section of the cylinder is 42 cm.

Ans. [2 cm, 1.05 atm]

2-33 Compute the temperature at which the rms speed is equal to the speed of escape from the surface of the earth for hydrogen and for oxygen. The temperature of the uper atmosphere is about 1000 K. Would you expect to find a lot of hydrogen there or a lot of oxygen ?

Ans. [1.01×10^4 K, 16.2×10^4 K, we would expect more oxygen]

2-34 A spherical vessel of radius $r = 5$ cm contains hydrogen (H_2) at a temperature $T = 300$ K and pressure $p = 10^5$ Pa. How many molecules collide on the vessel in 1 s ?

Ans. [3.37×10^{26}]

2-35 Air at 273 K and 1 atm pressure contains 2.70×10^{25} molecules per cubic metre. How many molecules per cubic metre will there be at a place where the temperature is 223 K and the pressure is 1.33×10^{-4} N m^{-2} ? (1 atm $= 1.01 \times 10^5$ N m^{-2})

Ans. [4.35×10^{16} m^{-3}]

2-36 Assume that air (molecular weight = 29) is under standard conditions close to the earth's surface. Find the air pressure at a height 5 km above the surface and in a mine at a depth 5 km below the surface. Assume that the temperature and the molar mass of air are independent of height.

Ans. [0.53 atm, 1.87 atm]

2-37 A cylindrical tube of uniform cross sectional area A is fitted with two frictionless pistons, as shown in figure-2.42. The pistons are connected to each other by a metallic wire. Initially the pressure of the gas is equal to atmospheric pressure P_0 and temperature is T_0. If the temperature of the gas is increased to $2T_0$, find the tension in the wire.

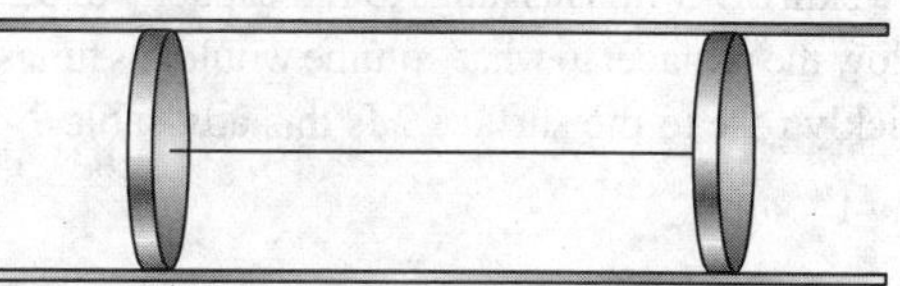

Figure 2.42

Ans. [P_0A]

2-38 Figure-2.43 shows a cylindrical container of radius 5 cm and a piston is fitted in it to enclose a length of 20 cm in it. The cylinder contains an ideal gas at a pressure of 1 atmosphere and 300 K temperature. The cylinder is slowly heated and it is found that the piston starts displacing when the gas temperature reaches 600 K. It is given that the friction coefficient between the piston sides and the container wall is 0.2. Find the normal force acting between piston sides and the container wall per unit length of its circumference.

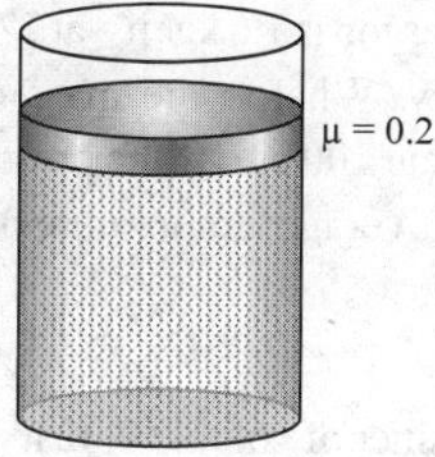

Figure 2.43

Ans. [1.25×10^4 Nt/m]

2-39 Two glass spheres of equal volume are connected by a small tube containing a small amount of mercury. The spheres are sealed at 20°C with exactly 1 litre of air in each side. If the cross sectional area of tube is 5×10^{-4} m^2, how far will the mercury be displaced if the temperature of one sphere is raised by 0.1°C while the other is maintained at 20°C.

Ans. [3.4 cm]

2-40 A planet of mass M and radius a is surrounding by an atmosphere of constant density consisting of a gas of molar mass μ. Find the temperature T of the atmosphere on the surface of the planet if the height of the atmosphere is $h << a$.

Ans. [$T = \frac{\mu GMh}{a^2R}$ where G = gravitational constant]

2-41 One mole of a gas at standard temperature and pressure (STP corresponds to $T = 273$ K and $\rho = 1.01 \times 10^5$ Pa) occupies a volume of 22.5 l. Suppose the container is in the shape of a cube. (a) Determine the length of the cube edge. (b) What force is exerted by the gas on each face of the container ?

Ans. [(0.282 m; (b) 8.03 kN]

2-42 If a skin diver fills his lungs to full capacity of 5.5 L when 12 m below the surface, to what volume would his lungs expand if he quickly rose to the surface ? Is this advisable ?

Ans. [11.9 L, No]

2-43 An air bubble at the bottom of a lake 16 m deep has a volume of 1.10 cm^3. If the temperature at the bottom is 5.5ºC and at the top it is 17.0ºC, what is the volume of the bubble just before it reaches the surface ?

Ans. [2.92 cm^3]

2-44 A vessel of volume V contains a mixture of hydrogen and helium at a temperature T and pressure p. The mass of the mixture is equal to m. Find the ratio of the mass of hydrogen to that of helium in the given mixture. Take molar masses of hydrogen and helium to be M_1 and M_2 respectively.

Ans. [$m_1/m_2 = (1 - a/M_2) / (a/M_1 - 1) = 0.50$, where $a = mRT/pV$]

2-45 The density of argon is 1.6 kg m^{-3} at 27ºC and at a pressure of 75 cm of mercury. What is the mass of the argon in an electric bulb of volume 100 cm^3 if the pressure inside is 75 cm of mercury when the average temperature of the gas is 150ºC ?

Ans. [1.135×10^{-4} kg]

2-46 A closed container of volume 0.02 m^3 contains a mixture of neon and argon gases, at a temperature of 27ºC and pressure of 1×10^5 N m^{-2}. The total mass of the mixture is 28 gm. If the gram molecular weights of neon and argon are 20 and 40 respectively, find the masses of the individual gases in the container, assuming them to be ideal. (Universal gas constant $R = 8.314$ J mol^{-1} K).

Ans. [23.928 g; 4.072 g]

2-47 A 20 cm long cylindrical test tube is inverted and pushed vertically down into water. When the closed end is at the water surface, how high has the water risen inside the tube ?

Ans. [0.374 cm]

2-48 A piece of dry ice, CO_2 is placed in a test tube, which is then sealed off. If the mass of dry ice is 0.36 g and the sealed test tube has a volume of 20 cm^3, what is the final pressure of the CO_2 in the tube if all the CO_2 vaporizes and reaches thermal equilibrium with the surroundings at 27ºC ?

Ans. [1.02 MPa]

2-49 Two vessels of volumes 5 and 3 litres contain air at pressure of 3 and 7 atmospheres, respectively. What will be the resultant pressure when they are connected through a small-bore tube ? Assume that the temperature remains constant throughout.

Ans. [4.5 atm]

2-50 At the top of a mountain, a thermometer reads 7ºC and a barometer reads 70 cm of *Hg*. At the bottom of the mountain, they read 27ºC and 76 cm of *Hg*. Calculate the ratio the density of the air at the top with that at the bottom.

Ans. [0.9868]

2-51 A thin walled cylinder of mass m, height h, cross-sectional area S is filled with a gas and floats part of the cylinder in water. As a result of the leakage of water from the lower part of the cylinder, the depth of submergence has increased by Δh. Determine the initial pressure of the gas in the cylinder, if the atmospheric pressure is p_0, and the temperature remains unchanged.

Ans. [$\left(p_0 + \frac{mg}{S}\right)\left(1 - \frac{\Delta h}{h}\right)$]

2-52 A thin tube of uniform cross-section is sealed at both ends. It lies horizontally, the middle 5 cm containing mercury and the two ends containing air at the same pressure P. When the tube is held at an angle of 60º with the vertical direction, the length of the air column above and below the mercury column are 46 cm and 44.5 cm respectively. Calculate the pressure P in cms of mercury. The temperature is kept at 30ºC.

Ans. [75.4 cm]

2-53 20 g of helium ($M = 4$) in a cylinder under a piston are transferred infinitely slowly from a state of volume $V_1 = 0.032$ m^3 and pressure $p_1 = 4.1$ atm to a state of volume $V_2 = 0.009$ m^3 and $p_2 = 15.5$ atm. What maximum temperature will the gas reach if the pressure decreases linearly with volume ?

Ans. [474.5 K]

2-54 In a high altitude cosmic station on a mountain at an altitude of 3250 m above sea level, calculate the pressure of air at this station. Take the temperature of the air constant and equal to 5ºC. The mass of one kilomole of air is 29 kg/kmole and the pressure at sea level is 760 mm of mercury.

Ans. [≈ 506.3 mm of *Hg*]

2-55 A vessel of volume V contains ideal gas at the temperature 0ºC. After a portion of the gas the been let out, the pressure in the vessel decreased by Δp (the temperature remaining constant). Find the mass of the released gas. The gas density under the normal conditions ρ.

Ans. [$m = \rho V \, \Delta p/p_0$, where p_0 is the standard atmospheric pressure]

2-56 Find the pressure in an air bubble of diameter $d = 4.0$ μm, located in weather at a depth h = 5.0 m. The atmospheric pressure has the standard value p_0.

Ans. [2.2 atm]

2-57 The mass of a 250 cm^3 flask is 287 mg more when it is filled with an unknown gas than when it is evacuated. When the flask is filled, the gas is at 20ºC and 1.00×10^5 Pa. What is the molecular mass of the gas molecules.

2-58 Both limbs of a 'U' tube are of equal length. One of the limbs is sealed and contains a column of 28 cm of air at atmospheric pressure. The air is separated from the atmosphere by mercury. What will be the height of air in the sealed limb, if the other limb is now filled to the top with mercury ? Atmospheric pressure is 76 cm of mercury.

Ans. [21.77 cm]

2-59 A glass tube sealed at one end and containing a quantity of air is immersed in mercury until the sealed end is 10 cm from the surface of mercury. At 0ºC the level of mercury in the tube is 5 cm above the level of mercury in the vessel. The length of the tube is 15 cm. To what temperature should the air in the tube be raised as to fill the tube completely ? The atmospheric pressure is 75 cm of *Hg*. Neglect any change in the level of mercury in the vessel.

Ans. [663ºC]

2-60 A column of mercury 10 cm long is contained in the middle of a narrow, horizontal 1 m long tube which is closed at both ends. Both the halves of the tube contain air at a pressure of 76 cm of mercury. By what distance will the column of mercury be displaced if the tube is held vertically ?

Ans. [by 3 cm downwards]

2-61 Modern vacuum pumps permit the pressures down to $p = 4.10^{-15}$ atm to be reached at room temperatures. Assuming that the gas exhausted is nitrogen, find the number of its molecules per 1 cm^3 and the mean distance between them at this pressure.

Ans. [$n = p/kT = 1.10^5$ cm^{-3}; $\langle l \rangle = 0.2$ mm.]

2-62 The diameter of a gas bubble formed at the bottom of a pond is $d = 4.0$ μm. When the bubble rises to the surface its diameter increases $n = 1.1$ times. Find how deep is the pond at that spot. The atmospheric pressure is standard, the gas expansion is assumed to be isothermal.

Ans. [5 m]

2-63 Determine the gas temperature at which

(a) the root mean square velocity of hydrogen molecules exceeds their most probable velocity by $\Delta v = 400$ m/s;

(b) the velocity distribution function $F(v)$ for the oxygen molecules will have the maximum value at the velocity $v = 420$ m/s.

Ans. [(a) 380 K; (b) 340 K]

2-64 At what temperature of a nitrogen and oxygen mixture do the most probable velocities of nitrogen and oxygen molecules differ by $\Delta v = 30$ m/s ?

Ans. [370 K]

* * * * *

Thermodynamics Laws & Specific Heats of Gases 3

FEW WORDS FOR STUDENTS

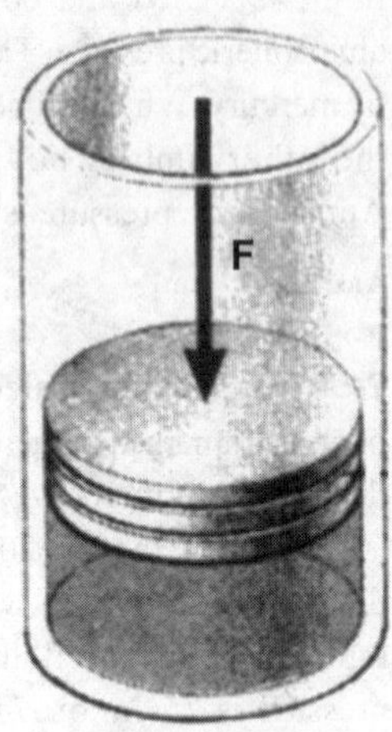

In this chapter we'll discuss the fundamental laws of thermodynamics. These laws are the basics for us to understand flow of heat and energy as in mechanics the fundamentals to understand motion are energy and momentum conservation laws. These thermodynamics laws are very useful in explaining the physical behaviour of a system when it responds to the flow of heat or thermal energy.

The two laws, first and second laws of thermodynamics completely govern the flow of thermal energy in nature.

CHAPTER CONTENTS

3.1 *Thermal Equilibrium and Zeroth Law of Thermodynamics*

3.2 *First Law of Thermodynamics*

3.3 *State of a Gas and Indicator Diagram*

3.4 *Molar Specific Heats of a Gas*

3.5 *Different Type of Thermodynamic Processes*

3.6 *Free Expansion of a Gas*

3.7 *Polytropic Process*

3.8 *Second Law of Thermodynamics*

COVER APPLICATION

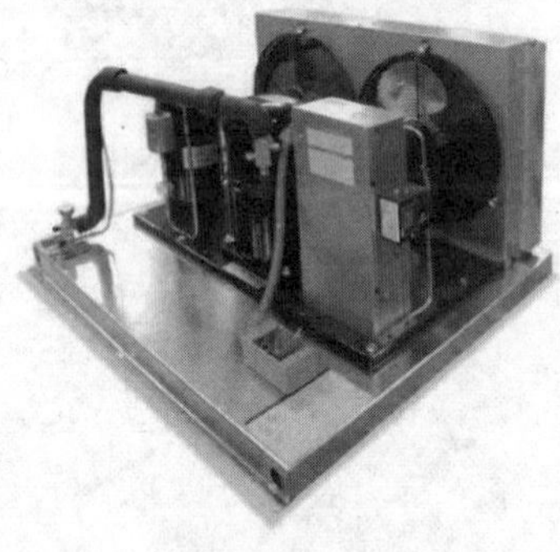

Figure (a)

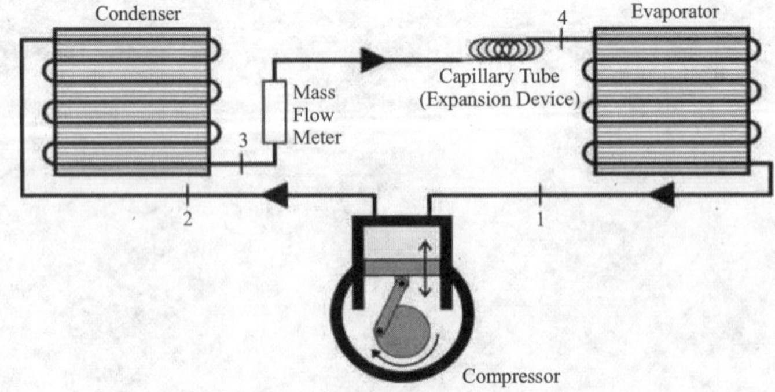

Figure (b)

Refrigeration, or cooling process, is the removal of unwanted heat from a selected object, substance, or space and its transfer to another object, substance, or space. The main components of the refrigeration system are condenser, evaporator and compressor. Removal of heat lowers the temperature and may be accomplished by use of ice, snow, chilled water or mechanical refrigeration. Figure-(a) is the industrial setup of a refrigeration system and Figure-(b) is the block diagram of different units and assembly of a refrigeration system.

The branch of physics thermodynamics is concerned with the relationships between heat and work. In previous chapters of calorimetry and kinetic theory of gases, we have discussed the measurements of heat or thermal energy in the form of kinetic energy of gas molecules. Thermodynamics is the study of thermal energy in different forms and it is based on two basic laws. First is that you can not get more energy out of a system than you put into it in all forms. That is the basic law of conservation of energy. Second law says that the transfer of energy by heat flow has a direction generally from high temperature region to a low temperature region or in other words we can say that processes in nature are not reversible.

The principles of thermodynamics were developed in eighteenth and nineteenth century and these are the most useful relations established between heat and work which are used very widely in different experiments and researches.

3.1 Thermal Equilibrium and Zeroth Law of Thermodynamics

In previous chapters we've discussed that two objects in thermal contact can exchange heat as long as they are at different temperatures. The hot object cools and colder one gets warm until they reach a common temperature at which no further change takes place. These two objects in this state are said to be in thermal equilibrium.

Based on thermal equilibrium earlier we've defined the zeroth law of thermodynamics as if two bodies are independently in thermal equilibrium with a third body then those two bodies are also in thermal equilibrium with each other. This is called zeroth law of thermodynamics because this is the logical basis of first and second laws of thermodynamics.

In further sections of this chapter we'll discuss about the concept of a thermodynamics system and about energy into or out of the system in the form of heat or work. A thermodynamic system is a collection of objects considered together and rest of the environment is called surrounding of system. A thermodynamic system interacts with its surrounding by exchange of energy in the form of heat transfer or work. As a result of this exchange of energy, the system's internal energy may change. We've discussed that by internal energy we mean the total kinetic energy and potential energy associated with the internal state of atoms composing the system. In addition to internal energy a system may have kinetic and potential energies due to the outside forces acting on system.

3.2 First Law of Thermodynamics

The first law of thermodynamics is based on the idea that energy is neither created nor destroyed in any thermodynamic system. In the usual formulation of first law, we consider the transfer of heat into a system, the work performed by the system and the change in the system's internal energy.

This law simply states that the total amount of heat supplied to a gaseous system is used in two parts. A part of supplied heat increases the kinetic energy of gas molecule or increases the temperature of system and the other part of supplied heat is used to do work against surrounding.

If dQ is the heat supplied to a gas during a heating process and due to this internal energy of a gas increases by dU and gas does a work dW against surrounding then according to first law of thermodynamics, we have

$$dQ = dU + dW \qquad \dots(3.1)$$

This equation-(3.1) is called differential form of first law of thermodynamics. If a gas is heated from an initial state to a final state by a process and if total heat supplied in the heating is ΔQ, total work done by the gas is ΔW and total change in internal energy of the gas is ΔU then we have

$$\Delta Q = \Delta W + \Delta U \qquad \dots(3.2)$$

Equation-(3.2) is state form of first law of thermodynamics and is used to relate the heat, work and change in internal energy of gas between initial and final states of a thermodynamics heating process.

3.2.1 Specific Heat Capacities of Gases

In solids and liquids we define specific heat as the amount of heat required for per degree rise in temperature of unit mass of substance. In the same sense we can define specific heat for a gas. Specific heat of a gas can be defined as the amount of heat required for a unit mass of a gas to raise its temperature by one degree. If instead of unit mass we take one mole of gas then it is termed as molar specific heat or molar heat capacity of the gas. It is denoted by C and if n moles of a gas is heated on dQ supply of heat, and if gas temperature increases by dT, then we have

$$dQ = n\,C\,dT \qquad \dots(3.3)$$

If temperature of gas charges from T_1 to T_2. Then total heat supplied is

$$Q = \int dQ = \int_{T_1}^{T_2} n\,C\,dT = n\,C\,(T_2 - T_1) \qquad \dots(3.4)$$

In solids and liquids generally specific heat remains constant for a material or varies slightly with temperature. But the case is not same for gases. In gases their specific heat also depends on the way of heating. If the process changes by which heat is supplied to a gas, it will also change the amount of heat required for a given amount of gas to change its temperature by a specific value. Before discussing the specific heats of a gas, we first discuss the phenomenon of heating a gas or how heat supplied to a gas is used by it.

3.2.2 Heating of a Gaseous System and Work done by a Gas

Figure-3.1(a) shows a cylindrical container in which a gas is enclosed and top of the container is closed by a light piston. Initially piston is in equilibrium as the pressure exerted by gas due to collisions of molecules is balanced by the atmospheric pressure due to air molecules outside. In this state if some heat is supplied to the gas by the burner as shown in figure-3.1 say a small amount dQ heat is supplied to the gas as shown in figure-3.1(b). If due to this dQ amount of heat, the temperature of gas is also slightly increased, say by amount dT. Thus this increase in temperature increases the kinetic energy of moving gas molecules due to which pressure exerted by gas on piston increases and piston will start displacing upward till again the pressure of gas becomes equal to atmosphere pressure. If the piston is displaced up by a distance dx, and this is due to the pressure of gas. We can say that in displacement of piston, work done by the gas is dW, which is given as

$$dW = P_{gas}\, S.\, dx \qquad [S = \text{area of piston}]$$

or

$$dW = P_{gas}\, dV \qquad \ldots(3.5)$$

$[dV = Sdx$ is the increase in volume of gas$]$

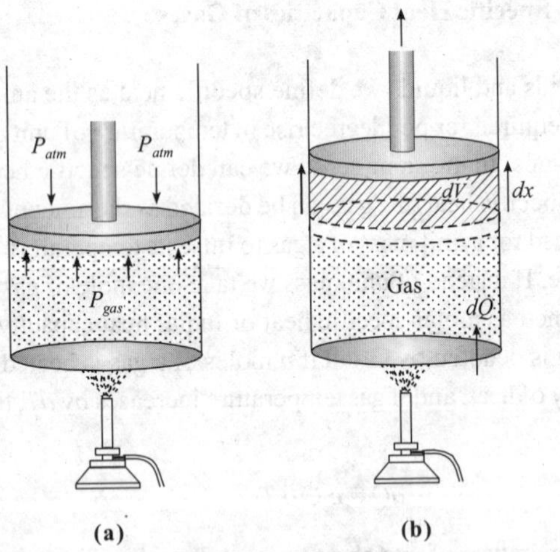

Figure 3.1

If during heating total volume of gas changes from V_1 to V_2 then the net work done in the heating process is

$$W = \int_{V_1}^{V_2} P_{gas}\, dV \qquad \ldots(3.6)$$

Equation-(3.5) gives the net work done in heating a gaseous system. In different cases during heating, pressure of gas may vary in different ways which results in different total work from integral in equation-(3.6) however the volume of initial and final state remain same.

As discussed, whenever volume of gas increases, we can say the work is done by the gas and when a gas is compressed, we say work is done on the gas by atmosphere or by some external agent responsible for the compression of gas.

3.2.3 Change in Internal Energy of a Gas on Heating

In previous section we've discussed that when heat is supplied to a system, it may be possible that gas expands. If it expands, we say gas does work against surrounding. It means some energy out of supplied heat goes to the surrounding in this work done. Similarly it may be possible that a part of supplied heat increases the kinetic energy of gas molecules. This means the temperature of gas increases. If temperature of gas increases by a small amount dT, we can say that the total internal energy of gas is also increased by a small amount, say dU, which can be given as

$$dU = \frac{f}{2} n R\, dT \qquad \ldots(3.7)$$

Similarly if in a case gas temperature decreases, then equation-(3.7) gives the decrement in internal energy and we write this equation with a negative sign on either side of equality.

If total change in temperature of gas is from T_1 to T_2 then total change in its internal energy from initial to final state is

$$\Delta U = \int dU = \int_{T_1}^{T_2} \frac{f}{2} n R\, dT$$

or

$$\Delta U = \frac{f}{2} n R\,(T_2 - T_1) \qquad \ldots(3.8)$$

 # Illustrative Example 3.1

One mole of an ideal gas is heated from 0 °C to 100 °C at a constant pressure of 1 atmosphere. Calculate the work done in the process.

Solution

One mole of gas occupies a volume of 22400 cm^3 at 0 °C and at 1 atmosphere pressure. Thus, the initial volume of the gas is $V_1 = 22400\text{ cm}^3 = 22400 \times 10^{-6}\text{ m}^3 = 0.0224\text{ m}^3$. The final volume V_2 can be calculated by using gas laws as

$$\frac{P_1 V_1}{T_1} = \frac{P_2 V_2}{T_2}$$

Here $T_1 = 0\,°\text{C} = 273\text{ K}$

$$T_2 = 100\,°\text{C} = 373\text{ K}$$

$$P = P_2 = 1\text{ atmosphere} = 0.76\text{ m of Hg}$$

$$= 0.76 \times 9.8 \times 13600\text{ Nm}^{-2}$$

$$= 1.013 \times 10^5\text{ Nm}^{-2}$$

or $$V_2 = V_1\frac{T_2}{T_1}$$

Thus we have $= 0.0224 \times \dfrac{373}{273}\text{ m}^3 = 0.0306\text{ m}^3$

We know work done in the process can be calculated as

$$W = \int_{V_1}^{V_2} PdV = P\int_{V_1}^{V_2} dV \text{ [As } P \text{ is constant]}$$

$$= P(V_2 - V_1)$$

$$= 1.013 \times 10^5 (0.0306 - 0.0224)$$

$$= 830.7\text{ J}$$

Here as gas expands, work is done by the gas.

Illustrative Example 3.2

In thermodynamic system internal energy decreases by 400 J while it is doing 250 J of work. What net heat is taken in by the system in the process.

Solution

Here it is given that

$$\Delta U = -400\text{ J}$$

and $$W = +250\text{ J}$$

Now from first law of thermodynamics, we have

$$Q = \Delta U + W$$

$$= (-400) + (+250) = -150\text{ J}$$

The amount of heat Q is negative thus in the process this thermodynamic system rejects 150 J of heat to the surroundings.

Illustrative Example 3.3

An ideal gas in a cylindrical vessel is confined by a piston at a constant pressure of 10^5 Pa. When 2×10^4 J of heat is added to it, the volume of gas expands from 0.15 m^3 to 0.25 m^3. (a) What is the work done by the system in this process. (b) What is the change in internal energy of the system.

Solution

(a) We know that work done by a gas in a process is given as

$$W = \int_{V_1}^{V_2} PdV = P(V_2 - V_1)$$

[As P = constant here]

$$= 10^5[0.25 - 0.15] = 10^4\text{ J}$$

(b) From first law of thermodynamics, in the process we have

$$Q = \Delta U + W$$

Here $$2 \times 10^4 = \Delta U + 10^4$$

or $$\Delta U = 10^4\text{ J}$$

Illustrative Example 3.4

A vertical hollow cylinder contains an ideal gas. The gas is enclosed by a 5 kg movable piston having a cross-sectional area of $5 \times 10^{-3}\text{ m}^2$. Now the gas is heated from 300 K to 350 K and the piston rises by 0.1 m. The piston is now clamped in this position and the gas is cooled back to 300 K. Find the difference between the heat energy added during heating and the heat energy lost during cooling. (1 atmospheric pressure = 10^5 Nm^{-2} and $g = 10\text{ ms}^{-2}$).

Solution

Given, mass of piston $M = 5$ kg, cross-sectional area of piston $A = 5 \times 10^{-3}\text{ m}^2$, $g = 10\text{ ms}^{-2}$ and atmospheric pressure $P_0 = 10^5\text{ Nm}^{-2}$.

The initial pressure of the gas in the cylinder is

P = atmospheric pressure + pressure due to weight Mg of piston

$$= P_0 + \frac{Mg}{A} \text{ or } P = 10^5 + \frac{5\times10}{5\times10^{-6}} = 1.1 \times 10^5\text{ Nm}^{-2}$$

When the piston rises by $x = 0.1$ m, the increase in the volume of the gas is

$$\Delta V = Ax = (5 \times 10^{-3}) \times 0.1 = 5 \times 10^{-4}\text{ m}^3$$

Thus work done by the gas is

$$W = \int_{V_1}^{V_2} PdV$$

or $$= P(V_2 - V_1)$$

$$= 1.1 \times 10^5 \times 5 \times 10^{-4} = 55\text{ J}$$

If ΔU is the increase in the internal energy during heating, then from the first law of thermodynamics, the heat energy supplied to the gas is given as

$$Q = \Delta U + W = (\Delta U + 55) \text{ joule}$$

Since the piston is clamped, the volume of the gas remains constant during cooling. Hence work done during cooling is zero.

As the gas is cooled back to the initial temperature, the change in the internal energy during cooling is

$$\Delta U' = -\Delta U$$

Thus heat energy lost by the gas during cooling is

$$Q' = \Delta U' + W' = -\Delta U + 0 = -\Delta U$$

The difference between heat energy added during heating and heat energy lost during cooling is

$$\Delta Q = Q - Q' = (\Delta U + 55) - \Delta U = 55 \text{ joule}$$

Illustrative Example 3.5

Gaseous hydrogen initially at STP in a container of volume 5×10^{-5} m^3 is cooled by 55 K. Find the change in internal energy and amount of heat lost by the gas.

Solution

Initially in standard conditions the gas pressure is

$$P = 10^5 \text{ Pa}$$

Gas temperature is $T = 273$ K

Gas volume is $V = 5 \times 10^{-3}$ m^3

If n moles of gas are there, then from gas law, we have

$$PV = nRT$$

or
$$n = \frac{PV}{RT} = \frac{10^5 \times 5 \times 10^{-3}}{8.314 \times 273} = 0.22 \text{ mole}$$

Thus change in internal energy in a process is given as

$$\Delta U = \frac{f}{2} nR\Delta T$$

$$= \frac{5}{2} \times 0.22 \times 8.314 \times 55 = 251.5 \text{ J}$$

As gas is enclosed in a container its volume remains constant during the process thus work done in this process is zero and according to first law of thermodynamics, we have

$$Q = \Delta U = -251.5 \text{ J}$$

Thus the decrease in internal energy is lost by the gas in the form of heat to the surrounding.

Web Reference at www.physicsgalaxy.com

Age Group - High School Physics | Age 17-19 Years
Section - HEAT & THERMODYNAMICS
Topic - Laws of Thermodynamics
Module Number - 1 to 6

Practice Exercise 3.1

(i) A gas undergoes a change of state during which 100 J of heat is supplied to it and it does 20 J of work. The system is brought back to its original state through a process during which 20 J of heat is rejected by the gas. Find the work done by the gas in the second process.

[60 J]

(ii) A sample of an ideal gas is taken through a process *ABCD*. It absorbs 50 J of energy during the process *AB* which is an isometric process, no heat during *BC* and it rejects 70 J of heat during isobaric process *CD*. It is also given that 40 J of work is done on the gas during the process *BC*. Internal energy of gas in state *A* is 1500 J. Find the internal energy of gas in state C.

[1590 J]

(iii) In a gaseous system, a gas expands from 10^{-4} m^3 to 2×10^{-4} m^3 while its pressure remains constant at 10^5 Nt/m^2. Calculate the amount of heat absorbed by the gas in the expansion. [$\gamma = 1.67$]

[24.92 J]

(iv) At atmospheric pressure, $m = 1$ g of water boils into steam which occupies a volume of $V_g = 1671$ cm^3. The latent heat of vaporisation of $L = 539$ cal/g and specific volume of water $V_L = 1$ cm^3. Find the increase in internal energy of the system. Atmospheric pressure is $p_0 = 1.013 \times 10^5$ Pa. Take 1 cal = 4.2 J

[2094.63 J]

(v) N_2 is confined in a cylindrical vessel with a movable piston exposed to open atmosphere. If 25 kcal of heat is added to it and the internal energy of the gas increases by 8 kcal, find the work done by the gas.

[17 kcal]

(vi) A sample of an ideal diatomic gas is heated at constant pressure. If an amount of 100 J of heat is supplied to the gas, find the work done by the gas.

[28.57 J]

3.3 *State of a Gas and Indicator Diagram*

When a gas is heated its thermodynamic parameters pressure, volume and temperature changes. These three parameters of a gas at an instant, pressure P, volume V and temperature T, combinedly define the state of a gas. Whenever the state of a gas (P, V, T) is changed, we say the gaseous system is undergone a thermodynamic process. The graphical representation of the change in state of a gas by a thermodynamic process is called indicator diagram. Indicator diagram is plotted generally in pressure and volume of a gas. Figure-3.2 shows a general PV indicator diagram. This indicator diagram representing the change of state of a gaseous system from state-1 $(P_1\ V_1\ T_1)$ to state-2 $(P_2\ V_2\ T_2)$. Each point on indicator diagram represents a unique state of gas. In the figure-3.2 shown when gas is in its state-1 its pressure, volume and temperature are P_1, V_1 and T_1 respectively. Now the gas state is to be changed to state-2 with pressure, volume and temperature P_2, V_2 and T_2 respectively. Figure-3.2 shows three different paths along which the gas can be taken from state-1 to state-2. In path-I, initially volume of gas is kept constant at V_1 and its pressure is increased from P_1 to P_2 then pressure P_2 is kept constant and volume is increased to V_2. In path-III first pressure is kept constant and volume is increased to V_2 then volume is kept constant at V_2 and pressure is increased to P_2. In path-II both pressure and volume are changed simultaneously along the curve shown to attain the desired values of pressure and volume of state-2. Here each path from which a gas is carried from initial to final state is called a thermodynamic process. There are infinite ways or thermodynamic processes by which state of a gas can be changed from given initial to final state. It can also be stated that when a gas is carried from one state to another, there are several adjacent intermediate states exist between initial and final states of the gas. Thus an indicator diagram curve represents the locus of all intermediate states between the two terminal states.

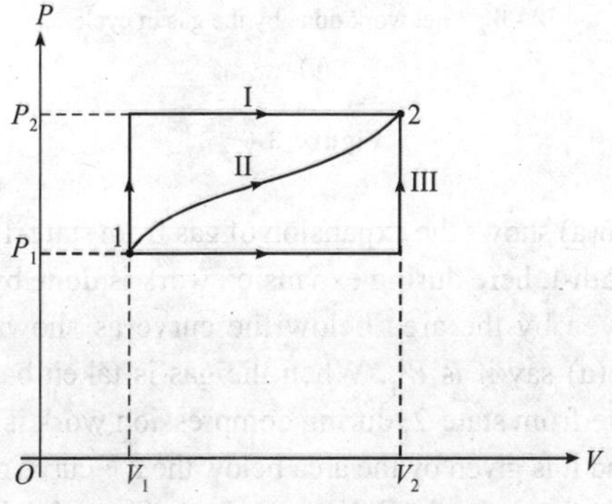

Figure 3.2

3.3.1 Properties of an Indicator Diagram

Figure-3.3 shows a general indicator diagram for a thermodynamic process for heating of a gas from state-1 to state-2. The path of this process is shown in figure-3.3 from initial to final state. Some standard characteristic of a P-V curve plotted for a thermodynamic process are

(i) Each point on an indicator diagram represents a unique state of a gas. In a P-V diagram, each points gives a specific value of pressure and volume of a gas and if number of moles are known, we can get its temperature using gas law. Hence a PV curve is the locus of the states of a gas during a thermodynamic process between initial and final states.

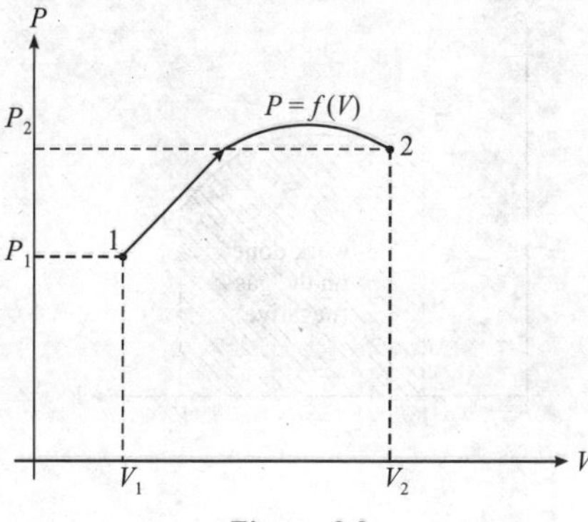

Figure 3.3

(ii) The path of a thermodynamic process on a P-V diagram relates pressure and volume of gas during the heating process. Each curve on P-V diagram has a characteristic function between P and V as $P = f(V)$. This function between pressure and volume is called as process equation or equation of the thermodynamic process between state-1 and state-2.

(iii) In a thermodynamic process, the work done by the gas, we've already discussed, is given as

$$W = \int_{V_1}^{V_2} P\,dV \quad \ldots (3.9)$$

If the process equation is known we can solve the integral in equation-(3.9) as

$$W = \int_{V_1}^{V_2} f(V)\,dV \quad \ldots (3.10)$$

This equation-(3.10) gives the work done by the gas during the process between state-1 and state-2 and mathematically this equation gives the area under the P-V curve on indicator diagram. As shown in figure-3.4(a) and 3.4(b), when final volume of gas is more then its initial volume, the area below the P-V curve gives the work done by the gas as it expands and when final volume of gas is lesser then its initial volume the curve is drawn from right to left as shown in figure and the area below the P-V curve gives the work done on the gas and is taken negative in numerical calculations.

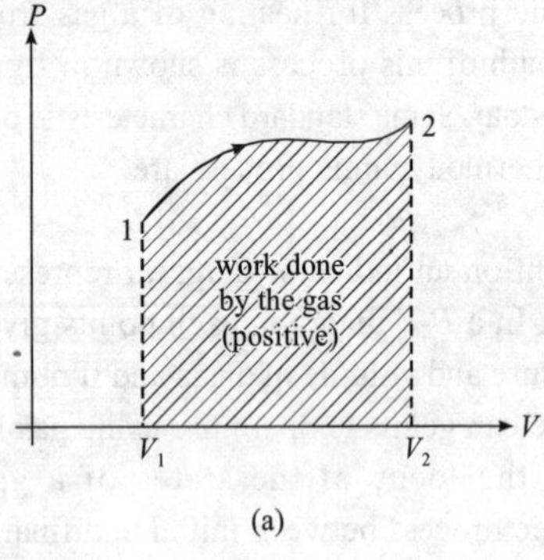

(a)

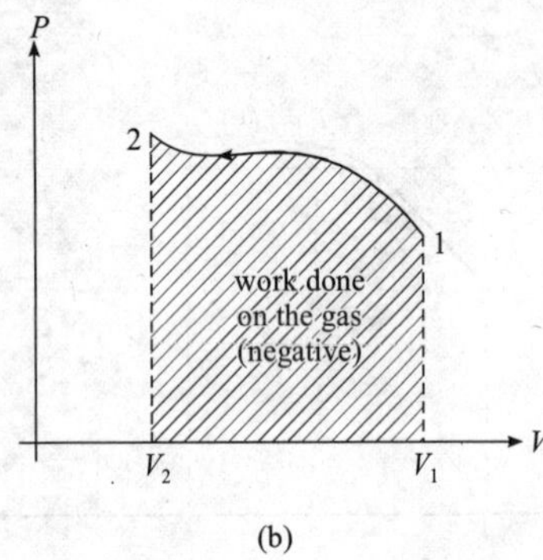

(b)

Figure 3.4

3.3.2 State Variable and Path Variables

When a gas is taken from its initial state (P_1, V_1, T_1) to a final state (P_2, V_2, T_2), out of the three thermodynamic variables, heat supplied Q and work done by the gas W, depend on the path along which the gas is taken from initial to final state. Dependency on path means it depends on the function $P = f(V)$ or the way how pressure and volume of gas are related during the process. Thus both Q and W are called path variables. Unlike to these internal energy of a gas only depends on its temperature or only on the initial and final state temperatures (T_1 and T_2) of the gas irrespective of how gas is heated to change its temperature from T_1 to T_2. Thus internal energy of a gas is called state variable.

If a gas is taken from a state-1 to another state-2 by several different paths and the heat supplied and work done in the respective paths are (Q_1, W_1), (Q_2, W_2), (Q_3, W_3) ... and so on then according to first law of thermodynamics, we have

$$\Delta U_{12} = Q_1 - W_1 = Q_2 - W_2 = \ldots \qquad \ldots(3.11)$$

3.3.3 Cyclic Processes

A thermodynamic process in which initial and final state are same are called cyclic processes. Figure-3.5 shows an indicator diagram of a cyclic process. A gas in state-1 is heated and is expand to change its state to state-2 shown in figure along path-I. Now it is compressed along path-II and taken back to its initial state to restore its pressure, volume and temperature to its initial values.

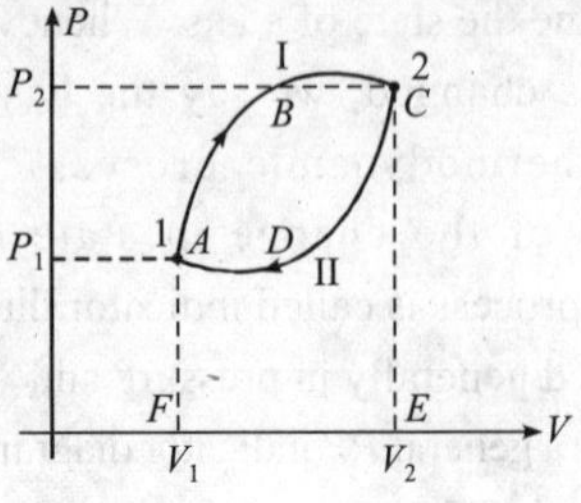

Figure 3.5

In a cyclic process we can say that no change in internal energy takes place as it is a state function and here also $\Delta T = 0$, thus $\Delta U = 0$. But as heat supplied and work done are path functions, we can numerically obtain these variables easily using first law of thermodynamics for paths I and II respectively.

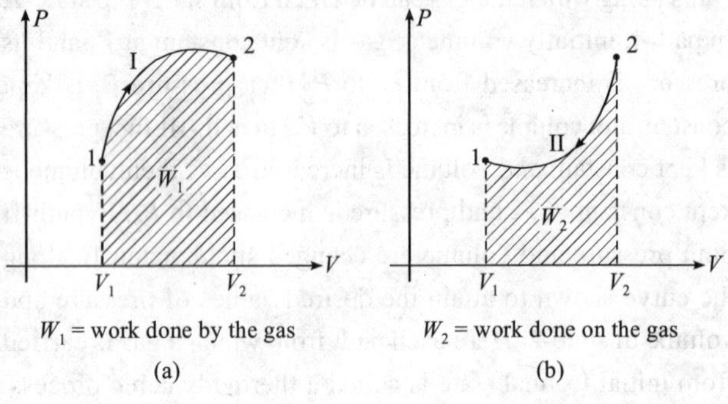

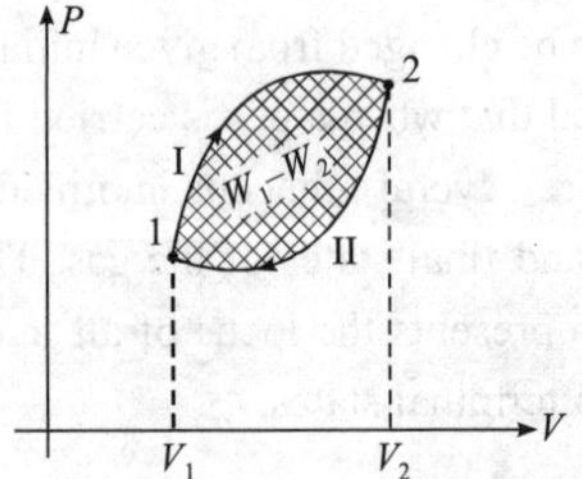

$W_1 - W_2$ = net work done by the gas in cycle

(c)

Figure 3.6

Figure-3.6(a) shows the expansion of gas from state-1 to state-2 along path-I, here during expansion work is done by the gas and is given by the area below the curve as shown in this figure-3.6(a) say it is W_1. When the gas is taken back to its initial state from state-2, during compression work is done on the gas and it is given by the area below the PV curve of path-II as shown in figure-3.6(b) say it is W_2. From figure-3.5 it is clear that W_1 is more then W_2 hence in the complete cycle net work is done by the gas and it is given by the area enclosed by the PV-curve of the complete cycle as shown in figure-3.6(c). Thus net work done by the gas in a cyclic process is

$W_1 - W_2$ = Area enclosed by the PV-curve of the cyclic process

As discussed initially that in a cyclic process net change in internal energy of gas is zero thus the total work done is equal to the total amount of heat supplied to the gas. In fact during first part of the cycle i.e. during expansion of gas, heat is supplied and work is done by the gas, say heat supplied to the gas is Q_1. In second part of the cycle i.e. during compression of gas, work is done on the gas and some heat is rejected by the gas to its surrounding say this amount is Q_2. As total work is done by the gas thus we generally have $Q_1 > Q_2$ so total heat supplied to the gas can be written as

$$\Delta Q = Q_1 - Q_2 \qquad \ldots(3.12)$$

This must be equal to the total work done by gas as $\Delta U = 0$ in the complete cycle. Thus

$$\Delta Q = Q_1 - Q_2 = \Delta W = W_1 - W_2 \qquad \ldots(3.13)$$

3.3.4 Positive and Negative Cycles

In previous section we have discussed that net work done by a gas in a cyclic process is equal to the area enclosed by its PV-curve on indicator diagram. We've taken example shown by the curve in figure-3.5 and figure-3.6. If we carefully look on the path of process, it is clockwise. Another cyclic process can also be realized of which PV curve can be anticlockwise. Such a process is shown in figure-3.7. There it can be clearly seen that during expansion the work done by the gas along path-I is less then the work done on the gas during its compression along path-II. Thus in cyclic processes having anticlockwise cycles, net work is done on the gas during the complete cycle and is again given by the area enclosed by the cyclic curve as shown by figure-3.7. Again as no net change in internal energy takes place in a cyclic process, in anticlockwise cycles net heat is rejected by the gas to the surrounding and is equal to the net work done on the gas.

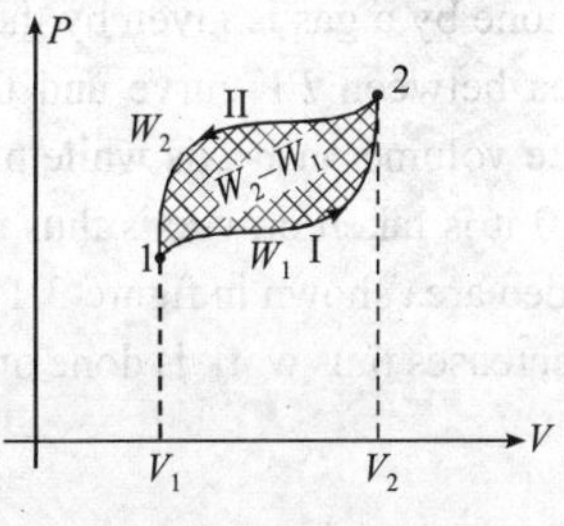

Figure 3.7

Cyclic processes in which PV curve is clockwise, net work is done by the gas, such cycles are called heat engine cycles. And those processes in which PV curve is anticlockwise, net work is done on the gas and heat is rejected by the gas to the surrounding, such cycles are called refrigeration cycles. In further sections we'll discuss these cycles in more details.

 # Illustrative Example 3.6

When a thermodynamic system is taken from an initial state I to a final state F along the path IAF, as shown in figure-3.8, the heat energy absorbed by the system is $Q = 55$ J and the work done by the system is $W = 25$ J. If the same system is taken along the path IBF, the value of $Q = 35$ J.

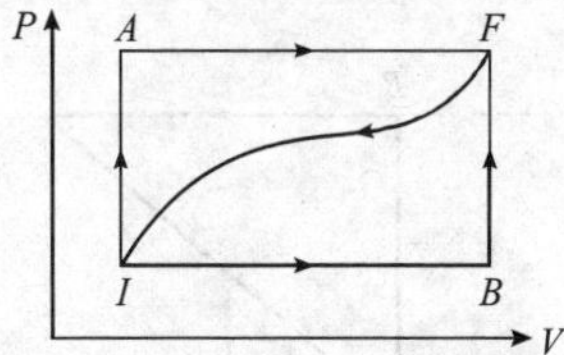

Figure 3.8

(a) Find the work done along the path IBF.

(b) If $W = -15$ J for the curved path FI, how much heat energy is lost by the system along this path ?

(c) If $U_I = 10$ J, what is U_F?

(d) If $U_B = 20$ J, what is Q for the processes BF and IB ?

Solution

The first law of thermodynamics states that

$$\Delta Q = \Delta U + \Delta W \text{ or } Q = (U_F - U_I) + W$$

Here U_I and U_F are the internal energies in the initial and the final state. Given that, for path IAF, $Q = 55$ J and $W = 25$ J. Therefore,

$$\Delta U = U_F - U_I = Q - W = 55 - 25 = 30 \text{ J}$$

The internal energy is independent of the path; it depends only on the initial and final states of the system. Thus the internal energy between I and F states is 30 J irrespective of the path followed by the system.

(a) For path IBF, $Q = 35$ J and $\Delta U = 30$ J. Therefore,

$$W = Q - \Delta U = 35 - 30 = 5 \text{ J}$$

(b) For path FI, $W = -15$ J, but $\Delta U = -30$ J

Therefore $Q = W + \Delta U = -15 - 30 = -45$ J

(c) Given $U_I = 10$ J. Therefore, $U_F = \Delta U + U_I = 30 + 10 = 40$ J

(d) The process BF is isochoric, i.e. the volume is constant. Hence $W = 0$. Therefore

$$Q = (\Delta U)_{BF} = U_F - U_B = 40 - 20 = 20 \text{ J}$$

The process IB is isobaric (constant pressure). Therefore,

$$Q = (Q)_{IBF} - (Q)_{BF} = 35 - 20 = 15 \text{ J}$$

Illustrative Example 3.7

Figure-3.9 shows an ideal gas changing its state from state A to state C by two different paths ABC and AC.

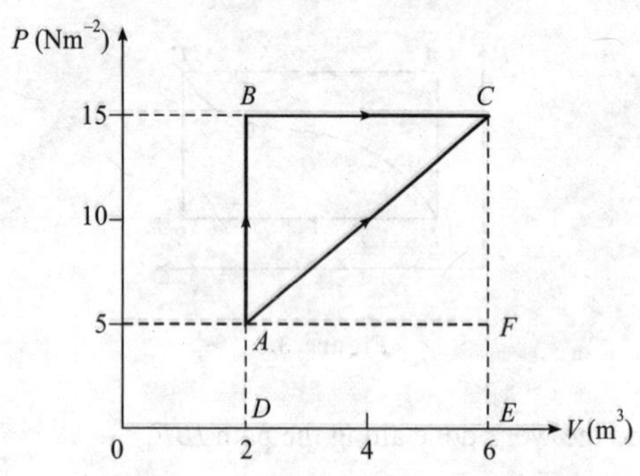

Figure 3.9

(a) Find the path along which the work done is the least.

(b) The internal energy of the gas at A is 10 J and the amount of heat supplied to change its state to C through the path AC is 200 J. Find the internal energy at C.

(c) The internal energy of the gas at state B is 20 J. Find the amount of heat supplied to the gas to go from state A to state B.

Solution

(a) We know work done is given by the area below PV curve thus by observing the two PV curves AC and ABC, we can say that work done in path AC is less then that in path ABC.

(b) Work done in path AC by the gas is

$$W_{AC} = \text{area of } ACFEDA$$

$$= \text{area of } ACF + \text{Area of } AFED$$

$$= \frac{1}{2} \times (15 - 5) \times (6 - 2) + (6 - 2) \times 5$$

$$= 20 + 20 = 40 \text{ J}$$

It is given that heat supplied in process AC is $Q_{AC} = 200$ T

Thus change in internal energy of gas in path AC is from first law of thermodynamics, given as

$$Q_{AC} = W_{AC} + \Delta U_{AC}$$

or $$\Delta U_{AC} = Q_{AC} - W_{AC} = 200 - 40 = 160 \text{ J}$$

As it is given that at state A, internal energy of gas is 10 J thus at state C, its internal energy is

$$\Delta U_{AC} = U_C - U_A$$

or $$U_C = \Delta U_{AC} + U_A = 160 + 10 = 170 \text{ J}$$

(c) As in process AB, no volume change takes place thus no work is done by or on the gas during path AB. Thus according to first law of thermodynamics, we have

$$Q_{AB} = \Delta U_{AB} + W_{AB}$$

or $$Q_{AB} = U_B - U_A + 0$$

or $$Q_{AB} = 20 - 10 = 10 \text{ J}$$

[As it is given that $U_B = 20$ J]

Illustrative Example 3.8

A gas is taken from state-1 to state-2 along the path shown in figure-3.10. If 70 cal of heat is extracted from the gas in the process, calculate the change in internal energy of the system.

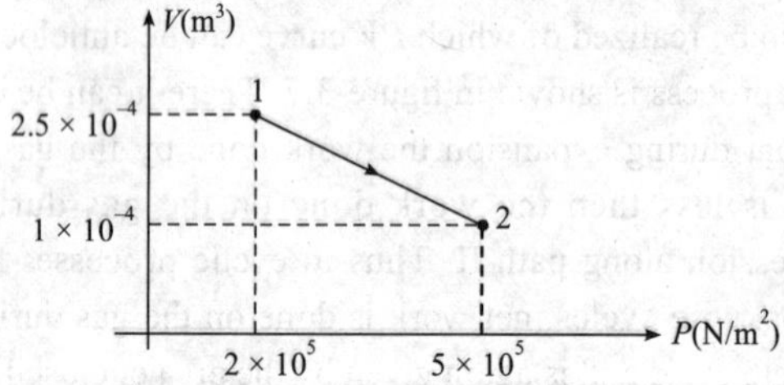

Figure 3.10

Solution

We know work done by a gas is given by the area under PV-curve or the area between PV-curve and the volume axis. Generally we take volume on x-axis while plotting PV-curve but in figure-3.10 it is taken on y-axis thus the work done is given by the shaded area shown in figure-3.11. In this process volume of gas decreases thus work is done on the gas and it is given as

$$W = -\frac{1}{2} \times 1.5 \times 10^{-4} \times (2 + 5) \times 10^5$$

$$= -52.5 \text{ J}$$

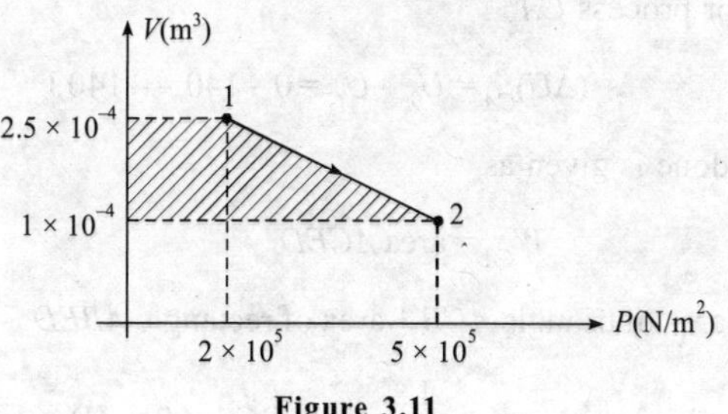

Figure 3.11

It is given that heat extracted in the process is 70 cal thus

$$Q = -70 \text{ cal} = 70 \times 4.2 \text{ J}$$

$$= -294 \text{ J}$$

Now from first law of thermodynamics, we have

$$Q = W + \Delta U$$

or $$\Delta U = Q - W$$

$$= (-294) - (-52.5)$$

$$= -241.5 \text{ J}$$

Thus in the process internal energy of gas decreases by 241.5 J

 # Illustrative Example 3.9

Figure-3.12 shows a process *ABCA* performed on one mole of an ideal gas. Find the net heat supplied to the gaseous system during the process.

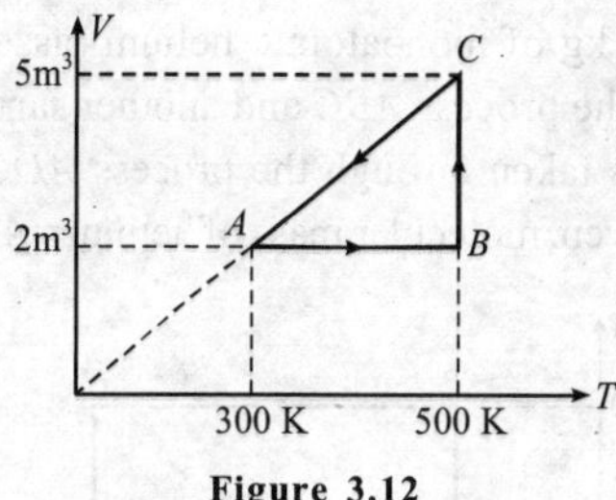

Figure 3.12

Solution

As we know in a cyclic process gas finally returns to its initial state hence total change in internal energy of gas is zero thus the total heat supplied to the gas is equal to the work done by the gas. Now we find the work done by the gas in different paths of the cycle.

In Process AB

As shown in graph during process *AB*, volume of gas remains constant thus work done by gas is zero

$$W_{AB} = 0$$

In Process BC

In process *BC*, volume of gas changes from $V_1 = 2 \text{ m}^3$ to $V_2 = 5 \text{ m}^3$ thus work done can be obtained as

$$W_{BC} = \int_2^5 P dV$$

As in process *BC*, temperature of gas remains constant at 500 K, thus we can write pressure of gas from gas law as

$$P = \frac{RT}{V} = \frac{500 R}{V} \qquad \text{[As } n = 1 \text{ mole]}$$

Now work done is

$$W_{BC} = \int_2^5 \frac{500 R}{V} dV$$

$$= 500 \text{ R } ln\left(\frac{5}{2}\right)$$

In Process CA

As in this process path is a straight line passing through origin thus $V \propto T$ or pressure of gas remains constant and we know if gas pressure is constant work done is given as

$$W_{CA} = nR(T_2 - T_1) = nR(300 - 500) = -200 \text{ R}$$

This is negative as gas is being compressed from volume 5 m³ to 2 m³ or work is done on the gas.

Now we can find the total work done by the gas in the complete cycle *ABCA* as

$$W_{ABCA} = W_{AB} + W_{BC} + W_{CA}$$

$$= 0 + 500 R \, ln\left(\frac{5}{2}\right) - 200 \text{ R}$$

$$= R(500 \, ln \, 5/2 - 200)$$

$$= 2146.22 \text{ J} = \text{heat supplied to the gas}$$

 # Illustrative Example 3.10

An ideal gas is taken round a cyclic thermodynamic process *ABCA* as shown in figure-3.13. If the internal energy of the gas at point *A* is assumed zero while at *B* it is 50 J. The heat absorbed by the gas in the process *BC* is 90 J.

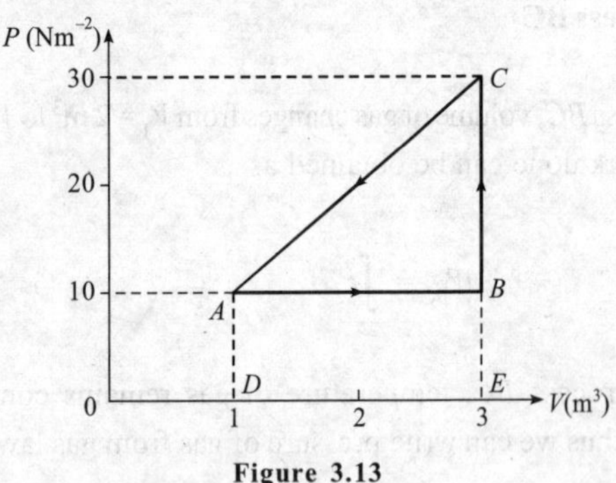

Figure 3.13

(a) What is the internal energy of the gas at point C?

(b) How much heat energy is absorbed by the gas in the process AB?

(c) Find the heat energy rejected or absorbed by the gas in the process CA.

(d) What is the net work done by the gas in the complete cycle $ABCA$?

Solution

Given that $U_A = 0$, $U_B = 50$ J and $Q_{BC} = 90$ J. Also

$$P_A = P_B = 10\ \text{Nm}^{-2}, P_C = 30\ \text{Nm}^{-2},$$

$$V_A = 1\ \text{m}^3 \text{ and } V_B = V_C = 3\ \text{m}^3$$

(a) In process BC as volume of gas remains constant, work done by gas in this process is zero, thus

$$W_{BC} = 0$$

Heat absorbed by the gas is $Q_{BC} = 90$ J. From the first law of thermodynamics.

$$(\Delta U)_{BC} = U_C - U_B = Q_{BC} - W_{BC} = 90\ \text{J} - 0 = 90\ \text{J}.$$

or $$U_C = (\Delta U)_{BC} + U_B = 90\ \text{J} + 50\ \text{J} = 140\ \text{J}$$

(b) In process AB, we have

$$(\Delta U)_{AB} = U_B - U_A$$

$$= 50 - 0 = 50\ \text{J}$$

Work done is given as

$$W_{AB} = \text{area under } AB \text{ in } P - V \text{ diagram}$$

$$= \text{area of rectangle } ABED$$

$$= AB \times AD = (3\ \text{m}^3 - 1\ \text{m}^3) \times 10\ \text{Nm}^{-2}$$

$$= 20\ \text{J}$$

Thus heat absorbed by the system is

$$Q_{AB} = (\Delta U)_{AB} + W_{AB} = 50 + 20 = 70\ \text{J}$$

(c) For process CA

$$(\Delta U)_{CA} = U_A - U_C = 0 - 140 = -140\ \text{J}$$

Work done is given as

$$W_{CA} = \text{area } ACED$$

$$= \text{area of triangle } ACB + \text{area of rectangle } ABED$$

$$= \frac{1}{2} \times AB \times BC + AB \times AD$$

$$= \frac{1}{2} \times (3-1)\ \text{m}^3 \times (30-10)\ \text{Nm}^{-2} + 20$$

$$= 20 + 20 = 40\ \text{J}$$

In this process, the volume decreases, the work is done on the gas. Hence, the work done is negative. Thus

$$W_{CA} = -40\ \text{J}$$

Thus heat rejected by the gas is

$$Q_{CA} = (\Delta U)_{CA} + W_{CA} = -140 - 40 = -180\ \text{J}$$

(d) Net work done in the complete cyclic process $ABCA$ is

$$W = \text{area of triangle } ABC = \frac{1}{2} \times 2 \times 20 = 20\ \text{J}$$

As the cycle is anticlockwise, net work is done on the gas.

Illustrative Example 3.11

A sample of 2 kg of monoatomic helium (assumed ideal) is taken through the process ABC and another sample of 2 kg of the same gas is taken through the process ADC as shown in figure-3.14. Given, molecular mass of helium = 4.

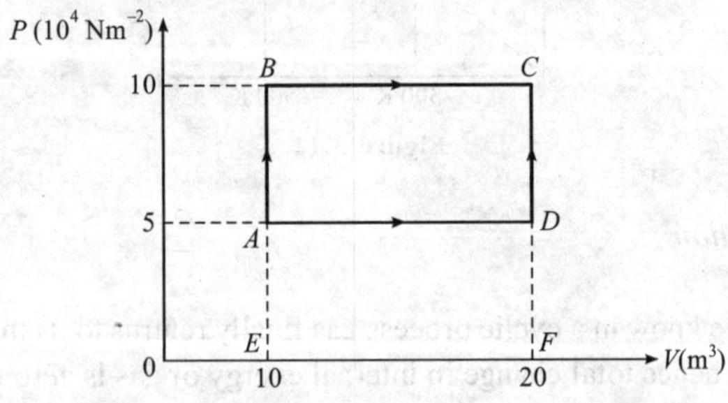

Figure 3.14

(a) What is the temperature of helium in each of the states A, B, C and D?

(b) Is there any way of telling afterwards which sample of helium went through the process ABC and which went through the process ADC? Write yes or no.

(c) How much is the heat involved in each of the process ABC and ADC?

Solution

Given that mass of helium used in the process is $m = 2$ kg thus number of moles can be given as

$$n = \frac{m}{M} = \frac{2}{4\times10^{-3}} = 500$$

At different states, the pressure and volume of gas are also given, from figure-3.14

$$P_A = P_D = 5\times10^4\ \text{N/m}^2$$

$$P_B = P_C = 10^5\ \text{N/m}^2$$

$$V_A = V_B = 10\ \text{m}^3$$

$$V_C = V_D = 20\ \text{m}^3$$

(a) From gas law, we have

$$T_A = \frac{P_A V_A}{nR} = \frac{5\times10^4\times10}{500\times8.314} = 120.3\ \text{K}$$

$$T_B = \frac{P_B V_B}{nR} = \frac{10^5\times10}{500\times8.314} = 240.6\ \text{K}$$

$$T_C = \frac{P_C V_C}{nR} = \frac{10^5\times20}{500\times8.314} = 481.11\ \text{K}$$

and $$T_D = \frac{P_D V_D}{nR} = \frac{5\times10^4\times20}{500\times8.314} = 120.3\ \text{K}$$

(b) Since the gas is taken from same initial state to same final state C no matters whatever be the path, the answer is No.

(c) In process ABC, the change in internal energy is

$$\Delta U_{ABC} = U_C - U_A = \frac{f}{2}\,nR\,(T_C - T_A)$$

$$= \frac{3}{2}\times500\times8.314\,(481.11 - 120.3)$$

$$= 2.25\times10^6\ \text{J}$$

Net work done in process ABC is

$$W_{ABC} = W_{AB} + W_{BC}$$

$$= 0 + \text{area below curve } BC$$

$$= 0 + 10^5\times10$$

$$= 10^6\ \text{J}$$

Thus from first law of thermodynamics, heat supplied in process ABC is

$$Q = W + \Delta U$$

or $$Q = 10^6 + 2.25\times10^6$$

$$= 3.25\times10^6\ \text{J}$$

Similarly in process ADC as being a state function change in internal energy remains same as initial and final states are same. Thus

$$\Delta U_{ADC} = 2.25\times10^6\ \text{J}$$

Thus work done by the gas in process ADC is

$$W_{ADC} = W_{AD} + W_{DC}$$

$$= \text{area below curve } AD + 0$$

$$= 5\times10^4\times10 + 0$$

$$= 0.5\times10^6\ \text{J}$$

Thus from first law of thermodynamics, heat supplied in the process ADC is given as

$$Q = W + \Delta U$$

or $$= 0.5\times10^6 + 2.25\times10^6$$

$$= 2.75\times10^6\ \text{J}$$

 # Illustrative Example 3.12

One mole of an ideal monatomic gas is taken round the cyclic process $ABCA$ as shown in figure-3.15. Calculate

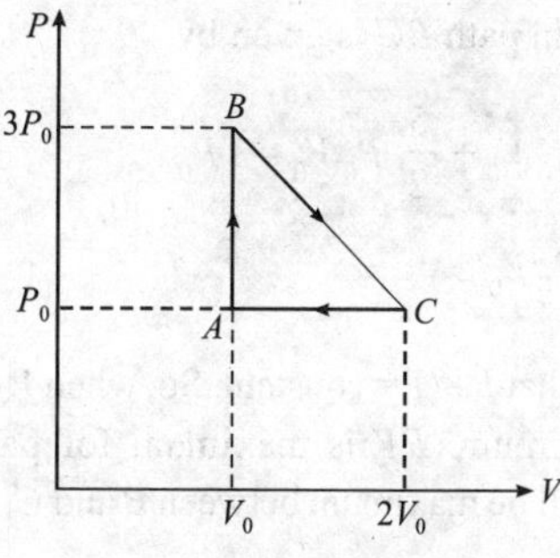

Figure 3.15

(a) the workdone by the gas

(b) the heat rejected by the gas in the path CA and the heat absorbed by the gas in the path AB

(c) the net heat absorbed by the gas in the path BC

(d) the maximum temperature attained by the gas during the cycle.

Solution

(a) The workdone by the gas is equal to the area under the closed curve. Thus workdone in cycle is

$$W=\frac{1}{2}(2V_0-V_0)(3P_0)(3P_0-P_0)$$

$$=\frac{1}{2}V_0\times 2P_0$$

$$=P_0V_0$$

(b) Heat rejected in path CA is given as

$$Q_{CA}=\eta C_p\Delta T=\eta C_p(T_C-T_A)$$

$$=1\times 5/2\,.\,R\left[\frac{P_0\,2V_0}{R}-\frac{P_0V_0}{R}\right]$$

$$=\frac{5}{2}P_0V_0 \qquad \text{[As } n=1 \text{ mole]}$$

Heat absorbed in path AC

$$Q_{AC}=\eta C_p(T_B-T_A)$$

$$=1\times\frac{3}{2}R\times\left[\frac{3P_0V_0}{R}-\frac{P_0V_0}{R}\right]$$

$$=3P_0V_0$$

(c) For cycle ABC, we have

Heat supplied = workdone by the gas

or $$=-\frac{5}{2}P_0V_0+3P_0V_0+Q_{BC}=P_0V_0$$

Heat supplied in path BC is given by

$$Q_{BC}=P_0V_0+\frac{5}{2}P_0V_0-3P_0V_0$$

$$=P_0V_0/2$$

(d) We know that $PV/T=$ constant. So, when PV is maximum, T is also maximum. PV is maximum for part BC. Hence temperature will be maximum between B and C.

Let equation of BC be as

$P=kV+k'$ satisfying both the point B and C

For point B, $\quad 3P_0=kV_0+k'$

For point C, $\quad P_0=k(2V_0)+k'$

Solving these equations, we get

$$k=-2(P_0/V_0) \text{ and } k'=5P_0$$

So, the equation for time BC is

$$P=-2\frac{P_0}{V_0}\times V+5P_0$$

or $$\frac{RT}{V}=-\frac{2P_0V}{V_0}+5P_0$$

or $$T=\frac{P_0}{R}\left[5V-2\frac{V^2}{V_0}\right] \qquad \ldots(3.14)$$

For maximum, $dT/dV=0$

So, $$\frac{dT}{dV}=\frac{P_0}{R}\left[5-\frac{4V}{V_0}\right]=0$$

Hence $5-\frac{4V}{V_0}=0$ or $5V_0-4V=0$

or $$V=\frac{5}{4}V_0 \qquad \ldots(3.15)$$

Substituting the value of V from equation-(3.15) in equation-(3.14), we get

$$T_{max}=\frac{P_0}{R}\left[5\times\left(\frac{5}{4}V_0\right)-2\left(\frac{5V_0}{4}\right)^2\frac{1}{V_0}\right]$$

$$=\frac{P_0}{R}\left[\frac{25V_0}{4}-\frac{25V_0}{8}\right]=\frac{P_0}{8}\times\frac{25V_0}{8}$$

$$=\frac{25P_0V_0}{8R}$$

Web Reference at www.physicsgalaxy.com
Age Group - High School Physics | Age 17-19 Years
Section - HEAT & THERMODYNAMICS
Topic - Laws of Thermodynamics
Module Number - 9 to 16

Practice Exercise 3.2

(i) A thermodynamic system undergoes cyclic process 1423451 as shown in figure-3.16. Find the work done by the system.

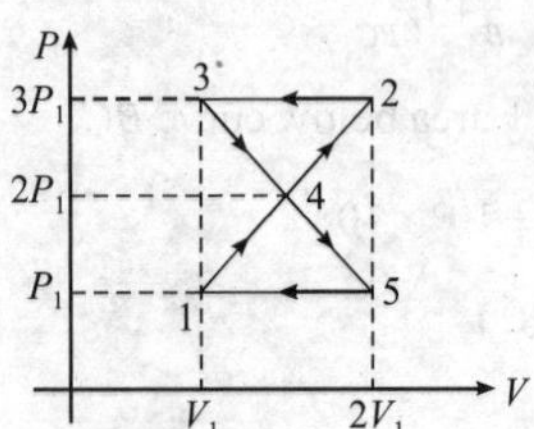

Figure 3.16

[0]

(ii) n moles of an ideal gas undergoes a thermodynamic process in which pressure of gas varies linearly with the volume of gas as shown in figure-3.17. Find the maximum temperature of the gas during the process.

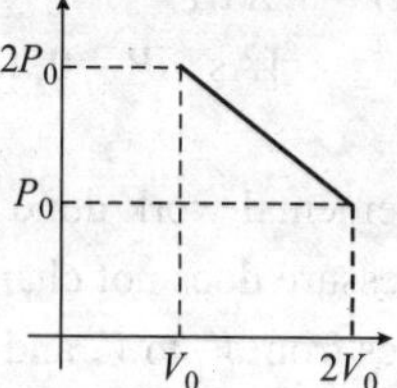

Figure 3.17

$\left[\frac{9P_0V_0}{4nR}\right]$

(iii) The PV diagram shown in figure-3.18 for a thermodynamic process is a semicircle. Find the work done on the gas in the process ABC.

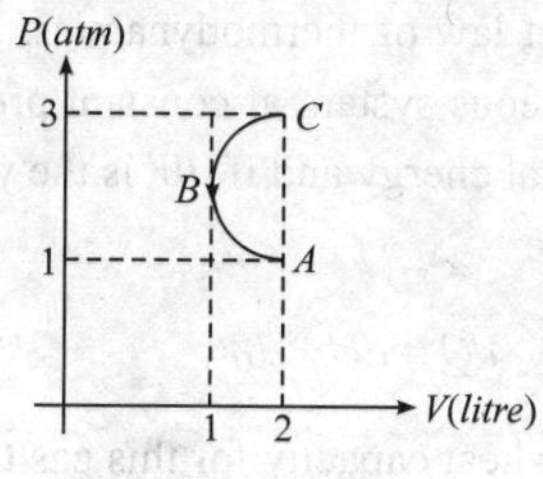

Figure 3.18

[$\pi/2$ atm-ltr]

(iv) The figure-3.19 shows p-V diagram of the thermodynamic process of an ideal gas. Compute from this graph : (a) work done in the processes $A \to B$, $B \to C$, $C \to D$, and $D \to A$. (b) work done in the complete cycle. 1 atm = 1.0×10^5 N/m^2.

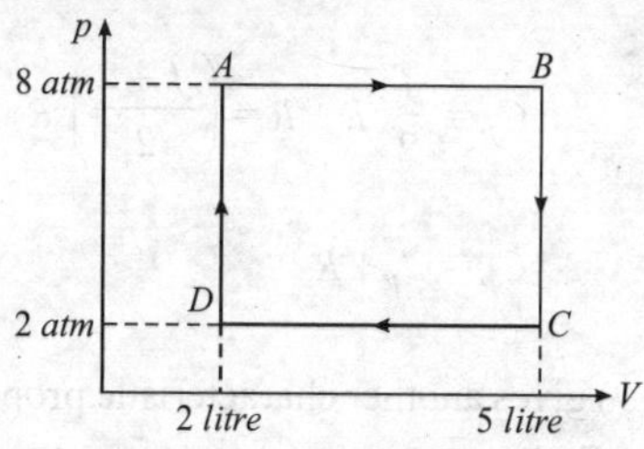

Figure 3.19

[2400 J, 0, –600 J, 0; 1800 J]

(v) A cyclic process $ABCA$ shown in V-T diagram (figure-3.20) is performed with a constant mass of an ideal gas. Show the same process on a P-V diagram.

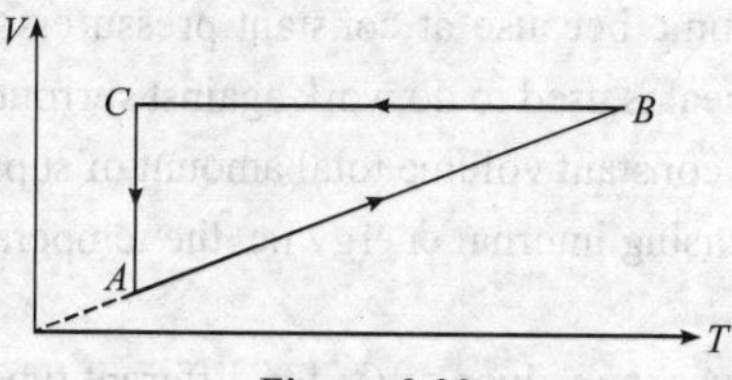

Figure 3.20

In the figure-3.20, CA is parallel to the V-axis and BC is parallel to the T-axis.

(vi) Figure-3.21 shows the PV diagram for a gas confined to a cylinder by a piston. How much work does the gas do as it expands from A to C along the curve ?

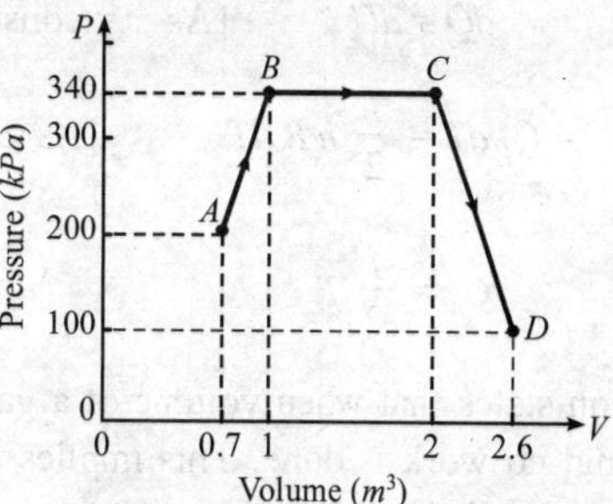

Figure 3.21

[421 kJ]

(vii) The volume of a monoatomic ideal gas increases linearly with pressure, as shown in the figure-3.22. Calculate (a) increase in internal energy, (b) work done by the gas, and (c) heat supplied to the gas.

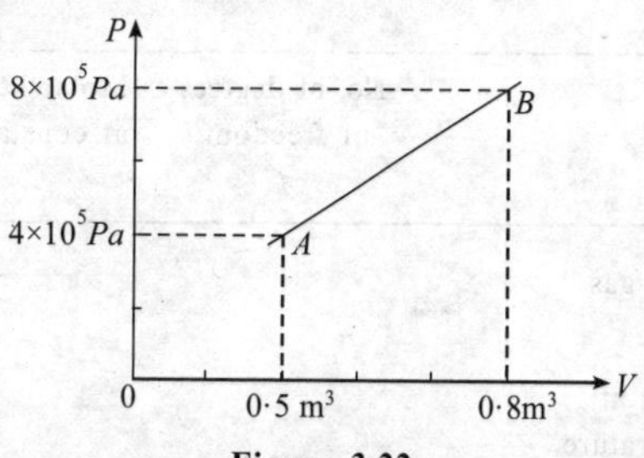

Figure 3.22

[6.6×10^5, 1.8×10^5, 8.4×10^5]

3.4 Molar Specific Heats of a Gas

As we have already discussed that depending on ways of supplying heat to a gas, it may have infinite different molar specific heats. But as a characteristic property a gas has two standard molar specific heats or molar heat capacities. These are

(i) Molar heat capacity at constant volume (C_V)

(ii) Molar heat capacity at constant pressure (C_P)

3.4.1 Molar Heat Capacity at Constant Volume (C_V)

This is the amount of heat required for one mole of a gas to raise its temperature by one degree at constant volume. This is denoted by C_V.

If a gas is heated at constant volume, we can simply state that no work is done by the gas or on the gas during heating. Thus if we apply first law of thermodynamics to such type of a heating process, we get

$$dQ = dU + dW$$

or $$dQ = dU \qquad [\text{As } v = \text{constant}, dW = 0]$$

or $$n\,C_V dT = \frac{f}{2}\,n\,R\,dT \qquad [\text{As } dQ = nC_V dT]$$

or $$C_V = \frac{f}{2}\,R \qquad \ldots(3.16)$$

Above relation states that when volume of a gas is constant during heating, no work is done. This implies that the total amount of heat supplied to the gas is used in increasing internal energy of gas, that is to raise the temperature.

Here equation-(3.16) gives the characteristic property of a gas, the molar specific heat at constant volume. For different types of gases values of C_V are listed in table-3.1

Table-3.1

Type of Gas	No. of degrees of freedom f	Molar heat capacity at constant volume C_V
Monoatomic gas	3	$\frac{3}{2}R$
Diatomic gas at lower temperature	5	$\frac{5}{2}R$
Diatomic gas at higher temperature	7	$\frac{7}{2}R$
Polyatomic gas linear molecule	5 + x (vib.)	$\left(\frac{5+x}{2}\right)R$
Polyatomic gas non linear molecule	6 + x (vib.)	$\frac{6+x}{2}R$

3.4.2 Molar Heat Capacity at Constant Pressure (C_P)

It is the amount of heat required for one mole of a gas to raise its temperature by one degree at constant pressure. It is denoted by C_P.

When a gas is heated at constant pressure, with rise in temperature volume of gas must increase by gas law as

$$PV = n\,R\,T$$

Differentiating gas law gives

$$PdV + VdP = n\,R\,d\,T \qquad \ldots(3.17)$$

This equation-(3.17) is called "*differential form of gas law*". If during heating pressure of gas is a constant, second term on left hand side of equality will be zero thus we have

$$P\,dV = n\,R\,dT$$

[As $dP = 0$, for constant pressure]

Which is also the elemental work done by the gas. This is a process when gas pressure does not change during heating, if volume of gas changes from V_1 to V_2 and temperature changes from T_1 to T_2, the total work done is given as

$$W = \int_{V_1}^{V_2} P.dV = \int_{T_1}^{T_2} n\,R\,dT$$

or $$W = P(V_2 - V_1) = nR(T_2 - T_1) \qquad \ldots(3.18)$$

According to first law of thermodynamics, if dQ is the heat supplied to a gaseous system at constant pressure, dU is the increase in internal energy and if dW is the work done by the gas, then we have

$$dQ = dU + dW$$

If C_P is the molar heat capacity for this gas then we have

$$n\,C_P dT = \frac{f}{2}\,n\,R\,dT + PdV \quad [\text{As } dQ = nC_P dT]$$

or $$n\,C_P dT = \frac{f}{2}\,n\,R\,dT + n\,R\,dT$$

[as $PdV = nRT$ for constant pressure]

or $$C_P = \frac{f}{2}\,R + R = \left(\frac{f+2}{2}\right)R \qquad \ldots(3.19)$$

or $$C_P = C_V + R \qquad \ldots(3.20)$$

Equation-(3.19) gives another characteristic property of a gas, the molar specific heat at constant pressure. Equation-(3.20) gives a relation among the molar specific heats of a gas. This relation is called Mayor's Relation. It shows that always values of C_P are higher then C_V for a gas because when a gas is heated at constant pressure, more heat is required to raise the temperature of gas as compared to the case when it is heated at constant volume because at constant pressure some amount of supplied heat is used to do work against surrounding where in heating at constant volume total amount of supplied heat is used in increasing internal energy i.e. the temperature of gas.

Table-3.2 gives the values of C_P for different types of gases.

Table 3.2

Type of Gas	No. of degrees of freedom f	Molar heat capacity at constant Pressure C_P
Monoatomic gas	3	$\frac{5}{2}R$
Diatomic gas at lower temperature	5	$\frac{7}{2}R$
Diatomic gas at higher temperature	7	$\frac{9}{2}R$
Polyatomic gas linear molecule	5 + x (vib.)	$\left(\frac{7+x}{2}\right)R$
Polyatomic gas non linear molecule	6 + x (vib.)	$\left(\frac{8+x}{2}\right)R$

3.4.3 Ratio of Heat Capacities of a Gas

In previous section we've obtained C_V and C_P as

$$C_V = \frac{f}{2} R$$

and $$C_P = \frac{f+2}{2} R$$

The values of C_P and C_V are the characteristic properties of a gas. One more characteristic property is widely used in analyzing the behaviour of gas. This is ratio of the two specific heats of a gas and is termed as adiabatic exponent of a gas. It is denoted by γ as

$$\gamma = \frac{C_P}{C_V} = \frac{f+2}{f} \quad \ldots(3.21)$$

Later we'll see that γ is very useful property of a gas in calculating different thermodynamic parameters of a gas when it undergoes a thermodynamic process. From equation-(3.21), we can find the values of γ for different types of gases.

Table-3.3 gives the values of γ for different types of gases

Table-3.3

Type of Gas	No. of degrees of freedom f	Ratio of specific heat γ
Monoatomic gas	3	$\frac{5}{3} = 1.67$
Diatomic gas at lower temperature	5	$\frac{7}{5} = 1.4$
Diatomic gas at higher temperature	7	$\frac{3}{7} = 1.28$
Polyatomic gas linear molecule	5 + x (vib.)	$\frac{7+x}{5+x}$
Polyatomic gas non linear molecule	6 + x (vib.)	$\frac{8+x}{6+x}$

From equation-(3.21), we can represent number of degrees of freedom in terms of γ as

$$f = \left(\frac{2}{\gamma - 1}\right) \quad \ldots(3.22)$$

Using equation-(3.22) we can represent C_P and C_V in terms of γ as

$$C_V = \frac{f}{2} R = \frac{R}{\gamma - 1} \quad \ldots(3.23)$$

and $$C_P = \gamma C_V = \frac{\gamma R}{\gamma - 1} \quad \ldots(3.24)$$

Equation-(3.23) and (3.24) are commonly used in wide range of numerical problems so students are advised to keep these results on their tips.

3.4.4 Ratio of Specific Heats for a Mixture of Gases

In previous chapter we've discussed that if N gases of n_1 n_2 ...... n_N moles are mixed at a common temperature T, the internal energy of the mixture remains constant. If these N gases have values of C_V as C_{V_1}, C_{V_2} ...... C_{V_N} then we have

$$n_1 C_{V_1} T + \cdots\cdots n_N C_{V_N} T$$

$$= (n_1 + n_2 + \cdots\cdots n_N)\, C_{V_{eq}} T \quad \ldots(3.25)$$

or $$C_{V_{eq}} = \frac{n_1 C_{V_1} + n_2 C_{V_2} + \cdots\cdots + n_N C_{V_N}}{n_1 + n_2 + \cdots\cdots n_N} \quad \ldots(3.26)$$

Where $C_{V_{eq}}$ is the equivalent molar specific heat for the mixture of gases at constant volume similarly $C_{P_{eq}}$ for the mixture of gases can be given as

or $$C_{P_{eq}} = \frac{n_1 C_{P_1} + n_2 C_{P_2} + \cdots\cdots + n_N C_{P_{eq}}}{n_1 + n_2 + \cdots\cdots n_N} \quad \ldots(3.27)$$

If $\gamma_1\, \gamma_2$ ...... γ_N are the ratio of specific heats for these independent gas then from equation-(3.25) we have

$$\frac{n_1 RT}{\gamma_1 - 1} + \frac{n_2 RT}{\gamma_2 - 1} + \cdots\cdots \frac{n_N RT}{\gamma_N - 1}$$

$$= (n_1 + n_2 + \cdots\cdots n_N)\left(\frac{R}{\gamma_{eq} - 1}\right) T \qquad \left[\text{As } C_V = \frac{R}{\gamma - 1}\right]$$

Here γ_{eq} is the equivalent adiabatic exponent for the mixture of gases and given by the equation

$$\frac{n_1}{\gamma_1 - 1} + \frac{n_2}{\gamma_2 - 1} + \ldots + \frac{n_N}{\gamma_N - 1} = \frac{n_1 + n_2 + \cdots + n_N}{\gamma_{eq} - 1} \quad \ldots(3.28)$$

Illustrative Example 3.13

Calculate the heat absorbed by a system in going through the cyclic process shown in figure-3.23.

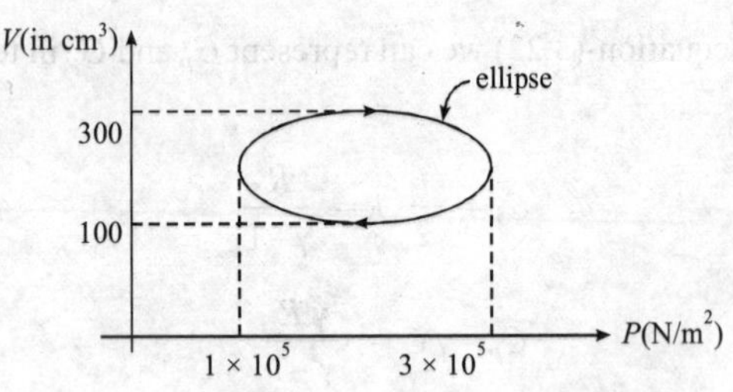

Figure 3.23

Solution

In the figure-3.23 shown, the cycle is clockwise, thus net work is done by the gas. As in a cyclic process no change in internal energy takes place thus heat supplied is equal to the work done by the gas in one complete cycle so in this case heat supplied to the gas is given as

$$Q = \text{Work done by the gas } W$$

$$= \text{Area of ellipse}$$

$$= \pi ab$$

Where a and b are semi major and semi-minor axis of the ellipse which are given from figure-3.23 as

$$a = 1.0 \times 10^5 \text{ N/m}$$

and $$b = 100 \times 10^{-6} \text{ m}^3$$

Thus area of ellipse is

$$Q = W = \pi \times 1.0 \times 10^5 \times 100 \times 10^{-6}$$

$$= 3.14 \times 10$$

$$= 31.4 \text{ J}$$

Illustrative Example 3.14

An ideal gas has a specific heat at constant pressure $C_P = (5\ R/2)$. The gas is kept in a closed vessel of volume 0.0083 m^3, at a temperature of 300 K and a pressure of 1.6×10^6 N/m^2. An amount of 2.49×10^4 J of heat energy is supplied to the gas. Calculate the final temperature and pressure of the gas.

Solution

Given that initial pressure, volume and temperature of gas is

$$P_1 = 1.6 \times 10^6 \text{ N/m}^2$$

$$V_1 = 0.0083 \text{ m}^3$$

$$T_1 = 300 \text{ K}$$

From gas law we can find the number of moles of gas in the container as

$$n = \frac{PV}{RT} = \frac{1.6 \times 10^6 \times 0.0083}{8.314 \times 300}$$

$$= \frac{16}{3} \text{ mole}$$

It is given that molar specific heat of gas at constant pressure is

$$C_P = \frac{5R}{2}$$

Thus gas is monoatomic, hence its molar specific heat at constant volume is given as

$$C_V = \frac{3R}{2}$$

As gas is heated in a closed vessel i.e. at constant volume, if its temperature is raised from T_1 to T_2 then, we have heat supplied to the gas is

$$Q = n\,C_V(T_2 - T_1)$$

or $$2.49 \times 10^4 = \frac{16}{3} \times \frac{3}{2} R(T_2 - 300)$$

or $$T_2 = 300 + \frac{3 \times 2 \times 2.49 \times 10^4}{16 \times 3 \times 8.314}$$

$$= 300 + 374.36$$

$$= 674.36 \text{ K}$$

For constant volume process, we have

$$\frac{P_2}{P_1} = \frac{T_2}{T_1}$$

Thus $$P_2 = \frac{T_2}{T_1} \times P_1$$

$$= \frac{674.36}{300} \times 1.6 \times 10^6$$

$$= 3.6 \times 10^6 \text{ N/m}^2$$

Illustrative Example 3.15

Figure-3.24 shows a cylindrical container containing oxygen gas and closed by a piston of mass 50 kg. Piston can slide smoothly in the cylinder. Its cross sectional area is 100 cm^2 and atmospheric pressure is 10^5 Pa. Some heat is supplied to the cylinder so that the piston is slowly displaced up by 20 cm.

Find the amount of heat supplied to the gas.

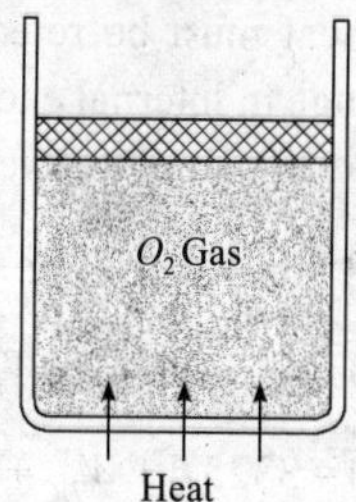

Figure 3.24

Solution

As here piston is open to atmosphere, the gas is under a constant pressure given as

$$P_{gas} = P_{atm} + \frac{Mg}{S}$$

$$= 10^5 + \frac{50 \times 10}{100 \times 10^{-4}} \text{ Pa}$$

$$= 10^5 + 5 \times 10^4 = 1.5 \times 10^5 \text{ Pa}$$

It is given that the piston moves out by 20 cm, thus increment is its volume is given as

$$\Delta V = S\Delta x$$

$$= 100 \times 10^{-4} \times 20 \times 10^{-2} \text{ m}^3$$

$$= 2 \times 10^{-3} \text{ m}^3$$

Thus in the process work done by gas is

$$W = P_{gas} \Delta V \qquad [\text{As } P_{gas} = \text{constant}]$$

$$= 1.5 \times 10^5 \times 2 \times 10^{-3}$$

$$= 300 \text{ J}$$

For a process is which gas pressure is constant, work done can also be given as

$$W = nR\Delta T = P_{gas} \Delta V$$

or $$nR\Delta T = 300 \text{ J}$$

As in the process gas pressure is constant thus heat supplied in raising the temperature by ΔT is given as

$$Q = n C_P \Delta T$$

$$= n\left(\frac{7}{2}R\right)\Delta T$$

$$[\text{As for } O_2 \text{ as being diatomic gas } C_P = \frac{7R}{2}]$$

$$Q = \frac{7}{2} \times 300$$

$$= 1050 \text{ J}$$

 # Illustrative Example 3.16

Two moles of an ideal monoatomic gas are confined within a cylinder by a massless spring loaded with a frictionless piston of negligible mass and of cross-sectional area 4×10^{-3} m². The spring is initially in its relaxed state. Now the gas is heated by a heater for some time. During this time the gas expands and does 50 J of work in moving the piston through a distance of 0.1 m. The temperature of the gas increases by 50 K. Calculate the spring constant and the heat supplied by the heater.

Solution

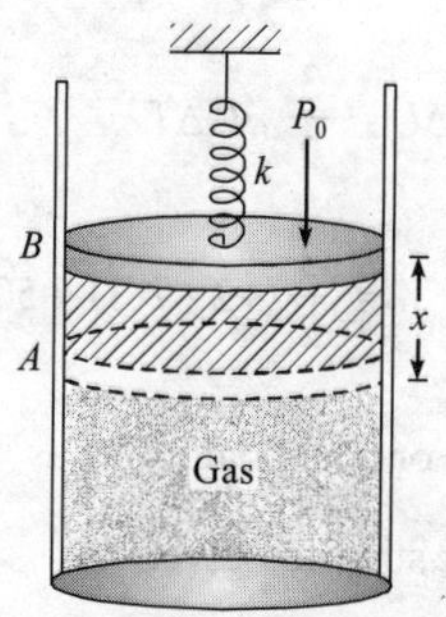

Figure 3.25

Refer to figure-3.25. A is the initial (equilibrium) position of the piston when the spring is relaxed. When the gas is heated, it expands and pushes the piston up by a distance, say, x. The spring is compressed, if k is the force constant of the spring and A the area of cross-section of the piston (which is equal to the cross-sectional area of the cylinder), the force in the spring is $F = kx$ and the pressure exerted on the gas by the spring is

$$P_s = \frac{F}{A} = \frac{kx}{A}$$

If P_0 is the atmospheric pressure, at equilibrium of piston the pressure of the gas in the cylinder is

$$P = P_0 + P_s = P_0 + \frac{kx}{A}$$

The increase in the volume of the gas by infinitesimal movement dx of the piston is

$$dV = Adx$$

Thus work done is given as

$$W = \int PdV = \int_0^x \left(P_0 + \frac{kx}{A}\right) Adx$$

$$= P_0 A \int_0^x dx + k \int_0^x xdx$$

or $$W = P_0 Ax + \frac{1}{2} kx^2$$

Given $A = 4 \times 10^{-3}$ m², $x = 0.1$ m, $W = 50$ J. The atmospheric pressure $P_0 = 0.76$ m of Hg $= 0.76 \times 9.8 \times 13600 = 1.013 \times 10^5$ Nm^{-2}. Using these values in above expression of work and solving for k, we get

$$k = 1896 \text{ Nm}^{-1}$$

To find heat energy Q supplied by the heater, we use the first law of thermodynamics.

$$Q = \Delta U + W$$

Now $$\Delta U = \frac{f}{2} nR\,\Delta T = nC_V \Delta T$$

$$\Delta U = \frac{3}{2} nR\,\Delta T$$

$$= \frac{3}{2} \times 2 \times 8.31 \times 50 = 1246.5 \text{ J}$$

[For a monoatomic gas we have $C_V = \frac{3}{2} R$]

Thus we have, heat supplied given as

$$Q = 1246.5 + 50 = 1296.5 \text{ J}$$

Illustrative Example 3.17

Consider the cyclic process *ABCA* shown in figure-3.26. An ideal gas of 2 moles is undergone this process. A total of 1200 J heat is rejected by the gas in the complete cycle. Find the work done by the gas during the process *BC*.

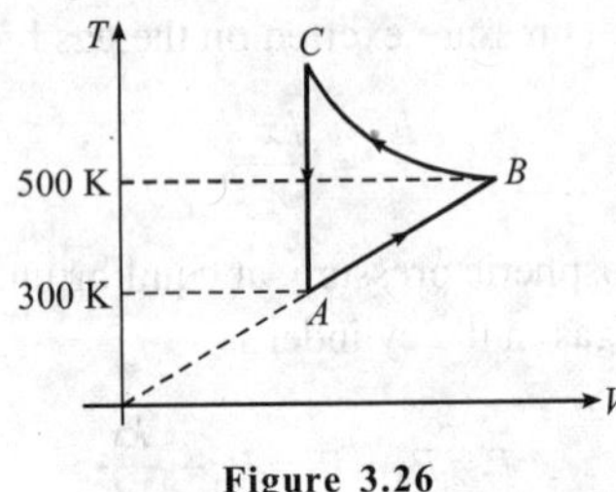

Figure 3.26

Solution

As we can see that in figure-3.26 *CA* is a process where gas volume remains constant thus no work is done in this process and in process *AB* gas pressure remains constant as $T \propto V$. Work done by the gas in this process can be given as

$$W_{AB} = nR(T_B - T_A)$$

[As if P = constant $W = P(V_2 - V_1) = nR(T_2 - T_1)$]

$$= 2 \times 8.314 \times (500 - 300)$$

$$= 2 \times 8.314 \times 200$$

$$= 3325.6 \text{ J}$$

As the cycle is anticlockwise, net work is done on the gas and the equal amount of heat must be rejected by the gas as in complete cycle no change in internal energy takes place. Thus heat rejected by the gas in complete cycle is given as

$$Q = \text{Net Work done on gas}$$

or $$-1200 = W_{AB} + W_{BC} + W_{CA}$$

$$-1200 = 3325.6 + W_{BC} + 0$$

or $$W_{BC} = -4525.6 \text{ J}$$

Illustrative Example 3.18

An ideal monoatomic gas is confined in a cylinder by a spring loaded piston of cross-section 8×10^{-3} m². Initially the gas is at 300 K and occupies a volume of 2.4×10^{-3} m³ and the spring is in its relaxed (unstretched, uncompressed) state (see figure-3.27). The gas is heated by a small electric heater until the piston moves out slowly by 0.1 m. Calculate the final temperature of the gas and the heat supplied (in joule) by the heater. The force constant of the spring is 8000 N/m, atmospheric pressure is 1×10^5 N/m². The cylinder and the piston are thermally insulated. The piston is massless and there is no friction between the piston and the cylinder. Neglect heat-loss through the lead wires of the heater. The heat-capacity of the heater coil is negligible. Assume the spring to be massless.

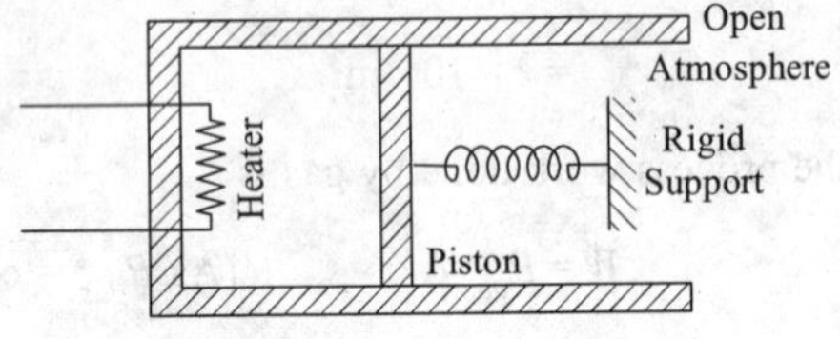

Figure 3.27

Solution

Initially, the pressure of the gas in the cylinder is atmospheric pressure as spring is in relaxed state. Therefore

$$P_1 = \text{atmospheric pressure} = 1.0 \times 10^5 \text{ N/m}^2$$

$$V_1 = \text{initial volume} = 2.4 \times 10^3 \text{ m}^3$$

$$T_1 = \text{initial temperature} = 300 \text{ K}$$

When heat is supplied by the heater, the piston is compressed by 0.1 m. The reaction force of compression of spring is equal to $k\,x$ which acts on the piston or on the gas as

$$F = kx = 8000 \times 0.1 = 800 \text{ Nt}$$

Pressure exerted on the piston by the spring

$$\Delta P = \frac{F}{A} = \frac{800}{8 \times 10^{-3}} = 1 \times 10^5 \text{ N/m}^2$$

The total pressure P_2 of the gas inside cylinder is

$$P_2 = P_{atm} + \Delta P = 1 \times 10^5 + 1 \times 10^5$$

$$= 2 \times 10^5 \text{ N/m}^2$$

Since the piston has moved outwards, there has been an increase ΔV in the volume of the gas

$$\Delta V = A \times x = (8 \times 10^{-3}) \times (0.1)$$

$$= 8 \times 10^{-4} \text{ m}^3$$

The final volume of the gas

$$V_2 = V_1 + \Delta V = 2.4 \times 10^{-3} + 8 \times 10^{-4}$$

$$= 3.2 \times 10^{-3} \text{ m}^3$$

Let T_2 be the final temperature of gas. Then

$$\frac{P_1 V_1}{T_1} = \frac{P_2 V_2}{T_2}$$

or $$T_2 = T_1 \frac{P_2 V_2}{P_1 V_1}$$

$$= 300 \times \frac{2 \times 10^5 \times 3.2 \times 10^{-3}}{10^5 \times 2.4 \times 10^{-3}}$$

$$= 800 \text{ K}$$

Let the heat supplied by the heater be Q. This is used in two parts : a part is used in doing external work W due to expansion of the gas and the other part is used in increasing the internal energy of the gas. Hence

$$Q = W + \Delta U$$

Now $$W = \int_{V_1}^{V_2} P\, dV = \int_0^x \left(P_{atm} + \frac{kx}{A}\right) A\, dx$$

[As pressure is $(P_{atm} + kx/A)$ and $dV = A\, dx$]

or $$W = P_{atm} A x + \frac{kx^2}{2}$$

$$= \left[10^5 \times (8 \times 10^{-3})(0.1) + \frac{8000 \times (0.1)^2}{2}\right]$$

$$= 120 \text{ joule}$$

Further $$U = nC_v \Delta T$$

Number of moles of gas can be obtained from initial conditions and gas law as

$$n = \frac{PV}{RT} = \frac{1 \times 10^5 \times 2.4 \times 10^{-3}}{8.314 \times 300}$$

$$= 0.096 \text{ mole}$$

Thus change in internal energy of gas is given as

$$\Delta U = n\left(\frac{3}{2}R\right)\Delta T$$

[As for monoatomic gas $C_V = \frac{3}{2}R$]

or $$U = 0.096 \times \frac{3}{2} \times 8.314 \times 500 = 598.6 \text{ Joule}$$

Heat supplied by heater

$$= (120 + 598.6)$$

$$= 718.6 \text{ joule}$$

Illustrative Example 3.19

A monoatomic ideal gas is taken through the process ABC as shown in figure-3.28. The temperature at the point A is 300 K. Find the temperatures at points B and C. Also find the work done and heat supplied to the gas in paths AB and BC.

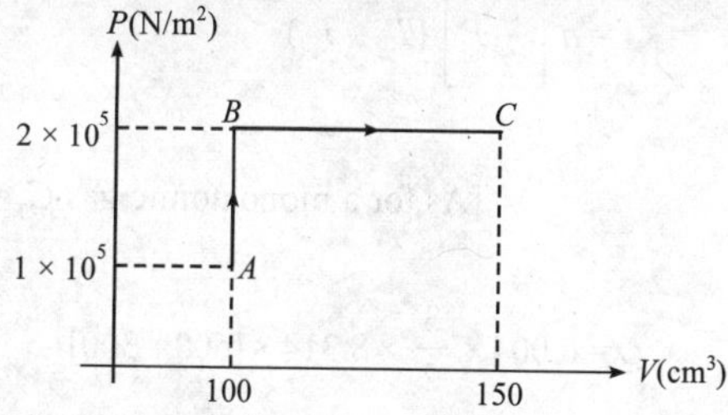

Figure 3.28

Solution

At initial state pressure, volume and temperature of gas is given as

$$P_A = 1 \times 10^5 \text{ Pa}$$

$$V_A = 100 \times 10^{-6} \text{ m}^3$$

$$T_A = 300 \text{ K}$$

Thus from gas law, we can find number of moles of gas, as

$$n = \frac{P_A V_A}{RT_A} = \frac{10^5 \times 10^{-4}}{8.314 \times 300} = 0.004 \text{ mole}$$

Thus at point B, gas temperature is given by

$$\frac{P_A}{T_A} = \frac{P_B}{T_B}$$

or $$T_B = \frac{P_B}{P_A} \times T_A$$

$$= \frac{2\times10^5}{10^5}\times300$$

$$=600\,\text{K}$$

Similarly at point C, gas temperature is given by

$$\frac{T_C}{V_C}=\frac{T_B}{V_B}$$

or $$T_C=\frac{V_C}{V_B}\times T_B$$

$$=\frac{150\times10^{-6}}{100\times10^{-6}}\times600$$

$$=900\,\text{K}$$

Now in process AB, gas volume is constant thus no work is done by the gas and heat supplied to the gas can be given as

$$Q=n\,C_V(T_B-T_A)$$

$$=n\left[\frac{3}{2}R\right](T_B-T_A)$$

[As for a monoatomic gas $C_V=\frac{3R}{2}$]

or $$Q=0.004\times\frac{3}{2}\times8.314\times[600-300]$$

$$=14.96\,\text{J}$$

In the process BC, gas pressure is constant thus work done by the gas can be given as

$$W=P_B(V_C-V_B)$$

$$=2\times10^5\,[150-100]\times10^{-6}$$

$$=10\,\text{J}$$

The heat supplied to the gas in this constant pressure process BC can be given as

$$Q=n\,C_P(T_C-T_B)$$

$$=n\left[\frac{5}{2}R\right](T_C-T_B)$$

[As for monoatomic gas the value of $C_P=\frac{5}{2}R$]

$$=0.004\times\frac{5}{2}\times8.314\times(900-600)$$

$$=24.94\,\text{J}$$

Web Reference at www.physicsgalaxy.com

Age Group - High School Physics | Age 17-19 Years
Section - HEAT & THERMODYNAMICS
Topic - Laws of Thermodynamics
Module Number - 7 to 8

3.5 Different Type of Thermodynamic Processes

We've already discussed that a thermodynamic process is a way of heating a gas or doing work on it by which state of a gas can be changed from one to another by a specific path. Each thermodynamic process can be represented by a specific $P=f(V)$ curve on a P-V indicator diagram. In each thermodynamic process, there are three variable related. Heat supplied to a gas, change in its internal energy and work done by a gas. According to first law of thermodynamics a part of supplied heat is used as rise in internal energy of gas and rest is used to do work against surrounding. As we change the process of heating, the fraction of heat supplied which is used to increase the internal energy of gas and the fraction of heat supplied consumed in doing work will change. These three variables heat supplied Q, change in internal energy of a gas ΔU and work done W are called thermodynamic variables for a process.

There are some standard thermodynamic processes, commonly used in practice, these are

(1) Isochoric or Isometric Process

(2) Isobaric Process

(3) Isothermal Process

(4) Adiabatic Process

We first discuss the above processes in detail, then we'll discuss about, some other thermodynamic processes as a special case.

3.5.1 Isochoric or Isometric Process

In this process volume of gas remains constant during heating or state changing process on a gas. Thus during the heating process, we have

$$dV=0 \quad \text{[During the process } V=\text{constant]}$$

and $$\Delta V=0 \qquad [\text{As } V_1=V_2]$$

As no change in volume is taking place, work done by the gas in the process is zero. Some time in few processes $\Delta V=0$ but $dV\neq0$. We can not treat these processes as isochoric because in such processes initial and final volume of the gas are same but during the process, volume change takes place. We can differentiate these processes easily by looking carefully on their PV diagrams as shown in figure-3.29.

Figure-3.29(a) shows a PV diagram of an isochoric process in which, when a gas is carried from state-1 to state-2, its volume V remains constant during heating, only increase in pressure takes place as shown and the effective area below the PV-curve is also zero which shows no work is done during the process.

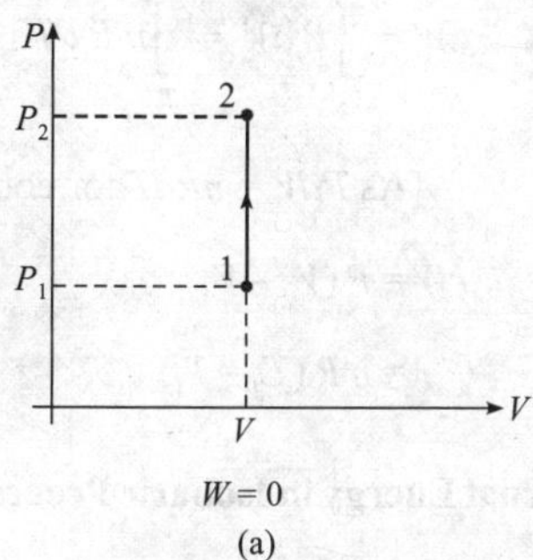

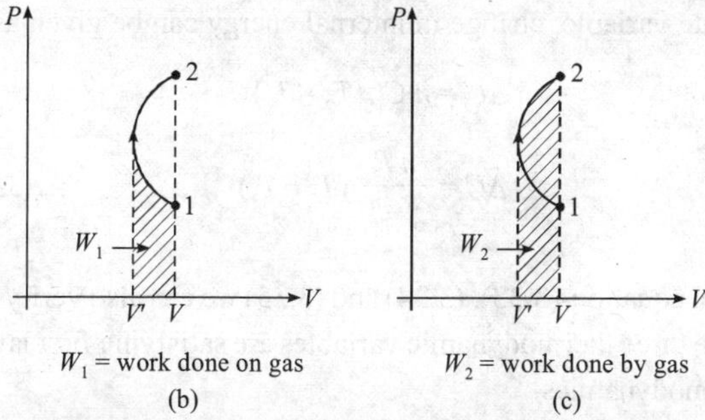

Figure 3.29

Figure-3.29(b) and (c) shows a process in which the state of gas is changed from same state-1 to state-2 and the volume of gas at both the states is same V. But we can see that during the process first the volume of gas is compressed from V to V' then it is expended from V' to V. Figure-3.29(b) shows the area below the graph during the process when gas is compressed from volume V to V'. This area represents the work W_1 done on the gas (-ve) upto this intermediate state with volume V' from initial state-1. Figure-3.29(c) shows the area below the graph during the process when gas is expanded from this intermediate state to the final state to restore the volume V of the gas. This area during expansion of gas represents the work W_2 done by the gas from this intermediate state with volume V to the final state-2. It is clear that $W_2 > W_1$ hence the total work in this process is done by the gas and is given as

$$W_{gas} = W_2 - W_1$$

Although in the process $\Delta V = 0$ but the process is not isochoric.

Heat supplied in Isochoric Process

If n moles of a gas is heated from temperature T_1 to T_2 keeping its volume constant during heating, the total amount of heat supplied to the gas can be obtained by using molar heat capacity of gas at constant volume as

$$dQ = n\,C_V dT$$

and
$$Q = \int dQ = \int_{T_1}^{T_2} n\,C_V\,dT$$

$$Q = n\,C_V(T_2 - T_1)$$

$$= \frac{nR}{\gamma - 1}(T_2 - T_1) \qquad \ldots(3.29)$$

Work done in Isochoric Process

As discussed earlier, no change in volume implies no work done, thus

$$W = 0 \qquad \ldots(3.30)$$

Change in Internal Energy in Isochoric Process

As discussed earlier, internal energy is a state variable so in all process if a gas is heated from temperature T_1 to T_2, change in internal energy is given by

$$\Delta U = \frac{f}{2}\,nR\,\Delta T = nC_V\Delta T$$

or
$$\Delta U = \frac{nR}{\gamma - 1}(T_2 - T_1) \qquad \ldots(3.31)$$

This is same as equation-(3.29) because according to first law of thermodynamics if no work is done in a process, whole of supplied heat to a gas will appear as increase in its internal energy.

As we know internal energy of a gas is a state function, in all the process the change in internal energy is always given by equation-(3.31). As in isochoric process, volume of gas during the process remains constant from gas law the pressure and temperature of gas between its initial and final state can be related as

$$\frac{P_1}{T_1} = \frac{P_2}{T_2} \qquad \ldots(3.32)$$

3.5.2 Isobaric Process

In this process during change of state of a gas, its pressure remains constant. Thus

$$dP = 0$$

and
$$\Delta P = 0$$

Again some process can be there in which $\Delta P = 0$ but $dP \neq 0$. Such process can not be taken as isobaric process. We can discuss these by their *PV*- diagrams shown in figure-3.30. Figure-3.30(a) represents an isobaric process in which a gas is taken from state-1 to state-2 and during the process only volume of gas is being changed from V_1 to V_2, pressure remains constant at P. Thus the area below the curve $P(V_2 - V_1)$ gives the work done in the process. But in figure-3.30(b) and (c), the gas is taken from same state-1 to state-2 by different paths in which during the process, the pressure of gas is not constant thus in these processes, even $\Delta P = 0$ but $dP \neq 0$ and due to this work done or area below these *PV* curves are either less or more than the case when the pressure remains constant i.e. in an isobaric process.

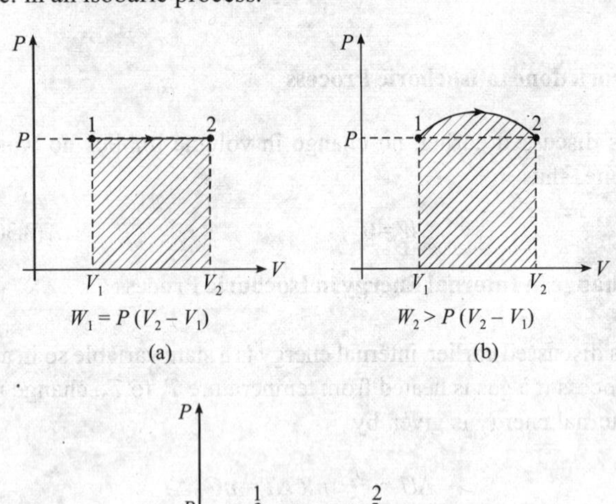

Figure 3.30

Heat Supplied in Isobaric Process

If n moles of a gas is heated at constant pressure from temperature T_1 to T_2 the amount of heat supplied can be easily calculated by using molar heat capacity of gas at constant pressure, thus

$$dQ = n\,C_P\,dT$$

$$Q = \int dQ = \int_{T_1}^{T_2} n\,C_P\,dT$$

or
$$Q = n\,C_P(T_2 - T_1)$$

or
$$Q = \frac{n\gamma R}{\gamma - 1}(T_2 - T_1) \quad \ldots(3.33)$$

Work Done by gas in Isobaric Process

At the beginning of chapter we've discussed that when a gas is heated from volume V_1 to V_2, work done can be calculated as

$$W = \int dW = \int_{V_1}^{V_2} P\,dV$$

As pressure of gas is constant, we have

$$W = \int_{V_1}^{V_2} P\,dV = \int_{T_1}^{T_2} n\,R\,dT$$

[As $PdV = nRdT$ for constant pressure]

or
$$W = P(V_2 - V_1)$$
$$= nR(T_2 - T_1) \quad \ldots(3.34)$$

Change in Internal Energy in Isobaric Process

If n moles of a gas is heated from temperature T_1 to T_2, as being a state variable, change in internal energy can be given as

$$\Delta U = n\,C_V(T_2 - T_1)$$

or
$$\Delta U = \frac{nR}{\gamma - 1}(T_2 - T_1) \quad \ldots(3.35)$$

From equation-(3.33), (3.34) and (3.35) we can also verify that these three thermodynamic variables are satisfying first law of thermodynamics.

3.5.3 Isothermal Process

In this process temperature of gas remains constant during heating. Thus during the process

$$dT = 0$$

and
$$\Delta T = 0$$

If temperature of gas does not change then it implies that there is no change in internal energy of gas during the process thus in an isothermal process, we also have

$$dU = 0$$

and
$$\Delta U = 0$$

As no change is there in internal energy of a gas, then according to first law of thermodynamics we can say that the total amount of heat supplied to a gas is used in doing work against surrounding i.e. in expending the gas.

Indicator diagrams for an Isothermal Process

To plot an indicator diagram we must require a process equation which can be given by gas law, in case of an isothermal process. According to gas law

$$PV = nRT$$

As in isothermal process gas temperature remains constant, thus, we have

$$P \alpha \frac{1}{V}$$

or $$P = \frac{k}{V} \quad \ldots(3.36)$$

Thus according to equation-(3.35), it is clear that PV curve on an indicator diagram is a rectangular hyperbola as shown in figure-3.31. Figure-3.32 shows a gas undergoes several isothermal processes at different temperatures. Here we can see that all curves for these processes are almost parallel to each other and no two curves can intersect as these are at different temperatures these curves are called "*Isotherms*". If a gas undergone a process in which $\Delta T = 0$ but $dT \neq 0$ then it is obvious that during the process gas temperature is changing. The PV curve for such a process must intersect with the series of isotherms shown in figure-3.32 such a process is shown in figure-3.33 this type of a process can never be taken as isothermal process, however in this process also internal energy of gas in its initial and final state are same.

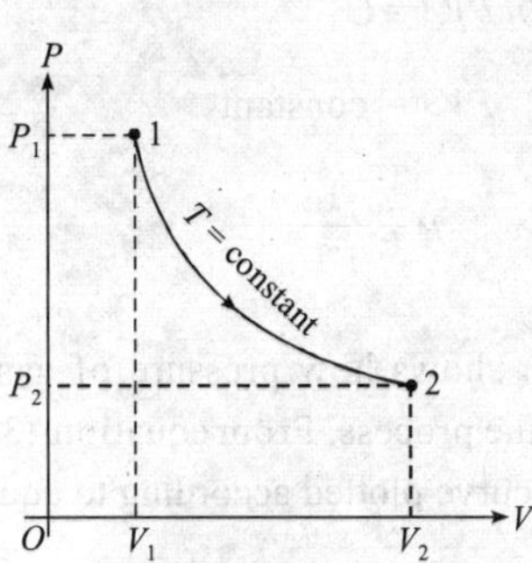

Figure 3.31

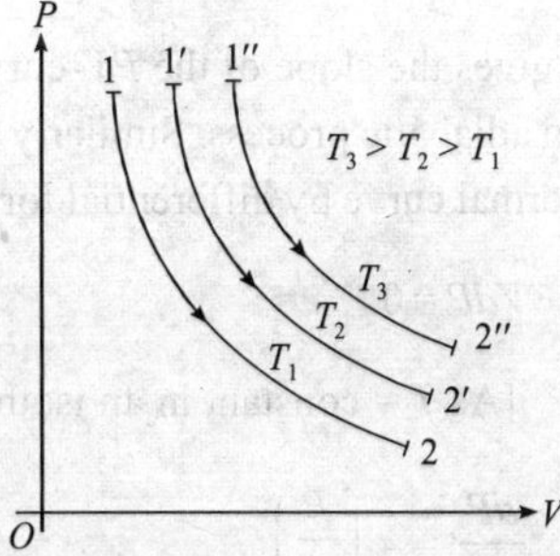

Figure 3.32

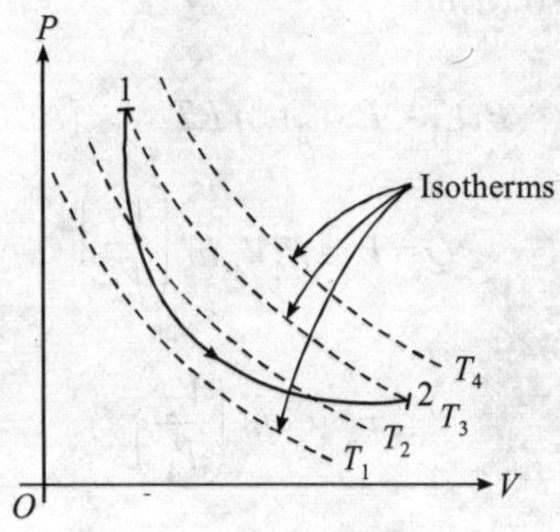

Figure 3.33

Heat Supplied and Work done in Isothermal Process

As discussed, in isothermal process temperature of gas does not change thus the total heat supplied to the gas is used in doing work against surrounding. If during the process volume of gas increases from V_1 to V_2 then pressure also very simultaneously with it and as temperature remains constant we can use Boyle's law to relate pressure and volume of the gas as

$$P_1V_1 = P_2V_2 \quad \ldots(3.37)$$

[If P_1 and P_2 are the initial and final pressures of gas]

Work done by the gas can be calculated as

$$W = \int_{V_1}^{V_2} PdV$$

$$W = \int_{V_1}^{V_2} \frac{nRT}{V} dV$$

[As $P = \frac{nRT}{V}$ at every intermediate state of gas during heating]

or $$W = nRT \ln\left(\frac{V_2}{V_1}\right)$$

$$= nRT \ln\left(\frac{P_1}{P_2}\right) \quad \ldots(3.38)$$

As change in internal energy in the process is zero, we have heat supplied

$$Q = W = nRT \ln\left(\frac{V_2}{V_1}\right)$$

$$= nRT \ln\left(\frac{P_1}{P_2}\right)$$

Here we can also write

$$P_1V_1 = P_2V_2 = nRT \quad \text{[As } T = \text{constant]}$$

$$Q = W = P_1V_1 \, ln\left(\frac{V_2}{V_1}\right)$$

$$= P_2V_2 \, ln\left(\frac{V_2}{V_1}\right) \quad \ldots(3.39)$$

3.5.4 Adiabatic Process

In this process no heat is supplied to the gaseous system during the process. More precisely the system remains thermally insulated so that no heat can be given to it or can be taken out from it during the process. Thus here $\Delta Q = 0$ as well as $dQ = 0$. If no heat is supplied to a gas then according to first law of thermodynamics, during the process we have

$$dW + dU = 0$$

or $$dW = -dU \quad \ldots(3.40)$$

Equation-(3.40) shows that if a gas expands in such a process or work is done by the gas, then by the same amount internal energy of gas decreases. It is obvious that if gas is doing work against surrounding then the amount of energy required in this work is extracted from the internal energy of gas as there is no external heat supply. This is called adiabatic expansion and in adiabatic expansion always the gas is cooled. Similarly when some external work is done on the gas, by the same amount its internal energy must increase as there is no rejection of heat in adiabatic process. Thus in adiabatic compression always gas temperature increases.

Indicator Diagram for an adiabatic process

To plot an indicator diagram we must have the relation in pressure and volume of a gas undergoing the process at one of its intermediate state during the process or the process equation for the process. In previous three standard thermodynamic processes, the process equations are directly given by the gas laws. Now we first discuss how to obtain the process equation in a general thermodynamic process.

How to derive the process equation for a thermodynamic process

In a general thermodynamic process to derive its process equation, we generally try to develop a relation in heat, work and change in internal energy for the process and then solve this relation with differential form of gas law to obtain the desired relation in any two of the thermodynamic parameters of a gas pressure, volume and its temperature. For example first we derive the process equation for an adiabatic process.

For adiabatic process the differential form of first law of thermodynamics can be written as

$$dW = -dU$$

or $$PdV = -nC_VdT$$

or $$PdV = -\frac{nR}{\gamma - 1}dT \quad \ldots(3.41)$$

Equation-(3.41) is the differential form of first law of thermodynamics in terms of gas parameters pressure, volume and temperature.

Differential form of gas law can be written as

$$PdV + VdP = nRdT \quad \ldots(3.42)$$

Now from equation-(3.41) and (3.42), we get

$$PdV + VdP = (1-\gamma)PdV$$

or $$VdP = -\gamma PdV \quad \ldots(3.43)$$

or $$\int \frac{dP}{P} = -\gamma \int \frac{dV}{V}$$

or $$ln\, P = -\gamma \, ln\, V + C$$

[$C \rightarrow$ constant of integration]

or $$ln\, PV^{\gamma} = C$$

or $$PV^{\gamma} = \text{constant} \quad \ldots(3.44)$$

or $$P \propto \frac{1}{V^{\gamma}}$$

Equation-(3.44) shows how pressure of gas vary with its volume during the process. From equation-(3.43) we can get the slope of PV curve plotted according to equation-(3.44) as

$$\frac{dP}{dV} = -\gamma\left(\frac{P}{V}\right) \quad \ldots(3.45)$$

Equation-(3.45) gives the slope of the PV-curve plotted for a gas undergone an adiabatic process. Similarly we can find the slope of an isothermal curve by differential form of gas law as

$$PdV + VdP = 0$$

[As T = constant in an isothermal process]

or $$\frac{dP}{dV} = -\left(\frac{P}{V}\right) \quad \ldots(3.46)$$

Comparing this with equation-(3.45). We can see that in magnitude slope of an adiabatic curve is γ times more then the slope of an isothermal curve as

$$\left|\frac{dP}{dV}\right|_{\substack{adiabatic\\process}} = \gamma \left|\frac{dP}{dV}\right|_{\substack{isothermal\\process}} \quad \dots(3.47)$$

From equation-(3.47) we can state qualitatively that an adiabatic curve is always steeper then an isothermal curve. If we note the values of γ for a gas then it is maximum for a monoatomic gas. If we compare the isothermal and adiabatic curves for different types of gases starting with same initial state of a gas, we can see that the curve of a monoatomic gas in adiabatic process is the steepest and the curve for an isothermal process (independent from γ) for a gas is having least slope. Figure-3.34 shows the comparison. We can also note that the work done, the area below the $P-V$ curve is minimum for the steepest graph.

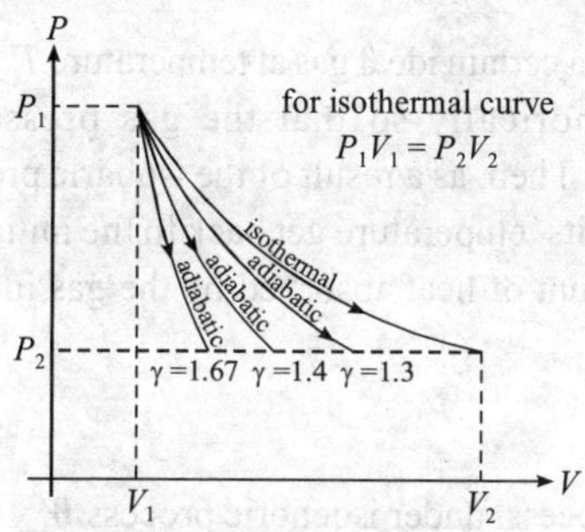

Figure 3.34

We have derived that the process equation for an adiabatic process, which can be written as

$$PV^{\gamma} = \text{constant} \quad \dots(3.48)$$

From gas law we can write

$$P = \frac{nRT}{V}$$

Thus $$\frac{nRT}{V} V^{\gamma} = \text{constant}$$

or $$TV^{\gamma-1} = \text{constant} \quad \dots(3.49)$$

Similarly volume of gas can be written as

$$V = \frac{nRT}{P}$$

or $$T^{\gamma}P^{1-\gamma} = \text{constant} \quad \dots(3.50)$$

Equation-(3.48), (3.49) and (3.50) represent the same process equation for an adiabatic process in terms of different gas parameters.

One more important point students should keep in mind that in nature if a process occurs very fast, like bursting of a tyre, sudden compression or expansion of a gas, these are regarded as approximately an adiabatic process as flow of heat is a slow and gradual process. It is assumed that in sudden thermodynamic changes, there is no sufficient time available so hardly any heat flow can take place. Similarly if a thermodynamic process is very slow and it is given that the system is in good thermal contact with the surrounding then in such processes it is assumed that during the process gas remains in thermal equilibrium with the surrounding and thus it can be regarded as an isothermal process.

Heat Supplied in Adiabatic Process

We've discussed that in an adiabatic process no heat flow takes place between system and surrounding during the process (expansion or compression) thus

$$Q = 0$$

Work done and change in internal energy in adiabatic process

As already discussed, according to first law of thermodynamics the amount of work done by gas in an adiabatic process is equal to the negative of change in internal energy between final and initial state of the process. We know that internal energy is a state function thus does not depend as to how the state of a gas is changed. If gas temperatures are T_1 and T_2 before and after the process or in its initial and final states then the change (increase) in internal energy can be given as

$$\Delta U = \int dU = \int_{T_1}^{T_2} \frac{nR}{\gamma-1} dT$$

$$= \frac{nR}{\gamma-1}(T_2 - T_1)$$

Thus is adiabatic process work done by the gas can be written as

$$W = -\Delta U = -\frac{nR}{\gamma-1}(T_2 - T_1)$$

or $$W = \left(\frac{P_1V_1 - P_2V_2}{\gamma-1}\right) \quad \dots(3.51)$$

[As $P_1V_1 = nRT_1$ and $P_2V_2 = nRT_2$]

These four process we've discussed are the most common processes realized in practice. But initially we've discussed that there can be infinite ways of heating a gas are there thus there is no limitation on number of thermodynamic processes for a gas. Now we first take few examples to understand the above discussed processes in details then we will discuss a general thermodynamic process named polytropic process, there after we'll see that the above four processes are also the special cases of polytropic process.

 # Illustrative Example 3.20

The volume of an ideal diatomic gas with $\gamma = 1.5$ is changed adiabatically from 16 litre to 12 litre. Find the ratio of the final and initial pressures and temperatures.

Solution

We know in an adiabatic process pressure and volume of different states of a gas are related as

$$P_1V_1^\gamma = P_2V_2^\gamma$$

Thus here $$\frac{P_2}{P_1} = \left(\frac{V_1}{V_2}\right)^\gamma$$

or $$= \left(\frac{16}{12}\right)^{1.5} = \left(\frac{4}{3}\right)^{1.5} = 1.533$$

Similarly in an adiabatic process gas volume and temperature of its different states are related as

$$T_1V_1^{\gamma-1} = T_2V_2^{\gamma-1}$$

or $$\frac{T_2}{T_1} = \left(\frac{V_1}{V_2}\right)^{\gamma-1}$$

$$= \left(\frac{16}{12}\right)^{0.5} = \left(\frac{4}{3}\right)^{0.5} = 1.153$$

 # Illustrative Example 3.21

A sample of diatomic gas with $\gamma = 1.5$ is compressed from a volume of 1600 cc to 400 cc adiabatically. The initial pressure of gas was 1.5×10^5 Pa. Find the final pressure and work done by the gas in the process.

Solution

We know in an adiabatic process, pressure and volume of gas of its different sates are related as

$$P_1V_1^\gamma = P_2V_2^\gamma$$

or $$P_2 = \left(\frac{V_1}{V_2}\right)^\gamma \cdot P_1$$

$$= \left(\frac{1600}{400}\right)^{1.5} \times 1.5 \times 10^5$$

$$= (4)^{1.5} \times 1.5 \times 10^5$$

$$= 1.2 \times 10^6 \text{ Pa}$$

For an adiabatic process work done by a gas is given as

$$W = \frac{P_1V_1 - P_2V_2}{\gamma - 1}$$

$$= \frac{1.5\times10^5 \times 1600\times10^{-6} - 1.2\times10^6 \times 400\times10^{-6}}{1.5-1}$$

$$= \frac{240-480}{0.5} = -480 \text{ J}$$

Here work done by gas comes out a negative value thus we can state that as gas is being compressed, work is done on the gas and so work done by gas is – 480 J.

 # Illustrative Example 3.22

Two moles of a certain ideal gas at temperature $T_0 = 300$ K were cooled isochorically so that the gas pressure reduced $\eta = 2.0$ times. Then, as a result of the isobaric process, the gas expanded till its temperature get back to the initial value. Find the total amount of heat absorbed by the gas in this process.

Solution

In the first process, under isochoric process $W = 0$ (as $\Delta V = 0$). From gas law, if the pressure is reduced to η times, then the temperature is also reduced to η times i.e., the new temperature becomes T_0/η.

Thus from first law of thermodynamics, we have

$$Q_1 = \Delta U_1 = nC_V\Delta T = \frac{nR}{\gamma-1}\Delta T$$

or $$Q_1 = \frac{nR}{\gamma-1}\left[\frac{T_0}{\eta} - T_0\right] = \frac{nRT_0(1-\eta)}{\eta(\gamma-1)}$$

During second process (under isobaric process), workdone is equal to $P\Delta V = nR\Delta T$. And from first law of thermodynamics, we have

$$Q_2 = \Delta U_2 + W_2 = \frac{nR\Delta T}{\gamma-1} + nR\Delta T$$

$$= nR\Delta T\left[\frac{1}{\gamma-1}+1\right] = nR\Delta T\left[\frac{\gamma}{\gamma-1}\right]$$

$$= \frac{nR\gamma}{\gamma-1}\left[T_0 - \frac{T_0}{\eta}\right] = \frac{nR\gamma(\eta-1)}{\eta(\gamma-1)}$$

Now total amount of heat supplied is

$$Q = Q_1 + Q_2$$

$$= \frac{nRT_0(1-\eta)}{\eta(\gamma-1)} + \frac{nR\gamma(\eta-1)}{\eta(\gamma-1)}$$

$$= nRT_0\left(1-\frac{1}{\eta}\right)$$

Here we have $n = 2, R = 8.3, T_0 = 300\,K$ and $\eta = 2$

Thus $$Q = 2 \times 8.3 \times 300\left(1-\frac{1}{2}\right)\text{J}$$

or $$= 2490\,\text{J} = 2.5\,\text{kJ}$$

Illustrative Example 3.23

One mole of a gas is isothermally expanded at 27°C till the volume is doubled. Then it is adiabatically compressed to its original volume. Find the total work done.
($\gamma = 1.4$ and $R = 8.4$ joule/mole/°K).

Solution

In case of isothermal expansion, the workdone is given by

$$dW_1 = RT\,.\,ln(V_f/V_i)$$

Here $R = 8.314, T = 27\,°C = 273 + 27 = 300\,°K,$

$$(V_f/V_i) = 2$$

or $$dW_1 = 8.314 \times 300 \times ln(2)$$

$$= 8.314 \times 300 \times 0.693$$

$$= 1728.48\,\text{J}$$

Now the gas is adiabatically compressed to its original volume. Initially at the beginning of adiabatic compression, the temperature of the gas is 300 K and at the end of adiabatic compression, the temperature becomes T_2 because the temperature is changed. The initial volume of the gas is $2V_1$ and after compression it again becomes the original volume *i.e.*, V_i. For an adiabatic process, we know temperature and volume are related as

$$T_1 V_1^{\gamma-1} = T_2 V_2^{\gamma-1}$$

or $$300 \times (2V_i)^{\gamma-1} = T_2 \times (V_i)^{\gamma-1}$$

or $$300 \times (2)^{1.4-1} = T_2(1)^{1.4-1}$$

or $$T_2 = 300 \times (2)^{0.4} = 395.85\,\text{K}$$

Workdone during adiabatic process is

$$W_2 = \frac{nR}{(\gamma-1)}(T_2 - T_1)$$

$$= \frac{8.314}{-(1.4-1)}(395.85 - 300)$$

$$= -1992.24\,\text{J}$$

Total workdone $= -1728.47 - 1992.24$

$$= -263.77\,\text{J}$$

Illustrative Example 3.24

Calculate the work done when one mole of an ideal monoatomic gas is compressed adiabatically. The initial pressure and volume of the gas are 10^5 N/m² and 6 litre respectively. The final volume of the gas is 2 litres. Molar specific heat of the gas at constant volume is $3R/2$.

Solution

For an adiabatic change

$$P_1 V_1^{\gamma} = P_2 V_2^{\gamma}$$

or $$P_2 = P_1\left(\frac{V_1}{V_2}\right)^{\gamma}$$

Here $P_1 = 10^5$ N/m², $V_1 = 6$ litre, $V_2 = 2$ litre and for a monoatomic gas, we have

$$C_V = \frac{3R}{2}$$

and $$C_P = \frac{3R}{2} + R = \frac{5R}{2}$$

or $$\gamma = \frac{C_P}{C_V} = \frac{5R/2}{3R/2} = \frac{5}{3}$$

Thus $$P_2 = 10^5 \times \left(\frac{6}{2}\right)^{5/3} = 10^5 \times (3)^{5/3}$$

We know that work done on gas ΔW in adiabatic change is given by

$$\Delta W = \frac{P_2V_2 - P_1V_1}{\gamma - 1}$$

$$= \frac{10^5 \times (3)^{5/3} \times (2\times10^{-3}) - 10^5 \times (6\times10^{-3})}{(5/3)-1}$$

[Here $V_2 = 2$ litre $= 2 \times 10^{-3}$ m³ and $V_1 = 6$ litre $= 6 \times 10^{-3}$ m³]

$$\frac{2\times10^2[(3)^{5/3} - 3]}{(2/3)}$$

$$= \frac{2\times10^2[6.19-3]}{(2/3)} = 3 \times 10^2 \times (3.19)$$

$$= 957\,\text{J}$$

Illustrative Example 3.25

An ideal gas at 75 cm mercury pressure is compressed isothermally until its volume is reduced to three quarters of its original volume. It is then allowed to expand adiabatically to a volume 20% greater than its original volume. If the initial temperature of the gas is 17 °C, calculate the final pressure and temperature ($\gamma = 1.5$).

Solution

First of all the gas is compressed isothermally. Using Boyle's law

$$P_1 V_1 = P_2 V_2$$

or $$P_2 = (P_1 V_1/V_2)$$

Here $P_1 = 75$ cm of mercury and $V_2 = \frac{3}{4} V_1$

Thus $$P_2 = \frac{75 V_1}{(3/4)V_1} = 100 \text{ cm of mercury}$$

The gas is now expanded adiabatically to 20% greater of its original value. Under adiabatic change the pressure and volume of gas are related as

$$P_2 V_2^{\gamma} = P_3 V_3^{\gamma}$$

or $$P_3 = P_2 \left(\frac{V_2}{V_3}\right)^{\gamma}$$

Here $$V_2 = \frac{3}{4} V_1 \text{ and } V_3 = \frac{120}{100} V_1$$

Thus $$P_3 = 100 \times \left(\frac{3V_1}{4}\right)^{1.5} \times \left(\frac{100}{120 V_1}\right)^{1.5}$$

$$= 100 \times \left(\frac{3}{4}\right)^{1.5} \times \left(\frac{5}{6}\right)^{1.5}$$

$$= 100 \times \left(\frac{5}{8}\right)^{1.5}$$

$$= 100 \times 0.494 = 49.4 \text{ cm of mercury}$$

Let the final temperature after adiabatic change be T_3 then from the relation of temperature and volume in an adiabatic process, we have

Now $$T_2 V_2^{\gamma-1} = T_3 V_3^{\gamma-1}$$

$$T_2 = 17\,°\text{C} = (273 + 27) = 290 \text{ K}$$

Now $$T_3 = T_2 \left(\frac{V_2}{V_3}\right)^{\gamma-1}$$

$$= 290 \times \left(\frac{3V_1}{4}\right)^{1.5-1} \times \left(\frac{100}{120 V_1}\right)^{1.5-1}$$

$$= 290 \times \left(\frac{5}{8}\right)^{0.5} = 229.3 \text{ K}$$

Hence the final temperature will be – 43.7 °C

Illustrative Example 3.26

One mole of a certain ideal gas is contained under a weightless piston of a vertical cylinder at a temperature *T*. The space over the piston opens into the atmosphere. What work has to be performed in order to increase isothermally the gas volume under the piston η times by slowly raising the piston ? The friction of the piston against the cylinder walls is negligibly small.

Solution

As gas expands from its initial volume (say *V*) to η time of initial volume (ηV) we can say that work is done by the gas in this expansion. As this expansion is isothermal, work done by the gas is simply given as

$$W = nRT \ln\left(\frac{V_2}{V_1}\right)$$

Here $n = 1$ mole, $V_2 = \eta V_1$ thus

$$W = RT \ln \eta \quad \ldots(3.52)$$

As gas is expanding, it is doing work and some external agent is pulling the piston up to increase the volume of gas we can say that gas is supporting the external agent and atmosphere is opposing this expansion thus work is done on atmosphere. As atmospheric pressure to be constant, and change in volume of gas is from *V* to ηV, the work done on atmosphere is

$$W_{atm} = -P(\Delta V)$$

$$= PV(1 - \eta)$$

Initially the piston was in equilibrium thus gas pressure was equal to atmospheric pressure so, we have

$$PV = RT \quad [\text{As } n = 1 \text{ mole}]$$

or $$W_{atm} = -RT(\eta - 1) \quad \ldots(3.53)$$

If W_{ext} is the work done by external agent in pulling the gas here we must have

$$|W_{ext}| + |W_{gas}| = |W_{atm}| \quad \ldots(3.54)$$

$$W_{ext} = W_{atm} - W_{gas}$$

$$W_{ext} = RT(\eta - 1) - RT \ln \eta$$

Here equation-(3.54) the basic equation we've encountered several times in mechanics as if some work is being done then at least two objects are to be involved in the system, one who is doing the work (energy supplier) and the other on which work is done (energy accepter). Only one body can never do any work. This we'll discuss in next section and then we'll take some more examples on such concepts.

3.6 Free Expansion of a Gas

When heat is added to a thermodynamics system, it undergoes a change of state which depends on the path from the initial state to final state. We take an example of it. Figure-3.35 shows an ideal gas contained in a cylinder with a piston having an initial volume of 5 litre at temperature 300 K. We want to increase its volume from 5 litre to 8 litre. We put this cylinder on to a heater at same temperature 300 K Heater supplies heat to the gas and the gas expands slowly and after expending in the slow and isobaric manner, the gas reaches its final volume of 8 litre. In this process gas absorbs a definite amount of heat.

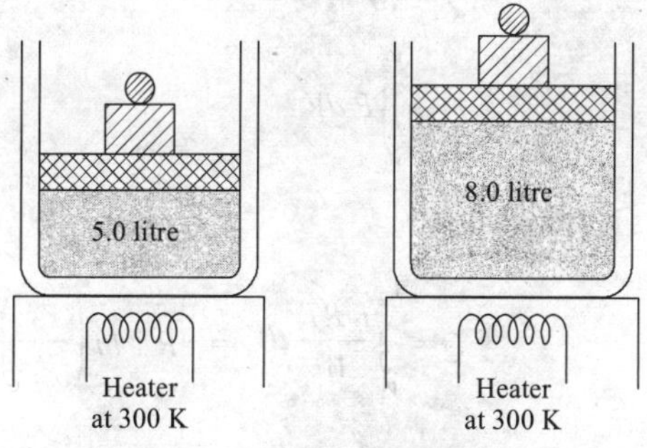

Figure 3.35

Figure-3.36 shows a different process leading to similar final state. In this case an insulated cylinder is divided in two parts by a thin massless fixed piston. The volume of lower compartment is 5.0 litre and that of upper is 3.0 litre. In the lower part we place the same amount of the same gas used in previous case at same temperature 300 K. The initial state is same as before. In the upper part there is vacuum or no pressure region. If we release the piston. It undergoes a sudden expansion due to vacuum on other side and the gas fills the whole space of 8.0 litre volume of cylinder rapidly. In this expansion we can see that no heat is supplied to the gas as walls are insulated. During such an expansion gas does no work because it is not pushing any thing during expansion or in this case there is nothing (vacuum) on which work can be done. Thus if no heat is supplied and no work is done by the gas, its internal energy will also remain constant. Such an expansion of gas is called "*free expansion*" of gas. As during free expansion temperature of gas remains constant, Boyle's law will remain valid in such cases; thus

$$P_1V_1 = P_2V_2$$

Here subscript 1 and 2 are used for the state of gas before and after the free expansion.

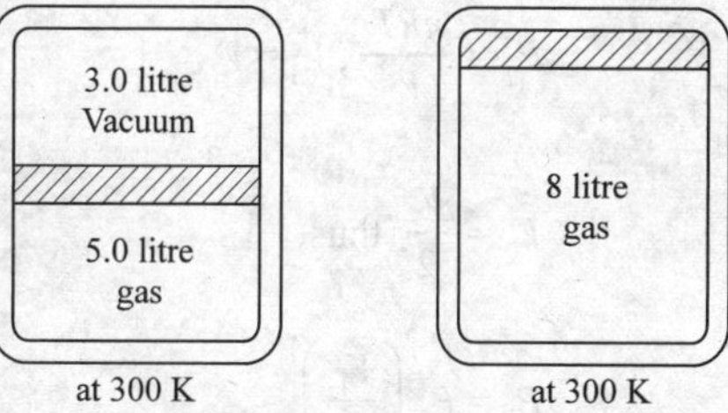

Figure 3.36

 # Illustrative Example 3.27

Figure-3.37 shows a cylindrical container of volume V. Whose walls are adiabatic. Initially a light adiabatic piston divides the container in two equal parts as shown. In left part there is n moles of an ideal gas with adiabatic exponent γ is filled at temperature T_A and in other part there is vacuum. If the piston is released, the gas fills the whole container uniformly. Find the final pressured and temperature of gas. Now if the piston is slowly displaced externally back to its initial position. Find the final pressure and temperature of gas.

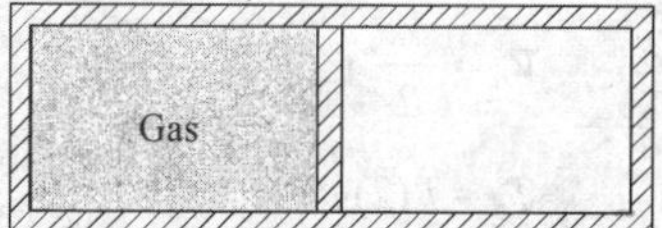

Figure 3.37

Solution

When the piston is released the gas expands to fill the complete volume of container. As there is nothing in the other part of cylinder, this is the free expansion of gas hence no work is done by the gas and as container is thermally insulated from surrounding, the gas temperature remains constant and thus according to Boyle's Law as the volume of gas is doubled so its final pressure is reduced to half. Thus

$$P_f = \frac{P_i}{2}$$

Initial pressure P_i of gas can be given by gas law as

$$P_i = \frac{nRT}{V/2}$$

Thus, we have $P_f = \frac{P_i}{2} = \frac{nRT}{V}$

Now if piston is displaced back to its initial position, this is adiabatic compression of gas in which gas volume decreases to half i.e. $V/2$. As we know in an adiabatic process, pressure and volume of gas in different states are related as

$$P_1 V_1^{\gamma} = P_2 V_2^{\gamma}$$

Here $P_1 = \frac{nRT}{V}, V_1 = V$

and $V_2 = \frac{V}{2}$ thus

$$P_2 = P_1 \left(\frac{V_1}{V_2}\right)^{\gamma}$$

$$= P_1 (2)^{\gamma}$$

$$= (2)^{\gamma} \frac{nRT}{V}$$

Similarly in adiabatic process, gas volume and temperature in different states are related as

$$T_1 V_1^{\gamma-1} = T_2 V_2^{\gamma-1}$$

or $T_2 = T_1 \left(\frac{V_1}{V_2}\right)^{\gamma-1}$

Here $T_1 = T, V_1 = V$

and $V_2 = \frac{V}{2}$ thus

$$T_2 = T(2)^{\gamma-1}$$

Illustrative Example 3.28

There are two thermally insulated vessel. One with 0.025 moles of helium and other with n moles of hydrogen. Initially both the gases are at room temperature. Now equal amount of heat is supplied to both the vessels. It is found that in both the gases temperature rises by same amount. Find the number of moles of hydrogen in second vessel

Solution

As the gases arc enclosed in closed vessels, the heating can be taken as isochoric heating and as heat supplied to both vessels are same, we have

$$Q = n_1 C_{V_1} \Delta T = n_2 C_{V_2} \Delta T$$

or $0.025 \times \frac{3}{2} R\Delta T = n \frac{5}{2} R\Delta T$

[As for He, $C_{V_1} = 3/2\ R$ and for H_2, $C_{V_2} = 5/2\ R$]

or $n = \frac{0.025 \times 3}{5} = 0.015$ mole

Illustrative Example 3.29

There are two vessels. Each of them contains one mole of a monatomic ideal gas. Initial volume of the gas in each vessel is 8.3×10^{-3} m^3 at 27°C, Equal amount of heat is supplied to each vessel. In one of the vessels, the volume of the gas is doubled without change in its internal energy, whereas the volume of the gas is held constant in the second vessel. The vessels are now connected to allow free mixing of the gas. Find the final temperature and pressure of the combined gas system.

Solution

According to first law of thermodynamics

$$\Delta Q = \Delta U + \Delta W$$

For vessel I, $\Delta U = 0$ [As no change in temperature]

or $\Delta Q = \Delta W$

or $Q = \int_{V_1}^{V_2} P\,dV$

From gas law, we have

$$Q = \int_{V_1}^{V_2} \frac{n\,RT}{V} dV = n\,R\,T\,ln\left(\frac{V_2}{V_1}\right)$$

$$= n\,R\,T\,ln(2) \quad [\text{As } V_2 = 2V_1] \quad \ldots(3.55)$$

For second vessel, $\Delta W = 0$ (as volume is constant)

Thus heat supplied is given as

$$Q = n\,C_V \Delta T = n\left(\frac{3}{2}R\right)\Delta T \quad \ldots(3.56)$$

[As for monoatomic gas $C_V = 3/2\ .\ R$]

From equation-(3.55) and (3.56), we get

$$n\,R\,T\,ln(2) = 2\,n\left(\frac{3}{2}R\right)\Delta T$$

or $$\Delta T = \frac{2}{3} \times 300 \times 0.693 = 138.6\,\text{K}$$

This is the change in the temperature of the gas of second vessel.

Now the final temperature of the gas in second vessel is

$$T' = T + \Delta T = 300 + 138.6 = 438.6\,\text{K}$$

Let after mixing, T_f and P_f be the final temperature and pressure respectively. Then as moles are equal, we have

$$T_f = \frac{T + (T + \Delta T)}{2} = \frac{300 + 438.6}{2}$$

$$= 369.3\,\text{K}$$

For a gas system from gas law, we have

$$P_f V_f = n R T_f$$

or $$P_f = \frac{n R T_f}{V_f} = \frac{2 \times 8.3 \times 369.3}{2 \times 8.3 \times 10^{-3} + 8.3 \times 10^{-3}}$$

$$= 2.46 \times 10^5\,\text{N/m}^2$$

Illustrative Example 3.30

Two moles of helium gas undergo a cyclic process as shown in figure-3.38. Assuming the gas to be ideal, calculate the following quantities in this process.

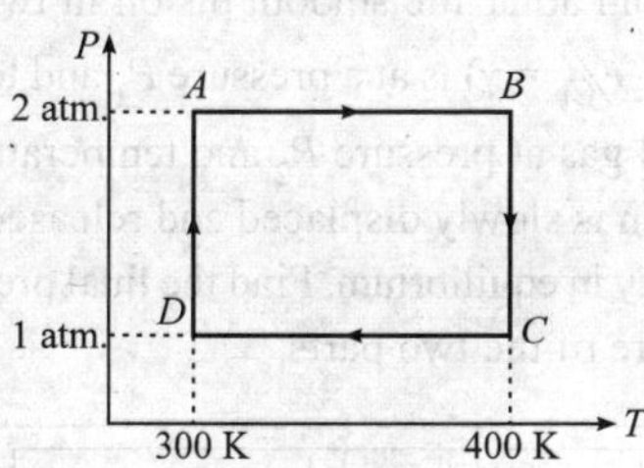

Figure 3.38

(a) The net change in the heat energy.

(b) The net work done.

(c) The net change in internal energy.

Solution

As we know in a cyclic process, the change in heat energy or heat supplied to the gas is equal to the net work done by the gas.

Here *AB* is isobaric process. Hence work done during this process from *A* to *B* is

$$W_{AB} = P(V_2 - V_1) = nR(T_2 - T_1)$$

or $$W_{AB} = 2 \times 8.314 \times (400 - 300) = 1662.8\,\text{joule}$$

Work done during isothermal process from *B* to *C*

$$W_{BC} = n R T_C \ln(V_2/V_1) = n R T_C \ln(P_1/P_2)$$

$$= 2 \times 8.314 \times 400 \times \ln(2)$$

$$= 2 \times 8.314 \times 400 \times 0.693$$

$$= 4610.2\,\text{joule}$$

Workdone during isobaric process from *C* to *D*

$$W_{CD} = nR(T_D - T_C) = 2 \times 8.314 \times (300 - 400)$$

$$= -1662.8\,\text{joule}$$

Workdone during isothermal process from *D* to *A*

$$W_{DA} = n R T_D \ln(P_D/P_A)$$

$$= n R T_D \ln(2)$$

$$= -2 \times 8.314 \times 300 \times 0.693$$

$$= -3457.7\,\text{joule}$$

Net workdone

$$= W_{AB} + W_{BC} + W_{CD} + W_{DA}$$

$$= 1662.8 + 4610.2 - 1662.5 - 3457.7$$

$$= 1152.5\,\text{joule}$$

Now from first law of thermodynamics

$$\Delta Q = \Delta U + \Delta W$$

Here $\Delta U = 0$, thus we have

$$\Delta Q = \Delta W = 1152.5\,\text{joule}$$

So the heat given to the system is 1152.5 joule

As the gas returns to its original state, hence there is no change in internal energy.

Illustrative Example 3.31

Two moles of helium gas ($\gamma = 5/3$) are initially at temperature 27 °C and occupy a volume of 20 litres. The gas is first expanded at constant pressure until the volume is doubled. Then it undergoes an adiabatic change until the temperature returns to its initial value.

(i) Sketch the process on a *P-V* diagram.

(ii) What are the final volume and pressure of the gas ?

(iii) What is the work done by the gas ?

Solution

For a perfect gas

$$PV = nRT$$

Given that $V = 20$ litres

$= 20 \times 10^{-3}\ m^3$

$T = 27\,°C = 300$ K and number of molecules

$n = 2$

Thus initial pressure is given as

$$P = \frac{nRT}{V} = \frac{2 \times 8.3 \times 300}{20 \times 10^{-3}}$$

$$= 2.5 \times 10^5\ N/m^2$$

(i) Figure-3.39 shows the indicator diagram of the complete process.

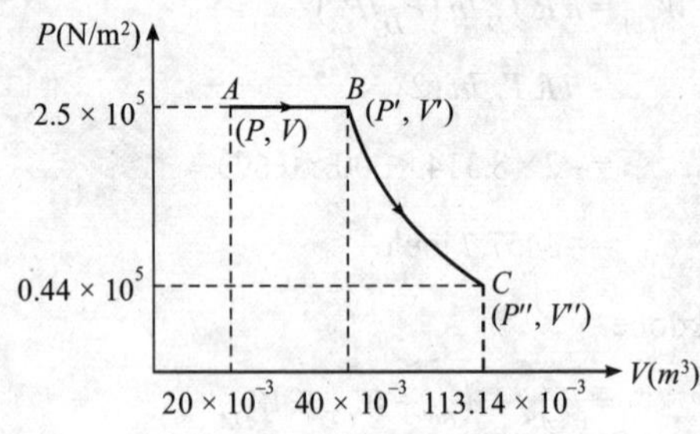

Figure 3.39

(ii) At point B,

Pressure $P' = P = 2.5 \times 10^5\ N/m^2$,

$V' = 2V = 40 \times 10^{-3}\ m^3$

As pressure is constant in the process AB, making its volume doubled, its temperature will also be doubled.

Thus temperature at point B is $T' = 600$ K

The gas now undergoes adiabatic expansion to cool down to

$T'' = T = 300$ K

We know for an adiabatic process $TV^{\gamma-1} =$ constant

$$T'(V')^{\gamma-1} = T''(V'')^{\gamma-1}$$

$$\left(\frac{V''}{V'}\right) = \left(\frac{T'}{T''}\right)^{1/(\gamma-1)} = \left(\frac{600}{300}\right)^{1/(\frac{5}{3}-1)}$$

$$= (2)^{3/2} = 2\sqrt{2}$$

Thus final volume is

$$V'' = (2\sqrt{2})\,V'$$

$$= 2 \times 1.414 \times 40 \times 10^{-3}$$

$$= 113.14 \times 10^{-3}\ m^3$$

Similarly final pressure is given by process equation as

$$P'V'^{\gamma} = P''V''^{\gamma}$$

or $$P'' = P'\left(\frac{V'}{V''}\right)^{\gamma}$$

$$= 2.5 \times 10^5 \times \left(\frac{40 \times 10^{-3}}{113.14 \times 10^{-3}}\right)^{5/3}$$

$$= 4.42 \times 10^4\ Pa$$

(iii) Work done under isobaric process AB is

or $W_1 = P\Delta V$

or $W_1 = 2.5 \times 10^5 \times (40 - 20) \times 10^{-3}$

or $= 4980$ J

Workdone during adiabatic process BC is given as

or $$W_2 = \frac{nR}{\gamma - 1}[T_1 - T_2]$$

or $$= \frac{2 \times 8.3}{[1-(5/3)]}[300 - 600] = 7470\ J$$

Total work done $= W_1 + W_2 = 4980 + 7470$

$= 12450$ J

Illustrative Example 3.32

Figure-3.40 shows on adiabatic cylindrical container of volume V_0 divided by an adiabatic smooth piston in two equal parts. An ideal gas ($C_P/C_V = \gamma$) is at a pressure P_1 and temperature T_1 in left part and gas at pressure P_2 and temperature T_2 in right part. The piston is slowly displaced and released at a position where it can stay in equilibrium. Find the final pressure, volume and temperature of the two parts.

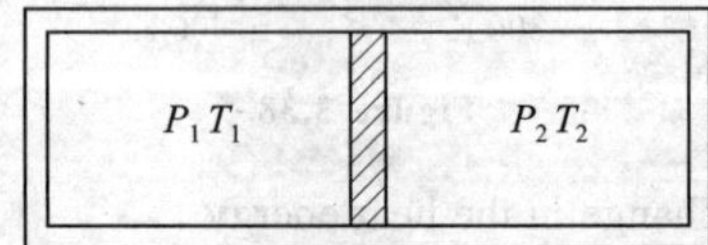

Figure 3.40

Solution

As finally the piston is in equilibrium, both the gases must be at same pressure P_f. Let the displacement of piston be in final state x and if A is the area of cross-section of the piston the final volumes of the left and right part finally can be given by figure-3.41 as

$$V_L = \frac{V_0}{2} + Ax$$

and $$V_R = \frac{V_0}{2} - Ax$$

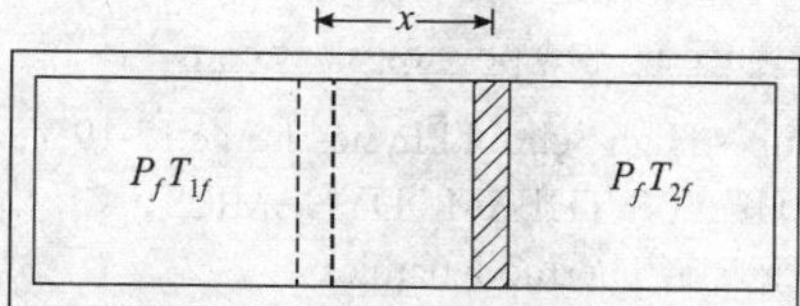

Figure 3.41

As it is given that the container walls and piston are adiabatic in left side the gas undergoes adiabatic expansion and on right side the gas undergoes adiabatic compressive. Thus we have for initial and final state of gas on left side

$$P_1\left(\frac{V_0}{2}\right)^{\gamma} = P_f\left(\frac{V_0}{2}+Ax\right)^{\gamma} \quad \ldots(3.57)$$

Similarly for gas on right side, we have

$$P_2\left(\frac{V_0}{2}\right)^{\gamma} = P_f\left(\frac{V_0}{2}-Ax\right)^{\gamma} \quad \ldots(3.58)$$

Dividing equation-(3.57) by (3.58), we get

$$\frac{P_1}{P_2} = \frac{\left(\frac{V_0}{2}+Ax\right)^{\gamma}}{\left(\frac{V_0}{2}-Ax\right)^{\gamma}}$$

or
$$\left(\frac{V_0}{2}-Ax\right)P_1^{1/\gamma} = \left(\frac{V_0}{2}+Ax\right)P_2^{1/\gamma}$$

or
$$Ax = \frac{V_0}{2}\frac{\left[P_1^{1/\gamma}-P_2^{1/\gamma}\right]}{\left[P_1^{1/\gamma}+P_2^{1/\gamma}\right]}$$

Now from equation-(3.57)

$$P_f = \frac{P_1\left(V_0/2\right)^{\gamma}}{\left[V_0/2+Ax\right]^{\gamma}}$$

or
$$P_f = \frac{P_1\left(V_0/2\right)^{\gamma}}{\left[\frac{V_0}{2}+\frac{V_0}{2}\left(\frac{P_1^{1/\gamma}-P_2^{1/\gamma}}{P_1^{1/\gamma}+P_2^{1/\gamma}}\right)\right]^{\gamma}}$$

or
$$P_f = \frac{P_1\left(P_1^{1/\gamma}+P_2^{1/\gamma}\right)^{\gamma}}{(2)^{\gamma}P_1}$$

or
$$P_f = \left[\frac{P_1^{1/\gamma}+P_2^{1/\gamma}}{2}\right]^{\gamma}$$

Similarly the final temperatures of the two parts are T_{1f} and T_{2f} respectively then for left part, we have

$$T_1\left(\frac{V_0}{2}\right)^{\gamma-1} = T_{1f}\left(\frac{V_0}{2}+Ax\right)^{\gamma-1} \quad \ldots(3.59)$$

or
$$T_{1f} = \frac{T_1\left(V_0/2\right)^{\gamma-1}}{\left[\frac{V_0}{2}+\frac{V_0}{2}\left(\frac{P_1^{1/\gamma}-P_2^{1/\gamma}}{P_1^{1/\gamma}+P_2^{1/\gamma}}\right)\right]^{\gamma-1}}$$

or
$$T_f = \frac{T_1}{P_1}\left[\frac{\left(P_1^{1/\gamma}+P_2^{1/\gamma}\right)}{2}\right]^{\gamma-1}$$

Similarly for right part of gas, we have

$$T_2\left(\frac{V_0}{2}\right)^{\gamma-1} = T_{2f}\left(\frac{V_0}{2}-Ax\right)^{\gamma-1} \quad \ldots(3.60)$$

or
$$T_{2f} = \frac{T_2\left(V_0/2\right)^{\gamma-1}}{\left[\frac{V_0}{2}-\frac{V_0}{2}\left(\frac{P_1^{1/\gamma}-P_2^{1/\gamma}}{P_1^{1/\gamma}+P_2^{1/\gamma}}\right)\right]^{\gamma-1}}$$

or
$$T_f = \frac{T_2}{P_2}\left[\frac{\left(P_1^{1/\gamma}+P_2^{1/\gamma}\right)}{2}\right]^{\gamma-1}$$

Illustrative Example 3.33

A piston can freely move inside a horizontal cylinder closed from both ends. Initially, the piston separates the inside space of the cylinder into two equal parts each of volume V_0, in which an ideal gas is contained under the same pressure P_0 and at the same temperature. What work has to be performed in order to increase isothermally the volume of one part of gas η times compared to that of the other by slowly moving the piston ?

Solution

As the piston is displaced externally some external work is done in the process. If piston is displaced toward right the gas on left side expands and does some work. Similarly gas on right is compressed and on it work is done. As discussed earlier, here we have

$$\left|W_{gas\ in\ left\ part}\right| + \left|W_{ext}\right| = \left|W_{gas\ in\ right\ part}\right| \quad \ldots(3.61)$$

Here $\left|W_{gas\ on\ left}\right|$ = magnitude of work done by gas in left part

$\left|W_{ext}\right|$ = magnitude of work done by external agent

$\left|W_{gas\ in\ right\ part}\right|$ = magnitude of work done on gas in right part

It is given that initial volume of both the parts is V_0 and in the process final volume of one part is η times that of the other part. If the final volume of right part is V then that of left part will become ηV. As total volume of container is $2V_0$, then we have

$$V + \eta V = 2V_0$$

or

$$V = \frac{2V_0}{\eta + 1}$$

For gas in left part work done by gas in isothermal expansion is

$$W_{by\ gas} = nRT\, ln \frac{V_2}{V_1}$$

$$\Rightarrow \quad = P_0 V_0\, ln \frac{\eta V}{V_0}$$

[As from gas law for gas on left part $P_0V_0 = nRT$]

$$\Rightarrow \quad = P_0 V_0\, ln \left(\frac{2\eta}{\eta + 1}\right) \quad \ldots(3.62)$$

Similarly for gas in right part, work done on the gas in isothermal compression is

$$W_{on\ gas} = nRT\, ln \frac{V_2}{V_1}$$

$$\Rightarrow \quad = P_0 V_0\, ln \frac{V}{V_0}$$

$$\Rightarrow \quad = P_0 V_0\, ln \left(\frac{2}{\eta + 1}\right)$$

$$\Rightarrow \quad = -P_0 V_0\, ln \left(\frac{\eta + 1}{2}\right)$$

Now from equation-(3.61), (3.62) and (3.63), we have

$$\left|W_{ext}\right| = \left|W_{by\ gas\ in\ left\ part}\right| + \left|W_{on\ gas\ in\ right\ part}\right|$$

$$= -P_0 V_0\, ln \frac{2\eta}{\eta + 1} + P_0 V_0\, ln \left(\frac{\eta + 1}{2}\right)$$

$$= P_0 V_0\, ln \left[\frac{(\eta + 1)^2}{4\eta}\right]$$

Web Reference at www.physicsgalaxy.com

Age Group - High School Physics | Age 17-19 Years

Section - HEAT & THERMODYNAMICS

Topic - Laws of Thermodynamics

Module Number - 17 to 28

Practice Exercise 3.3

(i) One mole of an ideal gas undergoes a process whose process equation is given as

$$P = \frac{P_0}{1 + \left(\frac{V_0}{V}\right)^2}$$

Here P_0 and V_0 are constant. When the volume of gas is changed from V_0 to $2V_0$, find the change in temperature of the gas.

$\left[\frac{11 P_0 V_0}{10 R}\right]$

(ii) For a thermodynamic system the pressure, volume and temperature are related as new gas law given as

$$P = \frac{\alpha T^2}{V}$$

Here α is a constant. Find the work done by the system in this process when pressure remains constant and its temperature changes from T_0 to $2T_0$.

[$3\,\alpha T_0^2$]

(iii) Temperature of 1 mole of an ideal gas is increased from 300 K to 310 K under isochoric process. Heat supplied to the gas in this process is 25 *R*. What amount of work has to be done by the gas if temperature of the gas decreases from 310 K to 300 K adiabatically.

[25 *R*]

(iv) During the adiabatic expansion of 2 moles of a gas, the increase in internal energy was found to be equal to –100 J. Find the work done by the gas in the process.

[100 J]

(v) One litre of an ideal gas ($\gamma = 1.5$) at 300 K temperature and 10^5 Pa pressure, is suddenly compressed to half of its original volume. Find the final temperature of the gas. It is then cooled to 300 K by isobaric process and then it is expanded isothermally to achieve its original volume of 1 litre. Calculate the work done by the gas in each process and also calculate the total work done in the cycle.

[424.26 K, – 82.84 J, – 41.4 J, 103.95 J, – 20.29 J]

(vi) Three identical diatomic gases ($\gamma = 1.5$) are enclosed in three identical containers but at different pressures and same temperatures. These gases are expanded to double their volumes. In first container the process is isothermal, in second container the process is adiabatic and in third container process is isobaric. If the final pressures are equal in the three containers, find the ratio of the initial pressures in the three containers.

[$2 : 2\sqrt{2} : 1$]

(vii) One mole of a gas is taken in a cylinder with a movable piston. A resistor R connected to a capacitor through a key is placed inside the gas as shown in figure-3.42 below. When the key is open, potential difference across the plates of the capacitor is equal to 640/3 V. When the key is closed for 2.5 ln(4) minutes, the gas expands isobarically and its temperature changes by 22 K.

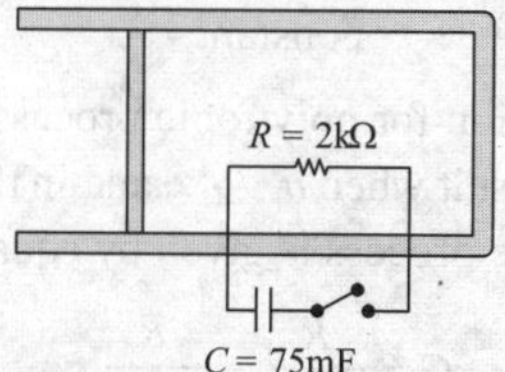

Figure 3.42

(a) Find the work done by the gas

(b) Increase in the internal energy of the gas

(c) The value of γ for gas

Ans. [(a) 0.183 kJ; (b) 1.417 kJ; (c) 1.13]

(viii) An ideal diatomic gas is heated at constant pressure such that it performs a work $W = 2.0$ J. Find the amount of heat supplied.

[7 J]

(ix) Two identical gases whose adiabatic exponent is γ are filled in two identical containers at equal pressures. In both the containers the volume of gas is doubled. In first container it is done by an isothermal process and in second container it is done by adiabatic process. Find the condition for which the work done by the gas in the two expansion process is same.

[$1 - 2^{1-\gamma} = (\gamma - 1)\ln 2$]

(x) A rectangular box shown in the figure-3.43 has a partition which can slide without friction along the length of the box. Initially each of the two chambers of the box has one mole of a monatomic gas $\left(\gamma = \frac{5}{3}\right)$ at a pressure P_0, volume V_0, and temperature T_0. The chamber on the left is slowly heated by an electric heater. The walls of the box and the partition are thermally insulated. Heat loss through the lead wires is negligible. The gas in the left chamber expands, pushing the partition until the final pressure in both chambers becomes $\frac{243p_0}{32}$. Determine : (a) the final temperature of the gas in each chamber, (b) the work done by the gas in the right chamber.

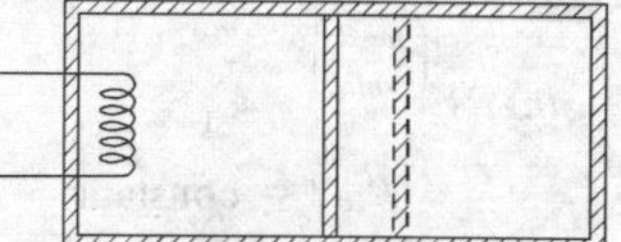

Figure 3.43

[(a) $\frac{9}{4}T_0$, $\frac{207}{16}T_0$ (b) $-\frac{15}{8}p_0V_0$]

(xi) One mole of oxygen, initially at temperature $T = 290$ K is compressed adiabatically so that its pressure increases $\eta = 10$ times. Find the final temperature and work done on it.

[559.90K, 5609.87J]

3.7 Polytropic Process

A polytropic process is one in which the molar specific heat of a gas during the process (heating) remains constant or does not change with the gas parameters pressure, volume or temperature. If for a polytropic process molar specific heat is taken C then according to first law of thermodynamics, we have

$$dQ = dU + dW$$

or
$$nC\,dT = \frac{nR\,dT}{\gamma - 1} + P\,dV$$

or
$$C = \frac{R}{\gamma-1} + \frac{P\,dV}{ndT} \quad \ldots(3.63)$$

From gas law

$$P\,dV + V\,dP = nR\,dT \quad \ldots(3.64)$$

From (3.63) and (3.64)

$$C = \frac{R}{\gamma-1} + \frac{RPdV}{PdV + VdP} \quad \ldots(3.65)$$

or
$$PdV\left(C - \frac{R}{\gamma-1} - R\right) = -\left(C - \frac{R}{\gamma-1}\right)VdP$$

or
$$\frac{dV}{V}\left(\frac{m-R}{m}\right) = -\frac{dP}{P}$$

[Where $m = C - \frac{R}{\gamma - 1}$ = constant]

Integrating the expression, we get

$$\left(\frac{m-R}{m}\right)\int\frac{dV}{V} = -\int\frac{dP}{P}$$

or $$\left(\frac{m-R}{m}\right) \ln V = -\ln P + C_1$$

[C_1 = integration constant]

or $$\ln PV^{\left(\frac{m-R}{m}\right)} = C_1$$

or $$PV^n = \text{constant} \qquad \ldots(3.66)$$

Where $n = \frac{m-R}{m}$ is another constant which is called *polytropic constant* whose value depends on γ of gas, gas constant R and the molar specific heat C of the process which is taken a constant equation-(3.66) shows that if the process equation of a process is represented in the form of PV^n = constant then it can be regarded as a polytropic process and the molar specific heat for a polytropic process can be defined by using first law of thermodynamics by equation-(3.65) as

$$C = \frac{R}{\gamma-1} + \frac{R\,PdV}{PdV+VdP} \qquad \ldots(3.67)$$

As PV^n = const we have

$$dPV^n + nPV^{n-1}\,dV = 0$$

or $$dP = -\frac{nP}{V}dV \qquad \ldots(3.68)$$

From (3.67) and (3.68) we have

$$C = \frac{R}{\gamma-1} + \frac{R\,PdV}{PdV + V\left(-\frac{nP}{V}dV\right)}$$

or $$C = \frac{R}{\gamma-1} + \frac{R}{1-n} \qquad \ldots(3.69)$$

or $$C = \frac{R(\gamma-n)}{(\gamma-1)(1-n)} \qquad \ldots(3.70)$$

Equation-(3.69) and (3.70) gives the molar heat capacity for a general polytropic process. If the polytropic constant n is known we can directly find the molar heat capacity C for the respective process using equation-(3.69) or (3.70) which directly gives the total amount of heat supplied to a gas as if n moles of gas are heated from a temperature T_1 to T_2 then the total heat supplied for the purpose is given as

$$Q = \int_{T_1}^{T_2} nC\,dT$$

$$Q = nC(T_2 - T_1) \qquad \ldots(3.71)$$

As internal energy change for any process can be given as

$$\Delta U = n\,C_V(T_2 - T_1) \qquad \ldots(3.72)$$

Thus work done in a polytropic process can be written from equation-(3.72) and (3.73) as

$$W = Q - \Delta U$$

$$W = n(C - C_V)(T_2 - T_1) \qquad \ldots(3.73)$$

3.7.1 Standard Processes as a Special Case of Polytropic Process

As discussed earlier the four standard processes are the special cases of general polytropic processes. Now we discuss these processes again in terms of polytropic process

(i) Isochoric Process

We know in an isochoric process, the process equation for the process is

$$V = \text{constant}$$

The general equation for polytropic process PV^n = constant, approaches this result when $n \to \infty$ and in this case the molar specific heat of the process is given by equation-(3.69) as

$$C = \frac{R}{\gamma-1} + \frac{R}{1-n}$$

As $n \to \infty$ $$C = \frac{R}{\gamma-1} = C_V$$

Which is in favour of the process

(ii) Isobaric process

Here in isobaric process the process equation is given as

$$P = \text{constant}$$

From the general equation of polytropic process PV^n = constant, above equation is obtained by substituting polytropic constant $n = 0$. Thus molar specific heat of this process can be given by equation-(3.69) as

$$C = \frac{R}{\gamma-1} + \frac{R}{1-n}$$

or $$C = \frac{R}{\gamma-1} + R = C_V + R = C_P$$

Hence it is also same as that used for constant pressure heating.

(iii) Isothermal process

Here during the process temperature of system remains constant thus the process equation is given as

$$PV = \text{constant}$$

From general equation of polytropic process here we can see that for an isothermal process the polytropic constant $n = 1$.

Thus if we find molar specific heat for isothermal process from equation-(3.65), we get

$$C = \frac{R}{\gamma - 1} + \frac{R}{1 - n}$$

or $$C \longrightarrow \infty$$

This is also obvious that in isothermal process temperature of gas never changes and molar heat capacity is the amount of heat required to change the temperature for one mole of gas by one degree. So if we continuously supply heat to a gas infinitely then also its temperature will not change then it is undergoing an isothermal process.

(iv) Adiabatic process

In previous section we've derived the process equation of an adiabatic process, given as

$$P V^{\gamma} = constant$$

Thus for an adiabatic process, the polytropic constant is equal to the adiabatic exponent of the gas, $n = \gamma$. Now from equation-(3.69) we can see that the molar heat capacity for a gas in adiabatic process is

$$C = \frac{R}{\gamma - 1} + \frac{R}{1 - n}$$

or $$C = 0$$

Again here it is obvious that in an adiabatic expansion or compression, temperature of gas changes without any supply of heat. Thus in this process no heat is required to raise the temperature of gas.

3.7.2 Indicator Diagram For a Polytropic Process

The general process equation is

$$PV^n = constant$$

or $$P \propto \frac{1}{V^n}$$

We know if $n = 1$, it becomes an isothermal process, PV-curve of which is a rectangular hyperbola and the slope of the curve is given as

$$\frac{dP}{dV} = -n\left(\frac{P}{V}\right)$$

or $$\left|\frac{dP}{dV}\right|_{\substack{Polytropic \\ Process}} = n\left|\frac{dP}{dV}\right|_{\substack{Isothermal \\ Process}} \qquad \ldots(3.74)$$

Thus for a process if polytropic constant n is more then unity then this curve will be steeper then isothermal curve and if $n < 1$ then its slope will be less then isothermal curve. Figure-3.44 shows various PV-curves for different value of n for some standard and general processes.

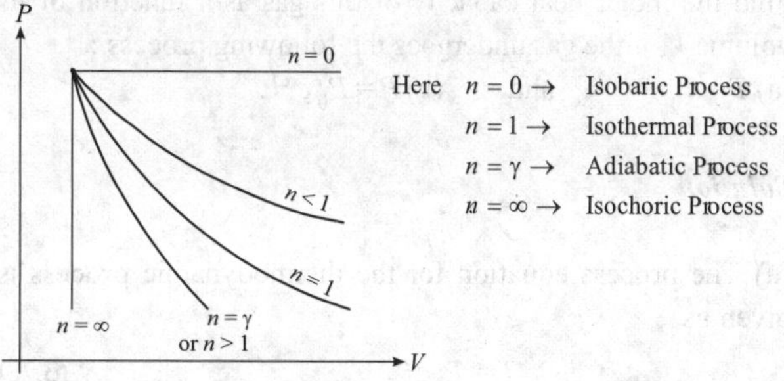

Figure 3.44

Illustrative Example 3.34

An amount Q of heat is added to a monoatomic ideal gas in a thermodynamic process. In the process gas expands and does a work $Q/2$ on its surrounding. Find the molar specific heat of gas in this process.

Solution

From first law of thermodynamics we have

$$Q = \Delta U + W$$

It is given that $$W = Q/2$$

Thus $$Q = \Delta U + Q/2$$

or $$\Delta U = Q/2 \qquad \ldots(3.75)$$

If C is the molar specific heat of the gas in this process then the amount of heat supplied can be given as

$$Q = nC\Delta T \qquad \ldots(3.76)$$

[If ΔT is rise in temperature of gas]

For change in internal energy of gas, we can write

$$\Delta U = nC_V\Delta T$$

or $$= n\left(\frac{3R}{2}\right)\Delta T \qquad \ldots(3.77)$$

[As for a monoatomic gas $C_V = \left(\frac{3R}{2}\right)$]

Thus from equation-(3.75), (3.76) and (3.77) we have

$$nC_V\Delta T = \frac{1}{2}(nC\Delta T)$$

or $$C = 2C_V = 3R$$

 # Illustrative Example 3.35

An ideal gas has a molar heat capacity C_V at constant volume. Find the molar heat capacity of this gas as a function of its volume V, if the gas undergoes the following process :
(a) $T = T_0 e^{\alpha V}$ and (b) $P = P_0 e^{\alpha V}$.

Solution

(a) The process equation for the thermodynamic process is given as

$$T = T_0 e^{\alpha V} \quad \ldots(3.78)$$

For a general thermodynamic process we know the molar heat capacity is given by

$$C = C_V + \frac{RPdV}{PdV + VdP} \quad \ldots(3.79)$$

From gas law we can relate pressure and volume of gas as

$$P = \frac{nRT}{V}$$

From equation-(3.74)

$$P = \frac{nRT_0}{V} e^{\alpha V} \quad \ldots(3.80)$$

Differentiating this equation, we get

$$PdV + VdP = nRT_0 \alpha e^{\alpha V} dV \quad \ldots(3.81)$$

From equation-(3.79), (3.80) and (3.81), we get

$$C = C_V + \frac{R\left(\frac{nRT_0}{V} e^{\alpha V}\right) dV}{nRT_0 \alpha e^{\alpha V} dV}$$

or $$C = C_V + \frac{R}{\alpha V} \quad \ldots(3.82)$$

Euqation-(3.82) gives the molar specific heat of the gas undergoing the given process and students should note that this molar specific heat is given a function of volume of gas thus this process is a nonpolytropic process.

(b) In this case the process equation is given as

$$P = P_0 e^{\alpha V} \quad \ldots(3.83)$$

Differentiating, we get

$$dP = P_0 \alpha e^{\alpha V} dV \quad \ldots(3.84)$$

If C is the molar specific heat of the gas in this process then from equation-(3.79), (3.83) and (3.84) we have

$$C = C_V + \frac{R(P_0 e^{\alpha V}) dV}{(P_0 e^{\alpha V}) dV + V(P_0 \alpha e^{\alpha V} dV)}$$

or $$C = C_V + \frac{R}{1 + \alpha V} \quad \ldots(3.85)$$

Equation-(3.85) gives the molar heat capacity of the gas in the given process and again we can say that this is also not a polytropic process.

 # Illustrative Example 3.36

An ideal gas is taken through a process in which the process equation is given as $P = kV^{\alpha}$, where k and α are positive constants. Find the value of α for which in this process molar heat capacity becomes zero.

Solution

For a given polytropic process PV^n = constant, we know the molar heat capacity is given as

$$C = \frac{R}{\gamma - 1} + \frac{R}{1 - n}$$

In this process equation can be rewritten as

$$PV^{-\alpha} = k \text{ (a constant)}$$

Thus in this process value of polytropic constant n is $-\alpha$. So molar heat capacity of gas in this process is directly given as

$$C = \frac{R}{\gamma - 1} \frac{R}{1 + \alpha}$$

Given that $C = 0$

or on solving we get

$$\alpha = -\gamma$$

 # Illustrative Example 3.37

n moles of a monoatomic ideal gas undergone in a thermodynamic process along the path shown in figure-3.45 from state-1 to state-2. The gas pressure in state-1 is P_0. Find the amount of heat supplied to the gas in this process and work done by the gas in the process.

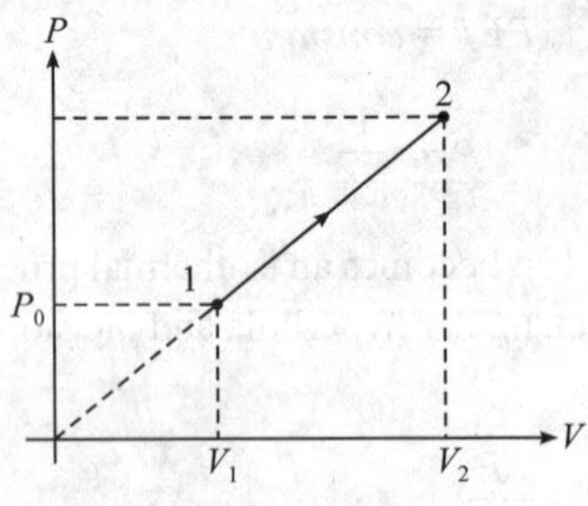

Figure 3.45

Solution

From indicator diagram shown in figure-3.34 at is clear that the process equation of this process can be written as

$$P = kV \quad \text{or} \quad PV^{-1} = k \text{ (constant)} \quad \ldots(3.86)$$

[As PV curve is a straight line passing through origin]

Thus here from equation-(3.86), we can say that the process is polytropic with the value of polytropic constant $n = -1$. So the molar heat capacity of the gas can be given as

$$C = C_V + \frac{R}{1-n}$$

or $$C = \frac{3R}{2} + \frac{R}{2} = 2R$$

$$\text{[As for a monoatomic gas } C_V = \frac{3R}{2}\text{]}$$

If in the process gas temperatures at state-1 and state-2 are T_1 and T_2 then these can be obtained by gas law as

$$PV = nRT$$

For state-1 $$T_1 = \frac{P_0 V_1}{nR}$$

For this process from equation-(3.86), we have

$$\frac{P_1}{V_1} = \frac{P_2}{V_2}$$

or $$P_2 = \frac{V_2}{V_1} P_0$$

Thus for state-2 from gas law

$$T_2 = \frac{P_2 V_2}{n R} = \frac{V_2^2 P_0}{n R V_1}$$

If heat supplied in the process in changing the gas state from 1 to 2 is Q, then it is given as

$$Q = n C (T_2 - T_1)$$

or $$Q = n(2R)\left[\frac{V_2^2 P_0}{nRV_1} - \frac{P_0 V_1}{nR}\right]$$

or $$Q = 2P_0\left(\frac{V_2^2 - V_1^2}{V_1}\right)$$

Work done in a polytropic process is given by

$$W = n(C - C_V)(T_2 - T_1)$$

or $$W = n\left(2R - \frac{3R}{2}\right)\left(\frac{V_2^2 P_0}{nRV_1} - \frac{P_0 V_1}{nR}\right)$$

or $$W = \frac{P_0}{2}\left(\frac{V_2^2 - V_1^2}{V_1}\right)$$

Work done in the process can also be obtained by the area below the PV curve (in figure-3.46, shaded area), can be given as

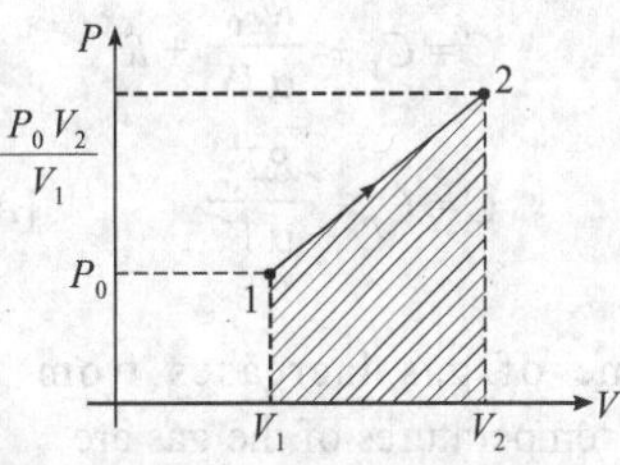

Figure 3.46

$$W = \frac{1}{2}\left(P_0 + P_0\frac{V_2}{V_1}\right)(V_2 - V_1)$$

or $$= \frac{P_0}{2}\left(\frac{V_2^2 - V_1^2}{V_1}\right)$$

 # Illustrative Example 3.38

One mole of an ideal gas with heat capacity at constant pressure C_P undergoes the process $T = T_0 + \alpha V$, where T_0 and α are constant. Find

(a) heat capacity of the gas as a function of its volume,

(b) the amount of heat transferred to the gas, if its volume increased from V_1 to V_2.

Solution

The process equation for the thermodynamic process is given as

$$T = T_0 + \alpha V \qquad \ldots(3.87)$$

From gas law we have

$$P = \frac{RT}{V} = \frac{R}{V}(T_0 + \alpha V) \qquad \ldots(3.88)$$

[As $n = 1$ mole]

(a) The heat capacity of a gas in a thermodynamic process is given as

$$C = C_V + \frac{RPdV}{PdV + VdP} \qquad \ldots(3.89)$$

Differentiating equation-(3.88), we get

$$PdV + VdP = \alpha RdV \qquad \ldots(3.90)$$

Now from equation-(3.88), (3.89) and (3.90), we have

$$C = C_V + \frac{R\left[\left(\frac{R}{V}\right)(T_0 + \alpha V)\right]dV}{\alpha\, RdV}$$

or $$C = C_V + \frac{R}{\alpha V}(T_0 + \alpha V)$$

or $$C = C_V + \frac{RT_0}{\alpha V} + R$$

or $$C = C_P + \frac{RT_0}{\alpha V} \qquad [\text{As } C_P = C_V + R]$$

(b) As volume of gas increases from V_1 to V_2, the corresponding temperatures of the gas are

$$T_1 = T_0 + \alpha V_1$$

and $$T_2 = T_0 + \alpha V_2$$

The amount of heat supplied to the gas can be given as

$$Q = \int dQ = \int_{T_1}^{T_2} C dT \qquad [\text{As } n = 1 \text{ mole}]$$

or $$Q = \int_{T_1}^{T_2} \left[C_P + \frac{RT_0}{\alpha V} \right] dT$$

From the given relation we have

$$V = \frac{T - T_0}{\alpha}$$

Thus $$Q = \int_{T_1}^{T_2} \left[C_P + \frac{RT_0}{T - T_0} \right] dT$$

$$= C_P (T_2 - T_1) + RT_0 \, ln \left(\frac{T_2 - T_0}{T_1 - T_0} \right)$$

$$= C_P \alpha (V_2 - V_1) + RT_0 \, ln \left(\frac{V_2}{V_1} \right)$$

Illustrative Example 3.39

One mole of an ideal gas with adiabatic exponent γ whose pressure changes with volume as $P = \alpha V$, where α is a constant, is expanded so that its volume increases η times. Find the change in internal energy and heat capacity of the gas. Initial volume of gas is V_0.

Solution

The process equation of the thermodynamic process in which gas is undergoing is given as

$$P = \alpha V \qquad \ldots(3.91)$$

Rearranging we can write

$$PV^{-1} = \alpha \text{ (a constant)} \qquad \ldots(3.92)$$

Equation-(3.92) shows that this is a polytropic process with the value of polytropic constant $n = -1$. Thus the molar heat capacity of gas in this process can be given as

$$C = \frac{R}{\gamma - 1} + \frac{R}{1 - n}$$

or $$= \frac{R}{\gamma - 1} + \frac{R}{2} \qquad [n = -1]$$

$$= \frac{R}{2} \left[\frac{\gamma + 1}{\gamma - 1} \right]$$

If during the process, temperature of gas changes from T_1 to T_2 then change in internal energy of gas is given as

$$\Delta U = C_V \Delta T \qquad [\text{As } n = 1 \text{ mole}]$$

$$= \frac{R}{\gamma - 1} (T_2 - T_1) \qquad [\text{As } C_V = \frac{R}{\gamma - 1}] \quad \ldots(3.93)$$

Here it is given that initial and final volumes of the gas are V_0 and $\eta\, V_0$. Thus the respective pressures in initial and final states are

$$P = \alpha V_0$$

and $$P = \alpha \eta V_0$$

Thus from gas law we can find initial and final temperatures as

$$T_1 = \frac{P_1 V_1}{R} = \frac{\alpha V_0 \cdot V_0}{R}$$

and $$T_2 = \frac{P_2 V_2}{R} = \frac{\alpha \eta V_0 \cdot \eta V_0}{R} \qquad [\text{As } n = 1 \text{ mole}]$$

Now from equation-(3.93), change in internal energy of gas is given as

$$\Delta U = \frac{R}{\gamma - 1} \left[\frac{\alpha \eta^2 V_0^2}{R} - \frac{\alpha V_0^2}{R} \right]$$

$$= \frac{\alpha V_0^2}{\gamma - 1} [\eta^2 - 1]$$

Illustrative Example 3.40

One mole of an ideal gas, whose adiabatic exponent equal to γ, is expanded so that the amount of heat transferred to the gas is equal to the decrease in internal energy. Find :

(a) the molar heat capacity of the gas in this process,

(b) the equation of the process in the variables T, V;

(c) the work performed by one mole of the gas when its volume increases η times if the initial temperature of gas is T_0.

Solution

(a) It is given that in the thermodynamic process amount of heat supplied is equal to the decrease in internal energy of gas thus we have in the process

$$dU = -dQ$$

or $\quad nC_V dT = -nCdT$

or $\quad C = -C_V = -\dfrac{R}{\gamma - 1}$ ...(3.94)

(b) Now from first law of thermodynamics, we have in this process

$$dQ = dU + dW$$

or $\quad 2dQ = dW$

or $\quad -\dfrac{2nR}{\gamma-1}\,dT = PdV$ ...(3.95)

We have differential form of gas law

$$PdV + VdP = \left(\frac{1-\gamma}{2}\right) PdV$$

or $\quad \left(\dfrac{1+\gamma}{2}\right) PdV = -VdP$

or $\quad \left(\dfrac{1+\gamma}{2}\right) \dfrac{dV}{V} = -\dfrac{dP}{P}$

Integrating this equation we get

$$\left(\frac{1+\gamma}{2}\right) \int \frac{dV}{V} = -\int \frac{dP}{P}$$

$$ln\, V^{\left(\frac{1+\gamma}{2}\right)} = -ln\, P + C$$

or $\quad PV^{\left(\frac{1+\gamma}{2}\right)} = \text{constant}$ ...(3.96)

As we require process equation in T and V, from gas law

$$P = \frac{nRT}{V}$$

Now from equation-(3)

$$\left(\frac{nRT}{V}\right) V^{\left(\frac{1+\gamma}{2}\right)} = \text{constant}$$

or $\quad TV^{\left(\frac{1-\gamma}{2}\right)} = \text{constant}$ ...(3.97)

[As nR = constant]

Process equation in P and V which is given in equation-(3.96) can be directly obtained by the molar heat capacity as from equation-(3.94). We can see that the value of C is a constant not depending on pressure, volume or temperature of gas thus we can say that this process is a polytropic process whose molar specific heat can be given as

$$C = \frac{R}{\gamma-1} + \frac{R}{1-n} = -\frac{R}{\gamma-1}$$

Where n is the polytropic constant of the process

or $\quad \dfrac{R}{1-n} = -\dfrac{2R}{\gamma-1}$

or $\quad (1-n) = -\dfrac{1}{2}(\gamma-1)$

or $\quad 2-2n = 1-\gamma$

or $\quad n = \left(\dfrac{1+\gamma}{2}\right)$

Thus now it is obvious that the process equation of this thermodynamic process in P and V can be simply given as

$$PV^n = \text{constant}$$

or $\quad PV^{\left(\frac{1+\gamma}{2}\right)} = \text{constant}$

Which is same as equation-(3.92)

(c) The work done by a gas in a polytropic process can be given as

$$W = n(C - C_V)(T_2 - T_1) \qquad ...(3.98)$$

Here initial temperature of gas is given as T_0 and the final temperature can be obtained from equation-(3.97) for initial and final state of gas as

$$T_1 V_1^{\left(\frac{\gamma-1}{2}\right)} = T_2 V_2^{\left(\frac{\gamma-1}{2}\right)}$$

Here $\quad T_1 = T_0$ and $V_2 = \eta V_1$, thus

$$T_2 = T_0 \left(\frac{V_1}{V_2}\right)^{\frac{\gamma-1}{2}} = T_0\, \eta^{\left(\frac{1-\gamma}{2}\right)}$$

Now from equation-(3.98), work done is

$$W = n(-C_V - C_V)(T_2 - T_1)$$

or $\quad W = -\dfrac{2R}{\gamma-1}\left[T_0 (\eta)^{\frac{1-\gamma}{2}} - T_0\right]$ [As $n = 1$ mole]

or $\quad W = \dfrac{2RT_0}{\gamma-1}\left[1 - (\eta)^{\frac{1-\gamma}{2}}\right]$

Web Reference at www.physicsgalaxy.com

Age Group - High School Physics | Age 17-19 Years

Section - HEAT & THERMODYNAMICS

Topic - Laws of Thermodynamics

Module Number - 29 to 34

Practice Exercise 3.4

(i) One mole of an ideal gas whose adiabatic exponent is γ undergoes a process in which the volume changes with temperatures as $V=\frac{\alpha}{T}$, where α is constant. Find the amount of heat required to raise its temperature by ΔT.

$[\frac{2-\gamma}{\gamma-1}\ R\Delta T]$

(ii) For the case of an ideal gas find the equation of the process (in the variables T, V) in which the molar heat capacity varies as :
(a) $C=C_V+\alpha T$;
(b) $C=C_V+\beta V$;
(c) $C=C_V+aP$, where α, β, and a are constants.

[(a) $Ve^{-\alpha T/R}$ = const; (b) $Te^{R/\beta V}$ = const; (c) $V-aT$ = const.]

(iii) A gas consisting of monatomic molecules (degrees of freedom = 3) was expanded in a polytropic process so that the rate of collisions of the molecules against the vessel's wall did not change. Find the molar heat capacity of the gas in the process.

[2 R]

(iv) A gas consisting of rigid diatomic molecules was expanded in a polytropic process so that the rate of collisions of the molecules against the vessel's wall did not change. Find the molar heat capacity of the gas in this process.

[3R]

(v) An ideal gas has an adiabatic exponent γ. In some process its molar heat capacity varies as $C=\alpha/T$, where α is a constant. Find :

(a) the work performed by one mole of the gas during its hating from the temperature T_0 to the temperature η times higher;

(b) the equation of the process in the variables p, V.

[(a) $\alpha\ \ln\eta - RT_0(\eta-1)/(\gamma-1)$; (b) $pV^{\gamma}e^{\alpha(\gamma-1)/pV}$ = const.]

(vi) The volume of a gas containing diatomic molecules was increased $\eta=2$ times in a polytropic process with molar heat capacity $C=R$. How many times will the rate of collision of molecules against the wall of vessel be reduced as a result of this process ?

[$2^{4/3}$ times]

(vii) One mole of an ideal gas whose adiabatic exponent equals γ undergoes a process in which the gas pressure relates to the temperature as $p=aT^{\alpha}$, where a and α are constants. Find :

(a) the work performed by the gas if its temperature gets an increment ΔT;

(b) the molar heat capacity of the gas in this process; at what value of α will the heat capacity be negative ?

[(a) $W=(1-\alpha)R\Delta T$; (b) $C=\frac{R}{(\gamma-1)}+R(1-\alpha)$; $C<0$ for $\alpha>\frac{\gamma}{(\gamma-1)}$]

(viii) A gas is taken from state-1 to state-2 from two different paths A and B as shown in figure-3.47. If molar heat capacities of the gas in the two paths are C_A and C_B respectively then which molar heat capacity is greater.

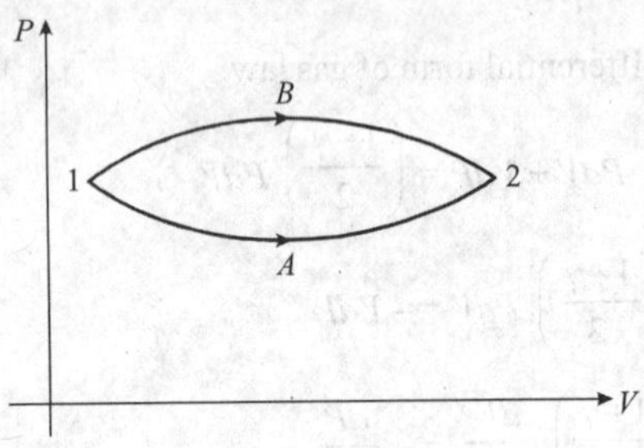

Figure 3.47

[C_B]

3.8 Second Law of Thermodynamics

Most of the thermodynamic processes in nature proceed in one direction but not in opposite direction, for example, we know heat always flows from a hot body to a colder body, never the reverse. There are so many examples in which mechanical energy is completely converted into heat and also so many devices exist which convert heat partially into mechanical energy. But till now there is no machine which can convert heat completely into mechanical energy. Why ? The answer to this question is the second law of thermodynamics. But before proceeding to second law of thermodynamics, we first discuss some basic things related to that.

3.8.1 Reversible Processes

Thermodynamic processes that occur in nature are all irreversible processes. This implies that if a gas is taken from its initial state to final state along a specified path, in practical nature it is not possible to carry the gas back to its initial state along the same path in reverse direction. Reversible processes are idealized in nature and can occur only when the system is in thermal equilibrium within itself and with its surroundings. When two systems are in thermal equilibrium, any change of state that take place can be reversed by making a very elemental change in the conditions of these systems. For example, heat flow between two bodies whose temperature differ by a very small amount can be reversed by making a very small variation in their temperatures. This we'll discuss in details later. Thus those processes which are reversible are also called equilibrium processes. We know when a system is in thermal equilibrium, no change of state takes place. As discussed, reversible process is an idealization that can never be possible in practical world.

But during a thermodynamic process if the process is carried out very slowly so that it can be considered to be in thermal equilibrium always or if it is of a quasi-static nature we can make such processes approximately reversible and these processes are called quasi-static processes. On the other hand all relatively fast processes or like heat flow with a temperature difference, free expansion of gas or conversion of work to heat are all irreversible processes, these are called, non equilibrium processes.

Now we'll discuss the second law of thermodynamics by considering two broad classes of devices. Heat engines and Refrigerators. Heat engines are partly successful in converting heat into work, and refrigerators are partly successful in transporting heat from colder to hotter bodies.

Earlier while discussing cyclic processes we've learned that the clockwise cycles are called the heat engine cycles and anticlockwise cycles are the refrigeration cycles. Now we discuss both in details.

3.8.2 Heat Engines

Any device that transforms heat partly into work or mechanical energy is called a heat engine. In a heat engine some quantity of a substance undergoes inflow and outflow of heat, expansion and compression and sometimes phase changes. This substance used in heat engine is called working substance or fuel.

The simplest heat engine is a thermodynamic system undergoes a clockwise cyclic process. If the cycle is repeated periodically it leaves the substance in the same state in which it started and during the process some heat is supplied in the expansion process and gas does some work and during compression part of cycle, some work (lesser then first part) is done on the gas and it rejects some heat to the surrounding, lesser then the amount absorbed during expansion. Thus according to first law of thermodynamics the total work done by the gas is equal to the amount of heat supplied to the gas minus the heat which is rejected by the gas during its compression to the initial state.

A heat engine does not use the same substance and over the cycles but it is changed after every cycle by some mechanism. All heat engine absorb heat from a source at a relatively high temperature, perform some mechanical work and reject some heat at relatively lower temperature. As engine is concerned, the rejected heat is wasted.

When we analyse the heat engine, it helps to think of two bodies with which the working substance of engine interact. One is the heat source and other is the heat sink. Heat source is the one which can supply large amount of heat to the working substance during first part of its cycle and heat sink is the one to which the working substance can reject heat after performing mechanical work during the second part of its cycle. As discussed heat source is at higher temperature and heat sink is at lower temperature.

Figure-3.48 shows the basic block diagram of a heat engine also called energy flow diagram of heat engine. In this diagram engine is represented by the circular block. During the cycle it takes a quantity of heat Q_1 from the heat source at high temperature T_1 and does mechanical work W and rejects a heat Q_2 to the heat sink at lower temperature T_2.

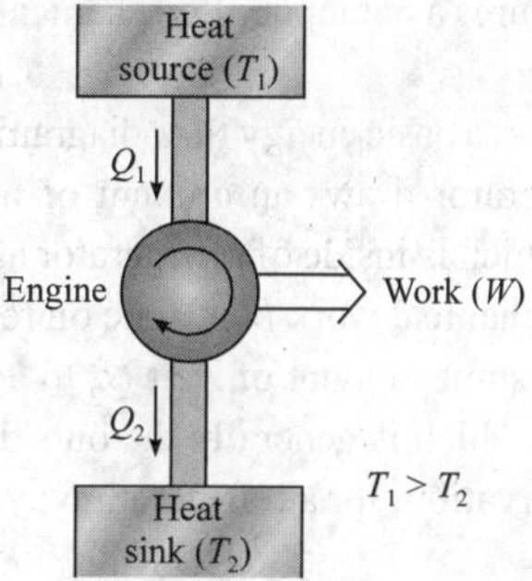

Figure 3.48

Here W is called useful power output of engine and Q_2 is the energy which is wasted. In a heat engine we would like to convert all input heat Q_1 into work but experiments show that it is impossible to have $Q_2 = 0$. According to conservation of energy we have

$$Q_1 = Q_2 + W \quad \text{...(3.99)}$$

3.8.3 Thermal Efficiency of a Heat Engine

Thermal efficiency of an engine gives the fraction of heat supplied to the engine which is transformed into the useful mechanical work. Thus thermal efficiency of a heat engine is given as

$$\eta = \frac{W}{Q_1} \quad \text{...(3.100)}$$

From equation-(3.99) we have

$$W = Q_1 - Q_2$$

Thus $$\eta = \frac{Q_1 - Q_2}{Q_1} = 1 - \frac{Q_2}{Q_1} \quad \dots (3.101)$$

or $$\eta = 1 - \left|\frac{Q_{out}}{Q_{in}}\right| \quad \dots (3.102)$$

At the time of designing of the engines, designers always try to develop a mechanism in which the amount of useful mechanical work is as wide as possible and to keep the rejected heat as narrow as possible. As Q_2 can never be zero and no engine is having efficiency equal to unity.

3.8.4 Refrigerators

Refrigerator is a device just like a heat engine operating in reverse fashion. A heat engine takes heat from a hot place and gives off heat to a colder place. A refrigerator does the opposite of this. It takes heat from a place at lower temperature and gives it off to a place at relatively higher temperature. A heat engine has a net output of mechanical work where as a refrigerator requires a net input of mechanical work.

Figure-3.49 shows a basic energy flow diagram of a refrigerator. Here the refrigerator draws an amount of heat Q_1 from the colder region which is inside of refrigerator at temperature T_1. An external mechanical work W is done on refrigerator due to which it rejects some amount of heat Q_2 to a region at higher temperature T_2, which is generally the outside air. According to energy conservation, for a refrigeration cycle we can write

$$Q_1 + W = Q_2 \quad \dots (3.103)$$

or $$W = Q_2 - Q_1 \quad \dots (3.104)$$

The best refrigeration cycle is one that removes the greatest amount of heat Q_1 from the inside of refrigerator for the least amount of mechanical work W. The ratio (Q_1/W), we call this ratio the coefficient of performance of a refrigerator, and it gives the quality of refrigeration cycle. The larger this ratio, the better the refrigerator.

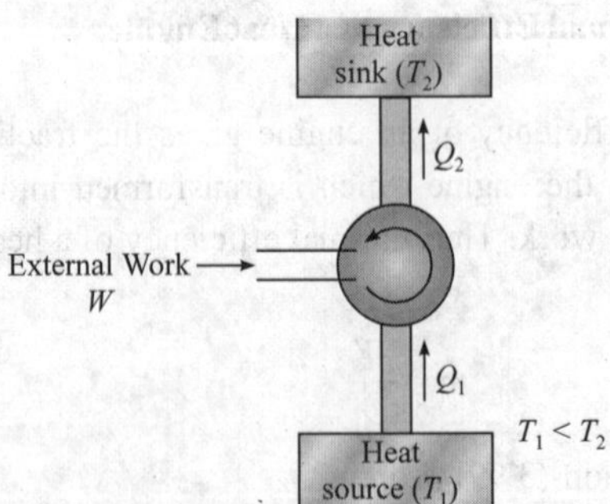

Figure 3.49

The coefficient of performance of a refrigeration cycle is

$$K = \frac{Q_1}{W} = \frac{Q_1}{Q_2 - Q_1} \quad \dots (3.105)$$

3.8.5 Statement of Second Law of Thermodynamics

We've discussed that experiments showed that it is impossible to build a heat engine that converts heat completely to work, that is an engine with 100% thermal efficiency. This leads to the basic statement of second law of thermodynamics. Stated as

"It is impossible for any system to absorb heat and convert it completely into mechanical work leaving the system in its initial state from which the process was started."

The analysis of refrigerator we've discussed in previous section forms the basis for an alternative statement of the second law of thermodynamics. We know heat always flows spontaneously from hotter to colder bodies, never the reverse. A refrigerator does take heat from a colder to a hotter region, but its operation requires an input of mechanical energy or work. Thus we state.

"It is impossible for any process to have only the heat flow from a colder to a hotter body without any involvement of an external agency."

3.8.6 Carnot Cycle

According to second law of thermodynamics, no heat engine can have 100% efficiency. Efficiency of a heat engine depends on the amount of heat taken in and outflow from the heat engine. In 1824, a French scientist Carnot developed a hypothetical, idealized heat engine that has maximum possible efficiency consistent with the second law. The cycle of this engine is called the Carnot Cycle. Now we'll discuss the basic theme of this cycle.

We know conversion of work to heat is an irreversible process and the purpose of a heat engine is a partial reversal of this process, the conversion of heat to work with a given efficiency. The higher the efficiency is, the better the engine will be. For maximum efficiency we must avoid the irreversible processes. This forms the basis of Carnot cycle.

Heat flow through a finite temperature drop is an irreversible process. In carnot cycle when engine takes heat from heat source at temperature T_1, the engine temperature or the temperature of working substance is also at same temperature T_1. Similarly when engine rejects heat to the sink at the lower temperature T_2 then during this rejection of heat, engine is also at the same temperature T_2. The cycle will be ideal if engine does not exchange any heat during the process when its temperature is changing thus in a single line we can state that every process in the idealized carnot cycle must be either isothermal or adiabatic.

An ideal Carnot cycle is accomplished in four steps, there are:

(1) The gas or working substance expands isothermally at temperature T_1 and absorbs an amount of heat Q_1 from heat source at temperature T_1.

(2) It expands adiabatically until its temperature drops to T_2 where T_2 is the temperature of heat sink.

(3) It is compressed isothermally at temperature T_2 and rejects an amount of heat Q_2 to the sink.

(4) Now it is compressed adiabatically back to its initial sate at temperature T_1.

Figure-3.50 shows an indicator diagram for an ideal gas undergoing in carnot cycle.

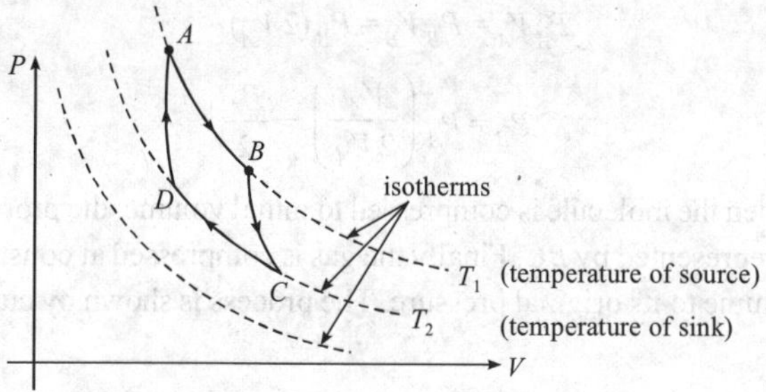

Figure 3.50

As shown in figure-3.49 in a carnot cycle, first gas starts from state-A and in its isothermal expansion upto state-B heat absorbed by the gas is

$$Q_1 = W_{ab} = n R T_1 \ln\left(\frac{V_B}{V_A}\right) \quad \ldots(3.106)$$

Here V_B and V_A are the volumes of the gas at state (A) and state (B) respectively. Similarly in isothermal compression of gas from state (C) to state (D), heat rejected by the gas is

$$Q_2 = W_{cd} = n R T_2 \ln\left(\frac{V_C}{V_D}\right) \quad \ldots(3.107)$$

In the adiabatic processes from state (B) to state (C) and from state (D) to state (A), we can relate temperatures and volumes of gas as

$$T_1 V_B^{\gamma-1} = T_2 V_C^{\gamma-1} \quad \ldots(3.108)$$

and $$T_1 V_A^{\gamma-1} = T_2 V_D^{\gamma-1} \quad \ldots(3.109)$$

From equation-(3.108) and equation-(3.109), we get

$$\frac{V_B}{V_A} = \frac{V_C}{V_D} \quad \ldots(3.110)$$

From equation-(3.106) and (3.107), we get

$$\frac{Q_2}{Q_1} = \frac{n R T_2 \ln\left(\frac{V_C}{V_D}\right)}{-n R T_1 \ln\left(\frac{V_B}{V_A}\right)} = -\frac{T_2}{T_1} \quad \ldots(3.111)$$

or $$\left|\frac{Q_2}{Q_1}\right| = \frac{T_2}{T_1}$$

Thus the efficiency of a carnot cycle can be given as

$$\eta = 1 - \left|\frac{Q_2}{Q_1}\right|$$

$$\eta = 1 - \frac{T_2}{T_1} \quad \ldots(3.112)$$

This shows that efficiency of a carnot cycle depends only on the temperatures of heat source and heat sink and is large when temperature difference of the two is large and it is very small when the temperatures are very close to each other.

Illustrative Example 3.41

One mole of oxygen undergoes a cyclic process in which volume of the gas changes 10 times within the cycle as shown in figure-3.51. The processes *AB* and *CD* are adiabatic while processes *BC* and *DA* are isochoric. What is the efficiency of the process ?

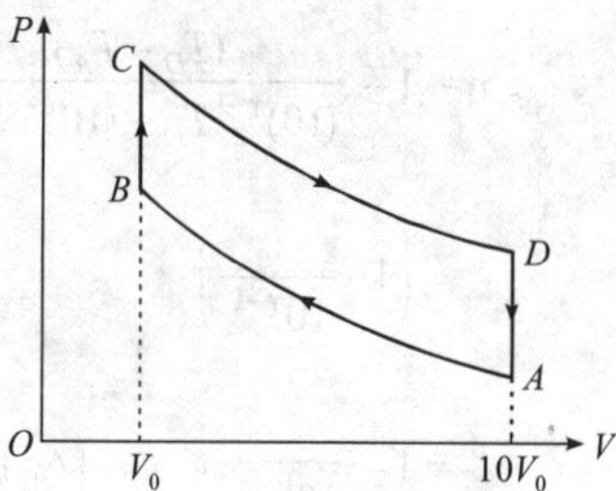

Figure 3.51

Solution

In the cyclic process the efficiency of cycle can be given as

$$\eta = 1 - \left|\frac{Q_{out}}{Q_{in}}\right| \quad \ldots(3.113)$$

As the process *CD* and *AB* are adiabatic, no heat exchange takes place in these processes. In isochoric process *BC* as temperature increases, the heat is taken in which is given as

$$Q_{in} = n\,C_V(T_C - T_B)$$

$$= \frac{5}{2} R(T_C - T_B) \quad \ldots(3.114)$$

[As $n = 1$ mole and for O_2 $C_V = \frac{5}{2}R$]

Similarly in isochoric process A as temperature decreases heat is rejected by the gas, which is given as

$$Q_{out} = n\,C_V(T_D - T_A)$$

[Magnitude of heat rejected]

$$= \frac{5}{2} R(T_D - T_A) \quad \ldots(3.115)$$

From equation-(3.113), (3.114) and (3.115), we have

Efficiency $$\eta = 1 - \frac{T_D - T_A}{T_C - T_B} \quad \ldots(3.116)$$

As we know in an adiabatic process the volume and temperature of gas in initial and final states are related as

$$T_1 V_1^{\gamma-1} = T_2 V_2^{\gamma-1}$$

Here we use the same relation for process CD and AB as

$$T_C V_0^{\gamma-1} = T_D (10\,V_0)^{\gamma-1}$$

or $$T_C = (10^{\gamma-1})\,T_D \quad \ldots(3.117)$$

and $$T_B V_0^{\gamma-1} = T_A (10\,V_0)^{\gamma-1}$$

or $$T_B = (10^{\gamma-1})\,T_A \quad \ldots(3.118)$$

Now from equation-(3.116), (3.117) and (3.118), we have

Efficiency $$\eta = 1 - \frac{(T_D - T_A)}{(10)^{\gamma-1}T_D - (10)^{\gamma-1}T_A}$$

or $$= \left(1 - \frac{1}{10^{\gamma-1}}\right)$$

$$= 1 - \frac{1}{10^{0.4}} \quad \text{[As for } O_2, \gamma = 1.4]$$

$$= 0.6 = 60\,\%$$

 # Illustrative Example 3.42

Three moles of an ideal gas ($C_P = \frac{7}{2}R$) at pressure P_A and temperature T_A is isothermally expanded to twice its initial volume. It is then compressed at constant pressure to its original volume. Finally the gas is compressed at constant volume to its original pressure P_A.

(a) Sketch P-V and P-T diagrams for the complete process.

(b) Calculate the new work done by the gas, and net heat supplied to the gas during the complete process.

Solution

(a) Sketch of P-V and P-T are shown in figure-3.52(a) and (b).

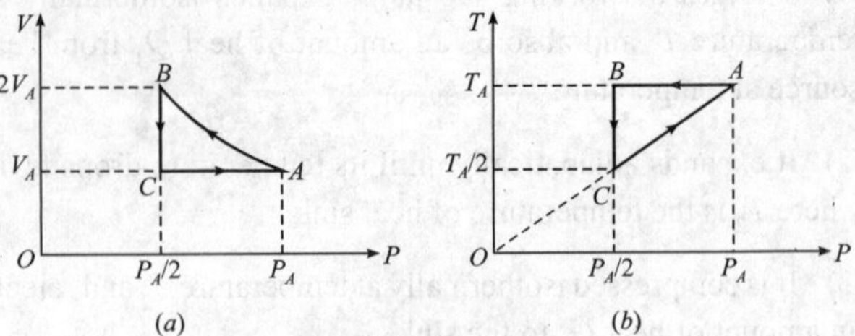

Figure 3.52

The initial state of isothermal expansion is represented by A where pressure is P_A and volume is V_A. Let the final state is represented by B where volume V_B is twice of V_A. Let the pressure be P_B. Then

$$P_A V_A = P_B V_B = P_B (2\,V_A)$$

or $$P_B = P_A \left(\frac{V_A}{2\,V_A}\right) = \frac{P_A}{2}$$

When the molecule is compressed to initial volume, the process is represented by BC. Finally the gas is compressed at constant volume to its original pressure. The process is shown by curve CA.

Similarly, P-T diagram can be drawn.

(b) Workdone in the process AB is given by

$$W_1 = nR\,T\,ln\,(V_B/V_A)$$

$$= 3 \times 8.314 \times T_A \times ln\,2$$

$$= 3 \times 8.314 \times T_A \times 0.693 = 17.29\,T_A$$

Workdone in the process BC is given by

$$W_2 = P\,\Delta V = P_B \times (V_C - V_B)$$

$$= \frac{P_A}{2} \times (V_A - 2V_A)$$

$$= -P_A V_A/2 = -n\,R\,T_A/2$$

$$= -3\,R\,T_A/2 = -3 \times 8.314\,T_A/2 = -12.471\,T_A$$

Workdone during process CA is given by

$$W_3 = P\,\Delta V = 0 \quad \text{[As } \Delta V = 0]$$

Network $$W = W_1 + W_2 + W_3$$

$$= 17.26\,T_A - 12.45\,T_A = 4.81\,T_A.$$

As initial and final states of the gas are same, hence

$$\Delta U = U_A - U_A = 0$$

From first law of thermodynamics

$$\Delta Q = \Delta U + \Delta W = 0 + \Delta W$$

$$Q = W \text{ joule}$$

Illustrative Example 3.43

One mole of a diatomic ideal gas ($\gamma = 1.4$) is taken through a cyclic process as shown in figure-3.53 starting from point A. In this cycle the process AB is an adiabatic compression. BC is isobaric, CD an adiabatic expansion and DA is isochoric. The volume ratios are $V_A/V_B = 16$ and $V_C/V_B = 2$ and the temperature at A to $T_A = 300°K$. Calculate the temperature of the gas at the point B and D and find the efficiency of the cycle.

Solution

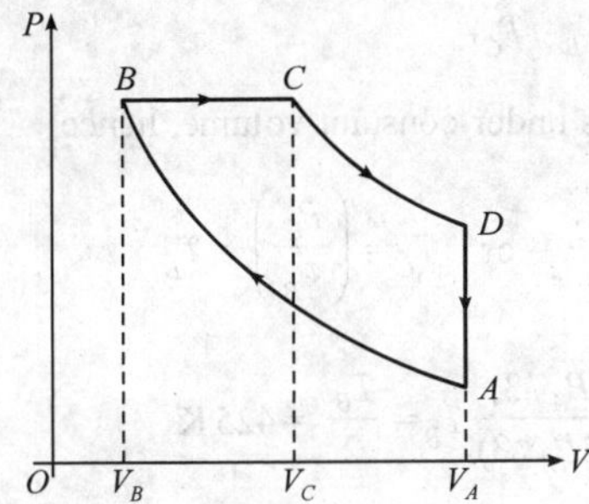

Figure 3.53

The respective cyclic process is shown in figure-3.53. The expansion and compression ratio are given as

$$\frac{V_A}{V_B} = 16 \quad \text{and} \quad \frac{V_C}{V_B} = 2$$

In adiabatic process AB, we have

$$T_A V_A^{\gamma-1} = T_B V_B^{\gamma-1}$$

or

$$T_B = T_A \left(\frac{V_A}{V_B}\right)^{\gamma-1}$$

$$= 300 \times (16)^{0.4}$$

$$= 909\text{ K}$$

Similarly for isobaric process BC, we have

$$\frac{T_C}{V_C} = \frac{T_B}{V_B}$$

or

$$T_C = T_B \left(\frac{V_C}{V_B}\right) \quad \ldots(3.119)$$

$$= 909 \times 2 = 1818\text{ K}$$

Similarly for adiabatic process CD we have

$$T_C V_C^{\gamma-1} = T_D V_D^{\gamma-1}$$

or

$$T_D = T_C \left(\frac{V_C}{V_D}\right)^{\gamma-1}$$

As we have $V_D = V_A$, thus

$$\frac{V_C}{V_D} = \frac{V_C}{V_A} = \frac{V_C}{V_B} \times \frac{V_B}{V_A}$$

$$= 2 \times \frac{1}{16} = \frac{1}{8}$$

Thus from equation-(3.119)

$$T_D = 1818 \times \left(\frac{1}{8}\right)^{0.4}$$

$$= 791.3\text{ K}$$

The efficiency of cycle can be given as

$$\eta = 1 - \left|\frac{Q_{out}}{Q_{in}}\right|$$

Here we know in process AB and CD, as being adiabatic processes no heat exchange takes place and in isobaric process BC as temperature of gas increases, heat is taken in (say Q_1) and it is given as

$$Q_1 = nC_P(T_C - T_B) \quad \ldots(3.120)$$

Similarly in isochoric process DA as temperature of gas decreases heat is rejected (say Q_2) and it can be given as

$$Q_2 = nC_P(T_D - T_A)$$

[A magnitude of rejected heat]

Now efficiency of this cycle can be given as

$$\eta = 1 - \left|\frac{Q_{out}}{Q_{in}}\right|$$

$$= 1 - \frac{Q_2}{Q_1}$$

$$= 1 - \frac{C_V(T_D - T_A)}{C_P(T_C - T_B)}$$

$$= \frac{T_D - T_A}{\gamma(T_C - T_B)}$$

$$= \frac{(791.3 - 300)}{(1.4)(1818 - 909)}$$

$$= 1 - \frac{491.3}{1272.6} = 0.614 = 61.4\%$$

NOTE : While solving the problems related to finding the efficiency of a cycle students are advised to first check in which of the path of cycle heat is taken in or heat is rejected and mansion it by arrows as for above problem Q_1 and Q_2 can be mentioned as shown in figure-3.54.

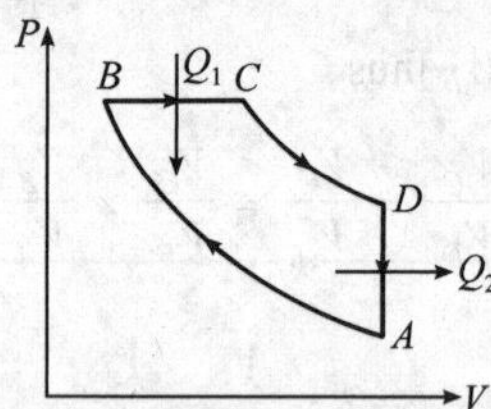

Figure 3.54

 # Illustrative Example 3.44

One mole of a monatomic ideal gas is taken through the cycle shown in figure-3.55.

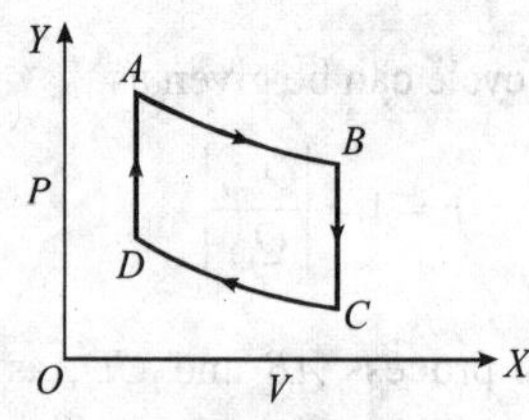

Figure 3.55

$A \rightarrow B$ adiabatic, expansion
$B \rightarrow C$ cooling at constant volume
$C \rightarrow D$ adiabatic compression
$D \rightarrow A$ heating at constant volume

The pressure and temperature at A, B etc. are denoted by P_A, P_B, ...; T_A, T_B, ..., etc. respectively. Given that

$T_A = 1000$ K, $P_B = (2/3)\,P_A$ and $P_C = (1/3)\,P_A$.

Calculate the following quantities :

(i) The work done by the gas in process $A \rightarrow B$

(ii) The heat lost by the gas in process $B \rightarrow C$

(iii) The temperature T_D

Given that $(2/3)^{2/5} = 0.85$

Solution

(i) The workdone in adiabatic process AB is given by

$$W_1 = \frac{R(T_A - T_B)}{\gamma - 1} = \frac{R(T_A - T_B)}{(5/3) - 1}$$

[As for monatomic gas $\gamma = 5/3$]

or $$W_1 = \frac{3}{2}\,R(T_A - T_B) \quad \ldots (3.121)$$

For adiabatic change

$$P_A^{\gamma-1}\,T_A^{-\gamma} = P_B^{\gamma-1}\,T_B^{-\gamma}$$

or $$\left(\frac{P_A}{P_B}\right)^{2/3} = \left(\frac{T_A}{T_B}\right)^{5/3} \text{ or } \left(\frac{T_A}{T_B}\right) = \left(\frac{P_A}{P_B}\right)^{2/5}$$

or $$\left(\frac{T_A}{T_B}\right) = \left(\frac{3}{2}\right)^{2/5} \quad [\text{As } P_B = (2/3)\,P_A]$$

or $$T_B = T_A\left(\frac{2}{3}\right)^{2/5} \quad \ldots (3.122)$$

$$= 1000 \times 0.85 = 850 \text{ K}$$

From equation-(3.121)

$$W_1 = \frac{3}{2} \times 8.31 \times (1000 - 850) = 1869.83 \text{ J}$$

(ii) Heat lost by the gas in process BC is given by

$$= C_V(T_B - T_C) = \frac{R}{\gamma - 1}\,(T_B - T_C)$$

$$= \frac{3}{2}\,R\,(T_B - T_C) \quad \ldots (3.123)$$

Process BC is under constant volume, hence

$$\frac{P_B}{T_B} = \frac{P_C}{T_C} \text{ or } T_C = \left(\frac{P_C}{P_B}\right) \times T_B$$

or $$T_C = \frac{(P_A/3)}{(2P_A/3)}\,T_B = \frac{T_B}{2} = 425 \text{ K} \quad \ldots (3.124)$$

From equation-(3.123)

$$\text{Heat lost} = \frac{3}{2} \times 8.31 \times (850 - 425) = 5297.63 \text{ J}$$

(iii) For path AB

$$P_A^{\gamma-1}\,T_A^{-\gamma} = P_B^{\gamma-1}\,T_B^{-\gamma}$$

or $$\left(\frac{P_A}{P_B}\right)^{\gamma-1} = \left(\frac{T_A}{T_B}\right)^{\gamma} \quad \ldots (3.125)$$

For path BC

$$\frac{P_B}{T_B} = \frac{P_C}{T_C} \text{ or } \left(\frac{P_B}{P_C}\right) = \left(\frac{T_B}{T_C}\right) \quad \ldots (3.126)$$

For path CD

$$\left(\frac{P_D}{P_C}\right)^{\gamma-1} = \left(\frac{T_D}{T_C}\right)^{\gamma} \quad \ldots (3.127)$$

For path AD

$$\left(\frac{P_A}{P_D}\right) = \left(\frac{T_A}{T_D}\right) \quad \ldots (3.128)$$

Dividing equation-(3.125) by (3.127), we get

$$\left(\frac{P_A}{P_B}\times\frac{P_C}{P_D}\right)^{\gamma-1}=\left(\frac{T_A}{T_B}\times\frac{T_C}{T_D}\right)^{\gamma} \qquad \ldots(3.129)$$

Dividing equation-(3.128) by equation-(3.126) we get

$$\left(\frac{P_A}{P_B}\times\frac{P_C}{P_D}\right)=\left(\frac{T_A}{T_B}\times\frac{T_C}{T_D}\right)$$

or

$$\left(\frac{P_A}{P_B}\times\frac{P_C}{P_D}\right)^{\gamma-1}=\left(\frac{T_A}{T_B}\times\frac{T_C}{T_D}\right)^{\gamma-1} \qquad \ldots(3.130)$$

From equation-(3.129) and (3.130)

$$\left(\frac{T_A}{T_B}\times\frac{T_C}{T_D}\right)^{\gamma}=\left(\frac{T_A}{T_B}\times\frac{T_C}{T_D}\right)^{\gamma-1}$$

$$T_A T_C = T_D T_B$$

$$1000\times 425 = T_D\times 850$$

$$T_D = 500\,\text{K}$$

Illustrative Example 3.45

Figure-3.56 shows three isothermals at temperature $T_1 = 4000$ K, $T_2 = 2000$ K, $T_3 = 1000$ K. When one mole of an ideal monatomic gas is taken through the paths AB, BC, CD and DA, find the change in internal energy ΔU, the workdone by the gas W and the heat Q absorbed by the gas in each path. Also find these quantities for complete cycle $ABCDA$.
Given $V_A = 1\ \text{m}^3$ and $V_B = 2\ \text{m}^3$.

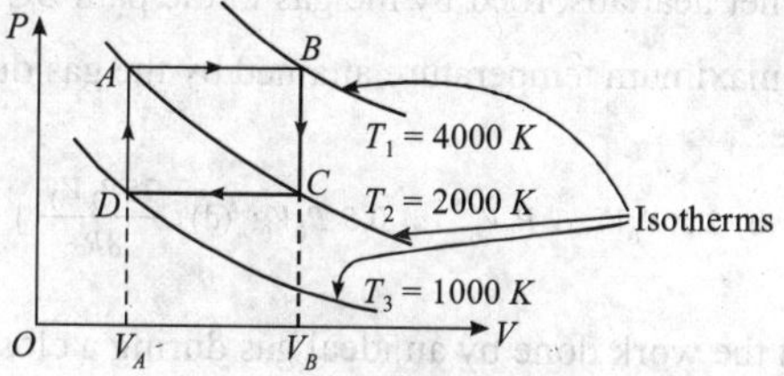

Figure 3.56

Solution

(i) When one mole of an ideal gas undergoes a change in temperature ΔT, the change in its internal energy equals $C_V\Delta T$, where C_V is the molar specific heat of the gas at constant volume. For monoatomic gas $C_V = (3/2)\,R$. Thus the change of internal energy is given by

$$\Delta U_{AB} = C_V(T_B - T_A)$$

$$= (3/2)\,R\,(4000 - 2000) = 3000\,\text{R}$$

$$= 3000\times 8.31 = 24.93\times 10^3\ \text{J}$$

$$\Delta U_{BC} = C_V(T_C - T_B)$$

$$= (3/2)\,R\,(2000 - 4000) = -3000\,R$$

$$= -24.93\times 10^3\ \text{J}$$

$$\Delta U_{CD} = C_V(T_D - T_C)$$

$$= (3/2)\,R\,(1000 - 2000) = -1500\,\text{R}$$

$$= -12.465\times 10^3\ \text{J}$$

$$\Delta U_{DA} = C_V(T_A - T_D)$$

$$= (3/2)\,R\,(2000 - 1000) = 1500\,\text{R}$$

$$= +12.465\times 10^3\ \text{J}$$

Total $\quad \Delta U = 0$

(ii) Workdone by gas during path AB under constant pressure

$$= P(V_2 - V_1) = R(T_1 - T_2) = 8.314\times 2000$$

$$= 16.62\times 10^3\ \text{J}$$

No work is done during BC and DA

Workdone on the gas during CD

$$= R(T_2 - T_1) = 8.314\times 1000 = 8.314\times 10^3\ \text{J}$$

Net workdone by the gas during the cycle

$$= (16.62\times 10^3 - 8.314\times 10^3) = 8.314\times 10^3\ \text{J}$$

(iii) Heat absorbed during

$$AB = C_P(T_1 - T_2)$$

$$= \frac{R\gamma}{\gamma-1}\times 2000 = \frac{8.314\times(5/3)}{(5/3)-1}\times 2000$$

[As $\gamma = 5/3$ for monoatomic gas]

$$= 8.314\times\frac{3}{2}\times 2000 = 41.55\times 10^3\ \text{J}$$

Heat released during

$$BC = C_V(T_1 - T_2)$$

$$= \frac{R}{\gamma-1}\times 2000$$

$$= 8.314\times\frac{3}{2}\times 2000 = 24.93\times 10^3\ \text{J}$$

Heat released during

$$CD = \frac{R\gamma}{\gamma-1}\times 1000$$

$$= 8.314\times\frac{5}{2}\times 1000$$

$$= 20.775\times 10^3\ \text{J}$$

Heat absorbed during

$$DA = \frac{R}{\gamma - 1} \times 1000$$

$$= 8.314 \times \frac{3}{2} \times 10^3 \text{ J}$$

$$= 12.465 \times 10^3 \text{ J}$$

Net heat absorbed by the gas during the cycle

$$= (12.465 + 41.55 - 20.775 - 24.93) \times 10^3 \text{ J}$$

$$= 8.314 \times 10^3 \text{ J}$$

Web Reference at www.physicsgalaxy.com

Age Group - High School Physics | Age 17-19 Years
Section - HEAT & THERMODYNAMICS
Topic - Laws of Thermodynamics
Module Number - 35 to 38

Practice Exercise 3.5

(i) An ideal gas undergoes in a thermodynamic cyclic process shown in figure-3.57. Find the work done by the gas in complete cycle.

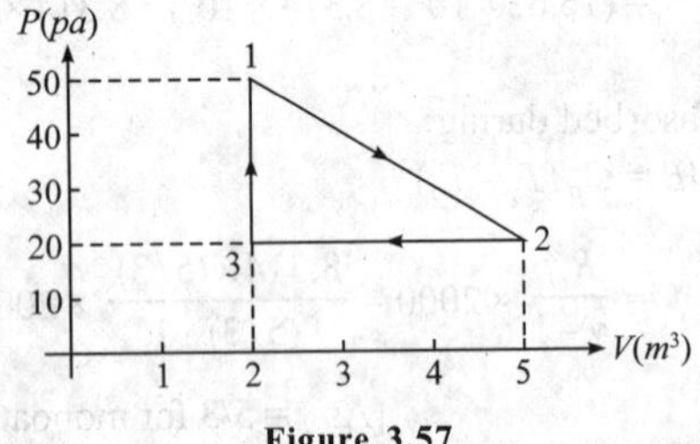

Figure 3.57

[45 J]

(ii) Figure-3.58 shows the *VT* graph of a thermodynamic process in which gas temperature changes from 300 K to 500 K during isochoric part of the cycle and volume of gas is doubled during isothermal part of the cycle. This graph is plotted for 2 mole of a gas. Find the total heat rejected by the gas in the complete cycle.

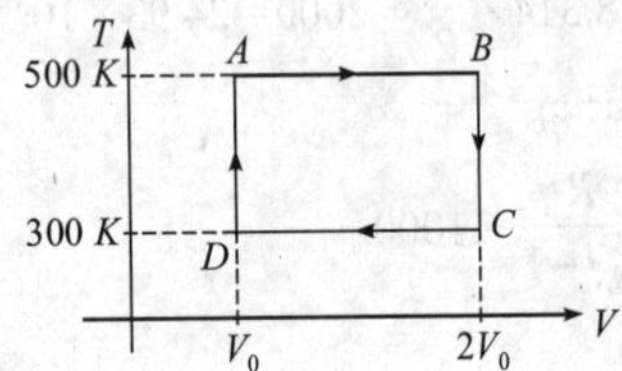

Figure 3.58

[– 2304.64 J]

(iii) Two moles of an ideal monoatomic gas is taken through a cycle *ABCA* as shown in the *PT* diagram in figure-3.59. During the process *AB*, pressure and temperature of the gas vary such that *PT* = constant. If T_0 = 300 K, calculate

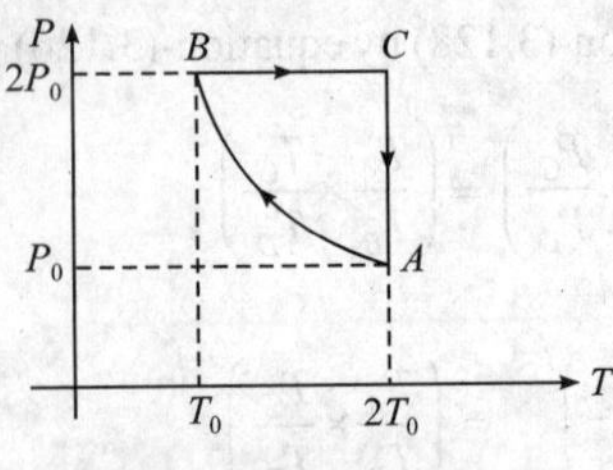

Figure 3.59

(a) The work done by the gas in the process *AB*

(b) The heat absorbed or released by the gas in each of the process.

[(a) – 1200 R; (b) – 2100 R, 1500 R, 831.6 R]

(iv) One mole of an ideal monoatomic gas is taken round the cyclic process *ABCA* as shown in figure-3.60. Calculate

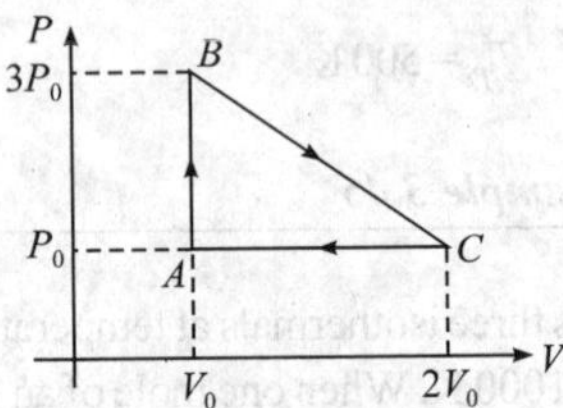

Figure 3.60

(a) The work done by the gas.

(b) The heat rejected by the gas in the path *CA* and the heat absorbed by the gas in the path *AB*.

(c) The net heat absorbed by the gas in the path *BC*.

(d) The maximum temperature attained by the gas during the cycle.

[(a) P_0V_0; (b) 2.5 P_0V_0, 3 P_0V_0; (c) 0.5 P_0V_0; (d) $\frac{25P_0V_0}{8R}$]

(v) Find the work done by an ideal gas during a closed cycle 1 – 4 – 3 – 2 – 1 as shown if $P_1 = 10^5$ Pa, $P_0 = 3 \times 10^5$ Pa, $P_2 = 4 \times 10^5$ Pa, $V_2 - V_1 = 100$ litre and segments 4 – 3 and 2 – 1 of the cycle are parallel to the *V*-axis.

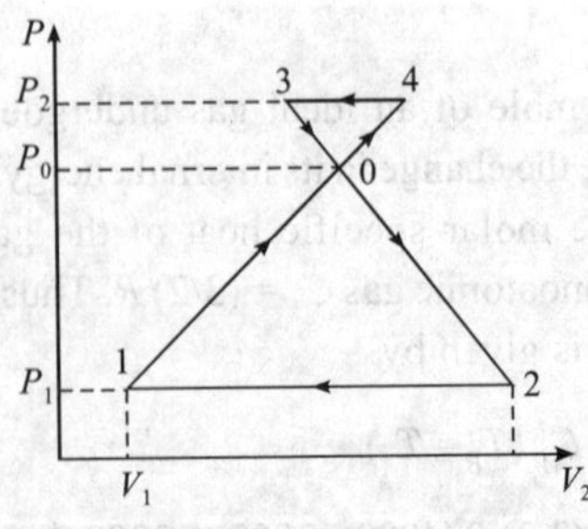

Figure 3.61

[7500 J]

(vi) Three moles of an ideal monoatomic gas perform a cyclic process as shown in the figure-3.62. The gas temperature in different states are $T_1 = 400\ K$, $T_2 = 800\ K$, $T_3 = 2400\ K$, and $T_4 = 1200\ K$. Find the work done during the cycle.

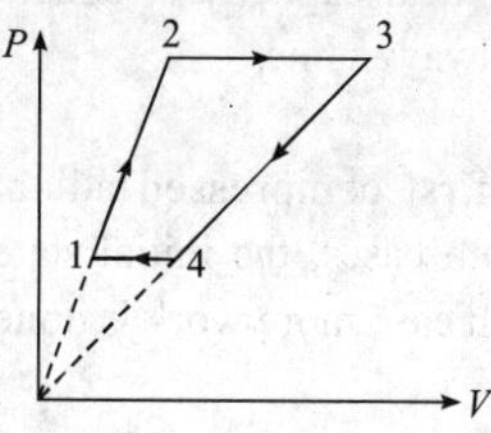

Figure 3.62

[9976.8 J]

(vii) An ideal gas with the adiabatic exponent γ goes a cycle (figure-3.63) within which the absolute temperature varies *n*-fold. Find the efficiency of this cycle.

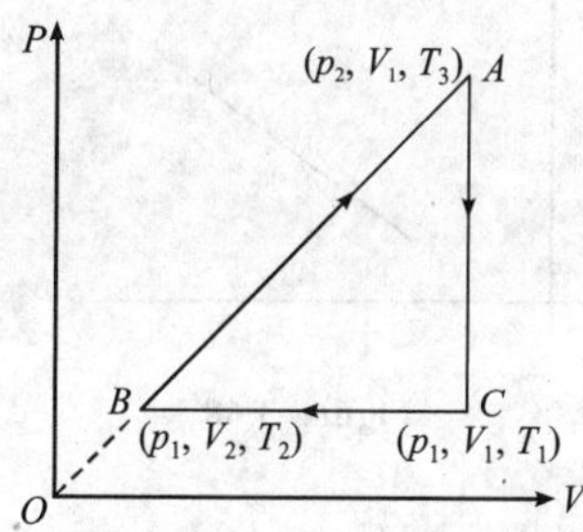

Figure 3.63

$[\left(\frac{\gamma-1}{\gamma+1}\right)\left(\frac{n-1}{n+1}\right)]$

(viii) An ideal gas with the adiabatic exponent γ goes through a direct (clockwise) cycle consisting of adiabatic, isobaric and isochoric lines. Find the efficiency of the cycle if in the adiabatic process the volume of the ideal gas increases *n*-fold.

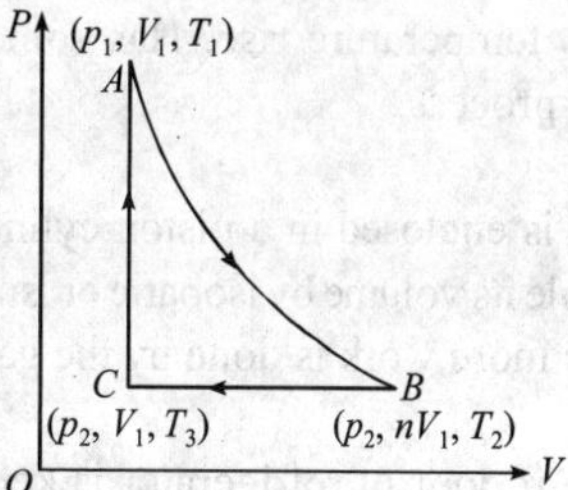

Figure 3.64

$[1 - \gamma\frac{n-1}{n^{\gamma}-1}]$

(ix) An ideal gas whose adiabatic exponent is equal to γ goes through a cycle consisting of two isochoric and two isobaric lines as shown in figure-3.65. Find the efficiency of such a cycle, if the absolute temperature of the gas rises *n* times both in isochoric heating and in isobaric expansion.

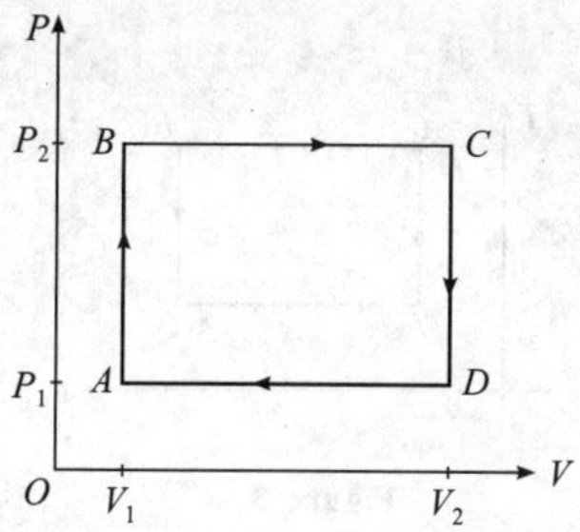

Figure 3.65

$[\frac{(\gamma-1)(n-1)}{1+n\gamma}]$

* * * * *

Discussion Question

Q3-1 When a thermos flask with some water in it is vigorously shaken. Does its temperature rise. Has some heat added to water during the process.

Q3-2 Some gas is enclosed in a piston-cylinder system. It is expanded to double its volume by isobaric or isothermal process. In which process more work is done by the gas.

Q3-3 In a room if door of refrigerator is kept open, will the room temperature decrease.

Q3-4 When a block moves in a straight line on a rough surface. Some heat is dissipated. Is this process reversible.

Q3-5 Can we convert mechanical work completely into heat.

Q3-6 Can we convert heat completely into mechanical work in a cyclic process.

Q3-7 Draw the *PV* diagram of the process shown in figure-3.66 in *VT* diagrams.

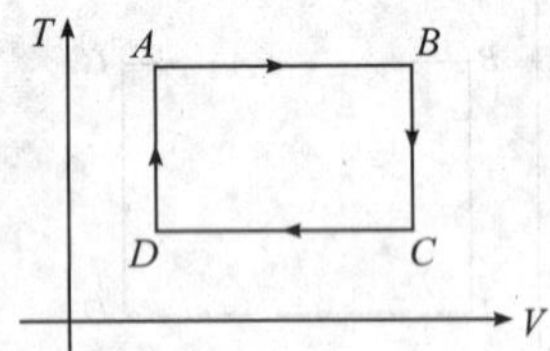

Figure 3.66

Q3-8 When a gas is compressed, it becomes more elastic. Explain.

Q3-9 When we whistle out air on to palm held close to mouth, the air feels cold, but when we blow air out from mouth, keeping it wide open, the air feels hot. Explain.

Q3-10 One mole of an ideal gas changes its state from state-1 to state-2 along the two paths I and II as shown in figure-3.67. In which of the process is the amount of heat absorbed by the gas more. Explain.

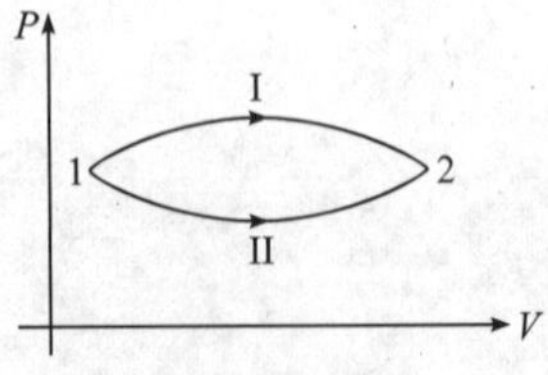

Figure 3.67

Q3-11 Plot approximate graphs between pressure and internal energy of a sample of gas for these processes, (a) isobaric, (b) isochoric, (c) isothermal and (d) adiabatic.

Q3-12 Represent the Carnot cycle on a *VT* diagram.

Q3-13 The molar heat capacity at constant pressure of all diatomic gases is always same.

Q3-14 A gas is first compressed adiabatically and then isothermally. In both cases, the initial state of the gas is the same. Find in which case more work is done on the gas.

Q3-15 In the polytropic process PV^2 = constant, is the gas cooled or heated with increase in volume.

Q3-16 In the following *PT*-graph shown in figure-3.68, find what happens to the volume of gas on increasing temperature of the gas.

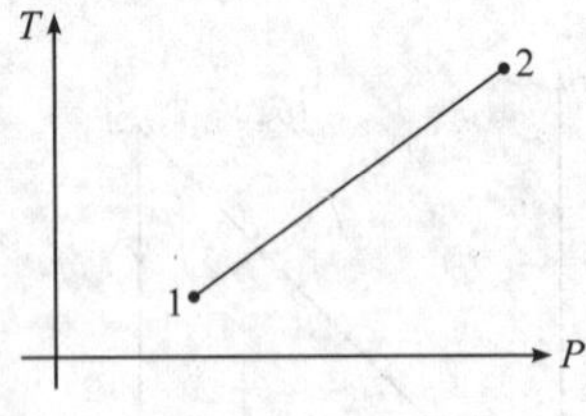

Figure 3.68

Q3-17 In the following *VT*-graph shown in figure-3.69, find what happens to the pressure of the gas on increasing temperature of the system.

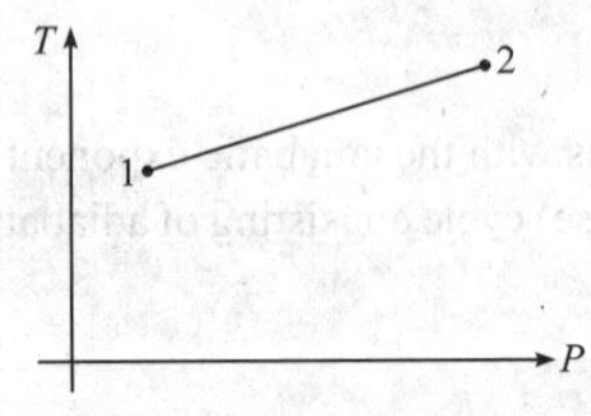

Figure 3.69

Q3-18 What happens to the internal energy of water vapour in the air that condenses on the outside of a cold glass of water ? Is work done or heat exchanged ?

Q3-19 When a mountaineer who eats food, gets warm a lot during a climb and does a lot of mechanical work in raising himself upwards. When he descents, again he also gets warm during descent. Is the source of this energy the same as during the ascent.

Q3-20 The temperature of a gas is increasing, hence its internal energy also increases. Just be observing initial and final states, can we determine whether the internal energy increment was due to work or by heat transfer.

Q3-21 When a hand pump is used to inflate the tires of a bicycle, the pump gets warm after a while. Why ?

Q3-22 There are few materials that contracts when their temperature is increased, such as water between 0ºC and 4ºC. Would you expect C_p for such materials to be greater or less than C_v ?

Q3-23 A disc rotated about its central axis and gently placed on another coaxial disc at rest. Due to friction between the two first disc retards and the second one starts rotating and after some time both with rotate with a common angular speed. In this process the total internal energy of the system of two discs does not change. State and justify whether this statement is true or false.

Q3-24 "When heat is added to a system, the internal energy of the system must increase". Justify this statement.

Q3-25 When in a thermally insulated container gas is filled at some temperature above room temperature on ground floor and it is taken to second floor of a building, will the temperature of the gas in it change. Is some work is done by or on the gas in the process.

Q3-26 The outer surface of a metallic cylinder is rubbed by a rough duster, after some. Due to this gas temperature increases. Is some work is done on the gas in the process or some heat is transferred to the gas.

Q3-27 When a tyre bursts, it cools down. Why ?

Q3-28 Consider two thermodynamic processes shown in figure-3.70. In both the processes volume of the gas in initial and final states are same. In which path work done by the gas is more.

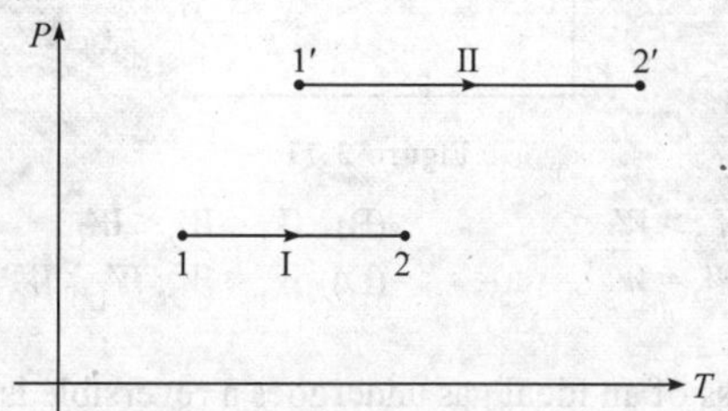

Figure 3.70

* * * * *

Conceptual MCQs Single Option Correct

3-1 A given mass of a gas expands from state A to B by three different paths 1, 2 and 3 as shown in the figure-3.71. If W_1, W_2 and W_3 respectively be the work done by the gas along the three paths, then :

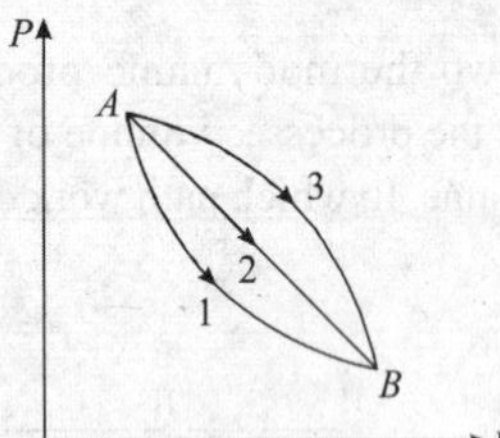

Figure 3.71

(A) $W_1 > W_2 > W_3$ (B) $W_1 < W_2 < W_3$
(C) $W_1 = W_2 = W_3$ (D) $W_1 < W_2; W_1 < W_3$

3-2 A mass of an ideal gas undergoes a reversible isothermal compression. Its molecules will then have compared with initial state, the same :
(i) Root mean square velocity
(ii) Mean momentum (iii) Mean kinetic energy
(A) (i), (ii) & (iii) are correct (B) (i) & (ii) are correct
(C) (ii) & (iii) are correct (D) only (i) is correct

3-3 Heat energy absorbed by a system in going through a cyclic process shown in figure-3.72, is :

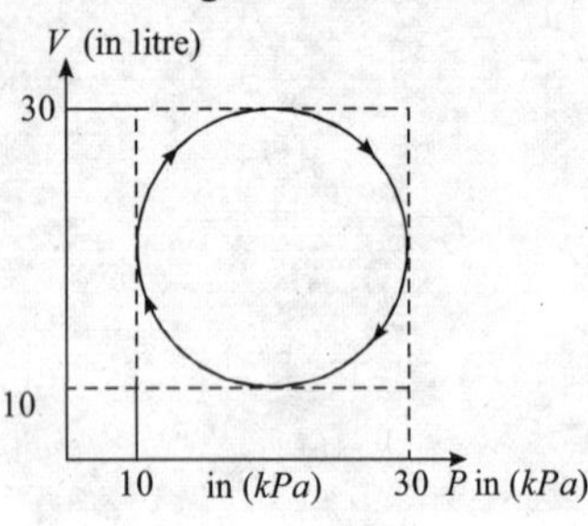

Figure 3.72

(A) $10^7 \pi$ joule (B) $10^4 \pi$ joule
(C) $10^2 \pi$ joule (D) $10^{-3} \pi$ joule

3-4 In figure-3.73, curves AB and CD represent the relation between pressure P and volume V of an ideal gas. One of the curves represents an isothermal expansion and the other represents an adiabatic expansion. Which curve represents an adiabatic expansion ?

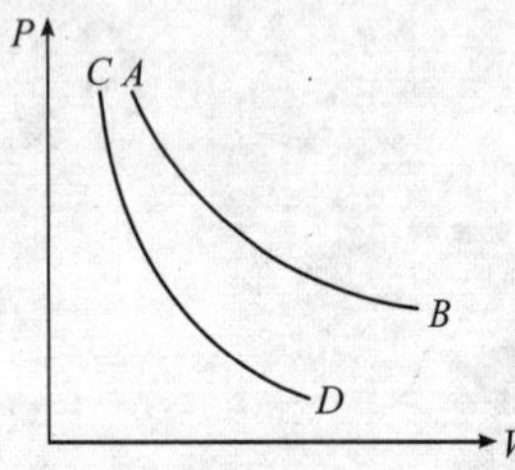

Figure 3.73

(A) Curve AB (B) Curve CD
(C) Both (D) Neither

3-5 In the isothermal expansion of an ideal gas. Select wrong statement :
(A) There is no change in the temperature of the gas
(B) There is no change in the internal energy of the gas
(C) The work done by the gas is equal to the heat supplied to the gas
(D) The work done by the gas is equal to the change in its internal energy

3-6 A gas is expanded from volume V_0 to $2V_0$ under three different processes. Process 1 is isobaric, Process 2 is isothermal and process 3 is adiabatic. Let ΔU_1, ΔU_2 and ΔU_3 be the change in internal energy of the gas in these three processes. Then :

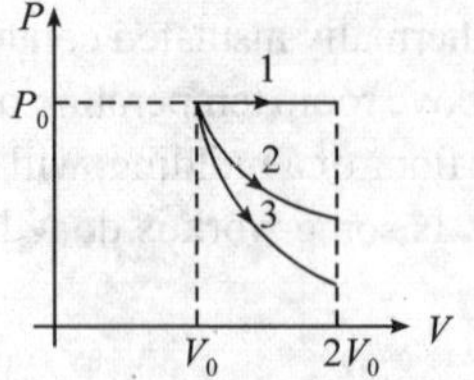

Figure 3.74

(A) $\Delta U_1 > \Delta U_2 > \Delta U_3$ (B) $\Delta U_1 < \Delta U_2 < \Delta U_3$
(C) $\Delta U_2 < \Delta U_1 < \Delta U_3$ (D) $\Delta U_2 < \Delta U_3 < \Delta U_1$

3-7 Heating of water under atmospheric pressure is an :
(A) Isothermal process (B) Isobaric process
(C) Adiabatic process (D) Isochoric process

3-8 Suppose a gas obeys pV^2 = constant in addition to the gas equation $pV = RT$. If on heating temperature is doubled, what will be the percentage change in volume ?
(A) Decreases by 50% (B) Increases by 50%
(C) Decreases by 100% (D) Increases by 100%

3-9 Figure-3.75 is the P-V diagram for a Carnot cycle. In this diagram :

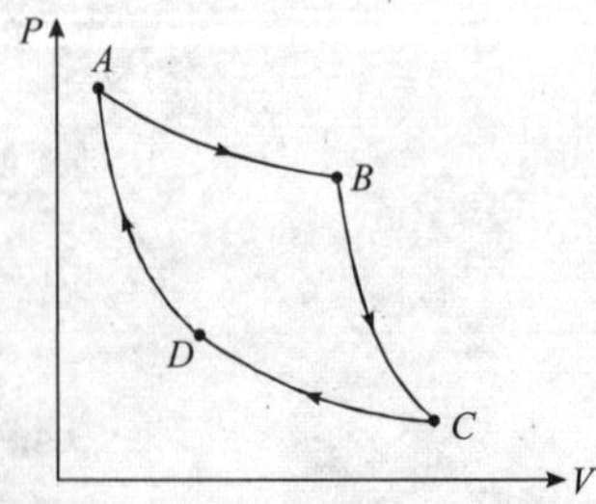

Figure 3.75

(A) Curve AB represents isothermal process and BC adiabatic process

(B) Curve AB represents adiabatic process and BC isothermal process
(C) Curves CD and DA represent isothermal processes
(D) Curves CD and DA represent adiabatic processes

3-10 A fixed mass of ideal gas undergoes changes of pressure and volume starting at L, as shown in figure-3.76.

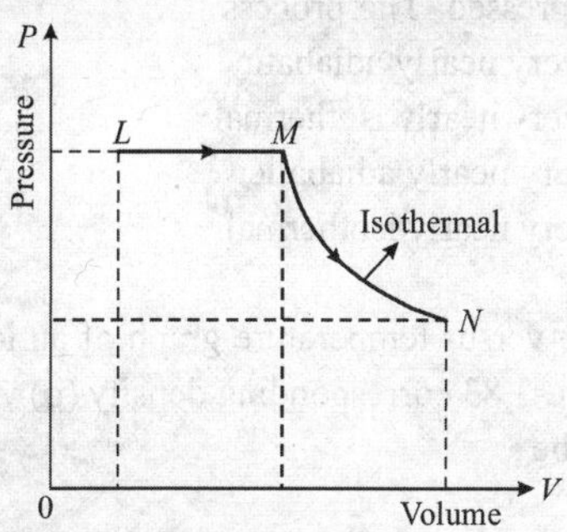

Figure 3.76

Which of the following is correct :

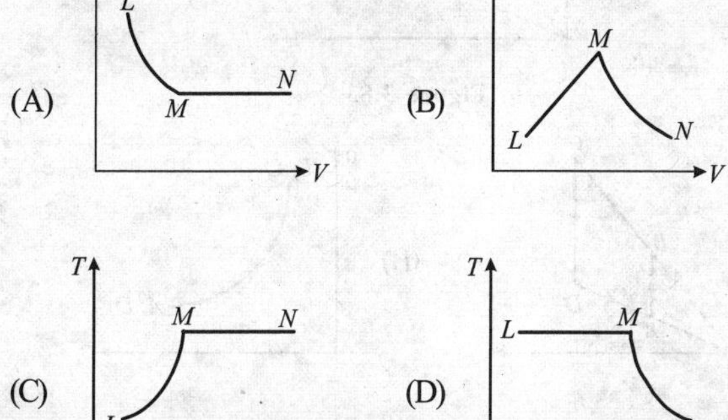

3-11 A fixed mass of gas undergoes the cycle of changes represented by $PQRSP$ as shown in figure-3.77. In some off the changes, work is done on the gas and in others, work is done by the gas. In which pair of the changes is work done on the gas ?

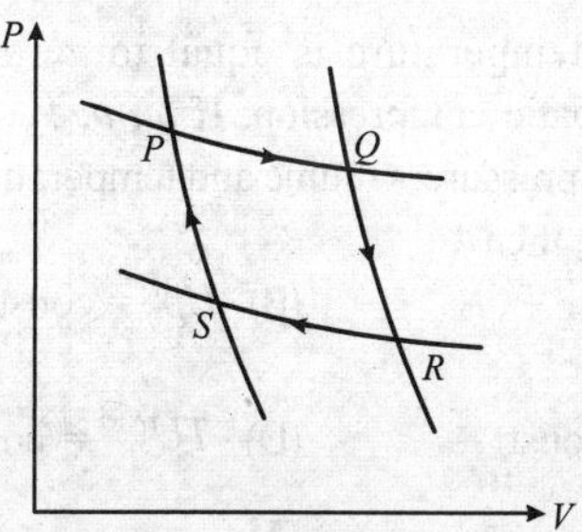

Figure 3.77

(A) PQ and RS (B) PQ and QR
(C) QR and RS (D) RS and SP

3-12 Figure-3.78 shows the P-V diagram for a fixed mass of an ideal gas undergoing cyclic process $ABCA$. AB represents isothermal process. Which of the graphs shown in figure represents the P-T diagram of the cyclic process ?

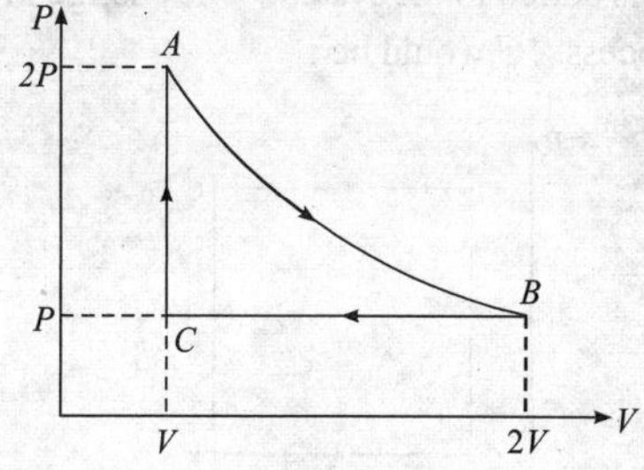

Figure 3.78

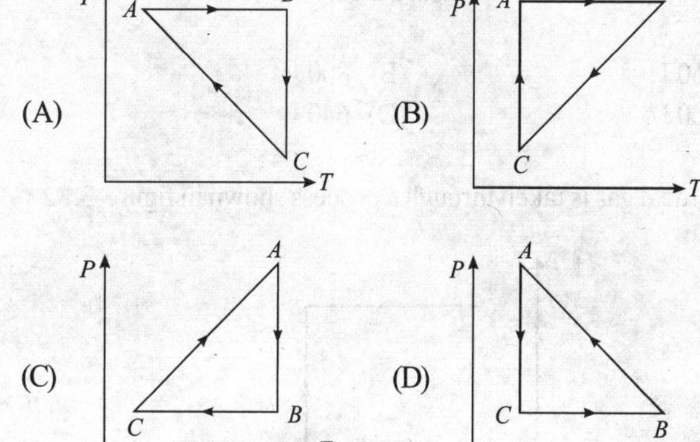

3-13 consider the process on a system shown in figure-3.79. During the process, the cumulative work done by the system :
(A) Continuously increases
(B) Continuously decreases
(C) First increases then decreases
(D) First decreases then increases

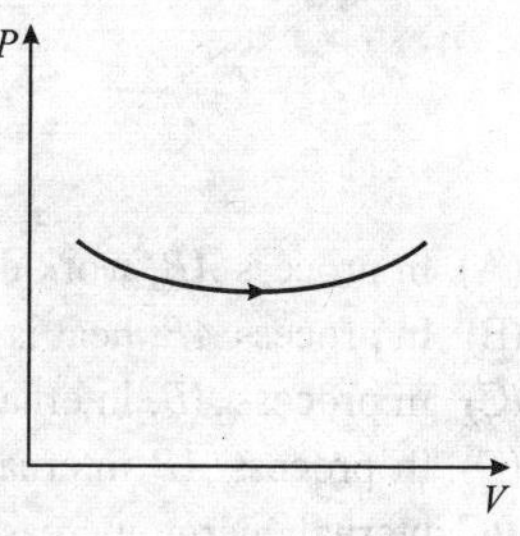

Figure 3.79

3-14 Volume versus temperature graph of two moles of helium gas is as shown in figure-3.80. The ratio of heat absorbed and the work done by the gas in process 1-2 is :

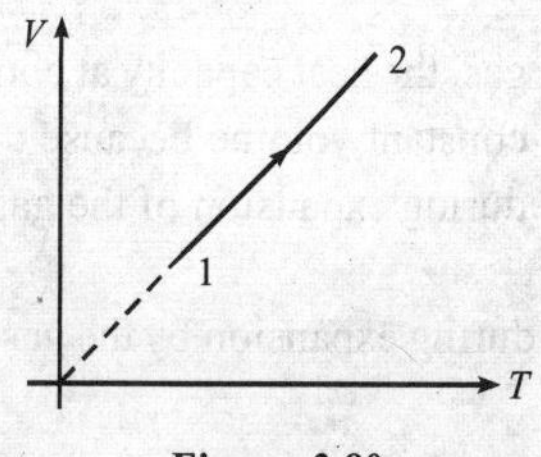

Figure 3.80

(A) 3 (B) 5/2
(C) 5/3 (D) 7/2

3-15 A thermodynamic process is shown in figure-3.81. The pressures and volumes corresponding to some points in the figure are, $P_A = 3 \times 10^4$ Pa, $V_A = 2 \times 10^{-3}$ m^3, $P_B = 8 \times 10^4$ Pa, $V_D = 5 \times 10^{-3}$ m^3. In process AB, 600 J of heat and in process BC, 200 J of heat is added to the system. The change in the internal energy in process AC would be :

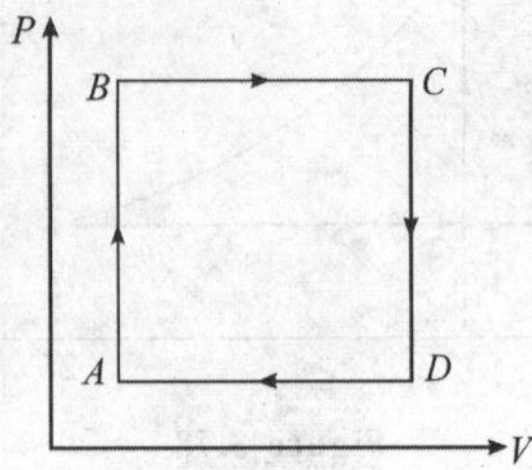

Figure 3.81

(A) 560 J (B) 800 J
(C) 600 J (D) 640 J

3-16 Ideal gas is taken through a process shown in figure-3.82 :

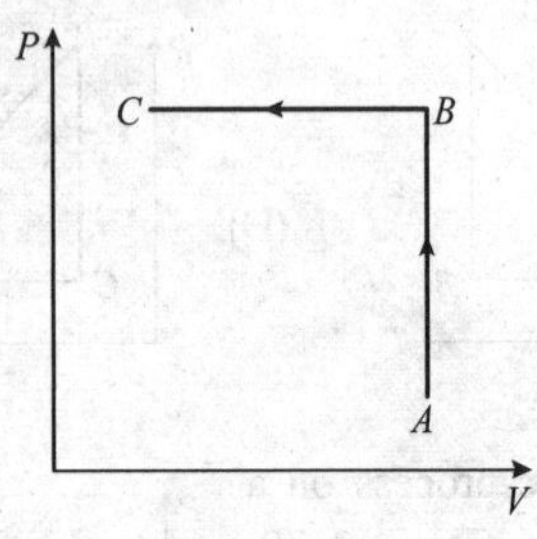

Figure 3.82

(A) In process AB, work done by system is positive
(B) In process AB, heat is rejected out of the system
(C) In process AB, internal energy increases
(D) In process AB internal energy decreases and in process BC internal energy increases

3-17 In which of the following processes the system always returns to the original thermodynamic state ?
(A) Adiabatic (B) Isobaric
(C) Cyclic (D) Reversible

3-18 For an ideal gas, the heat capacity at constant pressure is larger than that at constant volume because :
(A) Work is done during expansion of the gas by the external pressure
(B) Work is done during expansion by the gas against external pressure
(C) Work is done during expansion by the gas against intermolecular forces at attraction
(D) More collisions occur per unit time when volume is kept constant.

3-19 A gas has :
(A) One specific heat only
(B) Two specific heats only
(C) Infinite number of specific heats
(D) No specific heat

3-20 A gas kept in a container of finite low conductivity is suddenly compressed. The process :
(A) Must be very nearly adiabatic
(B) Must be very nearly isothermal
(C) May be very nearly adiabatic
(D) May be very nearly isothermal

3-21 Pressure versus temperature graph of an ideal gas is as shown in figure-3.83 corresponding density (ρ) versus volume (V) graph will be :

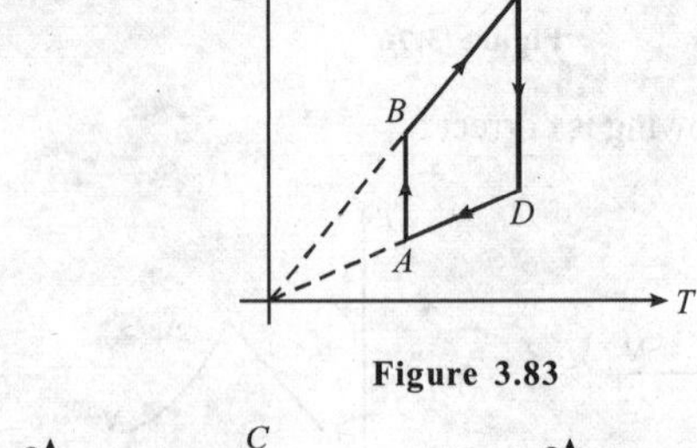

Figure 3.83

(A)

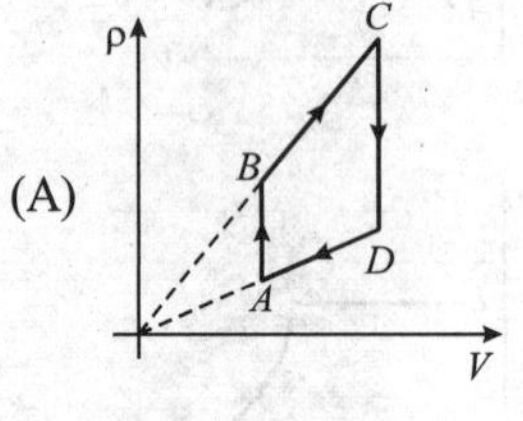

(B)

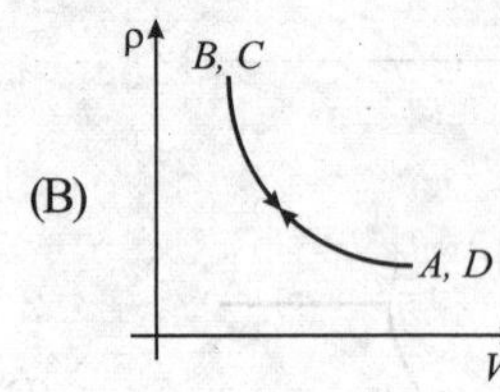

(C)

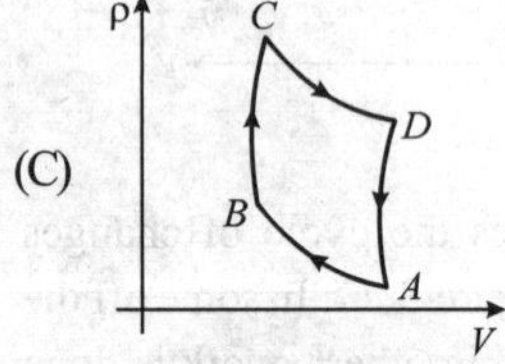

(D)

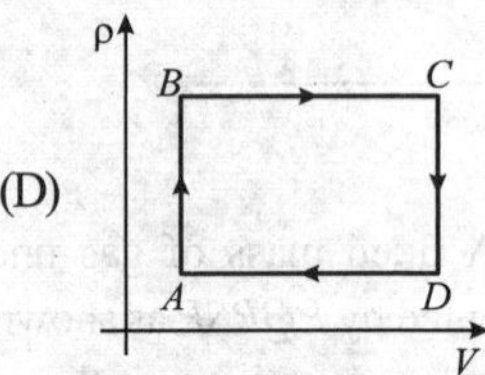

3-22 An ideal gas (whose $\frac{C_p}{C_v} = \lambda$, and internal energy U at absolute zero temperature is equal to zero) undergoes a reversible adiabatic compression. If U, p, V, T represent the internal energy, pressure, volume and temperature respectively of the ideal gas, then
(A) $UV^{\lambda} =$ const (B) $Up^{\lambda} =$ const
(C) $VU^{\frac{1}{\lambda-1}} =$ const (D) $TU^{\lambda-1} =$ const

3-23 For an adiabatic compression (for an ideal gas) the quantity PV :
(A) increases (B) decreases
(C) remains constant (D) depends on γ

3-24 Figure-3.84 below represents two processes a and b for a given sample of gas. Let ΔQ_1 and ΔQ_2 be the heat absorbed by the systems in the two cases respectively. Then which of the following relation is correct ?

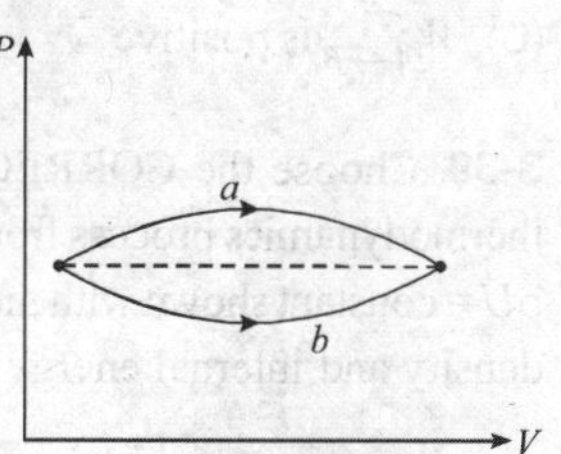

Figure 3.84

(A) $\Delta Q_1 = \Delta Q_2$
(B) $\Delta Q_1 < \Delta Q_2$
(C) $\Delta Q_1 > \Delta Q_2$ (D) $\Delta Q_1 \leq \Delta Q_2$

3-25 When an ideal gas undergoes an adiabatic change causing a temperature change ΔT :

(i) There is no heat gained or lost by the gas
(ii) The work done on system is equal to loss in internal energy
(iii) The change in internal energy per mole of the gas is $C_v \Delta T$, where C_v is the molar heat capacity at constant volume

(A) (i), (ii) & (iii) are correct (B) (i) & (ii) are correct
(C) (i) & (iii) are correct (D) only (i) is correct

3-26 The slopes of isothermal and adiabatic curves are related as :

(A) Slope of isothermal curve = slope of adiabatic curve
(B) Slope of isothermal curve = γ × slope of adiabatic curve
(C) Slope of adiabatic curve = γ × slope of isothermal curve
(D) Slope of adiabatic curve = $\frac{1}{2}$ × slope of isothermal curve

3-27 When a thermodynamic system is taken from state A to state B via path ACB (figure-3.85), 100 cal is given to the system and 60 cal worth work is done. Along the path ADB, the work done is worth 20 cal; the heat flowing into the system in this case would be :

(A) 120 cal
(B) 40 cal
(C) 140 cal
(D) 60 cal

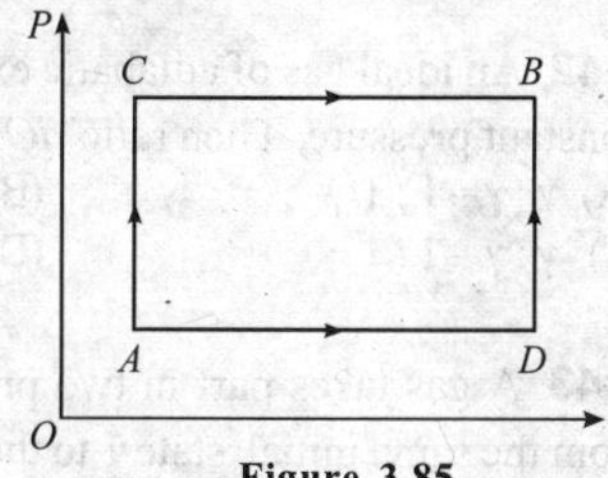

Figure 3.85

3-28 An ideal gas is allowed to expand freely against vacuum in a rigid insulated container. The gas undergoes :

(A) An increase in its internal energy
(B) A decrease in its internal energy
(C) Neither an increase or decrease in temperature or internal energy
(D) An increase in temperature

3-29 Which one of graphs below best illustrates the relationship between internal energy U of an ideal gas and temperature T of the gas in K ?

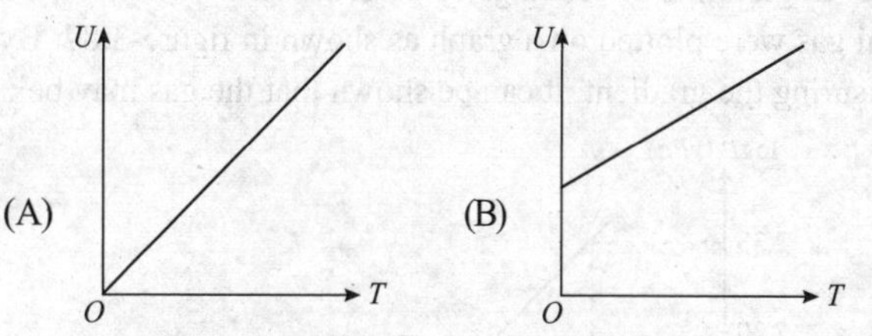

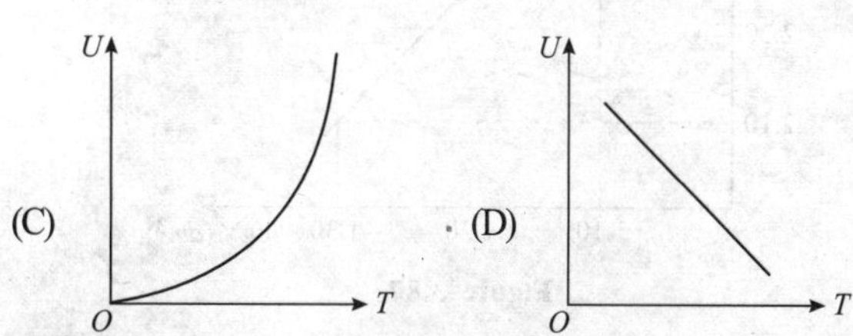

3-30 The value of $C_p - C_v$ is 1.00 R for a gas sample in state A and is 1.08 R in state B. Let p_A, p_B denote the pressure and T_A and T_B denote the temperature of the states A and B respectively. Most likely

(A) $p_A < p_B$ and $T_A > T_B$ (B) $p_A > p_B$ and $T_A < T_B$
(C) $p_A = p_B$ and $T_A < T_B$ (D) $p_A > p_B$ and $T_A = T_B$

3-31 The P-V graph for a thermodynamical system is shown in figure-3.86. The work done by the system in the process A to B is :

(A) 90 J
(B) 60 J
(C) 0 J
(D) 30 J

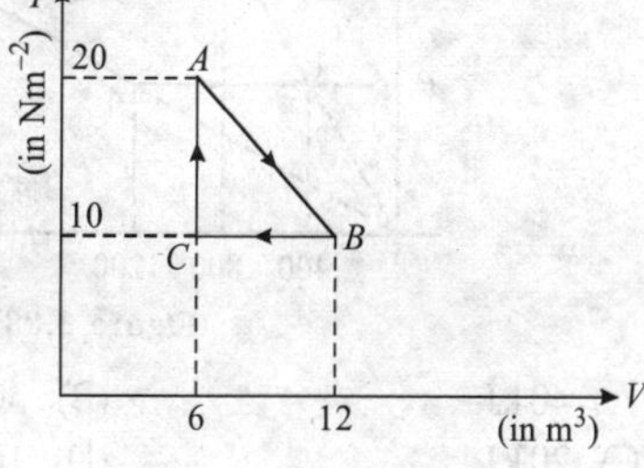

Figure 3.86

3-32 In Q. No. 3-31, the work done in the process B to C is :

(A) – 90 J (B) – 60 J
(C) 0 J (D) 30 J

3-33 A gas undergoes a process in which its pressure P and volume V are related as VP^n = constant. The bulk modulus of the gas in the process is :

(A) nP (B) $P^{1/n}$
(C) P/n (D) P^n

3-34 During free expansion of an ideal gas which of the following remains constant ?

(A) Pressure
(B) Temperature
(C) Both pressure and temperature
(D) Neither pressure nor temperature

3-35 Logarithms of readings of pressure and volume for an ideal gas were plotted on a graph as shown in figure-3.87. By measuring the gradient, it can be shown that the gas may be :

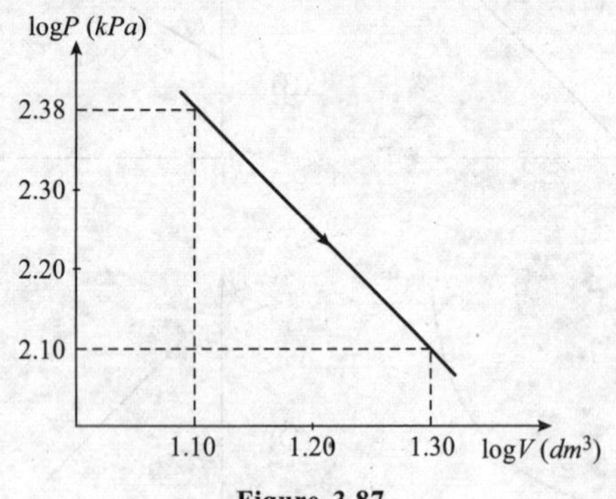

Figure 3.87

(A) Monoatomic and undergoing an adiabatic change
(B) Monoatomic and undergoing an isothermal change
(C) Diatomic and undergoing an adiabatic change
(D) Triatomic and undergoing an isothermal change

3-36 A thermal engine having three moles of monoatomic gas as its working fluid undergoes the cyclic process as shown in the figure-3.88. Find the mechanical work over one cycle approximately ($R = 8.314$ J/mole-K) :

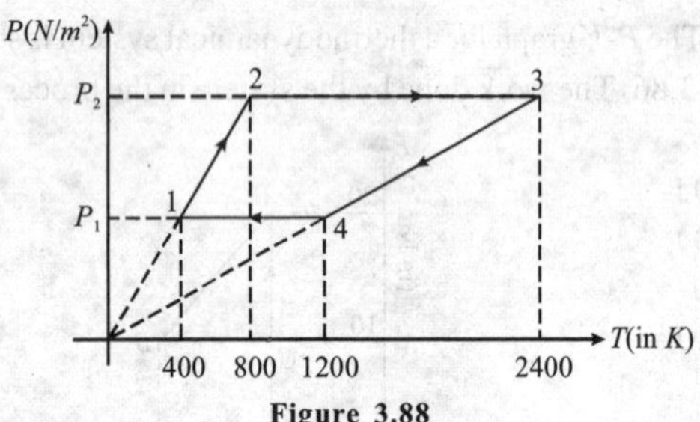

Figure 3.88

(A) 40 kJ (B) 30 kJ
(C) 20 kJ (D) 10 kJ

3-37 The internal energy of a gas is given by $U = 2PV$. It expands from V_0 to $2V_0$ against a constant pressure P_0. The heat absorbed by the gas in the process is :
(A) $2P_0V_0$ (B) $4P_0V_0$
(C) $3P_0V_0$ (D) P_0V_0

3-38 The density (ρ) versus temperature (T) graph of an ideal gas. Undergoing a process AB is as shown in the figure-3.89. Choose the incorrect option :

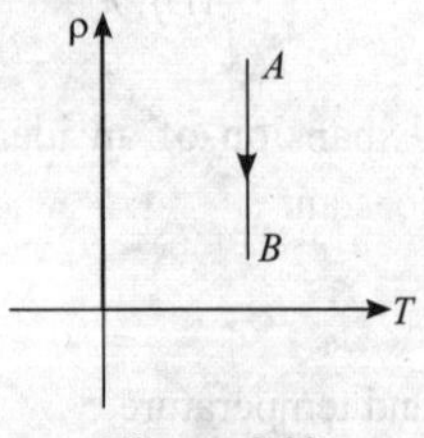

Figure 3.89

(A) $P_AV_A = P_BV_B$ (B) $P_B > P_A$
(C) $W_{A\to B}$ is positive (D) $DU_{AB} = 0$

3-39 Choose the CORRECT option for a gas undergoing a thermodynamics process from state A to B with process equation ρU = constant shown with the indicator diagram plotted between density and internal energy as given below :

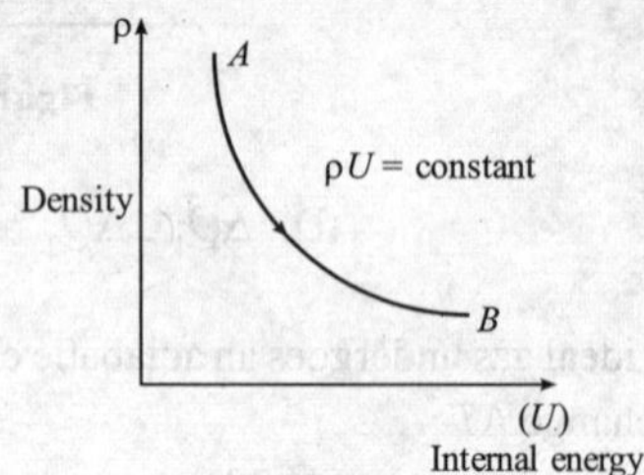

Figure 3.90

(A) Heat is expelled by gas (B) Heat is absorbed by gas
(C) Process $A \to B$ is adiabatic
(D) Temperature of the gas decreases from A to B

3-40 A gas is found to obey the law P^2V = constant. The initial temperature and volume are T_0 and T_0. If the gas expands to a volume $3V_0$, then the final temperature becomes :
(A) $\sqrt{3}T_0$ (B) $\sqrt{2}T_0$
(C) $\frac{T_0}{\sqrt{3}}$ (D) $\frac{T_0}{\sqrt{2}}$

3-41 An ideal gas has initial volume V and pressure P. In doubling its volume the minimum work done will be in the following process (of given processes)
(A) Isobaric process (B) Isothermal process
(C) Adiabatic process (D) None of the above

3-42 An ideal gas of adiabatic exponent γ is supplied heat at a constant pressure. Then ratio $dQ : dW : dU$ is equal to :
(A) $\gamma : \gamma - 1 : 1/\gamma$ (B) $1 : 1 : \gamma - 1$
(C) $\gamma : \gamma - 1 : 1$ (D) $\gamma : 1 : \gamma - 1$

3-43 A gas takes part in two processes in which it is heated from the same initial state 1 to the same final temperature. The processes are shown on the P-V diagram by the straight line 1 – 2 and 1 – 3.2 and 3 are the points on the same isothermal curve. Q_1 and Q_2 are the heat transfer along the two processes. Then :

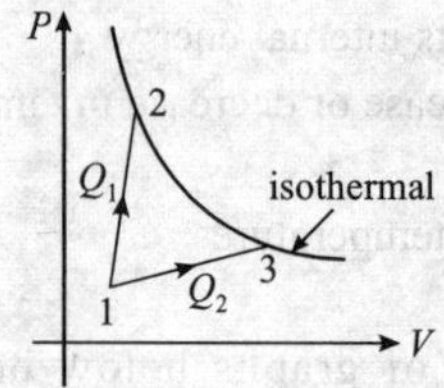

Figure 3.91

(A) $Q_1 = Q_2$ (B) $Q_1 < Q_2$
(C) $Q_1 > Q_2$ (D) insufficient data

3-44 *P-T* diagram is shown below then choose the corresponding *V-T* diagram

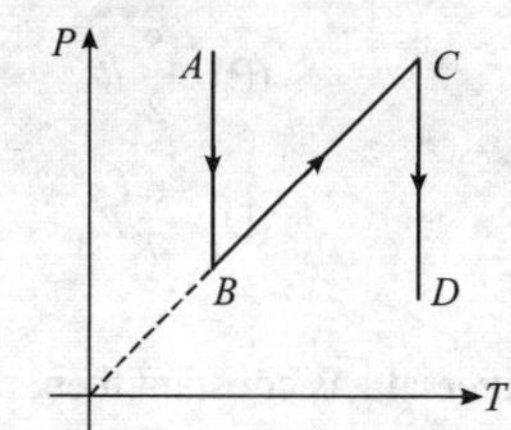

Figure 3.92

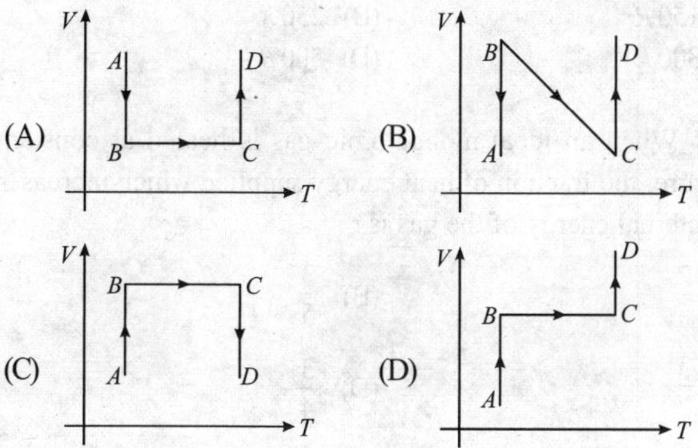

3-45 When an ideal gas is compressed isothermally then its pressure increases because :

(A) Its potential energy increases

(B) Its kinetic energy increases and molecules move apart

(C) Its number of collisions per unit area with walls of container increases

(D) Molecular energy increases

3-46 The figure shows two paths for the change of state of a gas from *A* to *B*. The ratio of molar heat capacities in path 1 and path 2 is :

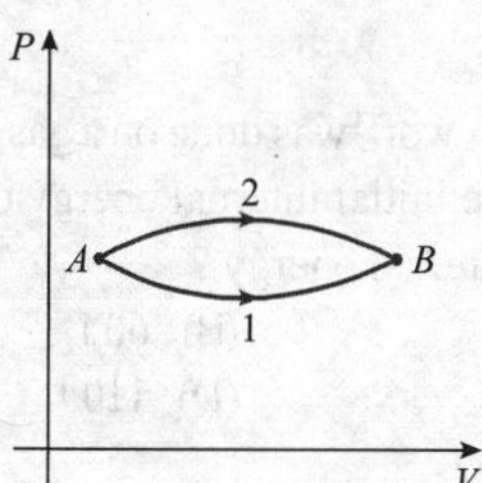

Figure 3.93

(A) >1 (B) <1
(C) 1 (D) Data insufficient

3-47 A gas has molar heat capacity $C = 24.9 \text{ J mol}^{-1}\text{ K}^{-1}$ in the process P^2T = constant. Then (R = 8.3 J/mol k)

(A) Gas is monoatomic (B) Gas is diatomic
(C) Gas is triatomic (D) Atomicity of gas is 4

3-48 Pressure versus temperature graph of an ideal gas are as shown in figure-3.94. Choose the wrong statement

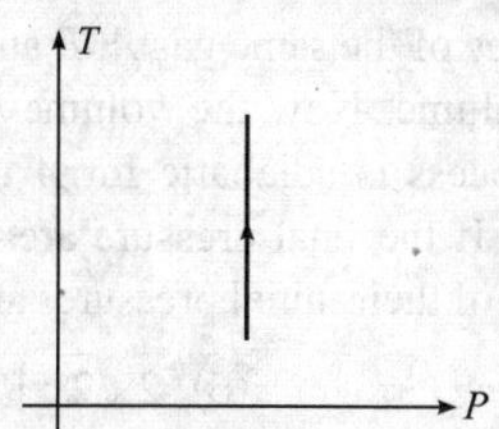

Figure 3.94

(A) Given process is isobaric

(B) Density of gas is constant

(C) Volume of gas is increasing

(D) None of these

3-49 Some of the thermodynamic parameters are state variables while some are process variables. Some grouping of the parameters are given. Choose the correct one.

(A) State variables : Temperature, No of moles
Process variables : Internal energy, work done by the gas.

(B) State variables : Volume, Temperature
Process variables : Internal energy, work done by the gas.

(C) State variables : Work done by the gas, heat rejected by the gas
Process variables : Temperature, volume.

(D) State variables : Internal energy, volume
Process variables : Work done by the gas, heat absorbed by the gas.

* * * * *

Numerical MCQs Single Options Correct

3-1 A gas is expanded adiabatically at an initial temperature of 300 K so that its volume is doubled. The final temperature of the gas is ($\gamma = 1.40$) :

(A) 227.3 K (B) 500.30 K
(C) 454.76 K (D) -47°C

3-2 Three samples of the same gas *A*, *B* and *C* ($\gamma = 3/2$) have initially equal volume. Now the volume of each sample is doubled. The process is adiabatic for *A* isobaric for *B* and isothermal for *C*. If the final pressure are equal for all three samples, the ratio of their initial pressures are :

(A) $2\sqrt{2} : 2 : 1$ (B) $2\sqrt{2} : 1 : 2$
(C) $\sqrt{2} : 1 : 2$ (D) $2 : 1 : \sqrt{2}$

3-3 An ideal gas at 27°C is compressed adiabatically to $\frac{8}{27}$ of its original volume. If $\gamma = \frac{5}{3}$, then the rise in temperature is :

(A) 450°C (B) 375°C
(C) 225°C (D) 405°C

3-4 One mole of an ideal gas at temperature *T* was cooled isochorically till the gas pressure fell from *P* to $\frac{P}{n}$. Then, by an isobaric process, the gas was restored to the initial temperature. The net amount of heat absorbed by the gas in the process is :

(A) nRT (B) $\frac{RT}{n}$
(C) $RT(1-n^{-1})$ (D) $RT(n-1)$

3-5 14 g of nitrogen is contained in a vessel at 300 K. How much heat should be taken out of the gas to half the rms speed of its molecules ? $R = 2$ cal/mol K :

(A) 500 cal (B) 562.5 cal
(C) 2000 cal (D) 2250 cal

3-6 A gas is enclosed in a vessel of volume 1000 cc at a pressure of 72.6 cm of Hg. It is being evacuated with the help of a piston pump, which expels 10% gas in each stroke. The pressure after the second stroke will be nearest to :

(A) 50 cm (B) 55 cm
(C) 60.0 cm (D) 66 cm

3-7 Certain amount of an ideal gas are contained in a closed vessel. The vessel is moving with a constant velocity *v*. The molecular mass of gas is *M*. The rise in temperature of the gas when the vessel is suddenly stopped is ($\gamma = C_P/C_V$) :

(A) $\frac{Mv^2}{2R(\gamma+1)}$ (B) $\frac{Mv^2(\gamma-1)}{2R}$
(C) $\frac{Mv^2}{2R\gamma}$ (D) $\frac{Mv^2\gamma}{2R(\gamma-1)}$

3-8 The molar heat capacity in a process of a diatomic gas if it does a work of $\frac{Q}{4}$ when a heat of *Q* is supplied to it is :

(A) $\frac{2}{5}R$ (B) $\frac{5}{2}R$
(C) $\frac{10}{3}R$ (D) $\frac{6}{7}R$

3-9 If *R* be the universal gas constant then, the amount of heat required to raise the temperature of 2 mole of monoatomic gas under isobaric conditions from 0°C to 100°C will be :

(A) 150 *R* (B) 250 *R*
(C) 300 *R* (D) 500 *R*

3-10 When an ideal monoatomic gas is heated at constant pressure, the fraction of heat energy supplied which increases the internal energy of the gas is :

(A) $\frac{2}{5}$ (B) $\frac{3}{5}$
(C) $\frac{3}{7}$ (D) $\frac{3}{4}$

3-11 A geyser, operating on LPG (liquefied petroleum gas) heats water flowing at the rate of 3.0 litres per minute, from 27°C to 77°C. If the heat of combustion of LPG is 4.0×10^4 J g^{-1} how much fuel in gram consumed per minute :

(A) 15.25 (B) 15.5
(C) 15.75 (D) 16

3-12 The ratio of adiabatic bulk modulus and isothermal bulk modulus of a gas is ($\gamma = C_p/C_v$) :

(A) 1 (B) γ
(C) $\frac{\gamma}{(\gamma-1)}$ (D) $\frac{(\gamma-1)}{\gamma}$

3-13 When 20 J of work was done on a gas, 40 J of heat energy was released. If the initial internal energy of the gas was 70 J, what is the final internal energy ?

(A) 50 J (B) 60 J
(C) 90 J (D) 110 J

3-14 *P-V* diagram of a diatomic gas is a straight line passing through origin. The molar heat capacity of the gas in the process will be :

(A) 4*R* (B) 2.5*R*
(C) 3*R* (D) $\frac{4R}{3}$

3-15 An ideal gas at pressure *P* is adiabatically compressed so that its density becomes n times the initial value. The final pressure of the gas will be ($\gamma = C_p/C_v$) :

(A) $n^{\gamma}P$ (B) $n^{-\gamma}P$
(C) $n^{(\gamma-1)}P$ (D) $n^{(1-\gamma)}P$

3-16 For an ideal monoatomic gas, the universal gas constant R is n times the molar heat capacity at constant pressure C_p. Here n is :

(A) 0.67 (B) 1.4
(C) 0.4 (D) 1.67

3-17 Unit mass of a liquid of volume V_1 completely turns into a gas of volume V_2 at constant atmospheric pressure P_0 and temperature T. The latent heat of vaporization is L. Then the change in internal energy of the gas is :

(A) L (B) $L + P_0(V_2 - V_1)$
(C) $L - P_0(V_2 - V_1)$ (D) Zero

3-18 The height of a waterfall is 84 m. Assuming that the entire kinetic energy of falling water is converted into heat, the rise in temperature of the water will be : ($g = 10$ m s^{-2}, J = 4.2 joule/cal)

(A) 0.2°C (B) 1.960°C
(C) 0.96°C (D) 0.0196°C

3-19 One mole of an ideal gas requires 207 J heat to raise its temperature by 10 K when heated at constant pressure. If the same gas is heated at constant volume to raise the temperature by the same 10 K, the heat required will be (R, the gas constant = 8.3 JK^{-1} mol^{-1}) :

(A) 198.7 J (B) 29 J
(C) 215.3 J (D) 124 J

3-20 A gas is expanded to double its volume by two different processes. One is isobaric and the other is isothermal. Let W_1 and W_2 be the respective work done, then :

(A) $W_2 = W_1 \ln(2)$ (B) $W_2 = \dfrac{W_1}{\ln(2)}$
(C) $W_2 = \dfrac{W_1}{2}$ (D) Data is insufficient

3-21 One mole of monoatomic gas and one mole of diatomic gas are mixed together. What is the molar specific heat at constant volume for the mixture ?

(A) $\dfrac{3}{2}R$ (B) $2R$
(C) $\dfrac{5}{2}R$ (D) $3R$

3-22 The equation of state for n moles of an ideal gas is $PV = nRT$, where R is a constant. The SI unit for R is :

(A) J K^{-1} per molecule (B) J kg^{-1} K^{-1}
(C) J K^{-1} mol^{-1} (D) J K^{-1} g^{-1}

3-23 In rising from the bottom of a lake to the top, the temperature of an air bubble remains unchanged, but its diameter is doubled. If h is the barometric height (expressed in metres of mercury of relative density ρ) at the surface of the lake, the depth of the lake is (in metres)

(A) 8 ρh (B) 4 ρh
(C) 7 ρh (D) 2 ρh

3-24 Heat is supplied to a diatomic gas at constant pressure. The ratio of $\Delta Q : \Delta U : \Delta W$ is :

(A) 5 : 3 : 2 (B) 5 : 2 : 3
(C) 7 : 5 : 2 (D) 7 : 2 : 5

3-25 A vessel contains 0.5 m^3 of hydrogen gas at 300 K and pressure 10^5 Pa. How much heat should be added to it to raise the temperature to 500 K ? Molar specific heat of hydrogen is 5 cal/mol K :

(A) 20 kcal (B) 10 kcal
(C) 5 kcal (D) 2.5 kcal

3-26 Given that the interatomic distance between the molecules of a diatomic gas remains constant, what is the value of molar specific heat of the gas ?

(A) $3R/2$ (B) $5R/2$
(C) $3R$ (D) $5R$

3-27 If a triatomic gas is heated isothermally, what percentage of the heat energy is used to increase the internal energy ?

(A) Zero (B) 14%
(C) 60% (D) 100

3-28 A monoatomic ideal gas expands at constant pressure, with heat Q supplied. The fraction of Q which goes as work done by the gas is :

(A) 1 (B) $\dfrac{2}{3}$
(C) $\dfrac{3}{5}$ (D) $\dfrac{2}{5}$

3-29 When an ideal diatomic gas is heated at constant pressure, the fraction of the heat energy supplied which increases the internal energy of the gas is :

(A) $\dfrac{2}{5}$ (B) $\dfrac{3}{5}$
(C) $\dfrac{3}{7}$ (D) $\dfrac{5}{7}$

3-30 If one mole of a monoatomic gas $\left(\gamma = \dfrac{5}{3}\right)$ is mixed with one mole of a triatomic gas $\left(\gamma = \dfrac{4}{3}\right)$, the value of γ for the mixture is :

(A) 1.40 (B) 1.44
(C) 1.53 (D) 3.07

3-31 One mole of an ideal gas ($C_p/C_v = \gamma$) at absolute temperature T_1 is adiabatically compressed from an initial pressure P_1 to a final pressure P_2. The resulting temperature T_2 of the gas is given by :

(A) $T_2 = T_1\left(\frac{P_2}{P_1}\right)^{\frac{\gamma}{\gamma-1}}$ (B) $T_2 = T_1\left(\frac{P_2}{P_1}\right)^{\frac{\gamma-1}{\gamma}}$

(C) $T_2 = T_1\left(\frac{P_2}{P_1}\right)^{\gamma}$ (D) $T_2 = T_1\left(\frac{P_2}{P_1}\right)^{\gamma-1}$

3-32 The pressure of the air inside the motor tyre is 2 atmosphere and the temperature is 27°C. If it suddenly bursts, the final temperature will be ($\gamma = 1.4$) :
(A) 27 K (B) – 150°C
(C) – 81°C (D) – 27°C

3-33 A certain mass of an ideal gas at pressure P_1 is adiabatically expanded from an initial volume V_1 to a final volume V_2. The resulting pressure P_2 of the gas is given by :

(A) $P_2 = P_1\left(\frac{V_1}{V_2}\right)^{\gamma}$ (B) $P_2 = P_1\left(\frac{V_1}{V_2}\right)^{1/\gamma}$

(C) $P_2 = P_1\left(\frac{V_1}{V_2}\right)^{\frac{\gamma-1}{\gamma}}$ (D) $P_2 = P_1\left(\frac{V_1}{V_2}\right)^{\frac{\gamma}{\gamma-1}}$

3-34 5 mol of oxygen is heated at constant volume from 10°C to 20°C. Given : $C_p = 8$ cal/mol/°C and $R = 8.36$ J/mol/°C. The amount of heat consumed by oxygen is :
(A) 100 cal (B) 200 cal
(C) 300 cal (D) 400 cal

3-35 In Q. No. 3-34, the change in internal energy is :
(A) 100 cal (B) 200 cal
(C) 300 cal (D) 400 cal

3-36 A gas at pressure P is adiabatically compressed so that its density becomes twice that of initial value. Given that the ratio of specific heats at constant pressure and constant volume is 7/5. What will be the final pressure of the gas ?
(A) P (B) $2P$
(C) $2.6P$ (D) $\frac{7P}{5}$

3-37 A monoatomic ideal gas, initially at temperature T_1, is enclosed in a cylinder fitted with a frictionless piston. The gas is allowed to expand adiabatically to a temperature T_2 by releasing the piston suddenly. If L_1 and L_2 are lengths of the gas column before and after expansion respectively, then T_1/T_2 is given by :

(A) $\left(\frac{L_1}{L_2}\right)^{2/3}$ (B) $\left(\frac{L_1}{L_2}\right)$

(C) $\left(\frac{L_2}{L_1}\right)$ (D) $\left(\frac{L_2}{L_1}\right)^{2/3}$

3-38 During the adiabatic expansion of 2 moi of a gas, the internal energy was found to have decreased by 100 J. The work done by the gas in this process is :
(A) zero (B) – 100 J
(C) 200 J (D) 100 J

3-39 In a thermodynamic process, the pressure of a fixed mass of gas is changed in such a manner that the gas molecules give out 30 J of heat and 10 J of work is done on the gas. If the initial internal energy of the gas was 40 J, then the final internal energy will be :
(A) 0 (B) 80 J
(C) 20 J (D) – 20 J

3-40 A freezer has coefficient of performance 5. When 3.6×10^6 J work is done on the freezer, what mass of water at 0°C is converted into ice cubes at 0°C :
(A) ≈ 5 kg (B) ≈ 3.6 kg
(C) ≈ 54 kg (D) ≈ 107 kg

3-41 An ideal gas undergoes a circular cycle as shown in the figure-3.95. Find the ratio of maximum temperature of cycle to minimum temperature of cycle :

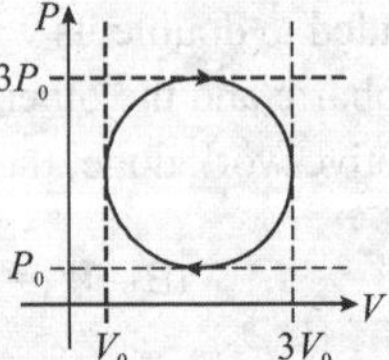

Figure 3.95

(A) $\left(\frac{1+\sqrt{2}}{\sqrt{2}-1}\right)^2$ (B) $\left(\frac{2+\sqrt{2}}{2-\sqrt{2}}\right)^2$

(C) $\left(\frac{3+\sqrt{2}}{3-\sqrt{2}}\right)^2$ (D) $\left(\frac{4+\sqrt{2}}{4-\sqrt{2}}\right)^2$

3-42 In a thermodynamic process helium gas obeys the law $TP^{-2/5}$ = constant. The heat given to the gas when the temperature of 2 moles of the gas is raised from T to $4T$ (R is the universal gas constant) is :
(A) $9RT$ (B) $18RT$
(C) Zero (D) Data insufficient

3-43 For adiabatic expansion of a monoatomic perfect gas, the volume increases by 2.4%. What is the percentage decrease in pressure ?

(A) 2.4% (B) 4.0%
(C) 4.8% (D) 7.1%

3-44 5 moles of gas were heated from 100ºC to 120ºC at constant volume. The internal energy was changed by 200 joule. What is the specific heat capacity of the gas ?

(A) 5 J mole^{-1} K^{-1} (B) 4 J mole^{-1} K^{-1}
(C) 2 J mole^{-1} K^{-1} (D) 1 J mole^{-1} K^{-1}

2-45 A monoatomic gas at 27ºC is suddenly compressed to one eighth of its original volume. The temperature of the gas sample is :

(A) 27ºC (B) 300ºC
(C) 327ºC (D) None of the above

2-46 An ideal gas with pressure p is compressed isothermally till the mean separation between molecules of the gas is reduced to half of the original value. The final pressure will be :

(A) p (B) $2p$
(C) $8p$ (D) $4p$

2-47 One mole of a monoatomic gas undergoes a linear process from state A to B as shown in $P - V$ diagram below. In this process shown in figure-3.96 find the volume of the gas when the rate of change of internal energy of gas is zero :

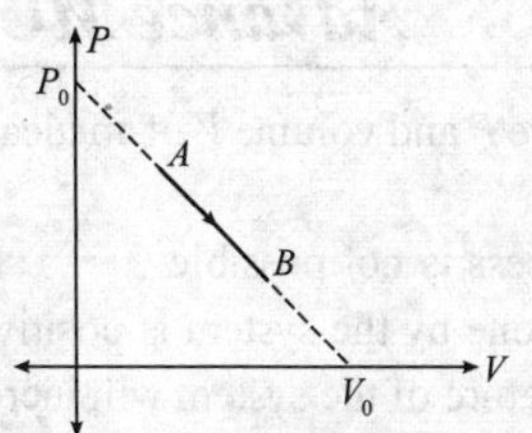

Figure 3.96

(A) $\frac{5}{8}V_0$ (B) $\frac{V_0}{2}$
(C) $\frac{8V_0}{15}$ (D) $\frac{3V_0}{5}$

2-48 In an adiabatic process, the density of a gas is found to be proportional to cube of temperature. The degree of freedom of gas molecule are :

(A) 6 (B) 5
(C) 4 (D) 3

2-49 A Cannot engine is operating between source temperatures T_1 and sink temperature T_2 has cycle efficiency 20%. When temperature T_2 is reduced by 50K, its efficiency increases to 40%. The temperatures T_1 and T_2 are :

(A) 200 K, 250 K (B) 250 K, 200 K
(C) 300 K, 250 K (D) 300 K, 200 K

* * * * *

Advance MCQs with One or More Options Correct

3-1 The pressure P and volume V of an ideal gas both increase in a process :

(A) Such a process is not possible
(B) The work done by the system is positive
(C) The temperature of the system will increase
(D) Heat supplied to the gas is equal to the change in internal energy

3-2 In a cyclic process, a gas is taken from state A to B via path-I as shown in the indicator diagram and taken back to state A from state B via path-II. In the complete cycle :

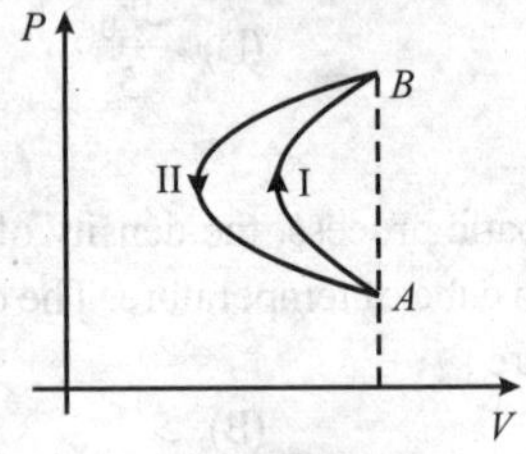

Figure 3.97

(A) Work is done on the gas
(B) Heat is rejected by the gas
(C) No work is done by the gas
(D) Nothing can be said about work as data is insufficient

3-3 In a process on a system in closed container, the initial pressure and volume are equal to the final pressure and volume :

(A) The initial temperature must be equal to the final temperature
(B) The initial internal energy must be equal to the final internal energy
(C) The net heat given to the system in the process must be zero
(D) The net work done by the system in the process must be zero

3-4 The internal energy of an ideal gas decreases by the same amount as the work done by the system :

(A) The process must be adiabatic
(B) The process must be isothermal
(C) The process must be isobaric
(D) The temperature must decrease

3-5 During the melting of a slab of ice at 273 K at atmospheric pressure:

(A) Positive work is done by the ice-water system on the atmosphere.
(B) Positive work is done on the ice-water system by the atmosphere
(C) The internal energy of ice-water system increases
(D) The internal energy of the ice-water system decreases

3-6 A partition divides a container having insulated walls into two compartments I and II. The same gas fills the two compartments whose initial parameters are given. The partition is a conducting wall which can move freely without friction. Which of the following statements is/are correct, with reference to the final equilibrium position ?

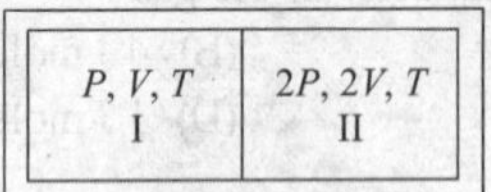

Figure 3.98

(A) The pressure in the two compartments are equal
(B) Volume of compartment I is $\frac{3V}{5}$
(C) Volume of compartment II is $\frac{12V}{5}$
(D) Final pressure in compartment I is $\frac{5P}{3}$

3-7 Three identical adiabatic containers A, B and C contain helium, neon and oxygen respectively at equal pressure. The gases are pushed to half their original volumes :

(A) The final temperature in the three containers will be the same
(B) The final pressures in the three containers will be the same
(C) The pressure of helium and neon will be the same but that of oxygen will be different
(D) The temperature of helium and neon will be the same but that of oxygen will be different

3-8 Which of the following statements is/are correct ?

(A) A gas has two specific heats only
(B) A material will have only one specific heat, if and only if its coefficient of thermal expansion is equal to zero.
(C) A gas has infinite number of specific heats.
(D) None of these

3-9 For an ideal gas :

(A) The change in internal energy in a constant pressure process from temperature T_1 to T_2 is equal to $nC_v(T_2 - T_1)$, where C_v is the molar specific heat at constant volume and n the number of moles of the gas.
(B) The change in internal energy of the gas and the work done by the gas are equal in magnitude in an adiabatic process.
(C) The internal energy does not change in an isothermal process
(D) No heat is added or removed in an adiabatic process.

3-10 A thermally insulated chamber of volume $2V_0$ is divided by a frictionless piston of area S into two equal parts A and B. Part A has an ideal gas at pressure P_0 and temperature T_0 and in part B is vacuum. A massless spring of force constant K is connected with the piston of cross sectional area S and the wall of the container as shown in figure-3.99. Initially the spring is unstretched. The gas in chamber A is allowed to expand. Let in equilibrium the spring is compressed by x_0. Then :

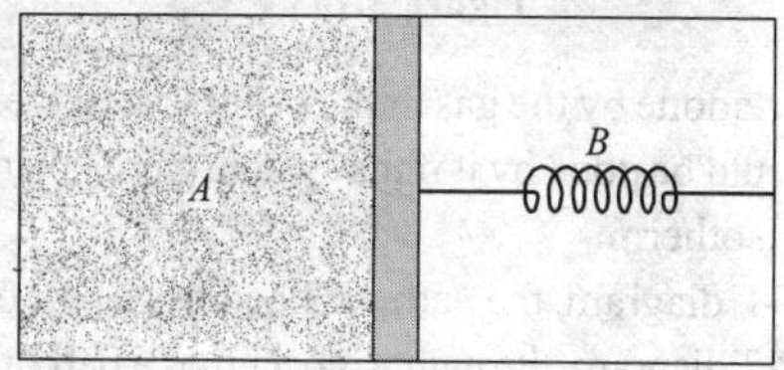

Figure 3.99

(A) Final pressure of the gas is $\dfrac{kx_0}{S}$

(B) Work done by the gas is $\dfrac{1}{2}kx_0^2$

(C) Change in internal energy of the gas is $\dfrac{1}{2}kx_0^2$

(D) Temperature of the gas is decreased

3-11 A sample of gas follows process represented by PV^2 = constant. Bulk modulus for this process is B, then which of the following graph is correct?

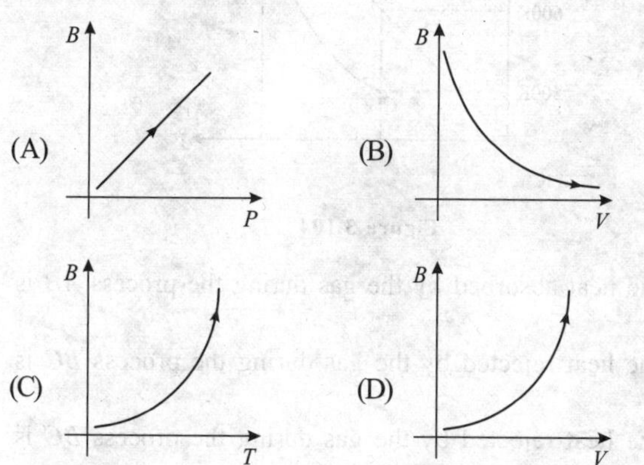

3-12 When a sample of a gas is taken from state i to state f along path 'iaf', heat supplied to the gas is 50 cal and work done by he gas is 20 cal. If it is taken by path 'ibf', then heat supplied is 36 cal :

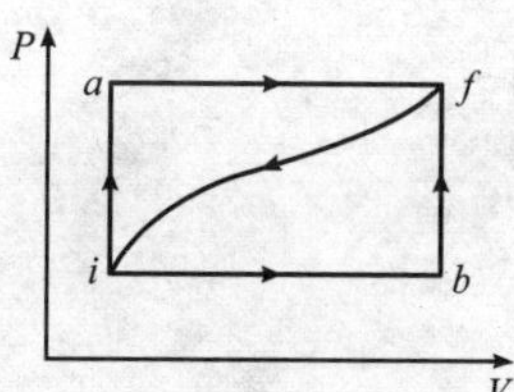

Figure 3.100

(A) Work done by the has along path ibf is 6 cal.

(B) If work done upon he gas is 13 cal for the return path 'fi', then heat rejected by the gas along path 'fi', is 43 cal.

(C) If internal energy of the gas at state i is 10 cal, then internal energy at state 'f' is 40 cal.

(D) If internal energy at state 'b' is 22 cal and at 'i' is 10 cal then heat supplied to the gas along path 'ib' is 18 cal.

3-13 Consider a thermodynamic cycle in a PV diagram shown in the figure performed on one mole of a monatomic gas. The temperature at A is T_0 and volume at A and B are related as $V_B = V_C = 2V_A$. Choose the correct option(s) from the following.

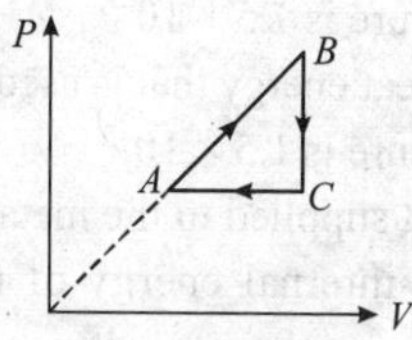

Figure 3.101

(A) The maximum temperature during the cycle is $4T_0$

(B) Net work done by the gas during the cycle is $0.5\ RT_0$

(C) The heat capacity of the process AB is $2R$

(D) The efficiency of the cycle is 8.33%

3-14 An ideal gas undergoes a process such that $\rho \propto \dfrac{1}{T}$. The molar heat capacity of this process is 33.24 J/mol K :

(A) The work done by the gas is $2R\Delta T$

(B) Degree of freedom of the gas is 4

(C) Degree of freedom of the gas is 3

(D) $Y\left(\dfrac{C_P}{C_V}\right)$

3-15 A rigid container of negligible heat capacity contains one mole of an ideal gas. The temperature of the gas increases by 1°C if 3.0 cal of heat is added to it. The gas may be :

(A) Helium (B) Argon

(C) Oxygen (D) Carbon dioxide

3-16 At ordinary temperatures, the molecules of an ideal gas have only translational and rotational kinetic energies. At higher temperatures, they may also have vibrational energy. As a result, at higher temperatures :

(A) $C_v = 3R/2$ for monatomic gas

(B) $C_v > 3R/2$ for monoatomic gas

(C) $C_v < 5R/2$ for diatomic gas

(D) $C_v > 5R/2$ for diatomic gas

3-17 When an enclosed perfect gas is subjected to an adiabatic process :

(A) Its total internal energy does not change
(B) Its temperature does not change
(C) Its pressure varies inversely as a certain power of its volume
(D) The product of its pressure and volume is directly proportional to its absolute temperature.

3-18 A metal bar of 1 kg is heated at atmospheric pressure ($P_{atm} = 10^5$ N/m²) from 20°C to 70°C. The coefficient of linear expansion, the specific heat and the density of metal are 20×10^{-6} per °C, 400 J/kg/°C and 10^4 kg/m³ respectively. Choose the correct statement(s)
(A) The fraction of heat energy that is used to do work against the atmospheric pressure is 1.5×10^{-6}
(B) The fraction of heat energy that is used to do work against the atmospheric pressure is 1.5×10^{-3}
(C) The quantity heat supplied to the metal is 20 kJ
(D) The increase in internal energy of the metal is 20 kJ approximately

3-19 The figure shows the *P-V* plot of an ideal gas taken through a cycle *ABCDA*. When drawn at a certain scale, the part *ABC* looks like a semi-circle and *CDA* looks like half of an ellipse. Then :

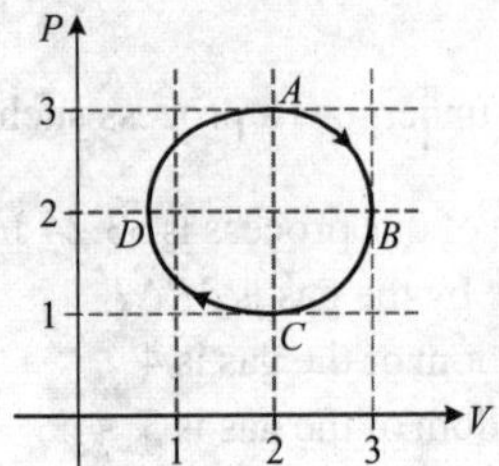

Figure 3.102

(A) The process during the path $A \to B$ is isothermal
(B) Heat flows out of the gas during the path $B \to C \to D$
(C) Work done during the path $A \to B \to C$ is zero
(D) Positive work is done by the gas in the cycle *ABCDA*

3-20 An ideal gas is taken from the state *A* (*P*, *V*) to the state *B* (*P*/2, 2*V*) along a straight line path in the *P-V* diagram. Select the correct statement (s) from the following :

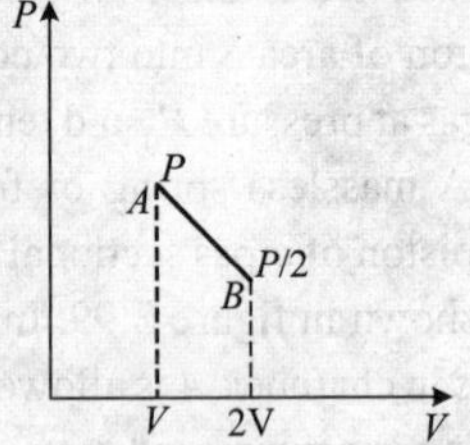

Figure 3.103

(A) The work done by the gas in the process *A* to *B* exceeds the work that would be done by it if the system were taken from *A* to *B* along the isotherm
(B) In the *T-V* diagram, the path *AB* becomes a part of parabola
(C) In the *P-T* diagram, the path *AB* becomes a part of hyperbola
(D) In going from *A* to *B* the temperature *T* of the gas first increases to a maximum value and then decreases

3-21 Two moles of an ideal monoatomic gas is taken through a cyclic process *ABCA* as shown in the *T-V* diagram. In the process *BC*, $T = \alpha V^2$ where α is a constant. Choose the correct statement(s) from the options given below :

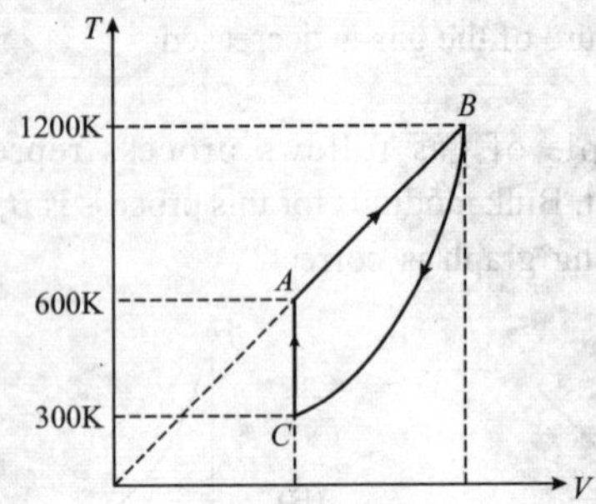

Figure 3.104

(A) The heat absorbed by the gas during the process *AB* is 3000*R*
(B) The heat rejected by the gas during the process *BC* is 3600*R*
(C) The heat rejected by the gas during the process *BC* is 1800*R*
(D) The total work done by the gas during the cyclic process is 300*R*

* * * * *

Unsolved Numerical Problems for Preparation of NSEP, INPhO & IPhO

For detailed preparation of INPhO and IPhO students can refer advance study material on www.physicsgalaxy.com

3-1 An ideal gas with adiabatic exponent 1.5 is expanded adiabatically. How many times has the gas to be expanded to reduce the rms velocity of the gas molecules to half.

Ans. [16 times]

3-2 Two diatomic gases are mixed in mole ratio 1 : 2. Find the value of adiabatic exponent for this mixture of gases.

Ans. [1.4]

3-3 A gas ($\gamma = 1.5$) is enclosed in a container of volume 150 cm^3. The initial pressure and the initial temperature are 1.5×10^5 Pa and 300K respectively. If the gas is adiabatically compressed to 50 cm^3, find the final pressure and temperature and the work done by the gas in the process. Also find the total change in internal energy of the gas in the process.

Ans. [7.8×10^5 Pa, 520 K, – 33 J, 33 J]

3-4 One mole of an ideal gas is heated at constant pressure so that its temperature rises by $\Delta T = 72\ K$. If the heat supplied is $Q = 1.6$ kJ, find the change in its internal energy and the work done by the gas.

Ans. [$\Delta U = Q - nR\,\Delta T = 1$ kJ; $\Delta W = n\,R\,\Delta T = 0.6$ kJ]

3-5 What work has to be done isobarically on a mole of diatomic gas to increase its rms speed $\eta = 3$ times from $T_0 = 300$ K ?

Ans. [$\frac{m}{M} RT_0 (\eta^2 - 1) = 1.8 \times 10^3$ J]

3-6 An engine that operates at half its theoretical (Carnot) efficiency, operates between 545°C and 310°C while producing work at the rate of 1000 kW. How much heat is discharged per hour ?

Ans. [2.15×10^{10} J/h]

3-7 A gas at 20°C and atmospheric pressure is compressed to a volume one-fifteenth as large as its original volume and an absolute pressure of 3000 kPa. What is the new temperature of the gas ?

Ans. [307°C]

3-8 A closed vessel 10 litres in volume contains air under a pressure of 10^5 N/m^2. What amount of heat should be imparted to the air to increase the pressure in the vessel five times ?

Ans. [10^4 J]

3-9 One cubic metre of air at 27°C and 10^5 N m^{-2} pressure weighs 1.18 kg. Calculate the value of the gas constant for 1 kg of the gas and calculate the C_p of air if 168 cal kg^{-1} K^{-1} and $J = 4.2$ J cal^{-1}.

Ans. [282.5 J kg^{-1} K^{-1}, 235.3 cal kg^{-1} K^{-1}]

3-10 As a result of heating one mole of an ideal gas at constant pressure by 72°C, 1600 J of heat is supplied in the process. Find the work performed by the gas, the increment of its internal energy and the value of γ for the gas.

Ans. [597.6 J, 1002.4 J, 1.6]

3-11 A gas at constant pressure P_1, volume V_1 and temperature T_1 is suddenly compressed to $V_1/2$ and then slowly expanded to V_1 again. Find the final temperature and pressure.

Ans. [$2^{\gamma-1} P_1$ and $2^{\gamma-1} T_2$]

3-12 A cubic metre of dry air at NTP is allowed to expand to 5 cubic metres (i) isothermally, (ii) adiabatically. Calculate, in each case, the pressure, temperature and work done. ($\gamma = 1.4$ and 1 atm $= 1.013 \times 10^5$ Nm^{-2})

Ans. [(i) 1/5 atm or 2.03×10^4 Nm^{-2}, 0°C and 3.6×10^3 (ii) 1.064×10^4 Nm^{-2}, – 129.6°C and 120×10^3 J]

3-13 A thermally insulated vessel containing an ideal gas ($M = 4$) at a temperature $t = 27$°C moves with velocity $v = 100$ m s^{-1}. How much (in per cent) will the gas pressure change on a sudden stoppage of the vessel ?

Ans. [0.54%]

3-14 As a result of the isobaric heating by $\Delta T = 72$ K one mole of a certain ideal gas obtains an amount of heat $Q = 1.60$ kJ. Find the work performed by the gas, the increment of its internal energy, and the value of $\gamma = C_p/C_v$.

Ans. [0.60 kJ, 1.00 kJ, 1.6]

3-15 What amount of heat is to be transferred to nitrogen in an isobaric beating process so that the gas may perform 2 J work ?

Ans. [7 J]

3-16 Five moles of neon gas (molecular weight = 20) at 2 atm and 27°C is adiabatically compressed to one-third its initial volume. Find the final pressure, the temperature and the work done on the gas.

Ans. [20.2 kJ]

3-17 Calculate the change in temperature when a gas ($\gamma = 1.4$) is suddenly allowed to expand to one hundredth of its original pressure, its original temperature being 37°C.

Ans. [227 K]

3-18 One mole of oxygen, initially at a temperature 290 K is adiabatically compressed so that its pressure increases ten fold. Find :

(a) the gas temperature after the compression, and

(b) the work that has been performed on the gas

Ans. [560 K, 5602 J]

3-19 A cylinder contains 0.15 kg of hydrogen. It is closed by a piston supporting a weight of 74 kg. What amount of heat should be supplied to lift the weight by 0.6 m ? Assume that the process is isobaric and that the heat capacity of the vessel and the external pressure are negligible.

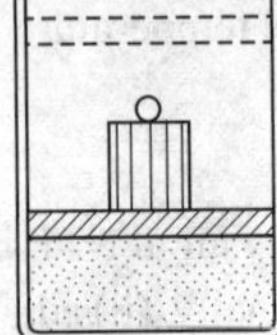

Figure 3.105

Ans. [1523 J]

3-20 Find the ratio of number of moles of a monoatomic and a diatomic gas whose mixture has a value of adiabatic exponent $\gamma = 3/2$.

Ans. [1]

3-21 10 J of heat is supplied to a gas enclosed in a cylindrical vessel in open atmosphere closed by a smooth piston of cross sectional area 4×10^{-4} m^2. It is observed that piston moves out by 10 cm. Find the amount by which the internal energy of the gas will increase. Given that the atmospheric pressure is 10^5 Pa.

Ans. [6 J]

3-22 Figure-3.106 shows a cycle under which two moles of an ideal gas undergoes. Find the efficiency of the cycle.

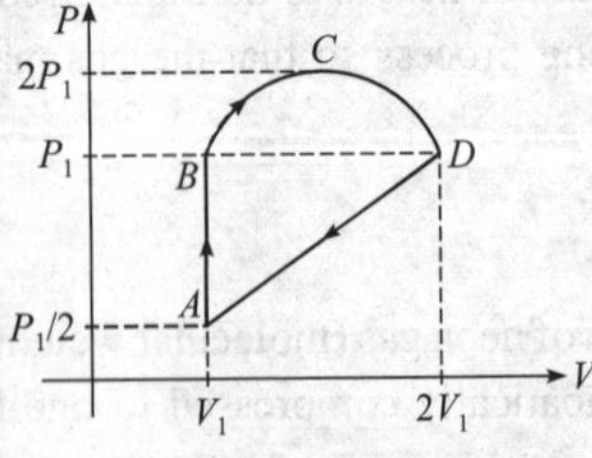

Figure 3.106

Ans. [25.8%]

3-23 A thermally insulated vessel contains a heat-insulating piston which can move in the vessel without friction. Initially the piston lies at the extreme left end and it is connected to a spring to the right wall of the vessel through a spring whose length is equal to the length of the cylinder. The right portion is completely evacuated and a mole of an ideal monatomic gas is introduced in the left portion. Find the heat capacity of this spring controlled monatomic gas system, neglecting the heat capacities of the vessel, piston, and spring.

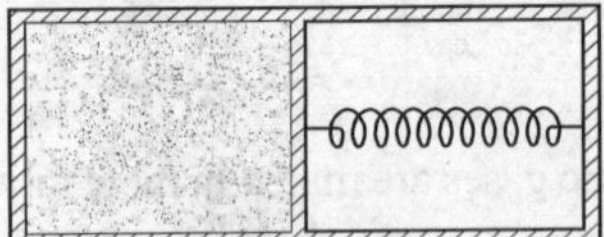

Figure 3.107

Ans. [2 R]

3-24 One cubic metre of hydrogen at 0°C and 76 cm of Hg weighs 0.0896 kg. The specific heat capacities of hydrogen at constant pressure and volume are 3409 and 2411 cal per kg per kelvin, respectively. Calculate the value of J. ($g = 9.81$ m s^{-2}, density of mercury $= 13.6 \times 10^3$ kg per cubic metre)

Ans. [4.15 J cal^{-1}]

3-25 A gas of given mass at a pressure of 10^5 Nm^{-2} expands isothermally until its volume is doubled and then adiabatically until its volume is again doubled. Find the final pressure of the gas. ($\gamma = 1.4$)

Ans. [1.89×10^4 Nm^{-2}]

3-26 Two different adiabatic paths for the same gas intersects two isothermals at T and T' as shown in the P-V as shown in figure-3.108. How does (V_a/V_d) compare with (V_b/V_c)?

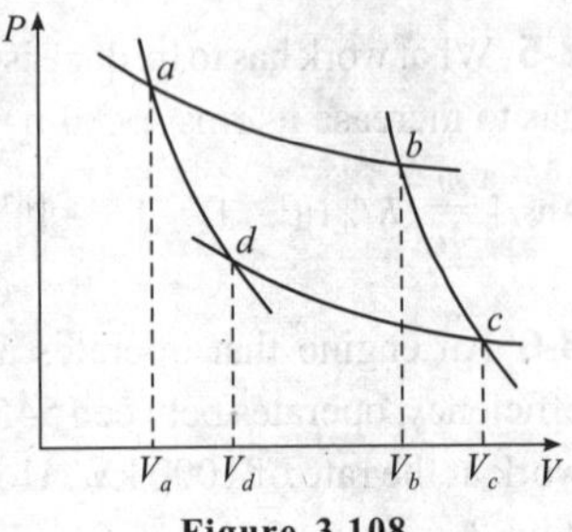

Figure 3.108

Ans. [$\frac{V_a}{V_d} = \frac{V_b}{V_c}$]

3-27 A vertical cylinder of cross-sectional area S contains one mole of an ideal monoatomic gas under a piston of mass M. At a certain instant a heater which supplies heat at the rate of q J/s is switched on under the piston. Determine the velocity v of the piston under the condition that the pressure remains constant and the gas under the piston is thermally insulated.

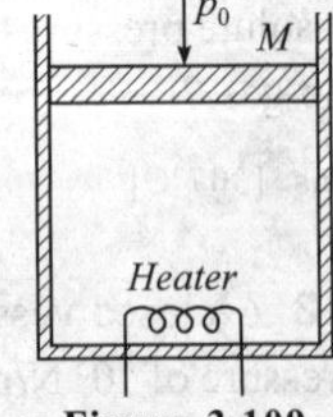

Figure 3.109

Ans. [$v = \frac{2}{5} \frac{q}{p_0 S + Mg}$]

3-28 A vessel containing one gram-mole of oxygen is enclosed in a thermally insulated vessel. The vessel is than moved with a constant speed v_0 and then suddenly stopped. The process results in a rise in the temperature of the gas by 1°C. Calculate the speed v_0.

Ans. [36.0 ms^{-1}]

3-29 An ideal gas with the adiabatic exponent γ undergoes a process in which its internal energy relates to the volume as $U = aV^{\alpha}$, where a and α are constants. Find :

(a) the work performed by the gas and the amount of heat to be transferred to this gas to increase its internal energy by ΔU;

(b) the molar heat capacity of the gas in this process.

Ans. [(a) $W = \Delta U\,(\gamma - 1)/\alpha$; $Q = \Delta U\,[1 + (\gamma - 1)/\alpha]$;
(b) $C = R/(\gamma - 1) + R/\alpha$]

3-30 Two moles of an ideal gas at temperature $T_0 = 300$ K was cooled isochorically so that the pressure was reduced to half. Then, in an isobaric process, the gas expanded till its temperature got back to the initial value. Find the total amount of heat absorbed by the gas in the process.

Ans. [2490 J]

3-31 Suppose that 5 g of helium gas is heated from – 30°C to 120°C. Find its change in internal energy and the work it does if the heating occurs (a) at constant volume and (b) at constant pressure. For helium, $C_v = 0.75$ cal/g · C° and $C_p = 1.25$ cal/g · C°.

Ans. [(a) 2350 J, Zero; (b) 2350 J, 1570 J]

3-32 10 gm of oxygen at a pressure 3×10^5 N/m² and temperature 10°C is heated at constant pressure and after heating it occupies a volume of 10 litres. (a) Find the amount of heat received by the gas and (b) the energy of thermal motion of gas molecules before heating.

Ans. [(a) 7.9×10^3 J (b) 1.8×10^3 J]

3-33 A gas expands adiabatically and its volume doubles while its absolute temperature drops 1.32 times. What number of degrees of freedom do the gas molecules have ?

Ans. [5 degrees of freedom]

3-34 The closed cylinder shown in figure-3.110 has a freely moving piston separating chambers 1 and 2. The chamber (1) contains 25 mg of N_2 gas and chamber (2) contains 40 mg of helium gas. When equilibrium is established, what is the ratio of $\frac{L_1}{L_2}$? What is the ratio of number of moles of N_2 to number of moles of He, given molecular weights of N_2 and He are 28 and 4 respectively ?

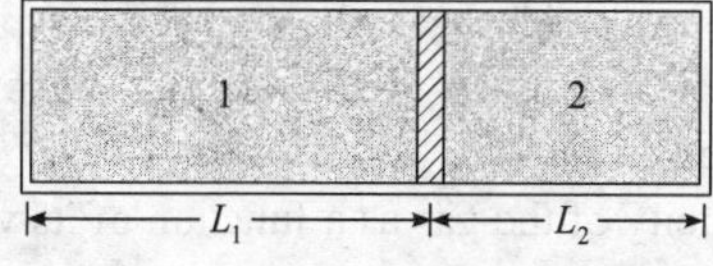

Figure 3.110

Ans. [$\frac{L_1}{L_2} = \frac{n_1}{n_2} = 0.089$]

3-35 A thermodynamic system undergoes a change of state during which it absorbs 100 kJ of heat and it does 50 kJ of work. Then the system is brought back to its original state through a process during which 120 kJ of heat is absorbed by it. Find the work done by the system in the second process.

Ans. [170 kJ]'

3-36 A certain volume of a gas (diatomic) expands isothermally at 20°C until its volume is doubled and then adiabatically until its volume is again doubled. Find the final temperature of the gas, given $\gamma = 1.4$ and that there is 0.1 mole of the gas. Also calculate the work done in the two cases. $R = 8.3$ J mole^{-1} K^{-1}.

Ans. [– 50.9°C, 1.47×10^2 J]

3-37 A cyclic process $ABCD$ is shown in the PV diagram in figure-3.111. Draw the VT graph for the same process.

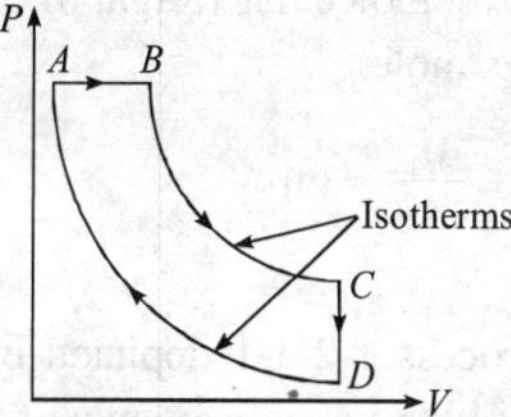

Figure 3.111

3-38 In a cyclic process initially a gas is at 10^5 Pa pressure and its volume is 2 m³. First it undergoes an isobaric expansion to increase its volume to 2.5 m³. The in an isochoric process its pressure is doubled. Now the gas is brought back to its initial state by changing the pressure of gas linearly with its volume. Find the total amount of heat supplied to the gas in the process.

Ans. [– 25000 J]

3-39 A certain volume of dry air at 20°C is expanded to three times of its initial volume (i) slowly, (ii) suddenly. Calculate the final pressure and temperature in each case. Atmospheric pressure = 10^5 N m^{-2}, γ of air = 1.4.

Ans. [3.3×10^4 Nm^{-2}, – 84.2°C, 2.15×10^4 Nm^{-2}]

3-40 Figure-3.112 shows two containers each of volume 2×10^{-4} m³ containing equal amount of an ideal gas. The two containers are connected by a U-tube containing some mercury in it as shown in figure. Initial pressure and temperature of the two containers are 75 cm of Hg and 300 K. If the two containers are supplied 5 J and 10 J heat respectively and the mercury level in the two sides of the U-tube was same before supplying heat to the containers, find the final difference in the heights of the mercury in the two sides of the U-tube. Neglect the volume of the connecting tubes and the U-tube. Given that the molar specific heat of gas at constant volume is $C_v = 12.5$ J/mole-K.

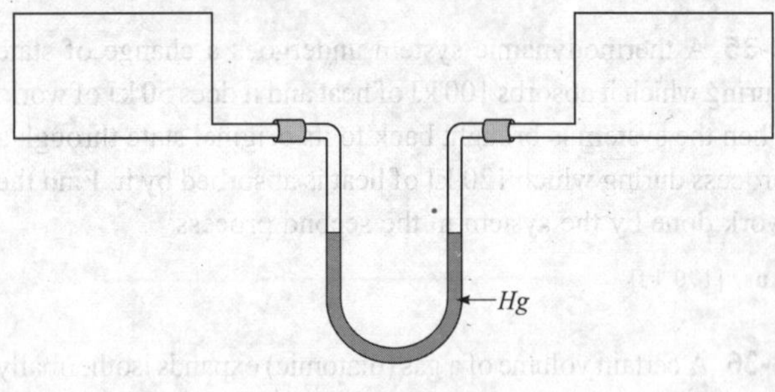

Figure 3.112

Ans. [12.5 cm]

3-41 A closed vessel impermeable to heat contains ozone (O_3) at a temperature of $t_1 = 527°C$. After some time the ozone is completely converted into oxygen (O_2). Find the increase of the pressure in the vessel if $q = 34$ kcal have to be spent to form one g-mole of ozone from oxygen. M_1 = molecular weight of ozone = 48 and M_2 = molecular weight of oxygen = 32, C_V of oxygen = 5 cal/deg. mole.

Ans. [$\frac{p_2}{p_1} = \frac{q}{C_V T_1} + \frac{M_1}{M_2} = 10$]

3-42 A cyclic process 1-2-3-1 depicted on *V-T* diagram is performed on a gas with a certain amount of an ideal gas. Show the same process on a *P-V* diagram and indicate the stages when the gas received and when it rejected heat.

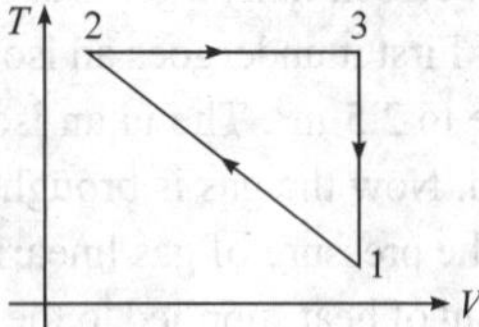

Figure 3.113

3-43 Figure-3.114 shows a horizontal cylindrical vessel of length 2 *l* is separated by a thin heat-insulating piston into two parts each of which contains *n* moles of an ideal monatomic gas at temperature *T*. The piston is connected to the end faces of the vessel by undeformed springs of stiffens *k*. When an amount of heat *Q* is supplied slowly to the gas in the right part, the piston is displaced by $x = l/2$. Find the amount of heat Q' given away at the temperature *T* to a thermostat with which the gas in left part is in thermal contact all the time.

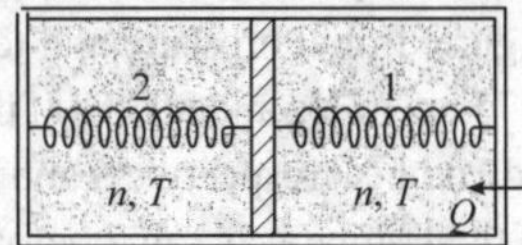

Figure 3.114

Ans. [$Q - 3\,nRT - \frac{5}{2}kl^2$]

3-44 Figure-3.115 shows three processes for an ideal gas. The temperature at '*a*' is 600 K, pressure 16 atm and volume 1 litre. The volume at '*b*' is 4 litre. Out of the two processes *ab* and *ac*, one is adiabatic and the other is isothermal. The ratio of specific heats of the gas is 1.5. Answer the following :

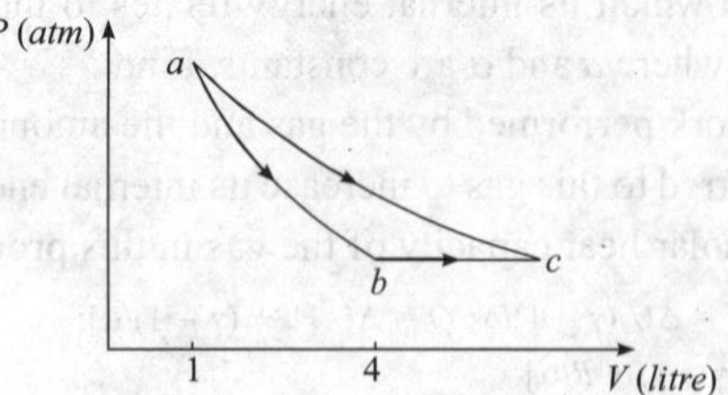

Figure 3.115

(i) Which of *ab* and *ac* processes is adiabatic - Why ?
(ii) Compute the pressures of the gas at *b* and *c*.
(iii) Compute the temperature at *b* and *c*.
(iv) Compute the volume at *c*.

Ans. [(ii) $P_b = P_c = 2$ atm (iii) $T_b = 300$ K; $T_c = 600$ K (iv) $V_c = 8$ litre]

3-45 A gas has a volume 1000 cm^2 at 80 cm of mercury pressure. It is expanded adiabatically to 1190 c.c. The pressure falls to 60 cm of Hg. Calculate the workdone by the gas.

Ans. [17.53 J]

3-46 A certain mass of a gas is taken at 0ºC in a cylinder whose walls are perfect insulators. The gas is compressed (a) slowly, (b) suddenly till its pressure is increased to 20 times the initial pressure ($\gamma = 1.4$). Calculate the final temperature in each case.

Ans. [In each case final temperature is 389.2 ºC]

3-47 In a polytropic process an ideal gas ($\gamma = 1.40$) was compressed from volume $V_1 = 10$ litres to $V_2 = 5$ litres. The pressure increased from $p_1 = 10^5$ Pa to $p_2 = 5 \times 10^5$ Pa. Determine : (a) the polytropic exponent *n*, (b) the molar heat capacity of the gas for the process.

Ans. [2.32, 1.74 R]

3-48 A diatomic ideal gas is heated at constant volume until its pressure is tripled. It is again heated at constant pressure until its volume is doubled. Find the molar heat capacity for the whole process.

Ans. [$\frac{31}{10}R$]

3-49 One mole of an ideal gas whose adiabatic exponent equals γ undergoes a process $p = p_0 + \alpha/V$, where p_0 and α are positive constants. Find :

(a) heat capacity of the gas as a function of its volume;
(b) the internal energy increment of the gas, the work

performed by it, and the amount of heat transferred to the gas, if its volume increased from V_1 to V_2.

Ans. [(a) $C = \gamma R/(\gamma - 1) + \alpha R/p_0V$; (b) $\Delta U = p_0(V_2 - V_1)/(\gamma - 1)$; $A = p_0(V_2 - V_1) + \alpha\, ln\,(V_2/V_1)$; $Q = \gamma\, p_0(V_2 - V_1)/(\gamma - 1) + \alpha\, ln\,(V_2/V_1)$]

3-50 One mole of argon is expanded polytropically, the polytropic constant being $n = 1.50$. In the process, the gas temperature changes by $\Delta T = -26$ K. Find :

(a) the amount of heat obtained by the gas;

(b) the work performed by the gas.

Ans. [(a) 0.11 kJ; (b) 0.43 kJ]

3-51 A reversible heat engine carries 1 mole of an ideal monoatomic gas around the cycle 1-2-3-1. Process 1-2 takes place at constant volume, process 2-3 is adiabatic, and process 3-1 takes place at constant pressure as shown in figure-3.116. Compute the values for the heat ΔQ, the change in internal energy ΔU, and the work done ΔW, for each of the three processes and for the cycle as a whole.

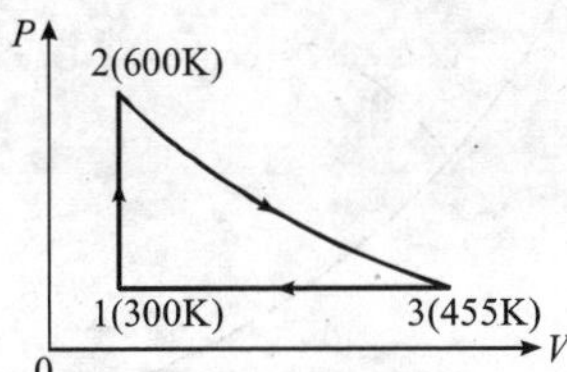

Figure 3.116

Ans. [$\Delta W = 0$, $\Delta U = 3735$, $\Delta Q = 3735$ J, $\Delta U = -1805$ J, $\Delta W = 1805$ J, $\Delta Q = 0$, $\Delta U = -1930$ J, $\Delta W = -1286$ J, $\Delta Q = -3216$ J]

3-52 Two identical containers *A* and *B* with frictionless pistons contain the same ideal gas at the same temperature and the same volume *V*. The mass of gas in cylinder *A* is m_1 and that in cylinder *B* is m_2. The gas in each cylinder is now allowed to expand isothermally to the same final volume 2*V*. Find the ratio of the two masses if the change in pressure in cylinder *B* is found to be 1.5 times higher than that of cylinder *A*.

Ans. [2/3]

3-53 An ideal gas undergoes a thermodynamic process, indicator diagram of which is shown in figure-3.117. Find the work done by the gas in going from state-1 to state-4.

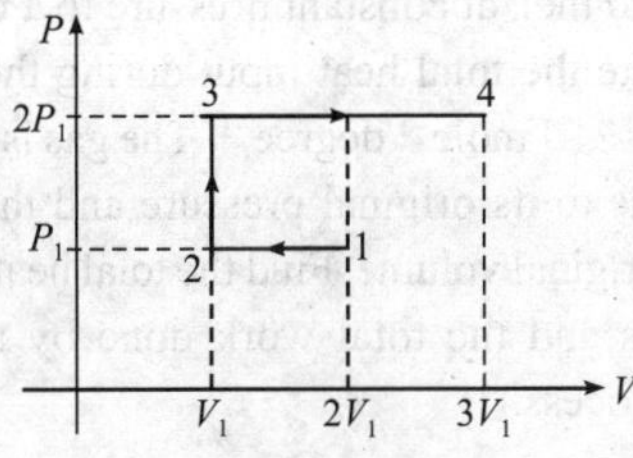

Figure 3.117

Ans. [3 PV]

3-54 A monoatomic ideal gas of two moles is taken through a cyclic process starting from A as shown in figure-3.118. The volume ratios are $V_B/V_A = 2$ and $V_D/V_A = 4$. If the temperature T_A at state A is 27°C, find :

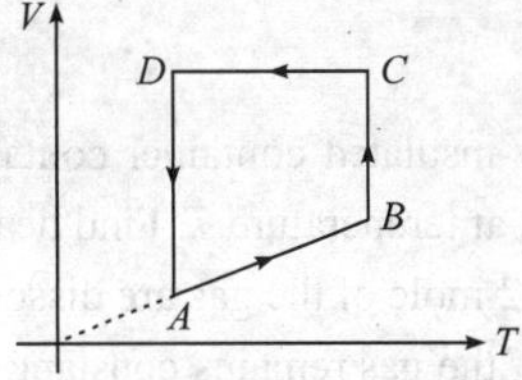

Figure 3.118

(a) The temperature of the gas at point *B*.

(b) Heat absorbed or released by the gas in each process.

(c) The total work done by the gas during the complete cycle.

Ans. [(a) 600 K (b) 1500 R, 831.6 R, – 900 R, – 831.6 R (c) 600 R]

3-55 Suppose that 30 g of highly compressed air ($C_V = 0.177$ cal/g · C°) is confined to a cylinder by a piston. Its volume is 2400 cm^3, its pressure is 10×10^5 Pa, and its temperature is 35°C. The air is expanded adiabatically until its volume is 24,000 cm^3. During the process, 4100 J of work is done by the air. What is its final temperature ?

Ans. [– 150°C]

3-56 A mole of a monatomic perfect gas is adiabatically compressed when its temperature rises from 27°C to 127°C. Calculate the work done.

Ans. [1246.5 J']

3-57 In a certain polytropic process the volume of argon is increased $\alpha = 4$ times and the pressure decreased $\beta = 8$ times. Find the molar heat capacity of argon in this process, assuming it to be a perfect gas.

Ans. [– 4.2 J K^{-1} mole^{-1} where $n = \dfrac{\ln\beta}{\ln\alpha}$]

3-58 Gaseous hydrogen contained initially under standard conditions in a sealed vessel of volume $V = 5.01$ was cooled by $\Delta T = 55$ K. Find how much the internal energy of the gas will change and what amount of heat will be lost by the gas.

Ans. [0.25 kJ, 0.25 kJ]

3-59 A cylinder contains 3 moles of oxygen at a temperature of 27°C. The cylinder is provided with a frictionless piston which maintains a constant pressure of 1 atm on the gas. The gas is heated until its temperature rises to 127°C.

(a) How much work is done by the gas in the process ?

(b) What is the change in the internal energy of the gas ?

(c) How much heat was supplied to the gas ?

Ans. [(a) 2523 J, (b) 1506 cal, (c) 2109 cal]

3-60 One mole of an ideal monoatomic gas at temperature T_0 expands slowly according to the law $P = kV$, where k is a constant. If the final temperature of the gas is $2T_0$, find the heat supplied to the gas.

Ans. [$2RT_0$]

3-61 A thermally insulated container contains 4 mole of an ideal diatomic gas at temperature T. Find heat supplied to this gas, due to which 2 mole of the gas are dissociated into atoms but temperature of the gas remains constant.

Ans. [RT]

3-62 A gaseous system is taken from state-1 to state-2 from three different paths I, II and III as shown in figure-3.119. Calculate the work done by the gas in the three paths I, II and III.

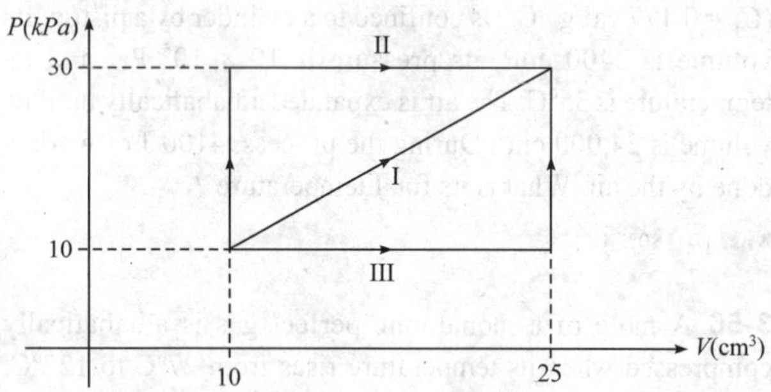

Figure 3.119

Ans. [0.3 J, 0.45 J, 0.15 J]

3-63 Two moles of an ideal monoatomic gas, initially at pressure P_1 and volume V_1, undergo an adiabatic compression until its volume is V_2. Then the gas is given heat Q at constant volume V_2.

(a) Sketch the complete process on a PV diagram.

(b) Find the total work done by the gas, the total change in internal energy and the final temperature of the gas.

Ans. [$-\frac{3}{2}P_1V_1\left[\left(\frac{V_1}{V_2}\right)^{2/3}-1\right]$, $Q+\frac{3}{2}P_1V_1\left[\left(\frac{V_1}{V_2}\right)^{2/3}-1\right]$, $\frac{Q}{3R}+\frac{P_1V_1}{3R}\left(\frac{V_1}{V_2}\right)^{2/3}$]

3-64 A cyclic process 1–2–3–4–1 consisting of two isobars 2–3 and 4–1, isochor 1–2, and a certain process 3–4 represented by a straight line on the P-V diagram involves n moles of an ideal gas as shown in figure-3.120. The gas temperatures in states 1, 2, and 3 are T_1, T_2 and T_3 respectively, and points 3 and 4 lie on the same isotherm. Find the work done by the gas during the cycle.

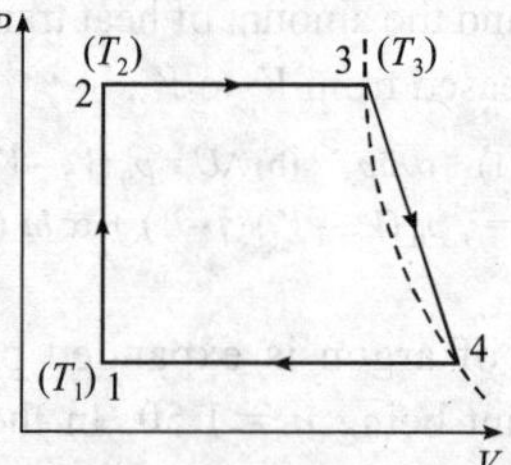

Figure 3.120

Ans. [$W = \frac{1}{2}nR(T_2 - T_1)\left(\frac{T_2}{T_1}+\frac{T_3}{T_2}-2\right)$]

3-65 For the cycle shown in the figure-3.121, find the net heat transfer if 100 g of air is contained in a piston-cylinder arrangement. For air $M = 20$.

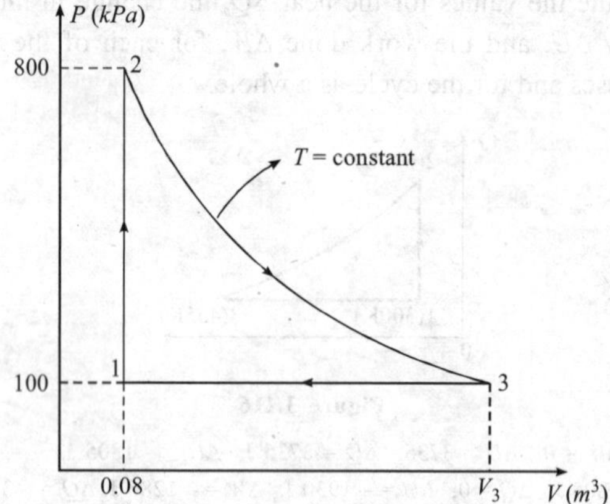

Figure 3.121

Ans. [77.1 KJ]

3-66 One mole of an ideal gas at 290 K temperature expands at constant pressure with volume ratio 2. Then the gas is cooled to its initial temperature at constant volume. Find the increment in internal energy of the gas and the work done by the gas.

Ans. [0, 2.4 kJ]

3-67 A cylinder contains an ideal gas at a pressure of two atmospheres, the volume being 5 litres at a temperature of 250 K. The gas is heated at constant volume to a pressure of 4 atmospheres and then at constant pressure to a temperature of 650 K. Calculate the total heat input during these processes. For the gas $C_v = 21$ J mole^{-1} degree^{-1}. The gas is then cooled at constant volume to its original pressure and then at constant pressure to its original volume. Find the total heat output during these processes and the total work done by the gas in the whole cyclic process.

Ans. [Total heat input = 4701 J, Total heat output = 4397 J, Work done = 304 J]

3-68 One mole of an ideal gas is taken from an initial state P_0, V_0 and temperature T_0 through the following cycle: (C_p/C_v for the gas is 1.4) :

(a) Heating at constant volume to a temperature $3T_0$

(b) Adiabatic expansion to a volume $2V_0$

(c) Cooling at constant volume

(d) Adiabatic compression so that it is returned to its initial state.

(i) Show this cycle on a PV diagram

(ii) Calculate efficiency of the cycle.

[Use $(2)^{-1.4} = 0.38$]

Ans. [(b) 25%]

3-69 A gram mole of a gas at 27°C expands isothermally until its volume is doubled. Calculate the amount of work done. ($R = 8$ J mol^{-1} K^{-1})

Ans. [1.66×10^3 J]

3-70 The temperature of 3 kg of nitrogen is raised from 10°C to 100°C. Compute the heat added, the work done and the change in internally energy if (a) this is done at constant volume and (b) if the heating is at constant pressure. For nitrogen $C_p = 1400$ J kg^{-1} K^{-1} and $C_v = 740$ J kg^{-1} K^{-1}.

Ans. [(a) 199800 J (b) 81000 J]

3-71 A heat-conducting piston can freely move inside a closed thermally insulated cylinder with an ideal gas. In equilibrium the piston divides the cylinder into two equal parts, the gas temperature being equal to T_0. The piston is slowly displaced. Find the gas temperature as a function of the ratio η of the volumes of the greater and smaller sections. The adiabatic exponent of the gas is equal to γ.

Ans. [$T = T_0\,[(\eta + 1)^2/4\eta]^{(\gamma - 1)/2}$]

3-72 A heat conducting piston can move freely inside a closed, thermally insulated cylinder with an ideal gas ($\gamma = 5/3$). At equilibrium, the piston divides the cylinder into two equal parts, the gas temperature being equal to 300 K. The piston is slowly displaced by an external agent. Find the gas temperature when the volume of the greater section is seven times the volume of the smaller section.

Ans. [395 K]

3-73 The atomic weight of iodine is 127. A standing wave in a tube filled with iodine gas at 400 K has nodes that are 6.77 cm apart when the frequency is 1000 Hz. Is iodine gas monoatomic or diatomic ?

Ans. [*diatomic*]

3-74 A cubical vessel of side 1 metre contains one gram molecule of nitrogen at pressure of 2 atmospheres and 300 K. If the molecules are assumed to move with their *rms* velocity find the number of collisions per second which he molecules can make with the wall of vessel. Further if the vessel now thermally isolated moved with a constant speed V and then suddenly results in a rise of temperature 2°C. Find V.

Ans. [222.5 K cals, $T_1 = 416.5$ K, $T_2 = 250$ K]

3-75 A gas consisting of rigid diatomic molecules of degree of freedom $r = 5$ was initially at standard pressure $p_0 = 1.013 \times 10^5$ Pa and $T_0 = 273$ K. Then the gas was compressed adiabatically $\eta = 5$ times. Find the mean kinetic energy of a rotating molecule in the final state.

Ans. [7.2×10^{-21} J]

3-76 A cylinder containing a gas is closed by a movable piston. The cylinder is submerged in an ice-bath as shown in figure-3.122. The piston is quickly pushed down from position 1 to position 2. The piston is held at position 2 until the gas is again at 0°C and then slowly raised back to position 1. Represent the whole process on p-V diagram. If $m = 100$ g of ice are melted during the cycle, how much work is done on the gas. Latent heat of ice = 80 cal/g.

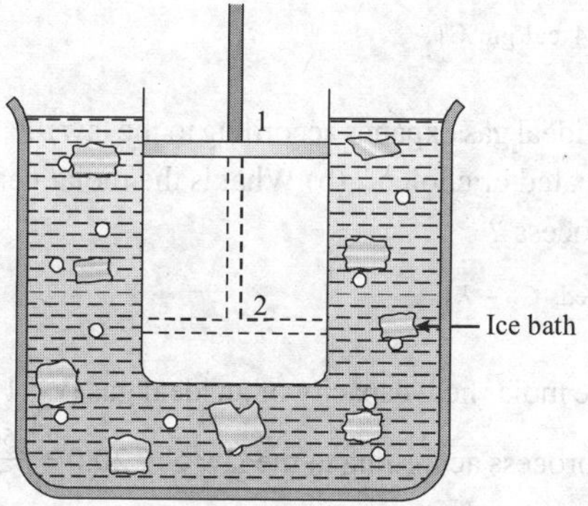

Figure 3.122

Ans. [8000 cal]

3-77 A gas is enclosed in a metallic container of volume V and its initial pressure is p. It is slowly compressed to a volume $V/2$ and then suddenly compressed to $V/4$. Find the final pressure of the gas. If from the initial state the gas is suddenly compressed to $V/2$ and then slowly compressed to $V/4$, what will be the final pressure now.

Ans. [$p(2)^{\gamma+1}$in both cases]

3-78 $1/R$ mole (where R is the magnitude of the gas constant in the SI system) of an ideal diatomic gas is enclosed in a container of volume 4 litres at a pressure of 2×10^5 Pa. The container is suddenly compressed to a volume of 2 litres. Then the gas is

given 200 J of heat at constant pressure.
(a) Plot the complete process on a PT diagram.
(b) Find the total work done by the gas
[Use $2^{1.4} = 2.63$]

Ans. [–583 J]

3-79 An ideal gas is expanding such that PT^2 = constant. The coefficient of volume expansion of the gas is $\frac{A}{T}$, where T is temperature in Kelvin & P is pressure. Calculate the value of A.

Ans. [3]

3-80 An ideal gas expands at a constant pressure of 7.0 atm from 280 mL to 630 mL. Heat then flows out of the gas, at constant volume, and the pressure and temperature are allowed to drop until the temperature reaches its original value. Calculate (a) the total work done by the gas in the process, and (b) the total heat flow into the gas.

Ans. [(a) 248 J; (b) 248 J]

3-81 Find the specific heat of a polyatomic gas at constant volume if the density of this gas in standard conditions is 7.95×10^{-4} gm/cm³. Express your result in cal/gm degree.

Ans. [0.334 cal/gm°C]

3-82 An ideal gas expands according to the law pV^2 = constant (a) Is it heated or cooled ? (b) What is the molar heat capacity in this process ?

Ans. [Cooled, $C_V - R$]

3-83 The molar heat capacity of an ideal gas ($\gamma = 1.40$) varies during a process according to the law $C = 20.0 + \frac{500}{T}$.
(a) Is the process polytropic ?
(b) Find the work done by a mole of the gas when heated from $T_1 = 200$ K to $T_2 = 544$ K.

Ans. [No, 230 J]

3-84 One cubic metre of argon at 27°C is adiabatically compressed so that the final temperature is 127°C. Calculate the new volume of the gas ($\gamma = 5/3$).

Ans. [0.65 m³]

3-85 The efficiency of a thermodynamic cycle 1-2-3-1 as shown in figure below is 20% and for another thermodynamic cycle shown in same figure 1-3-4-1, the efficiency is 10%. Determine the efficiency of the thermodynamic cycle 1-2-3-4-1. The gas is assumed to be ideal.

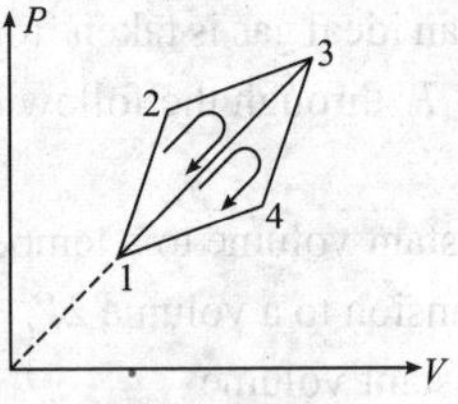

Figure 3.123

Ans. [28%]

3-86 Find the specific heat capacities C_v and C_p for a gaseous mixture consisting of 7.0 g of nitrogen and 20 g of argon. The gases are assumed to be ideal.

Ans. [C_v = 0.42 J/(g · K), C_p = 0.65 J/ (g · K)]

3-87 A gas($\gamma = 1.5$) is enclosed in a thermally insulated container of volume 4×10^{-4} m³ at 1 atmospheric pressure and at a temperature of 300K. If the gas is suddenly compressed to a volume of 10^{-4} m³, what will be the final pressure and the temperature of the gas. What will be your answers for final pressure and temperature if gas is slowly compressed to the same final volume.

Ans. [8 atm, 600 K, same answers]

3-88 The temperature of the sun's interior is estimated to be about 14×10^6 K. Protons ($m = 1.67 \times 10^{-27}$ kg) compose most of its mass. Compute the average speed of a proton by assuming that the protons act as particles in an ideal gas.

Ans. [5.89×10^5 m/s]

3-89 A horizontal insulated cylinder is provided with frictionless non-conducting piston. On each side of the piston there is 50 litres of air at a pressure of 1 atmosphere and 273 K. Heat is slowly supplied to the air at the left hand side, until the piston has compressed the air on the right hand side to 2.5 atmosphere. Find :
(i) Final temperature of air on the right hand side
(ii) Work done on the air on the right hand side
(iii) Final temperature of air on the left hand side
(iv) Heat added to air on the left hand side.

Ans. [(i) 354.7 K (ii) –3741.5 J (iii) 1010 K (iv) 3.749×10^4 J]

3-90 What work has to be done adiabatically to increase the root mean square speed of a mole of a diatomic gas $\eta = 5$ times from $T_1 = 300$ K ?

Ans. [1.5×10^{J4}]

3-91 A rectangular narrow U-tube has equal arm lengths and base length, each equal to $l = 250$ mm. The vertical arms are filled with mercury up to $l/2$ and then one end is sealed as shown in figure-3.124. By heating the enclosed gas all the mercury is expelled. Determine the work done by the gas if the atmospheric pressure $p_0 = 10^5$ Pa, the density of mercury $\rho = 13.6 \times 10^3$ kg/m^3 and cross-sectional area is $S = 1$ cm^2.

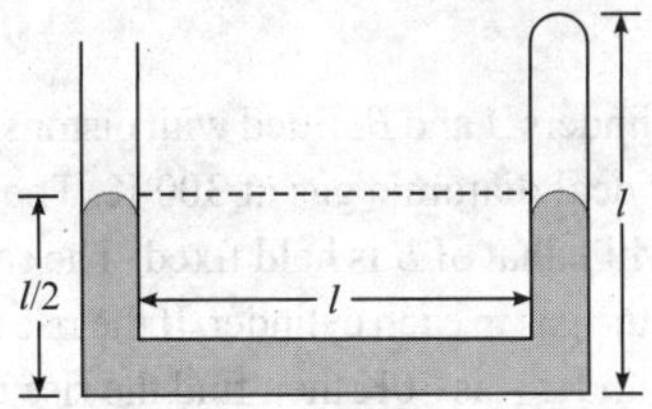

Figure 3.124

Ans. [7.71 J]

3-92 One mole of an ideal gas is contained in a vertical cylinder under a massless piston moving without friction. The piston is slowly raised so that the gas expands isothermally at temperature $T_0 = 300$ K. Find the amount of work done increasing the volume to $\eta = 2$ times. The outside pressure is atmospheric.

Ans. [764.5 J]

3-93 In an experiment with high energy beam, hydrogen ions each of 1.67×10^{-27} kg strike a stationary and thermally insulated target with a velocity of 2×10^7 m s^{-1}, at the rate of 10^{15} ions per second. If the mass of the target is 500 g and specific heat 0.09 cal g^{-1} °C^{-1}, find the time taken for the temperature of the target to rise by 100°C, assuming the whole energy of the ions is converted to heat and absorbed by the target.

Ans. [56.39 s]

3-94 Four moles of a certain ideal gas at 30°C are expanded isothermally to three times its volume and then heated at this constant volume until the pressure is raised to its initial value. In the whole process the heat supplied is 72 KJ. Calculate the ratio C_p/C_v for the gas and state whether it is monoatomic, diatomic or polyatomic gas.

Ans. [1.33]

3-95 One mole of a gas is put under a weightless piston of a vertical cylinder at temperature T. The space over the piston opens into atmosphere. How much work should be performed to increase isothermally the volume under the piston to twice the volume (neglect friction of piston) ?

Ans. [RT [1 – ln(2)]]

3-96 Two moles of a certain ideal gas at 300K is cooled at constant volume so that the pressure is reduced to half the original value. Now the gas is heated at constant pressure so that its temperature becomes equal to the initial temperature. Find the total amount of heat absorbed by the gas in the process.

Ans. [2500 J]

3-97 An ideal gas in a cylinder is slowly compressed to one-third of its original volume. During this process, the temperature of the gas remains constant and the work done in compression is 75 J. (a) How much does the internal energy of the gas change ? (b) How much heat flows into the gas ?

Ans. [(a) Zero; (b) – 75.0 J]

3-98 A diatomic gas initially occupying a volume 3 litres at 300 K and one atmospheric pressure is adiabatically compressed to 1/3 of the initial volume. It is then isobarically expanded till its temperature becomes 300 K, and finally isothermally expanded to restore it to the initial $P - V - T$ conditions. Find the work done during complete cycle of operations.

Ans. [271.6 J]

3-99 For air, $C_V = 0.177$ cal/g · °C. Suppose that air is confined to a cylinder by a movable piston under a constant pressure of 3.0 atm. How much heat must be added to the air if its temperature is to be changed from 27°C to 400°C ? The mass of air in the cylinder is 20 g, and its original volume is 5860 cm^3. *Hint:* Notice that $mc_v\Delta T$ is the internal energy one must add to the gas to change its temperature by ΔT.

Ans. [7730 J]

3-100 A given mass of monoatomic gas occupies a volume of 4 litre at 1 atmosphere pressure and 300 K. It is compressed adiabatically to 1 litre. Find :

(i) Final pressure and temperature

(ii) Increase in the internal energy

Ans. [(i) $P_2 = 10.08$ atm; $T_2 = 756$ K (ii) $\Delta u = 912$ J]

3-101 A sample of an ideal gas is enclosed in two cylindrical vessels of volume V, top of which are closed by identical light pistons. The walls of first vessel are diathermic and always in good thermal contact with the surrounding whereas the walls of second vessel are adiabatic. Initially both the vessels are at atmospheric pressure P_0 and atmospheric temperature T_0. Now in both the vessels the pistons are slowly pulled out to increase the volume of container to $2V$. Now the pistons are clamped and the two walls are connected by a thin tube of negligible volume. Find the final values of temperature and pressure in the containers after a long time.

Ans. [T_0, $\frac{1}{2}P_0$]

3-102 A cyclic process *ABCA* shown on $V-T$ diagram in figure-3.125 is performed with a constant mass m on an ideal gas. Show the same process on a $p-V$ diagram.

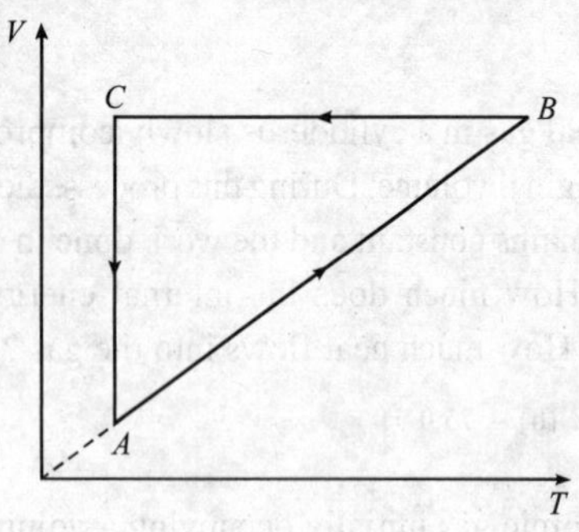

Figure 3.125

3-103 The average degrees of freedom per molecule of a gas are 6. The gas performs 25 J of work in a process when it is expanded at constant pressure. Find the amount of heat absorbed by the gas.

Ans. [100 J]

3-104 Two cylinders *A* and *B*, fitted with pistons, contain equal amounts of an ideal diatomic gas at 300 K. The piston of *A* is free to move, while that of *B* is held fixed. The same amount of heat is given to the gas in each cylinder. If the rise in temperature of the gas in cylinder *A* is 30K then find the rise in temperature of the gas in cylinder *B*.

Ans. [42 K]

* * * * *

Heat Transfer

4

FEW WORDS FOR STUDENTS

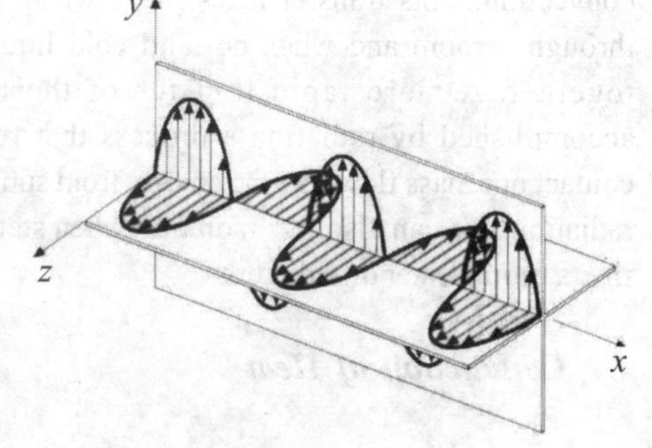

Upto now we've discussed about the effects of heat supply on different substances solids, liquids and gaseous systems. We've learnt how substances respond on absorbing thermal energy and the basic laws of conservation of energy conserved with thermal energy.

Now in this chapter we'll discuss the different ways how the transfer of energy takes places from one point (place) to another. This section is most essential for complete knowledge of thermal physics. In different situations the ways by which thermal energy transfer takes place depends on so many factors including the surrounding environment. Mainly these ways are classified in three broad categories conduction, convection and radiation. In previous chapters it is learnt that whenever heat is supplied to a body or a system, this is accomplished by either of these three ways.

CHAPTER CONTENTS

4.1 *Conduction of Heat*

4.2 *Convection of Heat*

4.3 *Radiation of Heat*

4.4 *Newton's Law of Cooling*

4.5 *Black Body Radiation Spectrum*

COVER APPLICATION

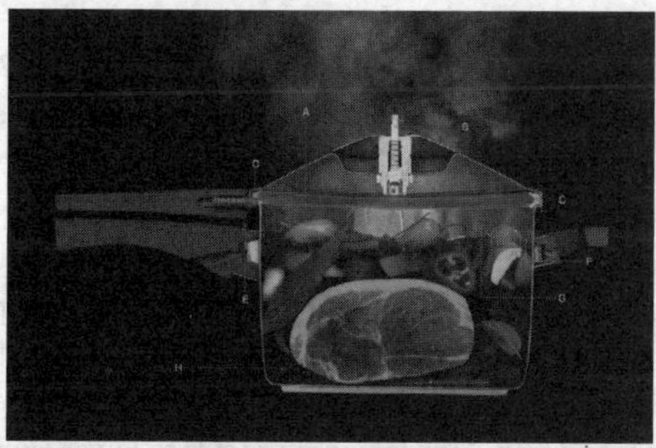

Figure (a)

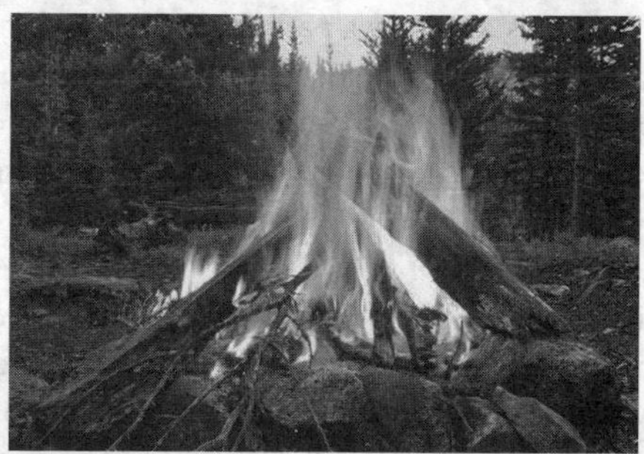

Figure (b)

Convection can only happen in fluids. This includes liquids and gases and is because the molecules have to be free to move. Heat energy can transfer by convection when there is a significant difference in temperature between two parts of a fluid. When this temperature difference exists, hot fluids rise and cold fluids sink, and then currents, or movements, are created in the fluid. Figure-(a) Shows a pressure cooker inside of which when its bottom is heated, due-to convection hot water flows up and heated the vegetables even in upper part of the cooker so it cooks uniformly. Figure-(b) shows a camp fire in which due to fire, hot air is lifted up and cold air from side is pulled and convection currents setup in the surrounding of fire that's why the region above fire is extremely hot compared to side region.

Heat energy can be transferred in three ways from one place to another, Conduction, Convection and Radiation. When one end of a metal rod is heated, the other end gets warm. This is an example of conduction, in which thermal energy is transferred without any net movement of the material itself. It is accomplished due to vibration and collisions of material particles. Conduction is a relatively slow process. A more rapid process of heat transfer is accomplished through the mass-motion or flow of some fluid, such as air or water and is called convection. This transfer takes place when warm air flows through a room and when hot and cold liquids are poured together. A more rapid transfer of thermal energy is accomplished by radiation a process that requires neither contact nor mass flow like the energy from sun comes to us by radiation. We can also feel radiation when standing near by a fire, a room heater or radiators.

4.1 Conduction of Heat

If one end of a metal rod is placed in a flame while the other is held in the hand, that part of the rod one is holding becomes hotter and hotter, although it is not itself in direct contact with the flame. Heat is said to reach the cooler end of the rod by "*thermal conduction*" through the material of the rod. The molecules at the hot end of the rod increase the energy of their vibration as the temperature increases. Then, as they collide with their more slowly moving neighbours on the rod toward colder end, some of their energy is shared with these neighbours, and they in turn pass it along those still farther from the flame. Hence energy of thermal motion is passed along from one molecule to the next, while each individual molecule remains at its original position.

Most of the metals are good conductors of electricity and also of heat. Conduction of electricity is by the free electrons in metal lattice which are detached from their parent molecules and are free to move in the lattice region called conduction band which is evenly spreaded in the whole lattice of the metal. The free electrons also play a part in conduction of heat, and the reason metals are such good heat conductors is that the free electrons provide an effective mechanism for carrying thermal energy from the hotter to the colder portions of the metal.

Conduction of heat can take place in a body only when different parts of body are at different temperatures, and the direction of heat flow is always from points of higher temperature to those at lower temperature. Figure-4.1 shows a metal bar connecting two bodies at temperature T_1 and T_2 ($T_1 > T_2$). The sides of the rod are covered by an insulating material, so that no heat flow takes place to the sides (surroundings). Practically even the best heat insulators also conduct heat to some extent. Perfect heat insulator is just an idealized concept.

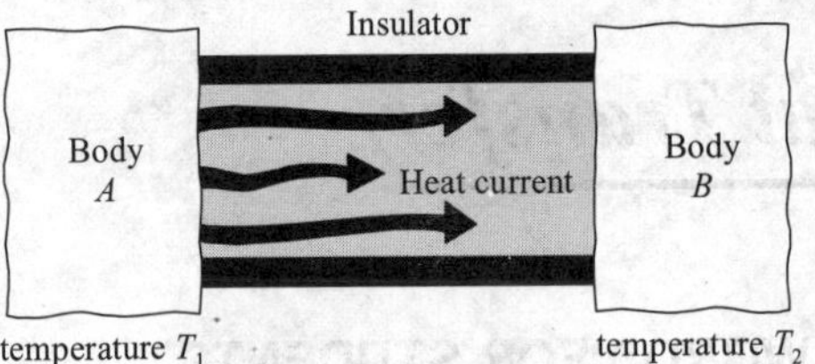

Figure 4.1

In the above example of heat conduction through a bar, after sufficiently long time, the temperature within the bar is found to decrease uniformly with distance from the hot to the cold face. When this uniform temperature gradient is established, at each point within the rod, the temperature remains constant with time. This condition is called steady state heat flow. In next section we'll discuss steady state conduction of heat in more details.

An objects usefulness as a thermal conductor depends in a number of things including its length, thickness and the material from which it is made. Initially we have discussed that when two bodies at different temperatures are connected by a thermally conducting material, heat flows from high temperature body to that which is at a lower temperature. The process by which this thermal energy is transferred through the material is called conduction of heat. Lets discuss conduction in detail step by step.

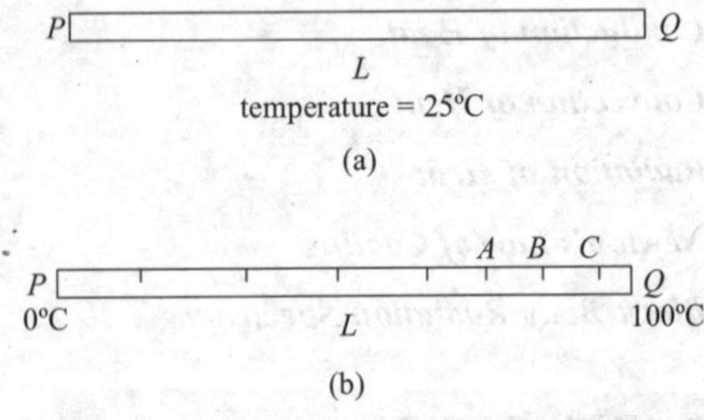

Figure 4.2

Consider an iron rod PQ of length L shown in figure-4.2(a). It is initially at room temperature 25°C. If at an instant left end P of the rod is submerged in an ice bath at 0°C and the other end Q is submerged in boiling water at 100°C. Just after this the temperature of different parts of rod will start changing with time. The part of rod near to end P will have its temperature falling with time and the part near to end Q will have its temperature rising with time. This happens due to heat flow through the rod from high temperature side to lower temperature side. Lets discuss is depth. Consider a part of rod near to end Q (marked as AB (in figure-4.2b) as shown in figure-4.3. If temperature to the right of point B is 90°C and that of segment AB and to the left of A are 82°C and 76°C respectively then due to temperature difference some heat say ΔQ_1 flows from end C

to end B then this heat increases the agitation of the molecules of the material in segment BC then due to the vibration and collision of these molecules with their adjacent atoms or molecules, some heat say ΔQ_2 is transferred to segment AB. Some of this ΔQ_1 was absorbed by segment BC, that will raise the temperature of BC by some value, hence ΔQ_2 will be less then ΔQ_1. Similarly when ΔQ_2 heat comes to segment AB, some of this increases the temperature of segment AB and rest is conducted to the next segments of the rod and in this manner heat is conducted to the other end of the rod for some time.

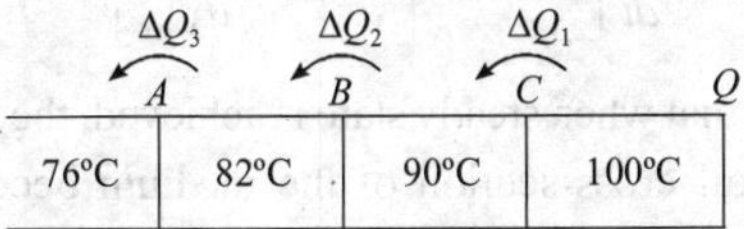

Figure 4.3

After some time we can observe that as the temperature of individual segments of the rod is increasing, the temperature difference between adjacent segments is approaching a constant value as in figure-4.3 the difference of temperature between BC and the end Q was 10°C and that between segments BC and AB was 8°C and after some time as shown in figure-4.4 temperature of the segments CQ, BC and AB are 95° C, 90°C and 86°C respectively the temperature difference is decreasing and hence as temperature difference decreases rate of heat flow becomes slower and ΔQ_1 and ΔQ_2 will be approximately same thus the amount of heat absorbed decreases with time.

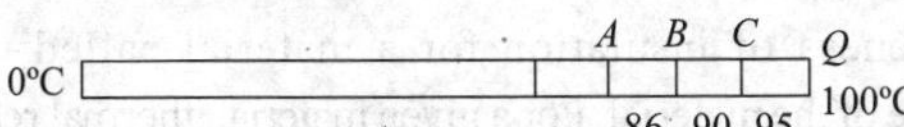

Figure 4.4

Now after a long time when temperature difference between different equally spaced segment of rod becomes equal the rate of heat taken by a segment will be equal to the rate of heat given to the next segment and at this stage no abortion of heat takes place by any segment of rod and temperature of every part of rod becomes constant. This is called steady state of thermal conduction. In steady state throughout the medium rate of flow of heat becomes constant and the amount of heat enters from one end is equal to the amount of heat leaving from the other end. Thus we state in steady state of thermal conduction, in the medium a constant temperature gradient is established and temperature of every part of the medium becomes constant as shown in figure-4.5 for the example we've discussed.

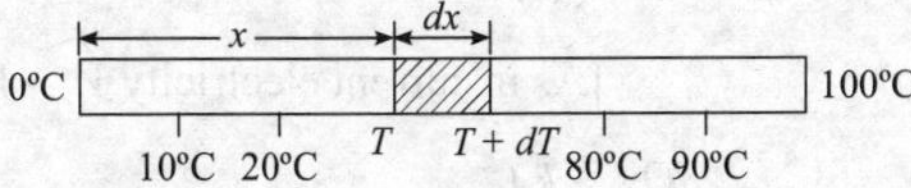

Figure 4.5

Thus in steady state if at a distance x from one end of the rod temperature is T and at a distance $x + dx$, temperature is $T + dT$ than the temperature gradient of the rod at a distance x is given as

$$\frac{dT}{dx} = \textit{constant throughout the rod in steady state}$$

This shows that in steady state, in the medium the temperature of medium varies linearly from one end to the other.

4.1.1 Analysis of Heat Conduction in Steady State

In steady state conduction of heat through a medium is uniform and very easy to understand compared to the case before steady state when continuous absorption of heat takes place by every part of the medium during conduction.

To understand the thermal conduction mathematically, we consider two bodies maintained at different temperature T_1 and T_2 respectively as shown in figure-4.6. The two bodies are connected by the thermally conducting rod of length l and area of cross-section A as shown. After connecting the two bodies, it will take some time to be in steady state. When steady flow of heat from one body to another starts. This heat flow rate dQ/dt is observed as

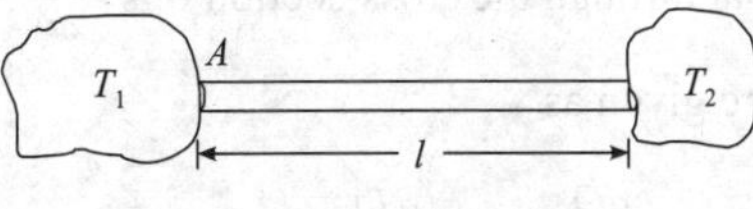

Figure 4.6

(i) Directly proportional to temperature difference

$$\frac{dQ}{dt} \propto (T_1 - T_2) \quad \ldots(4.1)$$

(ii) Directly proportional to area of cross-section, through which heat is flowing

$$\frac{dQ}{dt} \propto A \quad \ldots(4.2)$$

(iii) Inversely proportional to the length of the medium (rod) through which heat is flowing

$$\frac{dQ}{dt} \propto \frac{1}{l} \quad \ldots(4.3)$$

From the equations-(4.1), (4.2) and (4.3), we have

$$\frac{dQ}{dt} = k\frac{A(T_1 - T_2)}{l} \quad \ldots(4.4)$$

Here k is the proportionality constant and depends on material of the medium through which heat is flowing and it is termed as thermal conductivity of the medium. The *SI* units used for heat flow are J/sec or W. So the *SI* units of k are J/s-m°C or W/m°C. A high thermal conductivity indicates a good heat conductor and a low thermal conductivity indicates a good heat insulator. When we design a good insulator, the first requirement is to choose a material with a small thermal conductivity so from equation-(4.4) the heat flow is small. In addition by minimizing area of contact A and making the path length l as long as possible, we can further reduce the heat flow.

4.1.2 Heat Transfer Before Steady State

In previous section we've discussed that in steady state heat conduction through the material of a medium takes place in such a manner that no absorption of heat takes place and throughout the material the rate of flow of heat remains constant and a uniform temperature gradient exist in the medium.

As discussed earlier, before steady state the amount of heat transferred in the medium to further sections decreases as some amount of heat is absorbed by the intermediate sections of the material, this is explained in figure-4.7. This figure shows a section of material through which heat is conducted from high temperature end to low temperature end of the medium. Consider two cross-section A and B in the medium. Let at an instant the rate of flow of heat through the cross-section A is $\frac{dQ_1}{dt}$ and that through the cross-section B is $\frac{dQ_2}{dt}$. Then these flow rates are given as

$$\frac{dQ_1}{dt} = kA \left.\frac{dT}{dx}\right|_A$$

and
$$\frac{dQ_2}{dt} = kA \left.\frac{dT}{dx}\right|_B$$

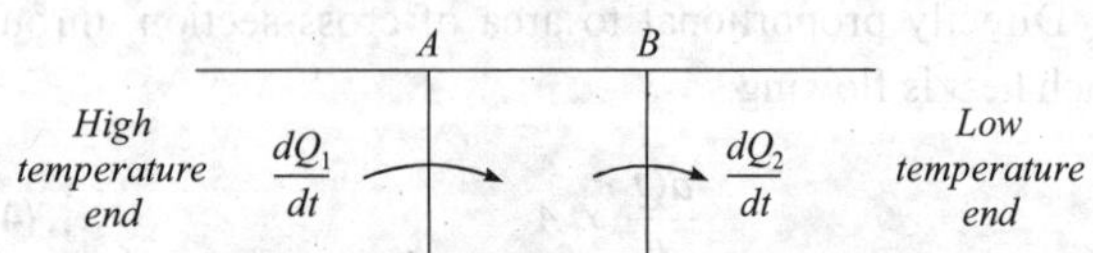

Figure 4.7

Here $\left.\frac{dT}{dx}\right|_A$ and $\left.\frac{dT}{dx}\right|_B$ are the temperature gradients at the location of cross sections A and B respectively.

Here it is obvious that if the medium steady state is not achieved $\frac{dQ_2}{dt}$ must be less than $\frac{dQ_1}{dt}$ as some amount of heat is absorbed by the section AB. Thus here we can say that the rate at which the section AB absorbs heat at this instant is given as

$$\left.\frac{dQ}{dt}\right|_{absorbed\ by\ AB} = \frac{dQ_1}{dt} - \frac{dQ_2}{dt}$$

or
$$= kA\left[\left.\frac{dT}{dx}\right|_A - \left.\frac{dT}{dx}\right|_B\right]$$

If the mass of section AB is m and s is the specific heat of the material of section AB, the rate at which temperature of section AB rises $\left.\frac{dT}{dt}\right|_{AB}$ can be given as

$$ms\left.\frac{dT}{dt}\right|_{AB} = kA\left[\left.\frac{dT}{dx}\right|_A - \left.\frac{dT}{dx}\right|_B\right]$$

As we know that when steady state is achieved, the temperature gradient at all cross-section of the medium becomes equal. Thus we can say that as the medium is approaching towards steady state the difference in temperature gradients at cross-section A and B decreases and hence the rate at which the temperature of segment AB is increasing also decreases and in steady state it becomes zero. This is the reason why we say that in steady state the temperature of all segments of the medium becomes constant at a steady value (linearly decreasing from one end to another) and no absorption of heat takes place when heat conduction takes place in steady state.

4.1.3 Thermal Resistance and Ohm's Law in Thermal Conduction

One more parameter can be defined to indicate the effectiveness of insulation for a material called thermal resistance of the material. For a given material, thermal resistance is given as

$$R_{th} = \frac{1}{k}\frac{l}{A} \qquad \ldots(4.5)$$

Here l is the path length for heat flow and A is the area of cross-section of material through which heat is flowing. Students should note that equation-(4.5) can only be used to find thermal resistance of those materials in which cross-sectional area A through which heat is conducted is uniform throughout the path length.

In thermal conduction ohm's law can be stated as "the heat current across a given thermal resistance is directly proportional to the thermal potential (temperature difference) difference across it." Analytically it is given as

$$(T_1 - T_2) = \left(\frac{dQ}{dt}\right)R_{th}$$

[As in current electricity $V_1 - V_2 = IR$]

Here
$$\frac{dQ}{dt} = \frac{kA}{L}(T_1 - T_2) \qquad \ldots(4.6)$$

Equation- (4.6) is exactly same as equation-(4.5). We use this analogy of current electricity in numerical calculations of thermal conduction. We take few examples to understand this analogy.

Illustrative Example 4.1

Consider two rods of equal cross-sectional area A, one of Aluminium and other of Iron joined end to end as shown in figure-4.8. Length of the two rods and their thermal conductivities are l_1, k_1 and l_2, k_2 respectively. If the ends of the rods are maintained at temperature T_1 and T_2, $(T_1 > T_2)$ find the temperature of the junction in steady state.

Figure 4.8

Solution

We know in steady state the rate of heat flow or the thermal current throughout the medium remains constant thus we have

$$\left(\frac{dQ}{dt}\right)_{Al} = \left(\frac{dQ}{dt}\right)_{Fe}$$

If junction temperature is assumed T_x then we have

$$\frac{k_1A(T_1 - T_x)}{l_1} = \frac{k_2A(T_x - T_2)}{l_2}$$

or $$T_x = \frac{\frac{k_1T_1}{l_1} + \frac{k_2T_2}{l_2}}{\frac{k_1}{l_1} + \frac{k_2}{l_2}} = \frac{k_1l_2T_1 + k_2l_1T_2}{k_1l_2 + k_2l_1}$$

Illustrative Example 4.2

A bar of copper of length 75 cm and a bar of steel of length 125 cm are joined together end to end. Both are of circular cross-section with diameter 2 cm. The free ends of the copper and steel bars are maintained at 100°C and 0°C respectively. The surfaces of the bars are thermally insulated. What is the temperature of the copper-steel junction ? What is the heat transmitted per unit time across the junction ? Thermal conductivity of copper 9.2×10^{-2} k cal m^{-1} °C^{-1} s^{-1} and that of steel is 1.1×10^{-2} k cal m^{-1} s^{-1} °C^{-1}.

Solution

Let T_x be the temperature of the junction of the copper and steel bars (Figure-4.9). In the steady state, the rate of flow of heat in the copper bar must be the same as that in the steel bar, i.e. (since their cross-sectional areas are equal)

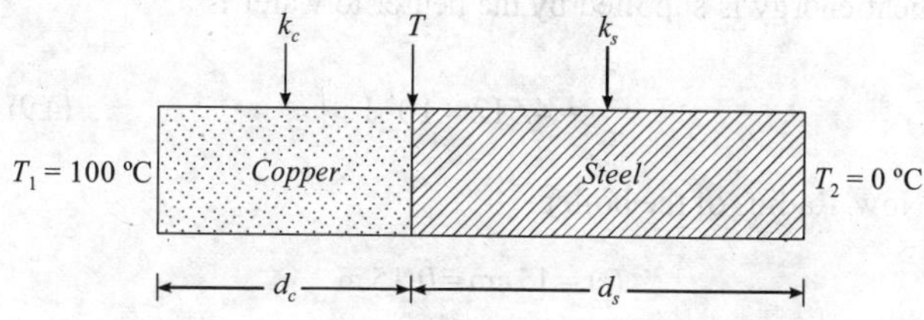

Figure 4.9

$$\frac{dQ}{dt} = \frac{k_cA(T_1 - T_x)}{d_c} = \frac{k_sA(T_x - T_2)}{d_s}$$

or $$\frac{k_c}{k_s} \times \frac{d_s}{d_c} = \frac{T_x - T_2}{T_1 - T_x} \quad \ldots(4.7)$$

Substituting the given values in equation (4.7), we have

$$\frac{9.2 \times 10^{-2}}{1.1 \times 10^{-2}} \times \frac{125}{75} = \frac{T_x - 0}{100 - T_x}$$

or $$T_x = 93.3\text{°C}$$

or Thus the temperature of the junction is 93.3 °C. The heat flowing through the junction per second is

$$\frac{dQ}{dt} = \frac{k_cA(T_1 - T)}{d_c} \quad \ldots(4.8)$$

Given $k_c = 9.2 \times 10^{-2}$ kcal m^{-1} s^{-1} °C^{-1}, $d_c = 75$ cm $= 0.75$ m, and $A = \pi r^2 = \pi \times (10 - 2\text{ m})^2 = 3.14 \times 10^4$ m^2. Also $T_1 = 100$°C and $T = 93.3$°C. Using these values in (4.8) we have

$$\frac{dQ}{dt} = \frac{9.2 \times 10^{-2} \times 3.14 \times 10^{-4} \times (100 - 93.3)}{0.75}$$

$$= 2.58 \times 10^{-4} \text{ J/s}$$

Illustrative Example 4.3

A cylindrical brass boiler of radius 15 cm and thickness 1.0 cm is filled with water and placed on an electric heater. If the water boils at the rate of 200 gm/s, estimate the temperature of the heater filament. Thermal conductivity of brass = 109 J s^{-1} m^{-1} °C^{-1} and heat of vaporisation of water = 2.256×10^3 J g^{-1}.

Solution

Rate of boiling of water = 200 gm/s. Since the heat of vaporisation of water is 2.256×10^3 J/gm, the amount of heat energy required to boil 200 g of water is

$$2.256 \times 10^3 \text{ J g}^{-1} \times 200 \text{ g} = 4.512 \times 10^5 \text{ J}$$

Since water is boiling at the rate of 200 gm/s, the rate at which heat energy is supplied by the heater to water is

$$\frac{Q}{t} = 4.512 \times 10^5 \text{ J s}^{-1} \quad \ldots(4.9)$$

Now, Radius of the boiler

$$(r) = 15 \text{ cm} = 0.15 \text{ m}$$

Base area of the boiler

$$(A) = \pi r^2 = 3.142 \times (0.15)^2 = 0.0707 \text{ m}^2$$

Thickness of brass

$$(d) = 1.0 \text{ cm} = 1.0 \times 10^{-2} \text{ m}$$

Thermal conductivity of brass

$$(k) = 109 \text{ J s}^{-1} \text{ m}^{-1} \text{ °C}^{-1}$$

Temperature of boiling water

$$(T_w) = 100 \text{ °C}$$

If T_f is the temperature of the filament, the rate at which heat energy is transmitted through the base is given by

$$\frac{Q}{t} = \frac{kA(T_f - T_w)}{d} \quad \ldots(4.10)$$

Substituting the values of k, A, T_w and d in (4.10) and equating with (4.9), we get

$$\frac{109 \times 0.0707(T_f - 100)}{1.0 \times 10^{-2}} = 4.512 \times 10^5$$

or $$T_f - 100 = 585.5$$

or $$T_f = 685.5 \text{ °C}$$

Illustrative Example 4.4

A slab of stone of area 3600 cm² and thickness 10 cm is exposed on the lower surface to steam at 100 °C. A block of ice at 0 °C rests on the upper surface of the slab. If in one hour 4.8 kg of ice is melted, calculate the thermal conductivity of the stone.

Solution

Assuming that heat loss from the sides of the slab is negligible, the amount of heat flowing through the slab is :

$$Q = \frac{kA(T_1 - T_2)t}{d} \quad \ldots(4.11)$$

If m is the mass of ice and L the latent heat of fusion, then

$$Q = mL \quad \ldots(4.12)$$

Equating (4.11) and (4.12), we have

$$mL = \frac{kA(T_1 - T_2)t}{d}$$

or $$k = \frac{mLd}{A(T_1 - T_2)t} \quad \ldots(4.13)$$

Given $m = 4.8$ kg,

$d = 10 \text{ cm} = 0.1 \text{ m}$,

$A = 3600 \text{ cm}^2 = 0.36 \text{ m}^2$

$T_1 = 100 \text{ °C}, T_2 = 0 \text{ °C}$ and $t = 1 \text{ hour} = (60 \times 60)\text{s}$

We know that $L = 80 \text{ cal g}^{-1} = 80{,}000 \text{ cal kg}^{-1}$

$= 80{,}000 \times 4.2 \text{ J kg}^{-1} = 3.36 \times 10^5 \text{ J kg}^{-1}$

Substituting these values in equation (4.13) and solving, we get

$$k = 1.24 \text{ J s}^{-1} \text{ m}^{-1} \text{ °C}^{-1} \text{ or } 1.24 \text{ W m}^{-1} \text{ K}^{-1}$$

Illustrative Example 4.5

Few rods of material X and Y are connected as shown in figure-4.10. The cross sectional area of all the rods are same. If the end A is maintained at 80°C and the end F is maintained at 10°C. Calculate the temperatures of junctions B and E in steady state. Given that thermal conductivity of material X is double that of Y.

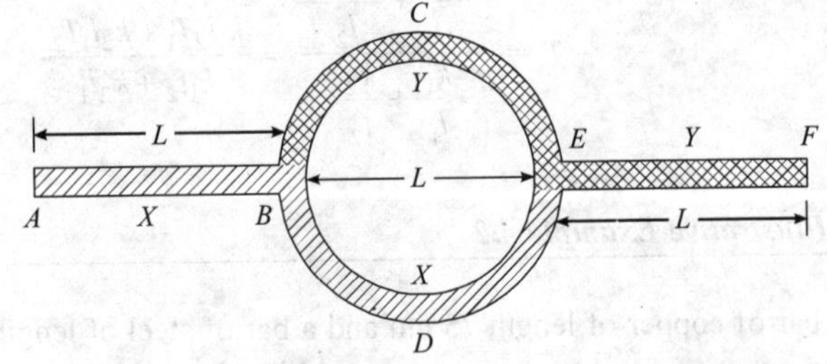

Figure 4.10

Solution

We first find the thermal resistances of the different rods shown in figure-4.10 these are given as

$$R_{AB} = \frac{1}{k_X} \cdot \frac{L}{A}$$

$$R_{BCE} = \frac{1}{k_Y} \cdot \frac{(\pi L/2)}{A}$$

$$R_{BDE} = \frac{1}{k_X} \cdot \frac{(\pi L/2)}{A}$$

$$R_{EF} = \frac{1}{k_Y} \cdot \frac{L}{A}$$

Now in steady state the amount of heat flow from end E to F remains constant as there is no absorption of heat. Then we must have that the amount of heat coming at junction B is equal to the amount of heat having B and same statement can be given for junction E. If temperature of junction B and E are taken as T_B and T_E then we have for junction B.

$$\frac{T_A - T_B}{R_{AB}} = \frac{T_B - T_E}{R_{BCE}} + \frac{T_B - T_E}{R_{BDE}}$$

or $$\frac{80 - T_B}{\frac{1}{k_X} \cdot \frac{L}{A}} = \frac{T_B - T_E}{\frac{1}{k_Y} \cdot \frac{\pi L}{2A}} + \frac{T_B - T_E}{\frac{1}{k_X} \cdot \frac{\pi L}{2A}}$$

or $$80 - T_B = \left(\frac{T_B - T_E}{\pi}\right) + \left(\frac{T_B - T_E}{2\pi}\right)$$

[As $k_X = 2k_Y$]

or $$80 - T_B = \frac{3}{2\pi}(T_B - T_E) \quad \ldots (4.14)$$

Similarly for junction E, we can write

$$\frac{T_B - T_E}{R_{BCE}} + \frac{T_B - T_E}{R_{BDE}} = \frac{T_E - 10}{R_{EF}}$$

or $$\frac{T_B - T_E}{\frac{1}{k_Y} \cdot \frac{\pi L}{2A}} + \frac{T_B - T_E}{\frac{1}{k_X} \cdot \frac{\pi L}{2A}} + \frac{T_E - 10}{\frac{1}{k_Y} \cdot \frac{L}{A}}$$

or $$\frac{2(T_B - T_E)}{\pi} + \frac{4(T_B - T_E)}{\pi} = T_E - 10$$

or $$\frac{3}{4\pi}(T_B - T_E) = T_E - 10 \quad \ldots (4.15)$$

Solving equation-(4.14) and (4.15), we get

$$T_E = 19.74\,°C$$

and $$T_B = 60.52\,°C$$

Illustrative Example 4.6

The space between two thin concentric metallic spherical shells of radii a and b is filled with a thermal conducting medium of conductivity k. The inner shell is maintained at temperature T_1 and outer is maintained at a lower temperature T_2. Calculate the rate of flow of heat in radially outward direction through the medium.

Solution

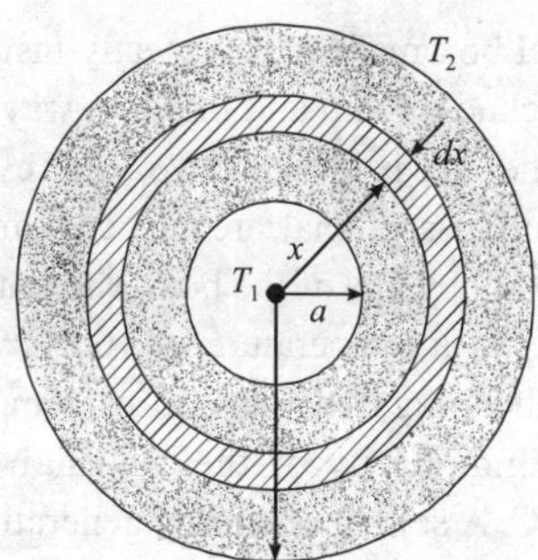

Figure 4.11

Figure-4.11 shows the situation. As we know according to Ohm's Law in thermal conduction, the rate of heat flow or thermal current is given as

$$\frac{dQ}{dt} = \frac{T_1 - T_2}{R_{th}}$$

Where R_{th} is the thermal resistance of the medium through which heat is conducted, which is given as

$$R_{th} = \frac{1}{k} \cdot \frac{L}{A}$$

Where L is the path length and A is the cross-sectional area of the medium through which heat is conducted. But this relation can be used to find thermal resistance only when throughout the path length, area of cross-section A is uniform. In this case in radial direction area is increasing so we can not use the above relation to find thermal resistance.

Here we consider an elemental shell of radius x and width dx in the medium as shown in figure-4.11. If dR be the thermal resistance of this shell then, we have

$$dR = \frac{1}{k} \cdot \frac{dx}{4\pi x^2}$$

Here between the two inner and outer shells, all such small dR resistances can be considered in series combination thus the net thermal resistance of the medium between inner and outer shells is given as

$$R = \int dR = \int_a^b \frac{1}{k} \cdot \frac{dx}{4\pi x^2}$$

or $$R = \frac{1}{4\pi k}\left[-\frac{1}{x}\right]_a^b = \frac{b-a}{4\pi kab}$$

Now rate of flow of heat from inner to outer shell in radial direction is given as

$$\frac{dQ}{dt} = \frac{T_1 - T_2}{R} = \frac{4\pi kab(T_1 - T_2)}{b-a}$$

Illustrative Example 4.7

A closed cubical box made of a perfectly insulating material has walls of thickness 8 cm and the only way for the heat to enter or leave the box is through two solid cylindrical metal plugs, each of cross-sectional area 12 cm^2 and length 8 cm fixed in the opposite walls of the box. The outer surface A of one plug is kept at a temperature of 100°C while the outer surface of the other plug is maintained at a temperature of 4°C. The thermal conductivity of the material of the plug is 0.5 cal/cm sec °C. A source of energy generating 36 cal s^{-1} is enclosed inside the box. Find the equilibrium temperature of the inner surface of the box assuming that it is the same at all points on the inner surface.

Solution

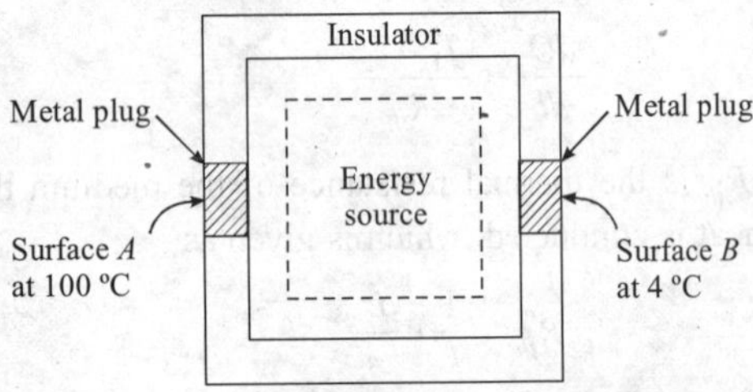

Figure 4.12

At equilibrium, the total energy generated by the source per second is equal to the heat leaving per second through the two metal plugs (Figure-4.12). Let T °C be the equilibrium temperature. Then heat leaving the box per second through surface A

$$= \frac{k(T-100)\times 12}{8} \text{ cal s}^{-1}$$

Heat leaving the box per second through the surface B

$$= \frac{k(T-4)\times 12}{8} \text{ cal s}^{-1}$$

Hence $$\frac{12k}{8}(T-100+T-4) = 36$$

or $$2T - 104 = \frac{36\times 8}{12k} = \frac{36\times 8}{12\times 0.5} = 48 \text{ or } T = 76\,°\text{C}$$

Illustrative Example 4.8

Figure-4.13 shows a water tank at a constant temperature. T_0 and a small body of mass m, and specific heat s at a temperature T_1. Given that $T_1 < T_0$. A metal rod of length L, cross-sectional area A whose thermal conductivity is K is placed between the tank and the body to connect than. Find the temperature of body as a function of time. Given that the heat capacity of rod is negligible.

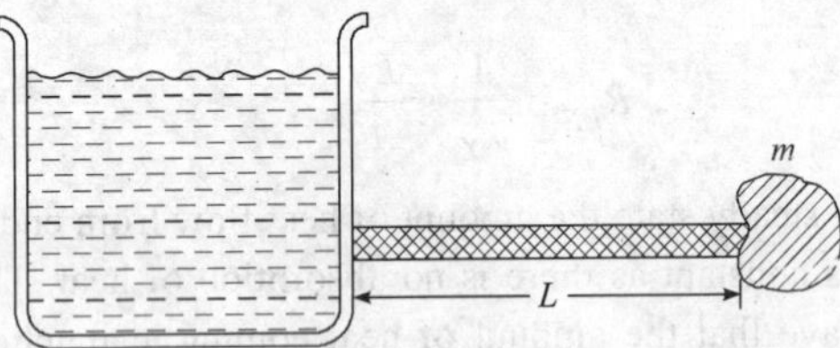

Figure 4.13

Solution

As temperature of water tank is constant at T_0 as it is very large, heat is conducted through the rod to the small body. If at an instant $t = t$, the temperature of small body is T, then the rate of heat flow through the rod can be written as

$$\frac{dQ}{dt} = \frac{KA(T_0 - T)}{L} \qquad \ldots(4.16)$$

Equation-(4.16) is used for heat conduction is steady state and here as the heat capacity of the rod through which heat is conducted is negligible, it does not absorb any heat thus we can assume that it is always in steady state.

If on dQ amount of heat absorption, let the temperature of small body rises by dT, then we have

$$dQ = msdT$$

Now from equation (4.16)

$$ms\frac{dT}{dt} = \frac{KA}{L}(T_0 - T)$$

or $$\frac{dT}{T_0 - T} = \frac{KA}{msL}dt$$

Now integrating the above expression in proper limits, we get

$$\int_{T=T_1}^{T} \frac{dT}{T_0 - T} = \frac{KA}{msL}\int_{t=0}^{t} dt$$

$$-\ln\left(\frac{T_0 - T}{T_0 - T_1}\right) = \frac{KA}{msL}t$$

or $$\frac{T_0 - T}{T_0 - T_1} = e^{-\frac{KAt}{msL}}$$

or $$T = T_0 - (T_0 - T_1)\, e^{-\frac{KAt}{msL}}$$

Illustrative Example 4.9

When two bodies of masses m_1 and m_2 with specific heats s_1 and s_2 at absolute temperatures T_{10} and T_{20} ($T_{10} > T_{20}$) are connected by a rod of length l and cross sectional area A with thermal conductivity k. Find the temperature difference of the bodies after time t. Neglect any heat loss due to radiation at any surface.

Solution

Let at time t after connecting the two bodies, they are at temperature, T_1 and T_2 respectively ($T_1 > T_2$). At this time, heat must be flowing from m_1 to m_2 as m_1 is at higher temperature if dQ is the amount of heat flown through the rod from m_1 to m_2 and due to this if dT_1 is fall in temperature of m_1 and dT_2 is rise in temperature of m_2 then we have

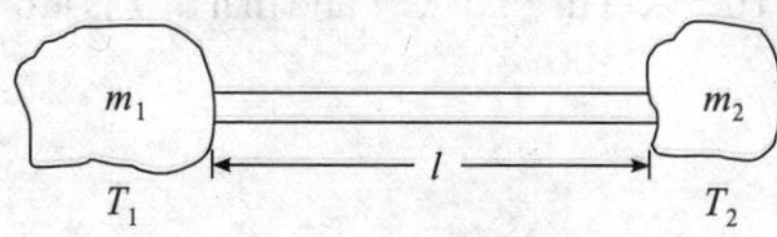

Figure 4.14

$$dQ = -m_1 s_1 dT_1 \qquad \dots(4.17)$$

Also
$$dQ = m_2 s_2 dT_2 \qquad \dots(4.18)$$

As this heat dQ is conducted through the rod, we have

$$\frac{dQ}{dt} = \frac{kA(T_1 - T_2)}{l}$$

or
$$dQ = \frac{kA}{l}(T_1 - T_2)\,dt \qquad \dots(4.19)$$

As in this expression dQ is given as a function of $(T_1 - T_2)$. Thus from (4.17) and (4.18), we can get

$$dQ\left[\frac{1}{m_1 s_1} + \frac{1}{m_2 s_2}\right] = -d(T_1 - T_2) \qquad \dots(4.20)$$

Now from (4.19) and (4.20)

$$\frac{kA(T_1 - T_2)}{l}\left[\frac{1}{m_1 s_1} + \frac{1}{m_2 s_2}\right] dt = -d(T_1 - T_2)$$

or
$$\frac{d(T_1 - T_2)}{(T_1 - T_2)} = -\frac{kA}{l}\left[\frac{1}{m_1 s_1} + \frac{1}{m_2 s_2}\right] dt$$

Integrating the expression within proper limits, we get

$$\int_{T_{10}-T_{20}}^{T_1-T_2} \frac{d(T_1 - T_2)}{(T_1 - T_2)} = -\int_0^t \frac{kA}{l}\left(\frac{1}{m_1 s_1} + \frac{1}{m_2 s_2}\right) dt$$

$$ln\frac{(T_1 - T_2)}{(T_{10} - T_{20})} = -\frac{kA}{l}\left(\frac{1}{m_1 s_1} + \frac{1}{m_2 s_2}\right) dt$$

or
$$(T_1 - T_2) = (T_{10} - T_{20})\, e^{-\frac{kA}{l}\left(\frac{1}{m_1 s_2} + \frac{1}{m_2 s_2}\right)t}$$

Illustrative Example 4.10

A cubical container of side a and wall thickness x ($x << a$) is suspended in air and filled n moles of diatomic gas (adiabatic exponent = γ) in a room where room temperature is T_0. If at $t = 0$ gas temperature is T_1 ($T_1 > T_0$), find the gas temperature as a function of time t. Assume the heat is conducted through all the walls of container.

Solution

As shown in figure-4.15 if at time $t = 0$, gas temperature is T_1 and after time t, its temperature is T, heat will be conducted through the walls of container, the rate of heat conducted to outside surrounding can be written as

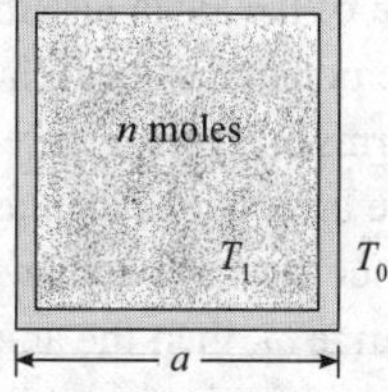

Figure 4.15

$$\frac{dQ}{dt} = \frac{k(6a^2)}{x}[T - T_0] \qquad \dots(4.21)$$

If dQ heat is conducted outside in a time dt and due to this if the temperature gas falls by dT, we have

$$dQ = -nC_v\,dt$$

[As volume of container is constant]

or
$$dQ = \frac{nR}{\gamma - 1}dT \quad [\text{as } C_V = \frac{R}{\gamma - 1}] \qquad \dots(4.22)$$

From equation (4.21) and (4.22) we have

$$\frac{nR}{\gamma - 1}\frac{dT}{dt} = -\frac{6ka^2}{x}(T - T_0)$$

or
$$\frac{dT}{T - T_0} = -\frac{6ka^2(\gamma - 1)}{nRx}dt$$

Integrating the above expression within proper limits from beginning ($t = 0$)

$$\int_{T_1}^{T} \frac{dT}{T-T_0} = -\int_{t=0}^{t} \frac{6ka^2(\gamma-1)}{nRx}\,dt$$

$$ln\left(\frac{T-T_0}{T_1-T_0}\right) = -\frac{6ka^2(\gamma-1)}{nRx}\,t$$

or $$T = T_0 + (T_1 - T_0)\,e^{-\frac{6ka^2(\gamma-1)}{nRx}t}$$

Illustrative Example 4.11

A layer of ice at 0°C of thickness x_1 is floating on a pond. If the atmospheric temperature is $-T$°C, show that the time taken for thickness of the layer of ice to increase from x_1 to x_2 is given by

$$t = \frac{\rho L}{2kT}(x_2^2 - x_1^2)$$

where ρ is the density of ice, k its thermal conductivity and L is the latent heat of fusion of ice.

Solution

When the temperature of the air is less than 0°C, the cold air near the surface of the pond takes heat (latent) from the water which freezes in the forms of layers. Figure-4.16. Consequently, the thickness of the ice layer keeps increasing with time. Let x be the thickness of the ice layer at a certain time. If the thickness is increased by dx in time dt, then the amount of heat flowing through the slab in time dt is given by (see figure-4.16)

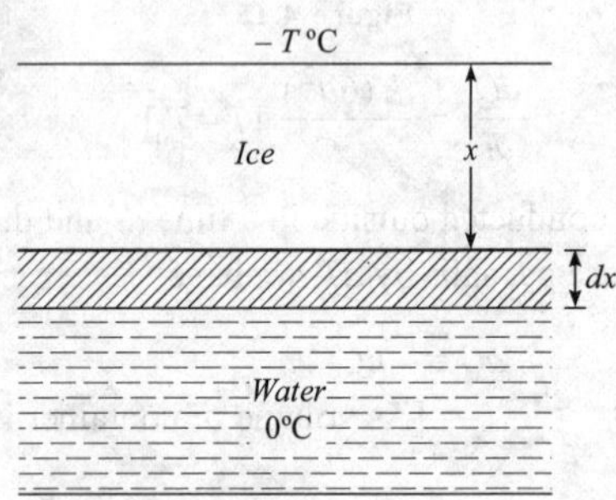

Figure 4.16

$$Q = \frac{kA[0-(-T)]\,dt}{x} = \frac{kATdt}{x} \quad \dots(4.23)$$

Where A is the area of the layer of ice and $-T$ °C is the temperature of the surrounding air. If dm is the mass of water frozen into ice, then $Q = dm \times L$. But $dm = A\rho dx$, where ρ is the density of ice. Hence

$$Q = A\rho L dx \quad \dots(4.24)$$

Equating (4.23) and (4.24), we have

$$\frac{kATdt}{x} = A\rho L dx \quad \text{or} \quad dt = \frac{\rho L}{kT}.xdx$$

Integrating, we have

$$\int_0^t dt = \frac{\rho L}{kT}\int_{x_1}^{x_2} xdx \quad \text{or} \quad t = \frac{\rho L}{kT}\left|\frac{x^2}{2}\right|_{x_1}^{x_2} = \frac{\rho L}{2kT}(x_2^2 - x_1^2)$$

Illustrative Example 4.12

Three rods of material X and three rods of material Y are connected as shown in figure-4.17. All the rods are of identical lengths and cross-sectional areas. If the end A is maintained at 60°C and the junction E at 10°C, calculate the temperature of junctions B, C and D. The thermal conductivity of X is 9.2×10^{-2} kcal m^{-1} s^{-1} °C^{-1} and that of Y is 4.6×10^{-2} kcal m^{-1} s^{-1} °C^{-1}.

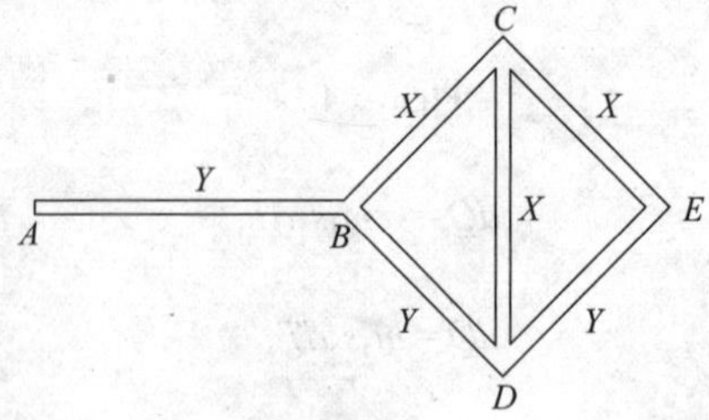

Figure 4.17

Solution

Let k_x and k_y be the thermal conductivities of X and Y respectively and let T_B, T_C and T_D be the temperatures of junctions B, C and D respectively. Given $T_A = 60$°C and $T_E = 10$°C.

In order to solve this problem, we will apply the principle that, in the steady state, the rate at which heat enters a junction is equal to the rate at which heat leaves that junction. In Figure-4.18 the direction of flow of heat is given by arrows.

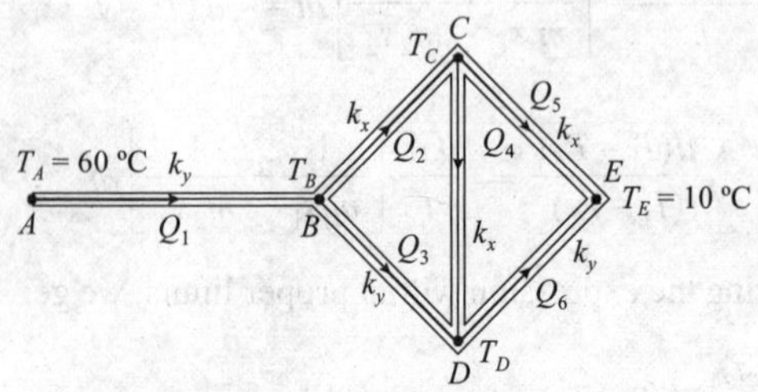

Figure 4.18

For junction B, we have

$$\frac{k_y A(T_A - T_B)}{d} = \frac{k_x A(T_B - T_C)}{d} + \frac{k_y A(T_B - T_D)}{d}$$

or $$k_y(T_A - T_B) = k_x(T_B - T_C) + k_y(T_B - T_D)$$

or $$(T_A - T_B) = \frac{k_x}{k_y}(T_B - T_C) + k_y(T_B - T_D)$$

Given $$\frac{k_x}{k_y} = \frac{9.2\times10^{-2}}{4.6\times10^{-2}} = 2$$

and $$T_A = 60°\text{C}$$

Therefore, $$(60 - T_B) = 2(T_B - T_C) + (T_B - T_D)$$

or $$4T_B - 2T_C - T_D = 60 \qquad \ldots(4.25)$$

For junction C, we have

$$\frac{k_x A(T_B - T_C)}{d} = \frac{k_x A(T_C - T_D)}{d} + \frac{k_x A(T_C - T_E)}{d}$$

Solving we get

$$-T_B + 3T_C - T_D = 10 \qquad [\text{At } T_E = 10°\text{C}] \ldots(4.26)$$

For junction D, we have

or $$\frac{k_y A(T_B - T_D)}{d} + \frac{k_x A(T_C - T_D)}{d} = \frac{k_y A(T_D - T_E)}{d}$$

or $$(T_B - T_D) + \frac{k_x}{k_y}(T_C - T_D) + (T_D - T_E)$$

Putting $\frac{k_x}{k_y} = 2$ and $T_E = 10°\text{C}$ in this equation, we have

$$(T_B - T_D) + 2(T_C - T_D) = (T_D - 10)$$

$$T_B + 2T_C - 4T_D = -10 \qquad \ldots(4.27)$$

Solving equation (4.25), (4.26) and (4.27), we get

$$T_B = 30°\text{C}$$

and $$T_C = T_D = 20°\text{C}$$

Web Reference at www.physicsgalaxy.com

Age Group - High School Physics | Age 17-19 Years

Section - HEAT & THERMODYNAMICS

Topic - Heat Transfer

Module Number - 1 to 11

Practice Exercise 4.1

(i) A wall has two layers A and B each made of different materials. Both the layers have the same thickness. Thermal conductivity of material A is twice that of B. Under thermal equilibrium the temperature difference across the wall is 36°C. What will be the temperature difference across the layer A ?

[12°C]

(ii) A 100 W heater is placed in a cubical container of edge length 6×10^{-2} m. The wall thickness of the container is 1 mm. If inside and outside temperature in steady state are 30°C and 25°C, find the thermal conductivity of the material of the box.

[0.926 W/m°C]

(iii) One end of metal rod of 1 m length and cross sectional area 10 cm^2 is immersed in boiling water and other end in an ice chamber. If the thermal conductivity of the metal is 92 cal/ms°C and the latent heat of fusion of ice is 80 cal/gm, find the amount of ice which will melt in one minute.

[6.9g]

(iv) Water is filled in a closed cylindrical vessel of 10 cm height and base radius $\sqrt{10/\pi}$ cm. The open ends of the cylinder are closed by two metal discs made of a material whose thickness is 10^{-3} m and having thermal conductivity 200 W/m °C. If water temperature inside the cylinder is 50°C and surrounding temperature is 20°C, find the time taken for the temperature to fall by 1°C. Given that the specific heat of water is 4200 J/kg °C and heat loss from water only takes place by the discs as the walls are made up of a thermally insulating material.

[0.035 s]

(v) A uniform steel rod of length 50 cm is insulated on its sides. There is a layer of water of thickness 0.2 mm at each end of the rod. If the ends of the rod are exposed to ice at 0°C and steam at 100°C, calculate the temperature gradient in the rod. Thermal conductivities of steel and water are 0.11 cal cm^{-1} s^{-1} °C^{-1} and 1.5×10^{-3} cal cm^{-1} s^{-1} °C^{-1}.

[0.945°C per cm]

(vi) Two plates of the same area and the same thickness having thermal conductivities k_1 and k_2 are placed one on top of the other. Show that the thermal conductivity of the composite plate for conduction of heat is given by

$$k = \frac{2k_1k_2}{(k_1 + k_2)}$$

(vii) Figure-4.19 shows a paddle wheel coupled with an agitator submerged in a water tank placed in an ice bath at 0°C. The thickness of the tank walls is 2 mm and with thermal conductivity 0.5 W/m°C. The surface area of tank in contact with water is 0.05 m^2. As the block of mass M attached to wheel goes down agitator rotates. It is found that in steady state the block goes down with a constant speed 0.1 m/s and the temperature of water in the tank remains constant at 1°C. Find the mass of the block. Take $g = 10$ m/s^2.

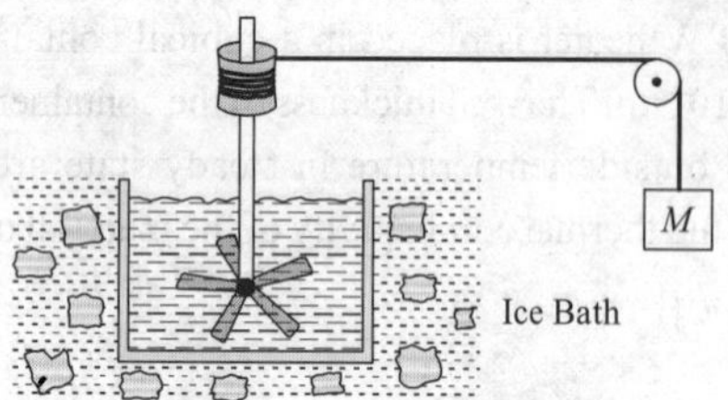

Figure 4.19

[12.5 kg]

(viii) Find the heat current through the frustum of a cone shown in figure-4.20. Temperature of its two ends are maintained at T_1 and T_2 ($T_2 > T_1$) respectively and the thermal conductivity of the material is k.

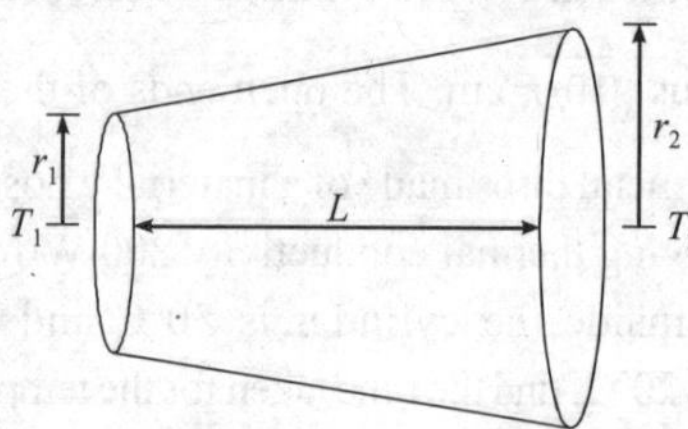

Figure 4.20

[$\dfrac{k\pi r_1 r_2 (T_2 - T_1)}{L}$]

(ix) Three rods of identical cross sectional area and made from the same metal form the sides of an isosceles triangle ABC right angled at B. The points A and B are maintained at temperatures T and $\sqrt{2}\,T$ respectively in the steady state. Assume heat flow only by conduction, find the temperature of point C.

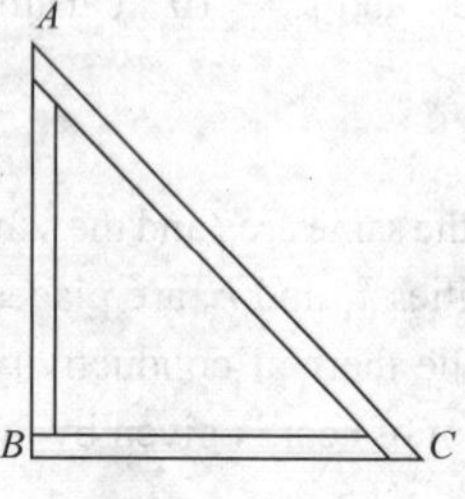

Figure 4.21

[$\dfrac{3T}{\sqrt{2}+1}$]

(x) Two identical rods AB and CD, each of length L are connected as shown in figure-4.22. Their cross-sectional area is A and their thermal conductivity is k. Ends A, C and D are maintained at temperatures T_1, T_2 and T_3 respectively. Neglecting heat loss to the surroundings, find the temperature at B.

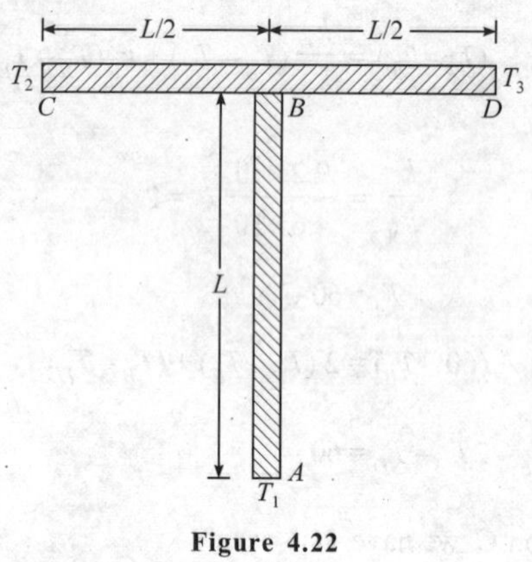

Figure 4.22

[$\dfrac{T_1 + 2T_2 + 2T_3}{5}$]

(xi) A room is maintained at 20°C by a heater of resistance 20 ohms connected to 200 V mains. The temperature is uniform throughout the room and the heat is transmitted through glass window of area 1 m^2 and thickness 0.2 cm. Calculate the temperature of outside. Thermal conductivity of glass is 0.2 cal/s m °C and mechanical equivalent of heat is 4.2 J/cal.

[15.24°C]

4.2 Convection of Heat

Convection is transfer of heat by actual motion of material. Hot air furnace, hot water heating system, and the flow of blood in the body are the examples. If the material is forced to move by a blower or pump, the process is called forced convection. If the material flows due to difference in density, is called natural or free convection.

Free convection in the atmosphere plays a dominant role to determine the daily weather and convection in oceans is also an important heat transfer mechanisms. To understand in a better way we discuss an example, consider the U-tube shown in figure-4.23. In this U-tube its left end A is open to atmosphere and at the other end C a stop X is placed. Initially some water is filled in the tube and temperature of both the arms are equal thus stands equally in both arms. If right arm of U-tube is heated, the water in this arm expends and its density will decrease, thus a larger column of water is needed to balance the pressure produced by the cold water in left column. When stop valve is opened, water starts flowing from the warmer column into the colder column. This increases the pressure at the bottom of U-tube produced by the cold column, and decreases the pressure at this point due to the hot column. Hence at the bottom of U-tube, water is forced from the cold to the hot side. If heat is continuously supplied to the hot side and removed from the cold side, the circulation continuous indefinitely. The net result is a continuous transfer of heat from hot to cold side of the column.

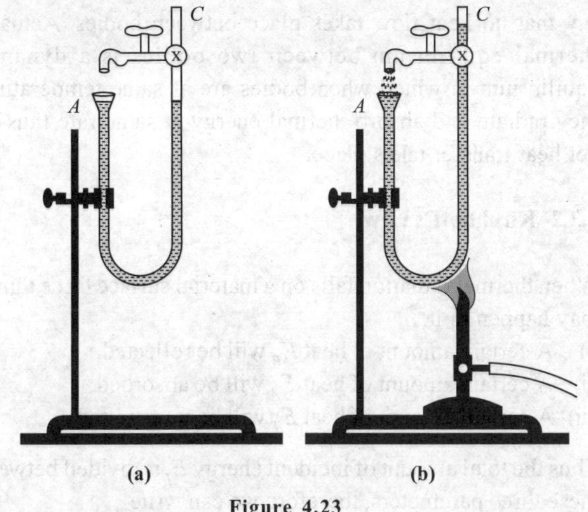

Figure 4.23

There is no simple equation for convective heat transfer as there is for conduction. The heat lost or gained by a surface at one temperature in contact with a fluid at another temperature depends on many factors, such as the shape and orientation of the surface, the mechanical and thermal properties of fluid, and the nature of the fluid flow, laminar or turbulent. Some experimental observations are taken for convection of heat, these are

(i) The heat current due to convection is directly proportional to the surface area of the main body of fluid in contact with the surface. This is the reason for the large surface areas of heat radiators and cooling fins used in transformers and heat sinks used in power electronic devices.

(ii) The heat current due to convection is found to be approximately proportional to the temperature difference between the surface and main body of fluid.

Thus we define the heat current due to a surface in contact with a fluid as :

$$\frac{dQ}{dt} = hA\Delta T \qquad \ldots(4.28)$$

Here A is the surface area in contact and ΔT is the temperature difference between the surface and main body of the fluid and h is a constant called convection coefficient. Values of h are determined experimentally, actually it is found not to be constant but depend on several factors, these are :

(i) Whether the surface in contact with fluid is flat or curved.
(ii) Whether the surface is horizontal or vertical.
(iii) Whether the fluid in contact is liquid or a gas.
(iv) The density, viscosity, specific heat and thermal conductivity of the fluid.
(v) Whether the speed of the fluid is small enough to give rise to laminar flow or large enough to cause turbulent flow.
(vi) Whether conduction or evaporation takes place during flow.

Another example of convection is our human body. The human body produces a great deal of thermal energy, of the food energy transformed within the body, at best 20 percent is used to do work, so over 80 percent appears as thermal energy. During light activity, for example, if this thermal energy were not dissipated, the body temperature would rise about 3°C per hour. Thus we can say that the heat generated by body must be transferred to the outside surrounding. Is this heat transferred by conduction ? The temperature of the skim at normal room temperature is 30 to 35°C where as the interior of body is 37°C. It can be easily proved that this small temperature difference along with low thermal conductivity of tissue, by conduction only a very small amount of heat can be dissipated. Instead the heat is carried to the surface by the blood. In addition to other important responsibilities, blood acts as a convective fluid to transfer heat to just beneath the surface of the skin. It is then conducted through the very small thickness of skin to the surface. Once at the surface, the heat is transferred to the environment by convection, evaporation and radiation.

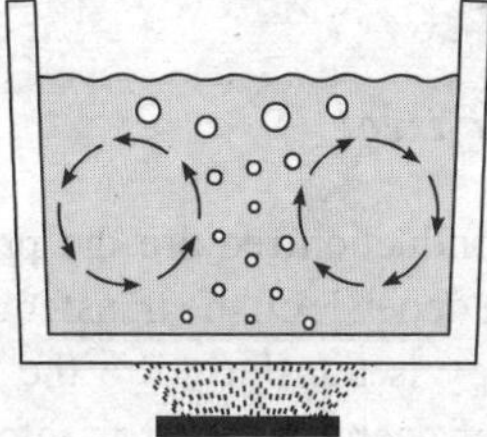
Figure 4.24

Another example of convection is heating water in a pot on a gas burner. When a pot of water is heated on a gas burner as shown in figure-4.24, convection currents are set up as the heated water at the bottom of pot rises because of its reduced density and is replaced by cooler water from above. In figure convection currents are shown in arrows. This principle is used in many heating systems, such as hot water radiator system in houses. Figure-4.25 shows internal diagram of a house having installed such a system. Cold water is heated in furnace, its temperature rises, it expands and start rising up to room-1 as shown. Hot water then enters in the radiators and heat is transferred to the surrounding air by conduction through the walls of radiator and cooled water returns to the furnace. Thus the water circulates because of convection, sometimes pumps are used to make the circulation fast. The air in the room also becomes uniformly heated as a result of convection. The air heated by radiator rises and is replaced by cooled air, resulting the convection air currents as shown in figure-4.25.

Some type of furnaces also depend on convection. Hot air furnaces have openings (called registers) near the floor often do not have fans but depend on natural convection.

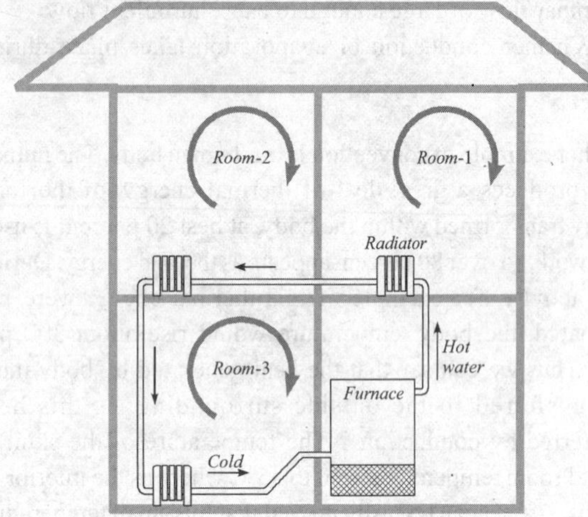

Figure 4.25

Web Reference at www.physicsgalaxy.com

Age Group - High School Physics | Age 17-19 Years
Section - HEAT & THERMODYNAMICS
Topic - Heat Transfer
Module Number - 12

4.3 Radiation of Heat

Convection and conduction require the presence of matter. Whole life on earth depends on the transfer of energy from the sun, and this energy is transferred to the earth over empty space. This form of energy transfer is referred as radiation. Similarly when a fire is lit and if we stand near by, feel the warmth called radiant energy. Most of the air heated by a fire rises up by convection in the surrounding of fire.

Thermal radiation are electromagnetic waves of several wavelengths (polychromatic radiation) which carry thermal energy. Radiation from the Sun to Earth consists of visible light plus many other wavelengths that the eye is not sensitive to. This includes infrared (*IR*) radiation which is mainly responsible for heating the earth.

4.3.1 Prevost Theory

In early ages it was assumed that only hot body emits radiation but later a theory of heat radiation was given by Prevost that every body which is at temperature above 0K temperature radiate thermal energy in the form of electromagnetic waves of several wavelengths. Simultaneously the body also absorbs thermal radiation from its surroundings. When a body at higher temperature is kept near one at lower temperature, it radiates energy more than what it absorbs from the one at lower temperature similarly the colder one absorbs more than what it radiates thus thermal energy is transferred from hot body to the cold body by means of thermal radiations. If two bodies are at same temperature kept close to each other, they radiate and absorbs heat at same rate, so we say that the bodies are in thermal equilibrium. Thus in thermal equilibrium we can not say that no heat flow takes place between bodies. Actually thermal equilibrium between two bodies is a dynamic equilibrium in which when bodies are at same temperature, they radiate and absorb thermal energy at same rate thus no net heat transfer takes place.

4.3.2 Kirchhoff's Law

When thermal radiation falls on a material surface three things may happen to it.

(i) A certain amount of heat E_R will be reflected,
(ii) A certain amount of heat E_A will be absorbed,
(iii) A certain amount of heat E_T will be transmitted

Thus the total amount of incident energy E_I is divided between these three parameters, therefore we can write

$$E_I = E_R + E_A + E_T \quad \ldots (4.29)$$

For a shiny surface such as silver, E_R is large and both E_T and E_A are small. For a black surface such as charcoal E_R is small, E_A is large and E_T is small. For a transparent medium like glass E_R is small, E_A small and E_T large.

The energy absorbed by a body can be emitted later or simultaneously along with absorption and clearly if a surface can not absorb radiation strongly it will be unable to emit strongly. Kirchhoff Law states the same that "*a good emitter is also a good absorber*".

When thermal radiation incident upon a body or emitted by a body equally in all directions, the radiation is said to be isotropic. Some of the radiation incident on a body may be absorbed, reflected and transmitted. In general, the incident radiation of all wavelengths that is absorbed depends on the temperature and the nature of the surface of the absorbing body. The fraction of the total incident power that is absorbed by a body is called its absorptivity. It can be given as

$$absorptivity = \frac{Total\ power\ absorbed\ by\ a\ body}{Total\ power\ incident\ on\ the\ body}$$

When a body is in thermal equilibrium, the process of absorption and emission of radiant power are equal and opposite. So the total emissivity is equal to total absorptivity. Total emissivity is defined as the fraction of power provided to a general body that is emitted through a material surface as thermal radiation, here the "total" includes all the wavelengths of electromagnetic radiation from the body. Practically it is easier to measure emissivity than absorptivity.

The emissivity of a body depends on both the temperature and the nature of emitting surface. Bodies of same temperature and size but different material emit different amount of total thermal radiation. According to Kirchhoff's Law good absorbers are good emitters. For Theoretical purpose we define an ideal substance capable either of absorbing all the thermal radiation falling on it or emitting all the energy provided to it in the form of thermal radiation. Such a substance is called Black Body.

Thus for a black body we can say that its emissivity is 1, as well as its absorptivity. We can compare different substances with black body and obtain the emissivity of respective substances. For example a polished shining steel piece emits only 9% of the thermal radiation as compared to a black body of same size and shape of same temperature, hence its emissivity is 0.09. Similarly emissivity of a rough oxidized steel surface is 0.81 and that of ocean water is 0.96 and some substances like lamp black, coal are there whose emissivity is very nearly unity that is, almost an ideal emitter. The emissivity of a general body is denoted by e and mathematically defined as

$$e = \frac{\textit{Radient power emitted by body at a given temperature}}{\textit{Radient power emitted by a Black Body of same geometry at same temperature}}$$

Thus total thermal radiation power emitted by a General Body is given as

$$\begin{pmatrix} \textit{Radiation Power} \\ \textit{from a} \\ \textit{General Body} \\ \textit{at a given temperature} \end{pmatrix} = e \begin{pmatrix} \textit{Radiation Power} \\ \textit{from a} \\ \textit{Black Body} \\ \textit{at same temperature} \end{pmatrix} \quad \ldots(4.30)$$

Experimentally a very good approximation to a black body is provided by a cavity enclosed by high temperature opaque walls regardless of the composition of the material of its interior walls.

4.3.3 Stefan Boltzmann Law

On the basis of experiments, Stefan concluded in 1879 that the total amount of thermal radiation power from a body is directly proportional to the fourth power of its absolute temperature. The mathematical result was derived later by Boltzmann that the total radiation power per unit surface area of a body is given as

$$P_R = \sigma T^4 \text{ J/s.m}^2 \quad \ldots(4.31)$$

If a body of surface area A is at temperature T, then total thermal power radiated by the body is

$$P_R = \sigma A T^4 \text{ J/s} \quad \ldots(4.32)$$

Later experimentally it is observed that equation-(4.32) does not give correct results in many cases, it gives approximately true results for substances with high emissivities and it was accepted that equation-(4.32) is only valid for black bodies or those having emissivity very close to unity. Thus for general bodies equation-(4.32) can be generalized as power radiated by a general body of surface area A, at temperature T and with emissivity e, can be given by equation-(4.30) as

$$P_R = e A \sigma T^4 \text{ J/s} \quad \ldots(4.33)$$

Any object not only emits energy by radiation, but it also absorbs energy radiated by other bodies in its surrounding. If an object of emissivity e and area A is at a temperature T, it radiates energy at a rate $e A \sigma T^4$. If the object is surrounded by an environment at temperature T_s. The rate at which the surrounding in immediate contact of the body surface radiate energy at a rate $\sigma A T_s^4$ if it is assumed to be a black body and if absorptivity of the body material is a, the amount of energy absorbed by the body is at a rate $a \sigma A T_s^4$. Thus the net heat flow from the object can be given as

$$\frac{dQ}{dt} = e A \sigma T^4 - a A \sigma T_s^4 \quad \ldots(4.34)$$

As good absorbers are good emitters we can approximately use $e \simeq a$ thus we have

$$\frac{dQ}{dt} = e A \sigma (T^4 - T_s^4) \quad \ldots(4.35)$$

When body and surrounding both are at same temperature equation-(4.35) shows that there is no net flow of heat takes place with the body. When $T > T_s$, net flow of heat takes place from body to surrounding and temperature of body decreases. Similarly if $T < T_s$, net flow of heat takes place from surrounding to body and temperature of body increases with time.

If mass of body is m and s is the specific heat of the material of body then we have

$$\frac{dQ}{dt} = ms \frac{dT}{dt} \quad \ldots(4.36)$$

Where $\frac{dT}{dt}$ is rate of change of temperature of body. If $\frac{dQ}{dt}$ is rate of heat loss from a body than $\frac{dT}{dt}$ will be the rate at which temperature of body falls and is termed as rate of cooling. Thus if a body of mass m and specific heat s at temperature T is placed in surrounding of temperature T_s then the rate of cooling of body can be given as

$$\frac{dT}{dt} = \frac{e A \sigma}{ms} (T^4 - T_s^4) \text{ K/s} \quad \ldots(4.37)$$

4.3.4 Solar Constant

It is defined as "*solar energy received per unit surface area of earth surface per unit time, when sun is overhead*". If radius of sun is R_s and its temperature T_s, the average rate at which it radiates energy is given as

$$E = \sigma (4\pi R_s^2) T_s^4 \quad \ldots(4.38)$$

This radiant power given by equation-(4.38) is isotropically radiated by sun in all direction. If d is the mean distance between earth and sun, the average energy intensity on earth surface for normal incidence of sun rays that is solar constant can be given as

$$s = \frac{E}{4\pi d^2}$$

or $$s = \frac{\sigma R_s^2 T_s^4}{d^2} \quad \ldots(4.39)$$

Now we take few examples to understand the applications of above concepts in details.

Illustrative Example 4.13

An electric heater of power 1 kW emits thermal radiations the surface area of heating element of heater is 200 cm^2. If this heating element is treated like a black body find the temperature at its surface. Assume its temperature is very much higher then its surroundings.

Solution

As it is given that the temperature of surrounding is very low as compared to that of heating element, we can ignore the amount of heat absorbed by the filament from its surroundings. Thus the power radiated by the heating element is given as

$$P = \sigma A T^4$$

or $$1000 = 5.67 \times 10^{-8} \times 0.02 \times T^4$$

or $$T^4 = 8.82 \times 10^{11}$$

or $$T = 969.3 \text{ K}$$

Illustrative Example 4.14

A cube of mass 1 kg and volume 125 cm^3 is placed in an evacuated chamber at 27ºC. Initially temperature of block is 227ºC. Assume block behaves like a black body, find the rate of cooling of block if specific heat of the material of block is 400 J/kg-k.

Solution

In this case the rate of loss of heat by the block is given as

$$\frac{dQ}{dt} = \sigma A (T^4 - T_S^4)$$

$$= 5.67 \times 10^{-8} \times 150 \times 10^{-4} \times [(500)^4 - (300)^4]$$

[surface area of cube is $6a^2 = 150$ cm^2]

If $\frac{dT}{dt}$ is rate of cooling of block then we have

$$\frac{dQ}{dt} = ms\,\frac{dT}{dt}$$

or $$\frac{dT}{dt} = \frac{1}{ms} \cdot \frac{dQ}{dt}$$

$$= \frac{1}{1 \times 400} \times 38.556$$

$$= 0.115\ ºC/S$$

Illustrative Example 4.15

One end A of a metallic rod of length 10 cm is inserted in a furnace whose temperature is 827ºC. The curved surface of the rod is insulated. The room temperature is 27ºC. When the steady state is attained, the temperature of the other end B of the rod is 702ºC. Find the thermal conductivity of the metal. Stefan's constant = 5.67×10^{-8} W m^{-2} K^{-4}.

Solution

Since the curved surface of the rod is insulated, heat is lost from the end B of the rod is by radiation. If T_B is the absolute temperature of end B, then the energy radiated per unit area per time from end B is, from Stefan's law,

$$E_1 = \sigma (T_B^4 - T_0^4) \quad \ldots(4.40)$$

Where T_0 is the room temperature, σ is Stefan's constant. Also, energy received at end B by conduction through the rod per unit area unit time is

$$E_2 = \frac{k\,(T_A - T_B)}{l} \quad \ldots(4.41)$$

Where T_A = temperature of end A of the rod, l is the length of the rod and k its thermal conductivity. In the steady state $E_1 = E_2$. Equating equation-(4.40) and (4.41) we have

$$\frac{k\,(T_A - T_B)}{l} = \sigma (T_B^4 - T_0^4)$$

or $$k = \frac{\sigma l (T_B^4 - T_0^4)}{(T_A - T_B)} \quad \ldots(4.42)$$

Given $\sigma = 5.67 \times 10^{-8}$ W m^{-2} K^{-4}, $l = 0.1$ m, $T_B = 702ºC = 975$ K, $T_0 = 27ºC = 300$ K and $T_A = 827ºC = 1100$ K. Using these values in equation-(4.42), we get

$$k = 36.6 \text{ J s}^{-1} \text{ m}^{-1} \text{ K}^{-4}$$

Illustrative Example 4.16

A solid metallic sphere of diameter 20 cm and mass 10 kg is heated to a temperature of 327ºC and suspended in a box in which a constant temperature of 27ºC is maintained. Find the rate at which the temperature of the sphere will fall with time. Stefan's constant = 5.67×10^{-8} W m^{-2} K^{-4} and specific heat of metal = 420 J kg^{-1} ºC^{-1}.

Solution

The rate of loss of heat by the sphere is given by

$$\frac{dQ}{dt} = \sigma A\,(T^4 - T_0^4)$$

Where A is the surface area of the sphere = $4\pi r^2$, with r=10 cm = 0.1 m, T=327°C = 600 K and T_0 = 27°C = 300 K.

Thus $$\frac{dQ}{dt} = 5.67 \times 10^{-8} \times 4\pi \times (0.1)^2 \times \{(600)^4 - (300)^4\}$$

$$= 866 \text{ J s}^{-1}$$

Now $dQ = msdT$, where dT is the fall in temperature in time dt.

$$\frac{dQ}{dt} = ms\,\frac{dT}{dt}$$

or $$866 = 10 \times 420 \times \frac{dT}{dt}$$

or $$\frac{dT}{dt} = \frac{866}{4200} = 0.206\text{°C/s}$$

 # Illustrative Example 4.17

A cylindrical rod of 50 cm length and having 1 cm^2 cross sectional area is used as a conducting material between an ice bath at 0°C and a vacuum chamber at 27°C as shown in figure-4.26. The end of rod which is inside the vacuum chamber behaves like a black body and is at temperature 17°C in steady state. Find the thermal conductivity of the material of rod and rate at which ice is melting in the ice bath. Given that latent heat of fusion of ice is 3.35×10^5 J/kg.

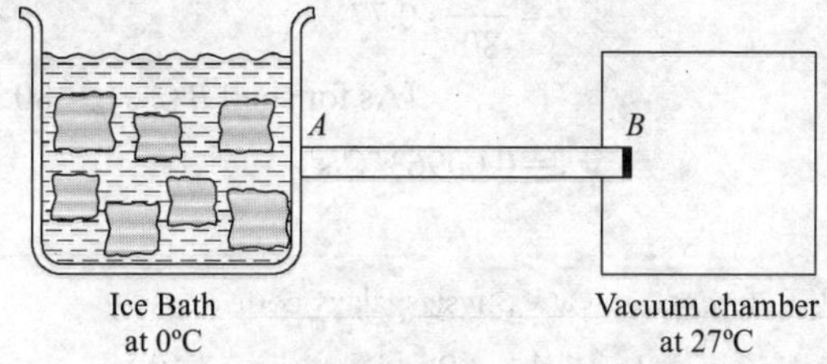

Figure 4.26

Solution

It is given that the system is in steady state. This means that any part of rod is not absorbing any heat. So heat absorbed by the end of the rod which is in vacuum chamber by radiation is fully conducted to the ice bath through the rod. Thus we have

Rate of that conduction through the rod =

Rate of heat absorption by radiation for the vacuum chamber

or $$\frac{kA\,(T_B - T_A)}{L}$$

$$= \sigma A\,(T_{vc}^4 - T_B^4)$$

or $$\frac{k\,(17\text{°C} - 0\text{°C})}{0.5} = 5.67 \times 10^{-8}\,[(300)^4 - (290)^4]$$

or $$k = \frac{5.67 \times 10^{-8}[(300)^4 - (290)^4] \times 0.5}{17}$$

$$= 1.713 \text{ W/m°C}$$

Using this value of k we can find the rate of heat obtained by the ice bath as

$$\frac{dQ}{dt} = \frac{kA\,(T_A - T_B)}{l}$$

$$= \frac{1.713 \times 1 \times 10^{-4} \times 17}{0.5}$$

$$= 5.82 \times 10^{-3} \text{ J/s}$$

This heat is used to melt the ice in ice bath. If m mass of ice is being melted per second, then we have

$$\frac{dQ}{dt} = mL$$

or $$5.82 \times 10^{-3} = m \times 3.35 \times 10^5$$

or $$m = 1.74 \times 10^{-8} \text{ kg/s}$$

 # Illustrative Example 4.18

The earth receives solar energy at the rate of 2 cal cm^{-2} per minute. Assuming the radiation to be black body in character, estimate the surface temperature of the sun. Given that $\sigma = 5.67 \times 10^{-8}$ W m^{-2} K^{-4} and angular diameter of the sun = 32 minute of arc.

Solution

Let surface temperature of Sun is T_s then total energy radiated by Sun per second is given as

$$E = \sigma T_s^4 \cdot (4\pi R_s^2)$$

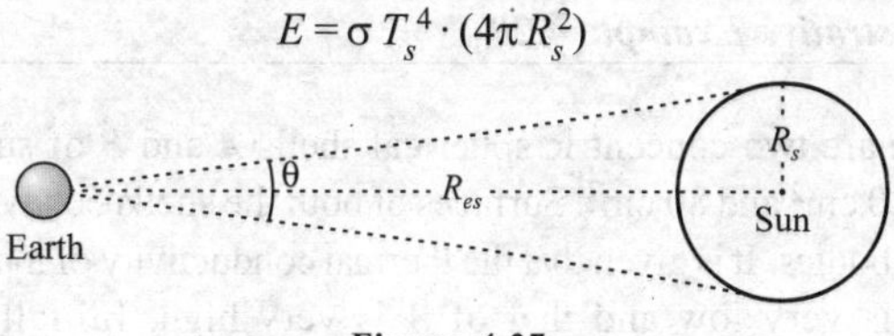

Figure 4.27

Energy received by earth per second per meter square is give as

$$\frac{dQ}{dt} = \frac{E}{4\pi R_{es}^2} = \sigma T_s^4 \left(\frac{R_s}{R_{es}}\right)^2 \qquad \ldots(4.43)$$

It is given that angular diameter of Sun as observed from earth is 32 min of arc thus, we have

$$\frac{R_s}{R_{es}} = \frac{\theta}{2} = \frac{1}{2} \times \frac{32}{60} = 4.655 \times 10^{-3}$$

and it is given that

$$\frac{dQ}{dt}=\frac{2\times 4.2\times 10^4}{60}\text{ J/s-m}^2 \qquad \ldots(4.44)$$

Now from equation-(4.43) and (4.44) we have

$$5.67\times 10^{-8}\times T_s^4\times[4.655\times 10^{-3}]^2=\frac{2\times 4.2\times 10^4}{60}$$

or $$T_s^4=\frac{2\times 4.2\times 10^4}{60\times 5.67\times 10^{-8}\times(4.655\times 10^{-3})^2}$$

or $$T_s^4=1.14\times 10^{15}$$

or $$T_s=5810.67\text{ K}$$

Illustrative Example 4.19

A spherical ball of radius 1 cm coated with a material having emissivity 0.3 is maintained at 1000 K temperature and suspended in a vacuum chamber whose walls are maintained at 300 K temperature. Find rate at which electrical energy is to be supplied to the ball to keep its temperature constant.

Solution

It is given that the temperature of ball is constant. This means that the rate at which it is loosing heat by radiation must be equal to the rate at which heat is supplied to this ball externally to keep its temperature constant.

The rate of heat loss by the ball is given as

$$\frac{dQ}{dt}=eA\sigma(T^4-T_s^4)$$

$$=0.3\times 4\pi(0.01)^2\times 5.67\times 10^{-8}\times[(1000)^4-(300)^4]$$

$$=21.1\text{ W}$$

Thus electrical energy must be supplied to the ball at a rate of 21.1 W.

Illustrative Example 4.20

There are two concentric spherical shells *A* and *B* of surface area 20 cm^2 and 80 cm^2. Surfaces of both the shells behave like black bodies. It is given that the thermal conductivity of material of *B* is very low and that of *A* is very high. Initially the temperature of *A* is 400 K and that of *B* is 300 K. Find the rate of change of temperature of *A* and *B*. Given that the heat capacities of *A* and *B* are 50 J/°C and 80 J/°C respectively.

Solution

It is given that the thermal conductivity of material of *A* is very high so we can assume that it will not absorb any heat, thus the rate of heat loss by *A* is given as

$$\frac{dQ}{dt}=A_A\sigma T_A^4$$

$$=20\times 10^{-4}\times 5.67\times 10^{-8}\times(400)^4$$

$$=2.9\text{ J/s}$$

If $\frac{dT}{dt}$ is rate of cooling of *A* then we have

$$\frac{dQ}{dt}=(ms)_A\left.\frac{dT}{dt}\right|_A$$

or $$\left.\frac{dT}{dt}\right|_A=\frac{1}{(ms)_A}\frac{dQ}{dt}$$

or $$\left.\frac{dT}{dt}\right|_A=\frac{1}{50}\times 2.9$$

[As for shall *A* $(ms)_A=50$ J/s]

$$=0.058\ ^\circ\text{C/s}$$

Now for *B* it is given that its thermal conductivity is very poor so it absorbs all the heat incident on it (as behaving like a black body). Thus rate of loss of heat from *B* can be written as

$$\frac{dQ}{dt}=A_B\sigma T_B^4-A_A\sigma T_A^4$$

or $$\frac{dQ}{dt}=80\times 10^{-4}\times 5.67\times 10^{-8}\times(300)^4-2.9$$

$$=3.67-2.9=0.77\text{ J/s}$$

If $\left.\frac{dT}{dt}\right|_B$ is the rate of cooling for shell *B*, we have

$$\frac{dQ}{dt}=(ms)_B\left.\frac{dT}{dt}\right|_B$$

or $$\left.\frac{dT}{dt}\right|_B=\frac{1}{(ms)_B}\frac{dQ}{dt}$$

$$=\frac{1}{80}\times 0.77$$

[As for shell *B* $(ms)_B=80$ J/°C]

$$=0.00963\ ^\circ\text{C/s}$$

Web Reference at www.physicsgalaxy.com

Age Group - High School Physics | Age 17-19 Years
Section - HEAT & THERMODYNAMICS
Topic - Heat Transfer
Module Number - 13 to 23

Practice Exercise 4.2

(i) A 500 W lamp loses all of its energy by emission of radiation from the surface. If the area of the surface of the filament is 2.0 cm^2 and its emissivity is 0.5, estimate the temperature of its filament. Given that Stefan constant, $\sigma=5.7\times 10^{-8}$ W/m^2 K^4. Neglect radiation received by lamp from surrounding.

[3060.37 K]

(ii) A white-hot metal wire at 3000 K has a radius of 0.075 cm. Calculate the rate per unit length at which it emits radiation if its emissivity is 0.35. Ignore the radiation it receives from the surroundings. Take stefan's constant $\sigma = 5.7 \times 10^{-8}$ W/m²K

[7611.12 W/m]

(iii) The temperature of the tungsten filament of a 60 W electric bulb is $T = 2000$ K. Find the surface area of the filament. The emissivity of the surface is $e = 0.30$. Neglect radiation received from surrounding. Take $\sigma = 5.7 \times 10^{-8}$ W/m²K

[2.192×10^{-4} m²]

(iv) A spherical black body with a radius of 12 cm placed in space radiates 450 W power at 500 K. If the radius were halved and the temperature doubled, find the power radiated.

[1800 W]

(v) A block having some emissivity is maintained at 500 K temperature in a surrounding of 300 K temperature. It is observed that, to maintain the temperature of the block, 210 W external power is required to be supplied to it. If instead of this block a black body of same geometry and size is used, 700 W external power is needed for the same. Find the emissivity of the material of the block.

[0.3]

(vi) A solid sphere of copper of radius R and a hollow sphere of the same material of inner radius r and outer radius R are heated to the same temperature and allowed to cool in the same environment. Which of the sphere will cool faster ?

[Hollow Sphere]

(vii) The shell of a space station is a blackened sphere in which a temperature $T = 500\ K$ is maintained due to the operation of appliances of the station. Find the temperature of the shell if the station is enveloped by a thin spherical black screen of nearly the same radius as the radius of the shell.

[594.6 K]

(viii) A copper ball of diameter d was placed in an evacuated vessel whose walls are kept at the absolute zero temperature. The initial temperature of the ball is T_0. Assuming the surface of the ball to be absolutely black, find how soon its temperature decreases η times. Take specific heat of copper c, density of copper ρ and emissivity e.

[$t = \dfrac{(\eta^3 - 1)\, c\, \rho d}{18\, \sigma\, T_0^3 e}$]

4.4 *Newton's Law of Cooling*

When a body radiates thermal energy in an environment at lower temperature, then equation-(4.37) can be used to find temperature of body as a function of time by integrating the expression

$$\int_{T_0}^{T} \frac{dT}{T^4 - T_s^4} = -\int_0^t \frac{e A \sigma}{ms}\, dt \qquad \ldots(4.45)$$

In equation-(4.45) limits of integration are applied for temperature of body at respective time instants as if at $t = 0$, temperature of body was T_0 and after time $t = t$, its temperature drops to T. Negative sign in equation-(4.45) shows that $\frac{dT}{dt}$ is negative and with time temperature is falling. In equation-(4.37), for using this equation for analytical purpose a negative sign must also be included.

Expression in equation-(4.45) is not easy to integrate and very bulky and time consuming for even problems of simple time calculations. The expression in equation-(4.37) can be approximated to a simple level for bodies at temperature not very high compared to their surroundings. Equation-(4.37) can be rewritten as

$$\frac{dT}{dt} = \frac{e A \sigma}{ms}(T^2 + T_s^2)(T + T_s)(T - T_s) \qquad \ldots(4.46)$$

Here if temperature of body is slightly higher then that of its surrounding then we can use $T \simeq T_s$ but not $T - T_s = 0$, thus equation-(4.46) becomes

$$\frac{dT}{dt} = -\frac{e A \sigma}{ms}(2T_s^2)(2T_s)(T - T_s)$$

or
$$\frac{dT}{dt} = -\frac{4 e A \sigma T_s^3}{ms}(T - T_s)$$

or
$$\frac{dT}{dt} = -k(T - T_s) \qquad \ldots(4.47)$$

Here $k = \frac{4 e A \sigma T_s^3}{ms}$ is a constant for bodies with small temperature difference with the surroundings. Equation-(4.47) can be stated as "*The rate of cooling for bodies having small temperature difference with the surrounding is directly proportional to the temperature difference of body with its surroundings.*" This is Newton's Law of cooling. From equation-(4.47) we can use this expression for further calculations of temperature as

$$\frac{dT}{T - T_s} = -k\, dt$$

Integrating within proper limits we have

$$\int_{T_0}^{T} \frac{dT}{T - T_s} = -\int_0^t k\, dt$$

or
$$ln\left(\frac{T - T_s}{T_0 - T_s}\right) = kt$$

or
$$T = T_s + (T_0 - T_s)\, e^{-kt} \qquad \ldots(4.48)$$

The above expression in equation-(4.48) gives the temperature of body after time t if at $t = 0$ body temperature was T_0. But this expression will be valid only if T_0 is very close to the surrounding temperature T_s.

According to Newton's Law of cooling. The rate of fall of temperature of a body is directly proportional to the temperature

4.4.1 Average Form of Newton's Law of Cooling

In previous article we've discussed that for bodies with small temperature difference with the surrounding the rate of cooling is directly proportional to the temperature difference of body with surrounding. As temperature difference is small, average rate of cooling of body $\left(\frac{\Delta T}{\Delta t}\right)$ can be taken approximately equal to the instantaneous rate of cooling $\left(\frac{dT}{dt}\right)$. This can be written according to Newton's Law of cooling as

$$\frac{dT}{dt} \simeq \frac{\Delta T}{\Delta t} = k(T - T_5)$$

Here T is the average temperature of body during cooling and T_s is the surrounding temperature. For example if a body is at temperature T_1 at $t = 0$ and after time t its temperature drops to T_2 then during cooling average temperature of body can be taken as

$$T = \frac{T_1 + T_2}{2} \qquad \ldots(4.49)$$

Now according to Newton's law of cooling, average rate at which body cools can be written as

$$\frac{\Delta T}{\Delta t} = \frac{T_2 - T_1}{t} = k\left(\frac{T_1 + T_2}{2} - T_s\right) \qquad \ldots(4.50)$$

Equation-(4.50) is known as average from of Newton's Law of cooling but is only applicable when T_1 and T_2 are very close to each other, otherwise the average temperature of body can not be given by equation-(4.49). Many times Newton's Law of cooling is used to compare the rate of two different substances. In such cases we slightly modify equation-(1.50) with the heat capacity of substance.

By Stefan's law rate of cooling is given as

$$\frac{dT}{dt} = -\frac{4eA\sigma T_s^3}{ms}(T - T_s)$$

Here if substance is changed the parameters e, A, m and s may change so for same emissivity and surface area it can be written as

$$\frac{dT}{dt} = -\frac{k}{ms}(T - T_s)$$

So equation-1.50 can be re written as

$$\frac{T_2 - T_1}{t} = -\frac{k}{ms}\left(\frac{T_1 + T_2}{2} - T_s\right)$$

And with variation of e or A you can modify this equation yourself. Lets take some examples to understand the applications of Newton's Law of Cooling.

 # Illustrative Example 4.21

The temperature of a body in a surrounding of temperature 16°C falls from 40°C to 36°C in 5 mins. Assume Newtons law of cooling to be valid and find the time taken by the body to reach temperature 32°C.

Solution

If we use average form of Newton's Law of cooling, we have

$$\left(\frac{T_2 - T_1}{t}\right) = k\left(\frac{T_2 + T_1}{2} - T_s\right)$$

Initially it is given that $T_2 = 40$°C, $T_1 = 36$°C, $t = 5$ min and $T_s = 16$°C

Thus we have

$$\frac{40 - 36}{5} = k\left[\frac{40 + 36}{2} - 16\right]$$

or
$$k = \frac{4}{5 \times 22} = 0.036\ \text{min}^{-1}$$

Now if body takes a time t' to come down to 32°C then again using the same relation we have

$T_2 = 36$°C, $T_1 = 32$°C, $t = t'$, $T_s = -16$°C and $k = 0.036\ \text{min}^{-1}$

Thus we have

$$\frac{36 - 32}{t'} = (0.036)\left[\frac{36 + 32}{2} - 16\right]$$

or
$$t' = \frac{4}{0.036 \times 18} = 6.173\ \text{min}$$

 # Illustrative Example 4.22

In a container some water is filled at temperature 50°C. It cools to 45°C in 5 minutes and to 40°C in next 8 minutes. If we assume Newton's law of cooling to be valid in this case, find the surrounding temperature.

Solution

According to average form of Newton's Law of cooling, initially we have

$T_2 = 50$°C, $T_1 = 45$°C, $t = 5$ min and let surrounding temperature be T_s, then we have

$$\left(\frac{T_2 - T_1}{t}\right) = k\left(\frac{T_2 + T_1}{2} - T_s\right)$$

or $$\left(\frac{50-45}{5}\right)=k\left(\frac{50+45}{2}-T_s\right)$$

or $$1=k(47.5-T_s) \quad \ldots(4.51)$$

Again when water cools, we have $T_2=45°C, T_1=40°C, t=8$ min and same surrounding temperature T_s, we have

or $$\left(\frac{45-40}{8}\right)=k\left(\frac{45+40}{2}-T_s\right)$$

or $$\frac{5}{8}=k(42.5-T_s) \quad \ldots(4.52)$$

Dividing equation-(4.51) by (4.52), we get

$$\frac{8}{5}=\frac{47.5-T_s}{42.5-T_s}$$

or $$8(42.5-T_s)=5(47.5-T_s)$$

or $$3T_s=340-237.5$$

or $$T_s=\frac{102-5}{3}=34.17\,°C$$

 # Illustrative Example 4.23

A solid body X of thermal capacity C is kept in an atmosphere whose temperature is $T_A=300$ K. At time $t=0$, the temperature of X is $T_0=400$ K. It cools according to Newton's law of cooling. At time t, the temperature is 350 K. At this time ($t=t_1$), the body X is connected to a large box Y at atmospheric temperature T_A, through a conducting rod of length L, cross-sectional area A and thermal conductivity K. The thermal capacity of Y is so large that any variation in its temperature may be neglected. The cross-sectional area A of the connecting rod is small compared to the surface area of X. Find the temperature of X at time $t=3t_1$.

Solution

If T is the temperature of body X at an instant of time t, then according to Newton's law of cooling, the rate of loss of heat by the body is given by

$$\frac{dQ}{dt}=-(T-T_A)$$

Where T_A is the temperature of the surrounding atmosphere and α is a constant which depends on the emissivity and the surface of the body. If C is the thermal capacity of body, we have

$$\frac{dQ}{dt}=C\frac{dT}{dt}$$

Thus $$C\frac{dT}{dt}=-\alpha(T-T_A) \quad \ldots(4.53)$$

or $$\frac{dT}{dt}=-k(T-T_A)$$

Where $k=\frac{\alpha}{C}$, is a constant of the body. Therefore,

$$\frac{dT}{(T-T_A)}=-kdt$$

Integrating we have

$$\int\frac{dT}{(T-T_A)}=-k\int dt$$

or $$ln(T-T_A)=-kt+c \quad \ldots(4.54)$$

Where c is a constant of integration. Given that at $t=0$, $T=T_0$ (= 400 K). Using this in equation-(4.54) we have

$$ln(T_0-T_A)=-k\times 0+c=c$$

Thus $$c=ln(T_0-T_A)$$

Using this value of c in equation-(4.54), we get

$$ln(T-T_A)=-kt+ln(T_0-T_A)$$

or $$ln\left(\frac{T-T_A}{T_0-T_A}\right)=-kt$$

$$\left(\frac{T-T_A}{T_0-T_A}\right)=e^{-kt}$$

Given $T_0=400$ K and $T_A=300$ K. Therefore,

$$\frac{T-300}{(400-300)}=e^{-kt} \text{ or } T-300=100\,e^{-kt}$$

or $$T=100(3+e^{-kt}) \quad \ldots(4.55)$$

Given that at $t=t_1$, $T=350$ K. Using this in equation-(4.55) we have

$$350=100(3+e^{-kt_1})$$

or $$e^{-kt_1}=\frac{1}{2} \text{ or } -kt_1=-ln(2) \text{ or } k=\frac{ln(2)}{t_1}$$

But $$k=\frac{\alpha}{C}. \text{ Therefore,}$$

$$\alpha=\frac{C\,ln(2)}{t_1} \quad \ldots(4.56)$$

Using (4.56) in (4.53), the rate of loss of heat due to radiation is given by

$$\left(\frac{dQ}{dt}\right)_r=C\left(\frac{dT}{dt}\right)_r=-\frac{C\,ln(2)}{t_1}\times(T-T_A) \quad \ldots(4.57)$$

When body X is connected to a box Y through a conducting rod, body X will lose heat also by conduction through the rod.

The rate of loss of heat by conduction through a rod of thermal conductivity K, area A and length L is given by

$$\left(\frac{dQ}{dt}\right)_c = -\frac{K\,A(T-T_A)}{L} \qquad \ldots(4.58)$$

Thus the total rate of loss of heat by body X at temperature T is

$$\left(\frac{dQ}{dt}\right)_t = \left(\frac{dQ}{dt}\right)_r + \left(\frac{dQ}{dt}\right)_c$$

As C is the thermal capacity of X, hence, using equation-(4.57) and (4.58) we get

$$C\frac{dT}{dt} = -\frac{C\,ln(2)}{t_1}\times(T-T_A) - \frac{K\,A(T-T_A)}{L}$$

or
$$\frac{dT}{(T-T_A)} = -\frac{1}{C}\left[\frac{C\,ln(2)}{t_1}dt + \frac{K\,A}{L}dt\right]$$

Integrating we have

$$\int_{350}^{T}\frac{dT}{(T-T_A)} = -\frac{1}{C}\left[\frac{C\,ln(2)}{t_1} + \frac{K\,A}{L}\right]\int_{t_1}^{3t_1}dt$$

or
$$\left|ln(T-T_A)\right|_{350}^{T} = -\frac{1}{C}\left[\frac{C\,ln(2)}{t_1} + \frac{K\,A}{L}\right]\times\left|t\right|_{t_1}^{3t_1}$$

or
$$ln(T-T_A) - ln(350-T_A) = -\left[\frac{ln(2)}{t_1} + \frac{K\,A}{L\,C}\right](3t_1 - t_1)$$

or
$$ln\left(\frac{T-T_A}{350-T_A}\right) = -\left[\frac{ln(2)}{t_1} + \frac{K\,A}{L\,C}\right](2t_1)$$

Given $T_A = 300$ K. Therefore,

$$ln\left(\frac{T-300}{350-300}\right) = -\left[\frac{ln(2)}{t_1} + \frac{K\,A}{L\,C}\right](2t_1)$$

or
$$\left(\frac{T-300}{50}\right) = e\left[-2t_1\left\{\frac{ln(2)}{t_1} + \frac{K\,A}{L\,C}\right\}\right]$$

$$= e\left[-2\,ln(2) - \frac{2\,K\,A\,t_1}{L\,C}\right]$$

or
$$T = 300 + 50\times\frac{1}{4}e\left(\frac{-2\,K\,A\,t_1}{L\,C}\right)$$

or
$$T = 300 + 12.5\,e\left(\frac{-2\,K\,A\,t_1}{L\,C}\right)$$

This is the temperature of body X at $t = 3t_1$.

Illustrative Example 4.24

A black walled metal container of negligible heat capacity is filled with water. The container has sides of length 10 cm. It is placed in an evacuated chamber at 27°C. How long will it take for the temperature of water to change from 30°C to 29°C.

Solution

As in this case temperature difference of water with its surrounding is not large, we can use Newton's Law of cooling. If t is the time taken in cooling water from 30°C to 29°C, we have the average from of Newton's law of cooling as

$$\frac{\Delta T}{\Delta t} = \left(\frac{T_2+T_1}{2} - T_5\right)$$

Where
$$k = \frac{4A\sigma T_5^3}{ms}$$

$$= \frac{4\times5.67\times10^{-8}\times6\times100\times10^{-4}\times(300)^3}{1\times4200}$$

$$= 8.75\times10^{-5}$$

or
$$\frac{30-29}{\Delta t} = 8.75\times10^{-5}[29.6-27]$$

or
$$\Delta t = \frac{1}{8.75\times10^{-5}\times2.5}$$

$$= 4571.43 \text{ s}$$

$$= 76.2 \text{ min}$$

$$= 1 \text{ hr } 16.2 \text{ min}$$

Illustrative Example 4.25

A calorimeter of water equivalent 100 gm cools in air in 18 minutes from 60°C to 40°C. When a block of metal of mass 60 gm is heated to 60°C and placed inside the calorimeter. Assume heat loss only by radiation and Newton's Law of cooling to be valid. Find the specific heat of metal if now the system cools from 60°C to 40°C in 20 minutes.

Solution

From average form of Newton's Law of cooling if a body cools from temperature T_2 to T_1 in time t, then we have

$$\frac{T_2-T_1}{t} = \frac{k}{ms}\left(\frac{T_2+T_1}{2} - T_s\right)$$

Where ms is the heat capacity of the body and k is the constant which depends on surrounding temperature and surface of body exposed to surrounding. Now in this case it is given that calorimeter alone takes 18 minutes to cool down from 60° to 40°C thus we have

$$\left(\frac{60-40}{18}\right)=\frac{k}{100}\left(\frac{60+40}{2}-T_s\right)$$

[As for calorimeter it is given that $ms = 100 \times 1 = 100$]

or $$\frac{20}{18}=k(50-T_s)$$

or $$\frac{10}{9}=\frac{k}{100}(50-T_s) \qquad \ldots(4.59)$$

Now when metal block is placed is it, it takes 20 minutes to cool down from 60°C to 40°C, thus we have

$$\frac{60-40}{20}=\frac{k}{100+60\times s}\left(\frac{60+40}{2}-T_s\right)$$

or $$1=\frac{k}{100+60s}(50-T_s) \qquad \ldots(4.60)$$

Dividing equation-(4.59) by (4.60)

$$\frac{10}{9}=\frac{100+60s}{100}$$

or $$1000 = 900 + 540\text{ s}$$

or $$s=\frac{100}{540}=0.185\text{ cal/gmK}$$

Illustrative Example 4.26

A metal ball of 1 kg mass is heated by a 20 W heater in a room at 20°C. After some time temperature of ball becomes steady at 50°C. Find the rate of loss of heat by the ball to surrounding when its temperature becomes 50°C. Also find the rate at which it looses heat to the surrounding when its temperature was 30°C.

Solution

It is given that when ball is at 50°C, its temperature becomes steady. This means that rate at which heat is being supplied to the ball, at the same rate, it is loosing heat. Thus when ball is at 50°C, the rate of loss of heat to the surrounding by ball is

$$\frac{dQ}{dt}=\text{Power of Heater}$$

$$=20\,W$$

When ball was at 30°C, using Newton's Law of cooling we can state that the sate of heat loss by ball is directly proportional to its temperature difference with surrounding, thus we have

$$\frac{dQ}{dt}=k(30-20)$$

$$\frac{dQ}{dt}=10\text{k} \qquad \ldots(4.61)$$

From the state when ball was at 50°C, we can write from Newton's Law of cooling

$$20 = k(50-20)$$

or $$k=\frac{2}{3}$$

Thus from equation-(4.61), we can write

$$\frac{dQ}{dt}=10\times\frac{2}{3}=\frac{20}{3}\text{ W}$$

Web Reference at www.physicsgalaxy.com

Age Group - High School Physics | Age 17-19 Years

Section - HEAT & THERMODYNAMICS

Topic - Heat Transfer

Module Number - 24 & 25

Practice Exercise 4.3

(i) The temperature of a body falls from 40°C to 36°C in 5 minutes. Find the time after which the temperature of the body will become 32°C. Take surrounding temperature to be 16°C.

[6.11 min]

(ii) A body initially at 80°C cools to 64°C in 5 minutes and to 52°C next 5 minutes. What will be its temperature after next 5 minutes and what is the temperature of the surroundings ?

[16°C, 43°C]

(iii) The excess temperature of a hot body above its surroundings is halved in $\tau = 10$ minutes. In what time will it be $\frac{1}{10}$ of its initial value. Assume Newton's law of cooling.

[33.23 min]

(iv) A body cools in a surrounding which is at a constant temperature T_0. Its temperature T is plotted with time t as shown in figure-4.28. Two tangents are drawn to the curve at the points A and B which meet the time axis at angles of θ_2 and θ_1 as shown. Assuming Newton's law of cooling to be valid show that

$$\frac{\tan\theta_2}{\tan\theta_1}=\frac{T_2-T_0}{T_1-T_0}$$

Figure 4.28

(v) A calorimeter of negligible heat capacity contains 100 gm water at 40°C. The water cools to 35°C in 5 minutes. If the water is now replaced by a liquid of same volume as that of water at same initial temperature, it cools to 35°C in 2 minutes. Given specific heats of water and that liquid are 4200 J/kg°C and 2100 J/kg°C respectively. Find the density of the liquid.

[800 kg/m^3]

4.5 *Black Body Radiation Spectrum*

Generally gaseous state spectrum of a substance is discrete lines, it is called line spectrum. In gases atoms are so far apart that interaction between them are negligible and each atom behaves as an isolated system. Hot matter in condensed state in form of solid or liquid always emits radiation with a continuous distribution of wavelengths rather than few particular wavelengths like a line spectrum. We have discussed that a black body is one which absorb all the wavelengths of electromagnetic radiation incident upon it. This is also the best possible emitter of electromagnetic radiation at any wavelength. The continuous spectrum radiation that it emits is called blackbody radiation spectrum.

Stefan-Boltzmann's Law states that the radiation energy emitted per unit surface area or average thermal power radiated per unit area of a black body is given as

$$E = \sigma T^4 \text{ W/m}^2$$

The above formula gives the total amount of energy radiated by the body in the form of electromagnetic radiation but it does not tell any thing about the wavelengths of emitted radiations. As we've discussed earlier that thermal radiation is a polychromatic radiation where total intensity of emitted radiation is distributed among a wide range of wavelengths. Here also this total energy σT^4 W/m^2 is not uniformly distributed over all the wavelengths. Its distribution can be measured and described by the intensity per wavelength interval denoted by E_λ, called spectral emittance. Here E_λ is defined as $E_\lambda\, d\lambda$ is the intensity of radiation emitted in the wavelength range from λ to $\lambda + d\lambda$. Thus the total intensity which is given by Stefan-Boltzmann's Law can be written as

$$E = \int_0^\infty E_\lambda d\lambda = \sigma T^4$$

If a variation graph is platted for spectral emittance E_λ with λ, it is shown in figure-4.29. Experiments show that each graph platted at a temperature has a peak value of spectral emittance at a wavelength λ_m at which these intensity per wavelength interval is maximum. It is also observed that as temperature of black body increases the wavelength at which spectral emittance is maximum decreases and experimental data shows that λ_m is inversely proportional to the absolute temperature of body given as

$$\lambda_m \propto \frac{1}{T}$$

or $$\lambda_m = \frac{b}{T}$$

or $$\lambda_m T = b \qquad \dots(4.62)$$

The above equation-(4.62) is called *Wein's Displacement Law* and here the proportionality constant b is called Wein's constant whose numerical value is

$$b = 2.89 \times 10^{-3} \text{ m-K}$$

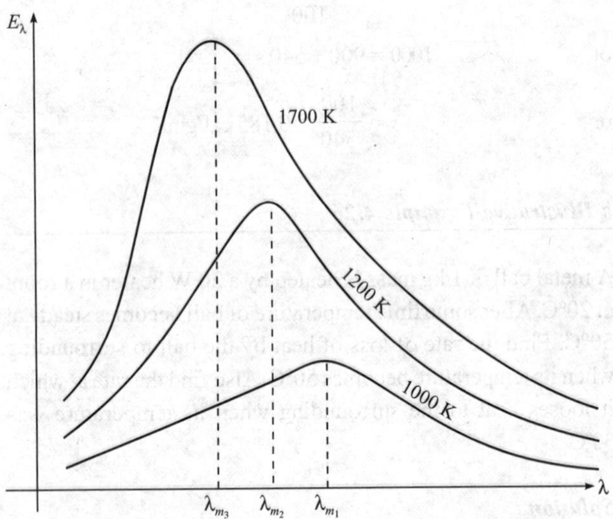

Figure 4.29

Thus as the temperature rises, the peak of E_λ becomes higher and shifts to shorter wavelengths. A body that glows yellow is hotter and brighter than one that glows red. Yellow light has shorter wavelengths then red light. Experiments also show that the shape of the distribution function is same for all the temperature, we can make a curve for one temperature fit any other temperature by only changing the scale on graph.

Several experiments were done by different scientists to develop some empirical expression for calculation of E_λ. The first best appropriate was found by Rayleigh. This result was

$$E_\lambda = \frac{2\pi ckT}{\lambda^4} \qquad \dots(4.63)$$

This formula given in equation-(4.63) was found valid only at high wavelengths but it is not valid for small wavelengths. Figure-4.29 shows that at low wavelengths curves fall toward zero but this expression is inversely proportional to λ^4 rises to infinite intensity at lower wavelengths approaching zero.

One more result can be obtained from expression in equation-(4.63). We've read that at maximum value of E_λ, wavelength is λ_m, thus

$$E_\lambda(max) = \frac{2\pi ckT}{\lambda_m^4}$$

From Wein's Displacement Law, we have

$$\lambda_m = b/T^5, \text{ thus}$$

$$E_\lambda(max) = \frac{2\pi ck}{b^4}T^5$$

or $$E_\lambda(max) \propto T^5 \quad \dots(4.64)$$

Equation-(4.61) states that the maximum spectral emittance from a black body at a given temperature is directly proportional to fifth power of absolute temperature of the body. This is called "*Wein's fifth power Law*". This was initially observed by Wein experimentally which is obtained by a partial correct Rayleigh relation. Later it was mathematically proven by Plank's Radiation theory.

4.5.1 Plank's Radiation Theory as a Proof of Wein's Law and Stefan Boltzmann's Law

In early years of twentieth century plank derived some mathematical expressions for his experiments on radiation and derived a formula for intensity distribution called Plank's Radiation Law. The final result is

$$E_\lambda = \frac{2\pi hc^2}{\lambda^5(e^{hc/\lambda kT}-1)} \text{ W/m}^3 \quad \dots(4.65)$$

Where h is plank's constant, c is speed of light, k is Boltzmann's constant, T is the absolute temperature and λ is the wavelength. This relation also agree well with the experimental Wein's curves shown in figure-4.29.

The Plank's Radiation Law also verifies Wein's displacement law and Stefan-Boltzmann's Law as consequences.

Proof of Wein's Displacement Law

From equation-(4.65) differentiating the expression and equating it to zero we can find the value of λ_m at which E_λ is maximum as

$$\frac{dE_\lambda}{d\lambda} = 0$$

Solving the above equation we get the value of λ_m as

$$\lambda_m = \frac{\text{hc}}{4.965\,\text{kT}} \quad \dots(4.66)$$

$$\lambda_m T = 2.89 \times 10^{-3}$$

Which agrees with the Wein's displacement law.

Proof of Wein's Fifth Power Law

Plank's Radiation Law gives the maximum value of E_λ as

$$E_\lambda(max) = \frac{2\pi hc^2}{\lambda_m^5(e^{hc/\lambda_m kT}-1)}$$

From Wein's displacement law we have $\lambda_m = \frac{b}{T}$, thus

$$E_\lambda(max) = \frac{2\pi hc^2 T^5}{b^5(e^{hc/kb}-1)}$$

or $$E_\lambda(max) \propto T^5$$

Proof of Stefan-Boltzmann's Law

Stefan-Boltzmann's Law gives the total amount of energy radiated by a black body at a given temperature which can be obtained by finding the area under the Wein's curve distributed from wavelength zero to infinity. This can be given as

$$E = \int_0^\infty E_\lambda d\lambda = \int_0^\infty \frac{2\pi hc^2}{\lambda^5(e^{hc/\lambda kT}-1)}d\lambda$$

On solving the above integral we get

$$E = \frac{2\pi^5 k^4}{15c^2h^3}T^4$$

This agrees with Stefan-Boltzmann Law and also verifies the numerical value of

$$\sigma = \frac{2\pi^5 k^4}{15c^2h^3} = 5.67 \times 10^{-8} \text{ w/m}^2\text{k}^4$$

Similarity with Rayleigh Expression

We've already discussed that Rayleigh's expression only agrees with the experimental curves at high wavelength. From Plank's Radiation law if we simplify the expression for high values of λ we get

$$E_\lambda = \frac{2\pi hc^2}{\lambda^5(e^{hc/\lambda kT}-1)}$$

For $x \ll 1$ we can use $e^x \simeq 1 + x$. Thus here for high values of λ we have $e^{hc/\lambda kT} = 1 + \frac{hc}{\lambda kT}$ which result

$$E_\lambda = \frac{2\pi\text{ckT}}{\lambda^4}$$

Which is Rayleigh Expression. Thus at high values of wavelengths both Plank's formula and Rayleigh expression approach to same value.

4.5.2 Practical Applications of Kirchhoff's Law

For deserts it is commonly heard that days are hot and nights are cold. This can be simply explained as sand is rough and can be approximated as a black body, so it is a good absorber and hence in deserts in day time sand absorbs radiation from sun and so day will be very hot. Now in accordance with Kirchhoff's Law, good absorber is a good emitter, so at night when send emits radiation, will be cold.

Another good example of Kirchhoff's law in practice can be seen when a metal ball with some black spots on its surface is heated to a high temperature and is taken in dark. In dark surroundings, the black spots shine brilliantly and the shining surfaces of the ball becomes dark. We can simply explain this as during heating black spots absorb radiation and so emit in dark surrounding while the shining parts reflects radiations and absorbs negligible radiation during heating and so does not emit radiation and becomes dull in dark surroundings.

In spectrum analysis Kirchhoff's law is useful in so many applications. When absorption spectrum of sodium vapours is formed, two dark lines are seen in yellow region in transmitted light due to absorption of these two wavelengths by sodium vapours. When emission spectrum of sodium vapours is obtained the above two bright lines are observed as these vapours emit those radiations which are absorbed initially. This is in accordance with Kirchhoff's Law i.e., a good emitter is a good absorber. When spectrum of sun is formed, Dark Fraunhofer lines are found which can be explained on the basis of Kirchhoff's Law. When white light is emitted from the central part of the sun (photosphere) passes through its atmosphere (chromosphere). Radiations of those wavelengths will be absorbed by the gases present there which they usually emit, as good emitter is a good absorber, which results dark lines in the spectrum of sun.

Another common example which can be realized in common practice is heating of a coloured glass. At normal temperature a piece of red glass appears red because from all the light falling it reflects red and absorbs other colours, when this glass is heated, it absorbs several wavelengths except red and when it is heated to a very high temperature and taken in dark it emits wavelengths which it was absorbing during heating thus at very high temperature red glass emits radiation other then red so it glows with colour complementary to red such as green or blue. Similarly when a blue glass is heated, it absorbs all radiation wavelengths other than blue and when at very high temperature it is taken in dark it emits all wavelengths other than blue thus it glows with a colour complementary to blue such as red or yellowish.

 # Illustrative Example 4.27

A black body at 1500 K emits maximum energy of wavelength 20000 Å. If sun emits maximum energy of wavelength 5500 Å, what would be the temperature of sun.

Solution

According to Wein's displacement law, we have

$$\lambda_m T = \text{constant}$$

or $$\lambda_{m_1} T_1 = \lambda_{m_2} T_2$$

Thus $$20000 \times 10^{-10} \times 1500 = 5500 \times 10^{-10} \times T_2$$

or $$T_2 = \frac{200}{55} \times 1500 = 5454.54\,\text{K}$$

 # Illustrative Example 4.28

If the filament of a 100 W bulb has an area 0.25 cm² and behaves as a perfect black body. Find the wavelength corresponding to the maximum in its energy distribution. Given that stefan's constant is $\sigma = 5.67 \times 10^{-8}$ J/m²s K⁴. $b = 2.89 \times 10^{-3}$ mk.

Solution

In the bulb filament given, the energy radiated per sec per m^2 of its surface area is given as

$$E = \frac{P}{A} = \frac{100}{0.25 \times 10^{-4}} = 4 \times 10^6 \text{ J/s m}^2$$

If T is the temperature of the filament then according to stefan's law, we have

$$E = \sigma T^4$$

or $$4 \times 10^6 = 5.67 \times 10^{-8} x T^4$$

or $$T^4 = \frac{4 \times 10^6}{5.67 \times 10^{-8}} = 7.055 \times 10^{13}$$

or $$T = [7.055 \times 10^{13}]^{1/4} = 2898.14\,\text{K}$$

If the filament radiates the maximum energy at a wavelength λ_m, from Wein's displacement law, we have

$$\lambda_m T = b$$

or
$$\lambda_m = \frac{b}{T}$$

$$= \frac{2.89\times10^{-3}}{2898.14} = 9971.9\ \text{Å}$$

Illustrative Example 4.29

A body emits maximum energy at 4253 Å and the same body at some other temperature emits maximum energy at 2342 Å. Find the ratio of the maximum energy radiated by the body in a short wavelength range.

Solution

If E_1 and E_2 are the maximum energy radiated by the body in short wavelength interval at temperature T_1 and T_2 then according to Wein's fifth power law, we have

$$\frac{E_1}{E_2} = \left(\frac{T_1}{T_2}\right)^5 \qquad \ldots(4.67)$$

According to Wein's displacement law, we have

$$\lambda_{m_1} T_1 = \lambda_{m_2} T_2$$

or
$$\frac{T_1}{T_2} = \frac{\lambda_{m_2}}{\lambda_{m_1}} \qquad \ldots(4.68)$$

Here λ_{m_1} and λ_{m_2} are the wavelength at temperatures T_1 and T_2 at which the energy radiated in a small internal of wavelength is maximum.

Now from equation-(4.67) and (4.68), we have

$$\frac{E_1}{E_2} = \left(\frac{\lambda_{m_2}}{\lambda_{m_1}}\right)^5$$

or
$$\frac{E_1}{E_2} = \left(\frac{234\times10^{-10}}{4253\times10^{-10}}\right)^5 = 0.0506$$

Web Reference at www.physicsgalaxy.com

Age Group - High School Physics | Age 17-19 Years

Section - HEAT & THERMODYNAMICS

Topic - Heat Transfer

Module Number - 26 to 29

Practice Exercise 4.4

(i) The maximum in the energy distribution spectrum of the sun is at wavelength 4753 Å and its temperature is 6050 K. What will be the temperature of the star whose energy distribution shows a maximum at wavelength 9506 Å.

[3025 K]

(ii) The power radiated by a black body is P, and it radiates maximum energy around the wavelength λ. If the temperature of the black body is now changed so that it radiates maximum energy around a wavelength $3\lambda/4$. By what factor the power radiated by it will increase.

[256/81]

(iii) A furnace is at a temperature of 2000 K. At what wavelength does it emit most intensively ?

[14450 Å]

(iv) A black body is at a temperature of 2880 K. The energy of radiation emitted by this object with wavelength between 4990 A and 5000 A is E_1 and that between 9990 A and 10000 A is E_2. Find the ratio of E_2 and E_1.

[4.67]

(v) The radiant emittance of a black body is $R = 250$ kW/m^2. At what wavelength will the emissivity of this black body be maximum ? ($b = 2.9 \times 10^{-3}$ m. K and $\sigma = 5.67 \times 10^{-8}$ W m^{-2} K^{-4})

[19944.7 Å]

* * * * *

Discussion Question

Q4-1 Explain why the surface of a lake freezes first.

Q4-2 Is temperature a conserved quantity in transfer of heat between two bodies at different temperatures.

Q4-3 When two identical object on touching feels hot and cold respectively, can we comment on the heat capacities of the objects.

Q4-4 A vessel is used to boil water. To boil water faster the thermal conductivity and specific heat of the material of vessel should be high or low.

Q4-5 Why is a clear night colder than a cloudy one ?

Q4-6 White clothing is more comfortable in summer but colourful clothing in winter. Explain.

Q4-7 Why a thermos flask has its interior surface mirror like polished.

Q4-8 If we put our hands above a fire or at the side of the fire to get warmth in a winter night. It feels hotter above a fire than by its side. Explain.

Q4-9 The body of a refrigerator is painted white, but the pipes and metal grid at its back are painted black. Why ?

Q4-10 Why are calorimeter made of metal, why not of glass ?

Q4-11 It is observed that if two blankets of same thickness x are used together, will keep more warm as compared to a single blanket of thickness $2x$. Why ?

Q4-12 A solid sphere of a material of radius R and a hollow sphere of the same material of inner radius r and outer radius R are heated to the same temperature and allowed to cool in the same surrounding. Which of them will have higher rate of cooling. Explain.

Q4-13 What is "*Green House Effect*" ?

Q4-14 A sphere, a cube and a circular disc, made of same material and of same mass are heated to same temperature and placed in same surrounding. Which one will have fastest rate of cooling and which one will have slowest ?

Q4-15 A black platinum wire, when heated, first appears dull red, then yellow, then blue and finally white. Explain.

Q4-16 Why it is advantageous to paint the outer walls and roof of a house white in hot weather ?

Q4-17 "Good thermal conductors are also good electrical conductors." Explain this statement.

Q4-18 Why do some materials, such as glass and metals, usually fell cold and other materials, such as cloth, usually feel warm ?

Q4-19 In air-conditioned compartments of a train windows are made-up of two panes of glass separated by an air space. Why ?

Q4-20 Explain why it is advisable to add water to an overheated automobile engine only slowly and only with the engine running.

Q4-21 A piece of wood lying in the sun absorbs more heat than a piece of shiny metal. Even after that the wood feels less hot than the metal when we touch it. Why ?

Q4-22 A person pours a cup of hot coffee, intending to drink it five minutes later. To keep it as hot as possible, should he put cream in it now or wait until just before he drinks it ?

Q4-23 Aluminium foil used for food cooking and storage sometimes has one shiny surface and one dull surface. When food is wrapped for baking, should the shiny side be in or out ?

Q4-24 Why must a room air conditioner be placed in a window ? Why can't it just be set on the floor and plugged in ?

Q4-25 When you step out of a shower bath, you feel cold. Bust as soon as you are dry, you feel warmer, even though the room temperature remains same. Explain.

Q4-26 Ice is slippery to walk on and is especially slippery if you wear ice skates. Why ?

Q4-27 Even when a lake freezes in winters, how do the animals survive deep inside the lake.

* * * * *

Conceptual MCQs Single Option Correct

4-1 A bottle of water at 0°C is opened on the surface of moon. Which of the following correctly expresses the behaviour of water in it ?
(A) It will freeze
(B) It will decompose into H_2 and O_2
(C) It will boil
(D) None of the above

4-2 The radiation power from a source at temperature T and 2 m away is 2 W/m^2. If the temperature of the source increases by 100% the radiation power at a distance 4 m from the source will increase by :
(A) 100% (B) 200%
(C) 600% (D) None of the above

4-3 Which one of the following statements is not true about thermal radiations ?
(A) All bodies emit thermal radiations at all temperature
(B) Thermal radiations are electromagnetic waves
(C) Thermal radiations are not reflected from a mirror
(D) Thermal radiations travel in free space with a velocity of 3×10^8 ms^{-1}

4-4 A metallic sphere of diameter D has a cavity of diameter d at its centre. If the sphere is heated, the diameter of the cavity will :
(A) Decrease
(B) Increase
(C) Remain unchanged
(D) Decrease if $d < D/2$ and increase if $d > D/2$

4-5 The wavelength of the radiation emitted by a body depends upon :
(A) The nature of its surface
(B) The area of its surface
(C) The temperature of its surface
(D) All the above factors

4-6 The amount of energy radiated by a body per unit time depends upon :
(A) The nature of its surface
(B) The area of its surface
(C) The temperature of its surface
(D) All the above factors

4-7 The top of a lake gets frozen at a place where the surrounding air is at a temperature of – 20°C. Then :
(A) The temperature of the layer of water in contact with the lower surface of the ice block will be at 0°C and that at the bottom of the lake will be 4°C
(B) The temperature of water below the lower surface of ice will be 4°C right up to the bottom of the lake
(C) The temperature of the water below the lower surface of ice will be 0°C right up to the bottom of the lake
(D) The temperature of the layer of water immediately in contact with the lower surface of ice will be – 20°C and that of water at the bottom will be 0°C

4-8 A solid sphere and a hollow sphere of the same material and size are heated to the same temperature and allowed to cool in the same surroundings. If the temperature difference between the surroundings and each sphere is T, then :
(A) The hollow sphere will cool at a faster rate for all values of T
(B) The solid sphere will cool at a faster rate for all values of T
(C) Both spheres will cool at the same rate for all values of T
(D) Both spheres will cool at the same rate only for small values of T

4-9 Ice starts forming on the surface of lake and takes 8 hours to form a layer of 1 cm thick. How much time will it take to increase the thickness of layer to 2 cm ?
(A) 8 hours (B) Less than 8 hours
(C) Between 8 to 16 hours (D) More than 16 hours

4-10 Why metals are good conductors of heat ?
(A) Their surfaces are good reflectors of heat
(B) Their atoms move very violently
(C) They contain large number of free electrons
(D) Because of some reason other than those mentioned above

4-11 Why the walls and roof of the green house are made of glass ?
(A) The glass absorbs most of the radiations coming from the sun
(B) The glass transmits the radiations coming from the sun but not those given out by the bodies inside
(C) The glass equally transmits the radiations from the sun as well as those from inside
(D) For some reason other than those mentioned above

4-12 A drop of water is sprinkled on a red hot iron plate. The drop forms a small sphere but does not vaporise immediately. This happens because :
(A) Red hot iron is a poor conductor of heat
(B) A layer of water vapour between the drop and plate prevents conduction of heat
(C) Boiling point of water is raised
(D) Of some other reason

4-13 Two ends of a conducting rod of varying cross-section are maintained at 200ºC and 0ºC respectively. There are two sections marked in the rod *AB* and *CD* of same thickness. In steady state :

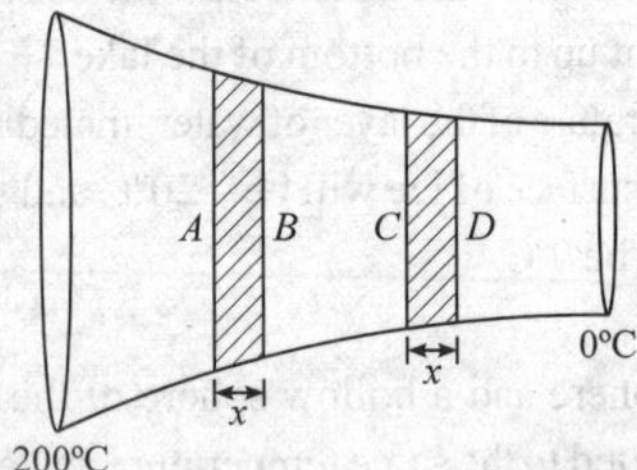

Figure 4.30

(A) Temperature difference across *AB* and *CD* are equal
(B) Temperature difference across *AB* is greater than that of across *CD*
(C) Temperature difference across *AB* is less than that of across *CD*
(D) Temperature difference may be equal or different depending on the thermal conductivity of the rod

4-14 Temperature of a body θ is slightly more than the temperature of the surrounding θ_0. Its rate of cooling (*R*) versus temperature of body (θ) is plotted, its shape would be :

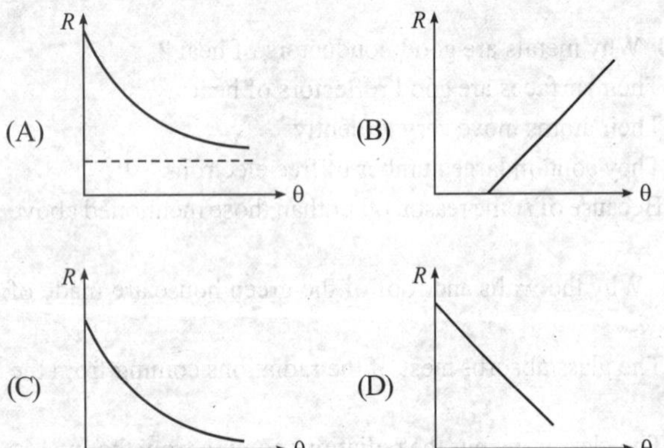

4-15 One end of a conducting rod is maintained at temperature 50ºC and at the other end ice is melting at 0ºC. The rate of melting of ice s doubled if :
(A) The temperature is made 200ºC and the area of cross-section of the rod is doubled
(B) The temperature is made 100ºC and length of the rod is made of four times
(C) Area of cross section of rod is halved and length is doubled
(D) The temperature is made 100ºC and area of cross-section of rod and length both are doubled

4-16 The diagram below shows rods of the same size of two different materials *P* and *Q* placed end to end in thermal contact and heavily lagged at their sides. The outer ends of *P* and *Q* are kept at 0ºC and 100ºC, respectively. The thermal conductivity of *P* is four times that of *Q*. What is the steady-state temperature of the interface ?

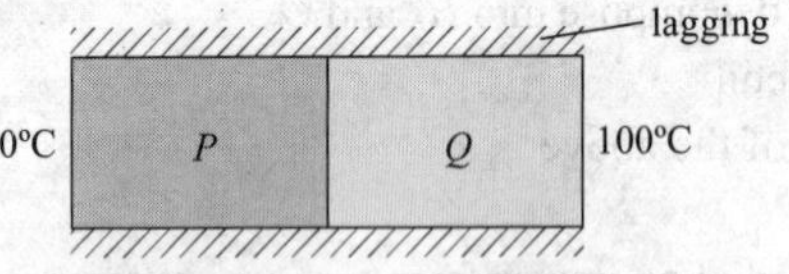

Figure 4.31

(A) 20ºC (B) 75ºC
(C) 25ºC (D) 80ºC

4-17 The lengths of the two rods made up of the same metal and having the same area of cross-section are 0.6 m and 0.8 m respectively. The temperatures of the ends of first rod are 90ºC and 60ºC and that for the ends of the other rod are 150ºC and 110ºC. For which rod, the rate of conduction will be greater ?
(A) First (B) Second
(C) Same for both (D) None of these

4-18 Why two thin blankets put together are warmer than one blanket of double the thickness ?
(A) Conductivity depends upon thickness
(B) Two blankets enclose a layer of air between them
(C) One blanket closes the pores in the other
(D) Because of some reason other than those mentioned above

4-19 λ_m is the wavelength of the radiations corresponding to maximum intensity of a very very hot body at temperature *T*. Which of the following correctly represents the relations between λ_m and *T* :
(A) λ_m decreases with increase in *T*
(B) λ_m increases with increase in *T*
(C) λ_m is independent of *T*
(D) None of the above

4-20 In designing a method for measuring the thermal conductivity of polystyrene, care must be taken to choose a specimen of appropriate dimensions as well as to decide whether or not the specimen requires lagging. Which of the following would be the correct choice ?

	Cross-sectional area of Specimen	*Thickness of Specimen*	*Lagging Required*
(A)	Small	Thin	No
(B)	Small	Thick	Yes
(C)	Large	Thin	No
(D)	Large	Thick	Yes

4-21 The graph shows how temperature varies with distance along a well-insulated metal rod which is conducting thermal energy at a steady rate. The slope of this graph is the temperature gradient. There is an analogy between electrical conduction and thermal energy conduction. If an equivalent electrical-graph were to be drawn, which electrical quantity, when plotted against distance along the rod, would have the slope shown ?

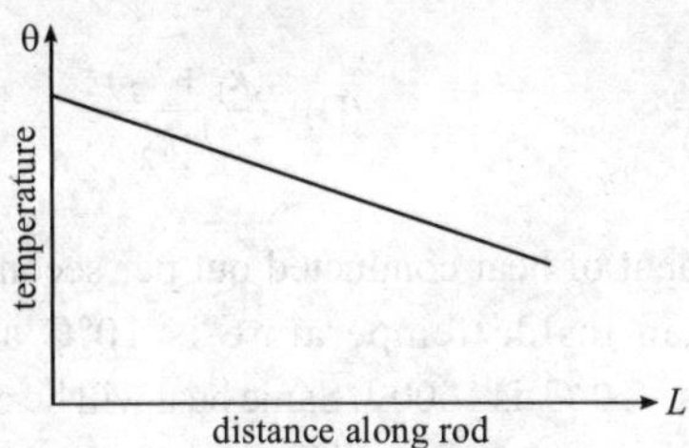

Figure 4.32

Electrical quantity	*Slope*
(A) Charge	Current
(B) Potential	Potential gradient
(C) Potential difference	Resistance
(D) Current	Current gradient

4-22 A composite rod of uniform cross-section has copper and aluminium sections of the same length in good thermal contact. The ends of the rod, which is well-lagged, are maintained at 100°C and at 0°C as shown in the diagram (Figure-4.33). The thermal conductivity of copper is twice that of aluminium.

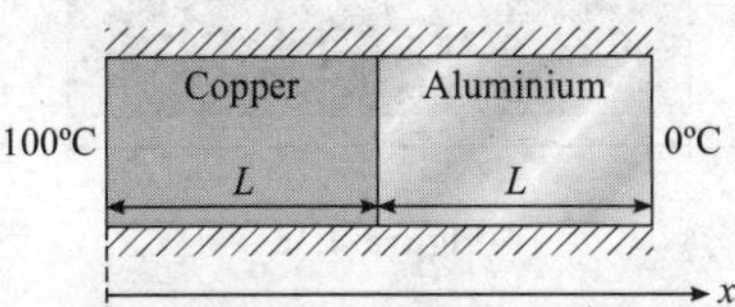

Figure 4.33

Which one of the following graphs represents the variation of temperature T with distance x along the rod in the steady state ?

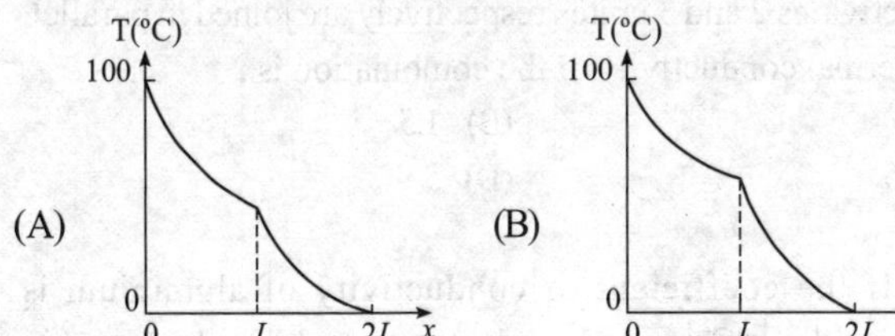

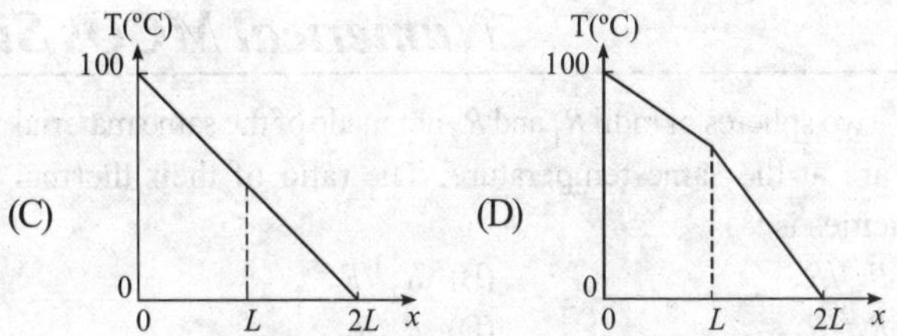

4-23 PQ is a fully-lagged metal bar, containing a section XY of a material of lower thermal conductivity. The thermal conductivities of the two materials are independent of temperature. Ends P and Q are maintained at different temperature.

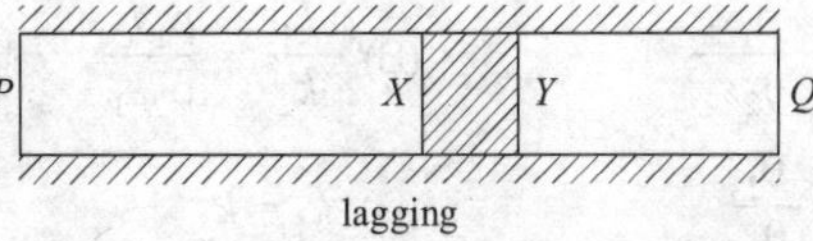

Figure 4.34

In the steady state, the temperature difference across XY would be independent of :

(A) The temperature difference between P and Q

(B) The metal of which the bar is made

(C) The thickness of the section XY

(D) The distance of the section XY from the end P

4-24 Two adiabatic vessels, each containing the same mass m of water but at different temperatures, are connected by a rod of length L, cross-section A, and thermal conductivity K. The ends of the rod are inserted into the vessels, while the rest of the rod is insulated so that there is negligible loss of heat into the atmosphere. The specific heat capacity of water is s, while that of the rod is negligible. The temperature difference between the two vessels reduces to $1/e$ of its original value after a time, Δt. The thermal conductivity (K) of the rod may be expressed by :

(A) $\frac{msL}{A\Delta t}$ (B) $\frac{emsL}{A\Delta t}$

(C) $\frac{msL}{2eA\Delta t}$ (D) $\frac{msL}{2A\Delta t}$

* * * * *

Numerical MCQs Single Options Correct

4-1 Two spheres of radii R_1 and R_2 are made of the same material and are at the same temperature. The ratio of their thermal capacities is :

(A) R_1^4/R_2^4 (B) R_1^3/R_2^3
(C) R_1^2/R_2^2 (D) R_1/R_2

4-2 Two different metal rods of equal lengths and equal areas of cross-section have their ends kept at the same temperature θ_1 and θ_2. if k_1 and k_2 are their thermal conductivities, ρ_1 and ρ_2 their densities and s_1 and s_2 their specific heats, then the rate of flow of heat in the two rods will be the same if :

(A) $\frac{k_1}{k_2} = \frac{\rho_1 s_1}{\rho_2 s_2}$ (B) $\frac{k_1}{k_2} = \frac{\rho_1 s_2}{\rho_2 s_1}$
(C) $\frac{k_1}{k_2} = \frac{\theta_1}{\theta_2}$ (D) $k_1 = k_2$

4-3 A slab of stone of area 0.34 m and thickness 10 cm is exposed on the lower face to steam at 100°C. A block of ice at 0°C rests on the upper face of the slab. In one hour, 3.6 kg of ice is melted. Assume that the heat loss from the sides is negligible. The latent heat of fusion of ice is 3.4×10^4 J kg^{-1}. What is the thermal conductivity of the stone in units of Js^{-1} m^{-1} °C^{-1} ?

(A) 0.1 (B) 0.15
(C) 0.2 (D) 0.25

4-4 The top of a lake is frozen as the atmospheric temperature is – 10°C. The temperature at the bottom of the lake is most likely to be :

(A) 4°C (B) 0°C
(C) –4°C (D) – 10°C

4-5 The tungsten filament of an electric lamp has a surface area A and a power rating P. If the emissivity of the filament is ε and σ is Stefan's constant, the steady temperature of the filament will be :

(A) $T = \left(\frac{P}{A\varepsilon\sigma}\right)^2$ (B) $T = \frac{P}{A\varepsilon\sigma}$
(C) $T = \left(\frac{P}{A\varepsilon\sigma}\right)^{1/2}$ (D) $T = \left(\frac{P}{A\varepsilon\sigma}\right)^{1/4}$

4-6 What are the dimensions of Stefan's constant ?

(A) $ML^{-2}T^{-2}K^{-4}$ (B) $ML^{-1}T^{-2}K^{-4}$
(C) $MLT^{-3}K^{-4}$ (D) $ML^0T^{-3}K^{-4}$

4-7 Two uniform brass rods A and B of lengths l and $2l$ and radii $2r$ and r respectively are heated to the same temperature. The ratio of the increase in the length of A to that of B is :

(A) 1 : 1 (B) 1 : 2
(C) 1 : 4 (D) 2 : 1

4-8 A slab consists of two parallel layers of two different materials of same thickness having thermal conductivities k_1 and k_2. The equivalent conductivity of the combination is :

(A) $k_1 + k_2$ (B) $\frac{k_1 + k_2}{2}$
(C) $\frac{2k_1k_2}{(k_1 + k_2)}$ (D) $\frac{(k_1 + k_2)}{2k_1k_2}$

4-9 The amount of heat conducted out per second through a window, when inside temperature is 10°C and outside temperature is – 10°C, is 1000 J. Same heat will be conducted in through the window, when outside temperature is – 23°C and inside temperature is :

(A) 23°C (B) 230 K
(C) 270 K (D) 296 K

4-10 A composite slab consists of two slabs A and B of different materials but of the same thickness placed one on top of the other. The thermal conductivities of A and B are k_1 and k_2 respectively. A steady temperature difference of 12°C is maintained across the composite slab. If $k_1 = k_2/2$, the temperature difference across slab A will be :

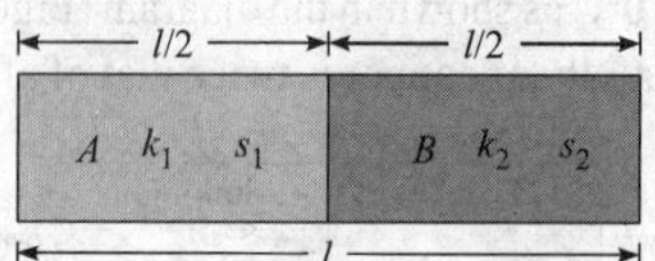

Figure 4.35

(A) 4°C (B) 8°C
(C) 12°C (D) 16°C

4-11 Two rods of equal length and diameter but of thermal conductivities 2 and 3 unites respectively are joined in parallel. The thermal conductivity of the combination is :

(A) 1 (B) 1.5
(C) 2.5 (D) 5

4-12 If the coefficient of conductivity of aluminium is 0.5 cal cm^{-1} s^{-1} °C^{-1}, then in order to conduct 10 cal s^{-1} cm^{-2} in the steady state, the temperature gradient in aluminium must be :

(A) 5°C/cm (B) 10°C/cm
(C) 20°C/cm (D) 10.5°C/cm

4-13 Wien's constant is 2892×10^{-6} SI unit and the value of λ_m for Moon is 14.46 micron. The surface temperature of Moon is :

(A) 100 K (B) 300 K
(C) 400 K (D) 200 K

4-14 The coefficients of thermal conductivity of copper, mercury and glass are respectively. K_c, K_m and K_g such that $K_c > K_m > K_g$. If the same quantity of heat is to flow per second per unit area of each and corresponding temperature gradients are X_c, X_m and X_g, then :

(A) $X_c = X_m = X_g$ (B) $X_c > X_m > X_g$
(C) $X_c < X_m < X_g$ (D) $X_m < X_c < X_g$

4-15 Two cylindrical rods of lengths l_1 and l_2, radii r_1 and r_2 have thermal conductivities k_1 and k_2 respectively. The ends of the rods are maintained at the same temperature difference. If $l_1 = 2l_2$ and $r_1 = r_2/2$, the rates of heat flow in them will be the same if k_1/k_2 is :

(A) 1 (B) 2
(C) 4 (D) 8

4-16 The amount of thermal radiations emitted from one square centimetre area of a black body in one second when at a temperature of 1000 K is :

(A) 5.67 J (B) 56.7 J
(C) 567 J (D) 5670 J

4-17 If the temperature of a black body increases from 7°C to 287°C, then the rate of energy radiation increases by :

(A) $\left(\frac{287}{7}\right)^4$ (B) 16
(C) 4 (D) 2

4-18 A body cools from 60°C to 50°C in 10 minutes. If the room temperature is 25°C and assuming newton's law of cooling to hold good, the temperature of the body at the end of next 10 minutes will be :

(A) 38.5°C (B) 40°C
(C) 42.85°C (D) 45°C

4-19 Given that p joule of heat is incident on a body and out of it q joule is reflected and transmitted by it. The absorption co-efficient of the body is :

(A) p/q (B) q/p
(C) $(q - p)/p$ (D) $(p - q)/p$

4-20 A black body radiates 3 joule per square centimeter per second when its temperature is 127°C. How much heat will be radiated per square centimetre per second when its temperature is 527°C ?

(A) 6 J (B) 12 J
(C) 24 J (D) 48 J

4-21 The rate of loss of heat by radiation from a body at 400°C is R. The radiation from it when the temperature rises to 800°C ?

(A) $2R$ (B) $4R$
(C) $16R$ (D) None of the above

4-22 Two rods of same length and material transfer a given amount of heat in 12 second, when they are joined as shown in figure-4.36(i). But when they are joined as shown in figure-4.36(ii), then they will transfer same heat in same conditions in :

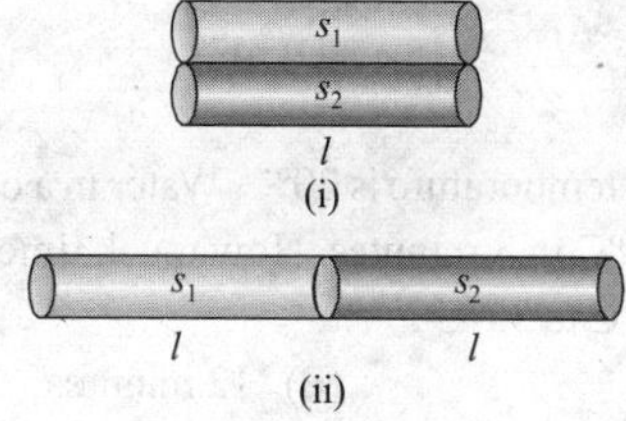

Figure 4.36

(A) 24 s (B) 13 s
(C) 15 s (D) 48 s

4-23 A body cools from 50.0°C to 49.9°C in 5 s. How long will it take to cool from 40.0°C to 39.9°C ? Assume the temperature of the surroundings to be 30.0°C and Newton's law of cooling to be valid :

(A) 2.5 s (B) 10 s
(C) 20 s (D) 5 s

4-24 Radiation from a black body at the thermodynamic temperature T_1 is measured by a small detector at distance d_1 from it. When the temperature is increased to T_2 and the distance to d_2, the power received by the detector is unchanged. What is the ratio d_2/d_1 ?

(A) $\frac{T_2}{T_1}$ (B) $\left(\frac{T_2}{T_1}\right)^2$
(C) $\left(\frac{T_1}{T_2}\right)^2$ (D) $\left(\frac{T_2}{T_1}\right)^4$

4-25 Two bars of equal length and the same cross-sectional area but of different thermal conductivities, k_1 and k_2, are joined end to end as shown in figure-4.37. One end of the composite bar is maintained at temperature T_h whereas the opposite end is held at T_c.

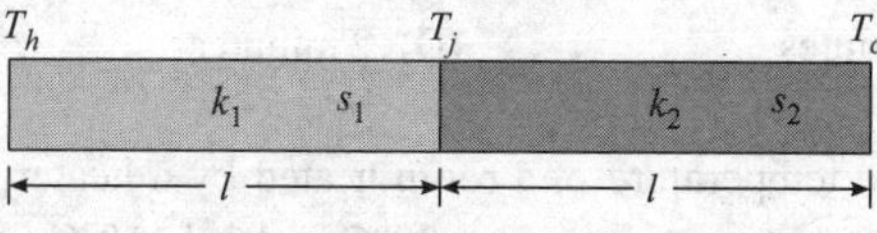

Figure 4.37

If there are no heat losses from the sides of the bars, the temperature T_j of the junction is given by :

(A) $\frac{k_2}{k_1}\frac{(T_h + T_c)}{2}$ (B) $\frac{k_2}{k_1 + k_2}(T_h + T_c)$
(C) $\frac{k_1 + k_2}{k_2}\frac{(T_h + T_c)}{2}$ (D) $\frac{1}{k_1 + k_2}(k_1 T_h + k_2 T_c)$

4-26 A composite slab consists of two parts of equal thickness. The thermal conductivity of one is twice that of the other. What will be the ratio of temperature difference across the two layers in the state of equilibrium ?

(A) 1 (B) 2
(C) 3 (D) 4

4-27 The room temperature is 20ºC. Water in a container cools from 55ºC to 45ºC in 8 minutes. How much time will it take in cooling from 45ºC to 35ºC ?

(A) 4 minutes (B) 12 minutes
(C) 16 minutes (D) 24 minutes

4-28 When the temperature difference between inside and outside of a room is 20ºC, the rate of heat flow through a window is 273 J s^{-1}. If the temperature difference becomes 20 K, the rate of flow of heat through the same window will be :

(A) 253 J s^{-1}
(B) 273 J s^{-1}
(C) 293 J s^{-1}
(D) Given by one of the above mentioned values

4-29 A wall has two layers *A* and *B*, each made of different materials. Both layers are of same thickness. But, the thermal conductivity of material *A* is twice that of *B*. If, in the steady state, the temperature difference across the wall is 24ºC, then the temperature difference across the layer *B* is :

(A) 8ºC (B) 12ºC
(C) 16ºC (D) 20ºC

4-30 You are given two spheres of same material and radii 10 cm and 20 cm. They are heated to the same temperature. They are placed in the same environment. The ratio of their rates of cooling will be :

(A) 1 : 2 (B) 2 : 1
(C) 1 : 4 (D) 4 : 1

4-31 An object is cooled from 75ºC to 65ºC in 2 minutes in a room at 30ºC. The time taken to cool the same object from 55ºC to 45ºC in the same room is :

(A) 5 minutes (B) 3 minutes
(C) 4 minutes (D) 2 minutes

4-32 The temperature of a room heated by a heater is 20ºC when outside temperature is – 20ºC and it is 10ºC when the outside temperature is – 40ºC. The temperature of the heater is :

(A) 80ºC (B) 100ºC
(C) 40ºC (D) 60ºC

4-33 The thermal conductivity of two materials are in the ratio 1 : 2. What will be the ratio of thermal resistances of rods of these materials having length in the ratio 1 : 2 and area of cross-section in the ratio 1 : 2 :

(A) 2 : 1 (B) 1 : 4
(C) 1 : 8 (D) 1 : 16

4-34 Two rods made of same material having same length and diameter are joined in series. The thermal power dissipated through then is $2W$. If they are joined in parallel, the thermal power dissipated under the same conditions on the two ends of the rods, will be :

(A) $16\,W$ (B) $8\,W$
(C) $4\,W$ (D) $2\,W$

4-35 The maximum radiations from two bodies correspond to 560 nm and 420 nm respectively. The ratio of their temperature is :

(A) 4 : 3 (B) 3 : 4
(C) 2 : 1 (D) 3 : 2

4-36 A ball is coated with lamp black. Its temperature is 327ºC and is placed in the atmosphere at 27ºC. Let the rate of cooling be *R*. If the temperature of the ball be 627ºC, what will be its rate of cooling ?

(A) $2R$ (B) $4R$
(C) $8R$ (D) $\frac{16}{3}R$

4-37 Two metallic rods are connected in series. Both are of same material of same length and same area of cross-section. If the conductivity of each rod be *k*, then what will be the conductivity of the combination ?

(A) $4\,k$ (B) $2\,k$
(C) k (D) $k/2$

4-38 A compound slab is made of two parallel plates of copper and brass of the same thickness and having thermal conductivities in the ratio 4 : 1. The free face of copper is at 0ºC. The temperature of the interface is 20ºC. What is the temperature of the free face of brass ?

(A) 0ºC (B) 20ºC
(C) 40ºC (D) 100ºC

4-39 Consider the two insulating sheets with thermal resistances R_1 and R_2 as shown in figure-4.38. The temperature θ is :

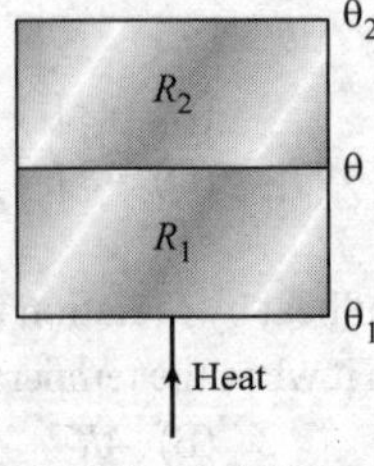

Figure 4.38

(A) $\dfrac{\theta_1\theta_2 R_1 R_2}{(\theta_1+\theta_2)(R_1+R_2)}$ (B) $\dfrac{\theta_1 R_1+\theta_2 R_2}{R_1+R_2}$

(C) $\dfrac{(\theta_1+\theta_2)R_1 R_2}{R_1^2+R_2^2}$ (D) $\dfrac{\theta_1 R_2+\theta_2 R_1}{R_1+R_2}$

4-40 Two cylindrical rods of the same material have the same temperature difference between their ends. The ratio of the rates of flow of heat through them is 1 : 8. The radii of the rods are in the ratio 1 : 2. What is the ratio of their lengths ?

(A) 2:1 (B) 4:1
(C) 1:8 (D) 1:32

4-41 An object is at temperature of 400°C. At what approximate temperature would it radiate energy twice as first ? The temperature of surroundings may be assumed to be negligible :

(A) 200°C (B) 200 K
(C) 800°C (D) 800 K

4-42 A wall is made of two equally thick layers *A* and *B* of different materials. The thermal conductivity of *A* is twice that of *B*. In the steady state, the temperature difference across the wall is 36°C. The temperature difference across the layer *A* will be :

(A) 6°C (B) 12°C
(C) 18°C (D) 24°C

4-43 The ratio of the coefficient of thermal conductivity of two different materials is 5 : 3. If the thermal resistance of the rods of the same thickness of these materials is same, then the ratio of the lengths of these rods is :

(A) $\frac{3}{5}$ (B) $\frac{5}{3}$

(C) $\frac{2}{7}$ (D) $\frac{7}{2}$

4-44 A cylindrical rod with one end in a steam chamber and the other end in ice results in melting of 0.1 g of ice per second. If the rod is replaced by another rod with half the length and double the radius of the first and if the thermal conductivity of material of the second rod is 0.25 times that of first, the rate at which ice melts in g s^{-1} will be :

(A) 0.1 (B) 0.2
(C) 1.6 (D) 3.2

4-45 There is ice formation on a tank of water of thickness 10 cm. How much time it will take to have a layer of 0.1 cm below it ? The outer temperature is – 5°C, the thermal conductivity of ice is 0.005 cal cm^{-1} °C^{-1} and latent heat of ice is 80 cal/g and the density of ice is 0.91 g cm^{-3} :

(A) 46.39 minute (B) 47.63 minute
(C) 48.78 minute (D) 49.31 minute

4-46 The rectangular surface of area 8 cm × 4 cm of a black body at temperature 127°C emits energy *E* per second. If length and breadth are reduced to half of the initial value and the temperature is raised to 327°C, the rate of emission of energy becomes :

(A) $\frac{3}{8}E$ (B) $\frac{81}{16}E$

(C) $\frac{9}{16}E$ (D) $\frac{81}{64}E$

4-47 The emissivity and surface area of tungsten filament of an electric bulb are 0.35 and 0.25 × 10^{-4} metre^2 respectively. The operating temperature of filament is 3000 K. If σ = 5.67 × 10^{-8} watt metre^{-2} K^{-4}, then power of bulb is approximately :

(A) 40 watt (B) 143 watt
(C) 3000 watt (D) 1050 watt

4-48 Ice starts forming in a lake with water at 0°C when the atmospheric temperature is – 10°C. If time taken for 1 cm of ice to be formed is 7 hour, the time taken for the thickness of ice to change from 1 cm to 2 cm is :

(A) 3.5 hour (B) 7 hour
(C) 14 hour (D) 21 hour

4-49 Which of the following cylindrical rods of the same metal has the highest rate of flow of heat ? The rods have equal difference of temperature between their ends :

(A) l = 2 m, r = 1 cm (B) l = 4 m, r = 2 cm
(C) l = 2 m, r = 2 cm (D) l = 2 m, r = 4 cm

4-50 In Q. No.4-49, the lowest rate of flow of heat is for :

(A) l = 2 m, r = 1 cm (B) l = 4 m, r = 2 cm
(C) l = 2 m, r = 2 cm (D) l = 2 m, r = 4 cm

4-51 Three rods made of the same material and having the same cross-section have been joined as shown in the figure-4.39. Each rod is of the same length. The left and right ends are kept at 0°C and 90°C respectively. The temperature of the junction of the three rods will be :

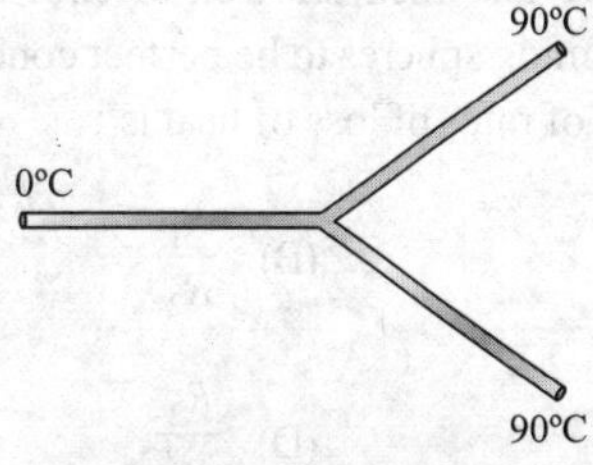

Figure 4.39

(A) 45°C (B) 60°C
(C) 30°C (D) 20°C

4-52 The intensity of radiation emitted by the Sun has its maximum value at a wavelength of 510 nm and that emitted by the North Star has the maximum value at 350 nm. If these Stars behave like black bodies, then the ratio of the surface temperatures of the Sun and the North Star is :

(A) 1.46 (B) 0.69
(C) 1.21 (D) 0.83

4-53 Two different metal rods of the same length have their ends kept at the same temperature θ_1 and θ_2 with $\theta_2 > \theta_1$. If A_1 and A_2 are their cross-sectional areas and k_1 and k_2 their thermal conductivities, the rate of flow of heat in the two rods will be the same it :

(A) $\frac{A_1}{A_2} = \frac{k_1}{k_2}$ (B) $\frac{A_1}{A_2} = \frac{k_2}{k_1}$

(C) $\frac{A_1}{A_2} = \frac{k_1\theta_1}{k_2\theta_2}$ (D) $\frac{A_1}{A_2} = \frac{k_2\theta_2}{k_1\theta_1}$

4-54 The heat is flowing through two cylindrical rods of same material. The diameters of the rods are in the ratio 1 : 2 and their lengths are in the ratio 2 : 1. If the temperature difference between their ends is the same, the ratio of rates of flow of heat through them will be :

(A) 1 : 1 (B) 2 : 1
(C) 1 : 4 (D) 1 : 8

4-55 The temperature gradient in a rod of 0.5 m length is 80ºC/m. If the temperature of hotter end of the rod is 30ºC, then the temperature of the cooler end is :

(A) 40ºC (B) – 10ºC
(C) 10ºC (D) 0ºC

4-56 A body at 300ºC radiates 10 J cm^{-2} s^{-1}. If Sun radiates 10^5 J cm^{-2} s^{-1}, then its temperature is :

(A) 3000ºC (B) 5457ºC
(C) 300 × 10^4 ºC (D) 5730ºC

4-57 Two solid spheres of radii R_1 and R_2 are made of same material and have similar surface. The spheres are raised to the same temperature and then allowed to cool under identical conditions. Assuming spheres to be perfect conductors of heat, their initial ratio of rates of loss of heat is :

(A) $\frac{R_1^2}{R_2^2}$ (B) $\frac{R_1}{R_2}$

(C) $\frac{R_2}{R_1}$ (D) $\frac{R_2^2}{R_1^2}$

4-58 Q. No 4-57, the ratio of their initial rates of cooling is :

(A) $\frac{R_1^2}{R_2^2}$ (B) $\frac{R_1}{R_2}$

(C) 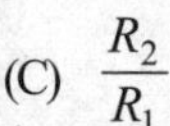 $\frac{R_2}{R_1}$ (D) $\frac{R_2^2}{R_1^2}$

4-59 Two identical vessels are filled with equal amounts of ice. The vessels are made from different materials. If the ice melts in the two vessels in times t_1 and t_2 respectively, then their thermal conductivities are in the ratio :

(A) $\frac{t_1}{t_2}$ (B) $\frac{t_2}{t_1}$
(C) $t_2^2 : t_1^2$ (D) $t_1^2 : t_2^2$

4-60 Two identical rods of a metal are welded as shown in figure-4.40(a). 20 cal of heat flows through them in 4 minute. If the rods are welded as shown in figure-4.40(b), then the same amount of heat will flow in :

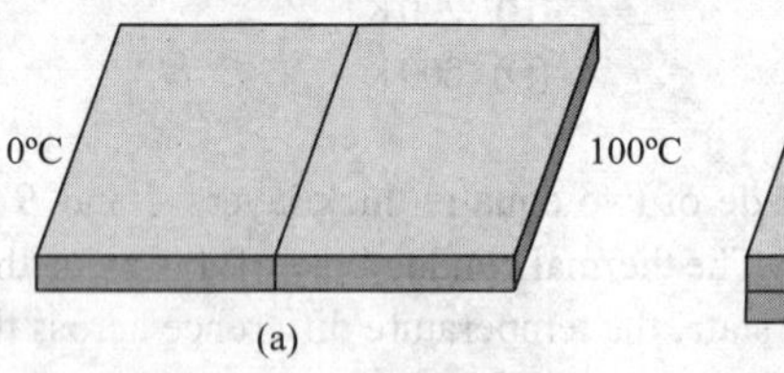

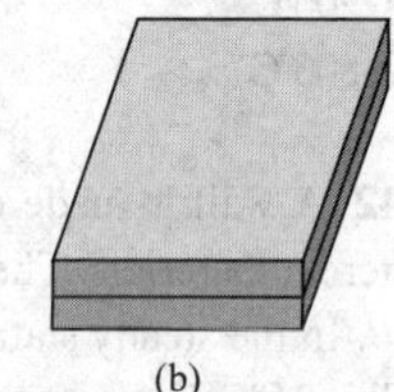

Figure 4.40

(A) 1 minute (B) 2 minute
(C) 4 minute (D) 16 minute

4-61 A small hole is made in a hollow enclosure whose walls are maintained at a temperature of 1000 K. The amount of energy being emitted per square metre per second is :

(A) 567 J (B) 5670 J
(C) 56700 J (D) 567000 J

4-62 The ends of the two rods of different materials with their lengths, diameters of cross-section and thermal conductivities all in the ratio 1 : 2 are maintained at the same temperature difference. The rate of flow of heat in the shorter rod is 1 cal s^{-1}. What is the rate of flow of heat in the larger rod :

(A) 1 cal s^{-1} (B) 4 cal s^{-1}
(C) 8 cal s^{-1} (D) 16 cal s^{-1}

4-63 The ratio of energy of radiation emitted by a black body at 27ºC and 927ºC is :

(A) 1 : 4 (B) 1 : 16
(C) 1 : 64 (D) 1 : 256

4-64 A pond of water at 0°C is covered with a layer of ice 4.00 cm thick. If the air temperature stays constant at – 10°C how long does it take the ice's thickness to increase to 8.00 cm. Thermal conductivity of ice is 2 W/m°C and latent heat of fusion is 80 cal/g. Density of ice is 900 kg/m^3 :

(A) 80.03 hr (B) 10.03 hr
(C) 11.03 hr (D) None of these

4-65 The energy emitted per second by a black body at 27°C is 10 J. If the temperature of the black body is increased to 327°C, the energy emitted per second will be :

(A) 20 J (B) 40 J
(C) 80 J (D) 160 J

4-66 The dimensional formula of thermal resistance is :

(A) $[M^{-1} L^{-2} T^3 K]$ (B) $[M L^2 T^{-2} K^{-1}]$
(C) $[M L^2 T^{-3} K]$ (D) $[M L^2 T^{-2} K^{-2}]$

4-67 Two vessels of different materials are similar in size in every respect. The same quantity of ice filled in them gets melted in 20 minute and 30 minute. The ratio of their thermal conductivities will be :

(A) 1.5 (B) 1
(C) $\frac{2}{3}$ (D) 4

4-68 The temperature of a body is increased by 50%. The amount of radiation emitted by it would be nearly :

(A) 50% (B) 225%
(C) 250% (D) 400%

4-69 A cylinder of radius R made of material of thermal conductivity K_1 is surrounded by a cylindrical shell of inner radius R and outer radius $3R$ made of a material of thermal conductivity K_2. The two ends of the combined system are maintained at two different temperatures. What is the effective thermal conductivity of the system ?

(A) $K_1 + K_2$ (B) $\frac{K_1 + 8K_2}{9}$
(C) $\frac{K_1 K_2}{K_1 + K_2}$ (D) $\frac{8K_1 + K_2}{9}$

4-70 The temperature of a body is increased from 27°C to 127°C. The radiation emitted by it increases by a factor of :

(A) $\frac{256}{81}$ (B) $\frac{15}{9}$
(C) $\frac{4}{5}$ (D) $\frac{12}{27}$

4-71 A metal ball of surface area 200 cm^2 and temperature 527°C is surrounded by a vessel a 27°C. If the emissivity of the metal is 0.4, then the rate of loss of heat from the ball is nearly ($\sigma = 5.67 \times 10^{-8}$ J/m^2-s-K^4) :

(A) 108 joule (B) 168 joule
(C) 186 joule (D) 192 joule

4-72 A plane very thick wall having uniform surface temperature along planes are 0 K and $T_0 = 300$ K at $x = 0$ and $x = x_0$ respectively. Thermal conductivity varies linearly with temperature according to the relation

$$K = K_0 (1 + T)$$

The temperature of wall at the plane $x = 2x_0$ is approximately :

(A) 300 K (B) 400 K
(C) 425 K (D) 450 K

4-73 Wires A and B have identical lengths and have circular cross-sections. The radius of A is twice the radius of B i.e. $R_A = 2R_B$. For a given temperature difference between the two ends, both wires conduct heat at the same rate. The relation between the thermal conductivities is given by :

(A) $K_A = 4K_B$ (B) $K_A = 2K_B$
(C) $K_A = K_B/2$ (D) $K_A = K_B/4$

4-74 The ratio of thermal conductivities of two rods of different material is 5 : 4. The two rods of same area of cross-section and same thermal resistance will have the lengths in the ratio :

(A) 4 : 5 (B) 9 : 1
(C) 1 : 9 (D) 5 : 4

4-75 The Sun radiates 480 nm wavelength radiation at maximum intensity. Assuming the Sun to be a black body and its radius is equal to $R = 7 \times 10^8$ m, the mass lost by the Sun per second due to radiation is given as :

Use: Stefan's constant $\sigma = 5.67 \times 10^{-8}$ Wm^{-2}K^{-4}
Wien's constant $b = 2.9 \times 10^{-3}$ m-K

(A) 2×10^9 kg/s (B) 6×10^8 kg/s
(C) 3×10^9 kg/s (D) 5×10^9 kg/s

4-76 In a steady state of thermal conduction, temperature of the ends A and B of a 20 cm long rod are 100°C and 0°C respectively. What will be the temperature of the rod at a point at a distance of 6 cm from the end A of the rod ?

(A) – 30°C (B) 70°C
(C) 5°C (D) None of these

4-77 A black metal foil is warmed by radiation from a small sphere at temperature T and at a distance d. It is found that the power received by the foil is 'P'. If both the temperature and the distance are doubled, the power received by the foil will be :

(A) 16 P (B) 4 P
(C) 2 P (D) P

4-78 A heat flux of 4000 J s^{-1} is to be passed through a copper rod of length 10 cm and area of cross-section 100 cm^2. The thermal conductivity of copper is 400 W/m°C. The two ends of this rod must be kept at a temperature difference of :

(A) 1°C (B) 10°C
(C) 100°C (D) 1000°C

4-79 The temperature of a liquid drops from 365 K to 361 K in 2 minute. The time during which temperature of the liquid drops from 344 K to 342 K is (Temperature of room is 293 K) :

(A) 84 s (B) 72 s
(C) 66 s (D) 60 s

4-80 Consider two hot bodies B_1 and B_2 which have temperature 100°C and 80°C respectively at $t = 0$. The temperature of the surroundings is 40°C. The ratio of the respective rates of cooling R_1 and R_2 of these two bodies at $t = 0$ will be :

(A) $R_1 : R_2 = 3 : 2$ (B) $R_1 : R_2 = 5 : 4$
(C) $R_1 : R_2 = 2 : 3$ (D) $R_1 : R_2 = 4 : 5$

4-81 The temperature of a perfect black body is 727°C and its area is 0.1 m^2. If Stefan's constant is 5.67×10^{-8} watt/m^2-s-K^4, then heat radiated by it in 1 minute is :

(A) 8100 cal (B) 81000 cal
(C) 810 cal (D) 81 cal

4-82 The temperature of a piece of metal is raised from 27°C to 51.2°C. The rate at which the metal radiates energy increases nearly :

(A) 2 times (B) 4 times
(C) 4.46 times (D) 1.36 times

4-83 The dimensions of the coefficient of thermal conductivity are :

(A) $ML^{-1}T^{-2}K^{-1}$ (B) $ML^{-2}T^{-3}K^{-1}$
(C) $ML^{-1}T^{-1}K^{-1}$ (D) $MLT^{-3}K^{-1}$

4-84 Six identical conducting rods are joined as shown in figure-4.41. Points A and D are maintained at temperatures 200°C and 20°C respectively. The temperature of junction B will be :

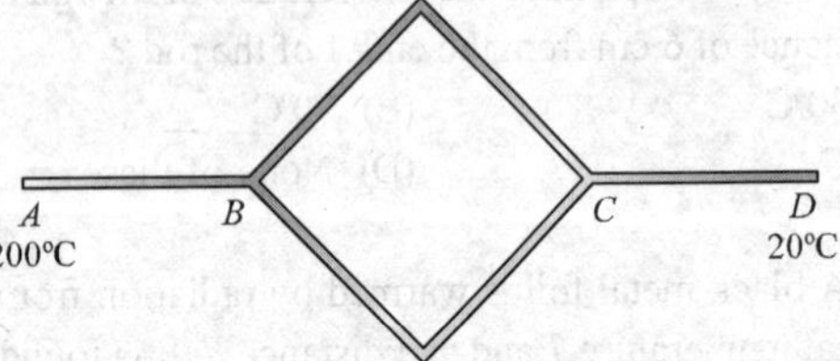

Figure 4.41

(A) 120°C (B) 100°C
(C) 140°C (D) 80°C

4-85 Two rods A and B of different materials are welded together as shown in figure-4.42. If their thermal conductivities are k_1 and k_2, the thermal conductivity of the composite rod will be :

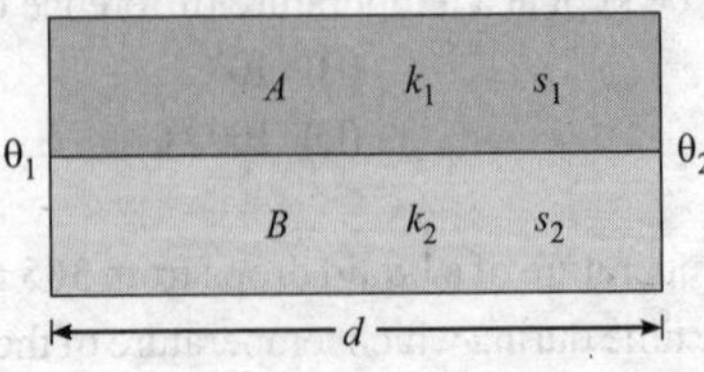

Figure 4.42

(A) $2(k_1 + k_2)$ (B) $\frac{3}{2}(k_1 + k_2)$
(C) $(k_1 + k_2)$ (D) $\frac{1}{2}(k_1 + k_2)$

4-86 A parallel-sided slab is made of two different materials. The upper half of the slab is made of material X, of thermal conductivity λ; the lower half is made of material Y, of thermal conductivity 2λ. In the steady state, the left hand face of the composite slab is at a higher, uniform temperature than the right-hand face, and the flow of heat through the slab is parallel to its shortest sides. What fraction of the total heat flow through the slab passes through material X ?

(A) $\frac{1}{4}$ (B) $\frac{1}{3}$
(C) $\frac{1}{2}$ (D) $\frac{2}{3}$

4-87 Metal rods X and Y of identical cross-sectional area, have lengths 60 cm and 30 cm respectively. They are made of metals of thermal conductivities λ_X and λ_Y. They are well-lagged and joined end-to-end as shown in the figure-4.43. One end of X is maintained at 100°C and the opposite end of Y is maintained at 0°C. When steady conditions have been reached, the temperature of the junction is found to be 25°C.

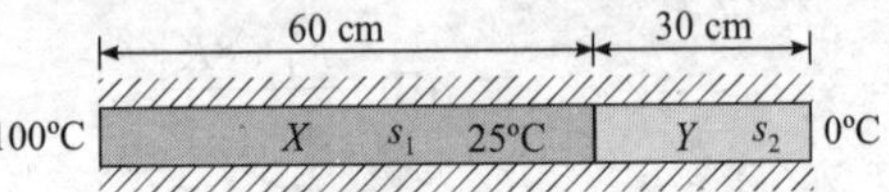

Figure 4.43

What is the value of $\frac{\lambda_X}{\lambda_Y}$?

(A) $\frac{1}{6}$ (B) $\frac{2}{3}$
(C) $\frac{25}{24}$ (D) $\frac{3}{2}$

4-88 When the centre of earth is at a distance of 1.5×10^{11} m from the centre of sun, the intensity of solar radiation reaching at the earth's surface is 1.26 kW/m^2. There is a spherical cloud of cosmic dust, containing iron particles. The melting point for iron particles in the cloud is 2000 K. Find the distance of iron particles from the centre of sun at which the iron particle starts melting. (Assume sun and cloud as a black body, $\sigma = 5.8 \times 10^{-8}$ W/m^2 K^4):

(A) 2.81×10^6 m (B) 2.81×10^{10} m
(C) 2.81×10^9 m (D) 1.40×10^{10} m

Paragraph for Question No. 89

Read the passage carefully and answer the following questions.

Imagine a system, that can keep the room temperature within a narrow range between 20°C to 25°C. the system includes a heat engine operating with variable power $P = 3KT$, where K is a constant coefficient, depending upon the thermal insulation of the room, the area of the walls and the thickness of the walls. T is temperature of the room in degree. When the room temperature drops lower than 20°C, the engine turns on, when the temperature increase over 25°C, the engine turns off, room looses energy at a ate of $K(T - T_0)$ is the outdoor temperature. The heat capacity of the room is C.

Given ($T_0 = 10$°C, $\ln\left(\frac{3}{2}\right) = 0.4$, $\ln\left(\frac{6}{5}\right) = 0.18$, $\frac{C}{K} = 750$ SI-unit)

4-89 Suppose at $t = 0$, the engine turns off, after how much time interval, again, the engine will turn on :

(A) 10 minute (B) 5 minute
(C) 1.125 minute (D) 2.25 minute

4-90 Two balls of same material and finish have their diameters in the ratio 2 : 1. Both are heated to the same temperature and allowed to cool by radiation. Rate of cooling of big ball as compared to smaller one will be in the ratio :

(A) 1 : 1 (B) 1 : 2
(C) 2 : 1 (D) 4 : 1

4-91 Three bars each of area of cross section A and length L are connected in series as shown in the figure. Thermal conductivities of their materials are K, $2K$ and $1.5K$. If the temperatures of free end of first and the last bar are 200°C and 18°C. The value of θ_1 and θ_2 are (in steady state) :

(A) 120°C, 80°C (B) 116°C, 80°C
(C) 116°C, 74°C (D) 120°C, 74°C

4-92 Four identical rods which have thermally insulated lateral surfaces are joined at point O. Points A, B, C and D are connected to furnaces maintained at constant temperatures. If the heat flows into the junction O from A at the rate of 2 J/s and from B at 4 J/s and flows out towards C at 8 J/s. Choose the correct relation(s) :

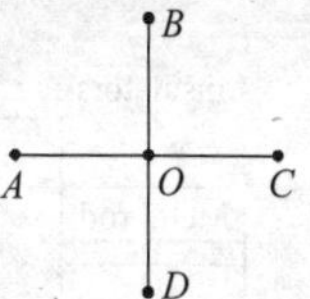

Figure 4.44

(A) $T_A < T_0$ (B) $T_0 < T_C$
(C) $T_A = T_D$ (D) $T_B = T_D$

4-93 In a room where temperature is 30°C, a body cools from 61°C to 59°C in 4 minutes. The time taken by the body to cool from 51°C to 49°C will be :

(A) 4 minute (B) 6 minute
(C) 5 minute (D) 8 minute

4-94 Two identical conducting rods AB and CD are connected to a circular conducting ring at two diametrically opposite points B and C. The radius of the ring is equal to the length of rods AB and CD. The area of cross-section, and thermal conductivity of the rod and ring are equal. Points A and D are maintained at temperatures of 100°C and 0°C. Temperature of point C will be :

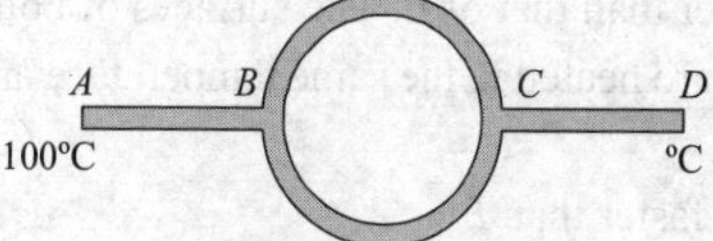

Figure 4.45

(A) 62°C (B) 37°C
(C) 28°C (D) 45°C

* * * * *

Advance MCQs with One or More Options Correct

4-1 An insulated container is filled with ice at 0ºC, and another container is filled with water that is continuously boiling at 100ºC. In series of experiments, the container connected by various, thick metal rods that pass through the walls of container as shown in the figure-4.46.

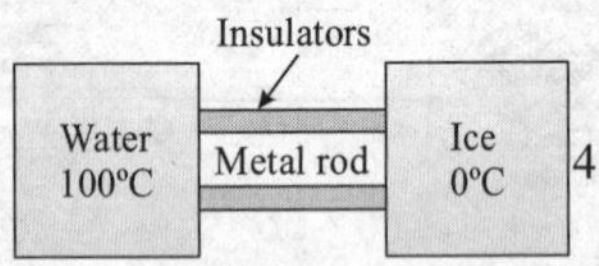

Figure 4.46

In the experiment-I: A copper rod is used and all ice melts is 20 minutes.

In the experiment-II: A steel rod of identical dimensions is used and all ice melts in 80 minutes.

In the experiment-III: Both the rods are used in series and all ice melts in t_{10} minutes.

In the experiment-IV: Both rods are used in parallel all ice melts in t_{20} minutes.

(A) The value of t_{10} is 100 minutes

(B) The value of t_{10} is 50 minutes

(C) The value of t_{20} is 16 minutes

(D) The value of t_{20} is 8 minutes

4-2 Two spheres A and B have same radius but the heat capacity of A is greater than that of B. The surfaces of both are painted black. They are heated to the same temperature and allowed to cool. Then :

(A) A cools faster than B

(B) Both A and B cool at the same rate

(C) At any temperature the ratio of their rates of cooling is a constant

(D) B cools faster than A

4-3 The two ends of a uniform rod of thermal conductivity k are maintained at different but constant temperatures. The temperature gradient at any point on the rod is $\frac{d\theta}{dl}$ (equal to the difference in temperature per unit length). The heat flow per unit time per unit cross-section of the rod is I then which of the following statements is/are correct:

(A) $\frac{d\theta}{dl}$ is the same for all points on the rod

(B) I will decrease as we move from higher to lower temperature

(C) $I \propto k \cdot \frac{d\theta}{dl}$

(D) All the above options are incorrect

4-4 A planet having surface temperature T K has a solar constant S. An angle θ is subtended by the sun at the planet :

(A) $S \propto T^2$

(B) $S \propto T^4$

(C) $S \propto \theta^0$

(D) $S \propto \theta^2$

4-5 Two ends of area A of a uniform rod of thermal conductivity k are maintained at different but constant temperatures. At any point on the rod, the temperature gradient is $\frac{dT}{dl}$. If I be the thermal current in the rod, then :

(A) $I \propto A$

(B) $I \propto \frac{dT}{dl}$

(C) $I \propto A^0$

(D) $I \propto \frac{1}{\left(\frac{dT}{dl}\right)}$

4-6 Two bodies A and B have thermal emissivities of 0.01 and 0.81, respectively. The outer surface areas of two bodies are the same. The two bodies emit total radiant power at the same rate. The wavelength λ_B corresponding to maximum spherical spectral radiance in the radiation from B is shifted from the wavelength corresponding to the maximum spectral radiance from A by 1.00 μm. If the temperature of A is 5802 K, then :

(A) The temperature of B is 1934 K

(B) $\lambda_B = 1.5\ \mu m$

(C) The temperature of B is 11604 K

(D) The temperature of B is 2901 K

4-7 Curved surface of a uniform rod is isolated from surrounding. Ends of the rod are maintained at temperatures T_1 and T_2 ($T_1 > T_2$) for a long time. At an instant, temperature T_1 starts to decrease at a constant and slow rate. If thermal capacity of material of the rod is considered, then which of the following statements is/are correct ?

(A) At an instant, rate of heat flow near the hotter end is equal to that near the other end

(B) Rate of heat flow through the rod starts to decrease near the hotter end and remains constant near the other end

(C) Rate of heat flow is maximum at mid section of the rod

(D) None of these

4-8 A thin spherical shell and a thin cylindrical shell (closed at both ends) have same volume. Both the shells are filled with water at the same temperature and are exposed to the same atmosphere. Initial temperature of water is slightly greater than that of surrounding. Then at initial moment :

(A) Rate of heat radiation from two shells will be same

(B) Rate of fall of temperature in both the shells will be same

(C) Rate of heat radiation and rate of fall of temperature, both, in cylindrical shell are less than those in spherical shell

(D) None of these

4-9 The gross radiation emitted by a perfectly black body is :
(A) Dependent on its temperature
(B) Dependent on the area of its surface
(C) Dependent on the temperature of the surroundings
(D) Independent of the temperature of the surroundings

4-10 The rates of fall temperature of two identical solid spheres of different materials are equal at a certain temperature if :
(A) Their specific heat capacities are equal
(B) Their heat capacities are equal
(C) Their specific heat capacities are proportional to their densities
(D) Their specific heat capacities are inversely proportional to their densities

4-11 A hollow sphere and a hollow cube, both made of the same metal, have same surface area and negligible thickness. The are filled with warm water of same temperature and placed in an enclosure of constant temperature, a few degrees below that of water. Then in the beginning the rate of :
(A) Energy lost by the sphere is less than that by the cube
(B) Energy lost by the sphere is more than that by the cube
(C) Energy lost by the two are equal
(D) Fall of temperature for sphere is less than that for the cube

4-12 The plots of intensity vs wavelength for two black bodies at temperature T_1 and T_2 such that $T_2 = 2T_1$ respectively are as shown. Let the energy radiated per second by body 1 and body 2 be E_1 and E_2 respectively. Pick up the correct statement(s).

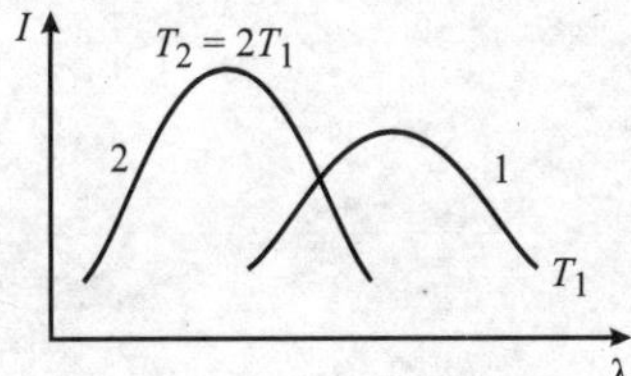

Figure 4.47

(A) $E_1 = 16 E_2$
(B) E_1 may be equal to 16 times of E_2
(C) The area under curve 1 and area under curve 2 will be same
(D) Area under curve 2 is larger than area under curve 1

4-13 A metal cylinder of mass 0.5 kg is heated electrically by a 12 W heater in a room at 15°C. The cylinder temperature rises uniformly to 25°C in 5 min and finally becomes constant at 45°C. Assuming that the rate of heat loss is proportional to the excess temperature over the surroundings :
(A) The rate of loss of heat of the cylinder to surrounding at 20°C is 2 W
(B) The rate of loss of heat of the cylinder to surrounding at 45°C is 12 W
(C) The rate of loss of heat of the cylinder to surrounding at 20°C is 5 W
(D) The rate of loss of heat of the cylinder to surrounding at 45°C is 30 W

4-14 A particle of mass 1 kg slides in a horizontal circle of radius 20 m with a constant speed of 1 m/s. The only forces in the vertical direction acting on the particle are its weight and the normal reaction, however no information is available about the forces in the horizontal plane. Over a period of time whole energy dissipated due to work done by friction is conducted to ground and simultaneously radiated to surround. If the coefficient of friction is $\mu = 0.5$. Then (Take $g = 10$ m/s^2) :
(A) The magnitude of frictional force acting on the block must be 5 N.
(B) The frictional force must be in tangential direction.
(C) The frictional force must be towards the centre.
(D) No comment can be made about the direction or magnitude of friction based on the given data.

4-15 In accordance with Kirchhoff's law (Assume transmissivity $a_t \to 0$ for all the cases) :
(A) Bad absorber is bad emitter
(B) Bad absorber is good reflector
(C) Bad reflector is good emitter
(D) Bad emitter is good absorber

4-16 A hollow and a solid sphere of same material and identical outer surface under identical condition are heated to the same temperature at the same time (both have same e, a) :
(A) In the beginning both will emit equal amount of radiation per unit time
(B) In the beginning both will absorb equal amount of radiation per unit time
(C) Both spheres will have same rate of fall of temperature (dT/dt)
(D) Both spheres will have equal temperatures at any moment

4-17 A heated body emits radiation which has maximum intensity at frequency ν_m. If the temperature of the body is doubled :
(A) The maximum intensity radiation will be at frequency $2\nu_m$
(B) The maximum intensity radiation will be at frequency ν_m
(C) The total emitted energy will increase by a factor 16
(D) The total emitted energy will increase by a factor 2

4-18 Two spherical black bodies A and B, having radii r_A and $r_B = 2r_A$ emit radiation with peak intensities at wavelength 400 nm and 800 nm respectively. If their temperature are T_A and T_B respectively in Kelvin scale, their emissive powers are E_A and E_B then :

(A) $\dfrac{T_A}{T_B} = 2$ (B) $\dfrac{T_A}{T_B} = 4$

(C) $\dfrac{E_A}{E_B} = 8$ (D) $\dfrac{E_A}{E_B} = 4$

4-19 Which of the following statements are true ?

(A) Hole in the wall of a cavity radiator behaves like a black body

(B) Hole in the wall of a cavity radiator does not act like a black body

(C) When a body is kept in a surrounding of low temperature it does not absorb any energy from the surroundings

(D) When a body is kept in surrounding of low temperature it simultaneously radiates heat to the surroundings and absorbs heat from the surroundings.

4-20 A 100 cm long cylindrical flask with inner and outer diameters 2 cm and 4 cm respectively is completely filled with ice as shown in the figure-4.48. The constant temperature outside the flask is 40ºC. (Thermal conductivity of the flask is 0.693 W/mºC, L_{ice} = 80 cal/gm)

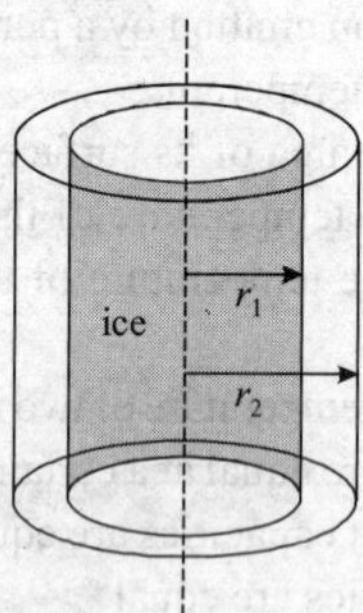

Figure 4.48

(A) Rate of heat flow from outside to the flask is 80π J/s

(B) The rate at which ice melts is $\frac{\pi}{4200}$ Kg/s

(C) The rate at which ice melts is 100π Kg/s

(D) Rate of heat flow from outside to flask is 40π J/s

* * * * *

Unsolved Numerical Problems for Preparation of NSEP, INPhO & IPhO

For detailed preparation of INPhO and IPhO students can refer advance study material on www.physicsgalaxy.com

4-1 A compound rod, 2 m long, is constructed of a solid steel core, 1 cm in diameter, surrounded by a copper casing whose outside diameter is 2 cm. The outer surface of the rod is thermally insulated. One end is maintained at 100°C, the other at 0°C.

(a) Find the heat current in the rod.

(b) What fraction is carried by each material ? Thermal conductivity of steel = 12 cal m^{-1} K^{-1} s^{-1} and that of copper = 92 cal m^{-1} K^{-1} s^{-1}

Ans. [(a) 1.13 cal s^{-1} (b) 96%]

4-2 A hollow glass sphere whose thickness is 2 mm and external radius is 10 cm is filled with ice and is placed in a bath containing boiling water at 100°C. Calculate the rate at which the ice melts. Thermal conductivity of glass = 1.1 J s^{-1} m^{-1} K^{-1} and L of ice = 336×10^3 J kg^{-1}.

Ans. [0.02 kg s^{-1}]

4-3 A steel boiler whose thickness is 3 cm is placed on a plate of area 1 m^2. The temperature of the plate is 300°C and that of the boiling water in the boiler is 100°C. How much water will evaporate per minute ? (Conductivity of steel = 63.0 J s^{-1} m^{-1} K^{-1} and sp. latent heat of vaporisation of water = 2251.2×10^3 Jkg^{-1}.)

Ans. [11.2 kg]

4-4 A certain double plane window consists of two glass sheets each 80 cm × 80 cm × 0.30 cm, separated by 0.3 cm stagnant air space between them (see figure-4.49). The indoor surface temperature is 20°C, while the outdoor surface temperature is 0°C. Find :

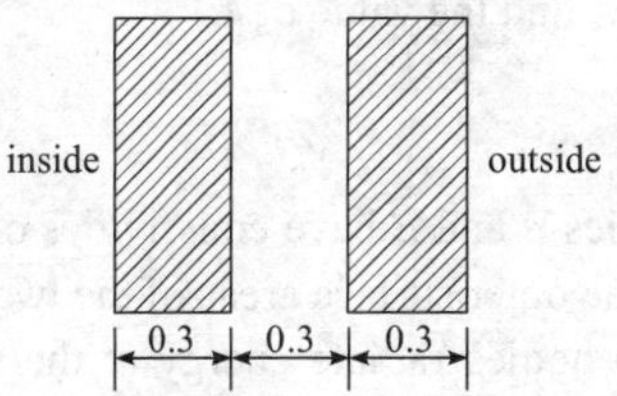

Figure 4.49

(i) the temperature of the surface of the sheets in contact with the stagnant air

(ii) the power transmitted from the inside to the outside.

Given that $K_{glass} = 2.0 \times 10^{-3}$ cal s^{-1} cm^{-1} °C^{-1}; $K_{air} = 2.0 \times 10^{-4}$ cal s^{-1} cm^{-1} °C^{-1}

Ans. [18.4°C, 1.67°C, 71.3 cal s^{-1}]

4-5 Water is being boiled in a flat bottom kettle placed on a stove. The area of the bottom is 300 cm^2 and thickness is 2 mm. If the amount of steam produced is 1 g/min, calculate the difference of temperature between the inner and outer surfaces of the bottom. The thermal conductivity of the material of kettle k = 0.5 cal/s cm °C and latent heat of steam L = 540 cal/g.

Ans. [0.012°C]

4-6 A spherical ball of surface area 2×10^{-3} m^2 is suspended in a room at temperature 330 K. If the temperature of the ball is 200°C, find the net rate of loss of heat from the ball if it behaves like a black body.

Ans. [4.6 W]

4-7 Some water is placed in a container made of a material of poor thermal conductivity. Temperature of water in it is 520 K. The total wall area of the container is 8000 cm^2. The surrounding temperature is 300 K. Find the rate at which heat current will flow from atmosphere to water.

Ans. [440 W]

4-8 Heat is conducted through a slab composed of parallel layers of two different materials of conductivities 134.4 SI units and 58.8 SI units and of thicknesses 3.6 cm and 4.2 cm, respectively. The temperature of the outer faces of the compound slab are 96°C and 8°C. Find (i) the temperature of the interface, (ii) temperature gradient in each section of the slab.

Ans. [(i) 72°C, (ii) 666.7°C per metre, (iii) 1523.8°C per metre]

4-9 Two bodies each of mass m, having specific heats s, are connected by a metal rod of negligible heat capacity of length l, area of cross section A and thermal conductivity k. Initially both bodies are at different temperatures, find the time taken for the temperature difference between the two bodies to become half of the initial value.

Ans. [$\dfrac{lms \ln(2)}{2kA}$]

4-10 A l = 2 m long wire of resistance R = 4 ohms and diameter d = 0.64 mm is coated with plastic of thickness. Δd = 0.06 mm. When a current of I = 5 A flows through the wire, find the temperature difference across the plastic insulation in steady state. Thermal conductivity of plastic is $k = 0.16 \times 10^{-2}$ cal/scm°C.

Ans. [2.05°C]

4-11 One end of a steel rod of length 1 m and area of cross section 4×10^{-6} m^2 is put in boiling water and the other end is kept in an ice bath at 0°C. If thermal conductivity of steel is 46 W/m°C, find the amount of ice melting per second if heat flow only by conduction. Given that the latent heat of fusion of ice is 3.36×10^5 J/kg.

Ans. [5.5×10^{-5} gm/s]

4-12 Figure-4.50 shows a thermal network of two metal rods of same cross section area. If the heat current from the ends *A* and *B* is 130 W, find the heat current through the curved metal rod.

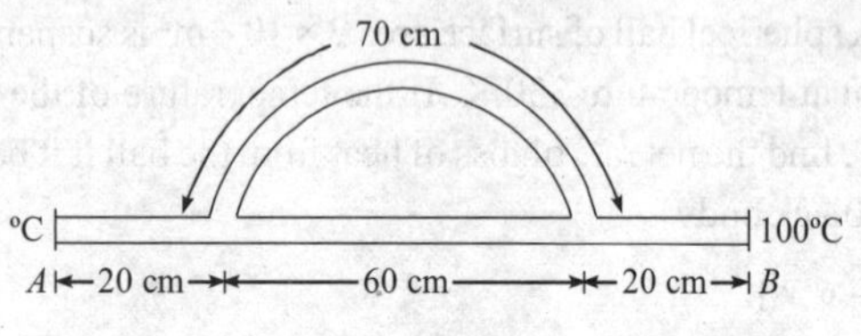

Figure 4.50

Ans. [60 W]

4-13 The heat generated by radioactivity within the earth is conducted outward through the oceans. Assuming the average temperature gradient within the solid earth beneath the ocean to be 0.07 °C^{-1} and the average thermal conductivity 0.2 cal m^{-1} s^{-1} °C^{-1}, determine the rate of heat transfer per square metre. Radius of the earth = 6400 km. Further, determine the quantity of heat transferred through the earth's surface each day.

Ans. [14×10^{-3} cal, 6.2×10^{17} cal]

4-14 Two rods whose lengths are l_1 and l_2 and heat conductivity coefficients x_1 and x_2 are placed end to end. Find the heat conductivity coefficient of a uniform rod of length $l_1 + l_2$ whose conductivity is the same as that of the system of these two rods. The lateral surfaces of the rods are assumed to be thermally insulated.

Ans. [$x = (l_1 + l_2)/(l_1/x_1 + l_2/x_2)$]

4-15 A solid copper sphere (density = 8900 kg m^{-3} and specific heat C = 390 J kg^{-1} °C^{-1}) of radius r = 10 cm is at an initial temperature T_1 200 K. It is then suspended inside a chamber whose walls are at almost 0K. Calculate the time required for the temperature of the sphere to drop to T_2 = 100 K. $\sigma = 5.67 \times 10^{-8}$ Wm^{-2} K^{-4}.

Ans. [165 h 19 min.]

4-16 A calorimeter of mass 100 g contains 100 cm^3 of water at 70°C. It cools down to 30°C in 12 minutes. When the same volume of glycerine is used in the same calorimeter, it takes 8 minutes to cool down through the same temperature range. Find the specific heat of glycerine of specific heat of the calorimeter is 0.1 cal g^{-1} °C^{-1} and specific gravity of glycerine = 1.27.

Ans. [0.498 cal g^{-1} °C^{-1}]

4-17 A vertical brick duct (tube) is filled with cast iron. The lower end of the duct is maintained at a temperature T_1 greater than the melting point T_m of cast iron and the upper end at a temperature T_2 less than the temperature of the melting point of cast iron. It is given that the conductivity of liquid cast iron is equal to *k* times the conductivity of solid cast iron. Determine the fraction of the duct filled with molten metal.

Ans. [$\frac{l_1}{l} = \frac{k(T_1 - T_m)}{k(T_1 - T_m) + (T_m - T_2)}$]

4-18 The gas between two long coaxial cylindrical surfaces is filled with a homogeneous isotropic substance. The radii of the surfaces are r_1 = 5.00 cm and r_2 = 7.00 cm. In the steady state the temperatures of the inner and outer surfaces are T_1 = 290 K and T_2 = 320 K respectively. Find the temperature of a coaxial surface of radius *r*.

Ans. [$T = 147 + 89 \ln r$]

4-19 The tungsten filament of an electric lamp has a length l = 0.25 m and diameter d = 0.04 mm. The power rating is P = 100 W. Assuming the radiation from the filament to be η = 80% of that of a black body radiator at the same temperature, estimate the temperature of the filament. Stefan constant = 5.7×10^{-8} W/m^{2}K^4.

Ans. [2044 K]

4-20 There are two concentric metallic shells of negligible thickness of radii 5 cm and 20 cm. The region between the two shells is filled with a medium of thermal conductivity *k*. The temperature of inner and outer sphere is maintained at 5°C and 10°C respectively. If the heat current flowing from inner to outer sphere is 100 W, find the value of *k*.

Ans. [3 W/m°C]

4-21 Two bodies *A* and *B* have emissivities of 0.01 and 0.81 respectively. The outer surface areas of the two bodies are the same. The two bodies radiate energy at the same rate. The wavelength λ, corresponding to the maximum spectral radiant power in the radiation from *B*, is shifted from the wavelength corresponding to the maximum spectral radiant power in the radiation from *A* by 10^{-6} m. If the temperature of *A* is 5802 K, find the temperature of body *B* and the wavelength of the radiation emitted from body *B* corresponding to maximum spectral radiant power.

Ans. [1934 K, 1.5×10^{-6} m]

4-22 A thin rectangular brass sheet of sides 15.0 cm and 12.0 cm is heated in a furnace to 600°C. How much electric power is needed to maintain the sheet at this temperature. Emissivity of brass surface at this temperature is 0.25 and Stefan constant = 5.67×10^{-8} Wm^{-2} K^{-4}.

Ans. [296 W]

4-23 A body which has a surface area 5.0 cm^2 and a temperature 727°C radiates 300 J of energy each minute. What is its emissivity ? Stefan constant = 5.67×10^{-8} W/m^2 K^4.

Ans. [0.18]

4-24 Over what distance must there be heat flow by conduction from the blood capillaries beneath the skin to the surface if the temperature difference is 0.50°C ? Assume 200 W must be transferred through the whole body's surface area of 1.5 m^2. Given that thermal conductivity of blood cells is 0.2 W/mK.

Ans. [0.75 mm]

4-25 A rod of length L with thermally insulated lateral surface is made of a material whose thermal conductivity varies as $K = C/T$, where C is a constant. The ends are kept at temperatures T_1 and T_2. Calculate the temperature at a distance x from the first end of the rod. Find the value of a.

T_1 ▬▬▬ T_2

Figure 4.51

Ans. [$T = T_1\left(\frac{T_2}{T_1}\right)^{x/L}$]

4-26 Assume that a planet radiates heat at a rate proportional to the fourth power of its surface temperature T and that the temperature of the planet is such that this loss is exactly compensated by the heat gained from the sun. Show that other things remaining the same, a planet's surface temperature will vary inversely as the square root of its distance from the sun.

4-27 The atmospheric temperature above a lake is below 0°C and constant. It is found that a 2 cm layer of ice is formed in four days. In how many days will the thickness increase to 3 cm ?

Ans. [Thickness increases from 2 cm to 3 cm in 5 days]

4-28 A hollow cube of metal has sides measuring 0.8 cm (internal) and thickness 0.5 cm. It is filled with ice at 0°C and immersed in boiling water at 100°C. How many kg of ice will melt in one minute ? Thermal conductivity of metal = 252 J m^{-1} s^{-1} °C^{-1} and latent heat capacity of ice = 336×10^3 J kg^{-1}.

Ans. [34.56 kg]

4-29 The walls of a closed cubical box of edge 50 cm are made of a material of thickness 1 mm and thermal conductivity 4×10^{-4} cal s^{-1} cm^{-1} °C^{-1}. The interior of the box is maintained 100°C above the outside temperature by a heater placed inside the box and connected across 400 V DC. Calculate the resistance of the heater.

Ans. [6.35 Ω]

4-30 A 300 W lamp loses all its energy by emission of radiation from the surface of its filament. If the area of surface of filament is 2.4 cm^2 and is of emissivity 0.4, estimate its temperature.
Given that $\sigma = 1.36 \times 10^{-12}$ cal cm^{-2} s^{-1} K^{-4}. J = 4.2 J cal^{-1}.
Neglect the absorption from the surroundings.

Ans. [2447°C]

4-31 A blackened solid copper sphere of radius 2 cm is placed in an evacuated enclosure whose walls are kept at 100°C. At what rate must energy be supplied to the sphere to keep its temperature constant at 127°C ? Stefan constant = 5.67×10^{-8} J m^{-2} K^{-4}.

Ans. [1.78 J s^{-1}]

4-32 Two identical solid bodies one of aluminium and other of copper are heated to the same temperature and are put in same surrounding. If the emissivity of the aluminium body is 4 times that of copper body, find the ratio of the thermal power radiated by the two bodies. If specific heat of aluminum is 900/kg°C and that of copper is 390 J/kg°C and density of copper is 3.4 times that of aluminum, find the ratio of rate of cooling of the two spheres.

Ans. [4:1, 5.9:1]

4-33 A solid copper sphere (density ρ and specific heat c) of radius r at an initial temperature 200 K is suspended inside a chamber whose walls are at almost 0K. Calculate the time required for the temperature of the sphere to drop to 100 K.

Ans. [$\frac{7\rho rc}{72\sigma}$ 10^{-6} s]

4-34 The thermal powered density u is generated uniformly inside a uniform sphere of radius R and thermal conductivity k. Find the temperature distribution in the sphere when the steady-state temperature at the surface is T_0.

Ans. [$T_0 + \frac{u(R^2 - r^2)}{6k}$]

4-35 A rod of length l with thermally insulated lateral surface and cross-sectional area A, consists of material whose heat conductivity coefficient varies with temperature as $k = \alpha/T$, where α is a constant. The ends of the rod are kept at temperatures T_1 and T_2 ($T_2 > T_1$). Find the function $T(x)$, where x is the distance from the end whose temperature is T and the heat flow density.

Ans. [$T(x) = T_1(T_2/T_1)^{x/l}$; $q = (\alpha/l)\ ln\ (T_2/T_1)$]

4-36 A hot water radiator at 310 K temperature radiates thermal radiation like a black body. Its total surface area is 1.6 m^2. Find the thermal power radiated by it.

Ans. [885 W]

4-37 A flat bottomed metal tank of water is dragged along a horizontal floor at the rate of 20 ms^{-1}. The tank is of mass 20 kg and contains 1000 kg of water and all the heat produced in the dragging is conducted to the water through the bottom plate of the tank. If the bottom plate has an effective area of conduction 1 m^2 and a thickness 5 cm and the temperature of the water in the tank remains constant at 50°C, calculate the temperature of the bottom surface of the tank, given the coefficient of friction between the tank and the floor is 0.343 and K for the material of the tank is 25 cal m^{-1} s^{-1} K^{-1}.

Ans. [82.84°C]

4-38 Two solid spheres, one of aluminium and the other of copper, of twice the radius are heated to the same temperature and are allowed to cool under the identical conditions. Given that specific heat of aluminium is 900 J/kg K and that of copper is 390 J/kg K. Specific gravity of aluminium and copper are 2.7 and 8.9 respectively.

(i) initial rates of fall of temperature, and

(ii) the initial rates of loss of heat

Ans. [2.856; 0.25]

4-39 Estimate the rate that heat can be conducted from the interior of the body to the surface. Assume that the thickness of tissue is 4.0 cm, that the skin is at 34°C and the interior at 37°C, and that the surface area is 1.5 m^2. Compare this to the measured value of about 225 W that must be dissipated by a person working lightly. This clearly shows the necessity of convective cooling by the blood. Given that the thermal conductivity of the blood cells is 0.2 W/mK

Ans. [22.5 W, 1/10]

4-40 The temperature of the filament of 100-watt lamp is 4000°C in the steady state and the radius of the glass bulb is 4 cm and the thickness of the wall is 0.4 mm. Assuming that there is no convection, calculate the thermal conductivity of glass. The temperature of the outside air is 27°C.

Ans. [5×10^{-4} J s^{-1} m^{-1} K^{-1}]

4-41 A thin pipe having outside diameter of 3 cm is to be covered with two layers of insulation each having thickness of 2.5 cm. The thermal conductivity of one material is five times that of the other. Assuming that the inner and outer surface temperatures of the composite wall are fixed, find the percentage reduction in heat transfer when the better insulating material is next to the thin pipe than when it is outside.

Ans. [36.6%]

4-42 A spherical metal ball of radius 1 cm is suspended in a room at 300 K temperature. Inside the sphere there is a battery operated heater which maintains the temperature of the ball at 1000 K. Find the power of the heater if emissivity of the metal ball is 0.3.

Ans. [22 W]

4-43 A block of copper of radius $r = 5.0$ cm is coated black on its outer surface. How much time is required for block to cool down from 1000 K to 300 K? Density of copper, $\rho = 9000$ kg/m^3 and its specific heat, $c = 4$ kJ/kg. K.

Ans. [1.27×10^5 s]

4-44 One end of a rod of length 20 cm is maintained at 800 K. The temperature of the other end of the rod is 750 K in steady state and this end is blackened to radiate thermal radiations like a black body. If temperature of the surrounding is 300 K, find the thermal conductivity of the rod. Assume no energy loss takes place through the lateral surface of the rod during conduction through its length.

Ans. [74 W/m°C]

4-45 In a pitcher 10 kg water is contained. Total surface area of pitcher walls is 2×10^{-2} m^2 and its wall thickness is 10^{-3} m. If surrounding temperature is 42°C, find the temperature of water in the pitcher when it attains a steady value. Given that in steady state 0.1 gm water gets evaporated per second from the outer surface of pitcher through its porous walls. The thermal conductivity of the walls of pitcher is 0.8 W/m°C and latent heat of vaporization of water is 2.27×10^6 J/kg.

Ans. [28°C]

4-46 A uniform copper rod 50 cm long is insulated on the sides, and has its ends exposed to ice and steam, respectively. If there is a layer of water 1 mm thick at each end, calculate the temperature gradient in the bar. The thermal conductivity of copper is 436 W m^{-1} K^{-1} and that of water is 0.436 W m^{-1} K^{-1}.

Ans. [40°C m^{-1}]

4-47 Find the temperature distribution in a substance placed between two parallel plates kept at temperatures T_1 and T_2. The plate separation is equal to l, the heat conductivity coefficient of the substance $k \propto \sqrt{T}$.

Ans. [$T = T_1\ \{1 + (x/l)\ [(T_2/T_1)^{3/2} - 1]\}^{2/3}$, where x is the distance from the plate maintained at the temperature T_1]

4-48 Four spheres *A*, *B*, *C* and *D* of different metals but of same radius are kept at same temperature. The ratio of their densities and specific heats are 2 : 3 : 5 : 1 and 3 : 6 : 2 : 4. Which sphere will show the fastest rate of cooling.

Ans. [*B*]

4-49 A closed cubical box made of perfectly insulating material has walls of thickness 8 cm and the only way for heat to enter or leave the box is through two solid, cylindrical, metallic plugs, each of cross-sectional area 12 cm^2 and length 8 cm in opposite walls of the box. The outer surface of one plug is kept at 100°C while the outer surface of the other plug is maintained at 4°C. The thermal conductivity of the plug is 50 cal s^{-1} m^{-1} K^{-1}. A source of energy generating 36 cal s^{-1} is enclosed inside the box. Find the equilibrium temperature of the inner surface of the box, assuming that it is the same at all points on the inner surface.

Ans. [76°C]

4-50 The solar energy received by the Earth per square metre per minute is 8.315×10^4 J m^{-2} min^{-1}. If the radius of the Sun is 7.5×10^5 km and the distance of the Earth from the Sun is 1.5×10^8 km, calculate the surface temperature of Sun. Assume the Sun as a perfect black body.
Given that Stefen constant $\sigma = 5.7 \times 10^{-8}$ Wm^{-2} K^{-4}.

Ans. [5584 K]

4-51 Two solid spheres are heated to the same temperature and allowed to cool under identical conditions. Compare : (i) initial rates of fall of temperature, and (ii) initial rates of loss of heat. Assume that all the surfaces have the same emissivity and ratios of their radii, specific heats and densities are respectively $1 : \alpha$, $1 : \beta$, $1 : \gamma$.

Ans. [$\alpha\beta\gamma : 1$; $1 : \alpha^2$]

4-52 A metal block with a heater in it is placed in a room at temperature 293 K. When the heater is switched on it is observed that the temperature of the block rises at the rate of 2°C/s and when its temperature rises to 30°C, it is switched off. Just after when heater is switched off, it is observed that the block cools at 0.2°C/s. If Newton's law of cooling is assumed to be valid, find the power of the heater. Also find the thermal power radiated by the block when it was at 30°C and at 25°C. Given that the heat capacity of the block is 80 J/°C.

Ans. [160 W, 16 W, 8 W]

4-53 In a cylindrical metallic vessel some water is taken and is put on a burner. The bottom surface area of the vessel is 2.5×10^{-3} m^2 and thickness 10^{-3} m. The thermal conductivity of the metal of vessel is 50 W/m°C. When water boils, it is observed that 100 gm water is vaporized per minute. Calculate the temperature of the bottom surface of the vessel. Given that the latent heat of vaporization of water is 2.26×10^6 J/kg.

Ans. [130°C]

4-54 A body receives heat continuously from an electrical heater of power 10 W. The temperature of the body becomes constant at 50°C when the surrounding temperature is 20°C. After the heater is switched off, body cools from 35.1°C to 34.9°C in 1 minute. Find the heat capacity of body.

Ans. [1500 J/°C]

4-55 In winters ice forms on the surface of a lake. Due to abnormal expansion of water the temperature of the water at the bottom of the lake remains constant at 4°C and we assume that the amount of heat required to maintain this temperature of the bottom layer of water may come from the bed of the lake. If surrounding temperature is – 10°C, Prove that ice formed from the surface of the lake attains a maximum thickness. Find the maximum depth from surface upto which ice is formed if the depth of lake is 1 m. Given that thermal conductivity of ice is 0.5 W/m°C.

Ans. [0.9 m]

4-56 Two spheres of the same material have radii 1 m and 4 m and temperatures 4000 K and 2000 K respectively. Will the energy radiated by per second by the first sphere be greater than that by the second ?

Ans. [Equal]

4-57 The temperature of the tungsten filament of a 40 watt lamp is 1655°C. The effective surface area of the filament is 0.85 cm^2. Assuming that the energy radiated from the filament is 60% of that of a black body radiator at the same temperature, find the value of Stefan's constant.

Ans. [5.67×10^{-8} Wm^{-2} K^{-4}]

4-58 A cubical tank of water of volume 1 m^3 is kept at a constant temperature of 65°C by 1 KW heater. At time $t = 0$, the heater is switched off. Find the time taken by the tank to cool down to 50°C, given the temperature of the room is steady at 15°C. Density of water = 10^3 kg m^{-3} and specific heat of water = 1.0 cal g^{-1} °C^{-1}. (Do not assume average temperature during cooling). Take 1 KW = 240 cal s^{-1}.

Ans. [20.64 hr]

4-59 Find the temperature distribution in the space between two coaxial cylinders of radii R_1 and R_2 filled with a uniform heat conducting substance if the temperatures of the cylinders are constant and are equal to T_1 and T_2 respectively.

Ans. [$T = T_1 + \dfrac{T_2 - T_1}{ln(R_2/R_1)} \ln\left(\dfrac{r}{R_1}\right)$]

4-60 A cube $a = 3.0$ cm on each side radiates energy at the rate of $P = 20$ J/s when its temperature is 727°C and surrounding temperature 27°C. Determine its emissivity.

Ans. [0.066]

4-61 Solve the foregoing problem for the case of two concentric spheres of radii R_1 and R_2 and temperature T_1 and T_2.

Ans. [$T = T_1 + \frac{T_2 - T_1}{1/R_1 - 1/R_2}\left(\frac{1}{R_1} - \frac{1}{r}\right)$]

4-62 A long tungsten heater wire is rated at 3 kWm^{-1} and is 5.0×10^{-4} m in diameter. It is embedded along the axis of a ceramic cylinder of diameter 0.12 m. When operating at the rated power, the wire is at 1500°C; the outside of the cylinder is at 20°C. Find the thermal conductivity of the ceramic.

Ans. [1.77 J s^{-1} m^{-1} K^{-1}]

4-63 A constant electric current flows along a uniform wire with cross-sectional radius R and heat conductivity coefficient k. A unit volume of the wire generates a thermal power ω. Find the temperature distribution across the wire provided the steady-state temperature at the wire surface is equal to T_0.

Ans. [$T = T_0 + (R^2 - r^2)\,\omega/4k$]

4-64 An iron boiler with walls 1.25 cm thick contains water at atmospheric pressure. The heated surface is 2.5 m^2 in area and the temperature of the underside is 120°C. Thermal conductivity of iron is 20 cal s^{-1} m^{-1} K^{-1} and the latent heat of evaporation of water 536×10^3 cal kg^{-1}. Find the mass of water evaporated per hour.

Ans. [537.3 kg per hour]

4-65 A thin wire of length $l = 50$ cm and area of cross-section $S = 3 \times 10^{-4}$ m^2 is heated to 727°C. How much electric power P is needed to maintain the wire at this temperature ? Assume that emissivity of the wire's surface is $e = 0.25$.

Ans. [4.2 watts]

4-66 In the figure-4.52 shown here, S is a source of heat supplying energy at a constant rate 75 J s^{-1} and S' is a sink maintained at 10°C. The two conductors joining S to S' are each 20 cm long, 1 cm^2 in cross-section and of thermal conductivity 385 W m^{-1} K^{-1} s^{-1}. Calculate the temperature of the point S.

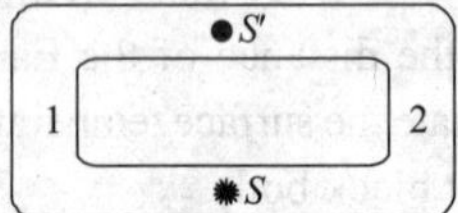

Figure 4.52

Ans. [400°C]

* * * * *

Oscillations and Simple Harmonic Motion 5

FEW WORDS FOR STUDENTS

As motion is concerned we've studied translational and rotational motion and we've applied them in different sections of Physics. There is one more important kind of motion, we introduce now and in further sections of this book we use it. This is oscillatory motion or vibrations. In such a motion it repeats itself and is also termed as periodic motion. The simplest type of oscillatory motion is Simple Harmonic Motion abbreviated as SHM on which we'll focus now in this chapter.

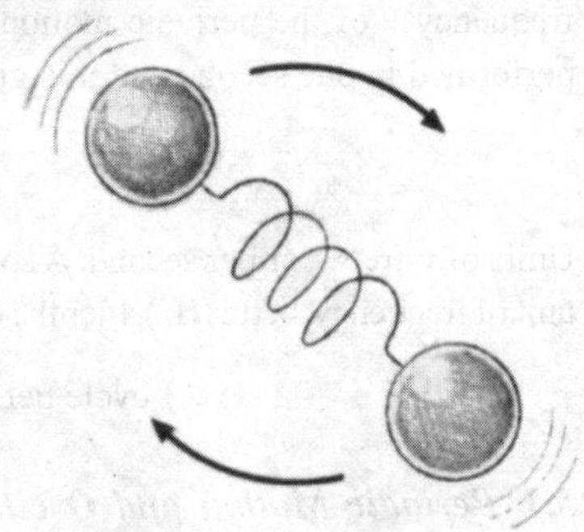

To describe SHM we'll use the basic laws of mechanics you've already covered. Further you'll see that the analysis of SHM is very useful in understanding the concepts of light and electronics.

CHAPTER CONTENTS

5.1 *Periodic Motion and Oscillations*

5.2 *Simple Harmonic Motion*

5.3 *Superpositions of Simple Harmonic Motions*

5.4 *Angular SHM*

5.5 *How to Find Time Period of SHM*

5.6 *Different Types of Pendulums*

5.7 *Phase Analysis of a Particle in SHM*

5.8 *Energy of a Particle in SHM*

5.9 *Energy Method to Find Frequency of SHM*

5.10 *Taylor's Method to Find Angular Frequency of a Particle in SHM*

5.11 *Equation of SHM with Shifting of Origin*

5.12 *SHM of Free Bodies in Absence of External Forces*

COVER APPLICATION

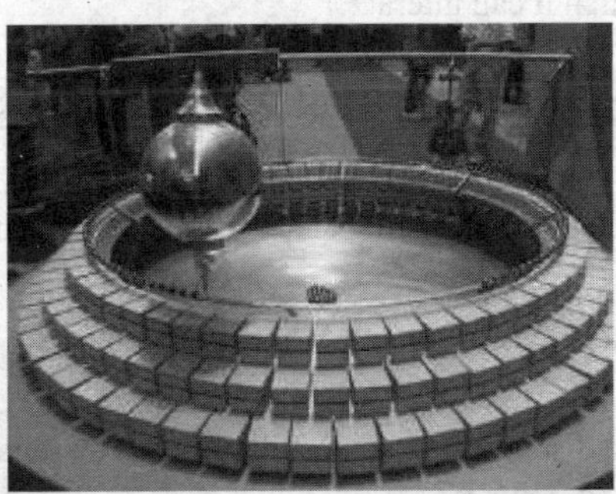

Figure (a)

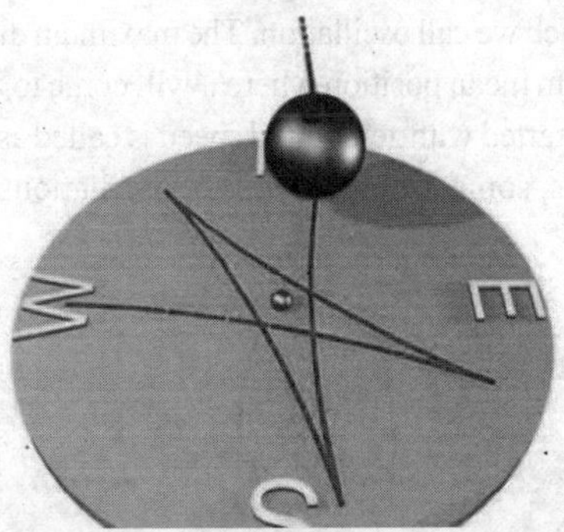

Figure (b)

Foucault's pendulum is an easy experiment which demonstrates the Earth's rotation. The concept that the Earth revolves was nothing new or radical; the pendulum's accomplishment was to provide a proof that did not require minute observations of the stars or other objects far away from Earth. Foucault's pendulum is a highly localized, easily prepared experiment whose result is clear, powerful, and accessible even to the nonscientist. Figure-(a) shows a Foucault's pendulum of which the plane of oscillations rotates with Earth's rotation with respect to a point relative the Earth and Figure-(b) shows the trajectory of pendulum bob on a flat surface above which it oscillates.

What is periodic motion, we all know the motion of a body or a particle which is repeated after a given period, is called periodic motion. The motion of a particle in a circle, all types of vibrations and any motion in which a particle repeatedly retraces its path of motion.

If T is the period of motion after which it repeats itself then the frequency ν of the periodic motion is the number of cycles performed in one second and it is given as

$$\nu = \frac{1}{T}$$

Units of ν are s^{-1} or per second. A special name is given to the unit of frequency, hertz (Hz) after the discoverer of radio waves.

$$1\text{ Hz} \equiv 1 \text{ cycle per second}$$

5.1 Periodic Motion and Oscillations

An oscillation is a special type of periodic motion in which a particle moves to and fro about a fixed point called mean position of particle. Oscillations are commonly seen in general life in our surrounding. As discussed, in all type of oscillations, there is always a mean position about which particle can oscillate. This is the position where particle is in equilibrium that is net forces on particle at this position is zero. If particle is displaced from mean position and due to this displacement some forces appear on it which act on particle in a direction directed toward its equilibrium position, these forces are called restoring forces as these forces tend particle to move towards its equilibrium position. Due to restoring forces, particle starts moving toward mean position and when it reaches mean position, it gains some KE due to work done by restoring forces and it will overshoot from this point with some velocity in other direction, again restoring forces appear on particle toward mean position and now particle is retarded and will stop after travelling some distance and will return toward mean position and starts accelerating & in such a way motion is continued which we call oscillation. The maximum displacement of particle from mean position where it will come to rest or from where it was started with zero initial speed is called as Amplitude of oscillations, some different types of oscillations are shown in figure-5.1.

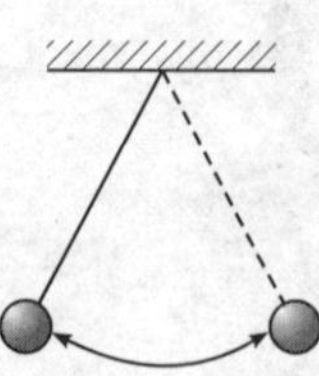

Simple Pendulum (Oscillation of bob)

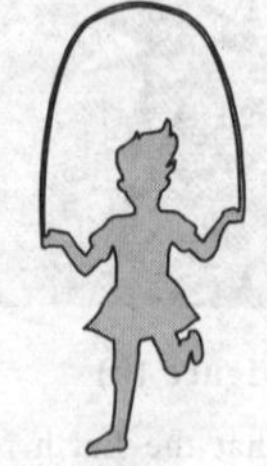

Skipping (Oscillation of girl)

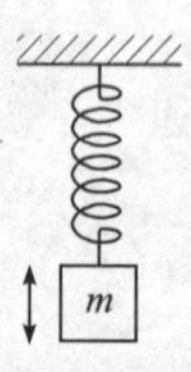

Spring-Block System (Oscillation of block)

Figure 5.1

5.1.1 Types of Oscillations

There are several different types of oscillations depending on the nature of restoring forces used in oscillations but oscillations are classified in three major categories

(a) Free oscillations

(b) Damped oscillations and

(c) Forced oscillations

Free oscillations are those in which once oscillation of a particle starts, it continues indefinitely till some external damping force appears in opposition to the restoring forces on it. Damped oscillations are those in which when a particle starts its oscillatory motion, due to friction or some other naturally acting opposing forces, the oscillation amplitude of particle start decreasing with time, this is called damping. Forced oscillations are those in which damping is not allowed by applying an external time varying force on particle which compensates the effect of the damping force acting on it, thus it is similar to free oscillations but naturally the oscillations are damped and by applying an external force these are made like free oscillations.

5.2 Simple Harmonic Motion

In this section we discuss a special type of oscillation called simple harmonic motion, abbreviated as SHM. A general oscillation can be regarded as SHM if it satisfies these basic conditions stated as

(i) The oscillation amplitude of particle must be very small compared to its surrounding dimensions (dimensions of bodies with which it can interact.)

(ii) During oscillation the acceleration of particle toward mean position due to net restoring forces must be directly proportional to its displacement from mean position.

5.2.1 Representation of SHM

We have discussed that an oscillation can be regarded as SHM if it satisfies the basic requirements to be SHM. Every SHM can be best represented as a projection of a particle in circular motion on its diameter. In fact the motion of projection of a uniform circular motion on its diameter satisfies both the conditions required to be SHM.

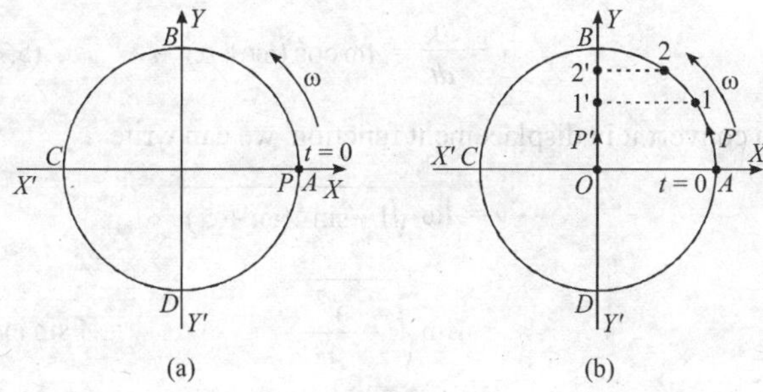

Figure 5.2

Let us analyze it from the figure-5.2 shown. *A* particle *P* is executing a uniform circular motion on the circle with a uniform angular velocity ω as shown. The particle is shown at its initial position *A* at $t = 0$. It starts in anticlockwise direction with uniform angular velocity ω. If we follow the motion of the projection of particle on its vertical diameter in figure-6.2 then we can see, along with *P*, its projection *P′* starts from mid point (centre of circle) in upward direction and the respective position of *P′* for position of *P* at point 1 and 2 are 1′ and 2′ as shown in figure. When *P* reaches the topmost position, *P′* will also be at this point and when *P* starts tracing the second quadrant of circle, *P′* starts coming down towards point *O*. Thus we can see, as point *P* traces its circular path *ABCD*, its projection on diameter *YY′* follows oscillatory motion along *OBODO* … and so on. This oscillatory motion of *P′* can be taken as SHM as it follows the conditions to be a SHM. We'll prove it in next section.

Here motion of particle is in a straight line with amplitude equal to the radius of circle.

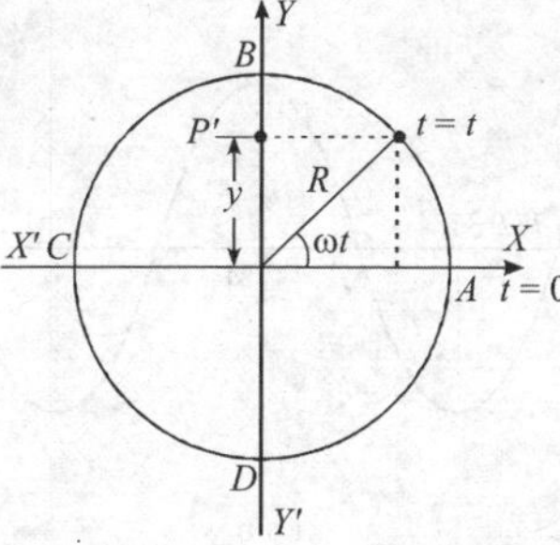

Figure 5.3

As shown in figure-5.3, the displacement of *P′* from point *O* as a function of time can be given as

$$y = R \sin \omega t \qquad \ldots(5.1)$$

As *P′* is going up, its velocity can be given as

$$v = \frac{dy}{dt} = R\omega \cos \omega t \qquad \ldots(5.2)$$

Its acceleration is

$$a = \frac{dv}{dt} = -R\omega^2 \sin \omega t$$

From equation (5.1), we have

$$a = -\omega^2 y \qquad \ldots(5.3)$$

Here ω is a constant thus the acceleration of *P′* is directly proportional to the displacement from its mean position *O* and negative sign in equation-(5.3) shows that direction of acceleration is opposite to y that is towards mean position *O*. Hence the motion of projection *P′* can be regarded as SHM.

5.2.2 Equation of SHM

Equation of an oscillation is the mathematical expression giving the displacement of oscillating particle from its mean position as a function of time.

If a particle is executing SHM with amplitude *A*, it can be regarded as the projection of a circular motion of radius *A* as shown in figure-5.4 if circular motion of point *P* is at a constant angular velocity ω then this is termed as angular frequency of the point *P′* which is in SHM.

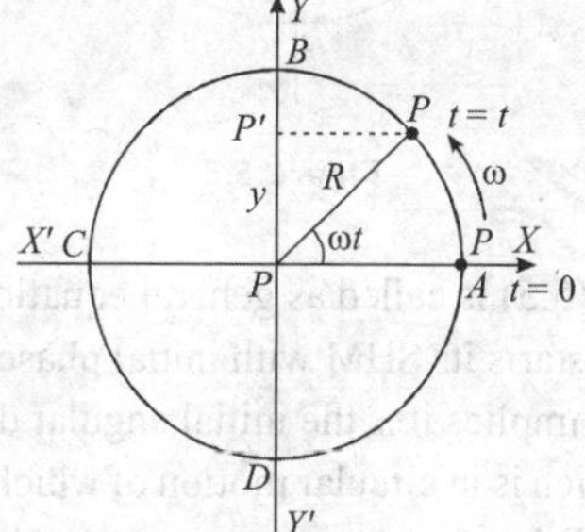

Figure 5.4

Let us consider at $t = 0$, *P* was at point *A* and starts in anticlockwise direction as shown in figure-5.4. Now in time *t*, point *P* traversed by an angle ωt (as shown) and *P′* reaches to a displacement *y* as shown, can be given as

$$y = A \sin \omega t \qquad \ldots(5.4)$$

This equation-(5.4) in this case is called as equation of SHM of point *P′* which is in SHM. Here ωt which is the angular displacement of point *P* (in circular motion) is called phase angle of point *P′* in SHM.

5.2.3 General Equation of SHM

In previous article we've discussed the SHM of point *P′* which was at its mean position at $t = 0$. But it is not necessary that particle starts its SHM from its mean position. It can start from any point on its path, thus equation-(5.4) can not be accepted as a general equation of SHM, this being the equation of those all SHMs where particle starts (at $t = 0$) their SHM from their mean position.

Now consider figure-5.5 where a particle P' starts its SHM with a point having initial phase angle α anticlockwise on the circle of point P of which it is the projection. Let at $t = 0$, point P was at an angular displacement α from its reference point (point A). Thus the point from which P' will start its SHM is shown in figure-5.5. At this position (projection of P at $t = 0$ on YY') α is called as initial phase of point P' in SHM, as α is the initial angular displacement of particle P which is in circular motion. Now after time t, the angular displacement of P is $(\alpha + \omega t)$ which is called the *instantaneous phase* of point P' at time $t = t$ and at this instant the displacement of point P' from mean position is

$$y = A \sin(\omega t + \alpha) \qquad \ldots (5.5)$$

Figure 5.5

This equation-(5.5) is called as general equation of SHM of a particle which starts its SHM with initial phase α. Here initial phase of SHM implies it is the initial angular displacement of the particle which is in circular motion of which the projection is executing SHM.

As equation-(5.4) gives the equation of SHM of those particles which starts their SHM from mean position. Similarly we can define an equation of SHM of those particles which start their SHM from their extreme position by substituting $\alpha = \pi/2$ in equation-(5.5). As if a particle starts from its extreme position, we can take its initial phase $\pi/2$ thus its equation of SHM from equation-(5.5) can be given as

$$y = A \cos \omega t \qquad \ldots (5.6)$$

In all type of problems in which a body or a particle execute SHM, we assume that this is the projection of an another particle who is in circular motion and its projection is executing SHM (that body or particle which is in SHM). Further we will take several examples to analyse this concept.

5.2.4 Velocity and Acceleration of a Particle in SHM

Equation-(5.5) gives the general expression for displacement from mean position of a particle executing SHM as a function of time. Thus velocity of this particle as a function of time can be given as

$$v = \frac{dy}{dt} = A\omega \cos(\omega t + \alpha) \qquad \ldots (5.7)$$

To convert it in displacement function, we can write

$$v = A\omega \sqrt{1 - \sin^2(\omega t + \alpha)}$$

$$= A\omega \sqrt{1 - \frac{y^2}{A^2}} \qquad [\text{As } y = A \sin \omega t]$$

$$v = \omega \sqrt{A^2 - y^2} \qquad \ldots (5.8)$$

Equation-(5.8) gives the velocity of a particle in SHM with amplitude A, and angular frequency ω as a function of its displacement from mean position. From equation-(5.8) we can state that in SHM, particle's velocity is maximum when $y = 0$ i.e. at its mean position and is given as

$$\text{at} \qquad y = 0,\ v_{max} = A\omega$$

At extreme positions of particle when $y = \pm A$, its velocity is zero where it returns towards its mean position. From equations-(5.5) and (5.8) we can plot the graphs of displacement and velocity as a function of time as shown in figure-5.6.

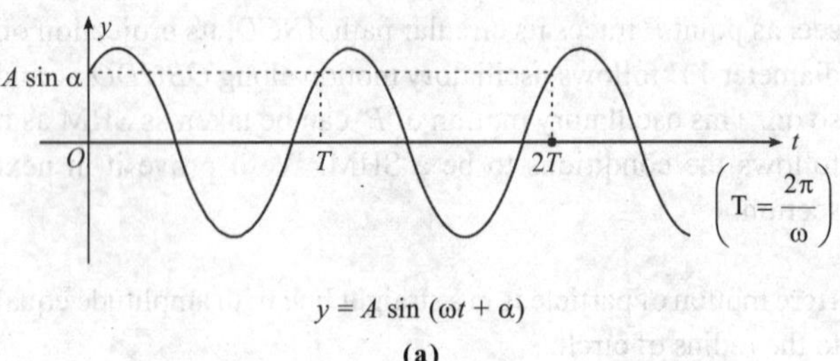

$y = A \sin(\omega t + \alpha)$

(a)

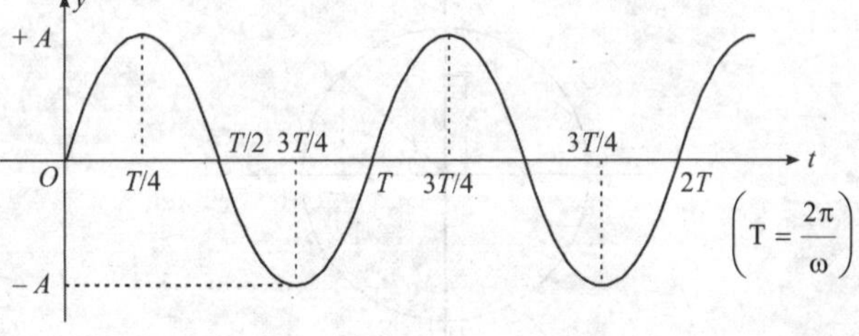

$y = A \sin wt$

(b)

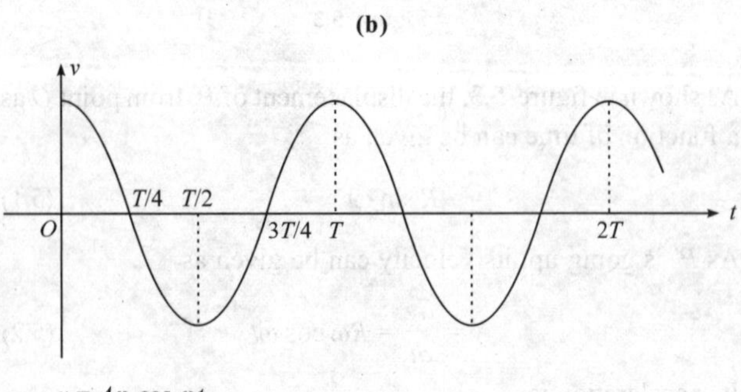

$v = A\omega \cos \omega t$

(c)

Figure 5.6

Similarly acceleration of particle in SHM can be given as

$$a = \frac{dv}{dt} = -A\omega^2 \sin(\omega t + \alpha) \quad \dots (5.9)$$

or $$a = -\omega^2 y \quad [\text{As } y = A\sin(\omega t + \alpha)] \quad \dots (5.10)$$

From equation-(5.10) we can see that at mean position ($y = 0$) when velocity of particle is maximum, its acceleration is zero and at extremities where $y = \pm$ A, acceleration of particle is maximum and its magnitude is given as

$$a_{max} = \omega^2 A \quad [\text{Towards mean position}]$$

It also shows that as particle moves away from mean position, its acceleration continuously increases till it reaches its extreme position (at amplitude) when its velocity becomes zero and it returns.

Equation-(5.10) can be rewritten in differential from as

$$\frac{d^2y}{dt^2} + \omega^2 y = 0 \quad \dots (5.11)$$

This equation-(5.11) is called "*Basic Differential Equation*" of motion of a particle in SHM. Every expression of displacement y as a function of time which satisfies this equation can also be regarded as an equation of SHM.

Illustrative Example 5.1

Prove that $y = Ae^{i\omega t}$ is an equation of SHM.

Solution

According to given equation in problem, differentiating with respect to time we get,

$$\frac{dy}{dt} = iA\omega e^{i\omega t}$$

Differentiating again with respect to time, we get

$$\frac{d^2y}{dt^2} = -\omega^2 Ae^{i\omega t} = -\omega^2 y \quad [\text{As } y = Ae^{i\omega t}]$$

Thus we have $\frac{d^2y}{dt^2} + \omega^2 y = 0$

This is the basic differential equation of SHM hence $y = Ae^{i\omega t}$ is an equation of SHM.

Illustrative Example 5.2

Find the amplitude and initial phase of a particle in SHM, whose motion equation is given as

$$y = A\sin\omega t + B\cos\omega t$$

Solution

Here in the given equation we can write

$$A = R\cos\phi \quad \dots (5.12)$$

and $$B = R\sin\phi \quad \dots (5.13)$$

Thus the given equation transforms to

$$y = R\sin(\omega t + \phi) \quad \dots (5.14)$$

Equation-(5.14) is a general equation of SHM and here R is the amplitude of given SHM and ϕ is the initial phase of the oscillating particle at $t = 0$.

Here R is given by squaring and adding equation-(5.12) & (5.13)

$$R = \sqrt{A^2 + B^2}$$

Initial phase ϕ can be given by dividing-(5.13) & (5.12) as

$$\tan\phi = \frac{B}{A}$$

$$\phi = \tan^{-1}\left(\frac{B}{A}\right)$$

NOTE : Equations $y = Ae^{i(\omega t + \phi)}$ and $y = A\sin\omega t + B\cos\omega t$, we can also represent the general equation of SHM.

Illustrative Example 5.3

A body of mass 1 kg is executing simple harmonic motion which is given by $y = 6.0\cos(100t + \pi/4)$ cm. What is the (i) amplitude of displacement, (ii) Angular frequency, (iii) initial phase, (iv) velocity, (v) acceleration, (vi) maximum kinetic energy ?

Solution

The given equation of SHM is

$$y = 6.0\cos(100t + \pi/4)\text{ cm.}$$

Comparing it with the standard equation of SHM, $y = A\sin(\omega t + \phi)$, we have

(i) Amplitude $A = 6.0$ cm.

(ii) Angular frequency $\omega = 100\text{ s}^{-1}$

(iii) Initial phase $\phi = \pi/4$

(iv) Velocity $v = \omega\sqrt{(A^2 - y^2)} = 100\sqrt{(36 - y^2)}$ cm/s

(v) Acceleration $= -\omega^2 y = -(100)^2 y = -10^4 y$

(vi) Kinetic energy $= \frac{1}{2}mv^2 = \frac{1}{2}m\omega^2(A^2 - y^2)$

The kinetic energy of a particle in SHM is maximum, when it passes its mean position i.e. at $y = 0$

$$(K.E.)_{max} = \frac{1}{2} mv^2_{max} = \frac{1}{2} mA^2\omega^2$$

$$= \frac{1}{2} \times 1 \times 10^4 \times (0.06)^2$$

$$= 18\,J$$

Illustrative Example 5.4

A particle of mass 0.8 kg is executing simple harmonic motion with an amplitude of 1.0 metre and periodic time 11/7 sec. Calculate the velocity and the kinetic energy of the particle at the moment when it displacement is 0.6 metre.

Solution

We know that, at a displacement y from mean position particle's velocity is given as

$$v = \omega\sqrt{(A^2 - y^2)}$$

or
$$v = \frac{2\pi}{T}\sqrt{(A^2 - y^2)}$$

$$= \frac{2 \times 3.14}{(11/7)}\sqrt{[(1.0)^2 - (0.6)^2]}$$

$$= 3.2\,m/s$$

Kinetic energy at this displacement is given by

$$K = \frac{1}{2} mv^2$$

$$= \frac{1}{2} \times 0.8 \times (3.2)^2$$

$$= 4.1\,J$$

Illustrative Example 5.5

A person normally weighing 60 kg stands on a platform which oscillates up and down harmonically at a frequency 2.0 s^{-1} and an amplitude 5.0 cm. If a machine on the platform gives the person's weight against time, deduce the maximum and minimum reading it will show, take $g = 10\,m/s^2$.

Solution

As shown in figure-5.7, platform is executing SHM with amplitude and angular frequency given as

$$A = 5.0\,cm$$

and
$$\omega = 2\pi n = 4\pi\,rad/s \qquad [\text{As } n = 2\,s^{-1}]$$

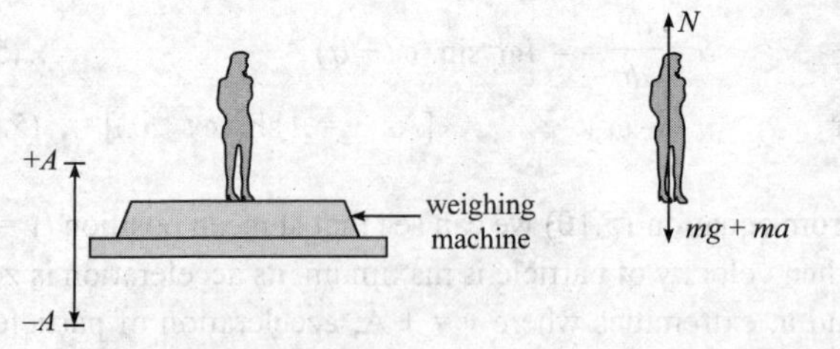

Figure 5.7 Figure 5.8

Here weighing machine will show weight more then that of man when it is below its equilibrium position when the acceleration of platform is in upward direction. In this situation the free body diagram of man relative to platform is shown in figure-5.8. Here *ma* is the pseudo force on man in downward direction relative to platform (or weighing machine). As weighing machine will read the normal reaction on it thus for equilibrium of man relative to platform, we have

$$N = mg + ma$$

or
$$N = mg + m(\omega^2 y) \qquad [\text{As } |a| = \omega^2 y]$$

Where y is the displacement of platform from its mean position. We wish to find the maximum weight shown by the weighing machine, which is possible when platform is at its lowest extreme position as shown in figure-5.8, thus maximum reading of weighing machine will be

$$N = mg + m\omega^2 A$$

$$= 60 \times 10 + 60 \times (4\pi)^2 \times 0.05$$

$$= 600 + 480$$

$$= 1080\,N = 108\,kg\,wt$$

Similarly the machine will show minimum reading when it is at its upper extreme position when pseudo force on man will be in upward direction, thus minimum reading of weighing machine will be

$$N = mg - m\omega^2 A$$

$$= 600 - 480 = 120\,N = 12\,kg\,wt$$

Web Reference at www.physicsgalaxy.com

Age Group - High School Physics | Age 17-19 Years
Section - OSCILLATION & WAVES
Topic - Simple Harmonic Motion
Module Number - 1 to 9

Practice Exercise 5.1

(i) The maximum velocity of a body undergoing simple harmonic motion is 0.04 m s^{-1} and its acceleration at 0.02 m from the mean position is 0.06 m s^{-2}. Find its amplitude and period of vibration.

[2.31×10^{-2} m, 3.625 s]

(ii) A man of mass 60 kg standing on a platform executing SHM in vertical direction. The displacement from the mean of platform varies as

$$y = 0.5 \sin(2\pi f t)$$

Find the minimum value of f, for which the man will feel weightless ness at the highest point. Take $g = 10$ m/s^2.
[0.712 Hz]

(iii) A point moves along the x axis according to the law $x = a \sin^2(\omega t - \pi/4)$. Find :

(a) the amplitude and period of oscillations; draw the plot $x(t)$;

(b) the velocity projection v_x as a function of the coordinate x; draw the plot $v_x(x)$.

[(a) The amplitude is equal to $a/2$, and the period is $T = \pi/\omega$,

Figure 5.9 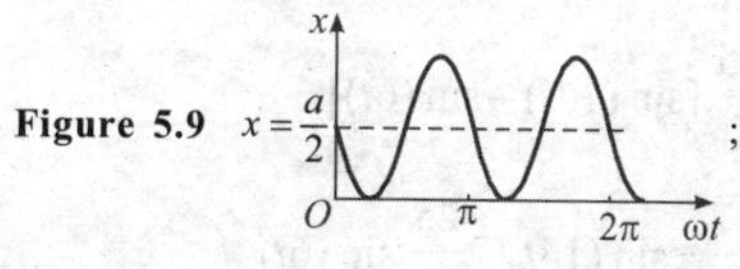

;

(b) $v_x^2 = 4\omega^2 x(a - x)$, see **Figure 5.10**]

(iv) (a) When a particle is executing SHM., what is the ratio of mean velocity during motion from one end of the path to the other and the maximum velocity ? (b) What is the ratio the average acceleration during motion from one extremity to the centre to the maximum acceleration ?

[(a) $\frac{2}{\pi}$; (b) $\frac{2}{\pi}$]

(v) A particle executes SHM in a straight line. The maximum speed of the particle during its motion is v_m. Find the average speed of the particle during its SHM.

[$\frac{2v_m}{\pi}$]

(vi) Equation of a particle in SHM is given as

$$x = 4 \sin \omega t + 3 \sin(\omega t + 63°)$$

Here x is in centimeters and t is in seconds. Find the amplitude of oscillation of the particle.

[6.277 cm]

(vii) Figure-5.11 shows the acceleration-displacement graph of a particle in SHM. Find the time period of its SHM.

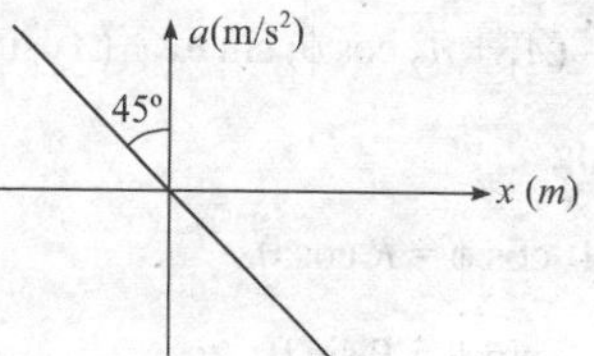

Figure 5.11

[6.28 s]

5.3 Superpositions of Simple Harmonic Motions

When a particle oscillates under the influence of two or more SHMs, its motion equation is not the simple one as discussed earlier for a common SHM equation. The equation of motion of a particle on which two or more than two SHMs are imposed, is given by the principal of superposition which is stated as

"When a particle oscillates under the influence of two or more SHMs then the resultant displacement of the particle is given by the vector sum of the individual displacements produced by the independent SHMs, which are being superposed on the particle."

If $y_1, y_2, y_3, \ldots\ldots y_N$ are the displacements of the particle when it is oscillating only under the N independent SHMs, then on superposing all these SHMs on same particle, its resultant displacement is given as

$$y_R = y_1 + y_2 + \ldots\ldots + y_N \quad \ldots(5.15)$$

These superposing SHMs may be of same or different frequencies. We will discuss this in detail.

5.3.1 Superposition of Same Frequency SHMs

First we discuss superposition of two SHMs, then we generalize the obtained result for more number of SHMs. Let two SHM equations be with amplitude A_1 and A_2 differing in phase by ϕ are producing independent displacements at a particle when acting independently, y_1 and y_2, which are given as

$$y_1 = A_1 \sin \omega t \quad \ldots(5.16)$$

$$y_2 = A_2 \sin(\omega t + \phi) \quad \ldots(5.17)$$

When both of these SHMs are superposed on the particle, the resultant displacement of the particle is given by principal of superposition as

$$y_R = y_1 + y_2$$

or $= A_1 \sin \omega t + A_2 \sin (\omega t + \phi)$

or $= A_1 \sin \omega t + A_2 \sin \omega t \cos \phi + A_2 \cos \omega t \sin \phi$

or $= (A_1 + A_2 \cos \phi) \sin \omega t + (A_2 \sin \phi) \cos \omega t$

Here substituting

$$A_1 + A_2 \cos \phi = R \cos \theta \quad \ldots(5.18)$$

and

$$A_2 \sin \phi = R \sin \theta \quad \ldots(5.19)$$

Now we get

$$y_R = R \sin (\omega t + \theta) \quad \ldots(5.20)$$

We can see that equation-(5.20) is also an equation of SHM with amplitude R and initial phase θ. Here R and θ can be obtained from equations-(5.18) and (5.19) as

$$R = \sqrt{(A_1 + A_2 \cos\phi)^2 + (A_2 \sin \phi)^2}$$

or

$$= \sqrt{A_1^2 + A_2^2 + 2A_1 A_2 \cos\phi} \quad \ldots(5.21)$$

and

$$\tan \theta = \frac{A_2 \sin \phi}{A_1 + A_2 \cos \phi}$$

or

$$\theta = \tan^{-1}\left(\frac{A_2 \sin \phi}{A_1 + A_2 \cos\phi}\right) \quad \ldots(5.22)$$

Thus we can say that when two SHMs of same frequency are superposed on a particle then also it executes SHM whose amplitude and initial phase are given by equation-(5.21) and (5.22) respectively.

By observing equation-(5.21) we can say that this result is similar to that used for resultant of two vectors of magnitudes A_1 and A_2 and having an angle ϕ between them. Similarly we can generalize this result for finding the amplitude of SHM of a particle which oscillates under the influence of more than two SHMs of same frequency.

5.3.2 Superposition of Different Frequency SHMs

If two SHMs of different frequencies are superposed on a particle which produces displacements y_1 and y_2 independently, where y_1 and y_2 are given as

$$y_1 = A \sin \omega_1 t \quad \ldots(5.23)$$

$$y_2 = A \sin \omega_2 t \quad \ldots(5.24)$$

Here we ignore the initial phase difference in the two SHMs as due to different frequencies, the phase difference between the two SHMs continuously change with time. Now according to principal of superposition, the resultant displacement of particle is given as

$$y_R = y_1 + y_2$$

$$= A \sin \omega_1 t + A \sin \omega_2 t$$

$$= 2A \sin\left(\frac{\omega_1 + \omega_2}{2}\right) t \cos\left(\frac{\omega_1 - \omega_2}{2}\right) t$$

In the resultant displacement function, here we can see that there are two sinusoidal functions of time with different arguments which on splitting gives the original SHM equations, superposition of which results this equation. Thus if displacement equation of a particle consists of two or more sinusoidal functions, the same number of independent SHMs are superposed for producing such equation. To understand this, look at the following equation

$$y = 25 \sin (4t) \cos^2 (5t) \quad \ldots(5.25)$$

This equation-(5.25) gives the displacement of an oscillating particle and we have to find the numbers of independent SHMs and their frequencies, superposition of which give rise to this displacement. For it we can split the given equation in the manner explained below.

$$y = 25 \sin 4t \left(\frac{1 + \cos(10t)}{2}\right)$$

or

$$y = \frac{25}{2} \sin 4t + \frac{25}{2} \sin (4t) \cos (10t)$$

or

$$y = \frac{25}{2} \sin 4t + \frac{25}{2} [\sin (14t) - \sin (6t)]$$

or

$$y = \frac{25}{2} \sin (4t) + \frac{25}{2} \sin (14t) - \frac{25}{2} \sin (6t)$$

or

$$y = \frac{25}{2} \sin (4t) + \frac{25}{2} \sin (14t) + \frac{25}{2} \sin (6t - \pi) \ldots(5.26)$$

From equation-(5.26) it is clear that equation-(5.25) is the resultant of superposition of three independent SHMs, given as

$$y_1 = \frac{25}{2} \sin (4t)$$

$$y_2 = \frac{25}{2} \sin (14t)$$

$$y_3 = \frac{25}{4} \sin (6t - \pi)$$

We can also observe in equation-(5.25) that there are three sinusoidal functions in equation-(5.25) so we can directly state that this equation is the superposition of three SHMs of different frequencies.

5.4 Analysis of Angular SHM

We have discussed the case of SHM of a simple pendulum when its bob oscillates with angular frequency $\omega = \sqrt{g/l}$.

Again consider the same case shown in figure-5.12. If the bob of a simple pendulum is thrown from its bottom most position at velocity v_0. If amplitude of its oscillation is A, we have

$$v_0 = A\omega = A\sqrt{\frac{g}{l}}$$

[As at mean position velocity of particle is $v = A\omega$]

or $$A = v_0\sqrt{\frac{l}{g}}$$

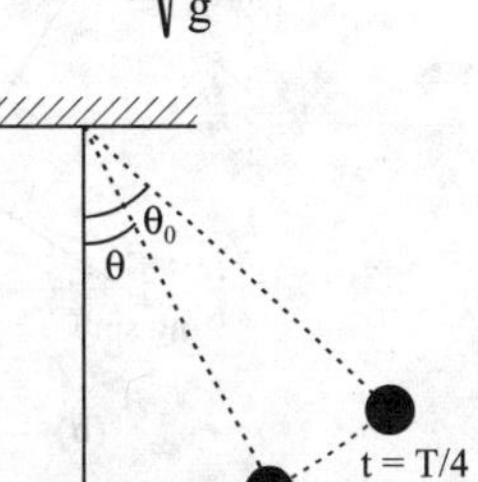

Figure 5.12

When ball is at its extreme position, if its angular displacement is θ_0, this can be regarded as the angular amplitude of oscillations. As the displacement of bob from its mean position is given as

$$x = A\sin(\omega t + \alpha) \quad \ldots(5.27)$$

[General equation of SHM]

If θ and θ_0 are angular displacement and angular amplitude of bob, we have

$$\theta = \frac{x}{l} \quad \text{and} \quad \theta_0 = \frac{A}{l}$$

Thus general equation of SHM of bob in angular from can be given by substituting values of x and A in equation-(5.27) as

$$\theta = \theta_0 \sin(\omega t + \alpha) \quad \ldots(5.28)$$

Using above equation we can find the angular velocity of the body which is in angular SHM as

$$\dot{\theta} = \frac{d\theta}{dt} = \theta_0\omega\cos(\omega t + \alpha) \quad \ldots(5.29)$$

or $$\dot{\theta} = \omega\sqrt{\theta_0^2 - \theta^2} \quad \ldots(5.30)$$

NOTE : Here we represent $\frac{d\theta}{dt}$ by $\dot{\theta}$ not ω as the notation ω is already being used for angular frequency of body in SHM.

Similarly angular acceleration of body is given as

$$\ddot{\theta} = \frac{d^2\theta}{dt^2} = -\theta_0\omega^2\sin(\omega t + \alpha) \quad \ldots(5.31)$$

or $$\ddot{\theta} = -\omega^2\theta \quad \ldots(5.32)$$

Thus restoring torque on body is given as

$$\tau_R = -I\ddot{\theta} = -I\omega^2\theta \quad \ldots(5.33)$$

Thus we can state in angular SHM, angular acceleration of body and the restoring torque on body is directly proportional to the angular displacement of body from its mean position and directed toward mean position. Similarly basic differential equation for angular SHM can be written as

$$\frac{d^2\theta}{dt^2} + \omega^2\theta = 0 \quad \ldots(5.34)$$

5.5 *How to Find Time Period of SHM*

We've discussed that SHM is a special type of oscillation in which the restoring force on the oscillating particle is directly proportional to its displacement from mean position and can be given as

$$F_R = ma = -m\omega^2 y \quad \ldots(5.35)$$

Where ω is the angular frequency of the particle in SHM. When a physical situation is given in which a particle can execute SHM, these are the steps to find the time period of particle in its SHM.

5.5.1 Steps to Find Angular Frequency or Time Period of SHM

Step I : When particle is in its equilibrium position, balance all forces acting on it and locate the equilibrium position mathematically. For rotational equilibrium balance all torques acting on body.

Step II : From the equilibrium position, displace the particle slightly by a displacement x and find the expression of net restoring force on it. For angular motion displace the body by a small angle θ and find expression of net restoring torque on it.

Step III : Try to express the net restoring force acting on particle as a proportional function of its displacement from mean position. The final expression should be obtained in the form.

$$F_R = -ky$$

For angular SHM it will be

$$\tau_R = -k\theta$$

Here we put –ve sign as direction of F_R is opposite to the displacement y or τ_R is opposite to θ. If a be the acceleration of particle at this displacement, we have

or $$a = -\left(\frac{k}{m}\right)y \quad \ldots(5.36)$$

Comparing this equation-(5.36) with the basic differential equation of SHM we get

$$\omega^2 = \frac{k}{m}$$

or $$\omega = \sqrt{\frac{k}{m}}$$

Similarly for angular SHM, angular acceleration of particle is given as

$$\beta = -\frac{\tau_R}{I} = -\left(\frac{k}{I}\right)\theta$$

Comparing with

$$\beta = -\omega^2\theta$$

we get $$\omega = \sqrt{\frac{k}{I}}$$

As ω is the angular frequency of the particle in SHM, its time period of oscillation can be given as

$$T = \frac{2\pi}{\omega} \quad \ldots(5.37)$$

Using the above steps we can find the oscillation period of particle in SHM in different physical situations.

To understand the concept in detail we first explain some different types of pendulums then we take some examples to discuss in details.

Web Reference at www.physicsgalaxy.com
Age Group - High School Physics | Age 17-19 Years
Section - OSCILLATION & WAVES
Topic - Simple Harmonic Motion
Module Number - 12 & 15

5.6 Different Types of Pendulums

There are four different types of pendulums are used in general practice. These are :

(1) Simple Pendulum

(2) Spring Block Pendulum

(3) Physical Pendulum or Compound Pendulum

(4) Torsional Pendulum

5.6.1 Simple Pendulum

This is the most fundamental oscillatory system as shown in figure-5.13(a) a bob of mass m is hanging from a string of length l. At this position as bob is in equilibrium so tension in string will be equal to weight of the bob, thus

$$T = mg$$

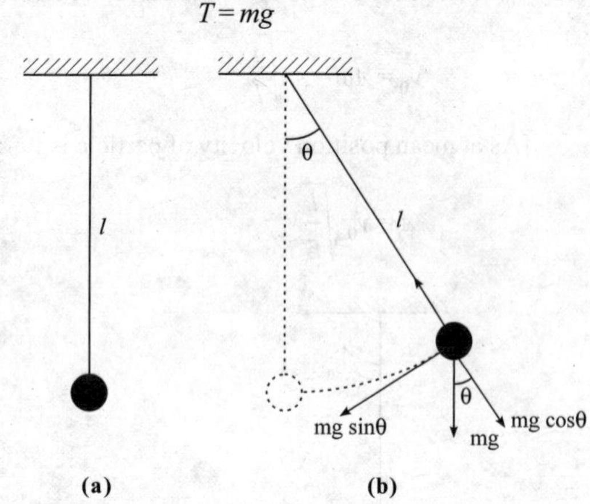

Figure 5.13

If bob is slightly displaced from its equilibrium position and released as shown in figure-5.13(b) by a small angular displacement θ. As still it is in equilibrium along radial direction, at this position, tension in string is

$$T = mg\cos\theta$$

Thus due to mg sin θ, bob will accelerate towards the equilibrium position thus we can say that in this case mg sin θ is behaving as restoring force and for motion of bob, so we have

$$F_R = -mg\sin\theta$$

[– ve sign for restoring nature]

or $$F_R = -mg\,\theta \quad \text{[As for small } \theta, \sin\theta \simeq \theta]$$

If bob is displaced by a distance x from mean position, we have

$$\theta = \frac{x}{l}$$

Now if acceleration of bob toward mean position is a, we have

$$F_R = ma = -mg\frac{x}{l}$$

or $$a = -\left(\frac{g}{l}\right)x \quad \ldots(5.38)$$

Comparing this equation with differential equation of SHM, we get

$$\omega = \sqrt{\frac{g}{l}} \quad \ldots(5.39)$$

Thus time period of oscillation of a simple pendulum is

$$T = \frac{2\pi}{\omega} = 2\pi\sqrt{\frac{l}{g}} \quad \ldots(5.40)$$

5.6.2 Spring Block Pendulum

This is another very simple and fundamental oscillating system. Figure-5.14 shows a spring block system in equilibrium. At equilibrium due to the weight of block spring is stretched from its natural length say by a distance h, such that

$$mg = kh \qquad \ldots(5.41)$$

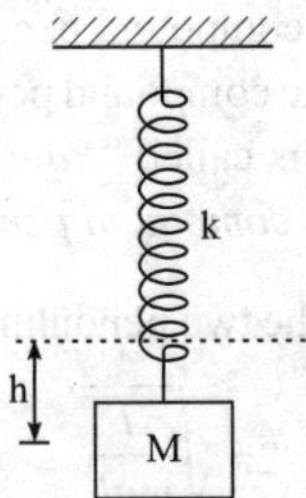

Figure 5.14

Now from this equilibrium position, block is slightly displaced down, say by a distance x and released, then due to spring force it will have a tendency to come back to its equilibrium position and due to this stable equilibrium position it will start oscillating.

When block is stretched down from its equilibrium position by a distance x, the restoring force on block can be written as

$$F_R = -[k(x+h) \quad - \quad mg]$$

upward force (towards mean position) — downward force (away from mean position)

or $\qquad F_R = -kx$

[As from equation-(5.41) $mg = kh$]

If acceleration of block toward mean position is a, we have

$$a = -\left(\frac{k}{m}\right)x \qquad \ldots(5.42)$$

Comparing this equation-(5.42) with standard differential equation of SHM, we get

$$\omega = \sqrt{\frac{k}{m}} \qquad \ldots(5.43)$$

Thus time period of oscillation is

$$T = \frac{2\pi}{\omega} = 2\pi\sqrt{\frac{k}{m}}$$

If shows that when a mass hanging from free end of a spring oscillates it executes SHM with angular frequency $\sqrt{k/m}$.

5.6.3 Compound Pendulum

This is made whenever a rigid body is hanging freely from a horizontally pivoted axis, as shown in figure-5.15. A body of mass m is pivoted at point O through a horizontal axis AA'. The body is hanging freely under gravity and in equilibrium position its centre of mass C is vertically below the suspension point O, at a distance l from O.

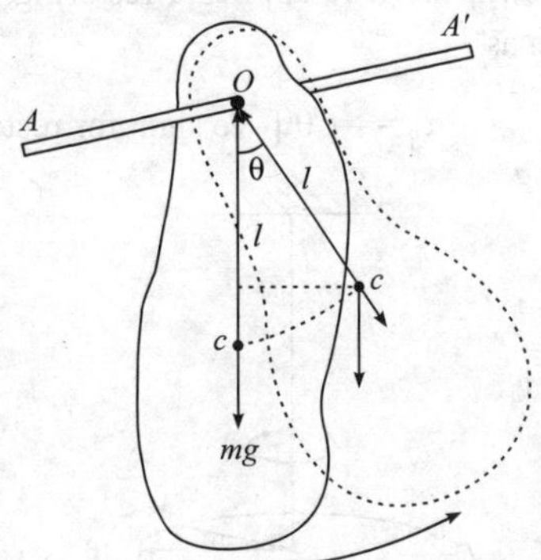

Figure 5.15

If the body is slightly tilted from its equilibrium position by an angle θ, mg will exert a restoring torque on it in opposite direction to restore the equilibrium position. Thus restoring torque on body in dotted position after tilting is

$$\tau_R = -mg \,.\, l\sin\theta$$

[– ve sign for restoring nature]

$$= -mgl\,\theta \qquad \text{[For small } \theta, \sin\theta \approx \theta]$$

If its angular acceleration is α, we have

$$I\alpha = -mgl\,\theta$$

[Here I is the momentum of inertia of body about axis AA']

or $$\alpha = -\frac{mgl}{I}\theta \qquad \ldots(5.44)$$

Comparing equation-(5.44) with standard differential equation of angular SHM we get

$$d = -\cos\theta$$

and $$\omega = \sqrt{\frac{mgl}{I}}$$

Thus its time period of oscillation is

$$T = \frac{2\pi}{\omega} = 2\pi\sqrt{\frac{I}{mgl}} \qquad \ldots(5.45)$$

5.6.4 Torsional Pendulum

In a Torsional Pendulum an object is suspended from a wire with rigidity coefficient C. If such a wire is twisted by an angle θ, due to its elasticity it exerts a restoring torque $\tau = C\theta$ on the twisted object attached to it.

A general torsional pendulum is shown in figure-5.16. Here a disc D of radius R and mass M is attached to a stiff wire whose other end is suspended from ceiling as shown.

From the equilibrium position of this disc if it is twisted by an angle θ as shown, the wire applies a restoring torque on it, which is given as

$$\tau_R = -C\theta \text{ [–ve sign, for restoring nature]}$$

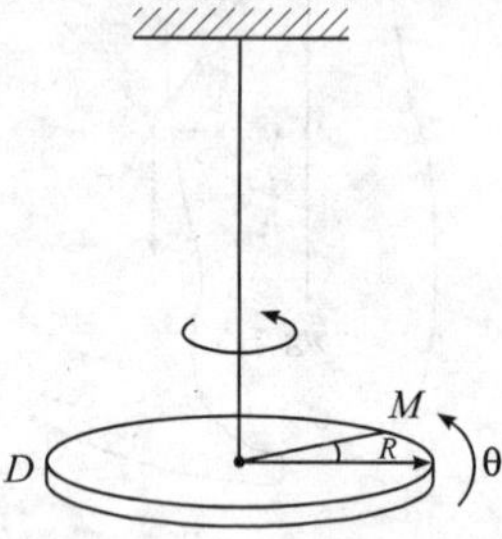

Figure 5.16

If during restoring motion the angular acceleration of disc is α, we can write $\tau = I\alpha$ where I is the moment of inertia of disc about its central axis, thus we have

$$I\alpha = -C\theta$$

or
$$\alpha = -\frac{C}{I}\theta \quad \ldots(5.46)$$

Equation-(5.46) resembles with the basic differential equation of SHM in angular form thus we can state the angular frequency of this SHM is

$$\omega = \sqrt{\frac{C}{I}} \quad \ldots(5.47)$$

Thus the period of SHM is

$$T = \frac{2\pi}{\omega} = 2\pi\sqrt{\frac{I}{C}}$$

In the above cases of some pendulums we've discussed, how to find the angular frequency and time period of a body in SHM. Now we take some similar examples of physical situations in which an object is in SHM.

5.6.5 Equivalent Length of a Simple Pendulum

We know that the time period of oscillations of a simple pendulum is given by

$$2\pi\sqrt{\frac{l}{g}} \quad \ldots(5.48)$$

Similarly we've also discussed that the time period of a compound pendulum is given as

$$2\pi\sqrt{\frac{I}{Mgl_c}} \quad \ldots(5.49)$$

Where I is the moment of inertia of the rigid body about the axis of rotation and l_c is the distance of centre of gravity of body from the suspension point (Axis of rotation). If we consider a simple pendulum of length l_{eq} which has a bob of same mass M as that of rigid body of compound pendulum and has the time period same as that of the compound pendulum then this length of simple pendulum l_{eq} is called "*Equivalent length of simple pendulum for the given compound pendulum*".

For the time periods of the two pendulums to be equal, we have

$$2\pi\sqrt{\frac{l}{g}} = 2\pi\sqrt{\frac{I}{mgl_c}} \quad \ldots(5.50)$$

If k be the radius of gyration of the rigid body about an axis passing through its centre of mass then the moment of inertia of the rigid body about point of suspension is given as

$$I = Mk^2 + Ml_c^2 \quad \ldots(5.51)$$

Now from equation-(5.50), we have

$$\sqrt{\frac{l_{eq}}{g}} = \sqrt{\frac{Mk^2 + Ml_c^2}{mgl_c}}$$

or
$$l_{eq} = l_c + \frac{k^2}{l_c} \quad \ldots(5.52)$$

Equation-(5.52) gives the equivalent length of simple pendulum for the given compound pendulum. One important point to be noted here is if in equation-(5.52) we replace l_c by k^2/l_c, we get

$$l_{eq} = \frac{k^2}{l_c} + \frac{k^2}{k^2/l_c}$$

or
$$l_{eq} = \frac{k^2}{l_c} + l_c \quad \ldots(5.53)$$

Which is same as that of equation-(5.52). Thus we can say that if the same rigid body, which is suspended from a point, situated at a distance l_c from centre of gravity of body, we suspend it from a point at a distance k^2/l_c from centre of gravity of the body and oscillate like a compound pendulum, its equivalent length of simple pendulum remains same or the time period of oscillation of body remains same. Consider figure-5.17, a rigid body is suspended at a point O through a horizontal axis AA'.

Here C is the centre of gravity of the body. If it oscillates then the time period of small oscillations can be given as

$$T = 2\pi\sqrt{\frac{l_c + \frac{k^2}{l_c}}{g}} = 2\pi\sqrt{\frac{l_{eq}}{g}} \quad \ldots(5.54)$$

As discussed in last section we can say that if the same body is suspended either from any point on circular arcs PQ or RS (as shown in figure-5.17(b)) of radius l_c with centre at C (circle M_1) or any point on the circle of radius k^2/l_c with centre at C (circle M_2), the time period of small oscillations of the body will remain same.

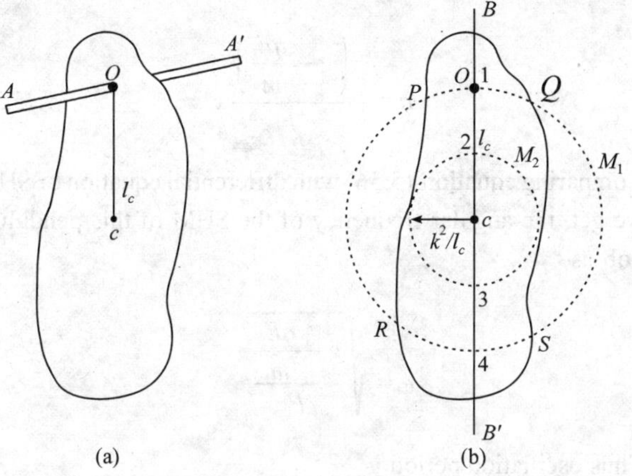

Figure 5.17

Here we can develop one property of the body when it is used as a compound pendulum. This is, when a straight line is drawn passing through the centre of gravity of body as in figure-5.17(b) a line BB' is drawn. There exist four points on this line (as here points 1,2,3 and 4) about which if body is suspended, the time period of small oscillation of body remains same. This we can also prove graphically as if we plot the time period of oscillation, the curve looks like as shown in figure-5.18

As shown in figure-5.18, if the body is suspended from C, from equation-(5.54), we can see that if $l_c = 0$, time period becomes ∞, and at $l_c = k$ i.e. if the body is suspended from a point at a distance equal to radius of gyration of body from C, the time period of oscillation is minimum and at all other suspension points the time period is higher and if we draw a horizontal line in graph at time period T_1 which is more than minimum period, it cuts the graph at four points as shown, which verifies the statement we've discussed earlier.

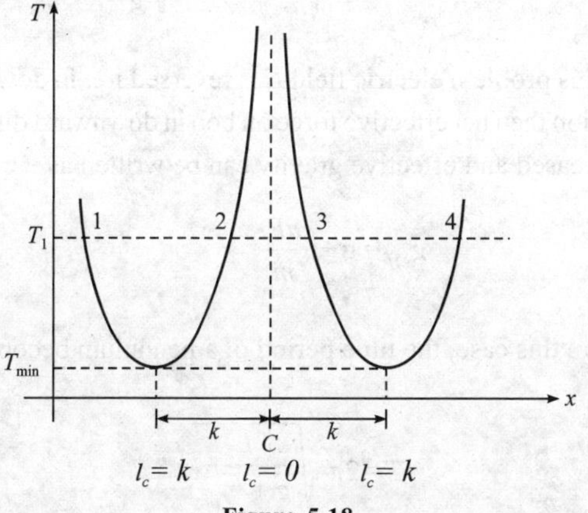

Figure 5.18

From equation-(5.54) we can also find the value of l_c at which this time period has a minimum value by equating $\frac{dT}{dl_c} = 0$, as

$$\frac{dT}{dl_c} = \frac{2\pi}{\sqrt{g}} \cdot \frac{1}{2\sqrt{l_c + \frac{k^2}{l_c}}}\left[1 - \frac{k^2}{l_c^2}\right] = 0$$

or $$l_c = \pm k$$

Which also verifies the experimental result obtained by graph shown in figure-5.18.

 # Illustrative Example 5.6

Find the period of small oscillations in a horizontal plane performed by a ball of mass $m = 40$ g fixed at the middle of a horizontally stretched string $l = 1.0$ m in length. The tension of the string is assumed to be constant and equal to $T = 10$ N.

Solution

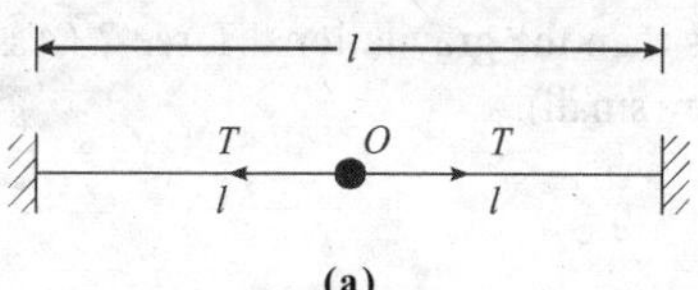

(a)

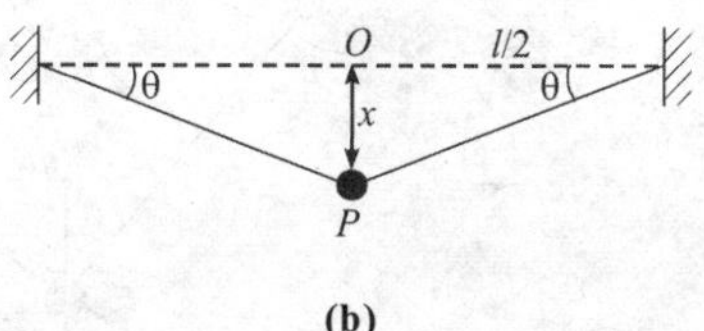

(b)

Figure 5.19

The situation is shown in figure-5.19. The ball is in equilibrium at point O as shown in figure-5.19(a). Now it is displaced from O by a distance x in horizontal plane to a position P as shown in figure-5.19(b). The components of tensions on ball toward O are $T \sin\theta$ and $T \sin\theta$, hence the restoring force on ball toward mean position is

$$F_R = -2T\sin\theta$$

[–ve sign for restoring tendency]

or $$F_R = -\frac{2T\,x}{\sqrt{x^2 + l^2/4}}$$

As x is very small compared to l, we can neglect its square compared to $l^2/4$, thus

$$F_R = -\frac{4T}{l}x$$

If a is the acceleration of ball toward mean position, we have

$$a = -\left(\frac{4T}{ml}\right)x$$

Here acceleration is directly proportional to x thus motion of ball is simple harmonic with angular frequency ω, given as

$$\omega = \sqrt{\frac{4T}{ml}}$$

Thus time period of its SHM be given as

$$T = \frac{2\pi}{\omega} = 2\pi\sqrt{\frac{ml}{4T}} = 3.14\sqrt{\frac{0.04\times 1}{10}} = 0.2\text{ s}$$

Illustrative Example 5.7

A simple pendulum consists of a small sphere of mass m suspended by a thread of length l. The sphere carries a positive charge q. The pendulum is placed in a uniform electric field of strength E directed vertically upwards. With what period will the pendulum oscillate, if the electrostatic force acting on the sphere is less than the gravitational force ? (Assume that the oscillations are small).

Solution

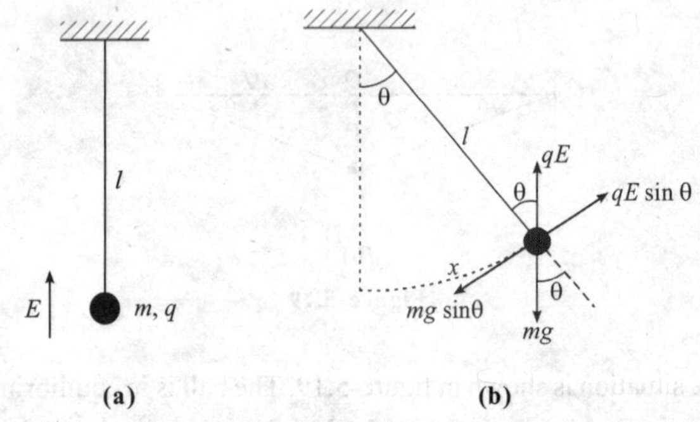

Figure 5.20

Figure-5.20(a) shows the simple pendulum with bob of mass m and charge q with electric field E in the region directed vertically upward.

When bob is in equilibrium, the tension in the string is

$$T = mg - qE \qquad \ldots(5.55)$$

If we displace this bob by a distance x from its mean position as shown in figure-5.20(b), the restoring force on it can now be written as

$$F_R = -(mg\sin\theta - qE\sin\theta)$$

[If θ is the angular displacement shown in figure]

or $\quad F_R = -[mg - qE]\,\theta$ [For small θ, $\sin\theta \simeq \theta$]

or $\quad F_R = (mg - qE)\dfrac{x}{l}$ $\quad$ [As $\theta = \dfrac{x}{l}$]

If a is the acceleration of bob in the situation shown in figure5.20(b), we have

$$a = -\frac{\left(g - \dfrac{qE}{m}\right)}{l}x \qquad \ldots(5.56)$$

Comparing equation-(5.56) with differential equation of SHM we get, the angular frequency of the SHM of this pendulum bob as

$$\omega = \sqrt{\frac{g - \dfrac{qE}{m}}{l}}$$

Thus oscillation period is

$$T = \frac{2\pi}{\omega} = 2\pi\sqrt{\frac{l}{g - \dfrac{qE}{m}}} \qquad \ldots(5.57)$$

The result in equation-(5.57) can also be directly obtained as we know the time period of a simple pendulum is given as $T = 2\pi\sqrt{l/g}$ and in a region where an electric field E exist in upward direction, the effective value of acceleration due to gravity for a positively charge particle with a charge q can be used as

$$g_{eff} = g - \frac{qE}{m}$$

Thus the time period of above pendulum can be directly written as

$$T = 2\pi\sqrt{\frac{l}{g_{eff}}} = 2\pi\sqrt{\frac{l}{g - {}^{qE}\!/_{m}}}$$

If in this problem electric field E is reversed i-e. in downward direction then net effective force on bob in downward direction is increased and effective gravity can be written as

$$g_{eff} = g + \frac{qE}{m}$$

Thus in this case, the time period of a pendulum becomes

$$T = 2\pi\sqrt{\frac{l}{g + {}^{qE}\!/_{m}}}$$

Illustrative Example 5.8

Calculate the period of small oscillations of a floating box as shown in figure-5.21 which was slightly pushed down in vertical direction. The mass of box is m, area of its base is A and the density of liquid is ρ. The resistance of the liquid is assumed to be negligible.

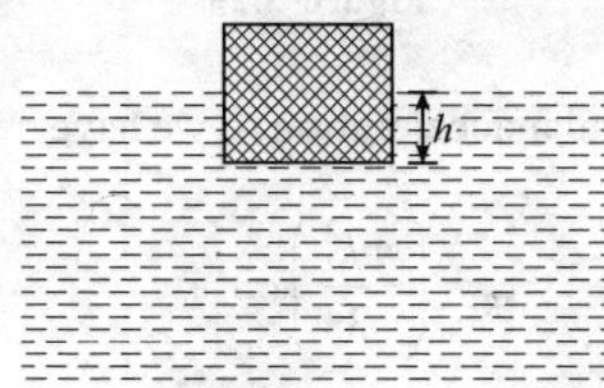

Figure 5.21

Solution

Initially when box is floating in liquid, if its h depth is submerged in liquid then buoyancy force on it is

$$F_B = \text{weight of liquid displaced}$$

$$= Ah\rho g$$

As the box is in equilibrium, we have

$$Ah\rho g = mg \quad \ldots(5.58)$$

Now if box is further pushed down by a distance x, net restoring force on it in upward (toward mean position) direction is

$$F_R = -[A(h+x)\rho g - mg]$$

$$= -Ax\rho g \qquad [\text{As } mg = Ah\rho g]$$

Figure 5.22

If a is the acceleration of box in upward direction we have

$$a = -\left(\frac{A\rho g}{m}\right)x \quad \ldots(5.59)$$

Equation-(5.59) shows that the box executes SHM with angular frequency ω given as

$$\omega = \sqrt{\frac{A\rho g}{m}}$$

Thus time period of its oscillation can be given as

$$T = \frac{2\pi}{\omega} = 2\pi\sqrt{\frac{m}{A\rho g}}$$

Illustrative Example 5.9

A mass M attached to a spring oscillates with a period of 2 s. If the mass is increased by 2 kg, the period increases by one second. Find the initial mass M.

Solution

We know that for a spring block system

$$T = 2\pi\sqrt{\left(\frac{M}{k}\right)}$$

Here k = spring constant.

In first case, $$2 = 2\pi\sqrt{\left(\frac{M}{k}\right)} \quad \ldots(5.60)$$

In second case, $$3 = 2\pi\sqrt{\left(\frac{M+2}{k}\right)} \quad \ldots(5.61)$$

Squaring of equation-(5.60) and (5.61) and then dividing (5.61) by (5.60), we have

$$\frac{9}{4} = \frac{M+2}{M} = 1 + \frac{2}{M}$$

Solving we get $M = 1.6\,\text{kg}$

Illustrative Example 5.10

Two masses m_1 and m_2 are suspended together by a massless spring of spring constant k as shown in figure-5.23. When the masses are in equilibrium, m_1 is removed without disturbing the system. Find the angular frequency and amplitude of oscillation.

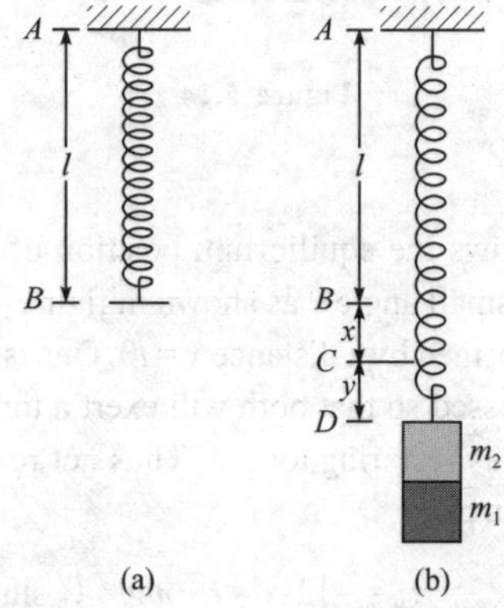

Figure 5.23

Solution

Let AB be the natural length l of the spring as shown in figure-5.23(a). When a mass m_2 is suspended, the spring is stretched to C *i.e.*, $BC = x$. Now on further loading by a mass m_1, let the spring is stretched to a point D *i.e.*, $CD = y$, then we have

$$kx = m_2 g \quad \ldots(5.62)$$

$$ky = m_1 g \quad \ldots(5.63)$$

When mass m_1 is removed, the spring block system of mass m_2 starts oscillating about the point C. It's motion is simple harmonic motion. The mass m_2 is executing simple harmonic motion with the angular frequency given as

$$\omega = \sqrt{\left(\frac{m_2}{k}\right)}$$

Thus its time period is

$$T = 2\pi\sqrt{\left(\frac{m_2}{k}\right)}$$

Amplitude of oscillation is given as

$$A = CD = y = \frac{m_1 g}{k}$$

Illustrative Example 5.11

Find the frequency of small oscillations of a thin uniform vertical rod of mass m and length l hinged at the point O (figure-5.24). The combined stiffness of each of the spring is equal to k. The mass of the spring is negligible.

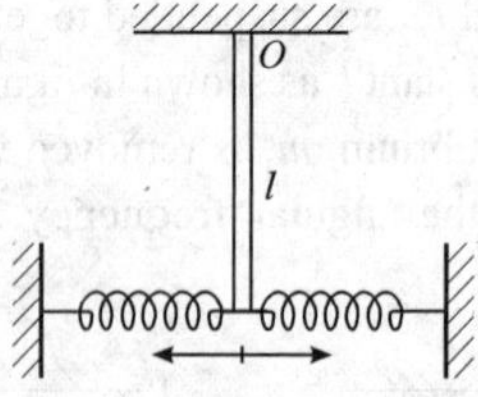

Figure 5.24

Solution

Figure-5.25 shows the equilibrium position of rod. If rod is displaced by a small angle θ as shown in figure-5.25, both the springs are deformed by a distance $x = l\theta$. One is stretched and other is compressed so that both will exert a torque on rod in same direction as restoring torque. Thus net restoring torque on rod is written as

$$\tau_R = -[2kx \times l + mg \times \tfrac{l}{2}\sin\theta]$$

[– ve sign for restoring nature]

or $$\tau_R = -[2kx \times l + mg \times \tfrac{l}{2}\theta]$$

[As for small θ, $\sin\theta \simeq \theta$]

or $$\tau_R = -(2kl^2 + \tfrac{mgl}{2})\,\theta \quad [x = l\theta]$$

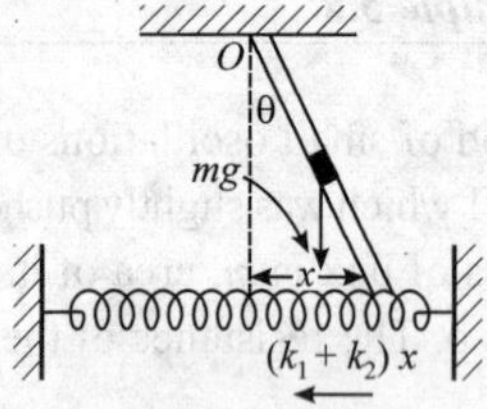

Figure 5.25

If rod has an angular acceleration α, we have, restoring torque

$$\tau_R = \left(\frac{ml^2}{3}\right)\alpha$$

Where $\tfrac{ml^2}{3}$ is the moment of inertia of rod about an axis passing through one of its end as in this case. Thus we have

$$\frac{ml^2}{3}\alpha = -\left(2kl^2 + \frac{mgl}{2}\right)\theta$$

or $$\alpha = -\left(\frac{2kl^2 + \frac{mgl}{2}}{\frac{ml^2}{3}}\right)\theta$$

or $$\alpha = -\left(\frac{12kl + 3mg}{2ml}\right)\theta \quad \ldots(5.64)$$

Comparing equation-(5.64) with the basic differential equation of SHM, we get

$$\omega = \sqrt{\frac{12kl + 3mg}{2ml}}$$

Thus the oscillation frequency of rod for its small oscillations can be given as

$$f = \frac{\omega}{2\pi} = \frac{1}{2\pi}\sqrt{\frac{12kl + 3mg}{2ml}}$$

Illustrative Example 5.12

A vertical U-tube of uniform cross-section contains water upto a height of 30 cm. Show that if the water on one side is depressed and then released, its motion up and down the two sides of the tube is simple harmonic. Calculate its period.

Solution

Figure-5.26 shows a U-tube of uniform cross-sectional area A. Let the liquid be depressed through the distance y in *a* limb, the difference of levels between two limbs will be $2y$ as shown in figure-2.26.

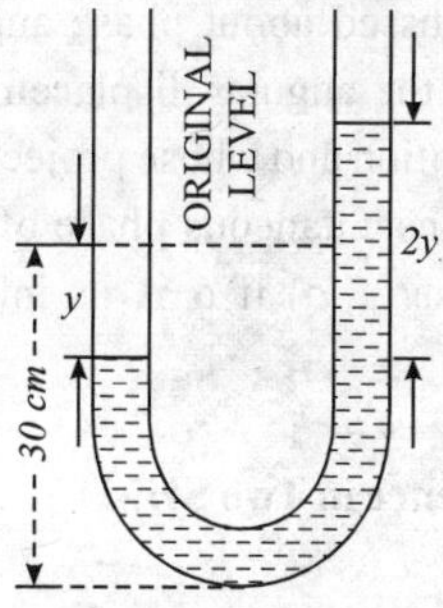

Figure 5.26

The liquid now oscillates about the initial positions.

Excess pressure on whole liquid = (excess height of the liquid column) (density) (g)

$$= 2y \times 1 \times g \quad [\text{As density of water} = 1]$$

Restoring Force on the liquid= Pressure × area of cross section

$$= 2ygA$$

Due to this force the liquid accelerates and if its acceleration is a, we have

$$ma = -2ygA$$

or $$(2 \times 30 \times A)\, a = -2ygA$$

or $$a = -\frac{g}{30}\, y$$

Hence acceleration is directly proportional to displacement, so the motion is simple harmonic motion. Thus the time period T is given by

$$T = \frac{2\pi}{\omega} = 2\pi\sqrt{\left(\frac{30}{g}\right)} = 2\pi\sqrt{\left(\frac{30}{980}\right)} \quad [\text{As } \omega = \sqrt{\frac{g}{30}}\,]$$

$$= 1.098 \text{ s}$$

Web Reference at www.physicsgalaxy.com

Age Group - High School Physics | Age 17-19 Years

Section - OSCILLATION & WAVES

Topic - Simple Harmonic Motion

Module Number - 13, 14, 16, 17, 18, 19, 22, 23, 24, 25

Practice Exercise 5.2

(i) A vertical spring block system executes SHM at a frequency of 10 osc/s. At the upper extreme position of the block the spring is unstretched. Find the maximum speed of the particle. Take $g = 10\text{ m/s}^2$.

[$\frac{1}{2\pi}$ m/s]

(ii) In the figure-5.27, the spring has a force constant 5000 N m^{-1}. The pulley is light and smooth. The spring and the string are light. The suspended block A is of mass 1 kg. If the block is slightly displaced vertically down from its equilibrium position and released, find the period of its vertical oscillations.

[0.1776 s]

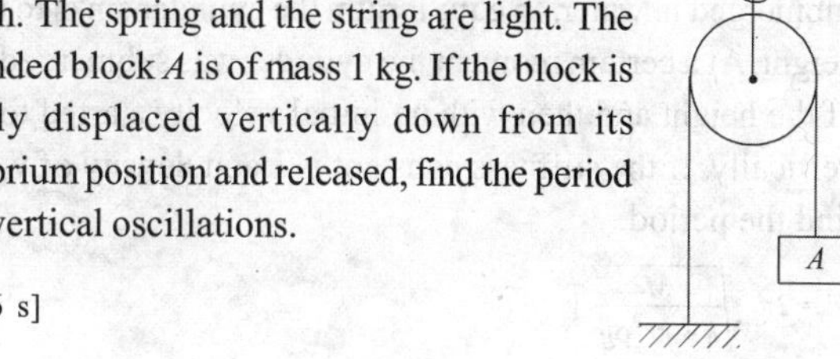

Figure 5.27

(iii) The bob of a simple pendulum is displaced by an small angle θ_0 from the vertical and released. If during its oscillation it is given that the maximum tension in the string is two times the minimum tension, find the value of θ_0.

[$\cos^{-1}\left(\frac{3}{4}\right)$]

(iv) Determine the period of small longitudinal oscillations of a body with mass m in the system shown in figure-5.28. The stiffness values of the springs are k_1 and k_2. The friction and the masses of the springs are negligible.

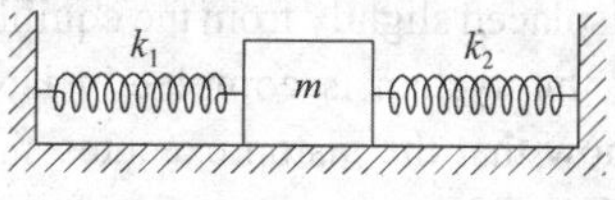

Figure 5.28

[$2\pi\sqrt{\frac{m}{k_1 + k_2}}$]

(v) Find the period of small vertical oscillations of a body with mass m in the system illustrated in figure-5.29. The stiffness values of the springs are k_1 and k_2, their masses are negligible.

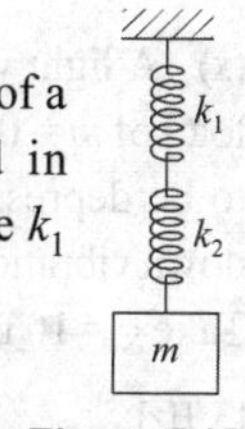

Figure 5.29

[$2\pi\sqrt{\frac{m(k_1 + k_2)}{k_1 k_2}}$]

(vi) A T-bar of uniform cross section and mass M is supported in a vertical plane by a hinge O and a spring of force constant k at A. Develop a formula for the period for small amplitude rotational oscillations in the plane of the figure-5.30.

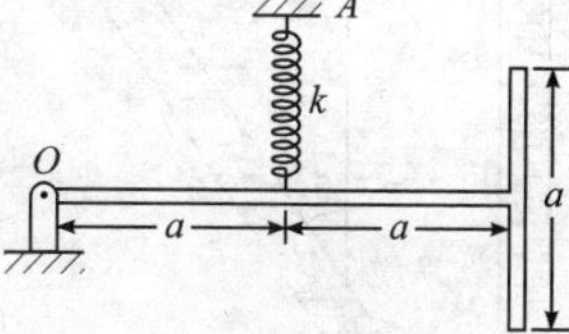

Figure 5.30

[$3\pi\sqrt{\frac{M}{k}}$]

(vii) A cylinder of mass M, radius r and height h is suspended by a spring where the upper end which is fixed is partly submerged in water. In equilibrium the cylinder sinks to half its height. At a certain moment the cylinder was submerged to 2/3 of the height and then with no initial velocity started to move vertically. If the stiffness constant is k and density of water ρ, find the period.

[$T = 2\pi\sqrt{\dfrac{M}{k+\pi r^2 \rho g}}$]

(viii) A point mass m is suspended at the end of a massless wire of length l and cross-section A. If Y is the Young's modulus of elasticity for the wire, obtain the frequency of oscillation for the simple harmonic motion along the vertical line.

[$\dfrac{1}{2\pi}\sqrt{\left(\dfrac{YA}{ml}\right)}$]

(ix) An ideal gas whose adiabatic exponents is γ, is enclosed in a vertical cylindrical container and supports a freely moving piston of mass M. The piston and the cylinder have equal cross-sectional area A. Atmospheric pressure is P_0 and when the piston is in equilibrium, the volume of the gas is V_0. The piston is now displaced slightly from the equilibrium position. Assuming that the system is completely isolated from its surrounding, show that the piston executes simple harmonic motion and find the frequency of oscillation.

[$\dfrac{1}{2\pi}\sqrt{\left(\dfrac{\gamma\,(p_0 + Mg/A)\,A^2}{M V_0}\right)}$]

(x) A light wooden rod fixed at one end is kept horizontal. A load of $m = 0.4$ kg tied to the free end of the rod causes that end to be depressed by $\delta = 2.8$ cm. If this load is set into up and down vibration will it oscillate ? Find its frequency of oscillation. Take $g = 10\ \text{m/s}^2$.

[3 Hz]

(xi) Determine the period of oscillations of mercury of mass m poured into a bent tube (Figure-5.31) whose right arm forms an angle θ with the vertical. The cross-sectional area of the tube is S. The viscosity of mercury is to be neglected.

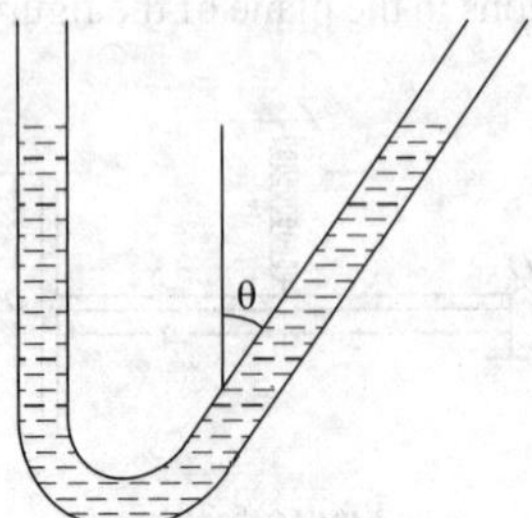

Figure 5.31

[$T = 2\pi\sqrt{m/S\rho g\,(1+\cos\theta)}$]

5.7 Phase Analysis of a Particle in SHM

We've already discussed about phase angle of a particle in SHM. It is actually the angular displacement of that particle who is in circular motion and whose projection is in SHM. At a general time t, the instantaneous phase of a particle in SHM can be written as $(\omega t + \alpha)$ if α is its initial phase (already discussed).

5.7.1 Phase Difference in Two SHM

Case I: When two SHMs are of same angular frequency

Figure-5.32 shows two particles P' and Q' in SHM with same angular frequency ω. P and Q are the corresponding particles in circular motion for SHM of P' and Q'.

Let P and Q both starts their circular motion at the same time at $t = 0$ then at the same instant P' and Q' starts their SHM in upward direction as shown. As frequency of both are equal, both will reach their extreme position (topmost point) at the same time and will again reach their mean position simultaneously at time $t = T/2$. [T = Time period of SHM = $2\pi/\omega$] and move in downward direction together or we can state that the oscillations of P' and Q' are exactly parallel and at every instant the phase of both P' and Q' are equal, thus phase difference in these two SHMs is zero. These SHMs are called same phase SHMs.

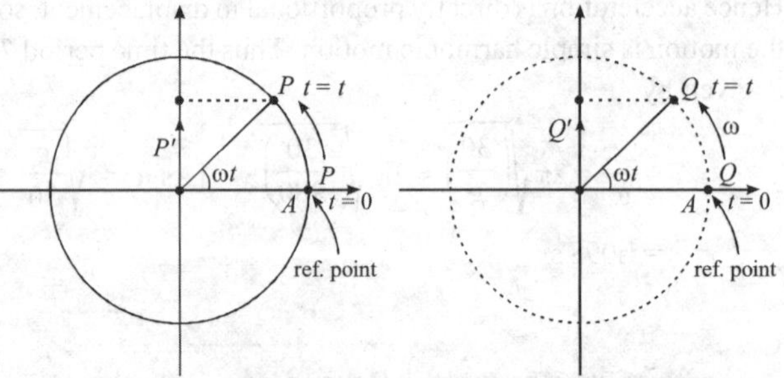

Figure 5.32

Now consider figure-5.32, where we assume if P' starts its SHM at $t = 0$ but Q' will start at time t_1. In this duration from t = 0 to $t = t_1$, P' will move ahead in phase by ωt_1 radians while Q' was at rest. Now Q' starts at time t_1 and move with same angular frequency ω. It can never catch P' as both are oscillating at same angular frequency. Thus here Q' will always lag in phase by ωt_1 then P' or we say P' is leading in phase by ωt_1 then Q' and as ω of both are constant their phase difference will also remains constant so keep it in mind that in two SHMs of same angular frequency, if they have some phase difference, it always remains constant.

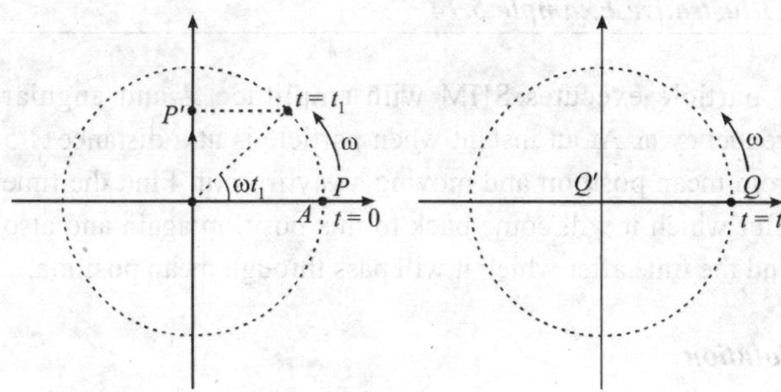

Figure 5.33

Now we consider a special case when time lag between the starting of two SHMs is $T/2$ i.e. half of oscillation period. Consider figure-5.34, here if we assume, particle P' starts at $t = 0$ and Q' at $t = T/2$ when P' completes its half oscillation. Here we can see that the phase difference in the two SHM is π by which Q' is lagging. Here when Q' starts its oscillation in upward direction P' moves in downward direction. As angular velocity of P and Q are same, both complete their quarter revolution in same time. Thus when P' reaches its bottom extreme position, Q' will reach its upper extreme position and then after Q' starts moving downward, P' starts moving upward and both of these will reach their mean position simultaneously but in opposite directions, P' has completed its one oscillation where as Q' is at half of its oscillation due to a phase lag of π.

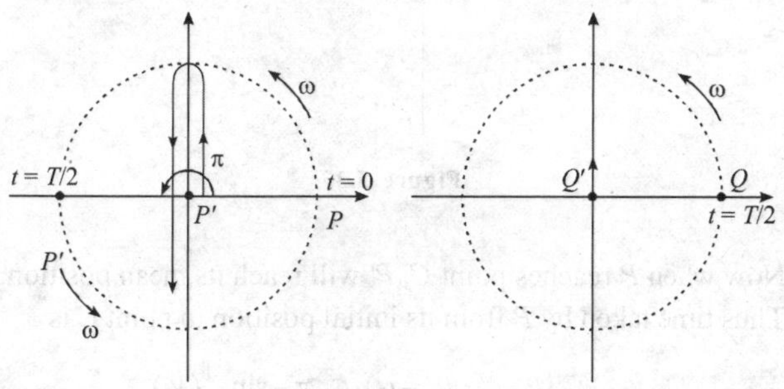

Figure 5.34

Thus if we observe both oscillations simultaneously we can see that oscillations of the two particles P' and Q' are exactly antiparallel i.e. when P' goes up, Q' comes down and at all instants of time their displacements from mean position are equal but in opposite direction if there amplitudes are equal. Such SHMs are called opposite phase SHMs.

Case II: When two SHMs are of different angular frequency

We've discussed that when two SHMs are of same angular frequency, their phase difference does not change with time. Consider two particles in SHM as shown in figure-5.35. Their corresponding particles for circular motion are A and B respectively as shown. If both A' and B' starts their SHM from mean position at $t = 0$ with angular frequencies ω_1 and ω_2, then we say at $t = 0$ their phase difference is zero but after time t, their respective phase are $\omega_1 t$ and $\omega_2 t$. Thus after time t, the phase difference in the two SHMs is

$$\phi = (\omega_1 - \omega_2)\, t \qquad \ldots(5.65)$$

Thus equation-(5.65) shows that if angular frequencies of the two SHMs are different their phase difference continuously changes with time.

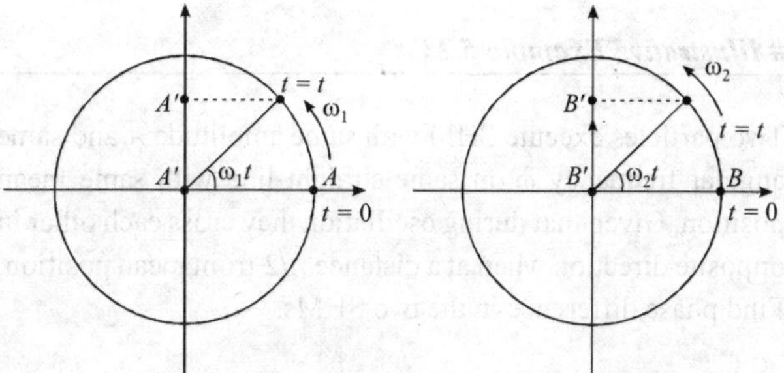

Figure 5.35

5.7.2 Same Phase and Opposite Phase SHMs

Same Phase SHMs

As discussed above two particles execute SHM in such a way that their oscillations are exactly parallel to each other or their phase difference during oscillation is zero, they are said to be in same phase we've seen that this happens when both SHMs are started at same time with same angular frequency. This can happen also when the time lag between starting of the two SHM is T or an integral multiple of time period of SHM. Because if one starts at $t = 0$ and other starts at $t = T$, in this duration first particle will complete its first oscillation and is going to start its second oscillations and the second particle will start in synchronization with the first. Hence the two oscillation will still be parallel or in same phase. There phase difference in the two SHMs will be 2π. Not only this even if the time lag in starting of the two SHMs is $2T, 3T \ldots nT$ or the phase difference in the two SHMs is $4\pi, 6\pi, 8\pi \ldots 2n\pi$, then also these SHMs can be treated in same phase.

Thus phase difference in two SHMs of same phase is

$$\phi = 2\pi, 4\pi, 6\pi \ldots\ldots 2n\pi \qquad \ldots(5.66)$$

Opposite Phase SHMs

As discussed in previous article, two SHMs are said to be in opposite phase when their oscillations are antiparallel this happens when two SHMs of same angular frequency start with a time lag of $T/2$ and phase difference among the two SHMs is π. By analyzing the situation it can also be stated that the same thing also happens when the time lag in starting of the two SHMs is $3T/2, 5T/2 \ldots\ldots (2n+1)T/2$ or the phase difference between the two is $3\pi, 5\pi \ldots\ldots (2n+1)\pi$.

Thus phase difference in two SHMs of opposite phase is

$$\phi = \pi, 3\pi, 5\pi \ldots\ldots, (2n+1)\pi \qquad \ldots(5.67)$$

To understand the concept of phase and phase difference in SHM, we take few examples.

Illustrative Example 5.13

Two particles execute SHM with same amplitude A and same angular frequency ω on same straight line with same mean position. Given that during oscillation they cross each other in opposite direction when at a distance $A/2$ from mean position. Find phase difference in the two SHMs.

Solution

Figure-5.36 shows that two respective particles P' and Q' in SHM along with their corresponding particles in circular motion. Let P' moves in upward direction when crossing Q' at $A/2$ as shown in figure-5.36(a), at this instant phase of P' is

$$\phi_1 = \sin^{-1}\left(\frac{1}{2}\right) = \frac{\pi}{6} \qquad \ldots(5.68)$$

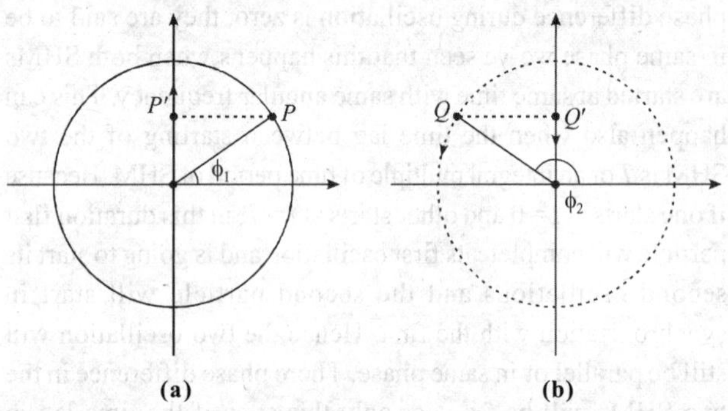

Figure 5.36

Similarly as shown in figure-5.36(b) we can take particle Q' is moving in downward direction (opposite P') at $A/2$, this implies its circular motion particle is in second quadrant thus its phase angle is

$$\phi_2 = \pi - \sin^{-1}\left(\frac{1}{2}\right) = \pi - \frac{\pi}{6} = \frac{5\pi}{6} \qquad \ldots(5.69)$$

As both are oscillating at same angular frequency their phase diff. remains constant which can be given from equation-(5.68) and (5.69), as

$$\Delta\phi = \phi_2 - \phi_1 = \frac{5\pi}{6} - \frac{\pi}{6} = \frac{2\pi}{3}$$

Illustrative Example 5.14

A particle executes SHM with amplitude A and angular frequency ω. At an instant when particle is at a distance $A/5$ from mean position and moving away from it. Find the time after which it will come back to this position again and also find the time after which it will pass through mean position.

Solution

Figure-5.37 shows the circular motion representation for the particle P' given in problem. The initial situation of particle is shown in figure. As P moves, its projection P' will go up and then come back to its initial position when P reaches to the corresponding position in second quadrant as shown. In this process P traversed an angular displacement θ with angular velocity ω, thus time taken in the process is

$$t = \frac{\theta}{\omega} = \frac{1}{\omega}\,[2\cos^{-1}(1/5)] = \frac{2\cos^{-1}(1/5)}{\omega}$$

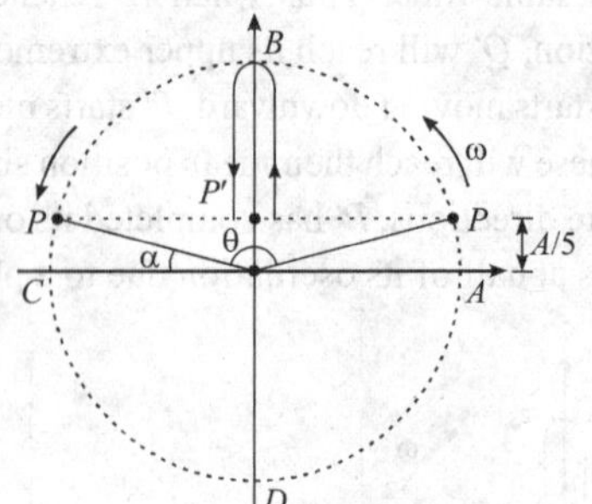

Figure 5.37

Now when P reaches point C, P' will reach its mean position. Thus time taken by P from its initial position to point C is

$$t = \frac{(\pi - \alpha)}{\omega} = \frac{\pi - \sin^{-1}(1/5)}{\omega}$$

The same time P' will take from $A/5$ position to mean position through its extreme position.

Illustrative Example 5.15

Two particles executing SHM with same angular frequency and amplitudes A and $2A$ on same straight line with same mean position cross each other in opposite direction at a distance $A/3$ from mean position. Find the phase difference in the two SHMs.

Solution

Figure-5.38 shows the two corresponding particles of circular motion for the two mentioned particles in SHM. Let particle P

is going up and particle Q is going down. From the figure shown, the respective phase differences of particles P' and Q' are

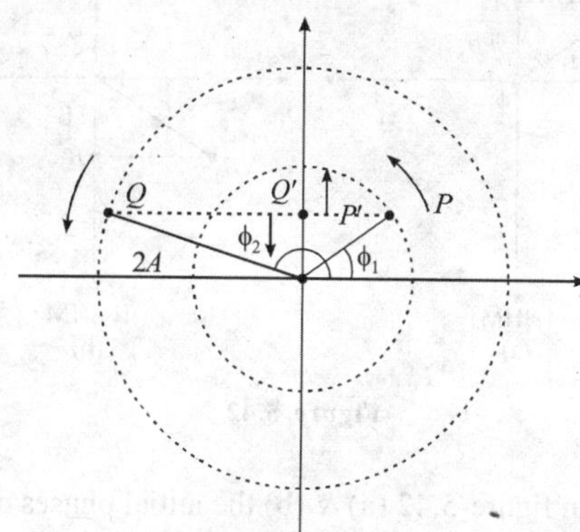

Figure 5.38

$$\phi_1 = \sin^{-1}\left(\frac{1}{3}\right) \quad \text{[Phase angle of } P'\text{]}$$

and

$$\phi_2 = \pi - \sin^{-1}\left(\frac{1}{6}\right) \quad \text{[Phase angle of } Q'\text{]}$$

Thus phase difference in the two SHMs is

$$\Delta\phi = \phi_2 - \phi_1 = \pi - \sin^{-1}\left(\frac{1}{6}\right) - \sin^{-1}\left(\frac{1}{3}\right)$$

 # Illustrative Example 5.16

A particle starts its SHM from mean position at $t = 0$. If its time period is T and amplitude A. Find the distance travelled by the particle in the time from $t = 0$ to $t = 5T/4$.

Solution

We know in one complete oscillation i.e. in period T, a particle covers a distance $4A$ and in first one quarter of its period it goes from its mean position to its extreme position as its starts from mean position thus the distance travelled by the particle in time $5T/4$ is $5A$.

 # Illustrative Example 5.17

Figure-5.39 shows two identical simple pendulums of length l. One is tilled at an angle α and imparted an initial velocity v_1 toward mean position and at the same time other one is projected away from mean position at a velocity v_2 at an initial angular displacement β. Find the phase difference in oscillations of these two pendulums.

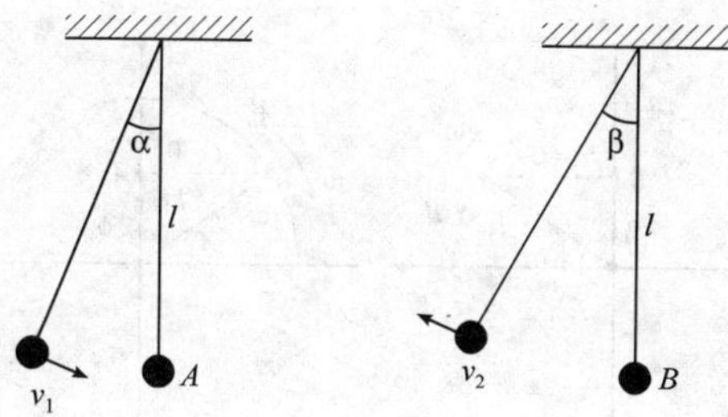

Figure 5.39

Solution

It is given that first pendulum bob is given a velocity v_1 at a displacement $l\alpha$ from mean position, using the formula for velocity we can find the amplitude of its oscillations as

$$V_1 = \omega\sqrt{A_1^2 - (l\alpha)^2}$$

[If A_1 is the amplitude of SHM of this bob.]

As for simple pendulum $\omega = \sqrt{\frac{g}{l}}$ we have

$$V_1^2 = \frac{g}{l}[(A_1^2 - (l\alpha)^2]$$

or

$$A_1 = \sqrt{l^2\alpha^2 + \frac{v_1^2 l}{g}} \quad \ldots(5.70)$$

Similarly if A_2 is the amplitude of SHM of second pendulum bob we have

$$V_2 = \omega\sqrt{A_2^2 - (l\beta)^2}$$

or

$$A_2 = \sqrt{l^2\beta^2 + \frac{v_2^2 l}{g}} \quad \ldots(5.71)$$

Now we represent the two SHMs by circular motion representation as shown in figure-5.40.

In first pendulum at $t = 0$ the bob is thrown from a displacement $l\alpha$ from mean position with a velocity v_1 toward mean position. As it is moving toward mean position, in figure-5.40(a), we consider the corresponding circular motion particle A_0 of the bob A is second quadrant, as the reference direction of ω, we consider anticlockwise. As shown in figure initial phase of bob A is given as

$$\phi_1 = \pi - \sin^{-1}\left(\frac{l\alpha}{A_1}\right) \quad \ldots(5.72)$$

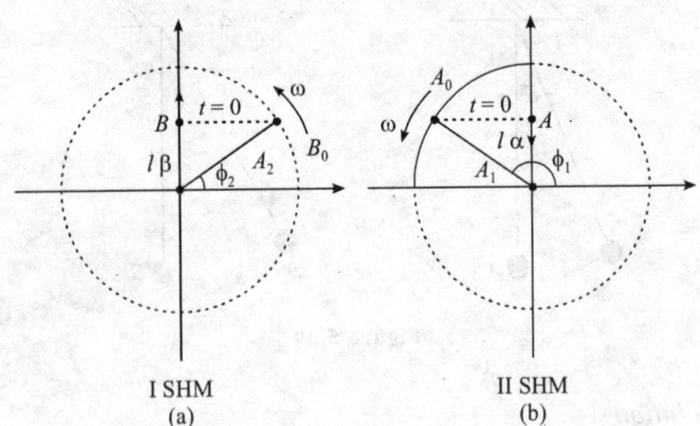

Figure 5.40

Similarly for second pendulum bob B, its corresponding circular motion particle B_0 at $t = 0$ is considered as shown in figure-5.40 (b) its initial base is given as

$$\phi_2 = \sin^{-1}\left(\frac{l\beta}{A_2}\right) \quad \ldots(5.73)$$

As both the pendulums are identical, their angular frequency for SHM must be same, so their phase difference will not change with time, hence their phase difference can be given as

$$\Delta\phi = \phi_2 - \phi_1 = \sin^{-1}\left(\frac{l\beta}{A_2}\right) + \sin^{-1}\left(\frac{l\alpha}{A_1}\right) - \pi$$

Illustrative Example 5.18

In previous question if second pendulum bob is thrown at velocity v_2 at an angle β from mean position but on other side of mean position. Find the phase difference in the two SHMs now as shown in figure-5.41.

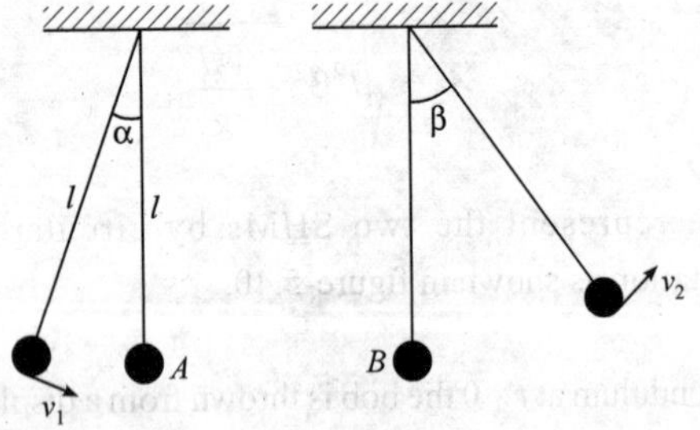

Figure 5.41

Solution

In this case still amplitudes of the two SHMs will remain same and are given by equation-(5.70) & (5.71) but when we represent the two SHMs on their corresponding circular motions, the position of the particle in circular motion in second pendulum is now different as shown in figure-5.42.

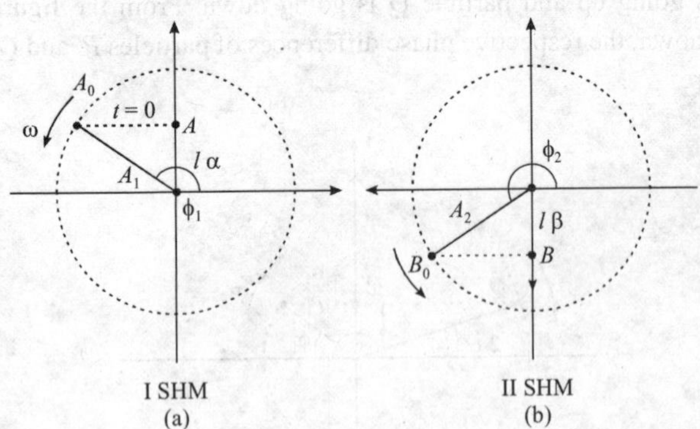

Figure 5.42

As shown in figure-5.42 (a) & (b) the initial phases of the two pendulum bobs are

$$\phi_1 = \pi - \sin^{-1}$$

and

$$\phi_2 = \pi + \sin^{-1}\left(\frac{l\beta}{A_2}\right)$$

As ω for both SHM are same, their phase difference remains constant so it is given as

$$\Delta\phi = \phi_2 - \phi_1 = \sin^{-1}\left(\frac{l\beta}{A_2}\right) + \sin^{-1}\left(\frac{l\alpha}{A_1}\right)$$

Illustrative Example 5.19

A spring block pendulum is shown in figure-5.43. The system is hanging in equilibrium. A bullet of mass $m/2$ moving at a speed u hits the block from downward direction and gets embedded in it. Find the amplitude of oscillation of the block now. Also find the time taken by the block to reach its upper extreme position after hit by bullet.

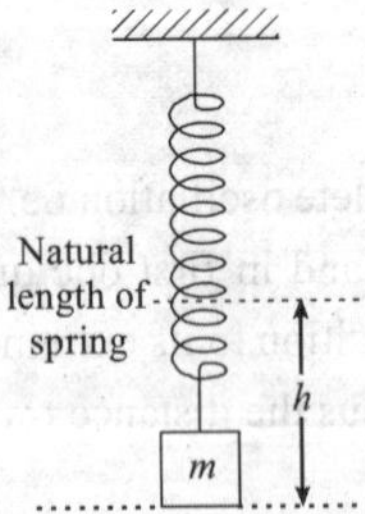

Figure 5.43

Solution

If block is in equilibrium then spring must be at some stretch if it is h, we have

$$mg = kh.$$

If a bullet of mass $m/2$ gets embedded in the block, due to this inelastic impact its new mass becomes $3m/2$ and now the new mean position of the block will be say at a dept. h_1 from old mean position then, we must have

$$\frac{3}{2}mg = k(h+h_1)$$

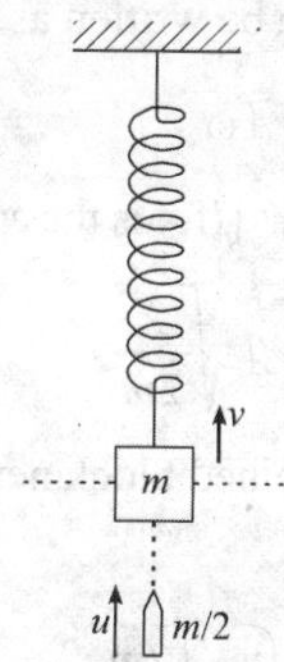

Figure 5.44

$$\frac{3m}{2}g = k(h+h_1)$$

$$\Rightarrow \quad h_1 = \frac{mg}{2k} \qquad [\text{As } mg = kh]$$

Just after impact due to inelastic collision if the velocity of block becomes v, we have according to momentum conservation

$$\frac{m}{2}u = \frac{3m}{2}v$$

or $$v = \frac{u}{3}$$

Now the block executes SHM and at $t = 0$ block is at a distance $h_1 = {}^{mg}/_{2k}$ above its mean position and having a velocity ${}^{u}/_{3}$. If amplitude of oscillation is A, we have

$$\frac{u}{3} = \omega\sqrt{A^2 - \left(\frac{mg}{2k}\right)^2}$$

or $$\frac{u^2}{9} = \frac{2k}{3m}\left[A^2 - \left(\frac{mg}{2k}\right)^2\right]$$

$$\left[\text{As for this spring block system } \omega = \sqrt{\frac{k}{(3m/2)}}\ \right]$$

$$\Rightarrow \quad A = \sqrt{\frac{mu^2}{6k} + \left(\frac{mg}{2k}\right)^2} \qquad \ldots(5.74)$$

Now time taken by particle to reach the topmost point can be obtained by circular motion representation as shown in figure-5.45. This figure shows the position of block P and its corresponding circular motion particle P_0 at the $t = 0$. Block P will reach its upper extreme position when particle P_0 will traverse the angle θ and reach the topmost point. As P_0 moves at constant angular velocity ω, it will take a time given as

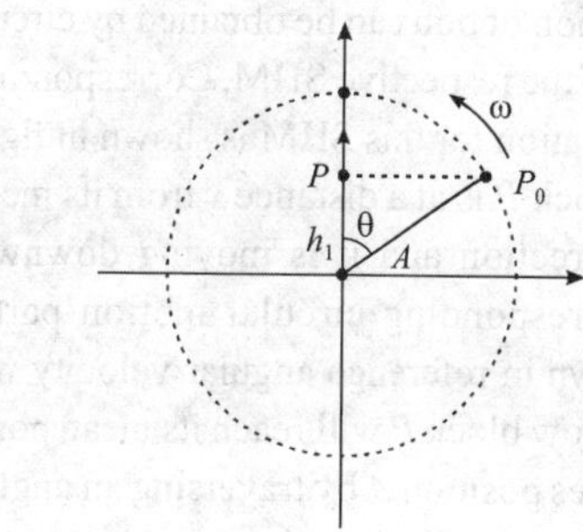

Figure 5.45

$$t = \frac{\theta}{\omega} = \frac{\cos^{-1}(h_1/A)}{\sqrt{\dfrac{k}{3m/2}}} = \sqrt{\frac{3m}{2k}}\cos^{-1}\left(\frac{mg}{2kA}\right).$$

Illustrative Example 5.20

Figure-5.46(a) shows a spring block system, hanging in equilibrium. The block of system is pulled down by a distance x and imparted a velocity v in downward direction as shown in figure-5.46(b). Find the time it will take to reach its mean position. Also find the maximum distance to which it will move before returning back towards mean position.

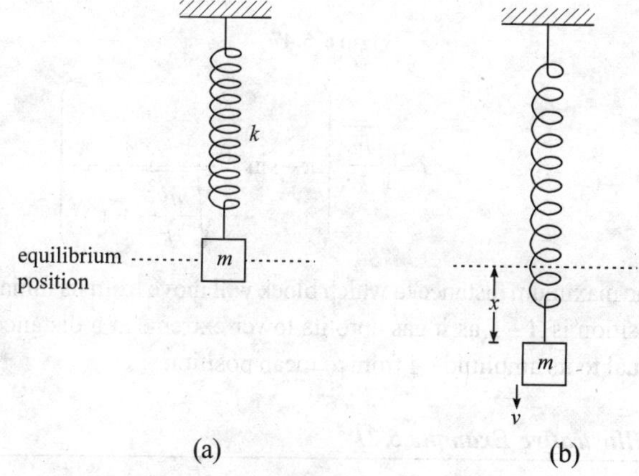

Figure 5.46

Solution

As shown in figure-5.46(b), when the block is pulled down by a distance x and thrown downward, it will start executing SHM. It will go further to a distance A (amplitude) from mean position before returning back which can be found by using the velocity of block v at a displacement x from its mean position as

$$v = \omega\sqrt{A^2 - x^2}$$

or $$v^2 = \frac{k}{m}(A^2 - x^2)$$

$$\left[\text{As for spring block system } \omega = \sqrt{\frac{k}{m}}\ \right]$$

or $$A = \sqrt{\frac{mv^2}{k} + x^2}$$

Now time of motion of bob can be obtained by circular motion representation of the respective SHM. Corresponding circular motion representation for this SHM is shown in figure-5.47 at $t = 0$. At $t = 0$, block P is at a distance x from its mean position in downward direction and it is moving downward so we consider its corresponding circular motion particle in III quadrant as shown in reference angular velocity we consider anticlockwise. Now block P will reach its mean position when particle P_0 reaches position A by traversing an angle θ. Shown in figure-5.47. Thus it will take a time given as

$$t = \frac{\theta}{\omega} = \frac{\pi - \sin^{-1}(x/A)}{\sqrt{\frac{k}{m}}}$$

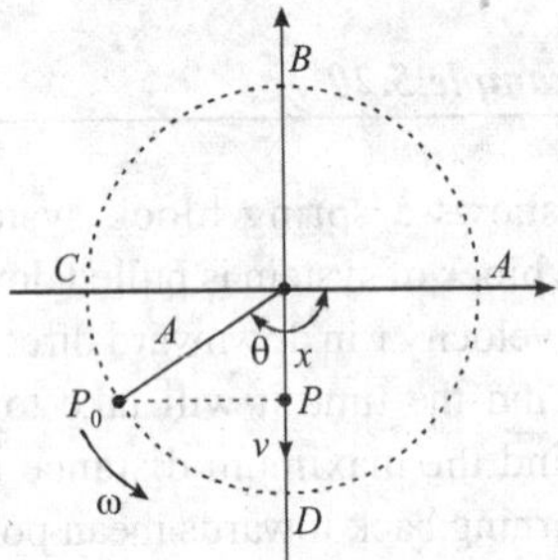

Figure 5.47

or $$t = \sqrt{\frac{m}{k}}\left(\pi - \sin^{-1}\frac{x}{\sqrt{\frac{mv^2}{k} + x^2}}\right)$$

The maximum distance to which block will move from its initial position is $A - x$ as it gas upto its lower extreme at a distance equal to its amplitude A from to mean position.

Illustrative Example 5.21

Figure-5.48 shows a block of mass m resting on a smooth horizontal ground attached to one end of a spring of force constant k in natural length. If another block of same mass and moving with a velocity u toward right is placed on the block which stick to it due to friction. Find the time it will take to reach its extreme position. Also find the amplitude of oscillations of the combined mass 2 m.

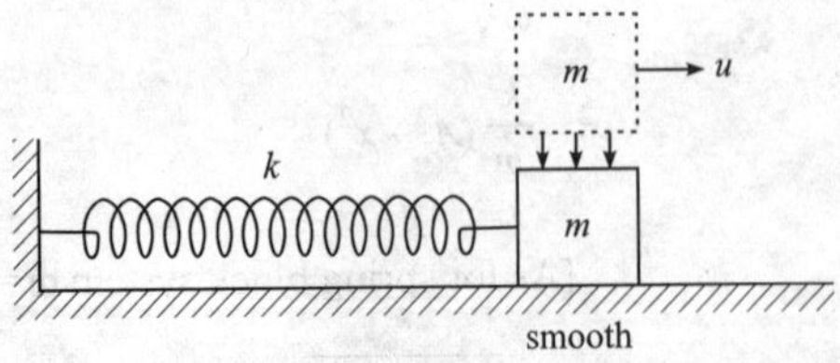

Figure 5.48

Solution

When second mass sticks to the lower mass, due to such an inelastic collision, the velocity of combined block is reduced by half that is $u/2$ to conserve momentum. Now at mean position the velocity of block can be written as

$$\frac{u}{2} = A\omega$$

[If A is the amplitude of oscillation]

or $$\frac{u}{2} = A\sqrt{\frac{k}{2m}}$$

[As here for combined block new angular frequency of SHM is $\omega = \sqrt{k/2m}$]

or $$A = \frac{u}{2}\sqrt{\frac{2m}{k}} = u\sqrt{\frac{m}{2k}}$$

As oscillation starts from mean position, in reaching its extreme position, particle has to cover a phase of $\pi/2$ radians, thus time taken by particle to reach its extreme position is

$$t = \frac{\pi/2}{\omega} = \frac{\pi}{2}\sqrt{\frac{k}{2m}}$$

Illustrative Example 5.22

In previous example if block is pulled toward right by a distance x_0 and released, when the block passes through a point at a displacement $x_0/2$ from mean position, another block of same mass is gently placed on it which sticks to it due to friction. Find the new amplitude of oscillation and find the time now it will take in reaching its mean position and extreme position on left side.

Solution

When block was released at x_0 from mean position, this will be the amplitude of oscillation and when it is passing through the position of half amplitude $\frac{x_0}{2}$, its velocity can be given as

$$v = \omega\sqrt{A^2 - \left(\frac{x_0}{2}\right)^2}$$

or $$v = \sqrt{\frac{k}{m}}\sqrt{x_0^2 - \frac{x_0^2}{4}}$$

$$= \frac{\sqrt{3}}{2}x_0\sqrt{\frac{k}{m}}$$

When another block of same mass is added to it, due to momentum conservation its velocity becomes half and ω of oscillation will, also change from $\sqrt{k/m}$ to $\sqrt{k/2m}$. Again using the formula for velocity of SHM at a distance $x_0/2$ from mean position, we get

$$v' = \frac{v}{2} = \omega\sqrt{A'^2 - \left(\frac{x_0}{2}\right)^2}$$

or $$\frac{\sqrt{3}}{4}x_0\sqrt{\frac{k}{m}} = \sqrt{\frac{k}{2m}}\sqrt{A'^2 - \frac{x_0^2}{4}}$$

[If A' is the new amplitude of oscillation]

$\Rightarrow$ $$A'^2 = \frac{3}{8}x_0^2 + \frac{x_0^2}{4} = \frac{5}{8}x_0^2$$

or $$A' = \frac{\sqrt{5}}{2\sqrt{2}}x_0$$

To find time of motion in SHM we use circular motion representation of the respective SHM. Thefigure-5.49 shows the corresponding circular motion. If at $t = 0$, the second mass is added to the oscillating block, it was at a position $x_0/2$ from mean position and moving towards it, and after adding the mass the new amplitude of oscillation changes to A' and ω changes from $\sqrt{k/m}$ to $\sqrt{k/2m}$. Figure-5.49 shows the corresponding position of particle in circular motion at $t = 0$ in II quadrant. When this particle P_0 will reach the position C after traversing the angle θ, particle P in SHM will reach its mean position and similarly when P_0 will reach position D, P will reach the extreme position on other side. Thus the time taken by P to reach mean position from a position of $x_0/2$ from mean position is given as

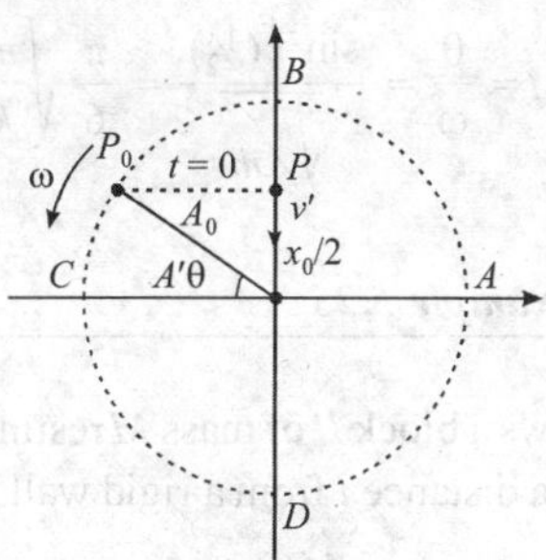

Figure 5.49

$$t_1 = \frac{\theta}{\omega'} = \frac{\sin^{-1}\left(\frac{x_0}{2A'}\right)}{\sqrt{\frac{k}{2m}}}$$

or $$t_1 = \frac{\sin^{-1}\left(\sqrt{\frac{2}{5}}\right)}{\sqrt{\frac{k}{2m}}} = \sqrt{\frac{2m}{k}}\sin^{-1}\left(\sqrt{\frac{2}{5}}\right)$$

Similarly time taken by P to reach the left end extreme position is

$$t_2 = \frac{\pi/2+\theta}{\omega'} = \sqrt{\frac{2m}{k}}\left[\frac{\pi}{2} + \sin^{-1}\left(\sqrt{\frac{2}{5}}\right)\right]$$

Illustrative Example 5.23

Figure-5.50 shows a block P of mass m resting on a smooth horizontal surface, attached to a spring of force constant k which is rigidly fixed on the wall on left side, shown in figure-5.34. At a distance l to the right of block there is a rigid wall. If block is pushed toward lift so that spring is compressed by a distance $5l/3$ and released, it will start its oscillations. If collision of block with the wall is considered to be perfectly elastic. Find the time period of oscillations of the block.

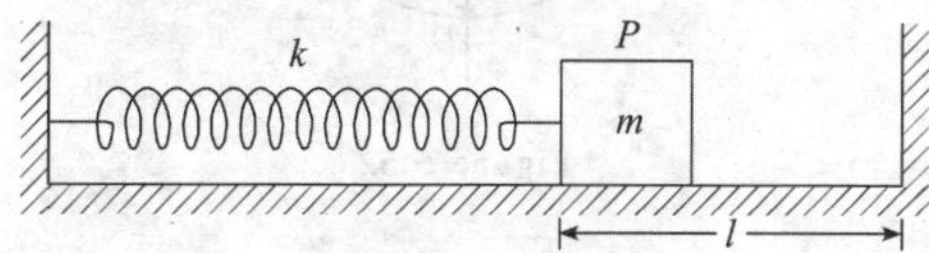

Figure 5.50

Solution

As shown in figure-5.50, as the block is released from rest at a distance $5l/3$ from its mean position, this will be the amplitude of oscillation. But on other side of mean position block can move only upto a distance l from mean position and then it will return from this point with equal velocity due to elastic collision. Consider figure-5.51. If no right wall is present during oscillation block P will executing complete SHM on right side of mean position also up to its amplitude $5l/3$. Thus we can observe the block P at a point X at a distance l from mean position (where in our case wall is present), if block passes this position at speed v (which is the speed with which block hits the wall in our case), after reaching its extreme position Y, it will return and during return path it will cross the position X with the same speed v (as displacement from mean position is same).

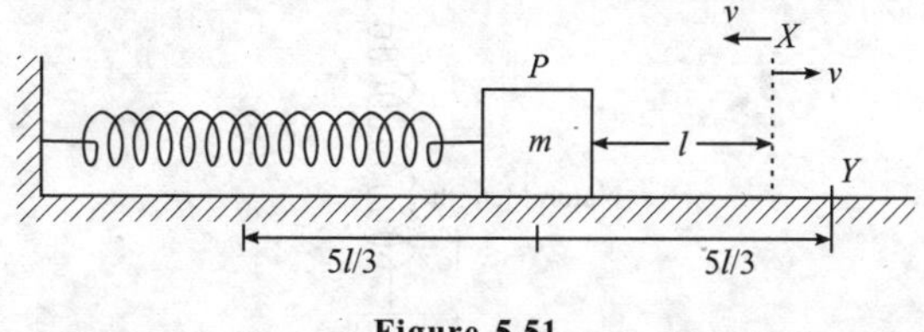

Figure 5.51

Thus we can state that in our case of given problem, block P is executing SHM but it skips a part XYX on right half of its motion due to electric collision of the block with the wall. If T_0 is the time period of this oscillation we look at figure-5.52, which shows the corresponding circular motion representation.

Here during oscillation of point P, particle P_0 covers its circular motion along $ECDAF$, and from F it instantly jumps to E (due to elastic collision of P with wall at X) and again carry out $ECDAF$ and so on, thus we can find the time of this total motion as

$$t = \frac{\pi + 2\theta}{\omega} = \frac{\pi + 2\sin^{-1}(3/5)}{\sqrt{\frac{k}{m}}}$$

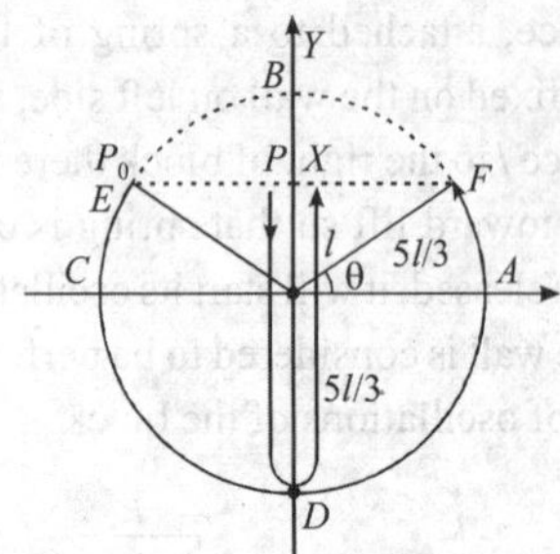

Figure 5.52

$$t = \sqrt{\frac{m}{k}}\,[\pi + 2\sin^{-1}(3/5)] \qquad \ldots(5.75)$$

We can also find the time period of this motion by subtracting the time of FYE from the total time period as

$$t = \frac{2\pi - 2\cos^{-1}(3/5)}{\omega}$$

or
$$t = \sqrt{\frac{m}{k}}\,[2\pi - 2\cos^{-1}(3/5)] \qquad \ldots(5.76)$$

These equation-(5.56) & (5.57) will result same numerical value.

Illustrative Example 5.24

Figure-5.53 shows a spring block system hanging in equilibrium. If a velocity v_0 is imparted to the block in downward direction. Find the amplitude of SHM of the block and the time after which it will reach a point at half of the amplitude of block.

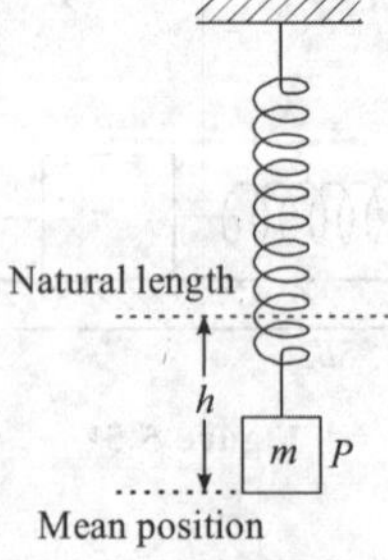

Figure 5.53

Solution

Initially in equilibrium if block is at a depth h below the natural length of spring then we have

$$mg = kh$$

If at mean position block is imparted a velocity v_0, this would be the maximum velocity of block during its oscillation. If its amplitude of oscillation is A, then it is given as

$$v_0 = A\omega \qquad \left[\text{Where } \omega = \sqrt{\frac{k}{m}}\,\right]$$

or
$$A = \frac{v_0}{\omega} = v_0\sqrt{\frac{m}{k}}$$

Now to find the time taken by block to reach its half of amplitude point we consider the corresponding circular motion of the SHM as shown in figure-5.54.

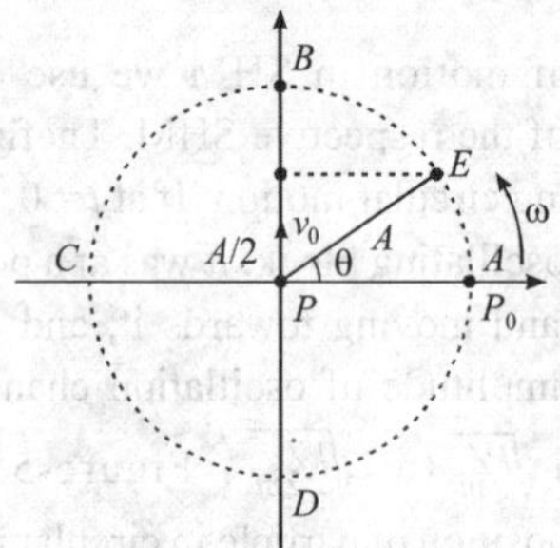

Figure 5.54

Here block P will reach to half of its amplitude when particle P_0 will reach point E shown in figure-5.54 at an angular displacement θ from mean position relative to point A, thus time taken by it is

$$t = \frac{\theta}{\omega} = \frac{\sin^{-1}(1/2)}{\sqrt{k/m}} = \frac{\pi}{6}\sqrt{\frac{m}{k}}$$

Illustrative Example 5.25

Figure-5.55 shows a block P of mass M resting on a horizontal smooth floor at a distance l from a rigid wall. Block is pushed toward right by a distance $3l/2$ and released, when block passes from its mean position another block of mass m_1 is placed on it which sticks to it due to friction. Find the value of m_1 so that the combined block just collides with the left wall.

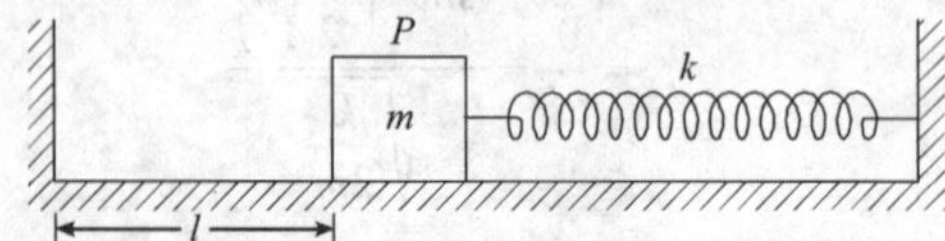

Figure 5.55

Solution

When block P is released from rest from a distance $3l/2$ toward right from mean position, this will be the amplitude of oscillation, so velocity of block when passing from its mean position is given as

$$v = A\omega = \frac{3l}{2}\sqrt{\frac{k}{m}} \qquad [\text{As } \omega = \sqrt{\frac{k}{m}}\,]$$

If mass m_1 is added to it and just after if velocity of combined block becomes v_1, from momentum conservation we have

$$mv = (m + m_1)\, v_1$$

or $$v_1 = \frac{m}{(m+m_1)}\left(\frac{3l}{2}\sqrt{\frac{k}{m}}\right)$$

If this is the velocity of combined block at mean position, it must be given as

$$v_1 = A\omega_1 \qquad [\text{Now } \omega_1 = \sqrt{\frac{k}{m+m_1}}\,]$$

Where A_1 and ω_1 are the new amplitude and angular frequency of SHM of the block. It is given that combined block just reaches the left wall thus the new amplitude of oscillation must be l so we have

$$\frac{m}{(m+m_1)} \cdot \frac{3l}{2}\sqrt{\frac{k}{m}} = l_1\sqrt{\frac{k}{m+m_1}}$$

or $$\frac{3\sqrt{m}}{2\sqrt{m+m_1}} = 1$$

or $$9m = 4m + 4m_1$$

or $$m_1 = \frac{5}{4}m$$

Practice Exercise 5.3

(i) A particle performing SHM is found at its equilibrium at $t = 1$ second and it is found to have a speed of 0.25 m s^{-1} at $t = 2$ seconds. If the period of oscillation is 6 seconds, calculate.

(a) amplitude of oscillation and initial phase

(b) velocity of particle at 6 seconds.

[(a) $\frac{3}{2\pi}$ m; $-\frac{\pi}{3}$ (b) 0.25 m/s]

(ii) Two light springs of force constant k_1 and k_2 and a block of mass m are in one line AB on a smooth horizontal table such that one end of each spring is fixed on rigid supports and the other end is free as shown in the figure-5.56. The distance between the free ends of the springs is d. If the block moves along AB with a velocity v in between springs, calculate the period of oscillation of the block.

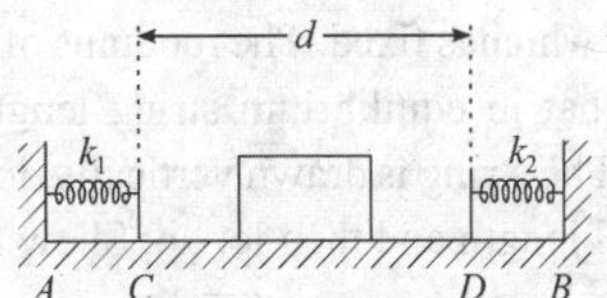

Figure 5.56

[$\pi\left\{\sqrt{\frac{m}{k_1}} + \sqrt{\frac{m}{k_2}}\right\} + \frac{2d}{v}$]

(iii) Find the phase difference between two particles executing simple harmonic motion with the same frequency if they are found in the states shown in the figure-5.57 at four different points of time.

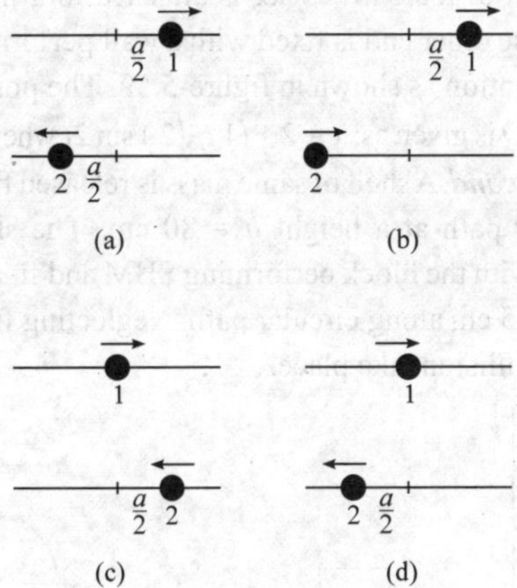

Figure 5.57

[(a) π; (b) $\frac{2\pi}{3}$; (c) $\frac{5\pi}{6}$; (d) $\frac{7\pi}{6}$]

(iv) A ball is suspended by a thread of length l at the point O on the wall, forming a small angle α with the vertical as shown in figure-5.58. Then the thread with the ball was deviated through a small angle β ($\beta > \alpha$) and set free. Assuming the collision of the ball against the wall to be perfectly elastic, find the oscillation period of such a pendulum.

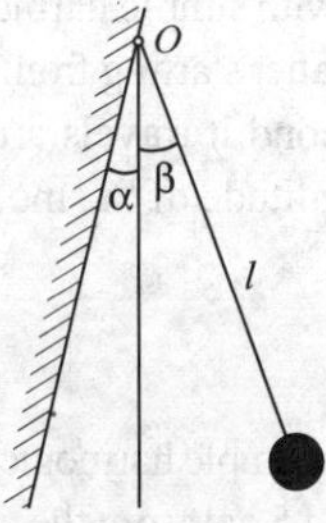

Figure 5.58

[$T = 2\sqrt{l/g}\ [\pi/2 + \sin^{-1}(\alpha/\beta)]$]

(v) A heavy particle is attached to one end of an elastic string, the other end of which is fixed. The modulus of elasticity of the string is such that in equilibrium string length is double its natural length. The string is drawn vertically down till it is four times its natural length and then let go. Show that the particle will return to this point in time $\sqrt{\frac{l}{g}}\left(2\sqrt{3}+\frac{4\pi}{3}\right)$ where l is the natural length of the string.

(vi) Two particles are in SHM with the same amplitude and frequency along the same line and about the same point. If the maximum separation between them is $\sqrt{3}$ times their amplitude, what is the phase difference between them?

[$2\pi/3$]

(vii) A block of mass m = 1 kg is attached to a free end of a spring whose other end is fixed with a wall performing simple harmonic motion as shown in figure-5.59. The position of the block from O is given as; $x = 2+(1/\sqrt{2})\sin 2t$ where x in *meter* and t is in *second*. A shell of same mass is released from smooth the circular path at a height h = 80 cm. The shell collide elastically with the block performing SHM and finally reaches upto height 5 cm along circular path. Neglecting friction, find where the collision take place.

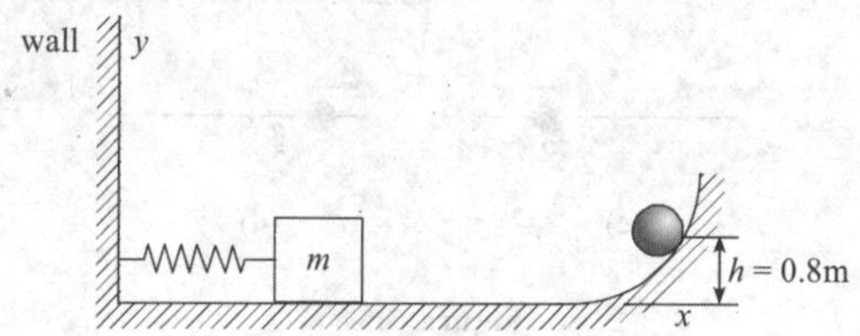

Figure 5.59

[At = x = 1.5 m or 2.5 m]

(viii) In a SHM the distances of a particle from the middle point of its path at three consecutive seconds are observed to be x, y and z. Show that the period of oscillation is $\frac{2\pi}{\cos^{-1}\left(\frac{x+z}{2y}\right)}$

(ix) A particle moves with simple harmonic motion in a straight line. In the first second after starting from rest, it travels a distance x_1, and in the next second it travels a distance x_2 in the same direction. Find the amplitude of the motion.

[$\frac{2x_1^2}{3x_1 - x_2}$]

(x) A particle moves in simple harmonic motion. If the velocities at distances of 4 cm and 5 cm from the equilibrium position are 13 cm per second and 5 cm per second respectively, find the period and amplitude.

[1.6 s, 5.02 cm]

(xi) At the moment $t = 0$ a particle starts moving along the x axis so that its velocity projection varies as $v_x = 35\cos \pi t$ cm/s, where t is expressed in seconds. Find the distance that this particle covers during t = 2.80 s after the start.

[60.29 cm]

5.8 Energy of a Particle in SHM

When a particle is in SHM, we know at its extreme position, *KE* of particle is zero and at mean position, particle's speed is maximum *i.e.*, its *K.E.* is maximum. We know at mean position particle is in stable equilibrium where potential energy of particle is minimum about which particle oscillates. During oscillation the total energy of a particle remains constant.

Figure-5.60 shows the graph which represents the variation of potential energy relative to the position of a particle in a force field. At position x_0 potential energy of particle is minimum and in the neighbourhood of x_0 its potential energy is more, thus force on particle is always toward mean position $x = x_0$ and is given by

$$\vec{F} = -\frac{dU}{dx}\hat{i} \qquad \ldots(5.77)$$

Figure-5.60 shows that at $x = x_0$, dU/dx is zero thus no force acts on particle and at $x > x_0$ from graph, dU/dx is + ve thus $\vec{F}$ is – ve according to equation-(5.77) and force on particle is toward x_0 and at points $x < x_0$, dU/dx is – ve and thus from equation-(5.77) $\vec{F}$ is + ve or towards x_0 thus in such a potential field, a particle can oscillate about $x = x_0$. The region of curve shown in figure is called potential well, in which if a particle is trapped, it can oscillate about the point of lowest potential energy i.e. the point of stable equilibrium.

If particle oscillates about $x = x_0$ with amplitude A, its kinetic energy is maximum at x_0 and as it moves away from x_0, its *PE* increases and kinetic energy decreases at extreme position the potential energy of particle becomes U_0 (as shown in graph) and obviously kinetic energy zero. Thus if at mean position its kinetic energy is K_0 we have

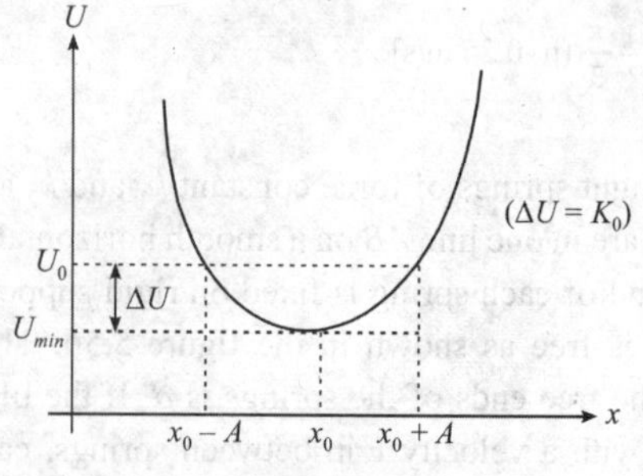

Figure 5.60

Total energy of SHM of particle is

$$E_T = U_{min} + K_0 = U_0$$

Which is also the maximum potential energy of particle when it is at its extreme position.

If particle is executing SHM with amplitude A and angular frequency ω, its velocity at mean position is given as

$$v_{max} = A\omega$$

Thus KE (maximum) of particle at mean position is

$$k_0 = \frac{1}{2}mv_{max}^2 = \frac{1}{2}m\omega^2A^2 \quad \text{...(5.78)}$$

If at mean position potential energy of particle is zero then equation-(5.78) represents the total energy of oscillations otherwise total energy of oscillation can be given as

$$E_T = U_{min} + \frac{1}{2}m\omega^2A^2 \quad \text{...(5.79)}$$

If $\quad U_{min} = 0$ then $\quad E_T = \frac{1}{2}m\omega^2A^2$

When particle is in SHM its displacement from mean position can be given as

$$x = A\sin(\omega t + \alpha)$$

At a displacement x from mean position velocity is given as

$$v_x = \omega\sqrt{A^2 - x^2}$$

Thus kinetic energy of particle during SHM at a displacement x from mean position is given as

$$K_x = \frac{1}{2}mv_x^2 = \frac{1}{2}m\omega^2(A^2 - x^2) \quad \text{...(5.80)}$$

Now using equation-(5.79), the potential energy of particle at a displacement x from mean position is given as

$$U_x = E_T - K_x \quad \text{[As total energy of particle } E_T \text{ is constant]}$$

$$U_x = U_{min} + \frac{1}{2}m\omega^2x^2 \quad \text{...(5.81)}$$

If potential energy of particle at mean position is taken as zero ($U_{min} = 0$). The value of U_x is

$$U_x = \frac{1}{2}m\omega^2x^2 \quad \text{...(5.82)}$$

From equation-(5.80) and (5.82) we can write the kinetic and potential energy of a particle in SHM as function of time as

$$U_t = \frac{1}{2}m\omega^2A^2\sin^2(\omega t + \alpha)$$

$$\text{[As } x = A\sin(\omega t + \alpha)\text{]}$$

and $\quad K_t = \frac{1}{2}m\omega^2A^2\cos^2(\omega t + \alpha)$

Thus at any instant total energy during oscillations is

$$E_T = K_t + U_t = \frac{1}{2}m\omega^2A^2$$

As we've discussed, the above result is valid if at mean position potential energy is zero ($U_{min} = 0$).

5.8.1 Energy of Oscillation in Angular SHM

When a body is in angular SHM its angular displacement is written as

$$\theta = \theta_0\sin(\omega t + \alpha)$$

There θ_0 is the angular amplitude and α is the initial phase of particle in SHM.

Similar to previous article here we can directly state that the total energy of oscillations can be given as

$$E_T = \frac{1}{2}I\omega^2\theta_0^2 \quad \text{...(5.83)}$$

In equation-(5.83) instead of mass, we use moment of inertia of body and instead of amplitude angular amplitude is used. If at mean position some potential energy U_{min} exist then total energy of body in angular SHM is given as

$$E_T = U_{min} + \frac{1}{2}I\omega^2\theta_0^2 \quad \text{...(5.84)}$$

Similarly kinetic and potential energies of the body at an angular displacement θ can be given as

$$K_\theta = \frac{1}{2}I\omega^2(\theta_0^2 - \theta^2) \quad \text{...(5.85)}$$

and $\quad U_\theta = \frac{1}{2}I\omega^2\theta^2 \quad \text{...(5.86)}$

Similar to previous article, equation-(5.85) and (5.86) are valid if at mean position $U_{min} = 0$.

5.9 Energy Method to Find Frequency of SHM

In previous articles we've read how to find angular frequency of a particle in SHM under some external forces. We first find the equilibrium position of particle then we displace it slightly from its equilibrium position and find the force acting on particle toward its equilibrium position i.e. the restoring force and we try to express this restoring force as a proportional function of displacement and then we compare the acceleration of particle during oscillation with the standard differential equation of SHM.

The above method is appropriate but using energy of oscillations also we can find the angular frequency of SHM of a particle. Some time this method is more useful in solving problem. To explain this method we take few example.

Illustrative Example 5.26

Find angular frequency of a spring block pendulum using energy of oscillations.

Solution

Figure-5.61 shows a spring block system in equilibrium which is at a depth h below the natural length of spring hence we have

$$mg = kh$$

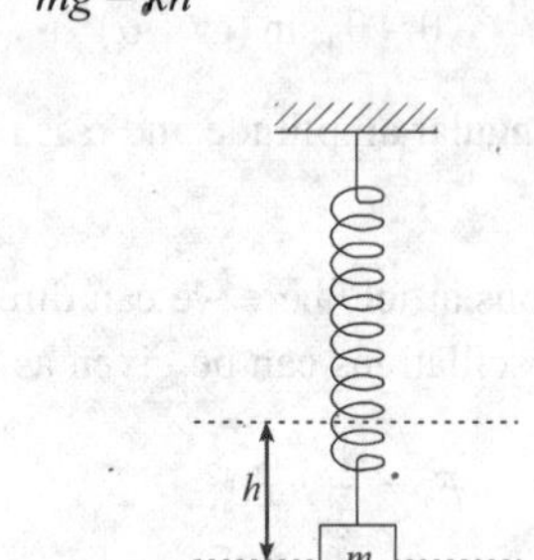

Figure 5.61

Now if the block is displaced down by a distance A below the equilibrium position and released. It starts its oscillation with amplitude A about the mean position. Now during oscillation, we consider the block at position P at a general displacement x from its mean position when it is moving at a speed v as shown in figure-5.62.

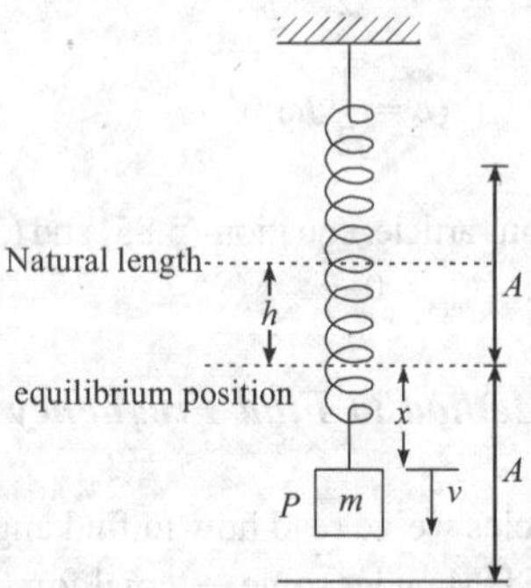

Figure 5.62

If we write the total energy of the oscillating system shown in figure-5.62 at this instant. This is given as

$$E_T = \frac{1}{2} mv^2 + \frac{1}{2} k(x+h)^2 - mgx$$

[Here gravitation work we've considered relative to mean position]

Here we know during oscillation the kinetic and potential energy changes into each other and the total energy of oscillation remains constant with time, thus we have

$$\frac{dE_T}{dt} = 0$$

or $$\frac{1}{2} m\left(2v\frac{dv}{dt}\right) + \frac{1}{2} k\left[2(x+h)\frac{dx}{dt}\right] - mg\left(\frac{dx}{dt}\right) = 0$$

Here we can write $v = \frac{dx}{dt}$ and $a = \frac{dv}{dt}$, thus

$$mva + k(x+h)v - mgv = 0$$

or $$ma + kx + kh - mg = 0$$

or $$a + \frac{k}{m}x = 0$$

[As from condition of equilibrium $mg = kh$]

Comparing this with standard differential equation of SHM, we have

$$\omega = \sqrt{\frac{k}{m}}$$

Above example explains the way how energy of oscillation can be used to determine the angular frequency of SHM. These are the steps to be followed for this :

Step I : Find equilibrium position of particle by making net force on it equal to zero.

Step II : From equilibrium position displace the particle by a distance A (amplitude of oscillation) and release and let it starts oscillation with amplitude A.

Step III : Consider the particle during oscillations at an intermediate position when its displacement from mean position is x and write the total energy E_T of oscillating system at this instant.

Step IV : Now differentiate this energy of oscillations with respect to time and equate it to zero as this energy does not vary with time.

In step IV when we differentiate this energy expression, we finally get the basic differential equation of SHM as we've seen in example 5.26. In general problems of SHM, if the physical situation involves the concept of mechanical forces, it is easier sometimes to deal the problem using energy expression other wise the conventional method of restoring forces are used. Now we take few more examples using the concept of energy.

Illustrative Example 5.27

Figure-5.63 shows a pulley block system in equilibrium. If the block is displaced down slightly from its equilibrium position and released. Find the time period of oscillation of the system. Assume there is sufficient friction present between pulley and string so that string will not slip over pulley surface.

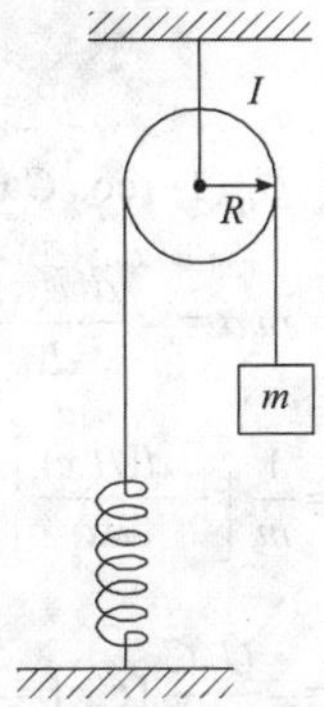

Figure 5.63

Solution

If m is in equilibrium, tension in string must be *mg* and spring is stretched by *h* so that $mg = kh$. If we displace the block downward by a distance *A* and released, it starts executing SHM with amplitude *A*. During its oscillation we consider the block at a displacement *x* below the equilibrium position, if it is moving at a speed *v* at this position, the pulley will be rotating at an angular speed ω given as

$$\omega = \frac{v}{r}$$

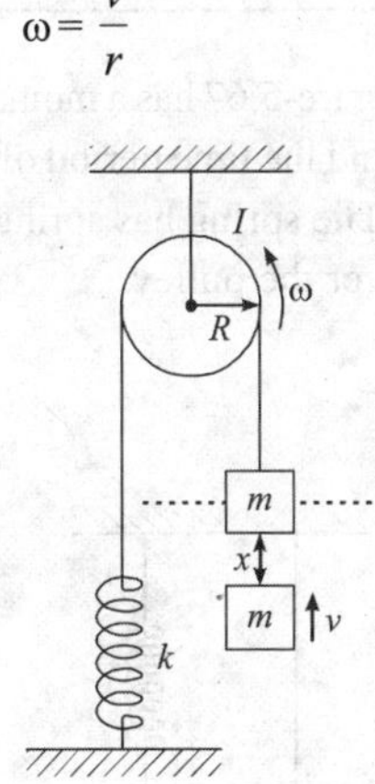

Figure 5.64

Thus at this position the total energy of oscillating system is

$$E_T = \frac{1}{2}mv^2 + \frac{1}{2}I\omega^2 + \frac{1}{2}k(x+h)^2 - mgx$$

Differentiating with respect to time, we get

$$\frac{dE_T}{dt} = \frac{1}{2}m\left(2v\frac{dv}{dt}\right) + \frac{1}{2}I\left(\frac{1}{r^2}\right)\left(2v\frac{dv}{dt}\right) + \frac{1}{2}k\left[2(x+h)\frac{dx}{dt}\right] - mg\left(\frac{dx}{dt}\right) = 0$$

or $$mva + \frac{I}{r^2}va + k(x+h)v - mgv = 0$$

or $$a + \left(\frac{k}{m + I/r^2}\right)x = 0 \qquad \ldots(5.87)$$

[As $mg = kg$]

Comparing above equation with standard differential equation of SHM we get

$$\omega = \sqrt{\left(\frac{k}{m + I/r^2}\right)}$$

Thus time period of oscillation is

$$T = \frac{2\pi}{\omega} = 2\pi\sqrt{\frac{m + I/r^2}{k}}$$

Illustrative Example 5.28

Figure-5.65 shows a pulley block system in which a block *A* is hanging on one side of pulley and on other side a small bead *B* of mass *m* is welded on pulley. The moment of inertia of pulley is *I* and the system is in equilibrium when bead is at an angle α from the vertical. If the system is slightly disturbed from its equilibrium position, find the time period of its oscillations.

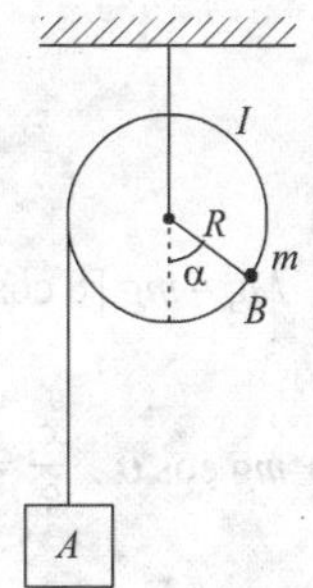

Figure 5.65

Solution

In equilibrium the net torque on pulley must be zero, thus we have

$$Mg\,R = mg\,R\sin\alpha$$

[If mass of block *A* is assumed to be *M*]

or $$M = m\sin\alpha \qquad \ldots(5.88)$$

Now if block is displaced down by distance *A* and released, it starts oscillating with amplitude *A*. Now consider the block at a distance x below the equilibrium position when it is going down at speed v. Figure-5.66 shows the corresponding situation at this instant and the total energy of oscillating system can be written as

$$E_T = \frac{1}{2}Mv^2 + \frac{1}{2}mv^2 + \frac{1}{2}I\left(\frac{v}{R}\right)^2 - Mgx + mgR$$
$$[\cos\alpha - \cos(\theta + \alpha)]$$

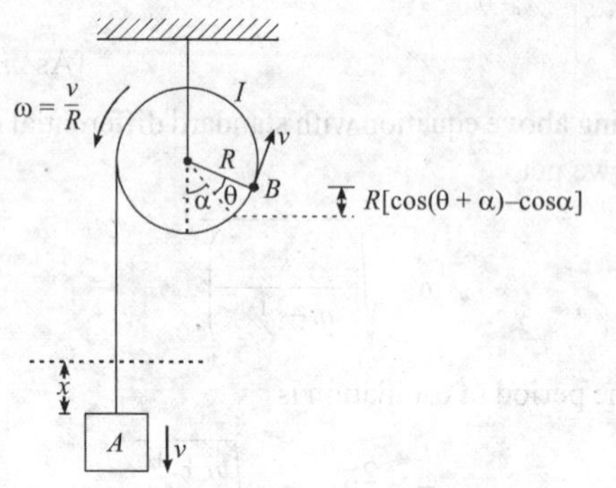

Figure 5.66

Differentiating the above equation w.r. to time, we get

$$\frac{dE_T}{dt} = \frac{1}{2}M\left(2v\frac{dv}{dt}\right) + \frac{1}{2}m\left(2v\frac{dv}{dt}\right) + \frac{1}{2}\frac{I}{R^2}\left(2v\frac{dv}{dt}\right)$$
$$- Mg\left(\frac{dx}{dt}\right) + mgR\left[-\sin(\theta+\alpha)\frac{d\theta}{dt}\right] = 0$$

or $$Mva + mva + \frac{I}{R^2}va - Mgv + mgR\sin(\theta+\alpha)\left(\frac{v}{R}\right) = 0$$

$$[\text{As } \frac{d\theta}{dt} = \omega = \frac{v}{R}]$$

$$\left(M + m + \frac{I}{R^2}\right)a - Mg - mg[\theta\cos\alpha + \sin\alpha] = 0$$

or $$\left(M + m + \frac{I}{R^2}\right)a + mg\cos\alpha \cdot \frac{x}{R} = 0$$

$$[\text{As } M = m\sin\alpha \text{ and } \theta = \frac{x}{R}]$$

or $$a = -\frac{mg\cos\alpha}{R(M + m + I/R^2)} \cdot x \qquad \ldots(5.89)$$

Comparing equation-(5.89) with basic differential equation of SHM, we get the angular frequency of SHM of system as

$$\omega = \sqrt{\frac{mg\cos\alpha}{R(M + m + I/R^2)}}$$

Thus its time period of oscillations is given as

$$T = \frac{2\pi}{\omega} = 2\pi\sqrt{\frac{R(M + m + I/R^2)}{mg\cos\alpha}}$$

Illustrative Example 5.29

A particle of mass m is located in a unidimensional potential field where the potential energy of the particle depends on the coordinate x as $U(x) = U_0(1 - \cos Cx)$; U_0 and C are constants. Find the period of small oscillations that the particle performs about the equilibrium position.

Solution

Given that $$U(x) = U_0(1 - \cos Cx)$$

We know that $$F = ma = -\frac{dU(x)}{dx}$$

or $$a = \frac{1}{m}\left[-\frac{dU(x)}{dx}\right] = \frac{1}{m}[-U_0 C\sin Cx]$$

or $$a = -\frac{U_0 C}{m}[Cx] = -\frac{U_0 C^2}{m}x$$

[For small x, we can take $\sin Cx \approx Cx$]

Here acceleration is directly proportional to the negative of displacement. So, the motion is SHM and its time period T is given by

$$T = \frac{2\pi}{\omega} = \frac{2\pi}{\sqrt{(U_0C^2/m)}} = 2\pi\sqrt{\frac{m}{U_0C^2}}$$

Illustrative Example 5.30

The pulley shown in figure-5.67 has a moment of inertia I about its axis and mass m. Find the time period of vertical oscillation of its centre of mass. The spring has spring constant k and the string does not slip over the pulley.

Solution

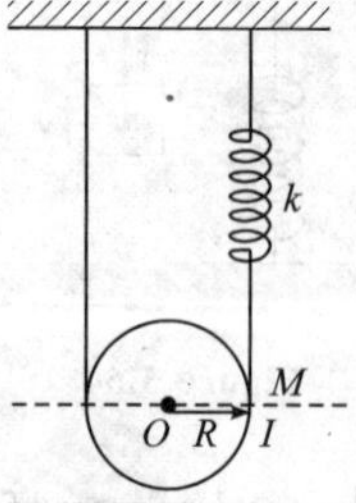

Figure 5.67

Figure-5.67 shows the system in equilibrium. As it is in equilibrium, if mass of pulley is m and tension in string is T, we have

$$T = kx_0$$

Thus $2kx_0 = mg$ ...(5.90)

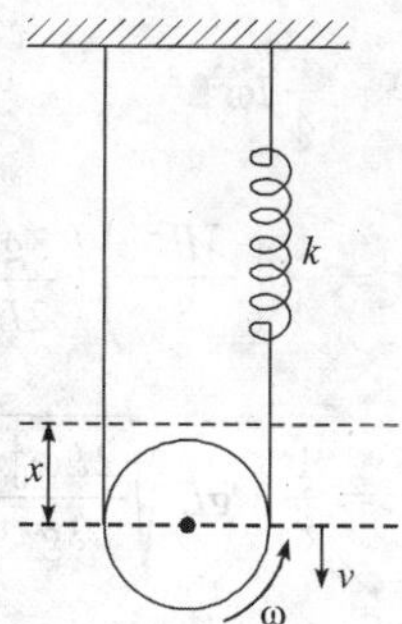

Figure 5.68

Now if the pulley is slightly displaced from its equilibrium position and released, to starts oscillating about the equilibrium position O. During its oscillations we consider the pulley at a depth x below the equilibrium position O as shown in figure-5.68. Due to a further pull by a distance x, total extension in the spring becomes $2(x + x_0)$. If at this instant it is going down with the velocity v and relating at angular speed ω which is given as $v/_R$, it is given that string does not slop over pulley surface. At this position we write the total energy of this oscillating system as

$$E_T = \frac{1}{2}Mv^2 + \frac{1}{2}I\omega^2 + \frac{1}{2}k[2(x_0 + 2x)]^2 - Mgx$$

differentiating with respect to time, we get

$$\frac{dE_T}{dt} = \frac{1}{2}M\left(2v\frac{dv}{dt}\right) + \frac{1}{2}(I)\left(\frac{2v}{R^2}\frac{dv}{dt}\right) + \frac{1}{2}k$$

$$[2(x_0 + 2x)^2 . 2\frac{dx}{dt}] - Mg\frac{dx}{dt} = 0$$

or $$Mva + \frac{Iv}{R^2}a + 2k(x_0 + 2x)v - Mgv = 0$$

or $$Ma + \frac{Iv}{R^2}a + 2kx_0 + 4kx - Mg = 0 \quad [\text{As } Mg = 2kx_0]$$

or $$\left(M + \frac{I}{R^2}\right)a + 4kx = 0$$

or $$a = -\left(\frac{4k}{M + I/_{R^2}}\right)x \quad ...(5.91)$$

Comparing equation-(5.91) with basic differential equation of SHM, we can say that angular frequency of SHM of pulley is

$$\omega = \sqrt{\frac{4k}{M + I/_{R^2}}}$$

Thus its time period of SHM is given as

$$T = \frac{2\pi}{\omega} = 2\pi\sqrt{\frac{M + I/_{R^2}}{4k}}$$

Illustrative Example 5.31

A solid uniform cylinder of mass M performs small oscillations in horizontal plane if slightly displaced from its mean position shown in figure-5.69. If it is given that initially springs are in natural lengths and cylinder does not slip on ground during oscillations due to friction between ground and cylinder. Force constant of each spring is k.

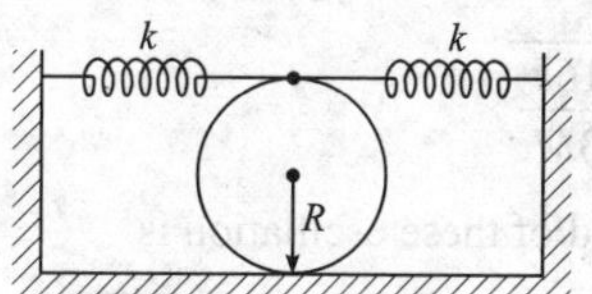

Figure 5.69

Solution

In the situation given in problem, the cylinder is in its equilibrium position when springs are unstrained. When it slightly rolled and released. It starts executing SHM and due to friction, the cylinder is in pure rolling motion. Now during oscillations we consider the cylinder when it is at a distance x from the mean position and moving with a speed v as shown in figure-5.70. As cylinder is in pure rolling, its angular speed of rotation can be given as

$$\omega = \frac{v}{R}$$

Figure 5.70

As centre of cylinder is at a distance x from the initial position, the springs which are connect at a point on its rim must be compressed and stretched by a distance $2x$. Thus at this intermediate position total energy of the oscillating system can be given as

$$E_T = \frac{1}{2}Mv^2 + \frac{1}{2}\left(\frac{1}{2}MR^2\right)\omega^2 + \frac{1}{2}k(2x)^2 \times 2$$

Differentiating with respect to time, we get

$$\frac{dE_T}{dt}=\frac{1}{2}M\left(2v\frac{dv}{dt}\right)$$

$$+\frac{1}{2}\left(\frac{1}{2}MR^2\right)\frac{1}{R^2}\left(2v\frac{dv}{dt}\right)+4k\left(2x\frac{dx}{dt}\right)=0$$

or $$Mva+\frac{1}{2}Mva+8kxv=0$$

or $$a=-\frac{16}{3}\frac{k}{M}x \quad \text{...(5.92)}$$

Comparing equation-(5.92) with basic differential equation of SHM, we get, the angular frequency of SHM as

$$\omega=\sqrt{\frac{16k}{3M}}$$

Thus time period of these oscillation is

$$T=\frac{2\pi}{\omega}=2\pi\sqrt{\frac{3M}{16k}}=\frac{\pi}{2}\sqrt{\frac{3M}{k}}$$

Illustrative Example 5.32

A uniform rod of mass m and length L performs small oscillations about a horizontal axis passing through its upper end. Find the mean kinetic energy of the rod during its oscillation period if at $t=0$ it is deflected from vertical by an angle θ_0 and imparted an angular velocity ω_0.

Solution

Here the rod oscillates like a physical pendulum whose angular frequency can be directly given as

$$\omega=\sqrt{\frac{Mgl}{I}}$$

Where $$I=\frac{Ml^2}{3} \quad \text{and} \quad l=\frac{1}{2}$$

Thus $$\omega=\sqrt{\frac{Mg(l/2)}{ML^2/3}}=\sqrt{\frac{3g}{2L}}$$

It is given that at $t=0$, rod is at an angular displacement θ_0 and has angular speed ω_0. If angular amplitude of rod is β then we have

$$\omega_0=\sqrt{\frac{3g}{2L}}\sqrt{\beta^2-\theta_0^2}$$

Thus $$\beta=\sqrt{\frac{2L\omega_0^2}{3g}+\theta_0^2}$$

We know the average kinetic energy of a body in angular SHM over its oscillation period is given by

$$<k_t>=\frac{1}{4}I\omega^2\beta^2$$

or $$=\frac{1}{4}\left(\frac{ML^2}{3}\right)\left(\frac{3g}{2L}\right)\sqrt{\frac{2L\omega_0^2}{3g}+\theta_0^2}$$

or $$=\frac{1}{8}MgL\sqrt{\frac{2L\omega_0^2}{3g}+\theta_0^2}$$

Illustrative Example 5.33

Figure-5.71 shows a torsional pendulum consists of a uniform disc D of mass M and radius R attached to a this rod of torsional constant C. Find the amplitude and the energy of small torsional oscillations of the disc, if initially the disc was imparted angular speed ω_0.

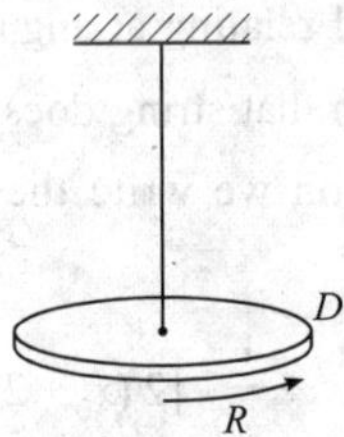

Figure 5.71

Solution

We know for a torsional pendulum angular frequency of small oscillations is given as

$$\omega=\sqrt{\frac{C}{I}}$$

Where $I=\frac{1}{2}MR^2$, thus

$$\omega=\sqrt{\frac{2C}{MR^2}}$$

As it is given that from mean position the disc is imparted an angular speed ω_0, if the angular amplitude of oscillations of disc is β, we have

$$\omega_0=\beta\omega$$

or $$=\beta\sqrt{\frac{2C}{MR^2}}$$

Thus angular amplitude is given as

$$\beta=\sqrt{\frac{MR^2}{2C}}\,\omega_0$$

For angular SHM the total oscillation energy is given as

$$E_T = \frac{1}{2} I\omega^2\beta^2 \qquad [\text{If } U_{min} = 0]$$

Thus here oscillation energy of the disc is given as

$$E_T = \frac{1}{2}\left(\frac{1}{2}MR^2\right)\left(\frac{2C}{MR^2}\right)\left[\frac{MR^2}{2C}\omega_0^2\right]$$

or

$$E_T = \frac{1}{4} MR^2\omega_0^2$$

Web Reference at www.physicsgalaxy.com

Age Group - High School Physics | Age 17-19 Years

Section - OSCILLATION & WAVES

Topic - Simple Harmonic Motion

Module Number - 10, 11, 20 & 26 to 31

Practice Exercise 5.4

(i) In an SHM, at the initial moment of time, the particle's displacement is 4.3 cm and its velocity is -3.2 m s^{-1}. The particle's mass is 4 kg and its total energy 79.5 J. Write down the equation of the SHM and find the distance travelled by the particle in 0.4 s from the start.

[$x = 0.05 \sin (126.33\, t + 2.1)$; 1.6 m]

(ii) A uniform rod of mass m and length l performs small oscillations about the horizontal axis passing through its upper end. Find the mean kinetic energy of the rod averaged over one oscillation period if at the initial moment it was deflected from the vertical by an angle θ_0 and then imparted an angular velocity $\dot{\theta}_0$.

[$\langle KE\rangle = \frac{1}{8} mgl\theta_0^2 + \frac{1}{12} ml^2\dot{\theta}_0^2$]

(iii) A point particle of mass 0.1 kg is executing SHM of amplitude of 0.1 m. When the particle passes through the mean position, its kinetic energy is 8×10^{-3} J. Obtain the equation of motion of this particle if this initial phase of oscillation is 45°.

[$x = 0.1 \sin (4\, t + \pi/4)$ m]

(iv) Equal charges +e are fixed at the four corners of a square of side $a\sqrt{2}$. A fifth charge +e, whose mass is m, is placed at the centre of the square and is free to move. Show that it is in equilibrium at this point that the equilibrium is stable for all small displacements in the plane of the charges. Find the period of small oscillations along the diagonals of square.

[$T = 2\pi\sqrt{\frac{2\pi\varepsilon_0 ma^3}{e^2}}$]

(v) Find the time period of oscillations of the system shown in the figure-5.72. The bar is rigid and light. Initially in equilibrium bar is horizontal.

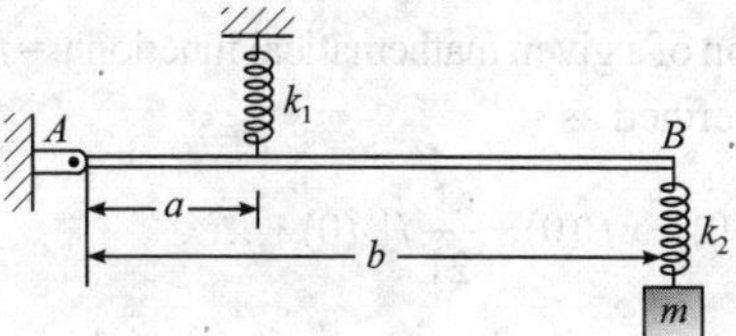

Figure 5.72

[$2\pi\sqrt{\frac{m}{k_1k_2}\left[k_1 + k_2\left(\frac{b}{a}\right)^2\right]}$]

(vi) Find the time period of small oscillations of the spring loaded pendulum. The equilibrium position is vertical as shown. The mass of the rod is negligible and treat mass as a particle.

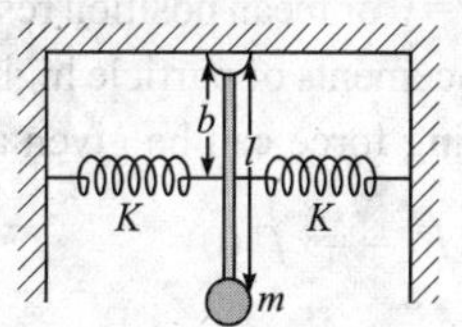

Figure 5.73

[$T = 2\pi\sqrt{\frac{ml^2}{mgl + 2Kb^2}}$]

(vii) A massless rod rigidly fixed at O. A string carrying a mass m at one end is attached to point A on the rod so that $OA = a$. At another point B ($OB = b$) of the rod, a horizontal spring of force constant k is attached as shown in figure-5.74. Find the period of small vertical oscillations of mass m around its equilibrium position. Consider rod in vertical position in equilibrium initially.

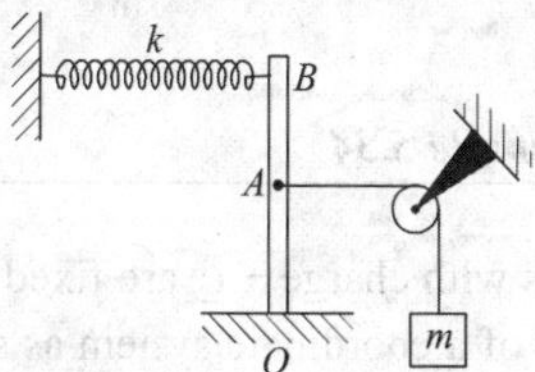

Figure 5.74

[$\frac{2\pi a}{b}\sqrt{\frac{m}{k}}$]

(viii) A particle of mass m is oscillating in SHM along X-axis about its mean position O with angular frequency ω and amplitude A. At the instant when the particle is passing the position $x = \sqrt{3}\,(A/2)$ and going away from O, an impulsive blow is given to it in the direction of motion. The impulse of this blow is of magnitude $J = m\omega A$. Calculate the new amplitude of vibration in terms of A.

[$A' = \sqrt{3}A$]

5.10 Taylor's Method to Find Angular Frequency of a Particle in SHM

For expression of a given mathematical function $y=f(x)$ Taylor's theorem is defined as

$$f(x)=f(0)+xf'(0)+\frac{x^2}{21}f''(0)+\ldots\ldots \qquad \ldots(5.93)$$

If x is taken as the displacement of a particle from its mean position and the restoring force on particle depends on this x by the function $F_R=f(x)$ then it can be given as

Restoring force on particle at a distance x from mean position is

$$F_R=f(x)=f(0)+xf(0)+\frac{x^2}{21}f''(0)+\ldots\ldots \qquad \ldots(5.94)$$

Here $f(0)=0$ as at $x=0$ or mean position restoring force is zero and for small displacements of particle higher powers of x can neglected so restoring force can be given as

$$F_R=-xf'(0)$$

[–ve sign shown the restoring nature]

Acceleration of particle during oscillation is

$$a=\frac{F_R}{m}=-\left(\frac{f'(0)}{m}\right)x \qquad \ldots(5.95)$$

Comparing this equation with general differential equation of SHM, we get

$$\omega=\sqrt{\frac{f'(0)}{m}} \qquad \ldots(5.96)$$

Hence time period of this SHM is $T=\frac{2\pi}{\omega}=2\pi\sqrt{\frac{\text{m}}{f'(0)}}$

Illustrative Example 5.34

Two point charges with charge $+Q$ are fixed at pts $(0, r)$ and $(0, -r)$ on -y axis of a coordinate system as shown in figure-5.75. Another small particle of mass m and charge $-q$ is placed at origin of system, where it stays in equilibrium. If this mass m is slightly displaced along $+x$ direction by a small distance x and released, show that it executes SHM and find its time period of oscillations.

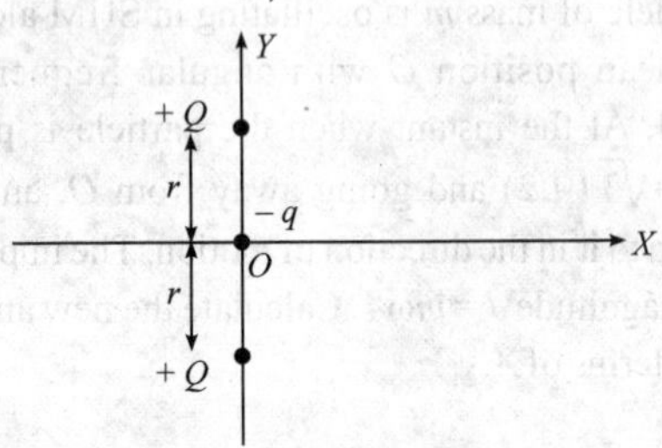

Figure 5.75

Solution

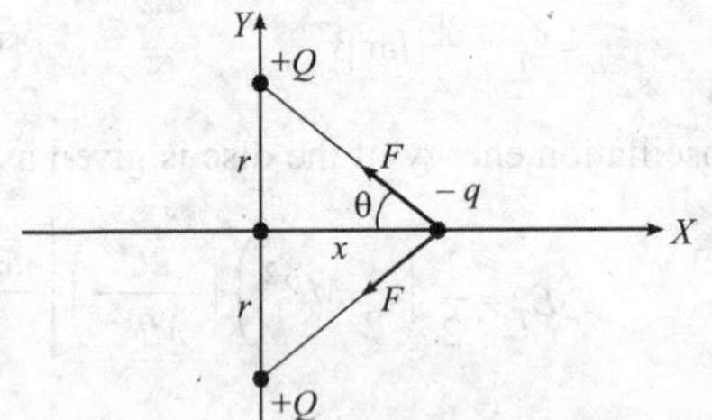

Figure 5.76

If we calculate the net force on particle after its displacement as shown in figure-5.76. The force due to each $+Q$ charge on $-q$ is given by coulomb's law as

$$F=\frac{kqQ}{(r^2+x^2)} \qquad \ldots(5.97)$$

Thus net restoring force on it is

$$F_R=-2F\cos\theta=-\frac{2kqQx}{(r^2+x^2)^{3/2}}$$

$$\left[\text{as } \cos\theta=\frac{x}{\sqrt{r^2+x^2}}\right]$$

As here $x \ll a$, we can neglect x^2, thus

$$F_R=-\frac{2kqQ}{r^3}x$$

If a is the acceleration of particle, we have

$$a=-\frac{2kqQ}{mr^3}x \qquad \ldots(5.98)$$

Comparing this equation with basic differential equation of SHM we get angular frequency of SHM of particle as

$$\omega=\sqrt{\frac{2kqQ}{mr^3}} \qquad \ldots(5.99)$$

Thus its time period is given as

$$T=\frac{2\pi}{\omega}=2\pi\sqrt{\frac{mr^3}{2kqQ}}$$

Alternative method by Taylor's theorem :

As we've get the restoring force on particle as

$$F_R=-\frac{2kqQx}{(a^2+x^2)^{3/2}}$$

We can directly write the angular frequency of SHM as

$$\omega=\sqrt{\frac{f'(0)}{m}} \qquad \ldots(5.100)$$

Where $\qquad f'(0)=\left.\frac{dF_R}{dx}\right|_{x=0}$

or $\quad = 2kqQ\left[\dfrac{(r^2+x^2)^{3/2}\cdot(1) - x(3/2[r^2+x^2]^{1/2})}{(r^2+x^2)^3}\right]_{x=0}$

or $\quad = 2kqQ\left[\dfrac{r^3}{r^6}\right] = \dfrac{2kqQ}{r^3}$

Thus from equation-(5.100)

$$\omega = \sqrt{\frac{2kqQ}{mr^3}}$$

Which is same as that of equation-(5.99)

Illustrative Example 5.35

Solve example(5.29) using Taylor's Method

Solution

In question it is given that potential energy of the oscillating particle is given as

$$U = U_0\,[1 - \cos(Cx)]$$

Thus force on particle can be given as

$$F = \left|\frac{dU}{dx}\right|$$

$$F = U_0 C \sin(Cx)$$

This force is given as a function of displacement of particle x from its mean position, thus angular frequency of its SHM can be directly given as

$$\omega = \sqrt{\frac{f'(0)}{m}} \qquad \ldots(5.101)$$

Where $\quad f'(0) = \left.\dfrac{dF}{dx}\right|_{x=0} = U_0C^2\cdot\cos(Cx)\Big|_{x=0}$

$$= U_0C^2$$

Thus from equation-(5.101)

$$\omega = \sqrt{\frac{U_0C^2}{m}}$$

Illustrative Example 5.36

In a given force field, the potential energy of a particle is given as a function of its x-coordinates as

$$U_{(x)} = \frac{p}{x^2} - \frac{q}{x}$$

where a and b are positive constants. Find the period of small oscillations of the particle about its equilibrium position in the field.

Solution

As potential energy of particle is given as

$$U_{(x)} = \frac{p}{x^2} - \frac{q}{x}$$

The force on particle can be given as

$$F = \left|\frac{dU}{dx}\right| = \left|-\frac{2p}{x^3} + \frac{q}{x^2}\right|$$

The equilibrium position of particle can be given for $F = 0$, as

$$-\frac{2p}{x^3} + \frac{q}{x^2} = 0$$

or $$x = \frac{2p}{q}$$

Thus at $x = {}^{2a}\!/_b$ position particle is in equilibrium. If we find restoring force on particle if it is displaced slightly by a distance z along $+x$ direction then it is given as

$$F_R = -\left[-\frac{2p}{({}^{2a}\!/_b + 2)^3} + \frac{q}{({}^{2a}\!/_b + 2)^2}\right]$$

[– ve sign for restoring nature]

For small z we have

$$F_R = -\left[-\frac{2p}{({}^{2p}\!/_q)^3}\left(1+\frac{qz}{2p}\right) + \frac{q}{({}^{2p}\!/_q)^2}\left(1+\frac{qz}{2p}\right)^{-2}\right]$$

or $$F_R = -\left[-\frac{q^3}{4p^2}\left(1-\frac{3qz}{2p}\right) + \frac{q^3}{4p^2}\left(1-\frac{bz}{p}\right)\right]$$

or $$F_R = -\left[\frac{3q}{2p} - \frac{q}{p}\right]\frac{q^3}{4p^2}\,z$$

or $$F_R = -\left(\frac{q^4}{8p^3}\right)z$$

If a is the acceleration of particle, we have

$$a = -\left(\frac{q^4}{8mp^3}\right)z \qquad \ldots(5.102)$$

Comparing equation-(5.102) with basic differential equation of SHM, we get the angular frequency of its oscillations as

$$\omega = \sqrt{\frac{q^4}{8mp^3}} = \frac{q^2}{2\sqrt{2m}\,p^{3/2}} \qquad \ldots(5.103)$$

This time period of its oscillations is

$$T = \frac{2\pi}{\omega} = 2\pi\left(\frac{2\sqrt{2m}\,p^{3/2}}{q^2}\right)$$

Alternative method by Taylor's theorem :

As we've got the restoring force on particle is given as

$$F_R = -\left(-\frac{2p}{x^3} + \frac{q}{x^2}\right)$$

[– ve sign for restoring nature]

Then the angular frequency of SHM of particle is given as

$$\omega = \sqrt{\frac{f'\left(\frac{2p}{q}\right)}{m}}$$

[Because now mean position of particle is at $x = \frac{2p}{q}$]

Here $$f'\left(\frac{2p}{q}\right) = \left.\frac{dF_R}{dx}\right|_{x=2p/q}$$

$$= \left.\frac{6p}{x^4} - \frac{2q}{x^3}\right|_{x=2p/q}$$

$$= \frac{6p}{(2p/q)^4} - \frac{2q}{(2p/q)^3}$$

$$= \frac{3q^4}{8p^3} - \frac{q^4}{4p^3} = \frac{q^4}{8p^3}$$

Thus angular frequency is given as

$$\omega = \sqrt{\frac{f'(2p/q)}{m}} = \sqrt{\frac{q^4}{8mp^3}} \qquad \ldots (5.104)$$

Which is same as that of equation-(5.103)

 # Illustrative Example 5.37

Figure-5.77 shows two identical balls of mass m and charge $+q$. Connected by an ideal spring of constant k. Ball-1 is fixed on a smooth surface as shown in figure. When balls are uncharged, the spring was in its natural length and as both the balls are charged, the spring length gets doubled in equilibrium position of the balls. Find the time period of small oscillations of the ball-2 about the new equilibrium position after charging the two balls.

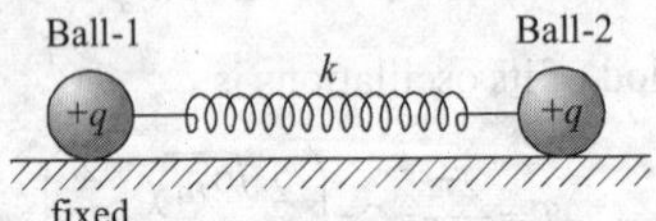

Figure 5.77

Solution

If initial length of spring is l and after charging it becomes $2l$, from coulomb's low we have for equilibrium of ball-2 as

$$\frac{kq^2}{(2l)^2} = kl$$

or $$k = \frac{kq^2}{4l^3} \qquad \ldots (5.105)$$

Now if ball is slightly displaced away from ball-1, formats equilibrium position such that the separation between two balls becomes x, then we have restoring force on ball-2 as

$$F_R = \left[k(x-l) - \frac{kq^2}{x^2}\right]$$

[As spring is stretched by $x = l$] ... (5.106)

Equation-(5.106) gives the restoring force as a function of distance x, here we can directly find the angular frequency of SHM of ball-2 using Taylor's Theorem as

$$\omega = \sqrt{\frac{f'(2l)}{m}}$$

[Because equilibrium position of ball-2 is at $x = 2l$]

Here $$f'(2l) = \left.\frac{dF_R}{dx}\right|_{x=2l}$$

$$= \left[k + \frac{2kq^2}{x^3}\right]_{x=2l}$$

$$= k + \frac{2kq^2}{8l^3} = 2k \qquad \left[\text{As } k = \frac{kq^2}{4l^3}\right]$$

Thus angular frequency of SHM of ball-2 can be given as

$$\omega = \sqrt{\frac{2k}{m}}$$

Thus the time period of SHM of ball-2 is

$$T = \frac{2\pi}{\omega} = 2\pi\sqrt{\frac{m}{2k}} \qquad \ldots (5.107)$$

NOTE : This problem can also be solved by the conventional method of restoring force. We leave this as an exercise for students to get equation-(5.107) by the conventional method.

5.11 Equation of SHM With Shifting of Origin

In previous articles we've discussed that a general equation of SHM of particle is given as

$$y = A\sin(\omega t + \alpha) \qquad \ldots (5.108)$$

Here mean position of particle is at $y=0$ and it oscillates between points $y=\pm A$. In all cases, it is not necessary that mean position of particle is at origin ($y=0$). If in some case mean position of particle is at $y=y_m$ and it executes SHM with amplitude A then the extreme position of the particle in SHM are y_m+A and y_m-A. In such a case the SHM equation can be given as

$$y=y_m+A\sin(\omega t+\alpha) \quad \ldots(5.109)$$

The differential equation for SHM can be written by differentiating equation-(5.109) twice as

$$\frac{d^2y}{dt^2}=-A\omega^2\sin(\omega t+\alpha)$$

or $$\frac{d^2y}{dt^2}=-\omega^2(y-y_m)$$

or $$\frac{d^2y}{dt^2}+\omega^2y=\omega^2y_m$$

or $$\frac{d^2y}{dt^2}+\omega y=C \quad \ldots(5.110)$$

Where $C=\omega^2y_m$ is a numerical constant, where mean position of particle can be given as

$$y_m=C/\omega^2 \quad \ldots(5.111)$$

In some cases of SHM, while solving using energy expression some time equation-(5.110) appears where instead of zero a constant appears on right side of equality, which implies that mean position of oscillation is not at $y=0$ but at $y=C/\omega^2$. Now we take few examples to understand the concept in a batter way.

Illustrative Example 5.38

Figure-5.78 shows block of mass m resting m a smooth horizontal plane attached with a spring of natural length l and force constant k. If at $t=0$ an external force F is applied on the block toward right, it starts executing oscillations. Analyse the motion of the block and write the equation of SHM of block by taking origin O at the left wall where spring is connected.

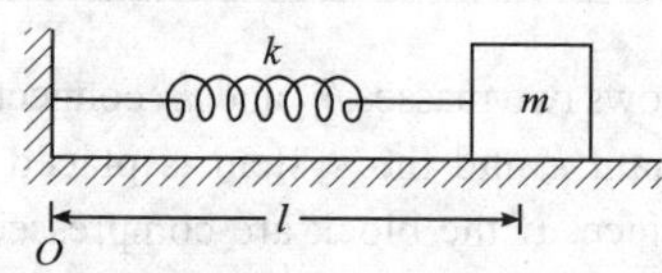

Figure 5.78

Solution

As F force is applied on block, its starts accelerating toward right and its acceleration during motion is given as

$$a=\frac{F-kx}{m}$$

[If x is the displacement of block from its initial position]

After some displacement at $x=F/x$, the block is in equilibrium but gained some velocity so it will move further but now $kx>F$ and it retards and say at $x=l$, it stops thus from work-energy theorem, we have

$$Fl-\frac{1}{2}kl^2=0$$

or $$l=\frac{2F}{k}$$

So it is clear that after equilibrium ($x=F/k$) position it travels a further distance F/k which can be regarded as the amplitude of the SHM of block and we can say that at $t=0$ block was started from its left extreme position i.e. at a distance F/k left of the equilibrium position. About the equilibrium position the SHM equation of block can be written as

$$y=\left(\frac{F}{k}\right)\cos\omega t$$

[As at $t=0$, particle starts from its left extreme position thus its initial phase is $\alpha=3\pi/2$]

If origin is taken at the point O then equation of SHM i.e. the displacement of block as time function about this origin can be written as

$$y=y_0-\frac{F}{k}\cos\omega t$$

Here y_0 is the distance coordinate of mean position of block from origin which is given by

$$y_0=l+\frac{F}{k}$$

Thus equation of SHM for origin O is

$$y=l+\frac{F}{k}(1-\cos\omega t)$$

Here it is important to note that angular frequency of SHM ω is still $\sqrt{\frac{k}{m}}$. There is no effect on the angular frequency due to the presence of external for F, because it is constant.

Always remember that on applying a constant external force on an oscillating system, there is no change in its oscillation frequency. The external force can only change the equilibrium position of oscillations.

Illustrative Example 5.39

Figure-5.79 shows, two balls having charges q_1 connected by a spring of force constant k first ball is fixed in the ceiling and second is hanging vertically in equilibrium. Taking origin at ceiling write the equation of SHM for the motion of hanging ball if at $t = 0$ is given a velocity v_0 in downward direction from equilibrium position. Given that in equilibrium ball with charge q_2 is at a depth y_0 below the ceiling.

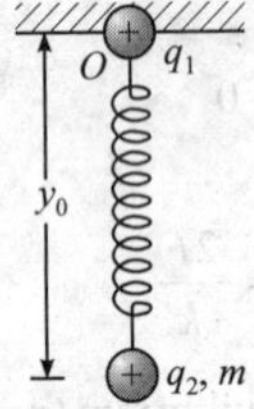

Figure 5.79

Solution

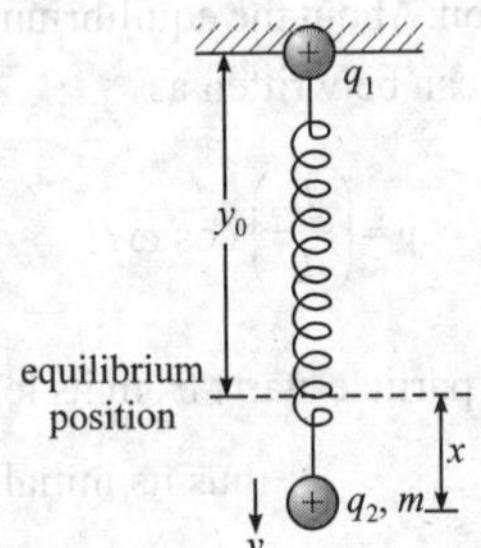

Figure 5.80

Here during oscillations of second ball, we consider it at an intermediate position at a depth x below the equilibrium position and moving downward at speed v, then the total energy of this oscillating system can be written as

$$E_T = \frac{1}{2}mv^2 + \frac{1}{2}k(x+y_0-l)^2 + \frac{kq_1q_2}{(y_0+x)} - mg(x+y_0)$$

[If l is the natural length of spring]

Differentiating with respect to the, we get

$$\frac{dE_T}{dt} = \frac{1}{2}m\left[2v\frac{dv}{dt}\right]$$

$$+\frac{1}{2}k\left(2(x+y_{0-l})\frac{dx}{dt}\right) - \frac{kq_1q_2}{(y_0+x)}\frac{dx}{dt} - mg\frac{dx}{dt} = 0$$

$$\text{or} \quad mva + k(x+y_0-l)v - \frac{kq_1q_2}{(y_0+x)}v - mgv = 0$$

$$\text{or} \quad ma + k(x+y_0-l) - \frac{kq_1q_2}{(y_0+x)^2} - mg = 0 \qquad \ldots(5.112)$$

We know at equilibrium position we have

$$k(y_0 - l) = mg + \frac{kq_1q_2}{y_0^2} \qquad \ldots(5.113)$$

In equation-(5.112) for small x, we have

$$ma + kx + k(y_0 - l) - \frac{kq_1q_2}{y_0^2}\left(1 - \frac{2x}{y_0}\right) - mg = 0 \quad \ldots(5.114)$$

From equation-(5.114) and (5.115)

$$ma + kx + \frac{2kq_1q_2}{y_0^3}x = 0$$

$$\text{or} \quad a = -\left(\frac{k}{m} + \frac{2kq_1q_2}{my_0^3}\right)x$$

Thus angular frequency of oscillations of second ball is given as

$$\omega = \sqrt{\frac{k}{m} + \frac{2kq_1q_2}{my_0^3}}$$

If amplitude of SHM is A then we have at mean position velocity of second ball is V_0, thus

$$V_0 = A\omega \quad \text{or} \quad A = \frac{V_0}{\omega} = \frac{V_0}{\sqrt{\frac{k}{m} + \frac{2kq_1q_2}{my_0^3}}}$$

As ball starts its SHM at $t = 0$ from its mean position, its equation can be given as

$$y = y_0 + A\sin\omega t$$

5.12 *SHM of Free Bodies in Absence of External Forces*

We know for oscillations of a body restoring force must be there due to which the body oscillates about its mean position. In some special cases, it is possible that a system oscillates due to only internal forces and internal forces of system provide the required centripetal force for oscillations. We take an Illustrative example to explain such situation.

Illustrative Example 5.40

Figure-5.81 shows two masses m_1 and m_2 connected by a spring of force constant k and the system is placed on a smooth horizontal surface. If the block are compressed slightly and released. Find the time period of such oscillations.

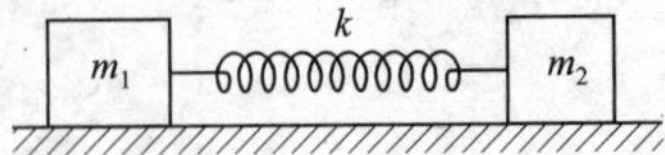

Figure 5.81

Solution

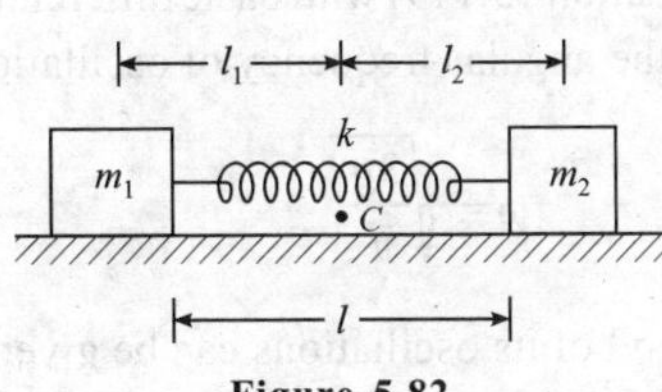

Figure 5.82

As during oscillations of the two blocks, there is no external force present, thus we can state that the centre of mass of the two block system remain at rest during oscillations. In figure-5.82 if C is the centre of mass of the blocks and l is the natural length of the system, then we can say that in this situation point C will remain at rest and with respect to this point m_1 and m_2 will oscillate independently. We can also split the spring in two parts of lengths l_1 and l_2 which are given by

$$l=\frac{m_2 l}{m_1+m_2} \quad \text{and} \quad l_2=\frac{m_1 l}{m_1+m_2}$$

Now if these two springs are assumed to be fixed at point C separately, the case still remains same as in absence of external forces centre of mass of system C remains at rest as shown in figure-5.83. The respective force constants can be given as

$$k_1=\frac{kl}{l_1}=\frac{k(m_1+m_2)}{m_2}$$

and $$k_2=\frac{kl}{l_2}=\frac{k(m_1+m_2)}{m_1}$$

Figure 5.83

Now the angular frequency and time period of oscillations can be directly given from that of a spring block system with one end of the spring fixed as

$$\omega=\sqrt{\frac{k}{m}}$$

Here for mass m_1, we have

$$\omega=\sqrt{\frac{k_1}{m_1}}=\sqrt{\frac{(m_1+m_2)k}{m_1 m_2}} \qquad \ldots(5.115)$$

For m_2, we have

$$\omega=\sqrt{\frac{k_2}{m_2}}=\sqrt{\frac{(m_1+m_2)k}{m_1 m_2}} \qquad \ldots(5.116)$$

Both are same thus both the blocks oscillates with same angular frequency given by equation-(5.115) or (5.116). Thus time period of oscillations of the system is given as

$$T=\frac{2\pi}{\omega}=2\pi\sqrt{\frac{m_1 m_2}{(m_1+m_2)k}}$$

or $$T=2\pi\sqrt{\frac{\mu}{k}} \qquad \ldots(5.117)$$

In equation-(5.117) $\mu=\frac{m_1 m_2}{m_1+m_2}$ is called reduced mass of the system. Reduced mass can also be regarded as mass of one body relative to the second body (assumed to be fixed) in absence of external forces.

Illustrative Example 5.41

Figure-5.84 shows a cart of mass M on which another mass m is placed and attached to a pole on cart by a spring of force constant k. If the friction between m and surface of cart as well as between cart and floor is neglected find the time period of small oscillation of cart-block system.

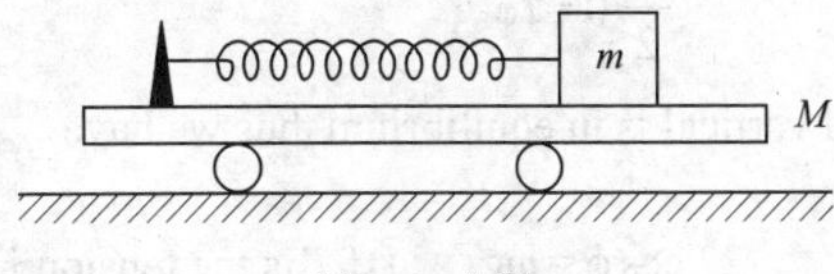

Figure 5.84

Solution

As in problem it is given that there is no friction present any where, this implies to external forces are acting on this system. If we assume cart is fixed at its position, we can consider only the block (with reduced mass μ) is oscillating on its surface, thus time period of oscillating of block can be given as

$$T=2\pi\sqrt{\frac{\mu}{k}} \quad \text{where} \quad \mu=\frac{mM}{m+M}$$

Now we take some more miscellaneous example to understand basic Simple Harmonic Motion in detail.

Illustrative Example 5.42

A uniform rod AB of mass m is suspended by two identical strings of length l as shown in figure-5.85. If this rod is turned by a small angle in horizontal plane about. The vertical axis passing through its centre C. In this process the strings are deviated by a small angle θ_0 from vertical. Then the rod is released to start performing angular oscillations. Find the period of oscillations and the rod's oscillation energy.

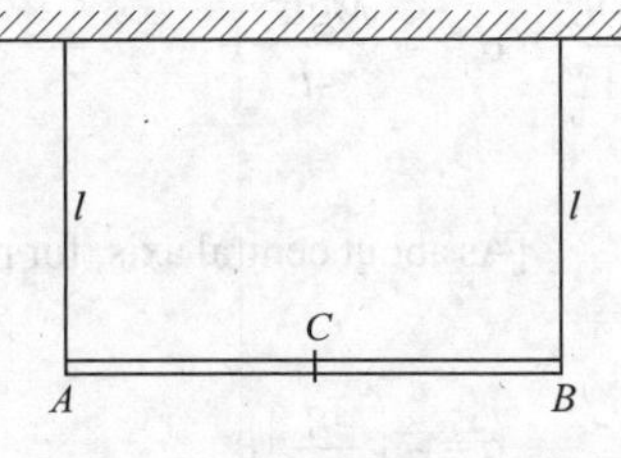

Figure 5.85

Solution

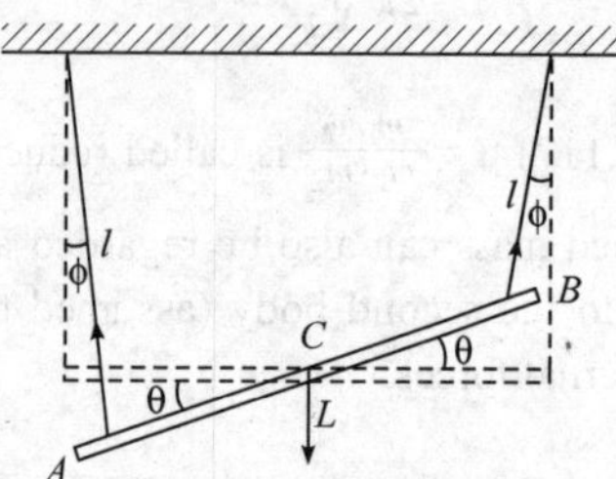

Figure 5.86

Figure-5.86 shows the situation when the rod is in twisted situation if rod is at an angular displacement θ, let string are at deviation φ, if length of rid is l, we have from figure-5.86

$$\frac{L}{2}\theta = l\phi \quad \text{...(5.118)}$$

As the rod vertical is in equilibrium thus we have

$$2T\cos\phi = mg \quad \text{[If } T \text{ is the tension in strings]}$$

For small φ, we have

$$T = \frac{1}{2}mg$$

From figure-5.86, we can see that $T\sin\phi$ on both the ends of rod produces a restoring torque on it which is given as

$$\tau_R = -2T\sin\phi \times \frac{L}{2}$$

[– ve sign for restoring nature]

or $$\tau_R = -\frac{1}{2}mgL\phi \quad \text{[As for small } \phi, \sin\phi \simeq \phi]$$

Now from equation-(5.118)

$$\tau_R = -\frac{1}{2}mgL\left[\frac{L}{2l}\theta\right]$$

If α be the angular acceleration of rod during oscillations, we have

$$\tau_R = I\alpha = -\frac{MgL^2}{4l}\theta$$

or $$\frac{ML^2}{12}\cdot\alpha = -\frac{MgL^2}{4l}\theta$$

[As about central axis, for rod, $I = \frac{ML^2}{12}$]

or $$\alpha = -\left(\frac{3g}{l}\right)\theta \quad \text{...(5.119)}$$

Comparing equation-(5.119) with basic differential equation of SHM, we get the angular frequency of oscillations as

$$\omega = \sqrt{\frac{3g}{l}} \quad \text{...(5.120)}$$

Thus time period of its oscillations can be given as

$$T = \frac{2\pi}{\omega} = 2\pi\sqrt{\frac{l}{3g}} \quad \text{...(5.121)}$$

If is given in the question that initially strings are deflected by an angle θ_0. If β is the angular amplitude of oscillations of rod then from equation-(5.119) we have

$$\frac{L}{2}\beta = l\theta_0$$

or $$\beta = \frac{2l}{L}\theta_0$$

Now we know that the total energy of oscillation of rod can be given as

$$E_T = \frac{1}{2}I\omega^2\beta^2$$

or $$E_T = \frac{1}{2}\left(\frac{ML^2}{12}\right)\left(\sqrt{\frac{3g}{l}}\right)^2\left(\frac{2l}{L}\theta_0\right)^2$$

or $$E_T = \frac{1}{2}Mgl\theta_0^2$$

 # Illustrative Example 5.43

Suppose a tunnel is dug through the earth from one side to the other side along a diameter. Show that the motion of a particle dropped into the tunnel is simple harmonic motion. Find the time period. Neglect all the frictional forces and assume that the earth has a uniform density.

$G = 6.67 \times 10^{-11}\,\text{Nm}^2\,\text{kg}^{-2}$; density of earth $= 5.51 \times 10^3\,\text{kg m}^{-3}$

Solution

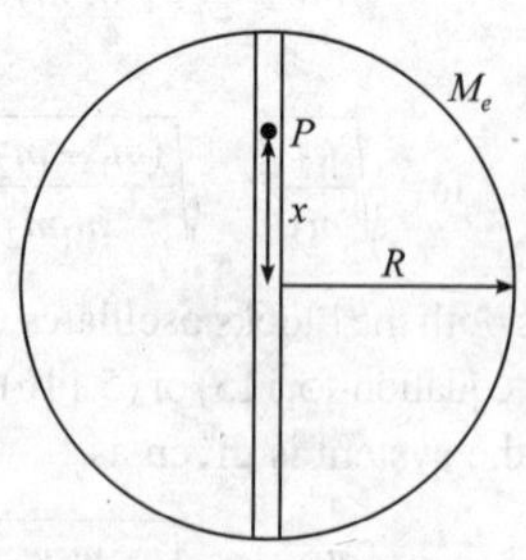

Figure 5.87

Figure-5.87 shows the particle P of mass m, dropped in the turned along diameter of earth at a distance x from the centre of earth.

We know intensity gravitational field inside the earth is given as

$$g_{in} = \frac{GM_e}{R_e^3} \cdot x \quad \dots (5.122)$$

Thus restoring force on particle P towards earth centre can be written as

$$F_R = -mg_{in} = -\frac{GM_e m}{R_e^3} x \quad \dots (5.123)$$

[– ve sign for restoring nature]

In equation-(5.123), restoring force on particle is always towards centre of earth and it is directly proportional to x, thus it shows that motion of particle is simple harmonic and during motion if its acceleration is a, we have

$$a = -\frac{GM_e}{R_e^3} \cdot x$$

Practice Exercise 5.5

(i) Find the angular frequency of SHM of block of mass m for small oscillation of light rod BD. Consider rod is vertical and springs relaxed in initial state.

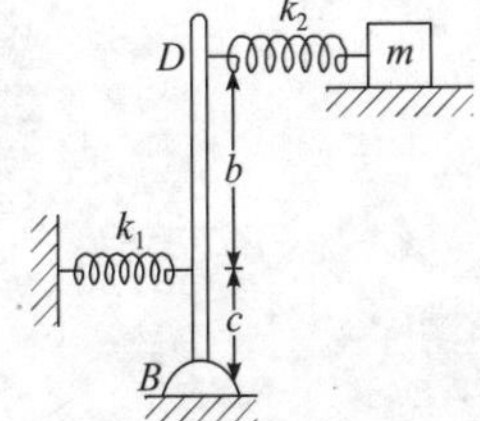

Figure 5.88

$[\omega = \sqrt{\frac{k_1 k_2 c^2}{m\{k_1 c^2 + k_2 (b+c)^2\}}}]$

(ii) A particle of mass m is suspended at the lower end of a thin rod of negligible mass. The upper end of the rod is free to rotate in the plane of the page about a horizontal axis through the point O. The spring is undeformed when the rod is vertical as in figure-5.89. Show that the motion of the particle is SHM if displaced from mean position and hence find the period of oscillation.

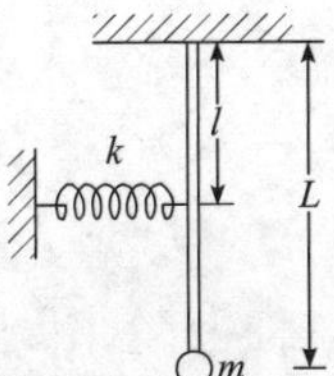

Figure 5.89

$[2\pi \sqrt{\frac{mL^2}{mgL + kl^2}}]$

(iii) The cord is light and inextensible in the spring-mass pulley system as in figure-5.90. Find the frequency of vibration if the mass m is displaced slightly and released. Assume that cord does not slip over pulley.

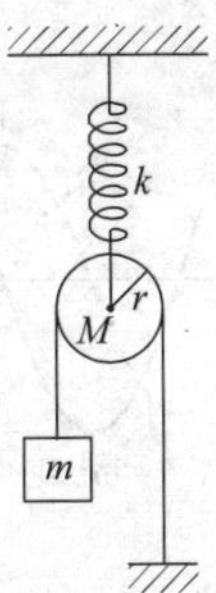

Figure 5.90

$[\omega = \sqrt{\frac{k}{4m + \frac{3M}{2}}}]$

(iv) A uniform semicircular cylinder of radius R and weight W is displaced through a small angle θ from its equilibrium position as shown in the figure-5.91. Find the period of small oscillations if it rolls without slipping when displaced slightly from its equilibrium position.

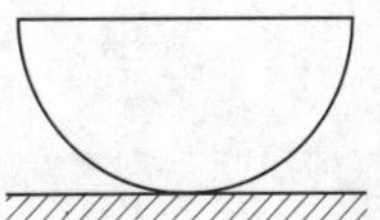
Figure 5.91

$[T = \pi \sqrt{\frac{(9\pi - 16)R}{2g}}]$

(v) In the figure-5.92 shown, the springs are unstretched. The left spring is compressed by $2A$ and then released with mass m which is always attached to it. Find the time to touch right spring. Find maximum compression in right spring and equilibrium position of mass m.

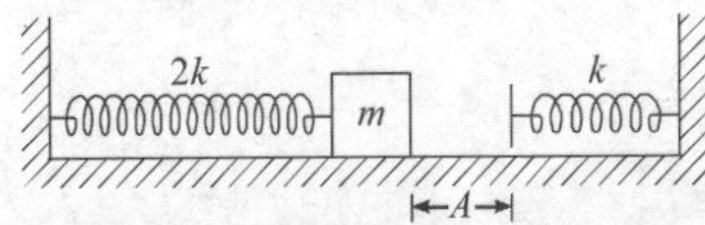

Figure 5.92

$[\frac{\pi}{3}\sqrt{\frac{m}{2k}}, \frac{\sqrt{22}+2}{3}A$; Equilibrium position is at $\frac{2A}{3}$ compression of right spring]

(vi) A point oscillates along the x-axis according to the law $x = a\cos(\omega t - \pi/4)$. Draw the approximate plots

(a) of displacement x, velocity projection v_x, and acceleration projection w_x as functions of time t;

(b) velocity projection v_x and acceleration projection w_x as function of the coordinate x.

[(a) See **Figure 5.93**

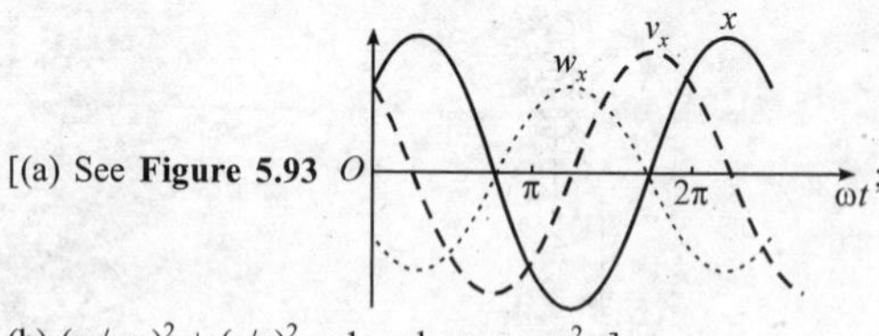

(b) $(v_x/a\omega)^2 + (x/a)^2 = 1$ and $w_x = -\omega^2 x$.]

(vii) A smooth horizontal disc rotates about the vertical axis O (Figure-5.94) with a constant angular velocity ω. A thin uniform rod AB of length l performs small oscillations about the vertical axis A fitted to the disc at a distance a from the axis of the disc. Find the angular frequency of these oscillations.

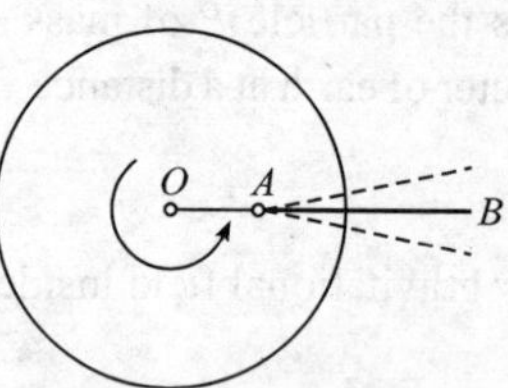

Figure 5.94

[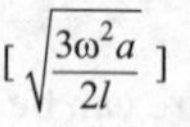 $\sqrt{\frac{3\omega^2 a}{2l}}$]

* * * * *

Discussion Question

Q5-1 A body of mass M is executing SHM on a rough horizontal plane having friction coefficient μ, Plot the variation graph of the restoring force acting on the body as a function of time.

Q5-2 If a body is in SHM of amplitude A and angular frequency ω in a horizontal straight line. If the frequency of SHM is to be changed to 5 ω, and for this we make amplitude of SHM $A/\sqrt{5}$, with supplying any extra energy to it. Will this method work for the required change in angular frequency.

Q5-3 We know during oscillation, a particle comes to rest at its extreme positions. Can we state that the resultant force on the particle becomes zero at this point ?

Q5-4 If a body in accelerated frame of reference experiences a force which is proportional to the displacement of the body from a fixed point and acting towards this point. Will the body executes SHM in this frame.

Q5-5 "In angular SHM, the angular momentum of oscillating body always remains constant". Is this statement true. Explain.

Q5-6 Justify the statement, "In SHM, the graph plotted between the speed of particle with displacement is a parabola".

Q5-7 A pendulum bob thrown from its bottom point in horizontal direction with a velocity sufficient to complete its vertical circle. Does its shadow formed by the sun on ground executes SHM. If bob performs vertical circular motion with a uniform speed the will this shadow executes SHM.

Q5-8 A spherical shell filled with water is suspended from a string to form a simple pendulum. What will be the effect on the time period of this pendulum if the water in the shell freezes. Will it make a difference if the size of the shell is changed.

Q5-9 In previous question if at the bottom of shell a small hole is made through which water start leaking during its oscillation. Find the effect on time period of oscillation during the time the shell will become empty.

Q5-10 Justify the statement, "Two particle in SHM with same mean position same angular frequency but different amplitude, when in same phase crosses their mean position at the same time in same direction".

Q5-11 "When two particles executes SHM with different angular frequencies, they will be in same phase periodically, with a constant time period". Explain.

Q5-12 A simple pendulum is attached to the ceiling of an elevator, at $t = 0$, the bob is in its equilibrium position and thrown horizontally. At the same instant the elevator is released to fall freely. Discuss about the motion followed by the bob now.

Q5-13 When the time period of a simple pendulum is measured by a stop watch, it is advisable to measure the time between consecutive passage through the mean position in the same direction instead of measuring the time between consecutive passage through an extreme position. Why ?

Q5-14 In SHM of a particle can total energy of a particle be negative.

Q5-15 When a pendulum clock is giving right time at equator. Find whether the it will show correct time, it will lose or gain time when it is situated at poles.

Q5-16 What time a pendulum clock will gain or lose when it is in an elevator and the cable supporting elevator is broken.

Q5-17 When the mean position of a particle in SHM with amplitude A, angular frequency ω, is moving along $+x$ direction with a velocity v_0. What would be the equation of SHM of particle with respect to origin. It is given that at $t = 0$, particle was started from origin.

Q5-18 Two clocks, one based on a spring mass pendulum and other based on a simple pendulum are taken to moon. Which clock will be slower there.

Q5-19 A particle is executing SHM with its displacement given as $y = \sin^2 \omega t$. What will be its amplitude and angular frequency of oscillations.

Q5-20 Try to collect at least 10 approximate SHM examples from your general life surroundings.

Q5-21 When the simple pendulum in SHM is damped due to air friction, its amplitude decreases with time which we call damping. Does time period of oscillation also decreases with time.

Q5-22 When a "*crazy ball*" is released from rest at a height 5 m above a hard floor. Can the repeated bounces of the ball be regarded as SHM.

Q5-23 At what points during the oscillations of a simple pendulum, the tension in its string is maximum or minimum ?

Q5-24 When pendulum clocks are made, the lengths used for the pendulums are approximately either 1 m or 0.25 m. What is the advantage of doing this ?

* * * * *

Conceptual MCQs Single Option Correct

5-1 Two particles undergo SHM along parallel lines with the same time period (T) and equal amplitudes. At a particular instant, one particle is at its extreme position while the other is at its mean position. They move in the same direction. They will cross each other after a further time :

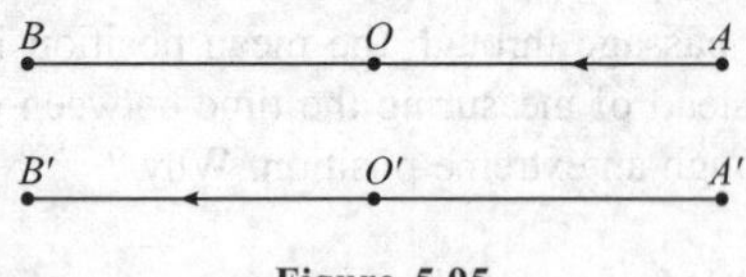

Figure 5.95

(A) T/8 (B) 3T/8
(C) T/6 (D) 4T/3

5-2 A particle of mass 10 gm moves in a field where potential energy per unit mass is given by expression $U = 8 \times 10^4 x^2$ erg/gm. If the total energy of the particle is 8×10^7 erg then the relation between x and time t is :
(A) $x = 10 \sin(400t + \phi)$ cm (B) $x = \sin(400t + \phi)$ m
(C) $x = 10 \sin(40t + \phi)$ cm (D) $x = 100 \sin(4t + \phi)$ m
[ϕ = constant]

5-3 In the resonating air column apparatus, when the air column is vibrated with a tuning fork, the first and the second resonating lengths are measured as l_1 and l_2. When tuning fork of relatively higher frequency is used, the measurement of :
(A) l_1 becomes more
(B) l_2 becomes more
(C) Both l_1 and l_2 become less but more sharp than earlier
(D) It doesnot make any difference in the sharpness

5-4 An accurate pendulum clock is mounted on the ground floor of a high building. How much time will it lose or gain in one day if it is transferred to top story of a building which is h = 200 m higher than the ground floor. Radius of earth is 6.4×10^6 m :
(A) It will lose 6.2 s (B) It will lose 2.7 s
(C) It will gain 5.2 s (D) It will gain 1.6 s

5-5 A child swinging on a swing in sitting position, stands up, then the time period of the swing will :
(A) increase
(B) decrease
(C) remain same
(D) increase if the child is long and decrease if the child is short

5-6 Displacement-time graph of a particle executing SHM is as shown below :

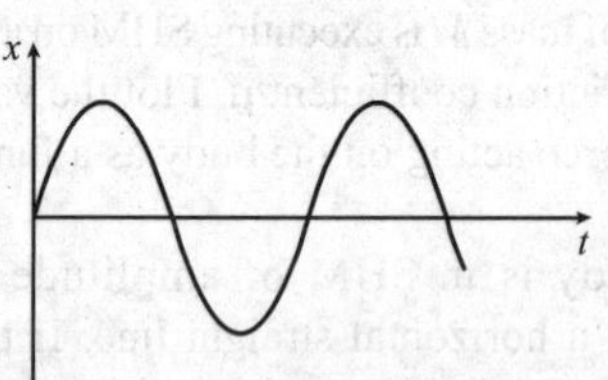

Figure 5.96

The corresponding force-time graph of the particle can be :

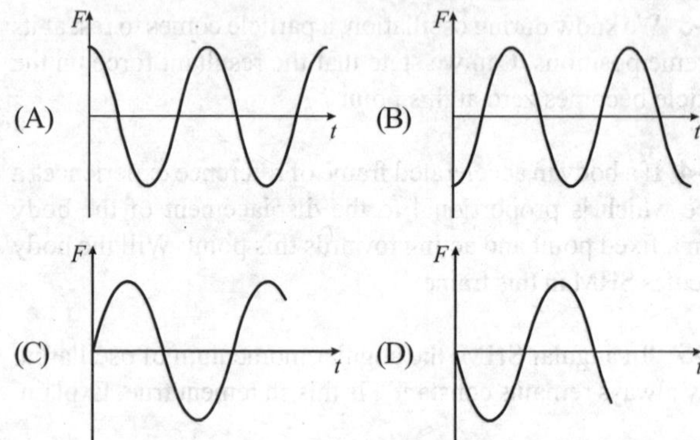

5-7 For a particle undergoing SHM, the velocity is plotted against displacement. The curve will be :
(A) A straight line (B) A parabola
(C) A circle (D) An ellipse

5-8 A body executes simple harmonic motion. The potential energy (PE), the kinetic energy (KE) and total energy (TE) are measured as function of displacement x. Which of the following statements is true ?
(A) KE is maximum when $x = 0$
(B) TE is zero when $x = 0$
(C) KE is maximum when x is maximum
(D) PE is maximum when $x = 0$

5-9 A simple pendulum of frequency n is taken up to a certain height above the ground and then dropped along with its support so that it falls freely under gravity. The frequency of oscillations of the falling pendulum will :
(A) Remains equal to n (B) Become greater than n
(C) Become less than n (D) Become zero

5-10 The function $\sin^2(\omega t)$ represents :
(A) a periodic, but not simple harmonic, motion with a period $2\pi/\omega$
(B) a periodic, but not simple harmonic, motion with a period π/ω
(C) a simple harmonic motion with a period $2\pi/\omega$
(D) a simple harmonic motion with a period π/ω

5-11 Two bodies performing SHM have same amplitude and frequency. Their phases at a certain instant are as shown in the figure-5.97. The phase difference between them is :

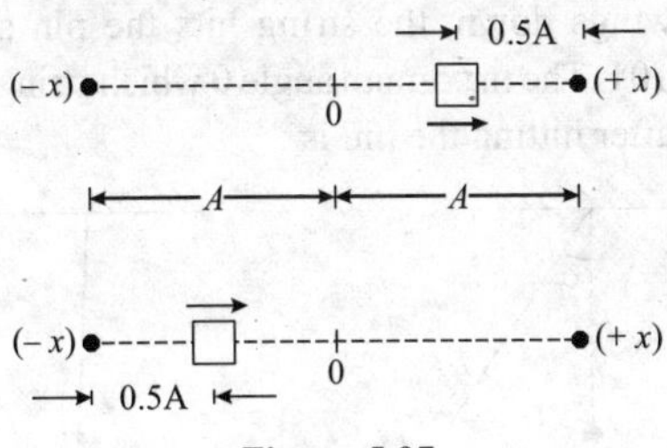

Figure 5.97

(A) $\frac{11}{6}\pi$ (B) π

(C) $\frac{5}{3}\pi$ (D) $\frac{3}{5}\pi$

5-12 A simple pendulum of frequency f has a metal bob. If the bob is charged negatively and is allowed to oscillate with a positively charged plate placed under it, the frequency will :

(A) Remain equal to f (B) Become less than f

(C) Become more than f (D) Become zero

5-13 Two blocks A and B, each of mass m, are connected by a massless spring of natural length L and spring constant k. The blocks are initially resting on a smooth horizontal floor with the spring at its natural length. A third identical block C, also of mass m, moving on the floor with a speed v along the line joining A and B, collides with A elastically (see figure-5.98). Then :

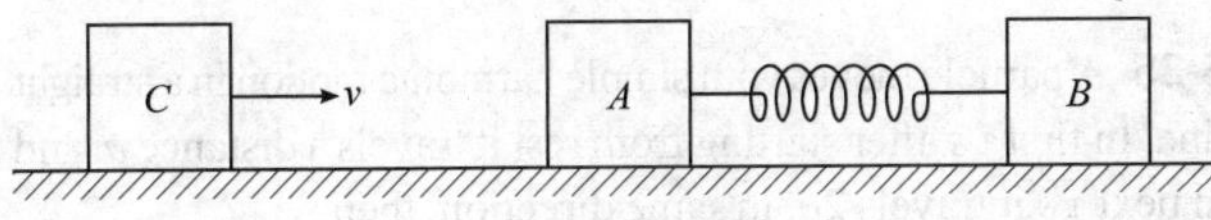

Figure 5.98

(A) The kinetic energy of $A-B$ system at maximum compression of the spring is zero

(B) The kinetic energy of $A-B$ system at maximum compression of the spring is $mv^2/4$

(C) The maximum compression of the spring is $v\sqrt{m/k}$

(D) The maximum compression of the spring is $v\sqrt{2m/k}$

5-14 The displacement y of a particle executing simple harmonic motion is given by

$$y = 4\cos^2\left(\frac{t}{2}\right)\sin(1000\, t)$$

This expression may be considered to be a result of the superposition of how many simple harmonic motions ?

(A) Two (B) Three

(C) Four (D) Five

5-15 A block of mass m is suspended by different springs of force constant shown in figure-5.99. Let time period of oscillation in these four position be T_1, T_2, T_3 and T_4. Then :

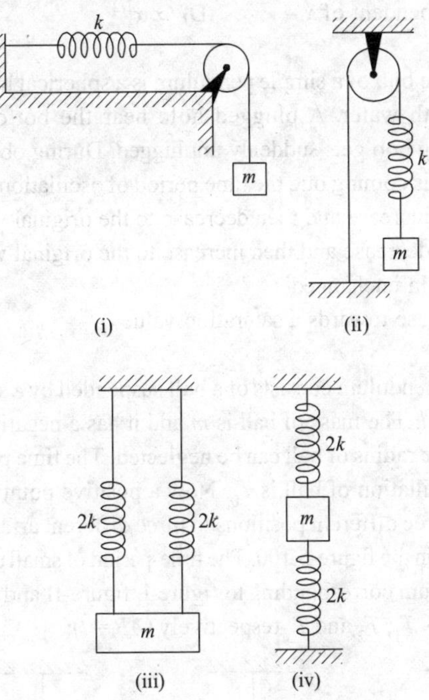

Figure 5.99

(A) $T_1 = T_2 = T_4$ (B) $T_1 = T_2$ and $T_3 = T_4$

(C) $T_1 = T_2 = T_3$ (D) $T_1 = T_3$ and $T_2 = T_4$

5-16 A particle of mass m is attached to a spring (of spring constant k) and has a natural angular frequency ω_0. An external force $F(t)$ proportional to $\cos\omega t(\omega \neq \omega_0)$ is applied to the oscillator. The time displacement of the oscillator will be proportional to :

(A) $\frac{m}{\omega_0^2 - \omega^2}$ (B) $\frac{1}{m(\omega_0^2 - \omega^2)}$

(C) $\frac{1}{m(\omega_0^2 + \omega^2)}$ (D) $\frac{m}{(\omega_0^2 + \omega^2)}$

5-17 A particle free to move along the x-axis has potential energy given by

$$U(x) = k[1 - \exp(-x^2)] \text{ for } -\infty \leq x \leq +\infty$$

where k is a constant of appropriate dimensions. Then :

(A) At points away from the origin, the particle is in unstable equilibrium

(B) For any finite nonzero value of x, there is a force directed away from the origin

(C) If its total mechanical energy is $k/2$, its has its minimum kinetic energy at the origin

(D) For small displacements from $x = 0$, the motion is simple harmonic

5-18 The total energy of a particle, executing simple harmonic motion is :

(A) $\propto x$ (B) $\propto x^2$
(C) independent of x (D) $\propto x^{1/2}$

5-19 The bob of a simple pendulum is a spherical hollow ball filled with water. A plugged hole near the bottom of the oscillating bob gets suddenly unplugged. During observation, till water is coming out, the time period of oscillation would :

(A) first increase and then decrease to the original value
(B) first decrease and then increase to the original value
(C) remain unchanged
(D) increase towards a saturation value

5-20 A pendulum consists of a ball suspended by a silk thread of length l. The mass of ball is m and it has a negative charge $(-Q)$. The radius of ball can be neglected. The time period of a small oscillation of ball is T_0. Now a positive point charge is kept at three different positions in three different arrangements as shown in the figure-5.100. The time-period of small oscillation of pendulum corresponding to figure-I, figure-II and figure-III has values T_1, T_2 and T_3 respectively ($AB = l$):

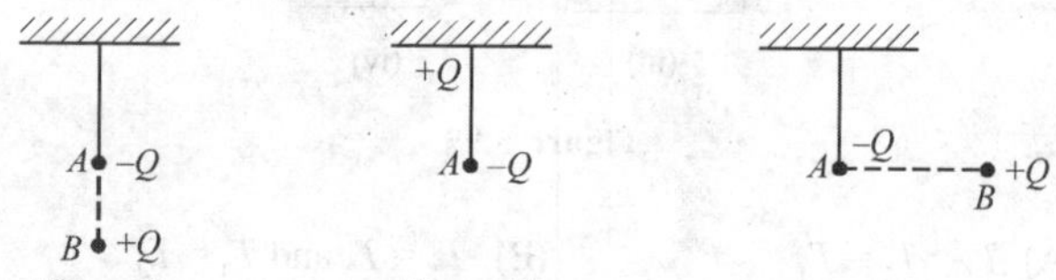

Figure 5.100

Choose the correct statement

(A) $T_0 < T_1 = T_2 < T_3$ (B) $T_2 < T_0 = T_3 < T_1$
(C) $T_1 < T_2 = T_0 < T_3$ (D) $T_3 < T_2 = T_0 < T_1$

5-21 Identify the correct statement:

(A) The fractional change in the time period of a pendulum on changing the temperature is independent of length of pendulum.
(B) As the length of the simple pendulum is increased, the maximum velocity of its bob during the oscillation will also increase.
(C) The greater the mass of pendulum bob the greater is the time period of oscillation.
(D) When the acceleration of the lift in which spring is oscillating is increased, the time period of oscillation also increases.

5-22 A particle at the end of a spring executes simple harmonic motion with a period t_1, while the corresponding period for another spring is t_2. If the period of oscillation with the two springs in series is T, then :

(A) $T = t_1 + t_2$ (B) $T^2 = t_1^2 + t_2^2$
(C) $T^{-1} = t_1^{-1} + t_2^{-1}$ (D) $T^{-2} = t_1^{-2} + t_1^{-2}$

5-23 A simple pendulum consisting of a mass M attached to a string of length L is released from rest at an angle α. A pin is located at a distance l below the pivot point. When the pendulum swings down, the string hits the pin as shown in the figure-5.101. The maximum angle θ which string makes with the vertical after hitting the pin is :

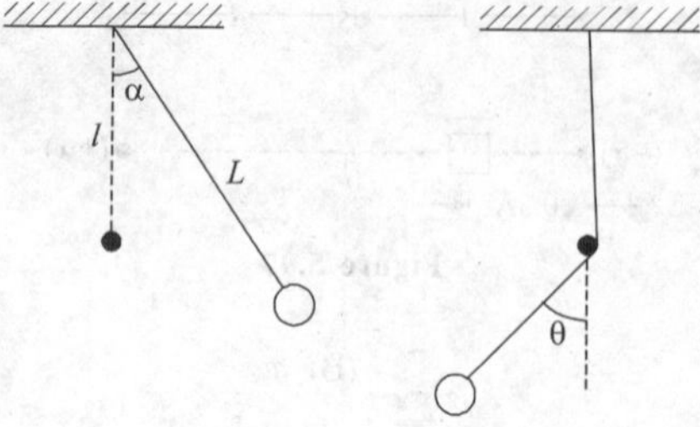

Figure 5.101

(A) $\cos^{-1}\left[\dfrac{L\cos\alpha + l}{L + l}\right]$ (B) $\cos^{-1}\left[\dfrac{L\cos\alpha + l}{L - l}\right]$

(C) $\cos^{-1}\left[\dfrac{L\cos\alpha - l}{L - l}\right]$ (D) $\cos^{-1}\left[\dfrac{L\cos\alpha - l}{L + l}\right]$

5-24 One end of a spring of force constant k is fixed to a vertical wall and the other to a body of mass m resting on a smooth horizontal surface. There is another wall at a distance x_0 from the body. The spring is then compressed by $2x_0$ and released. The time taken to strike the wall is :

(A) $\dfrac{\pi}{6}\sqrt{\dfrac{m}{k}}$ (B) $\sqrt{\dfrac{m}{k}}$

(C) $\dfrac{2\pi}{3}\sqrt{\dfrac{m}{k}}$ (D) $\dfrac{\pi}{4}\sqrt{\dfrac{m}{k}}$

5-25 A particle moves with simple harmonic motion in a straight line. In first τ s after starting from rest it travels a distance a, and in next τ s it travels $2a$, in same direction, then :

(A) amplitude of motion is $3a$
(B) time period of oscillations is 8τ
(C) amplitude of motion is $4a$
(D) time period of oscillations is 6τ

5-26 In a simple harmonic oscillator, at the mean position :

(A) kinetic energy is minimum, potential energy is maximum
(B) both kinetic and potential energies are maximum
(C) kinetic energy is maximum, potential energy is minimum
(D) both kinetic and potential energies are minimum

5-27 If a spring of stiffness 'k' is cut into two parts 'A' and 'B' of length ratio $l_A : l_B = 2 : 3$, then the stiffness of spring 'A' is given by :

(A) $\dfrac{5k}{2}$ (B) $\dfrac{3k}{5}$

(C) $\dfrac{2k}{5}$ (D) k

* * * * *

Numerical MCQs Single Options Correct

5-1 A particle is in a linear SHM. If the acceleration and the corresponding velocity of this particle are 'a' and 'v', then the graph relating to these values is :

(A) 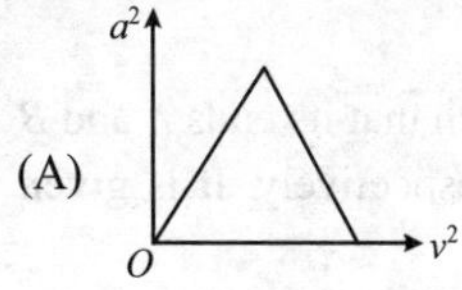

(B) 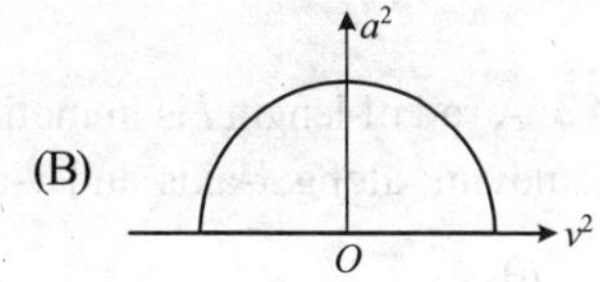

(C) 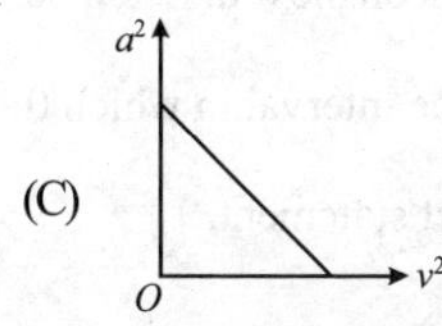

(D) 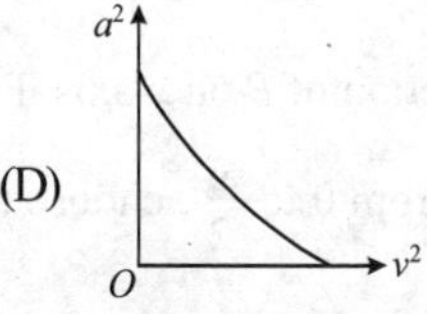

5-2 A particle performs SHM with a time period T and amplitude a. The magnitude of average velocity of the particle over the time interval during which it travels a distance $\frac{a}{2}$ from the extreme position is :

(A) $\frac{a}{T}$ (B) $\frac{2a}{T}$

(C) $\frac{3a}{T}$ (D) $\frac{a}{2T}$

5-3 Two particles P and Q describe SHM of same amplitude a, same frequency f along the same straight line. The maximum distance between the two particles is $a\sqrt{2}$. The phase difference between the particle is :

(A) zero (B) $\frac{\pi}{2}$

(C) $\frac{\pi}{6}$ (D) $\frac{\pi}{3}$

5-4 A particle performs SHM of amplitude A along a straight line. When it is at a distance $\frac{\sqrt{3}}{2}A$ from mean position, its kinetic energy gets increased by an amount $\frac{1}{2}m\omega^2A^2$ due to an impulsive force. Then its new amplitude becomes :

(A) $\frac{\sqrt{5}}{2}A$ (B) $\frac{\sqrt{3}}{2}A$

(C) $\sqrt{2}A$ (D) $\sqrt{5}A$

5-5 A particle of mass 10 gm is placed in a potential field given by $V = (50x^2 + 100)$ J/kg. The frequency of oscillation in cycle/sec is :

(A) $\frac{10}{\pi}$ (B) $\frac{5}{\pi}$

(C) $\frac{100}{\pi}$ (D) $\frac{50}{\pi}$

5-6 A street car moves rectilinearly from station A (here car stops) to the next station B (here also car stops) with an acceleration varying according to the law $f = a - bx$, where a and b are positive constants and x is the distance from station A. The distance between the two stations & the maximum velocity are :

(A) $x = \frac{2a}{b}; v_{max} = \frac{a}{\sqrt{b}}$ (B) $x = \frac{b}{2a}; v_{max} = \frac{a}{b}$

(C) $x = \frac{a}{2b}; v_{max} = \frac{b}{\sqrt{a}}$ (D) $x = \frac{2a}{b}; v_{max} = \frac{\sqrt{a}}{b}$

5-7 AOB is a swing suspended from vertical poles AA' and BB' as shown. If ropes OA' and OB of length l_1 and l_2 respectively are massless, and are perpendicular to each other with a point mass m hanging from O, the time period of the swing for small oscillations perpendicular to the plane of paper is :

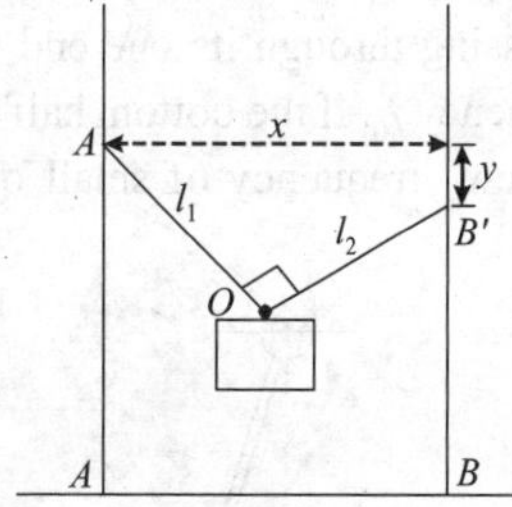

Figure 5.102

(A) $2\pi\sqrt{\frac{l_1l_2}{g\sqrt{x^2+y^2}}}$ (B) $2\pi\sqrt{\frac{(x^2+y^2)^{3/2}}{l_1l_2g}}$

(C) $2\pi\sqrt{\frac{x^2+y^2}{\sqrt{l_1l_2}g}}$ (D) $2\pi\sqrt{\frac{l_1l_2}{x \cdot g}}$

5-8 One end of a spring is tied to a wall and the other end moves at a speed v. If the mass of the spring is m then the kinetic energy of the spring is :

(A) $\frac{1}{2}mv^2$ (B) $\frac{1}{4}mv^2$

(C) $\frac{1}{6}mv^2$ (D) $\frac{1}{3}mv^2$

5-9 Four types of oscillatory systems; a simple pendulum; a physical pendulum; a torsional pendulum and a spring-mass system, each of same time period are taken to the Moon. If time periods are measured on the moon, which system or systems will have it unchanged ?

(A) only spring-mass system
(B) spring-mass system and torsional pendulum
(C) spring-mass system and physical pendulum
(D) None of these

5-10 The coefficient of friction between block of mass m and $2m$ is $\mu = 2\tan\theta$. There is no friction between block of mass $2m$ and inclined plane. The maximum amplitude of two block system for which there is no relative motion between both the blocks.

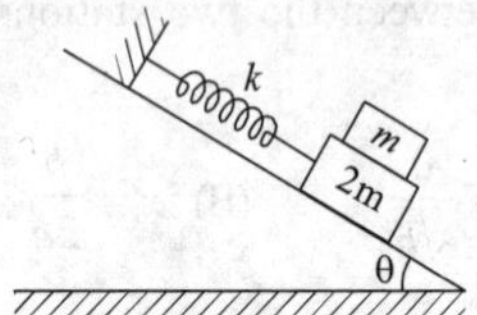

Figure 5.103

(A) $g\sin\theta\sqrt{\frac{k}{m}}$ (B) $\frac{mg\sin\theta}{k}$

(C) $\frac{3mg\sin\theta}{k}$ (D) None of these

5-11 A metre stick swinging in vertical plane about an fixed horizontal axis passing through its one end undergoes small oscillation of frequency f_0. If the bottom half of the stick were cut off, then its new frequency of small oscillation would become:

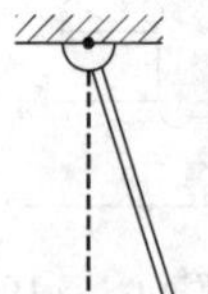

Figure 5.104

(A) f_0 (B) $\sqrt{2}f_0$

(C) $2f_0$ (D) $2\sqrt{2}f_0$

5-12 Find the natural frequency of oscillation of the system as shown in figure-5.105. Pulleys are massless and frictionless. Spring and string are also massless.

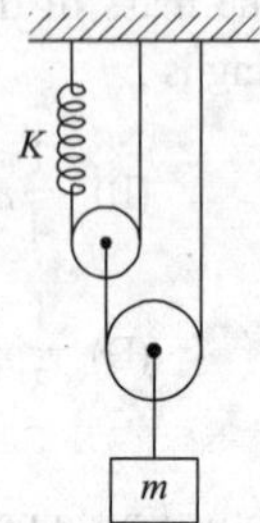

Figure 5.105

(A) $\frac{1}{7\pi}\sqrt{\frac{k}{m}}$ (B) $\frac{1}{2\pi}\sqrt{\frac{k}{m}}$

(C) $\frac{2}{\pi}\sqrt{\frac{k}{m}}$ (D) $\frac{1}{\pi}\sqrt{\frac{2k}{m}}$

5-13 A rod of length l is in motion such that its ends A and B are moving along x-axis and y-axis respectively. It is given that $\frac{d\theta}{dt} = 2$ rad/s always. P is a fixed point on the rod. Let M be the projection of P on x-axis. For the time interval in which θ changes from 0 to $\frac{\pi}{2}$, choose the correct statement,

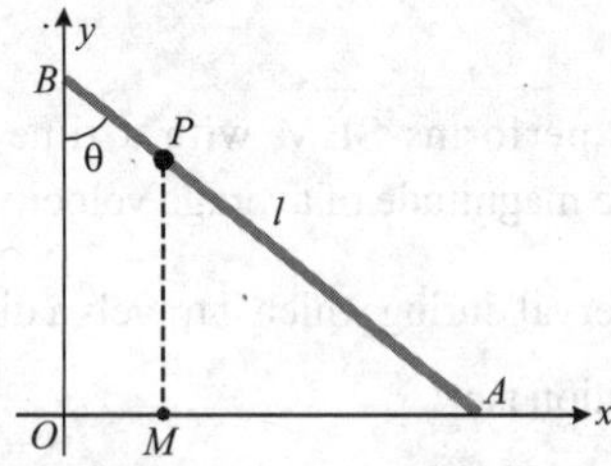

Figure 5.106

(A) The acceleration of M is always directed towards right
(B) M executes SHM
(C) M moves with constant speed
(D) M moves with constant acceleration

5-14 Which of the following is correct about a SHM, along a straight line?

(A) Ratio of acceleration to velocity is constant.
(B) Ratio of acceleration to potential energy is constant.
(C) Ratio of acceleration to displacement from the mean position is constant.
(D) Ratio of acceleration to kinetic energy is constant.

5-15 A body performs SHM along the straight line segment $ABCDE$ with C as the mid point of segment AE (A and E are the extreme position for the SHM). Its kinetic energies at B and D are each one fourth of its maximum value. If length of segment AE is $2R$, then the distance between B and D is:

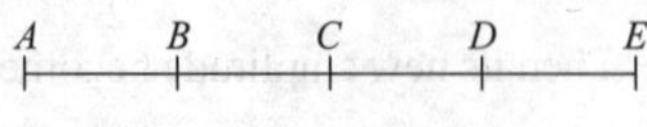

Figure 5.107

(A) $\frac{\sqrt{3}}{2}R$ (B) $\frac{R}{\sqrt{2}}$

(C) $\sqrt{3}R$ (D) $\sqrt{2}R$

5-16 The velocity v of a particle of mass m moving along a straight line changes with time 't' as $\frac{d^2v}{dt^2} = -Kv$ where 'K' is a positive constant. Which of the following statements is correct :

(A) The particle does not perform SHM

(B) The particle performs SHM with time period $2\pi\sqrt{\frac{m}{K}}$

(C) The particle performs SHM with frequency $\frac{\sqrt{K}}{2\pi}$

(D) The particle performs SHM with time period $\frac{2\pi}{K}$

5-17 A horizontal spring-block system of mass 2 kg executes SHM. When the block is passing through its equilibrium position, an object of mass 1 kg is put on it and the two move together. The new amplitude of vibration is (A being its initial amplitude):

(A) $\sqrt{\frac{2}{3}}A$ (B) $\sqrt{\frac{3}{2}}A$

(C) $\sqrt{2}\,A$ (D) $\frac{A}{\sqrt{2}}$

5-18 A uniform square plate of side 'a' is hinged at one of its corners. It is suspended such that it can rotate about horizontal axis. Find out its time period of small oscillation about its equilibrium position :

(A) $\pi\sqrt{\frac{2\sqrt{2}a}{g}}$ (B) $2\pi\sqrt{\frac{2a}{g}}$

(C) $2\pi\sqrt{\frac{\sqrt{2}a}{3g}}$ (D) $2\pi\sqrt{\frac{2\sqrt{2}a}{3g}}$

5-19 A constant force produces maximum velocity V on the block connected to the spring of force constant k as shown in the figure-5.108. When the force constant of spring becomes $4k$, the maximum velocity of the block is (block is at rest when spring is relaxed):

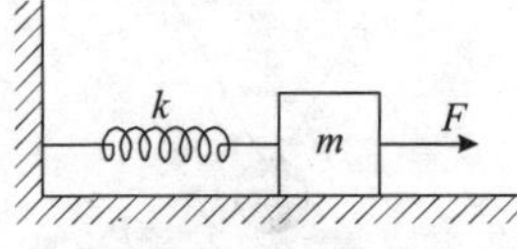

Figure 5.108

(A) $V/4$ (B) $2V$

(C) $V/2$ (D) V

5-20 A horizontal rod of mass m and length L is pivoted smoothly at one end. The rod's other end is supported by a spring of force constant k as shown in figure-5.109. The rod is rotated (in vertical plane) by a small angle θ from its horizontal equilibrium position and released. The angular frequency of the subsequent simple harmonic motion is :

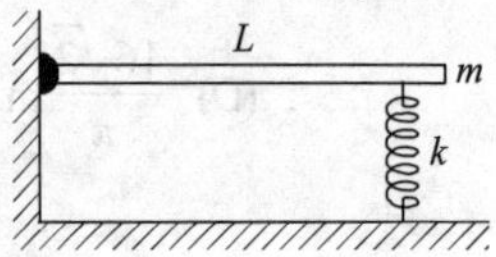

Figure 5.109

(A) $\sqrt{\frac{3k}{m}}$ (B) $\sqrt{\frac{k}{3m}}$

(C) $\sqrt{\frac{3k}{m}+\frac{3g}{2L}}$ (D) $\sqrt{\frac{k}{m}}$

5-21 The oscillations represented by curve 1 in the graph are expressed by equation $x = A \sin\omega t$. The equation for the oscillations represented by curve 2 is expressed as :

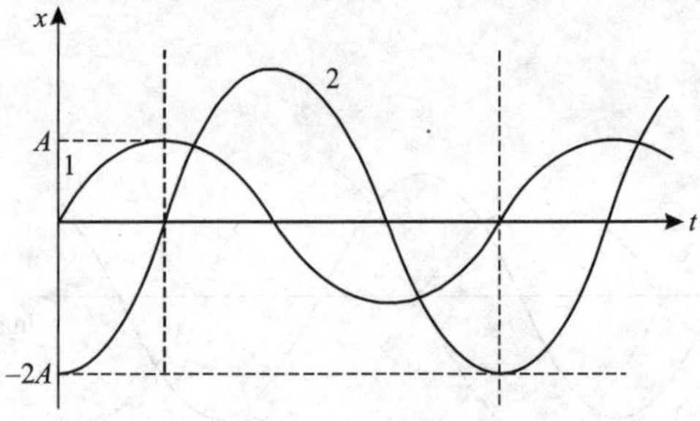

Figure 5.110

(A) $x = 2A \sin(\omega t - \pi/2)$ (B) $x = 2A \sin(\omega t + \pi/2)$

(C) $x = -2A \sin(\omega t - \pi/2)$ (D) $x = A \sin(\omega t - \pi/2)$

5-22 A particle is moving on x-axis has potential energy $U = 2 - 20x + 5x^2$ J along x-axis. The particle is released at $x = -3$. The maximum value of 'x' will be:

[x is in meters and U is in joule]

(A) 5 m (B) 3 m

(C) 7 m (D) 8 m

5-23 The potential energy of a particle executing SHM changes from maximum to minimum in 5 s. Then the time of SHM is :

(A) 5 s (B) 10 s

(C) 15 s (D) 20 s

5-24 A 4 kg particle is moving along the x-axis under the action of the force $F = -\left(\frac{\pi^2}{16}\right)xN$. At $t = 2$ sec, the particle passes through the origin and at $t = 10$ sec its speed is $4\sqrt{2}$ m/s. The amplitude of the motion is :

(A) $\frac{32\sqrt{2}}{\pi}$ m (B) $\frac{16}{\pi}$ m

(C) $\frac{4}{\pi}$ m (D) $\frac{16\sqrt{2}}{\pi}$ m

5-25 Two SHMs $y_1 = a \sin \omega t$ & $y_2 = b \sin \omega t$ are superimposed on a particle. The displacement y_1 & y_2 are along the directions which make angle 37° with each other :

(A) The particle will perform SHM
(B) The particle will not perform SHM
(C) The particle will perform periodic motion but not SHM
(D) The motion will not be oscillatory

5-26 Graph shows the $x(t)$ curves for three experiments involving a particular spring-block system oscillating in SHM. The kinetic energy of the system is maximum at $t = 4$ s for the experiment :

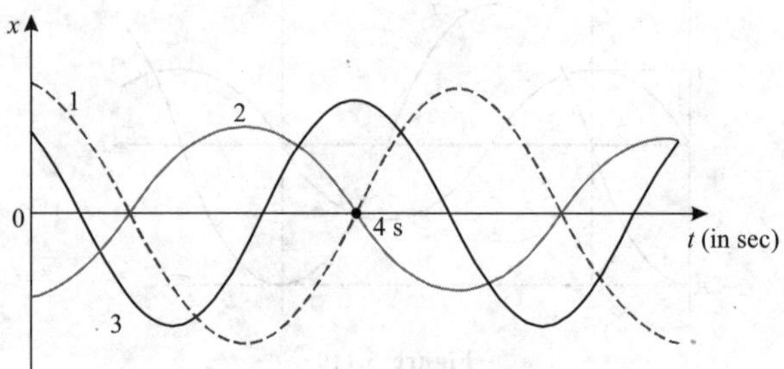

Figure 5.111

(A) 1 (B) 2
(C) 3 (D) Same in all

5-27 A particle is subjected to two simple harmonic motions along x and y directions according to, $x = 3 \sin 100 \pi t$; $y = 4 \sin 100 \pi t$:

(A) Motion of particle will be on ellipse traversing it in clockwise direction
(B) Motion of particle will be on a straight line with slope 4/3
(C) Motion will be a simple harmonic motion along x-axis with amplitude 5
(D) Phase difference between two motions is $\pi/2$

5-28 A small ball is suspended by a thread of length $l = 1$ m at the point O on the wall, forming a small angle $\alpha = 2°$ with the vertical (as shown in figure-5.112). Then the thread with ball was deviated through a small angle $\beta = 4°$ and set free. Assuming the collision of the ball against the wall to be perfectly elastic, find the oscillation period of such a pendulum. (Take $g = \pi^2$)

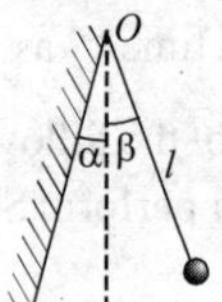

Figure 5.112

(A) $\frac{2}{3}$ sec (B) $\frac{4}{3}$ sec
(C) 2 sec (D) None of these

5-29 A simple pendulum 50 cm long is suspended from the roof of a cart accelerating in the horizontal direction with constant acceleration $\sqrt{3}$ g m/s^2. The period of small oscillations of the pendulum about its equilibrium position is ($g = \pi^2$ m/s^2):

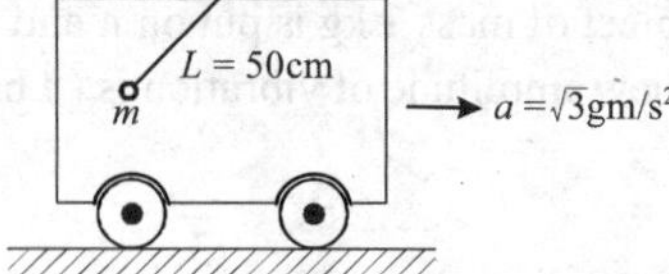

Figure 5.113

(A) 1.0 sec (B) $\sqrt{2}$ sec
(C) 1.53 sec (D) 1.68 sec

5-30 The amplitude of a particle due to superposition of following SHMs. Along the same line is $X_1 = 2 \sin 50 \pi t$; $X_2 = 10 \sin (50 \pi t + 37°)$ $X_3 = -4 \sin 50 \pi t$; $X_4 = -12 \cos 50 \pi t$:

(A) $4\sqrt{2}$ (B) 4
(C) $6\sqrt{2}$ (D) None of these

5-31 Two light strings, each of length l, are fixed at points A and B on a fixed horizontal rod xy. A small bob is tied by both strings and in equilibrium, the strings are making angle 45° with the rod. If the bob is slightly displaced normal to the plane of the strings and released then period of the resulting small oscillation will be :

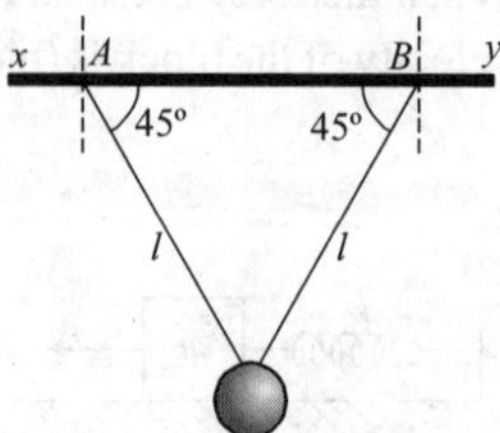

Figure 5.114

(A) $2\pi\sqrt{\frac{2\sqrt{2}l}{g}}$ (B) $2\pi\sqrt{\frac{\sqrt{2}l}{g}}$

(C) $2\pi\sqrt{\frac{l}{g}}$ (D) $2\pi\sqrt{\frac{l}{\sqrt{2}g}}$

5-32 In the figure shown, the time period and the amplitude respectively when m is released from rest when the spring is relaxed is : (the inclined plane is smooth)

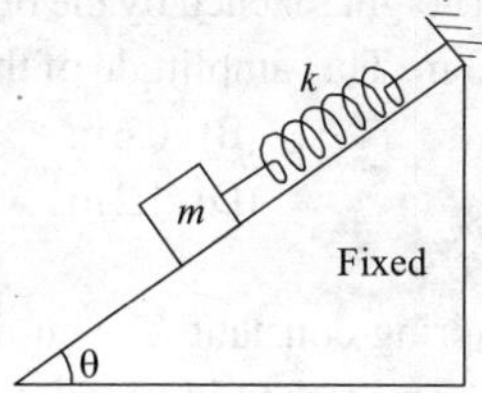

Figure 5.115

(A) $2\pi\sqrt{\frac{m}{k}}, \frac{mg\sin\theta}{k}$ (B) $2\pi\sqrt{\frac{m\sin\theta}{k}}, \frac{2mg\sin\theta}{k}$

(C) $2\pi\sqrt{\frac{m}{k}}, \frac{mg\cos\theta}{k}$ (D) None of these

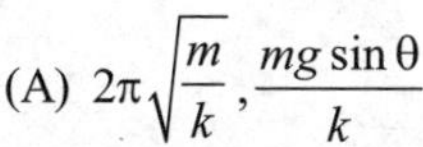

5-33 The acceleration of a certain simple harmonic oscillator is given by $a = -(35.28 \text{ m/s}^2) \cos 4.2t$. The amplitude of the simple harmonic motion is :

(A) 2.0 m (B) 8.4 m
(C) 16.8 m (D) 17.64 m

5-34 Figure shows the kinetic energy K of a simple pendulum versus its angle θ from the vertical. The pendulum bob has mass 0.2 kg. The length of the pendulum is equal to ($g = 10 \text{ m/s}^2$) :

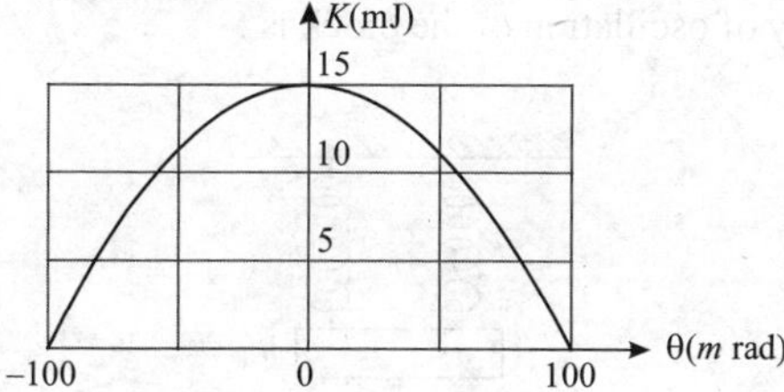

Figure 5.116

(A) 2.0 m (B) 1.8 m
(C) 1.5 m (D) 1.2 m

Comprehension for Q. No. 35 to 38

The acceleration of a particle moving along x-axis is $a = -100x + 50$. It is released from $x = 2$. Here 'a' and 'x' are in *S.I* units. Answer the following question about the motion of this particle :

5-35 The motion of particle will be :

(A) Periodic, oscillatory but not SHM
(B) Periodic but not oscillatory
(C) Oscillatory but not periodic
(D) Simple harmonic

5-36 The speed of the particle at origin will be :

(A) $10\sqrt{2}$ m/s (B) 1.5 m/s
(C) 10 m/s (D) None of these

5-37 The minimum time taken by particle to go from $x = 2$ to $x = 0.5$ is :

(A) $\frac{\pi}{10}$ s (B) $\frac{\pi}{5}$ s

(C) $\frac{\pi}{20}$ s (D) $\frac{\pi}{2}$ s

5-38 The maximum speed of the particle will be :

(A) 10 m/s (B) 20 m/s
(C) 15 m/s (D) Infinity

Comprehension for Q. No. 39 to 40

A particle is moving along the x-axis under the influence of a force given by $F = -5x + 15$. At time $t = 0$, the particle is located at $x = 6$ and is having zero velocity. It takes 0.5 seconds to reach the origin for the first time. Answer the following questions for the motion of this particle.

5-39 The equation of motion of the particle can be represented by :

(A) $x = 3 + 3\cos \pi t$ (B) $x = 3\cos \pi t$
(C) $x = 3 + 3\sin \pi t$ (D) $x = 3 + 3\cos(2\pi t)$

5-40 The mass of the particle is :

(A) $3\pi^2$ (B) $\frac{5\pi^2}{4}$

(C) $\frac{5}{4\pi^2}$ (D) $\frac{1}{3\pi^2}$

Comprehension for Q. No. 41 to 43

A large tank of cross-section area A contains liquid of density ρ. A cylinder of density $\rho/4$ and length l, and cross- section area a ($a << A$) is kept in equilibrium by applying an external vertically downward force as shown. The cylinder is just submerged in liquid. At $t = 0$ the external force is removed instantaneously. Assume that water level in the tank remains constant.

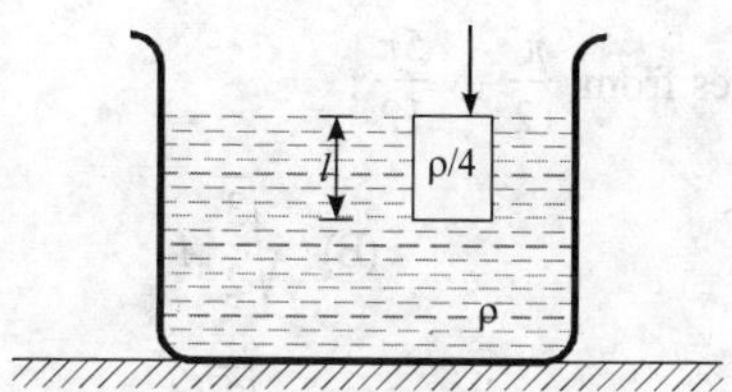

Figure 5.117

5-41 The acceleration of cylinder immediately after the external force is removed is :

(A) g (B) $2g$
(C) $3g$ (D) Zero

5-42 The speed of the cylinder when it reaches its equilibrium position is :

(A) $\frac{1}{2}\sqrt{gl}$ (B) $\frac{3}{2}\sqrt{gl}$
(C) $\sqrt{2gl}$ (D) $2\sqrt{gl}$

5-43 After its release at $t = 0$, the time taken by cylinder to reach its equilibrium position for the first time is :

(A) $\frac{\pi}{8}\sqrt{\frac{l}{g}}$ (B) $\frac{\pi}{3}\sqrt{\frac{l}{g}}$
(C) $\frac{\pi}{4}\sqrt{\frac{l}{g}}$ (D) $\frac{\pi}{2}\sqrt{\frac{l}{g}}$

5-44 Two particles P and Q describe simple harmonic motions of same period, same amplitude along the same line about the same equilibrium position O. When P and Q are on opposite sides of O at the same distance from O they have the same speed of 1.2 m/s in the same direction, when their displacements are same they have the same speed of 1.6 m/s in opposite directions. The maximum velocity in m/s of either particle is :

(A) 3 (B) 2.5
(C) 2.4 (D) 2

5-45 The equation of motion of a particle of mass 1 g is $\frac{d^2x}{dt^2} + \pi^2 x = 0$ where x is displacement (in m) from mean position. The frequency of oscillation is (in Hz):

(A) $\frac{1}{2}$ (B) 2
(C) $5\sqrt{10}$ (D) $\frac{1}{5\sqrt{10}}$

5-46 A particle executes SHM of amplitude A and time period T. The distance travelled by the particle in the duration its phase changes from $\frac{\pi}{12}$ to $\frac{5\pi}{12}$:

(A) $\frac{1}{\sqrt{2}}A$ (B) $\sqrt{\frac{3}{2}}A$
(C) $\frac{2}{\sqrt{3}}A$ (D) $\sqrt{\frac{2}{3}}A$

5-47 An object moves vertically with simple harmonic motion just behind a wall. From the other side of the wall the object is visible in each cycle for 2.0 s and hidden behind the wall for 6.0 s The maximum height reached by the object relative to the top of the wall is 0.3 m. The amplitude of the motion is :

(A) 0.5 m (B) 0.6 m
(C) 1.0 m (D) 1.2 m

5-48 A spring of spring constant K is cut into n equal parts, out of which r parts are placed in parallel & connected with mass M as shown in figure. The time period of oscillatory motion of mass M is:

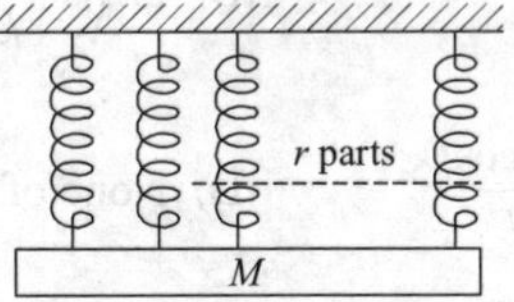

Figure 5.118

(A) $T = 2\pi\sqrt{\frac{M}{nrK}}$ (B) $T = 2\pi\sqrt{\frac{nrM}{K}}$
(C) $T = 2\pi\sqrt{\frac{rM}{nK}}$ (D) $T = 2\pi\sqrt{\frac{nM}{rK}}$

5-49 In the figure all springs are identical having spring constant k and mass m each. The block also has mass m. The frequency of oscillation of the block is :

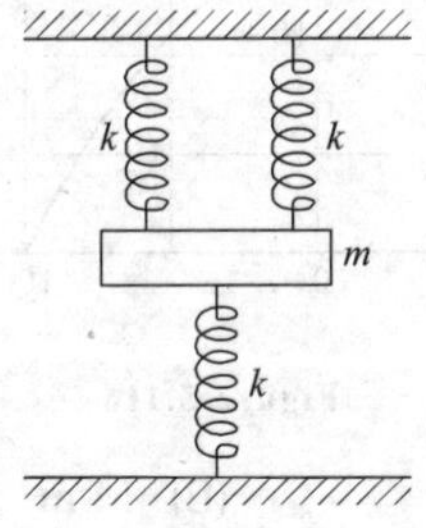

Figure 5.119

(A) $\frac{1}{2\pi}\sqrt{\frac{3k}{m}}$ (B) $\frac{1}{2\pi}\sqrt{\frac{3k}{2m}}$
(C) $2\pi\sqrt{\frac{3m}{3k}}$ (D) None of these

5-50 A block of mass 'm' is suspended from a spring and executes vertical SHM of time period T as shown in figure-5.120. The amplitude of the SHM is A and spring is never in compressed state during the oscillation. The magnitude of minimum force exerted by spring on the block is :

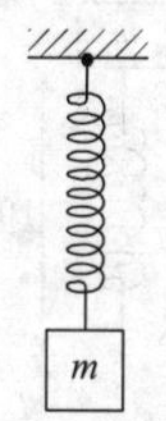

Figure 5.120

(A) $mg - \frac{4\pi^2}{T^2}mA$ (B) $mg + \frac{4\pi^2}{T^2}mA$

(C) $mg - \frac{\pi^2}{T^2}mA$ (D) $mg + \frac{\pi^2}{T^2}mA$

5-51 The spring block system as shown in figure is in equilibrium. The string connecting blocks A and B is cut. The mass of all the three blocks is m and spring constant of both the spring is k. The amplitude of resulting oscillation of block A is :

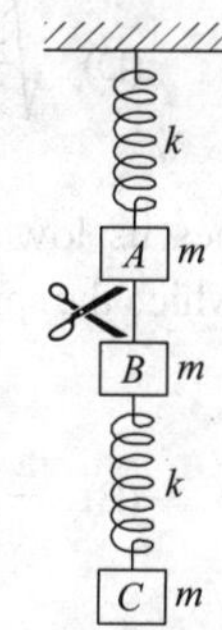

Figure 5.121

(A) $\frac{mg}{k}$ (B) $\frac{2mg}{k}$

(C) $\frac{3mg}{k}$ (D) $\frac{4mg}{k}$

5-52 The displacement y (in cm) produced by a simple harmonic wave is given by :

$y = \frac{10}{\pi}\sin\left[2000\pi t - \frac{\pi x}{17}\right]$. The time period and maximum velocity of the particles in the medium will respectively be :

(A) 10^{-3} s, 330 ms^{-1} (B) 10^{-4} s, 20 ms^{-1}

(C) 10^{-3} s, 200 ms^{-1} (D) 10^{-2} s, 2000 ms^{-1}

5-53 In a horizontal spring-mass system, mass m is released after being displaced towards right by some distance at $t = 0$ on a frictionless surface. The phase angle of the motion in radian when it is first time passing through the equilibrium position is equal to :

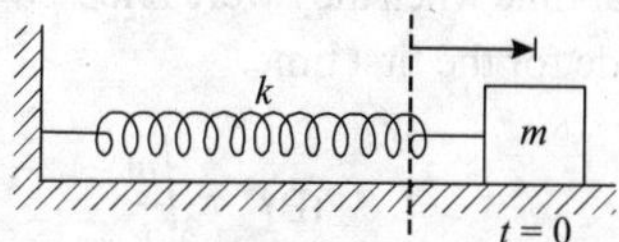

Figure 5.122

(A) $\pi/2$ (B) π

(C) $3\pi/2$ (D) 0

5-54 A system is shown in the figure-5.123. The time period for small oscillations of the two blocks will be.

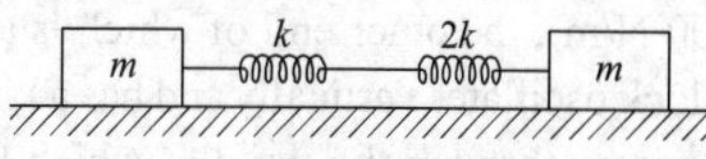

Figure 5.123

(A) $2\pi\sqrt{\frac{3m}{k}}$ (B) $2\pi\sqrt{\frac{3m}{2k}}$

(C) $2\pi\sqrt{\frac{3m}{4k}}$ (D) $2\pi\sqrt{\frac{3m}{8k}}$

Comprehension for Q. No. 55 to 57

Two identical blocks P and Q have mass m each. They are attached to two identical springs (of spring constant k) initially unstretched. Both the blocks are initially in contact as shown. Now the left spring (attached with block P) is compressed by $\frac{A}{2}$ and the right spring (attached with block Q) is compressed by A. Both the blocks are then released simultaneously.

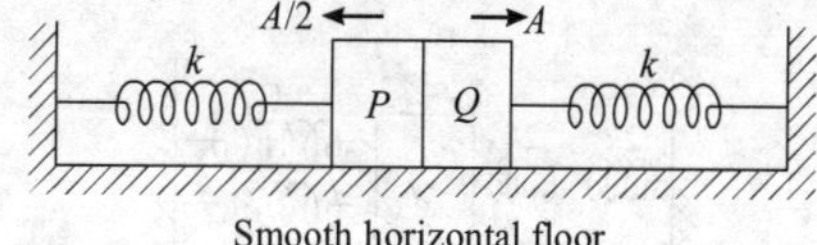

Figure 5.124

5-55 The speed of block P just before P and Q are about to collide for the first time.

(A) $\sqrt{\frac{k}{m}}\frac{A}{2}$ (B) $\sqrt{\frac{k}{m}}A$

(C) $\sqrt{\frac{k}{2m}}A$ (D) None of these

5-56 The speed of block Q just before P and Q are about to collide for the first time.

(A) $\sqrt{\frac{k}{m}}\frac{A}{2}$ (B) $\sqrt{\frac{k}{m}}A$

(C) $\sqrt{\frac{k}{2m}}A$ (D) None of these

5-57 After what time when they were released from rest, shall the blocks collide for the first time.

(A) $\frac{\pi}{2}\sqrt{\frac{m}{k}}$ (B) $\pi\sqrt{\frac{m}{k}}$

(C) $\frac{\pi}{3}\sqrt{\frac{m}{k}}$ (D) None of these

Comprehension for Q. No. 58 to 59

A block weighing 10 N is attached to the lower end of a vertical spring ($k = 200$ N/m), the other end of which is attached to a ceiling. The block oscillates vertically and has a kinetic energy of 2.0 J as it passes through the point at which the spring is unstretched. Answer the following questions for the motion of this block.

5-58 Maximum kinetic energy of the block as it oscillates is : ($g = 10$ m/s^2)

(A) 2.0 J (B) 2.25 J
(C) 2.5 J (D) 2.64 J

5-59 The amplitude of the oscillation of block is :

(A) $10\sqrt{2}$ cm (B) $5\sqrt{2}$ cm
(C) 15 cm (D) 20 cm

5-60 Four massless springs whose force constants are $2k$, $2k$, k and $2k$ respectively are attached to a mass M kept on a frictionless plane (as shown in figure). If the mass M is displaced in the horizontal direction, then the frequency of the system.

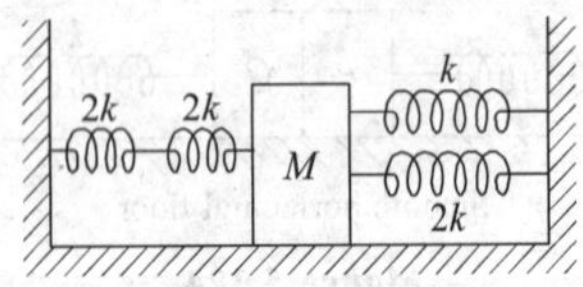

Figure 5.125

(A) $\frac{1}{2\pi}\sqrt{\frac{k}{4M}}$ (B) $\frac{1}{2\pi}\sqrt{\frac{4k}{M}}$

(C) $\frac{1}{2\pi}\sqrt{\frac{k}{7M}}$ (D) $\frac{1}{2\pi}\sqrt{\frac{7k}{M}}$

Comprehension for Q. No. 61 to 63

A small block of mass m is fixed at upper end of a massless vertical spring of spring constant $K = \frac{4mg}{L}$ and natural length '$10L$'. The lower end of spring is free and is at a height L from fixed horizontal floor as shown. The spring is initially unstressed and the spring-block system is released from rest in the shown position.

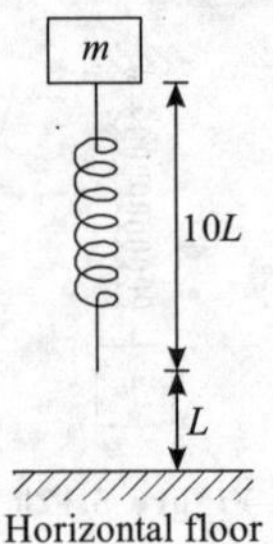

Figure 5.126

5-61 At the instant speed of block is maximum, the magnitude of force exerted by spring on the block is :

(A) $\frac{mg}{2}$ (B) mg
(C) Zero (D) None of these

5-62 As the block is coming down, the maximum speed attained by the block is :

(A) $\sqrt{gL}$ (B) $\sqrt{3gL}$

(C) $\frac{3}{2}\sqrt{gL}$ (D) $\sqrt{\frac{3}{2}gL}$

5-63 Till the block reaches its lowest position for the first time, the time duration for which the spring remains compressed is :

(A) $\pi\sqrt{\frac{L}{2g}} + \sqrt{\frac{L}{4g}}\sin^{-1}\frac{1}{3}$ (B) $\frac{\pi}{4}\sqrt{\frac{L}{g}} + \sqrt{\frac{L}{4g}}\sin^{-1}\frac{1}{3}$

(C) $\pi\sqrt{\frac{L}{2g}} + \sqrt{\frac{L}{4g}}\sin^{-1}\frac{2}{3}$ (D) $\frac{\pi}{2}\sqrt{\frac{L}{2g}} + \sqrt{\frac{L}{4g}}\sin^{-1}\frac{2}{3}$

5-64 The bob of a simple pendulum, which is in the shape of a hollow cylinder of mass M, radius r and length h is suspended by a long string (the mass of the base and lid of the cylinder are negligible). The cylinder is filled with a liquid of density ρ upto a height of x. Then the value of x for which the time period of the pendulum is maximum, is given by which of the following equations : ($\lambda = \pi r^2\rho$)

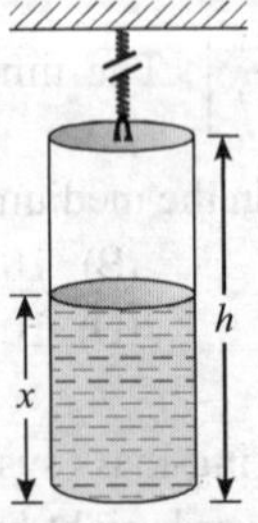

Figure 5.127

(A) $\lambda x^2 - 2Mx + Mh = 0$ (B) $\lambda x^2 + 2Mx + Mh = 0$
(C) $x = H/2$ (D) $\lambda x^2 + 2Mx - Mh = 0$

5-65 A block of mass 'm' is attached to a spring in natural length of spring constant 'k'. The other end A of the spring is moved with a constant velocity v away from the block. Find the maximum extension in the spring.

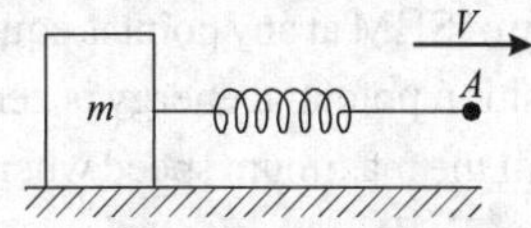

Figure 5.128

(A) $\frac{1}{4}\sqrt{\frac{mv^2}{k}}$ (B) $\sqrt{\frac{mv^2}{k}}$

(C) $\frac{1}{2}\sqrt{\frac{mv^2}{k}}$ (D) $2\sqrt{\frac{mv^2}{k}}$

5-66 A straight rod of negligible mass is mounted on a frictionless pivot and masses 2.5 kg and 1 kg are suspended at distances 40 cm and 100 cm respectively from the pivot as shown. The rod is held at an angle θ with the horizontal and released.

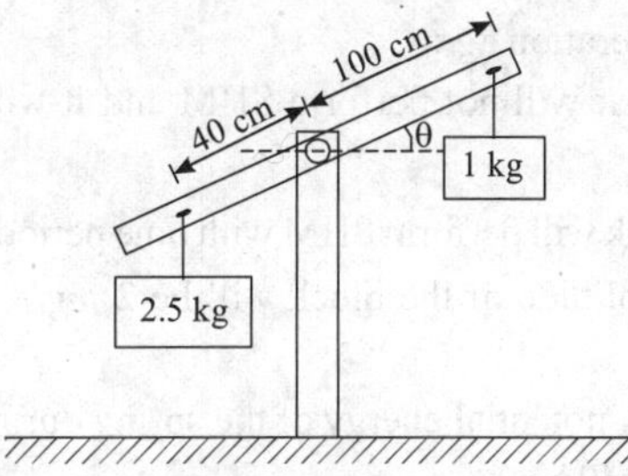

Figure 5.129

(A) The rod executes periodic motion about horizontal position after the release

(B) The rod remains stationary after the release

(C) The rod comes to rest in vertical position with 2.5 kg mass at the lowest point

(D) The rod executes periodic motion about vertical position after the release

5-67 A particle of mass $m = 2$ kg executes SHM in xy-plane between points A and B under action of force $\vec{F} = F_x\hat{i} + F_y\hat{j}$. Minimum time taken by particle to move from A to B is 1 sec. At $t = 0$ the particle is at $x = 2$ and $y = 2$. Then F_x as function of time t is :

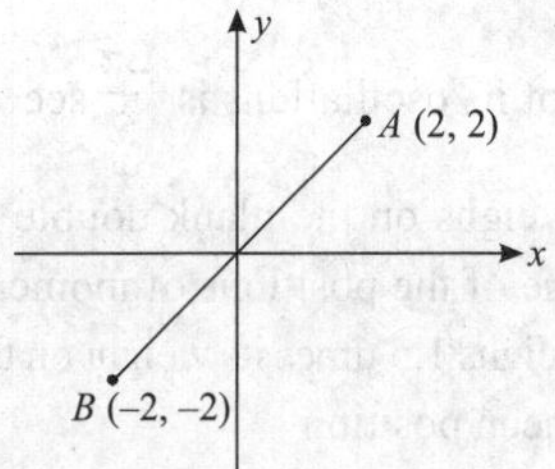

Figure 5.130

(A) $-4\pi^2 \sin \pi t$ (B) $-4\pi^2 \cos \pi t$

(C) $4\pi^2 \cos \pi t$ (D) None of these

5-68 A system of two identical rods (L-shaped) of mass m and length l are resting on a peg P as shown in the figure-5.131. If the system is displaced in its plane by a small angle θ, find the period of oscillations :

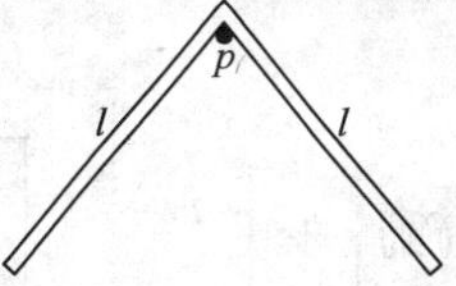

Figure 5.131

(A) $2\pi\sqrt{\frac{\sqrt{2}l}{3g}}$ (B) $2\pi\sqrt{\frac{2\sqrt{2}l}{3g}}$

(C) $2\pi\sqrt{\frac{2l}{3g}}$ (D) $3\pi\sqrt{\frac{1}{3g}}$

7-69 In this case one end of a long iron chain of linear mass density λ is fixed to a sphere of mass m and specific gravity 1/3 while the other end is free. The sphere along with the chain is immersed in a deep lake. If specific gravity of iron is 7 the sphere is slightly displaced vertically from its equilibrium position, the time period of the resulting SHM is :

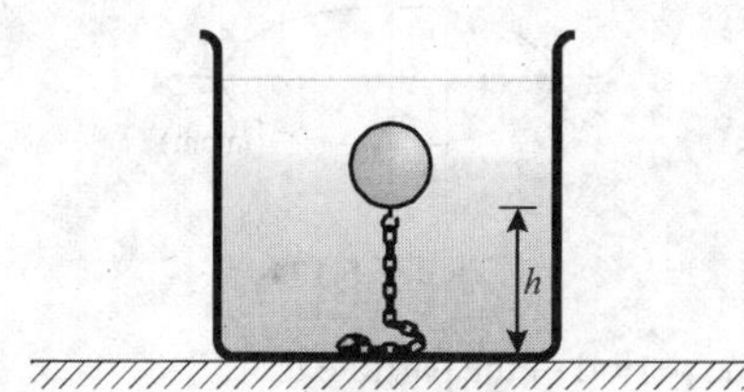

Figure 5.132

(A) $\frac{4\pi}{7}\sqrt{\frac{46m}{\lambda g}}$ (B) $\frac{2\pi}{3}\sqrt{\frac{35m}{\lambda g}}$

(C) $\frac{2\pi}{3}\sqrt{\frac{35\lambda}{mg}}$ (D) $\frac{4\pi}{7}\sqrt{\frac{46\lambda}{mg}}$

5-70 A particle undergoes SHM with a time period of 2 seconds. In how much time will it travel from its mean position to a displacement equal to half of its amplitude :

(A) 1/2 sec (B) 1/3 sec

(C) 1/4 sec (D) 1/6 sec

* * * * *

Advance MCQs with One or More Options Correct

5-1 Two blocks of masses 3 kg and 6 kg rest on a horizontal smooth surface. The 3 kg block is attached to a spring with a force constant $k = 900\ \text{Nm}^{-1}$ which is compressed 2 m from the equilibrium position as shown in figure-5.133. The 6 kg mass is at rest at 1 m from mean position. 3 kg mass strikes the 6 kg mass and the two stick together :

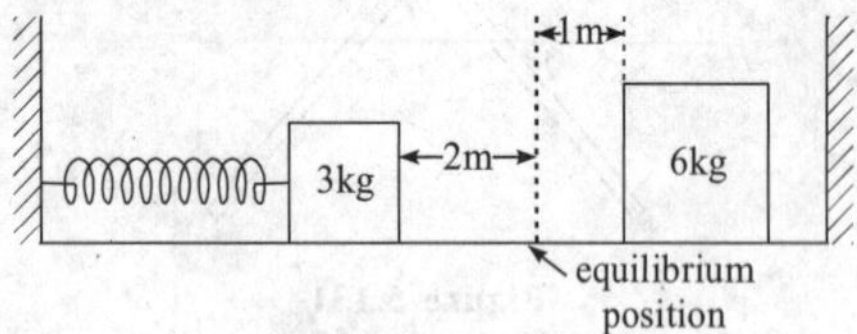

Figure 5.133

(A) Velocity of the combined masses immediately after the collision is $10\ \text{ms}^{-1}$

(B) Velocity of the combined masses immediately after the collision is $5\ \text{ms}^{-1}$

(C) Amplitude of the resulting oscillation is $\sqrt{2}$ m

(D) Amplitude of the resulting oscillation is $\sqrt{5/2}$ m

5-2 The figure-5.134 shows a graph between velocity and displacement (from mean position) of a particle performing SHM :

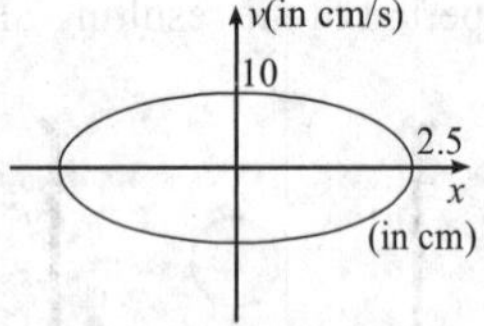

Figure 5.134

(A) The time period of the particle is 1.57 s

(B) The maximum acceleration will be $40\ \text{cm/s}^2$

(C) The velocity of particle is $2\sqrt{21}$ cm/s when it is at a distance 1 cm from the mean position.

(D) None of these

5-3 A particle moves in xy plane according to the law $x = a \sin \omega t$ and $y = a(1 - \cos \omega t)$ where a and ω are constants. The particle traces :

(A) A parabola

(B) A straight line equally inclined to x and y axes

(C) A circle

(D) A distance proportional to time

5-4 The amplitude of a particle executing SHM about O is 10 cm. Then :

(A) When the K.E. is 0.64 of its maximum K.E. its displacement is 6 cm from O.

(B) When the displacement is 5 cm from O its K.E. is 0.75 times its maximum K.E.

(C) Its total energy of SHM at any point is equal to its maximum K.E if at mean position potential energy is zero

(D) Its speed is half the maximum speed when its displacement is half the maximum displacement.

5-5 A linear harmonic oscillator of force constant 2×10^6 N/m and amplitude 0.01 m has a total mechanical energy of 160 J. Its :

(A) Maximum potential energy is 100 J

(B) Maximum kinetic energy is 100 J

(C) Maximum potential energy is 160 J

(D) Minimum potential energy is zero

5-6 A spring of spring constant K is fixed to the ceiling of a lift. The other end of the spring is attached to a block of mass m. The mass is in equilibrium. Now the lift accelerates downwards with an acceleration $2g$:

(A) The block will not perform SHM and it will stick to the ceiling.

(B) The block will perform SHM with time period $2\pi\sqrt{m/K}$.

(C) The amplitude of the block will be $2\ mg/K$ if it perform SHM.

(D) The min. potential energy of the spring during the motion of the block will be 0.

5-7 The potential energy U of a particle is given by $U = 20 + (x - 4)^2$ J. Total mechanical energy of the particle is 36 J. Select the correct alternative(s) :

(A) The particle oscillates about point $x = 4$ m

(B) The amplitude of the particle is 4 m

(C) The kinetic energy of the particle at $x = 2$ m is 12 J

(D) The motion of the particle is periodic but not simple harmonic.

5-8 A block is placed on a horizontal plank. The plank is performing SHM along a vertical line with amplitude of 40 cm. The block just loses contact with the plank when the plank is momentarily at rest. Then :

(A) The period of its oscillations is $\frac{2\pi}{5}$ sec

(B) The block weighs on the plank double its weight, when the plank is at one of the positions of momentary rest

(C) The block weighs 1.5 times its weight on the plank, halfway down from the mean position

(D) The block weighs is true weight on the plank, when velocity of the plank is maximum

5-9 Speed v of a particle moving along a straight line, when it is at a distance x from a fixed point on the line is given by $v^2 = 108 - 9x^2$ (all quantities in S.I. unit). Then :

(A) The motion is uniformly accelerated along the straight line

(B) The magnitude of the acceleration at a distance 3 cm from the fixed point is 0.27 m/s^2

(C) The motion is simple harmonic about the given fixed point

(D) The maximum displacement from the fixed point is 4 cm.

5-10 The system shown in the figure-5.135 can move on a smooth surface. The spring is initially compressed by 6 cm and then released :

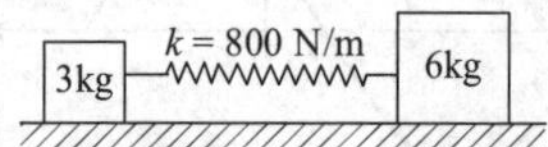

Figure 5.135

(A) The particles perform SHM with time period $\frac{\pi}{10}$ sec.

(B) The block of mass 3 kg perform SHM with amplitude 4 cm.

(C) The block of mass 6 kg will have maximum momentum 2.40 kgm/s

(D) Their time periods will be in the ratio of $1 : \sqrt{2}$

5-11 Two blocks A(5 kg) and B(2 kg) attached to the ends of a spring constant 1120 N/m are placed on a smooth horizontal plane with the spring undeformed. Simultaneously velocities of 3 m/s and 10 m/s along the line of the spring in the same direction are imparted to A and B then :

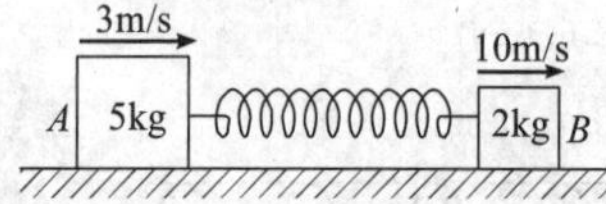

Figure 5.136

(A) When the extension of the spring is maximum the velocities of A and B are zero.

(B) The maximum extension of the spring is 25 cm.

(C) The first maximum compression occurs $3\pi/56$ seconds after start.

(D) Maximum extension and maximum compression occur alternately.

5-12 A simple pendulum of length 1 m with a bob of mass m swings with an angular amplitude 10°. Then : ($g = 10$ m/s$^2 = \pi^2$)

(A) Time period of pendulum is 2 s

(B) Tension in the string is greater than $mg \cos 5°$ at angular displacement 5°

(C) Rate of change of speed at angular displacement 5° is $g \sin 5°$

(D) Tension in the string is $mg \cos 5°$ at angular displacement 5°

5-13 A constant force F is applied on a spring block system as shown in figure-5.137. The mass of the block is m and spring constant is k. The block is placed over a smooth surface. Initially the spring was unstretched. Choose the correct alternative(s) :

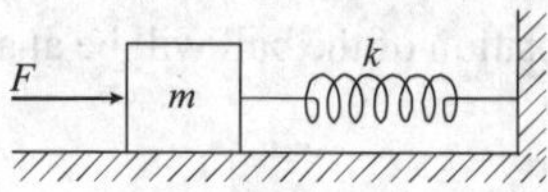

Figure 5.137

(A) The block will execute SHM

(B) Amplitude of oscillation is $\frac{F}{2k}$

(C) Time period of oscillation is $2\pi\sqrt{\frac{m}{k}}$

(D) The maximum speed of block is $\sqrt{\frac{2Fx - kx^2}{m}}$

5-14 Velocity-time graph of a particle executing SHM is shown in figure-5.138. Select the correct alternative(s) :

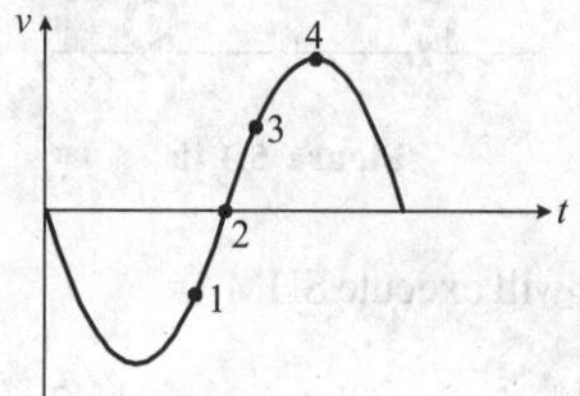

Figure 5.138

(A) At position 1 displacement of particle may be positive or negative

(B) At position 2 displacement of particle is negative

(C) At position 3 acceleration of particle is positive

(D) At position 4 acceleration of particle is zero

5-15 Acceleration-time graph of a particle executing SHM is as shown in figure-5.139. Select the correct alternative(s)

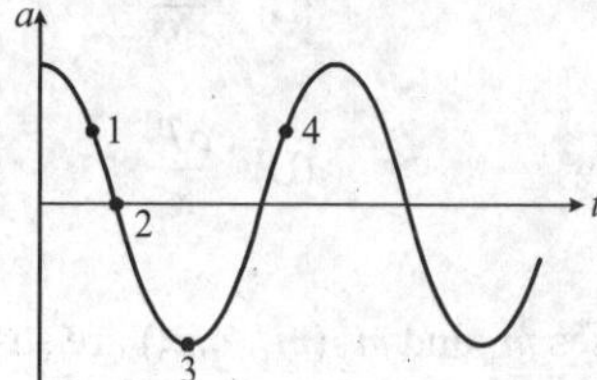

Figure 5.139

(A) Displacement of particle at 1 from mean position is negative

(B) Velocity of particle at 2 is positive

(C) Potential energy of particle at 3 is maximum

(D) Speed of particle at 4 is decreasing

5-16 Density of a liquid varies with depth as $\rho = \alpha h$. A small ball of density ρ_0 is released from the free surface of the liquid. Then :

(A) The ball will execute SHM of amplitude $\frac{\rho_0}{\alpha}$

(B) The mean position of the ball will be at a depth $\frac{\rho_0}{2\alpha}$ from the free surface

(C) the ball will sink to a maximum depth of $\frac{2\rho_0}{\alpha}$

(D) All of the above

5-17 A block of mass m is attached to a massless spring of force constant k, the other end of which is fixed from the wall of a truck as shown in figure-5.140. The block is placed over a smooth surface and initially the spring is unstretched. Suddenly the truck starts moving towards right with a constant acceleration a_0. As seen from the truck :

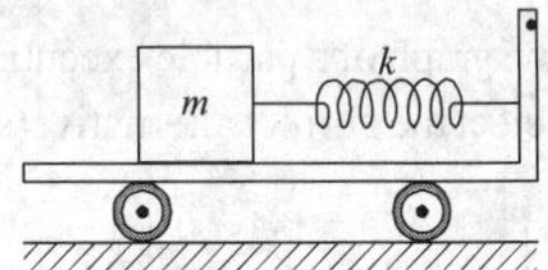

Figure 5.140

(A) The particle will execute SHM

(B) The time period of oscillations will be $2\pi\sqrt{\frac{m}{k}}$

(C) The amplitude of oscillations will be $\frac{ma_0}{k}$

(D) The energy of oscillations will be $\frac{m^2a_0^2}{k}$

5-18 If x, v and a denote the displacement, the velocity and the acceleration of a particle executing simple harmonic motion of time period T, then, which of the following does not change with time ?

(A) $aT + 2\pi v$ (B) $\frac{aT}{v}$

(C) $a^2T^2 + 4\pi^2v^2$ (D) $\frac{aT}{x}$

5-19 Two masses m_1 and m_2 ($m_1 > m_2$) are suspended by two springs vertically and are in equilibrium, extensions in the springs were same. Both the masses are displaced in the vertical direction by same distance and released. In subsequent motion T_1, T_2 are their time periods and E_1, E_2 are the energies of oscillations respectively then :

(A) $T_1 = T_2$; $E_2 < E$ (B) $T_1 > T_2$; $E_1 > E_2$

(C) $T_1 < T_2$; $E_1 > E_2$ (D) $T_1 = T_2$; $E_1 > E_2$

5-20 A particle is executing SHM between points $-X_m$ and X_m, as shown in figure-I. The velocity $V(t)$ of the particle is partially graphed and shown in figure-II. Two points A and B corresponding to time t_1 and time t_2 respectively are marked on the $V(t)$ curve:

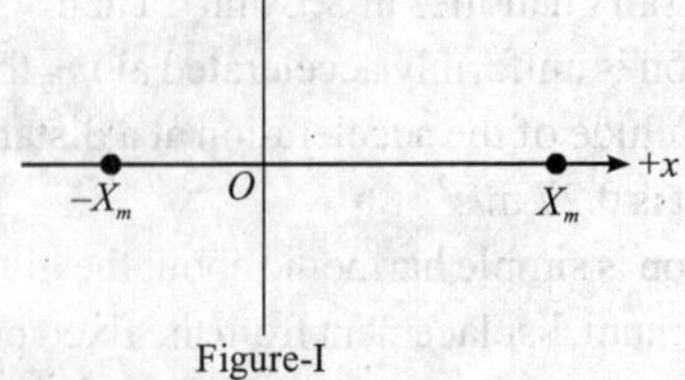

Figure-I

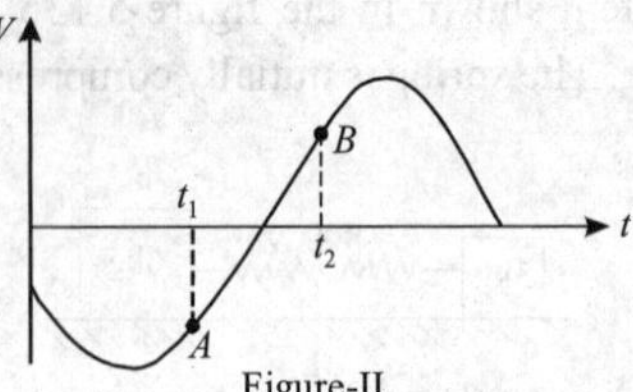

Figure-II

Figure 5.141

(A) At time t_1, it is going towards X_m

(B) At time t_1, its speed is decreasing

(C) At time t_2, its position lies in between $-X_m$ and O

(D) The phase difference Δf between points A and B must be expressed as $90° < \Delta f < 180°$

5-21 Kinetic energy of a particle of mass 2 kg executing simple harmonic motion changes with time according to the graph shown in figure below. Which of the following option(s) given below is/are correct :

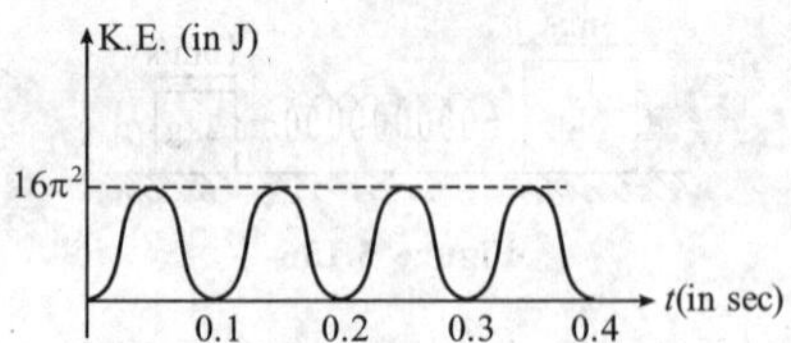

Figure 5.142

(A) Time period of oscillation is 0.1 s

(B) Frequency of oscillation is 5 Hz

(C) Amplitude of oscillation is 0.4 m

(D) Acceleration of the particle is zero at $t = 0.1$ s

5-22 The speed v of a particle moving along a straight line, when it is at a distance (x) from a fixed point on the line, is given by $v^2 = 144 - 9x^2$:

(A) Displacement of the particle ≤ distance moved by it

(B) The magnitude of acceleration at a distance 3 cm from the fixed point is 27 m/s²

(C) The motion is simple harmonic with $T = 2\pi/3$ units

(D) The maximum displacement from the fixed point is 4 units

5-23 An object of mass 0.8 kg is attached to one end of a spring and the system is set into simple harmonic motion. The displacement x of the object as a function of time t is shown in the figure-5.143 below. Which of the option(s) given below is/are correct about this SHM :

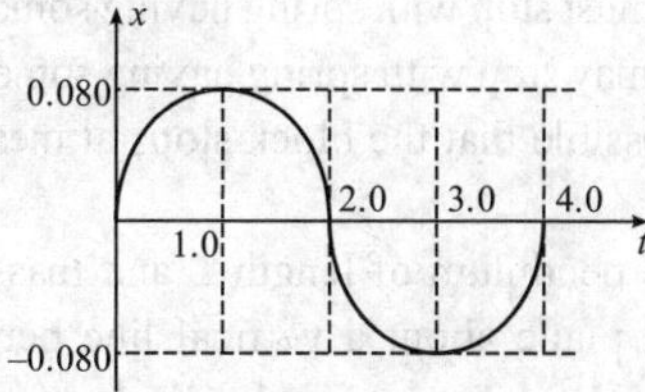

Figure 5.143

(A) Object velocity at $t = 3$ s is 0
(B) Object velocity at $t = 1$ s is 1.57 m/s
(C) Object acceleration at $t = 1$ s is 0.197 m/s^2
(D) Object acceleration at $t = 1$ s is 0.157 m/s^2

5-24 A simple pendulum is kept suspended vertically in a stationary bus. The bus starts moving with an acceleration a towards left. As observed inside the bus : (Neglect frictional forces on pendulum and assume size of the ball to be very small.)

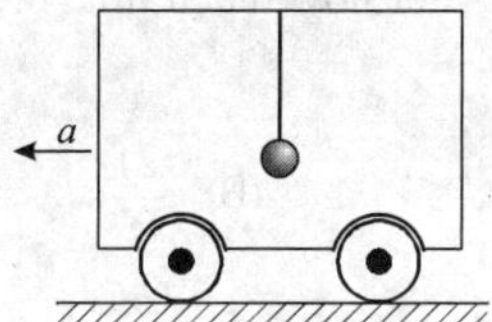

Figure 5.144

(A) Time period of oscillation of the pendulum will be $2\pi\sqrt{\frac{l}{\sqrt{a^2+g^2}}}$ for any value of a

(B) Time period of oscillation of the pendulum will be $2\pi\sqrt{\frac{l}{\sqrt{a^2+g^2}}}$ only when $a << g$

(C) Angular amplitude of oscillation will be $\tan^{-1}\left(\frac{a}{g}\right)$ for any value of a

(D) Angular amplitude of oscillation will be $\tan^{-1}\left(\frac{a}{g}\right)$ only when $a << g$

5-25 The position of a particle *w.r.* to origin varies according to the relation $x = 3 \sin 100t + 8 \cos^2 50t$. Which of the following is/are correct about this motion :
(A) The motion of the particle is not SHM
(B) The amplitude of the SHM of the particle is 5 units
(C) The amplitude of the resultant SHM is $\sqrt{73}$ units
(D) The maximum displacement of the particle from the origin is 9 units

5-26 A 20 gm particle is subjected to two simple harmonic motions

$x_1 = 2 \sin 10t, x_2 = 4 \sin (10t + \frac{\pi}{3})$. Where x_1 & x_2 are in metre & t is in sec.
(A) The displacement of the particle at $t = 0$ will be $2\sqrt{3}$ m
(B) Maximum speed of the particle will be $20\sqrt{7}$ m/s
(C) Magnitude of maximum acceleration of the particle will be $200\sqrt{7}$ m/s^2
(D) Energy of the resultant motion will be 28 J

5-27 A particle is executing SHM with amplitude A. At displacement $x = \frac{-A}{4}$, force acting on the particle is F, potential energy of the particle is U, velocity of particle is v and kinetic energy is Ka. Assuming potential energy to be zero at mean position. At displacement $x = \frac{A}{2}$:
(A) Force acting on the particle will be $2F$
(B) Potential energy of particle will be $4U$
(C) Velocity of particle will be $\sqrt{\frac{4}{5}}v$
(D) Kinetic energy of particle will be $0.8\,K$

5-28 A horizontal spring-mass system of mass M executes oscillatory motion of amplitude a_0 and time period T_0. When the mass M is passing through its equilibrium position another mass m is placed on it such that both move together. If a and T be the new amplitude and time period respectively then :

(A) $a = \sqrt{\frac{M}{M+m}}a_0$ (B) $a = \sqrt{\frac{M+m}{M}}a_0$

(C) $T = \sqrt{\frac{M}{M+m}}T_0$ (D) $T = \sqrt{\frac{M+m}{M}}T_0$

5-29 The potential energy of a particle of mass 2 kg, moving along the x-axis is given by $U(x) = 16(x^2 - 2x)$ J, where x is in metres. Its speed at $x = 1$ m is 2 ms^{-1} :
(A) The notion of the particle is uniformly accelerated
(B) The motion of the particle is oscillatory from $x = 0.5$ m to $x = 1.5$ m
(C) The motion of the particle is simple harmonic
(D) The period of oscillation of the particle is $\pi/2$s

5-30 A cylindrical block of density d stays fully immersed in a beaker filled with two immiscible liquids of different densities

d_1 and d_2. The block is in equilibrium with half of it in liquid 1 and the other half in liquid 2 as shown in the figure-5.145. If the block is given a displacement downwards and released, then neglecting frictional loses :

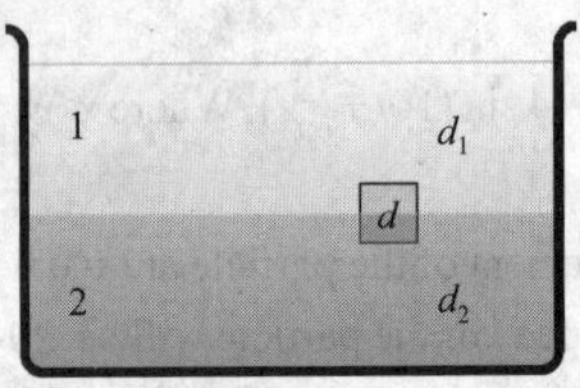

Figure 5.145

(A) It executes simple harmonic motion

(B) Its motion is periodic but not simple harmonic

(C) The frequency of oscillation is independent of the size of the cylinder

(D) The displacement of the centre of the cylinder is symmetric about its equilibrium position

5-31 A spring block system is placed on a rough horizontal floor as shown in figure-5.146. The block is pulled towards right to give spring some elongation and released. Then for the motion of block which of the following statement(s) is/are true:

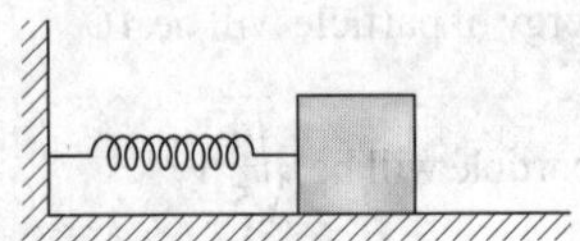

Figure 5.146

(A) The block may stop before the spring attains its mean position

(B) The block must stop with spring having some compression

(C) The block may stop with spring having some compression

(D) It is not possible that the block stops at mean position.

5-32 A simple pendulum of length L and mass of bob M is oscillating in a plane about a vertical line between angular amplitudes $-\phi$ and $+\phi$. For an angular displacement θ ($|\theta| < |\phi|$), the tension in the string and the velocity of the bob are T and v respectively. Which of the following relations are correct for this pendulum at θ :

(A) $T\cos\theta = Mg$

(B) $T = Mg\cos\theta$

(C) $T - Mg\cos\theta = MV^2/L$

(D) The magnitude of the tangential acceleration of the pendulum bob is $g\sin\theta$

5-33 Two simple pendulums of same amplitude but time period 3 s and 7 s start oscillating simultaneously from two opposite extreme positions. After how much time they will be in same phase :

(A) $\frac{21}{8}$ s (B) $\frac{21}{4}$ s

(C) $\frac{21}{2}$ s (D) $\frac{63}{8}$ s

* * * * *

Unsolved Numerical Problems for Preparation of NSEP, INPhO & IPhO

For detailed preparation of INPhO and IPhO students can refer advance study material on www.physicsgalaxy.com

5-1 A particle is executing SHM under the influence of a restoring force $F = -10x$ Nt. Find the amplitude of oscillation if its speed at mean position is 6 m/s.

Ans. [0.6 m]

5-2 A particle executes SHM and its acceleration as a function of displacement from its mean position is given as

$$a = -\omega(x - 2)$$

Find the time period of oscillation of the particle.

Ans. [$\frac{2\pi}{\sqrt{\omega}}$]

5-3 A particle starts its SHM from its equilibrium position at $t = 0$. The time period of its oscillation is T. Find the ratio of its kinetic and potential energy at time $t = T/12$.

Ans. [3 : 1]

5-4 A ball of mass 2 kg is hanging from a spring, oscillates with a time period 2 π seconds. If ball is removed when it is in equilibrium position, find the contraction in spring length.

Ans. [10 m]

5-5 A particle of mass m moves on a straight line under an attraction $m\omega^2 x$ towards a point O on the line where x is the distance from O. Show that, if $x = a$ and $x = u$ where $t = 0$, then at time t, $x = a\cos\omega t + \frac{u}{\omega}\sin\omega t$.

5-6 A particle of mass m executes SHM according to the equation $\frac{d^2x}{dt^2} + kx = 0$. Find its time period.

Ans. [$\frac{2\pi}{\sqrt{k}}$]

5-7 A point performs harmonic oscillations along a straight line with a period 0.60 s and an amplitude 10.0 cm. Find the mean velocity of the point averaged over the time interval during which it travels a distance $a/2$, starting from :

(a) the extreme position;

(b) the equilibrium position.

Ans. [(a) 0.50 m/s; (b) 1.0 m/s]

5-8 Two pendulums of time periods 3 s and 7 s respectively start oscillating simultaneously from two opposite extreme positions. Find the time after which they will be in phase.

Ans. [21/8 s]

5-9 A particle performs harmonic motion along the x-axis. The oscillation frequency is $\omega = 4$ rad/s. At a certain instant the particle has a coordinate $x' = 25$ cm and its velocity $v' = 100$ cm/s. Find the coordinate x and the velocity v of the particle at $t = 2.4$ s after that moment.

Ans. [–29 cm, – 81 cm/s]

5-10 A force $f = -10x + 2$ acts on a particle of mass 0.1 kg, where 'k' is in m and F in newton. If it is released from rest at $x = -2$ m, find :

(a) amplitude (b) time period (c) equation of motion.

Ans. [(a) $\frac{11}{5}$ m, (b) $\frac{\pi}{5}$ sec., (c) $x = 0.2 - \frac{11}{5}\cos\omega t$]

5-11 A seconds pendulum A (time period 2 second) and another simple pendulum B of slightly less length than A are made to oscillate at $t = 0$ in same phase. If they are again in the same phase first time, after 18 seconds, then the time period of B is ______.

Ans. [1.8 s]

5-12 A body is executing SHM under the action of force whose maximum magnitude is 50 N. Find the magnitude of force acting on the particle at the time when its energy is half kinetic and half potential.

Ans. [$25\sqrt{2}$ N]

5-13 A particle is executing SHM on a straight line. A and B are two points at which its velocity is zero. It passes through a certain point P ($AP < PB$) at successive intervals of 0.5 and 1.5 sec with a speed of 3 m/s. Determine the maximum speed and also the ratio AP/PB.

Ans. [$V_{max} = 3\sqrt{2}$ m/s, $AP/BP = \sqrt{2} - 1/\sqrt{2} + 1$]

5-14 A platform is executing simple harmonic motion in a vertical direction with an amplitude 5 cm and a frequency $10/\pi$ vibration per second. A block is placed on the platform at the lowest point of its path.

(a) At what point will the block leave the platform.

(b) How far will the block rise above the highest point reached by the platform.

Ans. [(a) 2.5 cm, (b) 1.25 cm]

5-15 A particle moves with simple harmonic motion in a straight line. When the distances of the particle from the equilibrium position are x_1 and x_2, the corresponding velocities are u_1 and u_2. Find the period of the motion.

Ans. [$2\pi\sqrt{\left(\frac{x_2^2 - x_1^2}{u_1^2 - u_2^2}\right)}$]

5-16 A thin rod of length L and having small area of cross-section A is pivoted at its lowest point P inside a stationary homogeneous and non-viscous liquid as shown in figure-5.147. The rod is free to rotate in a vertical plane about a horizontal axis passing through P. The density d_1 of the material of the rod is smaller than the density d_2 of the liquid. The rod is displace by small angle θ from its equilibrium position and then released. Show that the motion of the rod is simple harmonic and determine its angular frequency in terms of the given parameters.

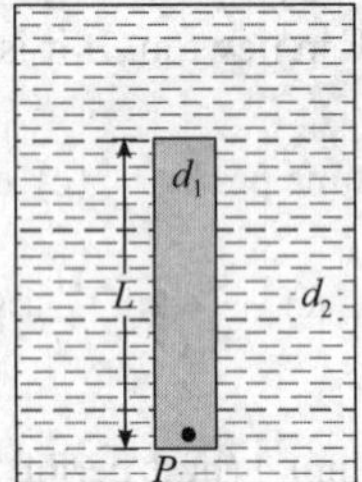

Figure 5.147

Ans. [$\omega = \sqrt{\frac{3}{2}\left[\frac{d_2 - d_1}{d_1 L}\right] g}$]

5-17 Two springs each of unstretched length 0.2 m but having different force constant K_1 and K_2 are attached to opposite ends of a block of mass m on a level frictionless surface as shown in figure-5.148. The outer ends of the springs are now attached to two pins P_1 and P_2, 10 cm from the original positions of the ends of springs. Let K_1 = 1 N/m, K_2 = 3 N/m m = 0.1 kg.

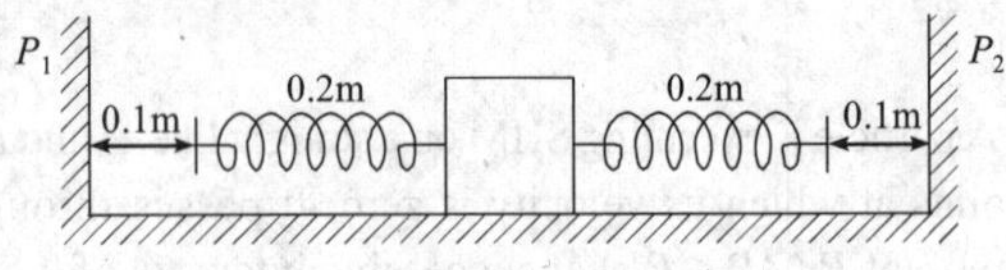

Figure 5.148

(i) Find the stretch of each spring when the block is in its new equilibrium position after the springs have been attached to the pins.

(ii) Find the period of the vibrations of the block if it is slightly displaced from its new equilibrium position and released. ($\pi^2 = 10$)

Ans. [(i) 0.15 m, 0.05 m, (ii) 1 sec]

5-18 A body of mass m = 0.5 kg is suspended from a rubber cord of co-efficient of elasticity (force constant) k = 10 N/m. Find the maximum distance through which the body can be pulled down for its oscillation to remain simple harmonic. What is the energy of oscillation in this case ?

Ans. [0.098 m, 0.24 J]

5-19 A point describes simple harmonic motion in a line 4 cm long. The velocity of the point while passing through the centre of the line is 12 cm per second. Find the period.

Ans. [1.047 s]

5-20 A bar of mass $m = \frac{1}{2}$ kg lying on a horizontal plane with a friction coefficient μ = 0.10 is attached to the wall by means of non-deformed spring as shown in figure-5.149. The stiffness of the spring is k = 2.45 Ncm^{-1}, its mass is negligible. The bar is displaced by x_0 = 3.0 cm, and then released. Find : (a) the period of oscillation of the bar, (b) the total number of oscillations that the bar performs until it stops completely.

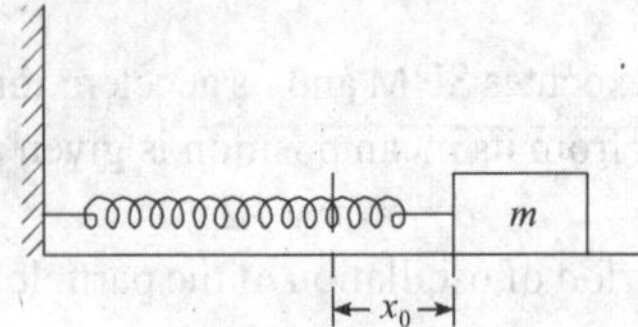

Figure 5.149

Ans. [$2\pi\sqrt{\frac{m}{k}}$, $\frac{kx_0}{2\mu mg}$]

5-21 A spring, of natural length l_0, is stretched on a smooth table between two fixed points at a distance $\eta\, l_0$ apart and a particle of mass m is attached to the middle of the spring. The particle is then displaced towards one of the fixed points through a distance not exceeding $\frac{1}{2}(\eta - 1)\, l_0$ and then liberated. Show that it will perform oscillations which is independent of η and of the distance through which it is displaced.

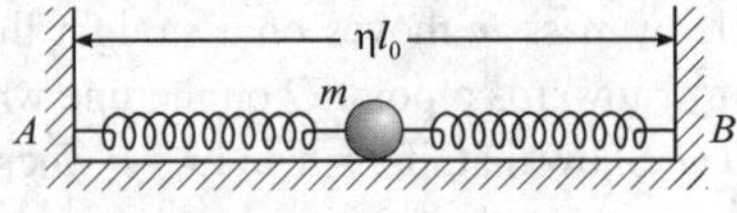

Figure 5.150

5-22 If the mass of a spring, m, is not negligible but small compared to the mass M suspended from it, show that the period of oscillations is given by $T = 2\pi\sqrt{\left(M + \frac{m}{3}\right)/k}$, where k is the force constant of the spring.

5-23 A point executes SHM about a fixed point O. Its distance from O at a certain time is 1 cm and 1 second later its distance from O is 5 cm. After yet another second its distance is again 5 cm. Find the time taken for a complete oscillation.

Ans. [$\frac{2\pi}{\cos^{-1} 3/5}$]

5-24 A particle performs harmonic oscillations along the x axis about the equilibrium position x = 0. The oscillation frequency is ω = 4.00 s^{-1}. At a certain moment of time the particle has a coordinate x_0 = 25.0 cm and its velocity is equal to v_{x0} = 100 cm/s. Find the coordinate x and the velocity v_x of the particle t = 2.40 s after that moment.

Ans. [– 29 cm, v_x = – 81 cm/s, where $a = \sqrt{x_0^2 + (v_{x0}/\omega)^2}$, $\alpha = \tan^{-1}(-v_{x0}/\omega_0 x_0)$]

5-25 At a given instant, the displacement of a particle from the equilibrium position O is x and it is moving away from O with speed v. Show that it next teaches O after a time $t = \frac{1}{\omega}\left(\pi - 2\tan^{-1}\frac{\omega x}{v}\right)$ where ω is the angular frequency of oscillation.

5-26 Two physical pendulums performs small oscillations about the same horizontal axis with frequencies ω_1 and ω_2. Their moments of inertia relative to the given axis are equal to I_1 and I_2 respectively. In a state of stable equilibrium the pendulums were fastened rigidly together. What will be the frequency of small oscillations of the compound pendulum ?

Ans. [$\omega = \sqrt{(I_1\omega_1^2 + I_2\omega_2^2)/(I_1 + I_2)}$]

5-27 Find the period of small oscillations of a mathematical pendulum of length l if its point of suspension O moves relative to the Earth's surface in an arbitrary direction with a constant acceleration w (as shown in figure-5.151). Find the time period of its small oscillations.

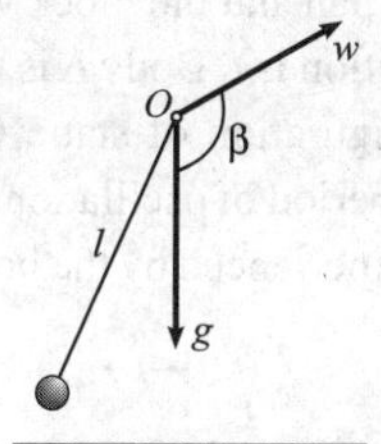

Figure 5.151

Ans. [$2\pi\sqrt{\frac{l}{\sqrt{g^2 + w^2 - 2gw\cos\beta}}}$]

5-28 A particle of mass m is executing oscillations in straight line about its mean position with amplitude A. The potential energy of the particle is given as $U = -ax^4$, where a is a positive constant and x is the displacement of the particle form its mean position. Find the displacement of the particle from its mean position where its potential energy is one third of its kinetic energy.

Ans. [$\frac{A}{\sqrt{2}}$]

5-29 A pendulum clock which shows right time is placed on the ground floor of a high building. How much time will it lose or gain in one day if it is transferred to top floor of the building at a height of 200 m from the ground floor. Given that radius of earth is 6400 km.

Ans. [2.7 s per day will be lost]

5-30 A box slides down on a smooth inclined plane of inclination θ with the horizontal. From the ceiling of the box a simple pendulum of length l is hanging. During its motion if the pendulum bob is slightly displaced from its mean position, find the time period of its oscillations.

Ans. [$2\pi\sqrt{\frac{l}{g\cos\theta}}$]

5-31 A particle performing SHM with amplitude A, undergoes displacement $A/2$ in one second. If at $t = 0$ the particle was located at mean position. Find the time period of SHM.

Ans. [12 s]

5-32 A particle executes SHM along a straight line with mean position at $x = 0$, with a period 20 s and amplitude 5 cm. Find the shortest time taken by the particle to go from $x = 4$ cm to $x = -3$ cm.

Ans. [5 s]

5-33 Determine the expression for the natural frequency of small oscillations of the L-shaped weighted rod as shown in figure-5.152 about O. The stiffness of the spring is K & its length is adjusted so that the rod is in equilibrium in the horizontal position shown. Neglect the mass of the spring & rod compared with m.

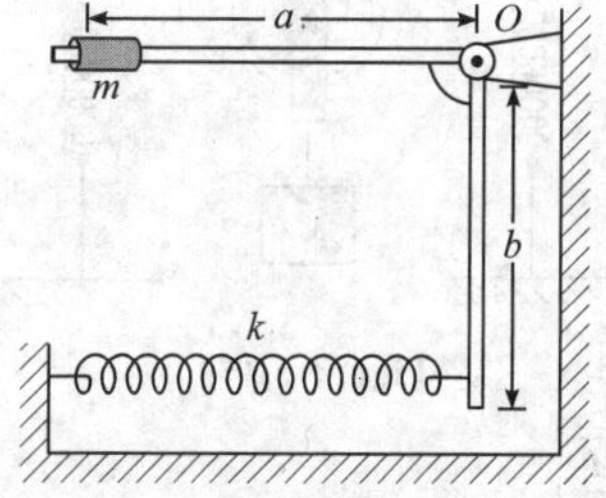

Figure 5.152

Ans. [$f = \frac{b}{2\pi l}\sqrt{\frac{k}{m}}$]

5-34 The figure-5.153 shows the displacement - time graph of a particle executing SHM. If the time period of oscillation is 2 s, find the equation of motion of its SHM

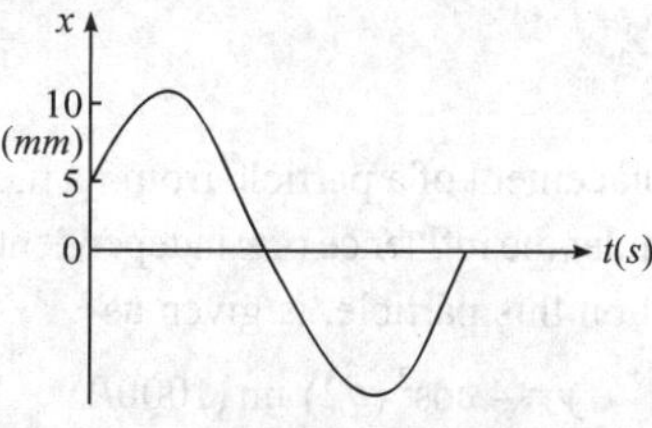

Figure 5.153

Ans. [$x = 10\sin(\pi t + \pi/6)$]

5-35 Two elastic strings obeying hooks law each of unstretched length l, each has one end attached to a particle of mass m lying on smooth horizontal floor. The other ends of the string are attached at points A & B which are at a distance $3l$ apart. Each would be doubled in length by a tension 2 mg. The particle is held at rest at A and then released. Show that after released that particle first reaches B at time

$$\sqrt{\frac{l}{g}}\left[\frac{\pi\sqrt{2}}{3}+\sin-1\sqrt{\frac{1}{7}}\right]$$

5-36 A uniform rod AB of mass m and length $4l$ is free to rotate in a vertical plane about a smooth horizontal axis through a point P, distant x from the centre of the rod of the rod and performs small oscillations about its equilibrium position find period of oscillation and also find the value of x for which time period is minimum.

Ans. [$2\pi\sqrt{\frac{4l^2+3x^2}{3gx}}$, $x=\frac{2l}{\sqrt{3}}$]

5-37 Find the time period of oscillation for the arrangement shown in the figure-5.154. The pulleys are smooth and massless.

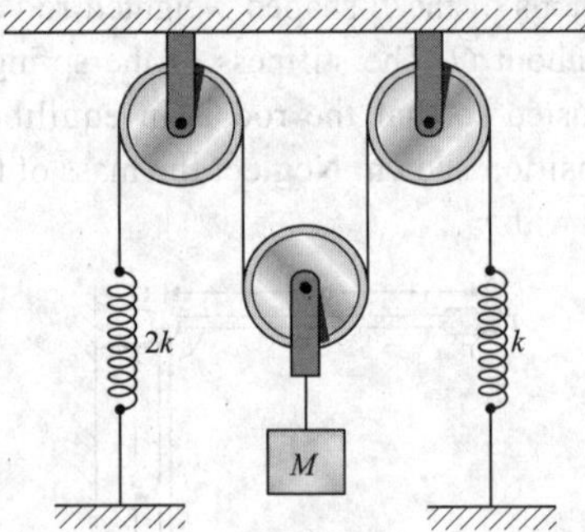

Figure 5.154

Ans. [$T=2\pi\sqrt{\frac{3M}{8k}}$]

5-38 A particle executing SHM in a straight line. During motion while moving from one extreme position it is at distances x_1, x_2 and x_3 from the centre at the end of three successive seconds. Find the time period of its oscillations.

Ans. [$\frac{2\pi}{\cos^{-1}\left(\frac{x_1+x_3}{2x_2}\right)}$]

5-39 The displacement of a particle from its mean position in an oscillation under the influence of n independent SHMs, which are superposed on this particle, is given as

$$y=4\cos^2(t/2)\sin(1000t)$$

Find n.

Ans. [3]

5-40 A uniform vertical cylinder of cross-sectional area a and length 80 cm floats with its 90% length submerged in a liquid inside a tank with cross-sectional area four times that of cylinder as shown in figure below. When cylinder is pushed down gently and released, it performs SHM. Calculate the maximum possible amplitude for this SHM.

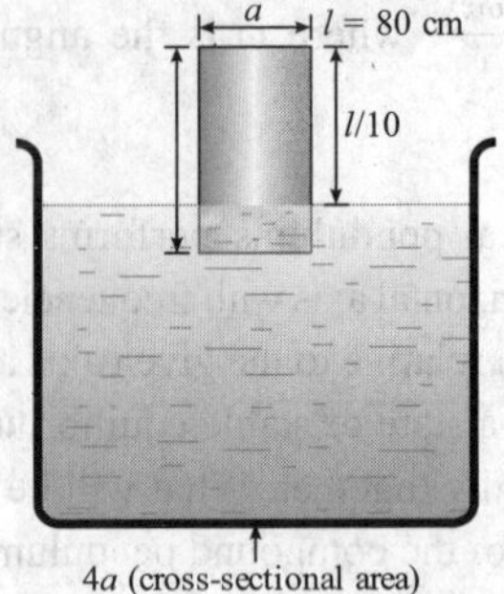

Figure 5.155

Ans. [6 cm]

5-41 A body A of mass m is connected to a light spring s_1 of spring constant k. At the right of 'A' there is a second light spring s_2 of spring constant 5 k and having a massless vertical pan (P) attached to its free end as shown in the figure-5.156. Distance between the pan and the block when both the springs are in the relaxed position is l. Body A is moved by 3 l distance to left from the configuration of static equilibrium and then released. What is the period of oscillation of the body ? What is the maximum force experienced by the body A ?

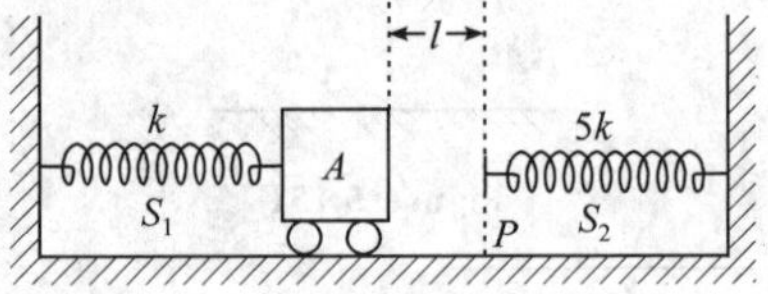

Figure 5.156

Ans. [$(m/k)^{1/2}$ [$\pi + 2\sin^{-1}(1/3)$] + $(m/6k)^{1/2}$ [$\pi - 2\sin^{-1}(1/7)$]; $F_{max} = 7kl$]

5-42 In the arrangement as shown in figure-5.157, pulleys are small and springs are ideal. K_1, K_2, K_3 and K_4 are force constants of the springs. Calculate period of small vertical oscillations of block of mass m.

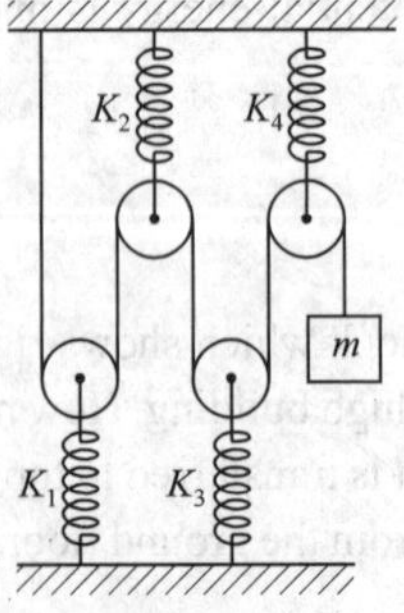

Figure 5.157

Ans. [$K_{eq}=\frac{1}{4\left[\frac{1}{K_1}+\frac{1}{K_2}+\frac{1}{K_3}+\frac{1}{K_4}\right]}$]

5-43 A particle executes SHM with time period 2 s. Find the time it will take to move from mean position to a position at a distance equal to half of amplitude from its mean position.

Ans. [$\frac{1}{6}$ s]

5-44 Two particle executes SHM in a straight line with same mean position, same amplitude A and same period of oscillation T. At time $t = 0$, one particle is at its extreme position on one side of mean position and other is at a distance $A/2$ from its mean position on the other side of the mean position. Find the time after which they cross each other.

Ans. [$\frac{T}{6}$]

5-45 A small bead of mass m is in equilibrium at the position shown in figure-5.158, on a smooth vertical ring of radius r. The ring revolves at some constant angular velocity about vertical diameter. Find :

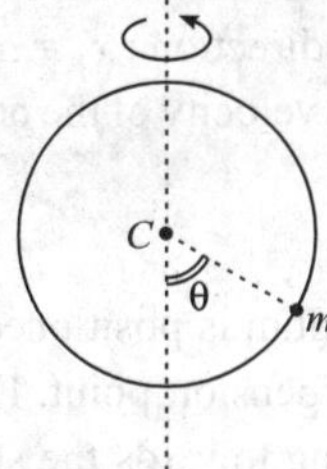

Figure 5.158

(i) Angular velocity of the ring.

(ii) If m is displaced slightly from its equilibrium position, prove that it will execute SHM on the ring. Find its time period.

Ans. [(i) $\sqrt{\frac{g}{r\cos\theta}}$; (ii) $2\pi\sqrt{\frac{r\cos\theta}{g\sin^2\theta}}$]

5-46 For a particle in SHM, What is the shape of the graph of velocity-displacement curve.

Ans. [ellipse]

5-47 Find the ratio of the time periods of a simple pendulum of length L and a physical pendulum consisting of a thin uniform rod of same length pivoted at one of its ends.

Ans. [$\sqrt{\frac{3}{2}}$]

5-48 Figure-5.159 shows a simple pendulum of length l whose bob is slightly displaced from vertical. A nail P is pivoted in the wall at a depth $3l/4$ below the suspension point of the string. If the bob is released, find the time after which bob will come to its initial position again for the first time.

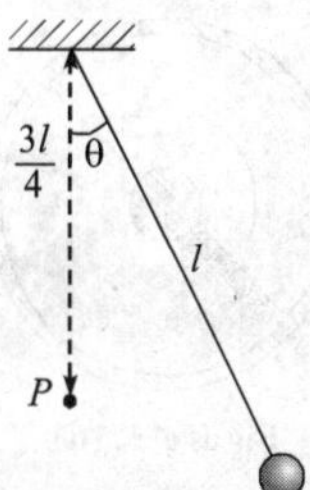

Figure 5.159

Ans. [$\frac{3\pi}{2}\sqrt{\frac{l}{g}}$]

5-49 A constant force applied to a block attached with an unstretched spring, produces a maximum velocity v. When the force constant of the spring is made four times the initial, now find the maximum velocity produced by the same force applied to it in unstretched position.

Ans. [$v/2$]

5-50 Two particles are in SHM in a straight line. Amplitude of particles is A and time period is T and both are oscillating about the same mean position. At $t = 0$, one particle is at its extreme position and other is at a distance $A/2$ from mean position on other side of it. Find the time after which they cross each other.

Ans. [$T/6$]

5-51 A small block of mass m is kept on a bigger block of mass M attached to one end of a vertical spring of force constant k as shown in figure-5.160. If this system is slightly displaced from its mean position, it starts executing SHM. Find the normal force on the smaller block when the two blocks are at a distance x above their equilibrium position. Also find the maximum possible amplitude of the two blocks so that they may oscillate without separation.

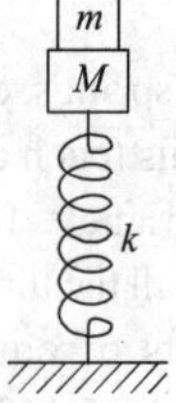

Figure 5.160

Ans. [$mg - \frac{mkx}{M+m}$, $\frac{(M+m)g}{k}$]

5-52 A small sleeve of mass m = 0. kg can move along the diameter of a horizontal disc, sliding without friction along a guide rod as shown in figure-5.161. The sleeve is tied to the end of the rod with the aid of a massless spring whose force constant is k = 10 Nm^{-1}. Find the angular frequency ω of the small amplitude oscillations of the sleeve, when the disc rotates about its axis at the angular speed ω equal to : (i) 6 rad/s, (ii) 11 rad/s.

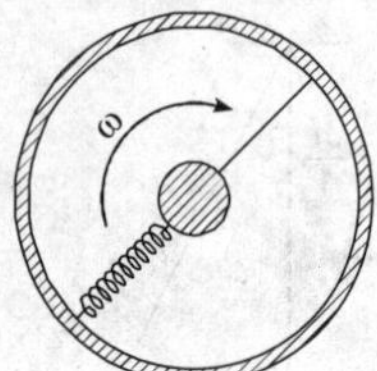

Figure 5.161

Ans. [8 rad/s]

5-53 A particle of mass m is a straight line with simple harmonic motion of amplitude a and frequency ω. At a distance x from the centre of motion the particle receives a blow of impulse I in the direction of motion. Find the new amplitude.

Ans. [$\sqrt{\left(\frac{I}{m\omega}+\sqrt{a^2-x^2}\right)^2+x^2}$]

5-54 Find the time dependence of angular displacement of an ideal simple pendulum, 80 cm in length, if at the initial moment, the pendulum was :

(1) displaced from its equilibrium position through in angle 3° and set free from rest.

(ii) in the equilibrium position, where the bob was imparted a horizontal velocity 0.22 m s^{-1}

(iii) deviated through 3° displacement and the bob was imparted a velocity of 0.22 m s^{-1} directed towards the equilibrium position.

Ans. [(i) θ = 3° cos (3.5 t); (ii) θ = 4.5° sin (3.5 t);
(iii) θ = 5.4° cos (3.5 t + 1)]

5-55 If for a particle executing SHM there is a sudden increase of 1% in the restoring force just as the particle is passing through the equilibrium position, what percentage increase will be given to (a) maximum velocity (b) amplitude (c) period ?

Ans. [(a) Zero, (b) $-\frac{1}{2}$%, (c) $-\frac{1}{2}$%]

5-56 Three identical ideal springs, each of force constant k are joined to three identical balls (each of mass m) as shown in the figure. O is centroid of the triangle. Initially, each of the springs is in its natural length. Now all the three balls are simultaneously given small displacements of equal magnitude along the directions shown in the figure-5.162. Calculate the oscillation frequency of balls.

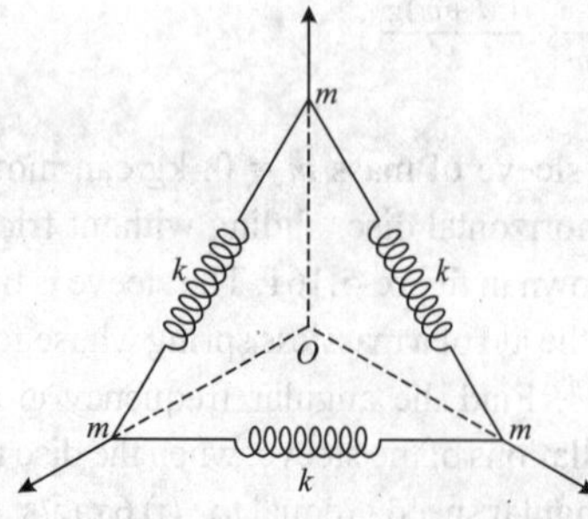

Figure 5.162

Ans. [$\frac{1}{2\pi}\sqrt{\frac{3k}{m}}$]

5-57 A block of mass M executes SHM with amplitude a and time period T. When it passes through the mean position, a lump of putty of mass m is dropped on it. Find the new amplitude and time period.

Ans. [$\sqrt{\frac{M}{M+m}}\cdot a$, $\sqrt{\frac{M+m}{M}}\cdot T$]

5-58 A pendulum clock is mounted in an elevator car which starts going up with a constant acceleration w, with $w < g$. At a height h the acceleration of the car reverses, its magnitude remaining constant. How soon after the start of the motion will the clock show the right time again ?

Ans. [$t = \sqrt{\frac{2h}{w}}\ \frac{\sqrt{1+\eta}-\sqrt{1-\eta}}{1-\sqrt{1-\eta}}$ where η = w/g]

5-59 A point participates simultaneously in two harmonic oscillations of the same direction : $x_1 = a\cos\omega t$ and $x_2 = a\cos 2\omega t$. Find the maximum velocity of the point.

Ans. [v_{max} = 2.73 aω]

5-60 A physical pendulum is positioned so that its centre of gravity is above the suspension point. From that position the pendulum started moving towards the stable equilibrium and passed it with an angular velocity ω. Neglecting the friction find the period of small oscillations of the pendulum.

Ans. [$T = 4\pi/\omega$]

5-61 In the figure-5.163 shown, initially the blocks are held at a height such that spring is in relaxed position. The block A is released. Find :

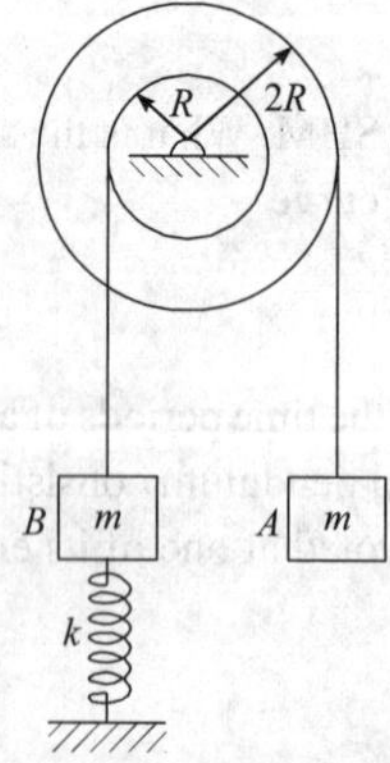

Figure 5.163

(a) the amplitude and maximum velocity of A during oscillations

(b) the frequency of the oscillation system

Ans. [(a) $a = \frac{2mg}{k}$, $v_A = \sqrt{\frac{mg^2}{k}}$; (b) ω $\sqrt{k/5m}$]

5-62 A body of mass 1 kg is suspended from a weightless spring having spring constant of 600 N/m. Another body of mass 0.5 kg moving vertically upwards with a velocity of 3 m/s hits the suspended body and gets itself embedded in it. Find the frequency of oscillations and the amplitude of the system.

Ans. [f = 3.18 Hz, a = 5 cm]

5-63 A diatomic molecule has atoms of masses m_1 and m_2. The potential energy of the molecule for the interatomic separation r is given by $U(r) = A + B(r - r_0)^2$, where r_0 is the equilibrium separation, and A and B are positive constants. The atoms are compressed towards each other from their equilibrium positions and released. What is the vibrational frequency of the molecule ?

Ans. [$\sqrt{\frac{2B(m_1+m_2)}{m_1 m_2}}$]

5-64 On a particle four SHMs are superimposed whose independent equations are given as

$$x_1 = 8 \sin \omega t$$
$$x_2 = 6 \sin (\omega t + \pi/2)$$
$$x_3 = 4 \sin (\omega t + \pi)$$
$$x_4 = 2 \sin (\omega t + 3\pi/2)$$

Find the resulting SHM amplitude of the particle and its phase difference with the first SHM given above.

Ans. [$4\sqrt{2}$, $\frac{\pi}{4}$]

5-65 A simple pendulum oscillates with time period 2 s. When this pendulum is submerged in a nonviscous liquid of density $\rho/2$ where ρ is the density of the pendulum bob. Now find the time period of the pendulum.

Ans. [$2\sqrt{2}$ s]

5-66 An object of mass 0.2 kg executes SHM along x-axis of a coordinate system with origin at mean position, with angular frequency 50 rad/s. At a position $x = 4$ cm from origin, the object has kinetic energy 0.5 J and potential energy 0.4 J. Find the amplitude of oscillation of object if at mean position potential energy of the object is zero.

Ans. [6 cm]

5-67 A second's pendulum is suspended in a car that is travelling with a constant speed of 10 m/s around a circle of radius 10 m. If the pendulum undergoes small oscillations about its equilibrium position, find its period of oscillation.

Ans. [$\sqrt{2\sqrt{2}}\,s$]

5-68 The time taken by a particle performing SHM to pass from point A to B where its velocities are same is 2 s. After another 2 s it returns to B. Find the time period of oscillations.

Ans. [8 s]

5-69 A mass at the end of a spring executes harmonic motion about an equilibrium position with an amplitude A. Its speed as it passes through the equilibrium position is v. If extended 2 A and released, find the speed of the mass passing through the equilibrium.

Ans. [2 v]

5-70 A block of mass 0.9 kg attached to a spring of force constant K is compressed by $\sqrt{2}$ cm and the block is at a distance $1/\sqrt{2}$ cm from the wall as shown in figure-5.164. When the block is released, it makes elastic collision with the wall and its period of motion is 0.2 s. Find the value of K.

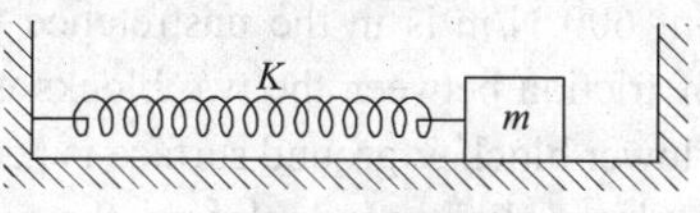

Figure 5.164

Ans. [100 N/m]

5-71 Two blocks of masses m_1 and m_2 are placed on a smooth horizontal surface as shown in figure-5.165. Block of mass m_1 is connected to one end of a light spring whose other end is attached to the vertical wall as shown. Now m_2 and m_1 both a brought in contact and pushed toward left so that the spring is compressed by a distance d. When the blocks are released, m_1 will start executing SHM, find the amplitude of this SHM.

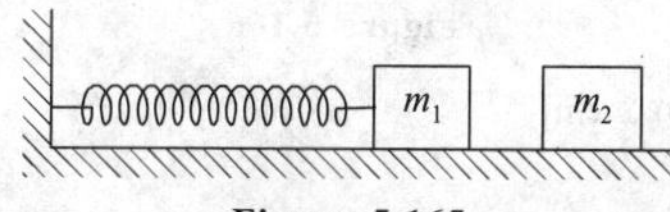

Figure 5.165

Ans. [$d\sqrt{\frac{m_1}{m_1+m_2}}$]

5-72 A spring block system oscillates with time period T. If the spring is slightly cut so that its length is decreased by 1%. Find the time period of the oscillations of the block now.

Ans. [0.995T]

5-73 24 A particle is executing SHM with amplitude A. At displacement $A/4$ from the mean position, its kinetic energy is K. Find the kinetic energy of the particle at a position when it is at a displacement $A/2$ from mean position.

Ans. [0.8K]

5-74 A particle of mass m is in a region of potential field $U(x) = 175 + 50x^2$. Find the frequency of the oscillation of the particle.

Ans. [$\left[\frac{10}{\sqrt{m}}\right]$]

5-75 The displacement of a particle varies according to the relation

$$x = 3 \sin 100\, t + 8 \cos^2 50\, t \text{ cm}$$

Find the amplitude of the oscillation of the particle and maximum displacement of the particle from origin.

Ans. [5 cm, 9 cm]

5-76 A small mass executes linear SHM about *O* with amplitude *A* and time period *T*. Find its displacement from *O* at time *T*/8 after passing through *O*.

Ans. [$A/\sqrt{2}$]

5-77 In the arrangement shown in figure-5.166, the spring of force constant 600 N/m is in the unstretched position. The coefficient of friction between the two blocks is 0.4 and that between the lower block & ground surface is zero. If both the blocks are displaced slightly and released, the system executes SHM.

(a) Find time period of their oscillation if they do not slip w.r.t. each other.

(b) What is the maximum amplitude of the oscillation for which sliding between them does not occur.

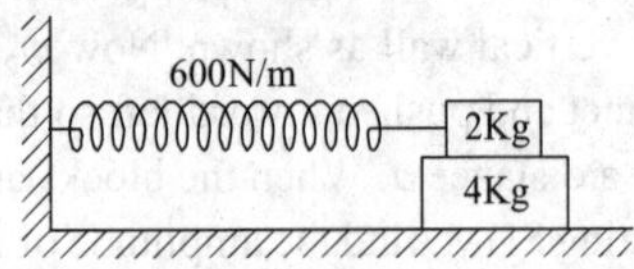

Figure 5.166

Ans. [(a) π/5, (b) 2 cm]

5-78 A block of mass *M* = 1 kg resting on a smooth horizontal surface, is connected to a horizontal light spring of spring constant *K* = 6 N/m whose other end is fixed to a vertical wall. Another block of mass *m* = 0.5 kg is mounted on the block *M*. If the coefficient of friction between the two blocks is μ = 0.4, find the maximum kinetic energy that the system can have for simple harmonic oscillations under the action of the spring.

Ans. [3 J]

5-79 A spring of force constant k is cut into two parts whose lengths are in the ratio 1 : 2. The two parts are now connected in parallel and a block of mass *m* is suspended at the end of the combined spring. Find the period of oscillation performed by the block.

Ans. [$T = 2\pi\sqrt{(2m/9k)}$]

5-80 A particle of mass m moves on a horizontal smooth line *AB* of length a such that when particle is at any general point *P* on the line two forces act on it. A force (*mg*/*a*) (*AP*) towards *A* and another force (2 *mg*/*a*) (*BP*) towards *B*. Show that particle performs SHM on the line when left from rest from midpoint of line *AB*. Find its time period and amplitude. Find the minimum distance of the particle from B during the motion. If the force acting towards *A* stops acting when the particle is nearest to *B* then find the velocity with which it crosses point *B*.

Ans. [$T = 2\pi\sqrt{a/3g}$, $A = a/6$, $a/6$, $1/6\sqrt{2ag}$]

5-81 A particle is oscillating in a straight line about a centre of force *O*, towards which when at a distance *x* the force is mn^2x where *m* is the mass, *n* a constant. The amplitude is *a* = 15 cm. When at a distance $a\sqrt{3}/2$ from *O* the particle receives a blow in the direction of motion which generates extra velocity *na*. If the velocity is away from *O*, find the new amplitude. What is the answer if the velocity of block was towards origin.

Ans. [$15\sqrt{3}$]

5-82 A lift operator hung an exact pendulum clock on the lift wall in a lift in a building to know the end of the working day. The lift moves with an upward & downward accelerations during the same time (according to a stationary clock), the magnitudes of the acceleration remaining unchanged. Will the operator work for more or less than required time.

Ans. [more]

5-83 A block of mass 1 kg hangs without vibrating at the end of a spring with a force constant 1 N/cm attached to the ceiling of an elevator. The elevator is rising with an upward acceleration of *g*/4. The acceleration of the elevator suddenly ceases. What is the amplitude of the resulting oscillations.

Ans. [2.5 cm]

5-84 A pendulum is suspended in a lift and its period of oscillation when the lift is stationary is T_0.

(i) What will the period *T* of oscillation of pendulum be if the lift begins to accelerate downwards with an acceleration equal to 3*g*/4 ?

(ii) What must be the acceleration of the lift for the period of oscillation of the pendulum to be $T_0/2$?

Ans. [(i) $T' = 2T_0 = 2\pi\sqrt{\dfrac{l}{g/4}}$, (ii) 3*g*↑]

5-85 Two blocks *A* (2 kg) and *B* (3 kg) rest up on a smooth horizontal surface are connected by a spring of stiffness 120 N/m. Initially the spring is undeformed. A is imparted a velocity of 2 m/s along the line of the spring away from *B*. Find the displacement of *A* t seconds later.

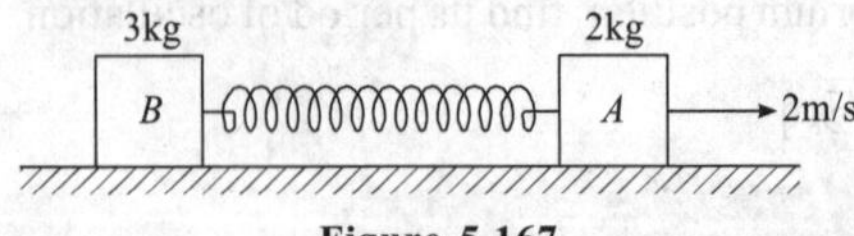

Figure 5.167

Ans. [0.8*t* + 0.12 sin 10*t*]

5-86 A rod of mass M, length l is hanged at its centre by a string as shown in figure-5.168. Torsional coefficient of the string is k. Two masses of mass m strike elastically with the rod perpendicularly at its ends with velocity v at time $t = 0$. Determine the expression for angular displacement of the rod as the function of time from the initial position.

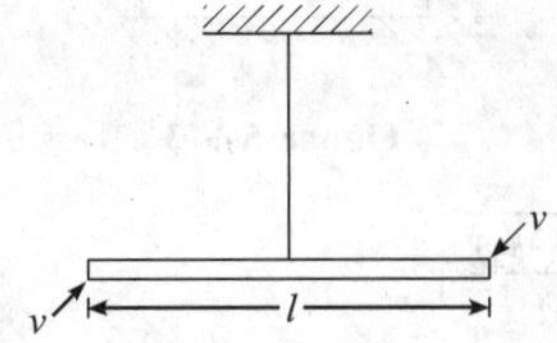

Figure 5.168

Ans. [$\frac{24mv}{(6m+m)l}\sqrt{\frac{I}{k}}\sin\left(\sqrt{\frac{k}{I}}\cdot t\right)$]

5-87 Suppose the mass m is attached to a long uniform spring of length L and observed to oscillate at a frequency f_0. Now the spring is cut into two pieces of lengths xL and $(1-x)L$. Mass m is divided into two pieces in this same ratio with $m_1 = xm$ and $m_2 = (1-x)m$. The larger mass is attached to the shorter spring and the smaller mass to the larger spring. Show that the frequency of oscillation for each of the two spring is.

$$f = \frac{f_0}{\sqrt{x(1-x)}}$$

5-88 A circular disc suspended from a torsional wire, oscillates with a time period T when twisted by a small angle θ from equilibrium and released. If another disc of same material but twice the radius and one fourth thickness is made to oscillate separately with the same wire, calculate its time period.

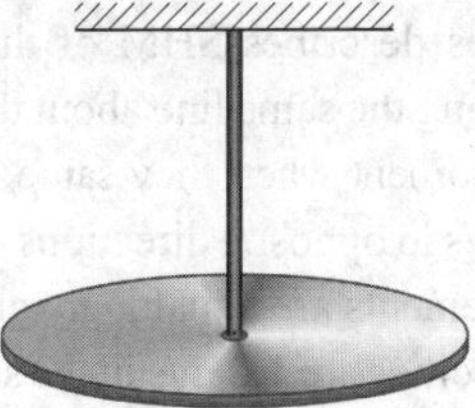

Figure 5.169

Ans. [$2T$]

5-89 Consider a fixed ring shaped uniform body of density ρ and radius R. A particle at the centre of ring is displaced along the axis by a small distance, show that the particle will execute SHM under gravitation at force of ring & find its time period neglecting other forces.

Ans. [$\sqrt{\frac{2\pi R^2}{G\rho}}$]

5-90 The acceleration versus time graph of a particle executing SHM is shown in figure-5.170. Plot the displacement versus time graph.

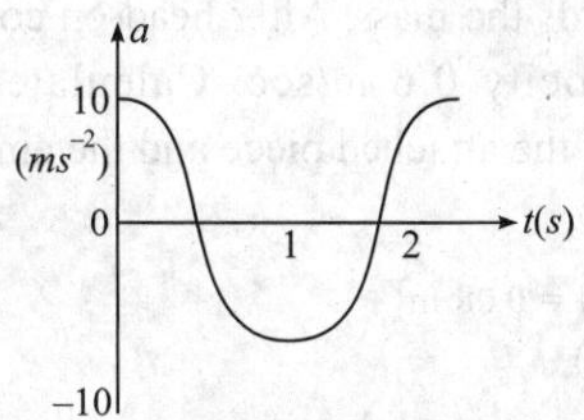

Figure 5.170

Ans. [
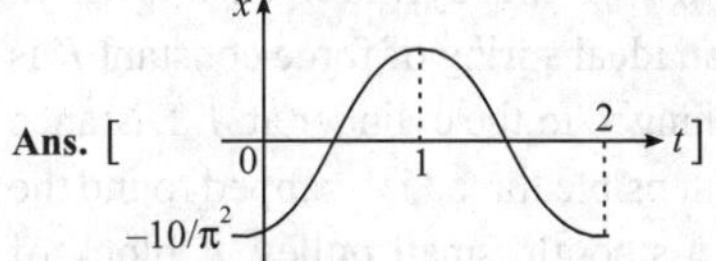

]

5-91 A square plate of mass m is held by eight springs, each of constant k in vertical plane. Knowing that each spring can act in either tension or compression, determine the frequency of the resulting vibration (a) if the plate is given a small vertical displacement and released, (b) if the plate is rotated through a small angle about G and released.

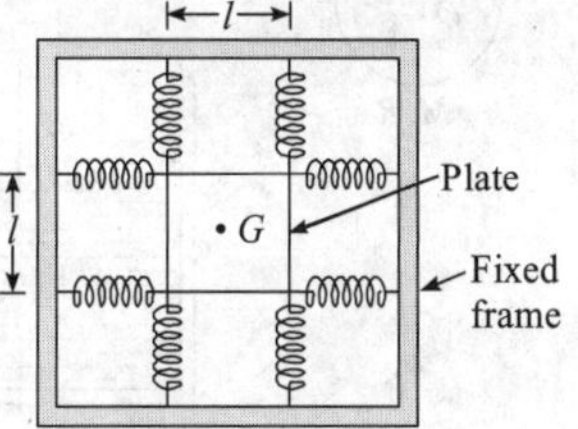

Figure 5.171

Ans. [$f = \frac{1}{2\pi}\sqrt{\frac{4k}{m}}$, $f = \frac{1}{2\pi}\sqrt{\frac{12k}{m}}$]

5-92 Two particles perform SHM with the same amplitude and same frequency about the same mean position and along the same line. If the maximum distance between them during the motion is A (A is the amplitude of either) then find phase difference between their SHMs.

Ans. [$\phi = \pi/3, 5\pi/3$]

5-93 Find the resultant amplitude due to superposition of these two SHMs

$$x_1 = 10\sin(\omega t + 30^\circ)$$

$$x_2 = -10\cos(\omega t - 60^\circ)$$

Ans. [0]

5-94 A spring of force constant 10 N/m is laying along the x-axis on a horizontal frictionless table. One of its ends is fixed. A piece of mass 0.1 kg is attached to the other end. Another piece of mass 0.1 kg is now sent with a velocity of 1 m/sec along the x-axis towards the mass. After head-on collision it returns back with velocity 0.6 m/sec. Calculate the maximum displacement of the attached piece and the amplitude of SHM set in.

Ans. [x_{max} = 0.1, a = 0.08 m]

5-95 Figure shows a solid uniform cylinder os radius R and mass M, which is free to rotate about a fixed horizontal axis O and passes through centre of the cylinder as shown in figure-5.172. One end of an ideal spring of force constant K is fixed and the other end is hinged to the cylinder at A. Distance OA is equal to $R/2$. An inextensible thread is wrapped round the cylinder and passes over a smooth, small pulley. A block of equal mass M and having cross sectional area A is suspended from free end of the thread. The block is partially immersed in a non-viscous liquid of density ρ.
If in equilibrium, spring is horizontal and line OA is vertical, calculate frequency of small oscillations of the system.

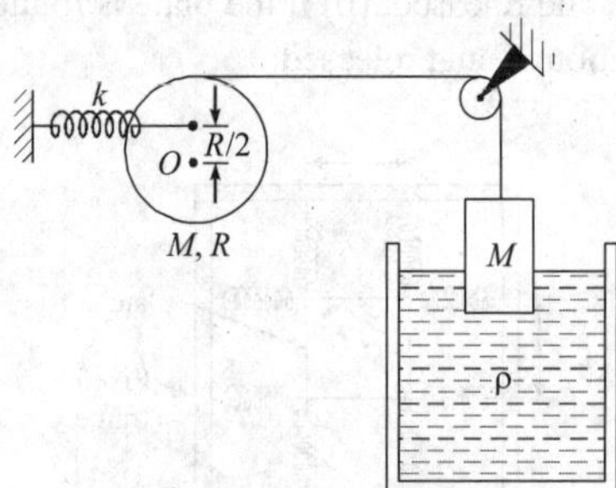

Figure 5.172

Ans. [$f = \left(\frac{1}{2\pi}\right)\sqrt{\frac{k+4A\rho g}{6m}}$]

5-96 A point moves in the plane xy according to the law $x = a \sin \omega t$, $y = b \cos \omega t$, where a, b, and ω are positive constants. Find :

(a) the trajectory equation $y(x)$ of the point and the direction of its motion along this trajectory;

(b) the acceleration w of the point as a function of its radius vector r relative to the origin of coordinates.

Ans. [(a) $x^2/a^2 + y^2/b^2 = 1$, clockwise; (b) $w = -\omega^2 r$.]

5-97 AB and CD are two ideal springs having force constant K_1 and K_2 respectively. Lower ends of these springs are attached to the ground so that the springs remains vertical. A light rod of length $3a$ is attached with upper ends B and C of springs as shown in figure-5.173. A particle of mass m is fixed with the rod at a distance a from end b and in equilibrium, the rod is horizontal. Calculate period of small vertical oscillations of the system. If rod has mass equal to particle then what will be the time period of small oscillation.

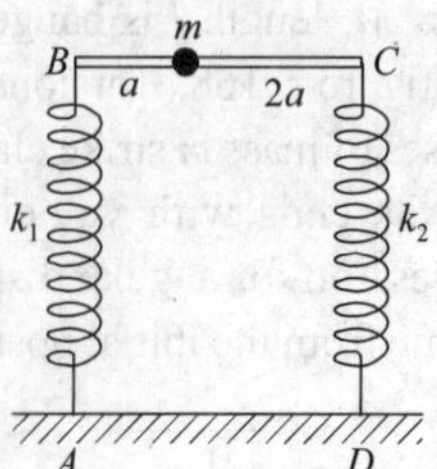

Figure 5.173

Ans. [$\sqrt{\frac{2\pi}{3}}\sqrt{\frac{m(k_1+4k_2)}{k_1k_2}}$]

5-98 Find the angular frequency of motion of block m as shown in figure-5.174, for small motion of rod AB. Spring constant are k_1 and k_2 Neglect friction forces and also neglect the mass of rod AB.

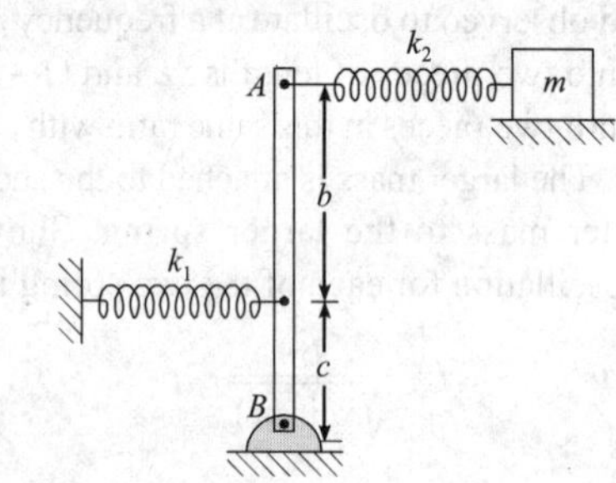

Figure 5.174

Ans. [$\omega = \sqrt{\frac{k_1k_2C^2}{m[k_1c^2 + k_2(b+c)^2]}}$]

5-99 Two particles describes SHM of the same period and same amplitude along the same line about the same equilibrium position O. At a moment when they same displacements their velocities are 1.6 m/s in opposite directions. At another moment when their displacements are equal in magnitude but on either side of O their velocities are 1.2 m/s in the same direction. Find the maximum speed of the particles and the phase difference between them.

Ans. [(a) 1.6 m/s; (b) 2 $\tan^{-1}$ (4/3)]

5-100 A spring mass system is hanging from the ceiling of an elevator in equilibrium as shown in figure-5.175. The elevator suddenly starts accelerating upwards with acceleration a find

(a) the frequency

(b) the amplitude of the resulting SHM

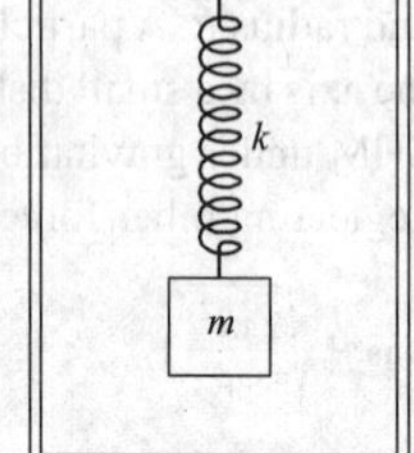

Figure 5.175

Ans. [(a) $\frac{1}{2\pi}\sqrt{\frac{k}{m}}$; (b) A = ma/k]

5-101 A physical pendulum performs small oscillations about the horizontal axis with frequency $\omega_1 = 15.0\ s^{-1}$. When a small body of mass $m = 50$ gm is fixed to the pendulum at a distance $l = 20$ cm below the axis, the oscillation frequency becomes equal to $\omega_2 = 10.0\ s^{-1}$. Find the moment of inertia of the pendulum relative to the oscillation axis.

Ans. [0.8 gm · m^2]

5-102 A uniform rod is placed on two spinning wheels as shown in figure-5.176. The axes of the wheels are separated by a distance $l = 20$ cm, the coefficient of friction between the rod and the wheels is $k = 0.18$. Demonstrate that in this case the rod performs harmonic oscillations. Find the period of these oscillations.

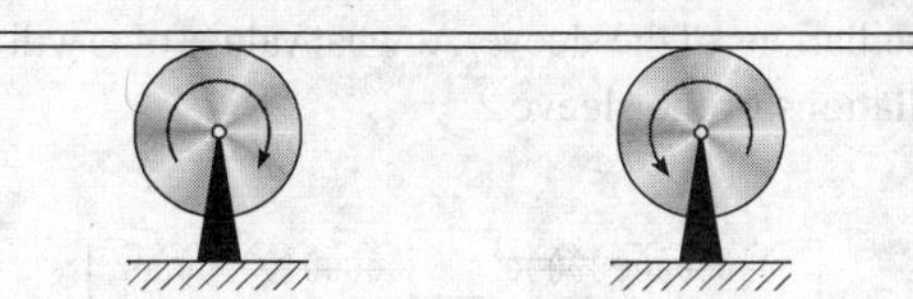

Figure 5.176

Ans. [1.5 s]

5-103 A pipe in the form of a half ring of radius r is placed on a horizontal surface as shown in figure-5.177. If is rotated through, a small angle, and then released. Assuming that it rolls without sliding determine the period of oscillations.

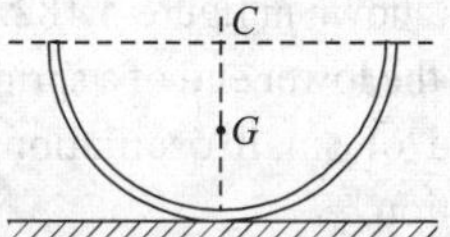

Figure 5.177

Ans. [$2\pi\sqrt{\frac{(\pi-2)r}{g}}$]

5-104 The balance wheel of a watch vibrates with an angular amplitude π radians and a period of 0.5 s. Find (a) the maximum angular speed of the wheel, (b) the angular speed of the wheel when its displacement is $\frac{\pi}{2}$ radians and (c) the angular acceleration of the wheel when its displacement is $\frac{\pi}{4}$ radians.

Ans. [39.5 rad/s, 34.2 rad/s, 124 rad/s^2]

5-105 When the displacement is one-half the amplitude, what fraction of the total energy is kinetic and what fraction is potential ? At what displacement is the energy half kinetic and half potential ?

Ans. [$\frac{3}{4}$, $\frac{1}{4}$, $\frac{a}{\sqrt{2}}$]

5-106 A block of mass $m_1 = 1$ kg is attached to a spring of force constant $k = 24$ N/cm at one end and to a string tensioned by mass $m_2 = 5$ kg at the other as shown in figure-5.178. Deduce the frequency of oscillations of the system. If m_2 is initially supported in hand and then suddenly released, find :

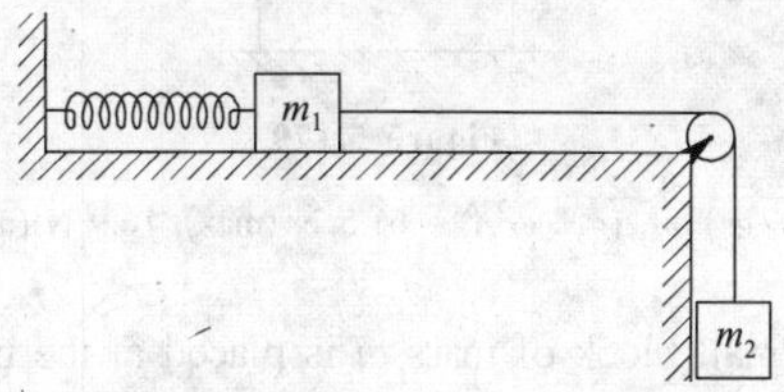

Figure 5.178

(i) the instantaneous tension just after m_2 is released,

(ii) the maximum displacement of m_1,

(iii) the maximum and minimum tension in the string during oscillations.

Ans. [$v = \frac{1}{2\pi}\sqrt{\frac{K}{m_1+m_2}} = \frac{10}{\pi}$ Hz, m_2g, $\frac{2m_2g}{k}$, $T_{max} = \frac{55g}{6}$, $T_{min} = \frac{5g}{6}$]

5-107 A rubber cord of force constant $k = 100$ N/m and $l = 1$ m is attached to a particle of mass $m = 1$ kg at one end and fixed to a vertical wall at the other. The body is displaced by $x_0 = 25$ cm so as to stretch the cord and then released. Calculate the time the particle takes to reach the wall.

Ans. [0.56 s]

5-108 A solid hemisphere of radius R is placed on a horizontal surface and is set into small oscillations in a vertical plane through a diameter. If no slipping occurs, find the period of these oscillations.

Ans. [$T = 2\pi\sqrt{\frac{26R}{15g}}$]

5-109 A thin fixed ring of radius 1 m has a positive charge 1×10^{-5} coulomb uniformly distributed over it. A particle of mass 0.9 g and having a negative charge of 1×10^{-6} coulomb is placed on the axis at a distance of 1 cm from the centre of the ring. Show that the motion of the negatively charged particle is approximately simple harmonic. Calculate the time period of oscillations.

Ans. [0.628 s]

5-110 A small body A of mass $m_1 = 1$ kg and a body B of mass $m_2 = 4$ kg are interconnected by a spring as shown in the figure-5.179. The body A performs free vertical harmonic oscillations with amplitude $A = 2$ cm and angular frequency $\omega = 25$ rad/s. Assuming mass of the spring to be negligible, find the maximum and minimum values of the normal reaction on the surface.

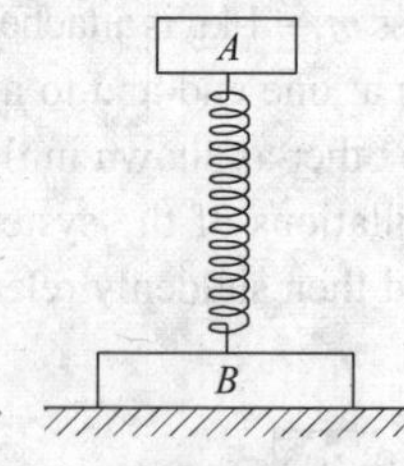

Figure 5.179

Ans. [$N = m_2 g + m_1 (g \pm \omega^2 A) = 61.5$ N (max), 16.9 N (min.)]

5-111 A small block of mass m is placed at the bottom of a smooth hemispherical cup of mass M and radius R as shown in figure-5.180. If it is displaced a little and released, show that the motion of both m and M is simple harmonic. Find the period of oscillations. Consider the case $M >> m$.

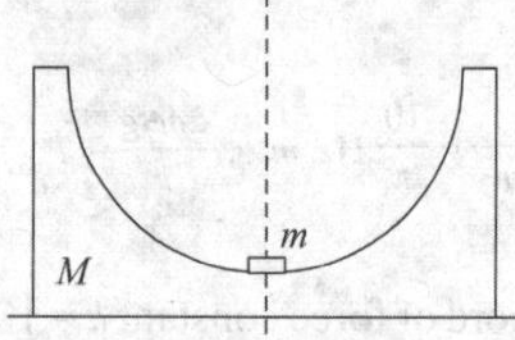

Figure 5.180

Ans. [$2\pi\sqrt{\frac{R}{g}}$]

5-112 A particle moves according to the equation $f + 4x = 0$, where x is its instantaneous displacement and f its instantaneous acceleration. The maximum value of x is 20×10^{-2} m. How much time will the particle take to move from $x = 0.02$ m to $x = 0.08$ m?

Ans. [0.157 s]

5-113 Determine the period of small oscillations of a mathematical pendulum, that is a ball suspended by a thread $l = 3.0$ times less then that of the ball. The resistance of the liquid is to be neglected.

Ans. [1.1 s]

5-114 A hoop of mass m and radius r rests at the bottom of a fixed hollow cylinder of radius R. If it is displaced a little and released, show that the centre of the hoop oscillates harmonically. Find the period of oscillation. Assume that the hoop rolls without slipping.

Ans. [$2\pi\sqrt{\frac{2R(R-r)}{g}}$]

5-115 Find the time dependence of the angle of deviation of a mathematical pendulum 80 cm in length if at the initial moment the pendulum :

(a) was deviated through the angle 3.0° and then set free without push;

(b) was in the equilibrium position and its lower end was imparted the horizontal velocity 0.22 m/s;

(c) was deviated through the angle 3.0° and its lower end was imparted the velocity 0.22 m/s directed toward the equilibrium position.

Ans. [(a) 3.0° cos 3.5t; (b) 4.5° sin 3.5t; (c) 5.4° cos (3.5t + 10)]

5-116 In the arrangement show in figure-5.181 the sleeve M of mass 0.20 kg is fixed between two identical springs whose combined stiffness is equal to 20 N/m. The sleeve can slide without friction over a horizontal bar AB. The arrangement rotates with a constant angular velocity 4.4 rad/s about a vertical axis passing through the middle of the bar. Find the period of small oscillations of the sleeve. At what values of ω will there be no oscillations of the sleeve ?

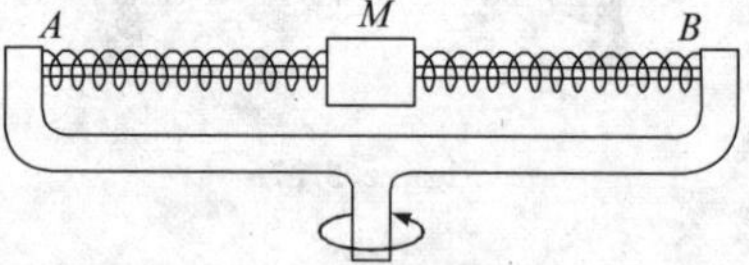

Figure 5.181

Ans. [0.7s, 10 rad/s.]

5-117 A block of mass m is tied to one end of a string which passes over a smooth fixed pulley A and under a light smooth movable pulley B as shown in figure-5.182. The other end of the string is attached to the lower end of a spring of spring constant k_2. Find the period of small oscillations of mass m about its equilibrium position.

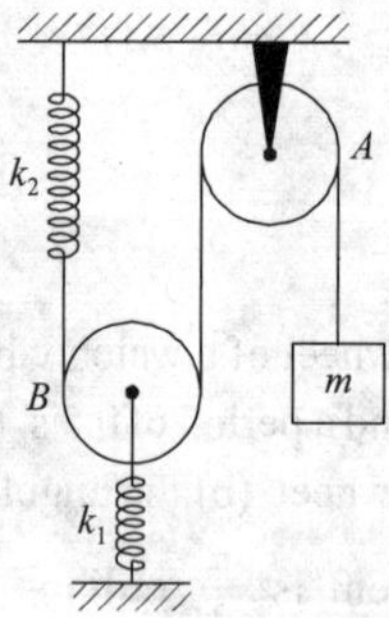

Figure 5.182

Ans. [$T = 2\pi\sqrt{\frac{m(k_1 + 4k_2)}{k_1 k_2}}$]

5-118 In the arrangement shown in figure-5.183, both the springs are in their natural lengths. The coefficient of friction between m_2 and m_1 is μ. There is no friction between m_1 and the ground surface. If the blocks are displaced slightly, they together perform simple harmonic motion. Obtain

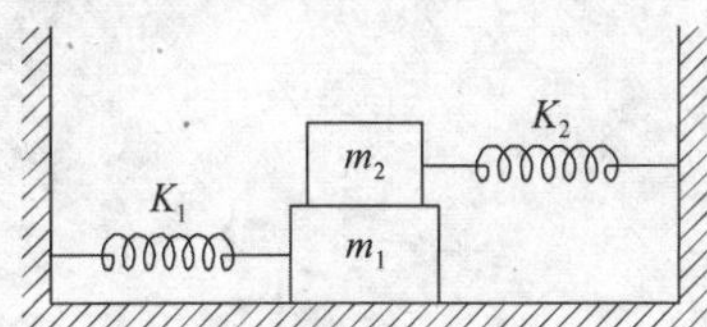

Figure 5.183

(a) Frequency of such oscillations.

(b) The condition if the direction of its displacement from mean position.

(c) If the condition obtained in (b) is met, what can be the maximum amplitude of their oscillations ?

Ans. [(a) $\frac{1}{2\pi}\sqrt{\frac{k_1+k_2}{m_1+m_2}}$; (b) $\frac{m_1}{m_2} > \frac{k_1}{k_2}$; (c) $A_m = \frac{\mu m_2\, g(m_1+m_2)}{m_1 k_2 - m_2 k_1}$]

5-119 In the arrangement shown in figure-5.184, AB is a uniform rod of length 90 cm and mass 2 kg. The rod is free to rotate about a horizontal axis passing through end A. A thread passes over a light, smooth and small pulley. One end of the thread is attached with end B of the rod and the other end carries a block of mass 1 kg. To keep the system in equilibrium one end of an ideal spring of force constant $K = 7500$ N/m is attached with mid point of the rod and the other end is fixed such that in equilibrium, the spring is vertical and the rod is horizontal. If in equilibrium, part of the thread between end B and pulley is vertical, calculate frequency of small oscillations of the system.

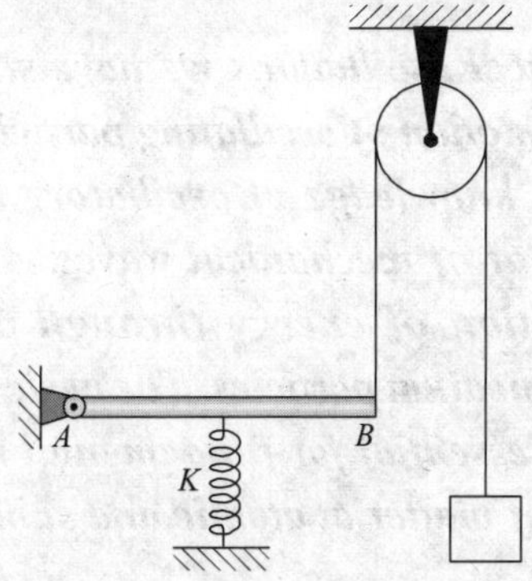

Figure 5.184

Ans. [$\frac{15\sqrt{5}}{2\pi}$ Hz]

* * * * *

Waves

6

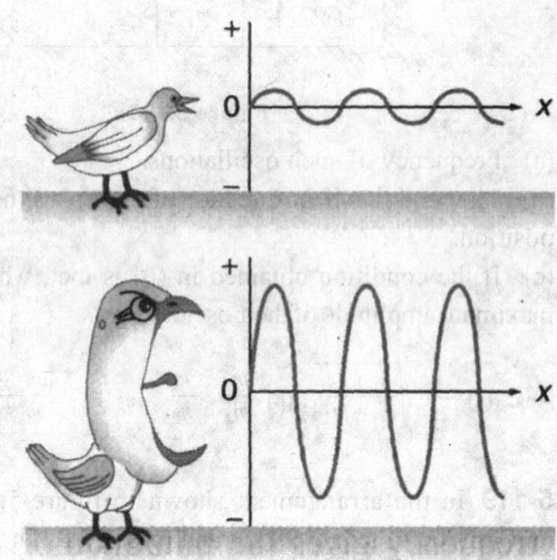

FEW WORDS FOR STUDENTS

In mechanical oscillations we have studied the detailed analysis of motion of oscillating particles. In this chapter we use our knowledge of oscillatory motion to explain the behaviour of mechanical waves. A mechanical wave is propagation of energy through a medium due to oscillating medium particles. The basic principles of wave motion are essential for fundamental understanding the behaviour of matter at atomic and subatomic level.

CHAPTER CONTENTS

6.1 *Properties of a Mechanical Wave*
6.2 *Equation of a Simple Harmonic Wave*
6.3 *Sound Waves*
6.4 *Velocity of a Wave*
6.5 *Principle of Superposition*
6.6 *Interference of Waves*
6.7 *Intensity of Wave*
6.8 *Compression Waves*
6.9 *Spherical and Cylindrical Waves*
6.10 *Measurements of Sound Levels*
6.11 *Stationary Waves*
6.12 *Standing Waves on Clamped String*
6.13 *Wave Resonance*
6.14 *Vibrations of Clamped Rod*
6.15 *Waves in a Vibrating Air Column*
6.16 *Beats*
6.17 *Doppler's Effect*
6.18 *Shock Waves*
6.19 *Reflection and Refraction of Waves*

COVER APPLICATION

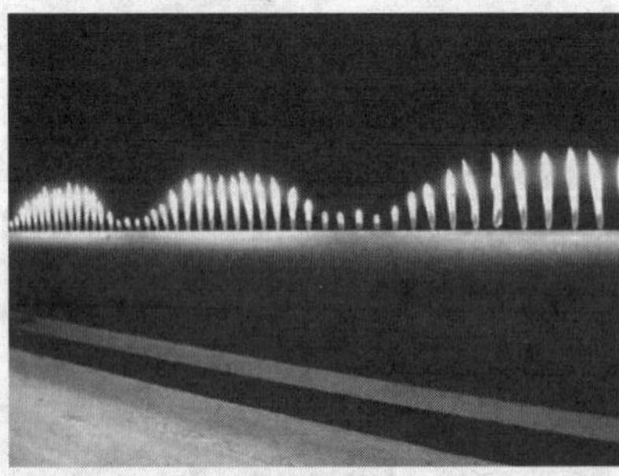

Figure (a)

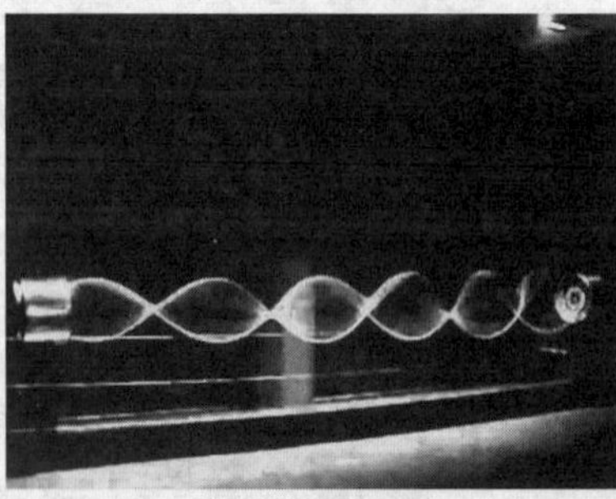

Figure (b)

Figure-(a) shows a Rubens' tube or flame tube experiment which is an apparatus for demonstrating acoustic standing waves in a tube. It graphically shows the relationship between sound waves and pressure. Above figure shows a tube in which propane gas is passed through a Bunsen burner and inside the tube due to variation of pressure by formation of standing waves the flame length changes with distance. At the position of constructive interference, antinodes are formed and at the points of destructive interference nodes are formed. In above figure it is very important to understand which points are node and which are antinodes in respect of flame length. Figure-(b) shows Melde's experiment setup demonstrating stationary wave in a stretched string.

In simple words a wave is the transfer of energy. We also experience the energy transferred by waves in many situations. We feel how much force an ocean wave can exert, our skin is warmed by the light waves from the sun, we hear sound waves and many more examples are there in our surroundings. Most of the information that we receive comes to us by waves. In this chapter we'll discuss in detail how energy (or information) is transmitted by a wave.

In a wave energy and momentum is transmitted by oscillations. A wave can be classified in two broad categories. Mechanical Waves and Non Mechanical or Electromagnetic waves. In mechanical waves, energy is transferred due to oscillations of medium particles and in non mechanical waves energy transfer takes place by the oscillations of electric and magnetic field vectors. In this chapter we'll mainly discuss all about mechanical waves which requires a physical medium for its propagation.

6.1 Properties of a Mechanical Wave

A wave has three basic properties which decide the characteristic behaviour of wave and these are

(i) Amplitude of wave (ii) Frequency of wave

(iii) Velocity of wave

(i) Amplitude : It is the maximum displacement of oscillating medium particle from their mean position. It depends on the source of oscillation or the wave generator. It may vary with the distance of medium particle from the oscillating source.

(ii) Frequency : It is the number of oscillations made by the medium particles per unit time. It also depends on the source of oscillations. Once a wave is produced by a source it is carried by the medium, no matters what the medium may be, the frequency of oscillation remains same wherever the wave will go.

Whenever a wave is produce by a source, it propagates in a medium and during propagations when it encounters another medium in its path then at boundary of the medium a part of wave is reflected into the same medium and a part is transmitted to the other medium. It is obvious that as the reflected and transmitted waves are produced by the initial propagating wave, the frequency of both of these waves must be same as that of the oscillating source of initial wave.

(iii) Velocity of wave : It is the speed with which energy transfers through a medium and it depends mainly on the physical properties of the medium. When a wave is transmitted through a medium, its frequency and amplitude depends on the source of oscillation which produces the wave but its speed is decided by the medium which carries energy.

6.1.1 Different Types of Mechanical Waves

We've discussed that mechanical waves carry energy through a physical medium by oscillations of the medium particles. Depending on the way how these medium particle oscillates and the nature of oscillations, there are several types of mechanical waves. Mainly mechanical waves are classified in two broad categories :

(i) Transverse waves, (ii) Longitudinal waves.

(i) Transverse Wave : During such type of wave propagation, medium particles oscillate in a plane normal to the direction of propagation of the wave energy as shown in figure-6.1.

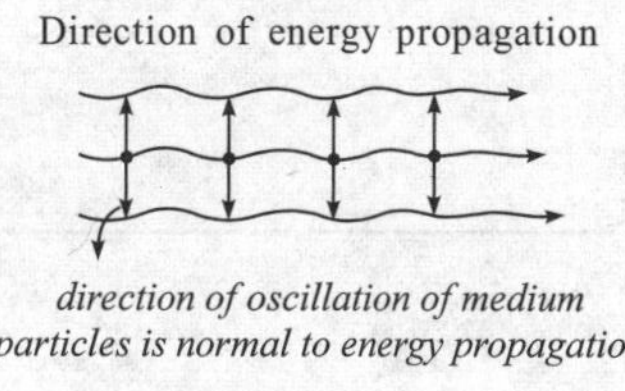

Figure 6.1

(ii) Longitudinal Waves : During such type of wave propagation, medium particles oscillate along the direction of propagation of the wave energy as shown in figure-6.2.

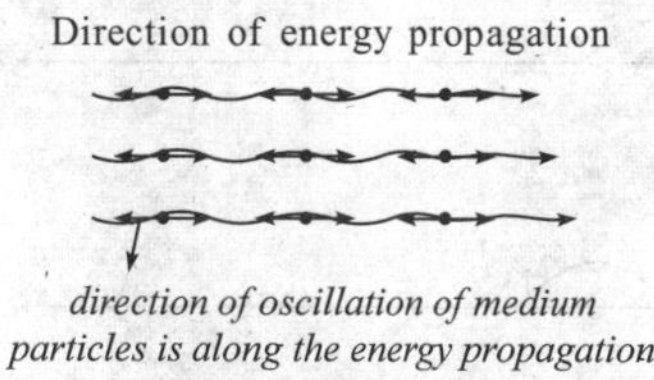

Figure 6.2

The most simple type of a wave is simple harmonic wave which exist in both longitudinal and transverse from. It is the one in which the medium particle oscillates simple harmonically. Now we'll discuss about simple harmonic waves in detail.

6.2 Equation of a Simple Harmonic Wave

We've discussed that in a simple harmonic wave, all medium particles execute SHM along or perpendicular to the direction of propagation of wave depending on whether wave is longitudinal or transverse. In the chapter of simple harmonic motion we've discussed that the equation of SHM of a particle gives its displacement from mean position as a function of time and can be written in general as

$$y = A \sin(\omega t + \phi) \qquad \ldots(6.1)$$

Here A is the amplitude of oscillations of the particle with angular frequency ω and ϕ gives the phase angle of particle (on circular projection) at time $t = 0$ when particle starts its SHM with respect to its reference position.

In a simple harmonic wave, all medium particles executes SHM and transfers energy from one particle to another and due to this the wave propagates. Equation of a simple harmonic wave is a mathematical expression similar to equation-(6.1) which gives the displacement of all the medium particles from their mean position as a function of time. Consider the situation shown in figure-6.3. A transverse wave is travelling on a stretched string along + X-direction.

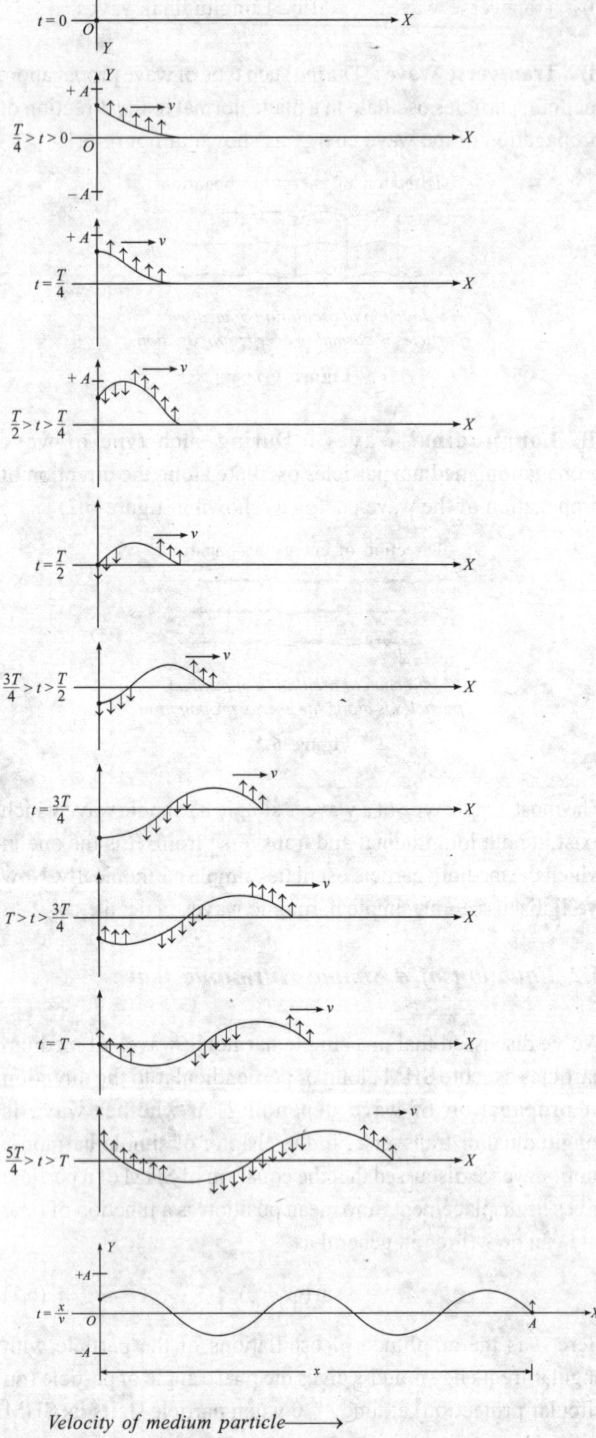

Figure 6.3

The oscillating source of the wave is at origin O, it starts its oscillations with amplitude A and angular frequency ω at $t = 0$ and the oscillations produced by the source is carried in + X direction by the medium with the wave speed v, as shown. If we consider a medium particle A at a distance x from the origin, will start its oscillations at time $t = x/v$ when wave will first reach this point and its oscillations are started from the mean position with amplitude A and same angular frequency ω. Here we can observe that if origin starts oscillations at $t = 0$ from its mean position, its SHM equation can be given as

$$y = A \sin \omega t \qquad \ldots(6.2)$$

Medium particle at point A also starts its SHM from its mean position but not at $t = 0$. It will start at time $t = x/v$ where x is the distance, wave covers from origin to point A. In this duration the source of wave or the medium particle at origin will move ahead in phase by an angle ϕ, which is given as

$$\phi = \omega t = \omega \frac{x}{v}$$

$$= \frac{2\pi n}{n\lambda} x$$

$$= \frac{2\pi}{\lambda} x$$

$$= kx \qquad \ldots(6.3)$$

Here $k = \frac{2\pi}{\lambda}$ is called angular wave number of the wave. In equation-(6.3) ϕ is the phase difference between point A and origin or this is the phase angle by which SHM of point A lagging with respect to SHM of particle at origin. Thus SHM equation of medium particle at point A can be written as

$$y = A \sin (\omega t - \phi)$$

or

$$y = A \sin (\omega t - kx) \qquad \ldots(6.4)$$

The expression in equation-(6.4) gives the displacement y of a medium particle from its mean position as a function of time, which is situated at a distance x from the source of oscillations of the wave. This equation-(6.4) is termed as the general equation of a simple harmonic wave propagating in positive x direction.

Equation-(6.4) can be written in different ways as

$$y = A \sin (\omega t - kx) \qquad \ldots(6.4a)$$

$$y = A \sin \omega \left(t - \frac{x}{v}\right) \qquad \left[\text{As } v = \frac{\omega}{k}\right] \qquad \ldots(6.4b)$$

$$y = A \sin \frac{2\pi}{\lambda} (vt - x) \qquad \left[\text{As } \frac{\omega}{v} = \frac{2\pi}{\lambda}\right] \qquad \ldots(6.4c)$$

$$y = A \sin 2\pi \left(\frac{t}{T} - \frac{x}{\lambda}\right) \qquad \left[\text{As } \frac{v}{\lambda} = \frac{1}{T}\right] \qquad \ldots(6.4d)$$

Above expressions in equations-(6.4a) to (6.4d) represent different forms of equations of a plane propagating wave in positive direction of X-axis. Students are advised to remember all these forms of wave equation in their mind for numerical applications.

6.2.1 Velocity and Acceleration of a Medium Particle in Wave Propagation

When a plane progressive wave propagates along positive x-axis with its source located at $x = 0$ and started at $t = 0$, the equation of motion of a particle at position x is given as

$$y = A \sin(\omega t - kx) \quad \ldots(6.5)$$

Equation-(6.5) is also termed as wave equation for the respective wave. Here the velocity of medium particle at position x is given as

$$v_p = \frac{\partial y}{\partial t} = A\omega \cos(\omega t - kx) \quad \ldots(6.6)$$

$$= A\omega\sqrt{A^2 - y^2} \quad \ldots(6.7)$$

Equation-(6.7) already we've covered in SHM. Here we can also see that during wave propagation the maximum speed of medium particles is given as

$$v_{p(\max)} = A\omega$$

When they cross their mean position, i.e. at $y = 0$.

Further from equation-(6.5), if we differentiate it w.r. to displacement of wave x then we get the slope of displacement curve of wave as

$$\frac{\partial y}{\partial x} = -AK \cos(\omega t - kx) \quad \ldots(6.8)$$

From equation-(6.6) and (6.8) we have

$$\frac{\partial y}{\partial x} = -\frac{k}{\omega}\frac{\partial y}{\partial t}$$

$$\frac{\partial y}{\partial x} = -\frac{1}{v}\frac{\partial y}{\partial t} \quad \left[\text{As wave velocity } v = \frac{\omega}{k}\right]$$

or $$v_p = -v \times (\text{slope}) \quad \ldots(6.9)$$

Thus in a propagating wave the speed of medium particle at a given position and at a given instant is the negative of the product of wave velocity and the slope of displacement curve of wave at that point and at that instant.

Similarly acceleration of a medium particle is given as

$$\frac{\partial^2 y}{\partial t^2} = -A\omega^2 \sin(\omega t - kx) \quad \ldots(6.10)$$

Now differentiating equation-(6.8) w.r. to x again, we get

$$\frac{\partial^2 y}{\partial x^2} = -Ak^2 \sin(\omega t - kx) \quad \ldots(6.11)$$

From equation-(6.10) and (6.11) we get

$$\frac{\partial^2 y}{\partial t^2} = \frac{\omega^2}{k^2}\frac{\partial^2 y}{\partial x^2}$$

or $$\frac{\partial^2 y}{\partial t^2} = v^2 \frac{\partial^2 y}{\partial x^2} \quad \ldots(6.12)$$

There $\frac{\partial^2 y}{\partial x^2}$ is the measure of curvature of the displacement curve, thus we can write that

Acceleration of a medium particle = $v^2 \times$ the curvature of the displacement curve

Here equation-(6.12) is termed as differential form of equation of a propagating wave.

6.2.2 Phase Difference and Path Difference of Medium Particles in Simple Harmonic Wave

We've discussed that when a wave propagates, only energy is transferred through the medium particles and these particles execute SHM at their position. From figure-6.3 it is also clear that as wave propagates, every medium particle follows the phase of its previous particle or in other words the instantaneous phase of a medium particle is same which was that of its previous particle just a moment before. Thus we can say that during wave propagation, phase also travels, that's why some times wave velocity is also termed as phase velocity.

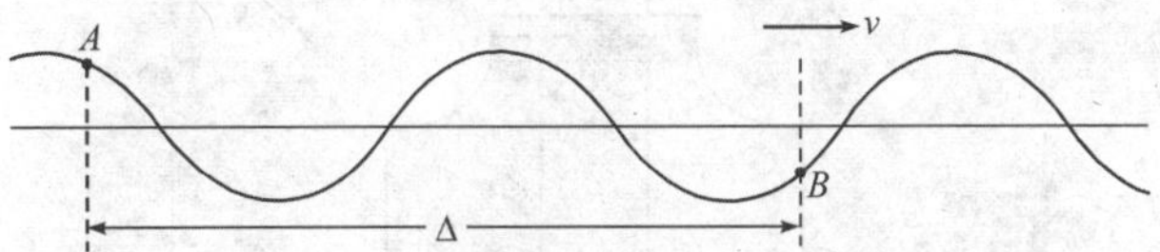

Figure 6.4

Here we can also mansion that as phase travels at some speed as that of wave, we can find the phase difference between SHMs of any two medium particles if their path difference is known. Consider figure-6.4 It shows a part of a stretched string carrying a transverse wave travelling at a speed v toward right. Consider two medium particles A and B at a path difference Δ apart. Here we can say that if at an instant A has some instantaneous phase, then the same phase B will be having after a time $t = \Delta/v$ as wave has to travel a distance Δ from A to B. In this duration A will move forward in phase by an angle

$\omega \Delta/v$, which is now the phase lead of A with respect to B. Thus phase difference between two oscillating medium particles having a path difference Δ is given as

$$\phi = \frac{\omega}{v}\Delta = \frac{2\pi}{\lambda}\Delta = k\Delta \quad \ldots(6.13)$$

Thus the relation in phase difference between the two points in a propagating wave is related to their path difference is given as

$$\text{Phase difference} = \frac{2\pi}{\lambda} \times \text{path difference} \quad \ldots(6.14)$$

The above relation is extremely useful in solving problems of wave motion as well as in problems concerned with principle of superposition, we'll discuss in next section.

6.3 Sound Waves

Sound is type of longitudinal wave. In general majority of longitudinal waves are termed as sound waves. Sound is produced by a vibrating source, like when a gong of a bell is struck with a hammer, sound is produced. The vibrations produced by gong are propagated through air. Through air these vibrations reach to the ear and ear drum is set into vibrations and these vibrations are communicated to human brain. By touching the gong of bell by hand, we can feel the vibrations.

Prongs of tuning fork when hit on a rubber pad vibrates and it is used as the most common source of sound in laboratory experiments. Similarly vibrating string, air column, and any vibrating body produces sound.

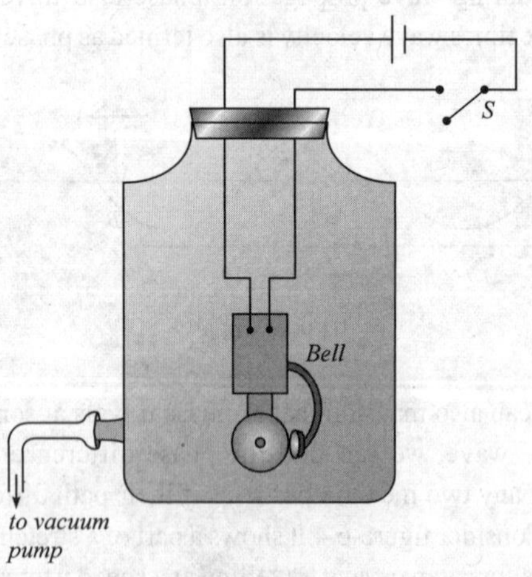

Figure 6.5

As being a mechanical wave sound requires material medium for its propagation. To understand this we discuss a simple experiment shown in figure-6.5. We take a jar and fix an electric bell in it. The jar is closed by an air light cork and a small opening at the bottom of jar is connected to a vacuum pump. When we close the switch S, the circuit is completed the bell rings and the sound is heard. Now the air in jar is removed gradually by the vacuum pump. We can listen that sound becomes fainter slowly. When pressure in jar becomes very low, almost no sound is heard, even the bell is vibrating at same pace. Hence we can say without material medium sound propagation is not possible. At normal atmospheric pressure and temperature it is observed hat sound travels at speed 332 m/s.

 # *Illustrative Example 6.1*

A harmonic oscillation is represented by

$$y = 0.34\cos(3000t + 0.74)$$

where y and t are in mm and second respectively. Deduce (i) amplitude, (ii) frequency and angular frequency, (iii) time period and (iv) initial phase.

Solution

We know that a simple harmonic oscillation can be represented by

$$y = A\cos(\omega t + \phi)$$

Where A is amplitude ω is angular frequency and ϕ is the initial phase. Comparing this equation with given equation, we have

(i) amplitude $A = 0.34$ mm

(ii) angular frequency $\omega = 3000$ Hz

Since $\quad \omega = 2\pi n \quad$ where n is the frequency

And thus we get $\quad n = \dfrac{\omega}{2\pi} = \dfrac{3000}{2\pi} = \dfrac{1500}{\pi}$ Hz

(iii) We know that $\quad T = \dfrac{1}{n} = \dfrac{1\times\pi}{1500} = \dfrac{\pi}{1500}$ sec

(iv) Initial phase $\phi = 0.74$ radian

 # *Illustrative Example 6.2*

An observer standing at sea coast observes 54 waves reaching the coast per minute. If the wavelength of the waves is 10 m, find the velocity. What type of waves did he observe ?

Solution

As 54 waves reach the shore per minute,

$$f = \frac{54}{60} = \frac{9}{10}\text{ Hz}$$

And as wavelength of waves is 10 m

$$v = f\lambda = \frac{9}{10} \times 10 = 9 \text{ m/s}$$

The waves on the surface of water are combined transverse and longitudinal called *'ripples'*. In case of surface waves the particles of the medium move in elliptical paths in a vertical plane so that the vibrations are simultaneously back and forth and up and down.

Illustrative Example 6.3

A progressive wave of frequency 500 Hz is travelling with a velocity of 360 m/s. How far apart are two points 60° out of phase ?

Solution

We know that for a wave $v = f\lambda$,

So $$\lambda = \frac{u}{f} = \frac{360}{500} = 0.72 \text{ m}$$

Now as in a wave path difference is related to phase difference by the relation.

phase difference

$$\Delta\phi = \frac{2\pi}{\lambda} \text{ (path difference } \Delta x)$$

Here, phase difference

$$\Delta\phi = 60^\circ = (\pi/180) \times 60 = (\pi/3) \text{ rad}$$

So path difference

$$\Delta x = \frac{\lambda}{2\pi}(\Delta\phi) = \frac{0.72}{2\pi} \times \frac{\pi}{3} = 0.12 \text{ m}$$

Illustrative Example 6.4

A person, standing between two parallel hills, fires a gun. He hears the first echo after 1.5 s and the second after 2.5 s. If the speed of sound is 332 m/s. Calculate the distance between the hills. When will he hear the third echo ?

Solution

Let the person P be at a distance x from hill H_1 and y from H_2 as shown in figure-6.6. The time interval between the original sound and echoes from H_1 and H_2 will be respectively

$$t_1 = \frac{2x}{v} \quad \text{and} \quad t_2 = \frac{2y}{v}$$

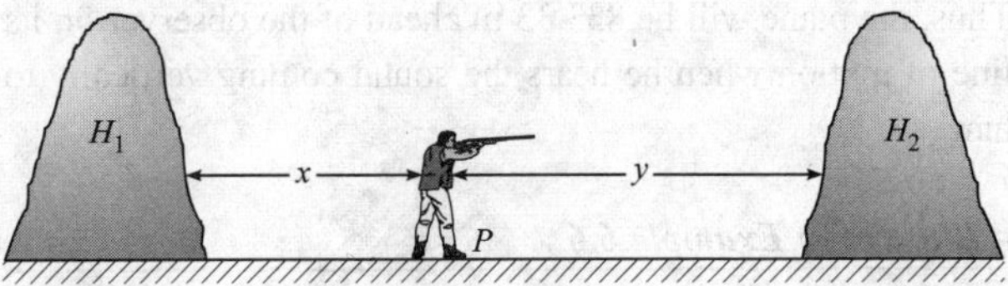

Figure 6.6

So the distance between the hills,

$$x + y = \frac{v}{2}[t_1 + t_2] = \frac{332}{2}[1.5 + 2.5] = 664 \text{ m}$$

Now as I echo will be from H_1 after time t_1 while II echo from H_2 after time t_2, III echo will be produced due to reflection of sound of I echo from H_2 or of II echo from H_1, thus we have

$$t_3 = t_1 + t_2 = 1.5 + 2.5 = 4 \text{ s}$$

Thus we can state that III echo will be produced after 4s and in it sound from both I and II echoes will reach simultaneously.

Illustrative Example 6.5

An aeroplane is going towards east at a speed of 510 km/h at a height of 2000 m. At a certain instant, the sound of the plane heard by a ground observer appears to becoming from a point vertically above him. Where is the plane at this instant ? Speed of sound in air = 340 m/s.

Solution

The situation is shown in figure-6.7. The sound reaching the ground observer P, was emitted by the plane when it was at the point Q vertically above his head. The time taken by the sound to reach the observer is

$$t = \frac{2000}{340} = \frac{100}{17} \text{ s}$$

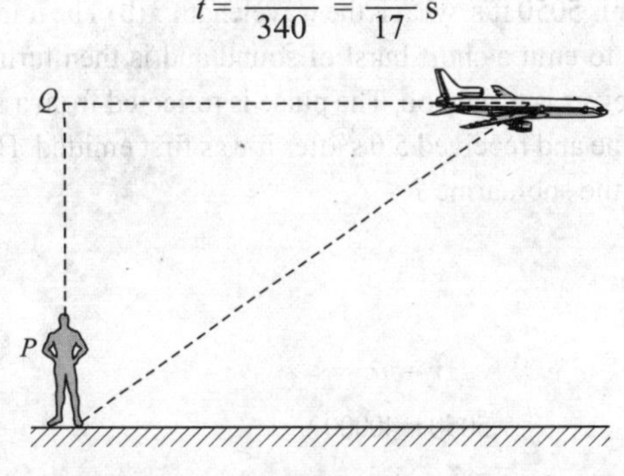

Figure 6.7

The distance moved by the plane during this period is

or $$d = vt$$

$$= \frac{510 \times 5}{18} \times \frac{100}{17}$$

$$= 833.33 \text{ m}$$

Thus, the plane will be 833.33 m ahead of the observer on its line of motion when he hears the sound coming vertically to him.

Illustrative Example 6.6

A light pointer fixed to one prong of a tuning fork touches a vertical plate. The fork is set vibrating and the plate is allowed to fall freely. Eight complete oscillations are counted when the plate falls through 10 cm. What is the frequency of the fork ?

Solution

During the time the plate falls through 10 cm from rest, the tuning fork makes 8 vibrations.

From speed equation we get

$$h = \frac{1}{2}gt^2$$

$$0.1 = \frac{1}{2} \times 9.8 \times t^2 \quad \text{or} \quad t = \frac{1}{7}\text{ s}$$

In $\frac{1}{7}$ s the fork makes 8 vibrations. Therefore in 1 s, the number of vibrations fork makes is

$$n = 8 \times 7 = 56$$

Thus frequency of fork is

$$n = 56\text{ Hz}$$

Illustrative Example 6.7

(a) An ultrasonic transducer used in sonar produces a frequency of 40 kHz. If the velocity of the sound wave in seawater is 5050 ft/s, what is the wavelength ? (b) The transducer is made to emit a short burst of sound and is then turned off. The receiver is turned on. The pulse is reflected from a lurking submarine and received 5.0 s after it was first emitted. How far away is the submarine ?

Solution

(a) $v = n\lambda$

or $5050 = 40000\,\lambda$

or $\lambda = 0.126\text{ ft}$

(b) $v = \frac{2d}{t}$

or $5050 = \frac{2d}{5.0}$

or $d = 12600\text{ ft}$

Illustrative Example 6.8

When a train of plane wave traverses a medium, individual particle execute periodic motion given by the equation

$$y = 4\sin\frac{\pi}{2}\left(2t + \frac{x}{8}\right)$$

where the lengths are expressed in cm and time in second. Calculate the amplitude, wavelength, (i) the phase difference for two positions of the same particle which are occupied at time intervals 0.4 second apart and (ii) the phase difference at any given instant of two particles 12 cm apart.

Solution

The equation of a wave motion is given by

$$y = A\sin\frac{2\pi}{\lambda}(vt + x) \quad \text{...(6.15)}$$

Here $y = 4\sin\frac{\pi}{2}\left(2t + \frac{x}{8}\right)$

This equation can be written as

$$y = 4\sin\frac{2\pi}{32}(16t + x) \quad \text{...(6.16)}$$

Comparing equation-(6.16) with equation-(6.15), we get amplitude $A = 4$ cm; wavelength $\lambda = 32$ cm; wave velocity $v = 16$ cm/s.

Here frequency is given as

$$n = \frac{v}{\lambda} = \frac{16}{32} = \frac{1}{2} = 0.5\text{ Hz.}$$

(i) Phase of a particle at instant t_1 is given by

$$\phi_1 = \frac{\pi}{2}\left(2t_1 + \frac{x}{8}\right)$$

The phase at instant t_2 is given by

$$\phi_2 = \frac{\pi}{2}\left(2t_2 + \frac{x}{8}\right)$$

The phase difference is given as

$$\phi_1 - \phi_2 = \frac{\pi}{2}\left[\left(2t_1 + \frac{x}{8}\right) - \left(2t_2 + \frac{x}{8}\right)\right]$$

$$= \pi(t_1 - t_2) = \pi(0.4) \quad [\text{As } t_1 - t_2 = 0.4]$$

$$= 180 \times 0.4 = 72^\circ \quad [\pi\text{ rad} = 180^\circ]$$

(ii) Phase different at an instant between two particles with path difference Δ is

$$\phi = \frac{2\pi}{\lambda} \times \Delta$$

$$= \frac{2\pi}{32} \times 12 \quad [\text{As } \Delta = 12\text{ cm}]$$

$$= \frac{3\pi}{4}$$

Illustrative Example 6.9

A rod runs midway between two parallel rows of buildings. A motorist moving with a speed of 36 kilometers per hour sounds the horn. He hears the echo one second after he has sounded the horn. Find the distance between the two rows of buildings. When will he hear the echo, a second time ? Velocity of sound in air is 330 m/s.

Solution

The situation is shown in figure-6.8.

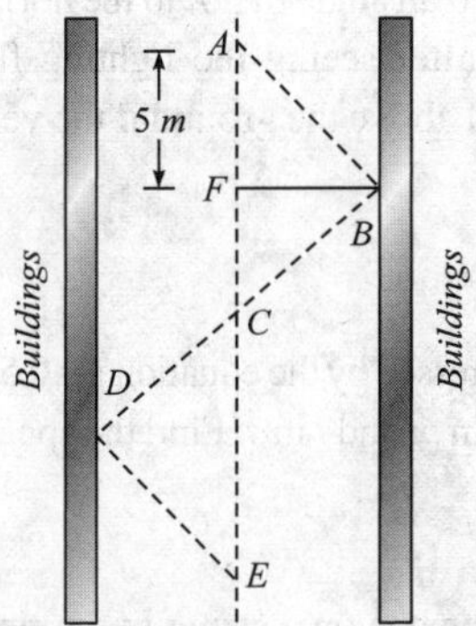

Figure 6.8

Given the velocity of motorist = 36 km/hour = 10 m/s.

So he travels a distance of 10 m in one second. He will hear the first echo after the sound had travelled 330 m through the least path *i.e.*, reflected at point *B*.

From figure-6.8, we have

$$AB = \sqrt{(AF^2 + BF^2)} = \sqrt{(5^2 + x^2)}$$

And $\qquad AB + BC = 2\sqrt{(5^2 + x^2)}$

But we also have $AB + BC = 330$ m

Thus $\qquad 2\sqrt{(5^2 + x^2)} = 330\,\text{m}$

Solving we get $\qquad x = 164.9\,\text{m}$

So the distance between the two rows of building $g = 2x = 329.8$ m. He will hear the second echo at *E* after the sound had travelled a further distance of 330 m, reflecting from the other row i.e., 2 seconds after the horn is sounded.

Illustrative Example 6.10

An engine approaches a hill with a constant speed. When it is at a distance of 0.9 km it blows a whistle, whose echo is heard by the driver after 5 s. If the speed of sound in air is 330 m/s, calculate the speed of the engine.

Solution

The situation is shown in figure-6.9.

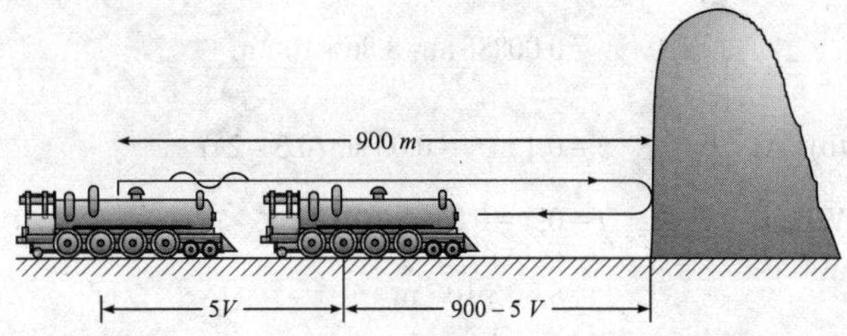

Figure 6.9

If the speed of the engine is *v*, the distance travelled by the engine in 5 s. will be 5 *v*. And hence, the distance travelled by sound in reaching the hill and coming back to the moving driver is given as

$$S = 900 + (900 - 5v) = (1800 - 5v)$$

Thus time interval between the original sound and its echo is

$$t = \frac{S}{v_{sound}}$$

$$5 = \frac{1800 - 5v}{330}$$

On solving we get $\qquad v = 30$ m/s

Illustrative Example 6.11

Given the equation for a wave in a string

$$y = 0.03 \sin(3x - 2t)$$

where *y* and *x* are in metres and *t* is in seconds, answer the following :

(a) At $t = 0$, what is the displacement at 0, 0.1 m.

(b) At $x = 0.1$ m, what is the displacement at $t = 0$ and $t = 0.2$ s.

(c) What is the equation for the velocity of oscillation of the particles of the string ? What is the maximum velocity of oscillation ?

(d) What is the velocity of propagation of the wave ?

Solution

Given that $\qquad y = 0.03 \sin(3x - 2t)$

(a) At $\qquad t = 0, y = 0.03 \sin 3x$

When $\qquad x = 0, y = 0.03 \sin 0 = 0$

When $\qquad x = 0.1, y = 0.03 \sin(0.3 \times \frac{180}{\pi})$

or $y = 0.03 \sin\left(\frac{54}{\pi}\right)$

$= 0.03 \times 0.2954$

$= 0.00886\,\text{m} = 8.86 \times 10^{-3}\,\text{m}$

(b) At $x = 0.1$ m, $y = 0.03 \sin(0.3 - 2t)$

When $t = 0, y = 0.03 \sin(0.3)$

$= 8.86 \times 10^{-3}$ m

When $t = 0.2, y = 0.03 \sin(0.3 - 0.4)$

$= -0.03 \sin 0.1$

$= -0.03 \sin(18/\pi)$

$= -0.03 \times 0.0999$

$= -2.997 \times 10^{-3}$ m

(c) Velocity of particle

$$v_p = \frac{dy}{dt}$$

$= -2 \times 0.03 \cos(3x - 2t)$

$= -0.06 \cos(3x - 2t)$

This is maximum when $\cos(3x - 2t) = 1$

or maximum velocity $= 0.06$ m/s $= 6 \times 10^{-2}$ m/s

(d) We know that the equation of a progressive wave is given by

$$y = a \sin 2\pi\left(\frac{x}{\lambda} - \frac{t}{T}\right)$$

Comparing the given equation, with this equation, we have

$$\frac{2\pi}{\lambda} = 3 \quad \text{and} \quad \frac{2\pi}{T} = 2$$

or $\lambda = \frac{2\pi}{3}$ and $2\pi n = 2$ or $n = \frac{1}{\pi}$

Now $v = n\lambda = \frac{1}{\pi} \times \frac{2\pi}{3} = 0.667$ m/s

Web Reference at www.physicsgalaxy.com

Age Group - High School Physics | Age 17-19 Years

Section - OSCILLATION & WAVES

Topic - Wave Motion

Module Number - 1 to 13

Practice Exercise 6.1

(i) The displacement of a wave is represented by

$$y = 0.25 \times 10^{-3} \sin(500t - 0.25x)$$

where y, t and x are in cm, sec and metre respectively. Deduce (a) amplitude (b) time period (c) angular frequency (d) wavelength (e) amplitudes of particle velocity and (f) particle acceleration.

[(a) 0.25×10^{-3} cm (b) $\frac{\pi}{250}$ s (c) 500 rad/s
(d) 8π cm (e) 0.125 cm/s (f) 6.25 cm/s^2]

(ii) From a cloud at an angle of 30º to the horizontal we hear the thunder clap 8 s after seeing the lighting flash. What is the height of the cloud above the ground if the velocity of sound in air is 330 m/s ?

[1.320 km]

(iii) A wave is expressed by the equation $y = 0.5 \sin \pi(0.01x - 3t)$, where y and x are in m and t in s. Find the speed of propagation.

[300 m/s]

(iv) A wave propagates on a string in the positive x-direction at a velocity v. The shape of the string at $t = t_0$ is given by $g(x, t_0) = A \sin(x/a)$. Write the wave equation for a general time t.

[$f(x, t) = A \sin\left(\frac{x - v(t - t_0)}{a}\right)$]

(v) A man seeing a lightning starts counting seconds, until he hears thunder. He then claims to have found an approximate but simple rule that if the count of second is divided by an integer, the result directly gives, in km, the distance of the lightning source. What is the integer ? (Velocity of sound in air = 330 m/s)

[3]

(vi) A man stands before a large wall at a distance of 50.0 m and claps his hands at regular intervals. Initially, the interval is large. He gradually reduces the interval and fixes it at a value when the echo of a clap merges with the next clap. If he has to clap 10 times during every 3 seconds, find the velocity of sound in air.

[333 m/s]

(vii) A simple harmonic wave has the equation $y = 0.30 \sin(314t - 1.57x)$ where t, x and a are in seconds, metres, and centimeters respectively. Find the frequency and wavelength of this wave. Another wave has the equation $y' = 0.10 \sin(314t - 1.57x + 1.57)$. Deduce phase difference and ratio of intensities of the two wave.

[90º, 9/1]

(viii) A plane elastic wave $y = A\cos(\omega t - kx)$ propagates in a medium K. Find the equation of this wave in a reference frame K' moving in the positive direction of x-axis with a constant velocity V relative to the medium K. Wave speed in medium K is v.

$[A \cos\left[\omega\left(1-\frac{V}{v}\right)t - kx'\right]]$

(ix) The equation of a travelling sound wave is $y = 6.0 \sin(600\,t - 1.8\,x)$ where y is measured in 10^{-5} m, t in second and x in metre. (a) Find the ratio of the displacement amplitude of the particles to the wavelength of the wave. (b) Find the ratio of the velocity amplitude of the particles to the wave speed.

[(a) 1.71×10^{-5}, (b) 1.08×10^{-4}]

(x) The equation of a travelling plane sound wave has the form $y = 50 \cos(1800\,t - 5.3\,x)$, where y is expressed in micrometers, t in seconds, and x in meters. Find :

(a) the ratio of the displacement amplitude, with which the particles of medium oscillate, to the wavelength;

(b) the velocity oscillation amplitude of particles of the medium and its ratio to the wave propagation velocity;

(c) the ratio of oscillation amplitude of relative deformation of the medium to the velocity oscillation amplitude of particles of the medium.

[(a) 4.22×10^{-5}, (b) 0.09 m/s, 2.65×10^{-4}, (c) 2.94×10^{-3} m]

(xi) A man standing in front of a mountain at a certain distance beats a drum at regular intervals. The drumming rate is gradually increased and he finds that the echo is not heard distinctly when the rate becomes 40 per minute. He then moves nearer to the mountain by 90 metres and finds that the echo is again not heard when the drumming rate becomes 60 per minute. Calculate

(a) the distance between the mountain and the initial position of the man,

(b) the velocity of sound.

[270 m and 360 m/s]

(xii) A sound wave of frequency 100 Hz is travelling in air. The speed of sound in air is 350 m/s. (a) By how much is the phase changed at a given point in 2.5 ms ? (b) What is the phase difference at a given instant between two points separated by a distance of 10.0 cm along the direction of propagation ?

[(a) $\pi/2$, (b) $2\pi/35$]

6.4 *Velocity of a Wave*

We have discussed that wave velocity is the velocity of energy propagation in the direction of wave motion. Wave velocity of a wave is also termed as its phase velocity as the phase of medium particles also travels along propagation direction with the wave with this speed. In different type of waves its velocity depends on medium properties in different manner, we will now discuss in detail.

6.4.1 Wave Speed of Transverse Waves on a Stretched String

When on a stretched string shown in figure-6.10, a transverse jerk is given, a pulse is created as shown in figure-6.10(b) and (c) which travels toward right with a wave speed v as shown. We start our analysis by looking at the pulse carefully as shown in enlarged view of figure-6.10(d). For convenience of our analysis we chose a reference frame in which the pulse remains stationary or we assume that our frame is moving along with the pulse at speed v.

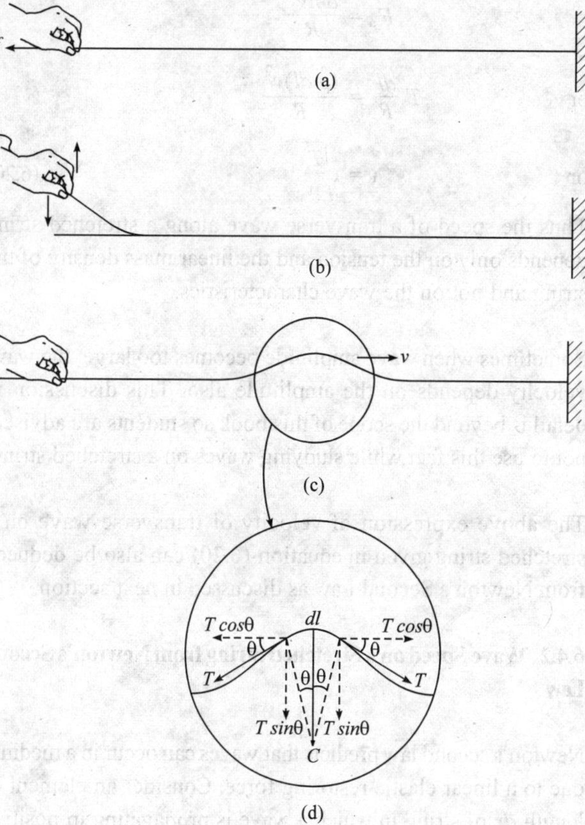

Figure 6.10

Now consider a small element of length dl on this pulse as shown. This element is forming an arc, say of radius R with centre at C and subtending an angle 2θ at C. We can see that two tensions T are acting on the edges of dl along tangential directions as shown. The horizontal components of these tensions cancels each other, but the vertical components add to form a radial restoring force in downward direction, which is given as

$$F_R = 2T \sin\theta$$

$$\simeq 2T\theta \qquad [\text{As } \sin\theta \simeq \theta]$$

$$= T\frac{dl}{R} \qquad [\text{As } 2\theta = \frac{dl}{R}] \quad \ldots(6.17)$$

If μ be the mass per unit length of the string, the mass of this element is given as

$$dm = \mu\, dl \quad \ldots(6.18)$$

In our reference frame if we look at this element, it appears to be moving toward left with speed v then we can say that the acceleration of this element in our reference frame is

$$a = \frac{v^2}{R} \quad \ldots(6.19)$$

Now from equation-(6.17), (6.18) and (6.19) we have

$$F_R = \frac{dmv^2}{R}$$

or
$$T\frac{dl}{R} = \frac{(\mu\, dl)v^2}{R}$$

or
$$v = \sqrt{\frac{T}{\mu}} \quad \ldots(6.20)$$

Thus the speed of a transverse wave along a stretched string depends only on the tension and the linear mass density of the string and not on the wave characteristics.

Sometimes when wave amplitude becomes too large, the wave velocity depends on the amplitude also. This discussion in detail is beyond the scope of this book so students are advised, not to use this fact while studying waves on a stretched string.

The above expression of velocity of transverse wave on a stretched string given in equation-(6.20) can also be deduced from Newton's Second Law as discussed in next section.

6.4.2 Wave Speed on a Stretched String from Newton's Second Law

Newton's second law predicts that waves can occur in a medium due to a linear elastic restoring force. Consider an element of length dx of string in which a wave is propagating in positive x-direction in the figure-6.11 shown.

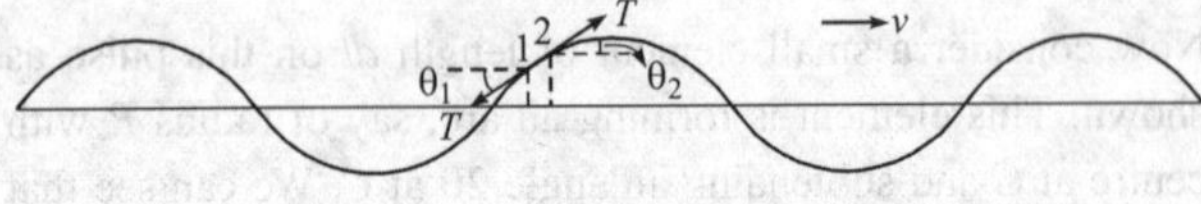

Figure 6.11

As tension in the string can be considered uniform, the restoring force on this element dx toward its mean position for its oscillation is given as

$$F_R = T\sin\theta_1 - T\sin\theta_2 \quad \ldots(6.21)$$

As here θ_1 and θ_2 are very small, we can use

$$\sin\theta_1 \simeq \tan\theta_1 = \left.\frac{\partial y}{\partial x}\right|_1$$

[Slope of displacement curve at point 1]

$$\sin\theta_2 \simeq \tan\theta_2 = \left.\frac{\partial y}{\partial x}\right|_2$$

[Slope of displacement curve at point 2]

From equation-(6.21) we have

$$F_R = +T\left[\left.\frac{\partial y}{\partial x}\right|_1 - \left.\frac{\partial y}{\partial x}\right|_2\right] \quad \ldots(6.22)$$

Here $\left.\frac{\partial y}{\partial x}\right|_2 - \left.\frac{\partial y}{\partial x}\right|_1$ is the change in slopes of displacement curve for a differential change in x by dx between points 1 and 2. Thus we can write

$$\left.\frac{\partial y}{\partial x}\right|_2 - \left.\frac{\partial y}{\partial x}\right|_1 = \frac{\partial^2 y}{\partial x^2}\, dx \quad \ldots(6.23)$$

Thus from equation-(6.22) and (6.23)

$$F_R = +T\frac{\partial^2 y}{\partial x^2}\, dx \quad \ldots(6.24)$$

If the element of string has mass dm, we have

$$dm = \mu\, dx \quad \ldots(6.25)$$

Where μ is the mass per unit length of string. Now from Newton's Second Law for this element, we can write

$$F_R = dm\frac{\partial^2 y}{\partial t^2} \quad \ldots(6.26)$$

From equation-(6.24), (6.25) and (6.26) we have

$$T\frac{\partial^2 y}{\partial x^2}\, dx = +(\mu\, dx)\frac{\partial^2 y}{\partial t^2}$$

or
$$\frac{\partial^2 y}{\partial x^2} = \frac{\mu}{T}\frac{\partial^2 y}{\partial t^2} \quad \ldots(6.27)$$

Equation-(6.27) is the wave equation, we have already discussed in previous sections of the chapter. Comparing it with equation-(6.12), we get the wave velocity as

$$v = \sqrt{\frac{T}{\mu}}$$

6.4.3 Velocity of Sound/Longitudinal Waves in Solids

Consider a section AB of medium as shown in figure-6.12(a) of cross-sectional area S. Let A and B be two cross section as shown. Let in this medium sound propagation is from left to right. If wave source is at origin O and when it oscillates, the oscillations at that point propagate along the rod.

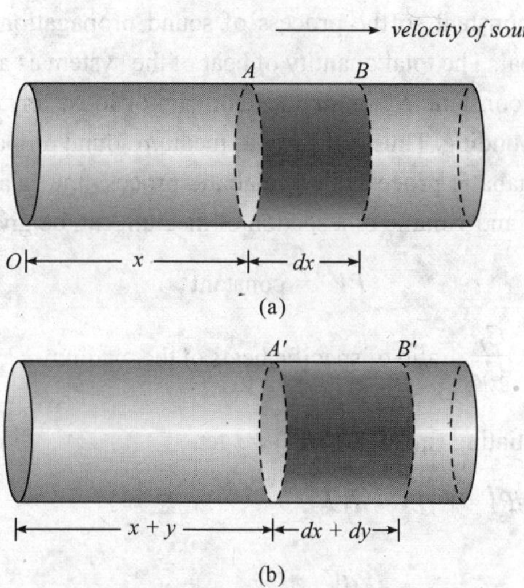

Figure 6.12

Here we say an elastic wave has propagated along the rod with a velocity determined by the physical properties of the medium. Due to oscillations say a force F is developed at every point of medium which produces a stress in rod and is the cause of strain or propagation of disturbance along the rod. This stress at any cross-sectional area can be given as

$$\text{Stress } \mathcal{S}_t = \frac{F}{S} \qquad \ldots(6.28)$$

If we consider the section AB of medium at a general instant of time t. The end A is at a distance x from O and B is at a distance $x + dx$ from O. Let in time dt due to oscillations, medium particles at A are displaced along the length of medium by y and those at B by $y + dy$. The resulting positions of section are A' and B' shown in figure-6.12(b). Here we can say that the section AB is deformed (elongated) by a length dy. Thus strain produced in it is

Strain in section AB

$$E = \frac{dy}{dx} \qquad \ldots(6.29)$$

If Young's modulus of the material of medium is Y, we have

Young's Modulus

$$Y = \frac{\text{Stress}}{\text{Strain}} = \frac{\mathcal{S}_t}{E}$$

From equation-(6.28) and (6.29), we have $Y = \dfrac{F/S}{dy/dx}$

or
$$F = YS\frac{dy}{dx} \qquad \ldots(6.30)$$

If net force acting of section AB is dF then it is given as

$$dF = dma \qquad \ldots(6.31)$$

Where dm is the mass of section AB and a be its acceleration, which can be given as for a medium of density ρ.

$$dm = \rho S dx \quad \text{and} \quad a = \frac{d^2y}{dt^2}$$

From equation-(6.31), we have

$$dF = (\rho S dx)\frac{d^2y}{dt^2}$$

or
$$\frac{dF}{dx} = \rho S\frac{d^2y}{dt^2} \qquad \ldots(6.32)$$

From equation-(6.30) on differentiating w.r. to x, we can write

$$\frac{dF}{dx} = YS\frac{d^2y}{dx^2} \qquad \ldots(6.33)$$

From equation-(6.32) and (6.33) we get

$$\frac{d^2y}{dx^2} = \left(\frac{Y}{\rho}\right)\frac{d^2y}{dx^2} \qquad \ldots(6.34)$$

Equation-(6.34) is the different form of wave equation, comparing it with equation-(6.12) we get the wave velocity in the medium can be given as

$$v = \sqrt{\frac{Y}{\rho}} \qquad \ldots(6.35)$$

6.4.4 Wave Velocity of Longitudinal Waves in Fluid/Gas

Similar to the case of a solid in fluid, instead of Young's Modulus we use Bulk modulus of the medium hence the velocity of longitudinal waves in a fluid medium is given as

$$v = \sqrt{\frac{B}{\rho}} \qquad \ldots(6.36)$$

Where B is the Bulk modulus of medium.

For a gaseous medium bulk modulus is defined as

$$B = \frac{dP}{(-dV/V)}$$

or
$$B = -V\frac{dP}{dV} \qquad \ldots(6.37)$$

6.4.5 Newton's Formula for Velocity of Sound in Gases

Newton assumed that during sound propagation temperature of medium remains same hence he stated that propagation of sound in a gaseous medium is an isothermal phenomenon, thus Boyle's law can be applied in the process. So for a section of medium we use

$$PV = \text{constant}$$

Differentiating we get

$$P\,dV + V\,dP = 0$$

or
$$-V\frac{dP}{dV} = P$$

or bulk modulus of medium can be given as

$$B = P \quad \text{(Pressure of medium)}$$

Newton found that during isothermal propagation of sound in a gaseous medium, bulk modulus of medium is equal to the pressure of the medium, hence sound velocity in a gaseous medium can be given as

$$v = \sqrt{\frac{B}{\rho}} = \sqrt{\frac{P}{\rho}} \quad \ldots(6.38)$$

From gas law we have

$$\frac{P}{\rho} = \frac{RT}{M} \quad \ldots(6.39)$$

From (6.38) & (6.39) we have

$$v = \sqrt{\frac{RT}{M}} \quad \ldots(6.40)$$

From the expression in equation-(6.38) if we find the sound velocity in air at normal temperature and atmospheric pressure we have

Normal atmospheric pressure is

$$P = 1.01 \times 10^5 \text{ Pa}$$

Density of air at NTP is

$$P = 1.293 \text{ kg/m}^3$$

Now from equation-(6.38)

$$v = \sqrt{\frac{P}{\rho}}$$

or
$$v = \sqrt{\frac{1.01 \times 10^5}{1.293}} = 279.48 \text{ m/s}$$

But the experimental value of velocity of sound determined from various experiments gives the velocity of sound at NTP, 332 m/s. Therefore there is a difference of about 52 m/s between the theoretical and experimental values. This large different can not be attributed to the experimental errors. Newton was unable to explain error in his formula. This correction was explained by a French Scientist Laplace.

6.4.6 Laplace Correction

Laplace explained that when sound waves propagate in a gaseous medium. There is condensation and rarefactions in the particles of medium. Where there is condensation, particles come near to each other and are heated up, where there is rarefaction, medium expends and there is fall of temperature. Therefore, the temperature of medium at every point does not remain constant so the process of sound propagation is not isothermal. The total quantity of heat of the system as a whole remains constant. Medium does not gain or loose any heat to the surrounding. Thus in a gaseous medium sound propagation is an adiabatic process. For adiabatic process the relation in pressure and volume of a section of medium can be given as

$$PV^{\gamma} = \text{constant} \quad \ldots(6.41)$$

Here $\rho = \frac{C_P}{C_V}$, ratio of specific heats of the medium.

Differentiating equation-(6.41) we get,

$$dPV^{\gamma} + \gamma V^{\gamma-1}\, dVP = 0$$

or
$$dP + \gamma \frac{PdV}{dV} = 0$$

or
$$-V\frac{dP}{dV} = \gamma P$$

Bulk modulus of medium

$$B = \gamma P \quad \ldots(6.42)$$

Thus Laplace found that during adiabatic propagation of sound, the Bulk modulus of gaseous mediums is equal to the product of ratio of specific heats and the pressure of medium. Thus velocity of sound propagation can be given as

$$v = \sqrt{\frac{B}{\rho}} = \sqrt{\frac{\gamma P}{\rho}} \quad \ldots(6.43)$$

From gas law
$$v = \sqrt{\frac{\gamma RT}{M}} \quad \ldots(6.44)$$

From equation-(6.43) if we find sound velocity in air at NTP, we have

Normal atmospheric pressure $P = 1.01 \times 10^5\ Pa$

Density of air at NTP $P = 1.293 \text{ kg/m}^3$

Ratio of specific heats of air $\gamma = \frac{C_P}{C_V} = 1.42$

Using equation-(6.43), we get

$$v = \sqrt{\frac{\gamma\rho}{\rho}}$$

or
$$v = \sqrt{\frac{1.42 \times 1.01 \times 10^5}{1.293}} = 333.04 \text{ m/s}$$

This value is in agreement with experimental value.

6.4.7 Effect of Temperature on Velocity of Sound

From equation-(6.43) we have velocity of sound propagation in a gaseous medium as

$$v = \sqrt{\frac{\gamma RT}{M}}$$

For a given gaseous medium γ, R and M remains constant, thus velocity of sound is directly proportional to square root of absolute temperature of the medium. Thus

$$v \propto \sqrt{T} \qquad \ldots(6.45)$$

If at two different temperatures T_1 and T_2, sound velocities in medium are v_1 and v_2 then from equation-(6.45), we have

$$\frac{v_1}{v_2} = \sqrt{\frac{T_1}{T_2}} \qquad \ldots(6.46)$$

6.4.8 Effect of Pressure on Velocity of Sound

We know form gas law

$$\frac{P}{\rho} = \frac{RT}{M}$$

If temperature of a medium remains constant then on changing pressure, density of medium proportionally changes so that the ratio $\frac{P}{\rho}$ remains constant.

Hence if in a medium, $T =$ constant

Then, $\frac{P}{\rho} =$ constant

Thus velocity of sound, $v = \sqrt{\frac{\gamma P}{\rho}} =$ constant

Therefore, the velocity of sound in air or in a gas in independent of change in pressure.

6.4.9 Effect of Humidity on Velocity of Sound

The density of water vapour at NTP is 0.8 kg/m^3 whereas the density of dry air at NTP is 1.293 kg/m^3. Therefore water vapour has a density less than the density of dry air. As atmospheric pressure remains approximately same, the velocity of sound is more in moist air then the velocity of sound in dry air

$$v_{\text{moist air}} > v_{\text{dry air}} \qquad \ldots(6.47)$$

6.4.10 Effect of Wind on Velocity of Sound

If wind is blowing in the direction of propagation of sound, it will increase the velocity of sound. On the other hand if wave propagation is opposite to the direction of propagation of wind, wave velocity is decreased. If wind blows at speed v_ω then sound velocity in the medium can be given as

$$\vec{v} = \vec{v}_s + \vec{v}_\omega \qquad \ldots(6.48)$$

Where $\vec{v}_s$ is the velocity of sound in still air.

6.4.11 Velocity of Longitudinal Waves in a Slinky Spring

Suppose a periodic disturbance is produced along a stretched slinky spring as shown in figure-6.13(a) and (b). The resulting wave consists in a series of compressions and expansions that propagate along the spring. In such a case the velocity of these longitudinal wave along the length of spring is given as

$$v = \sqrt{\frac{kL}{\mu}} \qquad \ldots(6.49)$$

Figure-3.16 shows how by holding a spring when hand oscillates forward and backward due to inertia of spring wave propagation take place.

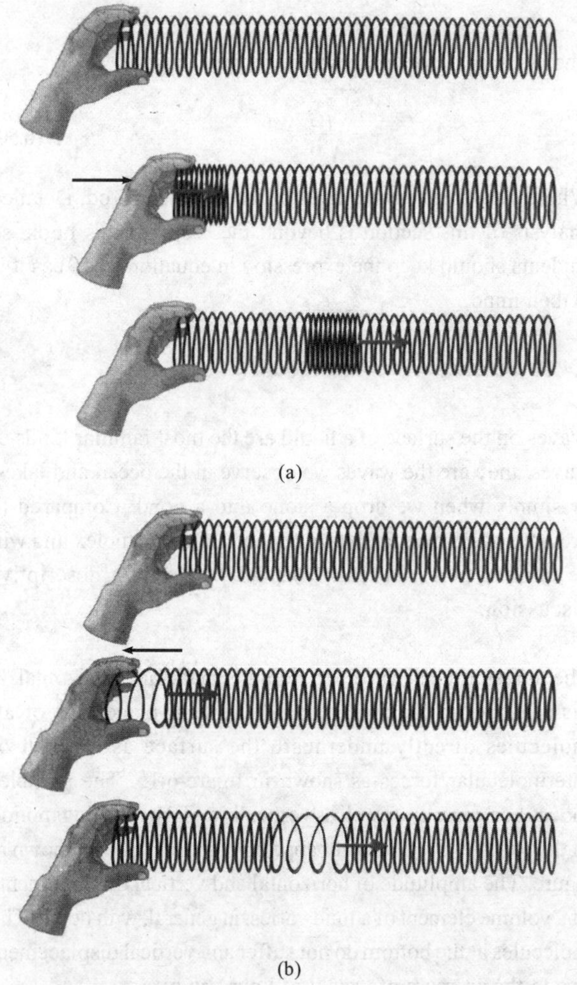

(a)

(b)

Figure 6.13

Here k is the force constant of the spring.

L is the length of the unstretched spring.

and μ is the linear density of the unstretched spring.

6.4.12 Velocity of Torsional Waves in a Rod

If a rod is damped at one end and other end is periodically twisted in angular oscillations, torsional waves are produced in the rod as shown in figure-6.14.

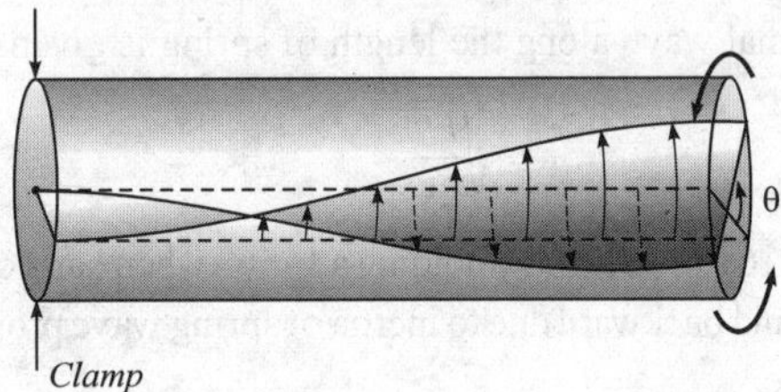

Figure 6.14

The velocity of torsional waves are given as

$$v = \sqrt{\frac{G}{\rho}} \quad \ldots(6.50)$$

Where G is the shear modulus of the material of rod. Detailed analysis of this section is beyond the scope of this book, so students should keep the expression in equation-(6.50) as it is in their mind.

6.4.13 Surface Waves in a Liquid

Waves on the surface of a liquid are the most familiar kinds of waves, they are the waves we observe in the ocean and lakes, or simply when we drop a stone into a pond. Compared to previous cases here analytical aspect is more complex and will be omitted here. We will consider here only a descriptive discussion.

The undisturbed surface of a liquid is plane and horizontal. A disturbance on the surface produces a displacement of all molecules directly underneath the surface as a result of intermolecular forces as shown in figure-6.15. The particles moves horizontally as well as vertically and the resulting motion of the particles is elliptical or approximately circular as shown in figure. The amplitude of horizontal and vertical displacements of a volume element of a fluid varies, in general, with depth. The molecules at the bottom do not suffer any vertical displacement due to the pressure of weight of liquid body.

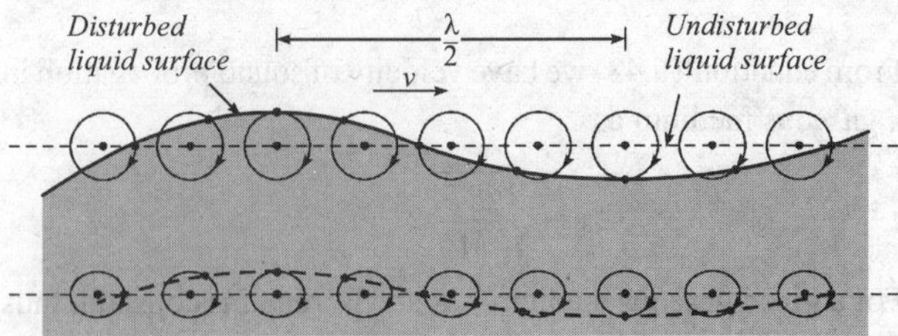

Figure 6.15

At the surface of liquid other forces are playing the role in oscillations. One force is the surface tension of the liquid which gives an upward or downward force on an element of the surface similar to the case of a string. Another force is the weight of the liquid above the undisturbed level of the liquids surface. The waves produced on the surface of liquid propagates with a velocity v given as

$$v = \sqrt{\frac{g\lambda}{2\pi} + \frac{2\pi\sigma}{\rho\pi}} \quad \ldots(6.51)$$

Where $g \rightarrow$ acceleration due to gravity

$\sigma \rightarrow$ surface tension of the liquid

$\rho \rightarrow$ density of the liquid

$\lambda \rightarrow$ wavelength of wave.

Here we can see that the velocity of propagation of surface wave depends on the wavelength λ of the waves. Students should note that this expression in equation-(6.51) is valid only when the depth of liquid is large compared to the wavelength λ.

If in a case wavelength λ is large enough so the second term in the expression of equation-(6.51) can be neglected then we have

$$v = \sqrt{\frac{g\lambda}{2\pi}} \quad \ldots(6.52)$$

The waves in this case are called gravity waves. In this approximation we can see in equation-(6.52), velocity of propagation is independent from the nature of liquid, since no factor related to the liquid appears in expression of equation-(6.52). Here we can say the longer the wavelength is, faster is the wave propagation. Such types of waves are produced by strong winds over a liquid surface, generally in oceans.

When the wavelength λ is very small so that the first term in equation-(6.51) can be neglected, the wave velocity of surface waves can be given as

$$v = \sqrt{\frac{2\pi\sigma}{\rho\pi}} \quad \ldots(6.53)$$

These waves are called ripples or capillary waves. These are the waves observed when a very gentle wind blows, over the surface of water or when a container is subject to vibrations of high frequency. In this case we can see from equation-(6.53), the longer the wavelength slower the wave propagation.

Now we take some examples on wave velocity in different mediums.

Illustrative Example 6.12

Calculate the increase in velocity of sound for 1°C rise of temperature, if the velocity of sound at 0°C is 332 m/s.

Solution

We know that $$\frac{v_t}{v_0} = \sqrt{\left(\frac{T_t}{T_0}\right)} = \sqrt{\left(\frac{237+t}{273}\right)}$$

or $$v_t = v_0\left(1+\frac{t}{273}\right)^{1/2}$$

$$= v_0\left(1+\frac{t}{2\times 273}\right) = v_0\left(1+\frac{t}{546}\right)$$

So, $$v_t - v_0 = v_0 \times \frac{t}{546}$$

Thus increase in velocity per °C is

$$\frac{\Delta v}{t} = \frac{v_0}{546}$$

or $$\frac{\Delta v}{t} = \frac{332}{546} = 0.61\text{ m/s}$$

Illustrative Example 6.13

A 4.0 kg block is suspended from the ceiling of an elevator through a string having a linear mass density of 19.2×10^{-3} kg/m. Find the speed (with respect to the string) with which a wave pulse can proceed on the string if the elevator accelerate up at the rate of 2.0 m/s^2. Take $g = 10$ m/s^2.

Solution

As elevator accelerates up at 2 m/s^2, tension in the string is

$$T = m(g+a)$$

$$= 4(10+2) = 48\text{ N}$$

Linear mass density of string is

$$\mu = 19.2 \times 10^{-3}\text{ kg/m}$$

Speed of transverse waves on string is

$$v = \sqrt{\frac{T}{\mu}}$$

$$= \sqrt{\frac{48}{19.2\times 10^{-3}}}$$

$$= 50\text{ m/s}$$

Illustrative Example 6.14

At what temperature will the speed of sound in air becomes double of its value at 0°C ?

Solution

We know that $$\frac{v_t}{v_0} = \sqrt{\left(\frac{T_t}{T_0}\right)}$$

Here $$v_t = 2\,v_0$$

or $$\frac{2\,v_0}{v_0} = \sqrt{\left(\frac{T_t}{273}\right)}$$

or $$4 = \frac{T_t}{273}$$

or $$T_t = 4\times 273 = 1092\text{ K}$$

or $$T(^\circ\text{C}) = 1092 - 273 = 819^\circ\text{C}$$

Illustrative Example 6.15

The planet Jupiter has an atmosphere mainly of methane at a temperature – 130°C. Calculate the velocity of sound on this planet assuming γ for the mixture to be 1.3 (Gas constant $R = 8.3$ joules/mol °C).

Solution

We know that $$v = \sqrt{\left(\frac{\gamma P}{d}\right)} = \sqrt{\left(\frac{\gamma R T}{M}\right)}$$

According to the given problem,

$$\gamma = 1.30,\ R = 8.3\times 10^3\text{ J/kg mol K},$$

and $$T = -130\,^\circ\text{C} = -130 + 273 = 143\text{ K}$$

$$M = \text{Molecular weight of methane } (CH_4)$$

$$= 12 + 4 = 16$$

Hence $$v = \sqrt{\left(\frac{1.3\times 8.3\times 10^3\times 143}{16}\right)}$$

$$= 311\text{ m/s}$$

Illustrative Example 6.16

How long will it take sound waves to travel the distance l between the points A and B if the air temperature between them varies linearly from T_1 to T_2? The velocity of sound propagation in air is equal to $v = \alpha\sqrt{T}$, where α is a constant.

Solution

For linear variation of temperature, we can write temperature at a distance x from point A is

$$T_x = T_1 + \frac{T_2 - T_1}{l}x$$

Thus velocity of sound at this point is given as

$$v = \alpha\sqrt{T_1 + \left(\frac{T_2 - T_1}{l}\right)x}$$

or $$\frac{dx}{dt} = \alpha\sqrt{T_1 + \left(\frac{T_2 - T_1}{l}\right)x}$$

or $$\alpha\frac{dx}{\sqrt{T_1 + \left(\frac{T_2 - T_1}{l}\right)x}} = dt$$

Integrating the above expression within proper limits, we get

or $$\int_0^l \frac{dx}{\alpha\sqrt{T_1 + \left(\frac{T_2 - T_1}{l}\right)x}} = \int_0^t dt$$

$$\frac{2l}{\alpha(T_2 - T_1)}\left[\sqrt{T_1 + \frac{T_2 - T_1}{l}x}\right]_0^l = t$$

or $$t = \frac{2l}{\alpha(T_2 - T_1)}\left[\sqrt{T_2} - \sqrt{T_1}\right]$$

or $$t = \frac{2l}{\alpha[\sqrt{T_2} + \sqrt{T_1}]}$$

Alternative solution :

Given that $v = \alpha\sqrt{T}$

or velocity at point A is $v_1 = \alpha\sqrt{T_1}$

Velocity at point B is $v_2 = \alpha\sqrt{T_2}$

The average velocity $\bar{v} = \frac{v_1 + v_2}{2}$

or $\bar{v} = \frac{\alpha(\sqrt{T_1} + \sqrt{T_2})}{2}$

Distance between A and $B = l$

Thus time from A to B is

$$t = \frac{\text{distance}}{\text{velocity}} = \frac{l}{[\alpha(\sqrt{T_1} + \sqrt{T_2})/2]}$$

$$= \frac{2l}{\alpha(\sqrt{T_1} + \sqrt{T_2})}$$

Illustrative Example 6.17

The speed of a transverse wave, going on a wire having a length 50 cm and mass 5.0 kg, is 80 m/s. The area of cross-section of the wire is 1.0 mm^2 and its Young's modulus is 16 × 10^{11} N/m^2. Find the extension of the wire over its natural length.

Solution

The linear mass density is

$$\mu = \frac{5\times10^{-3}}{50\times10^{-2}} = 1.0\times10^{-2}\text{ kg/m}$$

The wave speed is

$$v = \sqrt{\frac{T}{\mu}}$$

Thus, the tension is

$$T = \mu v^2$$

$$= (1.0\times10^{-2})\times6400 = 64\text{ N}$$

The Young's modulus is given by

$$Y = \frac{T/A}{\Delta L/L}$$

The extension is, therefore,

$$\Delta L = \frac{TL}{AY}$$

$$= \frac{64\times0.50}{1.0\times10^{-6}\times16\times10^{11}} = 0.02\text{ mm}$$

Illustrative Example 6.18

Two blocks each having a mass of 3.2 kg are connected by a wire CD and the system is suspended from the ceiling by another wire AB (figure-6.16). The linear mass density of the wire AB is 10 g/m and that of CD is 8 g/m. Find the speed of a transverse wave pulse produced in AB and in CD.

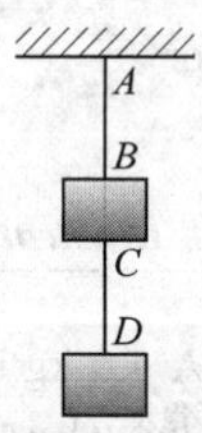

Figure 6.16

Solution

Tension in string AB is

$$T_{AB} = 6.4\,g = 64\text{ N}$$

Thus speed of transverse waves in string AB is

$$v_{AB} = \sqrt{\frac{T_{AB}}{\mu_{AB}}} = \sqrt{\frac{64}{10\times10^{-3}}}$$

$$= \sqrt{6400} = 80\text{ m/s}$$

Tension in strong CD is

$$T = 3.2\,g = 32\text{ N}$$

Thus speed of transverse waves in string CD is

$$v_{CD} = \sqrt{\frac{T_{CD}}{\mu_{DC}}} = \sqrt{\frac{32}{8\times10^{-3}}} = \sqrt{4000}$$

$$= 63.24 \text{ m/s}$$

Illustrative Example 6.19

A heavy but uniform rope of length L is suspended from a ceiling. (a) Write the velocity of a transverse wave travelling on the string as a function of the distance from the lower end. (b) If the rope is given a sudden sideways jerk at the bottom, how long will it take for the pulse to reach the ceiling ? (c) A particle is dropped from the ceiling at the instant the bottom end is given the jerk. Where will the particle meet the pulse ?

Solution

Let m be the mass of the hanging rope, then its linear mass density will be

$$\mu = \frac{M}{L} \quad \ldots(6.54)$$

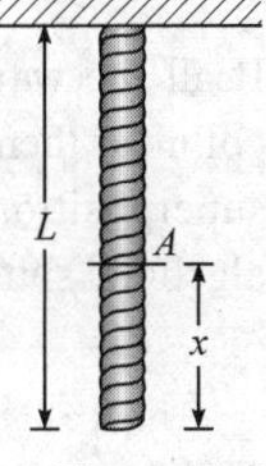

Figure 6.17

(a) At a distance x above the lower end if we consider a cross section A then tension at point A will be due to the weight of the lower part and it is given as

Tension at A is, $\quad T = \frac{M}{L}xg \quad \ldots(6.55)$

Now velocity of transverse waves at point A is given as

$$v = \sqrt{\frac{T}{\mu}} = \sqrt{\frac{\frac{M}{L}xg}{M/L}} = \sqrt{xg} \quad \ldots(6.56)$$

(b) If a jerk is given at the lower end of rope, it propagation in upward direction and its velocity at a distance x from lower end is given by equation-(6.56). We can find the time taken by pulse of jerk to reach the top by integration expression in equation-(6.56) as

$$\frac{dx}{dt} = \sqrt{xg}$$

or $$\frac{dx}{\sqrt{x}} = \sqrt{g}\,dt$$

Integrating this expression in proper limits we get

$$\int_0^L \frac{dx}{\sqrt{x}} = \int_0^t \sqrt{g}\,dt$$

or $$\left[2\sqrt{x}\right]_0^L = \sqrt{g}\,t$$

or $$t = 2\sqrt{\frac{L}{g}}$$

(c) When a particle is dropped from the top it falls by a distance $(L - x)$ in time t. When it will meet the pulse and if pulse has travelled a distance x, Thus time taken by pulse to travel a distance x from bottom is

$$t = 2\sqrt{\frac{x}{g}}$$

In this time the distance fallen by particle in its free fall motion is

$$(L - x) = \frac{1}{2}gt^2$$

or $$L - x = \frac{1}{2}g\left(2\sqrt{\frac{x}{g}}\right)^2$$

or $$L - x = 2x$$

or $$x = \frac{L}{3}$$

Thus particle and the pulse meet at a distance $\frac{L}{3}$ from the bottom.

Web Reference at www.physicsgalaxy.com

Age Group - High School Physics | Age 17-19 Years

Section - OSCILLATION & WAVES

Topic - Wave Motion

Module Number - 14 to 25

Practice Exercise 6.2

(i) A steel wire of length 64 cm weighs 5 g. If it is stretched by a force of 8 N, what would be the speed of a transverse wave passing on it?

[32 m/s]

(ii) A travelling wave is produced on a long horizontal string by vibrating an end up and down sinusoidally. The amplitude of vibration is 1.0 cm and the displacement becomes zero 200 times per second. The linear mass density of the string is 0.10 kg/m and it kept under a tension of 90 N. (a) Find the speed and the wavelength of the wave. (b) assume that the wave moves in the positive x-direction and at $t = 0$, the end $x = 0$ is at its positive extreme position. Write the wave equation. (c) Find the velocity and acceleration of the particle at $x = 50$ cm at time $t = 10$ ms.

[(a) 30 m/s, 30 cm (b) $y = (1.0 \text{ cm}) \cos 2\pi \left[100t - \frac{x}{0.3}\right]$

(c) – 5.45 m/s, 2.0 km/s]

(iii) Two wires of different densities but same area of cross section are soldered together at one end and are stretched to a tension T. The velocity of a transverse wave in one wire is double of that in the second wire. Find the ratio of the density of the first wire to that of the second wire.

[0.25]

(iv) A particle on a stretched string supporting a travelling wave, takes 5.0 ms to move from its mean position to the extreme position. The distance between two consecutive particles, which are at their mean positions, is 2.0 cm. Find the frequency, the wavelength and the wave speed.

[50 Hz, 4.0 cm, 2.0 m/s]

(v) The speed of sound as measured by a student in the laboratory on a winter day is 340 m/s when the room temperature is 17°C. What speed will be measured by another student repeating the experiment on a day when the room temperature is 32°C?

[348.68 m/s]

(vi) A string of length 40 cm and weighing 10 g is attached to a spring at one end and to a fixed wall at the other end. The spring has a spring constant of 160 N/m and is stretched by 1.0 cm. If a wave pulse is produced on the string near the wall, how much time will it take to reach the spring?

[0.05 s]

(vii) Find the change in the volume of 1.0 litre kerosene when it is subjected to an extra pressure of 2.0×10^5 N/m^2 from the following data. Density of kerosene = 800 kg/m^3 and speed of sound in kerosene = 1330 m/s.

[0.141 cm^3]

(viii) The constant γ for oxygen as well as for hydrogen is 1.40. If the speed of sound in oxygen is 470 m/s, what will be the speed in hydrogen at the same temperature and pressure?

[1880 m/s]

(ix) A tuning fork of frequency 440 Hz is attached to a long string of linear mass density 0.01 kg/m kept under a tension of 49 N. The fork produces transverse waves of amplitude 0.50 mm on the string. (a) Find the wave speed and the wavelength of the waves. (b) Find the maximum speed and acceleration of a particle of the string. (c) At what average rate is the tuning fork transmitting energy to the string?

[(a) 70 m/s, 15.9 cm, (b) 1.381 m/s, 3.872 km/s, (c) 0.667 W]

(x) Velocity of sound in a tube containing air at 27°C and at a pressure of 76 cm of Hg is 300 m/s. What will its velocity be when the pressure is increased to 100 cm of Hg and the temperature is kept constant ?

[Same 300 m/s]

(ix) A blast gives a sound of intensity 0.80 W/m^2 and frequency 1 kHz. If the density of air is 1.3 kg/m^3 and speed of sound in air is 330 m/s find the amplitude of the sound wave.

[9.656×10^{-6} m]

6.5 Principle of Superposition

This principle defines the displacement of a medium particle which is oscillating under the influence of two or more then two waves. The principle of superposition is stated as :

"When two or more waves superpose on a medium particle than the resultant displacement of that medium particle is given by the vector sum of the individual displacements produced by the component waves at that medium particle independently."

Let $\vec{y}_1$, $\vec{y}_2$, ... $\vec{y}_N$ are the displacements produced by N independent waves at a medium particle in absence of others then the displacement of that medium, when all the waves are superposed at that point, is given as

$$\vec{y} = \vec{y}_1 + \vec{y}_2 + \vec{y}_3 + ... + \vec{y}_N \quad ...(6.57)$$

If all the waves are producing oscillations at that point are collinear then the displacement of the medium particle where superposition is taking place can be simply given by the algebraic sum of the individual displacements. Thus we have

$$y = y_1 + y_2 + ... + y_N \quad ...(6.58)$$

The above equation is valid only if all individual displacements y_1, y_2 ...... y_N are along same straight line. In this book mainly we'll deal with the problems of superposition of this type.

A simple example of superposition can be understood by figure-6.18. Suppose two wave pulses are travelling simultaneously in opposite directions as shown. When they overlap each other the displacement of particle on string is the algebraic sum of the two displacements as the displacements of the two pulses are in same direction. Figure-6.18(b) also shows the similar situation when the wave pulses are in opposite sides.

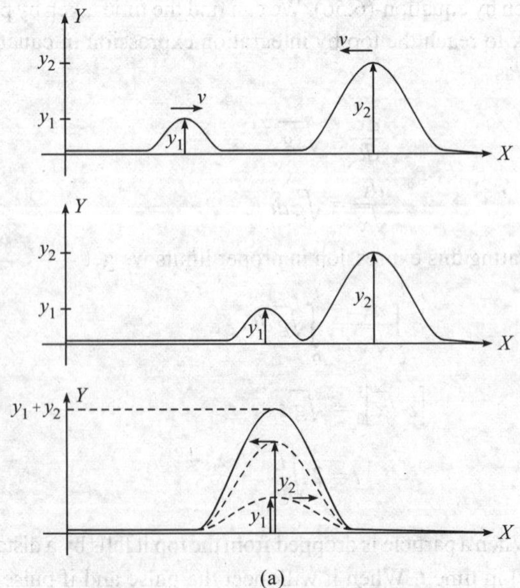

(a)

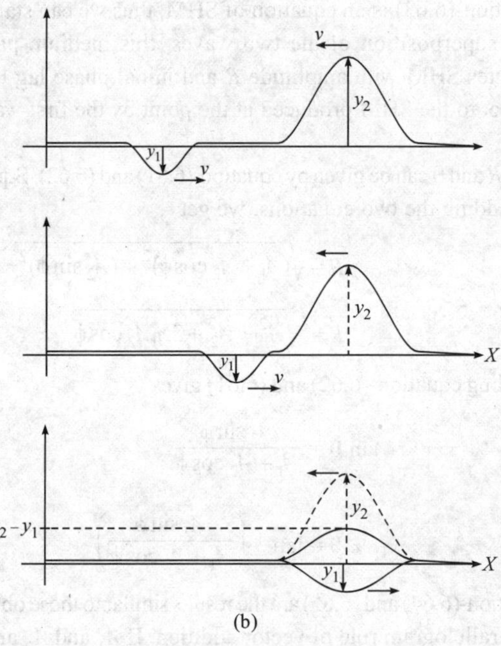

(b)

Figure 6.18

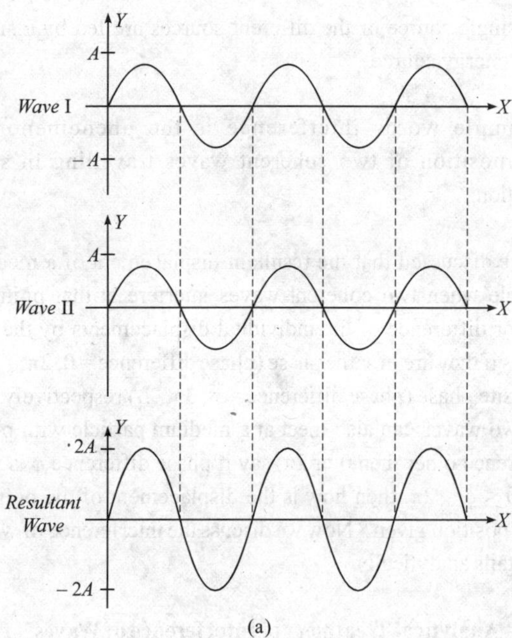

(a)

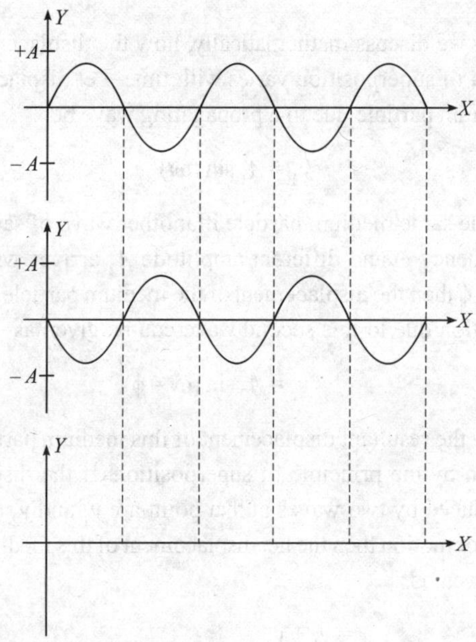

(b)

Figure 6.19

6.5.1 Application of Principle of Superposition of Waves

There are several different phenomenon which takes place during superposition of two or more waves depending on the wave characteristics which are being superposed. We'll discuss some standard phenomenons, and these are :

(1) Interference of Wave

(2) Stationary Waves

(3) Beats

(4) Lissajous Figures (Not discussed here in detail.)

Lets discuss these in detail.

6.6 Interference of Waves

Suppose two sinusoidal waves of same wavelength and amplitude travel in same direction along the same straight line (may be on a stretched string) then superposition principle can be used to define the resultant displacement of every medium particle. The resultant wave in the medium depends on the extent to which the waves are in phase with respect to each other, that is, how much one waveform is shifted from the other waveform. If the two waves are exactly in same phase, that is the shape of one wave exactly fits on to the other wave then they combine to double the displacement of every medium particle as shown in figure-6.19(a). This phenomenon we call as constructive interference. If the superposing waves are exactly out of phase or in opposite phase then they combine to cancel all the displacements at every medium particle and medium remains in the from of a straight line as shown in figure-6.19(b). This phenomenon we call destructive interference. Thus we can state that when two waves meet, they interfere constructively if they meet in same phase and destructively if they meet in opposite phase. In either case the wave patterns do not shift relative to each other as they propagates. Such superposing waves which have same form and wavelength and have a fixed phase relation to each other, are called coherent waves. Sources of coherent waves are called coherent sources. Two independent sources can never be coherent in nature due to practical limitations of manufacturing process. Generally all coherent sources are made either by spliting of the waveforms of a single source or the different sources are fed by a single main energy source.

In simple words interference is the phenomenon of superposition of two coherent waves travelling in same direction.

We've discussed that the resultant displacement of a medium particle when two coherent waves interfere at that point, as sum or difference of the individual displacements by the two waves if they are in same phase (phase difference = 0, 2π, …) or opposite phase (phase difference = π, 3π, …) respectively. But the two waves can also meet at a medium particle with phase difference other then 0 or 2π, say if phase difference ϕ is such that $0 < \phi < 2\pi$, then how is the displacement of the point of superposition given ? Now we discuss the interference of waves in details analytically.

6.6.1 Analytical Treatment of Interference of Waves

Now we discuss mathematically, how the displacement of the point of superposition varies with time. Let displacement of a medium particle due to a propagating wave be

$$y_1 = A_1 \sin(\omega t) \qquad \ldots(6.59)$$

At the same medium particle if another wave of same angular frequency ω and different amplitude A_2 arrives with a phase shift ϕ then the displacement of the medium particle from mean position due to this second wave can be given as

$$y_2 = A_2 \sin(\omega t - \phi) \qquad \ldots(6.60)$$

Now the resultant displacement of this medium particle can be given by the principle of superposition. If the displacements produced by two waves at that point are y_1 and y_2 along same line of motion then the net displacement of this medium particle is given as

$$y = y_1 + y_2$$

$$= A_1 \sin \omega t + A_2 \sin(\omega t - \phi)$$

$$= A_1 \sin \omega t + A_2 \sin \omega t \cos \phi - A_2 \cos \omega t \sin \phi$$

Rearranging the terms of $\sin \omega t$ and $\cos \omega t$ separately as

$$y = (A_1 + A_2 \cos \phi) \sin \omega t - (A_2 \sin \phi) \cos \omega t$$

Now substituting

$$R \cos \theta = A_1 + A_2 \cos \phi \qquad \ldots(6.61)$$

and $$R \sin \theta = A_2 \sin \phi \qquad \ldots(6.62)$$

We get $$y = R \cos \theta \sin \omega t - R \sin \theta \cos \omega t$$

or $$y = R \sin(\omega t - \theta) \qquad \ldots(6.63)$$

Equation-(6.63) is an equation of SHM, thus we can state that after superposition of the two waves, this medium particle executes SHM with amplitude R and initial phase lag θ with respect to the SHM produced at the point by the first wave.

Here R and θ can be given by equation-(6.61) and (6.62). Squaring and adding the two equations, we get

$$R = \sqrt{(A_1 + A_2 \cos\phi)^2 + (A_2 \sin\phi)^2}$$

$$R = \sqrt{A_1^2 + A_2^2 + 2A_1A_2 \cos\phi} \qquad \ldots(6.64)$$

Dividing equation-(6.62) and (6.61) gives

$$\tan \theta = \frac{A_2 \sin \phi}{A_1 + A_2 \cos \phi}$$

or $$\theta = \tan^{-1}\left(\frac{A_2 \sin \phi}{A_1 + A_2 \cos \phi}\right) \qquad \ldots(6.65)$$

Equation-(6.64) and (6.65) are the results similar to those obtained by parallelogram rule of vector addition. If A_1 and A_2 are two vectors and ϕ is the angle between their directions then the resultant vector of the two is given by equation-(6.63) and the direction of resultant with the first vector is given by equation-(6.64). Thus we can conclude that when two or more waves of same frequency which differ in phase, superpose on a medium particle then the resulting motion of that medium particle is also SHM with same frequency. Its amplitude can be given by treating the individual amplitudes as vectors with their phase differences as the angles between them and finding the resultant of these vectors.

6.6.2 Interference of two Coherent Waves of Same Amplitude

We've discussed in previous article that when two coherent waves of different amplitudes A_1 and A_2 with a phase difference ϕ superpose on a medium particle, the resulting amplitude of that medium particle is given as

$$R = \sqrt{A_1^2 + A_2^2 + 2A_1A_2 \cos\phi}$$

If the two waves are of equal amplitude $A_1 = A_2 = A$, then R is given as

$$R = \sqrt{A^2 + A^2 + 2A^2 \cos\phi}$$

$$= \sqrt{2A^2(1 + \cos\phi)}$$

$$= 2A \cos \phi/2 \qquad \ldots(6.66)$$

Here we can see that the resultants amplitude R of the medium particle after superposition, depends on the amplitudes of component waves and on the phase difference ϕ between the two component waves. Thus if the phase difference between the two waves changes at the point of superposition, the resulting amplitude of that medium particle also changes. From equation-(6.64). We can see that the amplitude at the point of interference is maximum when

$$\cos\phi = +1$$

or when $\phi = 2N\pi \quad [N \in I] \quad \ldots(6.67)$

Then the maximum value of R is given as

$$R_{max} = \sqrt{A_1^2 + A_2^2 + 2A_1A_2}$$

$$R_{max} = A_1 + A_2 \quad \ldots(6.68)$$

If $A_1 = A_2 = A$ then $R_{max} = 2A$

Thus when the phase difference between two superposition waves is an integral multiple of 2π i.e. when the two waves superpose on a medium particle in same phase then the resultant amplitude of that medium particle will be maximum given by equation-(6.68) and this situation is called constructive interference of waves at the medium particle.

Similarly from equation-(6.64) we can see that the amplitude at the point of superposition is minimum when

$$\cos\phi = -1$$

or when $\phi = (2N+1)\pi \quad [N \in I] \quad \ldots(6.69)$

Then the minimum amplitude is given as

$$R_{min} = \sqrt{A_1^2 + A_2^2 - 2A_1A_2}$$

$$= A_1 - A_2 \quad \ldots(6.70)$$

If $A_1 = A_2 = A$ then $R_{min} = 0$

Thus when the phase difference between two superposing waves is an odd multiple of π i.e., when the two waves superpose on a medium particle in opposite phase, then the resultant amplitude of that medium particle will be minimum and is given by equation-(6.70) and this situation is called destructive interference of the waves at the medium particle.

6.6.3 Condition on path difference at the point of interference

As we've already studied that two waves interfering at a point having their path difference Δ and phase difference ϕ are related as

$$\phi = \frac{2\pi}{\lambda} \cdot \Delta$$

For the case of constructive interference, waves must interfere in same phase for which $\phi = 2N\pi$ so for constructive interference the condition of path difference between waves at the point of interference is

$$\Delta = \frac{\lambda}{2\pi} \cdot 2N\pi = N\lambda$$

Thus if at a point path difference between interfering waves is an integral multiple of wavelength then waves superpose in same phase and constructive interference take place.

Similarly for the case of destructive interference, waves must interfere in opposite phase for which $\phi = (2N + 1)\pi$ so the condition of path difference between waves at the point of interference for destructive interference is

$$\Delta = \frac{\lambda}{2\pi} \cdot (2N+1)\pi = (2N+1)\frac{\lambda}{2}$$

Thus if at a point path difference between interfering waves is odd multiple of half wavelength then the waves superpose at the point in opposite phase and destructive interference take place.

6.7 *Intensity of Wave*

When a wave travels through a medium, energy is transferred from one part of medium to another part. The wave intensity is defined as the average amount of energy flow in the medium per unit time and per unit of its cross-sectional area. Thus intensity is measured in units of watt/m^2. Intensity of a wave can also be given as average power per unit cross-sectional area. Let us find mathematically the average power and intensity of a wave.

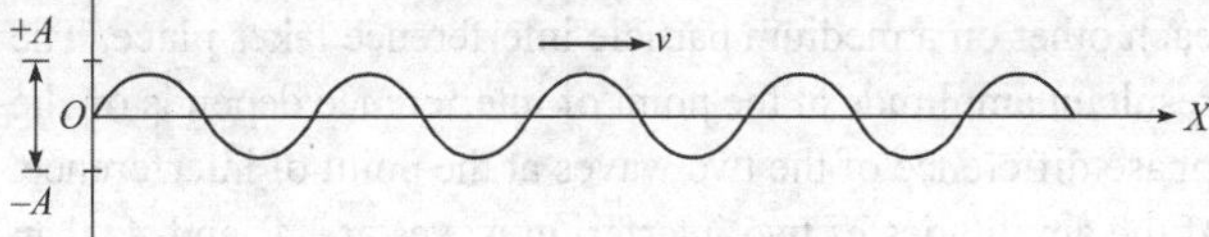

Figure 6.20

Consider a wave propagating along positive x-direction having angular frequency ω and amplitude A moving at speed v. We know wave speed is defined as the distance traveled by energy in one second. In one second wave imparts oscillation energy to all the medium particles in a length v meters. If ρ be the density of medium and S be the area of cross section through which energy flows, then the total oscillation energy of all the medium particles, oscillating with amplitude A and angular frequency ω is given as

$$E = \frac{1}{2} m\omega^2 A^2$$

$$= \frac{1}{2}(\rho S v)\omega^2 A^2 \qquad [\text{As } m = \rho S v]$$

$$P = E = 2\pi^2 n^2 A^2 \rho v S \quad \ldots(6.71)$$

Equation-(6.71) gives the oscillation energy of all the medium particles in a length v meter, which is the energy crossing a given cross section per unit time hence it can be regarded as the average power of wave. Now we can simply calculate the intensity of wave as

$$I = \frac{P}{S} = 2\pi^2 n^2 A^2 \rho v \quad \ldots (6.72)$$

If a wave is propagating in a medium then in the above equation the parameters frequency n, density ρ and velocity v remains constant and we can state that the intensity of a wave is directly proportional to the square of amplitude of the wave is

$$I \propto A^2$$

or $$I = k A^2 \quad \ldots (6.73)$$

Here k is a constant whose value can be obtained from equation-(6.72) as

$$k = 2\pi^2 n^2 \rho v \quad \ldots (6.74)$$

Web Reference at www.physicsgalaxy.com

Age Group - High School Physics | Age 17-19 Years

Section - OSCILLATION & WAVES

Topic - Wave Motion

Module Number - 26 to 29

6.7.1 Wave Intensity in Interference

We've discussed that when two coherent waves superpose each other on a medium particle interference takes place. The resultant amplitude at the point of interference depends on the phase difference of the two waves at the point of interference. If the amplitudes of two interfering waves are A_1 and A_2 than the resulting amplitudes of two interfering waves are A_1 and A_2 then the resulting amplitude R at the point of interference depends on their phase difference ϕ as

$$R = \sqrt{A_1^2 + A_2^2 + 2A_1A_2 \cos\phi} \quad \ldots (6.75)$$

If I_R be the intensity at the point of interference then it can be given as

$$I_R \propto R^2$$

or $$I_R = kR^2$$

or $$I_R = k(A_1^2 + A_2^2 + 2A_1A_2 \cos\phi)$$

or $$I_R = kA_1^2 + kA_2^2 + 2kA_1A_2 \cos\phi$$

or $$I_R = I_1 + I_2 + 2\sqrt{I_1 I_2} \cos\phi \quad \ldots (6.76)$$

Here $I_1 = kA_1^2$ and $I_2 = kA_2^2$ are the intensities of first and second wave respectively. The expression in equation-(6.76) gives the resultant intensity at the point of interference due to superposition of two coherent waves having independent intensities I_1 and I_2 respectively. Equation-(6.76) shows that the resultant intensity at the point of interference depends on the individual intensities I_1, I_2 and the phase difference ϕ between the two waves at that point. If the waves are of equal intensities $I_1 = I_2 = I_0$ then after interference the intensity at the point of interference is given by equation-(6.76) as

$$I_R = I_0 + I_0 + 2I_0 \cos\phi$$

or $$I_R = 2I_0(1 + \cos\phi)$$

or $$I_R = 4I_0 \cos^2\frac{\phi}{2} \quad \ldots (6.77)$$

We know when two coherent waves interfere constructively, phase difference between the two is zero or multiple of 2π. Thus from equation-(6.77) $\cos\phi = +1$ and maximum intensity at the point of constructive interference can be given as

$$I_{max} = I_1 + I_2 + \sqrt{I_1 I_2} \quad \ldots (6.78)$$

$$I_{max} = (\sqrt{I_1} + \sqrt{I_2})^2 \quad \ldots (6.79)$$

For waves of equal intensities if $I_1 = I_2 = I_0$ then we have

$$I_{max} = 4I_0 \quad \ldots (6.80)$$

Similarly for destructive interference as the phase difference between waves should be an odd multiple of π, we have

$$\cos\phi = -1$$

Thus from equation-(6.76), the maximum intensity at the point of destructive interference can be given as

$$I_{min} = I_1 + I_2 - 2\sqrt{I_1 I_2} \quad \ldots (6.81)$$

or $$I_{min} = (\sqrt{I_1} - \sqrt{I_2})^2 \quad \ldots (6.82)$$

For waves of equal intensities of $I_1 = I_2 = I_0$, then we have

$$I_{min} = 0 \quad \ldots (6.83)$$

From equation-(6.78) and (6.81) we can see that in constructive interference the resultant intensity is more than the sum of individual intensities of the component waves and in destructive interference the resultant intensity is less than the sum of individual intensities of the component waves.

6.7.2 Power of a Wave and Wave Energy Density of a Transverse Wave

As a transverse wave move along a string, it carries energy in the direction of wave travel. Consider an element of string of width dx as shown in figure-6.21, it oscillates in a direction perpendicular to wave propagation. During oscillation this element has both kinetic and potential energies. Kinetic energy due to its motion and potential energy due to the amount it is stretched. Its kinetic energy is given as

$$dk = \frac{1}{2}(\mu dx)\left(\frac{\partial y}{\partial t}\right)^2 \qquad \ldots(6.84)$$

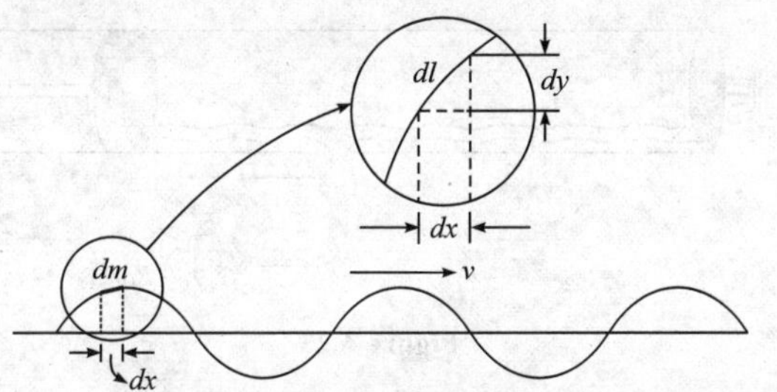

Figure 6.21

Here μ is the linear density of string and $\frac{\partial y}{\partial t}$ is the instantaneous velocity of the element. Therefore the kinetic energy per unit length of string can be given as

$$\frac{dK}{dx} = \frac{1}{2}\mu\left(\frac{\partial y}{\partial t}\right)^2 \qquad \ldots(6.85)$$

When the element goes from its mean position to a height *y*, its length changes to *dl*, which is given as

$$dl = \sqrt{\partial x^2 + \partial y^2} \qquad \ldots(6.86)$$

In stretching the element from *dx* to *dl*, work done by the tension *T* of the string will be stored in the form of potential energy in it, which is given as

$$dU = T(\partial l - \partial x)$$

or $$dU = T\,dx\left(\sqrt{1+\left(\frac{\partial y}{\partial x}\right)^2} - 1\right)$$

or $$dU = T\,dx\left(1+\frac{1}{2}\left(\frac{\partial y}{\partial x}\right)^2 - 1\right)$$

[Using binomial approximation]

or $$dU = \frac{1}{2}T\,dx\left(\frac{\partial y}{\partial x}\right)^2 \qquad \ldots(6.87)$$

Thus potential energy per unit length can be given as

$$\frac{dU}{dx} = \frac{1}{2}T\left(\frac{\partial y}{\partial x}\right)^2 \qquad \ldots(6.88)$$

Total energy of string carrying a wave per unit length is called its energy density and is given as

$$E = \frac{dK}{dx} + \frac{dU}{dx}$$

or $$E = \frac{1}{2}\mu\left(\frac{\partial y}{\partial t}\right)^2 + \frac{1}{2}T\left(\frac{\partial y}{\partial x}\right)^2 \qquad \ldots(6.89)$$

If we consider a wave propagating in positive *x* direction, its displacement equation can be given as

$$y = A\sin(\omega t - kx) \qquad \ldots(6.90)$$

From equation-(6.90) we get

$$\frac{\partial y}{\partial t} = A\omega\cos(\omega t - kx) \qquad \ldots(6.91)$$

And $$\frac{\partial y}{\partial x} = -Ak\cos(\omega t - kx) \qquad \ldots(6.92)$$

From equation-(6.89), (6.91) and (6.92) we have

$$E = \frac{1}{2}\mu A^2\omega^2\cos^2(\omega t - kx) + \frac{1}{2}TA^2k^2\cos^2(\omega t - kx) \ldots(6.93)$$

We have wave velocity

$$v = \sqrt{\frac{T}{\mu}} \quad \text{or} \quad T = \mu v^2$$

And we also have

$$v = \frac{\omega}{k}$$

or $$T = \frac{\mu\omega^2}{k^2} \qquad \ldots(6.94)$$

From equation-(6.93) and (6.94) we have

$$E = \mu A^2\omega^2\cos^2(\omega t - kx) \qquad \ldots(6.95)$$

Equation-(6.95) gives the total energy of string in a wave is propagating. The wave travels a distance *v* meter in one second thus power of a wave on string can be given as

$$P = Ev$$

$$= \mu A^2\omega^2 v\cos^2(\omega t - kx) \qquad \ldots(6.96)$$

For a string if ρ be the density and *S* be its cross sectional area, then we have

$$\mu = S\rho$$

Thus power of a wave can be given from equation-(6.96)

$$P = 4\pi^2n^2A^2\rho vS\cos^2(\omega t - kx) \quad \ldots(6.97)$$

Equation-(6.97) gives the instantaneous power transmitted by a wave during its propagation. Here average power transmitted can be obtained by substituting average value of time function $\cos^2(\omega t - kx)$ which is 1/2. Thus average power transmitted by a wave can be given as

$$P_{av} = 4\pi^2n^2A^2\rho vS\left(\frac{1}{2}\right)$$

or $$P_{av} = 2\pi^2n^2A^2\rho vS \qquad \ldots(6.98)$$

Equation-(6.98) is same as that of equation-(6.71) which we have already derived in section-*ABC*.

6.7.3 Quincke's Tube

This is an apparatus used to demonstrate the phenomenon of interference and also used to measure velocity of sound in air. This is made up of two U-tubes A and B as shown in figure-6.22. Here the tube B can slide in and out from the tube A. There are two openings P and Q in the tube A. At opening P, a tuning fork or a sound source of known frequency n_0 is placed and at the other opening a detector is placed to detect the resultant sound of interference occurred due to superposition of two sound waves coming from the tubes A and B.

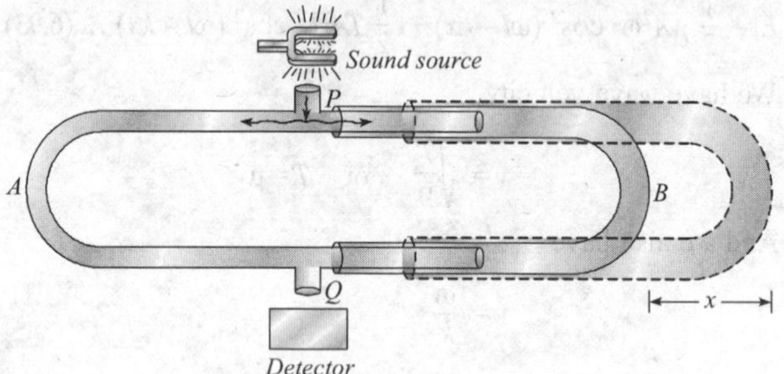

Figure 6.22

Initially tube B is adjusted so that detector detects a maximum. At this instant if length of paths covered by the two waves from P to Q from the side of A and side of B are l_1 and l_2 respectively then for constructive interference we must have

$$l_2 - l_1 = N\lambda \quad \dots(6.99)$$

If now tube B is further pulled out by a distance x so that next maximum is obtained and the length of path from the side of B is l_2' then we have

$$l_2' = l_2 + 2x \quad \dots(6.100)$$

Where x is he displacement of the tube. For next constructive interference of sound at point Q, we have

$$l_2' - l_1 = (N+1)\lambda \quad \dots(6.101)$$

From equation-(6.99), (6.100) and (6.101), we get

$$l_2' - l_2 = 2 \times Q = \lambda$$

or $$x = \frac{\lambda}{2} \quad \dots(6.102)$$

Thus by experiment we get the wavelength of sound as for two successive points of constructive interference, the path difference must be λ. As the tube B is pulled out by x, this introduces a path difference $2x$ in the path of sound wave through tube B. If the frequency of the source is known, n_0, the velocity of sound in the air filled in tube can be gives as

$$v = n_0 \lambda$$

$$= 2n_0 x \quad \dots(6.103)$$

6.7.4 Seebeck's Tube

This is also an apparatus used to demonstrate phenomenon of interference and it can also be used to find velocity of sound in air. This is a hollow tube with a freely moving piston as shown in figure-6.23.

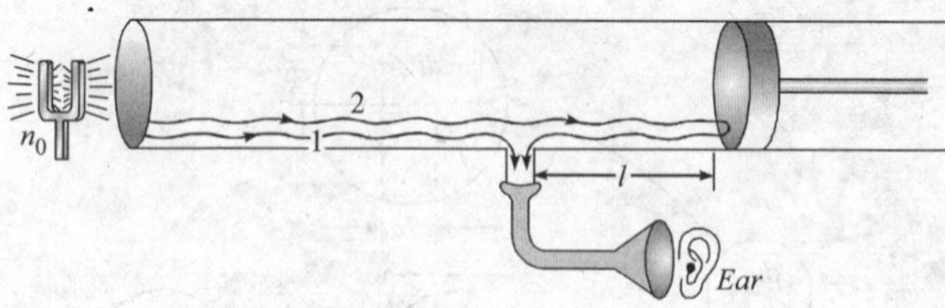

Figure 6.23

There is an opening in the tube which can be used as a point where sound can be detected directly by human ear or a detector as shown in figure. When a source of sound oscillates near the mouth of the tube (tuning fork as shown). At the opening two sound waves will interfere. One direct from the source and second, which is reflected from the piston. Here we can see that the path difference between direct wave and reflected wave at opening can be given as

$$\Delta = 2l \quad \dots(6.104)$$

Where l is the distance between opening and piston shown in figure-6.23.

In the experiment first the piston is adjusted so that a maximum sound is detected at opening. This implies that the path difference between the two waves must be an integral, multiple of wavelength λ.

Thus we have, $$\Delta = 2l = N\lambda \qquad (N \in I) \quad \dots(6.105)$$

Now the piston is slowly moved out so that the intensity of sound detected changed and again becomes maximum after some time. At this instant say if the distance of piston from opening becomes l', then we can say for next successive constructive interference the path difference of the two waves is

$$\Delta' = 2l' = (N+1)\lambda \quad \dots(6.106)$$

Here if displacement of piston is x, we have

$$x = l' - l$$

From equation-(6.105) & (6.106)

$$x = \frac{\lambda}{2}$$

or $$\lambda = 2x \quad \dots(6.107)$$

If the source frequency is known, n_0, then velocity of sound in air can be written as

$$v = n_0 \lambda$$

$$= 2xn_0 \quad \dots(6.108)$$

Illustrative Example 6.20

In a large room a person receives direct sound waves from a source 120 m away from him. He also receives waves from the same source which reach him, being reflected from the 25 m high ceiling at a point halfway between them. For which wavelength will these two sound waves interfere constructively?

Solution

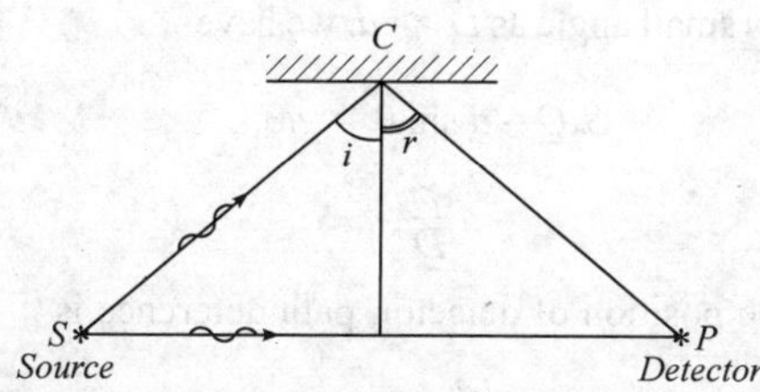

Figure 6.24

As shown in figure-6.24 for reflection from the ceiling

Path $SCP = SC + CP = 2SC$

[As $\angle i = \angle r$, $SC = CP$]

or Path $SCP = 2\sqrt{60^2 + 25^2} = 130\,\text{m}$

So path difference between interfering waves along paths SCP, and SP,

$$\Delta x = 130 - 120 = 10\,\text{m}$$

Now for constructive interference at P,

$$\Delta x = n\lambda, \quad \text{i.e.} \quad 10 = n\lambda$$

or $$\lambda = \frac{10}{n} \quad \text{with} \quad n = 1, 2, 3 \ldots$$

i.e., $\lambda = 10$ m, 5 m, (10/3) m and so on

Illustrative Example 6.21

Figure-6.25 shows a tube structure in which a sound signal is sent from one end and is received at the other end. The semicircular part has a radius of 20.0 cm. The frequency of the sound source can be varied electronically between 1000 and 4000 Hz. Find the frequencies at which maxima of intensity are detected. The speed of sound in air = 340 m/s.

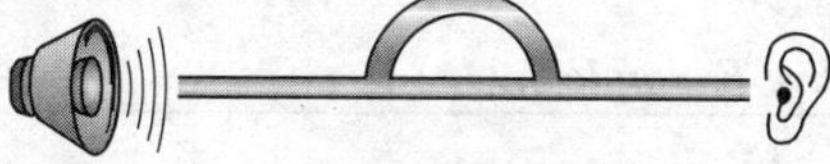

Figure 6.25

Solution

The sound wave reaches detector by two paths simultaneously by straight as well as semicircular track. The wave through the straight part travels a distance $l_1 = 2 \times 20$ cm and the wave through the curved part travels a distance $l_2 = \pi$ (20 cm) = 62.8 cm before they meet again and travel to the receiver. The path difference between the two waves received is, therefore,

$$\Delta l = l_2 - l_1 = 62.8\,\text{cm} - 40\,\text{cm}$$

$$= 22.8\,\text{cm} = 0.228\,\text{m}$$

The wavelength of either wave is $\frac{v}{n} = \frac{340}{n}$. For constructive interference, $\Delta l = N\lambda$, where N is an integer.

or, $$0.228 = N\left(\frac{340}{n}\right)$$

or, $$n = N\left(\frac{340}{0.228}\right) = N(1491.2)\,\text{Hz}$$

$$= N(1490)\,\text{Hz}$$

Thus, the frequencies within the specified range which cause maxima of intensity are 1490 Hz and 2980 Hz.

Illustrative Example 6.22

Two sources S_1 and S_2, separated by 2.0 m, vibrate according to equation $y_1 = 0.03 \sin \pi t$ and $y_2 = 0.02 \sin \pi t$ where y_1, y_2 and t are in M.K.S. units. They send out waves of velocity 1.5 m/s. Calculate the amplitude of the resultant motion of the particle colinear with S_1 and S_2 and located at a point (a) to the right of S_2 (b) to the left of S_2 and (c) in the middle of S_1 and S_2.

Solution

The situation is shown in figure-6.26.

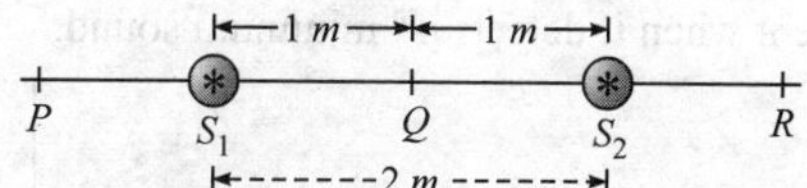

Figure 6.26

The oscillations y_1 and y_2 have amplitudes $A_1 = 0.03$ m and $A_2 = 0.02$ m respectively

The frequency of both sources is $n = \frac{\omega}{2\pi} = \frac{1}{2} = 0.5$ Hz

Now wavelength of each wave $\lambda = \frac{v}{n} = \frac{1.5}{0.5} = 3.0$ m

(a) The path difference for all points P_2 to the right of S_2 is

$$\Delta = (S_1P_2 - S_2P_2) = S_1S_2 = 2\,\text{m}$$

Phase difference $\phi = \frac{2\pi}{\lambda} \times$ Path difference

$$= \frac{2\pi}{3} \times 2.0 = \frac{4\pi}{3}$$

The resultant amplitude for this point is given by

$$R = \sqrt{A_1^2 + A_2^2 + 2A_1A_2\cos\phi}$$

$$= \sqrt{(0.03)^2 + (0.02)^2 + 2\times 0.03\times 0.02\times \cos(4\pi/3)}$$

Solving we get

$$R = 0.0265 \text{ m}$$

(b) The path difference for all points P, to the left of S_1

$$\Delta = (S_2P - S_1P) = S_1S_2 = 2.0 \text{ m}$$

Hence the resultant amplitude for all points to the left of S_1 is also 0.0265 m

(c) For a point Q, midway between S_1 and S_2, the path difference is zero i.e., $\phi = 0$. Hence constructive interference takes place at Q, thus amplitude at this point is maximum and given as

$$R = \sqrt{A_1^2 + A_2^2 + 2A_1A_2}$$

$$= A_1 + A_2$$

$$= 0.03 + 0.02$$

$$= 0.05 \text{ m}$$

Illustrative Example 6.23

Two point sources of sound are placed at a distance d and a detector moves on a straight line parallel to the line joining the sources as shown in figure-6.27 at a distance D away from sources. Initially Detector is situated on the line so that it is equidistant from both the sources. Find the displacement of detector when it detects n^{th} maximum sound and also find its displacement when it detects n^{th} minimum sound.

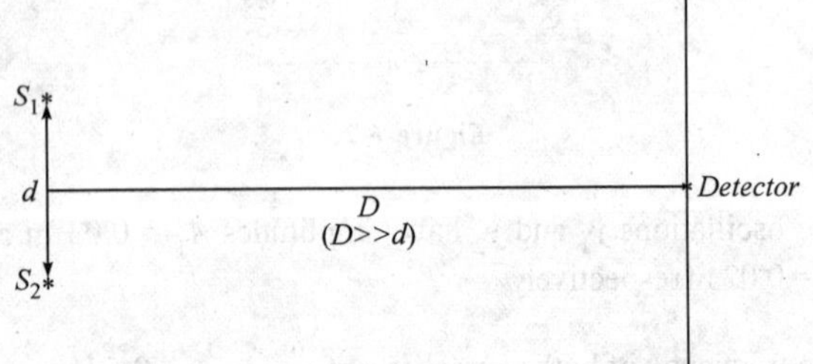

Figure 6.27

Solution

The situation is shown in figure-6.28.

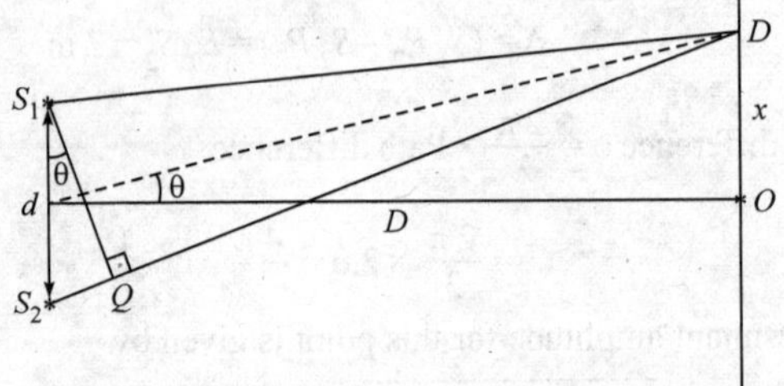

Figure 6.28

Let us consider the situation when detector move by a distance x as shown. Let at this position the path difference between the waves from S_1 and S_2 to detector be Δ then we have

$$\Delta = S_2D - S_1D$$

$$\simeq S_2Q$$

[Where S_1Q is perpendicular on line S_2D]

Here if θ is small angle as $D >> d$, we have

$$S_2Q = d\sin\theta \simeq d\theta$$

$$= d\frac{x}{D}$$

Thus at the position of detector, path deference is

$$\Delta = \frac{dx}{D} \qquad \ldots(6.109)$$

The expression for path difference in equation-(6.109) is an important formula for such problems. Students are advised to keep this formula in mind for future use.

When detector was at point O, path difference was zero and it detects a maxima, now if detector detects n^{th} maximum then its path difference at a distance x from O can be given as

$$\Delta = n\lambda$$

or $$\frac{dx}{D} = n\lambda$$

or $$x = \frac{n\lambda D}{d}$$

Similarly if detector detects n^{th} minima then the path difference between two waves at detector can be given as

$$\Delta = (2n-1)\frac{\lambda}{2}$$

or $$\frac{dx}{D} = (2n-1)\frac{\lambda}{2}$$

or $$x = \frac{(2n-1)\lambda D}{2d}$$

Illustrative Example 6.24

Two small loudspeakers A, B (1 m apart) are connected to the same oscillator so that both emit coherent sound waves of frequency 1700 Hz in phase. A sensitive detector, moving parallel to the line AB along LQ, 2.4 m away, detects a maximum wave at P on the perpendicular bisector MP of AB and another maximum wave when it first reaches a point Q directly opposite to B as shown in figure-6.29. Calculate the speed of the sound waves in air.

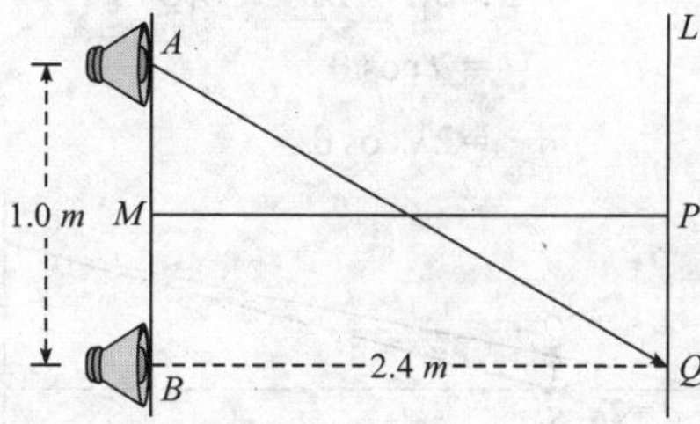

Figure 6.29

Solution

$AQ - BQ = \lambda$ for constructive interference of waves at Q

or $\sqrt{1.00^2 + 2.40^2} - 2.40 = \lambda$ or $\lambda = 0.2\text{ m}$

Thus we get $v = n\lambda$

or $v = 1700 \times 0.2 = 340\text{ m/s}$

 # Illustrative Example 6.25

A source emitting sound of frequency 180 Hz is placed in front of a wall at distance of 2 m from it. A detector is also placed in front of the wall at the same distance from it. Find the minimum distance between the source and the detector for which the detector detects a maximum of sound. Speed of sound in air = 360 m/s.

Solution

The situation is shown in figure-6.30.

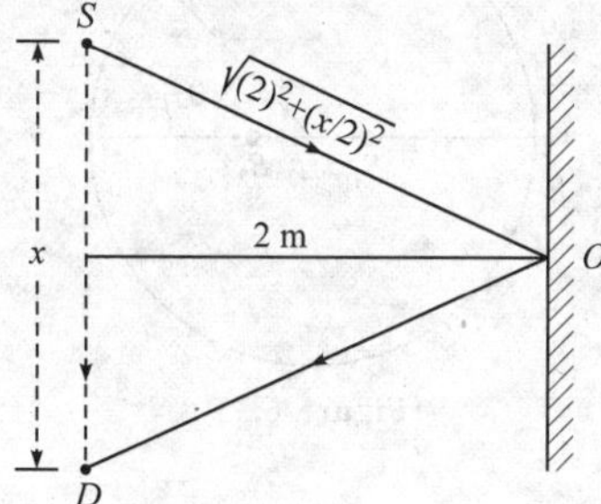

Figure 6.30

Suppose the detector is placed at a distance of x meter from the source. The direct wave received from the source travels a distance x meter. The wave reaching the detector after reflection from the wall has travelled a distance of $2[\sqrt{(2)^2 + x^2/4}]$ meter. Thus the path difference between the two waves at detector is

$$\Delta = \left\{2\sqrt{(2)^2 + \frac{x^2}{4}} - x\right\} \quad \ldots(6.110)$$

Constructive interference will take place when $\Delta = \lambda, 2\lambda, \ldots$ Thus the minimum distance x for which a maximum occurs at detector, the path difference will be

$$\Delta = \lambda \quad \ldots(6.111)$$

The wavelength is $\lambda = \frac{v}{n} = \frac{360}{180} = 2\text{ m}$

From equation-(6.110) and (6.111), we have

$$\Delta = 2\sqrt{2^2 + \frac{x^2}{4}} - x = 2$$

or, $\sqrt{4 + \frac{x^2}{4}} = 1 + \frac{x}{2}$

or, $4 + \frac{x^2}{4} = 1 + \frac{x^2}{4} + x$

or, $x = 3\text{ m}$

Thus, the detector should be placed at a distance of 3 m from the source to detect a maximum sound

 # Illustrative Example 6.26

Three plane sources of sound of frequency $n_1 = 400$ Hz, 401 Hz and $n_3 = 402$ Hz of equal amplitude a each, are sounded together. A detector receives waves from all the three sources simultaneously. It can detect signals of amplitude $\geq A$. Calculate

(a) period of one complete cycle of intensity received by the detector and

(b) time for which the detector remains idle in each cycle of intensity.

Solution

(a) We know that $y = A \sin \omega t = A \sin (2\pi n t)$

The displacements of the medium particles caused by these waves are given as

$$y_1 = A \sin (800\pi t) \quad \ldots(6.112)$$

$$y_2 = A \sin (802\pi t) \quad \ldots(6.113)$$

and

$$y_3 = A \sin (804\pi t) \quad \ldots(6.114)$$

The resultant displacement of medium particle at time t is given by

$$y = y_1 + y_2 + y_3$$

$$= A[\sin(800\pi t) + \sin(802\pi t) + \sin(804\pi t)]$$

$$= A[\{\sin(800\pi t) + \sin(804\pi t)\} + \sin(802\pi t)]$$

$$= A[1 + \cos 2\pi t] \sin 802\pi t$$

The resultant is also a plane wave. Let its amplitude be R. Then, $y = R \sin \omega t$

Here $R = A(1 + \cos 2\pi t)$ ...(6.115)

Equation-(6.115) shows that the resultant amplitude (or resultant intensity, $I \propto R^2$) varies with time.

The resultant amplitude is maximum, when

$$2\pi t = 0, 2\pi, 4\pi, \ldots\ldots$$

or $$t = 0, 1, 2, 3, \ldots\ldots$$

Hence period of one complete cycle of intensity is one second.

(b) Given that signal is detected when $A \geq a$

Thus $$\cos 2\pi t \geq 0$$

Thus $\cos 2\pi t$ should lie either in first quadrant or in fourth quadrant i.e., between either 0 to $\pi/2$ or $3\pi/2$ and 2π.

So, during first cycle of intensity, the signal is detected when

$$0 \leq t \leq \frac{1}{4} \text{ and } \frac{3}{4} \leq t \leq 1$$

This shows that detector remains ideal from

$$t = \frac{1}{4}\text{ s to } t = \frac{3}{4}\text{ s}$$

Therefore, in each cycle of intensity, the detector remains ideal for $\frac{3}{4} - \frac{1}{4} = \frac{2}{4} = 0.5$ s

Illustrative Example 6.27

Two coherent narrow slits emitting of wavelength λ in the same phase are placed parallel to each other at a small separation of 2λ. the sound is detected by moving a detector on the screen S at a distance D ($>> \lambda$) from the slit S_1 as shown in figure-6.31. Find the distance x such that the intensity at P is equal to the intensity at O.

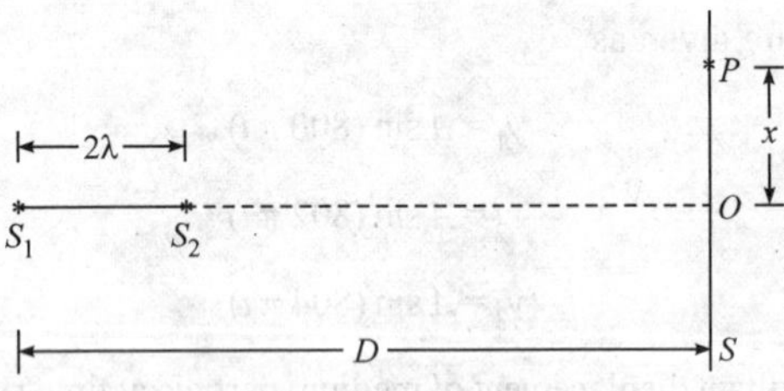

Figure 6.31

Solution

When detector is at O, we can see that the path difference in the two waves reaching O is $d = 2\lambda$ thus at O detector receives a maximum sound. When it reaches P and again there is a maximum sound detected at P the path difference between two waves must be $\Delta = \lambda$. Thus from figure-6.32 the path difference at P can be given as

$$\Delta = S_1P - S_2P \simeq S_1Q$$
$$= d\cos\theta$$
$$= 2\lambda\cos\theta$$

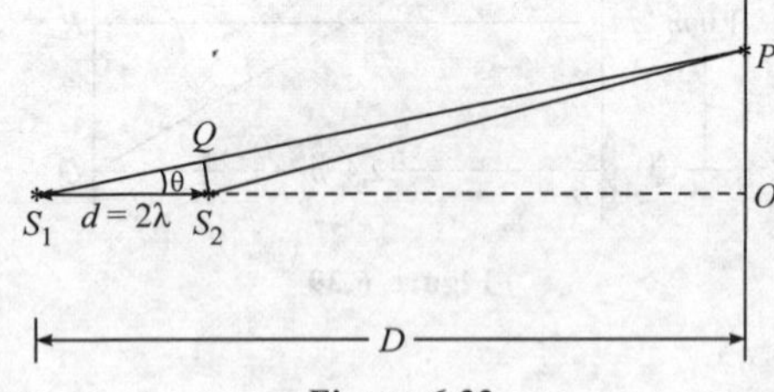

Figure 6.32

And we have at point P, path difference $\Delta = \lambda$, Thus

$$\Delta = 2\lambda\cos\theta = \lambda$$

or, $$\cos\theta = \frac{1}{2}$$

or, $$\theta = \frac{\pi}{3}$$

Thus the value of x can be written as

$$x = D\tan\theta = D\tan\left(\frac{\pi}{3}\right) = \sqrt{3}\,D$$

Illustrative Example 6.28

Figure-6.33 shows two coherent sources S_1 and S_2 which emit sound of wavelength λ in phase. The separation between the sources is 3λ. A circular wire of large radius is placed in such a way that S_1S_2 lies in its plane and the middle point of S_1S_2 is at the centre of the wire. Find the angular positions θ on the wire for which constructive interference takes place.

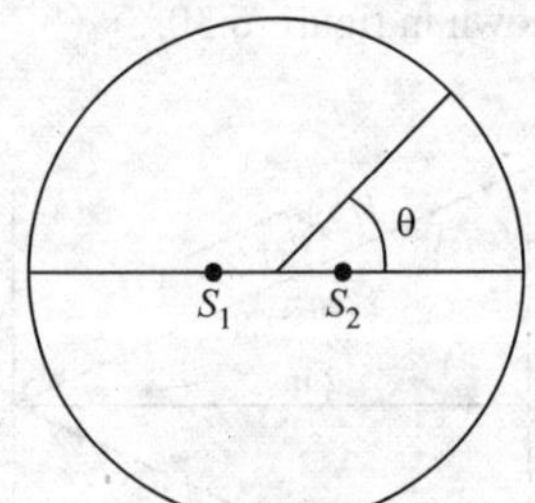

Figure 6.33

Solution

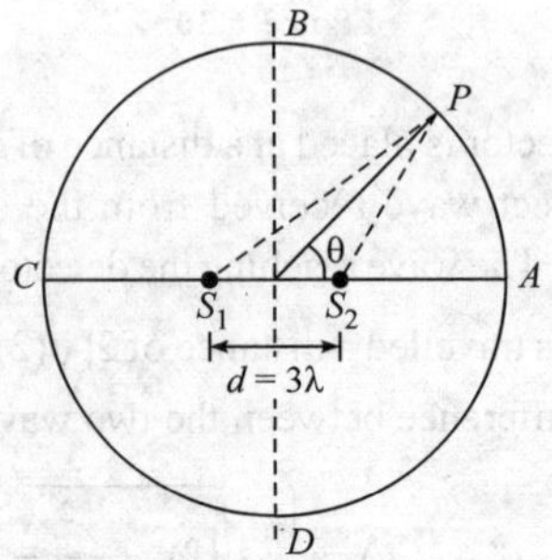

Figure 6.34

From previous question, we can say that for a point P on the circle shown in figure-6.34. The path difference in the two waves at P is

$$\Delta = S_1P - S_2P = d\cos\theta$$
$$= 3\lambda\cos\theta$$

We know for constructive interference at P. The path difference must be an integral multiple of wavelength λ. Thus for a maxima at P, we have

$$3\lambda\cos\theta = 0;\quad 3\lambda\cos\theta = \lambda;\quad 3\lambda\cos\theta = 2\lambda;\quad 3\lambda\cos\theta = 3\lambda$$

or, $\theta = \frac{\pi}{2}$ or $\theta = \cos^{-1}\frac{1}{3}$ or $\theta = \cos^{-1}\frac{2}{3}$ or $\theta = 0$

There are four points A, B, C and D on circle at which $\theta = 0$ or $\frac{\pi}{2}$ and there are two points in each quadrant at $\theta = \cos^{-1}\frac{1}{3}$ and $\theta = \cos^{-1}\frac{2}{3}$ at which constructive interference takes place. Thus there are total twelve points on circle at which maxima occurs.

Web Reference at www.physicsgalaxy.com

Age Group - High School Physics | Age 17-19 Years
Section - OSCILLATION & WAVES
Topic - Interference of Waves
Module Number - 1 to 17

Practice Exercise 6.3

(i) A source emitting sound of frequency 180 Hz is placed in front of an obstacle at a distance of 2 m from it. A detector is also placed at the position of source. (a) find the minimum distance between by which source and the detector are separated normal to the line passing through obstacle for which the detector detects a maximum of sound. (b) How much farther to the right must the obstacle be moved if the two waves are to be out of phase by 180°. (Speed of sound in air = 360 m/s).

[(a) 3 m; (b) 0.598 m]

(ii) Two audio speakers are kept some distance apart and are driven by the same amplifier system. A person is sitting at a place 6.0 m from one of the speakers and 6.4 m from the other. If the sound signal is continuously varied from 500 Hz to 5000 Hz, what are the frequencies for which there is a destructive interference at the place of the listener? Speed of sound in air = 320 m/s.

[1200 Hz, 2000 Hz, 2800 Hz, 3600 Hz and 4400 Hz]

(iii) Two points sources of sound are kept at a separation of 10 cm. They vibrate in phase to produce waves of wavelength 5.0 cm. What would be the phase difference between the two waves arriving a point 20 cm from one source

(a) on the line joining the source

(b) on the perpendicular bisector of the line joining the sources ?

[(a) zero, (b) zero]

(iv) Two sources of sound S_1 and S_2 vibrate at same frequency and are in phase (figure-6.35). The intensity of sound detected at a point P as shown in the figure-6.35 is I_0. If θ equals 45°, what will be the intensity of sound detected at this point if one of the sources is switched off ?

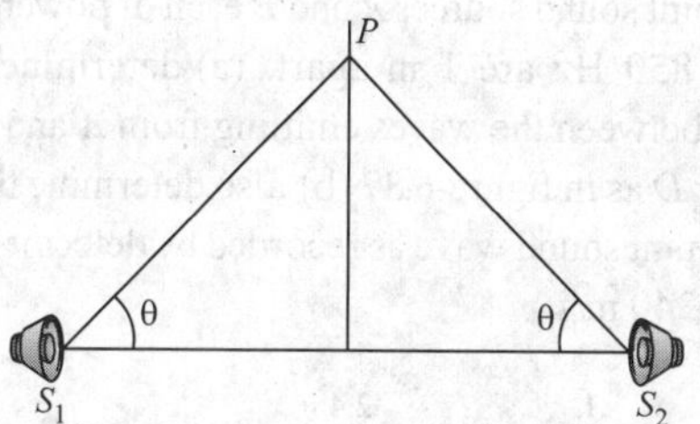

Figure 6.35

[$I_0/4$]

(v) Sound waves from a tuning fork A reach a point P by two separate paths ABP and ACP. When ACP is greater than ABP by 11.5 cm, there is silence at P. When the difference is increased to 23 cm the sound becomes loudest at P and again when it increases to 34.5 cm there is silence again and so on. Calculate the minimum frequency of the fork if the velocity of sound if taken to be 331.2 m/s.

[1440 Hz]

(vi) Three sources of sound S_1, S_2 and S_3 of equal intensity are placed in a straight line with $S_1S_2 = S_2S_3$ (figure-6.36). At a point P, far away from the sources, the wave coming from S_2 is 120° ahead in phase of that from S_1. Also, the wave coming from S_3 is 120° ahead of that from S_2. what would be the resultant intensity of sound at P ?

S_1 — S_2 — S_3 — P

Figure 6.36

[zero]

(vii) Sounds from two identical sources S_1 and S_2 reach a point P. When the sounds reach directly, and in the same phase, the intensity at P is I_0. The power of S_1 is now reduced by 64%, and the phase difference between S_1 and S_2 is varied continuously. The maximum and minimum intensities recorded at P are now I_{max} and I_{min}. Find I_{max}/I_{min}.

[I_{max}/I_{min} = 16]

(viii) At two points S_1 and S_2 on a liquid surface two coherent wave sources are set in motion at $t = 0$ with the same phase. The speed of the waves in the liquid $v = 0.5$ m/s, the frequency of vibration $\eta = 5$ Hz and the amplitude $A = 0.04$ m.
At a point P of the liquid surface which is at a distance $x_1 = 0.30$ m from S_1 and $x_2 = 0.34$ m from S_2 a piece of cork floats :
(a) Find the displacement of the cork at $t = 3$ s.
(b) Find the time t_0 that elapse from the moment the wave sources were set in motion until the moment that the cork passes through the equilibrium position for the first time.
[(a) $y = -0.02344$ m (b) $t_0 = 0.74$ s]

(ix) Two point sound sources A and B each of power 25 πW and frequency 850 Hz are 1 m apart. (a) determine the phase difference between the waves emitting from A and B received by detector D as in figure-6.37 (b) also determine the intensity of the resultant sound wave as recorded by detector D. Velocity of sound = 340 m/s.

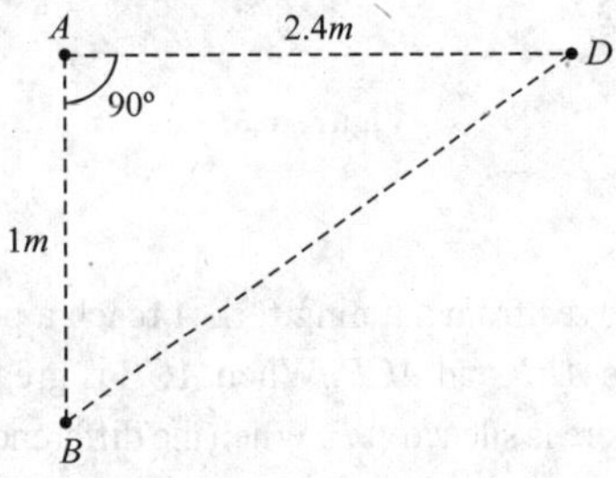

Figure 6.37

[(a) π, (b) 0.0064 W/m^2]

(x) Two sources of sound of the same frequency produce sound intensities I and $4I$ at a point P when used individually. If they are used together such that the sounds from them reach a point P with a phase difference of $2\pi/3$, find the intensity at point P.
[$3I$]

(xi) A source of sound S and a detector D are placed at some distance from one another. A big cardboard is placed near the detector and perpendicular to the line SD as shown in figure-6.38. It is gradually moved away and it is found that the intensity changes from a maximum to a minimum as the board is moved through a distance of 20 cm. Find the frequency of the sound emitted. Velocity of sound in air is 336 m/s.

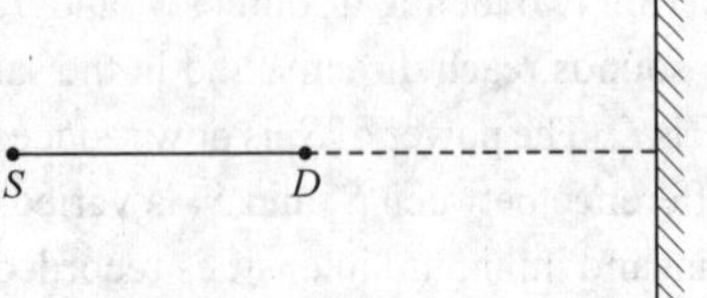

Figure 6.38

[420 Hz]

6.8 Compression Waves

When a longitudinal wave propagates in a gaseous medium, it produces compression and rarefaction in the medium periodically. The region where compression occurs, the pressure is more than the normal pressure of the medium and the region where rarefaction occurs, the pressure is lesser then the normal pressure of the medium. Thus we can also describe longitudinal waves in a gaseous medium as pressure waves and these are also termed as compression waves in which the pressure at different points of medium also varies periodically with their displacements. Let us discuss the propagation of excess pressure in a medium in longitudinal wave analytically.

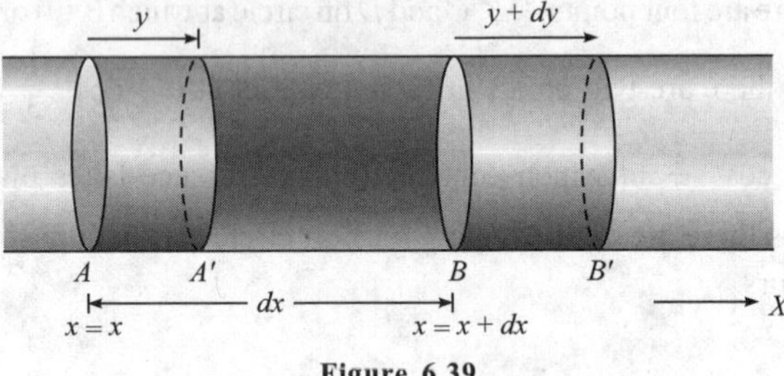

Figure 6.39

Consider a longitudinal wave propagating in positive x-direction as shown in figure-6.39. Figure shows a segment AB of the medium of width dx. In this medium let a longitudinal wave is propagating whose equation is given as

$$y = A \sin(\omega t - kx) \quad \ldots(6.116)$$

Where y is the displacement of a medium particle situated at a distance x from the origin, along the direction of propagation of wave. In figure-6.39 AB is the medium segment whose a medium particle is at position $x = x$ and B is at $x = x + dx$ at an instant. If after some time t medium particle at A reaches to a point A' which is displaced by y and the medium particle at B reaches to point B' which is at a displacement $y + dy$ from B. Here dy is given by equation-(6.116) as

$$dy = -Ak \cos(\omega t - kx)\, dx$$

Here due to displacement of section AB to $A'B'$ the change in volume of it's section is given as

$$dV = -S dy \quad [S \rightarrow \text{Area of cross-section}]$$

$$= S A k \cos(\omega t - kx)\, dx$$

The volume of section AB is

$$V = S\, dx$$

Thus volume strain in section AB is

$$\frac{dV}{V} = \frac{-SAk \cos(\omega t - kx) dx}{S\, dx}$$

or

$$\frac{dV}{V} = -Ax \cos(\omega t - kx)$$

If B is the bulk modulus of the medium, then the excess pressure in the section AB can be given as

$$\Delta P = B\left(\frac{dV}{V}\right) \quad \dots(6.117)$$

$$\Delta P = BAk \cos(\omega t - kx)$$

or $$\Delta P = \Delta P_0 \cos(\omega t - kx) \quad \dots(6.118)$$

Here ΔP_0 is the pressure amplitude at a medium particle at position x from origin and ΔP is the excess pressure at that point. Equation-(6.118) shows that excess pressure varies periodically at every point of the medium with pressure amplitude ΔP_0, which is given as

$$\Delta P_0 = BAk$$

$$= \frac{2\pi}{\lambda} AB \quad \dots(6.119)$$

Equation-(6.118) is also termed as the equation of pressure wave in a gaseous medium. We can also see that the pressure wave differs in phase by $\pi/2$ from the displacement wave and displacement maxima occur where the displacement is zero and displacement maxima occur where the pressure is at its normal level. Remember that pressure maxima implies that the pressure at a point is pressure amplitude times more or less then the normal pressure level of the medium.

Wave intensity for longitudinal waves at a point can also be expressed in terms of its pressure amplitude as from equation-(6.118)

$$I = 2\pi^2 n^2 A^2 \rho v$$

or $$I = \frac{1}{2}\,\frac{4\pi^2}{\lambda^2}\,A^2\,\rho\,v^3$$

or $$I = \frac{1}{2}\left(\frac{\Delta P_0}{B}\right)^2 \rho\,v^3$$

or $$I = \frac{\Delta P_0^2}{2\rho v} \quad \left[\text{As } v = \sqrt{\frac{B}{\rho}}\right] \quad \dots(6.120)$$

Expression in equation-(6.120) relates the wave intensity at a point and the pressure amplitude of the wave at that point for longitudinal waves.

6.9 Spherical and Cylindrical Waves

Till now we've discussed the longitudinal and transverse waves travelling in one direction only. Consider a source of sound which emits sound waves in all directions as shown in figure-6.40(a). When source vibrates, it emits oscillations in air in its surrounding space. It emits waves in the three dimensional spherical region in its surrounding and the oscillations produced by source in spherical region propagate radially with speed of sound in the medium (air). These waves which travel in three dimensional space in spherical form are called spherical waves. All the particles in the surrounding of the source where it produce oscillations on a spherical surface, we call spherical wave front. Once a wavefront is created, it expands with speed of sound and all wavefronts are in the form of concentric spherical shells.

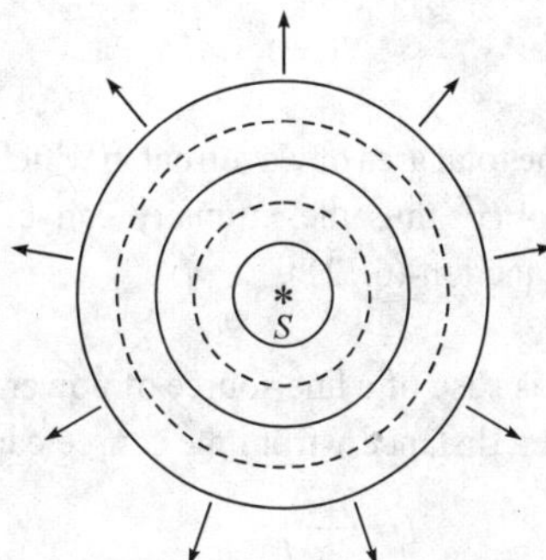

(a) Waves emitted by a point source

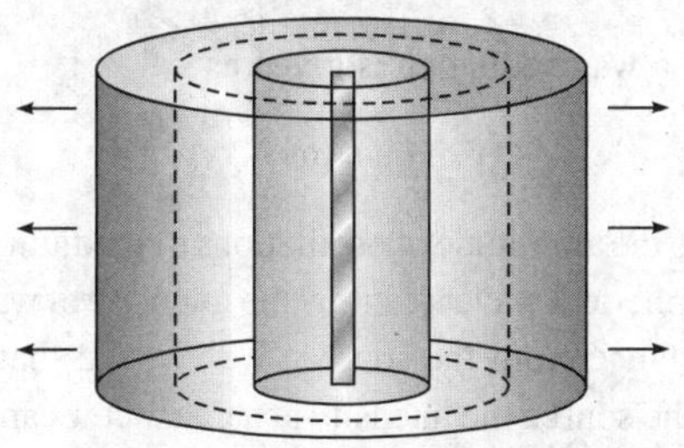

(b) Waves emitted by a line source

Figure 6.40

Similarly we can define cylindrical waves as shown in figure-6.40(b). As spherical waves are produced by a point source, cylindrical waves are produced by a line source. The best example to understand a cylindrical wave is a tube light, which is a source of cylindrical light waves. The wavefront produced by a line source is cylindrical and here also the radius of wavefront increases with speed of waves.

6.9.1 Intensity of Spherical and Cylindrical Waves

If a point source of power P watt produces a spherical wave then the power emitted by the source in its wavefronts is continuously spreaded in all directions. If we find the wave intensity at point A at a distance x from the source S, as shown in figure-6.41 then it can be directly given as

$$I_A = \frac{P}{4\pi x^2}\ \text{W/m}^2 \quad \dots(6.121)$$

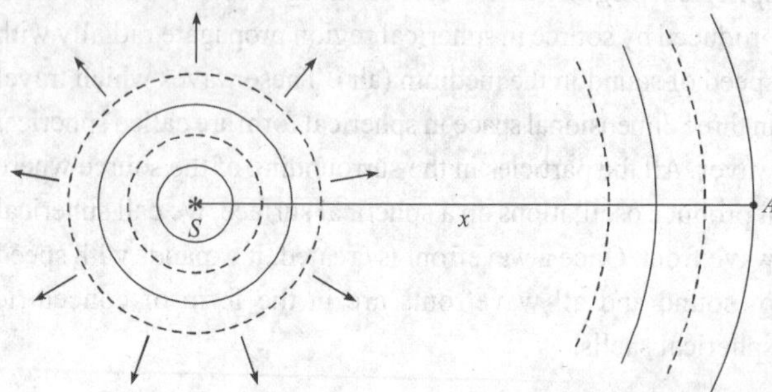

Figure 6.41

As at point A the total area of wavefront in which the power P is distributed is $4\pi x^2$ thus the intensity can be given by the expression in equation-(6.121).

Similar to this is case of a line source of power P and length l, the intensity at a distance x from the source can be given as

$$I = \frac{P}{2\pi x l} \quad \dots (6.122)$$

6.9.2 Equation of Spherical and Cylindrical Waves

In general a wave equation is given as

$$y = A \sin(\omega t - kx)$$

Where A is the amplitude of oscillations of medium particles. In case of a spherical wave we know the intensity of wave depends on the distance from the source. We've read that if P is the power of the source the intensity at a distance x can be given as

$$I = \frac{P}{4\pi x^2} \quad \dots (6.123)$$

We also know that the wave intensity is directly proportional to the square of amplitude of oscillations of medium particles thus in case spherical waves, we can say that the wave amplitude is inversely proportional to the distance from the source, as

$$A \propto \sqrt{I} \quad \dots (6.124)$$

or $$A \propto \frac{1}{x}$$

or $$A = \frac{A_0}{x} \quad \dots (6.125)$$

Here A_0 is a proportionality constant. Thus the wave equation of a spherical wave can be given as

$$y = \frac{A_0}{x} \sin(\omega t - kx) \quad \dots (6.126)$$

Similarly in case of cylindrical wave the intensity is inversely proportional to the distance from the source so we can say that here the wave amplitude is inversely proportional to the square root of the distance from the source these the amplitude of a cylindrical wave can be given as

$$A = \frac{A_0}{\sqrt{x}} \quad \dots (6.127)$$

Thus the equation of a cylindrical wave can be given as

$$y = \frac{A_0}{\sqrt{x}} \sin(\omega t - kx) \quad \dots (6.128)$$

6.10 Measurements of Sound Levels

The human ear is an extremely sensitive detector, capable of hearing sounds over an extremely large range of intensities. For example the sound produced by a thunder storm is 10^5 to 10^7 times greater then the sound intensity due to a buzzing mosquito, yet we can hear both sounds clearly. Our ears are sensitive to this enormous range of sound intensities. During observation people perceive a sound to be about twice as loud as a reference sound when its intensity is ten times as large as the reference sound. A sound perceived to be four times as loud as a reference requires an increase in sound intensity by a factor of 100. This relationship is approximately logarithmic, or we can state that loudness is proportional to the logarithm of the sound intensity.

The loudness of a sound is measured in units of decibel, *dB*. The decibel unit is one tenth of the size of the bel (a unit named in honor of Alexander Graham Bell). The intensity level in decibel is defined to be ten times the logarithm of the ratio of two intensities. If two sound intensities I_1 and I_2 are in W/m^2 then loudness level of I_2 with respect to I_1 can be given as

$$L\,(\text{in } dB) = 10 \log_{10} \frac{I_2}{I_1} \quad \dots (6.129)$$

Here we say second sound is L *dB* louder then first sound. If we fix a standard reference level I_0 then we can measure the loudness level of any sound with respect to the reference intensity I_0 as

$$L\,(\text{in } dB) = 10 \log_{10} \frac{I}{I_0} \quad \dots (6.130)$$

For example if a sound intensity exceeds the reference intensity I_0 by a factor of 4, then we have

$$L = 10 \log 4 = 10\,(0.6) = 6 \text{ dB}$$

Thus here we can say that intensity level of the sound is 6 dB above the reference sound level. We can see that the measure of sound intensity level in decibel is actually a comparison of loudness of two different sound levels. So a given sound level cannot be expressed in units of decibels unless the reference level is fixed. The standard reference level is taken $I_0 = 10^{-12}$ W/m^2, which is the sound intensity that can just be heard by a person with good hearing. This intensity 10^{-12} W/m^2 is called the threshold of hearing. Figure-6.42 shows the comparison of different loudness levels of different commonly heard sounds in day to day life.

Throshold of hearing, Very quite, Library silence, Average Home environment, Normal Conservation, Loud, Industrial or thunder sound (peinful)

0, 10, 20, 30, 40, 50, 60, 70, 80, 90, 100, 100 dB +

Sound level in dB

Figure 6.42

6.10.1 Comparison of Loudness Levels

Loudness of two sound waves are compared by their loudness levels as sound intensity is not a direct measure for perception of loudness of sound wave so comparison of two sound waves is done by measuring the difference in loudness levels of the two sounds.

If there are two waves having intensities I_1 and I_2, their loudness levels are given as

$$L_1 = 10 \log \frac{I_1}{I_0} \text{ dB}$$

and
$$L_2 = 10 \log \frac{I_2}{I_0} \text{ dB}$$

Difference in loudness level (in dB) is given as

$$\Delta L \text{ (in } dB) = L_2 - L_1 = 10 \log \frac{I_2}{I_0} - 10 \log \frac{I_1}{I_0}$$

$$= 10 \log \frac{I_2}{I_1}$$

Here we say sound of wave-2 is ΔL dB louder then sound of wave-1.

 # *Illustrative Example 6.29*

(a) The power of sound from the speaker of a radio is 20 mW. By turning the knob of volume control the power of sound is increased to 400 mW. What is the power increase in *dB* as compared to original power?
(b) How much more intense is an 80 dB sound than a 20 dB whisper?

Solution

(a) As intensity is power per unit area, for a given source $P \propto I$, if L_1 and L_2 are the in initial and final loudness levels then we have

$$L_2 - L_1 = 10 \log (I_2/I_1)$$

The increase in loudness level is

$$\Delta L = 10 \log \frac{P_2}{P_1} = 10 \log \frac{400}{20}$$

or
$$\Delta L = 10 \text{ [log 20]} \simeq 13 \text{ dB}$$

or

(b) Increase in loudness level of sound is

$$L_2 - L_1 = 10 \log (I_2/I_1)$$

So,
$$80 - 20 = 10 \log (I_2/I_1)$$

or
$$6 = \log (I_2/I_1)$$

or
$$(I_2/I_1) = 10^6$$

 # *Illustrative Example 6.30*

A dog while barking delivers about 1 mW of power. If this power is uniformly distributed over a hemispherical area, what is the sound level at a distance of 5 m? What would the sound level be if instead of 1 dog. 5 dog start barking at the same time delivering 1 mW of power?

Solution

As power is distributed uniformly in a hemisphere, intensity at a distance of 5 m from the source will be

$$I = \frac{P}{S} = \frac{P}{(1/2)4\pi r^2} = \frac{10^{-3}}{2 \times \pi \times 5^2} = 6.37 \ \mu\text{W/m}^2$$

Thus loudness level is

$$L = 10 \log \frac{I}{I_0} = 10 \log \frac{6.37 \times 10^{-6}}{(10^{-12})}$$

or
$$L = 10 \text{ [log } 6.37 + 6 \log 10] = 10 \text{ [}0.80 + 6]$$

or
$$L = 68 \text{ dB}$$

If there are 5 dogs barking at the same time and same level, $I_2 = 5I_1$. So

$$L_2 - L_1 = 10 \log \frac{I_2}{I_1} = 10 \log \frac{5I_1}{I_1}$$

or
$$L_2 = L_1 + 10 \log 5$$

or
$$L_2 = 68 + 10 \times 0.7 = 75 \text{ dB}$$

 # *Illustrative Example 6.31*

The sound level at a point is increased by 30 dB. By what factor is the pressure amplitude increased ?

Solution

The sound level in *dB* is

$$L = 10 \log_{10} \left(\frac{I}{I_0} \right)$$

If L_1 and L_2 are the sound levels and I_1 and I_2 are the corresponding intensities in the two cases,

$$L_2 - L_1 = 10\left[\log_{10}\left(\frac{I_2}{I_0}\right) - \log_{10}\left(\frac{I_1}{I_0}\right)\right]$$

or, $$30 = 10\log_{10}\left(\frac{I_2}{I_1}\right)$$

or, $$\frac{I_2}{I_1} = 10^3$$

As the intensity is proportional to the square of the pressure amplitude, thus we have

$$\frac{\Delta p_2}{\Delta p_1} = \sqrt{\frac{I_2}{I_1}} = \sqrt{1000} \approx 32$$

Illustrative Example 6.32

What is the maximum possible sound level in *dB* of sound waves in air? Given that density of air = 1.3 kg/m^3, v = 332 m/s and atmospheric pressure P = 1.01 × 10^5 N/m^2.

Solution

For maximum possible sound intensity, maximum pressure amplitude of wave can be at most equal to atmospheric pressure, so we have

$$\Delta p_0 = P = 1.01 \times 10^5 \text{ N/m}^2$$

So $$I = \frac{\Delta p_0^2}{2\rho v} = \frac{(1.01\times10^5)^2}{2\times1.3\times332} = 1.18 \times 10^7 \text{ W/m}^2$$

Thus loudness level is

$$L = 10\log\frac{I}{I_0} \approx 10\log\frac{10^7}{10^{-12}} = 190 \text{ dB}$$

Illustrative Example 6.33

A window whose area is 2 m^2 opens on street where the street noise result in an intensity level at the window of 60 dB. How much 'acoustic power' enters the window via sound waves. Now if an acoustic absorber is fitted at the window, how much energy from street will it collect in five hours?

Solution

Loudness level is given as

$$L = 10\log\left(\frac{I}{I_0}\right)$$

Thus $$10\log\frac{I}{I_0} = 60$$

or $$\frac{I}{I_0} = 10^6$$

or $$I = (10^{-12} \times 10^6) = 10^{-6} \text{ W/m}^2 = 1\ \mu\text{W/m}^2$$

And we have power of sound is

$$P = IS$$
$$= 1 \times 10^{-6} \times 2 = 2\ \mu\text{W}$$

Thus energy is given as

$$E = P \times t$$
$$= 2 \times 10^{-6} \times 5 \times 60 \times 60 = 36 \times 10^{-3} \text{ J}$$

Web Reference at www.physicsgalaxy.com
Age Group - High School Physics | Age 17-19 Years
Section - OSCILLATION & WAVES
Topic - Interference of Waves
Module Number - 30 to 42

Practice Exercise 6.4

(i) If the intensity of sound is doubled, by how many decibels does the sound level increase?

[3.01 dB]

(ii) A certain sound level is increased by an additional 30 dB. Find the factor by which (a) its intensity increases and (b) its pressure amplitude increases.

[(a) 10^3, (b) 31.62]

(iii) If the sound level in a room is increased from 50 dB to 60 dB, by what factor is the pressure amplitude increased?

[$\sqrt{10}$]

(iv) A typical loud sound wave with a frequency of 1 kHz has a pressure amplitude of about 10^{-4} atm. (a) At t = 0, the pressure is maximum at some point x_1. What is the displacement at that point at t = 0 ? (b) What is the maximum value of the displacement at any time and place? Consider air as diatomic ideal gas.

[(a) 0, (b) 3.753 × 10^{-6} m]

(v) A source of sound operates at 2.0 kHz, 20 W emitting sound uniformly in all directions. The speed of sound in air is 340 m/s and the density of air is 1.2 kg/m^2. (a) What is the intensity at a distance of 6.0 m from the source ? (b) What will be the pressure amplitude at this point ? (c) What will be the displacement amplitude at this point?

[(a) 44.2 mW/m^2, (b) 6.0 Pa, (c) 1.16 × 10^{-6} m]

(vi) The intensity of sound from a point source is 1.0 × 10^{-8} W/m^2 at a distance of 5.0 m from the source. What will be the intensity at a distance of 25 m from the source?

[4.0 × 10^{-10} W/m^2]

(vii) The noise level in a class-room in absence of the teacher is 50 dB when 50 students are present. Assuming that on the average each student outputs same sound energy per second, what will be the noise level if the number of students is increased to 100?

[53.01 dB]

(viii) At a distance $r_0 = 20.0$ m from a point isotropic source of sound the loudness level $L_0 = 30.0$ dB. Neglecting the damping of the sound wave, find :

(a) the loudness level at a distance $r = 10.0$ m from the source;

(b) the distance front the source at which the sound is not heard.

[(a) 36.02 dB; (b) 632.45 m]

(ix) In a good *FM* radio receiver, the radio signal detected may be as much as 65 dB greater than the noise signal. What is the ratio of signal intensity to noise intensity ?

[3.16×10^6]

(x) Two sound waves move in the same direction in a medium. If the average powers transmitted across a cross section by them are equal while their wavelength are in the ratio 1: 2. Find the ratio of their pressure amplitudes.

[1]

6.11 Stationary Waves

In previous sections we've discussed that when two coherent waves superpose on a medium particle, phenomenon of interference takes place. Similarly when two coherent waves travelling in opposite direction superpose then simultaneous interference at all the medium particles takes place. These waves interfere to produce a pattern on all the medium particles what we call, a stationary waves. If the two interfering waves which travel in opposite direction carry equal energies then no net flow of energy takes place in the region of superposition. Within this region redistribution of energy takes place between medium particles. There are some medium particles where constructive interference takes place and hence energy increases and on the other hand there are some medium particles where destructive interference takes place and energy decreases. Now we'll discuss the stationary waves in analytically.

Let two waves of equal amplitude travelling in opposite direction along x-axis. The wave equation of the two waves can be given as

$$y_1 = A \sin(\omega t - kx)$$

[Wave travelling in $+x$ direction]... (6.131)

and
$$y_2 = A \sin(\omega t + kx)$$

[Wave travelling in $-x$ direction]... (6.132)

When the two waves superpose on medium particles, the resultant displacement of the medium particles can be given as

$$y = y_1 + y_2$$

or
$$y = A \sin(\omega t - kx) + A \sin(\omega t + kx)$$

or
$$y = A$$
$$[\sin \omega t \cos kx - \cos \omega t \sin kx + \sin \omega t \cos kx + \cos \omega t \sin kx]$$

or
$$y = 2A \cos kx \sin \omega t \quad \text{...(6.133)}$$

Equation-(6.133) can be rewritten as

$$y = R \sin \omega t \quad \text{...(6.134)}$$

Where
$$R = 2A \cos kx \quad \text{...(6.135)}$$

Here equation-(6.134) is an equation of SHM. It implies that after superposition of the two waves the medium particles executes SHM with same frequency ω and amplitude R which is given by equation-(6.135). Here we can see that the oscillation amplitude of medium particles depends on x i.e. the position of medium particles. Thus on superposition of two coherent waves travelling in opposite direction the resulting interference pattern, we call stationary waves, the oscillation amplitude of the medium particle at different positions is different.

At some points in medium the resultant amplitude is maximum which are given as

R is maximum when

$$\cos kx = \pm 1$$

or
$$\frac{2\pi}{\lambda} x = N\pi \quad [N \in I]$$

or
$$x = \frac{N\lambda}{2}$$

or
$$x = 0, \frac{\lambda}{2}, \lambda, \frac{3\lambda}{2} \ldots\ldots$$

and the maximum value of R is given as

$$R_{max} = \pm 2A \quad \text{...(6.136)}$$

Thus in the medium at positions $x = 0, \lambda/2, \lambda, 3\lambda/2, \ldots\ldots$ the waves interfere constructively and the amplitude of oscillations becomes $2A$. Similarly at some points of the medium, the waves interfere destructively, the oscillation amplitude becomes minimum i.e. zero in this case. These are the points where R is minimum, when

$$\cos kx = 0$$

or
$$\frac{2kx}{\lambda} = (2N+1)\frac{\pi}{2}$$

or $$x=(2N+1)\frac{\lambda}{4} \qquad [N\in I]$$

or $$x=\frac{\lambda}{4},\frac{3\lambda}{4},\frac{5\lambda}{4}\ ......$$

and the minimum value of R is given as

$$R_{min}=0 \qquad \text{...(6.137)}$$

Thus in the medium at positions $x = \lambda/4, 3\lambda/4, 5\lambda/4$ ...... the waves interfere destructively and the amplitude of oscillation becomes zero. These points always remains at rest. Figure-6.43 shows the oscillation amplitude of different medium particles in a stationary wave.

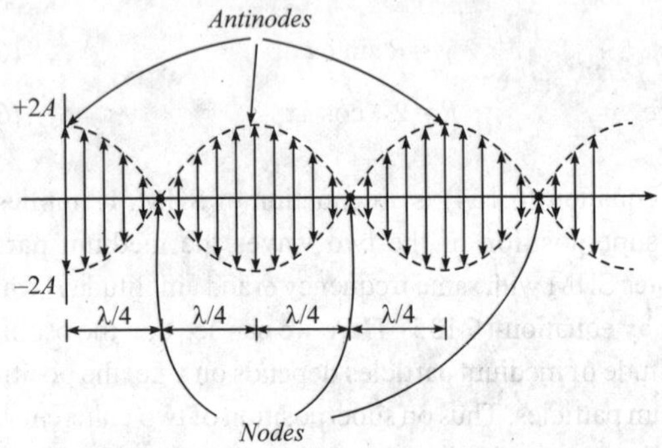

Figure 6.43

In figure we can see that the medium particles at which constructive interference takes place are called antinodes of stationary wave and the points of destructive interference are called nodes of stationary wave which always remain at rest.

Figure-6.44 explains the movement of medium particles with time in the region where stationary waves are formed. Let us assume that at an instant $t = 0$ all the medium particles are at their extreme positions as shown in figure-6.44(a). Here points $ABCD$ are the nodes of stationary waves where medium particles remains at rest. All other particles starts moving toward their mean positions and at $t = T/4$ all particles cross their mean position as shown in figure-6.44(c), you can see in the figure that the particles at nodes are not moving. Now the medium crosses their mean position and starts moving on other side of mean position toward the other extreme position. At time $t = T/2$, all the particles reach their other extreme position a shown in figure-6.44(e) and at time $t = 3T/4$ again all these particles cross their mean position is opposite direction as shown in figure-6.44(g). Finally at $t = T$, after completing oscillation all the medium particles are in their initial position as shown in figure-6.44(i).

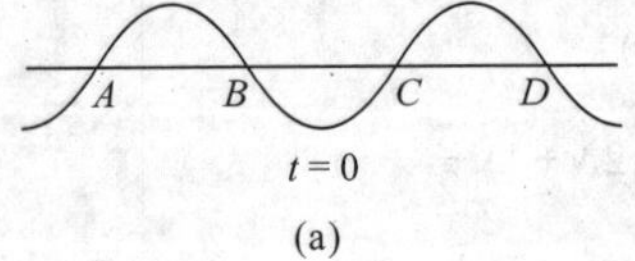

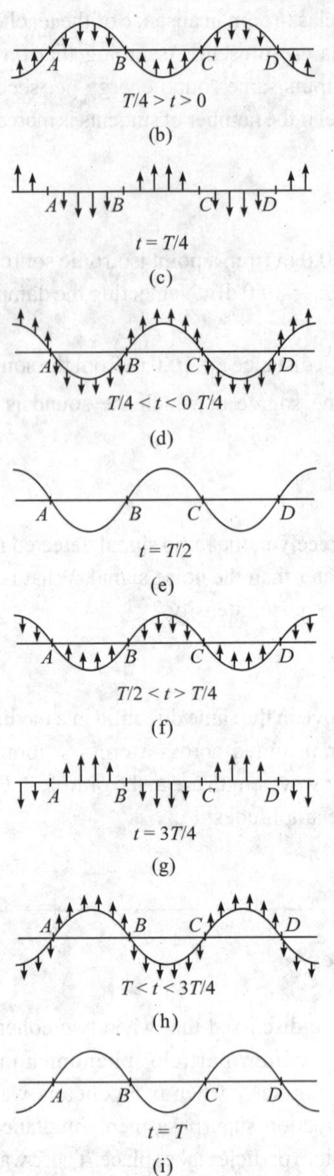

Figure 6.44

Based on the above analysis of one complete oscillations of the medium particles, we can make some inferences for a stationary wave. These are :

(i) In oscillations of a stationary wave in a region, some points are always at rest (nodes) and some oscillates with maximum amplitudes (antinodes). All other medium particles oscillate with amplitudes less then those of antinodes.

(ii) All medium particles between two successive nodes oscillate in same phase and all medium particles on one side of a node oscillate in opposite phase with those on the other side of the same node.

(iii) In the region of a stationary wave during one complete oscillation all the medium particles come in the form of a straight line twice.

(iv) If the component wave amplitudes are equal, then in the region where stationary wave is formed, no net flow of energy takes place, only redistribution of energy takes place in the medium.

When amplitudes of the two component waves are equal then the resultant amplitude at node is zero and these particles always remain at rest, which does not allow energy to propagate in any direction. But when the component waves have unequal amplitude say A_1 and A_2 then the medium particles situated at nodes also oscillate with amplitude $|A_1 - A_2|$ and in this case the amplitude of oscillations of medium particles at antinodes will be $|A_1 + A_2|$. Such an interference pattern is called partial stationary wave. Because in this case as the two component waves have unequal, amplitudes, their powers will also be different in opposite directions. Due to this after superposition there must be some flow of energy in the direction of propagation of wave having higher amplitude. The oscillation amplitude pattern of different medium particles in a pure stationary wave and a particle stationary wave is shown in figure-6.45

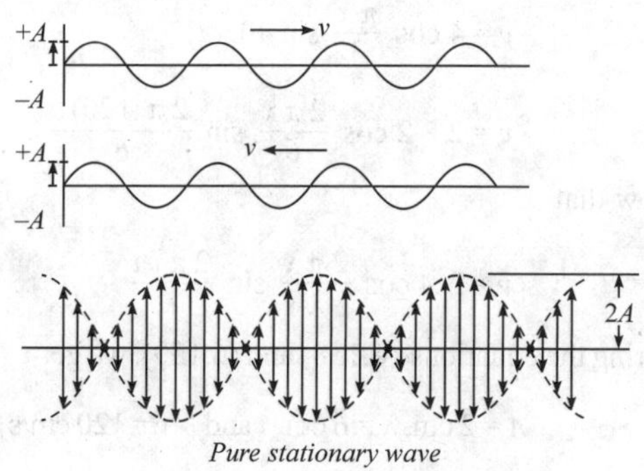

Pure stationary wave

(a)

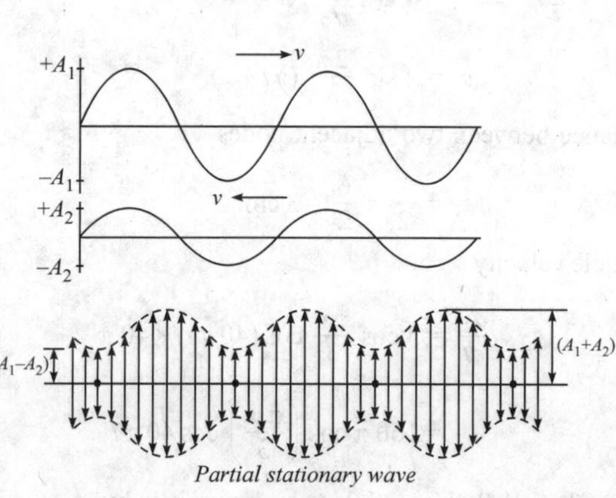

Partial stationary wave

(b)

Figure 6.45

A partial stationary wave can also be regarded as a superposition of a pure stationary wave with a propagating wave. Analytically we can discuss this. Let the two different amplitude coherent waves travelling in opposite direction be

$$y_1 = A_1 \sin(\omega t - kx) \quad \ldots(6.138)$$

[Travelling in $+x$ direction]

and $$y_2 = A_2 \sin(\omega t + kx) \quad [A_1 > A_2] \quad \ldots(6.139)$$

[Travelling in x-direction]

The region in which these waves will superpose the resultant displacement of medium particles can be given as

$$y = y_1 + y_2$$

$$= A_1 \sin(\omega t - kx) + A_2 \sin(\omega t + kx)$$

First term of the above equation can be split as

$$y = A_2 \sin(\omega t - kx) + (A_1 - A_2) \sin(\omega t - kx) + A_2 \sin(\omega t + kx)$$

$$y = 2A_2 \cos kx \sin \omega t + (A_1 - A_2) \sin(\omega t - kx) \quad \ldots(6.140)$$

The first term in the expression in equation-(6.140) is the equation of a pure stationary wave with antinode amplitude $2A_2$ and node amplitude zero and second term in equation-(6.140) is a propagating waves travelling in $+x$ direction with amplitude $A_1 - A_2$. Here we can state that net energy flow takes places in the medium due to the propagating wave in $+x$ direction as $A_1 > A_2$.

6.11.1 Different Equations for a Stationary Wave

Consider two equal amplitude waves travelling in opposite direction as

$$y_1 = A \sin(\omega t - kx) \quad \ldots(6.141)$$

and $$y_2 = A \sin(\omega t + kx) \quad \ldots(6.142)$$

The result of superposition of these two waves is

$$y = 2A \cos kx \sin \omega t \quad \ldots(6.143)$$

Which is the equation of stationary wave where $2A \cos kx$ represents the amplitude of medium particle situated at position x and $\sin \omega t$ is the time sinusoidal factor. This equation-(6.143) can be written in several ways depending on initial phase differences in the component waves given by equation-(6.141) and (6.142). If the superposing waves are having an initial phase difference π, then the component waves can be expressed as

$$y_1 = A \sin(\omega t - kx) \quad \ldots(6.144)$$

$$y_2 = -A \sin(\omega t - kx) \quad \ldots(6.145)$$

Superposition of the above two waves will result

$$y = 2A \sin kx \cos \omega t \quad \text{...(6.146)}$$

Equation-(6.146) is also an equation of stationary wave but here amplitudes of different medium particles in the region of interference is given by

$$R = 2A \sin kx \quad \text{...(6.147)}$$

Similarly the possible equations of a stationary wave can be written as

$$y = A_0 \sin kx \cos (\omega t + \phi) \quad \text{...(6.148)}$$

$$y = A_0 \cos kx \sin (\omega t + \phi) \quad \text{...(6.149)}$$

$$y = A_0 \sin kx \sin (\omega t + \phi) \quad \text{...(6.150)}$$

$$y = A_0 \cos kx \cos (\omega t + \phi) \quad \text{...(6.151)}$$

Here A_0 is the amplitude of antinodes. In a pure stationary wave it is given as

$$A_0 = 2A$$

Where A is the amplitude of component waves. If we care fully look at equation-(6.148) to (6.151), we can see that in equation-(6.148) and (6.150), the particle amplitude is given by

$$R = A_0 \sin kx \quad \text{...(6.152)}$$

Here at $x = 0$, there is a node as $R = 0$ and in equation-(6.149) and (6.151) the particle amplitude is given as

$$R = A_0 \cos kx \quad \text{...(6.153)}$$

Here at $x = 0$, there is an antinode as $R = A_0$. Thus we can state that in a given system of co-ordinates when origin of system is at a node we use either equation-(6.148) or (6.150) for analytical representation of a stationary wave and we use equation-(6.149) or (6.151) for the same when an antinode is located at the origin of system.

6.11.2 Velocity and Acceleration of Medium Particle in Stationary Wave

In a stationary wave we have discussed that the displacement of a medium particle from its mean position is given by either of equation (6.148) to (6.151) we take any one of these to represent a stationary wave in a medium as

$$y = A_0 \sin kx \cos \omega t \quad \text{...(6.154)}$$

Here velocity of a medium particle at a position x can be given by

$$v_p = \frac{\partial y}{\partial t} \equiv \omega A_0 \sin kx \cos \omega t \quad \text{...(6.155)}$$

Differentiating again equation-(6.155) only w.r. to time gives the acceleration of the medium particle at a position x as

$$a_p = \frac{\partial^2 y}{\partial t^2} = -\omega^2 A_0 \sin kx \sin \omega t \quad \text{...(6.156)}$$

Similarly we can find the slope of displacement curve of a stationary wave at a particular instant of time from equation-(6.154) as

$$\frac{\partial y}{\partial x} = kA_0 \cos kx \sin \omega t \quad \text{...(6.157)}$$

Illustrative Example 6.34

The following equation represents standing wave set up in a medium,

$$y = 4 \cos \frac{\pi x}{3} \sin 40 \pi t,$$

where x and y are in cm and t in sec. Find out the amplitude and the velocity of the two component waves and calculate the distance between adjacent nodes. What is the velocity of a medium particle at $x = 3$ cm at time 1/8 s ?

Solution

The given equation of stationary wave is

$$y = 4 \cos \frac{\pi x}{3} \sin 40 \pi t$$

or

$$y = 2 \times 2 \cos \frac{2 \pi x}{6} \sin \frac{2 \pi (120) t}{6} \quad \text{...(6.158)}$$

We know that

$$y = 2A \cos \frac{2 \pi x}{\lambda} \sin \frac{2 \pi v t}{\lambda} \quad \text{...(6.159)}$$

Comparing the equations-(6.158) and (6.159), we get

$$A = 2 \text{ cm}, \lambda = 6 \text{ cm} \quad \text{and} \quad v = 120 \text{ cm/s}$$

The component waves are

$$y_1 = A \sin \frac{2 \pi}{\lambda} (v t - x)$$

and

$$y_2 = A \sin \frac{2 \pi}{\lambda} (v t + x)$$

Distance between two adjacent nodes

$$= \frac{\lambda}{2} = \frac{6}{2} = 3 \text{ cm}$$

Particle velocity

$$\frac{dy}{dt} = 4 \cos \frac{\pi x}{3} \cos (40 \pi t) \times 40 \pi$$

$$= 160 \pi \cos \left(\frac{\pi x}{3}\right) \cos 40 \pi t$$

At $x = 3$, $t = 1/8$, the particle velocity is given by

$$= 160 \pi \cos \pi \cos \left(40\pi \times \frac{1}{8}\right) = 160 \pi \text{ cm/s}$$

Illustrative Example 6.35

A wave is given by the equation

$$y = 10 \sin 2\pi (100t - 0.02x) + 10 \sin 2\pi (100t - 0.02x)$$

Find the loop length, frequency, velocity and maximum amplitude of the stationary wave produced.

Solution

We know the equation of a stationary wave is given by

$$y = A \sin\left[\frac{2\pi}{\lambda}(vt - x)\right] + A \sin\left[\frac{2\pi}{\lambda}(vt + x)\right]$$

$$= 2A \cos\frac{2\pi x}{\lambda} \sin\frac{2\pi vt}{\lambda}$$

$$= R \sin\frac{2\pi}{\lambda} vt$$

Here $R = 2A \cos\frac{2\pi x}{\lambda}$ is the amplitude of medium particle situated at a distance x.

The given equation can be expressed as

$$y = 10 \sin\left[\frac{2\pi}{50}(5000t - x)\right] + 10 \sin\left[\frac{2\pi}{50}(5000t + x)\right]$$

$$= 2 \times 10 \cos\left(\frac{2\pi x}{50}\right) \sin\left(\frac{2\pi}{50} 5000t\right)$$

Comparing it with standard equation of stationary wave, we get wavelength

$$\lambda = 50 \text{ units}$$

Wave velocity $\quad v = 5000$ units

Thus amplitude $\quad R = 2 \times 10 \cos\frac{2\pi x}{50}$

and Maximum amplitude

$$R_{max} = 2 \times 10 = 20 \text{ units}$$

As wave velocity is

$$v = 5000 \text{ units,}$$

Frequency $\quad = \frac{v}{\lambda} = \frac{5000}{5} = 100$ units

and loop length is

$$\frac{\lambda}{2} = \frac{50}{2} = 25 \text{ units}$$

Illustrative Example 6.36

A progressive and a stationary simple harmonic wave each has the same frequency of 250 Hz, and the same velocity of 30 m/s. Calculate

(i) the phase difference between two vibrating points on the progressive wave which are 100 cm apart,

(ii) the equation of motion of the progressive wave if its amplitude is 0.03 m,

(iii) the distance between nodes in the stationary wave,

(iv) the equation of motion, the stationary wave if its amplitude is 0.01 m.

Solution

Given, $\quad n = 250$ Hz, $\quad v = 30$ m/s

or $\quad \lambda = \frac{v}{n} = \frac{3}{25}$ m $= 12$ cm

(i) Phase difference between two points at a distance $\lambda = 2\pi$

Phase difference between two points, unit distance apart $= \frac{2\pi}{\lambda}$

Thus phase difference for a distance of 10 cm

$$= \frac{2\pi}{\lambda} \times 10 = \frac{2\pi}{12} \times 10 = \frac{5}{3}\pi$$

(ii) Now $\quad A = 0.03, \lambda = (3/25)$ m

and $\quad \frac{1}{T} = n = 250$ Hz

The general equation of a plane progressive wave is given by

$$y = A \sin 2\pi\left(\frac{t}{T} - \frac{x}{\lambda}\right)$$

Here $\quad y = 0.03 \sin 2\pi (250t - 25x/3)$

(iii) The distance between nodes in stationary wave

$$= \frac{\lambda}{2} = \frac{12}{6} = 6 \text{ cm}$$

(iv) Equation of stationary wave is given by

$$y = 2A \cos\frac{2\pi x}{\lambda} \sin\frac{2\pi vt}{\lambda}$$

$$= 2A \cos\frac{2\pi x}{\lambda} \sin\frac{2\pi t}{T}$$

Here $\quad 2A = 0.01, \lambda = \frac{3}{25}$ m and $\frac{1}{T} = 250$ Hz

or $\quad y = 0.01 \cos\frac{5\pi x}{3} \sin 500\pi t$

Web Reference at www.physicsgalaxy.com

Age Group - High School Physics | Age 17-19 Years
Section - OSCILLATION & WAVES
Topic - Stationary Waves and Beats
Module Number - 1 to 8

6.12 Standing Waves on Clamped String

In previous sections we've discussed about the reflection of a wave pulse on a string when it arrives at a boundary point which may be a fixed or a free end. Now we'll discuss what happens when a propagating simple harmonic wave is reflected by a fixed end of a string. Consider the situation shown in figure-6.46.

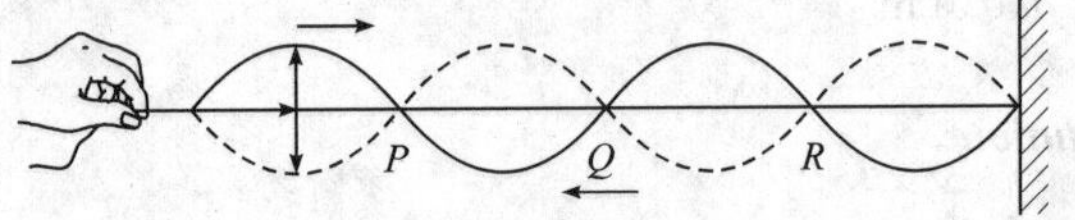

Figure 6.46

A stretched string is clamped at a point on a rigid vertical wall. The other end of string is given oscillations manually which creates a continuous propagating wave toward the wall from which it is reflected with a phase difference of π radians which start propagating in direction opposite to incident wave. If we assume ideal reflection from the wall then the reflected wave will also have the same amplitude as that of the incident wave. As here two coherent waves (as during reflection frequency does not change) travelling in opposite direction superpose each other, stationary waves are formed on the string. As we can see in figure-6.46. At points P, Q, R nodes are formed and between every two adjacent node an antinode is there. But this is not so simple that you move one end of a clamped string up and down and you'll see nodes and antinodes. This will happen only at some particular oscillation frequencies which depend on several factors like length of string, tension in string, linear mass density of string etc. Thus if a clamped string is oscillated like the way as shown in figure-6.46 stationary waves will be formed or not it depends on the frequency of source of oscillations (in our case it is hand) but theoretically when incident and reflected waves superpose, stationary waves must be formed then why does the practical situation differ. This we'll discuss now in detail.

First we discuss one more example of oscillations of a string clamped at both the ends as shown in figure-6.47. If we pluck the string at its mid point and release it will start oscillating as shown in figure-6.47(b). Actually when we pluck the string at its mid point and release, two transverse waves are generated and start moving toward the clamps C_1 and C_2 from middle portion of string. These are reflected from the clamps and superpose on the length of the string and stationary wave is formed between C_1 and C_2. As being rigid clamps the string particles are not allowed to oscillate at these points. Here at C_1 and C_2, nodes must be formed and there is one antinode at the mid point of the string. Similarly if at the mid point of the string we put a support and we pluck the left portion of the string a loop is formed and the wave of same frequency transmits to the right portion and another loop is formed there as shown in figure-6.47(c). Now if the support at the mid point is removed then also string oscillations remains same, it continues to oscillates in two loops as already there was a node at the point of support so it does not make any difference whether there is any support present or not. The support was required only to initiate the oscillations. In the same fashion we can make string to oscillate in three, four or more loops by placing a support at $\frac{1}{3}$ rd, $\frac{1}{4}$ th length from one clamp to initiate the oscillations in the beginning.

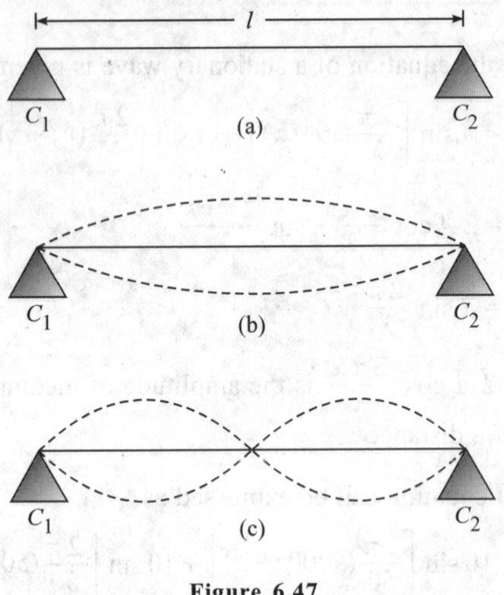

Figure 6.47

Here we can see that when there is no support, the string oscillates full length as one loop. In this case the separation between two nodes is the string length l i.e. $\lambda/2$. In second case we have $l/2 = \lambda/2$ and so on. This implies that as number of loops in the string increases the wavelength decreases and hence frequency of oscillations increases.

Thus in a clamped string oscillations, stationary waves are formed only when the string length is equally divided into loops otherwise there will not be a node at one of the clamps. So for the formation of stationary wave in a clamped string the string length must be an integral multiple of $\lambda/2$, where λ is the wave length of the wave on string.

6.12.1 Normal Modes of Oscillations of a Clamped String

We've discussed that stationary waves can be established in a clamped string and it can oscillate at different frequencies. These frequencies at which a stable stationary wave can be produced in a clamped string are called different modes of oscillations. Now we discuss these modes in detail.

When a string clamped at both the ends oscillates. The minimum frequency at which it can oscillate is called its fundamental frequency or the fundamental mode of its oscillations. This case is shown in figure-6.48 when only one antinode is formed between two nodes (clamps). In this case the wavelength is at its maximum possible value.

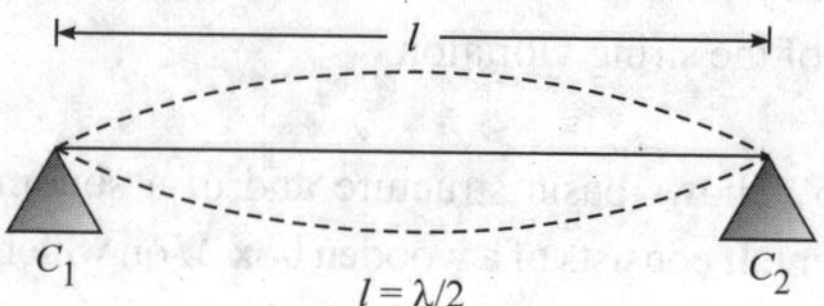

Figure 6.48

In this case oscillation frequency of string can be given as

$$n = \frac{v}{\lambda} = \frac{v}{2l} \qquad \left[\text{As here } \frac{\lambda}{2} = l\right]$$

$$= \frac{1}{2l}\sqrt{\frac{T}{\mu}} \qquad \ldots(6.160)$$

Here T is the tension at which string is stretched and μ is the linear mass density of the string. The next higher frequency at which string oscillates with stationary waves is the one when two loops are formed as shown in figure-6.49

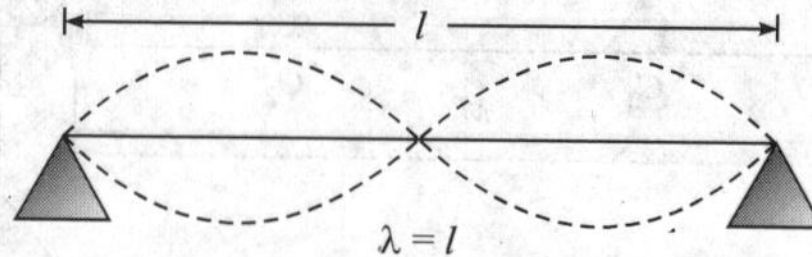

Figure 6.49

In this case oscillation frequency of string can be given as

$$n_2 = \frac{v}{\lambda} = \frac{v}{l} \qquad [\text{As here } \lambda = l]$$

$$= \frac{2}{2l}\sqrt{\frac{T}{\mu}} = 2n_1 \qquad \ldots(6.161)$$

This frequency n_2 is the next higher frequency after fundamental frequency at which stable stationary waves are formed in the string. This mode of oscillations is called first overtone. As this frequency is double that of fundamental frequency this is termed as second harmonic frequency of string oscillations. All the frequencies which are integral multiples of fundamental frequency are called harmonic frequencies.

If we come to the next mode of oscillations of this string it is the case when it vibrates in three loops as shown in figure-6.50.

Here $\qquad l = \frac{3\lambda}{2}$

or $\qquad \lambda = \frac{2l}{3}$

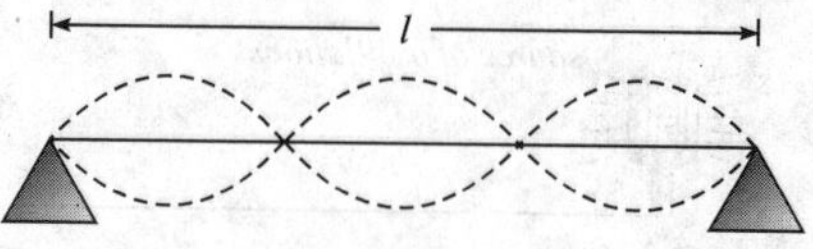

Figure 6.50

In this case the oscillation frequency of the string is given as

$$n_3 = \frac{v}{\lambda} = \frac{3v}{2l}$$

$$= \frac{3}{2l}\sqrt{\frac{T}{\mu}} = 3n_1 \qquad \ldots(6.162)$$

This mode of oscillation is called second overtone of the string oscillations and as the frequency is three times the fundamental frequency, it is also termed as third harmonic. Similarly if a string oscillates in P loops, its frequency can be written as

$$n_p = \frac{pv}{2l} = \frac{p}{2l}\sqrt{\frac{T}{\mu}} = pn_1$$

Where $\qquad p = 1, 2, 3, \ldots \qquad \ldots(6.163)$

The above frequencies n_p at which stationary waves can be formed are the harmonic frequencies and this series of these frequencies is called harmonic series.

6.13 Wave Resonance

When a pendulum or a block at the end of a spring is set into motion by a periodic force, the system moves with largest amplitude or with maximum energy when the frequency of force equals the frequency of natural vibrations of the free system. We can take a simple example to explain resonance. If we push a child on a swing periodically then the oscillations of swing become stronger if the pushing frequency is equal to the frequency of natural oscillations of the swing. Thus the concept of resonance is that the oscillations of a free system are most strong when the frequency of driving force is equal to the frequency of the system's free vibrations.

6.13.1 Resonance in Clamped String Oscillations

Resonance can also be observed in case of a clamped string oscillations consider a string of length l clamped between the two clamps C_1 and C_2. The length and tension in the string adjusted so that here we have the fundamental frequency of this string is 10 Hz, thus we have

$$n_1 = \frac{v}{2l} = 10\,\text{Hz} \qquad \ldots(6.164)$$

This implies that this string can sustain stationary waves at all frequencies which are multiple of 10 Hz (Harmonic frequencies). At frequencies other then 10 Hz the oscillation energy of string will be damped as its length will not be integral multiple of $\lambda/2$.

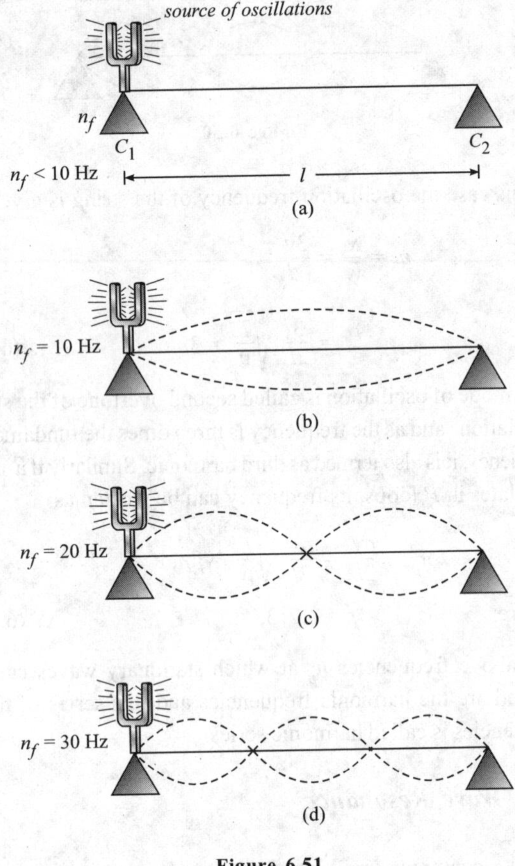

Figure 6.51

Let us use a tuning fork of frequency $n_f < 10$ Hz to establish oscillations in the string as shown in figure-6.51(a). As at frequencies less then 10 Hz, stationary waves can not be established in the string thus the energy supplied by the tuning fork will damp and string will oscillate very little or it appears motion less. But if the frequency of the tuning fork (driving agent) matches with any of the harmonic frequencies of the string, it starts oscillating widely and the amplitude of its oscillations is also so significant that it can be seen as shown in figure-6.51(b), (c) and (d). This is a common method of establishing stationary waves in a clamped string. Thus a string resonates whenever the external oscillating source frequency matches with any of the harmonic frequency of the string. In previous example if a tuning fork of frequency 43.2 Hz is used to setup oscillations in the string it will oscillate at 43.2 Hz but will appear almost straight as shown in figure-6.51(a) as the whole of supplied energy will clamp.

6.13.2 Sonometer

It is a device used to measure velocity of transverse mechanical wave in a stretched metal wire. The principle of sonometer is based on resonance of string vibrations. Working oscillations are induced in a clamped string by an external source like a tuning fork or an oscillator and the corresponding oscillations in string will become stronger when resonance takes place i.e. the frequency of oscillation of source matches with any of the harmonic of the string vibration.

Figure-6.52 shows basic structure and of a sonometer setup arrangement. It consists of a wooden box M on which a wire AB is stretched, by a hanging weight as shown in figure-6.52. On sonometer box there are two clamps C_1 and C_2 placed which can slide under the wire to change the length of wire between the clamps.

When on oscillating turning fork is placed in contact with the sonometer wire as shown in figure-6.52. Some oscillations are transferred to the wire. If tension in wire is T and n_0 be the frequency of tuning fork, the wavelength of wave in wire is

$$\lambda = \frac{v}{n_0} = \frac{1}{n_0}\sqrt{\frac{T}{\mu}} \quad \ldots (6.165)$$

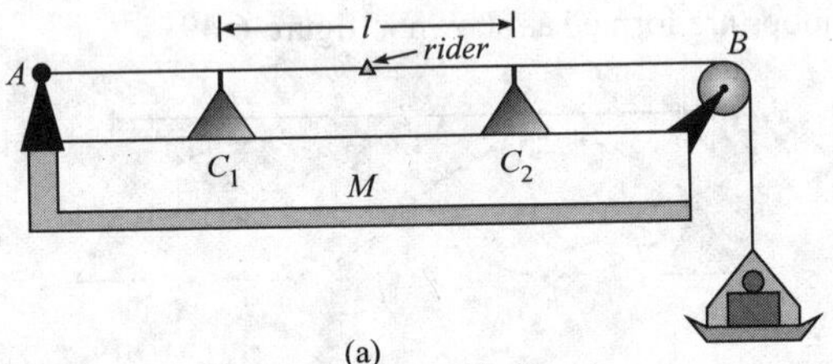

(a)

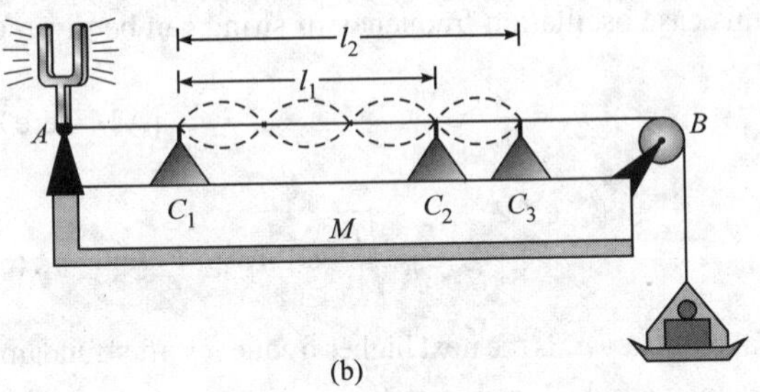

(b)

Figure 6.52

When the length between clamps is an integral multiple of $\lambda/2$ then stationary waves are established in the portion of wire between C_1 and C_2. To adjust this, clamp C_1 is fixed and C_2 is displaced so that a small rider (a piece of paper) on wire start jumping violently on wire and falls indicating that the oscillation amplitude of wire is increasing and stationary waves are established. Let in this situation the length between clamps is l_1. Now again C_2 is displaced away from C_1 so that again resonance is obtained. This will happen again when the clamp reaches the position C_3 and when next node of stationary waves is present as shown in figure-6.52(b). Let this length is l_2.

So we can say that if l_1 and l_2 are the two successive resonance lengths then we have

$$l_2 - l_1 = \frac{\lambda}{2}$$

or wavelength of wave is

$$\lambda = 2\,(l_2 - l_1)$$

As frequency n_0 of oscillating source is known, we can find the velocity of wave in wire as

$$v = n_0\lambda$$

$$= 2n_0\,(l_2 - l_1) \qquad \ldots(6.166)$$

Equation-(6.166) gives the practically measured value of velocity of transverse waves in stretched wire. This can be compared with the theoretical value of v given by $\sqrt{\frac{T}{\mu}}$.

6.13.3 Vibrations of Composite Strings

We have discussed the vibration of a clamped string in previous section, now we discuss the stationary waves in a string composed of two different strings as shown in figure-6.53. Here two strings S_1 and S_2 of different material and lengths are joined end to end and tied between two clamps as shown. Now when we induce oscillations in this composite string, stationary waves are established only at those frequencies which matches with any one harmonic of both the independent string S_1 and S_2.

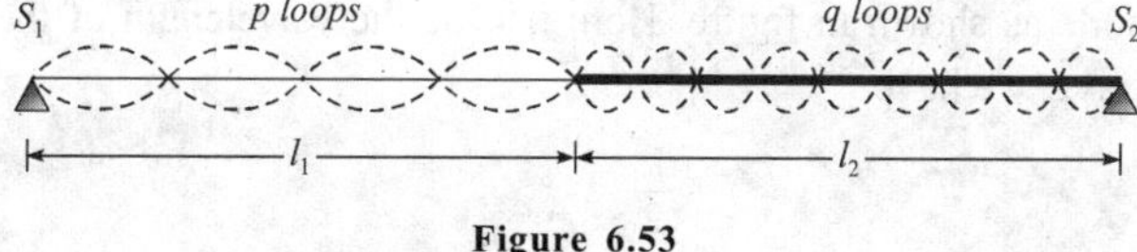

Figure 6.53

Let at a frequency stationary waves are established in this string so that string S_1 oscillates in p loops and strings S_2 oscillates in q loops as frequency of both the string is equal, we have

$$n_{ext} = n_{S_1} = n_{S_2}$$

or $$n_{ext} = \frac{p}{2l_1}\sqrt{\frac{T}{\mu_1}} = \frac{q}{2l_2}\sqrt{\frac{T}{\mu_2}} \qquad \ldots(6.167)$$

[As T = same in both the string]

or $$\frac{p}{q} = \frac{l_1}{l_2}\sqrt{\frac{\mu_1}{\mu_2}} \qquad \ldots(6.168)$$

In equation-(6.168) p and q must be integers, thus the minimum values of p and q which satisfies equation-(6.168) will decide fundamental frequency or the least frequency at which stationary waves can exist in this composite string and the oscillation frequency can be obtained from equation-(6.167).

6.13.4 Melde's Experiment

This is an experiment for demonstration of transverse stationary wave in a stretched string.

In Melde's experiment, one end of the string is connected to the prong of an electrically oscillated tuning fork. The other end of the string is connected to the scale pan. The string passes over a smooth friction less pulley. The distance between tuning fork and pulley can be adjusted. There are two different ways in which oscillations can be established in the string

Case-I : Transverse Mode of vibration

As shown in figure-6.54, tuning fork vibrates right angle to the length of the string. In this case frequency of vibration of string, is equal to the frequency of the tuning fork. First we adjust the length of string so that stationary waves are formed in string. In this case the vibrations of string are strong enough so that the loops can be seen in the string. If string vibrates in p loops as shown in figure, the frequency of string oscillations can be given as

$$n_s = \frac{p}{2l}\sqrt{\frac{T}{\mu}} \qquad \ldots(6.169)$$

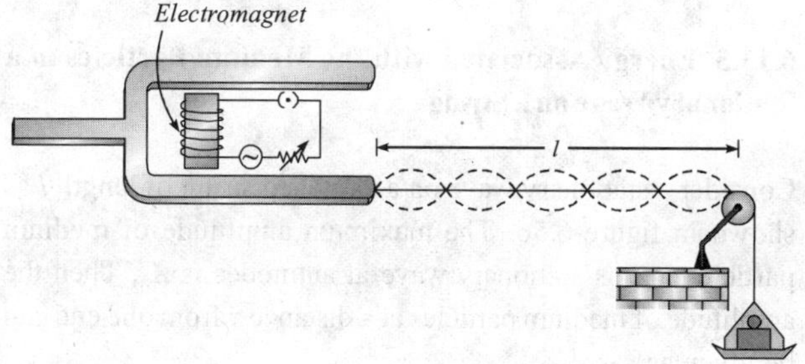

Figure 6.54

If n_f be the frequency of oscillation of tuning fork then we have

$$n_f = n_s = \frac{p}{2l}\sqrt{\frac{T}{\mu}} \qquad \ldots(6.170)$$

(2) Longitudinal Mode of vibrations

In this case the vibrations of tuning fork are along the length of the string. The orientation of tuning fork is shown in figure-6.55. In this case for one complete vibrations of the tuning fork, the string completes only half of its vibration so the frequency of vibration of string is half of that of the oscillation frequency of tuning fork. If string vibrates in p loops then we have,

$$\frac{n_f}{2} = n_s = \frac{p}{2l}\sqrt{\frac{T}{\mu}} \qquad \ldots(6.171)$$

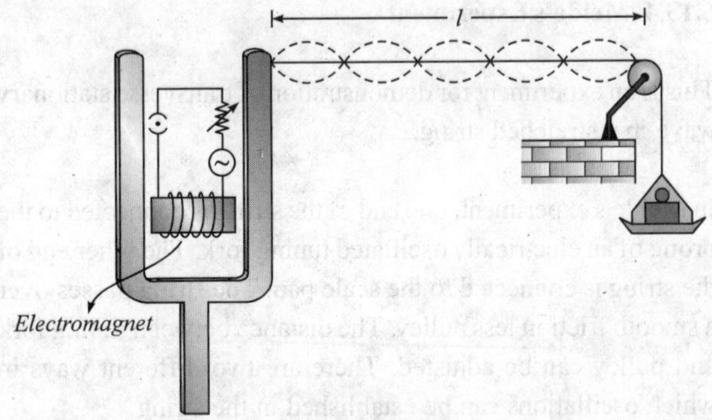

Figure 6.55

We can see if the frequency of tuning fork remains constant from equation-(6.170) and (6.171) we can write

$$p\sqrt{T} = \text{constant} \quad [\text{As } \mu = \text{constant}] \quad \ldots(6.172)$$

If the tension in the string is changed then number of loops in the stationary wave formed varies according to equation-(6.172). This is called as Melde's law.

Thus if in Melde's experiment stationary waves are formed at two different values of tension T_1 and T_2 at which p_1 and p_2 loops are formed in the string then we can write as

$$\frac{p_1}{p_2} = \sqrt{\frac{T_2}{T_1}} \quad \ldots(6.173)$$

6.13.5 Energy Associated with the Medium Particles in a Stationary Wave on a String

Consider a stationary wave on a stretched string of length l as shown in figure-6.56. The maximum amplitude of medium particles in this stationary wave at antinodes is A_0, Then the amplitude of medium particles at a distance x from one end can be given as

$$R = A_0 \sin kx$$

Now consider an element of length dx at a distance x from one end as shown. If frequency of oscillation of string in ω then the total energy contained in this element of length dx can be given as

$$dE = \frac{1}{2}\, dm\omega^2 R^2$$

or

$$dE = \frac{1}{2}(\mu dx)\, \omega^2 A_0^2 \sin^2 kx \quad \ldots(6.174)$$

Figure 6.56

Now total energy contained in the string can be string can be obtained by integrating the expression in equation-(6.174) for whole length of string as

$$E = \int dE = \int_0^L \frac{1}{2}\mu\omega^2 A_0^2 \sin^2 kx\, dx$$

$$= \frac{1}{2}\mu\omega^2 A_0^2 \int \left(\frac{1-\cos 2kx}{2}\right) dx$$

$$= \frac{1}{4}\mu\omega^2 A_0^2 \left[x - \frac{\sin 2kx}{2k}\right]_0^L$$

$$= \frac{1}{4}\mu\omega^2 A_0^2 [L]$$

$$= \frac{1}{4}\mu\omega^2 A_0^2 L \quad \ldots(6.175)$$

6.14 *Vibrations of Clamped Rod*

We have discussed the resonant vibrations of a string clamped at two ends. Now we discuss the oscillations of a rod clamped at a point on its length as shown in figure-6.57. Figure shows a rod AB clamped at its middle point. If we gently hit the rod at its one end, it begin to oscillate and in the natural oscillations the rod vibrates at its lowest frequency and maximum wavelength, which we call fundamental mode of oscillations. With maximum wavelength when transverse stationary waves setup in the rod, the free ends vibrates as antinodes and the clamped end as a node as shown in figure. Here if λ be the wavelength of the wave, we have

$$l = \frac{\lambda}{2}$$

or

$$\lambda = 2l \quad \ldots(6.176)$$

Figure 6.57

Thus the frequency of fundamental oscillations of a rod damped at mid point can be given as

$$n_0 = \frac{v}{\lambda} = \frac{1}{2l}\sqrt{\frac{Y}{\rho}} \quad \ldots(6.177)$$

Where Y is the Young's modulus of the material of rod and ρ is the density of the material of rod.

Next higher frequency at which rod vibrates will be then one when wave length is decreased to a value so that one node is inserted between mid point and an end of rod as shown in figure-6.58.

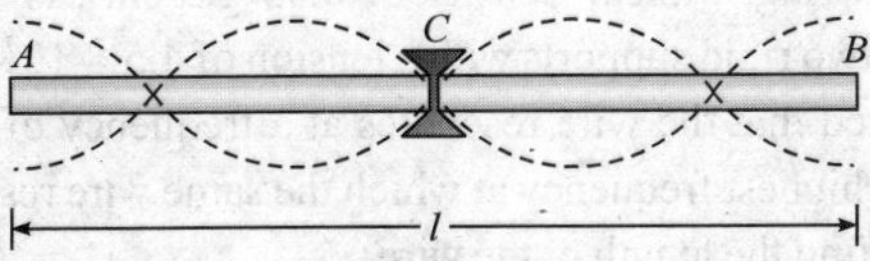

Figure 6.58

In this case if λ be the wavelength of the waves in rod, we have

$$l = \frac{3\lambda}{2}$$

or $$\lambda = \frac{2l}{3} \quad \ldots(6.178)$$

Thus in this case the oscillation frequency of rod can be given as

$$\nu_1 = \frac{v}{\lambda} = \frac{3}{2l}\sqrt{\frac{Y}{\rho}} = 3n_0 \quad \ldots(6.179)$$

This is called first overtone frequency of the damped rod or third harmonic frequency. Similarly, the next higher frequency of oscillation i.e. second overtone of the oscillating rod can be shown in figure-6.59. Here if λ be the wavelength of the wave then it can be given as

$$l = \frac{5\lambda}{2}$$

or $$\lambda = \frac{2l}{5} \quad \ldots(6.180)$$

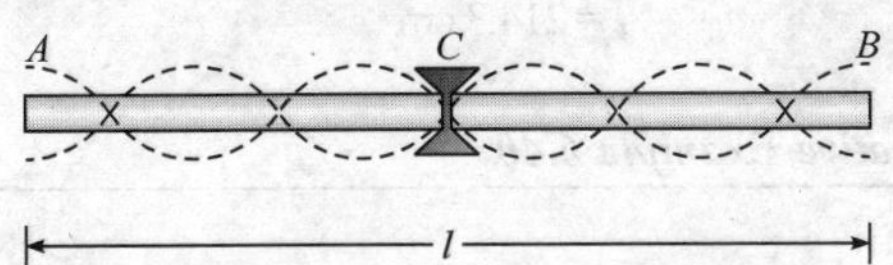

Figure 6.59

Thus the frequency of oscillation of rod can be given as

$$\nu_2 = \frac{v}{\lambda} = \frac{5}{2l}\sqrt{\frac{Y}{\rho}} = 5n_0 \quad \ldots(6.181)$$

Thus the second overtone frequency is the fifth harmonic of the fundamental oscillation frequency of rod. We can also see from the above analysis that the resonant frequencies at which stationary waves are setup in a damped rod are only odd harmonics of fundamental frequency.

Thus when an external source of frequency matching with any of the harmonic of the damped rod then stationary waves are setup in the rod.

 # Illustrative Example 6.37

A wire of density 9×10^3 kg/m³ is stretched between two clamps 1 m apart and is subjected to an extension of 4.9×10^{-4} m. What will be the lowest frequency of transverse vibration in the wire ? (Young's modulus of material = 9×10^{10} N/m²).

Solution

Let A be the area of cross-section of wire and T be the tension applied.

The lowest frequency of transverse vibration is given by

$$n = \frac{1}{2l}\sqrt{\left(\frac{T}{\mu}\right)} \quad \ldots(6.182)$$

Where m = mass per unit length of wire

$$= \text{Volume of unit length} \times \text{density}$$

$$= A \times 1 \times \rho$$

or $$n = \frac{1}{2l}\sqrt{\left(\frac{T}{A\rho}\right)} \quad \ldots(6.183)$$

We know that

Young's modulus

$$Y = \frac{\text{Stress}}{\text{Strain}} = \frac{T/A}{\Delta l/l}$$

or $$T = YA\left(\frac{\Delta l}{l}\right) \quad \ldots(6.184)$$

From equations-(6.183) and (6.184)

$$n = \frac{1}{2l}\sqrt{\left(\frac{YA\Delta l}{lA\rho}\right)} = \frac{1}{2l}\sqrt{\left(\frac{Y\Delta l}{l\rho}\right)}$$

Substituting the given values

$$n = \frac{1}{2\times1}\sqrt{\left(\frac{(9\times10^{10})\times(4.9\times10^{-4})}{1\times(9\times10^{3})}\right)}$$

$$= 35 \text{ Hz}$$

 # Illustrative Example 6.38

The fundamental frequency of a 1.5 m long, stretched steel wire is 175 Hz. The density of steel is 7.8×10^3 kg/m³. (i) Find the speed of transverse waves in the wire. (ii) Calculate the longitudinal stress of the wire. (iii) If the tension in the wire is increased by 3%, calculate the percentage change in the frequency of the wire.

Solution

(i) We know that the fundamental frequency of the wire is given by

$$n = \frac{1}{2l}\sqrt{\left(\frac{T}{\mu}\right)} \quad \ldots(6.185)$$

The speed of the transverse wave in the wire is

$$v = \sqrt{\left(\frac{T}{\mu}\right)} = n \times 2l \quad \ldots(6.186)$$

Substituting the given values, we have

$$v = 175 \times (2 \times 1.5) = 525 \text{ m/s}$$

(ii) Suppose the weight suspended from the wire be Mg. Then

$$T = Mg \quad \text{and} \quad \mu = \pi r^2 \rho$$

or $$v = \sqrt{\left(\frac{T}{\mu}\right)} = \sqrt{\left(\frac{Mg}{\pi r^2 \rho}\right)} \quad \ldots(6.187)$$

Now $$525 = \sqrt{\left(\frac{Mg}{\pi r^2 \rho}\right)} \quad [\text{As } v = 525 \text{ m/s}]$$

or $$\frac{Mg}{\pi r^2} = (525)^2 \times \rho = (525)^2 \times (7.5 \times 10^3)$$

$$= 2.15 \times 10^9 \text{ N/m}^2$$

(iii) When the tension of the wire is increased by 3%, then the new tension becomes

$$T' = T + \frac{3}{100}T = 1.03\,T$$

Now the new frequency

$$= n' = \frac{1}{2l}\sqrt{\left(\frac{T'}{\mu}\right)} \quad \ldots(6.188)$$

Dividing equation-(6.188) by equation-(6.185), we get

$$\frac{n'}{n} = \sqrt{\left(\frac{T'}{T}\right)} = \sqrt{\left(\frac{1.03T}{T}\right)}$$

$$= \sqrt{1.03}$$

or $$\frac{n'}{n} = 1.015$$

or $$n' = 1.015 \times n = n + 0.015\,n$$

$$= n + (3n/200)$$

Thus percentage change in frequency

$$\left(\frac{n' - n}{n}\right) \times 100 = \frac{3}{2} = 1.5$$

 # Illustrative Example 6.39

A wire having a linear density of 0.05 gm/cm^3. is stretched between two rigid supports with a tension of 4.5×10^7 dynes. It is observed that the wire resonates at a frequency of 420 Hz. The next highest frequency at which the same wire resonates is 490 Hz. Find the length of the wire.

Solution

Let the frequency 420 Hz corresponds to pth harmonic. The formula for pth harmonic is given by

$$n_p = \frac{p}{2l}\sqrt{\left(\frac{T}{\mu}\right)}$$

Hence, $$420 = \frac{p}{2l}\sqrt{\left(\frac{T}{\mu}\right)} \quad \ldots(6.189)$$

For the next higher frequency p is $(p + 1)$, hence

$$490 = \frac{p+1}{2l}\sqrt{\left(\frac{T}{\mu}\right)} \quad \ldots(6.190)$$

From equations-(6.189) and (6.190), we have

$$\frac{490}{420} = \frac{p+1}{p}$$

Solving we get, $p = 6$

Substituting the value p in equation-(6.189), we get

$$420 = \frac{6}{2l}\left(\frac{4.5 \times 10^7}{0.05}\right)^{1/2}$$

$$l = 214.3 \text{ cm}$$

 # Illustrative Example 6.40

In Melde's experiment it was found that the string vibrates in 3 loops when 8 gm were placed in the pan. What mass should be placed in the pan to make the string vibrate in 5 loops ? (Neglect the mass of string).

Solution

According to Melde's Law

$$P\sqrt{T} = \text{constant}$$

or $$P_1\sqrt{T_1} = P_2\sqrt{T_2}$$

$$3\sqrt{8} = 5\sqrt{T}$$

or $$T = \frac{9 \times 8}{25}$$

$$= 2.88 \text{ gm}$$

Illustrative Example 6.41

Find the ratio of the fundamental tone frequencies of two identical strings after one of them was stretched by $\eta_1 = 2.0\%$ and the other by $\eta_2 = 4.0\%$. The tension is assumed to be proportional to the elongation.

Solution

In case of a stretched string

$$n = \frac{1}{2l}\sqrt{\left(\frac{T}{\mu}\right)}$$

Where μ is the mass per unit length.

If M be the total mass of the wire, then

$$n = \frac{1}{2l}\sqrt{\left(\frac{Tl}{\mu}\right)} \quad \ldots(6.191)$$

It should be remembered that when the wire is stretched, the total mass of wire M remains constant.

If original length was l, then after elongation

$$l_1 = 1.02\,l \quad \text{and} \quad l_2 = 1.04\,l$$

Given that tension ∝ elongation

Hence $$\frac{T_1}{T_2} = \frac{\eta_1}{\eta_2} = \frac{2}{4} = 0.5 \quad \ldots(6.192)$$

The new frequencies are

$$n_1 = \frac{1}{2(1.02\,l)}\sqrt{\left[\frac{T_1(1.02\,l)}{M}\right]} \quad \ldots(6.193)$$

and $$n_2 = \frac{1}{2(1.04\,l)}\sqrt{\left[\frac{T_2(1.04\,l)}{M}\right]} \quad \ldots(6.194)$$

Dividing equation-(6.194) by equation-(6.193), we get

$$\frac{n_2}{n_1} = \sqrt{\left[\left(\frac{1.02}{1.04}\right)\left(\frac{T_2}{T_1}\right)\right]} = \sqrt{\left[\frac{1.02}{1.04} \times \frac{1}{0.5}\right]}$$

$$= 1.4$$

Illustrative Example 6.42

The fundamental frequency of a sonometer wire increases by 6 Hz if its tension is increased by 44% keeping the length constant. Find the change in the fundamental frequency of the sonometer wire, the length of the wire is increased by 20% keeping the original tension in the wire.

Solution

In case of vibration of a string, fundamental frequency is given by

$$f = \frac{1}{2L}\sqrt{\frac{T}{\mu}}$$

So if length of given wire is kept constant

$$(f'/f) = (T'/T)1/2$$

and as here $f' = f + 6$ and $T' = T + 0.44\,T = 1.44\,T$

$$\frac{(f+6)}{f} = \sqrt{\frac{1.44T}{T}}$$

or $$f = 30 \text{ Hz}$$

Now if keeping the original tension (T), the length wire is changed, we have

$$\frac{f''}{f} = \frac{l}{l''} = \frac{1}{1.20} \qquad [\text{As } l'' = l + 0.20\,l = 1.20l]$$

or $$f'' = \frac{30}{1.2} = 25 \text{ Hz}$$

Hence $$\Delta f = f'' - f = 25 - 30 = -5 \text{ Hz}$$

Thus, fundamental frequency will decrease by 5 Hz.

Illustrative Example 6.43

A sonometer wire fixed at one end has a solid mass M hanging from its other end to produce tension in it. It is found that a 70 cm length of the wire produces a certain fundamental frequency when plucked. When the same mass M is hanging in water, completely submerged in it, is found that the length of the wire has to be changed by 5 cm in order that it will produce the same fundamental frequency. Calculate the density of the material of the mass M hanging from the wire.

Solution

The fundamental frequency n_1 is given by

$$n_1 = \frac{1}{2l}\sqrt{\left(\frac{T}{\mu}\right)}$$

Here $l = 70$ cm, $T = Mg$ and μ, mass per unit length

$$n_1 = \frac{1}{2 \times 70}\sqrt{\left(\frac{Mg}{\mu}\right)} \quad \ldots(6.195)$$

When the mass M is submerged in water, the frequency remains the same for a length of 65 cm.

Hence we have $$n_1 = \frac{1}{2 \times 65}\sqrt{\left(\frac{M'g}{\mu}\right)} \quad \ldots(6.196)$$

Where $M'g$ is the effective weight of mass in water.

From equation-(6.195) and (6.196)

$$\frac{1}{2 \times 70}\sqrt{\left(\frac{Mg}{\mu}\right)} = \frac{1}{2 \times 65}\sqrt{\left(\frac{M'g}{\mu}\right)}$$

or $$\sqrt{\left(\frac{M}{M'}\right)} = \frac{14}{13} \qquad \ldots(6.197)$$

Now using the Archimedes principle, we shall calculate the value of M' in terms of M. Let ρ be the density of the material of the mass M.

Volume of mass $= (M/\rho)\ \text{cm}^3$

Volume of water displaced $= (M/\rho)\ \text{cm}^3$

or Upthrust $= (M/\rho)\, g$

Weight of mass M in water $M'g = Mg - \left(\frac{M}{\rho}\right) g$

or $$M' = M\left(1 - \frac{1}{\rho}\right) \qquad \ldots(6.198)$$

Substituting the value of M' in equation-(6.197), we get

$$\sqrt{\left(\frac{M}{M(1-1/\rho)}\right)} = \frac{14}{13}$$

Solving we get, $\rho = 7.26\ \text{gm/cm}^3 = 7.26 \times 10^3\ \text{kg/m}^3$

Illustrative Example 6.44

The length of the sonometer wire between two fixed ends is 100 cm. Where should the two bridges be placed so as to divide the wire into three segments whose fundamental frequencies are in the ratio of 1 : 2 : 3 ?

Solution

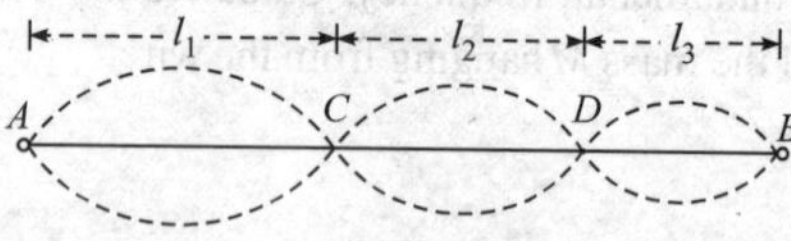

Figure 6.60

Figure-6.60 shows a sonometer wire AB between two fixed ends. Let the two bridges be placed at C and D such that the wire is divided into three segments (AC, CD and DB) of lengths l_1, l_2 and l_3 respectively whose frequencies are in the ratio of 1 : 2 : 3

For the length of string, we have

$$AC + CD + DB = 100\ \text{cm} \qquad \ldots(6.199)$$

Let n_1, n_2 and n_3 be the fundamental frequencies of these segments respectively, then

$$\frac{n_1}{n_2} = \frac{1}{2} \quad \text{and} \quad \frac{n_2}{n_3} = \frac{2}{3} \qquad \ldots(6.200)$$

We know that frequency is inversely proportional to the length of the segment because when tension remains constant

$$n \propto \frac{1}{l}$$

or $$n\, l = \text{constant}$$

or $$n_1\, l_1 = n_2\, l_2 = n_3\, l_3$$

or $$l_1 = \frac{n_2}{n_1}\, l_2 = 2\, l_2$$

and $$l_3 = \frac{n_2}{n_3}\, l_2 = \frac{2}{3}\, l_2 \qquad \ldots(6.201)$$

Substituting these values in equation-(6.199), we have

$$2\, l_2 + l_2 + \frac{2}{3}\, l_2 = 100$$

or $$l_2 = 27.27\ \text{cm}$$

From equation-(6.201),

$$l_1 = 2 \times 27.27 = 54.54\ \text{cm}$$

and $$l_3 = \frac{2}{3} \times 27.27 = 18.18\ \text{cm}$$

Illustrative Example 6.45

A uniform rope of length 12 m and mass 6 kg hangs vertically from a rigid support. A block of mass 2 kg is attached to the free end of the rope. A transverse pulse of wavelength 0.06 m is produced at the lower end of the rope. What is the wavelength of the pulse when it reaches the top of the rope?

Solution

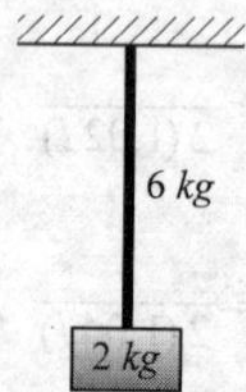

Figure 6.61

As the rope is heavy, its tension will be different at different points. The tension at the free end will be 2 g and that at the upper end it will be 8 g.

We have, $$v = n\lambda$$

or $$\sqrt{\frac{T}{\mu}} = n\lambda$$

or $$\frac{\sqrt{T}}{\lambda} = n\sqrt{\mu} \qquad \ldots(6.202)$$

The frequency of the wave pulse will be the same everywhere on the rope as it depends only on the frequency of the source. The mass per unit length is also the same throughout the rope as it is uniform. Thus, we have

As $\sqrt{\frac{T}{\lambda}}$ is constant, we have

$$\frac{\sqrt{2g}}{0.06m} = \frac{\sqrt{8g}}{\lambda_1}$$

Solving we get $\lambda_1 = 0.12\,\text{m}$

Where λ_1 is the wavelength at the top of the rope.

Illustrative Example 6.46

A metallic rod of length 1 m is rigidly clamped at its midpoint. Longitudinal stationary waves are set up in the rod in such a way that there are two nodes on either side of the midpoint. The amplitude of an antinode is 2×10^{-6} m. Write the equation of motion at a point 2 cm from the midpoint and those of the constituent waves in the rod. (Young's modulus = 2×10^{11} N/m², density = 800 kg/m³).

Solution

The situation is shown in figure-6.62.

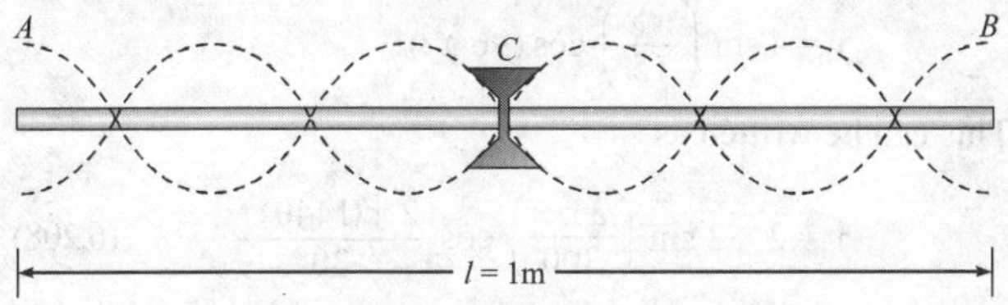

Figure 6.62

From figure, we can calculate the wavelength as

$$\lambda = 0.4\,\text{m} = 40\,\text{cm}$$

Velocity of longitudinal waves in the rod can be given as

$$v = \sqrt{\left(\frac{Y}{\rho}\right)}$$

$$= \sqrt{\left(\frac{2\times10^{11}}{8000}\right)} = \sqrt{\left(\frac{1\times10^{8}}{4}\right)} = \frac{10^4}{2} = 5000\,\text{m/s}$$

Now $n = \frac{v}{\lambda} = \frac{5000}{0.4} = 12500\,\text{Hz}$

Assuming left end of the rod as origin, the equation of stationary waves is given by

$$y = 2A\cos\frac{2\pi x}{\lambda}\sin(2\pi n t)$$

or $$y = 2A\cos\frac{2\pi x}{\lambda}\sin(2\pi\times 12500\,t) \quad \ldots(6.203)$$

Where amplitude at any instant t is given by

$$R = 2A\cos\left(\frac{2\pi x}{0.4}\right)$$

At $x = 0,\ R = 2A = 2\times10^{-6}\,\text{m}$

Thus, equation-(6.203) can be written as

$$y = 2\times10^{-6}\cos(5\pi x)\sin(25000\pi t) \quad \ldots(6.204)$$

At a point 2 cm from midpoint to the right

$$x = 50 + 2 = 52\,\text{cm} = 0.52\,\text{m}$$

$$y = 2\times10^{-6}\cos(5\pi\times0.52)\sin(25000\pi t)$$

or $$y = 2\times10^{-6}\cos(2.6\pi)\sin(25000\pi t) \quad \ldots(6.205)$$

This is the required equation of stationary waves in the rod. Now we can write the equations of constituents waves in the rod as

$$y_1 = 1\times10^{-6}\sin(25000\pi t - 5\pi x)$$

and $$y_2 = 1\times10^{-6}\sin(25000\pi t + 5\pi x)$$

Illustrative Example 6.47

A string 120 cm in length sustains a standing wave, with the points of the string at which the displacement amplitude is equal to 3.5 mm being separated by 15.0 cm. Find the maximum displacement amplitude. To which overtone do these oscillations correspond ?

Solution

We can see from figure-6.63, in a stationary wave two successive of equal amplitude, if separated by equal distances then this distance must be $\frac{\lambda}{4}$. Thus we have

$$\frac{\lambda}{4} = 15\,\text{cm}$$

or $$\lambda = 60\,\text{cm}$$

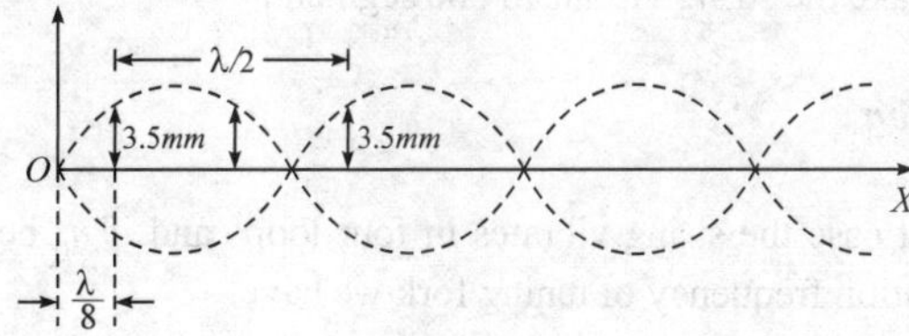

Figure 6.63

Thus there are four loops in 120 cm length of string. This corresponds to 3rd overtone oscillations. As shown in figure if we consider origin O is at a node then the amplitude of a general medium particle, at a distance x from O can be given as

$$R = A_0\sin kx$$

Where A_0 is the maximum displacement amplitude. First point from the origin where amplitude is 3.5 mm is at distance $\frac{\lambda}{8} = 7.5$ cm. Thus we have

$$3.5 = A_0 \sin\left(\frac{2\lambda}{60} \times 7.5\right)$$

or
$$A_0 = \frac{3.5}{\sin(\pi/4)} = 3.5\sqrt{2} \text{ mm}$$

Illustrative Example 6.48

A guitar string is 90 cm long and has a fundamental frequency of 124 Hz. Where should it be pressed to produce a fundamental frequency of 186 Hz?

Solution

The fundamental frequency of a string fixed at both ends is given by

$$n = \frac{1}{2L}\sqrt{\frac{T}{\mu}}$$

As F and μ are fixed,

$$\frac{n_1}{n_2} = \frac{L_2}{L_1}$$

or
$$L_2 = \frac{n_1}{n_2} L_1 = \frac{124}{186} \times 90 = 60 \text{ cm}$$

Thus, the string should be pressed at 60 cm from an end.

Illustrative Example 6.49

In a Melde's experiment when the tension is 100 gm and the tuning fork vibrates at right angles to the direction of the string, the later is thrown into four segments. If now the tuning fork is set to vibrate along the string, find what additional weight which will make the string vibrate in one segment.

Solution

In first case the string vibrates in four loops and if n_0 be the oscillation frequency of tuning fork we have

$$N = \frac{4}{2l}\sqrt{\frac{T_1}{\mu}} \qquad \ldots(6.206)$$

In second case if string vibrate in one segment, we have

$$\frac{N}{2} = \frac{1}{2l}\sqrt{\frac{T_2}{\mu}} \qquad \ldots(6.207)$$

From (6.206) and (6.207), we get

$$\sqrt{T_2} = 2\sqrt{T_1}$$

$$T_2 = 4T_1$$

As $T_1 = 100$ gm, we get

$$T_2 = 400 \text{ gm}$$

This additional weight required is 300 gm.

Illustrative Example 6.50

The vibrations of a string of length 600 cm fixed at both ends are represented by the equation

$$y = 4 \sin\left(\pi \frac{x}{15}\right) \cos(90\,\pi\, t)$$

where x and y are in cm and t in seconds.

(i) What is the maximum displacement of a point $x = 5$ cm ?
(ii) Where are the nodes located along the string ?
(iii) What is the velocity of the particle at $x = 7.5$ cm at $t = 0.25$ s.
(iv) Write down the equations of the component waves whose superposition gives the above wave

Solution

The given equation is

$$y = 4 \sin\left(\frac{\pi x}{15}\right) \cos(96\,\pi\, t)$$

This can be written as

$$y = 2 \times 2 \sin\left(\frac{2\pi x}{300}\right) \cos \frac{2\pi(1440)t}{30} \qquad \ldots(6.208)$$

Comparing equation-(6.208) with standard equation of stationary wave, we get

This shows that $A = 2$ cm $\lambda = 30$ cm and $v = 1440$ cm/s

(i) The maximum displacement is given by

$$y_{max} = 4 \sin \frac{2\pi x}{30}$$

(ii) For a point at $x = 5$ cm,

$$y_{max} = 4 \sin \frac{2\pi 5}{30} = \frac{4\sqrt{3}}{2} 2\sqrt{3} \text{ cm}$$

(iii) As $\lambda = 30$ cm, hence the nodes are located along the string at places

0, 15 cm, 30 cm, 45 cm, 60 cm

The velocity of the particle is given by

$$\frac{dy}{dt} = -4 \sin\left(\frac{\pi x}{15}\right) \sin(96\,\pi\, t)\, 96\,\pi$$

For $x = 7.5$ cm and $t = 0.25$ sec, we have

$$\frac{dy}{dt} = -4 \sin\left(\frac{\pi.7{\cdot}5}{15}\right) \sin(96\,\pi \times 0.25)\, 96\,\pi$$

$$= 0$$

(iv) The equations of component waves are

$$y_1 = A \sin \frac{2\pi}{\lambda}(x - vt) = 2 \sin \frac{2\pi}{30}(x - 1440\,t)$$

or $$y_1 = 2 \sin 2\pi\left(\frac{x}{30} - 48\,t\right) \quad \ldots(6.209)$$

and $$y_2 = A \sin \frac{2\pi}{\lambda}(x + vt) = 2 \sin \frac{2\pi}{30}(x + 1440\,t)$$

or $$y_2 = 2 \sin 2\pi\left(\frac{x}{30} + 48\,t\right) \quad \ldots(6.210)$$

Equations-(6.209) and (6.210) represent the equations of component waves superposition of which results the given stationary wave.

Web Reference at www.physicsgalaxy.com

Age Group - High School Physics | Age 17-19 Years
Section - OSCILLATION & WAVES
Topic - Stationary Waves and Beats
Module Number - 12 to 31

Practice Exercise 6.5

(i) A steel wire of length 1 m and density 8000 kg/m^3 is stretched tightly between two rigid supports. When vibrating in its fundamental mode, its frequency is 200 Hz.

(a) What is the velocity of transverse waves along this wire ?
(b) What is the longitudinal stress in the wire ?
(c) If the maximum acceleration of the wire is 800 m/s^2, what is the amplitude of vibration at the midpoint ?

[(a) 400 m/s, (b) 1.28×10^9 N/m^2, (c) 5×10^{-4} m]

(ii) A sonometer wire having a length of 1.50 m between the bridges vibrates in its second harmonic in resonance with a tuning fork of frequency 256 Hz. What is the speed of the transverse wave on the wire ?

[384 m/s]

(iii) The length of the wire shown in figure-6.64 between the pulleys is 1.5 m and its mass is 12.0 g. Find the frequency of vibration with which the wire vibrates in two loops leaving the middle point of the wire between the pulleys at rest. Take $g = 10$ m/s^2.

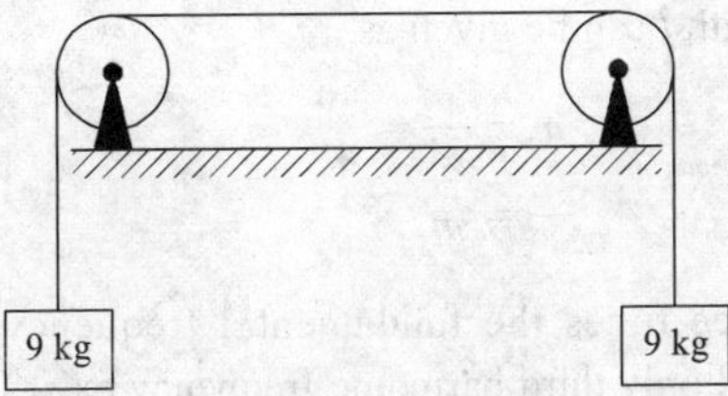

Figure 6.64

[70.71 Hz]

(iv) A steel wire fixed at both ends has a fundamental frequency of 200 Hz. A person can hear sound of maximum frequency 14 kHz. What is the highest harmonic that can be played on this string which is audible to the person?

[70]

(v) Figure-6.65 shows a string stretched by a block going over a pulley. The string vibrates in its tenth harmonic in unison with a particular tuning fork. When a beaker containing water is brought under the block so that the block is completely dipped into the beaker, the string vibrates in its eleventh harmonic. Find the density of the material of the block.

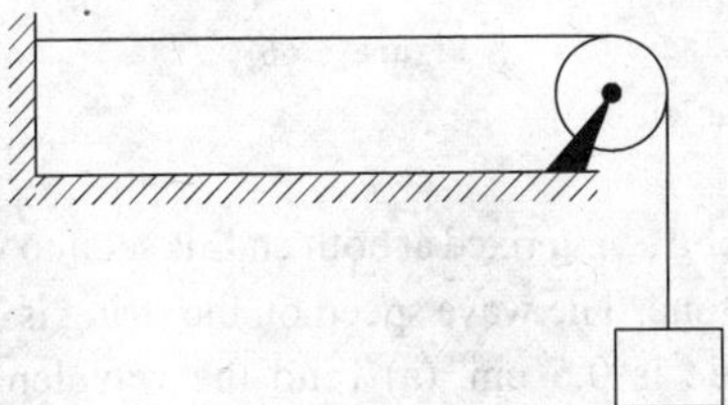
Figure 6.65

[5.76×10^3 kg/m^3]

(vi) A wire of diameter 0.04 cm and made of steel of density 8000 kg/m^3 is under a tension of 79 N. A fixed length of 50 cm is set into transverse vibrations. How would you cause vibrations of frequency 840 Hz to predominate in intensity ? Locate the support and plucking points on wire for this.

[$\frac{1}{6}$ point is to be plucked]

(vii) The displacement of the medium in sound wave is given by the equation

$$= A \cos(ax + bt)$$

where A, a and b are positive constants. The wave is reflected by an obstacle situated at $x = 0$. The intensity of the reflected wave is 0.64 times that of the incident wave.

(a) What is the wavelength and frequency of the incident wave?
(b) Write the equation for the reflected wave.
(c) In the resultant wave formed after reflection, find the maximum and minimum values of the particle speed in the medium.
(d) Express the resultant waves as a superposition of a standing wave and a travelling wave. What are the positions of the antinodes of the standing wave? What is the direction of propagation of the travelling wave?

[(a) $\frac{2\pi}{a}$, $\frac{b}{a}$, (b) $-0.8\,A\cos(bt - ax)$, (c) $1.8\,Ab$, $0.2\,Ab$,
(d) $2A \sin bt \sin ax + 0.2\,A\cos(bt - ax)$]

(viii) A uniform horizontal rod of length 40 *cm* and mass 1.2 kg is supported by two identical wires as shown in figure-6.66. Where should a mass of 4.8 kg be placed on the rod so that the same tuning fork may excite the wire on left into its fundamental vibrations and that on right into its first overtone? Take $g = 10$ m/s^2.

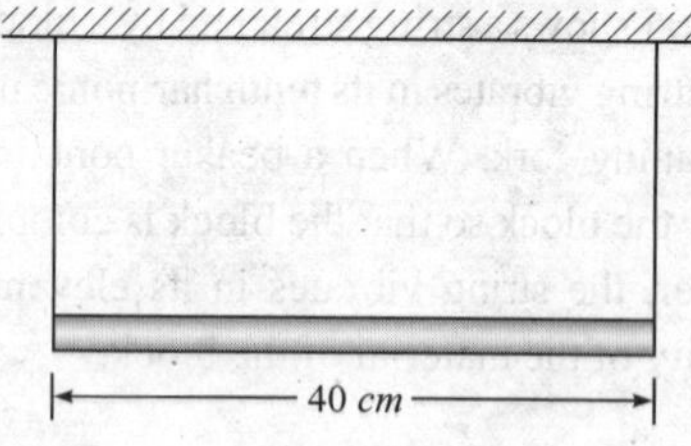

Figure 6.66

[5 cm from the left end]

(ix) A 2 m long string fixed at both ends is set into vibrations in its first overtone. The wave speed on the string is 200 m/s and the amplitude is 0.5 cm. (a) Find the wavelength and the frequency. (b) Write the equation giving the displacement of different points as a function of time. Choose the X-axis along the string with the origin at one end and $t = 0$ at the instant when the point $x = 50$ cm has reached its maximum displacement.

[(a) 2 m, 100 Hz, (b) (0.5 cm) sin (π x) cos (200 π t)]

(x) Three resonant frequencies of a string are 90, 150 and 210 Hz. (a) Find the highest possible fundamental frequency of vibration of this string. (b) Which harmonics of the fundamental are the given frequencies ? (c) Which overtones are these frequencies. (d) If the length of the string is 80 cm, what would be the speed of a transverse wave on this string ?

[(a) 30 Hz (b) 3rd, 5th and 7th (c) 2nd, 4th and 6th (d) 48 m/s]

6.15 Waves in a Vibrating air Column

Hollow pipes have long been used for making musical sounds. A hollow pipe we call organ pipe. To understand how these work, first we examine the behaviour of air in a hollow pipe that is open at both ends. If we blow air across one end, the disturbance due to the moving air at that end propagates along the pipe to the far end. When it reaches far end, a part of the wave is reflected, similar in the case when a wave is reflected along a string whose end point is free to move. Since the air particles are free to move at the open end, the end point is an antinode. If one end of the pipe is closed off, the air is not free to move any further in that direction and closed end becomes a node. Now the resonant behaviour of pipe is completely changed. Similar in the case of string, here also all harmonic frequencies are possible and resonance may take place if the frequency of external source matches with any of the one harmonic frequency of pipe. Let us discuss in detail.

6.15.1 Vibration of Air in a Closed Organ Pipe

When a tuning fork is placed near the open end of a pipe. The air in the pipe oscillates with the same frequency as that of tuning fork. Here the open end should be an antinode and closed end should be a node for perfect reflection of waves from either end or for formation of stationary waves. Since one end is a node and other is an antinode, the lowest frequency (largest wavelength) vibration has no other nodes or antinodes between ends as shown in fiugre-6.67(a). This is the fundamental (minimum) frequency at which stationary waves can be formed in a closed organ pipe. Thus if the wavelength is λ then we can see from figure-6.67(a), which shows the displacement wave of longitudinal waves in the closed organ pipe.

$$l = \frac{\lambda}{4} \quad \ldots(6.211)$$

or

$$\lambda = 4\,l$$

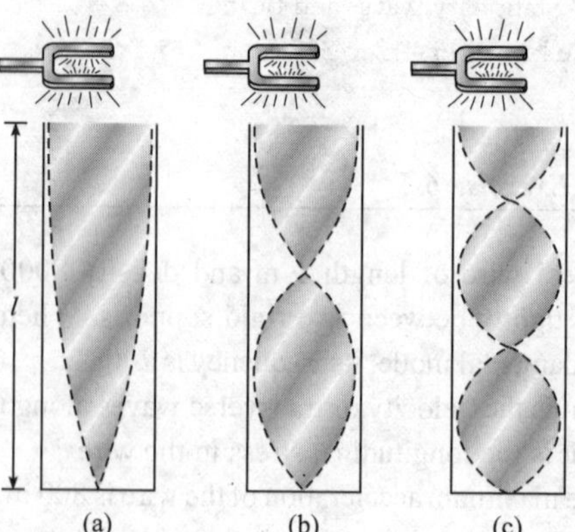

Figure 6.67

Thus fundamental frequency of oscillations of a closed organ pipe of length l be given as

$$n_1 = \frac{v}{\lambda} = \frac{v}{4l} \quad \ldots(6.212)$$

Similarly first overtone of closed pipe vibrations is shown in figure-6.67(b) here wavelength λ' and pipe length l are related as

$$l = \frac{3\lambda}{4} \quad \ldots(6.213)$$

or

$$\lambda = \frac{4l}{3}$$

Thus frequency of first overtone oscillations of a closed organ pipe of length l can be given as

$$n_2 = \frac{v}{\lambda'} = \frac{3v}{4l} \quad \ldots(6.214)$$

$$= 3n_1 \quad \ldots(6.215)$$

This is three times the fundamental frequency thus after fundamental only third harmonic frequency exist for a closed organ pipe at which resonance can take place or stationary waves can be formed in it.

Similarly next overtone, second overtone is shown in figure-6.67(c) Here the wavelength λ'' and pipe length l are related as

$$l=\frac{5\lambda}{4} \quad \ldots(6.216)$$

or

$$\lambda=\frac{4l}{5}$$

Thus the frequency of second overtone oscillation of a closed organ pipe of length l can be given as

$$n_3=\frac{v}{\lambda''}=\frac{5v}{4l}=5\,n_1 \quad \ldots(6.217)$$

This is fifth harmonic frequency of fundamental oscillations. From above analysis it is clear that the resonant frequencies of the closed organ pipe are only odd harmonics of the fundamental frequency. Thus when a timing fork is used to oscillate a closed organ pipe, the air in pipe oscillates with the some frequency as that of tuning fork but in pipe stationary waves are formed or resonance take place only when the frequency of fork matches with any of the odd harmonic of its fundamental frequency.

6.15.2 Vibration of Air in Open Organ Pipe

Figure-6.68 shows the resonant oscillations of an open organ pipe. The least frequency at which an open organ pipe resonates is the one with longest wavelength when at both the open ends of pipe antinodes are formed and there is one node is between as shown in figure-6.68(a). In this situation the wavelengths of sound in air λ is related to length of organ pipe as

$$l=\frac{\lambda}{2} \quad \ldots(6.218)$$

$$\Rightarrow \quad \lambda=2\,l$$

Thus the fundamental frequency of organ pipe can be given as

$$n_1=\frac{v}{\lambda}=\frac{v}{2l} \quad \ldots(6.219)$$

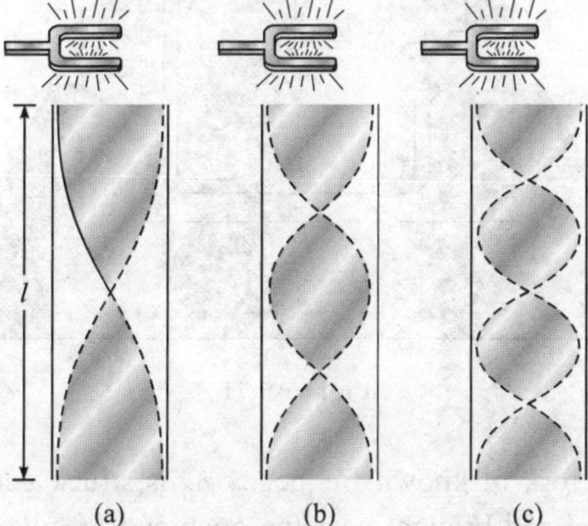

Figure 6.68

Similarly next higher frequency at which the open organ pipe resonate is shown in figure-6.68(b) which we call first overtone. Here the wavelength λ' is related to the length of pipe as

$$l=\lambda' \quad \ldots(6.220)$$

Thus here resonant frequency for first overtone is given as

$$n_2=\frac{v}{\lambda'}=\frac{v}{l} \quad \ldots(6.221)$$

$$=2n_1 \quad \ldots(6.222)$$

Which is second harmonic of fundamental frequency. Similarly as shown in figure-6.68(c), in second overtone oscillations, the wavelength λ'' of sound is related to the length of pipe as

$$l=\frac{3\lambda''}{2} \quad \ldots(6.223)$$

$$\Rightarrow \quad \lambda''=\frac{2l}{3} \quad \ldots(6.224)$$

Thus the frequency of second overtone oscillations of an open organ pipe can be given as

$$n_3=\frac{v}{\lambda''}=\frac{3v}{2l} \quad \ldots(6.225)$$

$$=3n_1 \quad \ldots(6.226)$$

Which is third harmonic of fundamental frequency. The above analysis shows that resonant frequencies for formation of stationary waves includes all the possible harmonic frequencies for an open organ pipe.

6.15.3 Natural Oscillations of Organ Pipes

When we initiate some oscillations in an organ pipe, which harmonics are excited in the pipe depends on how initial disturbance is produced in it. For example, if you gently blow across the top of an organ pipe it resonates softly at its fundamental frequency. But if you blow much harder you hear the higher pitch of an overtone because the faster airstream creates higher frequencies in the exciting disturbances. This sound effect can also be achieved by increasing the air pressure to an organ pipe.

6.15.4 Kundt's Tube

This is an apparatus used to find velocity of sound in a gaseous medium or in different materials. It consists of a glass tube as shown in figure-6.69 one end of which a piston B is fitted which is attached to a wooden handle H and can be moved inside and outside the tube and fixed, the rod M of the required material is fixed at clamp C in which the velocity of sound is required, at on end of rod a disc A is fixed as shown.

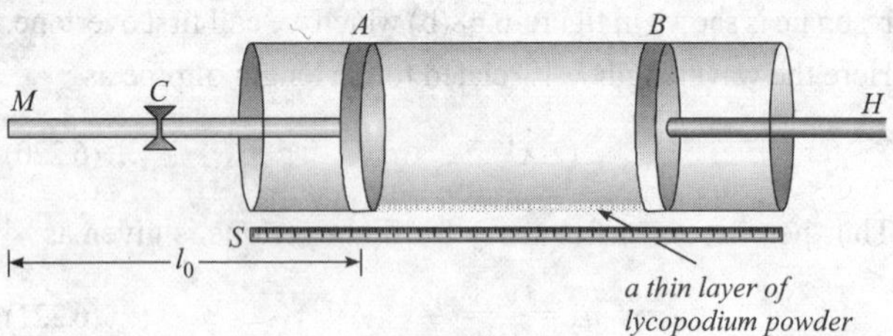

Figure 6.69

In the tube air is filled at room temperature and a thin layer of lycopodium powder is put along the length of the tube. It is a very fine powder particles of which can be displaced by the air particles also.

When rod M is gently rubbed with a resin cloth or hit gently, it starts oscillating in fundamental mode as shown in figure-6.70, frequency of which can be given as

$$n_{\text{rod}} = \frac{v}{\lambda} = \frac{1}{2l_0}\sqrt{\frac{Y}{\rho}} \qquad [\text{As } l_0 = \frac{\lambda}{2}] \qquad \ldots(6.227)$$

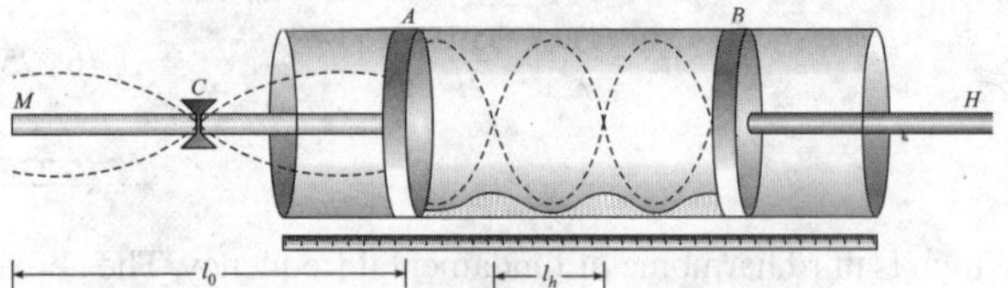

Figure 6.70

In fundamental mode, the free ends of the rod behaves as antinodes and the clamped point C acts as a node, we have also discussed earlier. These vibrations as transferred to the air column in the tube through the disc A and the air column starts oscillating at the same frequency. Now the piston B is adjusted so that the air column resonates with the vibrations of rod. In resonance condition the lycopodium powder sets itself in the form of heaps at the position of nodes as at antinodes the air particles vibrates with maximum amplitude and displaces the powder to the adjacent nodes. We can measure the length between successive heaps of powder, scale S attached with the tube, let it be l_h then we can write

$$l_h = \frac{\lambda_a}{2} \; [\lambda_a = \text{wavelength of sound in air}]$$

and we know that frequency of sound in air and rod is equal, thus

$$n_{rod} = n_{air}$$

$$\Rightarrow \quad \frac{v_{rod}}{\lambda_{rod}} = \frac{v_{air}}{\lambda_{air}}$$

$$\Rightarrow \quad v_{rod} = \left(\frac{\lambda_{rod}}{\lambda_{air}}\right) v_{\text{air}}$$

$$\Rightarrow \quad v_{rod} = \frac{2l_0}{2l_h} \times v_{air} = \left(\frac{l_0}{l_h}\right) \times v_{air} \qquad \ldots(6.228)$$

If the Young's modulus and density of material of rod is known then using equation-(6.227) and (6.228) we can find velocity of sound in air or in a gas which is filled in the tube, as

$$n_{rod} = n_{gas}$$

$$\frac{1}{2l_0}\sqrt{\frac{Y}{\rho}} = \frac{v_{gas}}{2l_h}$$

$$\Rightarrow \quad v_{gas} = \left(\frac{l_h}{l_0}\right)\sqrt{\frac{Y}{\rho}} \qquad \ldots(6.229)$$

6.15.5 Resonance Tube

This an apparatus used to determine velocity of sound in air experimentally and also to compare frequencies of two tuning forks.

Figure-6.71 shows the setup of a resonance tube experiment. There is a long tube T in which initially water is filled upto the top and the eater level can be change by moving a reservoir R up and down.

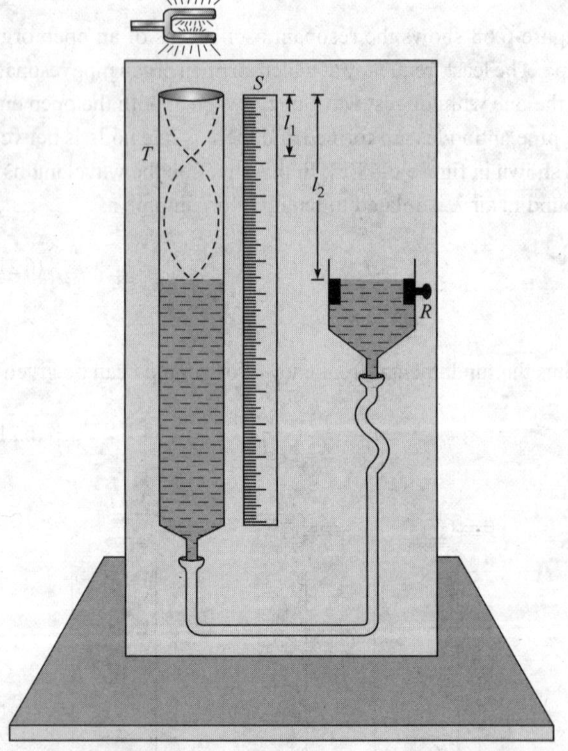

Figure 6.71

A tuning fork of known frequency n_0 is struck gently on a rubber pad and brought near the open end of tube T due to which oscillations are transferred to the air coloumn in the tube above water level. Now we gradually decrease the water level in the tube. This air column behaves like a closed organ pipe and the water level as closed end of pipe. As soon as water level reaches a position where there is a node of corresponding stationary wave, in air column, resonance takes place and maximum sound intensity is detected. Let at this position length of air column be l_1. If water level is further decreased, again maximum sound intensity is observed when water level is at another node i.e. at a length l_2 as shown in figure. Here if we find two successive resonance lengths l_1 and l_2, we can get the wavelength of the wave as

$$l_2 - l_1 = \frac{\lambda}{2}$$

or $$\lambda = 2(l_2 - l_1)$$

Thus sound velocity in air can be given as

$$v = n_0\lambda = 2n_0(l_2 - l_1)$$

6.15.6 End Correction in Organ Pipes

We have discussed, that in an organ pipe the incident and reflected waves superpose and give rise to establishment of stationary waves at harmonic frequencies. First we discuss how a wave is reflected from the open end of an organ pipe.

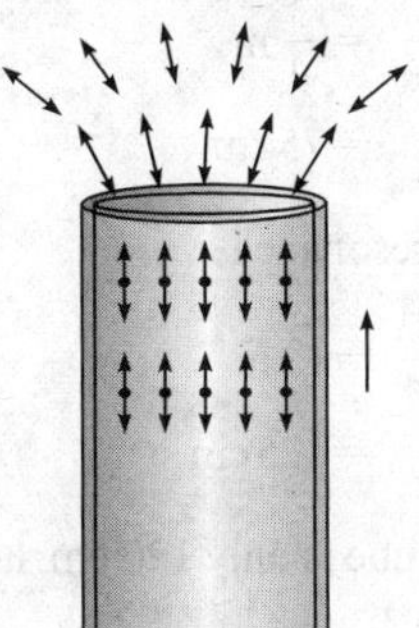

Figure 6.72

Consider an organ pipe shown in figure-6.72. Here we consider a wave is propagating towards its open end. As due to longitudinal wave medium (air) particles oscillates along the length of pipe as shown in figure-6.72. But the oscillations are along the length of the pipe within the boundaries of the pipe. When wave reaches the open end, due to collisions the medium particles outside the pipe scatters in the direction away from pipe and due to this medium (air) density reduces outside the pipe and from the region of this rarer medium the wave is reflected.

Here we can see that when a wave reaches the open end of a pipe it penetrates atmosphere upto to a small depth where the density is decreased and then it is reflected back into the pipe. Thus the wave is not exactly reflected from the open end of the pipe. Hence in the formation of stationary waves in organ pipe we say always there is an antinode at the open end of the pipe but in fact antinode is formed a little above the open end as shown in figure-6.73. The distance above the open end antinode formed is called end correction and is represented by e.

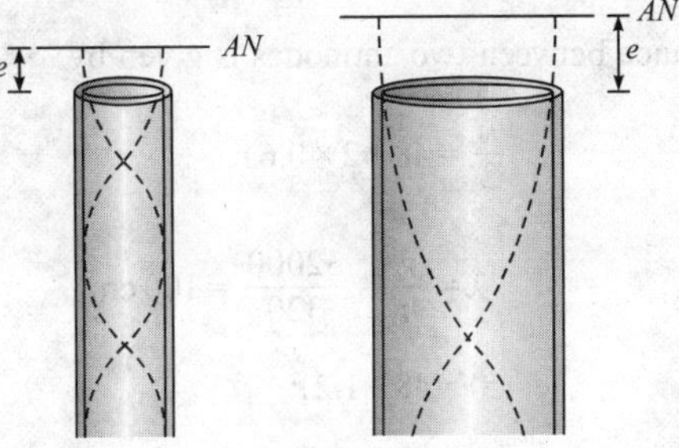

Figure 6.73

It is observed that end correction depends on the radius of organ pipe and is experimentally determined and expressed as

$$e = 0.6\,r \qquad \ldots(6.230)$$

Thus for a broad pipe end correction is more than a narrow pipe. When we find the different harmonic frequencies of oscillations of air column in organ pipe, we must account end corrections. Now taking into account end correction the fundamental frequency of a closed pipe of length l is taken as

$$n_0 = \frac{v}{4(l+e)} \quad \text{[One end open]} \qquad \ldots(6.231)$$

and fundamental frequency of an open pipe of length l is taken as

$$n_0 = \frac{v}{2(l+2e)} \quad \text{[Both ends open]} \qquad \ldots(6.232)$$

 # Illustrative Example 6.51

A tube of certain diameter and of length 48 cm is open at both ends. Its fundamental frequency of resonance is found to be 320 Hz. The velocity of sound in air is 320 m/s. Estimate the diameter of the tube. One end of the tube is now closed. Calculate the lowest frequency of resonance for the tube.

Solution

The displacement curves of longitudinal waves in a tube open at both ends is shown in figure-6.74(a) and (b).

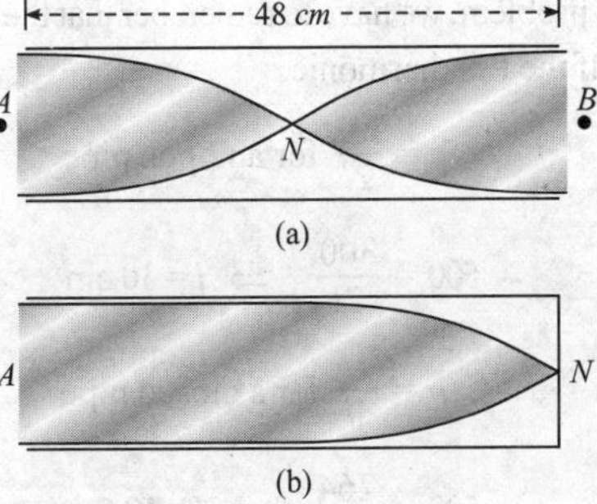

Figure 6.74

Let r be the radius of the tube. We know that antinodes occur slightly outside the tube at a distance 0.6 r from the tube end.

The distance between two antinodes is given by

$$\frac{\lambda}{2} = 48 + 2 \times 0.6\,r$$

We have $\lambda = \dfrac{v}{n} = \dfrac{32000}{320} = 100\text{ cm}$

$\Rightarrow$ $50 = 48 + 1.2\,r$

$\Rightarrow$ $r = \dfrac{2}{1.2}$

$\Rightarrow$ $r = 1.67\text{ cm}$

Thus diameter of the tube is

$$D = 2r = 3.33\text{ cm}$$

When one end is closed, then

$$\frac{\lambda}{4} = 48 + 0.6\,r$$

$$= 48 + 0.6 \times 1.67$$

$$= 49$$

or $\lambda = 4 \times 49$

$$= 196\text{ cm}$$

Now $n = \dfrac{v}{\lambda} = \dfrac{32000}{196} = 163.3\text{ Hz}$

 # Illustrative Example 6.52

An open organ pipe filled with air has a fundamental frequency of 500 Hz. The first harmonic of another organ pipe closed at one end and filled with CO_2 has the same frequency as that of the first harmonic of the open organ pipe. Calculate the length of each organ pipe. The velocity of sound in air and CO_2 are 300 m/s and 264 m/s, respectively.

Solution

To solve this problem, we have to remember that the fundamental mode is itself the first harmonic.

$n = \dfrac{c}{2l}$ for an open pipe

$\Rightarrow$ $500 = \dfrac{300}{2l} \Rightarrow l = 30\text{ cm}$

$n = \dfrac{c}{4l}$ for a closed pipe

$\Rightarrow$ $500 = \dfrac{264}{4l} \Rightarrow l = 13.2\text{ cm}$

 # Illustrative Example 6.53

A tuning fork having a frequency of 340 Hz is vibrated just above a cylindrical tube. The height of the tube is 120 cm. Water is slowly poured in it. What is the minimum height of water required for resonance ? Velocity of sound in air = 340 m/s.

Solution

In a closed tube, the first resonance takes place, when the length of air column = $\lambda/4$

The wavelength of sound in air

$$\lambda = \frac{v}{n} = \frac{340}{340}$$

$$= 1\text{ m} \quad [\text{As} \quad v = 340\text{ m/s and } n = 340]$$

Here length of first resonance can be given as

$$\frac{\lambda}{4} = 0.25\text{ m}$$

$$= 25\text{ cm}$$

The length of second resonance

$$\frac{3\lambda}{4} = \frac{3}{4}\text{ m}$$

$$= 75\text{ cm}$$

The length of third resonance

$$\frac{5\lambda}{4} = \frac{5}{4}\text{ m}$$

$$= 125\text{ cm}$$

As the length of the tube is only 120 cm, hence third resonance is not possible.

Therefore, the minimum height of water required for resonance

$$= 120 - 75 = 45\text{ cm}$$

 # Illustrative Example 6.54

The fundamental frequency of a closed organ pipe is equal to the first overtone frequency of an open organ pipe. If the length of the open pipe is 60 cm, what is the length of the closed pipe?

Solution

We know the fundamental frequency of a closed organ pipe is $\dfrac{v}{4l_1}$ and first overtone frequency of open pipe is $\dfrac{v}{l_2}$. Thus we have

$$\frac{v}{4l_1} = \frac{v}{60}$$

$$l_1 = \frac{1}{4} \times 60\text{ cm} = 15\text{ cm}$$

Illustrative Example 6.55

A pipe of length 1.5 m closed at one end is filled with a gas and it resonates in its fundamental with a tuning fork. Another pipe of the same length but open at both ends if filled with air and its resonates in its fundamental with the same tuning fork. Calculate the velocity of sound at 0°C in the gas, given that the velocity of sound in air is 360 m/s at 30°C, where the experiment is performed.

Solution

The frequency of the fundamental note emitted by an open pipe is given by

$$n = \frac{v}{2l} = \frac{360}{2\times1.5} \qquad [\text{As } v = 360\text{ m/s and } l = 1.5\text{ m}]$$

$$= 120\text{ Hz}$$

Let the velocity of sound in the gas at 30°C = v'.

Frequency of the fundamental note emitted by closed pipe filled with the gas is given by

$$n_1 = \frac{v'}{4l} = \frac{v'}{4\times1.5} = \frac{v'}{6}$$

But $n_1 = n$,

$\Rightarrow$ $120 = v'/6$ or $v' = 720$ m/s

If the velocity of sound in the gas at 0°C = v_0, then

$$\frac{v_0}{v'} = \sqrt{\left(\frac{T_0}{T}\right)}$$

Here, $T_0 = 0°\text{C} = 273°\text{K}$,

$$T = 30°\text{C} = 30 + 273 = 303°\text{K}$$

and $v' = 720$ m/s

$$\frac{v_0}{720} = \sqrt{\left(\frac{273}{300}\right)} \quad \text{or} \quad v_0 = 683.4\text{ m/s}$$

Illustrative Example 6.56

A certain organ pipe resonates in its fundamental mode at a frequency of 500 Hz in air. What will be the fundamental frequency if the air is replaced, by hydrogen at the same temperature? The density of air is 1.20 kg/m^3 and that of hydrogen is 0.089 kg/m^3.

Solution

Suppose the speed of sound in hydrogen is v_h and that in air is v_a. The fundamental frequency of an organ pipe is proportional to the speed of sound in the gas contained in it. If the fundamental frequency with hydrogen in the tube is ν, we have

$$\frac{\nu}{500} = \frac{v_h}{v_a} = \sqrt{\frac{\rho_a}{\rho_h}} = \sqrt{\frac{1.2}{0.089}} = 3.67$$

$\Rightarrow$ $\nu = 3.67 \times 500\text{ Hz} \approx 1840\text{ Hz}$

Illustrative Example 6.57

Clamped at the middle, a metal rod of length 1 metre and density 7.5 gm/cm^3 gives dust heaps at intervals of 8 cm. Calculate Young's modulus of the material of the rod. Velocity of sound in the gas used is 400 m/s.

Solution

The situation is shown in figure-6.75.

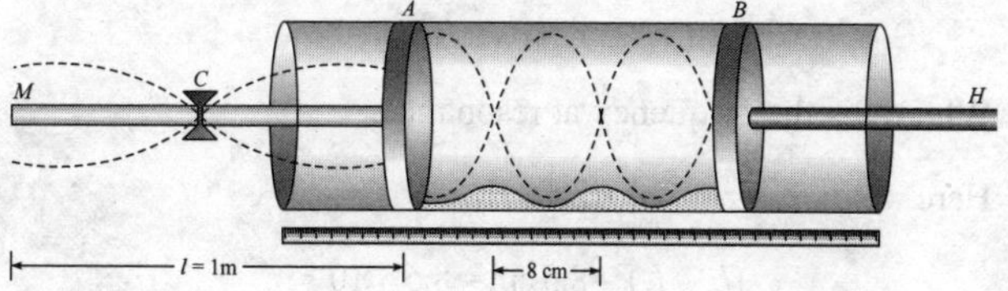

Figure 6.75

Let λ_r and λ_g be the wavelength in the rod and gas column respectively. Since the rod is clamped in the middle, it vibrates with a node in the middle and antinodes at the ends. Therefore

$$\frac{\lambda_r}{2} = 1\text{ m} = 100\text{ cm}, \qquad [\text{As } \lambda_r = 200\text{ cm}]$$

and

$$\frac{\lambda_g}{2} = 8\text{ cm} \qquad [\text{As } \lambda_g = 16\text{ cm}]$$

If v_r and v_g be the sound velocities in the rod and in the gas respectively and n be the frequency of vibration, then frequency of oscillations is given as

$$n = \frac{v_{rod}}{\lambda_{rod}} = \frac{v_{gas}}{\lambda_{gas}}$$

$$\Rightarrow \quad v_{rod} = \frac{\lambda_{rod}}{\lambda_{gas}} \times v_{gas}$$

$$\Rightarrow \quad = \frac{200}{16} \times 400$$

$$\Rightarrow \quad = 5000\text{ m/s}$$

Now velocity of longitudinal waves in a metal rod is given by

$$v_{rod} = \sqrt{\left(\frac{Y}{d}\right)}$$

or

$$Y = v_{rod}^2 \times d$$

or $Y = (500,0)^2 \times 7.5 \times 10^3$

$= 1.875 \times 10^{11}\ \text{N/m}^2$

Illustrative Example 6.58

To determine the sound propagation velocity in air by acoustic resonance technique one can use a pipe with a piston and a sonic membrane closing one of its ends. Find the velocity of sound if the distance between the adjacent positions of the piston at which resonance is observed at a frequency $n = 2000$ Hz is equal to $l = 8.5$ cm.

Solution

When the two positions of the resonance are obtained at distances l_1 and l_2 respectively, then the velocity v of sound is given by

$$v = 2n(l_2 - l_1)$$

Where n is the frequency at resonance.

Here $n = 2000$ Hz,

$$(l_2 - l_1) = 8.5\ \text{cm} = 8.5 \times 10^{-2}\ \text{m}$$

$$v = 2 \times 2000 \times 8.5 \times 10^{-2}$$

$$\Rightarrow \quad v = 340\ \text{m/s}$$

Illustrative Example 6.59

AB is a cylinder of length 1.0 m filled with a thin flexible diaphragm C (Figure-6.76) at the middle and two other thin flexible diaphragms A and B at the ends. The portions AC and BC contain hydrogen and oxygen gases respectively. The diaphragms A and B are set into vibrations of same frequency. What is the minimum frequency of these vibrations for which the diaphragm C is a node ? Under the conditions of the experiment, the velocity of sound in hydrogen is 1100 m/s and in oxygen is 300 m/s.

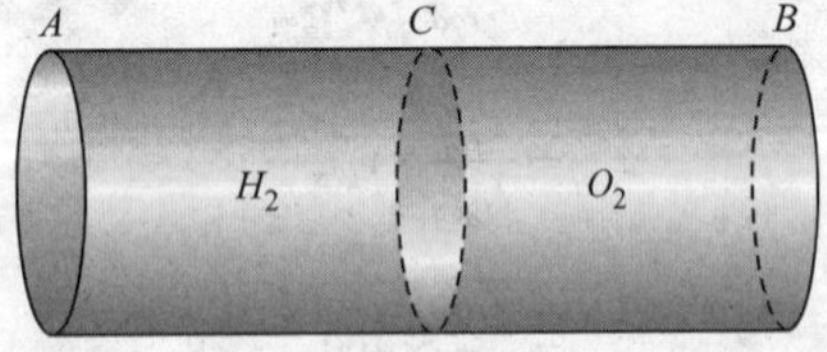

Figure 6.76

Solution

A and B are set in oscillation, hence antinodes are situated at these points. The portions of the cylinders i.e., AC and CB behaves as a close cylinder at the end C. Thus there is immediate node at C.

The fundamental frequency of each pipe corresponds to just one node and one antinode. Let n_1 and n_2 be the fundamental frequencies of gases in AC and BC respectively, then

$$n_1 = \frac{v_1}{4l} = \frac{1100}{4 \times 0.5} = 550\ \text{Hz}$$

or $AC = l = 0.5$

$$n_2 = \frac{v_2}{4l} = \frac{300}{4 \times 0.5} = 150\ \text{Hz}$$

Here v_1 and v_2 are the velocities of sound in hydrogen and oxygen respectively.

As the two frequencies are different and hence the two gas columns are not vibrating in the fundamental mode. In case of a closed pipe only odd harmonics with frequencies 3, 5, 7, 9, ..., etc. times the fundamental frequency are observed. Now the problem is to find out that which harmonics of n_1 and n_2 have the same frequency. We notice that

$$\frac{n_1}{n_2} = \frac{500}{150} = \frac{11}{3}$$

or $3n_1 = 11n_2$

This shows that third harmonic of n_1 and eleventh harmonic of n_2 have equal frequencies. Similarly, 6th harmonic of n_1 and 22th harmonic of n_2 have equal frequencies and so on.

Thus common minimum frequency is

$$= 3n_1 = 3 \times 500 = 1650\ \text{Hz}$$

$$= 11n_2 = 11 \times 150 = 1650\ \text{Hz}$$

Illustrative Example 6.60

In Kundt's tube experiment the following observations were made : Length of the brass rod is 100 cm; average length of a loop in air is 10.3 cm and in carbon-di-oxide = 8.0 cm. Calculate the velocity of sound in brass and in CO_2. What is the frequency of the note ?

(Given the velocity of sound in air at the temperature of the experiment to 350 m/s)

Solution

Let λ_r, λ_a and λ_g be the wavelengths in cm in the rod, in air and in gas respectively. Then

$$\frac{\lambda_r}{2} = 100 \quad \text{or} \quad \lambda_r = 200\ \text{cm},$$

$$\frac{\lambda_a}{2} = 10.3 \quad \text{or} \quad \lambda_a = 20.6\ \text{cm},$$

and $\frac{\lambda_g}{2} = 8.0$ or $\lambda_g = 16\,\text{cm}$,

Let v_r, v_a and v_g be the sound velocities in rod, air and gas respectively. Then

$$\frac{v_r}{v_a} = \frac{\lambda_r}{\lambda_a} \quad \text{or} \quad v_r = \frac{\lambda_r}{\lambda_a} \times v_a$$

$$\Rightarrow \qquad v_r = \frac{200}{20.6} \times 350$$

$$= 3.4 \times 10^3 \text{ m/s}$$

Similarly we have

$$v_g = 350 \times \frac{16}{20.6} = 271.8 \text{ m/s}$$

If n be frequency of the note, then we have

$$v_a = n\lambda_a$$

$$\Rightarrow \qquad n = \frac{v_a}{\lambda_a} = \frac{350}{0.206}$$

$$= 1699.02 \text{ Hz}$$

Illustrative Example 6.61

The air column in a pipe closed at one end is made to vibrate in its second overtone by a tuning fork of frequency 440 Hz. The speed of sound in air is 330 m/s. End corrections may be neglected. Let P_0 denote the mean pressure at any point in the pipe, and ΔP_0 the maximum amplitude of pressure variation.

(a) Find the length L of the air column.

(b) What is the amplitude of pressure variation at the middle of the column?

(c) What are the maximum and minimum pressure at the open-end of the pipe?

(d) What are the maximum and minimum pressure at the closed-end of the pipe?

Solution

(a) In case of closed organ pipe as fundamental frequency is $(v/4L)$ and only odd harmonics are present, second overtone will mean fifth harmonic and so

$$f = \frac{5v}{4L} = 440 \text{ Hz}$$

and hence $$L = \frac{5 \times 330}{4 \times 440} = \frac{15}{16} \text{ m}$$

(b) In terms of pressure as at the position of displacement antinode there is pressure node and vice-versa, the variation of pressure amplitude of standing pressure waves along the length of the column with $x = 0$ at its open end will be

$$p = \Delta p_0 \sin kx = \Delta p_0 \sin\left(\frac{2\pi}{\lambda}x\right) \qquad \left[\text{As } k = \frac{2\pi}{\lambda}x\right]$$

Now as for second overtone $L = (5/4)\lambda$, so at the middle.

$$x = \frac{L}{2} = \frac{5}{8}\lambda$$

and hence

$$p = \Delta p_0 \sin\frac{2\pi}{\lambda}\left(\frac{5}{8}\lambda\right) = \Delta p_0 \sin\left(\frac{5}{4}\pi\right)$$

$$\Rightarrow \qquad |p| = \Delta p_0 \times \frac{1}{\sqrt{2}} = \frac{\Delta p_0}{\sqrt{2}}$$

(c) For free end as $x = 0$, $p = 0$, *i.e.*, the amplitude of pressure wave is zero (as it is a node), so

$$p_{max} = p_{min} = p_0 \pm 0 = p_0$$

(d) For closed end $x + (5/4)\lambda$, so the amplitude of pressure wave

$$|p| = \left|\Delta p_0 \sin\frac{2\pi}{\lambda}\left(\frac{5}{4}\lambda\right)\right| = \Delta p_0$$

Thus maximum and minimum pressures are given as

$$p_{max} = p_0 + \Delta p_0 \quad \text{and} \quad p_{min} = p_0 - \Delta p_0$$

Illustrative Example 6.62

A pop-gun consists of a cylindrical barrel 3 cm^3 in cross-section closed at one end by a cork and having a well fitting piston at the other. If the piston is pushed slowly in, the cork is finally ejected, giving a pop, the frequency of which is found to be 512 Hz. Assuming that the initial distance between the cork and the piston was 25 cm and that there is no leakage of air, calculate the force required to eject the cork. Atmospheric pressure = 1 kg wt/cm^2, $v = 340$ m/s.

Solution

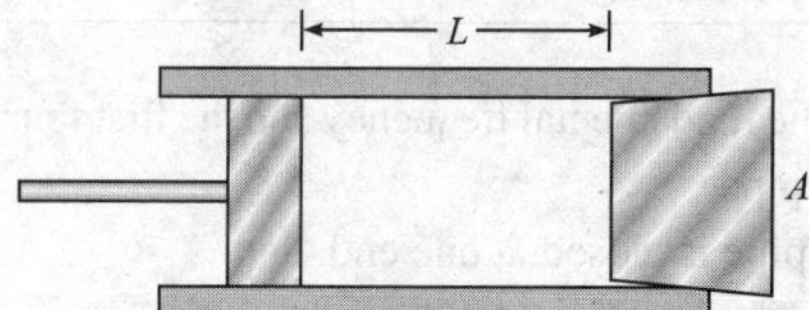

Figure 6.77

When the cork is ejected, the situation is shown in figure-6.77. Let the position of the piston from end A be L cm. So, this forms a closed pipe of length L. It produces a note of frequency 512 Hz. Now

$$n = \frac{v}{4L} \quad \text{or} \quad 512 = \frac{340}{4L}$$

or $$L = \frac{340}{512 \times 4} = 0.166 \text{ m} = 16.6 \text{ cm}$$

Before the piston is moved, $P = 1$ kg wt/cm^2 and $V = 25 \times 3$ cm^3. When the cork is ejected, let pressure be P'.

The volume of air inside

$$V' = 16.6 \times 3 \text{ cm}^3$$

From Boyle's law,

$$PV = P'V'$$

$$(1)(25 \times 3) = P' \times (16.6 \times 3)$$

$$P' = \left(\frac{25}{16.6}\right) \text{ kg wt/cm}^2$$

$$\Rightarrow \quad P' = 1.5 \text{ kg wt/cm}^2$$

Thus pressure inside the barrel = 1.5 kg wt/cm^2

Pressure difference = Pressure inside – Pressure outside

$$= (1.5 - 1) \text{ kg wt/cm}^2$$

[As Outside pressure = 1 kg wt/cm^2]

$$= 0.5 \text{ kg wt/cm}^2$$

Force on piston = Pressure × area

$$= 0.5 \times 3$$

$$= 1.5 \text{ kg wt}$$

Web Reference at www.physicsgalaxy.com

Age Group - High School Physics | Age 17-19 Years
Section - OSCILLATION & WAVES
Topic - Stationary Waves and Beats
Module Number - 32 to 46

Practice Exercise 6.6

(i) Find the fundamental frequency and the first four overtones of a 15 cm pipe :

(a) if the pipe is closed at one end, and
(b) if the pipe is open at both ends.
(c) How many overtones may be heard by a person of normal hearing in each of the above cases? Velocity of sound in air = 330 m/s.

[(a) 550, 1650, 2750, 3850, 4950 Hz (b) 1100, 2200, 3300, 4400, 5500 Hz (c) 17, 17]

(ii) The separation between a node and the next antinode in a vibrating air column is 25 cm. If the speed of sound in air is 340 m/s, find the frequency of vibration of the air column.

[340 Hz]

(iii) For a certain organ pipe, three successive resonance frequencies are observed at 425 Hz, 595 Hz and 765 Hz respectively. Taking the speed of sound in air to be 340 m/s.

(a) Explain whether the pipe is closed at one end or open at both ends
(b) Determine the fundamental frequency and length of the pipe.

[(a) closed-end, (b) 85 Hz, 1 m]

(iv) A pipe is closed at one end by a membrane which may be considered a seat of displacement node and provided with a piston at the other end. The membrane is set to sonic oscillations of frequency 2000 Hz. Find the velocity of sound if on moving the piston, resonance occurs at the interval of 8.5 cm.

[340 m/s]

(v) A '*pop*' gun consists of a tube 25 cm long closed at one end by a cork and at the other end by a tightly fitted piston. The piston is pushed slowly in. When the pressure rises to one and half times the atmospheric pressure, the cork is violently blown out. Calculate the frequency of the '*pop*' caused by its ejection. Speed of sound in air is 340 m/s.

[510 Hz]

(vi) A cylindrical metal tube has a length of 50 cm and is open at both ends. Find the frequencies between 1000 Hz and 2000 Hz at which the air column in the tube can resonate. Speed of sound in air is 340 m/s.

[1020 Hz, 1360 Hz and 1700 Hz]

(vii) A uniform tube of length 60 cm stands vertically with its lower end dipping into water. When the length above water successively taken at 14.8 cm and 48.0 cm, the tube responds to a vibrating tuning fork of frequency 512 Hz. Find the lowest frequency to which the tube will respond when it is open at both ends.

[283.30 Hz]

(viii) A tuning fork having frequency of 340 Hz is vibrated just above a cylindrical tube. The height of the tube is 120 cm. Water is slowly poured in. What is the minimum height of water required for resonance? (velocity of sound in air is $v = 340$ m/s).

[45 cm]

(ix) A tube closed at one end has a vibrating diaphragm at the other end, which may be assumed to be a displacement node. It is found that when the frequency of the diaphragm is 2000 Hz, a stationary wave pattern is set up in which the distance between adjacent nodes is 8 cm. When the frequency is gradually reduced, the stationary wave pattern disappears but another stationary wave pattern reappears at a frequency of 1600 Hz Calculate:

(a) The speed of sound in air,
(b) The distance between adjacent nodes at a frequency of 1600 Hz,
(c) The distance between the diaphragm and the closed end,
(d) The next lower frequencies at which stationary wave patterns will be obtained.

[(a) 320 m/s (b) 10 cm (c) 40 cm (d) 1200 Hz, 800 Hz and 400 Hz]

6.16 Beats

When two sources of sound that have almost the same frequency are sounded together, an interesting phenomenon occurs. A sound with a frequency average of the two is heard and the loudness of sound repeatedly grows and then decays, rather than being constant. Such a repeated variation in amplitude of sound are called "*beats*".

If the frequency of one of the wave source is changed, there is a corresponding change in the rate at which the amplitude varies. This rate is called beat frequency. As the frequencies come close together, the beat frequency becomes slower. A musician can tune a guitar to another source by listening for the beats while increasing or decreasing the tension in each string, eventually the beat frequency becomes very low so that effectively no beats are heard, and the two sources are then in tune.

We can also explain the phenomenon of beats mathematically. Let us consider the two superposing waves have frequencies n_1 and n_2 then their respective equations of oscillation are

$$y_1 = A \sin 2\pi n_1 t \quad \ldots(6.233)$$

and

$$y_2 = A \sin 2\pi n_2 t \quad \ldots(6.234)$$

On superposition at a point, the displacement of the medium particle is given as

$$y = y_1 + y_2$$

$$\Rightarrow \quad y = A \sin 2\pi n_1 t + A \sin 2\pi n_2 t$$

$$\Rightarrow \quad y = 2A \cos 2\pi \left(\frac{n_1 - n_2}{2}\right) t \sin 2\pi \left(\frac{n_1 + n_2}{2}\right) t \quad \ldots(6.235)$$

$$\Rightarrow \quad y = R \sin 2\pi \left(\frac{n_1 + n_2}{2}\right) t \quad \ldots(6.236)$$

There equation-(6.236) gives the displacement of medium particle where superposition takes place, it shows that the particle executes SHM with frequency $\frac{n_1 + n_2}{2}$, average of the two superposing frequencies and with amplitude R which varies with time, given as

$$R = 2A \cos 2\pi \left(\frac{n_1 - n_2}{2}\right) t \quad \ldots(6.237)$$

Here R becomes maximum when

$$\cos 2\pi \left(\frac{n_1 - n_2}{2}\right) t = \pm 1$$

$$\Rightarrow \quad 2\pi \left(\frac{n_1 - n_2}{2}\right) t = N\pi \quad [N \in I]$$

$$\Rightarrow \quad t = \frac{N}{n_1 - n_2} \quad \ldots(6.238)$$

$$\Rightarrow \quad t = 0, \frac{1}{n_1 - n_2}, \frac{2}{n_1 - n_2}, \ldots\ldots$$

At all the above time instants the sound of maximum loudness is heard, similarly we can find the time instants when the loudness of sound is minimum, it occurs when

$$\cos 2\pi \left(\frac{n_1 - n_2}{2}\right) t = 0$$

$$\Rightarrow \quad 2\pi \left(\frac{n_1 - n_2}{2}\right) t = (2N+1)\frac{\pi}{2} \quad [N \in I]$$

$$\Rightarrow \quad t = \frac{2N+1}{2(n_1 - n_2)} \quad \ldots(6.239)$$

$$\Rightarrow \quad t = \frac{1}{2(n_1 - n_2)}, \frac{3}{2(n_1 - n_2)}, \ldots\ldots$$

Here we can see that these time instants are exactly lying in the middle of the instants when loudest sound is heard. Thus on superposition of the above two frequencies at a medium particle, the sound will be increasing, decreasing, again increasing and decreasing and so on. This effect is called beats. Here the time between two successive maximum or minimum sounds is called beat period, which is given as

Beat Period T_B = time between two successive maxima = time between two successive maxima

$$= \frac{1}{n_1 - n_2} \quad \ldots(6.240)$$

Thus beat frequency or number of beats heard per second can be given as

$$F_B = \frac{1}{T_B} = n_1 - n_2 \quad \ldots(6.241)$$

The superposition of two waves of slightly different frequencies is graphically shown in figure-6.78. The resulting envelope of the wave formed after superposition is also shown in figure-6.78(b). Such a wave when propagates, produces *"beat"* effect at the medium particles.

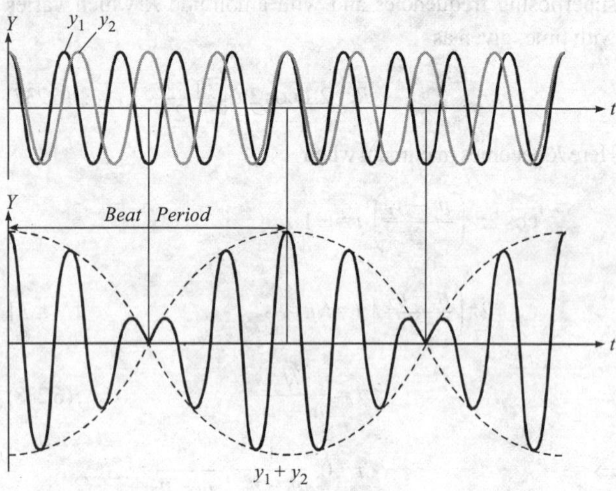

Figure 6.78

6.16.1 Echo

The repetition of sound produced due to reflection by a distant extended surface like a different, hill, well, building etc. is called an echo. The effect of sound on human ear remains for approximately one tenth of a second. If the sound is reflected back in a time less then 1/10 of a second, no echo is heard. Hence human ears are not able to distinguish a beat frequency of 10 Hz or more then 10 Hz.

Illustrative Example 6.63

Two identical sonometer wires have a fundamental frequency of 500 Hz when kept under the same tension. What fractional increase in the tension of one wire would cause an occurrence of 5 beats per second, when both wires vibrate together?

Solution

The fundamental frequency of wire is given as

$$n_0 = \frac{1}{2L}\sqrt{\frac{T}{\mu}}$$

On increasing tension by ΔT the new frequency will be

$$n_0' = \frac{1}{2L}\sqrt{\frac{T+\Delta T}{\mu}}$$

$$= n_0\sqrt{1+\frac{\Delta T}{T}}$$

$$\approx n_0\left(1+\frac{\Delta T}{2T}\right)$$

Now the fractional change in frequency will be

$$\frac{n_0'-n_0}{n_0} = \frac{1}{2}\frac{\Delta T}{T}$$

or $$\frac{\Delta T}{T} = 2\times\frac{5}{500}$$

$$= 0.02$$

Illustrative Example 6.64

Two wires are fixed on a sonometer wire. Their tensions are in the ratio 8 : 1, the lengths in the ratio 36 : 35, the diameters in the ratio 4 : 1 and the densities in the ratio 1 : 2. Find the frequency of the beats produced if the note of the higher pitch has frequency of 360 Hz.

Solution

For the two wires, we have

$$n_1 = \frac{1}{2l_1}\sqrt{\left(\frac{T_2}{\pi r_2^2\rho_2}\right)}\sqrt{\left(\frac{T_1}{\pi r_1^2\rho_1}\right)}$$

and $$n_2 = \frac{1}{2l_1}\sqrt{\left(\frac{T_2}{\pi r_2^2\rho_2}\right)}$$

$\Rightarrow$ $$n_2 = \frac{l_2}{l_1}\sqrt{\left[\frac{T_1}{T_2}\left(\frac{r_2}{r_1}\right)^2\frac{\rho_2}{\rho_1}\right]} \quad \dots(6.242)$$

According to the given problem

$$\frac{l_2}{l_1} = \frac{36}{35}\ ;\ \frac{T_1}{T_2} = \frac{8}{1}$$

and $$\frac{r_1}{r_2} = \frac{4}{1} \text{ and } \frac{\rho_1}{\rho_2} = \frac{1}{2}$$

Substituting these values in equation-(6.242)

$$\frac{n_1}{n_2} = \frac{35}{36}\sqrt{\left[\left(\frac{8}{1}\right)\left(\frac{1}{16}\right)\cdot\left(\frac{2}{1}\right)\right]} = \frac{35}{36} \quad \dots(6.243)$$

It is clear from equation-(6.243) that n_2 has higher pitch so

$$n_2 = 360$$

Now $$\frac{n_1}{360} = \frac{35}{36}$$

$\Rightarrow$ $$n_1 = 350\text{ Hz}$$

Thus beat frequency is given as

$$\Delta n = 360 - 350$$

$\Rightarrow$ $$\Delta n = 10\text{ Hz}$$

 # Illustrative Example 6.65

A tuning fork of frequency 300 Hz resonates with an air column closed at one end at 27°C. How many beats will be heard in the vibrations of the fork and the air column at 0°C ? End correction is negligible.

Solution

As the air column at 27°C resonates with a tuning fork of frequency 300 hertz and hence at 27°C its own frequency is also 300 Hz. Let l be the length of air column and v_2 be the speed of sound at 27°C, then frequency of air column at 27°C is

$$n = \frac{v_2}{4l} = 300\text{ Hz} \qquad \ldots(6.244)$$

Suppose the speed of sound at 0°C be v_0. We know that the speed is directly proportional to the square root of the absolute temperature, thus we have

$$\frac{v_0}{v_2} = \sqrt{\left(\frac{273}{27+273}\right)} = \sqrt{\left(\frac{273}{300}\right)} = 0.954$$

or $\quad v_0 = 0.954 \times v_2$

Thus frequency of air column at 0°C,

$$n' = \frac{v_0}{4l} = \frac{0.954 \times v_2}{4l} \qquad \ldots(6.245)$$

Substituting the value of $(v_2/4\,l)$ from equation-(6.244) in equation-(6.245), we get

$$n' = 0.954 \times 300 = 286\text{ Hz}$$

As the frequency of tuning fork is 300 Hz, the beat frequency is given as

$$\Delta n = 300 - 286$$
$$= 14\text{ Hz.}$$

 # Illustrative Example 6.66

A string under a tension of 129.6 N produces 10 beats per second when it is vibrated along with a tuning fork. When the tension in the string is increased to 160 N, it sounds in unison with the same tuning fork. Calculate the fundamental frequency of tuning fork.

Solution

Let n be the frequency of tuning fork. The frequency of string will be either $(n + 10)$ or $(n - 10)$. As the tension in the string increases, its frequency increases ($n \propto \sqrt{T}$) and becomes n. This shows that the initial frequency (at $T = 129.6$ N) of string will be $(n - 10)$. Hence

$$n - 10 = \frac{1}{2l}\sqrt{\left(\frac{129.6}{\mu}\right)} \qquad \ldots(6.246)$$

Finally, $\quad n = \frac{1}{2l}\sqrt{\left(\frac{160}{\mu}\right)} \qquad \ldots(6.247)$

Dividing equation-(6.246) by equation-(6.247), we get

$$\frac{n-10}{n} = \sqrt{\left(\frac{129.6}{160}\right)}$$

Solving we get $\quad n = 100\text{ Hz}$

 # Illustrative Example 6.67

Two forks A and B when sounded together produce 4 beats per second. The fork A is in unison with 30 cm length of a sonometer wire, and B is in unison with 25 cm length of the same wire at the same tension. Calculate the frequency of the forks.

Solution

As in case of vibrations of string under specific tension, we know that frequency $n \propto (1/L)$ or $n = (K/L)$. As forks A and B are in unison (*equal frequencies*) with 30 cm and 25 cm length of a given sonometer wire respectively. If n_A and n_B be the frequencies of the two tuning forks, we have,

$$n_A = \frac{K}{30} \quad\text{and}\quad n_B = \frac{K}{25}$$

or $$\frac{n_A}{n_B} = \frac{25}{30} \qquad \ldots(6.248)$$

Further as the forks A and B produce 4 beats when sounded together,

$$n_A \sim n_B = 4$$

But from equation-(6.248) it is clear that $n_A < n_B$

Thus we have $\quad n_B - n_A = 4 \qquad \ldots(6.249)$

Solving equation-(6.248) and (6.249) for n_A and n_B, we get

$$n_A = 20\text{ Hz} \quad\text{and}\quad n_B = 24\text{ Hz}$$

 # Illustrative Example 6.68

A column of air at 51°C and a tuning fork produce 4 beats per second when sounded together. As the temperature of air column is decreased, the number of beats per second tends to decrease and when the temperature is 16°C the two produce one beat per second. Find the frequency of tuning fork.

Solution

The frequency of air column is given by

$$n = \frac{v}{2l}$$

Neglecting end correction, we have

$$\frac{n_1}{n_2} = \frac{v_1}{v_2} = \sqrt{\left(\frac{T_1}{T_2}\right)}$$

$$= \sqrt{\left(\frac{273+51}{273+16}\right)} = \sqrt{\left(\frac{324}{289}\right)}$$

$$= 1.059$$

This shows that $n_2 < n_1$

As the number of beats with n_2 is less than the number of beats with n_1, hence the frequency of air column must be greater than the frequency of the tuning fork. If n be the frequency of tuning fork, then

$$n_1 = n + 4 \quad \text{and} \quad n_2 = n + 1$$

or $$\frac{n+4}{n+1} = 1.059$$

This gives $\quad n = 49.8 \text{ Hz}$

Illustrative Example 6.69

The first overtone of an open organ pipe beats with the first overtone of a closed organ pipe with a beat frequency of 2.2 Hz. The fundamental frequency of the closed organ pipe is 110 Hz. Find the lengths of the pipes.

Solution

Let the lengths of open and closed pipes be l_1 and l_2 respectively. We know that

first overtone of open organ pipe, $n_1 = \dfrac{v}{l_1}$

first overtone of closed organ pipe, $n_2 = \dfrac{3v}{4l_2}$

fundamental frequency of closed organ pipe $n = \dfrac{v}{4l_2}$

According to the given question, as n = 110 Hz, we have

$$110 = \frac{v}{4l_2} = \frac{330}{4l_2}$$

or $$l_2 = \frac{330}{4\times110} = 0.75 \text{ m}$$

Further, it is given that beat frequency is 2.2 Hz, we have

$$f_B = 2.2 = \frac{v}{l_1} - \frac{3v}{4l_2}$$

or $$2.2 = \frac{2\times330}{2l_1} - \frac{3\times330}{4\times0.75}$$

or $$2.2 = \frac{330}{l_1} - 330$$

or $$332.2 = \frac{330}{l_1}$$

or $$l_1 = \frac{330}{332.2} = 0.993 \text{ m}$$

Again, Beat frequency can also be given as

$$f_B = 2.2 = \frac{3v}{4l_2} - \frac{v}{l_1}$$

or $$2.2 = \frac{3\times330}{4\times0.75} - \frac{2\times330}{2l_1}$$

$$2.2 = 330 - \frac{330}{l_1}$$

Solving we get $\quad l_1 = 1.006 \text{ m}$

Illustrative Example 6.70

The vibration portion of a wire which is stretched with a weight of 6.48 kg weighs 0.5 gm. When sounding in fundamental note, it is found to give 20 beats in 5 seconds, with a vibrating tuning fork of frequency 256. If the length of the wire is slightly decreased, the note emitted by it is observed to be in unison with that of the fork. Calculate the original length of the wire.

Solution

When the length of the wire is l metre, the number of beats per second = 20/5 = 4.

If the length is decreased, the frequency increase and the beats disappear. The original frequency of the wire is less than 256 by 4.

So the frequency of the wire of length l is

$$n = 256 - 4 = 252 \text{ Hz}$$

Tension in wire is

$$T = 6.48 \times 9.8 \text{ N}$$

Linear mass density of wire is

$$\mu = \frac{0.5\times10^{-3}}{l} \text{ kg/m}$$

We know natural frequency of oscillations of the wire is given as

$$n_o = \frac{1}{2l}\sqrt{\frac{T}{\mu}}$$

or $$252 = \frac{1}{2l}\sqrt{\left(\frac{6.48\times 9.8\times L}{0.5\times 10^{-3}}\right)}$$

or $$(252)^2 = \frac{1}{4l^2}\times\frac{6.48\times 9.8\times L}{0.5\times 10^{-3}}$$

On solving we get

$$l = 0.5\text{ m} = 50\text{ cm}$$

Illustrative Example 6.71

When 0.98 m long metallic wire is stressed, an extension of 0.02 m is produced. An organ pipe 0.5 m long and open at both ends, when sounded with this stressed metallic wire, produces 8 beats in its fundamental mode. By decreasing the stress in the wire, the number of beats are found to decrease. Find the young's modulus of wire. The density of metallic wire is 10^4 kg/m^3 and sound velocity in air is 292 m/s.

Solution

We know the fundamental frequency of open pipe is given as

$$n_1 = \frac{v}{2l} = \frac{292}{2\times(0.5)} = 292\text{ Hz} \qquad \ldots(6.250)$$

Let L' be the stressed length of the wire. Then

$$L' = L + \Delta L,\text{ where } L = \text{initial length}$$

$$= 0.98 + 0.02 = 1.0\text{ m}$$

The fundamental frequency of stressed wire is

$$n = \frac{1}{2L'}\sqrt{\left(\frac{T}{\pi r^2\rho}\right)} \qquad \ldots(6.251)$$

Where r = radius of the wire and ρ = density of wire

Given that the wire produces 8 beats with pipe. Thus we have

$$n = n_1 \pm 8 = 292 \pm 8$$

$$= 300 \quad \text{or} \quad 284$$

As the number of beats decreases by decreasing the stress and hence

$$n = 300$$

From equation-(6.251), we have

$$\frac{T}{\pi r^2} = 4\,n^2\,\rho\,(L')^2$$

Now $$Y = \frac{(T/\pi r^2)}{(\Delta L/L)} = \frac{4n^2\rho(L')^2}{(\Delta L/L)}$$

$$\Rightarrow \quad Y = \frac{4\times(300)^2\times 10^4\times(1.0)^2}{(0.02/0.98)}$$

$$\Rightarrow \quad Y = 17.64\times 10^{10}\text{ N/m}^2$$

Illustrative Example 6.72

A string 25 cm long and having a mass of 2.5 gm is under tension. A pipe closed at one end is 40 cm long. When the string is set vibrating in its first overtone and the air in the pipe in its fundamental frequency, 8 beats per second are heard. It is observed that decreasing the tension in the string decreases the beat frequency. If the speed of sound in air is 320 m/s find the tension in the string.

Solution

Linear mass density of string is

$$\mu = \frac{m}{L} = \frac{2.5\times 10^{-3}}{0.25} = 0.01\text{ kg/m}$$

For first overtone (i.e., second harmonic) the frequency of the string is

$$n_1 = \frac{2}{2L}\sqrt{\frac{T}{\mu}} = \frac{2}{2\times 0.25}\sqrt{\frac{T}{0.01}} = 40\sqrt{T}$$

Fundamental frequency of closed organ pipe is given as

$$n_C = \frac{v}{4l} = \frac{320}{4\times 0.4} = 200\text{ Hz}$$

Now as the two produces 8 beats per second, we have

$$200 - 40\sqrt{T} = 8 \qquad \text{[case-I]}$$

or $$40\sqrt{T} - 200 = 8 \qquad \text{[case-II]}$$

Now as decreasing the tension decreases the beat frequency, case-I is not permissible. Thus we have

$$40\sqrt{T} = 208,$$

or $$T = \left[\frac{208}{40}\right]^2$$

$$= 27.04\text{ N}$$

Illustrative Example 6.73

A metal wire of diameter 1 mm is held on two knife edges separated by a distance of 50 cm. The tension in the wire is 100 N. The wire, vibrating with its fundamental frequency and a vibrating tuning fork together produces 5 beats per second. The tension in the wire is then reduced to 81 N. When the two are excited, beats are heard at the same rate. Calculate

(i) the frequency of the fork and

(ii) the density of the material of wire

Solution

Let the frequency of tuning fork be n, then in the first case the fundamental frequency of the wire will be $(n+5)$, which is given as

$$(n+5)=\frac{1}{2l}\sqrt{\left(\frac{T}{\mu}\right)}$$

Here $T=100$ N, $l=50$ cm $=0.5$ m, on substituting values, we get

$$(n+5)=\frac{1}{2\times0.5}\sqrt{\left(\frac{100}{\mu}\right)}=\frac{10}{\sqrt{\mu}} \quad \ldots(6.252)$$

In the second case, $T=81$ N. In this case the frequency of wire will be $(n-5)$. Thus we have

$$(n-5)=\frac{1}{2\times0.5}\sqrt{\left(\frac{81}{\mu}\right)}=\frac{9}{\sqrt{\mu}} \quad \ldots(6.253)$$

Subtracting equation-(6.253) from equation-(6.252), we get

$$10=\frac{10}{\sqrt{\mu}}-\frac{9}{\sqrt{\mu}}=\frac{1}{\sqrt{\mu}}$$

or $$\mu=\frac{1}{100}=0.01 \text{ kg/m}$$

But we know that linear mass density of a wire of cross sectional radius r and density ρ is given as

$$\mu=\pi r^2\rho$$

or $$\rho=\frac{m}{\pi r^2}=\frac{0.01}{3.14(5\times10^{-4})^2}$$

$$=12732.5 \text{ kg/m}^3$$

From equation-(6.252), we have

$$n+5=\frac{10}{\sqrt{0.01}}=100 \text{ Hz}$$

$$n=100-5$$

$$=95 \text{ Hz}$$

Web Reference at www.physicsgalaxy.com

Age Group - High School Physics | Age 17-19 Years

Section - OSCILLATION & WAVES

Topic - Stationary Waves and Beats

Module Number - 47 to 54

Practice Exercise 6.7

(i) A closed pipe and an open pipe sounding together produce 5 beats per second. If the length of the open pipe is 30 cm, find by how much the length of the closed pipe should be changed to bring the two pipes in unison. Take speed of sound in air is 330 m/s.

[0.1376 cm]

(ii) A tuning fork produces 4 beats per second with another tuning fork of frequency 256 Hz. The first one is now loaded with a little wax and the beat frequency is found to increase to 6 per second. What was the original frequency of the tuning fork?

[252 Hz]

(iii) If two sound waves, $y_1=0.3\sin 596\,\pi[t-x/330]$ and $y_2=0.5\sin 604\,\pi[t-x/330]$ are superimposed, what will be the (a) frequency of resultant wave (b) frequency at which beats are produced. (c) The ratio of maximum and minimum intensities of beats.

[(a) 300 Hz, (b) 4 Hz, (c) 16]

(iv) As set of 25 tuning forks is arranged in a series of decreasing frequencies. Each fork gives 3 beats with the succeeding one. The first fork is the octave of the last. Calculate the frequency of the first and the 16th tuning fork.

[144 Hz and 99 Hz]

(v) A piano wire *A* vibrates at a fundamental frequency of 600 Hz. A second identical wire *B* produces 6 beats per second with it when the tension in *A* is slightly increased. Find the ratio of the tension in *A* to the tension in *B*.

[1.02]

(vi) You are given four tuning forks; the lowest frequency of the fork is 300 Hz. By striking two tuning forks at a time, 1, 2, 3, 5, 7 and 8 Hz beat frequencies are heard. What are the possible frequencies of the other three forks ?

[301, 303 and 308 Hz]

(vii) There are three sources of sound of equal intensities with frequency 400, 401 and 402 Hz. What is the beat frequency heard if all are sounded simultaneously ?

[1 Hz]

(viii) A tuning fork of frequency 256 Hz produces 4 beats per second with a wire of length 25 cm vibrating in its fundamental mode. The beat frequency decreases when the length is slightly shortened. What could be the minimum length by which the wire be shortened so that it produces no beats with the tuning fork ?

[0.39 cm]

6.17 Doppler's Effect

When a car at rest on a road sounds its high frequency horn and you are also standing on the road near by, you'll hear the sound of same frequency it is sounding but when the car approaches you with its horn sounding, the pitch (frequency) of its sound seams to drop as the car passes. This phenomenon was first described by an Austrian Scientist Christian Doppler, is called the Doppler effect. He explained that when a source of sound and a listener are in motion relative to each other, the frequency of the sound heard by the listener is not the same as the source frequency. Lets discuss the Doppler effect in detail for different cases.

6.17.1 Stationary Source and Stationary Observer

Figure-6.79 shows a stationary sources of frequency n_0 which produces sound waves in air of wavelength λ_0 given as

$$\lambda_0 = \frac{v}{n_0} \qquad [v = \text{speed of sound in air}]$$

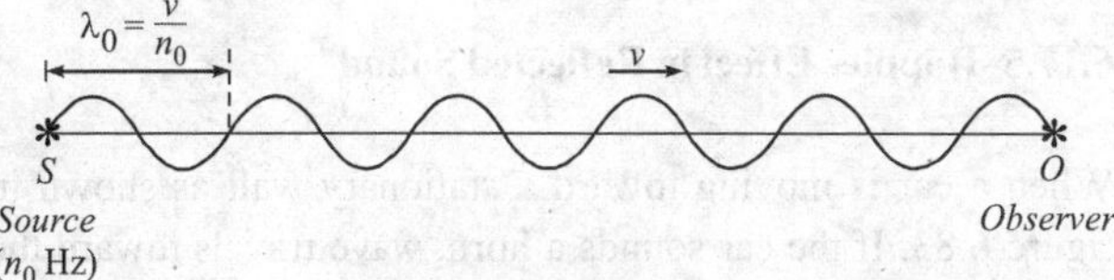

Figure 6.79

Although sound waves are longitudinal, here we represent sound weaves by the transverse displacement curve as shown in figure-6.79 to understand the concept in a better way. As source produces waves, these waves travel towards, stationary observer O in the medium (air) with speed v and wavelength λ_0. As observer is at rest here it will observe the same wavelength λ_0 is approaching it with speed v so it will listen the frequency n given as

$$n = \frac{v}{\lambda_0} = n_0 \qquad \ldots(6.254)$$

[Same as that of source]

This is why when a stationary observer listens the sound from a stationary source of sound, it detects the same frequency sound which the source is producing. Thus no Doppler effect takes place if there is no relative motion between source and observer.

6.17.2 Stationary Source and Moving Observer

Figure-6.80 shows the case when a stationary sources of frequency n_0 produces sound waves which have wavelength in air given as

$$\lambda_0 = \frac{v}{n_0}$$

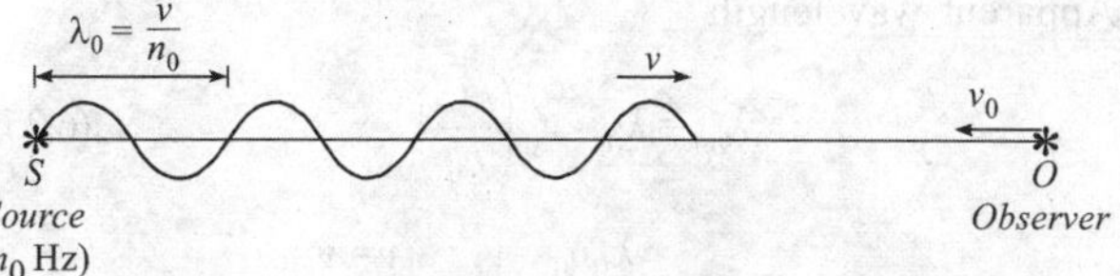

Figure 6.80

These waves travel toward moving observer with velocity v_0 towards, the source. When sound waves approach observer, it will receive the waves of wavelength λ_0 with speed $v + v_0$ (relative speed). Thus the frequency of sound heard by observer can be given as

Apparent frequency

$$n_{ap} = \frac{v + v_0}{\lambda_0}$$

$$= \frac{v + v_0}{\left(\frac{v}{n_0}\right)} = n_0\left(\frac{v + v_0}{v}\right) \qquad \ldots(6.255)$$

Similarly we can say that if the observer is receding away from the source the apparent frequency heard by the observer will be given as

$$n_{ap} = n_0\left(\frac{v - v_0}{v}\right) \qquad \ldots(6.256)$$

6.17.3 Moving Source and Stationary Observer

Figure-6.81 shows the situation when a moving source S of frequency n_0 produces sound waves in medium (air) and the waves travel toward observer with velocity v.

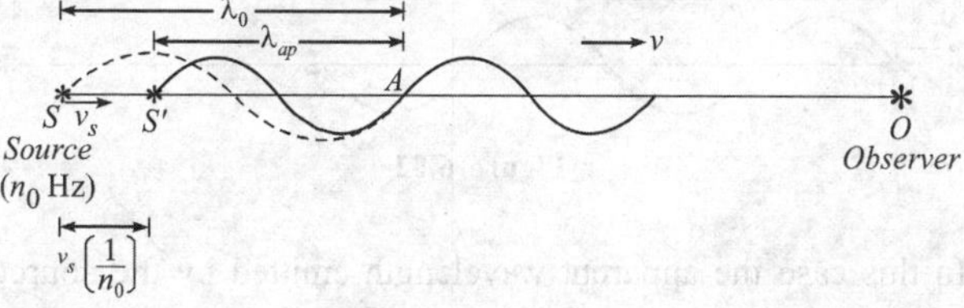

Figure 6.81

Here if we carefully look at the initial situation when source starts moving with velocity v_s as well as it starts producing waves. The period of one oscillation is $\left(\frac{1}{n_0}\right)$ sec and in this duration source emits one wavelength λ_0 in the direction of propagation of waves with speed v, but in this duration the source will also move forward by a distance $v_s\left(\frac{1}{n_0}\right)$. Thus the effective wavelength of emitted sound in air is slightly compressed by this distance as shown in figure-6.81. This we term as apparent wavelength of sound in medium (air) by the moving source. This is given as

Apparent wavelength

$$\lambda_{ap} = \lambda_0 - v_s\left(\frac{1}{n_0}\right) \quad \dots(6.257)$$

$$= \frac{\lambda_0 n_0 - v_s}{n_0} = \frac{v - v_s}{n_0}$$

Now this wavelength will approach observer with speed v (as O is at rest). Thus the frequency of sound heard by observer can be given as

Apparent frequency

$$n_{ap} = \frac{v}{\lambda_{ap}}$$

$$= \frac{v}{(v - v_s)/n_0}$$

$$= n_0\left(\frac{v}{v - v_s}\right) \quad \dots(6.258)$$

Similarly if source is receding away from observer, the apparent wavelength emitted by source in air toward observer will be slightly expanded and the apparent frequency heard by the stationary observer can be given as

$$n_{ap} = n_0\left(\frac{v}{v - v_s}\right) \quad \dots(6.259)$$

6.17.4 Moving Source and Moving Observer

Let us consider the situation when both source and observer are moving in same direction as shown in figure-6.82 at speeds v_s and v_0 respectively.

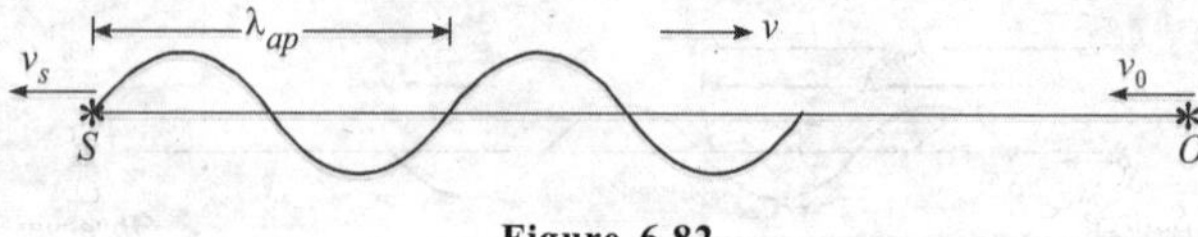

Figure 6.82

In this case the apparent wavelength emitted by the source behind it is given as

$$\lambda_{ap} = \frac{v + v_s}{n_0}$$

Now this wavelength will approach the observer at relative speed $v + v_0$, thus the apparent frequency of sound heard by the observer is given as

$$n_{ap} = \frac{v + v_0}{\lambda_{ap}}$$

$$= n_0\left(\frac{v + v_0}{v + v_s}\right) \quad \dots(6.260)$$

By looking at the expression of apparent frequency given by equation-(6.260), we can easily develop a general relation for finding the apparent frequency heard by a moving observer due to a moving source as

$$n_{ap} = n_0\left[\frac{v \pm v_0}{v \pm v_s}\right] \quad \dots(6.261)$$

Here + and – signs are chosen according to the direction of motion of source and observer. The sign convention related to the motion direction can be stated as :

(i) For both source and observer v_0 and v_s are taken in equation-(6.261) with – ve sign if they are moving in the direction of $\vec{v}$ i.e. the direction of propagation of sound from source to observer.

(ii) For both source and observer v_0 and v_s are taken in equation-(6.261) with + ve sign if they are moving in the direction opposite to $\vec{v}$ i.e. opposite to the direction of propagation of sound from source to observer.

6.17.5 Doppler Effect in Reflected Sound

When a car is moving toward a stationary wall as shown in figure-6.83. If the car sounds a horn, wave travels toward the wall and is reflected from the wall. When the reflected wave is heard by the driver, it appears to be of relatively high pitch. If we wish to measure the frequency of reflected sound then the problem must be handled in two steps.

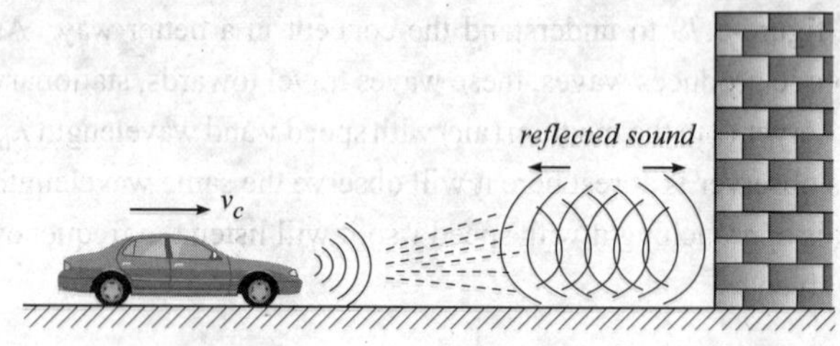

Figure 6.83

First we treat the stationary wall as a stationary observer and car as a moving source of sound of frequency n_0. In this case the frequency received by the wall is given as

$$n_1 = n_0\left(\frac{v}{v - v_c}\right) \quad \dots(6.262)$$

Now wall reflects this frequency and behaves like a stationary source of sound of frequency n_1 and car (driver) behave like a moving observer with velocity v_c. Here the apparent frequency heard by the car driver can be given as

$$n_{ap} = n_1\left(\frac{v + v_c}{v}\right)$$

or

$$= n_0\left(\frac{v}{v - v_c}\right) \times \left(\frac{v + v_c}{v}\right)$$

$$= n_0 \left(\frac{v+v_c}{v-v_c}\right) \quad \ldots(6.263)$$

Same problem can also be solved in a different manner by using method of sound images. In this procedure we assume the image of the sound source behind the reflector. In previous example we can explain this by situation shown in figure-6.84

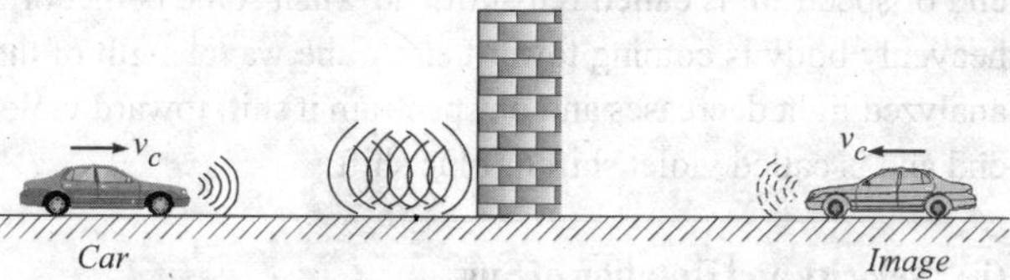

Figure 6.84

Here we assume that the sound which is reflected by the stationary wall is coming from the image of car which is at the back of it and coming toward it with velocity v_c. Now the frequency of sound heard by car driver can directly be given as

$$n_{ap} = n_0 \left[\frac{v+v_c}{v-v_c}\right] \quad \ldots(6.264)$$

This method of images for solving problems of Doppler effect is very convenient but is used only for velocities of source and observer which are very small compared to the speed of sound and it should not be used frequently when the reflector of sound is moving.

6.17.6 Doppler's Effect for Accelerated Motion

For the case of a moving source and a moving observer, we know the apparent frequency observer can be given as

$$n_{ap} = n_0 \left[\frac{v \pm v_0}{v \pm v_S}\right] \quad \ldots(6.265)$$

Here v is the velocity of sound and v_0 and v_S are the velocity of observer and source respectively.

When a source or observer has accelerated or retarded motion then in equation-(6.265) we use that value of v_0 at which observer receives the sound and for source, we use that value of v_S at which it has emitted the wave.

The alternative method of solving this case is by the traditional method of compressing or expending wavelength of sound by motion of source and using relative velocity of sound with respect to observer

6.17.7 Doppler's Effect when Source and Observer are not in Same Line of Motion

Consider the situation shown in figure-6.85. Two cars 1 and 2 are moving along perpendicular roads at speeds v_1 and v_2. When car-1 sound a horn of frequency n_0, it emits sound in all directions and say car-2 is at the position, shown in figure-6.85 when it receives the sound. In such cases we use velocity components of the cars along the line joining the source and observer thus the apparent frequency of sound heard by car-2 can be given as

$$n_{ap} = n_0 \left[\frac{v + v_2 \cos\theta_2}{v - v_1 \cos\theta_1}\right] \quad \ldots(6.266)$$

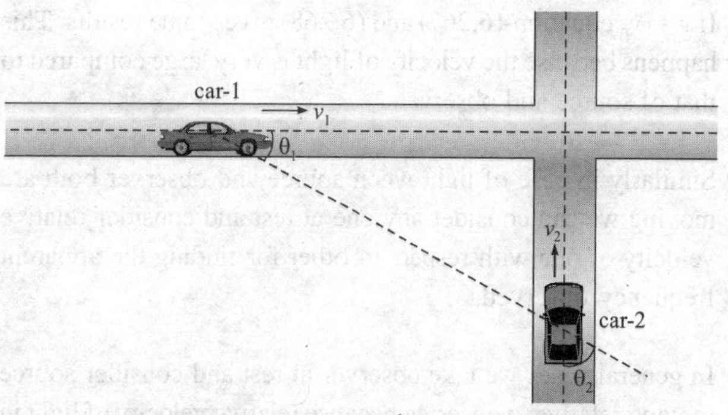

Figure 6.85

6.17.8 Doppler's Effect in Light

We've discussed the Doppler effect in sound. In case of light, the frequency of light radiation changes due to relative motion between light source and observer. According to the theory of electromagnetic waves, material medium is not necessary for the propagation of light, whereas for sound waves, material medium is necessary. In sound waves Doppler's effect is not symmetric i.e. the apparent frequencies are different when the source is moving toward a stationary observer and when the observer is moving toward a stationary source.

But the case is not same in light waves. In light, the Doppler effect is symmetric. The apparent frequency is same when either the source is moving or observer is moving. Let us consider an example, this will explain the concept in detail.

Consider a source of light with frequency ν_0 is moving toward a stationary observer at speed v_s then the frequency observed can be written as

$$\nu_{ap} = \nu_0 \left[\frac{c}{c - v_s}\right]$$

or

$$\nu_{ap} = \nu_0 \left[\frac{1}{1 - \frac{v_s}{c}}\right]$$

$$= \nu_0\left(1-\frac{v_s}{c}\right)^{-1} \simeq \nu_0\left(1+\frac{v_s}{c}\right) \quad \ldots(6.267)$$

$$\left[\text{As } \frac{v_s}{c} << 1\right]$$

Similarly if we consider an observer is moving at speed v_0 toward a stationary light source of frequency ν_0 then the apparent frequency observed by the observer can be given as

$$\nu_{ap} = \nu_0\left[\frac{c+v_0}{c}\right] = \nu_0\left(1+\frac{v_0}{c}\right) \quad \ldots(6.268)$$

If $v_s = v_0$ equation-(6.267) and (6.268) gives same results. This happens because the velocity of light is very large compared to that of source and observer.

Similarly in case of light when source and observer both are moving we can consider any one at rest and consider relative velocity of one with respect to other for finding the apparent frequency observed.

In general cases we take observer at rest and consider source moving relative to observer because relative velocity of light in any physical condition can not exceed c. If λ_0 and λ_{ap} be the actual and apparent wavelength of light then for a stationary observer and a moving source, we have

$$\nu_{ap} = \nu_0\left[\frac{c}{c-v_s}\right]$$

or $$\frac{c}{\lambda_{ap}} = \frac{c}{\lambda_0}\left[\frac{c}{c-v_s}\right]$$

or $$\lambda_0 c - \lambda_0 v_s = \lambda_{ap} c$$

or $$v_s = \frac{(\lambda_0-\lambda_{ap})}{\lambda_0}c$$

$$v_s = \frac{\Delta\lambda}{\lambda_0}c \quad \ldots(6.269)$$

Here $\Delta\lambda$ is the wavelength shift due to motion of source and this equation-(6.269) gives the relative velocity of source toward observer. Whenever we observe wavelength shift, if received wavelength (λ_{ap}) is less then actual wavelength (λ_0) or $\Delta\lambda$ is positive we say source is approaching the observer and when received wavelength (λ_{ap}) is more then the actual wavelength (λ_0) or $\Delta\lambda$ is negative we say source is moving away from observer. In the field of astronomy, Doppler effect is found to be very useful.

6.17.9 Applications of Doppler Effect in Light

(i) Doppler's Shift

When radiation coming from distant galaxies and nebulae are analyzed by radio telescopes and compared with their natural radiation wavelength focussed on mean wavelength on a visible spectrum, it is observed that the coming radiation has a shift toward red end of visible spectrum approximately by 200 Å i.e. The wave length of coming radiation is 200 Å more then their actual wavelength. This gives the idea that universe is expanding. The shifting of analyzed wavelength toward red end of spectrum is called red shift and when some comet or a heavenly body is coming toward earth, the wavelength of the analyzed light decreases and on spectrum it shift toward violet end and is called violet shift or blue shift.

(ii) Velocity and Rotation of Sun

When light coming from eastern and western edges of sun are observed and analyzed, Doppler's shift shows that the shift is due to a velocity of about 2×10^3 m/s. But when light from north and south edges is observed, no such shift is observed. This shows that the sun rotates about the north south axis.

(iii) Discovery of Double Stars

By the constant observation of the sky, it has been found that some of the stars that appear to be single are actually double stars and are known as spectroscopic binaries. These stars revolve about each other. When one is approaching the earth, and the other is going away from the earth, there is a shift in their spectral lines and a single spectral line is split up into two lines whose separation depends upon time and the time period is equal to the time-period of revolution of the starts. By this method a number of double-star systems have been found.

(iv) Saturn's Rings

The planet Saturn has been found to be surrounded by concentric rings. With the help of Doppler effect it has been found that these rings are not solids but consist of a number of 'satellites' moving around the Saturn in these orbits. If the rings were solids, the outer edge of the ring should have greater velocity than the inner edge. But, according to the principle of a satellite.

$$\frac{mv^2}{R} = \frac{GMm}{R^2}$$

or $$v^2 = \frac{GM}{R}$$

Thus, the velocity of the satellite in the inner orbit is more than that in the outer orbit. This fact has been established by the Doppler shift. Thus, the rings of the Saturn are not solids but there are a large number of satellites moving in these orbits called the rings of Saturn.

Illustrative Example 6.74

A locomotive whistle 256 Hz is moving towards a stationary observer with a velocity 1/20th that of sound. What will be the frequencies of the notes heard by observer before and after the engine passes it ?

Solution

We know that $n' = n\dfrac{(v-v_0)}{(v-v_s)}$

(i) When locomotive is approaching the stationary observer

$$n = 256, \quad v_s = \frac{v}{20} \quad \text{and} \quad v_0 = 0$$

or $$n' = 256\frac{v-0}{v-(v/20)} = 256\times\frac{20}{19}$$

$$= 269.5 \text{ Hz}$$

(ii) When locomotive passes the stationary observers

$$v_s = -v/20$$

or $$n' = 256\frac{v-0}{v-(-v/20)} = 256\times\frac{20}{21}$$

$$= 243.8 \text{ Hz}$$

Illustrative Example 6.75

Two tuning forks with natural frequencies of 340 Hz each move relative to a stationary observer. One fork moves away from the observer, while the other moves towards him at the same speed. The observer hears beats of frequency 3 Hz. Find the speed of this tuning fork.

Solution

Let the velocity of each tuning fork with respect to stationary observer be v_s. Apparent frequency of the tuning fork coming towards the stationary observer is given by

$$n_1 = \frac{nv}{v-v_s} \qquad \ldots(6.270)$$

Apparent frequency of the tuning fork moving away from the stationary observer is given by

$$n_2 = \frac{nv}{v+v_s} \qquad \ldots(6.271)$$

From equations-(6.270) and (6.272)

$$n_1 - n_2 = nv\left[\frac{1}{v-v_s} - \frac{1}{v+v_s}\right]$$

or $$n_1 - n_2 = nv\left[\frac{2v_s}{v^2-v_s^2}\right] \qquad \ldots(6.272)$$

Substituting the given values, we have

$$3 = 340\times 340\left[\frac{2v_s}{(340)^2 - v_s^2}\right]$$

or $$3[(340)^2 - v_s^2] = 2\times(340)^2 v_s$$

or $$3\times(340)^2 - 3v_s^2 = 2\times(340)^2 v_s$$

or $$3v_s^2 + 2\times(340)^2 v_s - 3\times(340)^2 = 0$$

or $$v_s = \frac{-2\times(340)^2 \pm\sqrt{4\times(340)^4 + 4\times3\times3\,(340)^2}}{2\times3}$$

Solving we get $v_s = 1.5$ m/s

Illustrative Example 6.76

A vibrating tuning fork tied to the end of a string 1.988 metre long is whirled round a circle. If it makes two revolutions in a second, calculate the ratio of the frequencies of the highest and the lowest notes heard by an observer situated in the plane of the tuning fork. Velocity of sound is 350 m/s.

Solution

Number of revolutions per second = 2

Radius of the circle = 1.988 m

As Linear velocity of the tuning fork is

$$v = 2\times2\pi r = 4\times\frac{22}{7}\times1.988 = 25 \text{ m/s}$$

(i) Apparent frequency when the tuning fork is approaching the listener

$$n_1 = \frac{vn}{v-v_s} = \frac{350n}{350-25} = \frac{14}{13}n \quad \text{[Highest note]}$$

(ii) Apparent frequency when the tuning fork is moving away from the listener

$$n_2 = \frac{vn}{v+v_s} = \frac{50n}{(350+25)} = \frac{14}{15}n \quad \text{[Lowest note]}$$

The ratio of highest note to the lowest note is given by

$$\frac{n_1}{n_2} = \frac{14n}{13}\times\frac{15}{14n} = \frac{15}{13} = 1.154$$

Illustrative Example 6.77

A sources of sonic oscillations with frequency $n = 1700$ Hz and a receiver are located on the same normal to a wall. Both the source and receiver are stationary, and the wall recedes from the source with velocity $u = 6.0$ cm/s. Find the beat frequency registered by the receiver. The velocity of sound is equal to $v = 340$ m/s.

Solution

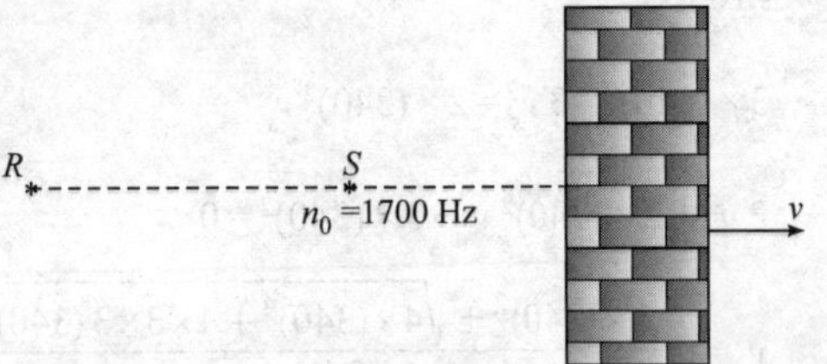

Figure 6.86

As both source and receiver are at rest the frequency of sound waves which directly reach to receiver, will be 1700 Hz and the frequency of sound which wall will receive as a moving observer is

$$n_1 = n_0\left[\frac{v}{v+u}\right]$$

The wall now behaves as a moving source of frequency n_1 which when received by receiver, the frequency observed is

$$n_2 = n_1\left[\frac{v-u}{v}\right]$$

$$= n_0\left(\frac{v-u}{v+u}\right)$$

$$= 1700\left[\frac{340-0.06}{340+0.06}\right]$$

$$= 1700\times\frac{339.94}{340.06}$$

$$= 1699.4\,\text{Hz}$$

Thus beat frequency received by detector is

$$\Delta n = 1700 - 1699.4 = 0.6\,\text{Hz}$$

Illustrative Example 6.78

If the earth is moving towards a stationary star at a speed of 30 kilometres per second, find the apparent wavelength of light emitted from the star. The real wavelength has the value 5875 Å.

Solution

Here earth (observer) is approaching the star and hence, the mutual distance is decreasing. So, the observer will notice an increase in frequency or decrease in wavelength. If v be the relative velocity of the source and c, the velocity of light, then the change in wavelength is given by

$$\Delta\lambda = \frac{v}{c}\times\lambda.$$

Substituting the given values, we have

$$\Delta\lambda = \frac{30\times10^3}{3\times10^8}\times 5875\,\text{Å}$$

$$= 5875\times10^{-4}\,\text{Å}$$

Altered wavelength

$$\lambda' = \lambda - \Delta\lambda$$

or $$\lambda' = 5875\,\text{Å} - (5875\times10^{-4}\,\text{Å})$$

or $$\lambda' = 0.9999\times5875\,\text{Å}$$

or $$\lambda' = 5874.4125\,\text{Å}$$

Illustrative Example 6.79

A source of sound of frequency 256 Hz is moving rapidly towards a wall with a velocity of 5 m/s. How many beats per second will be heard if sound travels at a speed of 330 m/s ?

Solution

Case-I : When observer is between wall and the source

In this case, the observer is stationary and the source in motion towards observer. The apparent frequency for stationary observer is given by

$$n' = n\left[\frac{v}{v-v_s}\right]$$

Here $n = 256$ Hz, $v = 330$ m/s

and $v_s = 5$ m/s

or $$n' = 256\left(\frac{330}{330-5}\right) = \frac{256\times330}{325} = 259.93\,\text{Hz}$$

In this case, the apparent frequency received by the observer from source is 259.93. The observer also receives the sound reflected from the wall. As reflection does not cause any change in frequency and hence the frequency of reflected sound is also 259.93 Hz.

Thus beats frequency is

$$\Delta n = 259.93 - 259.93 = 0$$

Case-II : When the sources is between wall and observer

For direct sound, source is moving away from the observer.

Hence $$n'' = n\left(\frac{v}{v+v_s}\right) = \frac{330}{330+5}\times256 = 252.2\,\text{Hz}$$

For reflected sound, source is moving towards wall. Hence

$$n' = n\left(\frac{v}{v-v_s}\right) = 259.9$$

Thus beat frequency is

$$\Delta n = n' - n'' = 259.9 - 252.2$$

$$= 7.7 \approx 8\text{ Hz}$$

Illustrative Example 6.80

A radar wave has a frequency of 7.8×10^9 s^{-1}. The reflected wave from an aeroplane shows a frequency difference of 2.7×10^3 s^{-1} on the higher side. Deduce the velocity of the aeroplane in the line of sight.

Solution

Suppose the aeroplane is approaching the observer with velocity v_a, then the velocity of image of source which is producing reflected wave will be $v_s = 2v_a$, (As in case of plane mirror, when the mirror moves with a velocity v, then the image moves with a velocity $2v$)

In this case, $$n' = n\left[\frac{c}{c - v_s}\right] = n\left[1 + \frac{v_s}{c}\right]$$

or $$n' = n + n\frac{v_s}{c}$$

Here $$n' - n = 2.7 \times 10^3\text{ s}^{-1},$$

or $$n = 7.8 \times 10^9\text{ s}^{-1} \text{ and } c = 3 \times 10^8\text{ m/s}$$

or $$2.7 \times 10^3 = 7.8 \times 10^9\left(\frac{v_s}{3 \times 10^8}\right) = \frac{78\,v_s}{3}$$

or $$v_s = \frac{3}{78} \times 2.7 \times 10^3\text{ m/s}$$

Now $$v_a = \frac{v_s}{2} = \left[\frac{3 \times 2.7 \times 10^3}{2 \times 78}\right] \times \frac{60 \times 60}{1000}$$

or $$= 1.87 \times 10^3\text{ km/hr}$$

Illustrative Example 6.81

Two distant sources situated together emit sound each of frequency 300 cycles per second. If one of them were to approach and the other to recede from a stationary observer each with a velocity of 1/100th the velocity of sound, calculate the number of beats per second heard by the observer.

Solution

The situation is shown in figure-6.87.

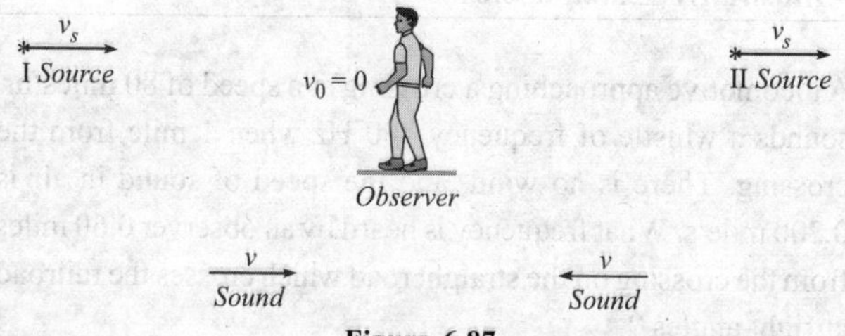

Figure 6.87

The first source is approaching the stationary observer. The frequency of the source n_1 as heard by observer is given by

$$n_1 = n\left(\frac{v}{v - v_s}\right)$$

Where n is the actual frequency of source

or $$n_1 = 300\left(\frac{v}{v - v/100}\right)$$

or $$n_1 = \frac{300 \times 100}{99}$$

or $$n_1 = 303.03\text{ Hz}$$

The second source is receding from the observer in the direction opposite to the sound. Hence the apparent frequency n_2

$$n_2 = \left(\frac{v}{v + 0.01v}\right) \times 300$$

or $$n_2 = \frac{300 \times 100}{101}$$

or $$n_2 = 297.03\text{ Hz}$$

Hence beat frequency detected by observer is

$$\Delta n = 303.03 - 297.03 = 6\text{ Hz}$$

Illustrative Example 6.82

A sources of sonic oscillations with frequency $n = 1700$ Hz and a receiver are located at the same point. At the moment $t = 0$, the source starts receding from the receiver with constant acceleration $a = 10.0$ m/s^2. Assuming the velocity of sound to be equal to $v = 340$ m/s, find the oscillation frequency registered by the stationary receiver $t = 10.0$ s after the start of motion.

Solution

In 10 second source will travel a distance

$$S_0 = \frac{1}{2}a(10)^2 = \frac{1}{2} \times 10 \times (10)^2 = 500\text{ m}$$

At this instant observer will receive that sound which source had emitted at time $t = t_1$. At time t_1 source was at a distance S from the source.

$$S = \frac{1}{2}at^2, = \frac{1}{2}(10)\,t_1^2 = 5\,t_1^2$$

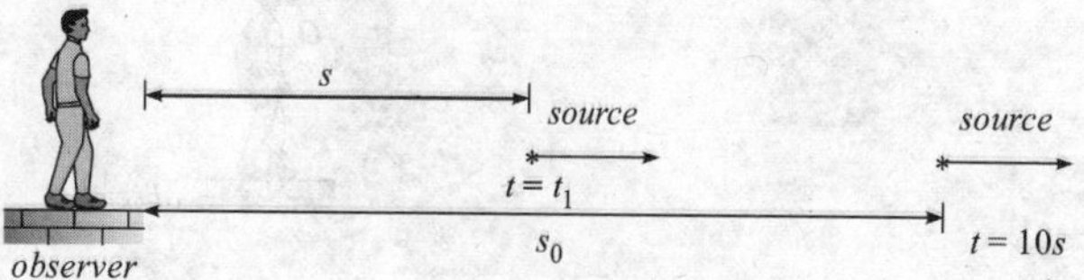

Figure 6.88

Now in a time $(10 - t_1)$ sound travels a distance S from source to observer. Thus, we have

$$St_1^2 = 340(10 - t_1)$$

or $$St_1^2 + 340t_1 - 3400 = 0$$

or $$t_1 = \frac{-340 \pm \sqrt{(340)^2 + 4(5)(3400)}}{2 \times 5}$$

$$= 8.85 \text{ s} \quad \text{[Ignoring negative root]}$$

Thus velocity of source at instant t_1 is

$$v = at_1 = 10 \times 8.85 = 88.5 \text{ m/s}$$

Thus frequency observed by observer at 10 sec is given as

$$n = n_0 \left[\frac{340}{340 + 88.5}\right]$$

$$= 1700 \times \frac{340}{428.5}$$

$$= 1350 \text{ Hz}$$

Illustrative Example 6.83

A source of sound with natural frequency $n = 1.8$ kHz moves uniformly along a straight line separated from a stationary observer by a distance $l = 250$ m. The velocity of the source is equal to $\eta = 0.80$ fraction of the velocity of sound. Find :

(a) the frequency of sound received by the observer at the moment when the source gets closest to him;

(b) the distance between the source and the observer at the moment when the observer receives a frequency $n_{ap} = n$.

Solution

The situation is shown in figure-6.89.

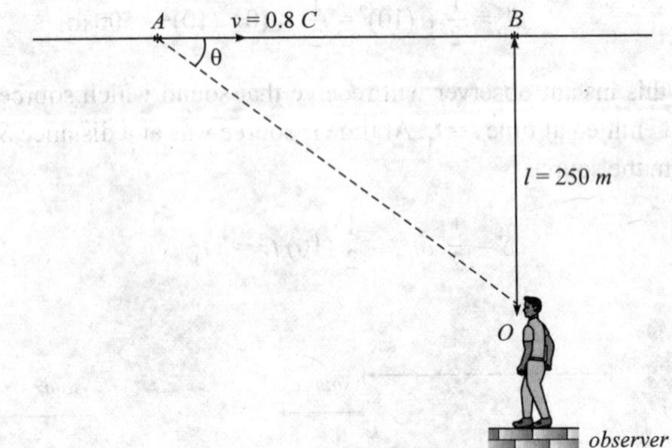

Figure 6.89

(a) Figure-6.89 shows the corresponding situation. Source gets closest to observer when it is at position B but at this instant observer receives those sound waves which source had emitted from an earlier position A shown in figure-6.89, so that when source reaches A to B, in the same time sound reaches A to O. Thus the apparent frequency heard by observer is

$$n_{ap} = n_0 \left[\frac{v}{v - v_s \cos\theta}\right] \quad \dots(6.273)$$

Here, we have

$$\cos\theta = \frac{AB}{AO} \quad \dots(6.274)$$

If sound takes t_1 time from A to O, we have

$$AB = v_s t_1 = 0.8\, t_1$$

and $$AO = vt_1$$

Now from equation-(6.274)

$$\cos\theta = 0.8$$

Now from equation-(6.273)

$$n_{ap} = n_0 0\left[\frac{v}{v - (0.8)^2 v}\right] = n_0\left[\frac{1}{0.36}\right] = \frac{1.8 \times 10^3}{0.36} = 5 \text{ kHz}$$

(b) Observer receives a frequency equal to original frequency of source corresponding to the waves emitted by source from position B, as in this case velocity component of source is there in the direction of observer.

In this case the time taken by sound to reach observer from B is

$$t_0 = \frac{l}{v}$$

In this direction distance travelled by source is

$$S = v_s t = 0.8\, vt = 0.8\, l$$

At the instant when observer receives this sound the separation between source and observer can be given as

$$x = \sqrt{l^2 + (0.8\, l)^2} = \sqrt{1.64} \times l$$

$$= \sqrt{1.16} \times 250$$

$$= 320 \text{ m}$$

Illustrative Example 6.84

A locomotive approaching a crossing at a speed of 80 miles/hr, sounds a whistle of frequency 400 Hz when 1 mile from the crossing. There is no wind, and the speed of sound in air is 0.200 mile/s. What frequency is heard by an observer 0.60 miles from the crossing on the straight road which crosses the railroad at right angles ?

Solution

The situation is shown in figure-6.90.

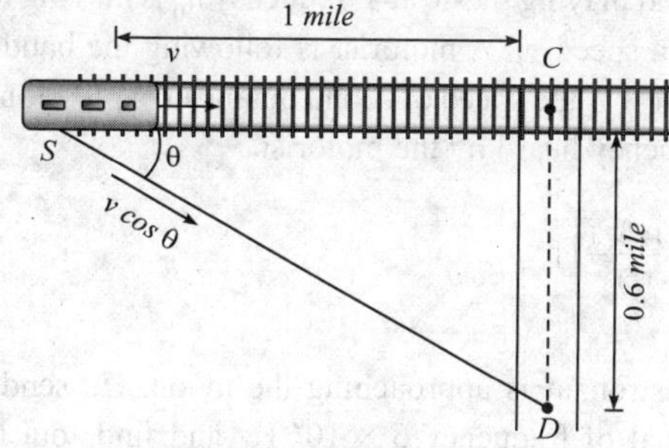

Figure 6.90

Here is $SD = \sqrt{1^2 + 0.6^2} = 1.166$ miles

$$\cos\theta = \frac{SC}{SD} = \frac{1}{1.166} = 0.857$$

Thus speed of source along the line of sight

$$v_S = v\cos\theta = \frac{80}{60\times 60}\times 0.857$$

$$= 0.019 \text{ mile/s}$$

Thus the apparent frequency observed is

$$n = n_0\left[\frac{v_{sound}}{v_{sound} - v_S}\right] = 400\left[\frac{0.2}{0.2 - 0.019}\right] = 442 \text{ Hz}$$

6.18 Shock Waves

The general equation, we've developed for finding the apparent frequency by Doppler's effect, is given as

$$n_{ap} = n_0\left(\frac{v \pm v_0}{v \pm v_s}\right) \qquad \ldots(6.275)$$

If a source is moving toward an observer at a speed equal to the speed of sound. That is $v_s = v$ then from equation-(6.275) the detected frequency n_{ap} will be infinitely high. This means that the source is moving so fast that the effective wavelength of produced sound in air is compressed to almost zero. This we can understand step by step as shown by figure-6.92.

Figure-6.91(a) shows the sound waves produced by a stationary source in three dimensional, space. The spherical region surrounding the source in which it creates oscillations in phase is called spherical wavefront produced by the source. These wavefronts propagate in radially outward direction with speed of sound as shown. All the spherical wavelengths with increasing size are concentric spherical shells with centre at source. If we look at figure-6.91(b) when source is moving toward right at speed v_s ($v_s < v$), here we can say that if initially a wavefront was emitted by source when it was at position s_1, then this wavefront will expend (sound propagates) continuously with centre located at point s_1, but source is now moved to another position s_2, s_3 and so on. In this case we can see that once if a wavefront is created (sound is produced), it is carried by the medium only and this propagation does not depend on source thus the wavefront will expand (sound travels) with its centre located at the same position from where it was created. Thus here it is clear that in front of source the separation between successive wavefronts is decreased (λ is compressed) and in the region behind the source the separation between successive wavefronts is increased (λ is expended). This is the same phenomenon of Doppler effect. Which we've described earlier in spherical waves.

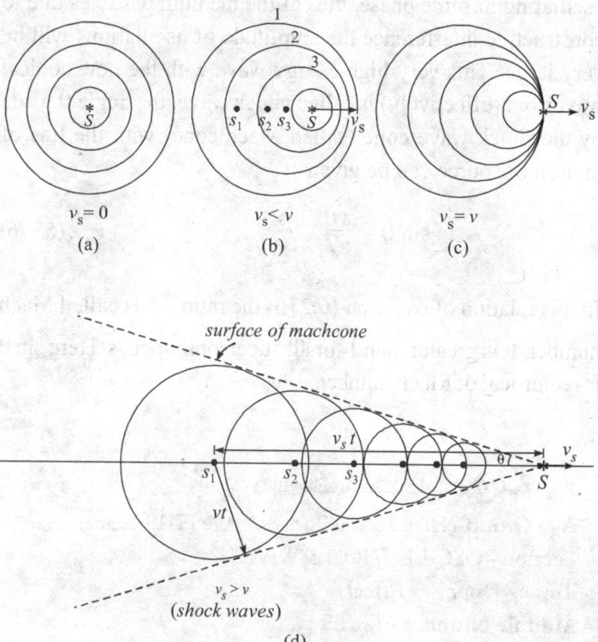

Figure 6.91

As the speed v_s of source approaches the speed of sound v, as shown in figure-6.91(c), then it keeps pace with its own spherical wavefronts, the wavelength approaches zero and the waves produced by the source from its different locations move together and pile up on each other. In such a case source must exert large force on medium particles to produce compressions and rarefaction in front of it. According to Newton's third Law, the medium exerts equally large force back on the source or we can say that when source speed approaches speed of sound then in the medium (air), there is a large increase in air resistance (aerodynamic drag) to its motion. This is called as "*sound barrier.*" This is the reason when a supersonic plane crosses its speed $v_s = v$ or sound barrier, it experiences a very high aerodynamic drag. When source speed v_s is greater in magnitude then v the source of sound is called supersonic. For supersonic sources the Doppler effect is no longer valid.

When sources speed is greater then speed of sound v, the situation is shown in figure-6.91(d). The source comes out of each spherical wavefront it produces as wavefronts expands at speed of sound v. We can see with time that a series of wavefronts are created by source during its motion and each spreads out in a sphere created at the position of source when it emitted the wavefront. After a time t, the wavefront emitted from a position s_1, has spread to a sphere of radius vt as shown in figure-6.91(c), and the source has moved a greater distance $v_s t$, here we can see that all the spreading wavefronts created from local intermediate position of the source bunch along a conical envelope as shown by dotted line in figure. At the surface of this cone we can say that all the wavefonts are oscillating in same phase, thus at the medium particles due to constructive interference the amplitude of oscillations will be very large. This very high energy wave with the new conical wavefront (effectively) is called shock wave, the angle θ made by the shock wave cone (called Mach cone) with the line of motion of source can be given as

$$\sin\theta = \frac{vt}{v_s t} = \frac{v}{v_s} \quad \ldots(6.276)$$

In this relation of equation-(6.276) the ratio $\frac{v_s}{v}$ is called Mach number. It is greater than 1 for all supersonic speeds. Here sin θ is reciprocal of Mach number.

> Web Reference at www.physicsgalaxy.com
>
> **Age Group** - High School Physics | Age 17-19 Years
> **Section** - OSCILLATION & WAVES
> **Topic** - Doppler's Effect
> **Module Number** - 1 to 25

Practice Exercise 6.8

(i) A policeman on duty detects a drop of 10% in the pitch of the horn of motion car as it crosses him. If the velocity of sound is 330 metres per second, calculate the speed of the car.

[17.37 m/s]

(ii) A car travelling at 10 m/s sounds its horn which has a frequency of 500 Hz and this is heard in another car which is travelling behind the first car in the same direction, with a velocity of 20 m/s. The sound can also be heard in the second car by reflection from a bridge head. What frequency will the driver of the second car hear ? (v = 340 m/s)

[545.45 Hz]

(iii) The wavelength of light coming from a distant galaxy is found to be 0.5% more than that coming from a source on earth. Calculate the velocity of the galaxy.

[1.5×10^6 m/s]

(iv) A band playing music at a frequency n_0 is moving towards a wall at a speed v_b. A motorist is following the band with a speed v_m. If v is the speed of sound obtain an expression for the beat frequency heard by the motorist.

[$n_0\left[\frac{(v+v_m)(2v_b)}{(v^2-v_b^2)}\right]$]

(v) An astronaut is approaching the moon. He sends out a radio signal of frequency 5×10^9 Hz and finds out that the frequency shift in echo received is 10^3 Hz. Find his speed of approach.

[30 m/s]

(vi) If a vibrating fork is rapidly moved towards a wall, beats may be heard between the direct and reflected sounds. Calculate beat frequency if the frequency of fork is 512 Hz and approaches the wall with a velocity of 300 cm/s. The velocity of sound is 330 m/s. Consider observer is behind the fork.

[9.3 Hz]

(vii) A train A crosses a station with a speed of 40 m/s and whistles a short pulse of natural frequency 596 Hz. Another train B is approaching towards the same station with the same speed along a parallel track. Two tracks are 99 m apart. When train A whistles train B is 152 m away from the station as shown in figure-6.92. If velocity of sound in air is 330 m/s, calculate the frequency of the pulse heard by driver of train B.

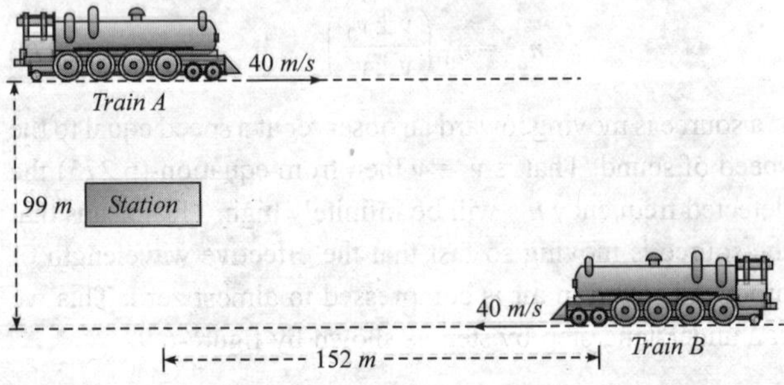

Figure 6.92

[724 Hz]

(viii) How fast would you have to go through a red light to have it appear green if the wavelengths of red and green light are respectively 620 nm and 540 nm ? Is it possible to achieve this speed on earth ?

[3.87×10^4 km/s, No]

6.19 Reflection and Refraction of Waves

Whenever a wave incident on the boundary of two different media, it splits in three parts (i) A part of incident wave bounces back into the same medium called reflected wave. (ii) A part of incident wave is transmitted into the other medium, called refracted wave (iii) A part of incident wave is absorbed by medium particles of both the medium at the boundary of media, called absorbed wave energy. If the incident wave amplitude is A; then the amplitudes of reflected, transmitted and absorbed waves can be given as

$$A_r = a_r A_i$$

$$A_t = a_t A_i$$

and $$A_a = a_a A_i$$

Where a_r, a_t and a_a are called reflection coefficient, transmission coefficient and absorption coefficient for the respective wave amplitudes and for the three we have

$$a_r + a_t + a_a = 1 \quad \ldots(6.277)$$

One more thing students should note that we have already discussed that whenever a wave is emitted from a source its frequency remains constant during propagation, no matters in which medium wave is propagating. Similarly here also we can state that the frequencies of reflected and transmitted waves must be same as that of incident wave.

Now we find corresponding reflection and transmission coefficients for the reflected and transmitted wave amplitudes.

Let us consider a wave propagating in medium-I (velocity = v_1) incident on a medium boundary as shown in figure-6.93(a). If displacement amplitude of incident wave is A; its equation can be written as

$$y_i = A_i \sin(\omega t - k_1 x) \quad [\text{Where } k_1 = \frac{\omega}{v_1}] \quad \ldots(6.278)$$

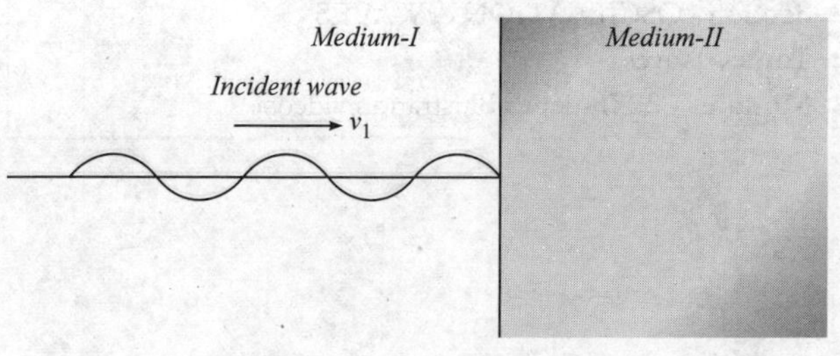

(a)

(b)

Figure 6.93

If A_r and A_t be the amplitudes of respective reflected and transmitted waves as shown in figure-6.93(b), the corresponding equations are

For reflected wave

$$y_r = A_r \sin(\omega t + k_1 x) \quad \ldots(6.279)$$

and for transmitted wave

$$y_t = A_t \sin(\omega t - k_2 x) \quad [\text{Where } k_2 = \frac{\omega}{v_2}] \quad \ldots(6.280)$$

As wave is continuous at the boundary i.e. at $x = 0$ the displacement of medium particles in the two mediums must be equal, thus we have

$$y_i + y_r = y_t$$

$$A_i + A_r = A_t \quad \ldots(6.281)$$

At the boundary, the slope of displacement curve must also be continuous thus at $x = 0$, we also have

$$\frac{dy_i}{dx} + \frac{dy_r}{dx} = \frac{dy_t}{dx}$$

Now from equation-(6.278), (6.279) and (6.280), we have

$$-A_i k_1 \cos \omega t + A_r k_1 \cos \omega t = -A_t k_2 \cos \omega t$$

or $$A_i - A_r = A_t\left(\frac{k_2}{k_1}\right) \quad \ldots(6.282)$$

Adding equation-(6.281) and (6.282) we get

$$2A_i = A_t\left(\frac{k_2}{k_1} + 1\right)$$

or $$A_t = \left(\frac{2k_1}{k_1 + k_2}\right) A_i \quad \ldots(6.283)$$

If a_t be the transmission coefficient for the boundary of the two media we have

$$A_t = a_t A_i \quad \ldots(6.284)$$

comparing equation-(6.283) and (6.284) we get

Transmission coefficient,

$$a_t = \frac{2k_2}{k_1 + k_2} = \frac{2v_2}{v_1 + v_2} \quad \ldots(6.285)$$

Now dividing equation-(6.282) and (6.281) we get

$$\frac{A_i - A_r}{A_i + A_r} = \frac{k_2}{k_1}$$

or $$\frac{A_i}{A_r} = \frac{k_1 + k_2}{k_1 - k_2}$$

or $$A_r = \left(\frac{k_1 - k_2}{k_1 + k_2}\right) A_i \quad \ldots(6.286)$$

If a_r be the reflection coefficient for the boundary of the two medium we have

$$A_r = a_r A_i \quad \ldots(6.287)$$

Comparing equation-(6.286) and (6.287) we get

Reflection coefficient,

$$a_r = \frac{k_1 - k_2}{k_1 + k_2} = \frac{v_2 - v_1}{v_1 + v_2} \quad \ldots(6.288)$$

From equation-(6.285) and (6.287) we can see that transmission coefficient is always positive but reflection coefficient can be negative when $v_2 < v_1$ or when a wave propagating in a rarer medium is reflected from the boundary of a denser medium.

The negative sign with reflection coefficient shows that whenever a wave is reflected from the boundary of a denser medium, there is always a phase addition of π radian takes place in reflected wave, due to this the wave is inverted on reflection if it is a transverse wave.

6.19.1 Reflection of a Wave Pulse in a Stretched String

Let us consider a case of reflection of a transverse wave pulse in a stretched string from a wall as shown. Here we can consider that the wave velocity in second medium (wall), $v_2 = 0$ as wall is rigid then we have from equation-(6.285) and (6.286)

$$a_r = -1 \text{ and } a_T = 0$$

This means that incident wave is completely reflected with a phase charge of π. As shown in figure-6.94.

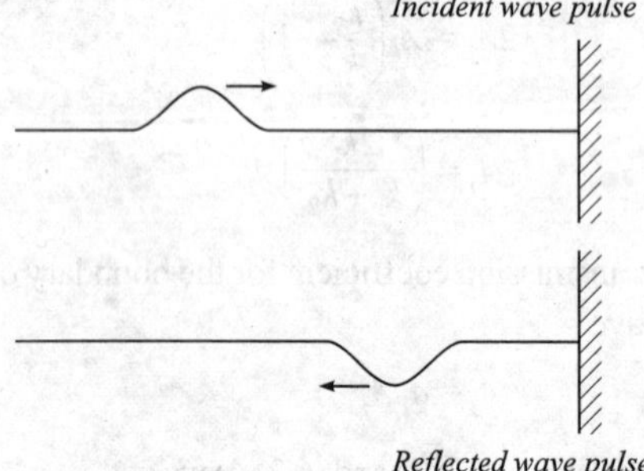

Figure 6.94

Now consider the case shown in figure-6.95. Two different strings are joined end to end stretched by a tension T. String 1 is lighter then string 2 so the wave speed in string 1 is more than that in string 2. When a wave pulse traveling from string 1 toward junction incident on the junction a part of energy is reflected and a part is transmitted to the other string. We can see as shown in figure-6.95(a) that when wave pulse travelling on lighter string (rarer medium) is reflected from heavier string (denser medium) the reflected pulse suffers a phase change of π radians and inverted. But if a wave pulse travelling from heavier string incident on the junction, during reflection no phase change occurs as we can see from figure-6.95(b)

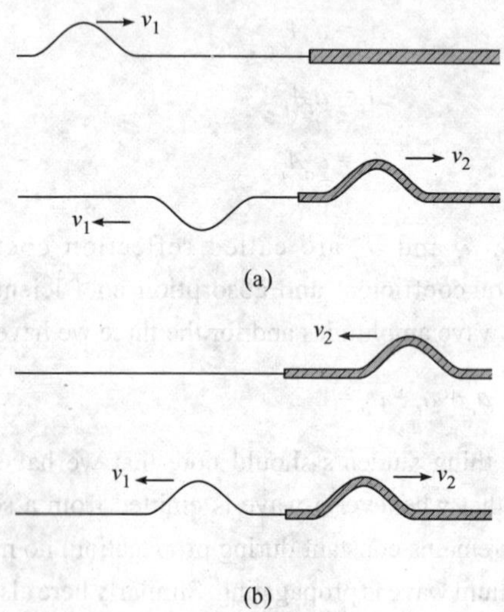

Figure 6.95

Web Reference at www.physicsgalaxy.com

Age Group - High School Physics | Age 17-19 Years
Section - OSCILLATION & WAVES
Topic - Stationary Waves and Beats
Module Number - 9, 10, 11

Advance Illustrations Videos at www.physicsgalaxy.com

Age Group - Advance Illustrations
Section - OSCILLATION & WAVES
Topic - Waves
Modules - 32 In-depth Illustration videos

* * * * *

Discussion Question

Q6-1 Will it be possible to monitor the temperature of a wire by measuring its vibrational frequency? Explain.

Q6-2 A wave propagates down a long rope which hangs freely from a support. As it propagates, what happens to the speed of the wave?

Q6-3 Show that the particle speed can never be equal to the wave speed in a sine wave if the amplitude is less than wavelength divided by 2π.

Q6-4 If the frequency of a harmonic wave on a rope is doubled and other factors are held fixed, how does the power of the wave change?

Q6-5 Two wave pulses identical in shape but inverted with respect to each other are produced at the two ends of a stretched string. At an instant when the pulses reach the middle, the string becomes completely straight. What happens to the energy of the two pulses?

Q6-6 the voice of a person, who has inhaled helium, has a remarkably high pitch. Explain on the basis of resonant vibration of vocal cord filled with air and with helium.

Q6-7 Which type of oscillations are produced when (a) an electric field vibrates in a light wave propagating in glass (b) a metallic strip oscillates in a magnetic field (c) the pendulum in a clock oscillates (d) the diaphragm of a microphone or loudspeaker vibrates (e) you tune your TV set to catch a desired station?

Q6-8 Distinguish between sound and radio waves of the same frequency (say 15 kHz).

Q6-9 Where will a person hear maximum sound at (displacement) node or antinode?

Q6-10 If you are walking on the moon, can you hear the sound of stones cracking behind you? Can you hear the sound of your own footsteps?

Q6-11 If oil of density higher than water is used in a resonance tube, how will the frequency change?

Q6-12 Two organ pipes of same length open at both ends produce sound of different pitch if their radii are different. Why?

Q6-13 Does the change in frequency due to Doppler effect depend (a) on distance between source and observer (b) on the fact that source is moving towards the listener or listener is moving towards the source?

Q6-14 Give an evidence in support of the fact that (a) sound is a wave (b) sound is a mechanical wave (c) sound waves are longitudinal.

Q6-15 The source of energy of sun is fusion of hydrogen which provides energy in the form of heat, light and sound. Explain why sound from sound from sun does not reach earth while heat and light do.

Q6-16 Explain clearly why the "*quality*" if sound from an open pipe is different than from a closed pipe of same fundamental frequency.

Q6-17 A graph of part of a wave pulse on a string at a particular instant is shown in figure-6.96, Which are the points marked with letters is instantaneously at rest? What are the directions of velocities of the points marked in figure. Do any of your answers depend on the direction of propagation ?

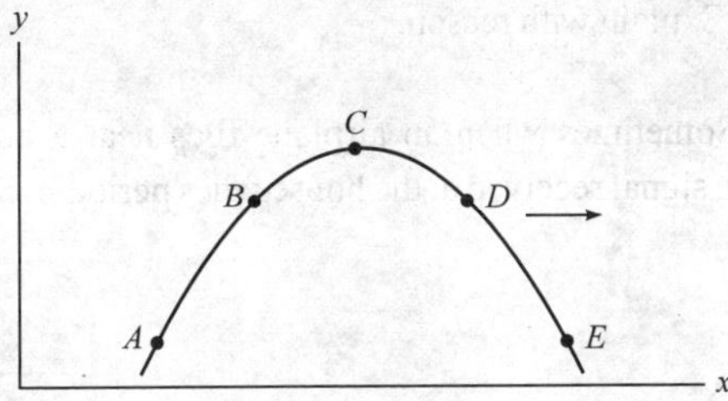

Figure 6.96

Q6-18 When two wave pulses traveling in opposite directions encounter each other, do they bounce off one another like billiard balls in head-on collision, or does each pulse pass through the other like a ghost in a cartoon? Which figure in this chapter best supports your answer?

Q6-19 The speed of sound waves in air depends on temperature but that of light does not. Why?

Q6-20 Two loudspeakers are arranged facing each other at some distance. Will a person standing behind the loudspeakers clearly hear the sound of the other loudspeaker or the clarity will be seriously damaged because of the 'collision' of the two sounds in between?

Q6-21 Two tuning forks vibrate with the same amplitude but the frequency of the first is double the frequency of the second. Which fork produces more intense sound in air?

Q6-22 Two harmonic waves are on different ropes and each rope has the same density and tension. The waves have the same frequency, but wave 1 has twice the amplitude of wave 2. Which wave has the larger speed? Which wave causes the larger maximum speed for the elements of the rope on which it travels?

Q6-23 Explain why (a) transverse mechanical waves cannot be propagated in liquids and gases while (b) waves on strings are always transverse.

Q6-24 Can we ever construct an organ pipe whose frequency does not change with temperature? If no why? If yes, under what condition?

Q6-25 What type of mechanical waves do you expect to exist in (a) vacuum (b) air (c) inside water (d) rock (e) on the surface of a liquid.

Q6-26 Why do the strings on a guitar have different diameters? Which strings produce the lower notes?

Q6-27 Can a great singer cause a glass object to shatter by his singing? Explain with reason.

Q6-28 Sometimes when an airplane flies near a house, the television signal received at the house fades periodically, Why?

Q6-29 State whether the following statement is true or false, giving reason in brief: "A plane wave of sound travelling in air is incident upon a plane water surface. The angle of incidence is 60°. Assuming Snell's law to be valid for sound waves, it follows that the sound wave will be refracted into water away from the normal.".

Q6-30 What factors determine the pitch of tuning fork?

Q6-31 The distance from the sun to *M*ars is about 3/2 that from the sun to the earth. Compare the intensity of sunlight at Mars with the intensity of sunlight at the earth.

Q6-32 If you twirl one end of a horizontally stretched rope in a circle in a plane perpendicular to the rope, a wave will propagate along the rope. Is this wave transverse, longitudinal, some combination of the two, or none of these?

Q6-33 Explain why (a) velocity of sound is generally greater in solids than in gases. (b) the velocity of sound in oxygen is lesser than in hydrogen.

Q6-34 The radio and TV programs, telecast at the studio, reach our antenna by wave motion. Is it a mechanical wave or non-mechanical ?

* * * * *

Conceptual MCQs Single Option Correct

6-1 Two stars P and Q have slightly different surface temperatures T_P and T_Q respectively, with $T_P > T_Q$. Both stars are receding from the earth with speeds v_P and v_Q relative to the earth. The wavelength of light at which they radiate the maximum energy is found to be the same for both :

(A) $v_P > v_Q$
(B) $v_P < v_Q$
(C) $v_P = v_Q$, and the size of $Q >$ the size of P
(D) Nothing can be said regarding v_P and v_Q from the given data

6-2 In the water a of a lake a blast occurs. The waves produced in water will be :

(A) Transverse
(B) Longitudinal
(C) Stationary
(D) Both transverse and longitudinal

6-3 Two sounding bodies are producing progressive wave given by $y_1 = 4 \sin (400 \pi t)$ and $y_2 = 3 \sin (404 \pi t)$, where t is in second which superpose near the ears of a person. The person will heat :

(A) 2 beats per second with intensity ratio $\frac{4}{3}$ between maxima and minima
(B) 2 beats per second with intensity ratio 49 between maxima and minima
(C) 4 beats per second with intensity ratio 7 between maxima and minima
(D) 4 beats per second with intensity ratio $\frac{4}{3}$ between maxima and minima

6-4 Two harmonic waves travelling in the same medium have frequency in the ratio 1 : 2 and intensity in the ratio 1 : 36. Their amplitude ratio is :

(A) 1 : 6 (B) 1 : 8
(C) 1 : 72 (D) 1 : 3

6-5 A pipe of length 20 cm is closed at one end. Which harmonic mode of the pipe is resonantly excited by a 425 Hz source ? The speed of sound = 340 ms^{-1} :

(A) First harmonic (B) Second harmonic
(C) Third harmonic (D) Fourth harmonic

6-6 The frequency of a wave is reduced to one quarter and its amplitude is made twice. The intensity of the wave :

(A) Increases by a factor of 2
(B) Decreases by a factor of 4
(C) Decreases by a factor of 2
(D) Remains unchanged

6-7 Radiowaves of frequency 600 MHz are sent by a radar towards an enemy aircraft. The frequency of the radiowaves reflected from the aircraft as measured at the radar station is found to increase by 6 kHz. It follows that the aircraft is :

(A) Approaching the radar station with a speed 1.5 kms^{-1}
(B) Going away from the radar station with a speed 1.5 kms^{-1}
(C) Approaching the radar station with a speed 3 kms^{-1}
(D) Going away from the radar station with a speed 3 kms^{-1}

6-8 The velocity of sound in dry air is V_d, and in moist air it is V_m. The velocities are measured under the same conditions of temperature and pressure. Which of the following statement is fully correct ?

(A) $V_d > V_m$ because dry air has lower density than moist air
(B) $V_d < V_m$ because moist air has lower density than dry air
(C) $V_d > V_m$ because the bulk modulus of dry air is greater than that of moist air
(D) $V_d < V_m$ because the bulk modulus of moist air is greater than that of dry air

6-9 A machine gun is mounted on a tank moving at a speed of 20 ms^{-1} towards a target with the gun pointing in the direction of motion of the tank. The muzzle speed of the bullet equals the speed of sound = 340 ms^{-1}. If, at the time of firing, the target is 500 m away from the tank, then :

(A) The sound arrives at the target later than the bullet
(B) The sound arrives at the target earlier than the bullet
(C) Both sound and bullet arrive at the target at the same time
(D) The bullet will never arrive at the target

6-10 Out of the four choices given in Q. No. 6-9 above, choose the correct choice, if the gun points in a direction opposite to the direction of motion of the tank.

(A) The sound arrives at the target later than the bullet
(B) The sound arrives at the target earlier than the bullet
(C) Both sound and bullet arrive at the target at the same time
(D) The bullet will never arrive at the target

6-11 When we hear a sound, we can identify its source from :

(A) The frequency of the sound
(B) The amplitude of the sound
(C) The wavelength of the sound
(D) The overtones present in the sound

6-12 The wavelength of light of a particular wavelength received from a galaxy is measured on earth and is found to be 5% more that its wavelength. It follows that the galaxy is :

(A) Approaching the earth with a speed 3×10^7 ms^{-1}
(B) Going away from the earth with a speed 1.5×10^7 ms^{-1}
(C) Approaching the earth with a speed 1.5×10^7 ms^{-1}
(D) Going away from the earth with a speed 1.5×10^7 ms^{-1}

6-13 Consider a wave represented by $y = a\cos^2(\omega t - kx)$ where symbols have their usual meanings. This wave has :
(A) An amplitude a, frequency ω and wavelength λ
(B) An amplitude a, frequency 2ω and wavelength 2λ
(C) An amplitude $\frac{1}{2}a$, frequency 2ω and wavelength $\frac{1}{2}\lambda$
(D) An amplitude $\frac{1}{2}a$, frequency 2ω and wavelength λ

6-14 A pipe of length 20 cm is open at both ends. Which harmonic mode of the pipe is resonantly excited by a 1700 Hz source ? The speed of sound = 340 ms^{-1} :
(A) First harmonic (B) Second harmonic
(C) Third harmonic (D) Fourth harmonic

6-15 A sine wave has an amplitude A and a wavelength λ. Let V be the wave velocity, and v be maximum velocity of particle in the medium :
(A) V cannot be equal to v (B) $V = v$, if $A = \lambda/2\pi$
(C) $V = v$, if $A = 2\pi\lambda$ (D) $V = v$, if $\lambda = A/\pi$

6-16 At $t = 0$, a transverse wave pulse in a wire is described by the function $y = \frac{6}{x^2 - 3}$ where x and y are in metre. The function $y(x, t)$ that describes the wave equation if it is travelling in the position x direction with a speed of 4.5 ms^{-1} is :
(A) $y = \frac{6}{(x+4.5t)^2 - 3}$ (B) $y = \frac{6}{(x-4.5t)^2 + 3}$
(C) $y = \frac{6}{(x+4.5t)^2 + 3}$ (D) $y = \frac{6}{(x-4.5t)^2 - 3}$

6-17 A motion is described by $y = 3e^x \cdot e^{-3t}$ where y, x are in metre and t is in second :
(A) This represents equation of progressive wave propagating along $-x$ direction with 3 ms^{-1}
(B) This represents equation of progressive wave propagating along $+x$ direction with 3 ms^{-1}
(C) This does not represent a progressive wave equation
(D) Data is insufficient to arrive at any conclusion of this short

6-18 Two waves of same frequency, constant phase difference but different amplitude superpose at a point :
(A) The resultant intensity varies periodically as a function of time
(B) There will be no interference
(C) There will be interference in which the minimum intensity will not be zero
(D) There will be interference in which the minimum intensity is zero

6-19 A wave equation is represented as

$$r = A\sin\left[\alpha\left(\frac{x-y}{2}\right)\right]\cos\left[\omega t - \alpha\left(\frac{x+y}{2}\right)\right]$$

where x and y are in metre and t is in second. Then,
(A) The wave is a stationary wave
(B) The wave is a progressive wave propagating along $+x$ axis
(C) The wave is a progressive wave propagating at right angle to the $+x$ axis
(D) All points lying on line $y = x + \frac{4\pi}{\alpha}$ are always at rest

6-20 A wave source of frequency ν and an observer are located a fixed distance apart. Both the source and observer are stationary. However, the propagation medium (through which the waves travel at speed v) is moving at a uniform velocity v_m in an arbitrary direction. If ν' is the frequency received by the observer then :
(A) $\nu' \neq \nu$
(B) $\nu' = \nu$ as the transit time from source to observer is the same for all wave fronts
(C) $\nu' < \nu$ as the transit time from source to observer is the same for all wave fronts
(D) Data Insufficient

6-21 Two wave functions in a medium along x-direction are given by,

$$y_1 = \frac{1}{2+(2x-3t)^2}\,m; \quad y_2 = -\frac{1}{2+(2x+3t-6)^2}\,m$$

where x is in metres and t is in seconds :
(A) There is no position at which resultant displacement will be zero at all times
(B) There is no time at which resultant displacement will be zero everywhere
(C) Both waves travel along the same direction
(D) Both waves travel in opposite directions

6-22 Mark correct statement(s) :
(A) Maximum pressure variation takes place at nodes
(B) In case of stationary wave, relative deformation at a point is given by $\Delta P = \frac{u}{v}$, where u is particle's velocity at that point
(C) When a stationary wave is established maximum intensity is obtained at antinodes
(D) None of these

6-23 A sine wave of wavelength λ is travelling in a medium. The minimum distance between the two particles, always having same speed, is :
(A) $\lambda/4$ (B) $\lambda/3$
(C) $\lambda/2$ (D) λ

6-24 The figure shows four progressive waves A, B, C & D. It can be concluded from the figure that with respect to wave A :

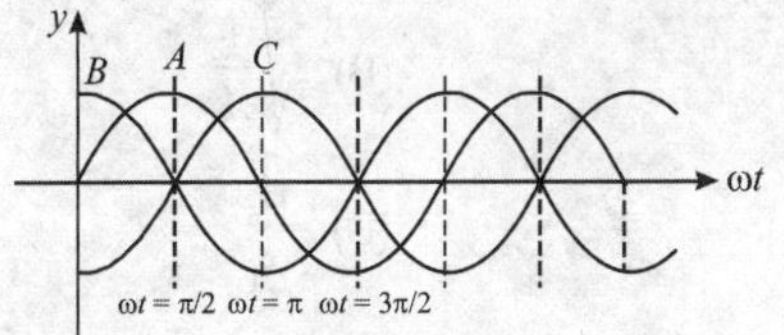

Figure 6.97

(A) The wave C is ahead by a phase angle of $\pi/2$ & the wave B lags behind by a phase angle $\pi/2$

(B) The wave C lags behind by a phase angle of $\pi/2$ & the wave B is ahead by a phase angle of $\pi/2$

(C) The wave C is ahead by a phase angle of π & the wave B lags behind by the phase angle of π

(D) The wave C lags behind by a phase angle of π & the wave B is ahead by a phase angle of π

6-25 Two radio frequency point sources S_1 and S_2, separated by distance 2.5 m are emitting waves of wavelength 1 m in same phase. A detector moves in a large circular path around the two sources in a plane containing them. The number of maxima that will be detected by it over the complete circular path, are (Assume the centre of circular path coincidence with the mid of the point sources) :

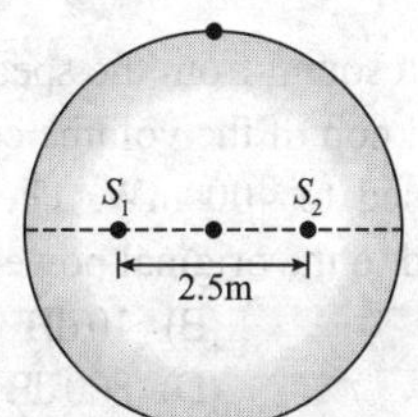

Figure 6.98

(A) 16 (B) 12
(C) 10 (D) 8

6-26 Two symmetric pulses in a stretched string whose centres are initially 8 cm apart are moving towards each other as shown in figure-6.99. The speed of each pulse is 2 cm/s. After 2 seconds the total energy of pulses will be :

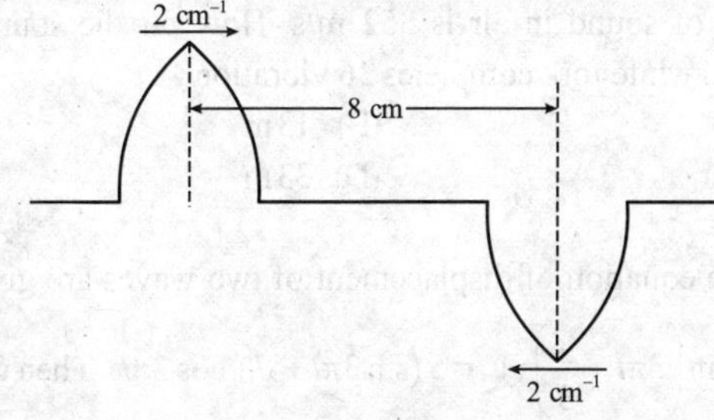

Figure 6.99

(A) Zero
(B) Purely kinetic
(C) Purely potential
(D) Partly kinetic & partly potential

6-27 The amplitude ratio of the two waves is 5 : 2. If all other conditions for the two waves are same, then what is the ratio of their energy densities ?

(A) 5:2 (B) 2:5
(C) 4:25 (D) 25:4

* * * * *

Numerical MCQs Single Options Correct

6-1 A man sets his watch by the sound of a siren placed at a distance 1 km away. If the velocity of sound is 330 m/s :
(A) His watch is set 3s faster (B) His watch is set 3s slower
(C) His watch is set correctly (D) None of the above

6-2 The frequency of a tuning fork is 384 per second and velocity of sound in air is 352 m/s. How far the sound has traversed while fork completes 36 vibration :
(A) 3 m (B) 13 m
(C) 23 m (D) 33 m

6-3 The equation of displacement of two waves are given as $y_1 = 10\sin\left(3\pi t + \frac{\pi}{3}\right)$; $y_2 = 5(\sin 3\pi t + \sqrt{3}\cos 3\pi t)$. Then what is the ratio of their amplitudes :
(A) 1 : 2 (B) 2 : 1
(C) 1 : 1 (D) None of these

6-4 Consider ten identical sources of sound all giving the same frequency but having phase angles which are random. If the average intensity of each source is I_0, the average of resultant intensity I due to all these ten sources will be :
(A) $I = 100\,I_0$ (B) $I = 10\,I_0$
(C) $I = I_0$ (D) $I = \sqrt{10}\,I_0$

6-5 The displacement-time graphs for two sound waves A and B are shown in the figure-6.100, then the ratio of their intensities I_A / I_B is equal to :

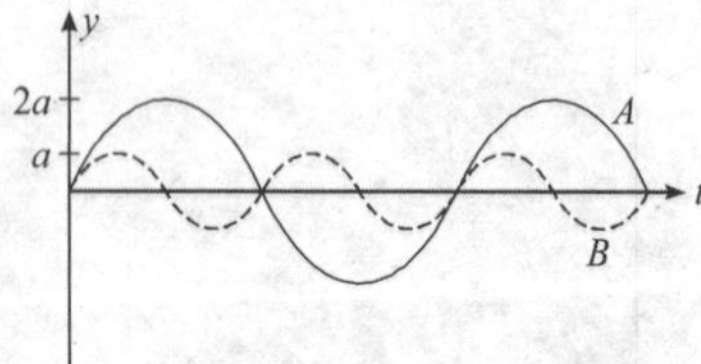

Figure 6.100

(A) 1 : 4 (B) 1 : 16
(C) 1 : 2 (D) 1 : 1

6-6 A tuning fork of frequency 340 Hz is vibrated just above the tube of 120 cm height. Water is poured slowly in the tube. What is the minimum height of water necessary for the resonance (speed of sound in the air = 340 m/sec):
(A) 15 cm (B) 25 cm
(C) 30 cm (D) 45 cm

6-7 Two monoatomic ideal gases 1 and 2 of molecular masses m_1 and m_2 respectively are enclosed in separate containers kept at the same temperature. The ratio of the speed of sound in gas 1 to that in gas 2 is given by:
(A) $\sqrt{\frac{A_1}{A_2}}$ (B) $\sqrt{\frac{A_2}{A_1}}$
(C) $\frac{A_1}{A_2}$ (D) $\frac{A_2}{A_1}$

6-8 An organ pipe is closed at one end has fundamental frequency of 1500 Hz. The maximum number of overtones generated by this pipe which a normal person can hear is :
(A) 14 (B) 13
(C) 6 (D) 9

6-9 The speed of a wave in a medium is 760 m/s. If 3600 waves are passing through a point, in the medium in 2 minutes, then its wavelength is:
(A) 13.8 m (B) 25.3 m
(C) 41.5 m (D) 57.2 m

6-10 A tuning fork sounded together with a tuning fork of frequency 256 emits two beats. On loading the tuning fork of frequency 256, the number of beats heard are 1 per second. The frequency of tuning fork is :
(A) 257 (B) 258
(C) 256 (D) 254

6-11 The power of a sound from the speaker of a radio is 20 mW. By turning the knob of the volume control, the power of the sound is increased to 400 mW. The power increase in decibels as compared to the original power is :
(A) 13 dB (B) 10 dB
(C) 20 dB (D) 800 dB

6-12 In the experiment for the determination of the speed of sound in air using the resonance column method, the length of the air column that resonates in the fundamental mode, with a tuning fork is 0.1 m. When this length is changed to 0.35 m, the same tuning fork resonates with the first overtone. Calculate the end correction:
(A) 0.012 m (B) 0.025 m
(C) 0.05 m (D) 0.024 m

6-13 An observer moves towards a stationary source of sound, with a velocity one-fifth of the velocity of sound. What is the percentage increase in the apparent frequency:
(A) 5% (B) 20%
(C) Zero (D) 0.5%

6-14 The intensity of sound from a radio at a distance of 2 metres from its speaker is $1 \times 10^{-2}\ \mu W/m^2$. The intensity at a distance of 10 meters would be :
(A) $0.2 \times 10^{-2}\ \mu W/m^2$ (B) $1 \times 10^{-2}\ \mu W/m^2$
(C) $4 \times 10^{-4}\ \mu W/m^2$ (D) $5 \times 10^{-2}\ \mu W/m^2$

6-15 A closed organ pipe of length L and an open organ pipe contain gases of densities ρ_1 and ρ_2 respectively. The compressibility of gases are equal in both the pipes. Both the pipes are vibrating in their first overtone with same frequency. The length of the open organ pipe is:

(A) $\frac{L}{3}$ (B) $\frac{4L}{3}$

(C) $\frac{4L}{3}\sqrt{\frac{\rho_1}{\rho_2}}$ (D) $\frac{4L}{3}\sqrt{\frac{\rho_2}{\rho_1}}$

6-16 In Melde's experiment, the string vibrates in 4 loops when a 50 gram weight is placed in the pan of weight 15 gram. To make the string to vibrates in 6 loops the weight that has to be removed from the pan is:

(A) 0.0007 kg wt (B) 0.0021 kg wt
(C) 0.036 kg wt (D) 0.0029 kg wt

6-17 The displacement due to a wave moving in the positive x-direction is given by $y = \frac{1}{(1+x^2)}$ at time $t = 0$ and by $y = \frac{1}{[1+(x-1)^2]}$ at $t = 2$ seconds, where x and y are in metres. The velocity of the wave in m/s is :

(A) 0.5 (B) 1
(C) 2 (D) 4

6-18 The equation of a progressive wave is given by $y = a \sin (628\,t - 31.4\,x)$. If the distances are expressed in cms and time in seconds, then the wave velocity will be :

(A) 314 cm/sec (B) 628 cm/sec
(C) 20 cm/sec (D) 400 cm/sec

6-19 Two waves are approaching each other with a velocity of 20 m/s and frequency n. The distance between two consecutive nodes is :

(A) $\frac{20}{n}$ (B) $\frac{10}{n}$

(C) $\frac{5}{n}$ (D) $\frac{n}{10}$

6-20 Consider the three waves z_1, z_2 and z_3 as $z_1 = A \sin (kx - \omega t)$, $z_2 = A \sin (kx + \omega t)$ and $z_3 = A \sin (ky - \omega t)$. Which of the following represents a standing wave :

(A) $z_1 + z_2$ (B) $z_2 + z_3$
(C) $z_3 + z_1$ (D) $z_1 + z_2 + z_3$

6-21 Equation of a progressive wave is given by $y = a \sin \pi\left[\frac{t}{2} - \frac{x}{4}\right]$, where t is in seconds and x is in meters. The distance through which the wave moves in 8 sec is (in meter):

(A) 8 (B) 16
(C) 2 (D) 4

6-22 The phase difference between two waves represented by $y_1 = 10^{-6} \sin [100\,t + (x/50) + 0.5]m$ and $y_2 = 10^{-6} \cos [100\,t + (x/50)]m$ where x is expressed in metres and t is expressed in seconds, is approximately :

(A) 1.5 rad (B) 1.07 rad
(C) 2.07 rad (D) 0.5 rad

6-23 Two waves are given by y_1 $a \sin (\omega t - kx)$ and $y_2 = a \cos (\omega t - kx)$ The phase difference between the two waves is:

(A) $\frac{\pi}{4}$ (B) π

(C) $\frac{\pi}{8}$ (D) $\frac{\pi}{2}$

6-24 Two similar sonometer wires given fundamental frequencies of 500 Hz. These have same tensions. By what amount the tension be increased in one wire so that the two wires produce 5 beats/sec :

(A) 1% (B) 2%
(c) 3% (D) 4%

6-25 A source of sound is travelling towards a stationary observer. The frequency of sound heard by the observer is of three times the original frequency. The velocity of sound is v m/s. The speed of source will be:

(A) $\frac{2}{3}v$ (B) v

(C) $\frac{3}{2}v$ (D) $3v$

6-26 A tuning fork of frequency 480 Hz produces 10 beats per second when sounded with a vibrating sonometer string. What must have been the frequency of the string if a slight increase in tension produces lesser beats per second than before :

(A) 460 Hz (B) 470 Hz
(C) 480 Hz (D) 490 Hz

6-27 A string is producing transverse vibration whose equation is $y = 0.021 \sin (x + 30t)$, Where x and y are in meters and t is in seconds. If the linear density of the string is 1.3×10^{-4} kg/m, then the tension in the string in N will be :

(A) 10 (B) 0.5
(C) 1 (D) 0.117

6-28 Two loudspeakers are emitting sound waves of wavelength λ with an initial phase difference of $\pi/2$. At what minimum distance from O on line AB will a detector detects a maxima :

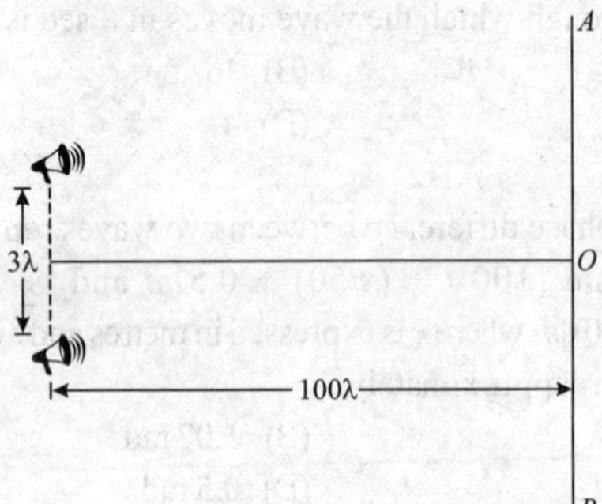

Figure 6.101

(A) 25 *l* (B) $\frac{100\lambda}{\sqrt{15}}$

(C) 50 *l* (D) $\frac{25\lambda}{3}$

6-29 A sound source is moving towards a stationary observer with 1/10 of the speed of sound. The ratio of apparent to real frequency is :

(A) 10/9 (B) 11/10

(C) $(11/10)^2$ (D) $(9/10)^2$

6-30 A string of length 0.4 m and mass 10^{-2} kg is tightly clamped at its ends. The tension in the string is 1.6 N. Identical wave pulses are produced at one end at equal intervals of time Δt. The minimum value of t which allows constructive interference between successive pulses is :

(A) 0.05 s (B) 0.10 s

(C) 0.20 s (D) 0.40 s

6-31 An earthquake generates both transverse (S) and longitudinal (P) sound waves in the earth. The speed of S waves is about 4.5 km/s and that of P waves is about 8.0 km/s. A seismograph records P and S waves from an earthquake. The first P wave arrives 4.0 min before the first S wave. The epicenter of the earthquake is located at a distance about:

(A) 25 km (B) 250 km

(C) 2500 km (D) 5000 km

6-32 Two waves are propagating to the point P along a straight line produced by two sources A and B of simple harmonic and of equal frequency. The amplitude of every wave at P is 'a' and the phase of A is ahead by $\frac{\pi}{3}$ than that of B and the distance AP is greater than BP by 50 cm. Then the resultant amplitude at the point P will be, if the wavelength is 1 meter:

(A) $2a$ (B) $a\sqrt{3}$

(C) $a\sqrt{2}$ (D) a

6-33 The superposing waves are represented by the following equations

$$y_1 = 5 \sin 2\pi(10t - 0.1x), y_2 = 10 \sin 2\pi(20t - 0.2x)$$

Ratio of intensities $\frac{I_{max}}{I_{min}}$ will be:

(A) 1 (B) 9

(C) 4 (D) 16

6-34 The correct graph between the frequency n and square root of density (ρ) of a wire, keeping its length, radius and tension constant, is

(A) 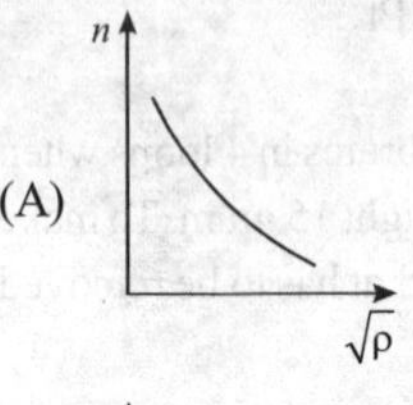

(B) 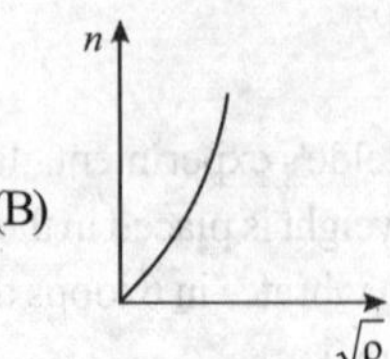

(C) 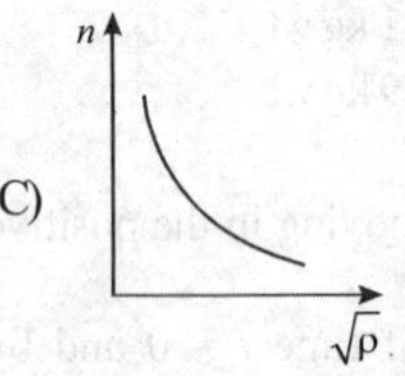

(D) 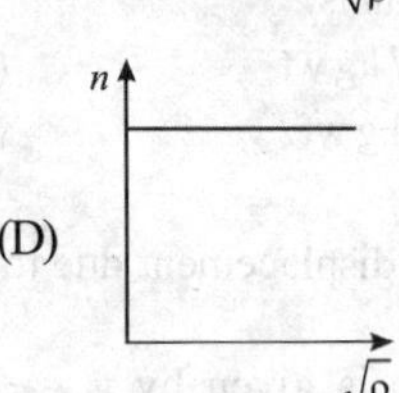

6-35 Two identical stringed instruments have frequency 100 Hz. If tension in one of them is increased by 4% and they are sounded together then the number of beats in one second is :

(A) 1 (B) 8

(C) 4 (D) 2

6-36 Which of the following function correctly represent the travelling wave equation for finite values of x and t :

(A) $y = x^2 - t^2$

(B) $y = \cos x^2 \sin t$

(C) $y = \log(x^2 - t^2) - \log(x - t)$

(D) $y = e^{2x} \sin t$

6-37 A violin string oscillating in its fundamental mode, generates a sound wave with wavelength λ. To generate a sound wave with wavelength $\lambda/2$ by the string, still oscillating in its fundamental mode, tension must be changed by the multiple :

(A) 2 (B) 1/2

(C) 4 (D) 1/4

6-38 Sinusoidal waves 5.00 cm in amplitude are to be transmitted along a string having a linear mass density equal to 4.00×10^{-2} kg/m. If the source can deliver a maximum power of 90 W and the string is under a tension of 100 N, then the highest frequency at which the source can operate is (take $\pi^2 = 10$) :

(A) 45.3 Hz (B) 50 Hz

(C) 30 Hz (D) 62.3 Hz

6-39 Wave pulse on a string shown in figure-6.102 is moving to the right without changing shape. Consider two particles at positions $x_1 = 1.5$ m and $x_2 = 2.5$ m. Their transverse velocities at the moment shown in figure are along directions :

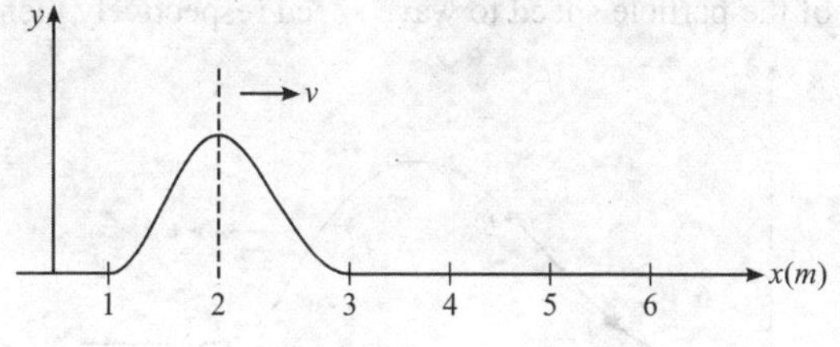

Figure 6.102

(A) positive y-axis and positive y-axis respectively
(B) negative y-axis and positive y-axis respectively
(C) positive y-axis and negative y-axis respectively
(D) negative y-axis and negative y-axis respectively

6-40 What is the percentage change in the tension necessary in a sonometer of fixed length to produce a note one octave lower (half of original frequency) than before :

(A) 25% (B) 50%
(C) 67% (D) 75%

6-41 Two identical coherent sources of wavelength λ are placed at $(100\lambda, 0)$ and $(-50\lambda, 0)$ respectively. A detector moves slowly from the origin to $(50\ \lambda, 0)$ along the x-axis. The number of minima detected are :

(A) 49 (B) 50
(C) 100 (D) 101

6-42 A 20 cm long rubber string obeys Hook's law. Initially when it is stretched to make its total length of 24 cm, the lowest frequency of resonance is n_0. It is further stretched to make its total length of 26 cm. The lowest frequency of resonance will now be :

(A) The same as n_0 (B) Greater than n_0
(C) Lower than n_0 (D) None of these

6-43 The equation of a wave is given by (all quantity expressed in *S.I.* units) $y = 5 \sin 10\pi\ (t - 0.01\ x)$ along the x-axis. The magnitude of phase difference between the points separated by a distance of 10 m along x-axis is :

(A) $\pi/2$ (B) π
(C) 2π (D) $\pi/4$

6-44 Which of the following travelling wave will produce standing wave, with node at $x = 0$, when superimposed on $y = A \sin(\omega t - kx)$:

(A) $A \sin(\omega t + kx)$ (B) $A \sin(\omega t + kx + \pi)$
(C) $A \cos(\omega t + kx)$ (D) $A \cos(\omega t + kx + \pi)$

6-45 Equation of a standing wave is generally expressed as $y = 2A \sin \omega t \cos kx$. In the equation, quantity ω/k represents :

(A) The transverse speed of the particles of the string
(B) The speed of either of the component waves
(C) The speed of the standing wave
(D) A quantity that is independent of the properties of the string

6-46 The figure shows at time $t = 0$ second, a rectangular and triangular pulse on a uniform wire are approaching each other. The pulse speed is 0.5 cm/s. The resultant pulse at $t = 2$ second is :

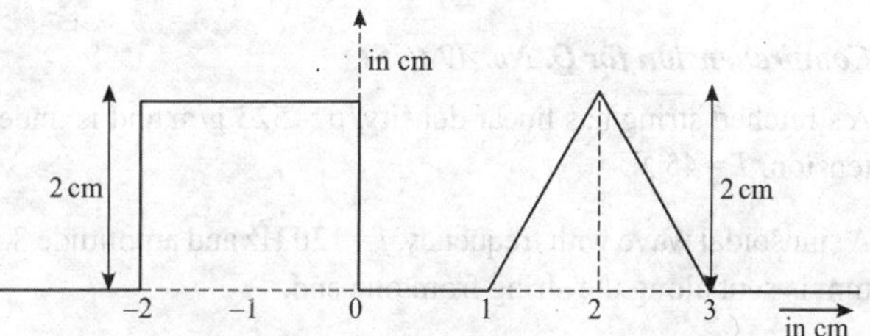

Figure 6.103

(A) (B) (C)

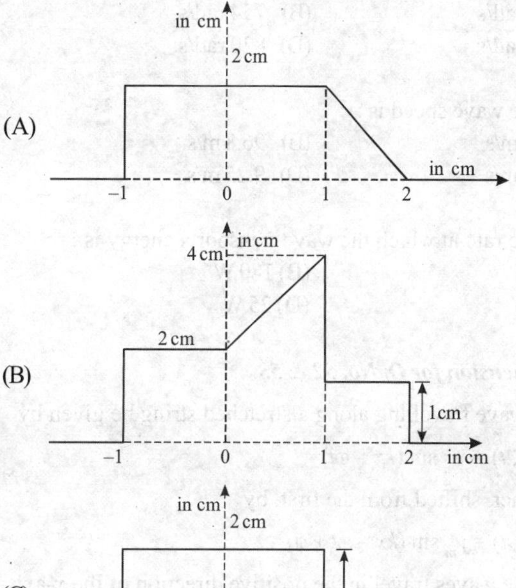

(D)

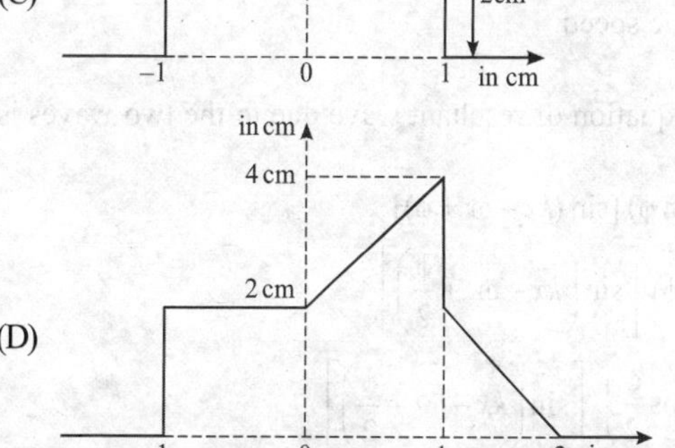

Comprehension for Q. No. 47 & 48

Difference in frequencies between 3rd overtone of closed pipe and 5th harmonic of the same pipe is 400 Hz. Further, 3rd harmonic of this closed pipe is equal to 6th harmonic of another organ pipe.

6-47 Fundamental frequencies of closed pipe and open pipe are :

(A) 200 Hz, 400 Hz (B) Hz, 75 Hz
(C) 200 Hz, 100 Hz (D) 400 Hz, 300 Hz

6-48 If speed of sound is 330 m/s. The lengths of closed pipe and open pipe are :

(A) 0.4125 m, 1.65 m (B) 3.3 m, 1.65 m
(C) 0.825 m, 0.825 m (D) 1.65 m, 0.825 m

Comprehension for Q. No. 49 to 51

A stretched string has linear density, $\mu = 525$ g/m and is under tension, $T = 45$ N.

A sinusoidal wave with frequency, $f = 120$ Hz and amplitude 8.5 mm is sent along the string from one end.

6-49 The angular frequency is :

(A) 120 rad/s (B) 754 rad/s
(C) 386 rad/s (D) 820 rad/s

6-50 The wave speed is :

(A) 62.9 m/s (B) 96.8 m/s
(C) 7.28 m/s (D) 9.25 m/s

6-51 The rate at which the wave transports energy is :

(A) 50 W (B) 180 W
(C) 100 W (D) 25 W

Comprehension for Q. No. 52 & 53

Let one wave travelling along a stretched string be given by

$$y_1(x, t) = y_m \sin(kx - \omega t)$$

and another, shifted from the first, by

$$y_2(x, t) = y_m \sin(kx - \omega t + \phi)$$

Both these waves travel in the positive direction of the x-axis, with the same speed.

6-52 The equation of resultant wave due to the two waves is $y'(x, t) =$

(A) $2ym(\sin\phi)[\sin(kx - \omega t + \phi)]$

(B) $y_m(\sin\phi)\left[\sin\left(kx - \omega t + \frac{\phi}{2}\right)\right]$

(C) $2y_m\left(\cos\frac{\phi}{2}\right)\left[\sin\left(kx - \omega t + \frac{\phi}{2}\right)\right]$

(D) $2y_m(\cos\phi)[\sin(kx - \omega t + \phi)]$

6-53 Out of the three wave equations $y_1(x, t)$, $y_2(x, t)$ and the resultant $y'(x, t)$, which wave would you actually see on the string?

(A) $y'(x, t)$ (B) $y_1(x, t)$
(C) $y_2(x, t)$ (D) All of these

6-54 A wave pulse is generated in a string that lies along x-axis. At the points A and B, as shown in figure-6.104, if R_A and R_B are ratio of the particle speed to wave speed respectively then :

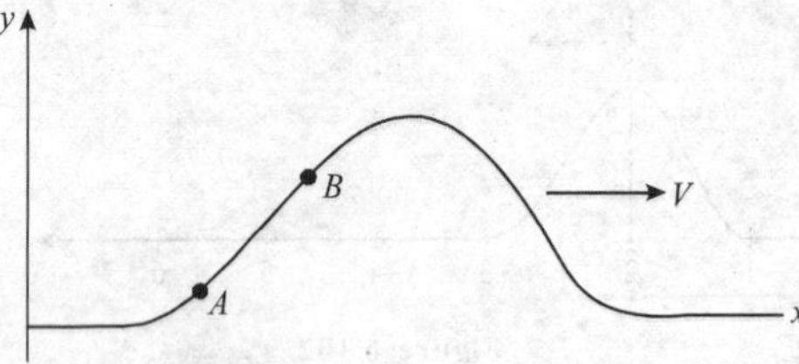

Figure 6.104

(A) $R_A > R_B$
(B) $R_B > R_A$
(C) $R_A = R_B$
(D) Information is not sufficient to decide

6-55 When a wave pulse travelling in a string is reflected from a rigid wall to which string is tied as shown in figure-6.105. For this situation two statements are given below :

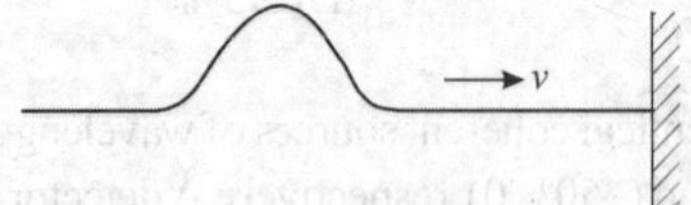

Figure 6.105

(1) The reflected pulse will be in same orientation of incident pulse due to a phase change of π radians
(2) During reflection the wall exert a force on string in upward direction

For the above given two statements choose the correct option given below.

(A) Only (1) is true (B) Only (2) is true
(C) Both are true (D) Both are wrong

6-56 A transverse wave described by equation $y = 0.02 \sin(x + 30t)$ (where x and t are in metres and sec. respectively) is travelling along a wire of area of cross-section 1 mm^2 and density 8000 kg/m^3. What is the tension in the string ?

(A) 20 N (B) 7.2 N
(C) 30 N (D) 14.4 N

6-57 Two vibrating strings of same material stretched under same tension and vibrating with same frequency in the same overtone have radii $2r$ and r. Then the ratio of their lengths is :

(A) 1 : 2 (B) 1 : 4
(C) 1 : 3 (D) 2 : 3

6-58 A wave moving with constant speed on a uniform string passes the point $x = 0$ with amplitude A_0, angular frequency ω_0 and average rate of energy transfer P_0. As the wave travels down the string it gradually loses energy and at the point $x = l$, the average rate of energy transfer becomes $\frac{P_0}{2}$. At the point

$x = l$, angular frequency and amplitude are respectively :

(A) ω_0 and $A_0/\sqrt{2}$ (B) $\omega_0/\sqrt{2}$ and A_0

(C) Less than ω_0 and A_0 (D) $\omega_0/\sqrt{2}$ and $A_0/\sqrt{2}$

6-59 A standing wave pattern is formed on a string. One of the waves is given by equation $y_1 = a\cos(\omega t - kx + \pi/3)$ then the equation of the other wave such that at $x = 0$ a node is formed :

(A) $y_2 = a\sin(\omega t + kx + \frac{\pi}{3})$

(B) $y_2 = a\cos(\omega t + kx + \frac{\pi}{3})$

(C) $y_2 = a\cos(\omega t + kx + \frac{2\pi}{3})$

(D) $y_2 = a\cos(\omega t + kx + \frac{4\pi}{3})$

6-60 The (x, y) coordinates of the corners of a square plate are $(0, 0)$ $(L, 0)$ (L, L) and $(0, L)$. The edges of the plate are clamped & transverse standing waves are set up in it. If $u(x, y)$ denotes the displacement of the plate at the point (x, y) at some instant of time, the possible expression for 'u' is : [a = positive constant]

(A) $a\cos\left(\frac{\pi x}{2L}\right)\cos\left(\frac{\pi y}{2L}\right)$ (B) $a\sin\left(\frac{\pi x}{L}\right)\sin\left(\frac{\pi y}{2L}\right)$

(C) $a\sin\left(\frac{\pi x}{L}\right)\sin\left(\frac{2\pi y}{L}\right)$ (D) $a\cos\left(\frac{2\pi x}{L}\right)\sin\left(\frac{\pi y}{L}\right)$

6-61 The particle displacement (in cm) in a stationary wave is given by $y(x, t) = 2\sin(0.1\pi x)\cos(100\pi t)$. The distance between a node and the next antinode is :

(A) 2.5 cm (B) 7.5 cm

(C) 5 cm (D) 10 cm

6-62 A wire of length 'l' having tension T and radius 'r' vibrates with fundamental frequency 'f'. Another wire of the same metal with length $2l$ having tension $2T$ and radius $2r$ will vibrate with fundamental frequency :

(A) f (B) $2f$

(C) $\frac{f}{2\sqrt{2}}$ (D) $\frac{f}{2}\sqrt{2}$

6-63 A transverse wave is propagating along $+x$ direction. At $t = 2$ sec, the particle at $x = 4$ m is at $y = 2$ mm. With the passage of time its y coordinate increases and reaches to a maximum of 4 mm. The wave equation is : (using ω and k with their usual meanings)

(A) $y = 4\sin[\omega(t+2) + k(x-2) + \frac{\pi}{6}]$

(B) $y = 4\sin[\omega(t+2) + k(x) + \frac{\pi}{6}]$

(C) $y = 4\sin[\omega(t-2) - k(x-4) + \frac{5\pi}{6}]$

(D) $y = 4\sin[\omega(t-2) - k(x-4) + \frac{\pi}{6}]$

6-64 In the figure shown strings AB and BC have masses m and $2m$ respectively. Both are of same length l. Mass of each string is uniformly distributed on its length. The string is suspended vertically from the ceiling of a room. A small jerk wave pulse is given at the end 'C'. It goes up to upper end 'A' in time 't'. If $m = 2$ kg, $l = \frac{9610}{1681}$ m, $g = 10$ m/s^2, $\sqrt{2} = 1.4$, $\sqrt{3} = 1.7$ then 't' is equal to :

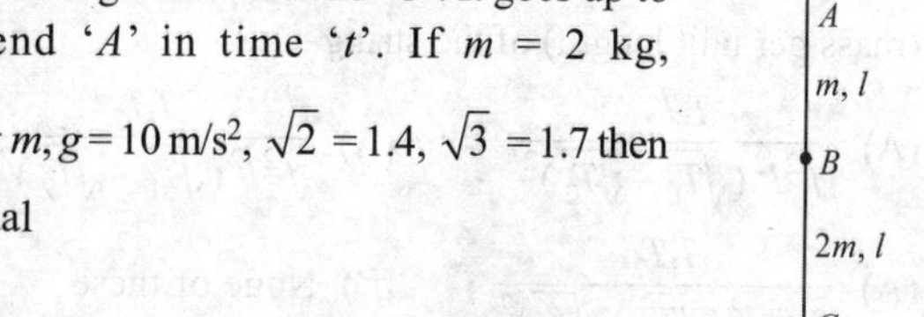

Figure 6.106

(A) $\frac{620}{697}$ s (B) $\frac{434}{205}$ s

(C) 2 s (D) None of these

6-65 A 75 cm string fixed at both ends produces resonant frequencies 384 Hz and 288 Hz without there being any other resonant frequency between these two. Wave speed for the string is :

(A) 144 m/s (B) 216 m/s

(C) 108 m/s (D) 72 m/s

6-66 A string of length 'l' is fixed at both ends. It is vibrating in its 3rd overtone with maximum amplitude 'a'. The amplitude at a distance $\frac{l}{3}$ from one end is :

(A) a (B) 0

(C) $\frac{\sqrt{3}a}{2}$ (D) $\frac{a}{2}$

6-67 A 40 cm long wire having a mass 3.2 gm and area of cross section 1 mm^2 is stretched between the support 40.05 cm apart. In its fundamental mode, it vibrates with a frequency 1000/64 Hz. Find the young's modulus of the wire in the form $X \times 10^9$ N-m^2 and fill value of X:

(A) 1 (B) 2

(C) 3 (D) 4

6-68 A string of length 1.5 m with its two ends clamped is vibrating in fundamental mode. Amplitude at the centre of the string is 4 mm. Minimum distance between the two points having amplitude 2 mm is :

(A) 1 m (B) 75 cm

(C) 60 cm (D) 50 cm

6-69 A string is fixed at both ends. The tension in the string and density of the string are accurately known but the length and the radius of cross section of the string are known with some error. If maximum errors made in the measurement of length and radius are 1% and 0.5% respectively then what is the maximum possible percentage error in the calculation of fundamental frequency of that string :

(A) 0.5% (B) 1.0%
(C) 1.5% (D) 2.0%

6-70 A string of length 'l' fixed at both ends vibrates in resonance with a tuning fork of frequency 'f' at two successive values of tension T_1 and T_2 in the string. Find the specific mass (mass per unit length) of the string :

(A) $\frac{T_1T_2}{f^2l^2(\sqrt{T_1}-\sqrt{T_2})^2}$ (A) $\frac{2T_1T_2}{f^2l^2(\sqrt{T_1}-\sqrt{T_2})^2}$

(A) $\frac{T_1T_2}{2f^2l^2(\sqrt{T_1}-\sqrt{T_2})^2}$ (D) None of these

Comprehension for Q. No. 71 to 73

A block of mass 2 m is hanging at the lower end of a rope of mass m and length the l, the other end being fixed to the ceiling. A pulse of wavelength λ_0 is produced at the lower end of the rope.

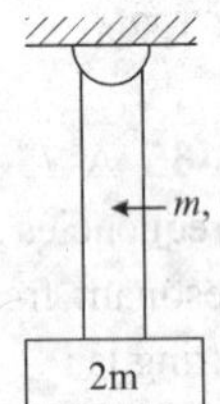

Figure 6.107

6-71 The wavelength of the pulse when it reaches the other end of the rope is :

(A) $\sqrt{3}\lambda_0$ (B) $\sqrt{\frac{3}{2}}\lambda_0$

(C) λ_0 (D) $\frac{\lambda_0}{2}$

6-72 The speed of the pulse at the mid point of rope is :

(A) $\sqrt{\frac{5}{2}gl}$ (B) $\sqrt{\frac{5}{3}gl}$

(C) $\sqrt{\frac{2}{5}gl}$ (D) $\sqrt{\frac{gl}{2}}$

6-73 The time taken by the pulse to reach the other end of the rope is :

(A) $2\sqrt{\frac{l}{g}}(\sqrt{3}-1)$ (B) $2\sqrt{\frac{l}{g}}(\sqrt{3}-2)$

(C) $2\sqrt{\frac{l}{g}}$ (D) $2\sqrt{\frac{l}{g}}(\sqrt{3}-\sqrt{2})$

Comprehension for Q. No. 74 to 76

A standing wave exists in a string of length 150 cm fixed at both ends. The displacement amplitude of a point at a distance of 10 cm from one of the ends if $5\sqrt{3}$ mm. The distance between two nearest points, within the same loop having the same displacement amplitude of $5\sqrt{3}$ is 10 nm.

6-74 The maximum displacement amplitude of the particle in the string is :

(A) 10 mm (B) $(20/\sqrt{3})$ mm
(C) $10\sqrt{3}$ mm (D) 20 mm

6-75 The mode of vibration of the string, i.e. the overtone produced is :

(A) 2 (B) 3
(C) 4 (D) 6

6-76 At what maximum distance from one end, is the potential energy of the string zero :

(A) $10\sqrt{3}$ cm (B) 15 cm
(C) 20 cm (D) 30 cm

Comprehension for Q. No. 77 to 79

A transverse sinusoidal wave is generated at one end of a long horizontal string by a bar that moves with an amplitude of 1.12 cm. The motion of the bar is continuous and is repeated regularly 120 times per second. The string has linear density of 117 g/m. The other end of the string is attached to a mass 4.68 kg. The string passes over a smooth pulley and the mass attached to the other end of the string hangs freely under gravity.

6-77 The maximum magnitude of the transverse speed is :

(A) 10.884 m/s (B) 8.44 m/s
(C) 844 m/s (D) None of these

6-78 The maximum magnitude of the transverse component of tension in the string is :

(A) Zero (B) 3.77 N
(C) 37.7 N (D) 377 N

6-79 The maximum power transferred along the string is :

(A) 3.845 kW (B) 34.85 kW
(C) 348.5 kW/d (D) None of these

6-80 The wave-function for a certain standing wave on a string fixed at both ends is $y(x, t) = 0.5 \sin(0.025\pi x) \cos 500t$ where x and y are in centimeters and t is in seconds. The shortest possible length of the string is :

(A) 126 cm (B) 160 cm
(C) 40 cm (D) 80 cm

6-81 A loop of a string of mass per unit length μ and radius R is rotated about an axis passing through centre perpendicular to the plane with an angular velocity ω. A small disturbance is created in the loop having the same sense of rotation. The linear speed of the disturbance for a stationary observer is :

(A) ωR (B) $2\omega R$
(C) $3\omega R$ (D) Zero

6-82 Graph shows three waves that are separately sent along a string that is stretched under a certain tension along *x*-axis. If ω_1, ω_2 and ω_3 are their angular frequencies respectively then :

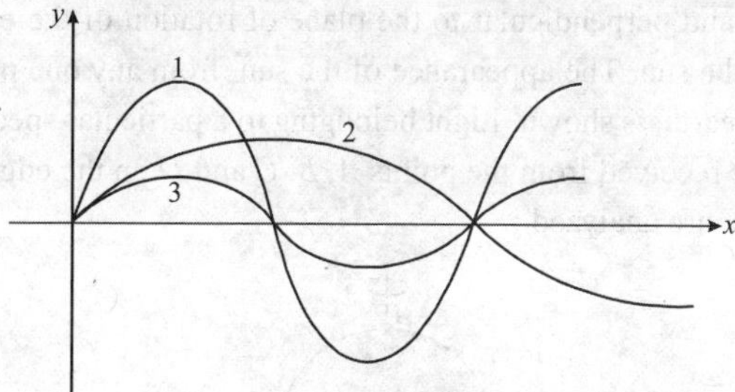

Figure 6.108

(A) $\omega_1 = \omega_3 > \omega_2$ (B) $\omega_1 > \omega_2 > \omega_3$
(C) $\omega_2 > \omega_1 = \omega_3$ (D) $\omega_1 = \omega_2 = \omega_3$

6-83 The same progressive wave is represented by two graphs I and II. Graph I shows how the displacement '*y*' varies with the distance *x*-along the wave at a given time. Graph II shows how *y* varies with time t at a given point on the wave. The ratio of measurements *AB* to *CD*, marked on the curves, represents :

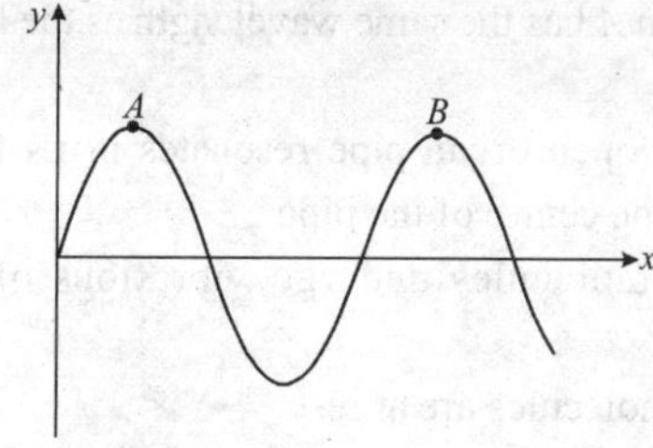

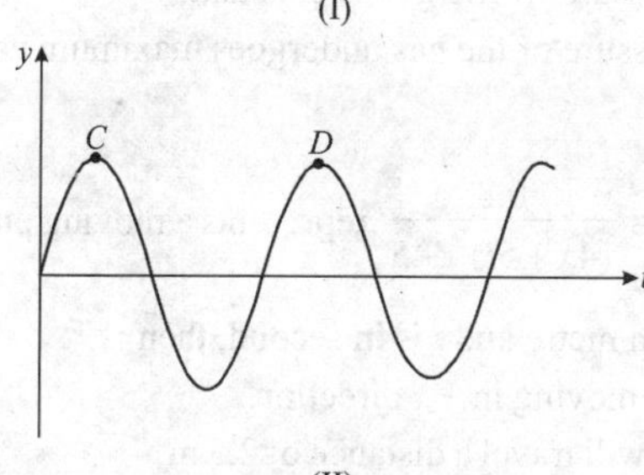

Figure 6.109

(A) Wave number *k* (B) Wave speed *V*
(C) Frequency ν (D) Angular frequency ω

6-84 A transverse periodic wave on a string with a linear mass density of 0.200 kg/m is described by the following equation $y = 0.05 \sin(420\,t - 21.0\,x)$ where *x* and *y* are in metres and *t* is in seconds. The tension in the string is equal to :
(A) 32 N (B) 42 N
(C) 66 N (D) 80 N

6-85 A certain transverse sinusoidal wave of wavelength 20 cm is moving in the positive *x*-direction. The transverse velocity of the particle at $x = 0$ as a function of time is shown. The amplitude of the motion is :

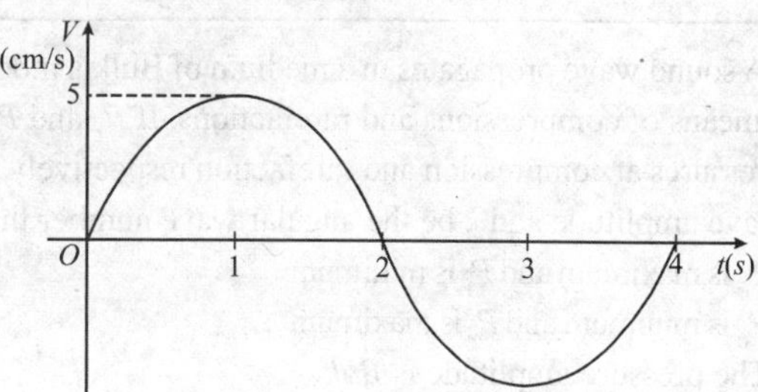

Figure 6.110

(A) $\frac{5}{\pi}$ cm (B) $\frac{\pi}{2}$ cm
(C) $\frac{10}{\pi}$ cm (D) 2π cm

6-86 Two particles of medium disturbed by the wave propagation are at $x_1 = 0$ and $x_2 = 1$ cm. The respective displacements (in cm) of the particles can be given by the equations :

$$y_1 = 2 \sin 3\pi t$$
$$y_2 = 2 \sin (3\pi t - \pi/8)$$

The wave velocity is :
(A) 16 cm/sec (B) 24 cm/sec
(C) 12 cm/sec (D) 8 cm/sec

6-87 A travelling wave $y = A \sin (kx - \omega t + \theta)$ passes from a heavier string to a lighter string. The reflected wave has amplitude 0.5 *A*. The junction of the strings is at $x = 0$. The equation of the reflected wave is :
(A) $y' = 0.5\,A \sin (kx + \omega t + \theta)$
(B) $y' = -0.5\,A \sin (kx + \omega t + \theta)$
(C) $y' = -0.5\,A \sin (\omega t - kx - \theta)$
(D) $y' = 0.5\,A \sin (kx + \omega t - \theta)$

6-88 In the above question, the displacement of particle at $t = 1$ sec and $x = 4$ cm is :
(A) 4 cm (B) 2 cm
(C) 1 cm (D) Zero

6-89 Spacing between two successive nodes in a standing wave on a string is *x*. If frequency of the standing wave is kept unchanged but tension in the string is doubled, then new spacing between successive nodes will become :
(A) $x/\sqrt{2}$ (B) $\sqrt{2}x$
(C) $x/2$ (D) $2x$

6-90 Two small boats are 10 m apart on a lake. Each pops up and down with a period of 4.0 seconds due to wave motion on the surface of water. When one boat is at its highest point, the other boat is at its lowest point. Both boats are always within a single cycle of the waves. The speed of the waves is :
(A) 2.5 m/s (B) 5.0 m/s
(C) 14 m/s (D) 40 m/s

* * * * *

Advance MCQs with One or More Options Correct

6-1 A sound wave propagates in a medium of Bulk's modulus B by means of compressions and rarefactions. If P_c and P_r are the pressures at compression and rarefaction respectively, a be the wave amplitude and k be the angular wave number then,
(A) P_c is maximum and P_r is minimum
(B) P_c is minimum and P_r is maximum
(C) The pressure amplitude is Bak
(D) If the displacement wave is $y = a \sin (\omega t - kx)$, the pressure wave at any instant is represented as $P = P_c \cos (\omega t - kx)$ which leads displacement wave by a phase angle of $\frac{\pi}{2}$

6-2 A driver in a stationary car blows a horn which produces monochromatic sound waves of frequency 1000 Hz normally towards a reflecting wall. The wall approaches the car with a speed of 3.3 ms^{-1} :
(A) The frequency of sound reflected from wall and heard by the driver is 1020 Hz
(B) The frequency of sound reflected from wall and heard by the driver is 980 Hz
(C) The percentage increase in frequency of sound after reflected from wall is 2%
(D) The percentage decrease in frequency of sound after reflected from wall is 2%

6-3 The equation of a wave is $y = 4 \sin \left[\frac{\pi}{2}\left(2t + \frac{1}{8}x\right)\right]$ where y and x are in cm and t is in second :
(A) The amplitude, wavelength, velocity and frequency of wave are 4 cm, 16 cm, 32 cms^{-1} and 1 Hz respectively with wave propagating along $+x$ direction
(B) The amplitude, wavelength, velocity and frequency of wave are 4 cm, 32 cm, 16 cms^{-1} and 0.5 Hz respectively with wave propagating along $-x$ direction
(C) Two positions occupied by the particle at time interval of 0.4 s have a phase difference of 0.4 π radian
(D) Two positions occupied by the particle at separation of 12 cm have a phase difference of 135°

6-4 A sinusoidal wave $y_i = a \sin (\omega t - kx)$ is reflected from a rigid support and the reflected wave superposes with the incident wave, y_i. Assume the rigid support to be at $x = 0$,
(A) Stationary wave are obtained with antinode at the rigid support
(B) Stationary wave are obtained with node at the rigid support
(C) Stationary waves are obtained with intensity varying periodically with distance
(D) Stationary wave are obtained with intensity varying periodically with time

6-5 Assume that the sun rotates about an axis through its centre and perpendicular to the plane of rotation of the earth about the sun. The appearance of the sun, from any one point on the earth, is shown. Light belonging to a particular spectral line, as received from the points A, B, C and D on the edge of the sun, are analyzed :

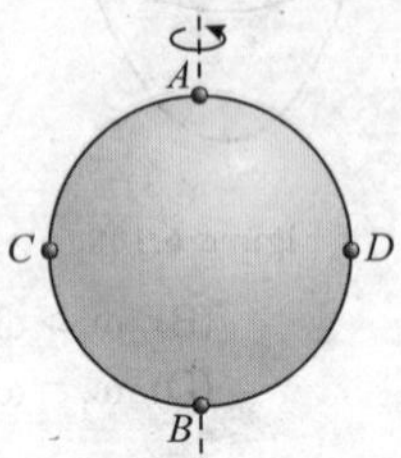

Figure 6.111

(A) Light from all four points have the same wavelength
(B) Light from C has greater wavelength than the light from D
(C) Light from D has greater wavelength than the light from C
(D) Light from A has the same wavelength as the light from B

6-6 When an open organ pipe resonates in its fundamental mode then at the centre of the pipe :
(A) The gas molecules undergo vibrations of maximum amplitude
(B) The gas molecules are at rest
(C) The pressure of the gas is constant
(D) The pressure of the gas undergoes maximum variation

6-7 $y(x, t) = \frac{0.8}{(4x + 5t)^2 + 5}$ represents a moving pulse, where x and y are in metre and t is in second, then :
(A) Pulse is moving in $+x$ direction
(B) In 2 s it will travel a distance of 2.5 m
(C) Its maximum displacement is 0.16 m
(D) It is a symmetric pulse

6-8 In a wave motion $y = a \sin (kx - \omega t)$, y can represent :
(A) Electric field
(B) Magnetic field
(C) Displacement
(D) Pressure

6-9 A wave travelling in a stretched string is described by the equation $y = A \sin (\omega t - kx)$. The maximum particle velocity is :
(A) $A\omega$
(B) $\frac{\omega}{k}$
(C) $\frac{d\omega}{dk}$
(D) $\frac{x}{t}$

6-10 In Q. No. 6-9,

(A) Wave velocity is $\frac{\omega}{k}$ (B) Group velocity is $\frac{d\omega}{dk}$

(C) Wave velocity is $A\omega$ (D) Group velocity is $A\omega$

6-11 As a wave propagates :

(A) The wave intensity remains constant for a plane wave

(B) The wave intensity decreases as the inverse of the distance from the source for a spherical wave

(C) The wave intensity decreases as the inverse square of the distance from the source for a spherical wave

(D) Total power of the spherical wave over the spherical surface centred at the source remains constant at all times

6-12 Any progressive wave equation in differential form is :

(A) $\frac{1}{\omega^2}\frac{\partial^2 y}{\partial t^2}=\frac{1}{k^2}\frac{\partial^2 y}{\partial x^2}$ (B) $\frac{1}{\omega}\frac{\partial y}{\partial t}=-\frac{1}{k}\frac{\partial y}{\partial x}$

(C) $\frac{1}{\omega^2}\frac{\partial^2 y}{\partial t^2}=-\frac{1}{k^2}\frac{\partial^2 y}{\partial x^2}$ (D) $\frac{1}{\omega}\frac{\partial y}{\partial t}=\frac{1}{k}\frac{\partial y}{\partial x}$

6-13 Two wave of nearly same amplitude, same frequency travelling with same velocity are superimposing to give phenomenon of interference. If a_1 and a_2 be their respective amplitudes, ω be the frequency for both, v be the velocity for both and $\Delta\phi$ is the phase difference between the two waves then,

(A) The resultant intensity varies periodically with time and distance

(B) The resultant intensity with $\frac{I_{\min}}{I_{\max}}=\left(\frac{a_1-a_2}{a_1+a_2}\right)^2$ is obtained for coherent waves travelling in the same direction.

(C) Both the waves must have constant phase difference at any point all the time.

(D) $I_R = I_1 + I_2 + 2\sqrt{I_1 I_2}\cos(\Delta\phi)$, where constructive interference is obtained for path differences that are odd multiple of $\frac{1}{2}\lambda$ and destructive interference is obtained for path differences that are even multiple of $\frac{1}{2}\lambda$

6-14 Two sine waves of slightly different frequencies f_1 and f_2 ($f_1 > f_2$) with zero phase difference, same amplitude, travelling in the same direction superimpose :

(A) Phenomenon of beats is always observed by human ear

(B) Intensity of resultant wave is a constant

(C) Intensity of resultant wave varies periodically with time with maximum intensity $4a^2$ and minimum intensity zero

(D) A maxima appears at a time $\frac{1}{2(f_1-f_2)}$ later (or earlier) than a minima appears

6-15 The displacement of a particle in a medium due to a wave travelling in the x-direction through the medium is given by $y = A\sin(\alpha t - \beta x)$, where t = time, and α and β are constants :

(A) The frequency of the wave is α

(B) The frequency of the wave is $\alpha/(2\pi)$

(C) The wavelength is $(2\pi)/\beta$

(D) The velocity of the wave is α/β

6-16 A wave is represented by the equation

$$y = a\sin\left(10\pi x + 15\pi t + \frac{\pi}{3}\right)$$

where x is in metre and t is in second. The expression represents :

(A) A wave travelling in the positive x-direction with a velocity of 1.5 ms^{-1}

(B) A wave travelling in the negative x-direction with a velocity of 1.5 ms^{-1}

(C) A wave travelling in the negative x-direction with a wavelength of 0.2 m

(D) A wave travelling in the positive x-direction with a wavelength of 0.2 m

6-17 Consider a harmonic wave travelling on a string of mass per unit length μ. The wave has a velocity v, amplitude A and frequency f. The power transmitted by a harmonic wave on the string is proportional to (take constant of proportionality as $2\pi^2$):

(A) μ (B) v

(C) A^2 (D) f^2

6-18 Standing wave can be produced :

(A) In a string clamped at both the ends

(B) In a string clamped at one end and free at the other

(C) When incident wave gets reflected from the wall superimpose

(D) When two identical waves with a phase difference of π are moving in the same direction superimpose

6-19 For a sine wave passing through a medium, let y be the displacement of a particle, v be its velocity and a be its acceleration :

(A) y, v and a are always in the same phase

(B) y and a are always in opposite phase

(C) Phase difference between y and v is $\pi/2$

(D) Phase difference between v and a is $\pi/2$

6-20 P, Q and R are three particles of a medium which lie on the x-axis. A sine wave of wavelength λ is travelling through the medium in the x-direction. P and Q always have the same speed, while P and R always have the same velocity. The minimum distance between :

(A) P and Q is $\lambda/2$ (B) P and Q is λ

(C) P and R is $\lambda/2$ (D) P and R is λ

6-21 A transverse simple harmonic wave is travelling on a string. The equation of the wave :

(A) Is the general equation for displacement of a particle of the string at any instant t

(B) Is the equation of the shape of the string at any instant t

(C) Must have sinusoidal form

(D) Is an equation of displacement for the particle at any one end at a particular time t

6-22 A sound wave passes from a medium A to a medium B. The velocity of sound in B is greater than in A. Assume that there is no absorption or reflection at the boundary. As the wave moves across the boundary :

(A) The frequency of sound will not change

(B) The wavelength will increase

(C) The wavelength will decrease

(D) The intensity of sound will not change

6-23 In a stationary wave system, all the particles of the medium :

(A) Have zero displacement simultaneously at some instant

(B) Have maximum displacement simultaneously at some instant

(C) Are at rest simultaneously at some instant

(D) Reach maximum velocity simultaneously at some instant

6-24 In the previous Q. No. 6-23, all the particles of the medium :

(A) Vibrate in the same phase

(B) In the region between two antinodes vibrate in the same phase

(C) In the region between two nodes vibrate in the same phase

(D) On either side of a node vibrate in opposite phase

6-25 Two simple harmonic waves are represented by the equations given as

$$y_1 = 0.3\sin(314t - 1.57x)$$
$$y_2 = 0.1\sin(314t - 1.57x + 1.57)$$

where x, y_1 and y_2 are in metre and t is in second, then we have:

(A) $v_1 = v_2 = 50$ Hz

(B) $\lambda_1 = \lambda_2 = 4$ m

(C) Ratio of intensity is 9

(D) y_2 leads y_1 by a phase angle of $\frac{\pi}{2}$

6-26 Two waves $y_1 = a\sin(\omega t - kx)$ and $y_2 = a\cos(\omega t - kx)$ superimpose at a point :

(A) The resultant amplitude is $\sqrt{2}a$

(B) If I is the intensity of each source then $I_{max} = 2I$

(C) The resultant wave leads y_1 by a phase angle of $\frac{\pi}{4}$

(D) Data insufficient to arrive at options (B) and (C)

6-27 Plane harmonic wave of frequency 500 Hz are produced in air with displacement amplitude of 10 micron. Given that density of air is 1.29 kgm^{-3} and speed of sound in air is 340 ms^{-1} :

(A) The pressure amplitude is 13.76 Nm^{-2}

(B) The energy density is 6.45×10^{-4} Jm^{-3}

(C) The energy flux is 0.22 Jm^{-2} s^{-1}

(D) Only (A) and (C) are correct

6-28 Two waves travelling in opposite directions produce a standing wave. The individual wave functions are given by $y_1 = 4\sin(3x - 2t)$ cm and $y_2 = 4\sin(3x + 2t)$ cm, where x and y are in cm :

(A) The maximum displacement of the motion at $x = 2.3$ cm is 4.63 cm

(B) The maximum displacement of the motion at $x = 2.3$ cm is 5.32 cm

(C) Nodes are formed at x values given by $0, \frac{\pi}{3}, \frac{2\pi}{3}, \pi, \frac{4\pi}{3}, \ldots$

(D) Antinodes are formed at x values given by $\frac{\pi}{6}, \frac{\pi}{2}, \frac{5\pi}{6}, \frac{7\pi}{6}, \ldots$

6-29 Two waves travelling in a medium in the x-direction are represented by $y_1 = A\sin(\alpha t - \beta x)$ and $y_2 = A\cos(\beta x + \alpha t - \pi/4)$, where y_1 and y_2 are the displacement of the particles of the medium, t is time, α and β are constant. The two waves have different :

(A) Speeds (B) Directions of propagation

(C) Wavelengths (D) Frequencies

6-30 Velocity of sound in air is :

(A) Faster in dry air than in moist air

(B) Directly proportional to pressure

(C) Directly proportional to temperature

(D) Independent of pressure of air

* * * * *

Unsolved Numerical Problems for Preparation of NSEP, INPhO & IPhO

For detailed preparation of INPhO and IPhO students can refer advance study material on www.physicsgalaxy.com

6-1 Write down the equation of a wave travelling in the negative direction along x-axis with an amplitude 0.01 m, a frequency 550 Hz and a speed 330 m/s.

Ans. [$y = 0.01 \sin (1100\ \pi t + 10\ \pi x/3)$]

6-2 Calculate the velocity of sound in a gas in which two waves of length 50 cm and 50.4 cm produce 6 beats per second.

Ans. [378 m/s]

6-3 Speed of sound in hydrogen is 1270 m/s. Calculate the speed of sound in the mixture of oxygen and hydrogen in which they are mixed in 1 : 4 ratio.

Ans. [635 m/s]

6-4 When a train is approaching the observer, the frequency of the whistle is 100 Hz when it has passed the observer, it is 50 Hz. Calculate the frequency when the observer moves with the train.

Ans. [66.6 Hz]

6-5 The speed of longitudinal wave is 100 times, then the speed of transverse wave in a brass wire. What is the stress in wire ? The Young's modulus of brass is 1.0×10^{11} N/m^2.

Ans. [1.0×10^7 N/m^2]

6-6 A copper wire is held at the two ends by rigid supports. At 30°C the wire is just taut, with negligible tension. Find the speed of transverse waves in this wire at 10°C ($\alpha = 1.7 \times 10^{-5}$°C^{-1}, $Y = 1.3 \times 10^{11}$ N/m^2, $d = 9 \times 10^3$ kg/m^3).

Ans. [70 m/s]

6-7 A train approaching a hill at a speed of 40 km/hr sounds a whistle of frequency 580 Hz when it is at a distance of 1 km from a hill. A wind with a speed of 40 km/hr is blowing in the direction of motion of the train. Find (i) the frequency of the whistle as heard by an observer on the hill, (ii) the distance from the hill at which the echo from the hill is heard by the driver and its frequency (Velocity of sound in air 1,200 km/hr)

Ans. [(i) 599.3 Hz, (ii) (29/30) km, 618.66 Hz]

6-8 A wave of frequency 500 Hz has a phase velocity of 350 m/s. (a) How far apart are two points 60° out of phase ? (b) What is the phase difference between two displacements at a certain point at time 10^{-3} s apart ?

Ans. [(a) 0.116 m, (b) π]

6-9 The velocity of sound in air at 14°C is 340 m/s. What will it be when the pressure of the gas is doubled and its temperature is raised to 157.5°C ?

Ans. [416.41 m/s]

6-10 A steel wire of length 1 metre, mass 0.1 kg and uniform cross sectional area 10^{-6} m^2 is rigidly fixed at both ends. The temperature of the wire is lowered by 20°C. If transverse wave are set up by plucking the string in the middle, calculate the frequency of the fundamental mode of vibration.
Young's modulus of steel = 2×10^{11} N/m^2, coefficient of linear expansion of steel = 1.21×10^{-5}°C^{-1}.

Ans. [11 Hz]

6-11 The equation $y = A \sin 2\pi (500\,t - x/\lambda)$ represents a wave. Speed of wave is 360 m/s. Calculate
(a) wavelength of wave
(b) distance between two points which are $\pi/3$ out of phase.

Ans. [0.72 m]

6-12 Which of the following represents (a) a progressive wave and (b) a stationary wave ?
(a) $y = 2 \cos 5x \sin 9t$, (b)
(b) $y = 2\sqrt{x - vt}$,
(c) $y = \sin (5x - 0.5t) + 4 \cos (5x - 0.5t)$
(d) $y = \cos x \sin t + \cos 2x \cdot \sin 2t$. If progressive, and its velocity

Ans. [(a) stationary, (b) not a wave, (c) progressive, $v = 0.1$ m/s, (d) stationary]

6-13 The velocity of sound in hydrogen is 1270 m/s at 0°C and the frequency of a fork is 335 Hz. Find the distance travelled by sound in hydrogen at 0°C and 30°C in the time in which the fork completes 71 vibrations.

Ans. [254 m, 267.6 m]

6-14 At what temperature is the velocity of sound in nitrogen equal to its velocity in oxygen at 20°C ? The atomic weights of oxygen and nitrogen are in the ratio 16 : 14.

Ans. [635 m/s]

6-15 Calculate the velocity of sound in a mixture of two gases obtained by mixing v_1 and v_2 volumes of them if the velocity of sound in them be c_1 and c_2. The atomicity of the gases is the same.

Ans. [$c_{mix} = c_1 c_2 \sqrt{\dfrac{v_1 + v_2}{v_1 c_1^2 + v_2 c_2^2}}$]

6-16 Calculate the velocity of sound in a mixture of two gases, obtained by mixing m_1 and m_2 of them if the velocity of sound in the two gases be c_1 and c_2 respectively. The atomicity of the two gases is the same.

Ans. [$\sqrt{\dfrac{m_1c_1^2 + m_2c_2^2}{m_1 + m_2}}$]

6-17 Calculate the frequency of a note emitted by a wire 20 cm in length when stretched by a weight 8 kg, if 2 m of the wire is found to weight 4 g. Also calculate the velocity of transverse wave along the string.

Ans. [495, 198 m/s]

6-18 In a spectrum of light a luminous heavenly body, the wavelength of a particular line is measured to be 3737 Å, while actual wavelength of the line is 3700 Å. What is the relative velocity of the heavenly body with respect to earth ?

Ans. [3×10^6 m/s]

6-19 A wire 50 cm long vibrates 100 times per second. If the length is shortened to 30 cm and the stretching force is quadrupled, what will be the frequency ?

Ans. [333.33 Hz]

6-20 A sensitive microphone with its receiving surface turned towards a long vertical wall is placed at a distance of 2 m from the wall. A strong source of sound of 500 Hz is placed between the wall and microphone on the line perpendicular to the wall and passing through the position of microphone. Find the position of the source where no sound will be heard in the microphone. (velocity of sound in air = 350 m/s)

Ans. [at distances 0.175 m, 0.525 m, 0.875 m, 1.225 m, 1.575 m and 1.925 m from the wall.]

6-21 A tuning fork with a frequency at 340 Hz is vibrated just above a cylindrical tube 1.20 m long. Water is slowly poured in the tube. At what lengths of the air column will resonance take place ? (Velocity of sound in air at room temperature = 340 m/s.

Ans. [0.25 m and 0.75 m]

6-22 A man sets his watch by the noon-whistle of a factory at a distance of 1.5 kilometres. By how many seconds is his watch slower than the clock of the factory ? (Velocity of sound in air is 332 m/s)

Ans. [4.52 s]

6-23 When two tuning forks are sounded together, 4 beats per second are heard. One of the forks is in unison with 0.96 metre length of sonometer wire and the other is in unison with 0.97 metre length of the same wire. Calculate the frequency of each fork.

Ans. [384 Hz, 388 Hz]

6-24 A bridge is placed under the string of a monochord at a point near the middle and it is found that the two parts produce 3 beats per second when the stretching force is 8 kg. If the load be then increased to 12 kg, determine the rate of beating of the two parts of the string.

Ans. [3.67]

6-25 A whistle emitting a sound of frequency 440 Hz is tied to a string of 1.5 m length and rotated with an angular velocity of 20 rad/s in the horizontal plane. Calculate the range of frequencies heard by an observer stationed at a large distance from the whistle.

Ans. [403 Hz to 484 Hz]

6-26 An under-water swimmer sends a sound signal to the surface. If it produces 5 beats per second when compared with the fundamental tone of a pipe of 20 cm length closed at one end, what is the wavelength of sound in water ? (v_{air} = 360 m/s and v_{water} = 1500 m/s)

Ans. [329 cm or 337 cm]

6-27 One end of a string of length 120 cm is tied to a peg and the other end is attached to a weightless ring that can slide along a frictionless vertical rod fixe at a distance slightly greater than 120 cm. Find the three longest possible wavelengths.

Ans. [480 cm, 160 cm, 96 cm]

6-28 The minimum intensity of audibility of a source is 10^{-12} W/m^2. If the frequency of the note is 1000 Hz, calculate the amplitude of vibrations of air particles. Density of air = 1.293 kg/m^3 and velocity of sound = 340 m/s.

Ans. [1.07×10^{-11} m]

6-29 A plane wave $y = A \cos(\omega t - kx)$ propagates in the reference frame S. Find the equation of this wave in a reference frame S' moving in the + ve direction of x-axis with a constant velocity V relative to S.

Ans. [$y = A \cos\left[\omega\left(1 - \frac{V}{v}\right)t - kx'\right]$]

6-30 The intensity of a sound wave 20 m away from the sound source is 3×10^{-9} W/m^2. Find the intensity of the wave 32 m away from the source, if the half-thickness for sound of this frequency is 120 m.

Ans. [2.8 nW/m^2]

6-31 A load of 20 kg is suspended by a steel wire as shown in figure-6.112. Velocity of wave when rubbed with a resigned cloth along the length is 20 times the velocity of the wave in the same string when it is plucked. Find the area of cross-section of the wire if Y for steel is 19.6×10^{10} N/m^2 and $g = 9.8$ m/s^2.

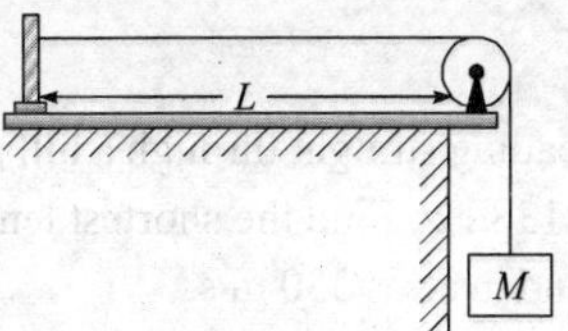

Figure 6.112

Ans. [0.004 cm^2]

6-32 A policemen blows a whistle of frequency 330 Hz as a car speeds and passed him with a velocity 18 km per hour. Find the change in frequency as heard by the driver of the car just as he passes the policeman. (Velocity of sound = 320 m/s).

Ans. [9.2 Hz]

6-33 A wire of uniform cross-section is suspended vertically from a fixed point; with a load attached at the lower end. Show that the change in frequency related to the altered frequency of the wire due to rise in temperature is $\approx \frac{1}{2}\alpha t$, where α is the linear coefficient of expansion of the wire and t°C is small rise in temperature.

6-34 Standing waves are produced by superposition of two waves

$$y_1 = 0.05 \sin(3\pi t - 2x),$$

and $$y_2 = 0.05 \sin(3\pi t + 2x),$$

where x and y are measured in metre and t in second. Find the amplitude of the particle at $x = 0.5$ m.

Ans. [0.054 m]

6-35 A ship steams towards a hill in the sea and sounds its siren and the echo is heard after 6 s. The siren is sounded again 3 minutes later after the first sounding and the echo is heard after 4 s. If the velocity of the ship is 6.87 km/hr, calculate the velocity of sound in air.

Ans. [341.6 m/s]

6-36 A source of sonic oscillations with frequency n_0 and a receiver are located on the same normal to the wall. Both the source and the receiver are stationary and the wall recedes from source with velocity u. Find the beat frequency registered by the receiver. The velocity of sound is equal to v.

Ans. [$\frac{2un_0}{u+v}$]

6-37 An organ pipe 17 cm long open at one end radiates a tone of frequency 1.5 kHz at temperature 16°C. What harmonic is this ? What is the fundamental frequency of these oscillations velocity of sound at NTP is $v = 330$ m/s.

Ans. [Third harmonic, 489.3 Hz]

6-38 A string is stretched between a pulley and a wave generator consisting of a plate vibrating up and down with small amplitude and frequency 120 Hz. The standing wave pattern has 4 nodes as shown. What should be the load required to produce a standing wave with 5 nodes.

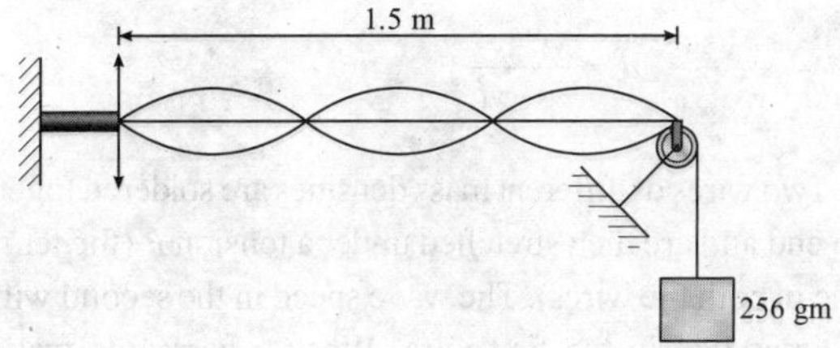

Figure 6.113

Ans. [144.00]

6-39 One end of each of two identical springs, each of force constant 0.5 N/m, are attached on the positive sides of a wooden block of mass 0.01 kg. The other ends of the springs are connected to separate rigid supports such that the springs are unstretched and are collinear in a horizontal plane. To the wooden pieces is fixed a pointer which touches a vertically moving plane paper. The wooden piece, kept on a smooth horizontal table is now displaced by 0.02 m along the line of spring and released. If the speed of the paper is 0.1 m/s. Find the equation of the path traced by the pointer on the paper and distance between two consecutive maxima of this path.

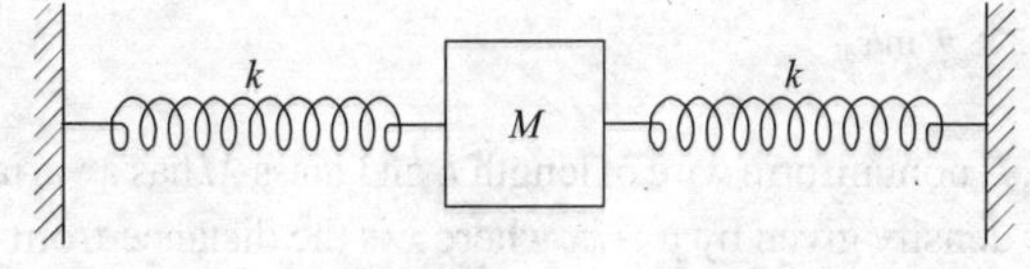

Figure 6.114

Ans. [$y = 0.02 \sin(10t - 100x)$]

6-40 A note of frequency 300 Hz has an intensity of 1 microwatt per square metre. What is the amplitude of the air vibrations caused by this sound ? (Density of air = 1.293 kg/m^3 and velocity of sound in air = 332 m/s)

Ans. [3.62×10^{-8} m]

6-41 A source of sound with natural frequency ν_0 moves uniformly along a straight line separated from a stationary observer by a distance l. The velocity of the source is equal to η fraction of velocity of sound. Find the frequency of sound received by the observer at the moment when the source gets closest to him and also find the distance between the source and the observer at the moment, when the observer receives a frequency $\nu = \nu_0$.

Ans. [$\nu = \frac{\nu_0}{1-\eta^2}$]

6-42 A wire when stretched by the weight of a solid, gives a fundamental frequency ν; when the solid is immersed in water it gives a frequency ν_1 and when immersed in liquid it gives a frequency of ν_2. Calculate the specific gravity of the solid and that of the liquid.

Ans. [$d_s = \frac{\nu^2}{\nu^2 - \nu_1^2}$; $d_l = \frac{\nu^2 - \nu_2^2}{\nu^2 - \nu_1^2}$]

6-43 Two wires of different mass densities are soldered together end to end and are then stretched under a tension F (the tension is same in both the wires). The wave speed in the second wire is three times that in the first wire. When a harmonic wave is travelling in the first wire, it is reflected at the junction of the wires; the reflected wave has half the amplitude of the incident wave. (a) If the amplitude of incident wave is A, what are the amplitudes of the reflected and transmitted waves ? (b) Assuming no loss in wire, what fraction of the incident power is reflected at the junction and what fraction is transmitted ? (c) Show that the displacement just to the left of the junction equals that just to the right of the junction.

Ans. [(a) $A_r = \frac{A}{2}$, $A_t = \frac{3A}{2}$; (b) $P_r = \frac{P_{in}}{4}$, $P_t = \frac{3P_{in}}{4}$; (c) $A_t = A + A_r = A_t$]

6-44 Calculate the velocity of sound in a mixture of oxygen, nitrogen and argon at 0°C when their masses are in the ratio 2 : 7 : 1. The molecular weights of gases are 32, 28 and 40 respectively.

Ans. [328.7 m/s]

6-45 A nonuniform wire of length L and mass M has a variable linear density given by $\mu = kx$ where x is the distance from one end of the wire and k is a constant. Find the time required for a pulse generated at one end of the wire to travel to the other end when tension in the wire is T.

Ans. [$\frac{2}{3}\sqrt{\frac{2ML}{T}}$]

6-46 Microwaves which travel with the speed of light are reflected from a distant aeroplane approaching the wave source radar. It is found that when the reflected waves are beat against the waves radiated from the source, the beat frequency is 990 Hz. If the microwaves are 0.1 m in wavelength, what is the approaching speed of the aeroplane.

Ans. [49.5 m/s]

6-47 A man walks towards a cliff while beating a drum at the rate of 5 beats per second till the echo of beating disappears completely. He walks at the rate of 8 kilometres per hour. Calculate the distance of the man from the cliff in the beginning if he walked for 5 minutes. (Velocity of sound in air = 350 m/s)

Ans. [702 m]

6-48 A tunnel leading straight through a hill greatly amplifies tones at 135 and 138 Hz. Find the shortest length of the tunnel if velocity of sound in air is 330 m/s.

Ans. [55 m]

6-49 A smoked plate falls vertically under gravity. A tuning fork traces wave on it. It is found that the lengths of two consecutive groups of 10 waves are 5.143 and 6.64 cm respectively. What is the frequency of the fork ?

Ans. [256 Hz]

6-50 A sonometer wire under tension of 64 newton vibrating in its fundamental mode is in resonance with a vibrating tuning fork. The vibrating portion of the sonometer wire has a length of 10 cm and a mass of one gm. The vibrating tuning fork is now moved a way from the vibrating wire with a constant speed and an observer standing near sonometer hears one beat per second. Calculate the speed with which the tuning fork is moved, if velocity of sound in air is 300 m/s.

Ans. [0.752 m/s]

6-51 Sources separated by 20 m vibrate according to equations $y_1' = 0.06 \sin \pi t$ metre and $y_2' = 0.02 \sin \pi t$ metre. They send out waves along a rod at speed 3 m/s. What is the equation of motion of a particle 12 m from the first source and 8 metre from the second ?

Ans. [$0.05 \sin \pi t - 0.0173 \cos \pi t$]

6-52 A wire of density 9 g/cm^3 is stretched between two clamps 100 cm apart. While subjected to an extension of 0.05 cm, what is the lowest frequency of transverse vibrations in the wire, assuming Young's modulus of the material to be 9×10^{11} dyne/cm^2.

Ans. [$25\sqrt{2} = 35.35$ Hz]

6-53 Ordinary cotton thread, 200 cm of which weighs 1 g, is used in Melde's experiment. It is attached at one end to a vibrator of frequency 100 Hz and at the other to a pan weighing 6 g. What length of the string will vibrate in 4 loops in the longitudinal arrangement if 10 g weight is put on the pan ?

Ans. [0.708 m]

6-54 A heavy ball is suspended from the ceiling of a motor car through a light string. A transverse pulse travels at a speed of 60 cm/s on the string when the car is at rest and 62 cm/s when the car acceleration on a horizontal road. Find the acceleration of the car. Take $g = 10$ m/s^2.

Ans. [3.7 m/s^2]

6-55 The difference between the apparent frequency of a source of sound as perceived by an observer during its approach and recession is 2% of the natural frequency of the source. Find the velocity of the source. Take the velocity of sound as 350 m/s.

Ans. [3.5 m/s]

6-56 Two wires are kept tight between the same pair of supports. The tension in the wires are in the ratio 2 : 1, the radii are in the ratio 3 : 1 and the densities are in the ratio 1 : 2. Find the ratio of their fundamental frequencies.

Ans. [2 : 3]

6-57 Three metal rods are located relative to each other as shown in figure-6.115, where $L_1 + L_2 = L_3$. Values of density and Young's modulus of the three materials are :

$\rho_1 = 2.7 \times 10^3$ kg/m^3, $Y_1 = 7 \times 10^{10}$ Pa,

$\rho_2 = 11.3 \times 10^3$ kg/m^3, $Y_2 = 1.6 \times 10^{10}$ Pa,

$\rho_3 = 8.8 \times 10^3$ kg/m^3, $Y_3 = 11 \times 10^{10}$ Pa,

If $L_3 = 1.5$ m, what must the ratio L_1/L_2 be if a sound wave is to travel the length of rods 1 and 2 in the same time as required to travel the length of rod 3 ?

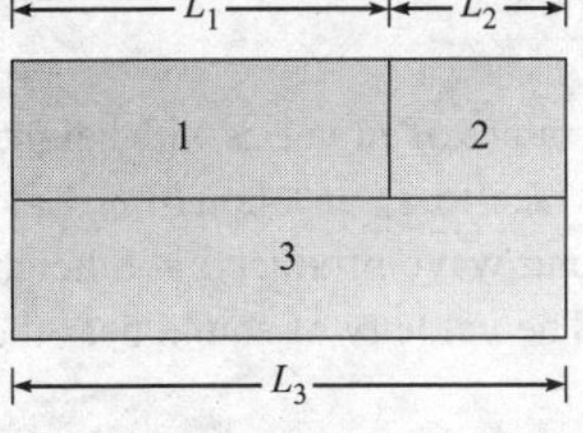

Figure 6.115

Ans. [$\frac{L_1}{L_2} = 6.258$]

6-58 Three second waves of frequencies 320, 344 and 280 are produced simultaneously. Find the number of beats per second, assuming the human ear's resolution as 10 beats per second.

Ans. [8]

6-59 State whether the following statement is true or false giving reason in brief : "A source of sound with frequency 256 Hz is moving with a velocity v towards a wall and an observer is stationary between the source and the wall. When the observer is between the source and the wall he will hear beats."

Ans. [False]

6-60 A siren emitting a sound of 1 kHz moves away from a stationary observer towards a cliff at a speed of 10 m/s. Calculate the frequency of the sound echoed off the cliff (speed of sound = 330 m/s). Will there be any beat frequency ? Will there be any beats heard by a man ?

Ans. [$f_2 = 1031.0$ Hz; $\Delta f = 60.4$ Hz, No]

6-61 S_1 and S_2 are two loudspeakers with the same frequency of 165 Hz and acoustic output 1.2×10^{-3} and 1.8×10^{-3} watts respectively. They vibrate in the same phase. P is a point at a distance 4 m from S_1 and 3 m from S_2.

(a) How are the phase of the two waves arriving at P related ?

(b) What is the intensity of P if S_1 is turned off (S_2 on) ?

(c) What is the intensity of sound at P if S_2 is turned off ?

(d) What is the intensity at P with S_1 and S_2 on ?

Ans. [(a) π, (b) 0.2×10^{-3} W, (c) 0.075×10^{-3} W, (d) 0.03×10^{-3} W]

6-62 A stretched sonometer wire gives 2 beats per second with a tuning fork when its length is 14.3 cm and also when its length is 14.5 cm. What is the frequency of the tuning fork ?

Ans. [288 Hz]

6-63 The sounding rod of a dust tube apparatus is made of brass and is 160 cm long. The distance between adjacent nodes in the wave tube was 11.35 cm. Calculate the Young's modulus of the rod assuming that velocity of sound in air at room temperature is 350 m/s and density of brass 9000 kg/m^3.

Ans. [2.2×10^{11} N/m^2]

6-64 If at $t = 0$ a travelling wave pulse on a string is described by the function :

$$y = \frac{6}{[x^2 + 3]}$$

what will be the amplitude and wave function representing the pulse at time t, if the pulse is propagating along positive x-axis with speed 4 m/s ?

Ans. [Amplitude = 2 m; $y = 6/[(x - 4t)^2 + 3]$]

6-65 A receiver and a source of sonic oscillation of frequency n = 2000 Hz are located on the x-axis. The source swings harmonically along that axis with a circular frequency ω and an amplitude $a = 50$ cm. At what value of ω will the frequency band width registered by the stationary receiver be equal to $\Delta n = 200$ Hz ? The velocity of sound is equal to $v = 340$ m/s.

Ans. [34 rad/s]

6-66 Calculate the velocity of sound in air saturated with moisture at 25°C and 745 mm pressure. The saturation pressure at 25°C is 23.76 mm of mercury and the velocity of sound at 0°C in dry air is 332 m/s.

Ans. [349 m/s]

6-67 Two long strings A and B, each having linear mass density 1.2×10^{-2} kg/m, are stretched by different tensions 4.8 N and 7.5 N respectively and are kept parallel to each other with their left ends at $x = 0$. Waves pulses are produced on the strings at the left ends at $t = 0$ on string A and at $t = 20$ ms on string B. When and where will the pulse on B overtake that on A ?

Ans. [at t = 100 ms at x = 2.0 m]

6-68 A source of sound is moving along circular orbit of radius 3 meters with an angular velocity of 10 rad/s. A sound detector located far away from the source is executing linear simple harmonic motion along the line BD (see figure-6.116) with an amplitude $BC = CD = 6$ meters. The frequency of oscillation of the detector is $5/\pi$ per second. The source is at the point A when the detector is at the point B. If the source emits a continuous sound wave of frequency 340 Hz, find the maximum and the minimum frequencies recorded by the detector.

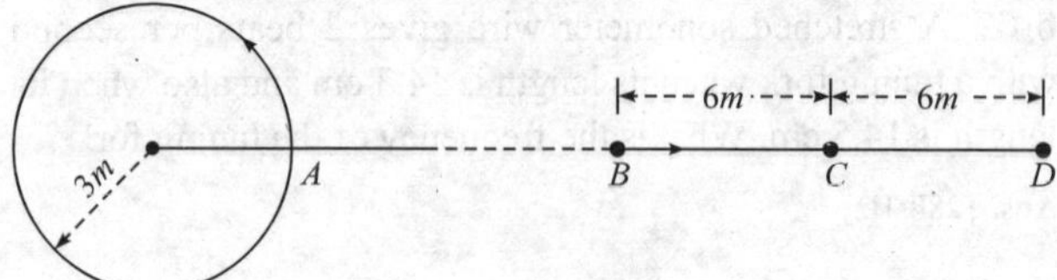

Figure 6.116

Ans. [(i) 442 Hz, (ii) 255 Hz]

6-69 A vibrator makes 150 cm of a string vibrate in 6 loops in the longitudinal arrangement when it is stretched by 15 g. The entire length of the string is then weighed and is found to weigh 500 mg. What is the frequency of the vibrator ? What is the distance between two nodes ?

Ans. [84 Hz, 25×10^{-2} m]

6-70 Find the radius vector defining the position of a point source of spherical waves if that source is known to be located on the straight line between the points with radius vector $\vec{r}_1$ and $\vec{r}_2$ at which the oscillation amplitudes of particles of the medium are equal to a_1 and a_2. The damping of wave is negligible, the medium is homogeneous.

Ans. [$\dfrac{a_1\vec{r}_1 + a_2\vec{r}_2}{a_1 + a_2}$]

6-71 A long string of length 1.5 m is made of steel. The tension in it produces an elastic strain of 1%. Calculate its fundamental frequency if density and elasticity of material of the wire are 7.7×10^3 kg/m^3 and 2.2×10^{11} N/m^2 respectively.

Ans. [178.174 Hz]

6-72 Fifty-six tuning forks are arranged in order of increasing frequencies so that each fork gives 4 beats per second with the next one. The last fork gives the octave of the first. Find the frequency of the first.

Ans. [220 Hz]

6-73 Two plane sonic waves of same frequency are travelling in a homogeneous medium. Loudness recorded by moving detector in the medium varies from $L_1 = 30\ dB$ to $L_2 = 43.974\ dB$. Calculate intensity of the two waves

Ans. [9×10^{-9} W/m^2, 4×10^{-9} W/m^2]

6-74 A column of air and a tuning fork produce 4 beats per sec when sounded together. The tuning fork gives the lower note. The temperature of air is 15ºC. When the temperature falls to 10ºC the two produce 3 beats per sec. Find the frequency of the fork.

Ans. [110.6 Hz]

6-75 A source of sonic oscillations with frequency $n = 1000$ Hz moves at right angles to the wall with a velocity $u = 0.17$ m/s. Two stationary receivers R_1 and R_2 are located on a straight line, coinciding with the trajectory of the source, in the following succession : R_1-source R_2-wall. Which receiver registers the beating and what is the beat frequency ? The velocity of sound is equal to $v = 340$ m/s.

Ans. [1.0 Hz]

6-76 A 200 Hz wave with amplitude 1 mm travels on a long string of linear mass density 6 g/m kept under a tension of 60 N. (a) Find the average power transmitted across a given point on the string. (b) Find the total energy associated with the wave in a 2.0 m long portion of the string.

Ans. [(a) 0.47 W, (b) 9.4 mJ]

6-77 The temperature of air varies with height linearly from T_1 at the earth's surface to T_2 at a height h. Calculate the time t needed for a sound wave produced at a height x to reach the earth's surface. The velocity of sound near the earth's surface is C.

Ans. [$\dfrac{2h}{C}\dfrac{\sqrt{T_1}}{T_1 - T_2}\left[\sqrt{T_1} - (T_1 - T_2)\dfrac{x}{h}\right]$]

6-78 The displacement of a wave disturbance propagating in the X-direction is given by

$$y = \frac{1}{\sqrt{(1+x^2)}} \quad \text{at } t = 0$$

$$\text{and} \quad y = \frac{1}{\sqrt{(2-2x+x^2)}} \quad \text{at } t = 1\text{ s}$$

where x and y are in metre. The shape of the wave disturbance does not change during propagation. Find the velocity of wave propagation.

Ans. [1 m/s]

6-79 A wire of density 9 gm/cm^3 is stretched between two clamps 100 cm apart. While subjected to an extension of 0.05 cm, what is the lowest frequency of transverse vibrations in the wire, assuming Young's modulus of the material to be 9×10^{11} dyne/cm^2.

Ans. [$25\sqrt{2} = 35.35$ Hz]

6-80 The following equations represent transverse waves

$$z_1 = A\cos(kx - \omega t)$$

$$z_2 = A\cos(kx + \omega t)$$

$$z_3 = A\cos(ky - \omega t)$$

Identify the combination (*s*) of the wave which will produce (i) standing wave (*s*), (ii) a wave travelling in the direction making an angle of 45 degrees with the positive *x* and positive *y* axis. In each case, find the positions at which the resultant intensity is always zero.

Ans. [(i) z_1 and z_2, $x = \frac{\pi}{2k}, \frac{3\pi}{2k}, \frac{5\pi}{2k}, \ldots\ldots \frac{(2n+1)\pi}{2k}$,

(ii) z_1 and z_3, $x = (x - y) = \frac{(2n+1)\pi}{2k}$,]

6-81 A wire of length *l* is kept just taut horizontally between two walls. A mass *m* hanging from its midpoint depresses it by δ. Calculate the time in which a pulse set up at one end will reach the other end. The mass of the wire per unit length of it is μ.

Ans. [$\sqrt{\frac{4\mu l\delta}{mg}}$]

6-82 Wavelength of two notes in air are 80/195 m and 80/193 m. Each note produces five beats per second with a third note of a fixed frequency. Calculate the velocity of sound in air.

Ans. [400 m/s]

6-83 A fork and a monochord string 100 cm long give 4 beats per second. The string is made shorter without any change of tension until it is in unison with the fork. If its length is now 99 cm, what is the frequency of the fork ?

Ans. [400 Hz]

6-84 A 40 cm wire having a mass of 3.2 g is stretched between two fixed supports 40.05 cm apart. In its fundamental mode, the wire vibrates at 220 Hz. If the area of cross-section of the wire is 1.0 mm^2, find its Young's modulus.

Ans. [1.98×10^{11} N/m^2]

6-85 A stationary observer receives sonic oscillations from two tuning forks one of which approaches, and the other recedes with the same velocity. As this takes place, the observer hears the beating with frequency 2.0 Hz. Find the velocity of each tuning fork if their oscillation frequency is $n = 680$ Hz and the velocity v of sound in air is 340 m/s.

Ans. [0.5 m/s]

6-86 A source plays a tone with frequency $f_0 = 440$ Hz. What is the speed of a car moving straight towards the source, if the driver hears a frequency of 462 Hz. Take speed of sound in the air is $v = 340$ ms^{-1}, the effects of the material of the car can be neglected.

Ans. [17 m/s]

6-87 The linear density of a wire under tension *T* varies linearly from μ_1 to μ_2. Calculate the time that a pulse would need to pass from one end to the other. The length of the wire is *l*.

Ans. [$\frac{2l(\mu_2^{3/2} - \mu_1^{3/2})}{3(\mu_2 - \mu_1)\sqrt{T}}$]

6-88 In a sonometer wire, the tension is maintained by suspending a 50.7 kg and from the free end of the wire. The suspended mass has a volume of 0.0075 m^3. The fundamental frequency of vibration of the wire is 260 Hz. What will be the fundamental frequency if the mass is completely submerged in water ?

Ans. [240 Hz]

6-89 Calculate the velocity of sound in air on a day when temperature is 30°C, pressure 0.74 m of mercury and relative humidity 60%. Velocity of sound at NTP = 330 m/s. Saturated vapour pressure at 30°C = 0.032 m of mercury.

Ans. [349.4 m/s]

6-90 If a loop of chain is spun at high speed, it will roll like a hoop without collapsing. Consider a chain of linear mass density μ that is rolling without slipping at a high speed v_0. (a) Show that the tension in the chain is $F = \mu v_0^2$. (b) If the chain rolls over a small hump, a transverse wave pulse will be generated in the chain. At what speed will it travel along the chain ? (c) How far around the loop (in degrees) will a transverse pulse travel in the time the hoop rolls through one complete revolution ?

Ans. [(a) $F = \mu v_0^2$; (b) $v_0 = \sqrt{F/\mu}$; (c) with respect to a fixed point on chain, the pulse travels through 360°.]

6-91 In a pipe closed at both ends the maximum amplitude of vibration is 5 mm and the amplitude of vibration at a distance 5 cm from one end is 4.33 mm. The length of the pipe is 120 cm. To what mode of vibration does it correspond ? What is the frequency of the note emitted by the pipe ? Velocity of sound in the gas enclosed in the pipe 336 m/s.

Ans. [8th harmonic, 140 Hz]

6-92 A 2.00 m long rope, having a mass of 80 g, is fixed at one end and is tied to a light string at the other end. The tension in the string is 256 N. (a) Find the frequencies of the fundamental and the first two overtones. (b) Find the wavelength in the fundamental and the first two overtones.

Ans. [(a) 10 Hz, 30 Hz, 50 Hz, (b) 8.00 m, 2.67 m, 1.60 m]

6-93 Calculate the velocity of sound in a medium where change in pressure and volume takes place according to the law $p = \frac{\alpha}{V_2}$ where α is a constant. Treat the medium as in ideal gas and assume ρ as its normal density.

Ans. [$\sqrt{\frac{2p}{\rho}}$]

6-94 A 2 m string is fixed at one end and is vibrating in its third harmonic with amplitude 3 cm and frequency 100 Hz. (a) Write an expression for the kinetic energy of a segment of the string of length dx at a point x at some time t. At what time is its kinetic energy maximum? What is the shape of the string at this time? (b) Find the maximum kinetic energy of the string by integrating your expression for part (a) over the total length of the string.

Ans. [(a) $dK = \frac{1}{2}\mu\left[6\pi \sin\left(\frac{3\pi}{4}\right)x \sin 200\pi t\right]^2 dx$; $t = 2.5 \times 10^{-3}$ s, straight line; (b) 89 mJ]

6-95 Show that if the rate of change of temperature with height dT/dh called lapse rate is a constant, a sound wave travelling horizontally is refracted along an arc of radius of curvature $\rho = 2T\frac{dT}{dh}$.

6-96 A transverse wave of amplitude 0.50 mm and frequency 100 Hz is produced on a wire stretched to a tension of 100 N. If the wave speed is 100 m/s, what average power is the source transmitting to the wire?

Ans. [49 mW]

6-97 An aluminium wire of length 0.6 m and cross-sectional area 10^{-6} m^2 is connected to a steel wire of the same cross-sectional area and length 0.866 m. The compound wire is loaded with 10 kg. Find the lowest frequency of excitation for which the joint in the wire is a node. Also find the number of nodes, excluding the two at the ends of the wire. The density of aluminium is 2600 kg/m^3 and that of steel is 7800 kg/m^3.

Ans. [323 Hz, 6]

6-98 Weak background noise from a classroom set up the fundamental stationary wave in a cardboard tube of length 80 cm with two open end. What frequency do you hear from the tube (a) If you jam your ear against one end? (b) If your move your ear away enough so that the tube has two open ends. Take $v = 320$ m/s.

Ans. [(a) 100 Hz, (b) 200 Hz]

6-99 Show that if $n_1, n_2, n_3, n_4, \ldots$ are the fundamental frequencies of the segments into which a string is divided by placing a number of bridges below it, the frequency of the string is given by

$$\frac{1}{n} = \frac{1}{n_1} + \frac{1}{n_2} + \frac{1}{n_2} + \ldots$$

6-100 A heavy string is tied at one end to a movable support and to a light thread at the other end as shown in figure-6.117. The thread goes over a fixed pulley and supports a weight to produce a tension. The lowest frequency with which the heavy string resonates is 120 Hz. If the movable support is pushed to the right by 10 cm so that the joint is placed on the pulley, what will be the minimum frequency at which the heavy string can resonate?

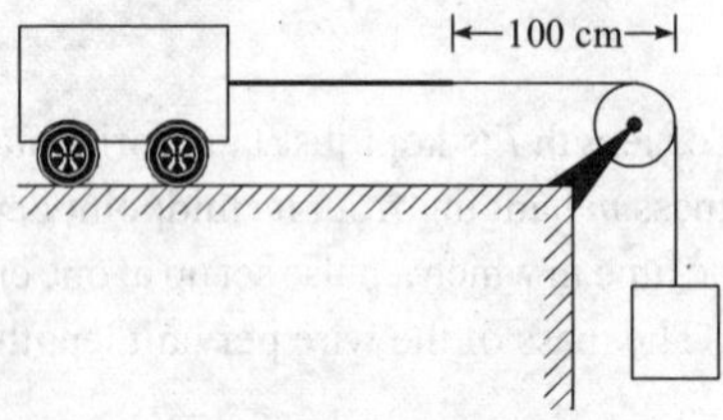

Figure 6.117

Ans. [240 Hz]

6-101 A uniform circular hoop of string is rotating clockwise in the absence of gravity. The tangential speed is v_0. If a disturbance is created in the string in this state what is the speed of disturbance along the string?

Ans. [v_0]

6-102 A long horizontal pipe is fitted with a piston of mass 10 kg which is connected to another mass 10.5 kg by a string passing over a frictionless pulley. A source of sound of frequency 512 Hz is placed in front of the piston. Initially the piston is almost in touch with the source and it moves away from the source when the hanging mass is released. Find the time/s when maximum sound is heard. Assume the string horizontal between pulley and piston. There is no friction. Velocity of sound = 340 m/s.

Ans. [0.83 s, 1.44 s, 1.85 s ...]

* * * * *

ANSWERS & SOLUTIONS

CONCEPTUAL MCQS Single Option Correct

1	(C)	2	(C)	3	(C)
4	(C)	5	(C)	6	(B)
7	(B)	8	(D)	9	(C)
10	(C)	11	(B)	12	(B)
13	(C)	14	(D)	15	(B)
16	(A)				

NUMERICAL MCQS Single Option Correct

1	(C)	2	(A)	3	(B)
4	(B)	5	(A)	6	(D)
7	(C)	8	(C)	9	(C)
10	(A)	11	(B)	12	(D)
13	(B)	14	(A)	15	(B)
16	(A)	17	(D)	18	(A)
19	(A)	20	(C)	21	(D)
22	(A)	23	(A)	24	(D)
25	(C)	26	(D)	27	(D)
28	(C)	29	(C)	30	(A)
31	(B)	32	(B)	33	(D)
34	(B)	35	(D)	36	(A)
37	(B)	38	(C)	39	(B)
40	(B)	41	(C)	42	(D)
43	(A)	44	(B)	45	(D)
46	(A)	47	(D)	48	(B)
49	(D)	50	(D)	51	(B)
52	(D)	53	(D)	54	(C)
55	(A)	56	(B)	57	(B)
58	(D)	59	(D)	60	(D)
61	(D)	62	(B)	63	(C)
64	(B)	65	(C)	66	(C)
67	(A)	68	(B)	69	(A)
70	(B)	71	(B)	72	(C)
73	(B)	74	(C)	75	(C)
76	(C)	77	(B)	78	(B)
79	(C)	80	(B)	81	(B)
82	(A)	83	(B)	84	(A)
85	(C)	86	(A)	87	(D)
88	(B)	89	(B)		

ADVANCE MCQs One or More Option Correct

1	(A, D)	2	(All)	3	(A, C)
4	(A, C)	5	(A, B)	6	(C, D)
7	(All)	8	(B, C, D)	9	(B, D)
10	(A, C, D)	11	(B, C)	12	(B, C)
13	(B, C)	14	(A, D)	15	(A, B, C)
16	(B, D)	17	(A, C)	18	(A, C, D)
19	(A, B, C)	20	(A, D)	21	(A, D)
22	(B, C, D)	23	(A, C, D)	24	(A)
25	(All)	26	(B, C)		

Solutions of PRACTICE EXERCISE 1.1

(i) (a) We use $T_C = \frac{5}{9}(T_F - 32) = \frac{5}{9}(68-32) = 20°C$

(b) We use $T_F = \frac{9}{5}T_C + 32 = \frac{9}{5} \times 1800 + 32$

$$= 3272°F$$

(ii) We use $\frac{T-100}{0-100} = \frac{25-0}{100-0}$

$$\Rightarrow \quad T - 100 = -25$$

$$\Rightarrow \quad T = 75°$$

(iii) (a) We use

$$\frac{T-0}{100-0} = \frac{15.0-12.45}{21.30-12.45} = \frac{2.65}{8.85}$$

$$\Rightarrow \quad T = \frac{2.65}{8.85} \times 100 = 29.94°C$$

(b) We use $\frac{T-0}{100-0} = \frac{22.95-12.45}{21.30-12.45} = \frac{10.5}{8.85}$

$$\Rightarrow \quad T = \frac{10.5}{8.85} \times 100 = 118.64°C$$

(iv) We use $\frac{T_C - 32}{212-32} = \frac{T_C - 0}{100-0}$

At $T_F = T_C = T_0$ we use

$$T_0 - 32 = 1.8T_0$$

$$-0.8T_0 = 32$$

$$\Rightarrow \quad T_0 = -40°F$$

Solutions of PRACTICE EXERCISE 1.2

(i) At $30°C$ length of copper rod is

$$l_{cu} = 90(1 + 1.7 \times 10^{-5} \times 20)$$

$$= 90.0306 \text{ cm}$$

Length of 1 cm of steel tap at

$$30° = 1(1 + 1.2 \times 10^{-5} \times 20)$$

$$= 1.00024 \text{ cm}$$

Reading at $30°C = \frac{l_{cu}}{l_{1cm} \text{ of tap}}$

$$= \frac{90.0306}{1.00024} = 90.01 \text{ cm}$$

(ii) For the given case

$$\Delta T = 30°C$$

Expansion of girders is

$$\Delta l = l \times \Delta T$$
$$= 12 \times 1.1 \times 10^{-5} \times 30$$
$$= 0.00396 \text{ m}$$

(iii) Thermal expansion in rod is

$$\Delta l = l \times \Delta T$$

due to clamps elastic strain in rod

$$= \frac{\Delta l}{l} = -\alpha\Delta T$$
$$= -1.2 \times 10^{-5} \times 30$$
$$= -3.6 \times 10^{-4}$$

(iv) Force by rod on wall is

$$F = YA \times \Delta T$$
$$= 2 \times 10^{11} \times 2 \times 10^{6} \times 1.2 \times 10^{-5} \times 80$$
$$= 384 \text{ N}$$

(v) For $\Delta T = 40°C$ dimensions of glass in winters is

$$l = 30(1 - 9 \times 10^{-6} \times 40) = 29.989$$
$$\omega = 20(1 - 9 \times 10^{-6} \times 40) = 19.993$$

dimensions of aluminimum frame at 40°C are

$$l_1 = 29.989 \times (1 + 2.4 \times 10^{-5} \times 40)$$
$$= 30.018 \text{ cm}$$
$$\omega_1 = 19.993\,(1 + 2.4 \times 10^{-5} \times 40)$$
$$= 20.012 \text{ cm}$$

(vi) Permissible error

$$= 10 \times 10^{-6} \text{ m} = 10^{-3} \text{ cm}$$

required diameter at 80°C is

$$d = 5.00(1 + 1.2 \times 10^{-5} \times 70)$$
$$= 5.0052 \text{ cm}$$

(vii) Time lost by clock per second is

$$\frac{\Delta t}{t} = \frac{1}{2}\alpha\Delta T = \frac{1}{2} \times 1.85 \times 10^{-5} \times 10$$
$$= 9.25 \times 10^{-5} \text{ s}$$

Total time lost in 24 hours is

$$= 9.25 \times 10^{-5} \times 24 \times 3600$$
$$= 7.992 \text{ s}$$

(viii) Time lost by clock per second is

$$\frac{\Delta t}{t} = \frac{1}{2}\alpha\Delta T = \frac{1}{2} \times 7 \times 10^{-7} \times 10$$
$$= 3.5 \times 10^{-6} \text{ s}$$

time lost by clock in 30 days is

$$= 3.5 \times 10^{-6} \times 30 \times 86400$$
$$= 9.072 \text{ s}$$

(ix) As temperature changes by ΔT, new length l' and moment of inertial I' is given as

$$l' = l(1 + \alpha\Delta T)$$
$$I' = I(1 + 2\alpha\Delta T)$$

Thus new time period is

$$T' = 2\pi\sqrt{\frac{I'}{mgl'}}$$
$$= 2\pi\sqrt{\frac{I}{mgl}\,\frac{(1 + 2\alpha\Delta T)^{1/2}}{(1 + \alpha\Delta T)^{1/2}}}$$

As $\alpha\Delta T << 1$, using binomial approximate we get

$$T' = 2\pi\sqrt{\frac{I}{mgl}}\left(1 + \frac{1}{2}\alpha\Delta T\right)$$

change in period is

$$T' - T = 2\pi\sqrt{\frac{I}{mgl}}\left(\frac{1}{2}\alpha\Delta T\right) = \pi\alpha\Delta T\sqrt{\frac{I}{mgl}}$$

(x) Natural elongation in x and y rods are

$$l_x = L(1 + \alpha_x\Delta T)$$
$$l_y = L(1 + \alpha_y\Delta T)$$

Due to pivots if final length is L_f we use strain in x and y rods as

$$(\text{strain})_x = \frac{L_f - l_x}{l_x} \simeq \frac{L_f - l_x}{L}$$
$$(\text{strain})_y = \frac{l_y - L_f}{l_y} \simeq \frac{l_y - L_f}{L}$$

There we can use $l_x \simeq l_y \simeq L$ as numerator is very small difference

Now stress on y is twice that of x so we use

$$Y_y(\text{strain})_y = 2Y_x(\text{strain})_x$$
$$\Rightarrow \quad Y_y(L(1 + \alpha_y\,\Delta T) - L_f) = 2Y_x(L_f - L(1 + \alpha_x\Delta T))$$
$$Y_yL + \alpha_yY_yL\Delta T - L_fY_y = 2Y_xL_f - 2Y_xL - 2Y_x\alpha_xL\Delta T$$
$$\Rightarrow \quad L_f = L\left[1 + \left(\frac{\alpha_yY_y + 2\alpha_xY_x}{Y_y + 2Y_x}\right)\Delta T\right]$$

Solutions of PRACTICE EXERCISE 1.3

(i) Volume expansion of mercury with respect to bulb is

$$\Delta V = V_0(\beta - 3\alpha)\,t$$

Find area of cross section of capillary is

$$A_f = A_0(1+2\alpha t)$$

height of mercury used in capillary

$$h = \frac{\Delta V}{A_f} = \frac{V_0(\beta-3\alpha)t}{A_0(1+2\alpha t)}$$

(ii) Let volume of glass vessel at 20°C is V_g and volume of mercury at 20°C is V_m. The volume of remaining space is given as

$$\Delta V = V_g - V_m$$

This volume should not change with temperature so we use

$$V_g - V_m = V'_g - V'_m$$

Where V'_g and V'_m are final volumes, so we use

$$V_g - V_m = V_g(1+\gamma_g\Delta\theta) - V_m(1+\gamma_{Hg}\Delta\theta)$$

$$\Rightarrow \quad V_g\gamma_g = V_m\gamma_{Hg}$$

$$\Rightarrow \quad V_m = \frac{100\times 9\times 10^{-6}}{1.8\times 10^{-4}}\text{ cc}$$

$$\Rightarrow \quad V_m = 50\text{ cc}$$

(iii) Let volume of silica balls is V_0

Thus at 0°C $\quad 340 = V_0\,\rho_{Hg}$ at 0°C

if V_1 is the volume of steel balls we use

$$255 = (V_0 - V_1)\,\rho_{Hg} \text{ at } 0°C$$

$$\Rightarrow \quad 85 = V_1\,\rho_{Hg} \text{ at } 0°C$$

at 100°C $\quad 250.2 = [V_0 - V_1(1+\gamma_s(100))]\,\dfrac{\rho_{Hg} \text{ at } 0°C}{1+\gamma_{Hg}(100)}$

$$250.2\,[1+\gamma_{Hg}(100)] = 255 - 85\,\gamma_s \times 100$$

$$254.7 = 255 - 8500\,\gamma_s$$

$$\Rightarrow \quad \gamma_s = 35.29\times 10^{-6}\,°C^{-1}$$

$$\Rightarrow \quad \alpha_s = \frac{\gamma_s}{3} = 11.76\times 10^{-6}\,°C^{-1}$$

(iv) If volume expansion of a liquid is ΔV, we use

$$\Delta V = V\gamma\,\Delta t$$

height raised by liquid in vessel is

$$h = \frac{\Delta V}{A} \qquad [A \to \text{constant}]$$

$$h = \frac{V\gamma\Delta t}{A} = h_i\gamma\,\Delta t$$

$[h_i \to$ initial level of liquid$]$

$\Rightarrow \gamma \to$ coefficient of linear expansion of liquid

(v) If vessel volume is V and its f fraction is filled with liquid, we use

$$V - fV = V(1+27\times 10^{-6}\,\Delta t) - fV(1+18\times 10^{-5}\,\Delta t)$$

$$\Rightarrow \quad f = \frac{27\times 10^{-6}}{18\times 10^{-5}} = \frac{3}{20}$$

(vi) For simple pendulum $T = 2\pi\sqrt{\dfrac{l}{g}}$

$$\Rightarrow \quad T \propto l^{1/2} \quad \Rightarrow \quad \frac{\Delta T}{T} = \frac{1}{2}\frac{\Delta l}{l} = \frac{1}{2}\alpha\Delta\theta$$

Assuming clock gives correct time at temperature θ_0

$$\Rightarrow \quad \frac{6}{24\times 3600} = \frac{1}{2}\alpha(\theta_0 - 20)$$

$$\& \quad \frac{6}{24\times 3600} = \frac{1}{2}\alpha(40 - \theta_0)$$

$$\Rightarrow \quad \theta_0 = 30°C$$

$$\Rightarrow \quad \alpha = 1.4\times 10^{-5}\,°C^{-1}$$

(vii) For the two vessels we can equate the coefficient of cubical expansion of liquid as

$$\gamma_L = \gamma_1 + 3\alpha_1 = \gamma_2 + 3\alpha_2$$

$$\Rightarrow \quad \alpha_2 = \frac{\gamma_1 - \gamma_2 + 3\alpha_1}{3}$$

(viii) All temperature T_1 if density of liquid is ρ_1 and that at temperature T_2 is ρ_2 we use

$$f_1V\rho_1 = f_2V_2\rho_2$$

$$\frac{f_1\rho_0}{1+\gamma T_1} = \frac{f_2\rho_0}{1+\gamma T_2}$$

$$\Rightarrow \quad f_1 + \gamma f_1 T_2 = f_2 + \gamma f_2 T_1$$

$$\Rightarrow \quad \gamma = \frac{f_2 - f_1}{f_1T_2 - f_2T_1}$$

(ix) Mixture forms globules when

$$\rho_{liq} = \rho_{water} \text{ at temperature } T°C$$

$$\Rightarrow \quad \frac{1021}{1+\gamma_L(T-20)} = \frac{998}{1+\gamma_\omega(T-20)}$$

$$1021 + 1021\,\gamma_\omega(T-20) = 998 + 998\times\gamma_L(T-20)$$

$$(998\times 85\times 10^{-5} - 1021\times 45\times 10^{-5})(T-20) = 23$$

$$0.38885\,(T-20) = 23$$

$$\Rightarrow \quad T - 20 = 59.15$$

$$\Rightarrow \quad T = 79.15°C$$

Solutions of PRACTICE EXERCISE 1.4

(i) Heat released by water

$$Q = 0.5 \times 10^{-3} \times 4200 \times 15 = mgh$$

$$h - \frac{0.5\times10^3\times4200\times15}{10\times10} = 3.15\times10^5 \text{ m}$$

(ii) When first and second liquid are mixed we use

$$ms_1(15-10) = ms_2(25-15)$$

$$\Rightarrow \quad s_1 = 2s_2 \quad \dots(1)$$

When second and third are mixed we use

$$ms_2(30-25) = ms_3(40-30)$$

$$\Rightarrow \quad s_2 = 2s_3 \quad \dots(2)$$

from (1) and (2) we get

$$s_1 = 4s_3$$

Thus on mixing first and third if equilibrium temperature is T_1 we use

$$ms_1(T-10) = ms_3(40-T)$$

$$4T-40 = 40-T$$

$$5T = 80$$

$$T = 16°\text{C}$$

(iii) Heat required to heat *m kg* water/hr is

$$m\times4200\times50 = 8500\times1000\times4.2$$

$$m = 170 \text{ kg/hr}$$

(iv) Heat supplied by iron = heat gained by glycerine + aluminimum

$$290\times470\times(180-38)$$

$$= 250\times S\times(38-10) + 100\times900\times(38-10)$$

$$\Rightarrow \quad 19354600 = 73000\,S + 2520000$$

$$\Rightarrow \quad S = 2405 \text{ J/kgK}$$

(v) Heat required is

$$H = \int msdT$$

$$= \int_0^{20} maT^3\,dT$$

$$= ma\left[\frac{T^4}{4}\right]_0^{20}$$

$$= 4\times10^4\,ma$$

(vi) Heat given by lead = Heat absorbed by (calorimeter + oil)

$$100\times0.0305\times(48-30)$$

$$= 4.9\times1\times(50-48) + 40\times s_{oil}(50-48)$$

$$\Rightarrow \quad 54.9 = 9.8 + 80\,s_{oil}$$

$$\Rightarrow \quad s_{oil} = 0.563 \text{ cal/g °C}$$

Solutions of PRACTICE EXERCISE 1.5

(i) Heat required by ice to raise its temperature to 100°C,

$$Q_1 = m_1L_1 + m_1c_1\Delta\theta_1 = 5\times80 + 5\times1\times100$$

$$= 400 + 500 + 900 = 1800 \text{ cal}$$

Heat given by steam when condensed

$$Q_2 = m_2L_2 = 5\times536 = 2680 \text{ cal}$$

As $Q_2 > Q_1$

This means that whole steam is not even condensed.

Hence temperature of mixture will remain at 100°C.

(ii) Work done by friction is

$$w = \frac{1}{2}mv^2 = \frac{1}{2}\times50\times(5)^2 = 625 \text{ J}$$

If *m* mass of ice will melt, we use

$$\frac{625}{4.2} = m(80)$$

$$m = \frac{625}{80\times4.2} = 1.86 \text{ g}$$

(iii) Supplied heat = (22) (0.5) (8) + (22) (80) + (22) (1) (16)

$$= 88 + 1760 + 352 = 2200 \text{ cal}$$

$$\text{Heat capacity of the body} = \frac{2200 \text{ cal}}{44°\text{C}} = 50 \text{ cal/°C}$$

Water equivalent of the body

$$= \frac{\text{Heat capacity of the body}}{\text{spcific heat capacity of water}} = \frac{50 \text{ cal/ °C}}{1 \text{ cal/ g°C}} = 50\text{g}$$

(iv) Heat supplied by steam

$$= 4\times10^{-3}\times2.25\times10^6 + 4\times10^{-3}\times4200\times100$$

$$= 9000 + 1680 = 10680 \text{ J}$$

Amount of ice melted by this heat is

$$m = \frac{Q}{L} = \frac{10680}{3.36\times10^5} = 0.03178 \text{ kg}$$

$$= 31.78 \text{ g}$$

Final mixture is = 70.78 g water + 3.22 g ice

As whole ice is not melted, equilibrium temperature will be 0°C.

(v) If bullet speed is *v*, we use

$$0.75\times\frac{1}{2}mv^2 = 37800 + 25200$$

$$\Rightarrow \quad v = 409.87 \text{ m/s}$$

(vi) Heat supplied in 4 min is

$$Q = 100 \times 4 \times 60 = 24000 \text{ cal}$$

$\Rightarrow$ $100 \times 0.215 \times (T+20) + 200 \times 0.5 \times 20 + 200 \times 80 + 200 \times 1 \times T = 24000$

$$221.5\,T = 2400 - 16000 - 2000 = 6000$$

$$\Rightarrow \quad T = 27.08\,°\text{C}$$

(vii) Mixture = 1 kg ice at °C + 1 kg steam at 100°C

Heat required to milt ice

$$Q_1 = 1 \times 3.36 \times 10^5 \text{ J}$$

Heat required to raise temperature of water to 100°C

$$Q_2 = 1 \times 4200 \times 100 = 4.2 \times 10^5 \text{ J}$$

Heat supplied ($Q_1 + Q_2 = 7.56 \times 10^5$ J) by steam mass m then

$$m = \frac{Q_1 + Q_2}{L_v} = \frac{7.56 \times 10^5}{2.27 \times 10^6} = 0.333 \text{ kg}$$

Thus final mixture is at 100°C and composition is

Mixture = 667 g steam + 1333 g water

(viii) Heat supplied by block = Heat gained by calorimeter and liquid

Here we consider water equivalent of calorimeter as m_ω

$$110 \times 0.1 \times 82 = m_\omega \times 1 \times 8 + 200 \times s_L \times 8 \quad \ldots(1)$$

Second case

$$110 \times 0.1 \times 85.5 = m_\omega \times 1 \times 4.5 + 400 \times s_L \times 4.5 \quad \ldots(2)$$

we use $(2) \times 8 - (1) \times 4.5$

$\Rightarrow$ $110 \times 0.1(85.5 \times 8 - 82 \times 4.5) = s_L (400 \times 4.5 \times 8 - 200 \times 4.5 \times 8)$

$$\Rightarrow \quad s_L = \frac{3150}{7200} = 0.481 \text{ cal/g °C}^{-1}$$

from equation-(1) we have

$$m_\omega = \frac{902 - 769.6}{8} = 16.55 \text{ g}$$

(ix) If after time t, temperature of inside water drops to 15°C we use

$$(10000 - 0.2t) \times 4200 \times 10^{-3} \times 5 = 0.2t \times 2.27 \times 10^3$$

Here $0.2t << 10000$ so we can use

$$\Rightarrow \quad 21 \times 1000 = 454t$$

$$\Rightarrow \quad t = 462 \text{ s approx}$$

(x) After time t mass of inside water is

$$m = 1000 - 50t \text{ at temperature } T°\text{C}$$

Then we use

$$(1000 - 50t) \times 1 \times dT = -50\,dt \times 540$$

$$\int_0^t \frac{27000\,dt}{1000 - 50t} = -\int_{40}^{30} dT$$

$$\frac{27000}{50} \ln\left(\frac{1000}{1000 - 50t}\right) = 10$$

$$\ln\left(\frac{1000}{100 - 50t}\right) = \frac{1}{54}$$

$$1000 = (1000 - 50t)\,e^{1/54}$$

$$t = 20(1 - e^{-1/54}) \text{ s}$$

Solutions of CONCEPTUAL MCQS Single Option Correct

Sol. 1 (C) At 4°C density of water is maximum so when heat is conducted and temperature of water at different regions becomes 4°C settles down at bottom and when temperature further falls below 4°C its density decreases and will float above so 0°C will attain first at the region in between and at top.

Sol. 2 (C) As mass and density (metal) is same the hollow sphere will have larger diameter hence on increasing temperature by same value hollow sphere will expand more but fractional increase in diameter is $(\Delta d/d) = \alpha\Delta T$ which is same for both spheres.

Sol. 3 (C) A part of liquid will evaporate immediately sucking latent heat from the bulk of liquid. Hence a part of liquid will freeze.

Sol. 4 (C) Specific heat capacity of a compound is measured in J/Kg-K and molar heat capacity of a compound is measured in J/Mole-K so the ratio of the two will give the molecular weight of the compound

Sol. 5 (C) On heating copper will expand more than iron so the strip will bend towards left.

Sol. 6 (B) Fractional change in density of a material is $\gamma\Delta T$ and that for radius and area are $\alpha\Delta T$ and $\beta\Delta T$ which are less than that of density.

Sol. 7 (B) The apparent weight of a body submerged in a liquid is given as $W_{app} = W[1 - (\rho_L/\rho_S)]$ where ρ_L is the density of liquid and ρ_S is the density of solid body. On increasing temperature water expands more than metal hence density of water decreases more so option (B) is correct.

Sol. 8 (D) In all the phenomenon as temperature increases the rate of variation increases due to increases in rate of collisions of molecules hence option (D) is correct.

Sol. 9 (C) During evaporation of a liquid as the external pressure increases rate of evaporation decreases hence statement given in option (C) is NOT correct.

Sol. 10 (C) As the volume of both are same, according the thermal expansion concept the change in volume is proportional to the total volume enclosed by the material hence it will be same for both spheres.

Sol. 11 (B) In portion AB a solid temperature increases then in portion BC it melts after which in portion CD liquid temperature increases and in portion DE liquid vaporises and after point E vapour temperature increases.

Sol. 12 (B) As α_A is greater it will expand more and due to this strip will bend with metal A on the convex outer side.

Sol. 13 (C) If A_1 is cross sectional area of silica cylinder, $(A_1 + A_2)$ is cross sectional area of glass cylinder, and h is the height of silica cylinder, then :

$$h(A_1 + A_2)(2\alpha)\,\Delta\theta = h(A_2)\gamma\Delta\theta$$

$$\Rightarrow \quad \frac{hA_1}{hA_2} = \left(\frac{\lambda}{2\alpha} - 1\right)$$

$$\Rightarrow \quad \frac{\text{volume of silica}}{\text{volume of mercury}} = \left(\frac{\lambda}{2\alpha} - 1\right)$$

Sol. 14 (D) The heat capacity of the solid is :

$$\frac{dQ}{d\theta} = 2a\theta + 4b\theta^3$$

Sol. 15 (B) $\quad \alpha_n = \alpha_1 + \left(\frac{\alpha_2 - \alpha_1}{L}\right)x$

$$\Delta L = \int_0^L \alpha_n dx \Delta t$$

$$L = \left(\frac{\alpha_1 + \alpha_2}{2}\right) L\Delta T$$

$$\alpha_{eff} = \frac{\alpha_1 + \alpha_2}{2}$$

Sol. 16 (A) $\frac{C}{5} = \frac{F - 32}{9}$

Solutions of NUMERICAL MCQS Single Option Correct

Sol. 1 (C) Both have same increase in their volume.

Sol. 2 (A) Length of rod 1 is given by,

$$l_1' = l_1(1 + \alpha_1\Delta T)$$

and length of rod 2 is given by,

$$l_2' = l_2(1 + \alpha_2\Delta T)$$

$$l_1' - l_2' = l_1 + \alpha_1 l_1 \Delta T - l_2 - \alpha_2 l_2 \Delta T$$

Since $l_1' - l_2'$ is independent of temperature,

$$\alpha_1 l_1 \Delta T - \alpha_2 l_2\, \Delta T = 0$$

$$\alpha_1 l_1 = \alpha_2 l_2$$

$$\frac{l_1}{l_2} = \frac{\alpha_2}{\alpha_1}$$

Sol. 3 (B) Upthrust, $\quad W_0 = V_s\,\rho_L g$

where, V_s = volume of solid at 0°C

and ρ_L = density of liquid at 0°C

As the temperature increases, V_s increases and ρ_L decreases.

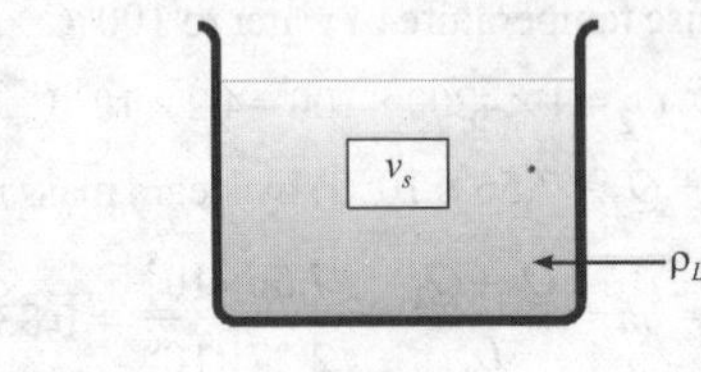

As $\quad W_0 \propto V_s\rho_L$

$$\frac{W}{W_0} = \frac{V_s'\rho_L'}{V_s\rho_L}$$

$$= \frac{(V_s + \Delta V_s)}{V_s} \times \frac{\rho_L(1 + \gamma_L\Delta T)^{-1}}{\rho_L}$$

$$\frac{W}{W_0} = (1 + \gamma_s\Delta T)\,(1 - \gamma_L\Delta T)$$

(By binomial approximation)

$$W = W_0(1 + \gamma_s\Delta T - \gamma_L\Delta T)$$

$$= W_0[1 + (\gamma_S - \gamma_L)\Delta T]$$

Sol. 4 (B) Heat lost by one liquid = Heat gained by another liquid

$$ms_1(40 - 32) = ms_2(32 - 20)$$

$$8s_1 = 12s_2$$

$$\frac{s_1}{s_2} = \frac{12}{8} = \frac{3}{2}$$

Thus, $\quad \frac{s_2}{s_1} = \frac{2}{3}$

Sol. 5 (A) $\quad \frac{\rho_x}{\rho_y} = \frac{1}{3}$

$$\frac{s_x}{s_y} = \frac{3}{1}$$

$$c = ms$$

$$\frac{c_1}{c_2} = \frac{m_x s_x}{m_y s_y} = \frac{V\rho_x s_x}{V\rho_y s_y} = \frac{1}{3} \times \frac{3}{1} = \frac{1}{1}$$

Sol. 6 (D) Given that $\quad c = 0.6t^2$

We use $dQ = mcdt$

$$\int_0^Q dQ = \int_0^{15} 10\times 0.6t^2 dt$$

$$Q = 6\left[\frac{t^3}{3}\right]_0^{15} = 2(15)^3 = 6750 \text{ cal}$$

Sol. 7 **(C)** Coefficient of cubical expansion of container,

$$\gamma_c = 3\alpha_c = 3\times 2\times 10^{-6}\,°\text{C}^{-1} = 6\times 10^{-6}\,°\text{C}^{-1}$$

Coefficient of cubical expansion of liquid,

$$\gamma_l = 6\times 10^{-6}\,°\text{C}^{-1}$$

Thus, both container and liquid will expand to same extent and level of liquid remain unchanged.

Sol. 8 **(C)** Change in length of composite rod

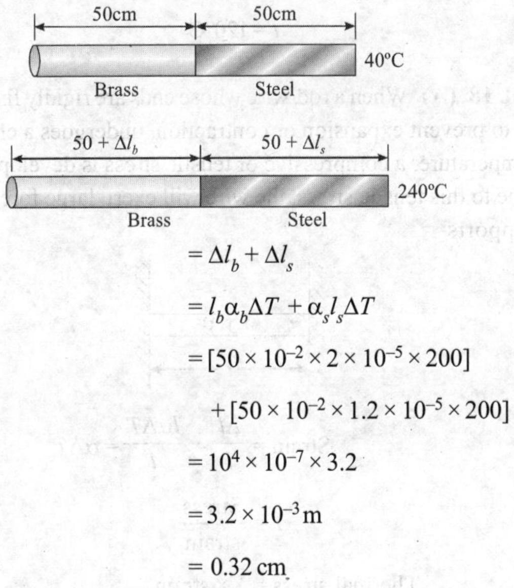

$$= \Delta l_b + \Delta l_s$$

$$= l_b\alpha_b\Delta T + \alpha_s l_s \Delta T$$

$$= [50\times 10^{-2}\times 2\times 10^{-5}\times 200]$$

$$+ [50\times 10^{-2}\times 1.2\times 10^{-5}\times 200]$$

$$= 10^4\times 10^{-7}\times 3.2$$

$$= 3.2\times 10^{-3}\text{m}$$

$$= 0.32 \text{ cm}$$

Sol. 9 **(C)** We use sphere volume

$$V = \frac{4}{3}\pi R^3 \quad \ldots(1)$$

when temperature is increased by 100°C

$$V' = \frac{4}{3}\pi R'^3$$

$$V(1+\gamma\Delta T) = \frac{4}{3}\pi R'^3$$

$$V[1+(8\times 10^{-5})(100)] = \frac{4}{3}\pi R'^3$$

$$V(1.008) = \frac{4}{3}\pi R'^3 \quad \ldots(2)$$

Dividing (1) by (2), we get

$$\frac{1}{1.008} = \frac{R^3}{R'^3}$$

$$R'^3 = 1.008R^3$$

$$R' = 1.00266R$$

Now, $I\omega = \text{constant}$

$$\frac{2}{5}MR^2\omega_0 = \frac{2}{5}MR'^2\omega$$

$$R^2\omega_0 = 1.0054R^2\omega$$

$$\omega = 0.996\omega_0$$

Sol. 10 **(A)** Since the measurement scale is expanded, the measured value (MV) decreases on increasing the temperature.

$$MV = l_1[1-\alpha_s\Delta T]$$

$$80 = l_1[1-(2.5\times 10^{-5})(40)]$$

$$80 = l_1\times 0.999$$

$$l_1 = 80.08 \text{ cm}$$

Sol. 11 **(B)** We use $l' = l(1+\alpha\Delta T)$

$$\frac{101l}{100} = l(1+\alpha(100))$$

$$0.01 = \alpha(100)$$

$$\alpha = 10^{-4}\,°\text{C}^{-1}$$

As we use $\beta = 2\alpha = 2\times 10^{-4}\,°\text{C}^{-1}$

For area we have $A' = A(1+\beta\Delta T)$

$$A' = A(1+(2\times 10^{-4})(100))$$

$$A' = 2l^2(1+2\times 10^{-2}) \quad (\because \; A = 2l^2)$$

$$A' = 2l^2(1.02)$$

$$A' = 2.04\, l^2$$

Percentage change in area $= \dfrac{A'-A}{A}\times 100$

$$= \frac{2.04l^2 - 2l^2}{2l^2}\times 100$$

$$= 2\%$$

Sol. 12 **(D)** (A) Let equilibrium temperature be T°C

$$20\times 1\times (T-30) = 20\times 1\times (40-T)$$

$$2T = 70$$

$$T = 35°\text{C}$$

(B) $20\times 1\times (T-30) = 40\times 1\times (35-T)$

$$T-30 = 70-2T$$

$$3T = 100$$

$$T = 33.3°\text{C}$$

(C) $20\times 1\times (T-30) = 10\times 1\times (50-T)$

$$2T-60=50-T$$
$$3T=110$$
$$T=36.67\,°C$$

(D) $20\times 1\times (T-30)=4\times 1\times (80-T)$
$$5T-150=80-T$$
$$6T=230$$
$$T=38.33°C$$

Thus, $4g$ water at 80°C raise temperature of $20g$ water at 30°C the most.

Sol. 13 (B)

$$\frac{\text{Reading of faulty thermomenter} - LFP}{UFP-LFP}=\frac{F-32}{180}$$
$$\frac{52-5}{99-5}=\frac{F-32}{180}$$
$$90=F-32$$
$$F=122°F$$

Sol. 14 (A) Given that $P_0=50$ cm of Hg
$$P_{100}=90\text{ cm of }Hg$$
$$P_t=60\text{ cm of }Hg$$
$$t=\frac{P_t-P_0}{P_{100}-P_0}\times 100°C$$
$$t=\frac{60-50}{90-50}\times 100$$
$$t=\frac{1000}{40}=25°C$$

Sol. 15 (B) We use $T_k=T_c+273$
$$T_k=\frac{5}{9}(T_F-32)+273$$
$$x=\frac{5}{9}x-\frac{5}{9}\times 32+273$$
$$0.44x=-14.08+273$$
$$0.44x=258.92$$
$$x=588.45$$

Sol. 16 (A) Time period of a simple pendulum is given as
$$T=2\pi\sqrt{\frac{l}{g}}$$
when the temperature is raised length changes to $l\,(1+\alpha\,\Delta T)$ and when the lift acceleration upwards, the effective gravity inside lift is given as
$$g_{\text{eff}}=g+a$$

New time period of pendulum is now given as
$$T'=2\pi\sqrt{\frac{l(1+\alpha\Delta T)}{g+a}}$$
For the pendulum to keep correct time, we use
$$T'=T$$
$$\Rightarrow\quad g\frac{(1+\alpha\Delta T)}{(g+a)}=1$$
$$\Rightarrow\quad a=g\,\alpha\,\Delta T=10\times 20\times 10^{-4}\times 50=1\text{ m/s}^2$$
Effective weight of operator is calculated as
$$W_{eff}=m\,(g+a)$$
$$W_{eff}=60\,(10+1)=660\text{ N}$$

Sol. 17 (D) We use $t=\dfrac{80-50}{75-50}\times 100°C$
$$t=\frac{30}{25}\times 100°C$$
$$t=120°C$$

Sol. 18 (A) When a rod/wire whose ends are rigidly fixed such as to prevent expansion or contraction, undergoes a change in temperature, a compressive or tensile stress is developed in it. Due to this tensile stress, the wire will exert large force on the supports

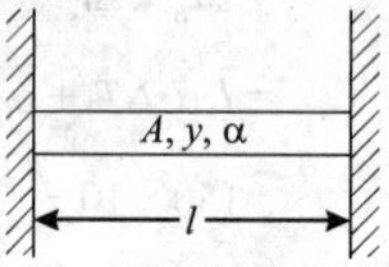

$$\text{Strain}=\frac{\Delta l}{l}=\frac{l\alpha\Delta T}{l}=\alpha\Delta T$$
$$Y=\frac{\text{Stress}}{\text{strain}}$$
$$\text{Thermal stress}=Y\times\text{strain}$$
$$=Y\alpha\Delta T$$
$$F=A(\text{stress})$$
$$F=YA\alpha\Delta T$$

Sol. 19 (A) Useful power available $=60\%$ of P
$$=0.6P$$
Energy consumed in T seconds,
$$E=0.6PT$$
$$Ms\Delta T=0.6PT$$
$$\Delta T=\frac{0.6PT}{Ms}$$

Sol. 20 (C) Let m kg of ice melts

Heat given out by copper block when it cools down from 500°C to 0°C

$$H_L = 2 \times 400 \times (500 - 0)$$

$$H_L = 4 \times 10^5 \text{ J}$$

This heat is absorbed by ice at 0°C

$$H_G = m \times 3.5 \times 10^5$$

Heat lost by block = Heat gained by ice

$$4 \times 10^5 = m \times 3.5 \times 10^5$$

$$m = \frac{8}{7} \text{kg}$$

Sol. 21 (D) Heat given out when 5*g* steam at 100°C converts to water at 100°C

$$H_1 = 5 \times 540 = 2700 \text{ cal}$$

Heat required by 6*g* ice at 0°C to reach water at 100°C

$$H_2 = (6 \times 80) + (6 \times 1 \times 100)$$
$$= (480 + 600) \text{ cal}$$
$$= 1080 \text{ cal}$$

As $H_2 < H_1$

The final temperature is 100°C

Sol. 22 (A) We use $\dfrac{\frac{1}{2} \times (m \times 9.8 \times 84)}{4.2} = m \times 1000 \times \Delta T$

$$\Delta T = 0.098°\text{C}$$

Sol. 23 (A) On expansion, volume of a given mass of a substance increases. So, density should decrease

$$\rho = \frac{m}{V}$$

$$\Rightarrow \quad \rho \propto \frac{1}{V}$$

$$\frac{\rho'}{\rho} = \frac{V}{V'} = \frac{V}{V + \Delta V} = \frac{V}{V + \gamma V \Delta T}$$

$$= \frac{1}{1 + \gamma \Delta T}$$

$$\frac{\rho'}{\rho} = \frac{1}{1 + \gamma \Delta T}$$

$$\Rightarrow \quad \rho' = \frac{\rho}{1 + \gamma \Delta T}$$

Change in density, $\rho' - \rho = \dfrac{\rho}{1 + \gamma \Delta T} - \rho$

$$= \frac{\rho - \rho - \rho\gamma\Delta T}{1 + \gamma \Delta T}$$

$$= \frac{-\rho\gamma\Delta T}{1 + \gamma \Delta T}$$

As Initial temperature = 0°C

$$\Rightarrow \quad \Delta T = T$$

$$\Rightarrow \quad \Delta\rho = \frac{-\rho\gamma T}{(1 + \gamma T)}$$

Sol. 24 (D) When a rod whose ends are rigidly fixed such as to prevent expansion or contraction, undergoes a change in temperature, a compressive or tensile stress is developed in it. Due to this tensile stress, rod will exert large force on the walls

$$\text{Strain} = \frac{\Delta l}{l} = \frac{l\alpha\Delta T}{l} = \alpha\Delta T$$

$$Y = \frac{\text{Stress}}{\text{Strain}}$$

$$\text{Thermal stress} = Y \times \text{strain}$$
$$= Y\alpha\Delta T$$

Force on supports, $F = \text{Stress} \times A$

$$= YA\alpha\Delta T$$

Since thermal stress developed in them are equal,

$$Y_1\alpha_1\Delta T = Y_2\alpha_2\Delta T$$

$$\frac{Y_1}{Y_2} = \frac{\alpha_2}{\alpha_1}$$

Sol. 25 (C) When temperature is increased, both glass vessel and mercury will expand

Here, apparent coefficient of expansion is

$$\gamma_a = \gamma_{Hg} - \gamma_g$$

$$\gamma_a = (182 \times 10^{-6}) - (30 - 10^{-6})$$

$$\gamma_a = 152 \times 10^{-6} \,°\text{C}^{-1}$$

Overflow volume is $\Delta V = V\gamma_a\Delta T$

$$= 1000 \times 152 \times 10^{-6} \times (100 - 0)$$

$$= 15.2 \text{ cm}^3$$

Sol. 26 (D) We use $\rho' = \rho(1 - \gamma\Delta T)$

$$998 = \rho(1 - 20\gamma) \quad \ldots(1)$$

$$992 = \rho(1 - 40\gamma) \quad \ldots(2)$$

Dividing (1) by (2), we get

$$\frac{499}{496} = \frac{1-20\gamma}{1-40\gamma}$$

$$499 - 19960\gamma = 496 - 9920\gamma$$

$$10040\gamma = 3$$

$$\gamma = 2.988 \times 10^{-4}\,°C^{-1}$$

Sol. 27 (D) We use $KE = \frac{1}{2}mv^2$

$$\frac{1}{2}mv^2 = mc\Delta\theta$$

$$v^2 = 2c\Delta\theta$$

$$v = \sqrt{2c\Delta\theta}$$

Sol. 28 (C) Heat given out when x grams of steam at 100°C is converted to water at 100°C

$$H_1 = 540x \quad \ldots(1)$$

Heat gained by ice at 0°C to convert to water at 100°C

$$H_2 = 80y + y \times 1 \times (100-0)$$

$$H_2 = 180y \quad \ldots(2)$$

According to principle of calorimetry,

$$H_1 = H_2$$

$$540x = 180y$$

$$\frac{y}{x} = 3$$

Sol. 29 (C) We use for heat absorbed by ice

$$H = (1 \times 80) + (1 \times 1 \times 100) + (1 \times 536)$$

$$= 80 + 100 + 536$$

$$= 716 \text{ cal}$$

Sol. 30 (A) Let volume of metal = V

density of metal = ρ

volume of metal inside mercury = V'

density of mercury = σ

In equilibrium, $V\rho g = V'\sigma g$

Fraction, $f = \frac{V'}{V} = \frac{\rho}{\sigma}$

New fraction on increase in temperature,

$$f' = \frac{\rho'}{\sigma'} = \frac{\rho}{1+\gamma_1\Delta T} \cdot \frac{1+\gamma_2\Delta T}{\sigma}$$

$$\frac{f'}{f} = \frac{1+\gamma_2\Delta T}{1+\gamma_1\Delta T}$$

Sol. 31 (B) We use $H = (60 \times 80)\text{ cal} = 4800 \text{ cal}$

$$P = \left(\frac{H}{t} \times 4.2\right) W$$

$$P = \frac{4800}{60} \times 4.2 = 336 \text{ W}$$

Sol. 32 (B) We use $\Delta l = \alpha l \Delta T$

For rod A,

$$0.075 = 20\,\alpha_A(100-0)$$

$$\alpha_A = 3.75 \times 10^{-5}\,°C^{-1}$$

For rod B,

$$0.045 = 20\,\alpha_B(100-0)$$

$$\alpha_B = 2.25 \times 10^{-5}\,°C^{-1}$$

Let portion of metal A is l cm and that of metal B is $(20 - l)$ cm

$$\Delta l_A + \Delta l_B = 0.06 \text{ cm}$$

$$\alpha_A l(100) + \alpha_B(20-l)(100) = 0.06$$

$$3.75 \times 10^{-5} l + 4.5 \times 10^{-4} - 2.25 \times 10^{-5} l = 6 \times 10^{-4}$$

$$1.5 \times 10^{-5} l = 1.5 \times 10^{-4}$$

$$l = 10 \text{ cm}$$

Sol. 33 (D) $\Delta l = \frac{0.05}{100} l = \alpha l(100-0)$

$$\alpha = 5 \times 10^{-6}\,°C^{-1}$$

Sol. 34 (B) New length of bar

$$l' = l + 0.05\% \text{ of } l$$

$$= l + \frac{0.05}{100}l$$

$$= \frac{2001}{2000}l$$

New volume, $V' = (l')^3$

$$V' = 1.0015 l^3$$

Original volume $= V = l^3$

Percentage increase in volume

$$= \frac{V'-V}{V} \times 100$$

$$= \frac{1.0015-1}{1} \times 100$$

$$= 0.15\%$$

Sol. 35 (D) Let original area of square plate is $A = l^2$

New length, $l' = l + \frac{l}{100} = \frac{101l}{100}$

New Area, $A' = (l')^2 = 1.0201 l^2$

Percentage increase in area

$$= \frac{A' - A}{A} \times 100$$

$$= \frac{1.0201 - 1}{1} \times 100$$

$$= 2.01\%$$

Sol. 36 **(A)** Heat released by 240g water at 40°C when it gets converted to 240g water at 0°C

$$H = 240 \times 1 \times (40 - 0)$$

$$H = 9600 \text{ cal}$$

According to principle of calorimetry,

$$mL_f = H$$

$$m \times 80 = 9600$$

$$\Rightarrow \quad m = 120g$$

Sol. 37 **(B)** Let temperature of mixture is T

Also, let us assume $\theta_1, \theta_2 < T < \theta_3$

$\Rightarrow$ Heat lost by liquids 1 and 2 = Heat gained by liquid 3

$$m_1s_1(\theta_1 - T) + m_2s_2(\theta_2 - T) = m_3s_3(T - \theta_3)$$

$$m_1s_1\theta_1 - m_1s_1T + m_2s_2\theta_2 - m_2s_2T = m_3s_3T - m_3s_3\theta_3$$

$$m_1s_1\theta_1 + m_2s_2\theta_2 + m_3s_3\theta_3 = T(m_1s_1 + m_2s_2 + m_3s_3)$$

$$T = \frac{m_1s_1\theta_1 + m_2s_2\theta_2 + m_3s_3\theta_3}{m_1s_1 + m_2s_2 + m_3s_3}$$

Sol. 38 **(C)** We use

$$\text{Power} = \frac{H}{t}$$

$$2kW = \frac{mL_v}{t}$$

$$\Rightarrow \quad t = \frac{1.5 \times 2000 \times 10^3}{2 \times 10^3} = 1500 \text{ s}$$

Sol. 39 **(B)** We use $T_C = \frac{5}{9}(T_F - 32)$

$$\Rightarrow \quad T_F = 3T_C$$

and

$$\frac{T_F}{3} = \frac{5}{9}(T_F - 32)$$

$$\Rightarrow \quad 3T_F = 5T_F - (32 \times 5)$$

$$\Rightarrow \quad 2T_F = 160$$

$$\Rightarrow \quad T_F = 80°\text{F}$$

Sol. 40 **(B)** We have $n_x = 3n_y$

$\Rightarrow$ Temperature on y-scale

$$= 3 \times 15° = 45°$$

Sol. 41 **(C)** We use $A_t = A_0[1 + \beta\Delta T]$

$$\beta = 2\alpha = 2.2 \times 10^{-5}\,°\text{C}^{-1}$$

For cylinder to be inserted into hole. The area of hole must be equal to area of cross-section of cylinder at T °C (let)

When the steel plate is heated, the hole expands too

$$\frac{\pi(1)^2}{4} = \frac{\pi(0.99967)^2}{4}[1 + (2.2 \times 10^{-5})(T - 30)]$$

$$1.000660327 = 1 + (2.2 \times 10^{-5})(T - 30)$$

$$\Rightarrow \quad 6.6 \times 10^{-4} = (2.2 \times 10^{-5})(T - 30)$$

$$\Rightarrow \quad 30 = T - 30$$

$$\Rightarrow \quad T = 60°\text{C}$$

Sol. 42 **(D)** We use

$$A_t = A_0[1 + \beta\Delta T]$$

Let diameter at 0°C is d_0 cm and at dry ice (– 60°C) is d cm

$$\frac{\pi(10.02)^2}{4} = \frac{\pi d_0^2}{4}[1 + (4 \times 10^{-5})(40 - 0)] \quad \ldots(1)$$

$$\Rightarrow \quad \frac{\pi d^2}{4} = \frac{\pi d_0^2}{4}[1 + (4 \times 10^{-5})(-60 - 0)] \quad \ldots(2)$$

Dividing (1) by (2), we get

$$\frac{(10.02)^2}{d^2} = \frac{1.0016}{0.9976}$$

$$\Rightarrow \quad d = 9.99997 \text{ cm} \approx 10 \text{ cm}$$

Sol. 43 **(A)** We use $P = \frac{\rho RT}{M}$

$$\Rightarrow \quad \frac{P_1}{P_2} = \frac{\rho_1}{P_2} \times \frac{T_1}{T_2}$$

$$\Rightarrow \quad \frac{68}{70} = \frac{\rho_1}{\rho_2}\left(\frac{260}{300}\right)$$

$$\Rightarrow \quad \frac{\rho_1}{\rho_2} = 1.12$$

Sol. 44 **(B)** We use

$$\frac{\text{Reading of new scale-}LFP}{UFP\text{ - }LFP} = \frac{C - 0}{100}$$

$$\frac{T - (-10)}{90 - (-10)} = \frac{40}{100}$$

$$T = 30°\text{X}$$

Sol. 45 (D) Heat given out by 300*g* water at 25°C to cool down to water at 0°C

$$H_1 = 300 \times 1 \times (25-0) = 7500 \text{ cal}$$

Heat required by 100g ice at 0°C to melt,

$$H_2 = 100 \times 80 = 8000 \text{ cal}$$

As $H_2 > H_1$ so, some of the ice will melt and temperature of mixture will be 0°C.

Sol. 46 (A) Heat given out by 100g water at 80°C when it cools to 0°C

$$H_1 = 100 \times 1 \times (80-0) = 8000 \text{ J}$$

Heat required by 100g ice at 0°C to melt,

$$H_2 = 100 \times 80 = 8000 \text{ J}$$

As $H_1 = H_2$ so, all of the ice will melt and temperature of mixture is 0°C.

Sol. 47 (D) Magnitude of *emf*

$$= [-4-(-20)] \times (100-0) \times 10^{-6}$$

$$\Rightarrow \quad = 1.6 \times 10^{-3} V$$

$$\Rightarrow \quad = 1.6\, mV$$

Sol. 48 (B) Given that $R_0 = 2.56\Omega$

$$R_{100} = 3.56\Omega$$

$$R_t = 5.06\Omega$$

$$t = \frac{R_t - R_0}{R_{100} - R_0} \times 100°C$$

$$\Rightarrow \quad t = \frac{5.06-2.56}{3.56-2.56} \times 100°C$$

$$\Rightarrow \quad t = 250°C$$

Sol. 49 (D) $T_c = \frac{5}{9}(T_F - 32)$

$$\Rightarrow \quad 90 = \frac{5}{9}(T_F - 32)$$

$$\Rightarrow \quad T_F = 194°F$$

Since the faulty thermometer reads 190°F, the correction to be made is +4°F.

Sol. 50 (D) Let reading of faulty thermometer and correct thermometer is T°F

$$\Rightarrow \quad \frac{T-34}{210-34} = \frac{T-32}{180}$$

$$\Rightarrow \quad 180T - 6120 = 176T - 5632$$

$$\Rightarrow \quad 4T = 488$$

$$\Rightarrow \quad T = 122°F$$

Sol. 51 (B) We use $l_1 = l_0(1+\alpha_1 \Delta T)$

$$l_2 = l_0(1+\alpha_2 \Delta T)$$

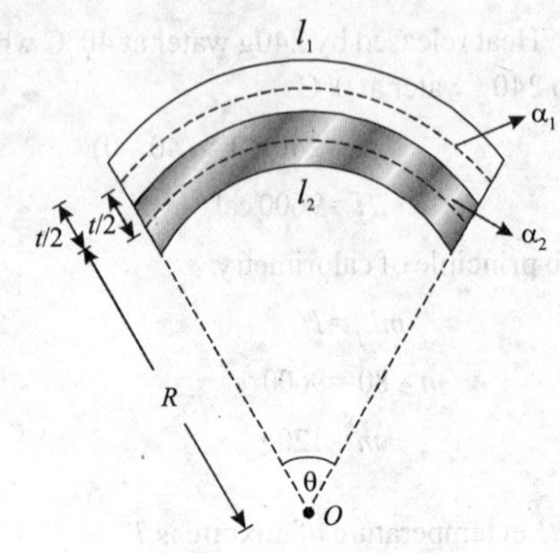

$$\because \quad \theta = \frac{l}{R}$$

$$\therefore \quad l_1 = \theta\left[R + \frac{t}{2}\right] \quad \ldots(1)$$

$$l_2 = \theta\left[R - \frac{t}{2}\right] \quad \ldots(2)$$

$$\theta\left(R + \frac{t}{2}\right) = l_0(1+\alpha_1 \Delta T) \quad \ldots(3)$$

$$\theta\left(R - \frac{t}{2}\right) = l_0(1+\alpha_2 \Delta T) \quad \ldots(4)$$

Dividing (3) by (4), we get

$$\frac{R+\frac{t}{2}}{R-\frac{t}{2}} = \frac{1+\alpha_1 \Delta T}{1+\alpha_2 \Delta T}$$

$$R + \alpha_2 R \Delta T + \frac{t}{2} + \frac{\alpha_2 \Delta T t}{2} = R + \alpha_1 R \Delta T - \frac{t}{2} - \frac{\alpha_1 \Delta T t}{2}$$

$$R(\alpha_2 - \alpha_1)\Delta T = -t - \frac{\Delta T t(\alpha_1 + \alpha_2)}{2}$$

$$R = \frac{2t + t\Delta T(\alpha_1 + \alpha_2)}{2(\alpha_1 - \alpha_2)\Delta T}$$

$$R = t\left[\frac{2 + (\alpha_1 + \alpha_2)\Delta T}{2(\alpha_1 - \alpha_2)\Delta T}\right]$$

Neglecting $(\alpha_1 + \alpha_2)$ in numerator,

$$R = \frac{t}{(\alpha_1 - \alpha_2)\Delta T}$$

Sol. 52 (D) We use $V_t = V_0[1 + \gamma\Delta T]$

$$\gamma = 3\alpha = 3 \times 2 \times 10^{-5}\,°C^{-1}$$

$$= 6 \times 10^{-6}\,°C^{-1}$$

When cube is heated from 0°C to 200°C,

$$\Delta V = V_0\gamma\Delta T$$

$$\Delta V = (10 \times 10^{-3})^3 \times (6 \times 10^{-5})(200)$$

$$\Delta V = 10^{-6} \times 6 \times 10^{-5} \times 200$$

$$\Delta V = 1.2 \times 10^{-8}\,\text{cm}^3$$

Percentage change in volume

$$= \frac{\Delta V}{V} \times 100$$

$$= \frac{1.2 \times 10^{-8}}{1 \times 10^{-6}} \times 100$$

$$= 1.2\%$$

Sol. 53 (D) Let reading of x is $T°$

$$\frac{T-20}{80} = \frac{120-30}{120}$$

$$\Rightarrow \quad T - 20 = 60$$

$$\Rightarrow \quad T = 80°$$

Sol. 54 (C) We convert all to °C so we have

$$100K = -173°C$$

and $$-13°F = \frac{9}{5}T_C + 32$$

$$\Rightarrow \quad -13°F = -25°C$$

Thus (C) – 20°C is the highest.

Sol. 55 (A) We use

$$T_{C_1} - T_{C_2} = \frac{5}{9}(T_{F_1} - T_{F_2})$$

$$\Rightarrow \quad 25 = \frac{5}{9}(T_{F_1} - T_{F_2})$$

$$\Rightarrow \quad T_{F_1} - T_{F_2} = 45°F$$

Sol. 56 (B) We use

$$\frac{\text{Reading of faulty thermometer} - LFP}{UFP - LFP} = \frac{C-0}{100}$$

$$\Rightarrow \quad \frac{60-(-10)}{U-(10)} = \frac{50}{100}$$

$$\Rightarrow \quad U = 130°C$$

Sol. 57 (B) We use directly

$$T_k = 273.16\left[\frac{p}{p_{tr}}\right]K$$

Sol. 58 (D) We use $T_C = \frac{5}{9}(T_F - 32)$

$$T_C = \frac{5}{9}T_F - \frac{160}{9}$$

Thus graph between °C and °F can be drawn as

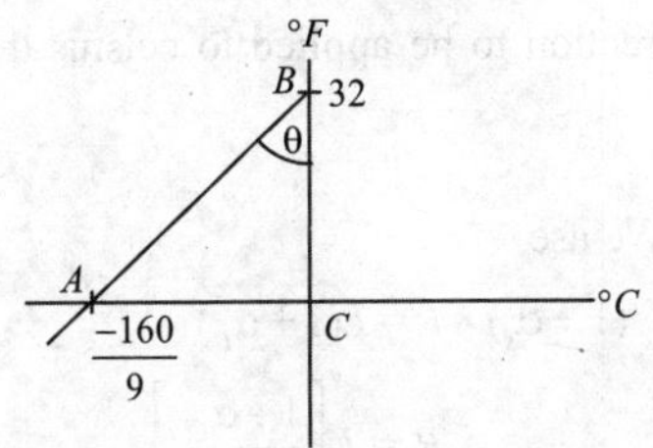

From graph we have $\sin\theta = \frac{AC}{AB} = \frac{160/9}{\sqrt{\left(\frac{160}{9}\right)^2 + (32)^2}}$

$$\Rightarrow \quad = \frac{160 \times 9}{9 \times 32\sqrt{106}} = \frac{5}{\sqrt{106}}$$

Sol. 59 (D) Kelvin and Reaumur scale do not agree to a common temperature

Sol. 60 (D) We use

$$\frac{\text{Reading of faulty thermometer} - LFP}{UFP - LFP} = \frac{T_C - 0}{100}$$

Let temperature on thermometer is T°C,

$$\Rightarrow \quad \frac{T-(-2)}{96-(-2)} = \frac{50-0}{100}$$

$$\Rightarrow \quad T = 47°C$$

Sol. 61 (D) We use $T_k = 273.16 \times \frac{30}{15}K$

$$\Rightarrow \quad T_k = 546.32\,K$$

Sol. 62 (B) We use $1ppm = 10^{-6}$m

$$\Delta l = l\alpha\Delta T$$

$$\Rightarrow \quad 10^{-6} = 1 \times 10^{-5} \times \Delta T$$

$$\Rightarrow \quad \Delta T = \pm 0.1\,K$$

Sol. 63 (C) We use

$$\frac{50-40}{120-40} = \frac{Y-(-30)}{130-(-30)}$$

$$\Rightarrow \quad \frac{10}{80} = \frac{Y+30}{160}$$

$$\Rightarrow \quad \frac{1}{8} = \frac{Y+30}{160}$$

$$\Rightarrow \quad Y+30 = 20$$

$$\Rightarrow \quad Y = -10°$$

Sol. 64 (B) We use $T_C = \frac{5}{9}(T_F - 32)$

$$\Rightarrow \quad T_C = \frac{5}{9}(113-32) = 45°C$$

Thus, the correction to be applied to celsius thermometer is +1°C.

Sol. 65 (C) We use

$$(1+\alpha_s) \times R = L(1+\alpha_C)$$

$$\Rightarrow \quad R = L\left[\frac{1+\alpha_C}{1+\alpha_S}\right]$$

Sol. 66 (C) We use $T = 2\pi\sqrt{\frac{l}{g}}$

$$T \propto \sqrt{l}$$

$$\frac{T'}{T} = \sqrt{\frac{l'}{l}} = \sqrt{\frac{l+\Delta l}{l}} = \sqrt{\frac{l+\alpha l\Delta\theta}{l}}$$

$$\Rightarrow \quad \frac{T'}{T} = (1+\alpha\Delta\theta)^{1/2}$$

$$\Rightarrow \quad T' = T(1+\alpha\Delta\theta)^{1/2}$$

As α is small,

$$\Rightarrow \quad T' = T\left[1+\frac{1}{2}\alpha\Delta\theta\right]$$

$$\Rightarrow \quad \Delta T = T' - T = \frac{1}{2}\alpha T\Delta\theta$$

Fraction change in time period,

$$\frac{\Delta T}{T} = \frac{1}{2}\alpha\Delta\theta$$

$$= \frac{1}{2}\alpha(\theta_2 - \theta_1)$$

Sol. 67 (A) We use $\rho_{100} = \rho_0(1-\rho\Delta T)$

$$9.7 = 10[1-3\alpha(100-0)]$$

$$\alpha = 1 \times 10^{-4}\,°C^{-1}$$

$$\alpha = 0.0001\,°C^{-1}$$

Sol. 68 (B) Let initial radius of sphere is R and after raising temperature by 100°C, its radius becomes R'

$$V = \frac{4}{3}\pi R^3 \quad \ldots(1)$$

and $$V' = \frac{4}{3}\pi R'^3$$

$$\Rightarrow \quad V+\Delta V = \frac{4}{3}\pi R'^3$$

$$\Rightarrow \quad V[1+(3\times 10^{-5})(100)] = \frac{4}{3}\pi R'^3 \quad \ldots(2)$$

Dividing (1) by (2), we get

$$\frac{1000}{1003} = \frac{R^3}{R'^3}$$

$$\Rightarrow \quad R' = 1.000999\,R$$

$$\Rightarrow \quad I = \frac{2}{5}MR^2 \quad \ldots(3)$$

$$\Rightarrow \quad I' = \frac{2}{5}MR'^2 = 1.001999\left[\frac{2}{5}MR^2\right] \quad \ldots(4)$$

Percentage increase in moment of inertia, $\frac{I'-I}{I}\times 100$

$$= 0.2\%$$

Sol. 69 (A) We use $V = V_0[1+\gamma\Delta T]$

$$\Rightarrow \quad 1016.2 = 1000[1+\gamma(320-20)]$$

$$\Rightarrow \quad 1.0162 = 1+300\gamma$$

$$\Rightarrow \quad 0.0162 = 300\gamma$$

$$\gamma = 5.4 \times 10^{-5}\,°C^{-1}$$

$$\alpha = \frac{\gamma}{3} = 1.8\times 10^{-5}\,°C^{-1}$$

$$\alpha = 18\times 10^{-6}\,°C^{-1}$$

Sol. 70 (B) Time lost, $\Delta T = \frac{1}{2}\alpha T\Delta\theta$

$$10 = \frac{1}{2}\alpha(86400)(20)$$

$$\Rightarrow \quad \alpha = \frac{1}{86400}\,°C^{-1}$$

Sol. 71 (B) We use $\Delta T = \frac{1}{2}\alpha T\Delta\theta$

$$\Rightarrow \quad \Delta T = \frac{1}{2}\times 1.9\times 10^{-5}\times 86400\times 25$$

$$\Rightarrow \quad \Delta T = 20.52\text{ s}$$

Sol. 72 (C) We use

$$\frac{59-5}{95-5} = \frac{T_C - 0}{100}$$

$$\Rightarrow \quad \frac{54}{90} = \frac{T_C}{100}$$

$$\Rightarrow \quad T_C = 60°$$

Sol. 73 (B) $T_C = \frac{5}{9}(T_F - 32)$

Let $T_C = x$

and $T_F = -x$

$\Rightarrow x = \frac{5}{9}[-x - 32]$

$\Rightarrow 9x = -5x - 160$

$\Rightarrow 14x = -160$

$\Rightarrow x = -11.43°C$ and and 11.43°F

Sol. 74 (C) Heat required to melt 10g ice

$$H = 80 \times 10 = 800 \text{ cal}$$

Heat supplied $= 0.93wh$

$$= \frac{0.93 \times 3600}{4.16} = 804.8 \text{ cal}$$

The entire block just melts.

Sol. 75 (C) $\Delta l = l\alpha\Delta\theta$

$\Rightarrow 1.1 \times 10^{-3} = 10 \times 0.000011[27 - T]$

$\Rightarrow 10 = 27 - T$

$\Rightarrow T = 17°C$

Sol. 76 (C) Energy stored per unit volume of the rod

$$= \frac{1}{2} \times \text{stress} \times \text{strain}$$

$$= \frac{1}{2} Y\alpha\Delta T \times \alpha\Delta T$$

$$= \frac{1}{2} Y[\alpha\Delta T]^2$$

$$= \frac{1}{2} \times 10^{11} \times (12 \times 10^{-6} \times 20)^2$$

$$= 2880 \text{ J/m}^3$$

Sol. 77 (B) Let final temperature is T°C

According to principle of calorimetry,

$$440 \times 1 \times (92 - T) = 200 \times 1 \times (T - 20) + 20 \times (T - 20)$$

$\Rightarrow 440(92 - T) = 220(T - 20)$

$\Rightarrow 184 - 2T = T - 20$

$\Rightarrow 3T = 240$

$\Rightarrow T = 68°C$

Sol. 78 (B) Upthrust = weight (just about to sink)

$$V_s \rho'_L g = mg$$

$\Rightarrow \frac{4}{3} \times \frac{22}{7} \times (3.5)^3 \times \left[\frac{1.527}{1 + \gamma(35)}\right] \times g = 266.5 \times g$

$\Rightarrow \gamma \approx 8.48 \times 10^{-4}°C^{-1}$

Sol. 79 (C) Apparent in coefficient of expansion is

$$\gamma_a = \gamma_l - \gamma_c$$

$$\gamma_l = 0.000597 \text{ °C}^{-1}$$

$$\gamma_c = 3\alpha_g = 3 \times 0.000009 = 2.7 \times 10^{-5} \text{ °C}^{-1}$$

$$\gamma_a = 0.00057 \text{ °C}^{-1}$$

Sol. 80 (B) Heat given out when 10g water at 50°C is converted to water at 0°C

$$H_1 = 10 \times 1 \times (50 - 0) = 500 \text{ cal}$$

Heat required by 10g ice at – 20°C to reach 0°C

$$H_2 = 10 \times 0.5 \times 20 = 100 \text{ cal}$$

Amount of heat remaining = 400 cal

$$mL_f = 400$$

$\Rightarrow m \times 80 = 400$

$$m = 5g$$

Hence, mass of ice left $= 10g - 5g = 5g$

Sol. 81 (B) According to principle of calorimetry,

Let final temperature is T

$$55 \times 1 \times (40 - T) = (10 \times 80) + 10 \times 1 \times (T - 0)$$

$\Rightarrow 2200 - 55T = 800 + 10T$

$\Rightarrow 65T = 1400$

$\Rightarrow T = 21.5°C$

Sol. 82 (A) Let mass of steam condensed is m

According to principle of calorimetry,

$$1.12 \times 10^3 \times 1 \times (80 - 15) = m \times 540 + m \times 1 \times (100 - 80)$$

$\Rightarrow 72800 = 540m + 20m$

$\Rightarrow m = 130 \text{ g} = 0.130 \text{ kg}$

Sol. 83 (B) Let specific heat of liquids A, B and C be s_A, s_B and s_C respectively,

According to principle of calorimetry,

$$ms_A(16 - 12) = ms_B(19 - 16)$$

$\Rightarrow 4s_A = 3s_B$ ...(1)

$$ms_B(23 - 19) = ms_C(28 - 23)$$

$\Rightarrow 4s_B = 5s_C$ ...(2)

When A and C are mixed, let final temperature is T

From (1) and (2),

$$16s_A = 12s_B = 15s_C$$

$$\Rightarrow \quad ms_C(28-T) = ms_A(T-12)$$

$$\Rightarrow \quad 15s_C(28-T) = 15s_A(T-12)$$

$$\Rightarrow \quad 16s_A(28-T) = 15s_A(T-12)$$

$$\Rightarrow \quad T = \frac{16\times 28+12\times 15}{16+15}$$

$$\Rightarrow \quad T = 20.26°C = 20.3°C$$

Sol. 84 **(A)** Let mass of hail stone that falls is $m kg$

$$K.E. = m(10)(1000) = 10^4 \text{mJ}$$

for m kg of ice to melt, heat required,

$$H = m\times 3.4\times 10^5 \text{J}$$

$$= 34 \text{m}\times 10^4 \text{J}$$

Fraction of ice that will melt

$$= \frac{10^4 m}{34m\times 10^4}$$

$$= \frac{1}{34}$$

Sol. 85 **(C)** Let reading of celsius scale $= x°$
As reading of Reaumur scale $= (x-3)°$

$$\frac{(x-3)-0}{80-0} = \frac{x-0}{100-0}$$

$$\Rightarrow \quad \frac{x-3}{80} = \frac{x}{100}$$

$$\Rightarrow \quad 5x-15 = 4x$$

$$\Rightarrow \quad x = 15°$$

Sol. 86 **(A)** Heat given out when 5g water at 30°C cools down to 5g water at 0°C

$$H_1 = 5\times 1\times 30 = 150 \text{ cal}$$

Heat required by 5g ice to melt to water at 0°C

$$H_2 = (5\times 0.5\times 20)+(5\times 80)$$

$$= 50+400$$

$$= 450 \text{ cal}$$

Since this much heat is not available, the temperature of mixture = 0°C.

Sol. 87 **(D)** 50 cal out of 150 cal available is used to bring temperature of ice from – 20°C to 0°C

Heat available = 150 cal – 50 cal = 100 cal

This 100 cal melts m grams of ice

$$100 = m\times 80$$

$$\Rightarrow \quad m = 1.25\text{g}$$

Sol. 88 **(B)** Heat given out by 5g water to cool down to 0°C

$$H_1 = 5\times 1\times (10-0) = 50 \text{ cal}$$

Heat required by 1g ice to melt,

$$H_2 = 1\times 80 = 80 \text{ cal}$$

Since only 50 cal is available, some of ice melts and temperature of mixture is 0°C.

Sol. 89 **(B)** Heat released when 1g steam at 100°C converts to 1g water at 100°C

$$H_1 = 1\times 540 = 540 \text{ cal}$$

Heat required by 1g ice at 0°C to reach 1g water at 100°C

$$H_2 = 1\times 80+1\times 1\times 100 = 180 \text{ cal}$$

As $H_2 < H_1$ whole steam will not condense so final temperature will be 100°C.

Solutions of ADVANCE MCQs One or More Option Correct

Sol. 1 **(A, D)** Fahrenheit scale has 180 divisions between LFP and UFP whereas in Celsius and Kelvin scale divisions are 100.

Sol. 2 **(All)** Due to polymer properties rubber contracts on heating and water has maximum density at 4°C and water expands on freezing.

Sol. 3 **(A, C)** Due to rise in temperature its radius increases and which causes its moment of inertia to increase and to conserve angular momentum its angular speed decreases as no external torque is acting on it.

Sol. 4 **(A, C)** As on increasing temperature a metal scale expands, the separation between the divisions increases so reading will be less than true value hence option (A) is correct. In case of pendulum clock the length of pendulum increases so time period also increase so pendulum clock gets slower hence option (B) is wrong. For a floating body the density of liquid will decrease more than that of solid so it will sink more hence option (C) is correct. Weight of a body is not affected by temperature hence option (D) is wrong.

Sol. 5 **(A, B)** As at 4°C temperature water density is maximum, on increasing or decreasing temperature density decreases so in both beakers the liquid level will rise.

Sol. 6 **(C, D)** Thermal capacity of a body is the product of its mass and specific heat. Specific heat of a body is a property which depends upon the specific molecular structure of the body material hence options (C) and (D) are correct.

Sol. 7 **(All)** Specific heat of a body is the measure of heat gain or loss by body by its unit mass when its temperature increases by unity. In different materials it can take up any value depending upon the amount of heat required by the molecular structure of the body. If body does not absorb heat then its specific heat is zero, if its temperature does not change its infinite and if it takes some heat then its finite and if it rejects heat in rise of temperature its negative. In case of negative specific heat body uses its internal energy for rise in temperature.

Sol. 8 (B, C, D) In general case of mixing the one which is at higher temperature will loose heat and will cool down and the one at lower temperature will gain heat and will heat up hence options (C) or (D) are correct. If either of the sample is at its boiling or melting point then final temperature may be at this level if after mixing its in same state hence option (B) is also correct.

Sol. 9 (B, D) For water in a test tube, it will boil only when the heat will continuously conduct into the tube and for this outer temperature must be more than the boiling point of water which cannot be possible if outside boiling water exist hence option (A) is not correct. By increasing pressure melting point increases hence option (C) is not correct. By basic definitions of heat and condensation options (B) and (D) are correct.

Sol. 10 (A, C, D) When temperature increases material as well as all the lengths and volumes enclosed by the material also increases due to increase in intermolecular separation of the material.

Sol. 11 (B, C) We can see the slope of second step (liquid heating) is less than that of first step (Solid heating) hence specific heat of liquid is greater than that of solid. We can also see that the horizontal portion of first part is smaller than that of second part which implies that solid melting is taking less time than liquid vaporization hence (C) is also correct.

Sol. 12 (B, C) As it is given that $L_1\alpha_1 = L_2\alpha_2$ the expansion in both the rods at same difference of temperature will be equal hence their difference in lengths will also remain equal.

Sol. 13 (B, C) When temperature increases of a bimetallic strip, the one which is having more value of coefficient of expansion will expand more so the strip will bend toward the metal with low value of coefficient of expansion and it will be bend toward high value of coefficient of expansion if it is cooled.

Sol. 14 (A, D) If $\alpha_b < \alpha_p$ then pipe will expand more than that of bolt and a tensile stress will be developed in the bolt and if $\alpha_b > \alpha_p$ then bolt will expand more than that of pipe and will remain loose so no stress will be developed in it.

Sol. 15 (A, B, C) We know that in case of a rotating body if no external torque is acting the angular momentum of the body remain conserved hence $I\omega$ = constant hence (B) is correct and for a cylinder we can use $I = (0.5)MR^2$ hence (A) is also correct. For the radius of the cylinder, on increasing its temperature by ΔT we can use $\Delta R = R\alpha\Delta T$ hence (C) is also correct.

Sol. 16 (B, D) As explained in Illustrative Example-1.5 (B) and (D) are correct.

Sol. 17 (A, C) Heat capacity of the body is the amount of heat required to raise the body temperature by 1°C so this is given as mc and water equivalent of the body is the amount of water which requires same amount of heat which the body requires for a specific rise in temperature, given as $w = mc/s_w = mc$ as $s_w =$ 1 cal/g °C.

Sol. 18 (A, C, D) When the bottle is shaken, we do work on the bottle and its contents which increases its internal energy as the bottle is thermally insulated so its temperature would rise.

Sol. 19 (A, B, C) When ice melts it absorbs heat $m \times 80$ and if equilibrium temperature of the mixture is T the water formed due to melting of ice will absorb heat $m \times 1 \times (T - 0)$ and initial water will release the heat $m \times 1 \times (100 - T)$ thus solving the equation of heat released = heat absorbed we get $T = 10°C$.

Sol. 20 (A, D) With the definition of thermal expansion for length and density options (A) and (D) are correct.

Sol. 21 (A, D) Kinetic energy of the rotating sphere is calculated as

$$K = \frac{1}{2} I\omega^2$$

$$\Rightarrow \quad K = \frac{1}{2} \times \frac{2}{5} MR^2(2\pi n)^2$$

$$\Rightarrow \quad K = \frac{4}{5} \pi^2 n^2 MR^2$$

Half of the kinetic energy used to raise, the temperature, which is given as

$$\frac{K}{2} = 0.5\left(\frac{4}{5}\pi^2 n^2 MR^2\right)$$

$$\Rightarrow \quad \frac{K}{2} = \frac{2}{5} \pi^2 n^2 mR^2$$

If the rise in temperature of the sphere is ΔT then we use

$$\frac{2}{5} \pi^2 n^2 mR^2 = mC\Delta T$$

$$\Rightarrow \quad \Delta T = \frac{2\pi^2 n^2 R^2}{5C}$$

Sol. 22 (B, C, D) Required heat Available heat

Required heat	Available heat
10 g ice (0ºC)	5 g steam (100ºC)
↓800 cal	↓ 2700 cal
10 g water (0ºC)	5 g water (100ºC)
↓ 1000 cal	
10 g water (100º)	

So available heat is more than required heat therefore final temperature will be 100ºC.

Mass of vapour condensed

$$=\frac{800+1000}{540}=\frac{10}{3}\text{ g}$$

Total mass of water

$$=10+\frac{10}{3}=\frac{40}{3}=13\frac{1}{3}\text{ g}$$

Total mass of steam

$$=5-\frac{10}{3}=\frac{5}{3}=1\frac{2}{3}\text{ g}$$

Sol. 23 (A, C, D) Length $l = l_0(1 + \alpha\Delta T) = l_0(1 + 20\alpha)$

Area

$A = A_0(1 + \beta\Delta T) = 6l_0^2(1 + 40\alpha)$

Volume

$$V = V_0(1 + \gamma\Delta T) = l_0^3(1 + 3\alpha\Delta T) = l_0^3(1 + 60\alpha)$$

Density

$$\rho = \frac{\rho_0}{1+\gamma\Delta T} = \frac{\rho_0}{1+60\alpha}$$

Sol. 24 (A) Due to internal pressure inside the pressure cooker the boiling point of water is raised thats why more heat supplied will be used in cooking food rather as latent heat in vaporization of water.

Sol. 25 (All) When a body is heated all dimension of the material as well as the enclosed lengths, areas and volumes also increase.

Sol. 26 (B, C) At very low pressure all gases behave like ideal. They follow ideal gas law $\rho v = nRT$ so option (B) and (C) are correct.

* * * * *

ANSWERS & SOLUTIONS

CONCEPTUAL MCQS Single Option Correct

1	(A)	2	(A)	3	(A)
4	(C)	5	(B)	6	(B)
7	(B)	8	(B)	9	(B)
10	(B)	11	(A)	12	(B)
13	(C)	14	(C)	15	(D)
16	(C)	17	(A)	18	(B)
19	(C)	20	(B)	21	(C)
22	(A)	23	(A)	24	(D)
25	(A)	26	(C)	27	(D)

NUMERICAL MCQS Single Option Correct

1	(D)	2	(D)	3	(C)
4	(C)	5	(B)	6	(A)
7	(A)	8	(A)	9	(D)
10	(B)	11	(D)	12	(D)
13	(B)	14	(A)	15	(D)
16	(D)	17	(B)	18	(B)
19	(B)	20	(B)	21	(B)
22	(D)	23	(B)	24	(B)
25	(C)	26	(D)	27	(C)
28	(B)	29	(C)	30	(A)
31	(B)	32	(A)	33	(B)

ADVANCE MCQs One or More Option Correct

1	(A, B, D)	2	(All)	3	(C, D)
4	(A, C)	5	(B, D)	6	(A, D)
7	(A, C, D)	8	(B, C)	9	(All)
10	(B, C)	11	(A, C)	12	(A, B, C)
13	(A, C, D)	14	(B, C, D)	15	(A, D)
16	(C, D)	17	(B, D)		

Solutions of PRACTICE EXERCISE 2.1

(i) We use initial moles = final moles

$$\frac{p_1V_1}{T_1} = \frac{p_2V_2}{T_2}$$

$$\Rightarrow \quad \frac{2\times10^5\times V}{293} = \frac{p\times1.02V}{313}$$

$$\Rightarrow \quad p = 2.095\times10^5\ \text{N/m}^2$$

(ii) We use initial moles = final moles

$$\frac{p_1V}{T_1}+\frac{p_2V}{T_2} = \frac{p_f(2V)}{T}$$

$$\Rightarrow \quad p_f = \frac{T}{2}\left[\frac{p_1}{T_1}+\frac{p_2}{T_2}\right]$$

(iii) By gas law we use

$$PV = nRT$$

$$2\times20 = \left(\frac{m_1}{2}+\frac{m_2}{4}\right)(0.082)(293)$$

$$\Rightarrow \quad 2m_1+m_2 = 6.66$$

and $\quad m_1+m_2 = 5$

Solving we get

$$m_1 = 1.66\ \text{g}$$

$$m_2 = 3.34\ \text{g}$$

$$\Rightarrow \quad \frac{m_1}{m_2} = \frac{1}{2}$$

(iv) If initial pressure k temperature are P and T we use

$$\frac{P}{T} = \frac{1.01P}{T+1}$$

$$\Rightarrow \quad T+1 = 1.01\,T$$

$$\Rightarrow \quad 0.01\,T = 1$$

$$\Rightarrow \quad T = 100\ \text{K}$$

(v) If vessel volume is V then partial pressures of N_2 and CO_2 are

$$P_{N_2} = \left(\frac{7}{28}\right)\frac{(8.314)(290)}{V}$$

and $$P_{CO_2} = \left(\frac{11}{44}\right)\frac{(8.314)(290)}{V}$$

Given that $\quad P_1+P_2 = 10^5$

$$\frac{8.314}{V}\left(\frac{290}{4}+\frac{290}{4}\right) = 10^5$$

$$\Rightarrow \quad V = 1.205\times10^{-2}\ \text{m}^3$$

Thus mixture density $P = \dfrac{m_1+m_2}{V} = \dfrac{18\times10^{-3}}{1.205\times10^{-2}}$

$$= 1.494\ \text{kg/m}^3$$

(vi) We use $\quad P_{H_2} = \left(\frac{30}{2}\right)\times\frac{8.314\times300}{30\times10^{-3}}$

$$= 12.471\times10^5\ \text{Pa}$$

$$P_{O_2} = \frac{160}{32}\times\frac{8.314\times300}{10\times10^{-3}}$$

$$= 12.471\times10^5\ \text{Pa}$$

$$P_{N_2} = \frac{70}{28}\times\frac{8.314\times300}{20\times10^{-3}}$$

$$= 3.118\times10^5\ \text{Pa}$$

$$P_{left} = P_{H_2} = 12.471\times10^5\ \text{Pa}$$

$$P_{middle} = P_{H_2}+P_{O_2}+P_{N_2} = 28.06\times10^5\ \text{Pa}$$

$$P_{right} = P_{H_2}+P_{N_2} = 15.589\times10^5\ \text{Pa}$$

(vii) At *STP* we use

$$P = \frac{PRT}{M}$$

$$\Rightarrow \quad 10^5 = \frac{1.3 \times 8.314 \times 273}{M}$$

$$\Rightarrow \quad M = 2.95 \times 10^{-3}\,\text{kg}$$

This for given conditions

$$\Delta P = \frac{\Delta hRT}{V}$$

$$\Rightarrow \quad 0.415 \times 10^5 = \frac{\Delta h \times 8.314 \times 336}{30 \times 10^{-3}}$$

$$\Rightarrow \quad \Delta h = 0.4456\,\text{mole}$$

$$\Rightarrow \quad m = \Delta h \times M = 13.14\,\text{g}$$

(viii) We use $\quad P = \frac{0.6 \times 8.314 \times 300}{8.3 \times 10^{-3}}$

$$= 1.8 \times 10^5\,\text{Pa}$$

equivalent molecular weight of mixture is

$$M_{eq} = \frac{0.1 \times 28 + 0.2 \times 32 + 0.35 \times 44}{0.6}$$

$$= 37.33$$

(ix) We use initial moles = final moles

$$\frac{76 \times 4}{303} = \frac{P \times 3}{373} + \frac{P \times 1}{303}$$

$$\Rightarrow \quad P = \frac{76 \times 4}{\left(\frac{303}{373} \times 3 + 1\right)} = \frac{304}{3.437}$$

$$= 88.45\,\text{am of Hg}$$

(x) We use pressure difference constant in upper and lower parts as weight of piston is constant.

Initial at 300 K, and finally at temperature *T* for upper part we use

$$\frac{P(4V)}{300} = \frac{P_f(2V_f)}{T} \quad \ldots(1)$$

and we use $\quad 3P = P_f \quad \ldots(2)$

and $\quad 5V = 3V_f \quad \ldots(3)$

Using equations (1), (2) and (3) we have

$$\Rightarrow \quad \frac{4}{300} = \frac{3 \times \frac{5}{3} \times 2}{T}$$

$$\Rightarrow \quad T = 750\,\text{K}$$

Solutions of PRACTICE EXERCISE 2.2

(i) We use $\quad P_1V_1 = P_2V_2$

$$\Rightarrow \quad (76 + 10) \times 10 = 76 \times l'$$

$$\Rightarrow \quad l' = 11.315\,\text{cm}$$

mass of air is $\quad m = \frac{PVM}{RT}$

$$= \frac{1.013 \times 10^5 \times 11.315 \times 10^{-2} \times 10^{-4} \times 29 \times 10^{-3}}{8.314 \times 300}$$

$$= 13.32\,\text{mg}$$

(ii) At 60° tilt we use

$$(76 - 10) \times 40 = (76 - 5) \times l_1$$

$$\Rightarrow \quad l_1 = 37.18\,\text{cm}$$

at 90° till we use

$$(76 - 10) \times 40 = 76 \times l_2$$

$$\Rightarrow \quad l_2 = 34.73\,\text{cm}$$

(iii) At depth 20 cm, of tube if air length is *x*, we use

$$10^5 \times 0.5 = [10^5 + (0.2 + x)\,8 \times 1000 \times 10] \times x$$

$$\Rightarrow \quad 5 \times 10^4 = 10^5 x + 0.2x \times 10^4 + x^2 \times 10^4$$

$$\Rightarrow \quad x^2 + 10.2x - 5 = 0$$

$$\Rightarrow \quad x = \frac{-10.2 \pm \sqrt{104.04 + 20}}{2} = 0.468\,\text{m}$$

Net upward force on tube is

$$F_{up} = F_{\text{Buoyoncy}} - mg$$

$$= 0.468 \times 0.5 \times 10^{-4} \times 1000 \times 10 - 0.015 \times 10$$

$$= 0.234 - 0.15$$

$$= 0.084\,\text{N}$$

(iv) At a height *y* we consider an elemental layer of width *dy*. If mass in this layer is *dm*, we use

$$dm = S\,dy\,\rho$$

$$\Rightarrow \quad dm = S\,dy\left(\frac{pM}{RT}\right)$$

$$dm = \frac{MS}{RT}\,p_0 e^{-\frac{Mgy}{RT}}\,dy$$

Total mass is $\quad m = \int dm = \frac{p_0 MS}{RT}\int_0^h e^{-Mgy/RT}\,dy$

$$= \frac{p_0 MS}{RT}\left(-\frac{RT}{Mg}\right)\left[e^{-Mgy/RT}\right]_0^h$$

$$= \frac{p_0 S}{g}\left(1 - e^{-Mgh/RT}\right)$$

(v) After tilting then tube by 60° we use

$$P_1V_1 = P_2V_2$$

$$(76+20)\times 43 = (76+10)\times l$$

$$\Rightarrow \quad l = 48 \text{ cm}$$

(vi) Centre of gravity of gas is given by

$$h_c = \frac{\int dm y}{\int dm}$$

where dm is mass of a layer of width dy at a height y

$$\Rightarrow \quad dm = Sdy\rho \qquad [S \text{ is base area of vessel}]$$

for uniform g and T we use

$$\rho = P_0 e^{-Mg\, y/RT}$$

where ρ_0 is density at base

$$\Rightarrow \quad h_c = \frac{\int_0^\infty S\rho_0 e^{-Mgy/RT}\, y dy}{\int_0^\infty S\rho_0 e^{-Mgy/RT}\, dy}$$

$$\Rightarrow \quad h_c = \frac{\left[y\dfrac{e^{-Mgy/RT}}{(-Mg/RT)} - \dfrac{e^{-Mgy/RT}}{(-Mg/RT)^2}\right]}{\left[\dfrac{e^{-Mgy/RT}}{-Mg/RT}\right]_0^\infty}$$

$$= \frac{0 - \left(\dfrac{RT}{Mg}\right)^2}{\left(-\dfrac{RT}{Mg}\right)} = \frac{RT}{Mg}$$

(vii) Initially air inside barometer

$$= 100 - 74.8 = 52.2 \text{ cm}$$

In second case air inside

$$= 100 - 73.6 \text{ cm} = 26.4 \text{ cm}$$

By gas law we use

$$(75.5 - l + 25.2)\times 25.2 = (74 - l + 26.4)\times 26.4$$

$$\Rightarrow \quad 2537.64 - 25.2l = 2650.56 - 26.4\, l$$

$$\Rightarrow \quad 1.2\, l = 112.92$$

$$\Rightarrow \quad l = 94.1 \text{ cm}$$

(viii) At a distance x from open end we consider an elemental layer of width dx and if pressure difference across this layer is dp we use

$$dp = dx(\omega^2 x)\,\rho = (\omega^2 x)dx\left(\frac{pM}{RT}\right)$$

$$\Rightarrow \quad \int_{p_0}^{p_x} \frac{dp}{p} = \frac{M\omega^2}{RT}\int_0^r x dx$$

$$\Rightarrow \quad \ln\frac{p_x}{p_0} = \frac{M\omega^2 r^2}{2RT}$$

$$\Rightarrow \quad p_x = p_0 e^{\frac{M\omega^2 r^2}{2RT}}$$

(ix) (a) For a layer of width dy at a height y we use

$$dp = -\,dy\rho g = -\left(\frac{pM}{RT}\right)gdy$$

$$\int_{p_0}^{p} \frac{dp}{p} = \frac{-Mg}{RT_0}\int_0^h \frac{dy}{1-ay}$$

$$\ln\frac{p}{p_0} = \frac{Mg}{RT_0}\ln(1-ah)$$

$$p = p_0(1-ah)^{Mg/aRT_0}$$

above relation is valid if

$$h < \frac{1}{a}$$

(b) Now we use

$$dp = -dyg\left(\frac{pM}{RT}\right)$$

$$\Rightarrow \quad \int_{p_0}^{p} \frac{dp}{p} = \frac{-Mg}{RT_0}\int_0^h \frac{dy}{(1+ay)}$$

$$\ln\frac{p}{p_0} = \frac{-Mg}{aRT_0}\ln(1+ah)$$

$$p = \frac{p_0}{(1+ah)^{Mg/aRT_0}}$$

Solutions of PRACTICE EXERCISE 2.3

(i) We use $\quad v_{\text{rms}} = \sqrt{\dfrac{3RT}{M}}$

$$\Rightarrow \quad \frac{v_1}{v_2} = \sqrt{\frac{T_1M_2}{T_2M_1}}$$

$$\Rightarrow \quad v_2 = v_1\sqrt{\frac{T_2M_1}{T_1M_2}} = 300 \times v_1\sqrt{\frac{2T_1M_1}{T_1\times(M_1/2)}}$$

$$= 600 \text{ m/s}$$

(ii) Number of molecules hitting per square meter of container wall is given as

$$N_c = \frac{1}{6}\, h_0 v_{\text{rms}} = \frac{1}{6}\times 10^{26}\times 2000$$

$$= 3.33\times 10^{28} \text{ per second}$$

and pressure is $\quad P = \dfrac{1}{3}\rho v_{rms}^2$

$$= \frac{1}{3}\times 3\times 10^{-27}\times 10^{26}\times (2000)^2$$

$$= 4\times 10^5 \text{ N/m}^2$$

(iii) If final pressure inside air is P_f we use

$$66 \times 40 = P_f \times 38$$

$$\Rightarrow \quad P_f = 69.47 \text{ cm of } Hg$$

For equilibrium of Hg pallet we use

$$P_f \times \pi r^2 + \frac{h}{2}\rho g \pi r^2 + f_r = P_{atm} \times \pi r^2$$

$$0.6947 \times 13600 \times 10 + 0.05 \times 13600 \times 10 + \frac{f_r}{\pi r^2}$$

$$= 0.76 \times 13600 \times 10$$

$$\Rightarrow \quad f_r = 3.14 \times (2 \times 10^{-3})^2 \times 0.0153 \times 13600 \times 10$$

$$= 0.026 \text{ N}$$

Alternative: This problem can be directly solved by finding the mercury pressure balanced by friction which is

$$76 - 5 - 69.47 = 1.53 \text{ cm of } Hg$$

$$\Rightarrow \quad f_r = 0.0153 \times 13600 \times 10 \times 3.14 \times (2 \times 10^{-3})^2$$

$$= 0.026 \text{ N}$$

(iv) Average translational kinetic energy of all gases remains same at same temperature and equal to $\frac{3}{2}kT$.

(v) Pressure of gas is given as

$$P = \frac{2}{3} \text{ (translational kinetic energy per unit volume)}$$

$$\Rightarrow \quad P = \frac{2}{3}\left(\frac{3}{2}kT \times n_0\right)$$

$$\Rightarrow \quad P = n_0 kT$$

$$\Rightarrow \quad n_0 = \frac{1.013 \times 10^5}{1.38 \times 10^{-23} \times 273}$$

$$= 2.688 \times 10^{25} \text{ m}^{-3}$$

average separation between molecules

$$d = \left(\frac{1}{n_0}\right)^{\frac{1}{3}} = 3.31 \times 10^{-9} \text{ m}$$

(iv) (a) We use $v_{mp} = \sqrt{\frac{2RT}{M}} = \sqrt{\frac{2 \times 8.314 \times 300}{2 \times 10^{-3}}}$

$$= 1579.3 \text{ m/s}$$

$$v_{mean} = \sqrt{\frac{8RT}{\pi M}} = \sqrt{\frac{8 \times 8.314 \times 300}{3.14 \times 2 \times 10^{-3}}}$$

$$= 1782.5 \text{ m/s}$$

$$v_{rms} = \sqrt{\frac{3RT}{m}} = \sqrt{\frac{3 \times 8.314 \times 300}{2 \times 10^{-3}}}$$

$$= 1934.25 \text{ m/s}$$

(b) We use $v_{mp} = \sqrt{\frac{2RT}{m}} = \sqrt{\frac{2 \times 8.314 \times 300}{32 \times 10^{-3}}}$

$$= 394.83 \text{ m/s}$$

$$v_{\text{mean}} = \sqrt{\frac{8RT}{\pi M}} = \sqrt{\frac{8 \times 8.314 \times 300}{32 \times 10^{-3}}}$$

$$= 445.63 \text{ m/s}$$

$$v_{rms} = \sqrt{\frac{8RT}{m}} = \sqrt{\frac{3 \times 8.314 \times 300}{32 \times 10^{-3}}}$$

$$= 483.56 \text{ m/s}$$

(vii) (a) $v_{mean} = \frac{5+2+2+6+0+4+1+3+5+1+7+3}{12}$

$$= 3.25 \text{ m/s}$$

(b)

$$v_{rms} = \sqrt{\frac{5^2+2^2+2^2+6^2+0^2+4^2+1^2+3^2+5^2+1^2+7^2+3^2}{12}}$$

$$= 3.86 \text{ m/s}$$

(viii) Temperature of nitrogen is

$$T = \frac{PV}{nR} = \frac{2.1 \times 8 \times 10^3}{1300 \times 0.082} = 157.6 \text{ k}$$

$$\Rightarrow \quad v_{rms} = \sqrt{\frac{3RT}{M}} = \sqrt{\frac{3 \times 8.314 \times 1576}{28 \times 10^{-3}}}$$

$$= 374.68 \text{ m/s}$$

Solutions of PRACTICE EXERCISE 2.4

Sol. (i) We use $\frac{K_T}{K_R} = \frac{\frac{3}{2}nRT}{\frac{(f-3)}{2}nRT} = \frac{3}{2}$

$$\frac{3}{f-3} = \frac{3}{2}$$

$$\Rightarrow \quad \sigma = 3f - 9 \quad \Rightarrow \quad f = 5$$

Now $U = \frac{f}{2}nRT$

$$= \frac{5}{2} \times 1 \times 8.3 \times 100 = 2075 \text{ J}$$

(ii) Rotational kinetic energy of a diatomic molecule is

$$E = kT = \frac{1}{2}I\omega_{rms}^2$$

$$\Rightarrow \quad \omega_{rms} = \sqrt{\frac{2kT}{I}}$$

$$= \sqrt{\frac{2 \times 1.38 \times 10^{-23} \times 300}{2.1 \times 10^{-39}}}$$

$$= 1.985 \times 10^9 \text{ rad/s}$$

(iii) (a) Average molecular energy of a gas is

$$= \frac{f}{2}kT = 6\,\text{kT}$$
$$= 6 \times 1.38 \times 10^{-23} \times 650$$
$$= 5.382 \times 10^{-20}\,\text{J}$$

(b) We use $v_{rms} = \sqrt{\frac{3RT}{M}} = \sqrt{\frac{3 \times 8.314 \times 650}{1.3 \times 10^{-25} \times 6.023 \times 10^{23}}}$

$$= 455.03\,\text{m/s}$$

(c) For a non linear polyatomic molecule there are 3 translational and 3 rotational degrees of freedom so vibrational degrees of freedom are

$$f_v = f_{total} - 6 = 6$$

(iv) For inelastic collisions of two atoms to excite both hydrogen atoms we use

$$\frac{3}{2}kT = 10.2 = V$$
$$T = \frac{10.2 \times 1.6 \times 10^{-19}}{1.5 \times 1.38 \times 10^{-23}}$$
$$= 7.88 \times 10^4\,\text{K}$$

(v) We use by gas law

$$\frac{p_1 V}{T_1} + \frac{p_2 V}{T_2} = \frac{p_{1f} V}{T_f} + \frac{p_{2f} V}{T_f} \quad \ldots(1)$$

by conservation of energy we use

$$\frac{f}{2}p_1 V + \frac{f}{2}p_2 V = \frac{f}{2}p_{1f} V + \frac{f}{2}p_{2f} V$$

$$\Rightarrow \quad p_{1f} + p_{2f} = p_1 + p_2 \quad \ldots(2)$$

from (1) and (2) we have

$$\frac{p_1}{T_1} + \frac{p_2}{T_2} = \frac{p_1 + p_2}{T_f}$$

$$\Rightarrow \quad T_f = \frac{T_1 T_2 (p_1 + p_2)}{(p_1 T_2 + p_2 T_1)}$$

for left and right part of gas

$$\frac{p_1}{T_1} = \frac{p_{1f}}{T_k} \text{ and } \frac{p_2}{T_2} = \frac{p_{2f}}{T_f}$$

$$\Rightarrow \quad p_{1f} = \frac{p_1 T_2 (p_1 + p_2)}{p_1 + T_2 + p_2 T_1}$$

$$\text{and} \quad p_{2f} = \frac{p_2 T_1 (p_1 + p_2)}{p_1 + T_2 + p_2 T_1}$$

(vi) That supplied from left part in

$$\Delta Q = U_i - U_f$$
$$= \frac{f}{2}p_1 V - \frac{f}{2}p_{1f} V$$
$$= \frac{f}{2}V\left[p_1 - \frac{p_1 T_2 (p_1 + p_2)}{(p_1 T_2 + p_2 T_1)}\right]$$
$$= \frac{f}{2}V\left[\frac{p_1 p_2 T_2 - p_1 p_2 T_2}{p_1 T_2 + p_2 T_1}\right]$$
$$= \frac{3}{2}\frac{p_1 p_2 V (T_2 - T_1)}{(p_1 T_2 + p_2 T_1)}$$

Solutions of CONCEPTUAL MCQS Single Option Correct

Sol. 1 (A) As RMS speed is inversely proportional to the square root of molecular mass of the gas, option (A) is correct.

Sol. 2 (A) At higher pressure boiling point of water increases so more heat will be used in cooking.

Sol. 3 (A) According to maxwell distribution curve as temperature increases the curve expands and its peak decreases as discussed in section 2.4 hence the number of molecules having most probable speed will decrease.

Sol. 4 (C) In evacuated chamber water evaporates fast and for evaporation it gains heat from the remaining water only due to which some water will vaporize and the rest will freeze due to loss of heat as it is loosing heat at melting point.

Sol. 5 (B) In thermal equilibrium at a constant temperature, according to Maxwells distribution of speed the average speed remain constant.

Sol. 6 (B) As total molecules in the container increases so it will increase the frequency of collision of molecules with each other as well as with container walls which increases the pressure of gas.

Sol. 7 (B) Average kinetic energy of a molecule is 0.5 fkT where f are the degrees of freedom of the molecule and it is independent of type of the gas.

Sol. 8 (B) The total kinetic energy of gas is given as

$$K = \frac{f}{2}NkT = \text{constant}$$

$$\Rightarrow \quad NT = \text{constant}$$

$$\Rightarrow \quad T_2 = \frac{T_1}{2}$$

Also as total kinetic energy of all the molecules of gas is kept constant we can use

$$PV = \text{constant}$$

As box is closed, its volume is constant so pressure will also remain constant, which gives

$$P_2 = P_1$$

Sol. 9 (B) Average speed of O_2 molecule will remain same as v_1 at same temperature.

Sol. 10 (B) From gas law $PV = nRT$ the slope of the curve will be nR/V hence option (B) is correct.

Sol. 11 (A) Based on explanation of previous question option (A) is correct.

Sol. 12 (B) Due to sudden compression gas pressure and temperature increases and now as it is maintained at this position due to metal cylinder heat is conducted out and its temperature decreases and hence pressure also decreases hence option (B) is correct.

Sol. 13 (C) The total kinetic energy of all the n moles of gas molecules at temperature T is given as

$$E = \frac{f}{2} nRT$$

At absolute zero temperature $T = 0$ K at which kinetic energy becomes zero hence all molecular motion of gas molecules will freeze.

Sol. 14 (C) From gas law $PV = mRT/M$ option (C) is correct.

Sol. 15 (D) As the air is saturated then on compression the volume the water vapours will condense and air remain saturated with water vapour and final pressure is maintained at same value.

Sol. 16 (C) As the slope of adiabatic curve is more than that of isothermal curve hence option (C) is correct.

Sol. 17 (A) For an ideal gas in case of free expansion as explained in section 3.6 the gas temperature remain constant and no work is done in expansion as there is no opposition for gas against its expansion. For a real gas the inertia of molecules will oppose the expansion even when the gas expands in vacuum or free space so in expansion the molecules will gain some kinetic energy due to pressure difference during expansion which is lost against collision so final internal energy of gas will be less compared to initial state hence the final temperature is less than initial temperature.

Sol. 18 (B) On heating the gas, it will expand due to which the whole system will move toward right.

Sol. 19 (C) According to barometric relation, the atmospheric pressure decreases with height above sea level exponentially so at great heights atmospheric pressure is much less compared to inside pressure of helium in balloon. The pressure difference when exceeds the minimum value at which the surface tension in balloon material exceeds its rupture strength, balloon bursts.

Sol. 20 (B) According to gas law the volume of gas is proportional to T/P hence it is decreased to 2/3 of the initial value hence density will increase to 3/2 of the initial value.

Sol. 21 (C) According to gas law we use $PV = NkT$ where N are the total number of molecules in the gas.

Sol. 22 (A) In the given expression dimensions of the term a/V^2 is that of pressure hence that of term a must be same that of PV^2 hence option (A) is correct.

Sol. 23 (A) $dP = g\rho dy$

$$\Rightarrow \int_{P_1}^{P_2} \frac{dP}{P} = \frac{Mg}{RT}$$

$$\Rightarrow H = \int_0^H dy \Rightarrow H = \frac{RT}{Mg} \ln \frac{P_1}{P_2}$$

Sol. 24 (D) According to kinetic theory of gases there is no intermolecular forces exist between molecules of an ideal gas, it can neither be liquefied or solidified.

Sol. 25 (A) As the inside gas pressure is equal to outside atmospheric pressure the rate of diffusion of gas outside and air inside will remain constant. So the inside pressure, volume and number of molecules will remain same hence gas temperature will remain constant.

Sol. 26 (C) According to phase transformation curve as explained in section 2.2.7, a gas can be liquefied below critical temperature only by applying a certain pressure to it. Critical temperature is the temperature above which a gas cannot be liquefied by applying any amount of pressure.

Sol. 27 (D).

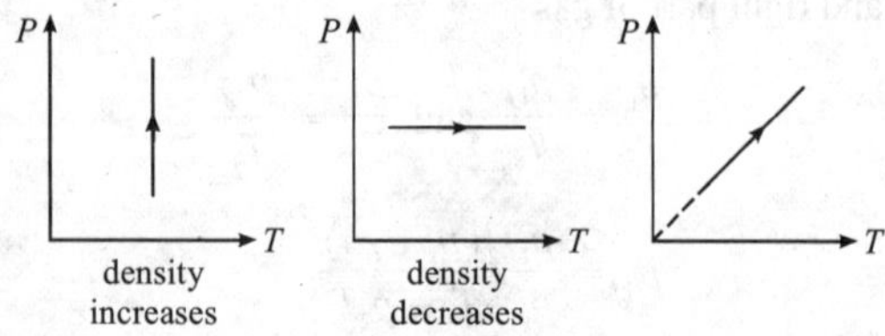

From gas law we have $P = \frac{\rho RT}{M}$

Thus at constant temperature we have $\rho \propto P$

In 1st graph $\rho \propto P$. At constant temperature thus density increases.

In 2nd graph at constant pressure, $\rho \propto \frac{1}{T}$.

In 3rd graph as $\frac{dP}{dT}$ = constant $\Rightarrow P \propto T$

$\Rightarrow$ density remain constant.

Solutions of NUMERICAL MCQS Single Option Correct

Sol. 1 (D) Work done in isothermal process is given by

$$W = 2.303\, nRT \log_{10}\left(\frac{V_f}{V_i}\right)$$

$$W = 2.303 \times 1 \times 8.314 \times 273 \times \log_{10}\left(\frac{11.2}{22.4}\right)$$

$$W = -1573.5 \text{ J}$$

$$W \approx -1570 \text{ J}$$

Sol. 2 (D) We have

$$E_{molecule} = \frac{1}{2}mv_{rms}^2 = \frac{1}{2}m\left(\frac{3kT}{m}\right)$$

$$= \frac{3}{2}kT$$

Sol. 3 (C) With the increase in molecular weight, the rms speed of gas molecule decreases.

$$v_{rms} \approx \frac{1}{\sqrt{M}}$$

$$\frac{(v_{rms})_{H_2}}{(v_{rms})_{O_2}} = \sqrt{\frac{M_{O_2}}{M_{H_2}}} = \sqrt{\frac{16}{1}} = 4$$

$$(v_{rms})_{H_2} = 4v$$

Sol. 4 (C) Kinetic energy of a gas molecule

$$= \frac{3}{2}kT$$

$$E \propto T$$

Molecular of different gases at same temperature will have same translational kinetic energy.

Sol. 5 (B) For gas G_1 $\quad pv = n_1RT \quad \ldots(1)$

for gas G_2 $\quad 2p\frac{v}{2} = n_2R(2T) \quad \ldots(2)$

Dividing (1) by (2), $\quad 1 = \frac{n_1}{2n_2}$

$$\frac{n_1}{n_2} = 2$$

Sol. 6 (A) The pressure will increase

$$p_1 + p_2 = p$$

From ideal gas equation,

$$pv = nRT$$

$$p = \frac{nRT}{v}$$

Volume remains same

$$\frac{2RT_0}{v} + \frac{4R(2T_0)}{v} = \frac{6RT}{v}$$

where T = temperature of mixture

$$10T_0 = 6T$$

$$T = \frac{5T_0}{3}$$

Sol. 7 (A) Total energy associated with each molecule,

$$E = \frac{f}{2}kT$$

Since both O_2 and N_2 are diatomic,

ratio of rotational KE per O_2 molecule to that per N_2 molecule $= 1:1$

Sol. 8 (A) We use $PV^c + aT^2 V^{c-1} = RT + b$

$$P = \frac{-aT^2V'^{c-1}}{V^c} + \frac{(RT+b)}{V^c}$$

$$p = (RT+b)V^{-c} - aT^2V^{-1}$$

$$m = -c \text{ and } n = -1$$

Sol. 9 (D) We use $\quad v_{rms} = \sqrt{\frac{3RT}{M}}$

For hydrogen, $\quad M = 1$

For oxygen, $\quad M = 16$

$$v = \sqrt{3RT}$$

$$v_{O_2} = \sqrt{\frac{3RT}{16}} = \frac{v}{4}$$

Sol. 10 (B) Let final pressure of mixture is p'

$$n_1 + n_2 = n$$

$$\frac{pV}{RT} + \frac{pV}{RT} = \frac{p'V}{RT}$$

$$p' = 2p$$

Sol. 11 (D) From ideal gas equation

$$pV = nRT$$

As $\quad n = 1$

$$p = \frac{RT}{V}$$

Both have same volume and temperature, thus, pressure of oxygen = pressure of hydrogen.

Sol. 12 (D) At equal temperature, the average kinetic energies are equal, therefore ratio is 1 : 1.

Sol. 13 (B) The average rotational kinetic energy of a diatomic molecule at temperature T is kT.

Sol. 14 (A) From ideal gas equation,

$$pV = nRT$$

$$p = \frac{nRT}{V} = \frac{nR(T_0 + aV^3)}{V}$$

$$p = \frac{nRT_0}{V} + nRaV^2$$

$$\frac{dp}{dV} = 0$$

$$\frac{-nRT_0}{V^2} + 2anRV = 0$$

$$\frac{T_0}{V^2} = 2aV$$

$$V^3 = \frac{T_0}{2a}$$

$$V = \left(\frac{T_0}{2a}\right)^{1/3}$$

Sol. 15 (D) From ideal gas equation,

$$p = \frac{nRT}{V}$$

$$p = \frac{nR(T_0 + aV^3)}{V}$$

$$p = \frac{nRT_0}{V} + anRV^2$$

$$p = \frac{nRT_0}{T_0^{1/3}}(2a)^{1/3} + anR.\frac{T_0^{2/3}}{(2a)^{2/3}}$$

for $n = 1$

$$\Rightarrow \quad p = RT_0^{2/3}(2)^{1/3}(a)^{1/3} + \frac{a^{1/3} \cdot RT_0^{2/3}}{2^{2/3}}$$

$$\Rightarrow \quad p = \frac{3RT_0^{2/3}a^{1/3}}{2^{2/3}}$$

$$\Rightarrow \quad p = \frac{3}{2}(a^{1/3}RT_0^{2/3})(2)^{1/3}$$

Sol. 16 (D) As we have

$$C_v = \frac{f}{2}R$$

From Mayer's formula,

$$C_p - C_v = R$$

$$\Rightarrow \quad C_p = \left(1 + \frac{f}{2}\right)R$$

$$\Rightarrow \quad \frac{C_p}{C_v} = \frac{\left(1 + \frac{f}{2}\right)R}{\frac{f}{2}R} = 1 + \frac{2}{f}$$

Sol. 17 (B) We use $p_0 = \frac{1}{3}\frac{mN}{V}v_{rms}^2$

$$\Rightarrow \quad p' = \frac{1}{3}\frac{mN}{2V}(4v_{rms}^2)$$

$$\Rightarrow \quad p' = 2p_0$$

Sol. 18 (B) rms speed of gas molecules does not depend on the pressure of gas (if temperature remain constant). According to Boyle's law,

$$P \propto \rho$$

If pressure is increased two times, density will also increase by 2 times, hence, v_{rms} remains constant.

Sol. 19 (B) Number of moles in first container,

$$n_1 = \frac{P_1V}{RT_1}$$

Number of moles in second container,

$$n_2 = \frac{P_2V}{RT_2}$$

If both vessels are joined

$$n_1 + n_2 = n$$

$$\Rightarrow \quad \frac{P(2V)}{RT} = \frac{P_1V}{RT_1} + \frac{P_2V}{RT_2}$$

$$\Rightarrow \quad \frac{P}{T} = \frac{1}{2}\left[\frac{P_1}{T_1} + \frac{P_2}{T_2}\right]$$

Sol. 20 (B) As we have

$$v_{rms} = \sqrt{\frac{3kT}{m}}$$

$$v_{rms} \propto \sqrt{T}$$

Sol. 21 (B) As the upper part of mercury column is at rest, the pressure in the air inside the column of mercury is equal to the weight of mercury over the air divided by the internal cross sectional area of the tube. When the temperature increases, the weight of the upper part of the mercury column does not change. That is why the pressure in the middle air column will also remain constant. The change in volume of this air column is proportional to the change in temperature at constant pressure. As expansion of tube is neglected, volume of this air column is proportional to its length so we use

$$\frac{l}{l_0} = \frac{T}{T_0}$$

$$\Rightarrow \quad l = \frac{l_0 T}{T_0} = 11 \text{ cm}$$

Sol. 22 (D) We use

$$\frac{C_{p_{mix}}}{C_{v_{mix}}} = \frac{\dfrac{\mu_1 C_{p_1} + \mu_2 C_{p_2}}{\mu_1 + \mu_2}}{\dfrac{\mu_1 C_{v_1} + \mu_2 C_{v_2}}{\mu_1 + \mu_2}}$$

$$= \frac{\mu C_{P_1} + \mu_2 C_{P_2}}{\mu_1 C_{v_1} + \mu_2 C_{v_2}}$$

$$= \frac{\left[\mu_1\left(\frac{\gamma_1}{\gamma_1 - 1}\right)R + \mu_2\left(\frac{\gamma_2}{\gamma_2 - 1}\right)R\right]}{\left[\mu_1\left(\frac{R}{\gamma_1 - 1}\right) + \mu_2\left(\frac{R}{\gamma_2 - 1}\right)\right]}$$

$$= \frac{\dfrac{\mu_1\gamma_1}{\gamma_1 - 1} + \dfrac{\mu_2\gamma_2}{\gamma_2 - 1}}{\dfrac{\mu_1}{\gamma_1 - 1} + \dfrac{\mu_2}{\gamma_2 - 1}}$$

$$= \frac{\mu_1\gamma_1(\gamma_2 - 1) + \mu_2\gamma_2(\gamma_1 - 1)}{\mu_1(\gamma_2 - 1) + \mu_2(\gamma_1 - 1)}$$

$$= \frac{3(1.4)(1.66 - 1) + 2(1.66)(1.4 - 1)}{3(1.66 - 1) + 2(1.4 - 1)}$$

$$= \frac{2.772 + 1.328}{1.98 + 0.8}$$

$$= \frac{4.1}{2.78} = 1.475$$

Sol. 23 (B) Energy given to person

$$= 10^5 \text{ cal}$$

$$= 418580 \text{ J}$$

Energy that can be utilized $= 418580 \times \dfrac{28}{100}$

$$E = 117202.4 \text{ J}$$

$$E = mgh$$

$$117202.4 = 60 \times 10 \times h$$

$$h = 195.34 \text{ m} \approx 196 \text{ m}$$

Sol. 24 (B) By gas law $p_f v_1 = n_1 R T_1$

$$p_f v_2 = n_2 R T_2$$

$$n_1 + n_2 = n$$

$$\Rightarrow \quad \frac{p_f v}{R T_0} + \frac{p_f v}{R(2T_0)} = \frac{p_0(2v)}{R T_0}$$

$$\Rightarrow \quad p_f + \frac{p_f}{2} = 2p_0$$

$$\Rightarrow \quad \frac{3p_f}{2} = 2p_0$$

$$p_f = \frac{4p_0}{3}$$

Sol. 25 (C) By gas law $n_2 = \dfrac{p_f v_0}{R(2T_0)} = \dfrac{4p_0 v_0}{3R(2T_0)} = \dfrac{2p_0 v_0}{3RT_0}$

Sol. 26 (D) We use $v_{rms} = \sqrt{\dfrac{(1)^2 + (2)^2 + (3)^2 + (4)^2}{4}}$

$$= \sqrt{\frac{1 + 4 + 9 + 16}{4}}$$

$$\Rightarrow \quad v_{rms} = \sqrt{\frac{30}{4}} = \sqrt{\frac{15}{2}} \text{ km/s}$$

Sol. 27 (C) Average $K.E. = \dfrac{3}{2}kT$

$$k_{avg} \propto T$$

Sol. 28 (B) Here we consider the temperature of lake remain constant. In this situation for bubble, we use

$$P_1 V_1 = P_2 V_2$$

As bubble rises, due to decrease in pressure if its size increases by k times, we use

$$P_1 \frac{4}{3}\pi r^3 = 10\left[\frac{4}{3}\pi(kr)^3\right]$$

Pressure at bottom of lake is related to the atmospheric pressure as

$$P_1 = P_2 + \text{depth of lake}$$

$$\Rightarrow \quad P_1 = 10 + 10^3 k$$

$$\Rightarrow \quad 10k^3 - 10^3 k - 10 = 0$$

$$\Rightarrow \quad k^3 - 10^2 k - 1 = 0$$

$$\Rightarrow \quad k = 10$$

Sol. 29 (C) $R = 8.31$ J/mole-K

S.I. unit of R is J mole^{-1} K^{-1}

Sol. 30 (A) $(76 - 73)\,V = (76 - H)\dfrac{V}{2}$

$$\Rightarrow \quad H = 70 \text{ cm}$$

31 (B); 32 (A); 33 (B)

Sol. 31-33 Let P_1 and P_2 be the initial pressure in lower chamber of gas and upper chamber of gas.

$$P_2 = P_0 + \frac{mg}{A} = 2P_0,\ V_2 = A \times 12 \times 10^{-2} \text{ m}^3$$

If P_2' and V_2' are final pressure and volume in upper chamber

$$V_2' = A \times (28 - l) \times 10^{-2}\ \text{m}^3$$

$$P_2V_2 = P_2'V_2'$$

$$\Rightarrow \quad P_2' = \frac{P_2V_2}{P_2'} = \frac{24P_0}{28-l}$$

Now consider lower chamber

$$P_1 = P_0 + \frac{2mg}{A} = 3P_0$$

and $V_1 = A \times 8 \times 10^{-2}\ \text{m}^3$

$$P_1' = P_2' + \frac{mg}{A} = P_0\left[\frac{52-l}{28-l}\right]$$

and $V_1' = A \times (8 + l) \times 10^{-2}\ \text{m}^3$

$$P_1V_1 = P_1'V_1'$$

$$3P_0A \times 8 \times 10^{-2} = P_0\left[\frac{52-l}{28-l}\right] \times A \times (8+l) \times 10^{-2}$$

$$24 = \left[\frac{52-l}{28-l}\right] \times (8+l)$$

Solving we get $l = 4$ cm

$$\Rightarrow \quad P_1' = 2P_0 = 2 \times 10^5\ \text{A/m}^2$$

$$\Rightarrow \quad P_2' = \frac{24P_0}{28-l} = P_0 = 1 \times 10^5\ \text{N/m}^2$$

$$\frac{V_2'}{V_1'} = \frac{28-l}{8+l} = \frac{24}{12} = 2$$

Solutions of ADVANCE MCQs One or More Option Correct

Sol. 1 (A, B, D) According to kinetic theory of gases, the gas pressure is due to the continuous collisions of gas molecules with the walls of container which is given as

$$P = \frac{1}{3}\rho v_{rms}^2 = \frac{2}{3}e$$

Where e is the kinetic energy per unit volume of the gas hence option (A) is incorrect. The product of gas pressure and volume is constant only when gas undergoes expansion or compression at constant temperature hence option (B) is incorrect. According to law of equipartition of energy, the average kinetic energy of gas molecules is given as

$$E = \frac{f}{2}NkT = \frac{f}{2}nRT$$

Hence option (C) is correct and option (D) is incorrect.

Sol. 2 (All) Average KE per molecule in A & $B = \frac{4KT}{\pi}$

$$(v_{rms})_A = \sqrt{\frac{3RT}{M_A}}\ ;\ (v_{rms})_B = \sqrt{\frac{3RT}{M_B}}$$

$$\Rightarrow \quad \frac{(v_{rms})_A}{(v_{rms})_B} = \sqrt{\frac{M_B}{M_A}} = \sqrt{\frac{M_B}{16M_B}} = \frac{1}{4}$$

No. of mole of $A = \frac{m_A}{M_A}$

No. of mole of $B = \frac{m_B}{M_B} = \frac{m_{A/2}}{M_{A/16}} = 8n_A$

Sol. 3 (C, D) According to gas law the given quantity is the product of pressure and molar mass of gas hence options (C) and (D) are correct.

Sol. 4 (A, C) Total molecules in 1 mole are always constant and equal to Avogadro number and at a given temperature translational kinetic energy of fix number of molecules is always constant for all gases.

Sol. 5 (B, D) $\quad \frac{P^2}{\rho} = \text{constant}$

$$P = \rho\frac{RT}{M} \text{ (Ideal gas equation)}$$

$$\Rightarrow \quad \frac{P^2}{\rho} = \frac{P}{\rho}\left(\frac{\rho RT}{M}\right) = PT\left(\frac{R}{M}\right) = \text{constant}$$

$\therefore$ The graph of the above process on the P–T diagram is hyperbola.

For the above process

$$\left(\frac{P^2}{\rho}\right)_1 = \left(\frac{P^2}{\rho}\right)_2$$

$$\Rightarrow \quad \frac{P^2}{\rho} = \frac{P_2^2}{\rho/2} \Rightarrow P_2 = \frac{P}{\sqrt{2}} \quad \ldots\text{(i)}$$

and $P_1T_1 = P_2T_2 \Rightarrow PT = \frac{P}{\sqrt{2}}T_2 \Rightarrow T_2 = \sqrt{2}\,T$ ...(ii)

Sol. 6 (A, D) The rms translational speed is only dependent upon the temperature of gas and not on gas quantity and it is directly proportional to the square root of absolute temperature of the gas. For a given temperature of gas its internal energy is constant and if P and V of gas varies such that PV = constant then option (D) is also correct.

Sol. 7 (A, C, D) For all gases co-efficient of expansion is $1/T$ so at a given temperature it is a constant hence option (A) is correct. In each degree of freedom always average energy is same and is equal to 0.5 kT hence option (C) is correct. As pressure of gas decreases, density of gas also decreases hence the intermolecular separation increases hence option (D) is correct.

Sol. 8 (B, C) As given in problem the gases are different hence their number of moles will also be different for same mass. Hence in this case option (B) and (C) are correct.

Sol. 9 (All) Area under the curve is equal to number of molecules of the gas sample.

Hence $N = \frac{1}{2} a V_0 \Rightarrow aV_0 = 2\text{N}$

$$V_{avg} = \frac{1}{N}\int_0^{\infty} vN(V)dV = \frac{1}{N}\int_0^{V_0} C.\left(\frac{a}{V_0}V\right)dV = \frac{2}{3}V_0$$

$$\Rightarrow \quad \frac{V_{avg}}{V_0} = \frac{2}{3}$$

$$V_{rms}^2 = \frac{1}{N}\int_0^{\infty} V^2 N(V)dV = \frac{1}{N}\int_0^{V_0} V^2\left(\frac{a}{V_0}V\right)dV = \frac{V_0^2}{2}$$

$$\Rightarrow \quad \frac{V_{rms}}{V_0} = \frac{1}{\sqrt{2}}$$

Area under the curve from $0.5V_0$ to V_0 is 3/4 of total area.

Sol. 10 (B, C) If the cylinder is in gravity free space then the inside pressure will be equal to that of the surrounding pressure. If gravity is there then in case when open end of cylinder is facing upward, gas pressure will be more than that of surrounding and if open end face downward then the gas pressure will be less than that of the surrounding.

Sol. 11 (A, C) Both H_2 and He molecules have same number of translational degrees of freedom so total translational kinetic energy of the two molecules will be same hence option (A) is correct. The molecules of H_2 have more total number of degrees of freedom which includes translational and rotational degrees of freedom. Speed of gas molecules depend on molar mass of gas, which is given as

$$v \propto \frac{1}{\sqrt{M}}$$

Hence option (D) is NOT correct. As hydrogen molecule has more total number of degrees of freedom, it has more total energy than helium molecule hence option (C) is correct and option (B) is NOT correct.

Sol. 12 (A, B, C) By definition of real gas behaviour option (A) and (C) are correct. As ideal gas molecules never interact with each other it can never be liquefied hence option (B) is correct.

Sol. 13 (A, C, D) *RMS* speed of a gas is directly proportional to square root of absolute temperature of the gas hence from gas law options (A), (C) and (D) are correct.

Sol. 14 (B, C, D) By gas law $PV = \frac{m}{M}RT$ we can directly find that option (B) is correct. Total translational kinetic energy of a gas depends upon the temperature of the gas and total number of molecules as $E = (3/2)NkT$ hence option (C) is correct. Total kinetic energy of a gas is given as $E_T = (f/2)kT$ hence option (D) is also correct.

Sol. 15 (A, D) The rate of collisions of the molecules with per square meter of the wall is $(1/6)n_0 v$ where n_0 is the molecular density and v is *RMS* speed of molecules and pressure exerted by the gas on wall is given by $(1/6)n_0 v \times 2m'v$ where m' is the mass of each molecule.

Sol. 16 (C, D) Using the concept of elastic collision between two particles, one light and other heavy we can conclude that options (C) and (D) are correct.

Sol. 17 (B, D)

(i) As PV^2 = Constant

$\Rightarrow$ TV = Constant

$\Rightarrow$ If volume expands temperature decreases.

(ii) As $P = KV^2$

$\Rightarrow$ $\frac{V^3}{T}$ = constant

$\Rightarrow$ If volume expands, temperature increases

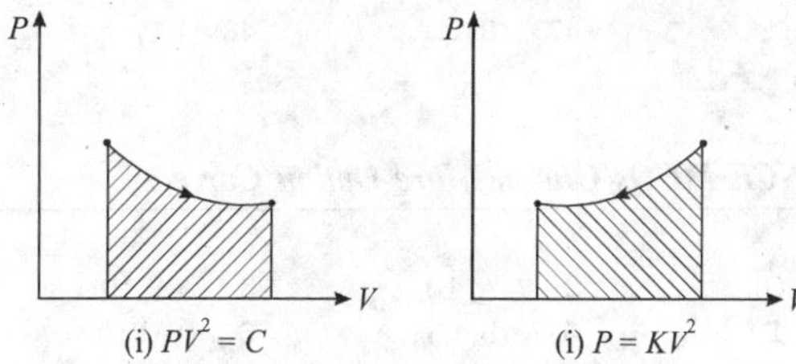

(i) $PV^2 = C$ (i) $P = KV^2$

By *FLT* we use $Q = \Delta U + W$

$\Rightarrow$ $Q_2 > Q_1$ as $W_2 > W_1$ & $\Delta U_2 > \Delta U_1$

* * * * *

ANSWERS & SOLUTIONS

CONCEPTUAL MCQS Single Option Correct

1	(B)	2	(A)	3	(C)
4	(B)	5	(D)	6	(A)
7	(B)	8	(A)	9	(A)
10	(B)	11	(D)	12	(C)
13	(A)	14	(B)	15	(A)
16	(C)	17	(C)	18	(B)
19	(C)	20	(A)	21	(B)
22	(C)	23	(A)	24	(C)
25	(C)	26	(C)	27	(D)
28	(C)	29	(A)	30	(A)
31	(A)	32	(B)	33	(C)
34	(B)	35	(C)	36	(C)
37	(C)	38	(B)	39	(B)
40	(A)	41	(C)	42	(C)
43	(B)	44	(D)	45	(C)
46	(B)	47	(A)	48	(C)
49	(D)				

NUMERICAL MCQS Single Option Correct

1	(A)	2	(B)	3	(B)
4	(C)	5	(B)	6	(C)
7	(B)	8	(C)	9	(D)
10	(B)	11	(C)	12	(B)
13	(A)	14	(C)	15	(A)
16	(C)	17	(C)	18	(A)
19	(D)	20	(A)	21	(B)
22	(C)	23	(C)	24	(C)
25	(A)	26	(B)	27	(A)
28	(D)	29	(D)	30	(B)
31	(B)	32	(D)	33	(A)
34	(C)	35	(C)	36	(C)
37	(D)	38	(D)	39	(C)
40	(C)	41	(D)	42	(C)
43	(B)	44	(C)	45	(D)
46	(C)	47	(B)	48	(A)
49	(B)				

ADVANCE MCQs One or More Option Correct

1	(B, C)	2	(A, B)	3	(A, B)
4	(A, D)	5	(B, C)	6	(All)
7	(C, D)	8	(B, C)	9	(All)
10	(All)	11	(A, B, C)	12	(All)
13	(All)	14	(A, B, D)	15	(A, B)
16	(A, D)	17	(C, D)	18	(A, C, D)
19	(B, D)	20	(A, B, D)	21	(A, B, D)

Solutions of PRACTICE EXERCISE 3.1

(i) Given that $\Delta Q_1 = 100\text{ J}$

$\Delta W_1 = -20\text{ J}$

$\Delta Q_2 = -20\text{ J}$

For a cyclic process we use

$$\Delta Q_1 - \Delta W_1 = -(\Delta Q_2 - \Delta W_2)$$

$$\Rightarrow \quad 100 - 20 = -(-20 - \Delta W_2)$$

$$\Rightarrow \quad \Delta W_2 = 80 - 20 = 60\text{ J}$$

(ii) Given that

$$\Delta Q_{A\to B} = 50\text{ J}$$

$$\Delta Q_{B\to C} = 0$$

$$\Delta Q_{C\to D} = -70\text{ J}$$

$$\Delta W_{B\to C} = 40\text{ J}$$

$$U_A = 1500\text{ J}$$

$$U_B = U_A + \Delta Q_{A\to B} = 1500 + 50 = 1550\text{ J}$$

$$U_C = B_B + W_{B\to C} = 1550 + 40 = 1590\text{ J}$$

(iii) Heat absorbed in isobaric process is

$$\Delta Q = nC_P\Delta T = \frac{n\gamma R}{\gamma - 1}\Delta T = \frac{\gamma P}{\gamma - 1}(V_2 - V_1)$$

$$= \frac{1.67}{0.67} \times 10^5 \times 10^{-4} = 24.92\text{ J}$$

(iv) Increase in internal energy

$$\Delta U = \Delta Q - \Delta W$$

$$= 1 \times 539 \times 4.2 - 1.013 \times 10^5 \times 1670 \times 10^{-6}$$

$$= 2263.8 - 169.171$$

$$= 2094.63\text{ J}$$

(v) By first law of thermodynamics we have

$$\Delta W = \Delta Q - \Delta U$$

$$= 25\text{ kcal} - 8\text{ kcal}$$

$$= 17\text{ kcal}$$

(vi) For isobaric process

$$W = P\Delta V = nR\Delta T$$

and $$\Delta Q = nC_P\Delta T = n\left(\frac{7}{2}R\right)\Delta T = 100\text{ J}$$

$$\Rightarrow \quad W = nR\Delta T = \frac{200}{7}\text{ J} = 28.57\text{ J}$$

Solutions of PRACTICE EXERCISE 3.2

(i) Work = Total area enclosed by cyclic curve = 0

(ii) Gas pressure is given as

$$(P-2P_0) = -\frac{P_0}{V_0}(V-V_0)$$

$$\Rightarrow \quad P = 3P_0 - \frac{P_0}{V_0}V$$

by gas law $\quad T = \frac{PV}{nR} = \frac{3P_0}{nR}V - \frac{P_0}{nRV_0}V^2$

T is maximum when $\frac{dT}{dV} = 0$

$$\Rightarrow \quad \frac{dT}{dV} = \frac{3P_0}{nR} - \frac{2P_0}{nRV_0}V = 0$$

$$\Rightarrow \quad V = \frac{3V_0}{2}$$

$$\Rightarrow \quad T_{max} = \frac{3P_0}{nR}\left(\frac{3V_0}{2}\right) - \frac{P_0}{nRV_0}\left(\frac{3}{2}V_0\right)^2$$

$$= \frac{9}{2}\frac{P_0V_0}{nR} - \frac{9}{4}\frac{P_0V_0}{nR} = \frac{9}{4}\frac{P_0V_0}{nR}$$

(iii) Work done on the gas is the area between semi circle which is given as

$$W = \frac{\pi(1)(1)}{2} = \frac{\pi}{2} \text{ ltr-atm}$$

(iv) (a) Work done are

$$W_{A\to B} = 8\times3\times10^5\times10^{-3} = 2400\text{ J}$$

$$W_{B\to C} = 0$$

$$W_{C\to D} = -2\times3\times10^5\times10^{-3} = -600\text{ J}$$

$$W_{D\to A} = 0$$

(b) Total work is

$$W_{cycle} = 2400-600 = 1800\text{ J}$$

(v) PV curve of given process is drawn using

$AB \to$ isobaric

$BC \to$ isochoric

$CA \to$ isothermal

$\Rightarrow$ Indicator diagram is drawn as

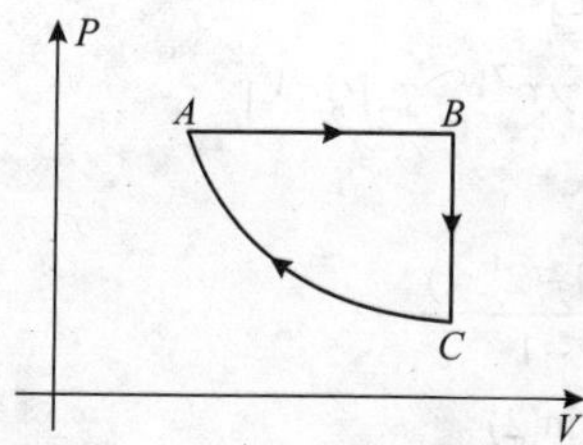

(vi) Work = area enclosed between PV curve and V-axis

$$= \frac{1}{2}(540)(0.3) + 340\times1$$

$$= 81 + 340$$

$$= 421\text{ kJ}$$

(vii) (a) Change in internal energy of gas

$$\Delta U = \frac{3}{2}(P_BV_B - P_AV_A)$$

$$= \frac{3}{2}(8\times10^5\times0.8 - 4\times10^5\times0.5)$$

$$= 6.6\times10^5\text{ J}$$

(b) Work done by gas

W = area under PV curve

$$= \frac{1}{2}(12\times10^5)(0.3)$$

$$= 1.8\times10^5\text{ J}$$

(c) Heat supplied $\quad Q = W + \Delta U$

$$= 8.4\times10^5\text{ J}$$

Solutions of PRACTICE EXERCISE 3.3

(i) At $V_1 = V_0$, $\quad P_1 = \frac{P_0}{2}$

and at $V_2 = 2V_0$, $\quad P_2 = \frac{4P_0}{5}$

change in temperature of gas is

$$\Delta T = \frac{P_2V_2}{nR} - \frac{P_1V_1}{nR}$$

$$= \frac{1}{nR}\left(\frac{8P_0V_0}{5} - \frac{P_0V_0}{2}\right) = \frac{11P_0V_0}{10R} \quad [\text{As } n=1]$$

(ii) Work done is calculated as

$$W = \int_{V_1}^{V_2} PdV = P(V_2 - V_1)$$

$$= P\left(\frac{\alpha(2T_0)^2}{P} - \frac{\alpha(T_0)^2}{P}\right)$$

$$= 3\alpha T_0^2$$

(iii) Given that $\Delta Q = nC_V(10) = 25R$

work done in adiabatic process is $W = -\Delta U$

$$= -nC_V\Delta T$$

$$= nC_V(10) = 25R$$

(iv) Given that $\Delta U = -100$ J

for adiabatic expansion we use $W = -\Delta U = 100$ J

(v) Sudden compression implies adiabatic process so we use

$$T_1V_1^{\gamma-1}=T_2V_2^{\gamma-1}$$

$$300\,(V_1)^{0.5}=T_2\left(\frac{V_1}{2}\right)^{0.5}$$

$$\Rightarrow \quad T_2=300(\sqrt{2})=424.26\,\text{K}$$

and $\quad P_2=P_1\left(\frac{V_1}{V_2}\right)^{1.5}=2\sqrt{2}\,P_1$

in isobaric process $T_3=300$ K

$$\Rightarrow \quad \frac{V_2}{T_2}=\frac{V_3}{T_3}$$

$$\Rightarrow \quad V_3=V_2\left(\frac{T_3}{T_2}\right)=\frac{V_1}{2}\left(\frac{300}{300\sqrt{2}}\right)=\frac{V_1}{2\sqrt{2}}$$

then in isothermal process $V_4=V_1$

$$\Rightarrow \quad P_3V_3=P_nV_4 \Rightarrow (2\sqrt{2}P_1)\left(\frac{V_1}{2\sqrt{2}}\right)=P_4V$$

$$\Rightarrow \quad P_4=P_1$$

work done by gas in first process is

$$W_{adiabatic}=\frac{P_1V_1-P_2V_2}{V-1}=\frac{P_1V_1-(2\sqrt{2}P_1)\left(\frac{V_1}{2}\right)}{0.5}$$

$$=\frac{1-\sqrt{2}}{0.5}\times10^5\times10^{-3}$$

$$=-82.84\,\text{J}$$

$$W_{isobaric}=P_2(V_3-V_2)=(2\sqrt{2}\,P_1)\left(\frac{V_1}{2\sqrt{2}}-\frac{V_1}{2}\right)$$

$$=P_1V_1(1-\sqrt{2})$$

$$=1-\sqrt{2}\times10^5\times10^{-3}$$

$$=-41.4\,\text{J}$$

$$W_{isobaric}=P_3V_3\ln\left(\frac{V_4}{V_3}\right)$$

$$=(2\sqrt{2}P_1)\left(\frac{V_1}{2\sqrt{2}}\right)\ln(2\sqrt{2})$$

$$=P_1V_1\ln(2)^{1.5}$$

$$=1.5\times10^5\times10^{-3}\times0.693$$

$$=103.95\,\text{J}$$

$$W_{total}=W_{adiabatic}+W_{isobaric}+W_{isobaric}$$

$$=-82.84-41.4+103.95=-20.29\,\text{J}$$

(vi) If initial pressure are P_1P_2 and P_3 we use in first container

$$P_1V=P_f(2V) \qquad \ldots(1)$$

in second container

$$P_2V_1^{1.5}=P_f(2V)^{1.5} \qquad \ldots(2)$$

in third container

$$P_3=P_f \qquad \ldots(3)$$

from (1), (2) and (3) we get

$$P_1:P_2:P_3=2:2\sqrt{2}:1$$

(vii) Initial charge on the capacitor is calculated as

$$q_0=CV_0=75\times10^{-3}\times\frac{640}{3}=16\,\text{C}$$

The charge on the capacitor decays according to the expression

$$q=q_0e^{-t/RC}$$

At $t=2.5\ln(4)$ minutes $=150\ln(4)$ seconds, the charge on capacitor left will be given as

$$q=16\times e^{-\ln(4)}=4\,\text{C}$$

Total heat dissipated in the resistor in this time duration is calculated as loss in energy of capacitor, given as

$$\frac{q_0^2-q^2}{2C}=1.6\,\text{kJ}=\text{Heat supplied to the gas}$$

(a) Work done by the gas at constant pressure is calculated as

$$W=P\Delta V=nR\Delta T\approx0.183\,\text{kJ}$$

(b) Increase in the internal energy is calculated as

$$\Delta U=Q-W=1.6-0.183=1.417\,\text{kJ}$$

(c) Ratio of specific heats of gas is calculated as

$$\gamma=\frac{C_P}{C_V}=\frac{nC_P\Delta T}{nC_V\Delta T}=\frac{Q}{\Delta U}=1.13$$

(viii) At constant pressure work done is

$$W=nR\Delta T=2\,\text{J}$$

and heat supplied to diatomic gas is

$$\Delta Q=\frac{7}{2}nR\Delta T=\frac{7}{2}\times2=7\,\text{J}$$

(ix) In first container work done is

$$W_1=nRT\ln(2) \qquad \ldots(1)$$

In second container work done is

$$W_2=\frac{nR(T-T_f)}{\gamma-1} \qquad \ldots(2)$$

where $T_f=T(2)^{1-\gamma}$ [using $T_1V_1^{\gamma-1}=T_2V_2^{\gamma-1}$]

using $W_1=W_2$ we get

$$nRT\ln(2)=\frac{nRT(1-2^{1-\gamma})}{\gamma-1}$$

$$\Rightarrow \quad (1-2^{1-\gamma})=(\gamma-1)\ln(2)$$

(x) **(a)** In right chamber we use for adiabatic process

$$P_0V_0^{6/3} = \frac{243}{32}P_0V_{fR}^{5/3}$$

$$\Rightarrow \quad V_{fR} = \left(\frac{32}{243}\right)^{3/5} V_0 = \frac{8}{27}V_0$$

$\Rightarrow$ Using gas law we have for right chamber

$$T_{fR} = \frac{\frac{243}{32}P_0 \cdot \frac{8}{27}V_0T_0}{P_0V_0} = \frac{9}{4}T_0$$

for left chamber volume is

$$V_{fL} = 2V_0 - \frac{8}{27}V_0 = \frac{46}{27}V_0$$

using gas law we have

$$T_{fL} = \frac{\frac{243}{32}P_0 \cdot \frac{46}{27}V_0T_0}{P_0V_0} = \frac{207}{16}T_0$$

(b) Work done by gas an right chamber is

$$W = \frac{P_0V_0 - \left(\frac{243}{32}P_0\right)\left(\frac{8}{27}V_0\right)}{\frac{5}{3}-1} = -\frac{15}{8}P_0V_0$$

(xi) We use $T_1^{\gamma}P_1^{1-\gamma} = T_2^{\gamma}P_2^{1-\gamma}$

$$\Rightarrow \quad T_2 = T_1\left(\frac{P_1}{P_2}\right)^{\frac{1-\gamma}{\gamma}}$$

$$= 290\left(\frac{1}{10}\right)^{\frac{1-1.4}{1.4}}$$

$$= 290(10)^{2/7} = 559.90\text{ K}$$

Work done on the gas is

$$W_{ext} = \frac{nR(T_2-T_1)}{\gamma-1} = \frac{8.314(559.90-290)}{0.4}$$

$$= 5609.87\text{ J}$$

Solutions of PRACTICE EXERCISE 3.4

(i) Given that $V = \frac{\alpha}{T}$

we use $\quad dV = -\frac{\alpha}{T^2}dT$

work done by gas is

$$W = \int PdV$$

$$= \int \frac{nRT}{V}\cdot\left(-\frac{\alpha}{T^2}dT\right)$$

$$= -nR\int_0^{\Delta T} dT = -nR\Delta T$$

Change in internal energy of gas is

$$\Delta U = n\left(\frac{R}{\gamma-1}\right)\Delta T$$

heat supplied $\quad \Delta Q = \Delta U + \Delta W$

$$= nR\Delta T\left(\frac{1}{\gamma-1}-1\right)$$

$$= \left(\frac{2-\gamma}{\gamma-1}\right)R\Delta T \qquad (\text{As } n=1)$$

(ii) (a) $C = C_V + \alpha T$

For a general polytropic process we use

$$C = C_V + \frac{PdV}{ndT}$$

$$\Rightarrow \quad \frac{PdV}{ndT} = \alpha T$$

$$\Rightarrow \quad \frac{RT}{V}\cdot\frac{dV}{dT} = \alpha T$$

$$\Rightarrow \quad \int\frac{dV}{V} = \int\frac{\alpha}{R}dT$$

$$\ln V = \frac{\alpha T}{R} + C$$

$$V = e^{\left(\frac{\alpha T}{R}+C\right)}$$

$$Ve^{-\frac{\alpha T}{R}} = \text{constant}$$

(b) $C = C_V + \beta V$

we use $\quad \frac{PdV}{ndT} = \beta V$

$$\Rightarrow \quad \frac{RT}{V}\frac{dV}{dT} = \beta V$$

$$\int\frac{dV}{V^2} = \frac{\beta}{R}\int\frac{dT}{T}$$

$$-\frac{1}{V} = \frac{\beta}{R}\ln T + C$$

$$T = e^{-\left(\frac{R}{\beta V}+C\right)}$$

$$Te^{R/\beta V} = \text{constant}$$

(c) $C = C_V + aP$

we use $\quad \frac{PdV}{ndT} = aP$

$$\int dV = \int an\, dT$$

$$V = an\, aT + C$$

$$V - aT = \text{constant} \qquad \text{[Taking } n = 1 \text{ mole]}$$

(iii) Rate of collisions with vessel wall is

$$N_C = \frac{1}{6} n_0 V_{rms} = \text{constant}$$

$$\Rightarrow \quad \frac{1}{6}\frac{N}{V}\cdot\sqrt{\frac{3RT}{m}} = \text{constant}$$

$$\Rightarrow \quad \frac{\sqrt{T}}{V} = \text{constant}$$

$$\Rightarrow \quad T = kV^2$$

$$\Rightarrow \quad \frac{dT}{dV} = 2kV$$

Molar heat capacity is

$$C = C_V + \frac{PdV}{ndT}$$

$$C = \frac{3R}{2} + \frac{RT}{V}\cdot\frac{dV}{dT}$$

$$C = \frac{3}{2}R + \frac{R(kV^2)}{V}\cdot\frac{1}{2kV} = 2R$$

(iv) Rate of collisions with vessel wall is

$$N_C = \frac{1}{6} n_0 V_{rms} = \frac{1}{6}\left(\frac{N}{V}\right)\sqrt{\frac{3RT}{M}}$$

$$\Rightarrow \quad N_C \,\alpha\, \frac{\sqrt{T}}{V} = \text{constant}$$

$$\Rightarrow \quad T = kV^2$$

$$\Rightarrow \quad \frac{dT}{dV} = 2kV$$

$\Rightarrow$ molar heat capacity is given as

$$C = C_V + \frac{RT}{V}\frac{dV}{dT}$$

$$\Rightarrow \quad C = \frac{5R}{2} + \frac{R(kV^2)}{V}\cdot\frac{1}{2kV} = 3R$$

(v) **(a)** Heat supplied to raise the temperature of gas from T_0 to ηT_0 is

$$\Delta Q = \int C dT = \int_{T_0}^{\eta T_0} \frac{\alpha}{T} dT = \alpha \ln(\eta)$$

Increase in internal energy of gas is

$$\Delta U = C_V(nT_0 - T_0) = \frac{RT_0}{\gamma - 1}(\eta - 1)$$

Work done is given by first law of thermodynamics

$$\Delta W = \Delta Q - \Delta U = \alpha \ln(\eta) - \frac{RT_0(\eta - 1)}{(\gamma - 1)}$$

(b) We use $\qquad C = C_V + \dfrac{PdV}{ndT}$

$$\Rightarrow \quad \frac{\alpha}{T} = \frac{R}{\gamma - 1} + \frac{RT}{V}\cdot\frac{dV}{dT}$$

$$\Rightarrow \quad \int \frac{dV}{V} = \int \frac{\alpha}{RT^2} dT - \frac{1}{\gamma - 1}\int \frac{dT}{T}$$

$$\Rightarrow \quad \ln V = -\frac{\alpha}{R}\cdot\frac{1}{T} - \frac{1}{\gamma - 1}\ln T + C$$

$$\Rightarrow \quad \ln(TV^{\gamma-1}) = -\frac{\alpha(\gamma - 1)}{RT} + C$$

$$TV^{\gamma-1} e^{\alpha(\gamma-1)/RT} = \text{constant}$$

$$\Rightarrow \quad PV^{\gamma} e^{\alpha(\gamma-1)/PV} = \text{constant}$$

(vi) For a polytropic process

$$C = C_V + \frac{PdV}{ndT} = C_V + \frac{RT}{V}\cdot\frac{dV}{dT}$$

$$\Rightarrow \quad R = \frac{5}{2}R + \frac{RT}{V}\frac{dV}{dT}$$

$$\Rightarrow \quad -\frac{3}{2}VdT = TdV$$

$$3\int \frac{dT}{T} + 2\int \frac{dV}{V} = 0$$

$$\ln T^3 + \ln V^2 = \text{constant}$$

$$T^3 V^2 = \text{constant}$$

$$T^{3/2} V = \text{constant}$$

If V changes to $2V$ then T becomes T' given as

$$T^{3/2} V = T'^{3/2}(2V)$$

$$T' = \frac{T}{(2)^{2/3}}$$

Rate of collision is proportional to $\dfrac{\sqrt{T}}{V}$

$\Rightarrow$ new rate becomes

$$N'_C = N_C \frac{\sqrt{\left(\dfrac{1}{2^{2/3}}\right)}}{2}$$

$$= \frac{N_C}{(2)^{4/3}}$$

(vii) **(a)** $P = aT^{\alpha}$

$$\Rightarrow \quad \left(\frac{RT}{V}\right) = aT^{\alpha} \Rightarrow V = \frac{R}{a}T^{1-\alpha}$$

$$\Rightarrow \quad dV = \frac{R}{a}(1-\alpha)T^{-\alpha}dT$$

we use work, done by gas

$$\Delta W = \int PdV$$

$$= \int (aT^{\alpha})\left(\frac{R}{a}(1-\alpha)T^{-\alpha}\right)dT$$

$$= R(1-\alpha)\Delta T$$

(b) Molar heat capacity is given as

$$C = C_V + \frac{RT}{V}\frac{dV}{dT}$$

$$\Rightarrow \quad C = \frac{R}{\gamma-1} + \frac{RT}{\left(\frac{R}{a}T^{1-\alpha}\right)} \cdot \frac{R}{a}(1-\alpha)T^{-\alpha}$$

$$= \frac{R}{\gamma-1} + R(1-\alpha)$$

(viii) As in both paths ΔU is same but work done is more in path B thus heat required in path B is more hence molar heat capacity in path B will be more.

Solutions of PRACTICE EXERCISE 3.5

(i) Work done = area enclosed by PV curve of angle

$$= \frac{1}{2} \times 3 \times 30 = 45 \text{ J}$$

(ii) Heat calculations in cycle are

$$\Delta Q_{AB} = 2(R)(500)\ln(2)$$

$$\Delta Q_{CD} = -2R(300)\ln(2)$$

$$\Delta Q_{BC} = -2(C_V)(200)$$

$$\Delta Q_{DA} = 2(C_V)(200) \quad \text{(cancel out with } \Delta Q_{BC})$$

Total heat supplied to gas is

$$\Delta Q_{Total} = \Delta Q_{AB} + \Delta Q_{CD}$$

$$= 2R(200)\ln 2$$

$$= 2 \times 8.314 \times 200 \times 0.693$$

$$= 2304.64 \text{ J}$$

Thus total heat rejected by gas is

$$-2304.64 \text{ J}$$

(iii) For process AB we use

$$PT = \text{constant}$$

$$T = k\sqrt{V}$$

$$\Rightarrow \quad dT = \frac{k}{2\sqrt{V}}dV$$

$$\Rightarrow \quad P\sqrt{V} = \text{constant}$$

$$\Rightarrow \quad PV^{1/2} = \text{constant}$$

Thus molar specific heat of gas is

$$C = C_V + \frac{R}{1-\frac{1}{2}} = C_V + 2R$$

$$= \frac{3}{2}R + 2R = \frac{7}{2}R$$

(a) Work done by gas in process AB is

$$W = \int PdV = \int \frac{2RT}{V}dV$$

$$= \int \frac{2R(k\sqrt{V})}{V} \cdot \frac{2\sqrt{V}}{k}dT$$

$$= 4R\int_{2T_0}^{T_0} dT = -4RT_0$$

$$= -1200\,R$$

(b) Heat supplied to gas is

$$\Delta Q_{AB} = 2C(T_0 - 2T_0) = -2CT_0$$

$$= -7RT_0 = -2100\,R$$

$$\Delta Q_{BC} = 2C_P(2T_0 - T_0) = 2\left(\frac{5R}{2}\right)T_0 = 1500\,R$$

$$\Delta Q_{CA} = 2(R)(2T_0)\ln(2)$$

$$= 1200\,R \times 0.693 = 831.6\,R$$

(iv) (a) Work done = area enclosed by angle

$$= \frac{1}{2} \times V_0 \times 2P_0 = P_0V_0$$

(b) Heat in path CA is

$$\Delta Q_{CA} = nC_P\Delta T = (1)\left(\frac{5}{2}R\right)\left(\frac{2P_0V_0}{R} - \frac{P_0V_0}{R}\right) = 2.5\,P_0V_0$$

$$\Delta Q_{AB} = nC_v\Delta T = 1\left(\frac{3}{2}R\right)(3P_0V_0 - P_0V_0)$$

$$= 3P_0V_0$$

(c) $\Delta Q_{\text{Total}} = \Delta Q_{AB} + \Delta Q_{BC} + \Delta Q_{CA}$

$$\Rightarrow \quad P_0V_0 = 3P_0V_0 + \Delta Q_{BC} - 2.5P_0V_0$$

$$\Rightarrow \quad \Delta Q_{BC} = 0.5\,P_0V_0$$

(d) Process equation of BC is

$$(P - 3P_0) = -\frac{2P_0}{V_0}(V - V_0)$$

$$P=-\frac{2P_0}{V_0}V+5P_0$$

Gas temperature is

$$T=\frac{PV}{R}=-\frac{2P_0}{RV_0}\cdot V^2+\frac{5P_0}{R}\cdot V$$

T is maximum when

$$\frac{dT}{dV}=0$$

$$\Rightarrow\quad -\frac{2P_0}{RV_0}(2V)+\frac{5P_0}{R}=0$$

$$\Rightarrow\quad \frac{4V}{V_0}=5$$

$$\Rightarrow\quad V=\frac{5V_0}{4}$$

$$\Rightarrow\quad T_{max}=-\frac{2P_0}{R\gamma_0}\left(\frac{25V_0^2}{16}\right)+\frac{5P_0}{R}\left(\frac{5V_0}{4}\right)$$

$$=-\frac{25}{8}\frac{P_0V_0}{R}+\frac{25}{4}\frac{P_0V_0}{R}$$

$$=\frac{25P_0V_0}{8R}$$

(v) Work done = Area 021 – Area 043

$$=\frac{1}{2}(V_2-V_1)(P_0-P_0)$$

$$-\frac{1}{2}(V_4-V_3)(P_2-P_0)$$

$$=\frac{1}{2}(100\times10^{-3})(2\times10^5)$$

$$-\frac{1}{2}\left[\frac{(P_2-P_0)}{(P_0-P_1)}(V_2-V_1)\right](P_2-P_0)$$

$$=10^4-\frac{1}{2}\left[\frac{10^5}{2\times10^5}\times100\times10^{-3}\right](10^5)\text{J}$$

$$=10^4-2500=7500\text{ J}$$

(vi) For processes 12 and 34 The process equation is $P=kV$

$\Rightarrow$ molar specific heat is

$$C=C_V+\frac{RPdV}{PdV+VdP}$$

$$=\frac{3}{2}R+\frac{R(kV)dV}{(kV)dV+V(kdV)}$$

$$=\frac{3}{2}R+\frac{R}{2}=2R$$

Heat supplied in processes of cycle are

$$\Delta Q_{12}=3(2R)(400)=2400\,R$$

$$\Delta Q_{23}=3\left(\frac{5}{2}R\right)(1600)=12000\,R$$

$$\Delta Q_{34}=3(2R)(-1200)=-7200\,R$$

$$\Delta Q_{41}=3\left(\frac{5R}{2}\right)(-800)=-6000\,R$$

Total work done = Total heat supplied

$$=2400\,R+12000\,R-7200\,R-6000\,R$$

$$=1200\,R$$

$$=9976.8\text{ J}$$

If we consider number of moles $=n_1$

(vii) Let temperature in states are

$$T_2=T;\ T_1=nT\ \&\ T_3=n^2T$$

process equation of BA is $P=kV$ for which specific heat is

$$C=C_V+\frac{R}{2}$$

$$=\frac{R}{\gamma-1}+\frac{R}{2}=\left(\frac{\gamma+1}{(\gamma-1)}\right)\frac{R}{2}$$

Heat supplied in process BA is

$$Q_{BA}=n_1\left(\frac{\gamma+1}{\gamma-1}\right)\frac{R}{2}T(n^2-1)$$

Work done by gas = area enclosed by cycle

$$=\frac{1}{2}(P_2-P_1)(V_1-V_2)$$

$$=\frac{n_1R}{2}[n^2T-nT-nT+T]$$

$$=\frac{n_1RT}{2}(n-1)^2$$

$$\text{Efficiency of cycle}\quad \eta=\frac{\text{work done}}{\text{heat import}}=\frac{W}{Q_{BA}}$$

$$\Rightarrow\quad \eta=\frac{\frac{n_1RT}{2}(n-1)^2}{\frac{n_1RT}{2}\left(\frac{\gamma+1}{\gamma-1}\right)(n^2-1)}$$

$$=\left(\frac{\gamma-1}{\gamma+1}\right)\left(\frac{n-1}{n+1}\right)$$

(viii) We consider n_1 moles of gas heat supplied in different processes of cycle are.

$$\Delta Q_{AB}=0$$

$$\Delta Q_{BC}=-n_1\left(\frac{\gamma R}{\gamma-1}\right)(T_2-T_3)$$

$$=-\frac{\gamma}{\gamma-1}(nP_2V_1-P_2V_1)$$

$$= -\frac{\gamma P_2 V_1}{\gamma - 1}(n-1)$$

$$\Delta Q_{CA} = n_1\left(\frac{R}{\gamma-1}\right)(T_1 - T_3)$$

$$= \frac{1}{\gamma-1}(P_1V_1 - P_2V_1)$$

For adiabatic process we use

$$P_1V_1^\gamma = P_2(nV_1)^\gamma$$

$$\Rightarrow \quad P_2 = \frac{P_1}{h^\gamma}$$

Thus cycle efficiency is given as

$$\eta = 1 - \left|\frac{Q_{out}}{Q_{in}}\right| = 1 - \frac{\frac{\gamma}{\gamma-1}P_2V_1(n-1)}{\frac{1}{\gamma-1}(P_1V_1 - P_2V_1)}$$

$$= 1 - \frac{\gamma P_2 V_1(n-1)}{P_2V_1(n^\gamma - 1)}$$

$$= 1 - \gamma\left(\frac{n-1}{n^\gamma - 1}\right)$$

(ix) If T is the temperature of state A we use

$$T_A = T;\; T_B = T_D = nT;\; T_C = n^2T$$

Total work done by gas in cycle for n_1 moles of gas

$$W = (P_2 - P_1)(V_2 - V_1)$$

$$= n_1R(n^2T - nT - nT + T)$$

$$= n_1RT(n-1)^2$$

Heat supplied to gas is

$$Q_{supp} = \Delta Q_{AB} + \Delta Q_{BC}$$

$$= n_1\left(\frac{R}{\gamma-1}\right)T(n-1) + n_1\left(\frac{\gamma R}{\gamma-1}\right)T(n^2-n)$$

$$= \frac{n_1RT}{\gamma-1}(n-1+\gamma n^2 - \gamma n) = \frac{n_1RT}{\gamma-1}(n-1)(1+\gamma n)$$

Cycle efficiency is

$$\eta = \frac{W}{Q_{supp}} = \frac{n_1RT(n-1)^2}{\frac{n_1RT}{\gamma-1}(n-1)(1+\gamma n)}$$

$$= \left(\frac{\gamma-1}{1+\gamma n}\right)(n-1)$$

Solutions of CONCEPTUAL MCQS Single Option Correct

Sol. 1 (B) Work done by the gas is the area under the P-V curve hence option (B) is correct.

Sol. 2 (A) All three quantities given above are dependent upon temperature of the gas and under isothermal compression temperature remain same hence option (A) is correct.

Sol. 3 (C) Work done by the gas in the given cyclic process will be the area enclosed by the cycle hence option (C) is correct.

Sol. 4 (B) Slope of adiabatic curve is more than that of isothermal curve.

Sol. 5 (D) In isothermal expansion temperature of gas remain constant and also the internal energy remain constant so heat supplied to the gas is equal to the work done by the gas.

Sol. 6 (A) On the PV diagram we can see that final temperature in process 1 is more than that in process 2 and that in process 2 is more than that in process 3 and internal energy change is directly proportional to the change in temperature hence option (A) is correct.

Sol. 7 (B) As atmospheric pressure is constant option (B) is correct.

Sol. 8 (A) pV^2 = constant it implies on using gas law we have TV = constant so if we double the temperature, volume will decrease to $V/2$ hence option (A) is correct.

Sol. 9 (A) In Carnot cycle there are two isothermal and two adiabatic processes complete the cycle in alternative manner and slope of isothermal curve is less than that of adiabatic curve hence option (A) is correct.

Sol. 10 (B) From point L to M as pressure is constant, by gas laws we use V is directly proportional to T so the curve in T and V will be a straight line passing through origin which is there only in option (B).

Sol. 11 (D) Work is done on the gas when in the process gas volume decreases which happens here only in processes RS and SP.

Sol. 12 (C) Process AB must be a vertical straight line as temperature is not changing in the process. Then Process BC is an isobaric process so here it must be a horizontal straight line and finally process CA is an isochoric process when volume remain constant so on P-T curve this will be a straight line passing through origin.

Sol. 13 (A) In the given process, as volume increases work done will be increasing with time.

Sol. 14 (B) In the above process pressure is a constant so the heat absorbed for a given temperature range can be given as

$\Delta Q = nC_P\Delta T$ and work done is $W = nR\Delta T$ and for a monoatomic gas C_P is $5R/2$.

Sol. 15 (A) For the process *AC* change in internal energy will be the difference of total heat supplied which is 800 J and the work done by the gas which can be calculated by the area under the *P-V* curve which is 240 J so it comes out to be 560 J.

Sol. 16 (C) In process *AB* as volume is constant no work is done and as at constant volume pressure increases so according to gas law temperature also increases and heat is absorbed by the system and its internal energy increases due to increase in temperature.

Sol. 17 (C) A cyclic process is one in which initial and final state are same or the gas always return to initial state after complete cycle.

Sol. 18 (B) When a gas is heated at constant volume, all the heat is used in raising the temperature of the gas whereas if it is heated at constant pressure, gas expands and some work is done against the external pressure.

Sol. 19 (C) Depending upon the thermodynamic process to be executed on a gas, its specific heat is different so it can have infinite number of specific heats.

Sol. 20 (A) For a container of finite low conductivity, heat cannot be instantly conducted through it so for sudden compression (In a very short time) no heat loss will be considered and the process will be taken as almost adiabatic. If the conductor is of very high conductivity then heat can be conducted in the short time also then the process may be isothermal as well if heat can be rejected by the gas to surrounding which is equal to the work done on the gas.

Sol. 21 (B) Processes *BC* and *AD* are isochoric so at these processes density as well as volume remain constant and for *AB* and *CD* volume and density inversely varies here option (B) is correct.

Sol. 22 (C) For an adiabatic process, $TV^{\gamma-1}$ = const; and $U(\text{ideal gas}) \propto T$.

Sol. 23 (A) In adiabatic compression, the temperature always increases and since $PV = nRT$, the quantity PV also increases.

Sol. 24 (C) As initial and final states of the gas are same, change in internal energy will be same but area under process *a* is more so work done by the gas is more in process *a* than process b so heat supplied in process which is the sum of change in internal energy and work will be more in process *a*.

Sol. 25 (C) As per definition of adiabatic process (i) is correct and change in internal energy in all processes is given by (iii) hence option. (ii) is wrong as if work is done on a system then in adiabatic process it is equal to increase in internal energy of the system.

Sol. 26 (C) Sole of isothermal curve is P/V and that of an adiabatic curve is $\gamma P/V$.

Sol. 27 (D) From state *A* to *B* total change in internal energy for all paths must be same so equating internal energy change in paths *ACB* and *ADB* we get heat absorbed by the system in path *ADB* is 60 cal.

Sol. 28 (C) Expansion of a gas in vaccum is free expansion in which no work is done and as container is insulated, no heat supply will take place so no change in internal energy of gas will occur.

Sol. 29 (A) Internal energy of gas in a state is given as $U = (1/2)fnRT$ hence option (A) is correct.

Sol. 30 (A) As per given data in state *B*, gas is not behaving like an ideal gas. As we know at very low pressure and very high temperature gases behave like ideal so in the given case option (A) is most likely to be correct.

Sol. 31 (A) For a given *P-V* curve work done is always the area under the curve.

Sol. 32 (B) As volume is decreasing in process *BC* the work done will be negative of area under the curve.

Sol. 33 (C) The bulk modulus is given as $B = -dP/(dV/V)$ which can be evaluated by the given process equation which gives option (C) is correct.

Sol. 34 (B) In free expansion of a gas internal energy of gas remain constant hence option (B) is correct.

Sol. 35 (C) As the graph of logarithm of *P* and *V* is a straight line the process must be adiabatic as the process equation will be $PV^\gamma = constant$ or $\log(P) = -\gamma\log(V) + K$ so the negative of slope of the curve gives the value of $\gamma = 7/5$ which is for a diatomic gas.

Sol. 36 (C) $W_{12} = W_{34} = 0$, (since the process is isochoric)

$$W_{23} = P_2(V_3 - V_2) = nR(T_3 - T_2),$$

$$W_{41} = P_1(V_2 - V_4) = nRT(T_1 - T_4)$$

$$W = nR[T_3 + T_1 - T_2 - T_4]$$

$$= 3 \times (2400 + 400 - 1200 - 800) + 8.314$$

$$\simeq 20\text{ kJ}$$

Sol. 37 (C) $W = P_0\Delta V = P_0V_0$

and $\Delta U = 2P_0(2V_0 - V_0) = 2P_0V_0$

$\Rightarrow$ $Q = W + \Delta U = 3P_0V_0$

Sol. 38 (B) By gas law $PV = \eta RT$

$\Rightarrow$ $\frac{PM}{\rho} = \eta RT$

$\Rightarrow$ $\frac{P}{\rho}$ = constant or

$\Rightarrow$ $\frac{P_B}{P_A} = \frac{\rho_B}{\rho_A} < 1$

Sol. 39 (B) From state *A* to *B* in the given diagram, we can see that the gas is expanding (density decreasing) and by the process equation it can be seen that volume of the gas is directly proportional to *T* and temperature is increasing so the process is isobaric, during expansion work is behind done by the gas thus heat is being absorbed by the gas.

Sol. 40 (A)

As P^2V = constant

$\Rightarrow$ T^2V^{-1} = constant

$\Rightarrow$ $T^2 = KV$

$\Rightarrow$ $T_0^2 = KV_0$ ... (A)

and $T_1^2 = K(3V_0)$ ... (B)

By (A) and (B) we get

$T_1 = \sqrt{3}T_0$

Sol. 41 (C)

In the diagram since adiabatic process curve for *P-V* diagram is steeper than isothermal *P-V* curve. So curve 3 will denote adiabatic process, curve 2 isothermal and curve 1 isobaric, i.e. the minimum area enclosed with v-axis will be for adiabatic process

Sol. 42 (C)

$$dQ = \frac{n\gamma R}{\gamma - 1}dT;\ dU = \frac{nR}{\gamma - 1}dT;\ dW = nR\,dT$$

$\Rightarrow$ $\frac{dQ}{\gamma} = \frac{dW}{\gamma - 1} = \frac{dU}{1}$

$\Rightarrow$ $\gamma : \gamma - 1 : 1$

Sol. 43 (B) Work done in process 1 – 3 is greater than that in process 1 – 2. While change in internal energy is same for both processes

$\Rightarrow$ $Q_2 > Q_1$

Sol. 44 (D) Process *AB* is isothermal so on *V-T* curve also it will remain a vertical straight line. Process *BC* is isochoric (as it is a straight line passing through origin) hence on *V-T* curve it will be a horizontal straight line and process *CD* is again isothermal so it will be a vertical straight line on *V-T* curve hence the curve will look like

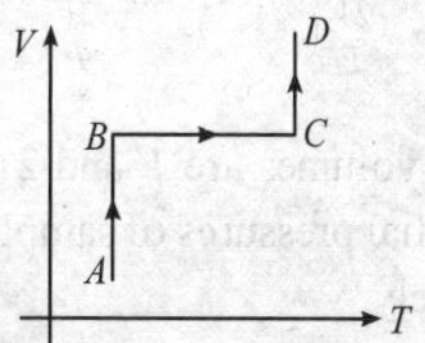

Sol. 45 (C) Under isothermal compression when a gas is compressed the separation between the gas molecules decreases due to which mean free path decreases and hence rate of collisions increase hence option (C) is correct.

Sol. 46 (B) As $Q_1 = \Delta U + W_1$

and $Q_2 = \Delta U + W_2$

Ratio of specific heats

$$\frac{C_1}{C_2} = \frac{\left(\frac{\Delta Q_1}{\Delta T}\right)}{\left(\frac{\Delta Q_2}{\Delta T}\right)} = \frac{\left(\frac{\Delta U}{\Delta T} + \frac{\Delta W_1}{\Delta T}\right)}{\left(\frac{\Delta U}{\Delta T} + \frac{\Delta W_2}{\Delta T}\right)} < 1 \quad (\text{As } W_2 > W_1)$$

Sol. 47 (A) As P^2T = constant

$\Rightarrow$ $P^2(PV)$ = constant

$\Rightarrow$ P^3V = constant

$\Rightarrow$ $PV^{1/3}$ = constant $\Rightarrow$ $(x = 1/3)$

$$C = \frac{fR}{2} + \frac{R}{1 - x}$$

After solving we get $f = 3$

$\Rightarrow$ So the gas is monoatomic.

Sol. 48 (C) As in the given process at constant pressure, temperature is increasing, gas volume is also increasing due to which gas density decreases.

Sol. 49 (D) Temperature, internal energy and volume depend upon states.

Solutions of NUMERICAL MCQS Single Option Correct

Sol. 1 (A) For adiabatic process

$TV^{\gamma-1}$ = constant

$\Rightarrow \quad 300V^{1.4-1} = T(2V)^{1.4-1}$

$\Rightarrow \quad 300 = T(2)^{0.4}$

$\Rightarrow \quad T = 227.3\text{K}$

Sol. 2 (B)

p_1 A, V → adiabatic → $2V$, P; p_2 B, V → isobaric → $2V$, P; p_3 C, V → isothermal → $2V$, P

Let initial and final volumes are V and $2V$ respectively. Final pressure is P and initial pressures of samples A, B and C be P_1, P_2 and P_3 respectively

The process is adiabatic for A,

$$PV^\gamma = \text{constant}$$

$$P_1V^{3/2} = P(2V)^{3/2}$$

$$P_1 = 2\sqrt{2}P \quad \ldots(1)$$

The process is isobaric for B, i.e. pressure remains same

$$P_2 = P \quad \ldots(2)$$

The process is isothermal for C,

$$PV = \text{constant}$$

$$P_3V = P(2V)$$

$$P_3 = 2P \quad \ldots(3)$$

$$P_1 : P_2 : P_3 = 2\sqrt{2} : 1 : 2$$

Sol. 3 (B) For adiabatic process

$$TV^{\gamma-1} = \text{constant}$$

$$(27+273)V^{\frac{5}{3}-1} = T\left(\frac{8}{27}\right)^{\frac{5}{3}-1}$$

$$300 = T\left(\frac{4}{9}\right)$$

$$T = 675\text{K} = 402°\text{C}$$

Rise in temperature $= 402°\text{C} - 27°\text{C}$

$= 375°\text{C}$

Sol. 4 (C) Since temperature remains unchanged,

(P–V diagram: A at (V, p); B at $(V, \frac{p}{n})$; C at $(nV, \frac{p}{n})$)

$$U_i = U_f$$

$$\Delta Q = \Delta W \qquad (\text{As } \Delta U = 0)$$

For isochoric process, $\Delta W = 0$

$$W = \frac{p}{n}(nV - V)$$

$$= pV\left(\frac{n-1}{n}\right) = RT(1 - n^{-1})$$

Sol. 5 (B) Number of moles of nitrogen

$$n = \frac{14}{28} = \frac{1}{2}$$

$$v_{rms}^2 \propto T$$

Thus to reduce *rms* speed to half, temperature has to be reduced by 4 times

$$T_f = \frac{300}{4} = 75\text{K}$$

$$\Delta T = 300 - 75 = 225\text{K}$$

$$\Delta Q = nC_p\Delta T$$

$$= \frac{1}{2} \times \frac{5}{2}R \times 225$$

$$= 562.5 \text{ cal}$$

Sol. 6 (C) Volume of vessel and hence the gas remains same.

$$p_1 = 72.6 \text{ cm of } Hg$$

$$n_1 = 1$$

After 2 strokes, let pressure $= p_2$

$$n_2 = 0.81$$

$$72.6V = 1\,RT \quad \ldots(1)$$

$$p_2V = 0.81\,RT \quad \ldots(2)$$

Dividing (2) by (1) we get,

$$\frac{p_2}{72.6} = \frac{0.81}{1}$$

$$p_2 = 58.8 \text{ cm of } Hg$$

$$\approx 60 \text{ cm of } Hg$$

Sol. 7 (B) Let mass of gas enclosed $= m$

Kinetic energy,

$$k = \frac{1}{2}mv^2$$

When vessel is stopped suddenly, its kinetic energy is converted into internal energy of gas molecules

$$\frac{1}{2}mv^2 = \Delta U = \frac{m}{M}C_v\Delta T$$

As $C_v = \frac{R}{\gamma - 1}$

$$\Rightarrow \quad \frac{1}{2}mv^2 = \frac{m}{M}\frac{R}{\gamma-1}\Delta T$$

$$\Rightarrow \quad \Delta T = \frac{Mv^2(\gamma-1)}{2R}$$

Sol. 8 **(C)** From first law of thermodynamics,

$$\Delta Q = \Delta U + \Delta W$$

$$\Delta U = \Delta Q - \Delta W$$

$$\Delta U = \frac{3Q}{4}$$

Let molar heat capacity of process is x

$$\Delta U = nC_v\Delta T$$

$$\Delta Q = nx\Delta T$$

$$nC_v\Delta T = \frac{3}{4}nx\Delta T$$

$$x = \frac{4C_v}{3}$$

For a diatomic gas, $C_v = \frac{5R}{2}$

$$x = \frac{4}{3} \times \frac{5R}{2} = \frac{10R}{3}$$

Sol. 9 **(D)** Given that $n = 2$

$$\Delta T = 100$$

$$\Delta Q = nC_p\Delta T$$

$$\Delta Q = 2 \times \frac{5}{2} R \times 100$$

$$\Delta Q = 500R$$

Sol. 10 **(B)** We use $\frac{\Delta U}{\Delta Q} = \frac{C_v}{C_p} = \frac{3}{5}$

Sol. 11 **(C)** Volume of water heated = 3l/minute

Mass of water heated = m = 3000g/minute

Increase in temperature,

$$\Delta T = 77°C - 27°C = 50°C$$

Amount of heat used, $Q = mc\Delta T$

$$= 3000 \text{ g/min} \times 4.2 \text{ J g}^{-1}\text{C}^{-1} \times 50°\text{C}$$

$$= 63 \times 10^4 \text{ J min}^{-1}$$

Rate of combustion of fuel = $\frac{63\times10^4}{4\times10^4}$ = 15.75 g min^{-1}

Sol. 12 **(B)** Adiabatic elasticity,

$$E_\phi = \gamma p$$

Isothermal elasticity, $E_\theta = p$

$$\frac{E_\phi}{E_\theta} = \frac{\gamma p}{p} = \gamma$$

Sol. 13 **(A)** Given that

$$\Delta W = 20 \text{ J}$$

$$\Delta Q = -40 \text{ J}$$

From first law of thermodynamics,

$$\Delta Q = \Delta U + \Delta W$$

$$-40 = U_f - 70 - 20$$

$$\Rightarrow \quad U_f = 50 \text{ J}$$

Sol. 14 **(C)** Given that $P \propto V$

$$PV^{-1} = \text{constant}$$

$$PV^x = \text{constant}$$

$$\Rightarrow \quad x = -1,$$

Molar heat capacity,

$$C = \frac{R}{\gamma-1} + \frac{R}{1-x}$$

For a diatomic gas, $\gamma = 1.4$

$$C = \frac{R}{1.4-1} + \frac{R}{1+1} = 3R$$

Sol. 15 **(A)** As we know

$$\text{Density} = \frac{\text{mass}}{\text{volume}}$$

$$\rho = \frac{m}{V}$$

$$V = \frac{m}{\rho}$$

New volume, $V' = \frac{m}{n\rho} = \frac{V}{n}$

Since the process is adiabatic,

$$PV^\gamma = \text{constant}$$

Let final pressure of gas is p'

$$PV^\gamma = P'\left(\frac{V}{n}\right)^\gamma$$

$$P' = n^\gamma P$$

Sol. 16 **(C)** Given that $R = nC_p$

$$R = \frac{n\gamma R}{\gamma - 1}$$

$$n = \frac{\gamma - 1}{\gamma}$$

For a monoatomic gas, $\gamma = 1.66$

$$n = \frac{1.66 - 1}{1.66} = 0.39 \approx 0.4$$

Sol. 17 (C) We use $\Delta Q = mL = L$ (As $m = 1$)

$$\Delta w = p_0(V_2 - V_1)$$

From first law of thermodynamics,

$$\Delta Q = \Delta U + \Delta w$$

$$\Delta w = \Delta Q - \Delta U$$

$$\Delta w = L - p_0(V_2 - V_1)$$

Sol. 18 (A) Kinetic energy of water is

$$\frac{m \times 9.8 \times 84}{4.2} = m \times 1000 \times \Delta T$$

$$\Delta T = 0.2°\text{C}$$

Sol. 19 (D) For constant pressure

$$H_1 = nC_p\Delta T$$

$$207 = 1 \times C_p \times 10$$

$\Rightarrow$ $C_p = 20.7\ \text{Jk}^{-1}\ \text{mole}^{-1}$

We use $C_p - C_v = R$

$\Rightarrow$ $C_v = C_p - R = 20.7 - 8.3$

$$= 12.4\ \text{Jk}^{-1}\ \text{mole}^{-1}$$

$\Rightarrow$ $H_2 = nC_v\Delta T$

$\Rightarrow$ $H_2 = 1 \times 12.4 \times 10$

$\Rightarrow$ $H_2 = 124\text{J}$

Sol. 20 (A) In isobaric process,

$$W_1 = p(2V - V) = pV$$

In isothermal process

$$W_2 = nRT\ \ln\left(\frac{2V}{V}\right) = nRT\ln(2)$$

$\Rightarrow$ $W_2 = pV\ln(2)$

$\Rightarrow$ $\frac{W_1}{W_2} = \frac{pV}{pV\ln(2)} = \frac{1}{\ln(2)}$

$\Rightarrow$ $W_2 = W_1\ln(2)$

Sol. 21 (B) For the mixture

$$C_{v_{mix}} = \frac{\eta_1 C_{v_1} + \eta_2 C_{v_2}}{\eta_1 + \eta_2}$$

$\Rightarrow$ $= \frac{\eta_1\left(\frac{R}{\gamma_1 - 1}\right) + \eta_2\left(\frac{R}{\gamma_2 - 1}\right)}{\eta_1 + \eta_2}$

$\Rightarrow$ $= \frac{R}{\eta_1 + \eta_2}\left(\frac{\eta_1}{\gamma_1 - 1} + \frac{\eta_2}{\gamma_2 - 1}\right)$

Here, $\eta_1 = 1, \eta_2 = 1$

$$\gamma_1 = 1.66, \gamma_2 = 1.4$$

$$C_{v_{mix}} = \frac{R}{1+1}\left[\frac{1}{1.66 - 1} + \frac{1}{1.4 - 1}\right]$$

$\Rightarrow$ $= \frac{R}{2}[4]$

$\Rightarrow$ $= 2R$

Sol. 22 (C) We use $R = 8.3\ \text{Jk}^{-1}\ \text{mole}^{-1}$

Sol. 23 (C) Volume $\propto$ (diameter)^3

Thus, as bubble goes up, its diameter is doubled and hence its volume becomes $(2)^3 = 8$ times

$$pV = \text{constant}$$

Pressure at bottom = 8 times pressure at top

$$H\rho_w g = (8h - h)\rho_m g$$

$$H = 7h\frac{\rho_m}{\rho_w} = 7h\rho$$

Sol. 24 (C) For isobaric process,

$$\Delta Q = nC_P\Delta T$$

$$\Delta U = nC_V\Delta T$$

From first law of thermodynamics,

$$\Delta Q = \Delta U + \Delta W$$

$$\Delta W = \Delta Q - \Delta U$$

$$= n(C_P - C_V)\Delta T$$

$$= nR\Delta T$$

$$\Delta Q : \Delta U : \Delta w = \frac{7}{2}R : \frac{5}{2}R : R = 7 : 5 : 2$$

Sol. 25 (A) $\Delta Q = nC\Delta T$

$$\Delta Q = \frac{pV}{RT} \times C \times \Delta T$$

$$= \frac{10^5 \times 0.5}{8.3 \times 300} \times 5 \times (500 - 300)$$

$$= 20080\ \text{cal} \approx 20\ \text{kcal}$$

Sol. 26 (B) Since the interatomic distance between molecules is same, it is molar specific heat at constant volume

For a diatomic gas,

$$C_V = \frac{5}{2}R$$

Sol. 27 (A) For an isothermal process,

$$\Delta U = 0$$

Sol. 28 (D) As we use

$$\Delta Q = nC_P\Delta T$$
$$\Delta U = nC_V\Delta T$$

From first law of thermodynamics

$$\Delta Q = \Delta U + \Delta W$$
$$\Delta W = \Delta Q - \Delta U$$
$$\Delta W = nR\Delta T \qquad (\text{As } C_P - C_V = R)$$
$$\frac{\Delta W}{\Delta Q} = \frac{nR\Delta T}{nC_P\Delta T} = \frac{R}{C_P} = \frac{R}{\frac{5}{2}R} = \frac{2}{5}$$

Sol. 29 (D) From previous problem solution we use

$$\frac{\Delta U}{\Delta Q} = \frac{nC_V\Delta T}{nC_P\Delta T} = \frac{C_V}{C_P} = \frac{5}{7}$$

Sol. 30 (B) For equivalent γ, we use

$$\Rightarrow \frac{n_1}{\gamma_1 - 1} + \frac{n_2}{\gamma_2 - 1} = \frac{n_1 + n_2}{\gamma_{mix} - 1}$$
$$\Rightarrow \frac{1}{\frac{5}{3} - 1} + \frac{1}{\frac{4}{3} - 1} = \frac{2}{\gamma_{mix} - 1}$$
$$\Rightarrow \frac{3}{2} + \frac{3}{1} = \frac{2}{\gamma_{mix} - 1}$$
$$\Rightarrow \frac{3+6}{2} = \frac{2}{\gamma_{mix} - 1}$$
$$\Rightarrow \gamma_{mix} - 1 = \frac{4}{9}$$
$$\Rightarrow \gamma_{mix} = \frac{13}{9} = 1.44$$

Sol. 31 (B) For adiabatic process we use

$$T^{\gamma}p^{1-\gamma} = \text{constant}$$
$$\Rightarrow T_1^{\gamma}P_1^{1-\gamma} = T_2^{\gamma}P_2^{1-\gamma}$$
$$\Rightarrow T_2^{\gamma} = T_1^{\gamma}\left(\frac{P_1}{P_2}\right)^{1-\gamma}$$
$$\Rightarrow T_2 = T_1\left(\frac{P_1}{P_2}\right)^{\frac{1-\gamma}{\gamma}}$$

Sol. 32 (D) Given that $P_1 = 2\text{atm}, P_2 = 1\text{ atm}$

$$T_1 = 27°\text{C},$$

As the process is sudden, it is considered adiabatic

$$T^{\gamma}P^{1-\gamma} = \text{constant}$$
$$\Rightarrow (300)^{1.4}(2)^{1-1.4} = (T_2)^{1.4}(1)^{1-1.4}$$
$$\Rightarrow T_2 = 300\left(\frac{2}{1}\right)^{\frac{1-1.4}{1.4}}$$
$$\Rightarrow T_2 = 300 \times 0.82$$
$$\Rightarrow T_2 = 246K$$
$$\Rightarrow T_2 = -27°\text{C}$$

Sol. 33 (A) For $PV^{\gamma} = \text{constant}$

$$P_1V_1^{\gamma} = P_2V_2^{\gamma}$$
$$P_2 = P_1\left(\frac{V_1}{V_2}\right)^{\gamma}$$

Sol. 34 (C) We use $R = 2\text{cal/mole/°C}$

$$C_p = 8\text{ cal/mole/°C}$$
$$C_v = C_p - R = 6\text{ cal/mole/°C}$$

and

$$\Delta Q = nC_v\Delta T$$
$$= 5 \times 6 \times 10$$
$$= 300\text{ cal}$$

Sol. 35 (C) As $\Delta W = 0$

$$\Rightarrow \Delta Q = \Delta U = 300\text{ cal}$$

Sol. 36 (C) As $\gamma = \frac{7}{5}$ and volume becomes half we use

$$PV^{\gamma} = \text{constant}$$
$$\Rightarrow PV^{7/5} = P'\left(\frac{V}{2}\right)^{7/5}$$
$$\Rightarrow P' = (2)^{7/5}P$$
$$\Rightarrow P' = 2.6P$$

Sol. 37 (D) For adiabatic process

$$T_1V_1^{\gamma-1} = T_2V_2^{\gamma-1}$$
$$\Rightarrow \frac{T_1}{T_2} = \left(\frac{V_2}{V_1}\right)^{\gamma-1}$$
$$\Rightarrow \frac{T_1}{T_2} = \left(\frac{L_2A}{L_1A}\right)^{\frac{5}{3}-1}$$
$$\Rightarrow \frac{T_1}{T_2} = \left(\frac{L_2}{L_1}\right)^{2/3}$$

Sol. 38 (D) Heat supplied in adiabatic process,

$$\Delta Q = 0$$

and $\qquad \Delta U = -100\text{ J}$

As work done by the gas,

$$\Delta W = -(-100\text{ J})$$
$$= 100\text{ J}$$

Sol. 39 (C) From first law of thermodynamics, we use

$$\Delta Q = \Delta U + \Delta W$$

$\Rightarrow \qquad -30 = U_f - 40 - 10$

$\Rightarrow \qquad U_f = 20\text{J}$

Sol. 40 (C) As $\qquad Q = \dfrac{5\times 3.6\times 10^6}{4.2}$ cal

and $\qquad Q = mL$

$\Rightarrow \qquad m = \dfrac{Q}{L} = \dfrac{5\times 3.6\times 10^6}{4.2\times 80\times 100} \approx 54\text{kg}$

Sol. 41 (D) The maximum temperature will occur at point A and minimum temperature will occur point B of the cycle, so. At point A, we use

$$\frac{P_A}{P_0} = \frac{V_A}{V_0} = 2 + \cos 45^\circ = \frac{2\sqrt{2}+1}{\sqrt{2}} = \frac{4+\sqrt{2}}{2}$$

$$nRT_A = P_A V_A = \left(\frac{4+\sqrt{2}}{2}\right)^2 P_0 V_0$$

Similarly at point B

$$\frac{P_B}{P_0} = \frac{V_B}{V_0} = 2 - \cos 45^\circ = \frac{4-\sqrt{2}}{2}$$

$$nRT_B = P_B V_B = \left(\frac{4-\sqrt{2}}{2}\right)^2 P_0 V_0$$

$\Rightarrow \qquad \dfrac{T_A}{T_B} = \left(\dfrac{4+\sqrt{2}}{4-\sqrt{2}}\right)^2$

Sol. 42 (C) $TP^{-2/5}$ = constant; Using gas equation was can write $PV^{5/3}$ = constant

It implies $\gamma = \dfrac{5}{3}$; The process is adiabatic, thus $Q = 0$.

Sol. 43 (B) For a monoatomic gas,

$$\gamma = 1.6$$

$$PV^\gamma = \text{constant}$$

$$PV^\gamma = P'\left(V + \frac{2.4}{100}V\right)^\gamma$$

$$P' = 0.96P$$

Percentage decrease in pressure

$$= \frac{P - 0.96P}{P} \times 100$$
$$= 4\%$$

Sol. 44 (C) $\qquad U = nC_v\Delta T$

$$200 = 5C_v(120-100)$$
$$C_v = 2\text{J mole}^{-1}\, k^{-1}$$

Change of temperature in degree celsius is same as temperature difference in kelvin.

Sol. 45 (D) Since the process is adiabatic (sudden) we use

$$TV^{\gamma-1} = \text{constant}$$

$\Rightarrow \qquad (273+27)V^{\frac{5}{3}-1} = T\left(\dfrac{V}{8}\right)^{\frac{5}{3}-1}$

$\Rightarrow \qquad 300 = T\left(\dfrac{1}{8}\right)^{2/3}$

$\Rightarrow \qquad T = 300\times 4 = 1200\text{K} = 927^\circ\text{C}$

Sol. 46 (C) We use $\quad pV$ = constant

$\Rightarrow \qquad p'\left(\dfrac{V}{8}\right) = pV$

$\Rightarrow \qquad p' = 8p$

Sol. 47 (B) In a linear process with negative slope, there exist a state (point on the straight line) at which temperature of gas is maximum. This point is denoted by point C as shown in figure below where the line is tangent to an isothermal curve. Upto point C the temperature of gas increase and then decreases so at point C being maximum temperature the rate of change of internal energy of gas will be zero.

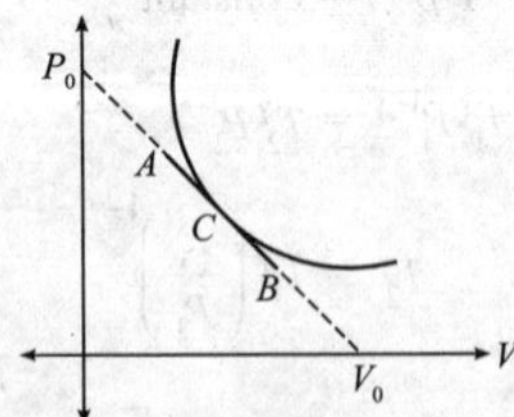

Pressure variation in the given process represented by the straight line can be written as

$$P = -\left(\frac{P_0}{V_0}\right)V + P_0$$

Gas temperature at any point on the straight line is given as

$$T=\frac{PV}{nR}=\frac{1}{nR}\left(-\frac{P_0V^2}{V_0}+P_0V\right)$$

Temperature will be maximum when $\frac{dT}{dV}=0$ which gives

$$\frac{dT}{dV}=\frac{1}{nR}\left(-\frac{2P_0V}{V_0}+P_0\right)=0$$

$$\Rightarrow \qquad V=\frac{V_0}{2}$$

Sol. 48 (A) For an adiabatic process, the process equation is $TV^{\gamma-1}=$ constant

In terms of mass and density, we can rewrite this equation as

$$T\left(\frac{m}{\rho}\right)^{\gamma-1}=\text{constant}$$

$$\Rightarrow \qquad \frac{T}{\rho^{\gamma-1}}=\text{constant}$$

$$\Rightarrow \qquad \rho\propto T^{1/(\gamma-1)}$$

According to the statement given in question, we have

$$\frac{1}{\gamma-1}=3$$

$$\Rightarrow \qquad \gamma=4/3$$

Thus degrees of freedom of gas molecule are

$$f=\frac{2}{\gamma-1}=\frac{2}{\left(\frac{4}{3}-1\right)}=6$$

Sol. 49 (B) For engines operating on Carnot cycle, efficiency is given as

$$\eta=1-\frac{T_2}{T_1}$$

In the given situation efficiency is changing from $\eta_1=0.2$ to $\eta_2=0.4$ so in the first case, we have

$$\eta_1=1-\frac{T_2}{T_1}$$

$$\Rightarrow \qquad 0.2=1-\frac{T_2}{T_1}=\frac{T_1-T_2}{T_1} \qquad \ldots(1)$$

For the second case, we have

$$\eta_2=1-\frac{T_2-50}{T_1}$$

$$\Rightarrow \qquad 0.4=\frac{T_1-T_2}{T_1}+\frac{50}{T_1}$$

$$\Rightarrow \qquad 0.4=\frac{T_1-T_2+50}{T_1}$$

$$\Rightarrow \qquad 0.4=\frac{T_1-T_2}{T_1}+\frac{50}{T_1}$$

$$\Rightarrow \qquad 0.4=0.2+\frac{50}{T_1}$$

$$\Rightarrow \qquad 0.4-0.2=\frac{50}{T_1}$$

$$\Rightarrow \qquad T_1=\frac{500}{2}=250\text{ K}$$

Substituting the value of T_1 in equation-(1) gives

$$0.2=\frac{T_1-T_2}{T_1}$$

$$\Rightarrow \qquad T_2=T_1-0.2T_1$$

$$\Rightarrow \qquad T_2=250-0.2\times 250$$

$$\Rightarrow \qquad T_2=250-50=200\text{ K}$$

Solutions of ADVANCE MCQs One or More Option Correct

Sol. 1 (B, C) As gas is expanding work done by the system is positive and as both p and V increase according to gas law T must also increase.

Sol. 2 (A, B) As the cycle is anticlockwise, the total work is done on the gas and in complete cycle heat is rejected by the gas.

Sol. 3 (A, B) As the process is carried out in a closed system for same pressure and volume, temperature must be equal and as internal energy is directly proportional to temperature will also be same in initial and final state. But as heat supplied and work done are path functions, no comment can be made on these hence options (A) and (B) are correct.

Sol. 4 (A, D) As work done by the system is equal to decrease in internal energy of system which implies heat supplied to system is zero hence the process is adiabatic and due to decrease in internal energy temperature decreases.

Sol. 5 (B, C) $Q=\Delta U+W$

$Q=$ +ve, as heat is absorbed from the atmosphere

$W=$ –ve as the volume decrease

As $\Delta U=Q-W=+\text{ve}-(-\text{ve})=+\text{ve}$

Thus internal energy increases.

Sol. 6 (All) For insulated chambers

$$n_1+n_2=n_1'+n_2'$$

(final pressures become equal)

$$\frac{PV}{RT}+\frac{2P.2V}{RT}=\frac{P}{RT}[3V]\Rightarrow P'=\frac{5P}{3}$$

For left chamber

$$PV = P'V' = \frac{5P}{3}V' \Rightarrow V' = \frac{3V}{5}$$

For right chamber

$$4PV = P'V' = \frac{5P}{3}V' \Rightarrow V' = \frac{12V}{5}$$

Sol. 7 (C, D) According to the process equation for adiabatic process PV^γ = constant for helium and neon which are monoatomic gases ratio of specific heats is same so final pressure will be same but for oxygen which is diatomic γ is different so its pressure will also be different.

Sol. 8 (B, C) Depending upon the type of thermodynamic process the specific of a material changes due to change in work done by the substance in different cases. If during heating a substance volume does not change then work done by it will be zero hence there will be a single specific heat exist for that substance.

Sol. 9 (All) By definition of First Law of thermodynamics and the standard process relations of isothermal and adiabatic process all options given are correct.

Sol. 10 (All) At equilibrium net force on piston is zero or the force on the two sides must be equal so we use $PS = kx_0$ and the energy stored by the spring is equal to work done by the gas as chamber is insulated and no heat supply is there. As chamber is insulated process will be nearly adiabatic so change in internal energy will be equal to work done by the gas and in adiabatic expansion temperature decreases.

Sol. 11 (A, B, C) PV^2 = constant

$$\Rightarrow P \propto V^{-2} \Rightarrow \frac{\Delta P}{P} = -2\frac{\Delta V}{V}$$

⇒ Bulk modulus

$$K = \frac{\Delta P}{-\frac{\Delta V}{V}} = 2P$$

As $PV = nRT$

So $K \propto \frac{1}{V^2}$ and $K \propto T^2$

Sol. 12 (All) In path *'iaf'* change in internal energy of gas is 50 – 20 = 30 cal which remain constant for all paths as it is a state function. Now in path *'ibf'*, it is given that heat supplied is 36 cal hence work done is = 36 – 30 = 6 cal. Then in return path *'fi'* the change in internal energy will be –30 cal and if work done is 13 cal on the gas then total heat supplied to the gas will be = –13 – 30 = –43 cal hence the rejected heat is 43 cal. If internal energy of state *'i'* is 10cal then internal energy at state *'f'* will be 10 + 30 = 40 cal. If internal energy at state *'b'* is 22 cal then total change in internal energy in process *'ib'* is 22 – 10 = 12 cal and as already calculated work done in process *'ibf'* or *'ib'* is 6 cal so heat supplied to the gas along path ib is 12 + 6 = 18 cal.

Sol. 13 (All) We use

$$P_AV_A = RT_0$$

As $P_B = 2P_A$

$$\Rightarrow \quad V_B = V_C = 2V_A$$

and $$T_B = \frac{P_BV_B}{R} = 4T_0$$

from graph work done is

$$\Delta W = \left(\frac{V_C - V_A}{2}\right)(P_B - P_C) = 0.5\,RT_0$$

and $$\Delta W_{AB} = \frac{1}{2}(P_A + P_B)(V_B - V_A) = \frac{3}{2}P_AV_A = 1.5RT_0$$

and $$\Delta U_{AB} = \frac{3}{2}R(T_B - T_A) = 4.5\,RT_0$$

and $$\Delta Q_{AB} = \Delta W_{AB} + \Delta U_{AB} = 6RT_0$$

$$\Rightarrow \quad C = \left(\frac{\Delta Q_{AB}}{T_B - T_A}\right) = 2R$$

Thus cycle efficiency is given as

$$\eta = \frac{\Delta W_{NET}}{\Delta Q_{AB}} = \frac{1}{12} = 8.33\%$$

Sol. 14 (A, B, D) Given PT = Constant

and $$PV = nRT$$

$$\Rightarrow \quad P^2V = \text{constant}$$

$$\Rightarrow \quad PV^{1/2} = k$$

From first law of thermodynamics

$$\Delta Q = \Delta U + \Delta O$$

$$\Rightarrow \quad C\Delta T = C_V T + \left(\frac{P_fV_f - P_iV_i}{1 - \frac{1}{2}}\right)$$

$$C = C_V + 2R$$

$$33.34 = \frac{R}{\gamma - 1} + 2R$$

$$\Rightarrow \quad \gamma = 1.5$$

and $$\gamma = 1 + \frac{2}{f}$$

$$\Rightarrow \quad f = 4$$

Sol. 15 (A, B) We use $Q = nC_v\Delta T$ which gives C_v = 3 cal hence the gas is monoatomic so options (A) and (B) can be correct.

Sol. 16 (A, D) Even at higher temperature monoatomic gas molecules will not have any vibrational energy as these do not have multiple atoms so dimensions of molecules is negligible and for diatomic gases at higher temperatures degrees of freedom will be more than 5 so options (A) and (D) are correct.

Sol. 17 (C, D) For an adiabatic Process we use the process equation $PV^{\gamma} = Constant$ so option (C) is correct and by gas law option (D) is also correct.

Sol. 18 (A, C, D)

We use $\Delta V = 3\alpha\, V\Delta T$

$$= 3\times 20\times 10^{-6}\times 50\times \frac{1}{10^4} = 3\times 10^{-7}\,\text{m}^{-3}$$

$\Rightarrow$ $W = P\Delta V = 10^5\times 3\times 10^{-7} = 3\times 10^{-2}$ J

$\Rightarrow$ $Q = mC\Delta T = 1\times 400\times 50 = 2\times 10^4$ J

$\Rightarrow$ $\Delta U \approx Q = 2\times 10^4$ J

Sol. 19 (B, D) In the curve shown in figure part AB is not rectangular hyperbola so it is not an isothermal process hence option (A) is NOT correct. In the process BCD, the volume and temperature decreases so work is done on the gas and internal energy of gas also decreases thus heat flows out of the gas hence option (B) is correct. In the path ABC, the area below the curve AB (positive work) is greater than the area below curve BC (negative work) thus total work done by gas during path ABC is positive hence option (C) is NOT correct. As overall cycle is clockwise total work done in cycle $ABCDA$ is positive.

Sol. 20 (A, B, D) Work done in a thermodynamic process is given by the area under PV curve. For the given indicator diagram, the work done in the process can be calculated as

$$W_1 = \left(P + \frac{P}{2}\right)(2V - V) = \frac{3}{2}PV$$

Work done under isothermal process from state A to state B is calculated as

$$W_2 = RT\ln\left(\frac{2V}{V}\right) = 0.693RT = 0.693\,\text{PV}$$

$\Rightarrow$ $W_1 > W_2$

Hence option (A) is correct.

We consider, P_0 and V_0 be the intercepts of the given curve on the P and V axes as shown in figure below.

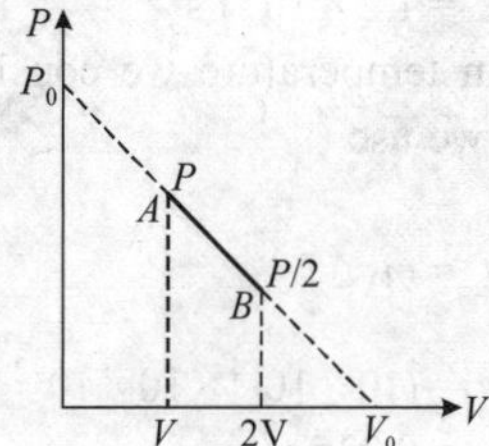

Now, the equation of straight line would be

$$P = -\left(\frac{P_0}{V_0}\right)V + P_0 \qquad \ldots(1)$$

Temperature of gas is given as

$$T = \frac{PV}{nR} = \frac{1}{nR}\left(-\frac{P_0V^2}{V_0} + P_0V\right) \qquad \ldots(2)$$

Above is a quadratic function in terms of V hence option (B) is correct. From equation-(1), P and T relation is written as

$$P^2 - PP_0 + \left(\frac{nRP_0}{V_0}\right)T = 0$$

Above is not an equation of hyperbola hence option (C) is NOT correct. In a linear process with negative slope on PV curve, there exist a state (point on the straight line) at which temperature of gas is maximum. This is the point where the straight line touches any isothermal curve. Thus in going from state A to B, first temperature will increase and after this point it will start decreasing hence option (D) is correct.

Sol. 21 (A, B, D) Heat absorbed by the gas in process AB is given as

$$\Delta Q_{AB} = nC_P\Delta T = 2\times\frac{5R}{2}(1200 - 600) = 3000R$$

Hence option (A) is correct. In the process BC, the process equation is given as

$$T = \alpha V^2$$

$\Rightarrow$ PV^{-1} = constant

This is a polytropic process so molar heat capacity in the process BC is calculated as

$$C = C_V + \frac{R}{(1-n)} = \frac{2R}{2} + \frac{R}{2}$$

$\Rightarrow$ $C = 2R$

The heat absorbed in the process BC is calculated as

$$\Delta Q_{BC} = nC\Delta T = 2\times 2R(300 - 1200) = -3600R$$

Thus heat is rejected in the process BC of value $3600R$. Hence option (B) is correct and option (C) is NOT correct. In process CA, which is an isochoric process work done is zero and heat absorbed is calculated as

$$\Delta Q_{CA} = nC_V\Delta T = 2\times\frac{3R}{2}(500 - 300) = 900R$$

The total heat absorbed by the gas in complete cycle or total work done by the gas during the cyclic process is given as

$$\Delta W_{\text{cycle}} = \Delta Q_{\text{cycle}} = 3000\,\text{R} - 3600\,\text{R} + 900\,\text{R} = 300R$$

Hence option (D) is correct.

* * * * *

ANSWERS & SOLUTIONS

CONCEPTUAL MCQS Single Option Correct

1	(C)	2	(D)	3	(C)
4	(B)	5	(C)	6	(D)
7	(A)	8	(A)	9	(D)
10	(C)	11	(C)	12	(B)
13	(C)	14	(B)	15	(D)
16	(A)	17	(C)	18	(B)
19	(A)	20	(C)	21	(B)
22	(D)	23	(D)	24	(D)

NUMERICAL MCQS Single Option Correct

1	(B)	2	(D)	3	(A)
4	(A)	5	(D)	6	(D)
7	(B)	8	(B)	9	(C)
10	(B)	11	(C)	12	(C)
13	(D)	14	(C)	15	(D)
16	(A)	17	(B)	18	(C)
19	(D)	20	(D)	21	(D)
22	(D)	23	(B)	24	(B)
25	(D)	26	(B)	27	(B)
28	(B)	29	(C)	30	(B)
31	(C)	32	(D)	33	(A)
34	(B)	35	(B)	36	(D)
37	(C)	38	(D)	39	(D)
40	(A)	41	(D)	42	(B)
43	(B)	44	(B)	45	(C)
46	(D)	47	(A)	48	(D)
49	(D)	50	(A)	51	(B)
52	(B)	53	(B)	54	(D)
55	(B)	56	(B)	57	(A)
58	(C)	59	(B)	60	(A)
61	(C)	62	(B)	63	(D)
64	(B)	65	(D)	66	(A)
67	(A)	68	(D)	69	(B)
70	(A)	71	(C)	72	(C)
73	(D)	74	(D)	75	(D)
76	(B)	77	(B)	78	(C)
79	(A)	80	(A)	81	(B)
82	(D)	83	(D)	84	(C)
85	(D)	86	(B)	87	(B)
88	(C)	89	(B)	90	(B)
91	(C)	92	(C)	93	(B)
94	(C)				

ADVANCE MCQs One or More Option Correct

1	(A, C)	2	(C, D)	3	(A, C)
4	(B, D)	5	(A, B)	6	(A, B)
7	(D)	8	(D)	9	(A, B, D)
10	(B, D)	11	(C, D)	12	(B)
13	(A, B)	14	(A, B)	15	(A, B, C)
16	(A, B)	17	(A, C)	18	(A, D)
19	(A, D)	20	(A, B)		

Solutions of PRACTICE EXERCISE 4.1

(i) Given that $k_A = 2k_B$

In steady state we use

$$\left.\frac{dQ}{dt}\right|_{net} = \left.\frac{dQ}{dt}\right|_A = \left.\frac{dQ}{dt}\right|_B$$

$$\Rightarrow \quad \frac{k_A A(\Delta T_A)}{x} = \frac{36}{\frac{1}{k_A}\cdot\frac{x}{A} + \frac{1}{k_B}\frac{x}{A}}$$

$$\Rightarrow \quad \Delta T_A = \frac{36}{3} = 12°\text{C}$$

(ii) In steady state

Heat power = Conduction rate

$$100 = \frac{k(6\times(6\times10^{-2})^2)}{10^{-3}}(5)$$

$$\Rightarrow \quad k = \frac{100\times10^{-3}}{1080\times10^{-4}} = 0.926\ \text{W/m°C}$$

(iii) Rate of heat conduction through rod is

$$\frac{dQ}{dt} = \frac{kA}{l}(100) = \frac{92\times10\times10^{-4}}{(1)}\times100$$

$$= 9.2\ \text{cal/s}$$

if m gm ice melt per second we use

$$\frac{dQ}{dt} = mL$$

$$9.2 = m\times80$$

$$m = \frac{9.2}{80}\ \text{g/s}$$

mass melt in one minute is

$$m' = \frac{9.2}{80}\times60 = 6.9\ \text{g}$$

(iv) Rate of heat condition through discs is

$$\frac{dQ}{dt} = 2\times\frac{200\times10\times10^{-4}}{10^{-3}}\times(30)$$

$$= 1.2\times10^4\ \text{J/s}$$

For just 1°C fall in temperature we consider almost same conduction rate so we use

$$\frac{dQ}{dt}\times t = ms\,\Delta T$$

$$1.2\times10^4\times t = (10\times10^{-4}\times10\times10^{-2}\times1000)\times4200\times1$$

$$t = 0.035\ \text{s}$$

(v)

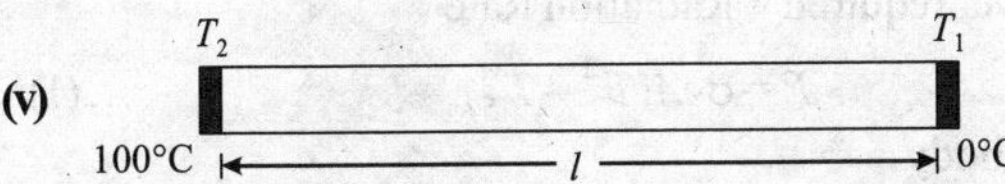

For steady state we use

$$\left.\frac{dQ}{dt}\right|_{net} = \left.\frac{dQ}{dt}\right|_{Rod}$$

$$\frac{100}{2\times\frac{1}{k_w}\cdot\frac{x}{A}+\frac{1}{k_{steel}}\cdot\frac{l}{A}} = k_{steel}A\left(\frac{T_2-T_1}{l}\right)$$

Thus temperature gradient in rod is

$$\frac{T_2-T_1}{l} = \frac{100}{\left(\frac{2\times0.2\times10^{-3}}{1.5\times10^{-3}}+\frac{0.5}{0.11}\right)\times0.11}$$

$$=94.517°\text{C/m}$$

$$=0.945°\text{C/cm}$$

(vi)

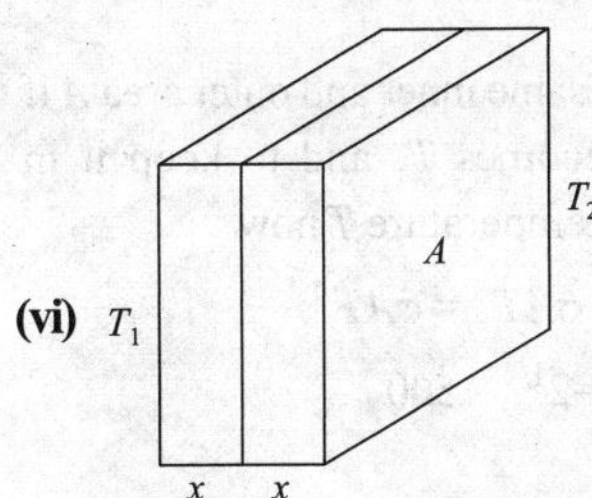

Total heat flow through plates is given as

$$\frac{dQ}{dt} = \frac{T_1-T_2}{\frac{1}{k_1}\cdot\frac{x}{A}+\frac{1}{k_2}\cdot\frac{x}{A}}$$

$$= \frac{k_1k_2}{k_1+k_2}\cdot\frac{A}{x}\,(T_1-T_2)$$

Above expression can be written as

$$\frac{dQ}{dt} = \frac{2k_1k_2}{k_1+k_2}\cdot\frac{A}{2x}\,(T_1-T_2)$$

$$\Rightarrow \quad \frac{dQ}{dt} = \frac{k_{eq}A}{2x}(T_1-T_2)$$

$$\Rightarrow \quad k_{eq} = \frac{2k_1k_2}{k_1+k_2}$$

(vii) In steady state we use

$$mgv = \frac{kA}{x}(T_2-T_1)$$

$$M(10)(0.1) = \frac{0.5\times0.05}{2\times10^{-3}}\times(1)$$

$$M = 12.5\text{ kg}$$

(viii)

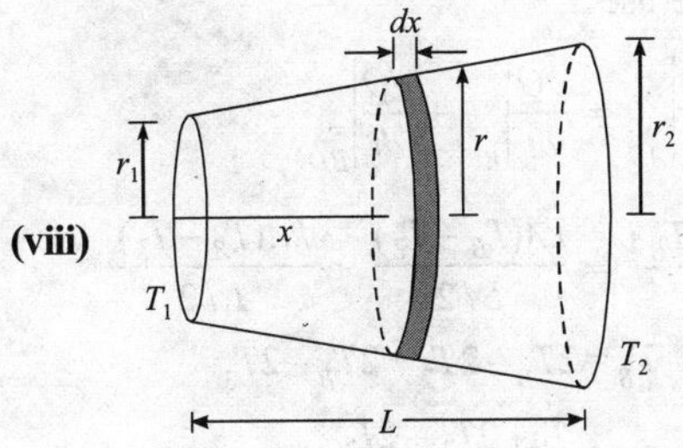

Here $\quad r = r_1 + \left(\frac{r_2-r_1}{L}\right)x$

As shown in figure we consider an elemental disc at a distance x from left face. Then thermal resistance of this elemental disc is given as

$$dR_{th} = \frac{1}{k}\cdot\frac{dx}{\pi\left(r_1+\frac{r_2-r_1}{L}x\right)^2}$$

Total thermal resistance of frustum is

$$R_{th} = \int dR_{th} = \frac{1}{k\pi}\int_0^l \frac{dx}{\left(r_1+\frac{r_2-r_1}{L}\cdot x\right)^2}$$

$$= \frac{L}{k\pi(r_2-r_1)}\left[-\frac{1}{\left(r_1+\frac{r_2-r_1}{L}\cdot x\right)}\right]_0^l$$

$$= \frac{L}{k\pi(r_2-r_1)}\left[\frac{1}{r_1}-\frac{1}{r_2}\right]$$

$$= \frac{L}{k\pi r_1 r_2}$$

Thus heat current through frustum is

$$\frac{dQ}{dt} = \frac{T_2-T_1}{R_{th}} = \frac{k\pi r_1 r_2(T_2-T_1)}{L}$$

(ix) If temperature of C is taken as T_C, and length of rods are l, l and $\sqrt{2}l$ we use in steady state

$$\left.\frac{dQ}{dt}\right|_{BC} = \left.\frac{dQ}{dt}\right|_{CA}$$

$$\Rightarrow \quad \frac{kA(\sqrt{2}T-T_C)}{l} = \frac{kA(T_C-T)}{\sqrt{2}l}$$

$$\Rightarrow \quad 2T-\sqrt{2}\,T_C = T_C - T$$

$$\Rightarrow \quad T_C = \frac{3T}{1+\sqrt{2}}$$

(x) In steady state we use

$$\left.\frac{dQ}{dt}\right|_{AB} = \left.\frac{dQ}{dt}\right|_{BC} + \left.\frac{dQ}{dt}\right|_{BD}$$

$$\Rightarrow \quad \frac{kA(T_1 - T_B)}{L} = \frac{kA(T_B - T_2)}{L/2} + \frac{kA(T_B - T_3)}{L/2}$$

$$\Rightarrow \quad T_1 - T_B = 2T_B - 2T_2 + 2T_B - 2T_3$$

$$\Rightarrow \quad T_B = \frac{T_1 + 2T_2 + 2T_3}{5}$$

(xi) Rate of heat generation is

$$\frac{V^2}{R} = \frac{(200)^2}{20} = 2 \times 10^3\ W$$

If outside temperature is T we use

$$2 \times 10^3 = \frac{0.2 \times 4.2 \times 1}{0.2 \times 10^{-2}}(20 - T)$$

$$\Rightarrow \quad T = 20 - 4.76 = 15.24°C$$

Solutions of PRACTICE EXERCISE 4.2

(i) If temperature of filament is T we use

$$500 = 5.7 \times 10^{-8} \times 2 \times 10^{-4} \times 0.5\, T^4$$

$$\Rightarrow \quad T^4 = 87.72 \times 10^{12}$$

$$\Rightarrow \quad T = 3060.37\text{ K}$$

(ii) Radiation rate $= \sigma eAT^4$ (here we use $A = 2\pi r$ as $l = 1$ m)

$$= 5.7 \times 10^{-8} \times 0.35 \times 2 \times 3.14 \times 0.075 \times 10^{-2} \times (3000)^4$$

$$= 7611.12\text{ W/m}$$

(iii) We use bulb power

$$P = \sigma eAT^4$$

$$\Rightarrow \quad A = \frac{P}{\sigma eT^4} = \frac{60}{5.7 \times 10^{-8} \times 0.3 \times (2000)^4}$$

$$= 2.193 \times 10^{-4}\text{ m}^2$$

(iv) Power radiated by black body is

$$P = \sigma e(4\pi r^2)T^4$$

$$\Rightarrow \quad P \propto r^2 T^4$$

$$\Rightarrow \quad \frac{P_1}{P_2} = \frac{r_1^2 T_1^4}{r_2^2 T_2^4}$$

As $T_2 = 2T_1$ and $r_2 = \frac{r_1}{2}$

$$\Rightarrow \quad P_2 = P_1 \times 4 = 450 \times 4 = 1800\text{ W}$$

(v) If emissivity of body is e we use

Power required = Radiation Rate

$$P = \sigma eA(T^4 - T_5^4) \qquad \ldots(1)$$

for a block body

$$P_B = \sigma A(T^4 - T_5^4) \qquad \ldots(2)$$

$$\frac{(1)}{(2)} \text{ gives} \quad \frac{P}{P_B} = e$$

$$\Rightarrow \quad e = \frac{210}{700} = 0.3$$

(vi) As outer radius is same at same temperature, radiation power will be same so we use

$$\frac{dQ}{dt} = ms\frac{dT}{dt}$$

$$\Rightarrow \text{ Rate of cooling } \frac{dT}{dt} = \frac{1}{ms}\frac{dQ}{dt}$$

Thus lower mass hollow sphere will cool faster

(vii) For space station if power generation is P we use

$$P = \sigma AT^4$$

After enveloping it with a shell of same inner and outer area A if temperature of space station becomes T_1 and to keep it in equilibrium outer shell will be at temperature T now

$$P = \sigma AT_1^4 - \sigma AT^4 = \sigma AT^4$$

$$\Rightarrow \quad T_1 = (2)^{1/4}T = 2^{1/4} \times 500$$

$$= 594.6\text{ K}$$

(viii) Radiation power of ball is

$$\frac{dQ}{dt} = \sigma e(\pi d^2)T^4$$

$$\rho\left(\frac{4}{3}\pi\frac{d^3}{8}\right)c\frac{dT}{dt} = -\sigma e\pi d^2 T^4$$

$$\frac{\rho dc}{6\sigma e} = \int_{T_0}^{T_0/\eta}\frac{dT}{T^4} = -\int_0^t dt$$

$$\Rightarrow \quad t = \frac{\rho dc}{18\sigma e}\left[\frac{\eta^3}{T_0^3} - \frac{1}{T_0^3}\right] = \frac{\rho dc(\eta^3 - 1)}{18\sigma e T_0^3}$$

Solutions of PRACTICE EXERCISE 4.3

(i) Using average form of Newton's law of cooling, we have

$$\frac{40 - 36}{5} = k\left(\frac{40 + 36}{2} - 16\right) \qquad \ldots(1)$$

and

$$\frac{36 - 32}{t} = k\left(\frac{36 + 32}{2} - 16\right) \qquad \ldots(2)$$

$\frac{(1)}{(2)}$ gives

$$\frac{t}{5} = \frac{22}{18}$$

$$\Rightarrow \quad t = 6.11 \text{ min}$$

(ii) Using average form of Newton's law of cooling, we have

$$\frac{80-64}{5} = k\left(\frac{80+64}{2} - T_S\right)$$

$$\Rightarrow \quad \frac{16}{5} = k(72 - T_S) \quad \ldots(1)$$

and
$$\frac{64-52}{5} = k\left(\frac{64+52}{2} - T_S\right)$$

$$\Rightarrow \quad \frac{12}{5} = k(58 - T_S) \quad \ldots(2)$$

$\frac{(1)}{(2)}$ gives

$$\frac{16}{12} = \frac{72 - T_S}{58 - T_S}$$

$$T = T_S + (T_0 - T_S)\, e^{-kt}$$

$$64 = T_S + (80 - T_S)\, e^{-k(5)}$$

$$8(58 - T_S) = 6(72 - T_S)$$

$$\Rightarrow \quad T_S = \frac{464 - 432}{2} = 16°\text{C}$$

from (1)

$$\frac{16}{5} = k(72 - 16)$$

$$\Rightarrow \quad k = 0.0571$$

Now if in 15 minutes temperature of body is T, we use

$$\frac{52 - T}{5} = 0.0571\left(\frac{52+T}{2} - 16\right)$$

$$\Rightarrow \quad 104 - 2T = 14.846 + 0.2855\,T - 9.136$$

$$\Rightarrow \quad T = 43°\text{C}$$

(iii) Using Newton's law of cooling we have

$$(T - T_S) = (T_0 - T_S)\, e^{-kt}$$

at $t = 10$ min $(T - T_S) = \frac{T_0 - T_S}{2}$

$$\Rightarrow \quad e^{-k(10)} = \frac{1}{2}$$

or
$$k = \frac{\ln(2)}{10}$$

Then at $t = t_0$

$$T - T_S = \frac{T_0 - T_S}{10}$$

$$\Rightarrow \quad e^{-kt_0} = \frac{1}{10}$$

$$t_0 = \frac{\ln(10)}{\ln(2)} \times 10$$

$$= 33.23 \text{ min}$$

(iv) Temperature as a function of time is given as

$$T = T_0 + (T_i - T_0)\, e^{-kt}$$

Slope of curve is

$$\frac{dT}{dt} = -k(T_i - T_0)\, e^{-kt} = -k(T - T_0)$$

if at $T = T_1$ slope is $\tan\theta_1$, we use

$$\tan\theta_1 = -k(T_1 - T_0) \quad \ldots(1)$$

and at $T = T_2$ slope is $\tan\theta_2$, we use

$$\tan\theta_2 = -k(T_2 - T_0) \quad \ldots(2)$$

$\frac{(2)}{(1)}$ gives

$$\frac{\tan\theta_2}{\tan\theta_1} = \frac{T_2 - T_0}{T_1 - T_0}$$

(v) Using average form of Newton's law of cooling, we use

For water
$$\frac{40-35}{5} = \frac{k}{0.1 \times 4200}\left(\frac{40+35}{2} - T_S\right) \ldots(1)$$

For liquid
$$\frac{40-35}{2} = \frac{k}{m \times 2100}\left(\frac{40+35}{2} - T_S\right) \ldots(2)$$

$\frac{(1)}{(2)}$ gives

$$\frac{2}{5} = \frac{m \times 2100}{0.1 \times 4200}$$

$$\Rightarrow \quad m = \frac{2 \times 420}{5 \times 2100} = 0.08 \text{ kg} = 80 \text{ gm}$$

As the volume of liquid is same that of water 100 cm^3, then density of liquid is

$$P = \frac{m}{V} = \frac{80 \times 10^{-3}}{100 \times 10^{-6}} = 800 \text{ kg/m}^3$$

Solutions of PRACTICE EXERCISE 4.4

(i) By wein's displacement law, we use

$$\lambda_m T = \text{constant}$$

$$\Rightarrow \quad \lambda_{m_1} T_1 = \lambda_{m_2} T_2$$

$$\Rightarrow \quad 4753 \times 6050 = 9506 \times T_2$$

$$\Rightarrow \quad T_2 = 3025 \text{ K}$$

(ii) Using stefan's law wein's displacement law we have

$$\frac{P_1}{P_2} = \left(\frac{T_1}{T_2}\right)^4 = \left(\frac{\lambda_{m_2}}{\lambda_{m_1}}\right)^4$$

$$\Rightarrow \quad \frac{P_1}{P_2} = \left(\frac{3\lambda/4}{\lambda}\right)^4$$

$$\Rightarrow \quad P_2 = P_1\left(\frac{4}{3}\right)^4 = \frac{256}{81}P_1$$

(iii) By Wein's displacement law, we use

$$\lambda_m T = b$$

$$\Rightarrow \quad \lambda = \frac{b}{T} = \frac{2.89\times10^{-3}}{2000} = 1.445\times10^{-6}\,\text{m}$$

$$= 14450\,\text{Å}$$

(iv) By plank's radiation law we use

$$E_\lambda = \frac{2\pi hc^2}{\lambda^5(e^{hc/\pi kT}-1)}$$

for two wavelengths heighbourhoods λ_1 & λ_2 we use

$$\frac{E_{\lambda_1}}{E_{\lambda_2}} = \frac{\lambda_2(e^{hc/\lambda_2 kT}-1)}{\lambda_1(e^{hc/\lambda_1 kT}-1)}$$

Here we use $\lambda_1 = 5000$ Å; $\lambda_2 = 10000$ Å & T = 2880 k we get

$$\frac{E_2}{E_1} = \frac{(5\times10^{-75})[e^{(6.63\times10^{-34}\times3\times10^8)/(5\times10^{-7}\times1.38\times10^{-23}\times2880)}-1]}{(10\times10^{-7})^5[e^{(6.63\times10^{-34}\times3\times10^8)/(10\times10^{-7}\times1.38\times10^{-23}\times2880)}-1]}$$

$$= \frac{1}{32}\left(\frac{e^{10}-1}{e^5-1}\right) = \frac{1}{32}\left[\frac{22002.64}{147.336}\right]$$

$$= 4.67$$

(v) Using Stefan's law we have

$$R = \sigma T^4$$

$$\Rightarrow \quad T = \left(\frac{R}{\sigma}\right)^{1/4}$$

$$= \left(\frac{250\times10^3}{5.67\times10^{-8}}\right)^{1/4}$$

$$= 1.449\times10^3$$

$$= 1449\,\text{K}$$

Now using Wein's displacement law, the maximum spectral radiance will be at wavelength λ_m given as

$$\lambda_m = \frac{b}{T} = \frac{2.89\times10^{-3}}{1449} = 19.9447\times10^{-7}\,\text{m}$$

$$= 19944.7\,\text{Å}$$

Solutions of CONCEPTUAL MCQS Single Option Correct

Sol. 1 (C) As on moon there is no atmospheric pressure, water starts boiling.

Sol. 2 (D) If temperature of the source is increased by 100% then at temperature $2T$ the radiation power of source is increased to 16 times (fourth power) and at a distance $2r$ the power received will be one fourth of the previous so the power per unit area received will be 16/4 = 4 times which is 300% increase.

Sol. 3 (C) Thermal radiations are electromagnetic waves and follow all characters of *EM* waves hence option (C) is NOT Correct.

Sol. 4 (B) Always if temperature of a material increases all dimensions of the material increase.

Sol. 5 (C) According to Plank's law of radiations, the wavelength of the radiation from a body depends upon its temperature.

Sol. 6 (D) Total radiation power from a body is given as $P = \sigma e A T^4$ where e is emissivity of the body surface, A is the surface area and T is its absolute temperature.

Sol. 7 (A) As water density is maximum at 4°C at the bottom of lake temperature of water will be 4°C and at the top from where it starts freezing temperature will be equal to that of atmosphere –20°C and at the top of water layer at the bottom of frozen part of lake temperature will be 0°C.

Sol. 8 (A) Rate of cooling of a body is the ratio of radiation power emitted by body and its heat capacity. As dimensions, surface material and temperature are equal the radiation power of both spheres will be same but heat capacity of hollow sphere is less so it will cool at a faster rate.

Sol. 9 (D) Time taken in freezing a lake is directly proportional to the square of thickness of ice frozen so in this case thickness is getting doubled so total time will be 32 hours and time to increase the layer thickness from 1 cm to 2 cm will be 32 – 8 = 24 hours.

Sol. 10 (C) Due to large number of free electrons in metals conductivity is high as heat is absorbed by free electrons as their kinetic energy $(3/2)kT$ and due to diffusion of electrons heat is quickly transferred to whole volume of metal.

Sol. 11 (C) Glass allows most of the solar radiation to pass through it which heats the greenhouse material and when this material radiates radiation most of this is absorbed by glass and heat is trapped inside which keeps the greenhouse warm hence option (C) is correct.

Sol. 12 (B) Due to sudden vaporization of a layer of water vapour is formed between drop and hot plate which blocks the conduction of heat hence option (B) is correct.

Sol. 13 (C) As area of cross section is different in the rod, the temperature gradient cannot be constant in the rod in steady state. In steady state the conduction rate is $kA(dT/dx)$ and area of cross section AB is more than that at CD, temperature difference across AB will be less.

Sol. 14 (B) According to Newton's law of cooling for small temperature difference between body and surrounding, rate of cooling is directly proportional to the temperature difference of the body with the surrounding.

Sol. 15 (D) In steady state of a rod the rate of heat conduction is given as $kA(\Delta T/l)$ so to double the rate option (D) is correct.

Sol. 16 (A) Thermal resistance of P is four times that of Q and in steady state rate of heat conduction is same in both so we can use

$$(T-0)/R_P = (100-T)/R_Q$$

which gives $T = 20°C$

Sol. 17 (C) In steady state heat conduction rate is given as $kA(\Delta T/l)$ which comes out to be equal for both rods.

Sol. 18 (B) Air is bad conductor of heat so the layer of air trapped between two thin blankets increases overall thermal resistance.

Sol. 19 (A) According to Wein's displacement law we have the product $\lambda_m T = constant$.

Sol. 20 (C) For high rate of heat conduction area of cross section should be large and thickness should be low and for a thin sample as heat will conduct quickly no lagging is required.

Sol. 21 (B) Electrical quantity analogous to the temperature is electric potential and the slope is rate of variation of potential with length which is potential gradient.

Sol. 22 (D) In steady state of condition, temperature gradient is constant but different in the two rods as their thermal conductivities are different hence option (D) is correct.

Sol. 23 (D) As the metal bar is of uniform cross section, through out the metal bar in steady state the temperature gradient will be constant hence for a given thickness of XY at every location in metal bar its temperature difference will be constant.

Sol. 24 (D) Suppose that the temperature of the water in the first vessel is $\theta_1(t)$ and that of the second is $\theta_2(t)$, then

$$ms\frac{d\theta_1}{dt} = -\frac{KA}{L}(\theta_1-\theta_2) \quad \ldots(1)$$

and

$$ms\frac{d\theta_2}{dt} = \frac{KA}{L}(\theta_1-\theta_2) \quad \ldots(2)$$

from (1) and (2), we get

$$\frac{d\theta}{dt} = \frac{-2KA}{msL}\theta,$$

where $\theta = \theta_1 - \theta_2$,

The time, in which the temperature difference reduces to $1/e$ of its initial value, is given by

$$\Delta t = \frac{msL}{2KA} \Rightarrow K = \frac{msL}{2A\Delta t}$$

Solutions of NUMERICAL MCQS Single Option Correct

Sol. 1 (B) We use $C = Mc$

$$\frac{C_1}{C_2} = \frac{M_1}{M_2} = \frac{V_1\rho}{V_2\rho}$$

$$= \frac{\frac{4}{3}\pi R_1^3\rho}{\frac{4}{3}\pi R_2^3\rho} = \frac{R_1^3}{R_2^3}$$

Sol. 2 (D) We use $Q = \frac{KA(\theta_1-\theta_2)t}{l}$

$$Q_1 = Q_2$$

$$\frac{k_1A(\theta_1-\theta_2)t}{l} = \frac{k_2A(\theta_1-\theta_2)t}{l}$$

$$k_1 = k_2$$

Sol. 3 (A) We use $\frac{Q}{t} = \frac{kA(\theta_1-\theta_2)}{l}$

$$\frac{3.6\times3.4\times10^4}{3600} = \frac{k(0.34)(100-0)}{0.1}$$

$$k = 0.1\ \text{Js}^{-1}\ \text{m}^{-1}\text{°C}^{-1}$$

Sol. 4 (A) The temperature of water in contact with ice is 0°C. The temperature at bottom of lake is most likely to be 4°C because at this temperature, water is most dense and settles at bottom due to natural convection.

Sol. 5 (D) We use $P = A\varepsilon\sigma T^4$

$$T = \left(\frac{P}{A\varepsilon\sigma}\right)^{1/4}$$

Sol. 6 (D) As stefan's constant is

$$\sigma = 5.67\times10^{-8}\ \text{W/m}^2\text{K}^4$$

The dimensions of σ is $[MT^{-3}\theta^{-4}]$ or $[ML°T^{-3}K^{-4}]$

Sol. 7 (B) $\Delta l \propto l$

(Both are made of same material)

$$\frac{\Delta l_1}{\Delta l_2} = \frac{l_1}{l_2} = \frac{1}{2}$$

Sol. 8 (B)

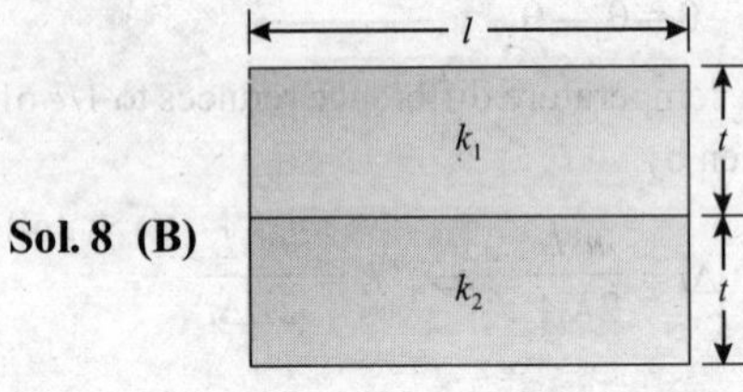

$$k = \frac{k_1A_1 + k_2A_2}{A_1 + A_2}$$

For two slabs of equal thickness and hence equal area,

$$k = \frac{k_1 + k_2}{2}$$

Sol. 9 (C) We use

$$\frac{kA[10-(-10)]}{L} = \frac{kA[T-(-23)]}{L}$$

$$20 = T + 23$$

$$T = -3°C = 270K$$

Sol. 10 (B)

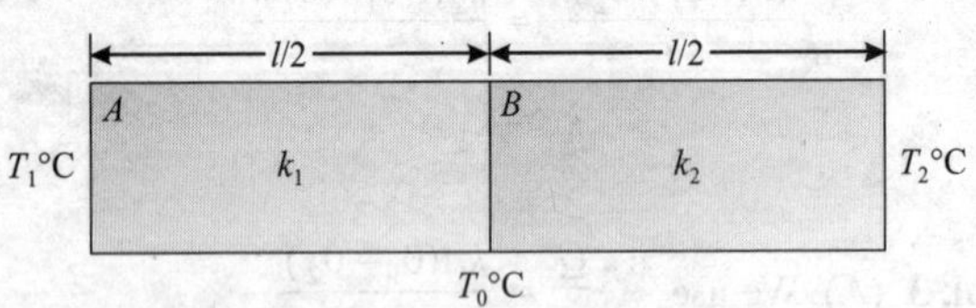

Let temperature of junction be T_0°C

Temperature difference across slab $A = (T_1 - T_0)$°C

Temperature difference across slab $B = (T_0 - T_2)$°C

Since both slabs are connected in series, heat current through both will be equal

$$\frac{k_1A(T_1 - T_0)}{l/2} = \frac{k_2A(T_0 - T_2)}{l/2}$$

As $k_1 = \dfrac{k_2}{2}$

$$\Rightarrow \quad \frac{k_2}{2}(T_1 - T_0) = (T_0 - T_2)\,k_2$$

$$T_1 - T_0 = 2T_0 - 2T_2$$

$$T_1 + 2T_2 = 3T_0 \quad \ldots(1)$$

As $T_1 - T_2 = 12°C$

$$\Rightarrow \quad T_2 = T_1 - 12 \quad \ldots(2)$$

From (1) and (2), we get

$$T_1 + 2(T_1 - 12) = 3T_0$$

$$3T_1 - 24 = 3T_0$$

$$T_1 - T_0 = 8°C$$

Sol. 11 (C) When two rods of same thickness and length are joined in parallel,

$$k_{eq} = \frac{k_1 + k_2}{2} = \frac{2+3}{2} = \frac{5}{2} = 2.5$$

Sol. 12 (C) We use $\dfrac{dQ}{dt} = -kA\dfrac{dT}{dx}$

$$\Rightarrow \quad \frac{\Delta T}{\Delta x} = \frac{dQ}{dt\,k} = \frac{10}{0.5} = 20°C/cm$$

Sol. 13 (D) By Wien's displacement law

$$\lambda_m T = b$$

$$\Rightarrow \quad T = \frac{b}{\lambda_m} = \frac{2892 \times 10^{-6}}{14.46 \times 10^{-6}}$$

$$\Rightarrow \quad T = 200K$$

Sol. 14 (C) We use $\dfrac{dQ}{dt} = -kA\dfrac{dT}{dx}$

$$\frac{dT}{dx} \propto \frac{1}{k}$$

As $\dfrac{dQ}{dt}$ = constant

$$\Rightarrow \quad X_g > X_m > X_c$$

Sol. 15 (D)

$$l_1 = 2l_2$$

$$r_1 = \frac{r_2}{2}$$

$$\frac{Q}{t} = \frac{kA(\Delta T)}{l}$$

$$\frac{k_1(\pi r_1^2)(\Delta T)}{l_1} = \frac{k_2(\pi r_2^2)(\Delta T)}{l_2}$$

$$\frac{k_1}{k_2} = \frac{r_2^2}{l_2} \times \frac{l_1}{r_1^2} = \frac{4r_1^2}{r_1^2} \times \frac{2l_2}{l_2} = 8$$

Sol. 16 (A) Radiation power is

$$\Rightarrow \quad P = Ae\sigma T^4$$

$$\Rightarrow \quad P = (10^{-4}\,\text{m}^2)(1)(5.67\times10^{-8}\,\text{W/m}^2\text{k}^4)(1000)^4$$

$$\Rightarrow \quad P = 5.67\,\text{J}$$

Sol. 17 (B) We use $P \propto T^4$

$$\frac{P_1}{P_2} = \frac{(7+273)^4}{(287+273)^4} = \frac{1}{16}$$

$$P_2 = 16P_1$$

Sol. 18 (C) We use $\dfrac{dT}{dt} = -k(T - T_0)$

$$\int_{60}^{50}\frac{dT}{T-T_0} = -k\int_0^{600} dt$$

Here $T_0 = 25°\text{C}$

$$\ln\left(\frac{50-25}{60-25}\right) = -k(600) \quad \dots(1)$$

In next 10 minutes, Let temperature of body is T °C

$$\int_{50}^{T}\frac{dT}{T-T_0} = -k\int_{600}^{1200} dt$$

$$\ln\left(\frac{T-25}{50-25}\right) = -k(1200-600)$$

$$= -600k \quad \dots(2)$$

From (1) and (2), we get

$$\ln\left(\frac{50-25}{60-25}\right) = \ln\left(\frac{T-25}{50-25}\right)$$

$$\frac{25}{35} = \frac{T-25}{25}$$

$$\Rightarrow \quad T = 42.85°\text{C}$$

Sol. 19 (D) As $a + r + t = p$

$$\Rightarrow \quad r + t = q$$

$$\Rightarrow \quad a = p - q$$

Absorption coefficient, $Q_a = \dfrac{a}{p} = \dfrac{p-q}{p}$

Sol. 20 (D) For a block body, $e = 1$

$$p = Ae\sigma T^4$$

$$3 = 10^{-4}\times1\times\sigma\times(127+273)^4$$

$$\sigma = 1.17\times10^{-6}$$

Now, $p' = Ae\sigma T'^4$

$$p' = 10^{-4}\times1\times1.17\times10^{-6}\times(527+273)^4$$

$$p' = 48\,\text{J}$$

Sol. 21 (D) We use $\dfrac{R}{P} = \dfrac{(400+273)^4}{(800+273)^4}$

$$\frac{R}{P} = 0.15$$

$$P = \frac{R}{0.15} \approx 6.5R$$

Sol. 22 (D) As we use

$$\frac{Q}{t} = \frac{kA(\Delta T)}{L}$$

$$\Rightarrow \quad \frac{Q}{12} = \frac{k(2A)(\Delta T)}{L} \quad \dots(1)$$

Let in second condition, same heat is transferred in t seconds,

$$\frac{Q}{t} = \frac{k(A)(\Delta T)}{2L} \quad \dots(2)$$

Dividing (1) by (2), we get

$$\frac{Q}{12}\times\frac{t}{Q} = \frac{k(2A)(\Delta T)}{L}\times\frac{2L}{k(A)(\Delta T)} = 4$$

$$t = 12\times4 = 48\,\text{s}$$

Sol. 23 (B) As we use

$$\frac{dT}{dt} = -k(T-T_0)$$

$$\Rightarrow \quad \frac{dT}{T-T_0} = -k\,dt$$

$$\Rightarrow \quad \int_{50}^{49.9}\frac{dT}{T-30} = -k\int_0^5 dt$$

$$\Rightarrow \quad \ln\left(\frac{49.9-30}{50-30}\right) = -k(5-0)$$

$$\Rightarrow \quad \ln\left(\frac{199}{200}\right) = -5k \quad \dots(1)$$

$$\Rightarrow \quad k = 10^{-3}$$

Let it takes t further seconds to cool down from 49.9 s to 40 s

$$\int_{49.9}^{40}\frac{dT}{T-30} = -k\int_5^t dt$$

$$\Rightarrow \quad \ln\left(\frac{40-30}{49.9-30}\right) = -k(t-5)$$

$$\Rightarrow \quad \ln\left(\frac{100}{199}\right) = -k(t-5) \quad \dots(2)$$

$$\Rightarrow \quad t = 693\,\text{s}$$

Let it takes t' further seconds to cool from 40°C to 39.9°C

$$\ln\left(\frac{39.9-30}{40-30}\right) = -k(t'-t)$$

$$\Rightarrow \quad t'-t = 10.05\text{ s}$$

Sol. 24 (B) We use $\quad I = \dfrac{p_1}{4\pi d_1^2} = \dfrac{A\sigma T_1^4}{4\pi d_1^2} \quad \ldots(1)$

$$\Rightarrow \quad I = \frac{p_2}{4\pi d_2^2} = \frac{A\sigma T_2^4}{4\pi d_2^2} \quad \ldots(2)$$

From (1) & (2), we get

$$\frac{T_1^4}{d_1^2} = \frac{T_2^4}{d_2^2}$$

$$\left(\frac{d_2}{d_1}\right)^2 = \left(\frac{T_2}{T_1}\right)^4$$

$$\frac{d_2}{d_1} = \left(\frac{T_2}{T_1}\right)^2$$

Sol. 25 (D) We use

$$\frac{k_1 A(T_h - T_j)}{l} = \frac{k_2 A(T_j - T_c)}{l}$$

$$k_1 T_h - T_j k_1 = k_2 T_j - k_2 T_c$$

$$T_j(k_1 + k_2) = k_1 T_h + k_2 T_c$$

$$T_j = \frac{k_1 T_h + k_2 T_c}{k_1 + k_2}$$

Sol. 26 (B) We use

$$\frac{k_1 A(\Delta T_1)}{l} = \frac{k_2 A(\Delta T_2)}{l}$$

$$\frac{\Delta T_1}{\Delta T_2} = \frac{k_2}{k_1} = \frac{2k_1}{k_1} = 2$$

Sol. 27 (B) From Newton's law of cooling,

$$\frac{dT}{dt} = -k(T - T_0)$$

$$T_0 = 20^\circ\text{C}$$

$$\Rightarrow \quad \int \frac{dT}{T - T_0} = -k\int dt$$

$$\Rightarrow \quad \int_{55}^{45} \frac{dT}{T-20} = -k\int_0^{480} dt$$

$$\Rightarrow \quad \ln\left(\frac{45-20}{55-20}\right) = -k(480-0)$$

$$k = 7 \times 10^{-4}$$

Now, $\quad \displaystyle\int_{45}^{35} \frac{dT}{T-20} = -(7\times 10^{-4})\int_{480}^{t} dt$

$$\Rightarrow \quad \ln\left(\frac{35-20}{45-20}\right) = -(7\times 10^{-4})(t-480)$$

$$\Rightarrow \quad -0.5 = -(7\times 10^{-4})(t-480)$$

$$(t-480) = 730s \approx 12\text{ min}$$

Sol. 28 (B) We use $\quad \dfrac{Q}{t} = \dfrac{kA\Delta T}{l}$

ΔT is same whether the scale is °C or K

$\Rightarrow$ rate of flow of heat remains same.

Sol. 29 (C) T_A k_A k_B T_B T_0

As $\quad T_A - T_B = 27^\circ\text{C} \quad \ldots(1)$

$$k_A = 2k_B$$

$$\Rightarrow \quad \frac{k_A A(T_A - T_0)}{L} = \frac{k_B A(T_0 - T_B)}{L}$$

$$\Rightarrow \quad 2T_A - 2T_0 = T_0 - T_B$$

$$\Rightarrow \quad 2T_A + T_B = 3T_0 \quad \ldots(2)$$

From (1) and (2),

$$2(24 + T_B) + T_B = 3T_0$$

$$\Rightarrow \quad 48 + 3T_B = 3T_0$$

$$\Rightarrow \quad T_B - T_0 = \frac{48}{3} = 16^\circ\text{C}$$

Sol. 30 (B) Rate of cooling,

$$\frac{dT}{dt} = \frac{eA\sigma}{mc}(T^4 - T_0^4)$$

$$\Rightarrow \quad \frac{dT}{dt} \propto \frac{A}{m}$$

$$\propto \frac{r^2}{r^3}$$

$$\propto \frac{1}{r}$$

$$\Rightarrow \quad \frac{\left(\frac{dT}{dt}\right)_1}{\left(\frac{dT}{dt}\right)_2} = \frac{20}{10} = \frac{2}{1}$$

Sol. 31 (C) From Newton's law of cooling,

$$\frac{dT}{dt} = -k(T - T_0)$$

$$\Rightarrow \quad \int_{75}^{65} \frac{dT}{T - T_0} = -k \int_0^{120} dt$$

Here, $T_0 = 30°C$

$$\ln\left(\frac{65-30}{75-30}\right) = -k(120-0)$$

$$k = 2.09 \times 10^{-3}$$

To cool from 55°C to 45°C

$$\int_{55}^{45} \frac{dT}{T-30} = -(2.09 \times 10^{-3}) \int_{t_1}^{t_2} dt$$

$$\Rightarrow \quad \ln\left(\frac{45-30}{55-30}\right) = -(2.09 \times 10^{-3})(t_2 - t_1)$$

$$\Rightarrow \quad t_2 - t_1 = 244 \text{ s} \approx 4 \text{ min}$$

Sol. 32 (D) Heat released to room = Heat dissipated out of room.

Let temperature of heater is T

$$T - 20 = 20 - (-20)$$

$$\Rightarrow \quad T - 20 = 40$$

$$T = 60°C$$

Also, $T - 10 = 10 - (-40)$

$$\Rightarrow \quad T - 10 = 50$$

$$\Rightarrow \quad T = 60°C$$

Sol. 33 (A) We use $R = \frac{l}{kA}$

$$\Rightarrow \quad \frac{k_1}{k_2} = \frac{1}{2}, \frac{l_1}{l_2} = \frac{1}{2}, \frac{A_1}{A_2} = \frac{1}{2}$$

$$\Rightarrow \quad \frac{R_1}{R_2} = \frac{l_1}{k_1 A_1} \times \frac{k_2 A_2}{l_2}$$

$$\Rightarrow \quad \frac{R_1}{R_2} = \left(\frac{l_1}{l_2}\right) \times \left(\frac{k_2}{k_1}\right) \times \left(\frac{A_2}{A_1}\right)$$

$$\Rightarrow \quad \frac{R_1}{R_2} = \frac{1}{2} \times \frac{2}{1} \times \frac{2}{1} = \frac{2}{1}$$

Sol. 34 (B)

$$\frac{kA(\Delta T)}{2l} = 2W \quad \ldots(1)$$

$$\Rightarrow \quad \frac{k(2A)(\Delta T)}{l} = x \quad \ldots(2)$$

Dividing (1) by (2), we get

$$x = 8W$$

Sol. 35 (B) By Wein's displacement law

$$\lambda_m T = \text{constant}$$

$$\Rightarrow \quad \frac{\lambda_{m_1}}{\lambda_{m_2}} = \frac{T_2}{T_1}$$

$$\Rightarrow \quad \frac{T_1}{T_2} = \frac{420 \text{ nm}}{560 \text{ nm}} = \frac{3}{4}$$

Sol. 36 (D) Rate of cooling, $\frac{dT}{dt} \propto (T^4 - T_0^4)$

$$\Rightarrow \quad \frac{R_1}{R_2} = \frac{[(327+273)^4 - (27+273)^4]}{[(627+273)^4 - (27+273)^4]}$$

$$\Rightarrow \quad \frac{R_1}{R_2} = \frac{1.215 \times 10^{11}}{6.48 \times 10^{11}} = \frac{3}{16}$$

$$\Rightarrow \quad R_2 = \frac{16}{3} R_1 = \frac{16}{3} R \quad (\because \ R_1 = R)$$

Sol. 37 (C) We use $k_{eq} = \frac{2k_1 k_2}{k_1 + k_2}$

As $k_1 = k_2 = k$

$$\Rightarrow \quad k_{eq} = \frac{2k^2}{k+k} = k$$

Sol. 38 (D)

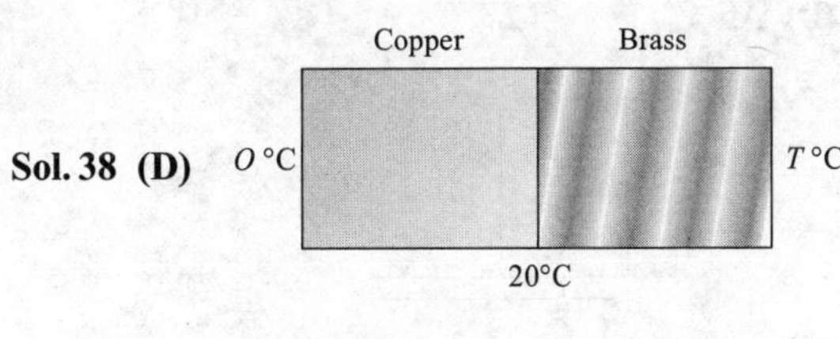

$$\frac{k_{cu}}{k_b} = \frac{4}{1}$$

Let temperature of free surface of brass is T °C

$$\frac{k_{cu} A(20-0)}{l} = \frac{k_b A(T-20)}{l}$$

$$\Rightarrow \quad 4k_b(20) = k_b(T-20)$$

$$\Rightarrow \quad 80 = T - 20$$

$$\Rightarrow \quad T = 100°C$$

Sol. 39 (D) $H = \dfrac{\Delta\theta}{R}$

is same through both sheets

$$\frac{\theta - \theta_2}{R_2} = \frac{\theta_1 - \theta}{R_1}$$

$$\Rightarrow \quad \theta R_1 - \theta_2 R_1 = \theta_1 R_2 - \theta R_2$$

$$\Rightarrow \quad \theta(R_1 + R_2) = \theta_2 R_1 + \theta_1 R_2$$

$$\Rightarrow \quad \theta = \frac{\theta_2 R_1 + \theta_1 R_2}{R_1 + R_2}$$

Sol. 40 (A) As $H = \dfrac{\Delta\theta}{R}$

$$\Rightarrow \quad H \propto \frac{1}{R} \propto \frac{kA}{l}$$

$$\Rightarrow \quad \frac{H_1}{H_2} = \frac{A_1}{A_2} \times \frac{l_2}{l_1}$$

$$\Rightarrow \quad \frac{1}{8} = \frac{1}{4} \times \frac{l_2}{l_1}$$

$$\Rightarrow \quad \frac{l_1}{l_2} = \frac{8}{4} = \frac{2}{1}$$

Sol. 41 (D) As we radiation power

$$P \propto T^4$$

$$\Rightarrow \quad P_1 \propto (400 + 273)^4$$

and $\quad P_2 \propto (T)^4$

As $\quad P_2 = 2P_1$

$$\Rightarrow \quad (T)^4 = 2(673)^4$$

$$\Rightarrow \quad T^4 = 4.1 \times 10^{11}$$

$$\Rightarrow \quad T = (4.1 \times 10^{11})^{1/4}$$

$$\Rightarrow \quad T \approx 800\,\text{K}$$

Sol. 42 (B) As $k_A = 2k_B$

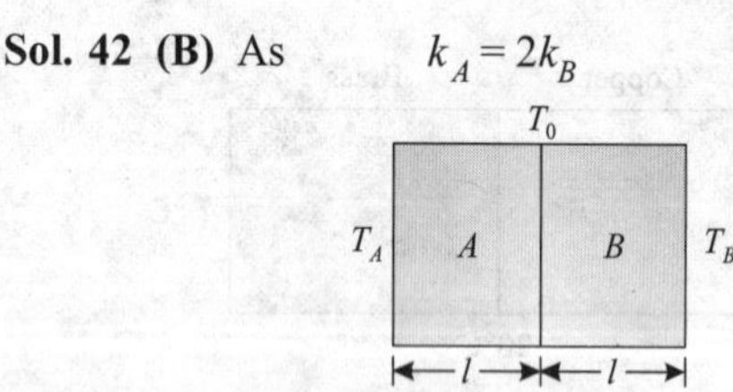

Let area of layers be A

$$T_A - T_B = 36°\text{C} \qquad \ldots(1)$$

$$\frac{k_A A(T_A - T_0)}{l} = \frac{k_B A(T_0 - T_B)}{l}$$

$$\Rightarrow \quad 2(T_A - T_0) = T_0 - T_B$$

$$\Rightarrow \quad 2T_A + T_B = 3T_0 \qquad \ldots(2)$$

From (1) and (2), we get

$$2T_A + T_A - 36 = 3T_0$$

$$\Rightarrow \quad 3T_A - 3T_0 = 36$$

$$\Rightarrow \quad T_A - T_0 = 12°\text{C}$$

Sol. 43 (B) As $\dfrac{k_1}{k_2} = \dfrac{5}{3}$

and $\quad A_1 = A_2$

and $\quad R_1 = R_2$

We use thermal resistance

$$R = \frac{l}{kA}$$

$$\Rightarrow \quad \frac{R_1}{R_2} = \frac{l_1}{k_1 A_1} \times \frac{k_2 A_2}{l_2}$$

$$\Rightarrow \quad \frac{l_1}{l_2} = \frac{k_1}{k_2} = \frac{5}{3}$$

Sol. 44 (B) 100°C —— l —— 0°C, A

Let length of rod $= l$

radius of rod $= r$

area of cross-section $= A$

and thermal conductivity $= k$

$$\frac{kA(100 - 0)}{l} = \frac{mL}{t}$$

$$\Rightarrow \quad \frac{kA(100 - 0)}{l} = \frac{(0.1g)L}{1s} \qquad \ldots(1)$$

For second rod,

$$\frac{0.25k \times (4A) \times (100 - 0)}{l/2} = \frac{mL}{1s} \qquad \ldots(2)$$

Dividing (1) by (2), we get

$$m = 2 \times 0.25 \times 4 \times 0.1$$

$$\Rightarrow \quad m = 0.2g$$

Sol. 45 (C) We use $mL = \dfrac{kA(\theta_1 - \theta_2)dt}{x}$

$$\Rightarrow \quad (A \times dx \times \rho) \times L = \frac{kA(\theta_1 - \theta_2)}{x} dt$$

$$\Rightarrow \quad dt = \frac{dx \rho L x}{k(\theta_1 - \theta_2)}$$

$$\Rightarrow \quad t = \int_0^t dt = \frac{\rho L}{k\theta} \int_{10}^{10.1} x\,dx$$

$$\Rightarrow \quad t = \frac{\rho L}{k\theta}\left[\frac{x^2}{2}\right]_{10}^{10.1}$$

$$\Rightarrow \quad t = \frac{0.91 \times 80}{2 \times 0.005 \times 5}[(10.1)^2 - (10)^2]$$

$$\Rightarrow \quad t = 2926.56\,\text{s} = 48.78\,\text{min}$$

Sol. 46 **(D)** By Stefen's law we use

$$P = Ae\sigma T^4$$

$$\Rightarrow \quad P = Ae\sigma(400)^4 \quad \ldots(1)$$

when length and breadth is reduced to half, area becomes $\frac{1}{4}$ times,

Let rate of emission is P'

$$P' = A'e\sigma(600)^4$$

$$\Rightarrow \quad P' = \frac{A}{4}e\sigma(600)^4 \quad \ldots(2)$$

Dividing (1) by (2), we get

$$\frac{P'}{P} = \frac{Ae\sigma(600)^4}{4} \times \frac{1}{Ae\sigma(400)^4}$$

$$\Rightarrow \quad \frac{P'}{P} = \frac{81}{4 \times 16}$$

$$\Rightarrow \quad P' = \frac{81}{64}P$$

Sol. 47 **(A)** Given that

$e = 0.35$

$A = 0.25 \times 10^{-4}\,\text{m}^2$

$\sigma = 5.67 \times 10^{-8}\,\text{Wm}^{-2}\text{K}^{-4}$

$T = 3000\,\text{K}$

We use $P = Ae\sigma T^4$

$\Rightarrow \quad P = 0.25 \times 10^{-4} \times 0.35 \times 5.67 \times 10^{-8} \times (3000)^4$

$\Rightarrow \quad P = 40.2\,\text{W}$

$\Rightarrow \quad P \approx 40\,\text{W}$

Sol. 48 **(D)** As we have $t = \frac{\rho L}{2k\theta}y^2$

$$\Rightarrow \quad (7 \times 3600) = \frac{(0.91)(80)}{2k(10)}(1)^2$$

$$\Rightarrow \quad k = \frac{72.8}{504000}$$

$$= 1.44 \times 10^{-4}\,\text{cal cm}^{-1}\,°\text{C}^{-1}$$

To change from 1 cm to 2 cm thickness,

$$t = \frac{\rho L}{k\theta}\int_1^2 y\,dy$$

$$\Rightarrow \quad t = \frac{0.91 \times 80}{2 \times 1.44 \times 10^{-4} \times 10}[2^2 - 1^2]$$

$$\Rightarrow \quad t = \frac{72.8}{2.88 \times 10^{-3}} \quad \ldots(3)$$

$$\Rightarrow \quad t = \frac{218.4}{2.88 \times 10^{-3}} = 75.8 \times 10^3\,\text{s}$$

$$\Rightarrow \quad t = 21.06\,h \approx 21\,\text{hour}$$

Sol. 49 **(D)** As $\frac{dQ}{dt} \propto \frac{A}{l}$

here we check all given options as

(A) $R_1 \propto \frac{r^2}{l}$

$\propto \frac{1}{2}$

$\propto 0.5$

(B) $R_2 \propto \frac{4}{4}$

$R_2 \propto 1$

(C) $R_3 \propto \frac{4}{2}$

$R_3 \propto 2$

(D) $R_4 \propto \frac{16}{2}$

$R_4 \propto 8$

Thus the rod of $l = 2$ cm and $r = 4$ cm has highest rate of flow of heat.

Sol. 50 **(A)** Lowest rate of heat is for rod of

$l = 2$ cm, $r = 1$ cm

Sol. 51 **(B)** Let temperature of junction is T °C

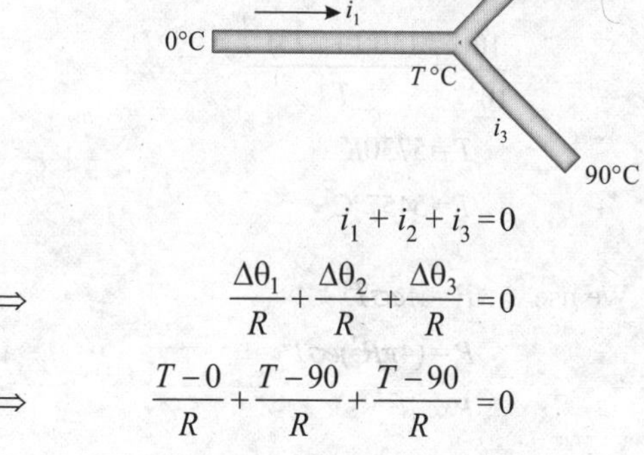

$$i_1 + i_2 + i_3 = 0$$

$$\Rightarrow \quad \frac{\Delta\theta_1}{R} + \frac{\Delta\theta_2}{R} + \frac{\Delta\theta_3}{R} = 0$$

$$\Rightarrow \quad \frac{T-0}{R} + \frac{T-90}{R} + \frac{T-90}{R} = 0$$

$$\Rightarrow \quad +T + T - 90 + T - 90 = 0$$

$$\Rightarrow \quad 3T = 180$$

$$\Rightarrow \quad T = 60°\text{C}$$

Sol. 52 **(B)** By Wein's displacement law

$$\lambda_m T = \text{constant}$$

$$\Rightarrow \quad \frac{\lambda_{m_{sun}}}{\lambda_{m_{star}}} = \frac{T_{star}}{T_{sun}}$$

$$\Rightarrow \quad \frac{T_{sun}}{T_{star}} = \frac{\lambda_{m_{star}}}{\lambda_{m_{sun}}} = \frac{350\text{nm}}{510\text{nm}}$$

$$\Rightarrow \quad \frac{T_{sun}}{T_{star}} = 0.69$$

Sol. 53 **(B)** As we use $Q = \frac{kA\Delta\theta t}{l}$

$$\Rightarrow \quad Q \propto kA$$

$$\Rightarrow \quad k_1A_1 = k_2A_2$$

$$\Rightarrow \quad \frac{A_1}{A_2} = \frac{k_2}{k_1}$$

Sol. 54 **(D)** As we use $Q = \frac{kA\Delta\theta}{l} = \frac{k(\pi r^2)\Delta\theta t}{l}$

$$\Rightarrow \quad \frac{Q_1}{Q_2} = \frac{r_1^2}{l_1} \times \frac{l_2}{r_2^2} = \left(\frac{1}{2}\right)^2 \times \left(\frac{1}{2}\right) = \frac{1}{8}$$

Sol. 55 **(B)** Temperature gradient

$$\frac{dT}{dx} = 80°\text{C/m}$$

$$\Rightarrow \quad \int_{30}^{T} dT = -80 \int_{0}^{0.5} dx$$

$$\Rightarrow \quad T - 30 = -80(0.5)$$

$$\Rightarrow \quad T - 30 = -40$$

$$\Rightarrow \quad T = -10°\text{C}$$

Sol. 56 **(B)** We use $E \propto T^4$

$$\Rightarrow \quad \frac{10}{10^5} = \frac{(300+273)^4}{T^4}$$

$$\Rightarrow \quad T = 5730K$$

$$\Rightarrow \quad T = 5457°\text{C}$$

Sol. 57 **(A)** We use $P = Ae\sigma T^4$

$$\Rightarrow \quad P = (4\pi R^2)e\sigma T^4$$

$$\Rightarrow \quad P \propto R^2$$

$$\Rightarrow \quad \frac{P_1}{P_2} = \frac{R_1^2}{R_2^2}$$

Sol. 58 **(C)** Rate of cooling is

$$R = \frac{dT}{dt} = \frac{eA\sigma}{mc}(T^4)$$

$$\Rightarrow \quad \frac{R_1}{R_2} = \frac{A_1}{m_1} \times \frac{m_2}{A_2}$$

$$\Rightarrow \quad \frac{R_1}{R_2} = \frac{R_1^2}{R_1^3} \times \frac{R_2^3}{R_2^2}$$

$$\Rightarrow \quad \frac{R_1}{R_2} = \frac{R_2}{R_1}$$

Sol. 59 **(B)** As we use

$$\frac{Q_1}{Q_2} = \frac{t_1k_1}{t_2k_2} \qquad \left(\text{As } Q = \frac{kA\Delta Tt}{l}\right)$$

As $\quad Q_1 = Q_2$

$$\Rightarrow \quad \frac{k_1}{k_2} = \frac{t_2}{t_1}$$

Sol. 60 **(A)** As we use $20 = \frac{kA(100-0)t_1}{2L}$ ...(1)

$$\Rightarrow \quad 20 = Q = \frac{k(2A)(100-0)t_2}{L} \quad ...(2)$$

$$\Rightarrow \quad \frac{t_1}{2} = 2t_2$$

$$\Rightarrow \quad t_2 = \frac{t_1}{4} = \frac{4}{4} = 1 \text{ min}$$

Sol. 61 **(C)** As we use $P = Ae\sigma T^4$

$$\Rightarrow \quad P = 1 \times 1 \times 5.67 \times 10^{-8} \times (1000)^4$$

$$\Rightarrow \quad P = 56700 \text{ J/s}$$

Sol. 62 **(B)** Given that

$$\frac{l_1}{l_2} = \frac{1}{2};\ \frac{r_1}{r_2} = \frac{1}{2};\ \frac{k_1}{k_2} = \frac{1}{2}$$

We use $\quad R = \frac{Q}{t} = \frac{kA\Delta T}{L}$

$$\Rightarrow \quad \frac{R_1}{R_2} = \frac{k_1A_1}{L_1} \times \frac{L_2}{k_2A_2}$$

$$\Rightarrow \quad \frac{R_1}{R_2} = \frac{1}{2} \times \frac{1}{4} \times \frac{2}{1} = \frac{1}{4}$$

$$\Rightarrow \quad R_2 = 4R_1 = 4 \text{ cal/s}$$

Sol. 63 **(D)** As we use

$$\frac{P_1}{P_2} = \frac{(27+273)^4}{(927+273)^4} = \left(\frac{300}{1200}\right)^4$$

$$\Rightarrow \quad \frac{P_1}{P_2} = \frac{1}{256}$$

Sol. 64 **(B)** If A be the area of the pond. Transfer of heat will take placed from bottom to top surface of pond. Figure below shows an intermediate situation when ice of thickness y is frozen and in time dt amount of heat dQ flows water to atmosphere through ice.

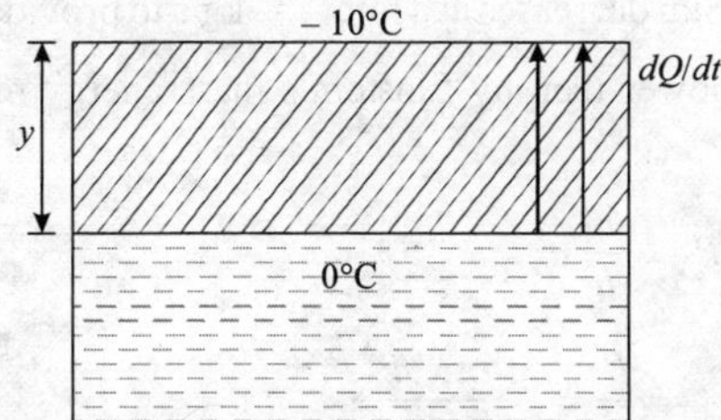

The rate of heat conduction through ice from water to atmosphere is given as

$$\frac{dQ}{dt} = L\cdot\left(\frac{dm}{dt}\right)$$

The heat flows through conduction, so rate of heat conduction is written as

$$\frac{KA(10)}{y} = L\left(\frac{\rho A dy}{dt}\right)$$

$$\Rightarrow \quad y.dy = \frac{10K}{L\rho}\cdot dt$$

$$\Rightarrow \quad dt = \frac{L\rho}{10K} ydy$$

$$\Rightarrow \quad \int_0^t dt = \frac{L\rho}{10K}\int_{4cm}^{8cm} ydy = \frac{L\rho}{10.K}\left(\frac{y^2}{2}\right)_{4\times10^{-2}m}^{8\times10^{-2}m}$$

$$\Rightarrow \quad t = \frac{L\rho}{10K}(64-16)\frac{(10^{-4})}{2}$$

Substituting the values, we have

$$t = \frac{80\times4.18\times(10^3)(48)(10^{-4})(900)}{10\times2\times2}\text{ s}$$

$$\Rightarrow \quad t = 36115.2\text{ s} = 10.03\text{ hr}$$

Sol. 65 (D) We use $P \propto T^4$

$$\Rightarrow \quad \frac{P_1}{P_2} = \frac{T_1^4}{T_2^4}$$

$$\Rightarrow \quad \frac{10}{P_2} = \frac{(27+273)^4}{(327+273)^4}$$

$$\Rightarrow \quad \frac{10}{P_2} = \left(\frac{300}{600}\right)^4 = \frac{1}{16}$$

$$\Rightarrow \quad P_2 = 160\text{ J/s}$$

Thus, energy emitted per second = 160 J

Sol. 66 (A) Unit of thermal resistance = °C s/cal

Dimensions: $[M^{-1}L^{-2}T^3K]$

Sol. 67 (A) As $Q_1 = Q_2$

$$\frac{k_1A(\Delta T)}{L}t_1 = \frac{k_2A(\Delta T)}{L}t_2$$

$$\Rightarrow \quad \frac{k_1}{k_2} = \frac{t_2}{t_1} = \frac{30}{20} = 1.5$$

Sol. 68 (D) As we use

$$\frac{P_1}{P_2} = \frac{T^4}{(1.5T)^4}$$

$$\Rightarrow \quad \frac{P_1}{P_2} = \frac{16}{81}$$

$$\Rightarrow \quad P_2 \approx 5P_1$$

Percentage change in rate is

$$\Delta P = \frac{P_2 - P_1}{P_1}\times100$$

$$\Rightarrow \quad \Delta P = 400\%$$

Sol. 69 (B) As we use

$$k_{eq} = \frac{K_1A_1 + K_2A_2}{A_1 + A_2}$$

$$\Rightarrow \quad k_{eq} = \frac{K_1[\pi R^2] + K_2[\pi(9R^2) - \pi R^2]}{\pi R^2 + \pi(9R^2 - R^2)}$$

$$\Rightarrow \quad k_{eq} = \frac{K_1 + 8K_2}{9}$$

Sol. 70 (A) As we use

$$\frac{P_1}{P_2} = \frac{(27+273)^4}{(127+273)^4} = \frac{(300)^4}{(400)^4}$$

$$\Rightarrow \quad \frac{P_1}{P_2} = \frac{81}{256}$$

$$\Rightarrow \quad \frac{P_2}{P_1} = \frac{256}{81}$$

Sol. 71 (C) As we use $P = Ae\sigma(T^4 - T_0^4)$

$\Rightarrow$ $P = (200\times10^{-4})\times(0.4)\times(5.67\times10^{-8})\times[(527+273)^4 - (27+273)^4]$

$\Rightarrow$ $P = (4.54\times10^{-10})\times(4.096\times10^{11} - 8.1\times10^9)$

$\Rightarrow$ $P = 4.54\times10^{-10}\times4.015\times10^{11}$

$\Rightarrow$ $P = 182.3\text{ J} \approx 186\text{ J}$

Sol. 72 (C) Through the wall at any elemental layer of thickness dx if the temperature difference across this layer is dT then rate of heat conduction or thermal power being conducted through this layer is given as

$$P = \frac{dQ}{dt} = KA\frac{dT}{dx}$$

$$\Rightarrow \quad \frac{P}{A}\int_0^x dx = K_0\int_0^T (1+T)\,dT$$

$$\Rightarrow \quad \frac{P}{A}x = K_0\left(T+\frac{T^2}{2}\right)_0^T = K_0\left(T+\frac{T^2}{2}\right)$$

At $x = x_0$ given that $T = 300$ K so we have

$$\frac{P}{A}x_0 = K_0\left(300+\frac{(300)^2}{2}\right)$$

$$\Rightarrow \quad K_0 = \frac{Px_0}{45300A}$$

Thus at $x = 2x_0$ temperature will be calculated as

$$\frac{P}{A}(2x_0) = \left(\frac{Px_0}{45300A}\right)\left(T+\frac{T^2}{2}\right)$$

$$\Rightarrow \quad T^2+2T-181200=0$$

$$\Rightarrow \quad T = \frac{-2\pm\sqrt{4+4(181200)}}{2} = -1\pm\sqrt{181201} = -1+425.67\text{ K}$$

$$\Rightarrow \quad T \approx 425\text{ K}$$

Sol. 73 (D) We use $\quad r = \frac{Q}{t} = \frac{kA\Delta T}{L}$

As $\quad r_A = r_B$

$$\Rightarrow \quad K_AA_A = K_BA_B$$

$$\Rightarrow \quad K_A\pi R_A^2 = K_B\pi R_B^2$$

$$\Rightarrow \quad K_A(2R_B)^2 = K_BR_B^2$$

$$\Rightarrow \quad K_A = \frac{K_B}{4}$$

Sol. 74 (D) Thermal resistance we use

$$R = \frac{l}{kA}$$

$$\Rightarrow \quad \frac{l_1}{k_1A_1} = \frac{l_2}{k_2A_2}$$

$$\Rightarrow \quad \frac{l_1}{l_2} = \frac{k_1}{k_2}\times\frac{A_1}{A_2}$$

$$\Rightarrow \quad \frac{l_1}{l_2} = \frac{5}{4}$$

Sol. 75 (D) By using Wien's displacement law, temperature of Sun can be calculated as

$$\lambda_m T = b$$

$$\Rightarrow \quad T = \frac{b}{\lambda_m}$$

Power radiated by the sun is given as

$$P = \sigma AT^4 = 4\pi R^2\sigma T^4$$

If mass of Sun decreases at a rate $\frac{dm}{dt}$ kg/s to provide the above radiation power then by Einstein's mass energy relationship, we use

$$P = \frac{dm}{dt}c^2$$

$$\Rightarrow \quad \frac{dm}{dt} = \frac{P}{c^2} = \frac{\sigma 4\pi R^2T^4}{c^2}$$

$$\Rightarrow \quad \frac{dm}{dt} = \frac{\sigma 4\pi R^2}{c^2}\left(\frac{b}{\lambda_m}\right)^4$$

$$\Rightarrow \quad \frac{dm}{dt} = \frac{5.67\times10^{-8}\times4\times3.14\times(7\times10^8)^2}{(3\times10^8)^2}\left(\frac{2.9\times10^{-3}}{480\times10^{-9}}\right)^4$$

$$\Rightarrow \quad \frac{dm}{dt} = 5.167\times10^9\text{ kg/s} \approx 5\times10^9\text{ kg/s}$$

Sol. 76 (B)

Let temperature of C is T°C

If k is thermal conductivity of rod and A be the area of cross-section,

$$\frac{kA(100-T)}{6} = \frac{kA(T-0)}{14}$$

$$\Rightarrow \quad \frac{100-T}{6} = \frac{T}{14}$$

$$\Rightarrow \quad 1400\ 14T = 6T$$

$$\Rightarrow \quad 20T = 1400$$

$$\Rightarrow \quad T = 70°\text{C}$$

Sol. 77 (B) We use $\quad s = \frac{P}{4\pi r^2} = \frac{4\pi R^2\sigma T^4}{4\pi r^2}$

$$\Rightarrow \quad \frac{s_1}{s_2} = \frac{T_1^4}{r_1^2}\times\frac{r_2^2}{T_2^4}$$

$$\Rightarrow \quad \frac{s_1}{s_2} = \left(\frac{T_1}{2T_1}\right)^4\times\left(\frac{2r_1}{r_1}\right)^2$$

$$\Rightarrow \quad \frac{s_1}{s_2} = \frac{1}{2^4}\times2^2$$

$$\Rightarrow \quad \frac{s_1}{s_2} = \frac{1}{4}$$

$$\Rightarrow \quad s_2 = 4s_1 = 4P$$

Sol. 78 (C) We use $\quad H = \frac{Q}{t} = \frac{kA(\Delta T)}{L}$

$\Rightarrow \quad 4000 = \dfrac{400\times(100\times10^{-4})\times\Delta T}{0.1}$

$\Rightarrow \quad \Delta T = 100°C$

Sol. 79 (A) From Newton's law of cooling,

$$\frac{dT}{dt} = -k(T-T_0)$$

$$\Rightarrow \int_{365}^{361}\frac{dT}{T-T_0} = -k\int_0^{120} dt$$

$$\Rightarrow \ln\left(\frac{361-293}{365-293}\right) = -k(120-0)$$

$$k = 4.76\times10^{-4}$$

To cool from 344 K to 342 K

$$\int_{344}^{342}\frac{dT}{T-293} = -k\int_{t_1}^{t_2} dt$$

$$\Rightarrow \ln\left(\frac{342-293}{344-293}\right) = -(4.76\times10^{-4})(t_2-t_1)$$

$$\Rightarrow t_2 - t_1 = 84 \text{ s}$$

Sol. 80 (A) From Newton's law of cooling,

$$R = \frac{dT}{dt} \propto (T-T_0)$$

$$\Rightarrow \frac{R_1}{R_2} = \frac{100-40}{80-40} = \frac{60}{40} = \frac{3}{2}$$

$$\Rightarrow R_1 : R_2 = 3:2$$

Sol. 81 (B) As we use

$$P = Ae\sigma T^4$$

$$\Rightarrow P = 0.1\times1\times5.67\times10^{-8}\times(727+273)^4$$

$$P = 5670W$$

and total heat $\quad H = P\times t$

$$\Rightarrow H = \frac{5670\times60}{4.2}\text{ cal}$$

$$\Rightarrow H = 81000 \text{ cal}$$

Sol. 82 (D) We use $\dfrac{P_1}{P_2} = \dfrac{(27+273)^4}{(51.2+273)^4} = 0.73$

$$\Rightarrow P_2 = \frac{P_1}{0.73} = 1.36p_1$$

Sol. 83 (D) Units of k is kcal/m s K

Dimensions: $[MLT^{-3}K^{-1}]$

Sol. 84 (C)

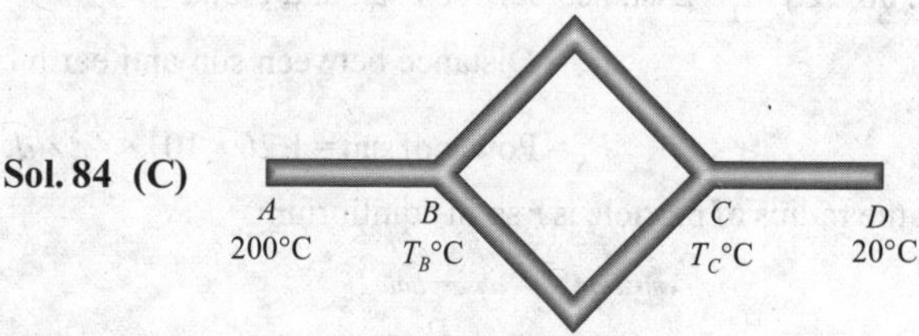

Let thermal resistance of each rod is R

Effective thermal resistance between B and $D = 2R$

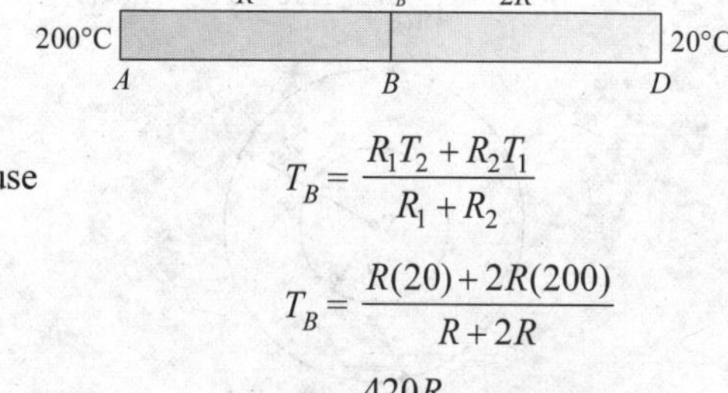

We use $\quad T_B = \dfrac{R_1T_2 + R_2T_1}{R_1+R_2}$

$$\Rightarrow T_B = \frac{R(20)+2R(200)}{R+2R}$$

$$\Rightarrow T_B = \frac{420R}{3R} = 140°C$$

Sol. 85 (D) As we use

$$k_{eq} = \frac{k_1A_1 + k_2A_2}{A_1+A_2}$$

$$\Rightarrow k_{eq} = \frac{k_1A + k_2A}{A+A} = \frac{k_1+k_2}{2}$$

Sol. 86 (B)

T_A | x → λ, y → 2λ | T_B

We use $\quad k_{eq} = \dfrac{k_1A_1+k_2A_2}{A_1+A_2} = \dfrac{\lambda+2\lambda}{2} = \dfrac{3\lambda}{2}$

Total heat flow through slab,

$$\Rightarrow H_1 = \frac{k_{eq}(2A)(\Delta T)}{L}$$

$$\Rightarrow H_1 = \frac{3\lambda(2A)\Delta T}{2L} \quad \ldots(1)$$

Heat flow through x,

$$H_2 = \frac{k_xA(\Delta T)}{L} \quad \ldots(2)$$

$$\Rightarrow \frac{H_2}{H_1} = \frac{\lambda A(\Delta T)}{L}\times\frac{2L}{3\lambda(2A)(\Delta T)} = \frac{1}{3}$$

Sol. 87 (B) We use for conduction rate

$$\frac{\lambda_x\times A(100-25)}{60} = \frac{\lambda_yA(25-0)}{30}$$

$$\Rightarrow \frac{\lambda_x}{\lambda_y} = \frac{25}{30}\times\frac{60}{75} = \frac{2}{3}$$

Sol. 88 (C) d_1– Distance between sun and cloud

d_2 – Distance between sun and earth

$$P_S = \text{Power of sun} = 1.26 \times 10^3 \times 4\pi \times d_2^2$$

Let the radius of particle is r so in equilibrium

$$P_{emission} = P_{absorption}$$

$$\Rightarrow \quad 4\sigma T^4 = \pi r^2 \times \frac{P_S}{4\pi d_1^2}$$

$$4\sigma T^4 = \frac{1}{4\pi d_1^2} \times 1.26 \times 10^3 \times 4\pi d_2^2$$

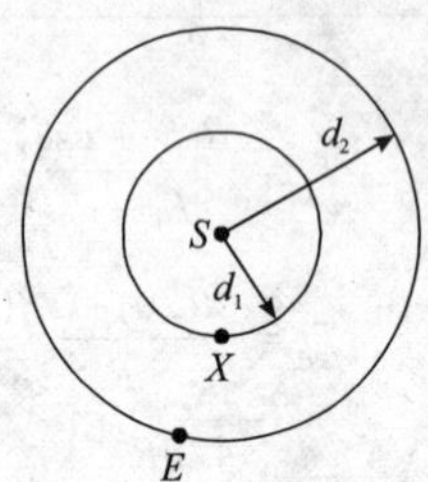

$$\Rightarrow \quad d_1 = \frac{d_2}{2T^2}\sqrt{\frac{1.26\times10^3}{5.6\times10^{-8}}}$$

$$\Rightarrow \quad d_1 = \frac{1.5\times10^{11}}{2\times4\times10^6}\times15\times10^4$$

$$\Rightarrow \quad d_1 \simeq 2.81 \times 10^9 \text{ m}$$

Sol. 89 (B) When engine turn off

$$\frac{dT}{dt} = -\frac{K}{C}(T - T_0)$$

$$\Rightarrow \quad \int_{25}^{20}\frac{dT}{T-10} = -\frac{k}{C}\int_0^t dt$$

$$\Rightarrow \quad \ln\frac{10}{15} = -\frac{K}{C}t$$

$$\Rightarrow \quad \ln(3) - \ln(2) = \frac{K}{C}t$$

$$\Rightarrow \quad t = 0.4 \times \frac{C}{k} = 5 \text{ min}$$

When engine turns on

$$\frac{dT}{dt} = -\frac{K}{C}(T - T_0) + \frac{P}{C}$$

$$\Rightarrow \quad = \frac{K}{C}[-T + T_0 + 3T]$$

$$\Rightarrow \quad \int_{20}^{25}\frac{dT}{2T+T_0} = \frac{+Kt}{C}$$

$$\Rightarrow \quad \ln\left(\frac{60}{50}\right) = \frac{K}{C}t$$

$$\Rightarrow \quad t = \frac{C}{2k}\ln\left(\frac{6}{5}\right)$$

$$= 1.125 \text{ min}$$

Sol. 90 (B) We use

$$ms\frac{dT}{dt} = A\sigma\varepsilon\frac{dT}{dx}$$

$$\Rightarrow \quad \frac{dT}{dt} \propto \frac{A}{m} \propto \frac{1}{d}$$

Sol. 91 (C)

K	2K	1.5K

200°C, θ_1, θ_2, 18°C

As we use
$$\frac{\Delta Q}{\Delta t} = \frac{KA(200-\theta_1)}{2L}$$

$$\Rightarrow \quad \frac{\Delta Q}{\Delta t} = (2K)\frac{A(\theta_1-\theta_2)}{2L}$$

$$\Rightarrow \quad \frac{\Delta Q}{\Delta t} = (1.5K)A\frac{(\theta_2-18)}{2L}$$

or,
$$200 - \theta_1 = 2\theta_1 - 2\theta_2 = 1.5\theta_2 - 27$$

$$\Rightarrow \quad \theta_1 = 116^\circ\text{C}, \theta_2 = 74^\circ\text{C}$$

Sol. 92 (C) As for steady state we use

$$\left.\frac{dQ}{dt}\right|_A + \left.\frac{dQ}{dt}\right|_B + \left.\frac{dQ}{dt}\right|_D = \left.\frac{dQ}{dt}\right|_C$$

$$2 + 4 + \left.\frac{dQ}{dt}\right|_D = 8$$

$$\Rightarrow \quad \left.\frac{dQ}{dt}\right|_D = 2 \text{ J/s}$$

$$\Rightarrow \quad T_D = T_A < T_B$$

Sol. 93 (B) Rate of cooling α difference in temperature

$$\frac{\Delta T}{\Delta t} \propto \Delta\theta$$

$$\Rightarrow \quad \frac{\Delta T}{\Delta t} = K\Delta\theta$$

$$\Rightarrow \quad \Delta T = K\Delta\theta.\Delta T$$

In first case :

$$\Delta T = 61 - 59 = 2$$

$$\Rightarrow \quad \Delta\theta = 60^\circ - 30^\circ = 30^\circ$$

$$\Delta t = 4 \text{ min}$$

$$\Rightarrow \quad K = \frac{\Delta T}{\Delta\theta\Delta t} = \frac{2}{30\times4} = \frac{1}{60}$$

For second case :

$$dT = 2$$

$$\Delta\theta = 50 - 30 = 20$$

$$\Rightarrow \quad dt = \frac{dT}{K\Delta\theta} = \frac{2}{\frac{1}{60}\times20} = 6 \text{ min}$$

Sol. 94 (C) For thermal resistance we use

$$R_{AB}=\frac{l}{KA}=R_{CD}$$

$$\Rightarrow \quad (R_{eq})_{BC}=\frac{\pi l}{2KA}$$

We have, $$\frac{100-0}{\frac{2l}{KA}+\frac{\pi l}{2KA}}=\frac{T_C-0}{\frac{l}{KA}},$$

$$\Rightarrow \quad T_C=28^{\circ}$$

Solutions of ADVANCE MCQs One or More Option Correct

Sol. 1 (A, C) $$P_1=\frac{K_1A(100-0)}{L}$$

As $$Q=P_1t_1$$

$$\Rightarrow \quad P_2=\frac{K_2A(100-0)}{L}$$

As $$Q=P_2t_2$$

$$\Rightarrow \quad P_3=\frac{P_1P_2}{P_1+P_2}=\frac{\frac{Q}{t_1}\times\frac{Q}{t_2}}{\frac{Q}{t_1}+\frac{Q}{t_2}}=\frac{Q}{t_1+t_2}$$

and $$Q=P_3(t_1+t_2)$$

$$\Rightarrow \quad t_{10}=t_1+t_2=100\text{ min}$$

$$\Rightarrow \quad P_2=P_1+P_2=\frac{Q}{t_1}+\frac{Q}{t_2}=\frac{Q(t_1+t_2)}{t_1t_2}$$

$$\Rightarrow \quad Q=P_4\left(\frac{t_1t_2}{t_1+t_2}\right)$$

$$\Rightarrow \quad t_{20}=\frac{t_1t_2}{t_1+t_2}=\frac{20\times 80}{100}=16\text{ min}$$

Sol. 2 (C, D) Rate of cooling = Radiation rate/heat capacity. As the heat capacity of both bodies are constant and radiation rate is same due to same surface area and same temperature, the ratio of rate of cooling of both will be a constant.

Sol. 3 (A, C) As the two ends of the rod are at constant temperature that means the rod is in steady state of thermal conduction hence throughout the length the temperature gradient will remain constant and in steady state of thermal conduction the rate of heat flow (heat current) is given by the product of thermal conductivity, cross sectional area and the temperature gradient.

Sol. 4 (B, D) This is explained in Illustrative Example-4.18 hence option (B) and (D) are correct.

Sol. 5 (A, B) As the two ends of the rod are at constant temperature that means the rod is in steady state of thermal conduction and in steady state of thermal conduction the rate of heat flow (heat current) is given by the product of thermal conductivity, cross sectional area and the temperature gradient.

Sol. 6 (A, B) By Wein's Law we use

$$\lambda_A=b/T_A \text{ and } \lambda_B=b/T_B$$

and given that

$$|\lambda_A-\lambda_B|=1\ \mu\text{m}$$

Solving the equations we get options (A) and (B) are correct.

Sol. 7 (D) When the temperature of one end (hotter) start to decrease, the rod will no longer be in steady state and continuously the temperature gradient as well as thermal current through the rod varies with time so non of the first three options can be correct.

Sol. 8 (D) As the surface area of both the volumes of water are unequal the rate of heat radiation as well as rate of cooling will be different. In case of cylinder area is more than that of spherical shell so for cylindrical case both will be more.

Sol. 9 (A, B, D) The total radiation emitted by a black body is given as $E=\sigma AT^4$ hence options (A), (B) and (D) are correct.

Sol. 10 (B, D) The rate of fall (cooling) of temperature is the ratio of radiation rate to the heat capacity of the body so rate of cooling will be equal only when their heat capacities are equal i.e. the product of their mass and specific heats (*ms*) will be equal. Hence options (B) and (D) are correct.

Sol. 11 (C, D) In this case as the surface areas of the two cases are same, the mass of water is different so for sphere the mass is less then that of cube. As temperatures are equal the radiation rate of both will be same but for sphere due to less heat capacity it will cool faster.

Sol. 12 (B) As in the situation surface area of the bodies is not specified we cannot comment on total energy radiated by the bodies which is given by the area under the spectral intensity curves. If the areas of the two bodies are equal then option (B) can be correct.

Sol. 13 (A, B) At 45°C we use

$$\left.\frac{dQ}{dt}\right|_{less}=k(45-75)=12$$

at 20°C $$\left.\frac{dQ}{dt}\right|_{less}=k(20-15)=0.4\times 5=2\text{W}$$

$$\Rightarrow \quad k=\frac{12}{30}=0.4$$

hence option (A) and (B) are correct.

Sol. 14 (A, B) Here there must be some force providing the centripetal acceleration for circular motion but we are not concerned about it any option. As the body is sliding the kinetic friction on the body must be $\mu mg = 5$ N and it will act in tangential direction i.e. opposite to direction of velocity.

Sol. 15 (A, B, C) For all bodies we know experimentally high emissivity implies high absorptivity and if absorption is less then radiation will be more reflected hence options (A), (B) and (C) are correct.

Sol. 16 (A, B) As initially they are at same temperature their radiation rates will be equal and their absorption rate from surrounding will also be equal but as time passes, due to the difference in masses of the two their temperature will differ and rates will also be changed at later instants and due to this rate of fall of temperatures will also be different at later instants.

Sol. 17 (A, C) According the Wein's displacement law the wavelength corresponding to maximum spectral intensity is inversely proportional to the temperature so the frequency is directly proportional to the temperature as $\lambda = c/\nu$. Thus option (A) is correct. As total emitted energy is directly proportional to fourth power of absolute temperature option (C) is also correct.

Sol. 18 (A, D) By wein's displacement law we use

$$\lambda_m T = \text{constant}$$

$$\Rightarrow \quad \frac{\lambda_{m_A}}{\lambda_{m_B}} = \frac{T_B}{T_A}$$

$$\Rightarrow \quad \frac{T_A}{T_B} = \frac{\lambda_{m_B}}{\lambda_{m_A}} = \frac{800}{400} = 2$$

By Stefan's law, we use

$$\frac{E_A}{E_B} = \frac{A_A T_A^4}{A_B T_B^4} = \frac{4\pi r_A^2}{4\pi r_B^2}\left(\frac{T_A}{T_B}\right)^4 = 4$$

Sol. 19 (A, D) A cavity radiator is a sealed heated enclosure with a small opening which allows radiation to escape or enter and the radiation falling into the opening gets absorbed inside by multiple reflections and absorptions hence option (A) & correct and by prevost theory option (D) is also correct.

Sol. 20 (A, B) Integrating we have

$$H = \frac{KAd\theta}{dr} = K(2\pi rL)\frac{d\theta}{dr}$$

$$\int_{r_1}^{r_2} \frac{dr}{r} = \frac{2\pi KL}{H}\int_{\theta_1}^{\theta_2} d\theta$$

$$\Rightarrow \quad \frac{dQ}{dt} = H = \frac{2\pi KL(\theta_2 - \theta_1)}{In\left(\frac{r_2}{r_1}\right)} = 80\theta$$

$$\Rightarrow \quad \frac{dm}{dt}L = 80\pi$$

$$\Rightarrow \quad \frac{dm}{dt} = \frac{8\pi}{L} + \frac{80\pi}{80 \times 4200}$$

$$= \frac{\pi}{4200} \text{ Kg/s}$$

* * * * *

ANSWERS & SOLUTIONS

CONCEPTUAL MCQS Single Option Correct

1	(B)	2	(A)	3	(C)
4	(B)	5	(B)	6	(D)
7	(D)	8	(A)	9	(D)
10	(D)	11	(C)	12	(C)
13	(B)	14	(B)	15	(B)
16	(B)	17	(D)	18	(C)
19	(A)	20	(C)	21	(A)
22	(B)	23	(C)	24	(C)
25	(D)	26	(C)	27	(A)

NUMERICAL MCQS Single Option Correct

1	(C)	2	(C)	3	(B)
4	(C)	5	(B)	6	(A)
7	(D)	8	(C)	9	(B)
10	(C)	11	(B)	12	(C)
13	(B)	14	(C)	15	(C)
16	(C)	17	(A)	18	(D)
19	(C)	20	(A)	21	(A)
22	(C)	23	(D)	24	(A)
25	(A)	26	(A)	27	(B)
28	(B)	29	(A)	30	(C)
31	(D)	32	(A)	33	(A)
34	(C)	35	(D)	36	(A)
37	(C)	38	(C)	39	(C)
40	(C)	41	(C)	42	(B)
43	(C)	44	(D)	45	(A)
46	(A)	47	(C)	48	(A)
49	(B)	50	(A)	51	(B)
52	(C)	53	(B)	54	(C)
55	(A)	56	(B)	57	(A)
58	(B)	59	(C)	60	(B)
61	(B)	62	(C)	63	(B)
64	(D)	65	(B)	66	(B)
67	(B)	68	(B)	69	(B)
70	(D)				

ADVANCE MCQs One or More Option Correct

1	(A, C)	2	(A, B, C)	3	(C, D)
4	(A, B, C)	5	(B, C)	6	(B, C, D)
7	(A, B, C)	8	(All)	9	(B, C)
10	(A, B, C)	11	(B, C, D)	12	(A, B, C)
13	(A, C, D)	14	(A, C, D)	15	(All)
16	(A, C)	17	(A, B, C)	18	(C, D)
19	(A, D)	20	(B, C)	21	(B, C)
22	(All)	23	(A, C)	24	(B, C)
25	(B, D)	26	(All)	27	(B, D)
28	(A, D)	29	(B, C, D)	30	(A, D)
31	(A, C)	32	(C, D)	33	(A, D)

Solutions of PRACTICE EXERCISE 5.1

(i) For SHM

$$v_{max} = A\omega \qquad \ldots(1)$$

and acceleration at position y is given as

$$a = -\omega^2 y$$

Here we use at $y = 0.02$ m; $a = 0.06$ m/s^2

$$\Rightarrow \quad 0.06 = \omega^2 \times 0.02$$

$$\Rightarrow \quad \omega^2 = 3$$

$$\Rightarrow \quad \omega = \sqrt{3} = 1.732 \text{ rad/s}$$

from equation-(1) $\quad A = \dfrac{v_{max}}{\omega} = \dfrac{0.04}{1.732} = 2.31 \times 10^{-2}$ m

Thus time period is $\quad T = \dfrac{2\pi}{\omega} = \dfrac{2 \times 3.14}{1.732} = 3.625$ s

(ii) Given equation of SHM is

$$y = 0.5 \sin(2\pi f t)$$

man will feel weightless ness when $\omega^2 A = g$

$$\Rightarrow \quad \omega^2 = \frac{g}{A} = \frac{10}{0.5} = 20$$

$$\Rightarrow \quad \omega = 4.472 \text{ rad/s}$$

$$\Rightarrow \quad f = \frac{\omega}{2\pi} = 0.712 \text{ Hz}$$

(iii) (a) Equation given is

$$x = a \sin^2\left(\omega t - \frac{\pi}{4}\right)$$

rearranging the equation

$$x = a\left(\frac{1 - \cos(2\omega t - \pi/2)}{2}\right)$$

$$\Rightarrow \quad x = \frac{a}{2} - \frac{a}{2}\cos(2\omega t - \pi/2) \qquad \ldots(1)$$

from equation-(1) the amplitude of SHM is $a/2$ and time period is $\dfrac{\pi}{\omega}$.

Plot of equation-(1) can be seen in figure blow with mean position $x = \dfrac{a}{2}$

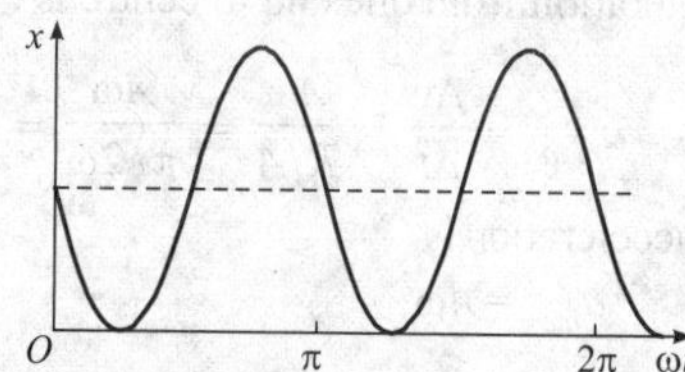

(b) Differentiating equation-(1) gives

$$v = \frac{a}{2} \times 2\omega \sin\left(2\omega t - \frac{\pi}{2}\right)$$

$$= a\omega \sin\left(2\omega t - \frac{\pi}{2}\right)$$

$$\Rightarrow \quad v = a\omega\sqrt{1 - \cos^2(2\omega t - \pi/2)}$$

$$= a\omega\sqrt{1-\frac{\left(\frac{a}{2}-x\right)^2}{\left(\frac{a}{2}\right)^2}}$$

$$\Rightarrow \qquad v_x = 2\omega\sqrt{\left(\frac{a}{2}\right)^2-\left(\frac{a}{2}-x\right)^2}$$

$$\Rightarrow \qquad v_x^2 = 4\omega^2 x(a-x)$$

rearranging terms we get

$$\left(\frac{v_x}{2\omega}\right)^2+\left(\frac{a}{2}-x\right)^2=\left(\frac{a}{2}\right)^2$$

$$\frac{v_x^2}{(a\omega)^2}+\left(\frac{\frac{a}{2}-x}{\frac{a}{2}}\right)^2=1 \qquad \ldots(2)$$

equation (2) is an equation of ellipse. Plotted as shown in figure below

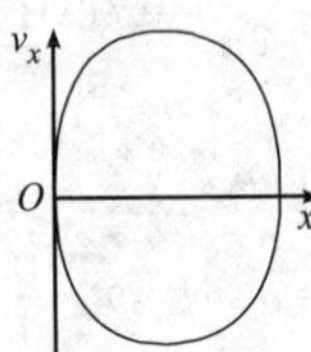

(iv) (a) Time taken in SHM from one end to other is

$$\Delta t = \frac{T}{2} = \frac{\pi}{\omega}$$

mean velocity is $v_{mean} = \frac{\Delta s}{\Delta t} = \frac{2A}{\pi/\omega} = \frac{2A\omega}{\pi}$

maximum velocity in SHM is

$$v_{max} = A\omega$$

$$\frac{v_{mean}}{v_{max}} = \frac{2}{\pi}$$

(b) Mean acceleration from one end to centre is

$$a_{mean} = \frac{\Delta v}{\Delta t} = \frac{A\omega}{T/4} = \frac{A\omega}{\pi/2\omega} = \frac{2A\omega^2}{\pi}$$

and maximum acceleration is

$$a_{max} = A\omega^2$$

Thus $\quad \frac{a_{mean}}{a_{max}} = \frac{2}{\pi}$

(v) Maximum speed of particle in SHM is

$$v_{max} = A\omega$$

mean speed in SHM is

$$v_{mean} = \frac{4A}{T} = \frac{2A\omega}{\pi} = \frac{2v_{max}}{\pi}$$

(vi) SHM equation is

$$x = 4\sin\omega t + 3\sin(\omega t + 63°)$$

$$\Rightarrow \qquad x = 4\sin\omega t + 3\sin\omega t\left(\frac{3}{5}\right) + 3\cos\omega t\left(\frac{4}{5}\right)$$

$$\Rightarrow \qquad x = \frac{29}{5}\sin\omega t + \frac{12}{5}\cos\omega t$$

we can rewrite this equation as

$$x = A\sin(\omega t + \theta)$$

where $\quad A = \sqrt{\left(\frac{29}{5}\right)^2+\left(\frac{12}{5}\right)^2}$

$$= \frac{1}{5}\sqrt{841+144} = 6.277 \text{ cm}$$

(vii) In SHM we use

$$a = -\omega^2 x$$

from graph $\quad \omega^2 = \tan 45° = 1$

$$\Rightarrow \qquad \omega = 1$$

$$\Rightarrow \qquad T = \frac{2\pi}{\omega} = 2\pi = 6.28 \text{ s}$$

Solutions of PRACTICE EXERCISE 5.2

(i) For a spring block system angular frequency is given as

$$\omega = \sqrt{\frac{k}{m}} = 20\pi$$

$$\Rightarrow \qquad \frac{k}{m} = (20\pi)^2$$

If A is oscillation amplitude, here we use

$$mg = kA$$

$$\Rightarrow \qquad A = \frac{mg}{k} = \frac{g}{(20\pi)^2}$$

maximum speed is

$$v_{max} = A\omega = \frac{g}{(20\pi)^2}\times(20\pi) = \frac{1}{2\pi} \text{ m/s}$$

(ii) At equilibrium if spring extension is h we use

$$mg = kh$$

after displacing the block down by x spring further stretches by $\frac{x}{2}$ so its equation of motion is given as

$$T - mg = ma$$

$$\frac{k\left(h+\frac{x}{2}\right)}{2} - mg = ma$$

$$\Rightarrow \qquad \frac{kh}{2}+\frac{kx}{4} - mg = ma$$

$$\Rightarrow \qquad a = \frac{k}{4m}x$$

for restoring acceleration we write it as

$$a = -\frac{k}{4m}x$$

Comparing with $a = -\omega^2 x$

we get $\omega = \sqrt{\frac{k}{4m}}$

Time period is $T = \frac{2\pi}{\omega} = 2\pi\sqrt{\frac{4m}{k}}$

$$= 2 \times 3.14\sqrt{\frac{4 \times 1}{5000}}$$

$$= 0.1776 \text{ s}$$

(iii) Maximum tension is at lowest position given as

$$T_{max} = mg + \frac{mv_{max}^2}{l} \quad \dots(1)$$

maximum tension is at extreme position given as

$$T_{rim} = mg \cos \theta_0 \quad \dots(2)$$

we use $mg + \frac{mv_{max}^2}{l} = 2mg \cos \theta_0$

and we use $v_{max} = \sqrt{2gl(1-\cos\theta_0)}$

$\Rightarrow \quad mg + 2mg(1 - \cos \theta_0) = 2mg \cos \theta_0$

$\Rightarrow \quad \cos \theta_0 = \frac{3}{4}$

$\Rightarrow \quad \theta_0 = \cos^{-1}\left(\frac{3}{4}\right)$

(iv) In the given situation when mass is displaced in either direction, restoring force on it is given as

$$(k_1 + k_2)x = ma$$

$\Rightarrow \quad a = \left(\frac{k_1 + k_2}{m}\right)x$

for restoring nature $a = -\left(\frac{k_1 + k_2}{m}\right)x$

comparing with $a = -\omega^2 x$

we get $\omega = \sqrt{\frac{k_1 + k_2}{m}}$

Thus time period is $T = \frac{2\pi}{\omega} = 2\pi\sqrt{\frac{m}{k_1 + k_2}}$

(v) In given system we can consider the two springs in series combination of which equivalent force constant is given as

$$k_{eq} = \frac{k_1 k_2}{k_1 + k_2}$$

hence time period of SHM of body is

$$T = 2\pi\sqrt{\frac{m}{k_{eq}}}$$

$$= 2\pi\sqrt{\frac{m(k_1 + k_2)}{k_1 k_2}}$$

(vi) For equilibrium of T-shaped rod, if h is initial elongation in spring, we balance the torque about point O as

$$\frac{2Mg}{3} \times a + \frac{Mg}{3} \times 2a = kha$$

$$4Mg = 3kh \quad \dots(1)$$

On slightly displacing the rod by θ we use

$$k(h + a\theta).a - \frac{4Mg}{3}a$$

$$= \left[\frac{\left(\frac{2M}{3}\right)(2a)^2}{3} + \frac{\left(\frac{M}{3}\right)a^2}{12} + \left(\frac{M}{3}\right)(2a)^2\right] \cdot \alpha$$

$\Rightarrow \quad ka^2\theta = \left(\frac{8}{9} + \frac{1}{36} + \frac{4}{3}\right)Ma^2 \cdot \alpha$

$\Rightarrow \quad \alpha = \frac{4k}{9M} \cdot \theta$

Due to restoring tendency we write

$$\alpha = -\frac{4k}{9M}\theta$$

Comparing with $\alpha = -\omega^2\theta$

we get $\omega = \sqrt{\frac{4k}{9M}}$

Thus time period is

$$T = \frac{2\pi}{\omega} = 3\pi\sqrt{\frac{M}{k}}.$$

(vii) In equilibrium as cylinder is submerged at a depth $\frac{h}{2}$ and if spring elongation is x_0 we use

$$kx_0 + \frac{h}{2}S\rho g = Mg \quad \dots(1)$$

if cylinder is displacement down further by x and released, its equation of motion will be

$$k(x_0 + x) + \left(\frac{h}{2} + x\right) S\rho g - Mg = Ma$$

$\Rightarrow \quad a = \frac{k + S\rho g}{M}x$

for restoring acceleration, we use

$$a = -\frac{k + S\rho g}{M} \cdot x$$

Comparing with $a = -\omega^2 x$

we get $\omega = \sqrt{\dfrac{k+\pi r^2\rho g}{M}}$ [As base area $S = \pi r^2$]

Thus time period is

$$T = \frac{2\pi}{\omega} = 2\pi\sqrt{\frac{M}{k+\pi r^2\rho g}}$$

(viii) For the elastic wire its equivalent spring constant is given as

$$k = \frac{YA}{l}$$

Thus frequency of oscillations we use

$$f = \frac{1}{2\pi}\sqrt{\frac{k}{m}} = \frac{1}{2\pi}\sqrt{\frac{YA}{ml}}$$

(ix) At equilibrium if gas pressure is P_{go} we use

$$P_{go} = \frac{Mg}{A} + P_0$$

If piston is displaced down by a distance x, volume becomes

$$V = V_0 - Ax$$

As system is isolated, gas pressure P is given as

$$P(V_0 - Ax)^\gamma = P_{go}V_0^\gamma$$

$$\Rightarrow \quad P = \frac{P_{go}V_0^\gamma}{(V_0 - Ax)^\gamma}$$

$$= P_{go}\left(1 - \frac{Ax}{V_0}\right)^{-\gamma} = P_{go}\left(1 + \frac{\gamma Ax}{V_0}\right)$$

For motion of piston we use

$$PA - Mg - P_0A = Ma$$

$$\Rightarrow \quad P_{go}\left(1 - \frac{\gamma Ax}{V_0}\right)A - Mg - P_0A = Ma$$

$$\Rightarrow \quad a = \frac{\gamma A^2 P_{go}}{MV_0}\cdot x = \frac{\gamma A^2\left(\frac{Mg}{A} + P_0\right)}{MV_0}x$$

For restoring acceleration we use

$$a = -\frac{\gamma A^2\left(\frac{Mg}{A} + P_0\right)}{MV_0}\cdot x$$

This shows that piston executes SHM and comparing with

$$a = -\omega^2 x$$

we get $\omega = \sqrt{\dfrac{\gamma A^2\left(\frac{Mg}{A} + P_0\right)}{MV_0}}$

frequency $f = \dfrac{\omega}{2\pi} = \dfrac{1}{2\pi}\sqrt{\dfrac{\gamma A^2\left(\frac{Mg}{A} + P_0\right)}{MV_0}}$

(x) Due to elasticity in rod it sags by weight of load. If its shear modulus of elasticity is η for equilibrium of system we use

$$\eta = \frac{F/A}{S/l}$$

[where A is area of cross section and is its length]

$$\Rightarrow \quad \frac{Mg}{A} = \frac{\eta S}{l} \quad \ldots(1)$$

If load is depressed by x we use

$$F - Mg = Ma \quad \ldots(2)$$

where $\eta = \dfrac{F/A}{(\delta + x)/l}$

$$\Rightarrow \quad F = \frac{\eta A}{l}(\delta + x)$$

from (2) we use

$$\frac{\eta A}{l}(\delta + x) - Mg = Ma$$

$$\Rightarrow \quad a = \frac{\eta A}{lM}\cdot x$$

From (1) we use $a = \dfrac{g}{\delta}\cdot x$

for restoring acceleration

$$a = -\frac{g}{\delta}x$$

This shows that load executes SHM.

Comparing with

$$a = -\omega^2 x$$

we get $\omega = \sqrt{\dfrac{g}{\delta}}$

$\Rightarrow$ frequency $f = \dfrac{\omega}{2\pi} = \dfrac{1}{2\pi}\sqrt{\dfrac{10}{2.8\times10^{-2}}} = 3\text{ Hz}$

(xi) If mercury is displaced in tube by a distance x, as shown in figure, the excess pressure done to level difference is

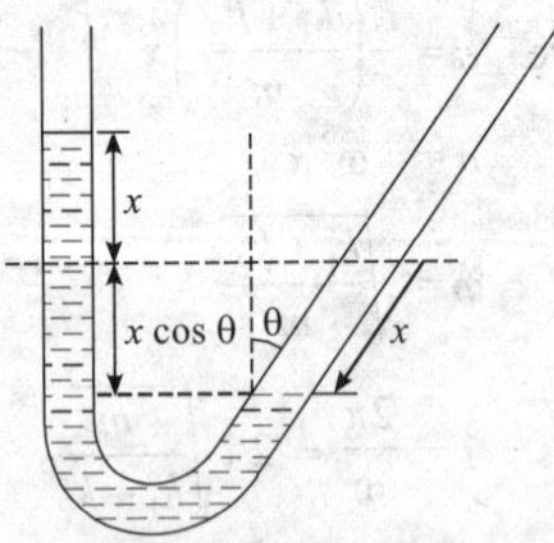

$$\Delta P = (x + x\cos\theta)\rho g$$

Thus restoring force on mercury is given as

$$F_R = \Delta P_S = ma$$

for restoring acceleration we use

$$a = -\frac{x\rho g S}{m}(1 + \cos\theta)$$

Comparing with $a=-\omega^2 x$

we get $\omega=\sqrt{\frac{\rho g S}{m}(1+\cos\theta)}$

$\Rightarrow$ time period $T=\frac{2\pi}{\omega}=2\pi\sqrt{\frac{m}{S\rho g(1+\cos\theta)}}$

Solutions of PRACTICE EXERCISE 5.3

(i) (a) Angular frequency ω we use from figure

$$v_0=A\omega \qquad \left[\text{where } \omega=\frac{\pi}{3}\text{ rad/s}\right]$$

$$\alpha=\omega(1)$$

$$0.25=A\omega\cos(\alpha) \qquad \ldots(1)$$

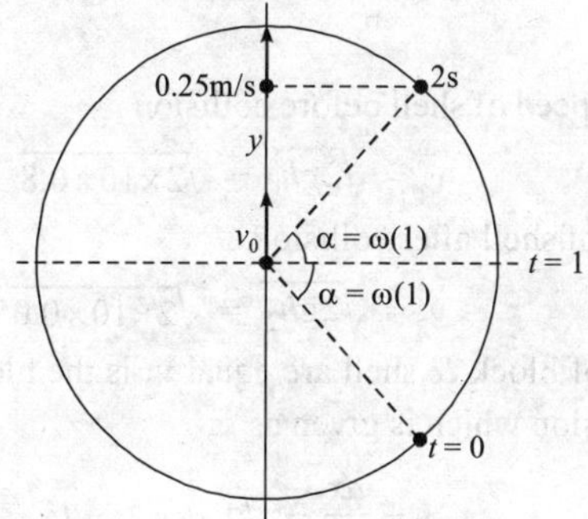

Here initial phase

$$\alpha=-\omega=-\frac{\pi}{3}$$

and from equation (1)

$$0.25=A\left(\frac{\pi}{3}\right)\left(\frac{1}{2}\right)$$

$$\Rightarrow \qquad A=\frac{3}{2\pi}m$$

(b) Velocity at $t=6s$ is

$$v=A\omega\cos(5\omega)$$

$$=\frac{3}{2\pi}\times\frac{\pi}{3}\cos\left(\frac{5\pi}{3}\right)$$

$$=0.5\times0.5=0.25\text{ m/s}$$

(ii) During motion the block oscillates as spring block system while in contact with both left and right springs for half oscillations so the time it is in contact with either spring is given by sum of half time period of both springs.

$$\Delta t_1=\pi\sqrt{\frac{m}{k_1}}+\pi\sqrt{\frac{m}{k_2}}$$

Between point C and D it moves uniformly so for one oscillation its motion time is

$$\Delta t_2=\frac{2d}{v}$$

Total period $T=\Delta t_1+\Delta t_2$

$$=\pi\left(\sqrt{\frac{m}{k_1}}+\sqrt{\frac{m}{k_2}}\right)+\frac{2d}{v}$$

(iii) (a)

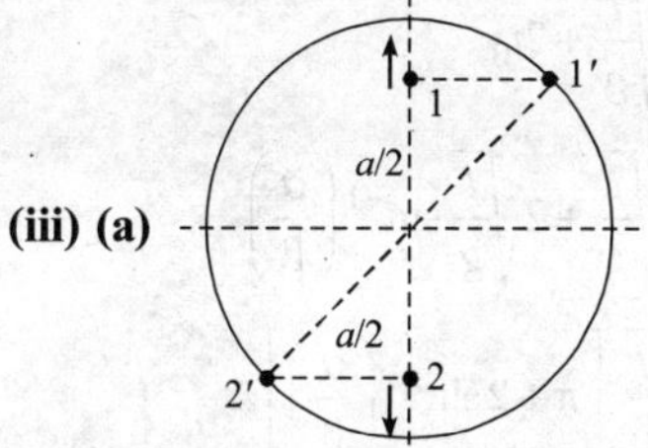

Here we can see from figure that $\phi=\pi$

(b)

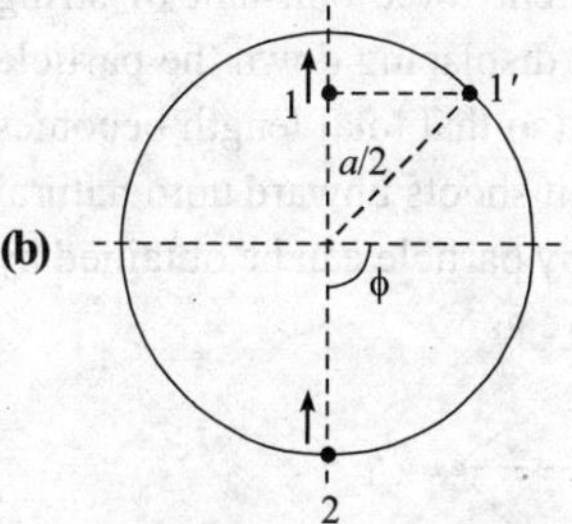

from figure $\phi=\frac{\pi}{2}+\frac{\pi}{6}=\frac{2\pi}{3}$

(c)

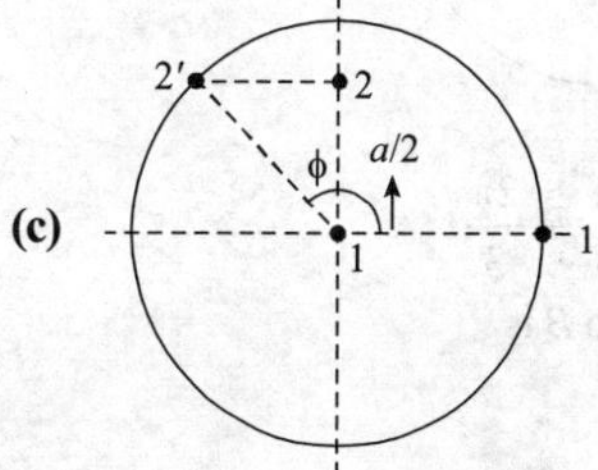

from figure $\phi=\frac{\pi}{2}+\frac{\pi}{3}=\frac{5\pi}{6}$

(d)

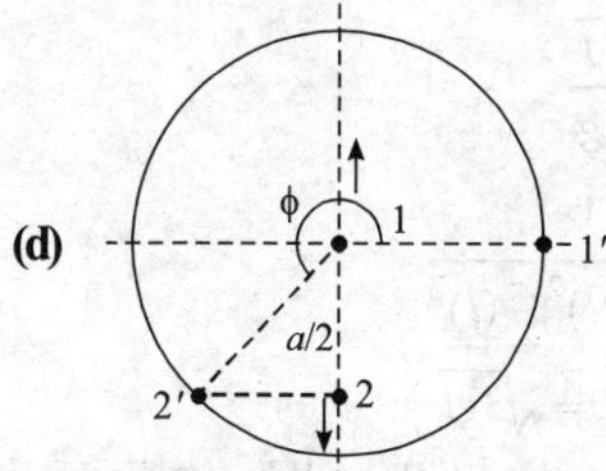

from figure $\phi=\pi+\frac{\pi}{6}=\frac{7\pi}{6}$

(iv) Time required to move from equilibrium position to wall for bob is given as

$$\alpha=\beta\sin\left(\sqrt{\frac{g}{l}}\cdot t_0\right)$$

$$\Rightarrow \qquad t_0 = \sqrt{\frac{l}{g}}\left[\sin^{-1}\left(\frac{\alpha}{\beta}\right)\right]$$

As collision is elastic ball will return at same speed so total oscillation period is

$$T = \pi\sqrt{\frac{l}{g}} + 2t_0$$

$$= \pi\sqrt{\frac{l}{g}} + 2\sqrt{\frac{l}{g}}\sin^{-1}\left(\frac{\alpha}{\beta}\right)$$

$$= \sqrt{\frac{l}{g}}\left[\pi + 2\sin^{-1}\left(\frac{\alpha}{\beta}\right)\right]$$

(v) It we consider k as equivalent force constant of string then at equilibrium we use after displacing down the particle $Mg = k(l)$ further by distance $2l$ (so that total length becomes $4l$) when we release the particle it shoots upward upto natural length of spring and time taken by particle can be obtained by phase diagram as shown in figure as

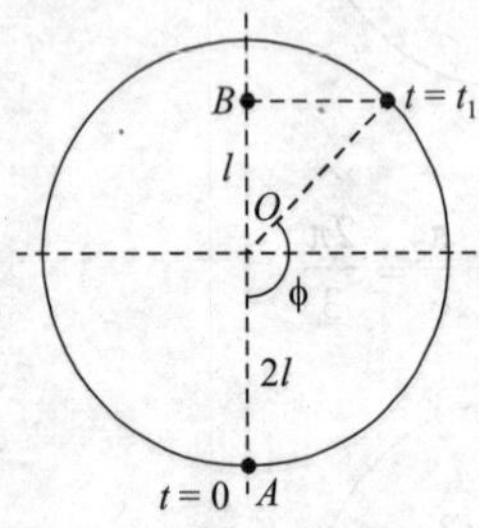

Here $\qquad \phi = \frac{\pi}{2} + \frac{\pi}{6} = \frac{2\pi}{3}$

Time for particle to go from A to B is

$$t_1 = \frac{\phi}{\omega}$$

where $\qquad \omega = \sqrt{\frac{k}{m}} = \sqrt{\frac{g}{l}}$

$$\Rightarrow \qquad t_1 = \frac{2\pi}{3}\sqrt{\frac{l}{g}}$$

At position B speed of particle is

$$v = \omega\sqrt{(2l)^2 - (l)^2}$$

$$= \sqrt{3}\omega l = \sqrt{3gl}$$

After point B string will slack and particle will be in free fall motion so time taken by it to go up and come back to point B is given as

$$t_2 = \frac{2\sqrt{3gl}}{g} = 2\sqrt{3}\sqrt{\frac{l}{g}}$$

Thus total time after which particle will come back to point A is

$$T = 2t_1 + t_2 = \sqrt{\frac{l}{g}}\left(\frac{4\pi}{3} + 2\sqrt{3}\right)$$

(vi) As shown in figure the phase difference between SHMs of A and B is given as

$$\phi = 2\sin^{-1}\left(\frac{\sqrt{3}}{2}\right) = 2 \times \frac{\pi}{3} = \frac{2\pi}{3}$$

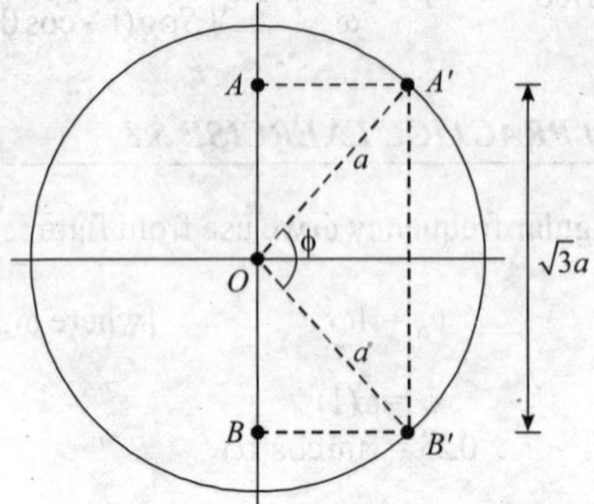

(vii) Initial speed of shell before collision

$$v_1 = \sqrt{2gh_1} = \sqrt{2 \times 10 \times 0.8} = 4 \text{ m/s}$$

Find speed of shell after collision

$$v_2 = \sqrt{2gh_2} = \sqrt{2 \times 10 \times 0.05} = 1 \text{ m/s}$$

As masses of block & shell are equal v_2 is the block velocity before collision which is given as

$$v = \frac{dx}{dt} = \sqrt{2}\cos 2t = 1$$

$$\Rightarrow \qquad \cos 2t = \frac{1}{\sqrt{2}}$$

$$\Rightarrow \qquad 2t = \frac{\pi}{4} \text{ or } \frac{7\pi}{4}$$

$$\Rightarrow \qquad t = \frac{\pi}{8} \text{ or } \frac{7\pi}{8}$$

position at $t = \frac{\pi}{8}$ is

$$x = 2 + \frac{1}{\sqrt{2}}\sin\left(\frac{\pi}{4}\right) = 2 + \frac{1}{2} = 2.5 \text{ m}$$

or at $t = \frac{7\pi}{8}$

$$x = 2 + \frac{1}{\sqrt{2}}\sin\left(\frac{7\pi}{8}\right) = 2 - \frac{1}{2} = 1.5 \text{ m}$$

(viii) We can use $\quad x = A\sin\omega$

$$y = A\sin 2\omega$$

$$z = A\sin 3\omega$$

we use $\qquad x + z = A(\sin\omega + \sin 3\omega)$

$$\Rightarrow \qquad x + z = 2A\sin 2\omega\cos\omega$$

$$\Rightarrow \qquad x + z = 2y\cos\omega$$

$$\Rightarrow \qquad \omega = \cos^{-1}\left(\frac{x+z}{2y}\right)$$

$$\Rightarrow \quad T = \frac{2\pi}{\omega} = \frac{2\pi}{\cos^{-1}\left(\frac{x+z}{2y}\right)}$$

(ix) From figure we use

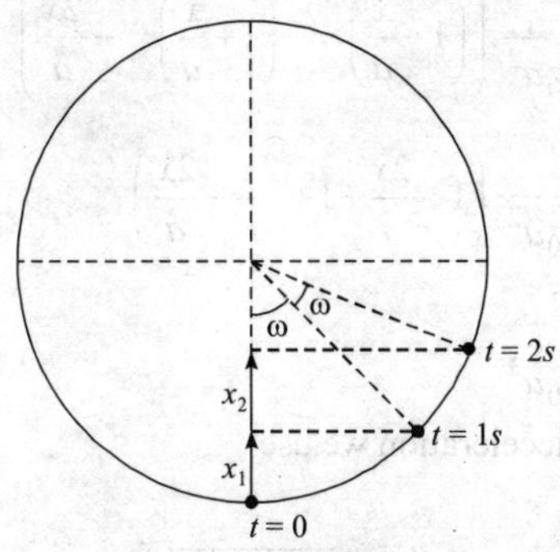

$$x_1 = A(1 - \cos\omega) \quad \ldots(1)$$

$$x_1 + x_2 = A(1 - \cos 2\omega) \quad \ldots(2)$$

from (1) $\quad \cos\omega = \frac{A - x_1}{A}$

from (2) $\quad x_1 + x_2 = 2A\sin^2\omega$

$$\Rightarrow \quad \sin^2\omega = \frac{x_1 + x_2}{2A}$$

we use

$$\sin^2\omega + \cos^2\omega = \frac{x_1 + x_2}{2A} + \left(\frac{A - x_1}{A}\right)^2 = 1$$

$$\Rightarrow \quad Ax_1 + Ax_2 + 2A^2 + 2x_1^2 - 4Ax_1 = 2A^2$$

$$\Rightarrow \quad A = \frac{2x_1^2}{3x_1 - x_2}$$

(x) We use $\quad v = \omega\sqrt{A^2 - x^2}$

at $x = 4$ cm; $v = 13$ cm/s

$$\Rightarrow \quad 13 = \omega\sqrt{A^2 - 16} \quad \ldots(1)$$

and at $x = 5$ cm; $v = 5$ cm/s

$$\Rightarrow \quad 5 = \omega\sqrt{A^2 - 25} \quad \ldots(2)$$

$\frac{(1)}{(2)}$ gives

$$\left(\frac{13}{5}\right)^2 = \frac{A^2 - 16}{A^2 - 25}$$

$$\Rightarrow \quad 169A^2 - 4225 = 5A^2 - 80$$

$$\Rightarrow \quad 164A^2 = 4145$$

$$\Rightarrow \quad A^2 = 25.2$$

$$\Rightarrow \quad A = 5.02 \text{ cm}$$

from (1)

$$13 = \omega\sqrt{A^2 - 16}$$

$$13 = \omega\sqrt{25.274 - 16}$$

$$\Rightarrow \quad \omega = \frac{13}{3.312} = 3.925 \text{ rad/s}$$

$$\Rightarrow \quad T = \frac{2\pi}{\omega} = \frac{6.28}{3.925} = 1.6 \text{ s}$$

(xi) Time period of particle is

$$T = \frac{2\pi}{\omega} = 2 \text{ s}$$

So in 2.5 s particle covers distance $5A$

Here maximum speed is $35 = A\omega$

$$\Rightarrow \quad A = \frac{35}{\omega} = \frac{35}{3.14} = 11.14 \text{ cm}$$

In remaining 0.3 sec particle covers is

$$S = 5A + x_0 = 55.7 + 4.59$$

$$= 60.29 \text{ cm}$$

Solutions of PRACTICE EXERCISE 5.4

(i) Total energy of particle is

$$\frac{1}{2}m\omega^2A^2 = 79.5$$

$$\Rightarrow \quad A\omega = \sqrt{\frac{79.5 \times 2}{4}} = 6.304 \quad \ldots(1)$$

we use $\quad v^2 = \omega^2A^2 - \omega^2x^2$

$$\Rightarrow \quad (3.2)^2 = (6.304)^2 - \omega^2(0.043)^2$$

$$\Rightarrow \quad \omega^2 = \frac{39.75 - 10.24}{(0.043)^2} = 15960$$

$$\Rightarrow \quad \omega = 126.33 \text{ rad/s}$$

from (1) we use $\quad A = \frac{6.304}{126.33} = 0.05 \text{ m}$

Initial phase of SHM can be calculated from phase diagram shown in figure so equation of SHM is

$$x = 0.05\sin(126.33t + 2.1) \text{ m}$$

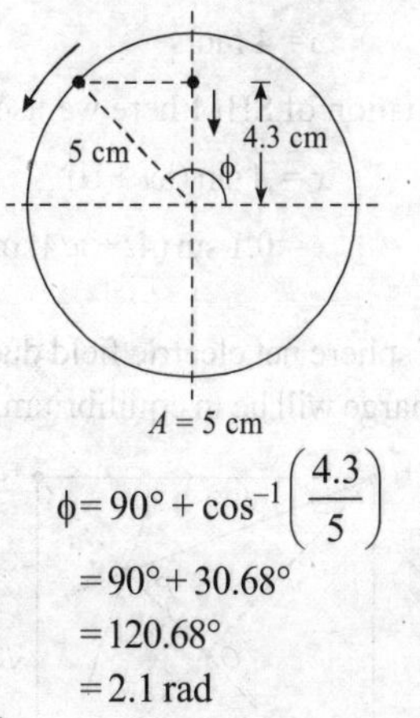

$$\phi = 90^\circ + \cos^{-1}\left(\frac{4.3}{5}\right)$$

$$= 90^\circ + 30.68^\circ$$

$$= 120.68^\circ$$

$$= 2.1 \text{ rad}$$

Oscillation period is

$$T = \frac{2\pi}{\omega} = \frac{6.28}{126.33} = 0.05 \text{ s}$$

Thus number of oscillation in 0.4 s are

$$N=\frac{0.4}{0.05}=8$$

Thus total distance travelled by particle is

$$8\times 4A=32A=32\times 0.05=1.6\text{ m}$$

(ii) Angular frequency of rod as compound pendulum is

$$\omega=\sqrt{\frac{mgl}{I}}=\sqrt{\frac{mg\left(\frac{l}{2}\right)}{\frac{ml^2}{3}}}=\sqrt{\frac{3g}{2l}}$$

If Rods angular amplitude is ϕ_0 we use

$$\dot{\theta}_0=\omega\sqrt{\phi_0^2-\theta_0^2}$$

$$\Rightarrow\qquad \phi_0^2=\frac{\dot{\theta}_0^2}{\omega^2}+\theta_0^2$$

Mean kinetic energy of rod is given as

$$<KE>=\frac{1}{4}I\omega^2\phi_0^2$$

$$=\frac{1}{4}\left(\frac{ml^2}{3}\right)\left(\frac{3g}{2l}\right)\left(\frac{\dot{\theta}_0^2(x)}{3g}+\theta_0^2\right)$$

$$=\frac{1}{8}mgl\theta_0^2+\frac{1}{12}ml^2\dot{\theta}_0^2$$

(iii) At mean position, KE is maximum so we use

$$\frac{1}{2}m\omega^2A^2=8\times10^{-3}$$

$$\Rightarrow\qquad \frac{1}{2}\times0.1\times\omega^2\times(0.1)^2=8\times10^{-3}$$

$$\Rightarrow\qquad \omega^2=16$$

$$\Rightarrow\qquad \omega=4\text{ rad/s}$$

Thus general equation of SHM here we use

$$x=A\sin(\omega t+\alpha)$$

$$\Rightarrow\qquad x=0.1\sin(4t+\pi/4)\text{ m}$$

(iv) At centre of sphere net electric field due to charges is zero hence the fifth charge will be in equilibrium.

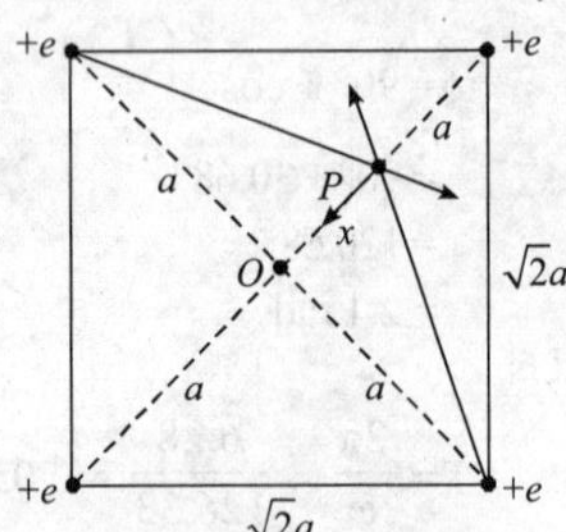

As shown in figure we find restoring force on central charge at position P.

$$F_R=\frac{1}{4\pi\varepsilon_0}\left(\frac{e^2}{(a-x)^2}-\frac{e^2}{(a+x)^2}-\frac{2e^2x}{(x^2+a^2)^{3/2}}\right)$$

$$\Rightarrow\qquad F_R=\frac{e^2}{4\pi\varepsilon_0a^2}\left(\left(1-\frac{x}{a}\right)^{-2}-\left(1+\frac{x}{a}\right)^{-2}-\frac{2x}{a}\right)$$

$$=\frac{e^2}{4\pi\varepsilon_0a^2}\left(1+\frac{2x}{a}-1+\frac{2x}{a}-\frac{2x}{a}\right)$$

$$F_R=\frac{e^2}{2\pi\varepsilon_0a^3}\cdot x$$

for restoring acceleration we use

$$a=-\frac{e^2}{2\pi\varepsilon_0ma^3}\cdot x$$

Comparing with $\qquad a=-\omega^2x$

we get $\qquad \omega=\sqrt{\frac{e^2}{2\pi\varepsilon_0ma^3}}$

$\Rightarrow$ time period $\qquad T=\frac{2\pi}{\omega}=2\pi\sqrt{\frac{2\pi\varepsilon_0ma^3}{e^2}}$

(v) For equilibrium of bar we consider the initial extensions in springs are h_1 and h_2 then we use

$$k_1h_1a=k_2h_2b \qquad \ldots(1)$$

and $\qquad k_2h_2=mg \qquad \ldots(2)$

If mass m is displaced down by x we consider further extensions in springs are x_1 and x_2 respectively so as bar is height we use

$$k_1(h_1+x_1)a=k_2(h_2+x_2)b$$

and by geometry we have

$$\left(\frac{x_1}{a}\right)b+x_2=x$$

$$\Rightarrow\qquad \frac{b}{a}\left(\frac{k_2b}{k_1a}\right)x_1+x_2=x$$

$$\Rightarrow\qquad x_2=\frac{x}{\frac{k_2b^2}{k_1a^2}+1}$$

we use equation of motion of mass as

$$k_2x_2-mg=ma$$

for restoring acceleration we use

$$a=-\frac{k_2}{m\left(\frac{k_2b^2}{k_1a^2}+1\right)}x+g$$

Comparing with $\qquad a=-\omega^2x+C$

we get $\omega = \sqrt{\dfrac{k_1 k_2}{m\left(k_2\left(\dfrac{b^2}{a^2}\right)+k_1\right)}}$

$\Rightarrow$ Time period $T = \dfrac{2\pi}{\omega} = 2\pi\sqrt{\dfrac{m}{k_1 k_2}\left(k_2\left(\dfrac{b^2}{a^2}\right)+k_1\right)}$

(vi) At a displacement θ from initial position, restoring torque is given as

$$\tau_R = mg(l\theta) + 2K(b\theta)(b)$$

Restoring angular acceleration is given as

$$\alpha = -\frac{\tau_R}{I} = -\frac{(Mgl + 2Kb^2)}{ml^2}\cdot\theta$$

Comparing with $\alpha = -\omega^2\theta$

we get $\omega = \sqrt{\dfrac{mgl + 2Kb^2}{ml^2}}$

$\Rightarrow$ Time period

$$T = \frac{2\pi}{\omega} = 2\pi\sqrt{\frac{ml^2}{mgl + 2Kb^2}}$$

(vii) If at equilibrium spring elongation is h, we use

$$kh(b) = mg(a) \qquad \ldots(1)$$

If mass is displaced down by x then its equation of motion is given as

$$T - mg = ma_1 \qquad \ldots(2)$$

and for massless rod

$$T(a) = k\left(h + x\left(\frac{b}{a}\right)\right)(b) \qquad \ldots(3)$$

from (1) and (2) we use

$$\frac{k\left(h + \dfrac{xb}{a}\right)b}{a} - mg = ma_1$$

$$\Rightarrow \qquad a_1 = \frac{kb^2}{ma^2}x$$

for restoring tendency we use

$$a_1 = -\frac{kb^2}{ma^2}x$$

Comparing with

$$a_1 = -\omega^2 x$$

we get $\omega = \sqrt{\dfrac{k}{m}}\cdot\dfrac{b}{a}$

$\Rightarrow$ Time period $T = \dfrac{2\pi}{\omega} = \dfrac{2\pi a}{b}\sqrt{\dfrac{m}{k}}$

(viii) At position $x = \dfrac{\sqrt{3}}{2}A$, particle velocity is

$$v = \omega\sqrt{A^2 - \frac{3A^2}{4}} = \frac{\omega A}{2}$$

Using impulse momentum equation we have

$$\frac{m\omega A}{2} + m\omega A = mv_f$$

$$\Rightarrow \qquad v_f = \frac{3}{2}A\omega$$

if new amplitude is A' we use

$$v_f = \omega\sqrt{A'^2 - x^2}$$

$$\frac{3}{2}A\omega = \omega\sqrt{A'^2 - \frac{3}{4}A^2}$$

$$\Rightarrow \qquad A'^2 = \left(\frac{9}{4} + \frac{3}{4}\right)A^2$$

$$\Rightarrow \qquad A' = \sqrt{3}A$$

Solutions of PRACTICE EXERCISE 5.5

(i) If mass m is displaced to right by x and due to this extensions in springs are x_1 and x_2 respectively, we use

$$k_1 x_1(c) = k_2 x_2(b + c)$$

and by geometry we have

$$\left(\frac{x_1}{c}\right)(b + c) + x_2 = x$$

$$\Rightarrow \qquad \frac{k_2 x_2 (b + c)^2}{k_1 c^2} + x^2 = x$$

$$\Rightarrow \qquad x_2 = \frac{x}{1 + \dfrac{k_2}{k_1}\left(\dfrac{b + c}{c}\right)^2}$$

Restoring force on block is

$$F_R = k_2 x_2 = k_2\left(\frac{x}{1 + \dfrac{k_2}{k_1}\left(\dfrac{b + c}{c}\right)^2}\right)$$

restoring acceleration is given as

$$a = -\frac{F_R}{m} = -\frac{k_2}{m\left(1 + \dfrac{k_2}{k_1}\left(\dfrac{b + c}{c}\right)^2\right)}\cdot x$$

Comparing with $a = -\omega^2 x$

we get $\omega = \sqrt{\dfrac{k_2 k_1 c^2}{m(k_1 c^2 + k_2 (b + c)^2)}}$

(ii) After displacement of rod by a small angle θ we use restoring torque on it is given as

$$\tau_R = mg(l\theta) + k(l\theta).l$$

Restoring angular acceleration is given as

$$\alpha = -\frac{\tau_R}{I} = -\frac{(mgL + Rl^2)}{ml^2}\theta$$

This verifies that system executes SHM and comparing with

$$\alpha = -\omega^2\theta$$

we get $\omega = \sqrt{\dfrac{mgL + kl^2}{mL^2}}$

⇒ Time period $T = \dfrac{2\pi}{\omega} = 2\pi\sqrt{\dfrac{mL^2}{mgL + kl^2}}$

(iii) In equilibrium if spring extension is h, we use

$$Mg + 2mg = kh \quad \ldots(1)$$

After displacing mass m down by x its equation of motion will be

$$T_1 - mg = ma \quad \ldots(1)$$

for pulley we write

$$k(h + x/2) - T_1 - T_2 - Mg = Ma/2 \quad \ldots(2)$$

and $(T_2 - T_1)r' = \dfrac{1}{2}Mr^2\left(\dfrac{a}{2r}\right)$

from equation-(1)

$$T_2 = \frac{Ma}{4} + ma + mg$$

from equation-(2)

$$kh + k\frac{x}{2} - ma - mg - \frac{Ma}{4} - ma - mg - Mg = \frac{Ma}{2}$$

$$\Rightarrow \quad a = \frac{\frac{kx}{2}}{2m + \frac{3}{4}M}$$

for restoring tendency we use

$$a = -\left(\frac{k}{4m + \frac{3}{2}M}\right)x$$

Comparing with $a = -\omega^2 x$

we get $\omega = \sqrt{\dfrac{k}{4m + \frac{3}{2}M}}$

(iv) In figure $OC = \dfrac{4R}{3\pi} = r$

at a displacement θ, restoring torque on half cylinder is given as

$$\tau_R = Wr\theta$$

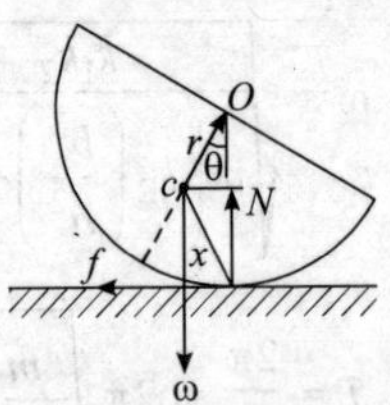

restoring angular acceleration is given as

$$\alpha = -\frac{\tau_R}{I} = -\frac{Wr}{\left(\frac{3}{2} - \frac{8}{3\pi}\right)\frac{W}{g}R^2}\theta$$

$$\alpha = -\frac{\left(\frac{4R}{3\pi}\right)g}{\left(\frac{9\pi - 16}{6\pi}\right)R^2}\theta$$

$$\alpha = -\frac{8}{9\pi - 16}\cdot\frac{g}{R}\cdot\theta$$

we use $I = \dfrac{1}{2}mR^2 - mr^2 + m(R - r)^2$

$$= mR^2\left[\frac{1}{2} - \frac{16}{9\pi^2} + \left(1 - \frac{4}{3\pi}\right)^2 + 1 + \frac{16}{9\pi^2} - \frac{8}{3\pi}\right]$$

$$= mR^2\left(\frac{3}{2} - \frac{8}{3\pi}\right)$$

comparing with

$$\alpha = -\omega^2\theta$$

we get $\omega = \sqrt{\dfrac{8g}{(9\pi - 16)R}}$

time period $T = \dfrac{2\pi}{\omega} = \pi\sqrt{\dfrac{(9\pi - 16)R}{2g}}$.

(v) As left spring is compressed by $2A$, this will be its amplitude so before it strikes the right spring its phase will change by $\theta = \pi/3$ hence time taken is

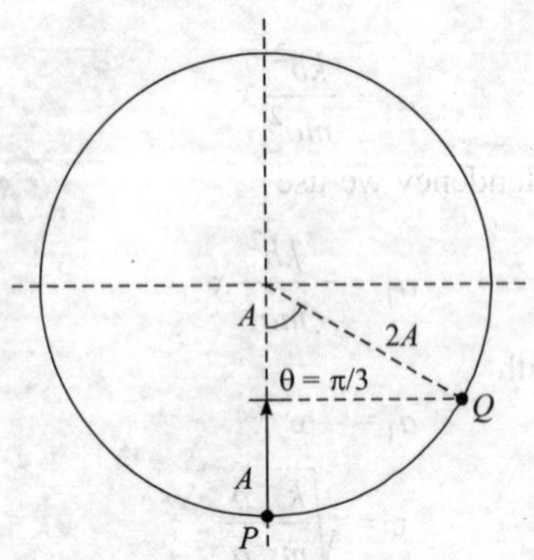

$$t = \frac{\theta}{\omega} = \frac{\pi/3}{\sqrt{2k/m}} = \frac{\pi}{3}\sqrt{\frac{m}{2k}}$$

After mass strikes right spring it moves in influence of both springs and let it comes in equilibrium after compressing the right spring by x_0, we use

$$2k(A - x_0) = kx_0$$

$$\Rightarrow \quad 2kA = 3kx_0$$

$$\Rightarrow \quad x_0 = \frac{2A}{3}$$

If y_0 is maximum compression in right spring, by work-energy theorem we write

$$\frac{1}{2}(2k)(2A)^2 - \frac{1}{2}ky_0^2 = \frac{1}{2}(2k)(A - y_0)^2$$

$$\Rightarrow \quad 8kA^2 - ky_0^2 = 2kA^2 + 2ky_0^2 - 4kAy_0$$

$$\Rightarrow \quad 3y_0^2 - 4Ay_0 - A^2 = 0$$

$$\Rightarrow \quad y_0 = \frac{2+\sqrt{22}}{3}A$$

(vi) (a) As $x = a\cos\left(\omega t - \frac{\pi}{4}\right)$

and $\quad v = -a\omega\sin\left(\omega t - \frac{\pi}{4}\right)$

and $\quad \omega = a\omega^2\cos\left(\omega t - \frac{\pi}{4}\right)$

plats are shown in figure

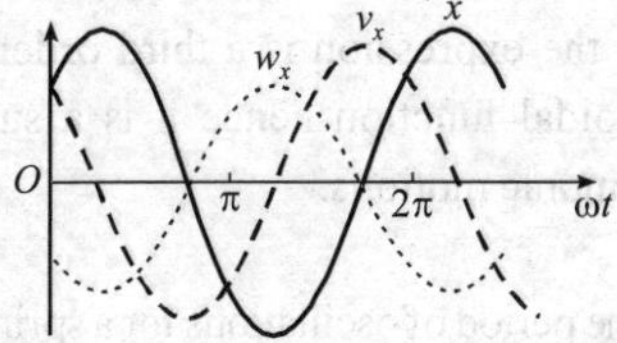

(b) We use $\quad v = \omega\sqrt{a^2 - x^2}$

$$\Rightarrow \quad \frac{v^2}{\omega^2 a^2} + \frac{x^2}{a^2} = 1$$

Thus plot will be an ellipse shown in figure

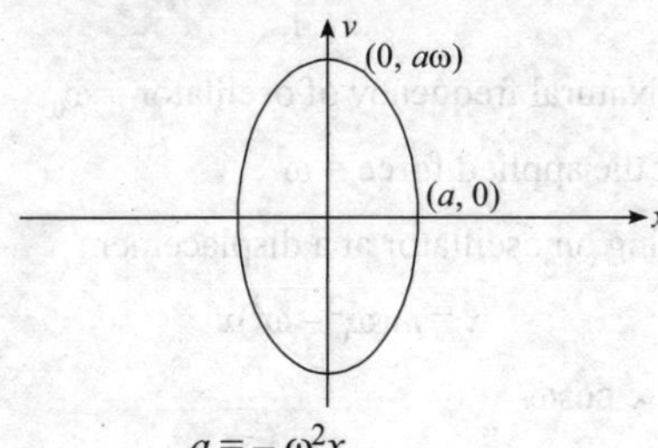

and $\quad a = -\omega^2 x$

Thus plot will be a straight line as shown in figure

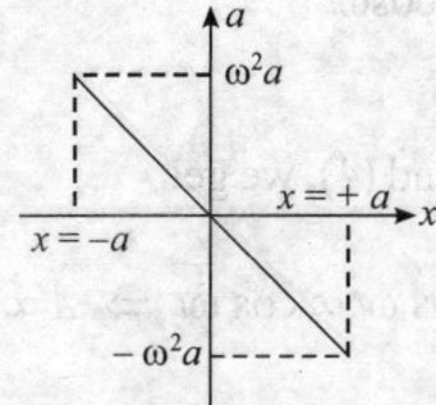

(vii) In from of disc when rod is slightly tilled by an angular θ, we use restoring torque on rod as

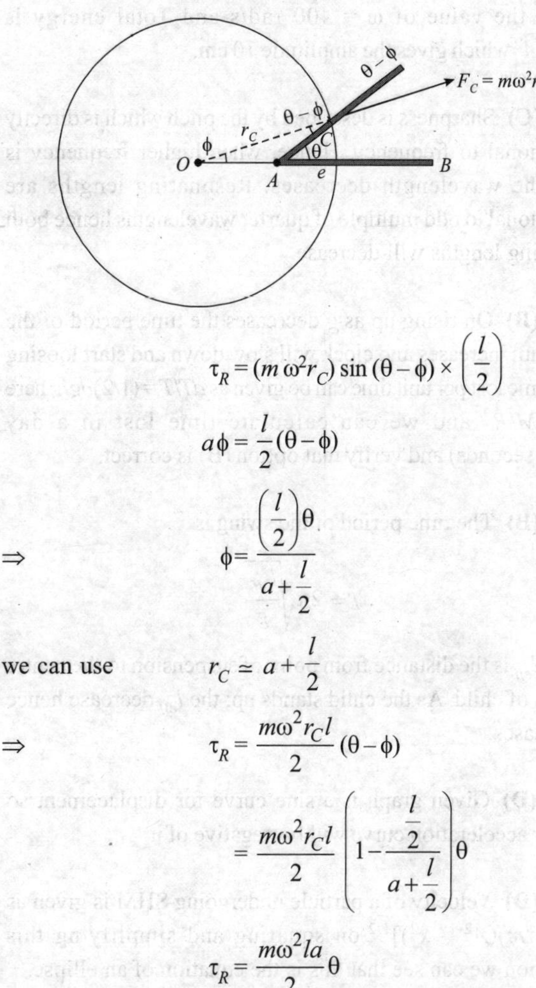

$$\tau_R = (m\omega^2 r_C)\sin(\theta - \phi) \times \left(\frac{l}{2}\right)$$

$$a\phi = \frac{l}{2}(\theta - \phi)$$

$$\Rightarrow \quad \phi = \frac{\left(\frac{l}{2}\right)\theta}{a + \frac{l}{2}}$$

we can use $\quad r_C \simeq a + \frac{l}{2}$

$$\Rightarrow \quad \tau_R = \frac{m\omega^2 r_C l}{2}(\theta - \phi)$$

$$= \frac{m\omega^2 r_C l}{2}\left(1 - \frac{\frac{l}{2}}{a + \frac{l}{2}}\right)\theta$$

$$\tau_R = \frac{m\omega^2 la}{2}\theta$$

Restoring angular acceleration is

$$\alpha = -\frac{\tau_R}{I} = -\frac{\frac{m\omega^2 la}{2}}{\frac{ml^2}{3}}\cdot\theta$$

$$\Rightarrow \quad \alpha = -\frac{3\omega^2 a}{2l}\theta$$

Comparing with $\quad \alpha = \omega_0^2\theta$

we get $\quad \omega_0 = \sqrt{\frac{3\omega^2 a}{2l}}$

Solutions of CONCEPTUAL MCQS Single Option Correct

Sol. 1 (B) We can map the two SHMs as projections of two uniform circular motions and find the phase angle of the position where the two particles will cross each other. This will happen at a phase angle 135° from initial positions hence the time to cover 135° is T(135/360) = 3T/8.

Sol. 2 (A) Potential energy per unit mass of a particle is given as $(1/2)\omega^2x^2$ and equating the given value with this expression we get the value of ω = 400 rad/s and Total energy is $(1/2)\omega^2A^2$ which gives the amplitude 10 cm.

Sol. 3 (C) Sharpness is described by the pitch which is directly proportional to frequency. Hence, when higher frequency is used, the wavelength decreases. Resonating lengths are proportional to odd multiple of quarter wavelengths hence both resonating lengths will decrease.

Sol. 4 (B) On rising up as g decreases the time period of the pendulum increases and clock will slow down and start loosing time. Time lost per unit time can be given as $dT/T = (1/2)dg/g$ here $g = GM/R^2$ and we can calculate time lost in a day (86400 seconds) and verify that option (B) is correct.

Sol. 5 (B) The time period of the swing is

$$T = 2\pi\sqrt{\frac{l_{eff}}{g}}$$

Where l_{eff} is the distance from point of suspension to the centre of mass of child. As the child stands up; the l_{eff} decrease hence T decreases.

Sol. 6 (D) Given graph is a sine curve for displacement so force or acceleration curve will be negative of it.

Sol. 7 (D) Velocity of a particle undergoing SHM is given as $v = [(k/m)(A^2 - x^2)]^{1/2}$ on squaring and simplifying this expression we can see that this is the equation of an ellipse.

Sol. 8 (A) A harmonic oscillator crosses the mean position with maximum speed hence kinetic energy is maximum at mean position (i.e., $x = 0$)
Total energy of the harmonic oscillator is a constant.
PE is maximum at the extreme position.

Sol. 9 (D) As in free fall effective gravity with respect to support of pendulum will be zero, it will not oscillate and frequency will be zero.

Sol. 10 (D) Given function can be written as

$$y = \sin^2 \omega t = \frac{1-\cos 2\omega t}{2} = \frac{1}{2} - \frac{1}{2}\cos 2\omega t$$

$\Rightarrow$ motion is SHM with time period $= \frac{2\pi}{2\omega} = \frac{\pi}{\omega}$

Sol. 11 (C) From the given figure if we draw the phase diagram on circular motion representation it looks like

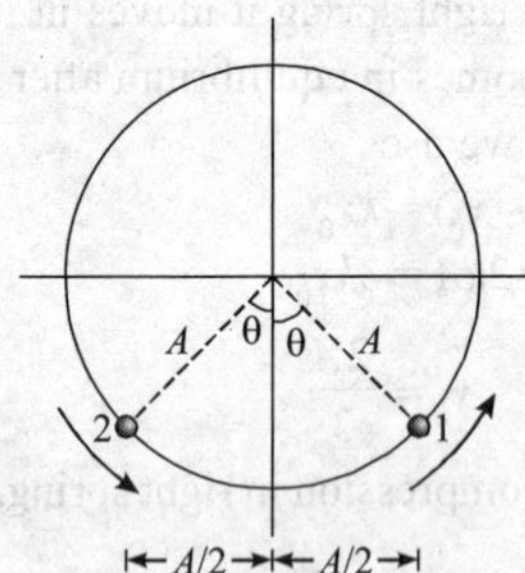

from figure phase difference between 1 & 2 is given as

$$\cos\theta = \frac{A/2}{A} = \frac{1}{2} \Rightarrow \theta = \frac{\pi}{3} \text{ or } 2\pi - \frac{\pi}{3} = \frac{5\pi}{3}$$

Sol. 12 (C) As positive plate under the bob will exert net downward force on it, this will increase the effective gravity acting on the bob due to which frequency increases as frequency is directly proportional to square root of the acceleration due to gravity.

Sol. 13 (B) When block C hits block A, as masses are same velocities will swap and when the spring compression is maximum both blocks A and B would be moving at same speed $v/2$ so that total momentum will remain conserved.

Sol. 14 (B) As the expression is a third order expression in degree of sinusoidal function hence it is a superposition of three simple harmonic motions.

Sol. 15 (B) Time period of oscillations for a spring block system is given by $2\pi(m/K)^{1/2}$ where K is the equivalent force constant of the spring system. Here in first and second figure equivalent force constant is only k whereas in third and fourth figure springs are taken in parallel combination because in both springs deformations are always equal on displacing the block so force constant is $4k$ hence option (B) is correct.

Sol. 16 (B) Natural frequency of oscillator = ω_0

Frequency of the applied force = ω

Net force acting on oscillator at a displacement

$$x = m(\omega_0^2 - \omega^2)x \quad \ldots(1)$$

Given that $F \propto \cos\omega t$ ...(2)

From equations (1) and (2) we get

$$m(\omega_0^2 - \omega^2)\, x \propto \cos\omega t \quad \ldots(3)$$

Also, $x = A \cos \omega t$ ...(4)

From equations-(3) and (4), we get

$$m(\omega_0^2 - \omega^2)A \cos\omega t \propto \cos\omega t \Rightarrow A \propto \frac{1}{m(\omega_0^2 - \omega^2)}$$

Sol. 17 (D) The restoring force on the particle can be given by $F = -dU/dx$ and using displacement very small we can see that the force is directly proportional to the displacement under which particle will execute SHM hence option (D) is correct.

Sol. 18 (C) The total energy of a harmonic oscillator is a constant and it is expressed as

$$E = \frac{1}{2}m\omega^2 \text{ (Amplitude)}^2$$

E is independent to instantaneous displacement x.

Sol. 19 (A) The expression of time period of a simple pendulum is

$$T = 2\pi\sqrt{\frac{l_{eff}}{g_{eff}}}$$

Where l_{eff} is the distance between point of suspension and centre of gravity of bob. As the hole is suddenly unplugged, l_{eff} first increases then decrease because of shifting of CM due to which the time period first increases and then decreases to the original value.

Sol. 20 (C) Figure-I: When the charge is placed below the bob of pendulum in vertical line with the point of suspension, the ball will subjected to the force of attraction to the positive charge as well as the force of gravity. The presence of electrostatic force will increases the restoring torque about point of suspension, so effective g will increases, hence the time period will decreases,

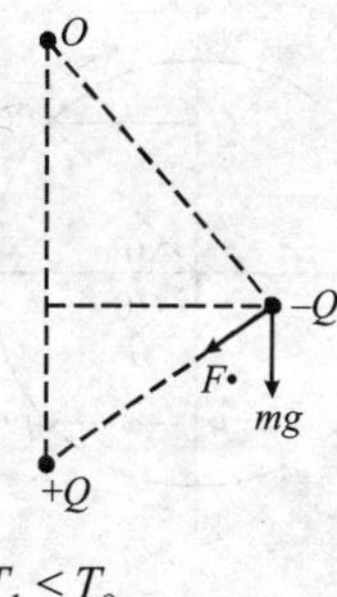

$$\Rightarrow \quad T_1 < T_0$$

Figure-II: When point charge is placed at the point of suspension, the presence of electrostatic force will not change restoring torque about point of suspension, so time-period will not alter.

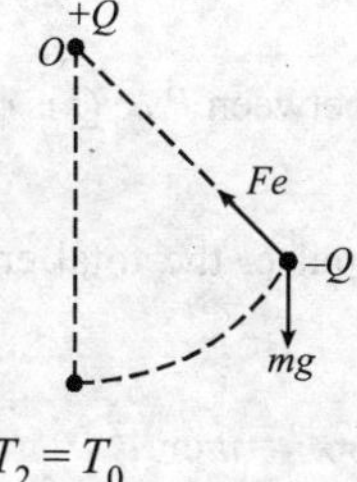

$$T_2 = T_0$$

Figure-III: Presence of electrostatic force first shifts the position of the equilibrium. Here, point C is the new equilibrium position. When the charge is placed at point B adjacent to the point A, the ball will subjected to the force of attraction to the positive charge as well as the force of gravity. The presence of electrostatic force will decrease the restoring torque about point of suspension, so effective g will decrease, hence the time period will increase,

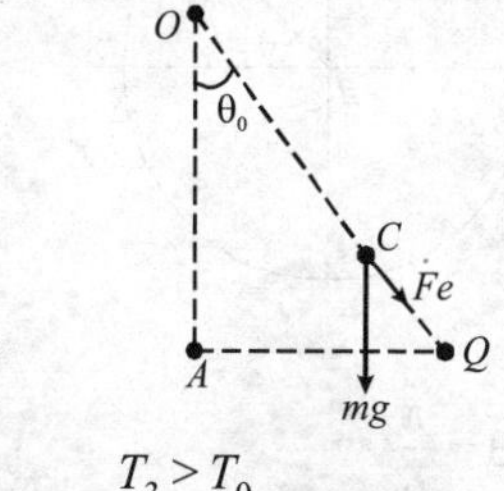

$$\Rightarrow \quad T_3 > T_0$$

Sol. 21 (A) $T = 2\pi\sqrt{l/g}$

$$\frac{\Delta T}{T} = \frac{1}{2}\frac{\Delta l}{l} = \frac{1}{2}a.\Delta t$$

So, the fractional change in the time period of a pendulum on changing the temperature is independent of length of pendulum.

Sol. 22 (B) For a spring block system time period is given as

$$T = 2\pi\sqrt{\frac{m}{k}} \Rightarrow T^2 \propto \frac{1}{k}$$

For the two given springs, we use

$$t_1^2 \propto \frac{1}{k_1} \;\&\; t_2^2 \propto \frac{1}{k_2} \Rightarrow t_1^2 + t_2^2 \propto \frac{1}{k_1} + \frac{1}{k_2}$$

But $\frac{1}{k_1} + \frac{1}{k_2} = \frac{1}{k_{eq}} \propto T^2$

$$\Rightarrow \quad t_1^2 + t_2^2 = T^2$$

Sol. 23 (C) Since, the pendulum started with no kinetic energy, conservation of energy implies that the potential energy at extreme position must be equal to the original potential energy, so the vertical position will be same at other extreme position, so we use

$$\Rightarrow \quad L\cos\alpha = l + (L - l)\cos\theta$$

$$\Rightarrow \quad \cos\theta = \frac{L\cos\alpha - l}{L - l}$$

$$\Rightarrow \quad \theta = \cos^{-1}\left[\frac{L\cos\alpha - l}{L - l}\right]$$

Sol. 24 (C) The total time from A to C

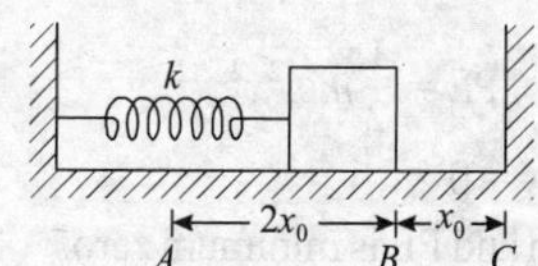

$$t_{AC} = t_{AB} + t_{BC} = \frac{T}{4} + t_{BC}$$

Where T = Time period of oscillation of spring-mass system and t_{BC} can be given by the figure shown as

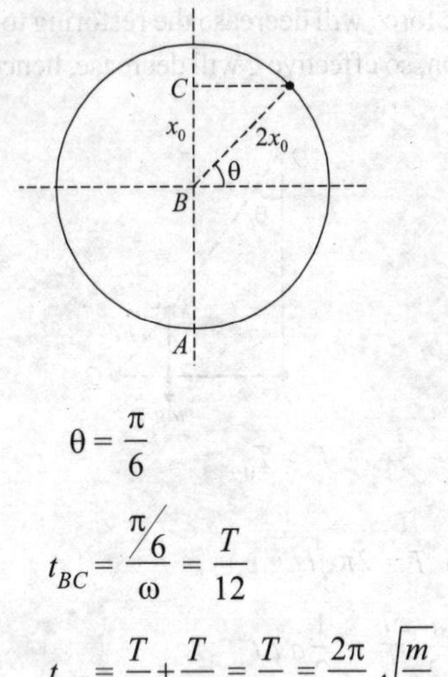

$$\theta = \frac{\pi}{6}$$

$$t_{BC} = \frac{\pi/6}{\omega} = \frac{T}{12}$$

$$\Rightarrow \quad t_{AC} = \frac{T}{4} + \frac{T}{12} = \frac{T}{3} = \frac{2\pi}{3}\sqrt{\frac{m}{k}}$$

Sol. 25 (D) We use equation of SHM as

$$x = A\cos\omega\tau$$

$$A - a = A\cos\omega\tau \qquad \ldots(1)$$

$$A - 3a = A\cos 2\omega\tau \qquad \ldots(2)$$

using $\quad \cos 2\omega\tau = 2\cos^2\omega\tau - 1$

$$\Rightarrow \quad \frac{A-3a}{A} = 2\left(\frac{A-a}{A}\right)^2 - 1$$

$$\Rightarrow \quad \frac{A-3a}{A} = \frac{2A^2 + 2a^2 - 4Aa}{A^2} - 1$$

$$\Rightarrow \quad A^2 - 3Aa = A^2 + 2a^2 - 4Aa$$

$$\Rightarrow \quad 2a^2 = Aa$$

$$\Rightarrow \quad A = 2a \qquad \ldots(3)$$

from equation-(1) $a = 2a\cos\omega\tau$

$$\cos\omega\tau = \frac{1}{2}$$

$$\Rightarrow \quad \omega\tau = \frac{\pi}{3}$$

$$\Rightarrow \quad \frac{2\pi}{T}.\tau = \frac{\pi}{3}$$

$$\Rightarrow \quad T = 6\tau$$

Sol. 26 (C) We use

$$\text{KE} = \frac{1}{2}m\omega^2(A^2 - x^2)$$

$$\text{PE} = \frac{1}{2}m\omega^2x^2$$

At mean position $x = 0$

So KE is maximum and PE is minimum zero.

Sol. 27 (A) We use for spring parts

$$k_A = \frac{kl}{l_A} = \frac{k(5l)}{2l} = \frac{5k}{2}$$

Solutions of NUMERICAL MCQS Single Option Correct

Sol. 1 (C) The equation giving relation between acceleration and speed as function of distance from mean position is

$$a = -\omega^2 x \qquad \ldots(1)$$

$$v = \omega\sqrt{a^2 - x^2} \qquad \ldots(2)$$

from equation (1) and (2) we get

$$a^2 = \omega^4\left(A^2 - \frac{v^2}{\omega^2}\right)$$

Hence the correct option is (C).

Sol. 2 (C) The magnitude of displacement in the given time interval is $\frac{a}{2}$ and time taken by the particle to cover a distance $\frac{a}{2}$ starting from rest is $\frac{T}{6}$.

Hence the magnitude of average velocity over given time interval is

$$v_{mean} = \frac{a/2}{T/6} = \frac{3a}{T}$$

Sol. 3 (B) For two particles in SHM along same line below figure shows the state of maximum separation.

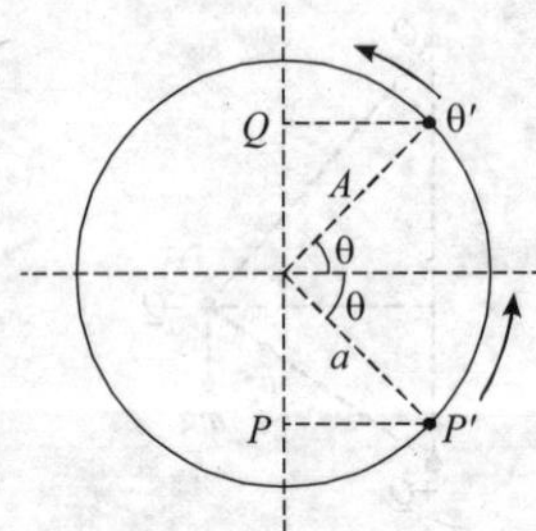

Here we use

$$PQ = a\sqrt{2} = 2a\sin\theta$$

$$\Rightarrow \quad \sin\theta = \frac{1}{\sqrt{2}}$$

$$\Rightarrow \quad \theta = \sin^{-1}\left(\frac{1}{\sqrt{2}}\right) = \frac{\pi}{4}$$

Thus phase difference between P & Q is $\phi = 2\theta = \frac{\pi}{2}$

Sol. 4 (C) Due to impulse, the total energy of the particle becomes

$$\frac{1}{2}m\omega^2A^2 + \frac{1}{2}m\omega^2A^2 = m\omega^2A^2$$

Let; A' be the new amplitude.

$$\Rightarrow \quad \frac{1}{2}m\omega^2(A')^2 = m\omega^2A^2$$

$$\Rightarrow \quad A' = \sqrt{2}A$$

Sol. 5 (B) Given that potential energy is $U = mV$

$$\Rightarrow \quad U = (50x^2 + 100)10^{-2}$$

$$F = -\frac{dU}{dx} = -(100x)\,10^{-2}$$

$$\Rightarrow \quad m\omega^2x = -(100 \times 10^{-2})\,x$$

$$10 \times 10^{-3}\,\omega^2x = 100 \times 10^{-2}x$$

$$\Rightarrow \quad \omega^2 = 100$$

$$\Rightarrow \quad \omega = 10 \text{ rad/s}$$

$$\Rightarrow \quad f = \frac{\omega}{2\pi} = \frac{10}{2\pi} = \frac{5}{\pi}$$

Sol. 6 (A) Given that acceleration of car is

$$f = a - bx$$

For maximum velocity, acceleration should be zero.

$$\Rightarrow \quad a - bx = 0$$

$$\Rightarrow \quad x = \frac{a}{b}$$

At $x = \frac{a}{b}$, the particle has its maximum velocity.

We use $\quad f = \frac{vdv}{dx} = a - bx$

$$\Rightarrow \quad \frac{v^2}{2} = ax - \frac{bx^2}{2} + c$$

At $\quad x = 0;\ v = 0$

$$\Rightarrow \quad c = 0$$

Substituting $x = \frac{a}{b}$ gives maximum velocity as

$$v_{max} = \frac{a}{\sqrt{b}}$$

Also, the velocity of the car should become zero at station B.

$$\Rightarrow \quad ax - \frac{bx^2}{2} = 0$$

$$\Rightarrow \quad x = 0;\ x = \left(\frac{2a}{b}\right)$$

$\Rightarrow$ Distance between the stations is $\frac{2a}{b}$.

Alternate : $f = a - bx$ means particle will execute SHM.

At mean position; $f = 0$

A |← a/b →| C ——— | B

x = 0   x = a/b

$$\Rightarrow \quad x = \frac{a}{b}$$

In the figure shown, 'C' is the mean position and A & B are extreme positions

$$\Rightarrow \quad x_{max} = \frac{2a}{b}$$

$$\& \ V_{max} = \omega A = \sqrt{b}\cdot\frac{a}{b} = \frac{a}{\sqrt{b}}$$

Sol. 7 (D) The system acts as a pendulum of length l acting under effective gravity of $g\cos\theta$ as shown in figure

Now, $l_1 l_2 = AB.l = \sqrt{x^2+y^2}\cdot l$

$$\cos\theta = \frac{x}{\sqrt{x^2+y^2}}$$

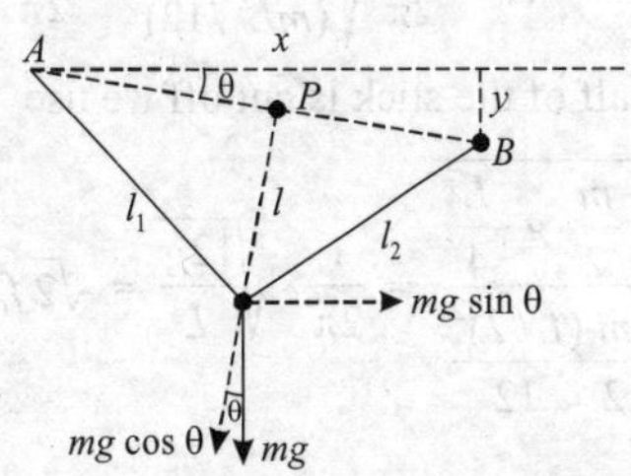

$$\Rightarrow \quad T = \sqrt{\frac{l_1l_2\sqrt{x^2+y^2}}{\sqrt{x^2+y^2}\cdot gx}} = 2\pi\sqrt{\frac{l_1l_2}{gx}}$$

Sol. 8 (C) Assuming the speed of the spring increases linearly with distance from O, the speed of a small element at a distance 'x' of spring as shown in figure is

$$u = \frac{v}{L}x$$

considering a small element:

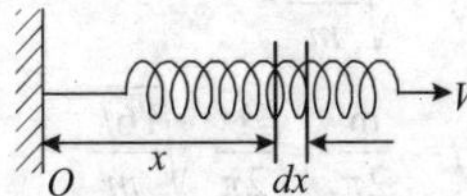

Total kinetic energy of spring is

$$K.E. = \int\frac{1}{2}\cdot dmu^2 = \int_0^L\frac{1}{2}\cdot\left(\frac{m}{L}\cdot dx\right)\cdot\left(\frac{v^2}{L^2}\cdot x^2\right) = \frac{1}{6}mv^2$$

Sol. 9 (B) Both the spring-mass system & torsional pendulum have no dependence on gravitational acceleration for their time periods.

Sol. 10 (C) The maximum static frictional force is

$$f = \mu mg\cos\theta = 2\tan\theta\, mg\cos\theta = 2\,mg\sin\theta$$

Applying Newton's second law to block at lower extreme position, we have

$$f - mg\sin\theta = m\omega^2A$$

$\Rightarrow \omega^2 A = g\sin\theta$ As $\omega = \sqrt{\dfrac{k}{3m}}$

$$\Rightarrow A = \frac{3mg\sin\theta}{k}$$

Sol. 11 (B) We use

$$f_0 = \frac{1}{2\pi}\sqrt{\frac{mgl}{I}}$$

where, l is distance between point of suspension and centre of mass of the body.

Thus, for the stick of length L and mass m frequency is

$$f_0 = \frac{1}{2\pi}\sqrt{\frac{m.g.\frac{L}{2}}{(mL^2/12)}} = \frac{1}{2\pi}\sqrt{\frac{6g}{L}}$$

when bottom half of the stick is cut off we use

$$f_0 = \frac{1}{2\pi}\sqrt{\frac{\frac{m}{2}\cdot g\cdot\frac{L}{4}}{\frac{m}{2}\frac{(L/2)^2}{12}}} = \frac{1}{2\pi}\times\sqrt{\frac{12g}{L}} = \sqrt{2}f_0$$

Sol. 12 (C) Let mass 'm' falls down by x so spring extends by $4x$; which causes an extra tension T in lowest string

$$\Rightarrow \frac{T}{4} = k(4x)$$

$$T = (16k)x$$

Thus equation of motion of mass m is

$$T = ma$$

$$\Rightarrow a = -\frac{16k}{m}x$$

Comparing with $a = -\omega^2 x$

we get $\omega = \sqrt{\dfrac{16k}{m}}$

$$\Rightarrow f = \frac{\omega}{2\pi} = \frac{1}{2\pi}\sqrt{\frac{16k}{m}}$$

$$= \frac{2}{\pi}\sqrt{\frac{k}{m}}$$

Sol. 13 (B) Given that $\dfrac{d\theta}{dt} = 2$ rad/s

$\Rightarrow \theta = 2t$

Let $BP = a$

$\Rightarrow x = OM = a\sin\theta = a\sin(2t)$

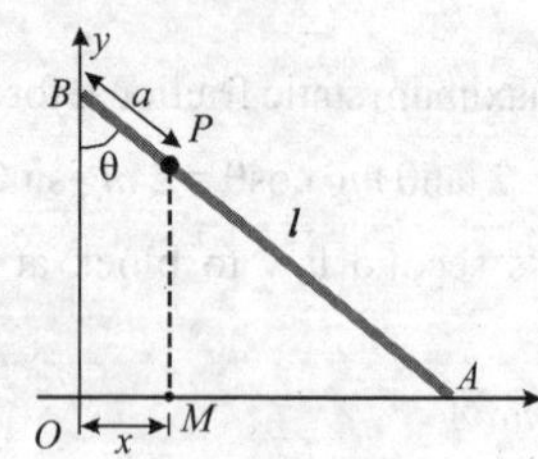

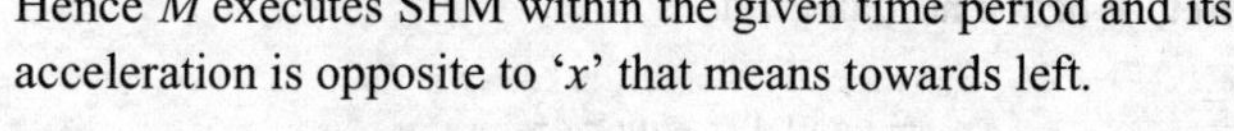

Hence M executes SHM within the given time period and its acceleration is opposite to 'x' that means towards left.

Sol. 14 (C) We use $V = \pm\,\omega\sqrt{A^2 - x^2}$

$$PE = \frac{1}{2}kx^2$$

$$a = -\omega^2 x$$

$$KE = \frac{1}{2}m\omega^2(A^2 - x^2) = \frac{1}{2}k(A^2 - x^2)$$

Ratio of acceleration to displacement $= \dfrac{-\omega^2 x}{x} = -\omega^2$ (constant)

Sol. 15 (C) When the particle crosses point D, its speed is half of the maximum speed. Given that amplitude is $2R$

$$\Rightarrow v = \frac{v_{max}}{R}\sqrt{R^2 - x^2}$$

or $\dfrac{v_{max}}{2} = \dfrac{v_{max}}{R}\sqrt{R^2 - x^2}$

or $x = \dfrac{\sqrt{3}}{2}R$

$\Rightarrow$ Distance $BD = 2x = \sqrt{3}R$

Sol. 16 (C) Given that $\dfrac{d^2v}{dt} = -Kv^2$

this equation has standard solution $v = v_0\sin(\sqrt{K}t + \theta)$ where $\omega = \sqrt{K}$. Hence the particle executes SHM with angular frequency $\omega = \sqrt{K}$

or frequency $f = \dfrac{\sqrt{K}}{2\pi}$.

Sol. 17 (A) By conservation of momentum, we use

$$2V = 3V'$$

$$\Rightarrow V' = \frac{2}{3}V$$

Initially $E_i = \dfrac{1}{2}m_1V_1^2 = \dfrac{1}{2}\cdot 2\cdot V^2 = V^2$

If A is initial amplitude we use

$$\Rightarrow \frac{1}{2}KA^2 = V^2$$

Finally $E_f = \dfrac{1}{2}\cdot m_2V'^2 = \dfrac{1}{2}\cdot 3\cdot\dfrac{2}{3}\cdot\dfrac{2}{3}V^2 = \dfrac{2}{3}V^2$

If A' is final amplitude, we use

$$\Rightarrow \frac{1}{2}KA'^2 = \frac{2}{3}V^2$$

$$\Rightarrow \frac{1}{2}KA'^2 = \frac{2}{3}\left(\frac{1}{2}KA^2\right)$$

$$\Rightarrow A' = \frac{2}{3}A$$

Sol. 18 (D)

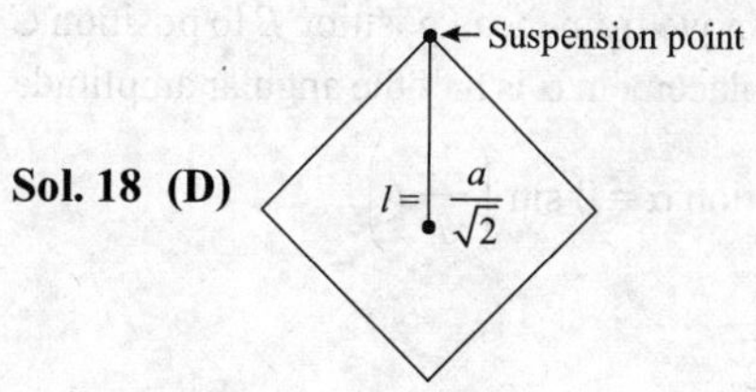

Time period of a compound pendulum is given as

$$T = 2\pi\sqrt{\frac{I}{mgl}} = 2\pi\sqrt{\frac{m\frac{(a^2+a^2)}{12} + m\left(\frac{a}{\sqrt{2}}\right)^2}{mg.\frac{a}{\sqrt{2}}}}$$

$$= 2\pi\sqrt{\frac{\left(\frac{a}{6}+\frac{a}{2}\right).\sqrt{2}}{g}} = 2\pi\sqrt{\frac{2\sqrt{2}a}{3g}}.$$

Sol. 19 (C) By work energy theorem at a displacement x_1 and x_2 we have

$$Fx_1 - \frac{1}{2}k x_1^2 = \frac{1}{2}mV^2 \quad \ldots(1)$$

and $$Fx_2 - \frac{1}{2}k' x_2^2 = \frac{1}{2}mv'^2 \quad \ldots(2)$$

where x_1, x_2 are initial and final extensions and V, v' are initial and final velocities.

In both cases : force applied is same, and velocity becomes maximum when $F = kx$, after which the mass will decelerate

$\Rightarrow$ $$F = kx_1 = (4k)x_2$$

$\Rightarrow$ $$x_2 = \frac{x_1}{4}$$

Substituting in equation-(2), we get

$$\frac{Fx_1}{4} - \frac{1}{2}(4k)\left(\frac{x_1}{4}\right)^2 = \frac{1}{2}mv'^2$$

$\Rightarrow$ $$\frac{1}{4}[Fx_1 - \frac{1}{2}k x_1^2] = \frac{1}{2}mv'^2 \quad \ldots(3)$$

Dividing (3)/(1); we get:

$$\frac{1}{4} = \frac{v'^2}{V^2}$$

$\Rightarrow$ $$v' = \frac{V}{2}$$

Sol. 20 (A) Restoring torque on rod after small angle tilt is

$\tau_R = -ky\,L = -KL^2\theta$ (Since $y \cong L\theta$ from figure)

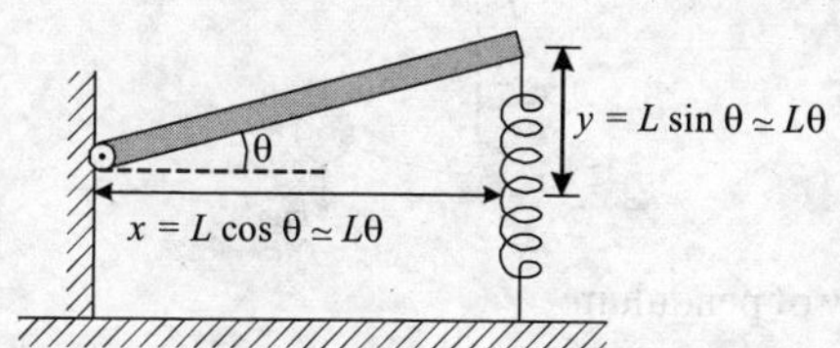

$\Rightarrow$ $$kL^2\theta = -\frac{mL^2}{3}.\alpha$$

$\Rightarrow$ $$\alpha = -\frac{3k}{m}.\theta$$

comparing with $\alpha = -\omega^2\theta$

We get $$\omega = \sqrt{\frac{3k}{m}}$$

Note: Torque due to mg was already balanced so it is not taken in calculation.

Sol. 21 (A) Oscillations represented by curve 2 lags in phase by $\pi/2$ and the periods are same. Amplitude of curve 2 is double that of 1.

Sol. 22 (C) Given that

$$U = 2 - 20x + 5x^2$$

Interaction force on particle is given as

$$F = -\frac{dU}{dx} = 20 - 10x$$

As F is linearly varying with $-x$, particle is executing SHM

At equilibrium position $F = 0$

$\Rightarrow$ $$20 - 10x = 0$$

$\Rightarrow$ $$x = 2$$

Since particle is released at $x = -3$, therefore amplitude of particle is 5

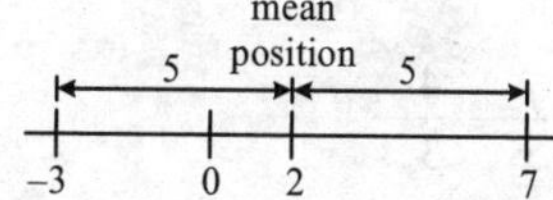

It will oscillate about $x = 2$ with an amplitude of 5

$\Rightarrow$ maximum value of x will be 7.

Sol. 23 (D) *P.E.* is maximum at extreme position and minimum at mean position

Time to go from extreme position to mean position is, $t = \frac{T}{4}$; where T is time period of SHM. Given that

$$\frac{T}{4} = 5\text{s}$$

$\Rightarrow$ $$T = 20\text{s}$$

Sol. 24 (A) Acceleration of particle is

$$a = -\left(\frac{\pi^2}{64}\right)x$$

comparing with $a = -\omega^2 x$ we get

$\Rightarrow$ $$\omega = \sqrt{\frac{\pi^2}{64}} = \frac{\pi}{8}$$

$\Rightarrow$ $$T = \frac{2\pi}{\omega} = 16\text{ s}$$

There is a time difference of $\frac{T}{2}$ between $t = 2$s to $t = 10$s. Hence particle is again passing through the mean position of SHM where its speed is maximum at $t = 10$s

$$\Rightarrow \quad V_{max} = A\omega = 4\sqrt{2}$$

$$\Rightarrow \quad A = \frac{4\sqrt{2}}{\pi/8} = \frac{32\sqrt{2}}{\pi} \text{ m.}$$

Sol. 25 (A) Resultant displacement will be the vector sum of two displacements :

$$y = \sqrt{y_1^2 + y_2^2 + 2y_1y_2 \cos 37°}$$

$$= \sqrt{a^2 \sin^2 \omega t + b^2 \sin^2 \omega t + 2ab \sin^2 \omega t \times \frac{4}{5}}$$

$$y = \sqrt{a^2 + b^2 + \frac{8ab}{5}} \sin\omega t$$

Which shows that the particle will perform SHM.

Sol. 26 (A) The slope of x-t graph is the speed.
From graph, the slope of curve 1 is greatest, hence (A)

Sol. 27 (B) $x = 3 \sin 100\,\pi t$
$y = 4 \sin 100\,\pi t$

Equation of path is

$$\frac{y}{x} = \frac{4}{3}$$

$$\Rightarrow \quad y = \frac{4}{3}x$$

Above is an equation of a straight line having slope $\frac{4}{3}$ thus equation of resulting motion is $\vec{r} = x\hat{i} + y\hat{j} = (3\hat{i} + 4\hat{j}) \sin 100\pi t$.

$\Rightarrow$ Amplitude is $\sqrt{3^2 + 4^2} = 5$

Sol. 28 (B) The time period of free oscillation of pendulum

$$T = 2\pi\sqrt{\frac{l}{g}} = 2 \text{ s}$$

Time taken by bob to go from extreme position A to mean position B is $= \frac{T}{4}$

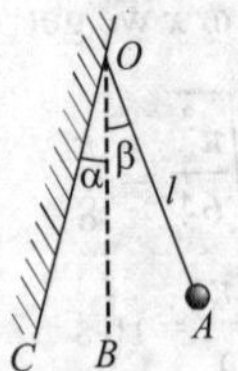

Time taken by bob to move from mean position B to position C (where its angular displacement α is half the angular amplitude β) is found from equation $\alpha = \beta \sin\left(\frac{2\pi}{T}t\right)$.

Solving we get $t = \frac{T}{12}$

$\Rightarrow$ Total time period of oscillation is

$$= 2\left[\frac{T}{4} + \frac{T}{12}\right] = \frac{2}{3}T = \frac{4}{3} \text{ s}$$

Sol. 29 (A) With respect to the cart, equilibrium position of the pendulum is shown. If displaced by small angle θ from this position, then it will execute SHM about this equilibrium position, time period of which is given by

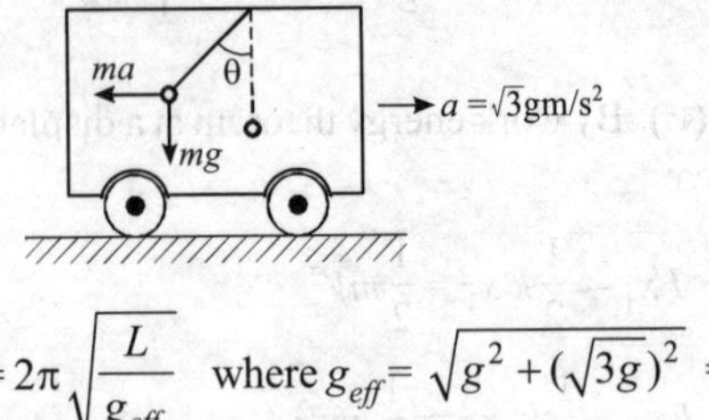

$$T = 2\pi\sqrt{\frac{L}{g_{eff}}} \quad \text{where } g_{eff} = \sqrt{g^2 + (\sqrt{3}g)^2} = 2g$$

$$\Rightarrow \quad T = 1.0 \text{ s}$$

Sol. 30 (C) Amplitude phasor diagram after super position of all four SHMs is shown in figure 1 and further simplification in figure-2&3

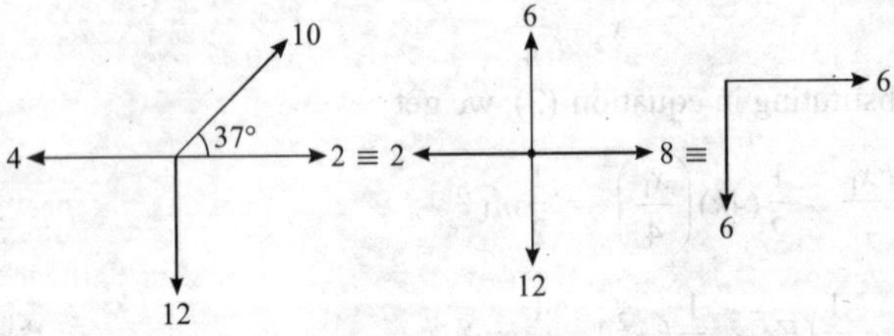

Figure-(1) Figure-(2) Figure-(3)

$\Rightarrow$ Resultant amplitude $= 6\sqrt{2}$.

Sol. 31 (D) In given situation if we look at pendulum from side its effective oscillating length is $\frac{l}{\sqrt{2}}$

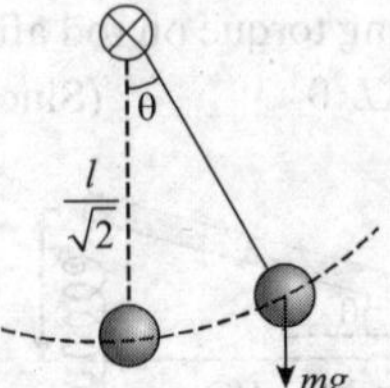

Side view of pendulum

Thus angular frequency of oscillations is

$$\omega = \sqrt{\frac{g}{l_{eff}}} = \sqrt{\frac{\sqrt{2}g}{l}}$$

$$\Rightarrow \quad T = 2\pi\sqrt{\frac{l}{\sqrt{2}g}}$$

Sol. 32 (A) At equilibrium

$$mg\sin\theta = kA$$

$$\Rightarrow \quad A = \frac{mg\sin\theta}{K}$$

As $mg \sin\theta$ is constant the time period for spring block system is given as

$$T = 2\pi\sqrt{\frac{m}{k}}$$

Sol. 33 (A) Given $\omega^2 A = 35.28$

$$\omega = 4.2$$

$$\Rightarrow \quad A = \frac{\omega^2 A}{(\omega)^2} = \frac{35.28}{(4.2)^2} = 2.0 \text{ m}$$

Sol. 34 (C) Given that from graph

$$\frac{1}{2}mV_m^2 = 15\times 10^{-3}$$

$$V_m = \sqrt{0.150} \text{ m/s}$$

$$A\omega = \sqrt{0.150} \text{ m/s}$$

$$L\theta_m\sqrt{\frac{g}{L}} = \sqrt{0.150} \text{ m/s}$$

$$\Rightarrow \quad \sqrt{gL} = \frac{\sqrt{0.150}}{100\times 10^{-3}}$$

$$\Rightarrow \quad L = \frac{0.150}{0.1} = 1.5 \text{ m}$$

Sol. 35 (D) The equation $a = -100x + 50$ shows that the particle performs SHM with mean position at $x \neq 0$.

Sol. 36 (A) We use

$$v\frac{dv}{dx} = -100x + 50$$

$$\Rightarrow \quad \int v\,dv = \int(50 - 100x)dx$$

$$\Rightarrow \quad \frac{v^2}{2} = 50x - \frac{100x^2}{2} + c$$

At $\quad x = 2; v = 0$

$$\Rightarrow \quad 0 = 100 - 200 + c$$

$$\Rightarrow \quad c = 100$$

$$\Rightarrow \quad v^2 = 2\left[50x - \frac{100x^2}{2} + 100\right]$$

At $\quad x = 0; v = \sqrt{2[100]}$

$$v = 10\sqrt{2} \text{ m/s}$$

Sol. 37 (C) We use

$$a = -100x + 50$$

$$\Rightarrow \quad \omega^2 = 100$$

$$\Rightarrow \quad \omega = 10 \text{ rad/s}$$

$$\Rightarrow \quad T = \frac{2\pi}{\omega} = \frac{\pi}{5} \text{ seconds}$$

$x = 0.5$ is the mean position (as $a = 0$ at $x = 0.5$)

From $x = 2$ to 0.5 m; time required $= \frac{T}{4} = \frac{\pi}{20}$ seconds.

Sol. 38 (C) Velocity will be maximum where $F = 0$

$$\Rightarrow \quad -100x + 50 = 0$$

$$\Rightarrow \quad x = 1/2$$

From previous question at $x = 1/2$

$$v = \sqrt{2\left(50\cdot\frac{1}{2} - 50\left(\frac{1}{4}\right) + 100\right)} = \sqrt{2\left(125 - \frac{25}{2}\right)}$$

$$= \sqrt{225} = 15 \text{ m/s}$$

Sol. 39 (C) The mean position of particle can be found by setting $F = -5x + 15 = 0$, so the mean position lies at $x = 3$. One extreme position is at $x = 6$. Hence the other extreme position for this particle undergoing SHM should be at $x = 0$. Time taken by particle to reach from $x = 6$ to $x = 0$ is 0.5 s, that is $\frac{T}{2} = 0.5$ s, hence $T = 1$ second. Hence the equation of motion is $x = 3 + A(\sin\omega t + \phi_0)$ where $A = 3$, $\omega = 2\pi \times 1$ and $\phi_o = \frac{\pi}{2}$. So $x = 3 + 3\cos(2\pi t)$.

Sol. 40 (C) From previous solution as $\omega = 2\pi$ we use

$$\Rightarrow \quad T = \frac{2\pi}{\omega} = 1 \text{ s}$$

and we use $\quad T = 2\pi\sqrt{\frac{m}{k}}$

$$\Rightarrow \quad m = \frac{T^2k}{4\pi^2} = \frac{1\times 5}{4\pi^2} = \frac{5}{4\pi^2}$$

Sol. 41 (C)

Upthrust (4mg)

a

mg

$$\Rightarrow \quad a = 3g$$

Sol. 42 (B) The density of liquid is four times that of cylinder, hence in equilibrium position one fourth of the cylinder will remain submerged. So as the cylinder is released from initial position, it moves distance $\frac{3l}{4}$ to reach its equilibrium position. The upward motion in this duration is SHM.

Therefore attained velocity is $v_{max} = \omega A$

Where $\omega = \sqrt{\frac{4g}{l}}$ and $A = \frac{3l}{4}$

Thus $v_{max} = \frac{3}{2}\sqrt{gl}$

Sol. 43 (C) The require time is one fourth of time period of SHM. Therefore $t = \frac{\pi}{2\omega} = \frac{\pi}{4}\sqrt{\frac{l}{g}}$.

Sol. 44 (D) From the given data we use

$$A\omega \sin\theta = 1.6$$

and $$A\omega\cos\theta = 1.2$$

$$\Rightarrow \quad A\omega = 2 \text{ m/s}$$

Sol. 45 (A) From given equation of SHM we have

$$\omega^2 = \pi^2$$

$$\Rightarrow \quad \omega = \pi$$

$$\Rightarrow \quad f = \frac{\omega}{2\pi} = \frac{1}{2}\text{ s}$$

Sol. 46 (A) Distance travelled by the particle is given as

$$l = A\sin\frac{5\pi}{12} - A\sin\frac{\pi}{12} = \frac{A}{\sqrt{2}}$$

Sol. 47 (C) Time period of motion = 6 + 2 = 8s from mean position to the highest point of the wall, it takes 1s and covers distance $\frac{A}{\sqrt{2}}$

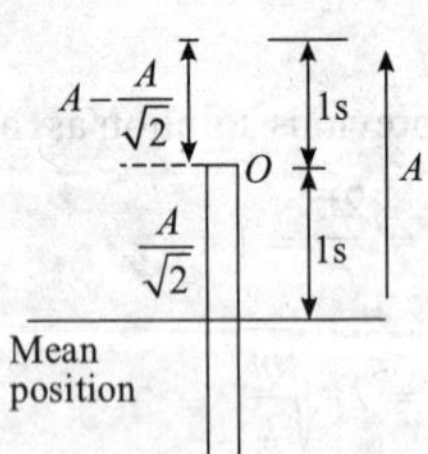

Thus $$A - \frac{A}{\sqrt{2}} = 0.3\text{ m}$$

$$\Rightarrow \quad A = 1.0\text{ m}$$

Sol. 48 (A) Force constant of each of springs made by cutting in n part is $K' = nK$

Now r part are taken in parallel so equivalent force constant is

$$K_{eq} = nrK$$

$$\text{Time period} = 2\pi\sqrt{\frac{m}{K_{eq}}} = 2\pi\sqrt{\frac{m}{nrK}}$$

Sol. 49 (B) If spring has the mass then we use oscillation frequency as

$$f = \frac{1}{2\pi}\sqrt{\frac{k}{m + \frac{M_{spring}}{3}}}$$

Equivalent force constant of spring

= $3k$ (As all are taken in parallel)

$$\Rightarrow \quad f = \frac{1}{2\pi}\sqrt{\frac{3k}{m + \frac{(3m)}{3}}}$$

$$\Rightarrow \quad f = \frac{1}{2\pi}\sqrt{\frac{3k}{2m}}$$

Sol. 50 (A) The spring is never compressed. Hence spring shall exert least force on the block when the block is at topmost position.

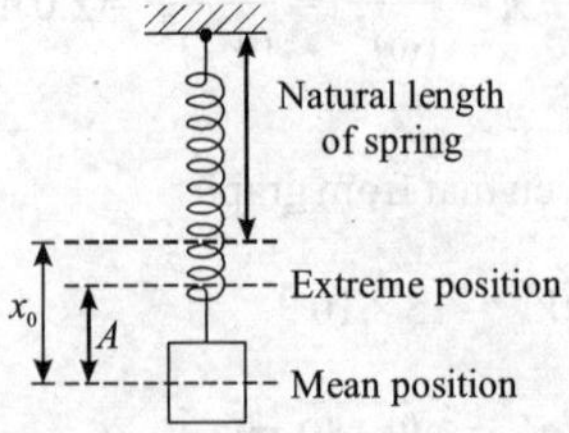

$$F_{least} = kx_0 - kA = mg - m\omega^2 A = mg - 4\frac{\pi^2}{T^2}mA$$

Sol. 51 (B) Just after cutting the string extension in spring = $\frac{3mg}{k}$ and extension in the spring when block is in mean position = $\frac{mg}{k}$

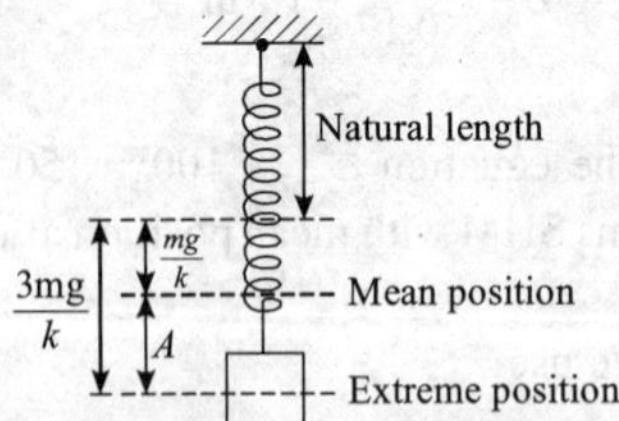

$\Rightarrow$ Amplitude of oscillation is given as

$$A = \frac{3mg}{k} - \frac{mg}{k} = \frac{2mg}{k}$$

Sol. 52 (C) Comparing given equation with $y = A\sin(\omega t - kx)$ we get

$$A = \frac{10}{\pi}\text{ cm},$$

$\omega = 2000\pi s^{-1}$

$T = \frac{2\pi}{\omega} = 10^{-3}$ s

Maximum velocity $= \omega A = \frac{10}{\pi.100} \times 2000\pi = 200$ ms^{-1}

Sol. 53 (B) Phase of the motion is $(\omega t + \phi)$
Using $x = A\sin(\omega t + \phi)$ and $v = A\omega\cos(\omega t + \phi)$ for conditions at $t = 0 \rightarrow x = A$ and $V = 0$ then $\phi = \pi/2$

When it passes equilibrium position for the first time $t = \frac{T}{4}$.

Phase $= \frac{2\pi}{T}\cdot\frac{T}{4} + \frac{\pi}{2} = \pi$

Sol. 54 (C) Both the spring are in series

$\Rightarrow \quad K_{eq} = \frac{K(2K)}{K+2K} = \frac{2K}{3}$

Time period

$T = 2\pi\sqrt{\frac{\mu}{K_{eq}}}$ where $\mu = \frac{m_1 m_2}{m_1 + m_2}$

Here $\quad \mu = \frac{m}{2}$

$\Rightarrow \quad T = 2\pi\sqrt{\frac{m}{2}\cdot\frac{3}{2K}} = 2\pi\sqrt{\frac{3m}{4K}}$

Sol. 55 (A) Just before collision, both P & Q arrive at their equilibrium position

$\Rightarrow \quad V_P = \omega\frac{A}{2} = \sqrt{\frac{k}{m}}\frac{A}{2}$

Sol. 56 (B) Speed of Q just before collision is

$V_Q = \omega A = \sqrt{\frac{k}{m}}A$

Sol. 57 (A) The block shall meet after time $t = \frac{T}{4}$, where T is time period of either isolated spring block system,

$t = \frac{T}{4} = \frac{1}{4}2\pi\sqrt{\frac{m}{k}} = \frac{\pi}{2}\sqrt{\frac{m}{k}}$

Sol. 58 (B) Maximum KE is acquired by the block when it passes the mean position of SHM where $\Sigma F = 0$ or $mg = kx$.

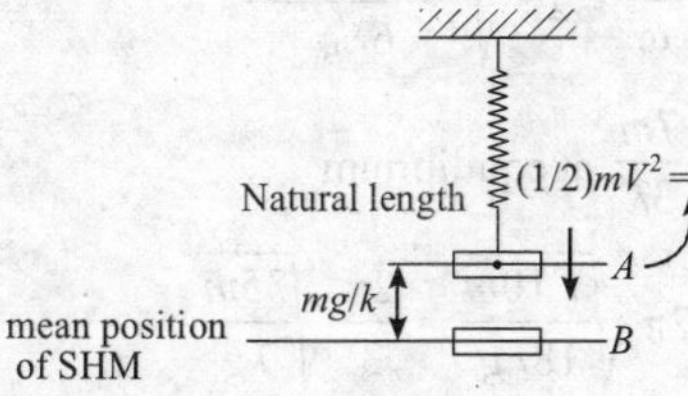

$x = mg/k = \frac{10}{200} = \frac{1}{20}$ m

Applying work energy theorem from position A to B on the block $K_f - K_i = W_{gravity} + W_{spring}$

$\Rightarrow \quad K_f - 2\text{J} = 10\text{N}\left(\frac{1}{20}m\right) + \left[-\frac{1}{2}\times 200\times\left(\frac{1}{20}\right)^2\right]$

$\Rightarrow \quad k_f = 2.25$ J

Sol. 59 (C) $KE_{\max} = \frac{1}{2}kA^2$

$A = \sqrt{\frac{2(KE_{\max})}{k}} = \sqrt{\frac{2\times(2.25)}{200}} = \sqrt{\frac{9}{400}} = \frac{3}{20}$ m $= 15$ cm

Sol. 60 (B) Spring on the left of the block are in series, hence there equivalent is

$k_1 = \frac{(2k)(2k)}{2k+2k} = k$

Springs on the right of the block are in parallel, hence there equivalent is

$k_2 = k + 2k = 3k$

Now again both k_1 and k_2 are in parallel

$\Rightarrow \quad k_{eq} = k_1 + k_2 = k + 3k = 4k$

Hence, frequency of oscillation is

$f = \frac{1}{2\pi}\sqrt{\frac{k_{eq}}{M}} = \frac{1}{2\pi}\sqrt{\frac{4k}{M}}$

Sol. 61 (B) When speed of block is maximum, net force on block is zero. Hence at that instant spring exerts a force of magnitude 'mg' on block.

Sol. 62 (C) At the instant block is in equilibrium position, its speed is maximum and compression in spring is x given by

$kx = mg \quad \ldots(1)$

From conservation of energy

$mg(L+x) = \frac{1}{2}kx^2 + \frac{1}{2}mv_{max}^2 \quad \ldots(2)$

from (1) and (2) we get $v_{max} = \frac{3}{2}\sqrt{gL}$

Sol. 63 (B) $V_{max} = \frac{3}{2}\sqrt{gL}$ and $\omega = \sqrt{\frac{k}{m}} = 2\sqrt{\frac{g}{L}}$

$\Rightarrow \quad A = \frac{V_{max}}{\omega} = \frac{3}{4}$L

Hence time taken t, from start of compression till block reaches mean position is given by

$x = A\sin\omega t_0$ where $x = \frac{L}{4}$

$$\Rightarrow \quad t_0 = \sqrt{\frac{L}{4g}} \sin^{-1}\frac{1}{3}$$

Time taken by block to reach from mean position to bottom most position is $\dfrac{2\pi}{4\omega} = \dfrac{\pi}{4}\sqrt{\dfrac{L}{g}}$

Hence the required time $= \dfrac{\pi}{4}\sqrt{\dfrac{L}{g}} + \sqrt{\dfrac{L}{4g}} \sin^{-1}\dfrac{1}{3}$

Sol. 64 (D) Centre of mass of system is

$$x_{cm} = \frac{(\lambda x)\dfrac{x}{2} + M\left(\dfrac{h}{2}\right)}{M + \lambda x}$$

Time period is maximum when

$$\frac{dx_{cm}}{dx} = 0$$

$$\Rightarrow \quad (M + \lambda x)\lambda x - \left(\frac{\lambda x^2}{2} + \frac{Mh}{2}\right)\lambda = 0$$

$$(Mx + \lambda x^2) - \frac{\lambda x^2}{2} - \frac{Mh}{2} = 0$$

$$\lambda x^2 + 2Mx - Mh = 0$$

Sol. 65 (B) Consider an observer moving with speed v with point A in the same direction.

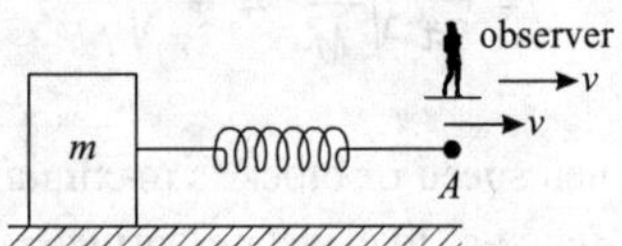

In the frame of observer, block will have initial velocity v towards left.

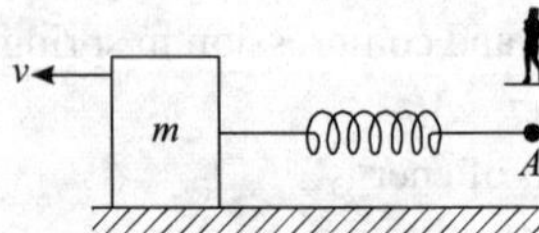

During maximum extension, the block will come to rest with respect to the observer. Now, by energy conservation,

$$\frac{1}{2}mv^2 = \frac{1}{2}k x_{max}^2$$

$$\Rightarrow \quad x_{max} = \sqrt{\frac{mv^2}{k}}$$

Sol. 66 (B) Torque about hinge

$$2.5\,g.\,4\cos\theta - 1g.100\cos\theta = 0$$

So rod remains stationary after the release.

Sol. 67 (B) Let the line joining AB represents axis 'r'. By the conditions given 'r' coordinate of the particle at time t is

$$r = 2\sqrt{2}\cos\omega t$$

$$\omega = \frac{2\pi}{T} = \frac{2\pi}{2} = \pi$$

$$\Rightarrow \quad r = 2\sqrt{2}\cos\pi t$$

$$x = r\cos 45° = \frac{r}{\sqrt{2}} = 2\cos\pi t$$

$$\Rightarrow \quad a_x = -\omega^2 x = -\pi^2\, 2\cos\pi t$$

$$\Rightarrow \quad F_x = ma_x = -4\pi^2\cos\pi t$$

Sol. 68 (B) The period of small oscillations of a hinged/pivoted rigid body is given by the expression of time period of a compound pendulum given as $T = 2\pi(I/mgd)^{1/2}$ where I is the moment of inertia and d is the distance of center of mass from the hinge. Here we use $I = 2\left(\dfrac{m}{2}\right)\dfrac{l^2}{3} = \dfrac{ml^2}{3}$ and $d = \dfrac{l}{2\sqrt{2}}$.

Sol. 69 (B) If sphere is displaced by x in upward direction) from is equilibrium position then increase in weight is λxg due to mass of chain.

Increase in buoyant force due to this is

$$= \frac{\lambda xg}{7}$$

$\Rightarrow$ excess force on chain will be $(\lambda xg - \dfrac{\lambda xg}{7})$ in down ward direction.

If a is acceleration of system then its motion equation is

$$\Rightarrow \quad \frac{6\lambda g}{7}x = (m + \lambda h)a$$

$$a = -\frac{6\lambda g}{7(m + \lambda h)}\cdot x$$

[–ve sing shows restoring tendency]

Comparing this with acceleration of SHM $a = -\omega^2 x$, we get

$$\omega = \frac{6\lambda g}{7(m + \lambda h)}$$

$$\& \quad T = \frac{2\pi}{\omega} = 2\pi\sqrt{\frac{7(m + \lambda H)}{6\lambda g}}$$

using $\quad h = \dfrac{7m}{3\lambda}$ at equilibrium

$$T = 2\pi\sqrt{\frac{7.10m}{18\lambda g}} = \frac{2\pi}{3}\sqrt{\frac{35m}{\lambda g}}$$

Sol. 70 (D) We use displacement equation of SHM as

$$x = A\sin\frac{2\pi}{T}t;\quad \text{for } x = \frac{A}{2}$$

$$\Rightarrow \quad \frac{A}{2} = A\sin\frac{2\pi}{T}t$$

Solving we get $t = \frac{1}{6}$ s

Solutions of ADVANCE MCQs One or More Option Correct

Sol. 1 (A, C) When 3kg mass is released the amplitude of its oscillations is 2m and at a distance 1m from the equilibrium position we can find the speed of it using the relation $v = [(k/m)(A^2 - x^2)]^{1/2}$ then by conservation of momentum we can find the resulting speed of the combined mass and the new amplitude using the above relation which gives options (A) and (C) are correct.

Sol. 2 (A, B, C) Comparing the graph with the relation in velocity and displacement $v = [(k/m)(A^2 - x^2)]^{1/2}$ we get option (A) and (C) are correct and maximum acceleration of the particle is given by $a_{max} = kA/m$ which gives option (B) is also correct.

Sol. 3 (C, D) Eleminating term of time t from the two equations we get the relation in x and y as locus of the curve traced by the particle.

Sol. 4 (A, B, C) At KE 0.64 times that of maximum KE the velocity would be 0.8 times that of maximum velocity, now we can use the relation of velocity and displacement $v = [(k/m)(A^2 - x^2)]^{1/2}$ to verify that options (A) and (B) are correct. Option (C) is correct by conservation of energy.

Sol. 5 (B, C) The maximum potential energy of linear harmonic oscillator is equal to the total mechanical energy at extreme positions of the oscillations hence option (C) is correct. The maximum kinetic energy of the oscillator is $(1/2)kA^2 = 100$J hence option (B) is also correct.

Sol. 6 (B, C, D) Due to the Pseudo force on block (considered external) its mean popsition will shift to a distance mg/K above natural length of spring as net force now is mg in upward direction so total distance of block from new mean position is 2mg/K which will be the amplitude of oscillations hence option (C) is correct. During oscillations spring will pass through the natural length hence option (D) is correct. As block is oscillating under spring force and other constant forces which do not affect the SHM frequency hence option (B) is correct.

Sol. 7 (A, B, C) By finding restoring force on particle using $F = -dU/dx$ we can see that force is a linear function of x which verifies that particle is executing SHM hence option (D) is wrong. From the given expression we have at $x = 4$ potential energy is minimum so this is the mean position of the oscillating particle hece option (A) is correct. If in this expression we put $U = 36$J which will happen at $x = 8$m or $x = 0$m which are the extreme positions of the oscillations so amplitude of oscillations is 4m hece option (B) is correct. At $x = 2$m we can use the velocity expression $v = [(k/m)(A^2 - x^2)]^{1/2}$ and find the kinetic energy and verify that option (C) is also correct.

Sol. 8 (All) Block loses contact at the highest point. Then

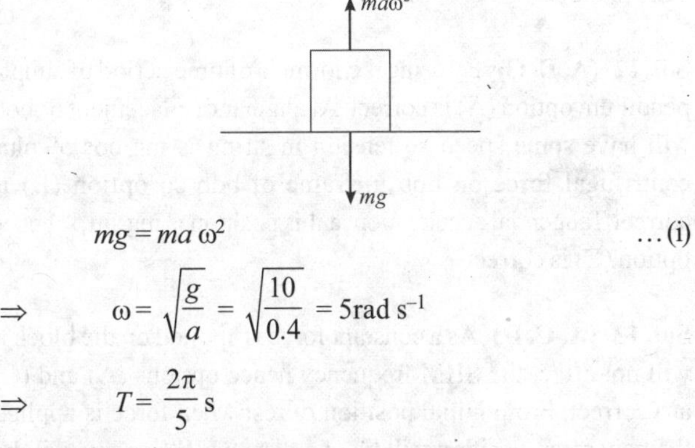

$$mg = ma\,\omega^2 \qquad \ldots(i)$$

$$\Rightarrow \quad \omega = \sqrt{\frac{g}{a}} = \sqrt{\frac{10}{0.4}} = 5\text{rad s}^{-1}$$

$$\Rightarrow \quad T = \frac{2\pi}{5}\text{ s}$$

At lowest point

$$N = mg + ma\,\omega^2$$

$$N = 2mg \text{ (from(1))}$$

Halfway down from mean position,

$$N = mg + k\left(\frac{a}{2}\right)$$

$$= mg + \frac{m\omega^2 a}{2}$$

$$= 1.5\text{ mg}$$

Block has maximum velocity when displacement (and thus acceleration) is zero, and thus has $N = mg$.

Sol. 9 (B, C) Differentiating the velocity expression we can verify that the particle is executing SHM hence option (C) is correct and substituting the displacement in expression of acceleration and verify that option (B) is correct.

Sol. 10 (A, B, C) As no external force is acting on the system both blocks will oscillate about their center of mass. If compression is 6cm then by mass moment property of center of mass we use $m_1\Delta x_1 = m_2\Delta x_2$ so the amplitude of 3kg mass is 4cm and that of 6kg mass is 2cm hence option (B) is correct. The time period can be obtained either by using concept of reduced mass or by splitting the spring in two parts about center of mass of the two blocks in series combination which gives the 3kg block oscillates with a spring constant 1200 N/m for which time period is $T = 2\pi\,(m/k)^{1/2} = \pi/10$sec hence option (A) is correct. The maximum momentum of 6kg block will be when it will pass through mean position and given as $mA\omega = 2.4$ kgm/s hence option (C) is correct.

Sol. 11 (B, C, D) when the spring has maximum extension by conservation of momentum we use $5(3) + 2(10) = 7(v)$ which gives $v = 5$m/s and by energy conservation we can obtain the maximum extension of spring. Both particles are executing SHM about their center of mass and in the frame of center of mass by any one particle's phase analysis we can find the time of maximum compression which is an extreme position of the blocks. velocity of center of mass here is 5m/s and with respect to center of mass 5kg block is moving at 2m/s away from it and the force constant of split spring for 5kg mass can be taken as $1120(5+2)/2 = 3920$ N/m.

Sol. 12 (A, B, C) By using the formula of time period of simple pendulum option (A) is correct. At angular displacement 5° bob will have some speed so tension in string is mg cos 5° plus centrifugal force on bob in frame of bob so option (B) is correct.Tangential acceleration at this position is mg sin 5° hence option (C) is correct.

Sol. 13 (A, C, D) As a constant force is applied on the block it will not affact the SHM frequency hence options (A) and (C) are correct. From initial position of rest when force is applied the new mean position will be at a distance *F*/*k* so this will be the amplitude of oscillations hence option (B) is wrong. Maximum speed of oscillations is at mean position which is given by $v_{max} = A\omega$ so option (D) is not correct.

Sol. 14 (A, C, D) The graph is showing variation of velocity so we cannot predict whether particle is oscillating on +ve or -ve axis hence option (A) is correct. At position 3 velocity of particle is positive and with time increasing so acceleration is in the direction of velocity hence option (C) is correct. At position 4 velocity becomes maximum which happens at mean position where acceleration is zero hence option (D) is correct.

Sol. 15 (All) As at position 1 acceleration is positive and displacement from mean position is opposite to direction of acceleration in SHM hence option (A) is correct. At position 2 acceleration is changing from positive to negative, particle is at mean position and moving in positive direction hence option (B) is correct. At position 3 acceleration magnitude is maximum so this is the extreem position of SHM so potential energy of particle is maximum here hence option (C) is correct. At position 4 acceleration is increasing that means particle is moving toward extreme position so its speed will be decreasing hece option (D) is correct.

Sol. 16 (A, C) Net force on ball will be zero at a depth where buoyant force balances its weight where $\rho_0 = \alpha h$ hence mean position of SHM will be at a depth ρ_0/α so this will be the amplitude of SHM hence option (A) is correct and other extreme position of the ball will be at a distance twice the amplitude from the free surface hence option (C) is correct.

Sol. 17 (A, B, C) Due to constant pseudo force on block it will execute SHM with same time period $2\pi\sqrt{\frac{m}{k}}$ as constant external force never changes the frequency of SHM hence options (A) and (B) are correct. Mean position of SHM is the position where pseudo force balances the spring force hence option (C) is correct. Total energy of oscillation is given by (1/2)mw^{2}A^2 with which you can verify that option (D) is not correct.

Sol. 18 (C, D) $a = -\omega^2 x,\ v = \omega\sqrt{A^2 - x^2}$

$$a^2T^2 + 4\pi^2v^2 = \omega^4x^2T^2 + 4\pi^2\omega^2(A^2 - x^2)$$

$$= \frac{4\pi^2}{T^2}\omega^2x^2T^2 + 4\pi^2\omega^2(A^2 - x^2)$$

$$= 4\pi^2\omega^2A^2 = \text{constant}$$

$$\frac{aT}{x} = -\frac{\omega^2 xT}{x} = -\omega^2 T = \text{constant}$$

Sol. 19 (A, D) $K_1 = m_1\frac{g}{x}$; $k_2 = m_2\frac{g}{x}$

Thus, Using $T = 2\pi\sqrt{\frac{m}{k}}$

$$T_1 = 2\pi\sqrt{\frac{m_1}{(m_1 g/x)}}$$

$$T_2 = 2\pi\sqrt{\frac{m_2}{(m_2 g/x)}}$$

$\Rightarrow\ T_1 = T_2$

Energy of oscillation

$$E = \frac{1}{2}m\omega^2A^2$$

Since ω and A are same for both and $m_1 > m_2$

$\Rightarrow\ E_1 > E_2$

Sol. 20 (B, C) At time t_1, velocity of the particle is negative i.e. going towards $-X_m$. From the graph, at time t_1, its speed is decreasing. Therefore particle lies in between $-X_m$ and 0.

At time t_2, velocity is positive and its magnitude is less than maximum i.e. it has yet not crossed *O*.

It lies in between $-X_m$ and 0.

Phase of particle at time t_1 is $(180 + \theta_1)$

Phase of particle at time t_2 is $(270 + \theta_2)$

Phase difference is $90 + (\theta_2 - \theta_1)$

$\theta_2 - \theta_1$ can be negative making $\Delta f < 90°$ but can not be more than 90°.

Sol. 21 (B, C) The maximum kinetic energy of particle is given as

$$K_{max} = 16\pi^2$$

The kinetic energy oscillates with double the frequency of

oscillation in SHM so the time period of SHM is given as 0.2 s hence option (A) is NOT correct. The frequency of oscillations is given as

$$f = \frac{1}{T} = 5\text{Hz}$$

Hence option (B) is correct. The maximum kinetic energy of particle is written as

$$K_{max} = \frac{1}{2}mv_{max}^2$$

$$\Rightarrow \quad v_{max} = 4\pi \text{ m/s}$$

Maximum speed during SHM is given as

$$v_{max} = A\omega = A\left(\frac{2\pi}{0.2}\right) = 4\pi$$

$$A = 0.4 \text{ m}$$

Hence option (C) is correct. From the given graph it is clear that at $t = 0.1$ s the particle is at extreme so acceleration is not zero hence option (D) is NOT correct.

Sol. 22 (All) We have

$$v = \sqrt{144 - 9x^2}$$

$$\Rightarrow \quad v = 3\sqrt{4^2 - x^2}$$

This is SHM (compare to $v = \omega\sqrt{a^2 - x^2}$)
we have $a = 4, \omega = 3$

$$\Rightarrow \quad T = \frac{2\pi}{3} \text{ units}$$

Amplitude $a = 4$ units.

Acceleration when displacement is 3 units is

$$a = \omega^2 x$$

$$= 3^2.3 = 27 \text{ units.}$$

Obviously in SHM, displacement $\leq$ distance.

Sol. 23 (A, C) From the graph shown in figure, the time period of oscillation is given as

$$T = 4 \text{ s}$$

Angular frequency of SHM is calculated as

$$\omega = \frac{2\pi}{T} = \frac{\pi}{2} = 1.57 \text{ rad/s}$$

At $t = 3$ s object is at extreme position at which velocity is zero hence option (A) is correct. At $t = 1$ s also object is at extreme position so its velocity is zero hence option (B) is NOT correct. At $t = 1$ s acceleration of object is given as

$$a = \omega^2 A = (0.8)\left(\frac{\pi}{2}\right)^2 = 0.197 \text{ m/s}^2$$

Hence option (C) is correct and (D) is NOT correct.

Sol. 24 (B, C) Bob will oscillate about equilibrium position with amplitude $\theta = \tan^{-1}\left(\frac{a}{g}\right)$ for any value of a

If $a << g$, motion will be SHM, and then

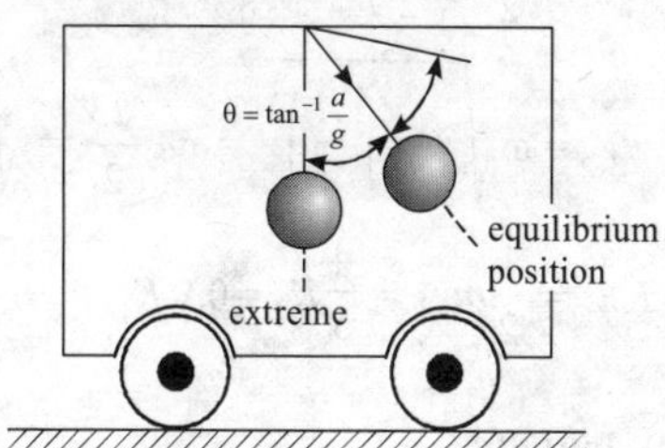

time period will be $2\pi\sqrt{\dfrac{l}{\sqrt{a^2+g^2}}}$

Sol. 25 (B, D) $x = 3 \sin 100t + 8 \cos^2 50t$

$$= 3 \sin 100t + \frac{8[1 + \cos 100t]}{2}$$

$$x = 4 + 3 \sin 100t + 4 \cos 100t$$

$$(x - 4) = 5 \sin (100t + f)$$

$$\left\{\tan\phi = \frac{4}{3}\right\}$$

Amplitude = 5 units
Maximum displacement = 9 units

Sol. 26 (All) At $t = 0$

Displacement $x = x_1 + x_2 = 4 \sin \frac{\pi}{3} = 2\sqrt{3}$ m

Resulting Amplitude $A = \sqrt{2^2 + 4^2 + 2(2)(4)\cos\pi/3}$

$$= \sqrt{4+16+8} = \sqrt{28} = 2\sqrt{7} \text{ m}$$

Maximum speed = $A\omega = 20\sqrt{7}$ m/s

Maximum acceleration = $A\omega^2 = 200\sqrt{7}$ m/s²

Energy of the motion = $\frac{1}{2}m\omega^2 A^2 = 28$ J

Sol. 27 (B, D) When $x = -\frac{A}{4}$

$$F_1 = -Kx = -K\left(\frac{-A}{4}\right) = \frac{KA}{4}$$

and $$U_1 = \frac{1}{2}K\left(\frac{A}{4}\right)^2 = \frac{KA^2}{32}$$

$$\Rightarrow \quad V_1 = \omega\sqrt{A^2 - \left(\frac{A}{4}\right)^2} = \frac{\omega A\sqrt{15}}{4}$$

$$\Rightarrow \quad K_1 = \frac{1}{2}mv_1^2 = \frac{1}{2}\frac{m\omega^2 A^2 15}{16} = \frac{m\omega^2 A^2 15}{32}$$

When $x = A/2$

$$F_2 = -kx = -\frac{kA}{2} = 2F \text{ (Magnitude)}$$

and $$U_2 = \frac{1}{2}k\left(\frac{A}{2}\right)^2 = \frac{kA^2}{8} = 4U$$

$\Rightarrow$ $$V_2 = \omega\sqrt{A^2 - \left(\frac{A}{2}\right)^2} = \omega A\frac{\sqrt{3}}{2} = \sqrt{\frac{4}{5}}\, v_1$$

$\Rightarrow$ $$KE_2 = \frac{1}{2}mv_2^2 = \frac{4}{5}K_1 = 0.8\,K_1$$

Sol. 28 (A, D) Initially,

amplitude $= a_0$

time period $= T_0$

Now, by conservation of momentum,

$$Mv_1 = (M+m)v_2 \quad \ldots(1)$$

$$Ma_0\omega_0 = (M+m)a'\omega' \quad \ldots(2)$$

Now $$\omega_0 = \sqrt{\frac{k}{M}}$$

$$\omega' = \sqrt{\frac{k}{M+m}}$$

$\therefore$ $$T' = T_0\sqrt{\frac{M+m}{M}} \quad \ldots(3)$$

Using (3) and (2), we have

$$a = a_0\sqrt{\frac{M}{M+m}}$$

Sol. 29 (B, C, D) $F = \dfrac{-\partial U}{\partial x}$

$\Rightarrow$ $F = -32(x-1)N$

As motion is simple harmonic and $x = 1$ is equilibrium position.

$$m\omega^2 = 32$$

$\Rightarrow$ $$\omega^2 = \frac{32}{2} \Rightarrow \omega = 4 \text{ rad s}^{-1}$$

At $x = 1, v = 2\text{ ms}^{-1}$ ($= a\omega$ (maximum))

As $$a\omega = 2$$

$\Rightarrow$ $$a = \frac{2}{4} = \frac{1}{2}\text{m}$$

As oscillation is from 0.5 to 1.5 m

$$\omega = 4$$

$\Rightarrow$ $$\frac{2\pi}{T} = 4$$

$\Rightarrow$ $$T = \frac{\pi}{2}\text{ s}$$

Sol. 30 (A, D) When block is displaced downwards by x, it experiences an upward force of

$$F = -(d_2Ax - d_1Ax)$$

$$F = -xA(d_2 - d_1)$$

This force is proportional to x, and hence block executes SHM Displacement will be symmetric about equilibrium position.

Sol. 31 (A, C) When block starts moving the potential energy of spring starts converting into kinetic energy of the block which will be lost during motion due to work against friction. Due to retardation by friction the block may stop before reaching mean position if the kinetic enery attained upto any instant becomes equal to the work done by friction and at that position of block all forces on it are also balanced hence option (A) is correct. This may happen anywhere in oscillations so block may also stop at mean position hence options (B) and (D) are NOT correct and option (C) is correct.

Sol. 32 (C, D) Motion of pendulum is in a circular arc. In circular motion at angle θ, all the forces acting on the bob are resolved in two perpendicular directions, along radial direction and along tangential direction, as shown in figure below.

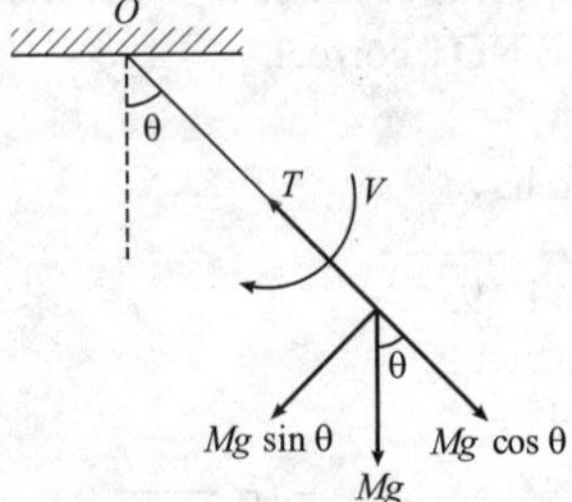

Along radial direction net force toward centre should be equal to $\dfrac{mv^2}{R}$ and along tangent it should be equal to Ma_T, where a_T is the tangential acceleration of the bob's motion. This gives

$$T - Mg\cos\theta = \frac{mv^2}{L}$$

and $$Mg\sin\theta = Ma_T$$

$\Rightarrow$ $$a_T = g\sin\theta$$

Hence options (C) and (D) are correct.

Sol. 33 (A, D) It is specified that the two pendulums starts from two opposite ends which means the initial phase difference between the two oscillations is π radians. They will be in same phase periodically after a time when the pendulum with lower time period will exceed in phase by π, 3π, 5π.... (2n+1)π radians. If it happens after time t, we use

$$\omega_1 t = \pi + \omega_2 t$$

$\Rightarrow$ $$t = \frac{\pi}{\omega_1 - \omega_2} = \frac{\pi}{\frac{2\pi}{3} - \frac{2\pi}{7}} = \frac{21}{8}\text{ s}$$

Hence option (A) is correct. It also happens at all odd multiples of this time hence option (D) is also correct.

* * * * *

ANSWERS & SOLUTIONS

CONCEPTUAL MCQS Single Option Correct

1	(A)	2	(D)	3	(B)
4	(D)	5	(A)	6	(B)
7	(A)	8	(B)	9	(A)
10	(B)	11	(D)	12	(D)
13	(C)	14	(B)	15	(B)
16	(D)	17	(B)	18	(C)
19	(D)	20	(B)	21	(D)
22	(A)	23	(C)	24	(B)
25	(C)	26	(B)	27	(D)

NUMERICAL MCQS Single Option Correct

1	(B)	2	(D)	3	(C)
4	(B)	5	(D)	6	(D)
7	(B)	8	(C)	9	(B)
10	(D)	11	(A)	12	(B)
13	(B)	14	(C)	15	(C)
16	(C)	17	(A)	18	(C)
19	(B)	20	(A)	21	(B)
22	(B)	23	(D)	24	(B)
25	(A)	26	(B)	27	(D)
28	(D)	29	(A)	30	(B)
31	(C)	32	(D)	33	(B)
34	(C)	35	(D)	36	(C)
37	(C)	38	(C)	39	(B)
40	(D)	41	(C)	42	(B)
43	(B)	44	(B)	45	(B)
46	(D)	47	(C)	48	(A)
49	(B)	50	(D)	51	(C)
52	(C)	53	(A)	54	(A)
55	(D)	56	(B)	57	(A)
58	(A)	59	(D)	60	(C)
61	(C)	62	(C)	63	(D)
64	(C)	65	(A)	66	(C)
67	(A)	68	(A)	69	(C)
70	(D)	71	(B)	72	(A)
73	(D)	74	(A)	75	(C)
76	(B)	77	(B)	78	(C)
79	(B)	80	(C)	81	(B)
82	(A)	83	(B)	84	(D)
85	(C)	86	(B)	87	(D)
88	(B)	89	(B)	90	(B)

ADVANCE MCQs One or More Option Correct

1	(A, C, D)	2	(A, C)	3	(B, C, D)
4	(B, C)	5	(C, D)	6	(B, D)
7	(B, C)	8	(A, B, C)	9	(A)
10	(A, B)	11	(A, C, D)	12	(A, B)
13	(B, C)	14	(C, D)	15	(B, C, D)
16	(B, C)	17	(All)	18	(A, C)
19	(B, C, D)	20	(A, D)	21	(A, B)
22	(A, B, D)	23	(All)	24	(C, D)
25	(All)	26	(A, B, C)	27	(A, B, C)
28	(A, C, D)	29	(B)	30	(D)

Solutions of PRACTICE EXERCISE 6.1

(i) In the given equation

$$y = 0.25 \times 10^{-3} \sin(500t - 0.25x)$$

Comparing with

$$y = A\sin(\omega t - kx)$$

we get

(a) Amplitude

$$A = 0.25 \times 10^{-3}\,\text{cm}$$

(b) Time period

$$T = \frac{2\pi}{\omega} = \frac{2\pi}{500} = \frac{\pi}{250}\,\text{s}$$

(c) Angular frequency

$$\omega = 500\,\text{rad/s}$$

(d) Wavelength

$$\lambda = \frac{2\pi}{k} = \frac{2\pi}{0.25} = 8\pi\,\text{cm}$$

(e) Particle velocity amplitude

$$v_{max} = A\omega = 0.25 \times 10^{-3} \times 500 = 0.125\,\text{cm/s}$$

(f) Particle acceleration amplitude

$$a_{max} = \omega^2 A = (500)^2 \times 0.25 \times 10^{-3} = 6.25\,\text{cm/s}^2$$

(ii) In h is cloud height then distance travelled by sound is

$$l = h\,\text{cosec}(30°) = 2h$$

we use $t = \dfrac{2h}{v}$

$\Rightarrow$ $8 = \dfrac{2h}{330}$

$\Rightarrow$ $h = 330 \times 4 = 1320\,\text{m} = 1.320\,\text{km}$

(iii) Wave equation is $y = 0.5 \sin \pi(0.01x - 3t)$

Comparing with standard wave equation

$$y = A \sin(\omega t - kx)$$

we get

$$A = 0.5\,\text{m}$$
$$\omega = 3\pi\,\text{rad/s}$$
$$k = 0.01\,\pi\,\text{m}^{-1}$$

wave speed is given as

$$v = \frac{\omega}{k} = \frac{3\pi}{0.01\pi} = 300\,\text{m/s}$$

(iv) String shape at time t_0 is

$$g(x, t_0) = A \sin\left(\frac{x}{a}\right)$$

As wave is propagating in positive x direction at speed v, origin shifts with respect to displacement curve in $-x$ direction at same speed so we replace x by $x - vt'$ where t' is time elapsed upto a general time t which is given as

$$t' = t - t_0$$

Thus wave equation is

$$f(x, t) = A \sin\left(\frac{x - v(t - t_0)}{a}\right)$$

(v) If distance of lighting source is l, time taken by sound to reach listener is

$$t = \frac{l}{v_s} = \frac{l}{330}$$

If l is measured in *km* we use

$$t = \frac{l(1000)}{330}$$

$$\Rightarrow \qquad l(\text{in } km) \cong \frac{t}{3}$$

so if total seconds are divided by 3 it directly gives the distance of lightning source in *km*.

(vi) When echo merges with clap the time between two claps is

$$\Delta t = \frac{3}{10} = 0.3 \text{ s}$$

in this time clap sound goes to wall and reflects back so we use

$$\Delta t = \frac{2d}{v}$$

$$\Rightarrow \qquad v = \frac{2d}{\Delta t} = \frac{100}{0.3} = 333 \text{ m/s}$$

(vii) Wave equations are

$$y = 0.3 \sin(314t - 1.57x)$$

and $$y' = 0.1 \sin(314t - 1.57x + 1.57)$$

phase difference between these waves is 1.57 rad = 90°

And ratio of intensities is

$$\frac{I_1}{I_2} = \left(\frac{A_1}{A_2}\right)^2 = \frac{9}{1}$$

(viii) In frame k wave equation is

$$y = A \cos(\omega t - kx)$$

In frame k' waves velocity is $v - V$

So motion equation for a point P is

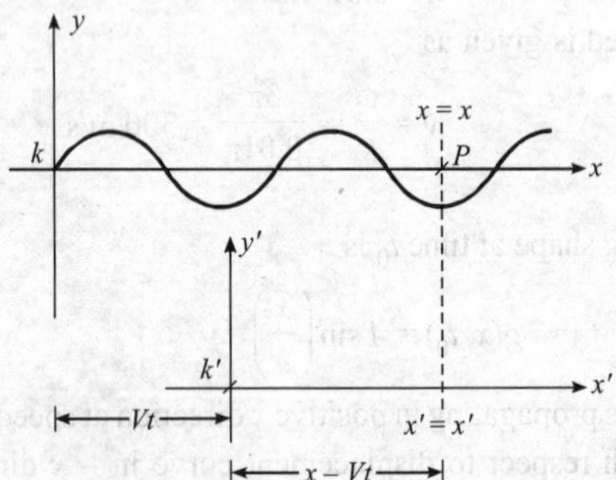

$$y' = A \cos[\omega t - k(x' + Vt)]$$

$$y' = A \cos[\omega t - kx' - kVt]$$

$$y' = A \cos\left[\omega\left(1 - \frac{V}{v}\right)t - kx'\right] \qquad \left(\text{as } k = \frac{\omega}{v}\right)$$

(ix) (a) In given equation displacement amplitude and wavelength are

$$A = 6 \times 10^{-5} \text{ m}$$

$$\frac{2\pi}{\lambda} = 1.8$$

$$\Rightarrow \qquad \lambda = \frac{6.28}{1.8} = 3.5 \text{ m}$$

Thus $$\frac{A}{\lambda} = \frac{6}{3.5} \times 10^{-5} = 1.71 \times 10^{-5}$$

(b) Velocity amplitude here is

$$v_{max} = A\omega = 6 \times 10^{-5} \times 600 = 3.6 \times 10^{-2} \text{ m/s}$$

Wave speed is $$v = \frac{\omega}{k} = \frac{600}{1.8} = 333.33 \text{ m/s}$$

Thus $$\frac{v_{max}}{v} = \frac{3.6 \times 10^{-2}}{333.33} = 1.08 \times 10^{-4}$$

(x) For the given equation

$$y = 50 \cos(1800t - 53x)$$

(a) Displacement Amplitude is

$$A = 50 \times 10^{-6} \text{ m}$$

Wavelength $$\lambda = \frac{2\pi}{k} = \frac{2\pi}{5.3} = 1.185 \text{ m}$$

Thus $$\frac{A}{\lambda} = \frac{50 \times 10^{-6}}{1.185} = 4.22 \times 10^{-5}$$

(b) Velocity amplitude is

$$v_{max} = A\omega = 50 \times 10^{-6} \times 1800$$

$$= 9 \times 10^{-2} \text{ m/s}$$

Wave velocity $$v = \frac{\omega}{k} = \frac{1800}{5.3} = 339.62 \text{ m/s}$$

Thus $$\frac{v_{max}}{v} = \frac{9 \times 10^{-2}}{339.62} = 2.65 \times 10^{-4}$$

(c) Relative deformation of medium is

$$\frac{\partial y}{\partial x} = 50 \times 5.3 \sin(1800t - 5.3x)$$

Thus $$\frac{\left(\frac{\partial y}{\partial x}\right)_{max}}{v_{max}} = \frac{50 \times 5.3}{9 \times 10^{-2}} = 2.94 \times 10^3$$

(xi) When rate is 40 per minute, duration between two beats is

$$\Delta t = \frac{60}{40} = 1.5 \text{ s}$$

$$\Rightarrow \quad 1.5 = \frac{2l}{v} \quad \ldots(1)$$

When rate is 60 per minute

$$\Delta t' = 1 \text{s}$$

$$\Rightarrow \quad 1 = \frac{2(l-90)}{v} \quad \ldots(2)$$

$$\frac{(1)}{(2)} \text{ gives} \quad 1.5 = \frac{l}{l-90}$$

$$\Rightarrow \quad 1.5l - 135 = l$$

$$\Rightarrow \quad 0.5l = 135$$

$$\Rightarrow \quad l = 270 \text{ m}$$

From (1) we use

$$1.5 = \frac{540}{v}$$

$$\Rightarrow \quad v = \frac{540}{1.5} = 360 \text{ m/s}$$

(xii) Angular frequency is

$$\omega = 2\pi n = 200\,\pi \text{ rad/s}$$

(a) Phase change $\quad \phi = \omega\delta t = 200\,\pi \times 2.5 \times 10^{-3}$

$$= \frac{\pi}{2}$$

(b) Phase difference

$$\phi = \frac{2\pi}{\lambda}\cdot\Delta$$

$$= \frac{200\pi}{350} \times 0.1 = \frac{2\pi}{35} \text{ rad}$$

Solutions of PRACTICE EXERCISE 6.2

(i) Wave speed on a wire is

$$v = \sqrt{\frac{I}{\mu}} = \sqrt{\frac{\tau l}{m}}$$

$$= \sqrt{\frac{8 \times 0.64}{5 \times 10^{-3}}} = 32 \text{ m/s}$$

(ii) (a) As displacement becomes zero zoo times per second, frequency is 100 Hz

Wave speed is $\quad v = \sqrt{\frac{T}{\mu}} = \sqrt{\frac{90}{0.1}} = 30 \text{ m/s}$

Wavelength $\quad \lambda = \frac{v}{n} = 0.3 \text{ m}$

(b) Wave equation is

$$y = A\sin(\omega t - kx + \phi)$$

As at $t = 0$, particle starts from positive extreme position, we use

$$\phi = \frac{\pi}{2}$$

$$\Rightarrow \quad y = 0.01\cos\left(200\pi t - \frac{2\pi}{0.3}x\right)$$

$$\Rightarrow \quad y = 0.01\cos 2\pi\left(100t - \frac{x}{0.3}\right)$$

(c) Velocity and acceleration of medium particles is given as

$$v = \frac{\partial y}{\partial t} = -0.01 \times 200\pi\sin 2\pi\left(100t - \frac{x}{0.3}\right)$$

$$\equiv 2\pi\sin 2\pi\left(1 - \frac{5}{3}\right) = -2\pi\sin\left(\frac{4\pi}{3}\right)$$

$$= -\sqrt{3}\pi = -5.45 \text{ m/s}$$

$$a = \frac{\partial v}{\partial t} = -0.01 \times (200\pi)^2\cos 2\pi\left(100t - \frac{x}{0.3}\right)$$

$$= -4000\cos\left(\frac{4\pi}{3}\right) = 2000 \text{ m/s}^2$$

(iii) Given that $\quad v_1 = 2v_2$

$$\sqrt{\frac{T}{P_1 S}} = 2\sqrt{\frac{T}{P_2 S}}$$

$$\Rightarrow \quad \frac{P_1}{P_2} = \frac{1}{4} = 0.25$$

(iv) Given that time period

$$T = 5 \times 4 = 20 \text{ m/s}$$

$$\Rightarrow \text{ frequency} \quad n = \frac{1}{T} = \frac{1000}{20} = 50 \text{ Hz}$$

$$\text{and} \quad \frac{\lambda}{2} = 2 \text{ cm}$$

$$\Rightarrow \quad \lambda = 4 \text{ cm}$$

Wave speed $\quad v = n\lambda = 50 \times 0.04 = 2 \text{ m/s}$

(v) We use $\quad v \propto \sqrt{T}$

$$\Rightarrow \quad \frac{v_1}{v_2} = \sqrt{\frac{T_1}{T_2}}$$

$$\Rightarrow \quad v_2 = v_1\sqrt{\frac{T_2}{T_1}} = 340\sqrt{\frac{305}{290}} = 348.68 \text{ m/s}$$

(vi) Tension in string is

$$T = kx = 160 \times 0.01 = 1.6 \text{ N}$$

Wave speed is $v = \sqrt{\frac{T}{\mu}} = \sqrt{\frac{Tl}{m}}$

$$= \sqrt{\frac{1.6 \times 0.4}{0.01}} = 8 \text{ m/s}$$

Time taken by pulse $t = \frac{l}{v} = \frac{0.4}{8} = 0.05 \text{ s}$

(vii) Sound speed $v = \sqrt{\frac{B}{P}}$

$$\Rightarrow \quad B = Pv^2$$

$$= 800 \times (1330)^2 = 1.415 \times 10^9 \text{ N-m}$$

We use $B = \left| \frac{\Delta P}{\frac{\Delta V}{V}} \right|$

$$\Rightarrow \quad \Delta V = \frac{\Delta PV}{B} = \frac{2 \times 10^5 \times 10^{-3}}{1.415 \times 10^9}$$

$$= 1.413 \times 10^{-7} \text{ m}^3$$

$$= 0.141 \text{ cm}^3$$

(viii) Sound speed in gases is given as

$$v = \sqrt{\frac{\gamma RT}{M}}$$

$$\Rightarrow \quad \frac{v_1}{v_2} = \sqrt{\frac{M_2}{M_1}}$$

$$\Rightarrow \quad v_{H_2} = v_{O_2}\sqrt{\frac{m_{O_2}}{M_{H_2}}} = 470 \times \sqrt{\frac{32}{2}}$$

$$= 1880 \text{ m/s}$$

(ix) (a) Wave speed

$$v = \sqrt{\frac{T}{\mu}} = \sqrt{\frac{49}{0.01}} = 70 \text{ m/s}$$

Wavelength $\lambda = \frac{v}{n} = \frac{70}{440} = 0.159 \text{ m}$

(b) Maximum particle speed is

$$v_{max} = A\omega = 0.5 \times 10^{-3} \times 2\pi \times 440$$

$$= 1.381 \text{ m/s}$$

Maximum particle acceleration is

$$a_{max} = A\omega^2 = 0.5 \times 10^{-3} \times (880\pi)^2$$

$$= 3872 \text{ m/s}$$

(c) Wave power is $P = 2\pi^2 n^2 A^2 \mu v$

$$= 2 \times 10 \times (440)^2 \times (0.5 \times 10^{-3}) \times (0.01) \times 70$$

$$= 0.667 \text{ W}$$

(x) No effect occurs on sound speed due to pressure change at same temperature

(xi) Sound intensity is given as

$$I = 2\pi^2 n^2 A^2 P v$$

$$0.8 = 2 \times 10 \times (1000)^2 \times A^2 \times 1.3 \times 330$$

$$\Rightarrow \quad A^2 = \frac{0.8}{2 \times 10^7 \times 1.3 \times 330} = 93.24 \times 10^{-12}$$

$$\Rightarrow \quad A = 9.656 \times 10^{-6} \text{ m}$$

Solutions of PRACTICE EXERCISE 6.3

(i) For a maxima minimum path difference should be λ

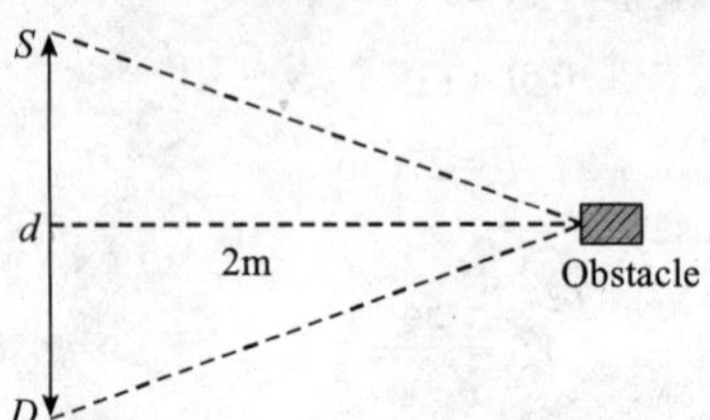

Wavelength

$$\lambda = \frac{v}{n} = \frac{360}{180} = 2 \text{ m}$$

If S and D are separated by d, we use

Path difference

$$\Delta = 2\sqrt{4 + \frac{d^2}{4}} - d$$

for maxima we use

$$\Delta = \lambda = 2 \text{ m}$$

$$2\sqrt{4 + \frac{d^2}{4}} - d = 2$$

$$4\left(4 + \frac{d^2}{4}\right) = 4 + d^2 - 4d$$

$$16 = 4 - 4d$$

$$\Rightarrow \quad d = 3 \text{ m}$$

(b) New path difference after displacing the obstacle should become

$$\Delta = \frac{3\lambda}{2} \text{ for minima}$$

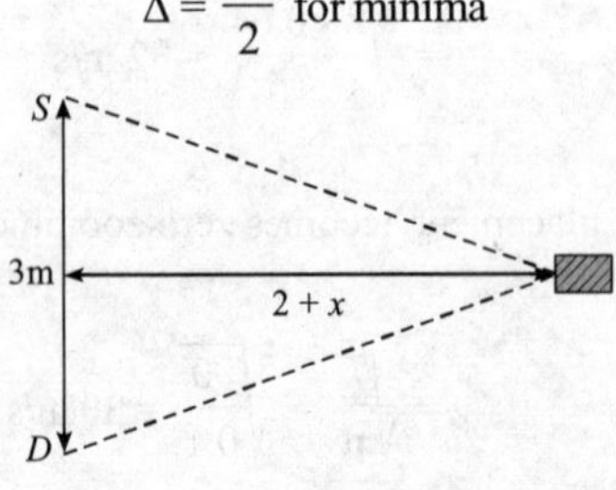

$$\Delta = 2\sqrt{(1.5)^2 + (2 + x)^2} - 3 = 3$$

$\Rightarrow \quad 4(2.25 + 4 + x^2 + 4x) = 36$

$$x^2 + 4x - 2.75 = 0$$

$$\Rightarrow \quad x = \frac{-4 + \sqrt{16 + 11}}{2} = 0.598 \text{ m}$$

(ii) Path difference $= 6.4 - 6 = 0.4$ m

High wavelength $= \dfrac{v}{n_L} = \dfrac{320}{500} = 0.64$ m

Low wavelength $= \dfrac{v}{n_H} = \dfrac{320}{5000} = 0.064$ m

Destructive interference occurs when

$$\Delta = (2n+1)\frac{\lambda}{2}$$

It happens when $\quad 0.4 = (2n+1)\dfrac{\lambda}{2}$

$$\Rightarrow \quad \lambda = \frac{0.8}{2n+1}$$

Thus corresponding frequencies are

$$n = \frac{320}{\lambda} = \frac{320}{0.8} \times (2n+1)$$

$$= 400(2n+1)$$

$$= 400 \text{ Hz}, 1200 \text{ Hz}, 2000 \text{ Hz}, 2800 \text{ Hz},$$

$$4400 \text{ Hz}, 5200 \text{ Hz} \ldots$$

Frequency in given range are 1200 Hz, 2000 Hz, 2800 Hz, 3600 Hz & 4400 Hz.

(iii) (a) S_1 — 10cm — S_2 — 20cm — P

Path difference 20 cm which is four times the wavelength so being an integral multiple of wavelength, phase difference is zero.

(b)

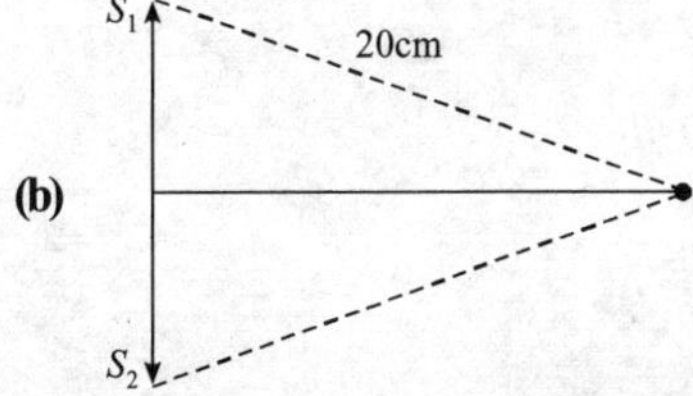

Due to symmetry phase difference at P is zero.

(iv) Due to symmetry phase difference at P is zero.
So waves will constructively interfere at P so intensity at P becomes four times that of individual intensity of each source. Now if one source is switched off the intensity at P will be only due to remaining source so it will be one fourth of resulting intensity.

(v) Given that

$$\Delta_1 = 11.5 \text{ cm} = (2n+1)\lambda/2 \quad \text{(Destructive)}$$

$$\& \quad \Delta_2 = 23 \text{ cm} = (2n+1)\lambda \quad \text{(Constructive)}$$

$$\Delta_3 = 34.5 \text{ cm} = (2n+1)\frac{3\lambda}{2} \quad \text{(Destructive)}$$

If there is no maxima or minima between Δ_1, Δ_2 and Δ_3 that means $n = 0$ for maximum wavelength or minimum frequency.

$$\Rightarrow \quad \frac{\lambda}{2} = 11.5 \text{ cm}$$

$$\Rightarrow \quad \lambda = 23 \text{ cm}$$

$$\Rightarrow \quad n = \frac{v}{\lambda} = \frac{331.2}{0.23} = 1440 \text{ Hz}$$

(vi) At point P we use three waves with then amplitude given as

$$\bar{R}_1 = A\angle 0^\circ$$

$$\bar{R}_2 = A\angle 120^\circ$$

$$\bar{R}_3 = A\angle 240^\circ$$

If we find the resultant we can see from the diagram symmetry that

$$\bar{R} = \bar{R}_1 + \bar{R}_2 + \bar{R}_3 = 0$$

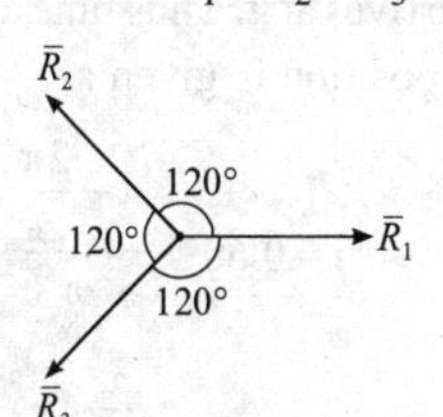

(vii) When waves are in phase resultant intensity is $I_0 = 4I_1$ where I_1 is intensity by each source.
If $I_2 = 0.36\, I_1$. Then we use

$$\frac{I_{max}}{I_{min}} = \left(\frac{\sqrt{I_1} + \sqrt{I_2}}{\sqrt{I_1} - \sqrt{I_2}}\right)^2$$

$$= \left(\frac{1.6}{0.4}\right)^2 = 16$$

(viii) (a) Path difference between waves at P is

$$\Delta = 0.04 \text{ m}$$

wavelength $\quad \lambda = \dfrac{v}{n} = \dfrac{0.5}{5} = 0.1$ m

$$= 2\pi \times 0.04 = \frac{4\pi}{5}$$

The waves from S_1 and S_2 arrive at point P at different time t_1 and t_2 given as

$$t_1 = \frac{0.3}{0.5} = 0.6 \text{ s and}$$

$$t_2 = \frac{0.34}{0.5} = 0.68 \text{ s}$$

equation of motion of cork it $t_0 = 3$ s is

$$y = y_1 + y_2$$
$$= A\sin(\omega + t_0 - t_1) A\sin(\omega + (t_0 - t_2))$$
$$= A[\sin(10\pi(2.4)) + \sin(10\pi(2.32))]$$
$$= 0.04 \times \sin(23.2\pi)$$
$$= -0.02344 \text{ m}$$

(b) If we consider $t = 0$ the time when cork starts it motion then the resulting oscillation at cork is given as

$$y = A\sin\omega t + A\sin(\omega t - \frac{4\pi}{5})$$
$$= R\sin(\omega t - \theta)$$

Where $$\theta = \tan^{-1}\left(\frac{A\sin(4\pi/5)}{A + A\cos(4\pi/5)}\right)$$

$$= 72° = \frac{2\pi}{5} \text{ rad}$$

Here initial phase of 72° (or $\frac{2\pi}{5}$ rad) will be there in cork motion when second wave arrives at it. Thus time after which cork will pass through mean position is given as

$$t = 0.68 + \frac{\pi - \frac{2\pi}{5}}{\omega}$$

$$= 0.68 + \frac{\frac{3\pi}{5}}{10\pi}$$

$$= 0.68 + 0.06 = 0.74 \text{ s}$$

(ix) (a) Path difference is

$$\Delta = \sqrt{(2.4)^2 + (1)^2} - 2.4$$
$$= 0.2 \text{ m}$$

wavelength $$A = \frac{v}{n} = \frac{340}{850} = 0.4 \text{ m}$$

phase difference $$\phi = \frac{2\pi}{\lambda} \times \Delta$$

$$= \frac{2\pi}{0.4} \times 0.2 = \pi$$

(b) Intensity of a point source is

$$I = \frac{P}{4\pi x^2}$$

Intensity of wave from A at D is

$$I_1 = \frac{25\pi}{4\pi(2.4)^2}$$

Intensity of wave from B at D is

$$I_2 = \frac{25\pi}{4\pi(2.6)^2}$$

Thus resulting intensity at D is

$$I = (\sqrt{I_1} - \sqrt{I_2})^2$$

$$= \left(\sqrt{\frac{25}{4(2.4)^2}} - \sqrt{\frac{25}{4(2.6)^2}}\right)^2 \text{ W/m}^2$$

$$= \left(\frac{5}{4.8} - \frac{5}{5.2}\right)^2 \text{ W/m}^2$$

$$= (1.0416 - 0.9615)^2 \text{ W/m}^2$$

$$= 0.0064 \text{ W/m}^2$$

(x) We use $$I_R = I_1 + I_2 + 2\sqrt{I_1 I_2}\cos\phi$$

$$= I + 4I + 4I\cos\left(\frac{2\pi}{3}\right)$$

$$= 3I$$

(xi) When board is moved through 20 cm, path difference will be 40 cm

Phase difference $$\phi = \frac{2\pi}{\lambda} \times 0.4 = \pi$$

$$\lambda = 0.8 \text{ m}$$

Wave frequency $$n = \frac{v}{\lambda} = \frac{336}{0.8} = 420 \text{ Hz}$$

Solutions of PRACTICE EXERCISE 6.4

(i) Loudness level ΔL (in dB) $= 10\log\frac{I_2}{I_1}$

if $I_2 = 2I_1$ we use

$$\Delta L(\text{in } dB) = 10\log(2)$$

$$= 10 \times 0.301 = 3.01\, dB$$

(ii) (a) Given that

$$\Delta L = 30\, dB$$

$$\Rightarrow \quad 30 = \log\frac{I_2}{I_1}$$

$$\Rightarrow \quad \frac{I_2}{I_1} = 10^3$$

(b) We use sound intensity in a medium is related to pressure amplitude as

$$I = \frac{\Delta P_0^2}{2\rho v}$$

$$\Rightarrow \quad \Delta P_0 = \sqrt{I}$$

$$\Rightarrow \quad \frac{\Delta P_2}{\Delta P_1} = \sqrt{\frac{I_2}{I_1}} = \sqrt{10^3} = 31.62$$

(iii) As loudness level increases by 10 *dB* we use

$$10 = 10 \log \frac{I_2}{I_1}$$

$$\Rightarrow \quad \frac{I_2}{I_1} = 10$$

$$\Rightarrow \quad \frac{\Delta P_2}{\Delta P_1} = \sqrt{\frac{I_2}{I_1}} = \sqrt{10}$$

(iv) (a) When pressure is maximum at a point, displacement is zero as pressure and displacement oscillate in phase difference of $\pi/2$.

(b) Pressure amplitude is related to displacement amplitude as

$$\Delta P_0 = \frac{2\pi}{\lambda} AB$$

$$\Rightarrow \quad A = \frac{\Delta P_0 \lambda}{2\pi B} = \frac{(10^{-4}\, atm).(330/1000)}{2 \times 3.14 \times 1.4 \times (1atm)}$$

$$= 3.753 \times 10^{-6}\,\text{m}$$

(v) (a) Intensity of sound due to a point source is

$$I = \frac{P}{4\pi r^2} = \frac{20}{4 \times 3.14 \times (6)^2}$$

$$= 0.0442\ \text{W/m}^2$$

(b) Pressure amplitude is given as

$$\Delta P_0 = \sqrt{2\rho v I}$$

$$= \sqrt{2 \times 1.2 \times 340 \times 0.0442}$$

$$= 6\ \text{Pa}$$

(c) Displacement amplitude is related to intensity as

$$I = 2\pi^2 n^2 A^2 \rho v$$

$$\Rightarrow \quad A = \sqrt{\frac{I}{2\pi^2 n^2 \rho v}}$$

$$= \sqrt{\frac{0.0442}{2 \times 10 \times (2000)^2 \times 1.2 \times 340}}$$

$$= 1.16 \times 10^{-6}\,\text{m}$$

(vi) For a point source we use

$$I = \frac{P}{4\pi x^2}$$

$$\Rightarrow \quad I_1 x_1^2 = I_2 x_2^2$$

$$\Rightarrow \quad I_2 = \frac{I_1 x_1^2}{x_2^2}$$

$$= \frac{10^{-8} \times 25}{625} = 4 \times 10^{-10}\ \text{W/m}^2$$

(vii) If sound intensity due to each student is I, given that

$$50 = 10 \log \frac{50I}{I_0}$$

When student count be comes 100 we use

$$L = 10 \log \frac{100I}{I_0}$$

$$= 10 \log \frac{50I}{I_0} + 10 \log (2)$$

$$= 50 + 3.01 = 53.01\ dB$$

(viii) (a) Intensity of wave at 20m from point source is

$$I_1 = \frac{P}{4\pi(20)^2}$$

Intensity at 10 m from source is

$$I_2 = \frac{P}{4\pi(10)^2} = 4I_1$$

Loudness level of I_2 is

$$L_2 = 10 \log \left(\frac{I_2}{I_0}\right)$$

$$= 10 \log \frac{4I_1}{I_0}$$

$$= 10 \log \left(\frac{I_1}{I_0}\right) + 10 \log 4$$

$$= 30 + 6.02$$

$$= 36.02\ dB$$

(b) Sound will not be heard when intensity goes below reference level so soddens becomes 0 *dB*

$$I_0 = 10^{-12}\ \text{w/m}^2$$

Given that at 20m distance loudness level is $30dB$

$$\Rightarrow \quad 30 = 10 \log \frac{I_1}{I_0}$$

$$\Rightarrow \quad I_1 = 10^{-3}\ \text{w/m}^2$$

Now for point sources we use

$$I_1 x_1^2 = I_2 x_2^2$$

$$\Rightarrow \quad 10^{-9}(20)^2 = 10^{-12}(x_2^2)$$

$$\Rightarrow \quad x_2^2 = (20)^2 \times 10^3$$

$$\Rightarrow \quad x_2^2 = 400 \times 10^3$$

$$\Rightarrow \quad x_2 = \sqrt{4 \times 10^5} = 632.45\ \text{m}$$

(ix) We use

$$\Delta L = 10 \log \frac{I_R}{I_N}$$

$$\Rightarrow \quad 65 = 10 \log \frac{I_R}{I_N}$$

$$\Rightarrow \quad \frac{I_R}{I_N} = 10^{6.5} = 3.16 \times 10^6$$

(x) Pressure amplitude is given as

$$\Delta P_0 = \sqrt{2\rho I v}$$

As $P.I$ and v are same for both waves so their pressure amplitudes will be equal.

Solutions of PRACTICE EXERCISE 6.5

(i) **(a)** If velocity of waves on wire is v, we use fundamental frequencies

$$n_0 = \frac{v}{2l}$$

$$\Rightarrow \quad v = 2l\, n_0 = 2 \times 1 \times 200 = 400 \text{ m/s}$$

(b) Wave velocity on wire is also given as

$$v = \sqrt{\frac{T}{\mu}} = \sqrt{\frac{T}{\rho S}}$$

$\Rightarrow$ longitudinal stress

$$\frac{T}{S} = \rho v^2$$

$$= 8000 \times (400)^2 \text{ N/m}^2$$

$$= 1.28 \times 10^9 \text{ N/m}^2$$

(c) Maximum acceleration in fundamental mode is at mid point given as

$$a = A\omega^2$$

$$\Rightarrow \quad A = \frac{a}{\omega^2} = \frac{800}{(2 \times 200)^2}$$

$$= \frac{800}{16 \times 10^5} = \frac{1}{2000} = 5 \times 10^{-4} \text{ m}$$

(ii) For second harmonic we use

$$n_f = \frac{2v}{2l}$$

$$\Rightarrow \quad v = n_f l = 256 \times 1.5 = 384 \text{ m/s}$$

(iii) For two loops vibrations, its second harmonic. Its frequency is given as

$$n = \frac{2v}{2l} = \frac{1}{l}\sqrt{\frac{T}{\mu}} = \frac{1}{1.5}\sqrt{\frac{90 \times 1.5}{12 \times 10^{-3}}}$$

$$= 70.71 \text{ Hz}$$

(iv) For n^{th} harmonic audible by person we use

$$1400 = x(200)$$

$$\Rightarrow \quad n = 70$$

(v) Initially we use frequency of force,

$$n_f = \frac{10}{2l}\sqrt{\frac{mg}{\mu}} \quad \ldots(1)$$

after block is dipped in water we use

$$n_f = \frac{11}{2l}\sqrt{\frac{mg(1-\rho_\omega/\rho_b)}{\mu}} \quad \ldots(2)$$

from (1) & (2) we use

$$10 = 11\sqrt{1-\rho_\omega/\rho_b}$$

$$\Rightarrow \quad 100\rho_b = 121\rho_b - 121\rho_\omega$$

$$\Rightarrow \quad \rho_b = \frac{121\rho_\omega}{21} = 5.76 \times 10^3 \text{ kg/m}^3$$

(vi) Fundamental frequency of wire is

$$h_0 = \frac{1}{2l}\sqrt{\frac{T}{\rho S}}$$

$$= \frac{1}{2 \times 0.5} \times \sqrt{\frac{79 \times 4}{8000 \times 3.14 \times (0.04 \times 10^{-2})^2}}$$

$$= 280 \text{ Hz}$$

Thus to setup 840 Hz, wire should setup in third harmonic for which wire must be supported at $l/3$ point from one end and plucked at $l/6$ point to setup oscillations.

(vii) Given wave is

$$y = A \cos(ax + bt)$$

(a) We use $\omega = b$ and $\frac{2\pi}{\lambda} = a$

$$\Rightarrow \quad \lambda = \frac{2\pi}{a} \text{ and } n = \frac{b}{2\pi}$$

$\Rightarrow$ Wave speed

$$v = n\lambda = \frac{b}{a}$$

(b) Equation of reflected wave is

$$y_r = 0.8\, A \cos(bt - ax - \pi) = 0.8A \cos(bt - ax)$$

Here phase of π is added due to reflection by an obstacle.

(c) After superposition maximum and minimum amplitudes are

$$A_{max} = 1.8\, b \text{ and } A_{min} = 0.2\, b$$

Thus maximum and minimum particle speeds are

$$v_{max} = A_{max}\,\omega = 1.8Ab$$

and

$$v_{min} = A_{min}\,\omega = 0.2\, Ab$$

(d) Resulting wave is given as

$$y_R = y + y_r$$
$$= A\cos(bt+ax) - 0.8\,A\cos(bt-ax) + [0.2\,A\cos(bt-ax) - 0.2A\cos(bt-ax)]$$
$$= 2A\sin bt \sin ax + 0.2\,A\cos(bt-ax)$$

(viii) For the given condition we must have

$$T_2 = 4T_1$$

if T_1 & T_2 are tensions in left and right strings. So if 4.8 kg mass is supported at a distance x from left we use for equilibrium of rod.

$$T_1 + T_2 = 60$$
$$\Rightarrow \quad 5I_1 = 60$$
$$\Rightarrow \quad T_1 = 12\,N$$

For torque about right and of rod we use

$$48(x) + 12(0.2) = 12(0.4)$$
$$\Rightarrow \quad 48x = 4.8 - 2.4 = 2.4$$
$$\Rightarrow \quad x = \frac{2.4}{48} = 0.05\text{ m}$$

(ix) (a) In first overtone we use

$$\lambda = l = 2\text{ m}$$

and frequency is

$$n_1 = \frac{v}{l} = \frac{200}{2} = 100\text{ Hz}$$

(b) As left end is node, we consider it as origin so we use equation of stationary wave as

$$y = A_0 \sin(kx)\cos\omega t$$

we choose cos ωt as at x = 50 cm there is an antinode in this case (first overtone) so wire start from extreme position.

Here $\quad k = \frac{2\pi}{\lambda} = \pi$ and $\omega = 2\pi n = 200\,\pi$

$$\Rightarrow \quad y = (0.5)\sin(\pi x)\cos(200\,\pi t)\text{ cm}$$

(x) (a) As the three resonant frequencies of a string are 90 Hz, 150 Hz and 210 Hz.

The height possible fundamental frequency in their *MCF* which is 30 Hz.

(b) Harmonics are $\frac{90}{30} = 3^{rd}$; 5th and $\frac{210}{30} = 7^{th}$

(c) These are 2nd, 4th and 6th overtones after fundamental frequencies

(d) For fundamental frequency we use

$$n_0 = \frac{v}{2l}$$
$$\Rightarrow \quad v = 2n_0 l = 2 \times 30 \times 0.8 = 48\text{ m/s}$$

Solutions of PRACTICE EXERCISE 6.6

(i) (a) For a closed pipe, we use

$$n_0 = \frac{v}{4l} = \frac{330}{4\times 0.15} = 550\text{ Hz}$$

As in closed pipe only odd harmonics are present, we use

$$n_{1_{OT}} = 3n_0 = 1650\text{ Hz}$$
$$n_{2_{OT}} = 5n_0 = 2750\text{ Hz}$$
$$n_{3_{OT}} = 7n_0 = 3850\text{ Hz}$$
$$n_{4_{OT}} = 9n_0 = 4950\text{ Hz}$$

(b) For an open pipe, we use

$$n_0 = \frac{v}{2l} = \frac{330}{2\times 0.15} = 1100\text{ Hz}$$

As in open pipe all harmonics are present, we use

$$n_{1_{OT}} = 2n_0 = 2200\text{ Hz}$$
$$n_{2_{OT}} = 3n_0 = 3300\text{ Hz}$$
$$n_{3_{OT}} = 4n_0 = 4400\text{ Hz}$$
$$n_{4_{OT}} = 5n_0 = 5500\text{ Hz}$$

(c) For closed pipe last overtone below audible frequency 20000 Hz is 17th overtone, given as

$$n_{17_{OT}} = 35 \times n_0 = 35 \times 550 = 19250\text{ Hz}$$

and for open pipe last one is 17th overtone given as

$$n_{17_{OT}} = 18\,n_0 = 18 \times 1100 = 19800\text{ Hz}$$

(ii) Given that $\frac{\lambda}{4} = 25$ cm

$$\Rightarrow \quad \lambda = 100\text{ cm}$$

Vibration frequency is

$$n = \frac{v}{\lambda} = \frac{340}{(1)} = 340\text{ Hz}$$

(iii) (a) As three successive frequencies 425 Hz, 595 Hz and 765 Hz. Then differences are 170 Hz so we can see these are 5th, 7th and 9th harmonics of 85 Hz frequency thus pipe is a closed one.

(b) As fundamental frequency is 85 Hz we use for a closed pipe

$$n_0 = \frac{v}{4l}$$
$$\Rightarrow \quad l = \frac{v}{4n_0} = \frac{340}{4\times 85} = 1\text{ m}$$

(iv) Resonating positions are separated by 8.5 cm displacement of piston so we use

$$\frac{\lambda}{2} = 8.5\text{ cm}$$
$$\Rightarrow \quad \lambda = 17\text{ cm}$$

wave speed is $v = n\lambda = 2000 \times 0.17 = 340$ m/s

(v) 'Pop' causes the closed pipe to oscillate in fundamental mode, so we use

$$n_0 = \frac{v}{4l} \qquad \ldots(1)$$

where l is such that pressure becomes 1.5 time so by Boyle's law

$$P(0.25) = 1.5\,P.l$$

$$\Rightarrow \qquad l = \frac{0.25}{1.5}$$

So from equation-(1)

$$n_0 = \frac{340 \times 1.5}{4 \times 0.25} = 510\,\text{Hz}$$

(vi) Fundamental frequency of tube is

$$n_0 = \frac{v}{2l} = \frac{340}{2 \times 0.5} = 340\,\text{Hz}$$

An open pipe resonates at all harmonics of fundamental frequency so the resinating frequencies are

$$n_R = 340\,\text{N}$$

frequencies between 1000 Hz & 2000 Hz are for $N = 3, 4, 5$

$$n_R = 1020\,\text{Hz},\ 1360\,\text{Hz}\ \&\ 1700\,\text{Hz}$$

(vii) From the given resonating lengths we can use

$$\Rightarrow \qquad 48 - 14.8 = \left(\frac{\lambda}{2}\right)$$

$$\Rightarrow \qquad \lambda = 66.4\,\text{cm}$$

Thus for given situation wavelength is $\lambda = 66.4$ cm so speed of sound is

$$v = n\lambda = 512 \times 0.664 = 339.97\,\text{m/s}$$

$\Rightarrow$ Fundamental frequency of tube is

$$n_0 = \frac{v}{2l} = \frac{339.97}{2 \times 0.6} = 283.30\,\text{Hz}$$

(viii) Sound wavelength is

$$\lambda = \frac{v}{n} = \frac{340}{340} = 1\,\text{m}$$

Resonance occurs when length of tube from open and is $\frac{\lambda}{4}$, $\frac{3\lambda}{4}$, $\frac{5\lambda}{4}$,.... and so on. Thus for this tube it is at 25 cm, 75 cm, 125 cm ... Here minimum length water is such that empty length becomes 75 cm hence

$$l = 120 - 75 = 45\,\text{cm}$$

(ix) (a) Given that

$$\frac{\lambda}{2} = 8\,\text{cm}$$

$$\Rightarrow \qquad \lambda = 16\,\text{cm}$$

Wave speed is

$$v = n\lambda = 2000 \times 0.16 = 320\,\text{m/s}$$

(b) At frequency 1600 hz wavelength is

$$\lambda = \frac{v}{n} = \frac{320}{1600} = 0.2\,\text{m}$$

$\Rightarrow$ distance between adjacent nodes is

$$\frac{\lambda}{2} = 0.1\,\text{m}$$

(c) For tube closed at both ends all harmonics of fundamental tube resonates so here fundamental frequency is

$$n_0 = 2000 - 1600 = 400\,\text{Hz}$$

$$\Rightarrow \qquad n_0 = \frac{v}{2l}$$

$$\Rightarrow \qquad l = \frac{v}{2n_0} = \frac{320}{2 \times 400} = 0.4\,\text{m}$$

(d) All resonating frequency will be from fundamental to 2000 Hz

$\Rightarrow$ $n_R = 400$ Hz, 800 Hz, 1200 Hz, 1600 Hz & 2000 Hz

Solutions of PRACTICE EXERCISE 6.7

(i) Given that

$$\frac{v}{2l_0} - \frac{v}{4l_c} = 5$$

$$\Rightarrow \qquad \frac{330}{2 \times 0.3} - \frac{330}{4l_c} = 5$$

$$\Rightarrow \qquad \frac{330}{4l_c} = 545$$

$$\Rightarrow \qquad l_c = 0.151376\,\text{m}$$

When the two pipes are in unison we use

$$\frac{v}{2l_0} = \frac{v}{4l'_c}$$

$$\Rightarrow \qquad l'_c = \frac{l_0}{2} = 0.15\,\text{m}$$

$$l_c - l'_c = 0.001376\,\text{m} = 0.1376\,\text{cm}$$

(ii) Initially we use

$$256 - n_0 = 4$$

because after loading wax on first fork of frequency n_0 it reduces so beat frequency will increases thus we use

$$n_0 = 252\,\text{Hz}$$

(iii) (a) The angular frequency of resulting wave will be of average frequency given as

$$\omega_R = \frac{\omega_1 + \omega_2}{2} = \frac{596\pi + 604\pi}{2} = 600\pi$$

Thus frequency is

$$f_R = \frac{\omega_R}{2\pi} = 300\text{ Hz}$$

(b) Beat frequency is given as

$$f_B = f_1 - f_2 = 302 - 298 = 4\text{ Hz}$$

(c) Ratio of maximum of minimum intensities is

$$\frac{I_{max}}{I_{min}} = \left(\frac{A_1 + A_2}{A_1 - A_2}\right)^2 = \left(\frac{0.8}{0.2}\right)^2 = 16$$

(iv) Given that $n_1 = 2n_{25}$

and $n_1 - n_{25} = 24 \times 3$

$\Rightarrow$ $n_{25} = 72\text{ Hz}$

$\Rightarrow$ $n_1 = 2 \times 72 = 144\text{ Hz}$

and $n_{16} = n_1 - 3 \times 15 = 99\text{ Hz}$

(v) When tension in A is increased its frequency increases and becomes 606 Hz

Thus $$\frac{n_A}{n_B} = \frac{606}{600} = 1.01$$

& we use $$\frac{n_A}{n_B} = \sqrt{\frac{T_A}{T_B}} = 1.01$$

$$\Rightarrow \quad \frac{T_A}{T_B} = 1.02$$

(vi) By making combination of frequency differences for the given beat frequencies then frequencies are 301 Hz, 303 Hz and 308 Hz

(vii) Let the SHM equations of these given frequencies are

$$y_1 = A\sin(800\,\pi t)$$
$$y_2 = A\sin(802\,\pi t)$$
$$y_3 = A\sin(804\,\pi t)$$

Resulting oscillation displacement is given as

$$y_R = y_1 + y_2 + y_3$$
$$= A[\sin(800\,\pi t) + \sin(802\,\pi t) + \sin(804\pi t)]$$
$$= A[(\sin 802\,\pi t) + 2\sin(802\pi t)(\cos 2\pi t)]$$
$$= A[1 + 2\cos(2\pi t)]$$
$$= R\sin(802\,\pi t)$$

Thus resulting sound is of average frequency 401 Hz and time varying amplitude given as

$$R = A(1 + 2\cos(2\pi t))$$

Here R will be maximum when

$$\cos 2\pi t = +1$$

$$\Rightarrow \quad 2\pi t = 2N\pi$$

$$\Rightarrow \quad t = N$$

Thus at $t = 0, 1, 2, \ldots$ time instants maxima occurs so beat period here is 1s so beat frequency is given as

$$f_B = \frac{1}{T_B} = 1\text{ Hz}$$

(viii) On decreasing length of wire its frequency increases thus frequency of wire initially was 252 Hz.

Thus we use

$$252 = \frac{1}{2(0.25)}\sqrt{\frac{T}{\mu}} \quad \ldots(1)$$

On changing wire length to l' its frequency becomes 256 Hz and beats becomes zero

Thus $$256 = \frac{1}{2(l')}\sqrt{\frac{T}{\mu}} \quad \ldots(2)$$

$\frac{(1)}{(2)}$ gives

$$\frac{l'}{0.25} = \frac{252}{256}$$

$$\Rightarrow \quad l' = 0.246\text{ m}$$

Difference

$$0.25 - 0.246 = 0.0039\text{ m} = 0.39\text{ cm}$$

Solutions of PRACTICE EXERCISE 6.8

(i) While car is approaching apparent frequency is

$$n_{\text{ap1}} = n_0\left(\frac{v}{v - v_c}\right)$$

while recording away apparent frequency is

$$n_{\text{ap2}} = n_0\left(\frac{v}{v + v_c}\right)$$

Given that percentage drop in pitch is 10%. Thus we use

$$\frac{n_{ap1} - n_{ap2}}{n_{ap1}} \times 100 = 0$$

$$\frac{\frac{v}{v - v_c} - \frac{v}{v + v_c}}{\frac{v}{v - v_c}} = 0.1$$

$$10\left(\frac{2v_c}{v + v_c}\right) = 1$$

$$20v_c = v + v_c$$

$$v_c = \frac{v}{19} = \frac{330}{19} = 17.37\text{ m/s}$$

(ii) As both cars are travelling in same direction, we use for reflected sound

$$n_{ap} = 500\left(\frac{340+20}{340-10}\right)$$

$$= 545.45\,\text{Hz}$$

(iii) We use $v = \frac{\Delta\lambda}{\lambda}c$

$$= \frac{0.5}{100} \times 3 \times 10^8 = 1.5 \times 10^6\,\text{m/s}$$

(iv) Apparent frequency received by motorist directly from ban is

$$n_1 = n_0\left(\frac{v+v_m}{v+v_b}\right)$$

Apparent frequency received by motorist from reflected sound by wall is

$$n_2 = n_0\left(\frac{v+v_m}{v-v_b}\right)$$

Beat frequency

$$n_B = n_2 - n_1$$

$$= (v+v_m)\left(\frac{1}{v-v_b} - \frac{1}{v+v_b}\right)$$

$$= \frac{2v_b(v+v_m)}{(v^2-v_b^2)}n_0$$

(v) If speed of astronaut is v

The apparent frequency received in echo is

$$n_{ap} = n_0\left(\frac{c+v}{c-v}\right)$$

$$\Rightarrow \quad n_{ap} = n_0\left(1+\frac{v}{c}\right) n_0\left(1-\frac{v}{c}\right)^{-1} \quad [\text{As } v << c]$$

$$\Rightarrow \quad n_{ap} = n_0\left(1+\frac{2v}{c}\right)$$

$$\Rightarrow \quad n_{ap} - n_0 = \frac{2n_0 v}{c}$$

$$\Rightarrow \quad v = \frac{c(\Delta h)}{2n_0} = \frac{3\times10^8 \times 10^3}{2\times5\times10^9} = 30\,\text{m/s}$$

(vi) Apparent frequency of direct sound from fork is

$$n_{ap_1} = n_0\left(\frac{v}{v+v_F}\right)$$

Apparent frequency of reflected sound from wall is

$$n_{ap_2} = n_0\left(\frac{v}{v-v_F}\right)$$

Beat frequency

$$n_B = n_{ap_2} - n_{ap_1}$$

$$= n_0 v\left(\frac{1}{v-v_F} - \frac{1}{v+v_F}\right)$$

$$= \frac{2n_0 vF}{v^2 - v_F^2}$$

$$= \frac{2\times512\times330\times3}{(330)^2-(3)^2}$$

$$= 9.3\,\text{Hz}$$

(vii)

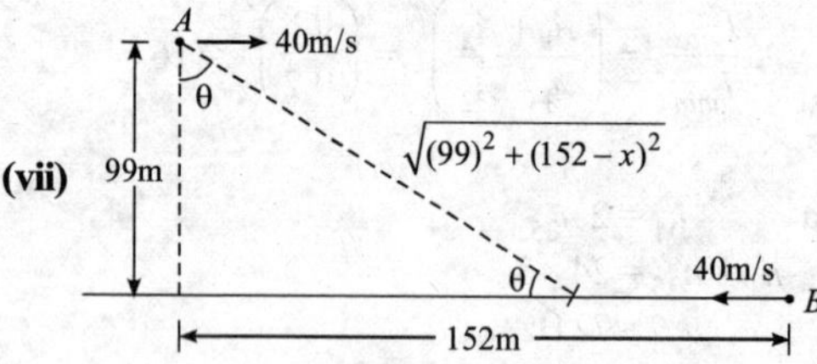

From figure id driver of train B receives the sound at point P, we use

$$\frac{\sqrt{(99)^2+(152-x)^2}}{330} = \frac{x}{40}$$

$$\Rightarrow \quad (4)^2[(99)^2+(152)^2+(x)^2-304x] = (33)^2x^2$$

$$1073x^2 + 4864x - 526480 = 0$$

$$\Rightarrow \quad x = \frac{-4864+\sqrt{(4864)^2+4(1073)(526480)}}{2\times1073}$$

$$= \frac{-4864+47784}{2\times1073} = 20\,\text{m}$$

Thus is figure

$$\cos\theta = \frac{132}{\sqrt{(99)^2+(132)^2}} = \frac{132}{165} = 0.8$$

Apparent frequency is

$$n_{ap} = 596\left[\frac{330+40\times\cos\theta}{330-40\cos\theta}\right]$$

$$= 596\left[\frac{330+32}{330-32}\right] = 724\,\text{Hz}$$

(viii) Apparent wavelength becomes

$$\lambda_{ap} = \lambda_0 - v\left(\frac{\lambda_0}{c}\right)$$

$$\lambda_{app} = \lambda_0\left(1-\frac{v}{c}\right)$$

$$540 = 620\left(1-\frac{v}{c}\right)$$

$$\Rightarrow \quad 1-\frac{v}{c}=\frac{27}{31}$$

$$\Rightarrow \quad \frac{v}{c}=\frac{4}{31}$$

$$\Rightarrow \quad v=\frac{4}{31}\times 3\times 10^8=3.87\times 10^7 \text{ m/s}$$

As this speed in much higher then escape velocity on earth. This is not attainable.

Solutions of CONCEPTUAL MCQS Single Option Correct

Sol. 1 (A) As $T_P > T_Q$ wavelength of maximum energy by Q will be more than that of P and as on earth both wavelengths received are same hence P is receding with more speed as the received wavelength by the observer behind a moving source will increase with the speed.

Sol. 2 (D) Longitudinal at the bottom of lake in the volume of water and both longitudinal and transverse at the surface of lake as due to surface tension particles move in elliptical path.

Sol. 3 (B) When the two waves superpose then the maximum amplitude will be 4 + 3 = 7 and minimum will be 4 – 3 = 1 hence the ratio of maximum to minimum intensity will be 49 and as the frequencies of the two waves are 200 Hz and 202 Hz the beat frequency will be 2 Hz.

Sol. 4 (D) As we know that intensity of a wave is directly proportional to square of frequency as well as square of amplitude hence in this case option (D) is correct.

Sol. 5 (A) The fundamental frequency of closed pipe is $v/4L = 425$ Hz. Hence option (A) is correct.

Sol. 6 (B) Wave intensity is directly proportional to square of frequency as well as square of its amplitude hence option (B) is correct.

Sol. 7 (A) Frequency received by aircraft is

$$n_a = n_0\left(\frac{v+v_a}{v}\right)$$

then frequency of reflected waves received back by radar is

$$n_R = n_a\left(\frac{v}{v-v_a}\right)=n_0\left(\frac{v+v_a}{v-v_a}\right)=600\left(\frac{v+v_a}{v-v_a}\right)$$

$$\Rightarrow \quad n_R(v-v_a)=n_0(v+v_a)$$

$$\Rightarrow \quad (n_R-n_0)\,v=(n_0+n_R)\,v_a$$

$$\Rightarrow \quad v_a=\frac{6\times 10^3}{12\times 10^8}\times 3\times 10^8=1.5\times 10^3 \text{ m/s}$$

$$= 1.5 \text{ km/s}$$

Sol. 8 (B) As density of moist air is less than that of dry air and speed of sound is inversely proportional to the square root of the density of air, option (B) is correct.

Sol. 9 (A) Here relative to ground the speed of bullet is more than that of sound so bullet will arrive earlier than the sound.

Sol. 10 (B) In this case the speed of bullet relative to ground is less than that of sound so it will arrive later than sound.

Sol. 11 (D) The quality of sound is detected by the overtones present in the sound. As overtones change in a specific device the sound quality changes by which we can differentiate same frequency sound from two different types of sound sources.

Sol. 12 (D) As wavelength is more that means galaxy is receding away from earth at speed given as

$$v=\frac{\Delta\lambda}{\lambda}\times C=0.05\times 3\times 10^8=1.5\times 10^7 \text{ m/s.}$$

Sol. 13 (C) The wave function can be expressed as

$$y=(a/2)[1+\cos(\omega t-kx)]$$

So here option (C) is correct

Sol. 14 (B) For an open pipe, fundamental frequency is $v/2L = 850$ Hz hence the given frequency will resonate with second harmonic of the fundamental frequency.

Sol. 15 (B) The maximum particle velocity is given by $v = A\omega$ and the wave velocity is given as $V = \omega/k$ and the two will be equal when $A = 1/k = \lambda/2\pi$.

Sol. 16 (D) At time t in the given equation we can replace x by $(x\text{-}vt)$ by shifting of origin due to propagation of wave.

Sol. 17 (B) The given function can be given as a function of $(x - 3t)$ which can be expressed as a wave pulse travelling at a speed of 3 m/s in positive x direction.

Sol. 18 (C) As the waves are coherent (same frequency and constant phase difference) interference will take place but as amplitudes are not equal minimum amplitude will be non zero hence minimum intensity will be more than zero.

Sol. 19 (D) From the given equation we can see that option (D) is correct.

Sol. 20 (B) As both source and observer are at rest the number of wavefronts / oscillations reaching to observer per unit time so frequency received will be same.

Sol. 21 (D) Resultant Displacement

$y = y_1 + y_2$

for y to be zero

$(2x - 3t)^2 = (2x + 3t - 6)^2$

on solving $(x - \frac{3}{2})(t - 1) = 0$

Therefore at $x = \frac{3}{2}$, resultant displacement is zero for all values of t.

Sol. 22 (A) Maximum pressure variation takes place at nodes. [Slope of the wave function is maximum at nodes]

Sol. 23 (C) The minimum distance between the two particles having same speed is $\lambda/2$.

Sol. 24 (B) In figure, 'C' reaches the position where 'A' already reached after $\omega t = \frac{\pi}{2}$ and 'A' reaches the position where 'B' already reached after $\omega t = \frac{\pi}{2}$.

Sol. 25 (C) In the figure shown below, at point A, the path difference is 2.5 λ and at B, path difference is zero. While moving from A to B, path difference changes from 2.5λ to zero, making two maxima corresponding to path differences 2λ and λ (excluding point B). Including point B, in upper half of circle there are five maxima thus detector will detect total 10 maxima in one circular movement.

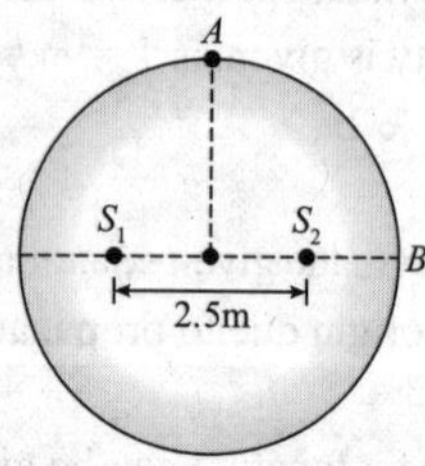

Sol. 26 (B) For the situation shown in figure given in question, after two seconds pulse will overlap each other. According to super position principle the string will not have any distortion and will be straight and when string is straight, it will not have any potential energy and total energy is kinetic energy.

Sol. 27 (D) Energy density of wave is given as

$$u = 2\pi^2 n^2 \rho a^2$$

If wave frequency and medium density are same, we have

$$u \propto a^2$$

$$\Rightarrow \quad \frac{u_1}{u_2} = \frac{a_1^2}{a_2^2} = \frac{5^2}{2^2}$$

$$\Rightarrow \quad u_1 : u_2 = 25 : 4$$

Solutions of NUMERICAL MCQS Single Option Correct

Sol. 1 (B) $\text{Time} = \frac{\text{Distance}}{\text{Velocity}} = \frac{1000}{330} = 3.03 \text{ s}$

Sound will be heard after 3.03 s. So his watch is set 3 s, slower.

Sol. 2 (D) $\lambda = \frac{v}{n} = \frac{352}{384}$ m thus during 1 vibration of fork sound will travel $\frac{352}{384}$ m so during 36 vibration of fork sound will travel $\frac{352}{384} \times 36 = 33$ m.

Sol. 3 (C) Wave equations are

$$y_1 = 10 \sin\left(3\pi t + \frac{\pi}{3}\right) \quad \ldots(1)$$

and $\quad y_2 = 5[\sin 3\pi t + \sqrt{3}\cos 3\pi t]$

$$\Rightarrow \quad y_2 = 5 \times 2\left[\frac{1}{2} \times \sin 3\pi t + \frac{\sqrt{3}}{2} \times \cos 3\pi t\right]$$

$$\Rightarrow \quad y_2 = 10\left[\cos\frac{\pi}{3}\sin 3\pi t + \sin\frac{\pi}{3}\cos \pi t\right]$$

$$\Rightarrow \quad y_2 = 10\left[\sin\left(3\pi t + \frac{\pi}{t}\right)\right] \quad \ldots(2)$$

Using $\sin(A + B) = \sin A \cos B + \cos A \sin B$

Comparing equation-(1) and (2) we get ratio of amplitude 1 : 1.

Sol. 4 (B) In case of interference of two waves resultant intensity is give as

$$I_R = I_1 + I_2 + 2\,2\sqrt{I_1 I_2}\cos\phi$$

$\Rightarrow$ If ϕ varies randomly with time, so $(\cos\phi)_{av} = 0$

$\Rightarrow$ $I = I_1 + I_2$

For n identical waves, $I = I_0 + I_0 + \ldots = n I_0$ here $I = 10 I_0$.

Sol. 5 (D) Intensity $\propto a^2\omega^2$ here $\frac{a_A}{a_B} = \frac{2}{1}$ and $\frac{\omega_A}{\omega_B} = \frac{1}{2}$

$$\Rightarrow \quad \frac{a_A}{a_B} = \left(\frac{2}{1}\right)^2 \times \left(\frac{1}{2}\right)^2 = \frac{1}{1}$$

Sol. 6 (D) Because the tuning fork is in resonance with air column in the pipe closed at one end, the frequency is $n = \frac{(2N-1)v}{4l}$ where $N = 1, 2, 3 \ldots$ corresponds to different mode of vibration putting $n = 340$ Hz, $v = 340$ m/s, the length of air column in the pipe can be

$$l = \frac{(2N-1)340}{4 \times 340} = \frac{(2N-1)}{4} m = \frac{(2N-1) \times 100}{4} \text{ cm}$$

For $N = 1, 2, 3, \ldots$ we get $l = 25$ cm, 75 cm, 125 cm ...

As the tube is only 120 cm long, length of air column after water is poured in it may be 25 cm or 75 cm only, 125 cm is not possible, the corresponding length of water column in the tube will be (120 – 25) cm = 95 cm or (120 – 75) cm = 45 cm.
Thus minimum length of water column is 45 cm.

Sol. 7 **(B)** Speed of sound in gases is given by $v = \sqrt{\frac{\gamma RT}{M}}$

$$\Rightarrow \quad v \propto \frac{1}{\sqrt{M}} \quad \Rightarrow \quad \frac{v_1}{v_2} = \sqrt{\frac{A_2}{A_1}}$$

Sol. 8 **(C)** Critical hearing frequency for a person is 20,000 Hz. If a closed pipe vibration in N^{th} mode then frequency of vibration

$$n = \frac{(2N-1)v}{4l} = (2N-1)n_1$$

(where n_1 = fundamental frequency of vibration)
Hence 20,000 = (2N – 1) × 500 ⇒ $N = 7.1 \approx 7$
Also, in closed pipe we use
Number of over tones = (No. of mode of vibration) – 1
= 7 – 1 = 6

Sol. 9 **(B)** We use frequency of wave is

$$n = \frac{3600}{2\times 60}\text{Hz}$$

$$\Rightarrow \quad \lambda = \frac{v}{n} = \frac{760}{30} = 25.3\text{ m}$$

Sol. 10 **(D)** Let n_A = Known frequency = 256 Hz beat frequency β = 2 Hz, which is decreasing after loading tuning fork A. Thus we use

$$n_A - n_B = \beta$$

$$\Rightarrow \quad 256 - n_B = 2$$

$$\Rightarrow \quad n_B = 254\text{ Hz}$$

Sol. 11 **(A)** We use

$$L_1 = 10\log_{10}\left(\frac{I_1}{I_0}\right) \text{ and } L_2 = 10\log_{10}\left(\frac{I_2}{I_0}\right)$$

So $\quad L_2 - L_1 = 10\log_{10}\left(\frac{I_2}{I_1}\right)$

As sound power ∝ intensity, we use

$$L_2 - L_1 = 10\log_{10}\left(\frac{P_2}{P_1}\right)$$

$$= 10\log_{10}\left(\frac{400}{20}\right)$$

$$= 10\log_{10}20$$

$$= 10\log(2\times 10)$$

$$= 10(0.301 + 1) = 13\text{ dB}$$

Sol. 12 **(B)** Let e be the end correction then according to the given situation

$$\frac{v}{4(l_1+e)} = \frac{3v}{4(l_2+e)}$$

$$\Rightarrow \quad e = 2.5\text{ cm} = 0.025\text{ m}$$

Sol. 13 **(B)** When observer moves towards stationary source then apparent frequency

$$n' = \left[\frac{v+v_0}{v}\right]n = \left[\frac{v+v/5}{v}\right]n = \frac{6}{5}n = 1.2n$$

Increment in frequency = $0.2n$ so percentage change in frequency = $\frac{0.2n}{n}\times 100 = 20\%$

Sol. 14 **(C)** For an isotropic source we use

$$I \propto \frac{1}{r^2}$$

$$\Rightarrow \quad \frac{I_2}{I_1} = \frac{r_1^2}{r_2^2}$$

$$\Rightarrow \quad \frac{I_2}{1\times 10^{-2}} = \frac{2^2}{10^2} = \frac{4}{100}$$

$$\Rightarrow \quad I_2 = \frac{4\times 10^{-2}}{100} = 4\times 10^{-4}\ \mu\text{W/m}^2$$

Sol. 15 **(C)** Frequency of first over tone of closed organ pipe = Frequency of first over tone of open organ pipe

$$\Rightarrow \quad \frac{3v}{4L_1} = \frac{v}{L_2}$$

$$\Rightarrow \quad \frac{3}{4L_1}\sqrt{\frac{\gamma P}{\rho_1}} = \frac{1}{L_2}\sqrt{\frac{\gamma P}{\rho_2}} \quad \left[\text{As } v = \sqrt{\frac{\gamma P}{\rho}}\right]$$

$$\Rightarrow \quad L_2 = \frac{4L_1}{3}\sqrt{\frac{\rho_1}{\rho_2}} = \frac{4L}{3}\sqrt{\frac{\rho_1}{\rho_2}}$$

Sol. 16 **(C)** Frequency of vibration of string in 'p' loops is given as

$$n = \frac{p}{2l}\sqrt{\frac{T}{m}}$$

From Melde's law

$$p\sqrt{T} = \text{constant}$$

$$\Rightarrow \quad \frac{p_1}{p_2} = \sqrt{\frac{T_2}{T_1}}$$

Hence $\frac{4}{6} = \sqrt{\frac{T_2}{(50+15)\text{gm-force}}} \quad \Rightarrow \quad T_2 = 28.8\text{ gm-}f$

Hence weight removed from the pan

$$= T_1 - T_2 = 65 - 28.8 = 36.2\text{ gm-force} \cong 0.036\text{ kg-}f$$

Sol. 17 (A) We rewrite the given equations as $y = \dfrac{1}{1+(x-vt)^2}$

For $t = 0$, this becomes $y = \dfrac{1}{(1+x^2)}$, and

For $t = 2$ s, this becomes $y = \dfrac{1}{[1+(x-2v)^2]} = \dfrac{1}{[1+(x-1)^2]}$

$\Rightarrow\ 2v = 1$ or $v = 0.5$ m/s

Sol. 18 (C) We use

$$v = \frac{\text{Co-efficient of } t}{\text{Co-efficient of } x} = \frac{628}{31.4} = 20 \text{ cm/s}$$

Sol. 19 (B) Distance between the consecutive node $= \dfrac{\lambda}{2}$

We use $\quad \lambda = \dfrac{v}{n} = \dfrac{20}{n}$

$$\Rightarrow \quad \frac{\lambda}{2} = \frac{10}{n}$$

Sol. 20 (A) Waves $Z_1 = A \sin(kx - \omega t)$ is travelling towards positive x-direction.

Wave $Z_2 = A \sin(kx + \omega t)$, is travelling towards negative x-direction.

Wave $Z_3 = A \sin(ky - \omega t)$ is travelling towards positive y-direction.

Since waves Z_1 and Z_2 are travelling along the same line so they will produce stationary wave.

Sol. 21 (B) We use

$$v = \frac{\text{Coefficent of } t}{\text{Coefficent of } x} = \frac{1/2}{1/4} = 2 \text{ m/s}$$

Hence $\quad d = vt = 2 \times 8 = 16$ m

Sol. 22 (B) We have

$$y_1 = 10^{-6} \sin[100\,t + (x/50) + 0.5]$$

$$y_2 = 10^{-6} \sin\left[100t + \left(\frac{x}{50}\right) + \left(\frac{\pi}{2}\right)\right]$$

Phase difference ϕ

$= [100\,t + (x/50) + 1.57] - [100t + (x/50) + 0.5] = 1.07$ radians.

Sol. 23 (D) We have

$$y_1 = a \sin(\omega t - kx)$$

and $\quad y_2 = a\cos(\omega t - kx) = a \sin\left(\omega t - kx + \dfrac{\pi}{2}\right)$

Hence phase difference between these two is $\dfrac{\pi}{2}$.

Sol. 24 (B) To produce 5 beats/sec. Frequency of one wire should be increase up to 505 Hz. i.e. increment of 1% in basic frequency

$$n \propto \sqrt{T} \text{ or } T \propto n^2$$

$$\Rightarrow \quad \frac{\Delta T}{T} = 2\frac{\Delta n}{n}$$

$\Rightarrow$ percentage change in Tension = 2(1%) = 2%

Sol. 25 (A) We use

$$n' = n\left(\frac{v}{v - v_S}\right) \Rightarrow \frac{n'}{n} = \frac{v}{v - v_S}$$

$$\Rightarrow \quad \frac{v}{v - v_S} = 3 \Rightarrow v_s = \frac{2v}{3}$$

Sol. 26 (B) If suppose n_s = frequency of string $= \dfrac{1}{2l}\sqrt{\dfrac{T}{m}}$

n_f = Frequency of tuning fork = 480 Hz

x = Beats heard per second = 10

as tension T increases, so n_s increases (↑)

Also it is given that number of beats per sec decreases (i.e. $x\downarrow$)

Hence $n_s\uparrow - n_f = x\downarrow$ ...(i) ⟶ Wrong

$n_f - n_s\uparrow = x\downarrow$ ... (ii) ⟶ Correct

$\Rightarrow\ n_s = n_f - x = 480 - 10 = 470$ Hz

Sol. 27 (D) We use

$$y = 0.021 \sin(x + 30t)$$

Wave speed is given as

$$v = \frac{\omega}{k} = \frac{30}{1} = 30 \text{ m/s}$$

Using, $\quad v = \sqrt{\dfrac{T}{m}}$

$$\Rightarrow \quad 30 = \sqrt{\frac{T}{1.3 \times 10^{-4}}}$$

$$\Rightarrow \quad T = 0.117 \text{ N}$$

Sol. 28 (D) To detect a maxima, phase difference at the location of detector (At point P as shown in figure below) should be

$$\Delta\phi = 2n\pi$$

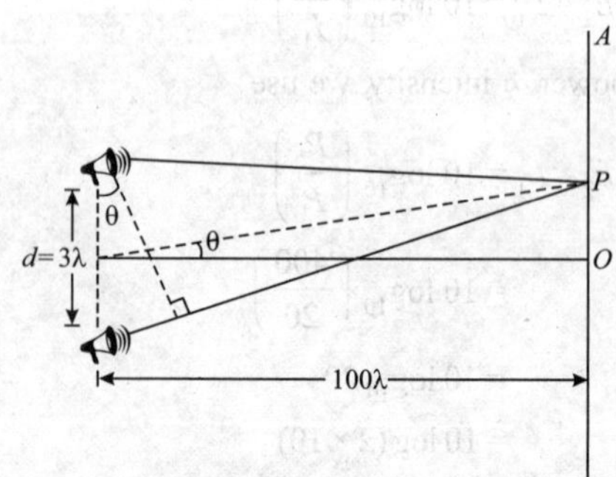

Physical path difference at a point P is calculated as illustrated in illustrative example 6-23 which is $d\sin\theta$. Initial phase difference between the sources is given as $\pi/2$ hence for a maxima at detector, the phase difference at

$$\Rightarrow \frac{2\pi}{\lambda}d\sin\theta - \frac{\pi}{2} = 2n\pi$$

$$\Rightarrow \frac{2\pi}{\lambda}d\sin\theta = \left(2n+\frac{1}{2}\right)\pi$$

$$\Rightarrow \sin\theta = \left(2n+\frac{1}{2}\right)\frac{\lambda}{2d}$$

For first maxima, we use $n = 0$ and using θ as very small angle, it gives

$$\sin\theta \approx \theta = \frac{1}{2}\times\frac{\lambda}{2\times 3\lambda} = \frac{1}{12}$$

$$\Rightarrow \frac{y}{100\lambda} = \frac{1}{12}$$

$$\Rightarrow y = \frac{100\lambda}{12} = \frac{25\lambda}{3}$$

Sol. 29 (A) We use

$$n' = n\left(\frac{v}{v-v_S}\right) = n\left(\frac{v}{v-v/10}\right)$$

$$\Rightarrow \frac{n'}{n} = \frac{10}{9}$$

Sol. 30 (B) For string mass per unit length is

$$\frac{10^{-2}}{0.4} = 2.5\times 10^{-2}\ \text{kg/m}$$

$$\Rightarrow \text{Wave Velocity } v = \sqrt{\frac{T}{m}} = \sqrt{\frac{16}{2.5\times 10^{-2}}} = 8\ \text{m/s}$$

For constructive interference between successive pulses

$$\Delta t_{min} = \frac{2l}{v} = \frac{2(0.4)}{8} = 0.1\ \text{s}$$

(After two reflections, the wave pulse is in same phase as it was produced since in one reflection it's phase changes by, and if at this moment next identical pulse is produced, then constructive interference will be obtained.

Sol. 31 (C) Suppose d = distance of epicenter of Earth quake from point of observation

v_s = Speed of S-wave and v_p = Speed of P-wave then $d = v_P t_P = v_S t_S$ or $8t_P = 4.5 t_S$

$$\Rightarrow t_P = \frac{45}{8}t_S, \text{ given that } t_S - t_P = 240$$

$$\Rightarrow t_S - \frac{4.5}{8}t_S = 240 \Rightarrow t_S = \frac{240\times 8}{3.5} = 548.5\ \text{s}$$

$$\Rightarrow d = v_S t_S = 4.5\times 548.5 = 2468.6 \approx 2500\ \text{km}$$

Sol. 32 (D) Path difference $(\Delta x) = 50\ \text{cm} = \frac{1}{2}\ \text{m}$

$$\Rightarrow \text{Phase difference } \Delta\phi = \frac{2\pi}{\lambda}\times\Delta x \Rightarrow \phi = \frac{2\pi}{1}\times\frac{1}{2} = \pi$$

$$\text{Total phase difference} = \pi - \frac{\pi}{3} = \frac{2\pi}{3}$$

$$\Rightarrow A = \sqrt{a^2 + a^2 + 2a^2\cos(2\pi/3)} = a$$

Sol. 33 (B) Given that

$a_1 = 5, a_2 = 10$

$$\Rightarrow \frac{I_{max}}{I_{min}} = \frac{(a_1+a_2)^2}{(a_1-a_2)^2} = \left(\frac{5+10}{5-10}\right)^2 = \frac{9}{1}.$$

Sol. 34 (C) We know frequency $n = \frac{p}{2l}\sqrt{\frac{T}{\pi r^2\rho}} \Rightarrow n \propto \frac{1}{\sqrt{\rho}}$

i.e., graph between n and $\sqrt{\rho}$ will be hyperbola.

Sol. 35 (D) Frequency of vibration in tight string

$$n = \frac{p}{2l}\sqrt{\frac{T}{m}} \Rightarrow n \propto \sqrt{T}$$

$$\Rightarrow \frac{\Delta n}{n} = \frac{\Delta T}{2T} = \frac{1}{2}\times(4\%) = 2\%$$

$$\Rightarrow \text{Number of beats} = \Delta n = \frac{2}{100}\times n = \frac{2}{100}\times 100 = 2$$

Sol. 36 (C) Analyzing option (C) we have

$$y = \log\frac{x^2-t^2}{x-t} = \log(x+t)$$

$$\left[\text{As } \log a - \log b = \log\frac{a}{b}\right]$$

$$\Rightarrow \frac{\partial y}{\partial x} = \frac{1}{(x+t)}$$

$$\Rightarrow \frac{\partial^2 y}{\partial x^2} = -\frac{1}{(x+t)^2} \text{ and } \frac{\partial y}{\partial t} = \frac{(\partial x/\partial t)}{(x+t)} = \frac{v}{(x+t)}$$

$$\Rightarrow \frac{\partial^2 y}{\partial t^2} = -\frac{v^2}{(x+t)^2}$$

$$\Rightarrow \frac{\partial^2 y}{\partial x^2} = \frac{1}{v^2}\frac{\partial^2 y}{\partial t^2}$$

Which is the general form of wave equation.

Sol. 37 (C) $v \propto \sqrt{T}$; and as there is no change in length

$$\Rightarrow \lambda \propto \frac{1}{\sqrt{T}}$$

$$\frac{\lambda'}{\lambda} = \frac{\sqrt{T}}{\sqrt{T'}}$$

$$\Rightarrow \sqrt{T'} = \frac{\lambda}{\lambda'}\sqrt{T}$$

$$\Rightarrow T' = (2)^2 T = 4T$$

Sol. 38 (C) We use power transmitted is given as

$$P = \frac{1}{2}\mu\omega^2 A^2 V \text{ using } V = \sqrt{\frac{T}{\mu}}$$

$$\Rightarrow P = \frac{1}{2}\omega^2 A^2 \sqrt{T\mu}$$

$$\Rightarrow \omega = \sqrt{\frac{2P}{A^2\sqrt{T\mu}}}$$

$$\Rightarrow f = \frac{\omega}{2\pi} = \frac{1}{2\pi}\sqrt{\frac{2P}{A^2\sqrt{T\mu}}} = 30 \text{ Hz}$$

Sol. 39 (B)

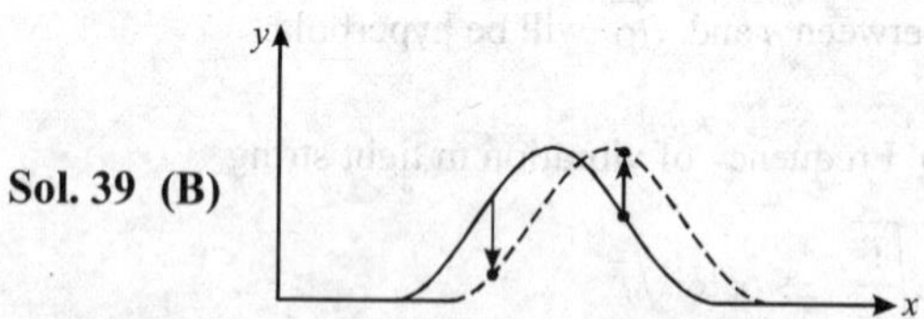

Dotted shape shows pulse position after a short time interval. Direction of the velocities are decided according to direction of displacements of the particles.

Sol. 40 (D) In Sonometer

$$n \propto \sqrt{T}$$

$$\Rightarrow \frac{n_1}{n_2} = 2 = \sqrt{\frac{T_1}{T_2}}$$

$$\Rightarrow T_2 = \frac{T_1}{4}$$

$$\Rightarrow \frac{T_1 - T_2}{T_1} \times 100 = \frac{T_1 - \frac{T_1}{4}}{T_1} \times 100 = 75\%$$

Sol. 41 (C) Figure below shows the situation described in question.

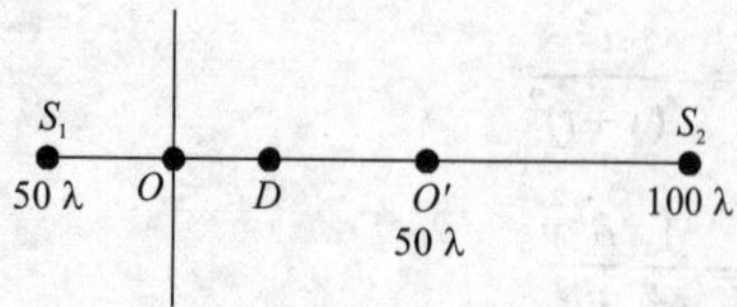

Due to detector movement, the path difference between two waves reaching the detector changes and it gives maxima for all the points at which the path difference is equal to $\Delta x = n\lambda$. At the location of detector D, the path difference is given as

$$\Delta x = S_2D - S_1D$$

At point O, we use

$$\Delta x_1 = 50\lambda$$

At point O', we use

$$\Delta x_2 = -50\lambda$$

Thus in going from origin to $(50\lambda, 0)$ the path difference changes from 50λ to -50λ and at some point in between path difference will also be zero. Thus total maxima detected are $50 + 1 + 50 = 101$ and between adjacent maxima there is one minima so total minima will be 100.

Sol. 42 (B) As we know

$$n_0 = \frac{1}{2L}\sqrt{\frac{T}{\mu}}$$

Initially $L = 24$ cm, $T = kx = k(4 \text{ cm})$; $\mu = \frac{m}{24}$

$$n_0 = \frac{1}{2\times 24}\sqrt{\frac{4k}{(m/24)}} = 0.20\sqrt{\frac{k}{m}}$$

When it is stretched to the length 26 cm

$$L = 26 \text{ cm}; T = K(6 \text{ cm}); \mu = \frac{m}{26}$$

$$n_0' = \frac{1}{2\times 26}\sqrt{\frac{6k}{(m/26)}} = 0.24\sqrt{\frac{k}{m}}$$

$$\Rightarrow n_0' > n_0$$

Sol. 43 (B) The magnitude of phase difference between the points separated by distance 10 metres

$$= k \times 10 = [10\pi \times 0.] \times 10 = \pi$$

Sol. 44 (B) Substituting $x = 0$ we have given wave $y = A \sin \omega t$ at $x = 0$ other should have $y = -A \sin \omega t$ equation so displacement may be zero at all the time.

Sol. 45 (B) Equation of the component waves are :

$$y = A\sin(\omega t - kx) \text{ and } y = A\sin(\omega t + kx)$$

where; $\omega t - kx$ = constant or $\omega t + kx$ = constant

Differentiating w.r.t. 't';

$$\omega - k\frac{dx}{dt} = 0 \text{ and } \omega + k\frac{dx}{dt} = 0$$

$$\Rightarrow v = \frac{dx}{dt} = \frac{\omega}{k} \text{ and } v = -\frac{\omega}{k}$$

This represents the speed of component waves.

Sol. 46 (D) At $t = 2$ second, the position of both pulses are separately given by figure-(a) and figure-(b); the superposition of both pulses is given by figure-(c).

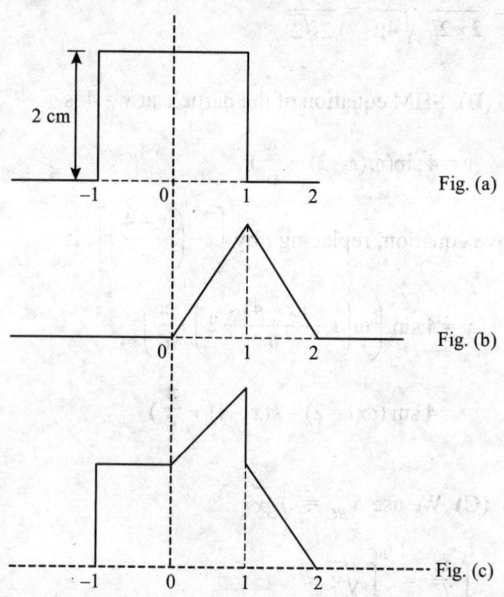

Sol. 47 (C); Sol. 48 (A)

Sol. (47 & 48)

For closed pipe,

3rd overtone = 7th harmonic = $n_7 = \frac{7v}{4l_c}$

5th harmonic $n_5 = \frac{5v}{4l_c}$

$n_7 - n_5 = \frac{2v}{4l_c} = 400$ Hz

$\Rightarrow$ $n_0 = \frac{v}{4l_c} = 200$ Hz (fundamental frequency of closed pipe)

Now 3rd harmonic of closed pipe is equal to 6th harmonic of open pipe

$\Rightarrow$ $\frac{v}{4l_c} = \frac{6v}{2l_0}$

$\Rightarrow$ $\frac{v}{l_0} = \frac{v}{4l_c} = 200$ Hz

Fundamental frequency of open pipe = $\frac{v}{2l_0} = 100$ Hz

Further, $l_c = \frac{330}{4 \times 200} = 0.4125$ m

$l_0 = \frac{330}{2 \times 100} = 1.65$ m

Sol. 49 (B) Given $\mu = 525$ g/m, $T = 45$ N

$f = 120$ Hz

$A = 8.5$ mm

Angular frequency $\omega = 2\pi f = 2\pi(120) = 754$ rad/s.

Sol. 50 (D) Wave speed $v = \sqrt{\frac{T}{\mu}} = \sqrt{\frac{45}{(0.525)}} = 925$ ms^{-1}

Sol. 51 (C) Power $P = \frac{1}{2}\mu\omega^2 A^2 v$

$= \frac{1}{2} \times 0.525 \times (754)^2 \times (8.5 \times 10^{-3})^2 \times 9.25$

$= 100$ W

Sol. 52 (C) $y_1 = y_m \sin(kx - \omega t)$

$y_2 = y_m \sin(kx - \omega t + \phi)$

Resultant is obtained by superposition

$y' = y_1 + y_2$

$= y_m \left[2\sin\left(kx - \omega t + \frac{\phi}{2}\right)\cos\left(\frac{\phi}{2}\right)\right]$

Sol. 53 (A) By superposition principle, we will always see the resultant $y' = (y_1 + y_2)$ on the string.

Sol. 54 (A) Slope at any point on the string in wave motion represents the ratio of particle speed to wave speed

$\Rightarrow$ slope $B >$ slope A

hence $R_A > R_B$

Sol. 55 (D) Reflected pulse will be inverted as it is reflected by a denser medium. The wall exerts force in downward direction.

Sol. 56 (B) We use

$y = 0.02 \sin(x + 30t)$ for the given wave :

$v = \frac{dx}{dt} = -30$ (As $x + 30t$ = constant)

we have wave speed $v = \sqrt{\frac{T}{\mu}}$

$\Rightarrow$ $T = \mu v^2 = A.\rho V^2$

$= (10^{-6}\, m^2)(8 \times 10^3\, \frac{kg}{m^3})(30)^2$

$\Rightarrow$ $T = 7.2$ N

Sol. 57 (A) We use

$n_1 = \frac{1}{2l_1}\sqrt{\left(\frac{T}{4\pi r^2 l}\right)}$ and $n_2 = \frac{1}{2l_2}\sqrt{\left(\frac{T}{4\pi r^2 s}\right)}$

$n_1 = n_2$

$\Rightarrow$ $\frac{1}{2l_1}\sqrt{\frac{T}{4\pi r^2 l}} = \frac{1}{2l_2}\sqrt{\frac{T}{\pi r^2 l}}$

$$\Rightarrow \quad \frac{1}{2l_1} \times \frac{1}{2} = \frac{1}{2l_2}$$

$$\Rightarrow \quad l_1 : l_2 = 1 : 2$$

Sol. 58 (A) We have power of a wave is given as $P = \frac{1}{2}\mu\omega^2 A^2 v$ and $v = \sqrt{\frac{T}{\mu}}$ will not change as both T and μ are constant. ω will also not change as it is property of the source only that is causing the wave motion. Hence to make power half the amplitude reduces to $A_0/\sqrt{2}$.

Sol. 59 (D) At $x = 0$ the phase difference should be π for destructive interference

Alternate solution

We use $y_2 = a\cos(\omega t + kx + \phi_0)$

Resultant after superposition is

$$y = y_1 + y_2 = a\cos\left(\omega t - kx + \frac{\pi}{3}\right) + a\cos(\omega t + kx + \phi_0)$$

$$= 2a\cos\left[\omega t + \frac{\frac{\pi}{3} + \phi_0}{2}\right] \times \cos\left[kx + \frac{\phi_0 - \frac{\pi}{3}}{2}\right]$$

$\Rightarrow \quad y = 0$ at $x = 0$ for any t

$$\Rightarrow \quad kx + \frac{\phi_0 - \frac{\pi}{3}}{2} = \frac{\pi}{2} \text{ at } x = 0$$

$$\Rightarrow \quad \phi_0 = \frac{4\pi}{3}. \text{ Hence } y_2 = a\cos\left(\omega t + kx + \frac{4\pi}{3}\right)$$

Sol. 60 (C) The possible expression will be one which gives zero displacement at $x = 0, X = L, y = 0$ and $y = L$.

Sol. 61 (C) We use

$y(x, t) = 2\sin(0.1\,\pi x)\cos(100\,\pi t)$ compare with $y = A\sin(Kx)\cos\omega t$

$$K = 0.1\,\pi = \frac{2\pi}{\lambda}$$

$$\lambda = 20 \text{ cm}$$

Distance between closet node and antinode is

$$\frac{\lambda}{4} = \frac{20}{4} = 5 \text{ cm}$$

Sol. 62 (C) As we have

$$f = \frac{1}{2l}\sqrt{\frac{T}{\mu}}$$

If radius is doubled and length is doubled, mass per unit length will become four times. Hence

$$f' = \frac{1}{2\times 2l}\sqrt{\frac{2T}{4\mu}} = \frac{f}{2\sqrt{2}}$$

Sol. 63 (D) SHM equation of the particle at $x = 4$ is

$$y = 4\sin\left(\omega(t-2) + \frac{\pi}{6}\right)$$

$\Rightarrow$ Wave equation, replacing t by $\left[t - \left(\frac{x-4}{v}\right)\right]$, is

$$y = 4\sin\left(\omega\left(t - \frac{(x-4)}{v} - 2\right) + \frac{\pi}{6}\right)$$

$$= 4\sin\left(\omega(t-2) - k(x-4) + \frac{\pi}{6}\right)$$

Sol. 64 (C) We use $v_{BC} = \sqrt{gx}$

$$\int_0^l \frac{dx}{\sqrt{x}} = \int_0^{t_{BC}} \sqrt{g}\, dt$$

$$2\sqrt{l} = g t_{BC}$$

$$t_{BC} = 2\sqrt{\frac{l}{g}}$$

$$v_{AB} = \sqrt{\frac{\left(2m + \frac{m}{l}x\right)g}{\frac{m}{l}}} = \sqrt{\left(2 + \frac{x}{l}\right)gl}$$

$$\int_0^l \frac{dx}{\sqrt{2 + \frac{x}{l}}} = \int_0^{t_{AB}} \sqrt{gl}\, dt$$

$$2l\sqrt{2 + \frac{x}{l}} = \sqrt{gl}\, t_{AB}$$

$$2l(\sqrt{3} - \sqrt{2}) = \sqrt{gl}\, t_{AB}$$

$$t_{AB} = 2(\sqrt{3} - \sqrt{2})\sqrt{\frac{l}{g}}$$

$$t = t_{BC} + t_{AB} = 2\sqrt{\frac{l}{g}}\,(1 + \sqrt{3} - \sqrt{2})$$

$$= 1.3 \times 2\sqrt{\frac{961}{1181}} = 2.6 \times \frac{31}{41} = 1.96\text{s} \simeq 2\text{s}$$

Sol. 65 (A) $\Delta n = 384 - 288 = 96$ Hz

Thus 288 Hz and 384 Hz (96 × 3; 96 × 4) are third and fourth harmonics

$\Rightarrow$ For fundamental mode

$$\frac{\lambda}{2} = 0.75$$

$\lambda = 1.5$ m

$\eta = 96$

$\Rightarrow \quad v = 96 \times 1.5 = 144$ m/s

Sol. 66 (C) For a string vibrating in its nth overtone ($(n+1)^{th}$ harmonic)

$$y = 2A\sin\left(\frac{(n+1)\pi x}{L}\right)\cos\omega t$$

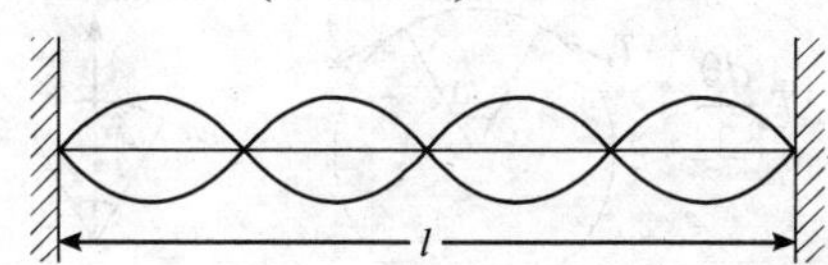

For $x = \frac{l}{3}$, $2A = a$ and $n = 3$; $y = \left[a\sin\left(\frac{4\pi}{l}.\frac{l}{3}\right)\right]\cos\omega t$

$$= a.\sin\frac{4\pi}{3}\cos\omega t = -a.\left(\frac{\sqrt{3}}{2}\right)\cos\omega t$$

i.e. at $x = \frac{l}{3}$; the amplitude is $\frac{\sqrt{3}a}{2}$

Sol. 67 (A) As linear mass density is

$$\mu = \frac{3.2\text{gm}}{40\text{ cm}} = \frac{3.2\times10^{-3}}{40\times10^{-2}} = \frac{3.2}{40} = \frac{32}{4000}\text{kg/m}$$

$$l = \frac{\lambda}{2}$$

$$\Rightarrow \lambda = 2l \qquad \ldots(1)$$

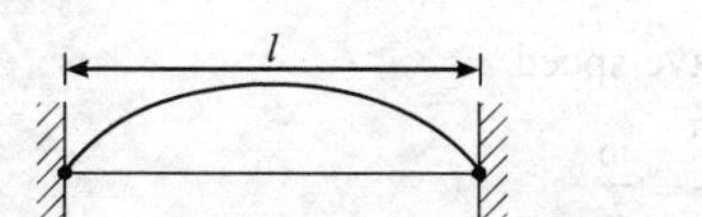

We use fundamental frequency

$$n_0 = \frac{v}{\lambda} = \frac{1}{2l}\sqrt{\frac{T}{\mu}}$$

$$\Rightarrow \frac{1000}{64} = \frac{1}{2\times40\times10^{-2}}\sqrt{\frac{T}{32/4000}}$$

$$\Rightarrow \left[\frac{1000}{64}\times2\times40\times10^{-2}\right]^2\frac{32}{4000} = T$$

$$\frac{1000}{64}\times\frac{32}{4000} = T$$

$$\Rightarrow T = \frac{10}{8}\text{N}$$

$$\text{now, } y = \frac{\frac{10/8}{10^{-6}}}{\frac{.05\times10^{-2}}{40\times10^{-2}}} = \frac{10^7}{8}\frac{40}{(.05)} = 10^9\text{ N/m}^2$$

Sol. 68 (A) As we use $\lambda = 2l = 3$ m

Equation of standing wave

$y = 2A\sin kx\cos\omega t$

$y = A$ as amplitude is $2A$

$A = 2A\sin kx$

$$\frac{2\pi}{\lambda}x = \frac{\pi}{6}$$

$$\Rightarrow x_1 = \frac{1}{4}\text{m and } \frac{2\pi}{\lambda}.x = \frac{\pi}{2} + \frac{\pi}{3}$$

$\Rightarrow x_2 = 1.25$ m

$\Rightarrow x_2 - x_1 = 1$ m

Sol. 69 (C) We use

$$n_0 = \frac{1}{2l}\sqrt{\frac{T}{\mu}} = \frac{1}{2l}\sqrt{\frac{T}{\rho s}} = \frac{1}{2l}\sqrt{\frac{T}{\rho\cdot\pi r^2}} = \frac{1}{2lr}\sqrt{\frac{T}{\rho\pi}}$$

$$\Rightarrow \frac{\Delta n_0}{n} = -\frac{\Delta l}{l} - \frac{\Delta r}{r}\left(\frac{\Delta f}{f}\right)_{max} = 1 + 0.5 = 1.5\%$$

Sol. 70 (D) We use

$$f = \frac{n}{2l}\sqrt{\frac{T_1}{\mu}} \qquad \ldots(1)$$

$$f = \frac{n+1}{2l}\sqrt{\frac{T_2}{\mu}} \qquad \ldots(2)$$

From equation (1) and (2) eliminate 'n' to get μ

$$\mu = \frac{T_1T_2}{4f^2l^2(\sqrt{T_1} - \sqrt{T_2})^2}$$

Sol. 71 (B) We use $v_1 = \sqrt{\frac{T_1}{\mu}} = \sqrt{\frac{2mg}{\mu}} = v\lambda_0$

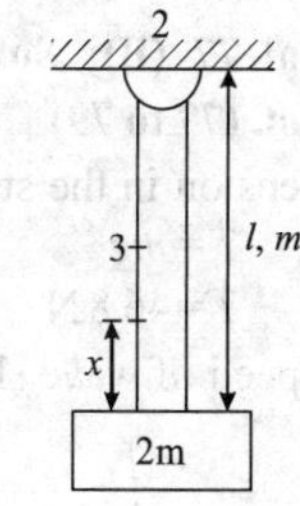

$$v_2 = \sqrt{\frac{3mg}{\mu}} = v\lambda_2$$

Comparing, we get

$$\lambda_2 = \sqrt{\frac{3}{2}}\lambda_0$$

Sol. 72 (A) Tension at midpoint $T_3 = \frac{5}{2}$mg

$$v = \sqrt{\frac{T_3}{\mu}} = \sqrt{\frac{5mg}{2(m/l)}}$$

$$v = \sqrt{\frac{5}{2}gl}$$

Sol. 73 (D) Let v_x be speed of pulse x distance from bottom of rope

Then $v_x = \sqrt{\left(2m + \frac{mx}{l}\right)\frac{g}{(m/l)}} = \sqrt{(2l+x)g}$

Then time taken to go from bottom to top will be

$$T = \int_0^L \frac{dx}{\sqrt{(2l+x)g}} = 2\sqrt{\frac{l}{g}}(\sqrt{3}-\sqrt{2})$$

Sol. 74 (A); Sol. 75 (C); Sol. 76 (B)
Sol. (74 to 76)

150 cm

Given displacement amplitude of a point 10 cm from end is $5\sqrt{3}$ mm.

Also distance with same loop between two point with displacement amplitude $5\sqrt{3}$ is also 10 cm.

Then

By symmetry, $\frac{\lambda}{2} = 30$ cm

$\lambda = 60$ cm

Now $\lambda \to 2p \to 60$ cm

$$10\text{ cm} \to \frac{\lambda}{6} = \frac{2\pi}{6} = \frac{\pi}{3}$$

$$\Rightarrow A \sin\frac{\pi}{3} = 5\sqrt{3}$$

$$\Rightarrow A = \frac{5\sqrt{3}}{\sqrt{3}/2} = 10\text{ mm}$$

Since there will be 5 loops in string, string is in 4th overtone. Potential energy of string will be zero at antinodes, which will be 15 cm from one end.

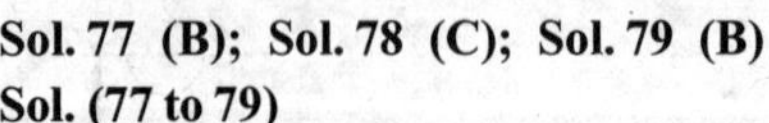

Sol. 77 (B); Sol. 78 (C); Sol. 79 (B)
Sol. (77 to 79)

Tension in the string should be

$T = mg$

$T = 46.8$ N

Speed of wave should be

$$v = \sqrt{\frac{t}{\mu}} = \sqrt{\frac{46.8}{0.117}} = 20\text{ ms}^{-1}$$

Power of wave on string is given as

$$P = \frac{1}{2}A^2\omega^2\mu v$$

$$= \frac{1}{2} \times (1.12 \times 10^{-2})^2 \times (2\pi \times 120)^2 \times 0.117 \times 10^{-3} \times 20$$

$= 0.0834$ W

Sol. 80 (C) We use $k = \frac{2\pi}{\lambda} = 0.025\,\pi$

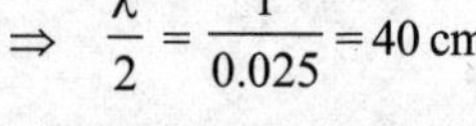

$$\Rightarrow \frac{\lambda}{2} = \frac{1}{0.025} = 40\text{ cm}$$

The shortest possible length will be $L_{min} = \frac{\lambda}{2} = 40$ cm

Sol. 81 (B) For equilibrium of mass dm we use

$$dm.\omega^2 R = 2T\sin\frac{d\theta}{2}$$

$$\Rightarrow \mu R d\theta\,\omega^2 R = 2T\frac{d\theta}{2}$$

$$\Rightarrow \mu\omega^2 R^2 = T$$

$$\Rightarrow v_w = \sqrt{\frac{T}{\mu}} = \sqrt{\omega^2 R^2} = \omega R$$

Also speed of string is ωR

$\Rightarrow$ The velocity of disturbance w.r.t. ground $= \omega R + \omega R = 2\omega R$.

Sol. 82 (A) As $v = \sqrt{\frac{T}{\mu}}$ is same for all, wave with maximum wavelength will have minimum angular frequency (by $v = n\lambda$). Also as $\lambda_1 = \lambda_3$ thus $\omega_1 = \omega_3$

Sol. 83 (B) $AB = \lambda$

$CD = T$

$$\frac{AB}{CD} = \frac{\lambda}{T} = v\lambda = V$$

i.e. wave speed.

Sol. 84 (D) We use wave speed

$$v = \sqrt{\frac{T}{\mu}} = \frac{\omega}{k}$$

$$\Rightarrow T = \frac{\omega^2\mu}{k^2} = \left(\frac{420}{21}\right)^2 \times 0.2 = 80\text{ N}$$

Sol. 85 (C) We use maximum particle velocity

$v_{max} = A\omega = 5$ cm/s; $T = 4$ s

$$\Rightarrow \omega = \frac{2\pi}{4} = \frac{\pi}{2}$$

$$\Rightarrow A = \frac{5}{\pi/2} = \frac{10}{\pi}\text{ cm}$$

Sol. 86 (B) We use $\omega = 3\pi$

$$\Rightarrow f = \frac{\omega}{2\pi} = 1.5,$$

Also $\Delta x = 1.0$ cm

Given, $\phi = \frac{2\pi}{\lambda}\Delta x$

$$\Rightarrow \frac{\pi}{8} = \frac{2\pi}{\lambda} \times 1$$

$\Rightarrow \quad \lambda = 16$ cm

$\Rightarrow \quad v = f\lambda = 16 \times 1.5 = 24$ cm/s

Sol. 87 (D) As wave has been reflected from a rarer medium, therefore there is no change in phase. Hence equation for the opposite direction can be written as

$$y = 0.5\,A \sin(-kx - \omega t + \theta)$$
$$= -0.5\,A \sin(kx + \omega t - \theta)$$

Sol. 88 (B) We use $y = a \sin \frac{2\pi}{\lambda}(vt - x)$

$$y = 2 \sin \frac{2\pi}{\lambda}(24t - x)$$

For $\quad t = 1, x = 4$ cm

$$y = 2\sin\left(\frac{2\pi}{16} \times 20\right)$$
$$= 2 \sin\left(2\pi + \frac{\pi}{2}\right) = y = 2 \text{ cm}$$

Sol. 89 (B) Spacing between successive nodes $= \frac{\lambda}{2}$ using $V = n\lambda$

$$\lambda \propto V \propto \sqrt{\frac{T}{\mu}}$$

New $\quad \frac{\lambda'}{\lambda} = \frac{\sqrt{2T}}{\sqrt{T}}$

$\Rightarrow \quad \lambda' = \sqrt{2}\,\lambda$

$$\frac{\lambda'}{2} = \sqrt{2} \cdot \frac{\lambda}{2} = \sqrt{2}\,x$$

Sol. 90 (B) Distance between beats $= \frac{\lambda}{2} = 10$ m

$\Rightarrow \quad \lambda = 20$ m time period, $T = 4$ s

$\Rightarrow \quad V = \lambda/T = 20$ m/4 s $= 5$ m/s

Solutions of ADVANCE MCQs One or More Option Correct

Sol. 1 (A, C, D) At points of compressor the pressure is more than that at rarefaction points hence option (A) is correct. The pressure amplitude in the medium in sound wave is given by the expression mentioned in option (C) hence it is correct and at any point the variation of pressure is ahead in phase compared to displacement variation by an angle $\pi/2$ hence option (D) is correct.

Sol. 2 (A, C) First by using Doppler's effect we can obtain the frequency of sound received by the wall considering it as a moving observer then we consider it as a moving source of this frequency and then we can find the frequency received by the driver as an observer. The analysis will result in option (A) and (C) correct.

Sol. 3 (B, C, D) Comparing the equation with the general equation of the wave $y = A \sin[2\pi(t/T - x/\lambda)]$ we get option (B) is correct and as wavelength is 4 cm we can calculate the phase difference between two positions of the medium particle by using the relation $(2\pi/\lambda)\Delta$ which gives option (C) and (D) are correct.

Sol. 4 (B, C) As the support is rigid, the wave is reflected in opposite phase hence at the support destructive interference takes place and node will be obtained. Due to nodes and antinodes at different positions, intensity of wave varies periodically with distance.

Sol. 5 (C, D) As point D is moving away from earth the light from this point will have a greater wavelength and point C is moving toward earth, light from this point will have a short wavelength. Point A and B are at rest in the observer's frame so light from both of these points will have same wavelength.

Sol. 6 (B, D) In fundamental mode of open pipe, at its center there is displacement node so gas molecules are at rest and pressure variation will be maximum.

Sol. 7 (B, C) From the equation given the function of x and t when compared to $(x + vt)$ we get the wave speed as 1.25 m/s and the wave has an amplitude of $0.8/5 = 0.16$ m.

Sol. 8 (A, B, C) Here y can represent all except pressure as in pressure waves y is the pressure difference not pressure at a point. If it represents pressure then according to this equation pressure can be negative and pressure below vaccum is not possible.

Sol. 9 (A) Maximum speed of a particle in SHM is $A\omega$.

Sol. 10 (A, B) Wave velocity of a simple harmonic propagating wave is given as $v = \omega/k$ and group velocity is the speed with which envelope of amplitude travels which is given as $v_g = \frac{d\omega}{dk}$.

Sol. 11 (A, C, D) For a plane wave (One dimensional) the wave amplitude and intensity remains constant during propagation. For a point source of spherical wave the wave intensity is given as $I = P/4\pi r^2$ where P is the source Power which remain constant for the whole spherical wavefront of the wave all the time.

Sol. 12 (A, B) By definition as explained in article 6.2.1, here options (A) and (B) are correct.

Sol. 13 (B, C) For interference of the waves, these must be travelling in same directions and coherent and the relation of maximum and minimum intensities is already explained in article 6.7.1.

Sol. 14 (C, D) By definitions of constructive and destructive interference of equal amplitude waves option (C) is correct and by definition of beats option (D) is also correct.

Sol. 15 (B, C, D) Here comparing the given equation with the standard equation of Simple Harmonic Wave $y = A\sin(\omega t - kx)$ we can have options (B), (C) and (D) are correct.

Sol. 16 (B, C) By comparing the given equation with the standard equation of a simple harmonic wave $y = A\sin(\omega t - kx + \phi)$ we have option (B) and (C) are correct.

Sol. 17 (All) Power transmitted on a string is given by

$$P = 2\pi^2 f^2 A^2 \rho v s = 2\pi^2 f^2 A^2 \mu v$$

Sol. 18 (A, C) Standing waves can be produced by superposition of two coherent waves travelling in opposite direction. Here on a clamped string incident and reflected wave can produce stationary wave by superposition on each other.

Sol. 19 (B, C, D) By the standard wave equation $y = A\sin(\omega t - kx)$ we can differentiate it twice to obtain v and a and by the expressions we can see that options (B), (C) and (D) are correct.

Sol. 20 (A, D) From the situation it is clear that particles P and Q are in opposite phase so there path difference must be odd multiple of half the wavelength and particles P and R are in same phase so there path difference must be a multiple of wavelength hence option (A) and (D) are correct.

Sol. 21 (A, B) The equation of a simple harmonic wave is given as

$$y = A\sin(\omega t - kx)$$

This equation gives the displacement curve (shape of a string in which transverse wave is propagating) as well as it gives the displacement of a particle at position x as a function of time t.

Sol. 22 (A, B, D) As we know that in transmission of a wave from one medium to another frequency of wave always remain same so with increase in speed wavelength increases. As there is no absorption or reflection of wave at the boundary, it means full wave energy is transmitted hence intensity remain same.

Sol. 23 (All) With the definition of stationary wave as explained in article 6.11, all given options are correct.

Sol. 24 (C, D) With the definition of stationary wave as explained in article 6.11, options (C) and (D) are correct.

Sol. 25 (All) Comparing given equations with the standard wave equations, all given options are correct.

Sol. 26 (A, B, C) As the two given waves have a phase difference $\pi/2$ we can use the vector superposition principal for the wave amplitudes to find the resulting amplitude and obtain that options (A), (B) and (C) are correct.

Sol. 27 (A, B, C) Given that

$$n = 500 \text{ Hz}$$
$$A = 10 \times 10^{-6} \text{ m}$$
$$\rho = 1.29 \text{ kg/m}^3$$
$$v = 340 \text{ m/s}$$

We use $v = \sqrt{\dfrac{B}{\rho}}$

$$\Rightarrow \quad B = \rho v^2 = 1.29 \times (340)^2 = 1.49 \times 10^5 \text{ N/m}^2$$

Wavelength $\lambda = \dfrac{v}{\lambda} = \dfrac{340}{500} = 0.68 \text{ m}$

Pressure amplitude

$$\Delta P = \frac{2\pi}{\lambda} AB$$
$$= \frac{2\pi}{0.68} \times 10 \times 10^{-6} \times 1.49 \times 10^5 = 13.76 \text{ m}$$

Energy density $\dfrac{P}{Sv} = 2\pi^2 n^2 A^2 \rho$

$$= 2 \times 10 \times (500)^2 \times (10 \times 10^{-6})^2 \times 1.29$$
$$= 6.45 \times 10^{-4} \text{ J/m}^3$$

Energy flux $u_\phi = \dfrac{P}{S} = 2\pi^2 n^2 A^2 \rho v = 0.22 \text{ J/m}^2\text{-s}$

Sol. 28 (A, C, D) Resulting wave equation will be

$$y = 8\sin 3x \cos 2t = R\cos 2t$$

at $x = 2.3$ we use $R = 8\sin(6.9) = 4.63$ cm

Nodes ($R = 0$) are obtained where $\sin(3x) = 0$

$$\Rightarrow x = 0, \frac{\pi}{3}, \frac{2\pi}{3}, \ldots$$

Antinodes ($R = 8$ cm) are obtained where $\sin(3x) = \pm 1$

$$\Rightarrow \quad x = \frac{\pi}{6}, \frac{\pi}{2}, \frac{5\pi}{6}, \ldots$$

Sol. 29 (B) In the given equations of the two waves are travelling in opposite directions, rest all parameters are same.

Sol. 30 (D) As $v = \sqrt{\dfrac{\gamma P}{\rho}}$; as P changes, ρ also changes. Hence $\dfrac{P}{\rho}$ remains constant so speed remains constant.

* * * * *